2·F

AN INTRODUCTION TO
THE OLD TESTAMENT IN GREEK

AN INTRODUCTION TO
THE OLD TESTAMENT
IN GREEK

BY

HENRY BARCLAY SWETE D D., F.B.A.

HON. D.LITT. OXFORD   HON. LITT.D. DUBLIN   HON. D.D. GLASGOW
FELLOW OF GONVILLE AND CAIUS COLLEGE, CAMBRIDGE
REGIUS PROFESSOR OF DIVINITY

REVISED BY

RICHARD RUSDEN OTTLEY, M.A.

SOMETIME SCHOLAR OF TRINITY COLLEGE

*WITH AN APPENDIX CONTAINING THE LETTER
OF ARISTEAS EDITED BY*

H. St J. THACKERAY, M.A.

SOMETIME SCHOLAR OF KING'S COLLEGE

KTAV PUBLISHING HOUSE, INC.
NEW YORK
1968

FIRST PRINTED 1902
REPRINTED BY PERMISSION OF CAMBRIDGE UNIVERSITY PRESS

LIBRARY OF CONGRESS CATALOG CARD NUMBER: 68-31420
MANUFACTURED IN THE UNITED STATES OF AMERICA

PREFACE TO THE FIRST EDITION.

THIS book is an endeavour to supply a want which has been felt by many readers of the Greek Old Testament. The literature of the subject is enormous, and its chief points have been compendiously treated in Biblical Dictionaries and similar publications. But hitherto no manual has placed within the student's reach all the information which he requires in the way of general introduction to the Greek versions.

A first attempt is necessarily beset with uncertainties. Experience only can shew whether the help here provided is precisely such as the student needs, and whether the right proportion has been preserved in dealing with the successive divisions of the subject. But it is hoped that the present work may at least meet the immediate wants of those who use *The Old Testament in Greek*, and serve as a forerunner to larger and more adequate treatises upon the same subject.

Such as it is, this volume owes more than I can say to the kindness of friends, among whom may especially be mentioned Principal Bebb, of St David's College, Lampeter, and Grinfield Lecturer at Oxford; Mr Brooke and Mr McLean, editors of the Larger Cambridge Septuagint; Mr Forbes Robinson, and Dr W. E. Barnes. But my acknowledgements are principally due to Professor Eberhard Nestle, of Maulbronn, who has added

PREFACE TO THE SECOND EDITION.

WHEN some two years ago it became clear that a reprint of this *Introduction* would shortly be required, the Syndics of the Press at my request put the revision, which I was unable to undertake, into the hands of a scholar already known to students of the Greek Old Testament by his *Book of Isaiah according to the Septuagint.* Mr Ottley, while leaving intact the form and even the pagination of the *Introduction*, has made every endeavour to bring the contents up to the present state of knowledge. This has been done partly by a careful revision of the text and the occasional rewriting of a paragraph, partly by writing new footnotes and a large number of valuable additional notes, and by expanding the bibliographical lists that follow each chapter, which after the lapse of so many years were necessarily defective.

I cannot sufficiently express my gratitude to Mr Ottley for the unremitting labour which he has expended on my book, and I am confident that future readers will share my sense of obligation. I venture to hope that, thus revised, the *Introduction* may continue for some years to be of service to those who are entering on the study of the Greek Old Testament.

H. B. S.

CAMBRIDGE,
May 11, 1914.

to the obligations under which he had previously laid me by reading the whole of this Introduction in proof, and suggesting many corrections and additions. While Dr Nestle is not to be held responsible for the final form in which the book appears, the reader will owe to him in great measure such freedom from error or fulness in the minuter details as it may possess. Mr Thackeray's work in the Appendix speaks for itself. Both the prolegomena to Aristeas and the text of the letter are wholly due to his generous labours, and they will form a welcome gift to students of the Septuagint and of Hellenistic Greek.

Free use has been made of all published works dealing with the various branches of learning which fall within the range of the subject. While direct quotations have been acknowledged where they occur, it has not been thought desirable to load the margin with references to all the sources from which information has been obtained. But the student will generally be able to discover these for himself from the bibliography which is appended to almost every chapter.

In dismissing my work I desire to tender my sincere thanks to the readers and workmen of the Cambridge University Press, whose unremitting attention has brought the production of the book to a successful end.

H. B. S.

CAMBRIDGE,
September 1, 1900.

CONTENTS.

PART I.

THE HISTORY OF THE GREEK OLD TESTAMENT AND OF ITS TRANSMISSION.

PART II.

PART III.

PART I.

THE HISTORY OF THE GREEK OLD TESTAMENT AND OF ITS TRANSMISSION.

PART I.

CHAPTER I.

THE ALEXANDRIAN GREEK VERSION.

1. A Greek version of any portion of the Old Testament presupposes intercourse between Israel and a Greek-speaking people. So long as the Hebrew race maintained its isolation, no occasion arose for the translation of the Hebrew Scriptures into a foreign tongue. As far as regards the countries west of Palestine, this isolation continued until the age of Alexander[1]; it is therefore improbable that any Greek version of the Scriptures existed there before that era. Among the Alexandrian Jews of the second century before Christ there was a vague belief that Plato and other Greek philosophical writers were indebted for some of their teaching to a source of this kind[2]. Thus Aristobulus (*ap.* Clem. Al. *strom.* i. 22 ; cf. Eus. *praep. ev.* xiii. 12) writes : κατηκολούθηκε δὲ καὶ ὁ Πλάτων τῇ καθ᾽

---

[1] Individual cases, such as that of the Jew mentioned by Clearchus (*ap.* Jos. *c. Ap.* 1, 22), who was Ἑλληνικὸς οὐ τῇ διαλέκτῳ μόνον ἀλλὰ καὶ τῇ ψυχῇ, are exceptions to a general rule. How numerous and prosperous were the Jewish colonies in Asia Minor at a later period appears from the Acts of the Apostles; see also Ramsay, *Phrygia* I. ii. p. 667 ff.

[2] This belief was inherited by the Christian school of Alexandria; see Clem. *strom.* v. 29, Orig. *c. Cels.* iv. 39, vi. 19; and cf. Lact. *inst.* IV. 2.

ἡμᾶς νομοθεσίᾳ, καὶ φανερός ἐστι περιεργασάμενος ἕκαστα τῶν ἐν αὐτῇ λεγομένων. διηρμήνευται δὲ πρὸ Δημητρίου ὑφ' ἑτέρου[1], πρὸ τῆς Ἀλεξάνδρου καὶ Περσῶν ἐπικρατήσεως, τά τε κατὰ τὴν ἐξ Αἰγύπτου ἐξαγωγὴν τῶν Ἑβραίων τῶν ἡμετέρων πολιτῶν καὶ ἡ τῶν γεγονότων ἁπάντων αὐτοῖς ἐπιφάνεια καὶ κράτησις τῆς χώρας καὶ τῆς ὅλης νομοθεσίας ἐπεξήγησις—words which seem to imply the existence before B.C. 400 of a translation which included at least the Books of Exodus, Deuteronomy, and Joshua. A similar claim has been found in the statement attributed by Pseudo-Aristeas to Demetrius of Phalerum : τοῦ νόμου τῶν Ἰουδαίων βιβλία...οὐχ ὡς ὑπάρχει σεσήμανται, καθὼς ὑπὸ τῶν εἰδότων προσαναφέρεται[2]. But no fragments of these early translations have been produced, and it is more than probable that the story arose out of a desire on the part of the Hellenistic Jews to find a Hebrew origin for the best products of Greek thought[3].

2. The earliest and most important of the extant Greek versions of the Old Testament was an offspring of the 'Greek Dispersion' (ἡ διασπορὰ τῶν Ἑλλήνων, Jo. vii. 35), which began with the conquests of Alexander the Great[4].

The Hebrew Prophets foresaw that it was the destiny of their race to be scattered over the face of the world (Deut. xxviii. 25, xxx. 4, Jer. xv. 4, xxxiv. 17). The word διασπορά (O.L. *dispersio*) employed by the Greek translators in these and similar passages (cf. 2 Esdr. xi. 9, Ps. cxxxviii. (cxxxix.) tit. (codd. A^a T), cxlvi. (cxlvii.) 2, Judith v. 19, Isa. xlix. 6, Jer. xiii. 14 (cod. א*), Dan. xii. 2 (LXX.), 2 Macc. i. 27) became the technical Greek term for Jewish communities in foreign lands, whether planted there by forcible deportation, or

---

[1] δι' ἑτέρων, Eus.
[2] See Tischendorf, *V. T. Gr.* (1879) *prolegg.* p. xiii. n.
[3] Cf. Walton (ed. Wrangham), p. 18; Frankel, *Vorstudien*, p. 14 f.; Buhl, *Kanon u. Text*, p. 108 f.
[4] See art. *Diaspora* in suppl. vol. of Hastings' *D.B.*

by their own free agency (Jo. vii. 35, Jas. i. 1, 1 Pet. i. 1)[1]. Such settlements were at first compulsory, and limited to countries east of Palestine. Between the eighth and sixth centuries B.C. the bulk of the population of both the Northern and Southern Kingdoms was swept away by Assyrian and Babylonian conquerors (2 Kings xvii. 6, xxiv. 14 ff., xxv. 11 f., 21 f.). A part of the Babylonian captivity returned (Ezra i. ii.), but Babylonia and Mesopotamia continued to be the home of a large body of Jewish settlers (Tob. i. 14 ff., 4 Esdr. xiii. 39 ff., Philo *ad Cai.* 36, Acts ii. 9, Joseph. *Ant.* xi. 5. 2, xv. 3. 1, xviii. 9. 1 ff.). This 'Eastern' Dispersion need not detain us here. No Biblical version in the stricter sense[2] had its origin in Babylonia; there, as in Palestine, the services of the synagogue interpreter (מְתוּרְגְּמָן) sufficed for the rendering of the lections into Aramaic, and no desire was manifested on the part of the Gentile population to make themselves acquainted with the Hebrew scriptures. It was among the Jews who were brought into relation with Hellenic culture that the necessity arose for a written translation of the books of the canon. Egypt was the earliest home of the Hellenistic Jew, and it was on Egyptian soil that the earliest Greek version of the Old Testament was begun.

3. Long before the time of Alexander Egypt possessed the nucleus of a Jewish colony. Shashanq, the Shishak of 1 K. xiv. 25 f., 2 Chr. xii. 2 f., who invaded Palestine[3] in the tenth century B.C., may have carried into Egypt captives or hostages from the conquered cities whose names still appear upon the

---

[1] The later Hebrew term was גּוֹלָה, 'exile'; see Dr Hort on 1 Pet. *l. c.*

[2] The 'Babylonian' Targum is of Palestinian origin (Buhl, p. 173). On early Aramaic translations arising out of the synagogue interpretations, see *ib.*, p. 168 f. ; and for the traditional account of the origin of the Syriac O. T. see Nestle, *Urtext u. Übersetzungen der Bibel* (Leipzig, 1897), p. 229.

[3] Professor Driver in D. G. Hogarth's *Authority and Archaeology*, p. 87 f.

walls of the temple at Karnak.   Isaiah (xix. 19 f.) foresaw[1] that
a time must come when the religious influence of Israel would
make itself felt on the banks of the Nile, while he endeavoured
to check the policy which led Judah to seek refuge from
Assyrian aggression in an Egyptian alliance (xxx. 1 ff.). Jewish
mercenaries are said to have fought in the expedition of
Psammetichus I. against Ethiopia *c.* B.C. 650 (cf. Ps.-Arist.:
ἑτέρων ξυμμαχιῶν ἐξαπεσταλμένων πρὸς τὸν τῶν Αἰθιόπων βασιλέα
μάχεσθαι σὺν Ψαμμιτιχῷ).   The panic which followed the
murder of Gedaliah drove a host of Jewish fugitives to Egypt,
where they settled at Migdol (Μάγδωλος), Tahpanhes (Ταφνάς
= Δάφνη)[2], Noph (Memphis), and Pathros (Παθούρη)[3], i.e.
throughout the Delta, and even in Upper Egypt; and the
descendants of those who survived were replenished, if we may
believe Pseudo-Aristeas, by others who entered Egypt during
the Persian period (ἤδη μὲν καὶ πρότερον ἱκανῶν εἰσεληλυθότων
σὺν τῷ Πέρσῃ).   These earlier settlers were probably among
the first to benefit by Alexander's policy, and may have been
partly hellenised before his birth.

4.   Alexander's victory at Issos in B.C. 333 opened the
gate of Syria to the conqueror.   In the next year he received
the submission of Tyre and Gaza and, according to Josephus,
was on the point of marching upon Jerusalem when the
statesmanship of the High Priest turned him from his purpose[4].
Whether the main features of this story be accepted or not,
it is certain that the subsequent policy of Alexander was
favourable to the Jews.   His genius discovered in the Jewish

---

[1] The passage is thought by some scholars to belong to the Ptolemaean
age; see Cheyne, *Intr. to Isaiah*, p. 105.
[2] Cf. *Authority and Archaeology*, p. 117.
[3] Jer. li. = xliv. 1 ff. ἅπασιν τοῖς Ἰουδαίοις τοῖς κατοικοῦσιν ἐν γῇ Αἰγύπτου
κτλ.   Many of these refugees, however, were afterwards taken prisoners by
Nebuchadnezzar and transported to Babylon (Joseph. *ant.* x. 9. 7).
[4] *Ant.* xi. 8. 4 f.   The story is rejected by Ewald and Grätz, and the
details are doubtless unhistorical : cf. Droysen, *l'histoire de l'Hellenisme,*
i. p. 300.

people an instrument well fitted to assist him in carrying out his purpose of drawing East and West together. Jews served in his army (Hecataeus *ap.* Joseph. *c. Ap.* i. 22 ἔτι γε μὴν ὅτι καὶ Ἀλεξάνδρῳ τῷ βασιλεῖ συνεστρατεύσαντο καὶ μετὰ ταῦτα τοῖς διαδόχοις αὐτοῦ μεμαρτύρηκεν); and such was his sense of their loyalty and courage that when Alexandria was founded (B.C. 332), although the design of the conqueror was to erect a monument to himself which should be essentially Greek [1], he not only assigned a place in his new city to Jewish colonists, but admitted them to full citizenship.

> Joseph. *ant.* xix. 5. 2 ἐπιγνοὺς ἀνέκαθεν τοὺς ἐν Ἀλεξανδρείᾳ Ἰουδαίους...ἴσης πολιτείας παρὰ τῶν βασιλέων τετευχότας : *c. Ap.* ii. 4 οὐ γὰρ ἀπορίᾳ γε τῶν οἰκησόντων τὴν μετὰ σπουδῆς ὑπ᾽ αὐτοῦ κτιζομένην Ἀλέξανδρος τῶν ἡμετέρων τινὰς ἐκεῖ συνήθροισεν, ἀλλὰ πάντας δοκιμάζων ἐπιμελῶς ἀρετῆς καὶ πίστεως τοῦτο τοῖς ἡμετέροις τὸ γέρας ἔδωκεν. *B. J.* ii. 18. 7 χρησάμενος προθυμοτάτοις κατὰ τῶν Αἰγυπτίων Ἰουδαίοις Ἀλέξανδρος γέρας τῆς συμμαχίας ἔδωκεν τὸ μετοικεῖν κατὰ τὴν πόλιν ἐξ ἴσου μοίρας πρὸς τοὺς Ἕλληνας.

Mommsen indeed (*Provinces*, E. T. ii. p. 162 n.) expresses a doubt whether the grant of citizenship [2] was made before the time of Ptolemy I., but in the absence of any direct evidence to the contrary the repeated statement of Josephus justifies the belief that it originated with Alexander [3].

5. The premature death of Alexander (B.C. 323) wrecked his larger scheme, but the Jewish colony at Alexandria continued to flourish under the Ptolemies, who succeeded to the government of Egypt.

It may be convenient to place here for reference the names and dates of the earlier Ptolemies. I. Lagi, or Soter (B.C. 322 —285). II. Philadelphus (B.C. 285—247). III. Euergetes I. (B.C. 247—222). IV. Philopator I. (B.C. 222—205). V. Epiphanes

---

[1] Plutarch *Alex.* 26 ἐβούλετο πόλιν μεγάλην καὶ πολυάνθρωπον Ἑλληνίδα συνοικίσας ἐπώνυμον ἑαυτοῦ καταλιπεῖν.

[2] See Mahaffy, *Empire of the Ptolemies*, p. 86.

[3] On the relations in which the Jews stood to Alexander and his successors see Wellhausen, *Isr. u. jüd. Geschichte*, c. xvi.

(B.C. 205—182). VI. Eupator (B.C. 182). VII. Philometor (B.C. 182—146). VIII. Philopator II. (B.C. 146). IX. Euergetes II., also known as Physkon (B.C. 146—117). Of the brief reigns of Eupator and the younger Philopator nothing is known.

The first Ptolemy added considerably to the Jewish population of Alexandria. His expeditions to Palestine and capture of Jerusalem placed in his hands a large number of Jewish and Samaritan captives, and these were conveyed to Alexandria, where many of them acquired civic rights. The report of the King's liberality towards his captives, and of their prosperity in Egypt, attracted other Palestinians to Alexandria, and many came thither as voluntary settlers.

Joseph. *ant.* xii. 1. 1 ὁ δὲ Πτολεμαῖος πολλοὺς αἰχμαλώτους λαβὼν ἀπό τε τῆς ὀρεινῆς Ἰουδαίας καὶ τῶν περὶ Ἱεροσόλυμα τόπων καὶ τῆς Σαμαρείτιδος καὶ τῶν ἐν Γαριζείν, κατῴκισεν ἅπαντας εἰς Αἴγυπτον ἀγαγών· ἐπεγνωκὼς δὲ τοὺς ἀπὸ τῶν Ἱεροσολύμων περὶ τὴν τῶν ὅρκων φυλακὴν καὶ τὰς πίστεις βεβαιοτάτους ὑπάρχοντας . πολλοὺς αὐτῶν τοῖς Μακεδόσιν ἐν Ἀλεξανδρείᾳ ποιήσας ἰσοπολίτας· οὐκ ὀλίγοι δὲ οὐδὲ τῶν ἄλλων Ἰουδαίων εἰς τὴν Αἴγυπτον παρεγίγνοντο, τῆς τε ἀρετῆς τῶν τόπων αὐτοὺς καὶ τῆς τοῦ Πτολεμαίου φιλοτιμίας προκαλουμένης.

A separate quarter of the city was assigned to the colony (Strabo *ap.* Joseph. *ant.* xiv. 7. 2 τῆς Ἀλεξανδρείας πόλεως ἀφώρισται μέγα μέρος τῷ ἔθνει τούτῳ[1]); it lay in the north-east of Alexandria, along the shore, near the royal palace. Here the Jews lived under their own ethnarch[2], who exercised judicial authority in all cases between Jew and Jew. They were permitted to follow their own religion and observe their national customs without molestation. Synagogues sprang up not only in the Jewish quarter, but at a later time in every part of the city

[1] In Philo's time the Jews occupied two districts out of five (*in Flacc.* 8). Droysen, iii. p. 59.
[2] Strabo *ap.* Jos. *ant.* xiv. 7. 2; cf. Schürer *Gesch. d. jüd. Volkes*[3], iii. 40; Lumbroso, *Recherches*, p. 218; Droysen, iii. p. 40 n. On the ἀλαβάρχης (ἀραβάρχης) who is sometimes identified with the ethnarch see Schürer iii. 88.

(Philo *ad Cai.* 20, *in Flacc.* 6[1]).   In the time of Philometor the
Jews stood so high in the royal favour that they were suffered
to convert a disused Egyptian temple at Leontopolis into
a *replica* of the Temple at Jerusalem, and the Jewish rite was
celebrated there until after the fall of the Holy City, when the
Romans put a stop to it (Joseph. *ant.* xii. 9. 7, xiii. 3. 1, *B. J.*
vii. 10. 4)[2].   Under these circumstances it is not surprising
that shortly after the Christian era the Jewish colony in Egypt
exceeded a million, constituting an eighth part of the population (Philo *in Flacc.* 6, Joseph. *c. Ap.* ii. 4).   In the Fayûm
villages were founded by Jews, and they lived on equal terms
with the Greeks[3].   Nor were the Jewish settlers on the African
coast limited to the Delta or to Egypt.   A daughter colony
was planted in Cyrenaica by the first Ptolemy, and at Cyrene
as at Alexandria the Jews formed an important section of the
community.   The Jew of Cyrene meets us already in the days
of the Maccabees (1 Macc. xv. 23, 2 Macc. ii. 23), and he was
a familiar figure at Jerusalem in the Apostolic age (Mt. xxvii.
32, Acts ii. 10, vi. 9[4], xi. 20, xiii. 1; cf. Strabo *ap.* Joseph. *ant.*
xiv. 7. 2).

6.   The Jews of the Dispersion everywhere retained their
religion and their loyalty to national institutions.   In each of
these settlements among Gentile peoples the Holy City
possessed a daughter, whose attachment to her was not less
strong than that of her children at home.   " Jerusalem," in
the words of Agrippa[5], " was the mother city, not of a single
country, but of most of the countries of the world, through the

[1] On the magnificence of the principal synagogue see Edersheim,
History of the Jewish Nation (ed. White), p. 67.
[2] Temporary checks seem to have been sustained by the Alexandrian
Jews under Philopator I. and Physcon; see 3 Macc. ii. 31, and cf. Mahaffy,
pp. 267 ff., 381, 390.
[3] See Mahaffy, *Empire, &c.*, p. 86 n.; cf. Philo *de sept.* 6.
[4] Where Blass (*Philology of the Gospels*, p. 69 f.) proposes to read
Λιβυστίνων for Λιβερτίνων.
[5] Philo *ad Cai.* 36.

colonies which she sent forth at various times." No colony
was more dutiful than the Alexandrian. The possession of a
local sanctuary at Leontopolis did not weaken its devotion to
the temple at Jerusalem[1]; pilgrimages were still made to
Jerusalem at the great festivals (Philo *ap.* Eus. *praep. ev.* viii.
14. 64; cf. Acts ii. 10); the Temple tribute was collected in
Egypt with no less punctuality than in Palestine (Philo *de
monarch.* ii. 3). But it was impossible for Jews who for
generations spent their lives and carried on their business in
Greek towns to retain their Semitic speech. In Palestine
after the Return, Aramaic gradually took the place of Hebrew
in ordinary intercourse, and after the time of Alexander Greek
became to some extent a rival of Aramaic. In Alexandria a
knowledge of Greek was not a mere luxury but a necesssity
of common life[2]. If it was not required by the State as a
condition of citizenship[3], yet self-interest compelled the in-
habitants of a Greek capital to acquire the language of the
markets and the Court. A generation or two may have
sufficed to accustom the Alexandrian Jews to the use of the
Greek tongue. The Jewish settlers in Lower Egypt who were
there at the coming of Alexander had probably gained some
knowledge of Greek before the founding of his new city[4];
and the children of Alexander's mercenaries, as well as many
of the immigrants from Palestine in the days of Soter, may
well have been practically bilingual. Every year of residence
in Alexandria would increase their familiarity with Greek and
weaken their hold upon the sacred tongue[5]. Any prejudice

---

[1] See Schürer[3], iii. 97 ff.

[2] Droysen, iii. p. 35.

[3] Mommsen, *Provinces*, ii. p. 163 f. On the whole question see Hody,
de Bibl. textibus, p. 224 f.; Caspari, *Quellen zur Gesch. d. Taufsymbols*,
iii. p. 268 ff.; Deissmann, *Bibelstudien*, p. 61 ff.; Kennedy, *Sources of
N. T. Gk.*, p. 21 ff.

[4] There was a large Greek settlement on the Pelusiac arm of the Nile
at an early period; see Herod. ii. 163.

[5] Cf. Streane, *Double Text of Jeremiah*, p. 11 f.

which might have existed against the use of a foreign language would speedily disappear under a rule which secured full liberty in worship and faith. The adoption of the Greek tongue was a tribute gladly paid by the Alexandrian Jews to the great Gentile community which sheltered and cherished them.

The Greek which they learnt was the κοινή as colloquially used in Alexandria : based on the less elevated kind of Attic, with some loss of the niceties; but less exclusive in its vocabulary, retaining many old Ionic and Homeric words, and adopting, but less freely, others of foreign origin. When the Jews employed this tongue, now common to the regions of Greek life and Greek conquest, to translate the Old Testament, they naturally used forms of expression which matched the original as closely as possible; though many of them were more or less prevalent, or paralleled, in the κοινή. Their ingrained habits of thought, and their native speech, even if partly forgotten, led them to give constant prominence to these expressions, which correspond with Semitisms, as well as, to some extent, with the current Greek speech and colloquial writings.

7. The 'Septuagint[1],' or the Greek version of the Old Testament which was on the whole the work of Alexandrian Jews, is, written in full, the *Interpretatio septuaginta virorum* or *seniorum*, i.e. the translation of which the first instalment was attributed by Alexandrian tradition to seventy or seventy-two Jewish elders. In the most ancient Greek MSS. of the Old

---

[1] Irenaeus (iii. 21. 3) speaks of the *seniorum interpretatio*; Tertullian (*Apol.* 18) of the *septuaginta et duo interpretes*; Jerome, of the *LXX. interpretes*, or *translatores* (*praeff. in Esdr., Isai.*), *LXX. editio* (*praef. in Job, ep. ad Pammach.*), *editio LXX.* (*praef. in Paralipp.*). Augustine, *de civ. Dei*, xviii. 42, remarks: "quorum interpretatio ut *Septuaginta* vocetur iam obtinuit consuetudo."

Testament it is described as the version 'according to the
LXX.' (κατὰ τοὺς ἑβδομήκοντα, παρὰ ἑβδομήκοντα, *O. T. in Greek*,
i. p. 103, ii. p. 479), and quoted by the formula οἱ ο' or οἱ οβ'.
All forms of the name point back to a common source, the
story of the origin of the version which is told in the
pseudonymous letter entitled Ἀριστέας Φιλοκράτει. See App.

> LITERATURE. The text of the letter of Aristeas is printed
> in the Appendix to this volume. It will be found also in Hody
> *de Bibl. text. orig.* (Oxon. 1705), and in Constantinus Oeconomus
> περὶ τῶν ο' ἑρμηνευτῶν βιβλία δ' (Athens, 1849); a better text was
> given by M. Schmidt in Merx, *Archiv f. wissensch. Erforschung*
> *a. A. T.* i. p. 241 ff.; the latest separate edition appeared in 1900
> under the title: *Aristeae ad Philocratem epistula cum ceteris de*
> *origine versionis LXX. interpretum testimoniis. Ludovici Men-*
> *delssohn schedis usus ed. Paulus Wendland.* A trans. by Mr H. St J.
> Thackeray appeared in *J. Q. R.* Ap. 1903 (since reprinted). For
> the earlier editions see Fabricius-Harles, iii. 660 ff.; the *editio*
> *princeps* of the Greek text was published at Basle in 1561.
>
> The controversies raised by the letter may be studied in
> Hody or in Fabricius-Harles; cf. Rosenmüller, *Handbuch f. d.*
> *Literatur d. bibl. Kritik u. Exegese;* Dähne, *gesch. Darstellung*
> *d. jüdisch Alex. Religions-Philosophie,* ii. p. 205 ff.; Papageor-
> gius, *Über den Aristeasbrief;* Lumbroso, *Recherches sur l'éco-*
> *nomie politique de l'Égypte,* p. 351 f. and in *Atti di R. Accademia*
> *della Scienza di Torino,* iv. (1868−9). Fuller lists will be found
> in Schürer[3], iii. 472 f., and in Nestle (*Real-encyklopädie f. p. Th.*
> *u. K.*[3] 3, p. 2), and Hastings (*D.B.* iv. 438 f., where much interest-
> ing information is collected); cf. Van Ess, *Epilegg.* p. 29 f.

8.   The writer professes to be a courtier in the service of
Philadelphus, a Greek who is interested in the antiquities
of the Jewish people[1]. Addressing his brother Philocrates, he
relates the issue of a journey which he had recently made
to Jerusalem. It appears that Demetrius Phalereus[2], who is

---

[1] From the mention of Cyprus as 'the island' (§ 5) it has been inferred
that Aristeas was a Cypriot. The name occurs freely in inscriptions from
the islands of the Aegean and the coast of Caria (*C. I. G.* 2262, 2266, 2349,
2399, 2404, 2655, 2693, 2694, 2723, 2727, 2781, 2892), and was borne by
a Cyprian sculptor (see *D. G. and R. B.*, i. 293). Wendland, however,
thinks 'the island' is Pharos, as certainly in § 301. The Aristeas who
wrote περὶ Ἰουδαίων (Euseb. *praep. ev.* ix. 25) was doubtless an Alexandrian
Jew who, as a Hellenist, assumed a Greek name.

[2] See Ostermann, *de Demetrii Ph. vita* (1857); Susemihl, *Gesch. d. gr.*

described as librarian of the royal library at Alexandria, had in conversation with the King represented the importance of procuring for the library a translation of the Jewish laws (τὰ τῶν Ἰουδαίων νόμιμα μεταγραφῆς ἄξια καὶ τῆς παρὰ σοὶ βιβλιο-θήκης εἶναι). Philadelphus fell in with the suggestion, and despatched an embassy to Jerusalem with a letter to the High Priest Eleazar, in which the latter was desired to send to Alexandria six elders learned in the law from each of the tribes of Israel to execute the work of translation. In due course the seventy-two elders, whose names are given, arrived in Egypt, bringing with them a copy of the Hebrew Law written in letters of gold on rolls[1] composed of skins (σὺν...ταῖς διαφόροις διφθέραις ἐν αἷς ἡ νομοθεσία γεγραμμένη χρυσογραφίᾳ τοῖς Ἰουδαικοῖς γράμμασι). A banquet followed, at which the King tested the attainments of the Jewish elders with hard questions. Three days afterwards the work of translation began. The translators were conducted by Demetrius along the Heptastadion[2] to the island of Pharos, where a building conveniently furnished and remote from the distractions of the city was provided for their use. Here Demetrius, in the words of Aristeas, 'exhorted them to accomplish the work of transla-tion, since they were well supplied with all that they could want. So they set to work, comparing their several results and making them agree; and whatever they agreed upon was suitably copied under the direction of Demetrius....In this way the transcription was completed in seventy-two days, as if that period had been pre-arranged.'

The completed work was read by Demetrius to the Jewish community, who received it with enthusiasm and begged that a copy might be placed in the hands of their leaders; and

---

Litt. in d. Alexandrinerzeit, i. p. 135 ff. On the royal library at Alexandria see Susemihl, i. p. 335 ff., and the art. *Bibliotheken* in Pauly-Wissowa, *Real-Encyclopädie*, v. 409 f.

[1] See Birt, *Die Buchrolle in der Kunst* (Leipzig, 1907), p. 21 f.

[2] The mole which connected the Pharos with the city: see art. *Alexandria* in Smith's *Dict. of Gr. and Rom. Geography*, pp. 96 f.

a curse was solemnly pronounced upon any who should presume to add to the version or to take from it. After this the Greek Pentateuch was read to the King, who expressed delight and surprise, greeted the book with a gesture of reverence (προσκυνήσας), and desired that it should be preserved with scrupulous care (ἐκέλευσε μεγάλην ἐπιμέλειαν ποιεῖσθαι τῶν βιβλίων καὶ συντηρεῖν ἀγνῶς).

9. The story of Aristeas is repeated more or less fully by the Alexandrian writers Aristobulus and Philo, and by Josephus.

Aristobulus *ap.* Eus. *praep. ev.* xiii. 12. 2 : ἡ δὲ ὅλη ἑρμηνεία τῶν διὰ τοῦ νόμου πάντων ἐπὶ τοῦ προσαγορευθέντος Φιλαδέλφου βασιλέως σοῦ δὲ προγόνου [he is addressing Philometor] προσενεγκαμένου μείζονα φιλοτιμίαν, Δημητρίου τοῦ Φαληρέως πραγματευσαμένου τὰ περὶ τούτων[1]. Philo, *vit. Moys.* ii. 5 ff.: Πτολεμαῖος ὁ Φιλάδελφος ἐπικληθεὶς...ζῆλον καὶ πόθον λαβὼν τῆς νομοθεσίας ἡμῶν εἰς Ἑλλάδα γλῶτταν τὴν Χαλδαικὴν μεθαρμόζεσθαι διενοεῖτο, καὶ πρέσβεις εὐθὺς ἐξέπεμπε πρὸς τὸν τῆς Ἰουδαίας ἀρχιερέα.. ὁ δέ, ὡς εἰκός, ἡσθεὶς καὶ νομίσας οὐκ ἄνευ θείας ἐπιφροσύνης περὶ τὸ τοιοῦτον ἔργον ἐσπουδακέναι τὸν βασιλέα...ἀσμένως ἀποστέλλει...καθίσαντες δ᾽ ἐν ἀποκρύφῳ καὶ μηδενὸς παρόντος...καθάπερ ἐνθουσιῶντες ἐπροφήτευον, οὐκ ἄλλα ἄλλοι, τὰ δὲ αὐτὰ πάντες ὀνόματα καὶ ῥήματα ὥσπερ ὑποβολέως ἑκάστοις ἀοράτως ἐνηχοῦντος κτλ. Josephus, *ant.* i. *prooem.* 3 : Πτολεμαίων μὲν ὁ δεύτερος μάλιστα δὴ βασιλεὺς περὶ παιδείαν καὶ βιβλίων συναγωγὴν σπουδάσας ἐξαιρέτως ἐφιλοτιμήθη τὸν ἡμέτερον νόμον καὶ τὴν κατ᾽ αὐτὸν διάταξιν τῆς πολιτείας εἰς τὴν Ἑλλάδα φωνὴν μεταλαβεῖν κτλ. In *ant.* xii. 2. 1—15 Josephus gives a full account obviously based on Aristeas (whom he calls Ἀρισταῖος), and to a great extent verbally identical with the letter.

The testimony of Josephus establishes only the fact that the letter of Aristeas was current in Palestine during the first century A.D. Philo, on the other hand, represents an Alexandrian tradition which was perhaps originally independent of the letter, and is certainly not entirely consistent with it. He

---

[1] In defence of the genuineness of this testimony see Schürer, *G. J. V.*[3] iii. 384—392. On the other hand cf. L. Cohn in *Neue Jahrbücher f. d. Klass. Alterthum* i. 8 (1895), and Wendland in *Byzantinische Zeitschrift* vii. (1898), 447—449. For Aristobulus see Susemihl, p. 630 f.

states (*l. c.*) that the completion of the work of the LXX. was
celebrated at Alexandria down to his own time by a yearly
festival at the Pharos (μέχρι νῦν ἀνὰ πᾶν ἔτος ἑορτὴ καὶ πανήγυρις
ἄγεται κατὰ τὴν Φάρον νῆσον, εἰς ἣν οὐκ Ἰουδαῖοι μόνον ἀλλὰ καὶ
παμπληθεῖς ἕτεροι διαπλέουσι, τό τε χωρίον σεμνύνοντες ἐν ᾧ πρῶτον
τὸ τῆς ἑρμηνείας ἐξέλαμψε κτλ.). A popular anniversary of this
kind can scarcely have grown out of a literary work so artificial
and so wanting in the elements which ensure popularity as the
letter of Aristeas. The fragment of Aristobulus carries us
much further back than the witness of Philo and Josephus.
It was addressed to a Ptolemy who was a descendant of Philadelphus, and who is identified both by Eusebius (*l. c.*) and by
Clement[1] (*strom.* i. 22) with Philometor. Whether Aristobulus
derived his information from Aristeas is uncertain, but his
words, if we admit their genuineness, establish the fact that the
main features of the story were believed by the literary Jews of
Alexandria, and even at the Court, more than a century and a
half before the Christian era and within a century of the date
assigned by Aristeas to the translation of the Law.

10. From the second century A.D. the letter of Aristeas is
quoted or its contents are summarised by the fathers of the
Church, who in general receive the story without suspicion, and
add certain fresh particulars.

Cf. Justin, *apol.* i. 31, *dial.* 68, 71, 'cohort. ad Graecos' 13 ff. ;
Iren. iii. 21. 2 f. ; Clem. Alex. *strom.* i. 22, 148 f. ; Tertullian,
apol. 18 ; Anatolius *ap.* Eus. *H. E.* vii. 32 ; Eusebius, *praep. ev.*
viii. 1—9, ix. 38 ; Cyril of Jerusalem, *catech.* iv. 34 ; Hilary, *prol.
ad Psalmos, tract. in Pss.* ii., cxviii.; Epiphanius, *de mens. et pond.*
§§ 3, 6 ; Philastrius *de haer.* 138 ; Jerome, *praef. in Gen., praef.
in libr. quaest. Hebr.;* Augustine, *de civ. Dei* xvii. 42 f., *de doctr.
Chr.* ii. 22 : Theodore of Mopsuestia *in Habakk.* ii., *in Zeph.* i.;
Chrysostom, *or.* i. *adv. Jud.*, c. 6, *hom.* iv. *in Gen.*, c. 4; Theo-

---

[1] Clement of Alexandria identifies this Aristobulus with the person
named in 2 Macc. i. 10 Ἀριστοβούλῳ διδασκάλῳ Πτολεμαίου τοῦ βασιλέως.
See Valckenaer *diatribe de Aristobulo* (printed at the end of Gaisford's
edition of Eus. *praep. ev.* iv.).

doret, *praef. in Psalmos ;* Cyril of Alexandria, *adv. Julian. or.*
1 ; Pseudo-Athanasius, *synops. scr. sacr.* § 77 ; the anonymous
dialogue of Timothy and Aquila (ed. Conybeare, Oxford, 1898,
p. 90 f.).

Most of these Christian writers, in distinct contradiction
to the statement of Aristeas, represent the Seventy as having
worked separately, adding that when the results were compared at the end of the task they were found to be identical
(so Irenaeus, Clement of Alexandria, Cyril of Jerusalem,
Augustine, &c.). The author of the *Cohortatio ad Graecos*[1]
declares that at Alexandria he had been shewn the vestiges of
the cells in which the translators had worked (αὐτοὶ ἐν τῇ ᾿Αλεξ-
ανδρείᾳ γενόμενοι καὶ τὰ ἴχνη τῶν οἰκίσκων ἐν τῇ Φάρῳ ἑωρακότες
ἔτι σωζόμενα, καὶ παρὰ τῶν ἐκεῖ ὡς τὰ πάτρια παρειληφότων ἀκηκο-
ότες ταῦτα ἀπαγγέλλομεν). This story of the cells therefore
was probably of Alexandrian origin, and had grown out of
the local belief in the inspiration of the Seventy which appears
already in the words of Philo quoted above[2]. The Fathers
generally accept both the belief and the legend which it
generated, though the latter sometimes undergoes slight modification, as when Epiphanius groups the LXXII. in pairs (ζύγη
ζύγη κατ᾿ οἰκίσκον). Jerome is an honourable exception; he
realises that the tale of the cells is inconsistent with the earlier
tradition (*prol. in Gen.* "nescio quis primus auctor LXX cel-
lulas Alexandriae mendacio suo exstruxerit, quibus divisi eadem
scriptitarint, quum Aristeas...et Josephus nihil tale retulerint"),
and rightly protests against the doctrine which was at the root of
the absurdity ("aliud est enim vatem, aliud est esse inter-
pretem")[3].

---

[1] On the date of this treatise, which is commonly ascribed to Justin,
see Krüger, *Hist. of Chr. Literature* (E. T.), p. 112 f., and cf. Harnack-
Preuschen, p. 107.

[2] Cf. *ib.* οὐχ ἑρμηνεῖς ἐκείνους ἀλλ᾿ ἱεροφάντας καὶ προφήτας προσαγο-
ρεύοντες.

[3] The story of the cells is not peculiar to Christian writers ; it is
echoed by the Talmud (Bab. Talm. *Megillah* 9ª, Jerus. Talm. *Meg.* c. i. ;
cf. *Sopherim*, c. i.).

11. Doubts as to the genuineness of the Aristeas-letter were first expressed by Ludovicus de Vives in his commentary on Aug. *de civ. Dei*, xviii. 4 (published in 1522), and after him by Joseph Scaliger. Ussher and Voss defended the letter, but its claim to be the work of a contemporary of Philadelphus was finally demolished by Humphry Hody, Regius Professor of Greek at Oxford (1698—1706)[1]. A few later writers have pleaded in its favour (e.g. Grinfield *Apology for the LXX.*, and Constantinus Oeconomus, *op. cit.*); but the great majority of modern scholars, and perhaps all living experts, recognise the unhistorical character of much of the story of Aristeas.

Indeed it scarcely needed the massive learning of Hody to convict the letter of Aristeas of being pseudonymous, and to a large extent legendary. The selection of the elders from all the tribes of Israel awakens suspicions; their names are clearly imaginary; the recurrence of the number seventy-two seems to have struck even the writer as open to remark[2]; the letters of Philadelphus and Eleazar are of the same stamp as the confessedly fictitious correspondence between the Egyptian and the Palestinian Jews in 2 Maccabees[3]. Above all, whereas the letter professes to have been written by a Greek and a pagan, its purpose proclaims it to be the work of a Jew; while it addresses itself to Gentile readers, its obvious aim is to glorify the Jewish race, and to diffuse information about their sacred books. On the other hand, though the story as 'Aristeas' tells it is doubtless a romance, it must not be hastily inferred that it has no historical basis. That the writer was a Jew who lived in Egypt under the Ptolemies seems to be

---

[1] In his *Contra historiam LXX. interpretum Aristeae nomine inscriptam dissertatio*, originally published in 1684, and afterwards included in *De Bibliorum textibus originalibus, versionibus Graecis, et Latina vulgata libri iv.* (Oxon. 1705). For other writers on both sides cf. Buhl, p. 117 (E. T. p. 115).

[2] On the Rabbinical partiality for this number, cf. Ewald, *Hist. of Israel*, v 252 n. (E. T.); Schürer II. i. p. 174; Buhl, p. 117 (=116, E. T.).

[3] Or the letters of Philopator in 3 Maccabees.

demonstrated by the knowledge which he displays of life at the Alexandrian Court[1]. There is also reason to suppose that he wrote within fifty years of the death of Philadelphus, and his principal facts are endorsed, as we have seen, by a writer of the next generation[2]. It is difficult to believe that a document, which within a century of the events relates the history of a literary undertaking in which the Court and the scholars of Alexandria were concerned, can be altogether destitute of truth. Detailed criticism is impossible in this place, but it is necessary to examine the credibility of the chief features of the romance so far as they affect questions relating to the date and origin of the LXX. There are certain points in the letter of Aristeas which demand investigation, especially the statements (1) that the translation of the Law was made in the time of Philadelphus; (2) that it was undertaken at the desire of the King, and for the royal library; (3) that the translators and the Hebrew rolls which they used were brought from Jerusalem; and (4) that their translation when completed was welcomed both by Jews and Greeks[3].

12. There is no improbability in the first of these statements. The personal tastes of Philadelphus, if by no means purely literary, included a fancy for the society of scholars and the accumulation of books[4]. He founded a second library at the Serapeion to receive the overflow of that which Soter had established near the Museum and the Palace[5]. His syncretistic temperament disposed him to listen to the representatives of various creeds. A Buddhist mission from the Ganges found a welcome at his court[6]; and the reign which produced

[1] See the remarks of Wilcken in *Philologus* liii. (1894), p. 111 f., and cf. Lumbroso, p. xiii.   [2] See Schürer[3], iii. p. 468 f.

[3] See Mr I. Abrahams in *J.Q.R.* xiv. 2, pp. 321 ff., *Recent Criticisms of the Letter of Aristeas.*

[4] Tertullian exaggerates his literary merits (*apol.* 18 Ptolemaeorum eruditissimus...et omnis litteraturae sagacissimus).

[5] Cf. Mahaffy, *Empire of the Ptolemies*, p. 164 ff. On the character of Philadelphus see also Droysen, iii., p. 254 f.   [6] Mahaffy, pp. 163 f., 170.

Manetho's Greek history of Egyptian institutions may well have yielded also a translation into Greek of the Hebrew sacred books. The presence of a large Jewish colony at Alexandria could hardly have failed to awaken in the King and his scholars of the Museum an interest in the ancient laws and literature of the Jewish race. For these reasons modern scholars have for the most part shewn no desire to disturb the tradition which assigns the Alexandrian version of the Law to the days of Philadelphus.

One exception must be noted. The late Professor Grätz maintained with much ingenuity that the Greek Pentateuch was a work of the reign of Philometor, thus transferring the inception of the LXX. from the middle of the third century to the middle of the second[1].

His opinion was based partly on the fact that the Jewish colony at Alexandria touched the zenith of its influence under Philometor, partly on internal grounds. Under the latter head he insisted on the translation in Lev. xxiii. 11 of the phrase מִמָּחֳרַת הַשַּׁבָּת by τῇ ἐπαύριον τῆς πρώτης. The Pharisees understood the word שַׁבָּת in that context to refer to the day after the Paschal Sabbath i.e. Nisan 15, while the Sadducees adhered to the usual meaning. Grätz argued with much force that, since the rendering of the LXX. shews evident signs of Pharisaic influence, the version itself must have been later than the rise of the Pharisees[2]. But *v.* 15 renders the same words by ἀπὸ τῆς ἐπαύριον τοῦ σαββάτου, and as it is not likely that a translator who had of set purpose written τῆς πρώτης in *v.* 11 would have let τοῦ σαββάτου escape him a little further down, we must suppose that τοῦ σ. stood originally in both verses and that τῆς πρ. is due to a Pharisaic corrector who left his work incomplete. But a partial correction of the passage in the interests of Pharisaism points to the version being pre-Maccabean, a conclusion quite opposite to that which Dr Grätz desired to draw.[3]

There is, moreover, positive evidence that the Alexandrian version of Genesis at least was in existence considerably before the beginning of Philometor's reign. It was used by the Hellenist Demetrius, fragments of whose treatise Περὶ τῶν ἐν

---

[1] *Gesch. Juden*[3], iii. p. 615 ff.
[2] He also notes the rendering ἄρχων in Deut. xvii. 14—20.
[3] See *Expository Times*, ii. pp. 209, 277 f.

τῇ Ἰουδαίᾳ βασιλέων are preserved by Clement (*strom.* i. 21) and Eusebius (*praep. ev.* ix. 21, 29). The following specimens may suffice to prove this assertion.

<table>
<tr><td>Demetrius.</td><td>Genesis (LXX.).</td></tr>
<tr><td>ἀντὶ τῶν μήλων τοῦ μανδρα-
γόρου.</td><td>εὗρεν μῆλα μανδραγόρου...
ἀντὶ τῶν μανδραγορῶν (xxx.
14 f.).</td></tr>
<tr><td>ἄγγελον τοῦ θεοῦ παλαῖσαι
καὶ ἅψασθαι τοῦ πλάτους τοῦ
μηροῦ τοῦ Ἰακώβ.</td><td>ἐπάλαιεν...καὶ ἥψατο τοῦ
πλάτους τοῦ μηροῦ Ἰακώβ
(xxxii. 25).</td></tr>
<tr><td>λέγειν κτηνοτρόφους αὐτοὺς
εἶναι.</td><td>ἐρεῖτε Ἄνδρες κτηνοτρόφοι
ἐσμέν (xlvi. 34).</td></tr>
</table>

As Demetrius carries his chronology no further than the reign of Philopator, it may be assumed that he lived under the fourth Ptolemy[1]. He is thus the earliest of the Alexandrian Hellenistic writers; yet equally with the latest he draws his quotations of the Book of Genesis from the LXX. It may fairly be argued that a version, which at the end of the third century B.C. had won its way to acceptance among the literary Jews of Alexandria, probably saw the light not later than the reign of Philadelphus.

13.   Both 'Aristeas' and Aristobulus associate with the inception of the LXX. the name of Demetrius Phalereus[2]. Aristobulus merely represents Demetrius as having 'negociated the matter' (πραγματευσαμένου τὰ περὶ τούτων), but Aristeas states that he did so (1) in the capacity of head of the royal library (κατασταθεὶς ἐπὶ τῆς τοῦ βασιλέως βιβλιοθήκης), and (2) in the days of Philadelphus, with whom he appears to be on intimate terms. Both these particulars are certainly unhistorical. Busch[3] has shewn that the office of librarian was

---

[1] Cf. Freudenthal, *hellen. Studien*, p. 41.

[2] The *Dialogue of Timothy and Aquila* strangely says: ἦν δὲ οὗτος ὁ Δημήτριος τῷ γένει Ἑβραῖος.

[3] *De bibliothecariis Alexandrinis* (1884), p. 1 ff.; cf. Droysen, iii. p. 256; Mahaffy, p. 115.

filled under Philadelphus by Zenodotus of Ephesus, and on the decease of Zenodotus by Eratosthenes. Moreover Demetrius, so far from being intimate with Philadelphus, was sent into exile soon after the accession of that monarch, and died a little later on from the bite of an asp, probably administered at the King's instigation (*c.* B.C. 283) [1]. Thus, if Demetrius took part in the inception of the LXX., he must have done so during the reign of Soter. This is not in itself improbable. He had taken refuge in Egypt as early as B.C. 307, and for many years had been a trusted adviser of the first Ptolemy; and it is not unlikely that the project of translating the Jewish Law was discussed between him and the royal founder of the Alexandrian library, and that the work was really due to his suggestion [2], though his words did not bear fruit until after his death. The point is of importance to the student of the LXX. only in so far as it has to do with the question whether the version was made under official guidance. The breakdown of the chronology of this part of the story of Aristeas leaves us free to abandon the hypothesis of direct intervention on the part of the King, and internal evidence certainly justifies us in doing so. An official version would assuredly have avoided such barbarisms as γειώρας, εἴν, σάββατα [3], when such Greek equivalents as προσήλυτος, δίχουν, ἀνάπαυσις, were available. The whole style of the version is alien from the purpose of a book intended for literary use, nor is it conceivable that under such circumstances Jewish translators, Palestinian or Alexandrian, would have been left without the advice and help of experts in the Greek tongue.

Thus everything points to the conclusion that the version

---

[1] Diog. Laert. v. 78. The statement rests on the authority of Hermippus Callimachus (*temp.* Ptolemy III.).

[2] Cf. Plutarch, *Apophthegm.* viii. Δημήτριος ὁ Φαληρεὺς Πτολεμαίῳ τῷ βασιλεῖ παρῄνει τὰ περὶ βασιλείας καὶ ἡγεμονίας βιβλία κτᾶσθαι καὶ ἀνα-γινώσκειν.

[3] Frankel, *Vorstudien,* p. 8 f.

arose out of the needs of the Alexandrian Jews. Whilst in Palestine the Aramaic-speaking Jews were content with the interpretation of the *Methurgeman*, at Alexandria the Hebrew lesson was gladly exchanged for a lesson read from a Greek translation, and the work of the interpreter was limited to exegesis[1]. In the closing paragraphs of the letter of Aristeas which describe the joy with which the work of the LXXII. was welcomed by the Greek-speaking Jews of Alexandria, the writer unconsciously reveals the true history of the version, when he represents the Jews as having heard and welcomed the Greek Pentateuch before it was presented to the King[2]. But it is not improbable that the King encouraged the work of translation with the view of promoting the use of the Greek language by the settlers[3] as well as for the purpose of gratifying his own curiosity.

14. The Greek of the Alexandrian Pentateuch is Egyptian, and, as far as we can judge, not such as Palestinian translators would have written. Instances are not indeed wanting of translations executed in Egypt by Palestinians; the most noteworthy[4] is the Wisdom of the Son of Sirach, which, as the prologue tells us, was turned into Greek by the grandson of the writer after a prolonged visit to the banks of the Nile (παραγενηθεὶς εἰς Αἴγυπτον καὶ συγχρονίσας); but the clumsy Greek of the prologue, and the stiff artificiality of the book, offer a

---

[1] Cf. Philo *ap.* Eus. *praep. ev.* viii. 7 τῶν ἱερέων δέ τις παρών, ἢ τῶν γερόντων εἷς, ἀναγινώσκει τοὺς ἱεροὺς νόμους αὐτοῖς καὶ καθ᾽ ἕκαστον ἐξηγεῖται. But ἐξηγεῖται is ambiguous.

[2] The hope of winning converts may have been among the motives which inspired the translators and gained a ready welcome for their work ; cf. the prol. to Sirach: οὐ μόνον αὐτοὺς τοὺς ἀναγινώσκοντας δέον ἐστὶν ἐπιστήμονας γίνεσθαι, ἀλλὰ καὶ τοῖς ἐκτὸς δύνασθαι τοὺς φιλομαθοῦντας χρησίμους εἶναι καὶ λέγοντας καὶ γράφοντας—where however the influence of the Jewish Scriptures on pagans is regarded as indirect, and not immediate.

[3] Cf. Mommsen, *Provinces*, ii. p. 164.

[4] Another example is offered by the Greek Esther, if the note at the end of the book is to be trusted (ἔφασαν...ἑρμηνευκέναι Λυσίμαχον Πτολεμαίου τῶν ἐν Ἰερουσαλήμ).

marked contrast to the simple style of the Pentateuch. That
the latter is mainly the work of Alexandrian Jews appears from
more than one consideration. An older generation of Biblical
scholars pointed to the occurrence in the LXX., and especially in
the Pentateuch, of such words of Egyptian origin as ἄχει (Gen.
xli. 2 ff.), κόνδυ (Gen. xliv. 2 ff.), ἶβις (Lev. xi. 17 ; Deut. xiv. 16),
βύσσος (Exod. xxv.—xxxix. *passim*) and such characteristically
Egyptian terms as δίδραχμον, ἀλήθεια (= םימֻּתּ), ἀρχιμάγειρος,
ἀρχιοινοχόος and the like. The argument is not conclusive,
since after the time of Alexander the κοινή contained elements
drawn from various localities[1]. But recent discoveries in Egypt
have yielded a criterion of Egyptian Greek which has been
applied to the LXX. with definite results. In 1892 Prof. Mahaffy
was able to write : "in the vocabulary of the papyri we find a
closer likeness to the Greek of the LXX. than to any other book
I could name[2]." This statement has been abundantly justified
by the publication of Deissmann's *Bibelstudien* (Marburg, 1895),
and *Neue Bibelstudien* (1897), where a number of the peculiar
or characteristic words and forms of the LXX. are shewn to
have been in common use among Egyptian Greeks of the third
and second centuries B.C.[3] The vocabulary and style of the LXX.
will be treated in a later chapter ; for the present it is enough
to say that they are such as to discredit the attribution of the
Greek Pentateuch to a company consisting exclusively or chiefly
of Palestinian Jews. The LXX. as a whole, or at any rate
the earlier part of the collection, is a monument of Alexandrian
Greek as it was spoken by the Jewish colony in the Delta
under the rule of the Ptolemies[4].

[1] See Hody, ii. 4; Eichhorn, p. 472; H. A. A. Kennedy, *Sources of
N. T. Greek*, p. 24 f. ; on the other hand, cf. Frankel, *Vorstudien*, p. 40 ff.

[2] *Exp. Times*, iii. p. 291 ; cf. Mahaffy, *Greek life*, p. 198 f.

[3] Evidence of this kind will doubtless accumulate as new volumes of
papyri are issued. The verbal indices which usually accompany such
collections offer a rich field for the Biblical student who will be at the
pains to explore them.

[4] See however Buhl, p. 124.

The story of the rolls being written in letters of gold and sent to the King by the High Priest may be dismissed at once; it belongs to the picturesque setting of the romance. But there is nothing improbable in the statement that the Hebrew rolls were freshly brought from Jerusalem[1], for communication between Jerusalem and Alexandria was frequent during the reigns of the earlier Ptolemies. Yet the legend may be intended to represent the loyalty of the colony towards the μητρόπολις, and the conviction of the Alexandrian Jews that in their Greek version they possessed the same sacred texts which their brethren in Judaea read in Hebrew. Nothing was further from their intention than to create an Alexandrian canon, or an Alexandrian type of text. The point is one which it is important to remember.

The welcome accorded to the Greek version by the Jews of Alexandria was doubtless, as Aristeas represents, both cordial and permanent; nor need we doubt that Philadelphus and his scholars approved what had been done. Insignificant and even intolerable as a literary work, the version promised to supply the Greek scholars of Alexandria with a trustworthy account of Hebrew origins. There is however little or no trace of the use of the LXX. by pagan writers[2]; the style was probably enough to deter them from studying it, and the Hellenistic Jews of a somewhat later date rendered the task unnecessary by presenting the history of their country in more attractive forms. As to the preservation of the original in the Alexandrian libraries, we have no evidence beyond Tertullian's scarcely trustworthy statement, "Hodie apud Serapeum Ptolemaei bibliothecae cum ipsis Hebraicis litteris exhibentur[3]."

---

[1] According to Epiphanius (*de mens. et pond.* 10 f.) the rolls only were sent in the first instance, and the interpreters followed in consequence of a second application from Philadelphus. This form of the story suggests that the desire for a translation may have been stimulated by the arrival of MSS. from Jerusalem.

[2] See, however, Mahaffy, *Hist. of Gk. class. literature*, 1. ii. p. 195.

[3] *Apol.* 18; cf. Justin, *apol.* i. 31, Chrys. *or.* 1 *adv. Jud.*, and Epiph.

15. It has been stated (p. 11) that the letter of Aristeas does not profess to describe the origin of any part of the Alexandrian Bible except the Pentateuch[1]. This was evident to Josephus : *ant.* i. *prooem.* 3 οὐδὲ γὰρ πᾶσαν ἐκεῖνος (sc. Πτολεμαῖος ὁ δεύτερος) ἔφθη λαβεῖν τὴν ἀναγραφήν, ἀλλὰ μόνα τὰ τοῦ νόμου παρέδοσαν οἱ πεμφθέντες ἐπὶ τὴν ἐξήγησιν εἰς Ἀλεξάνδρειαν. Christian writers, however, failed to notice this limitation; the whole Greek Bible was familiarly known as the version of the LXX., and no misgivings were felt upon the matter except by Jerome, whose intercourse with the Rabbis had opened his eyes on this and other matters about which the Jews were better informed : "tota schola Judaeorum (he writes) quinque tantum libros Moysis a LXX. translatos asserunt[2]." Epiphanius goes so far as to apportion the books of the Hebrew canon among thirty-six pairs of translators[3]. Nevertheless the Jews were unquestionably right; Aristeas has nothing to say about the translation of any books beyond the first five.   His silence as to the Prophets and the Hagiographa is entirely consistent with the conditions of the period in which he fixes his story.   The canon of the Prophets seems to have scarcely reached completion before the High-Priesthood of Simon II. (219—199 B.C.)[4]. If this was so in Palestine, at Alexandria certainly there would be no recognised body of Prophetic writings in the reign of the second Ptolemy.   The Torah alone was ready for translation, for it was complete, and its position as a collection of sacred books was absolutely secure.

16.   But when the example had once been set of rendering sacred books into Greek, it would assuredly be followed as often as fresh rolls arrived from Jerusalem which bore the stamp

de mens. et pond. § 11.   The library in the Brucheion perished in the time of Julius Caesar ; that of the Serapeion is said to have been destroyed by Omar, A.D. 640.

[1] See, e.g., §§ 3, 10, 46, 171, 176.
[2] *In Ezech.* v.; cf. *in Gen.* xxxi., *in Mich.* ii.   See the Talmudical passages cited by Hody, p. 296.   [3] *de mens. et pond.* 3 sq.
[4] Ryle, *Canon of the O. T.*, p. 113.   Cf. Buhl, p. 12.

of Palestinian recognition, if a bilingual Jew was found ready
to undertake the task. A happy accident enables us to estimate
roughly the extent to which this process had gone by the sixth
or seventh decade of the second century. The writer of the
prologue to Sirach, who arrived in Egypt in the 38th year of
Euergetes—i.e. in the year 132 B.C. if, as is probable, the
Euergetes intended was the second of that name—incidentally
uses words which imply that "the Law, the Prophets, and the
rest of the books" were already current in a translation (οὐ
γὰρ ἰσοδυναμεῖ αὐτὰ ἐν ἑαυτοῖς Ἑβραϊστὶ λεγόμενα, καὶ ὅταν
μεταχθῇ εἰς ἑτέραν γλῶσσαν· οὐ μόνον δὲ ταῦτα, ἀλλὰ καὶ αὐτὸς
ὁ νόμος καὶ αἱ προφητεῖαι καὶ τὰ λοιπὰ τῶν βιβλίων οὐ μικρὰν
τὴν διαφορὰν ἔχει ἐν ἑαυτοῖς λεγόμενα). This sentence reveals
the progress which had been made in the work of translation
between the second Ptolemy and the ninth. Under Euergetes II.
the Alexandrian Jews possessed, in addition to the original
Greek Pentateuch, a collection of prophetic books, and a
number of other writings belonging to their national literature[1]
which had not as yet formed themselves into a complete
group. The latter are doubtless the books which are known as
כְּתוּבִים or Hagiographa. Since the author of the prologue was
a Palestinian Jew, we may perhaps assume that under αἱ
προφητεῖαι and τὰ λοιπὰ τῶν βιβλίων he includes such books of
both classes as were already in circulation in Palestine. If this
inference is a safe one, it will follow that all the 'Prophets' of
the Hebrew canon, 'former' and 'latter,' had been translated
before B.C. 132.

With regard to the Hagiographa, in some cases we have
data which lead to a more definite conclusion. Eupolemus,
who, if identical with the person of that name mentioned in
1 Macc. viii. 17, wrote about the middle of the second century,
makes use of the Greek Chronicles, as Freudenthal has

---

[1] Cf. *prol. supra*: τοῦ νόμου καὶ τῶν προφητῶν καὶ τῶν ἄλλων πατρίων
βιβλίων.

clearly shewn[1]. Ezra-Nehemiah, originally continuous with Chronicles, was probably translated at the same time as that book. Aristeas (not the pseudonymous author of the letter, but the writer of a treatise περὶ Ἰουδαίων) quotes the book of Job according to the LXX., and has been suspected[2] of being the author of the remarkable codicil attached to it (Job xlii. 17 *b—e*). The footnote to the Greek Esther, which states that that book was brought to Egypt in the 4th year of "Ptolemy and Cleopatra" (probably i.e. of Ptolemy Philometor), may have been written with the purpose of giving Palestinian sanction to the Greek version of that book ; but it vouches for the fact that the version was in circulation before the end of the second century B.C.[2] The Psalter of the LXX. appears to be quoted in 1 Macc. vii. 17 (Ps. lxxviii. = lxxix. 2), and the Greek version of 1 Maccabees probably belongs to the first century B.C. At what time the Greek Psalter assumed its present form there is no evidence to shew, but it is reasonable to suppose that the great Palestinian collections of sacred song did not long remain unknown to the Alexandrian Jews[3] ; and even on the hypothesis of certain Psalms being Maccabean, the later books of the Greek Psalter may be assigned to the second half of the second century.

17. On the whole, though the direct evidence is fragmentary, it is probable that before the Christian era Alexandria possessed the whole, or nearly the whole, of the Hebrew Scriptures in a Greek translation. For the first century A.D. we have the very important evidence of Philo, who uses the LXX. and quotes largely from many of the books. There are indeed some books of the Hebrew canon to which he does not seem to refer, i.e. Ruth, Ecclesiastes, Canticles, Esther, Lamentations, Ezekiel, Daniel[4]. But, as Professor Ryle points out,

---

[1] Pp. 108, 119; cf. p. 185.   [2] *Ib.* p. 138 f.
[3] Cf. Cheyne, *Origin of the Psalter*, pp. 12, 83.
[4] Ryle, *Philo and Holy Scripture*, p. xxxi. f.

"it may be safely assumed that Ruth and Lamentations were, in Philo's time, already united to Judges and Jeremiah in the Greek Scriptures"; and Ezekiel, as one of the greater Prophets, had assuredly found its way to Alexandria before A.D. I. Ecclesiastes, Canticles, Esther, Daniel, which "seem to have been among the latest books to be received into the Sacred Canon[1]," may have been purposely neglected by Philo, as not possessing canonical authority.   But it would be precarious to conclude that they had not been as yet translated into Greek; the Book of Esther, as we have seen, was probably current at Alexandria during the second century B.C.   Two other Jewish, but not Alexandrian, authorities assist us to ascertain the contents of the Greek Bible in the first century A.D.   (*a*) The New Testament shews a knowledge of the LXX. version in most of the books which it quotes, and it quotes all the books of the Old Testament except Ezra, Nehemiah, Esther, Ecclesiastes, the Song of Solomon, and certain of the Minor Prophets[2].   As in the case of Philo, it is possible, though scarcely probable, that Esther, Ecclesiastes and the Song were passed by as not having received the stamp of canonicity; but the silence of the Apostolic writers about them does not in any case prove that Greek translations of these books were not yet in circulation among Palestinian Jews.   (*b*) Josephus, who knew and used the LXX., unfortunately has no explicit statement as to the extent of the Greek version; but his list of the Hebrew books is practically identical with our own, and, as it occurs in a treatise intended for Gentile readers, it is perhaps safe to assume that he speaks of books accessible in a translation; "in other words, that he writes with the LXX. version before him[3]."

Thus while the testimony of the first century A.D. does not absolutely require us to believe that all the books of the

[1] Ryle, *Philo and Holy Scripture*, p. xxxiii.
[2] Ryle, *Canon*, p. 151.   [3] *Ib.* p. 163.

Hebrew canon had been translated and were circulated in a Greek version during the Apostolic age, such a view is not improbable; and it is confirmed by the fact that they are all contained in the canon of the Greek Bible which the Christian Church received from its Jewish predecessors. It is another question whether the versions were all of Alexandrian origin, or the only Greek translations which claimed to represent the corresponding Hebrew books. In a few cases there were certainly rival interpretations or recensions of the same book (e.g. in Judges, Daniel, Tobit). But as a whole the work of translation was doubtless carried out at Alexandria, where it was begun; and the Greek Bible of the Hellenistic Jews and the Catholic Church may rightly be styled the Alexandrian Greek version of the Old Testament.

LITERATURE. The following list embraces a mere fraction of the vast literature of the Alexandrian Version. The selection has been made with the purpose of representing the progress of knowledge since the middle of the seventeenth century.

L. Cappellus, *critica sacra*, 1651; J. Pearson, *praefatio paraenetica*, 1655; Ussher, *Syntagma*, 1655; Walton, *prolegomena*, 1657; Hottinger, *disertationum fasciculus*, 1660; I. Voss, *de LXX. interpretibus*, 1661—1663; J. Morinus, *Exercitationes*, 1669; R. Simon, *histoire critique du Vieux Testament*[2], 1685; H. Hody, *de Bibl. textibus originalibus*, 1705; H. Owen, *Enquiry into the text of the LXX.*, 1769; *Brief account of the LXX.*, 1787; Stroth, in Eichhorn's *Repertorium*, v. ff., 1779 ff.; White, *Letter to the Bp of London*, 1779; Fabricius-Harles, iii. 658 ff., 1793; R. Holmes, *Episcopo Dunelm. epistola*, 1795; *praefatio ad Pentateuchum*, 1798; Schleusner, *opuscula critica*, 1812; Töpler, *de Pentateuchi interpretat. Alex. indole*, 1830; Dähne, *jüd.-alexandr. Philosophie*, 1834; Grinfield, *Apology for the LXX.*, 1850; Frankel, *Vorstudien zu der LXX.*, 1841; *über den Einfluss d. paläst. Exegese auf die alexandr. Hermeneutik*, 1851; do., *über paläst. u. alexandr. Schriftforschung*, 1854; Thiersch, *de Pentateuchi vers. Alexandr.*, 1841; Constantinus Oeconomus, περὶ τῶν ο' ἑρμηνευτῶν, 1849; Churton, *The Influence of the LXX. upon the progress of Christianity*, 1861; Ewald, *Gesch. des Volkes Israel*[3], 1868; E. Nestle, *Septuaginta-Studien*, i. 1886, ii. 1896, iii. 1899, iv. 1903, v. 1907; S. R. Driver, *Notes on Samuel* (*Introd.* § 3f.), 1890; P. de Lagarde, *Septuaginta-Studien*,

i. 1891, ii. 1892; A. Rahlfs, *Septuaginta-Studien*, i. 1904, ii. 1907, iii. 1911; Buhl, *Kanon u. Text der A. T.*, 1891; A. Loisy, *histoire critique du texte et des versions de la Bible*, 1892; Hatch, *Essays on Biblical Greek*, 1892; W. Robertson Smith, *O. T. in the Jewish Church*[2], 1892; E. Klostermann, *Analecta zur LXX^{ta}*, 1895; Nestle, *Urtext u. Übersetzungen der Bibel*, 1897. Monographs on special books or particular aspects of the subject will be enumerated elsewhere.

The student should also consult the best Introductions to the O.T., especially those of Eichhorn (1777 ff.), De Wette-Schrader (1869), Bleek-Wellhausen[6] (1893), König (1893); and the Encyclopedias and Bible Dictionaries, especially the articles on the Septuagint in Smith's *D. B.* iii. (Selwyn), the *Encyclopædia Britannica*[2] (Wellhausen), the *Real-Encykl. f. prot. Theologie u. Kirche*[3] (Nestle; also published in a separate form, under the title *Urtext u. Übersetzungen, &c.*), and Nestle's art. *Septuagint* in Hastings' *D.B.* iv.; the arts. *Septuaginta* (Hoberg) in Wetzer-Welte's Encyklopaedie[2] xi. (1899), 147—159, and *Text and Versions* (Burkitt) in Cheyne and Black's *Encyclop. Biblica*.

CHAPTER II.

LATER GREEK VERSIONS.

1. AT Alexandria and in Egypt generally the Alexandrian version was regarded, as Philo plainly says, with a reverence scarcely less than that which belonged to the original. It was the Bible of the Egyptian Jews, even of those who belonged to the educated and literary class. This feeling was shared by the rest of the Hellenistic world. In Palestine indeed the version seems to have been received with less enthusiasm, and whether it was used in the synagogues is still uncertain. But elsewhere its acceptance by Greek-speaking Jews was universal during the Apostolic age and in the next generation.

On the question of the use of the LXX. in the synagogues see Hody iii. 1. 1, Frankel, *Vorstudien*, p. 56 ff., König, *Einleitung*, p. 105 ff.; the negative is stoutly maintained by J. Lightfoot, *hor. Hebr.* (add. to 1 Cor. xiv.). If the Ep. to the Hebrews was addressed to the Church of Jerusalem, the preponderating use of the LXX. in its quotations from the O.T. is strong evidence, so far as it goes, for the acceptance of the LXX. by Palestinian Hellenists. Its use by St Paul vouches for the practice of the Hellenists of Asia Minor and Europe; no rival version had gained circulation at Antioch, Ephesus, or Rome. In the next century we have the evidence of Justin (*apol.* i. 31 ἔμειναν αἱ βίβλοι [the translated books] καὶ παρ' Αἰγυπτίοις μέχρι τοῦ δεῦρο καὶ πανταχοῦ παρὰ πᾶσίν εἰσιν Ἰουδαίοις: *dial.* 72 αὕτη ἡ περικοπὴ ἡ ἐκ τῶν λόγων τοῦ Ἰερεμίου ἔτι ἐστὶν ἐγγεγραμμένη ἔν τισιν ἀντιγράφοις τῶν ἐν συναγωγαῖς Ἰουδαίων), Tertullian (*apol.* 18 "Judaei palam lectitant"), Pseudo-Justin (*cohort. ad Gr.* 13 τὸ δὲ παρ' Ἰουδαίοις ἔτι καὶ νῦν τὰς τῇ ἡμετέρᾳ θεοσεβείᾳ

διαφερούσας σώζεσθαι βίβλους, θείας προνοίας ἔργον ὑπὲρ ἡμῶν
γέγονεν...ἀπὸ τῆς τῶν Ἰουδαίων συναγωγῆς ταύτας ἀξιοῦμεν προκο-
μίζεσθαι).

2. When the LXX. passed into the hands of the Church
and was used in controversy with Jewish antagonists, the Jews
not unnaturally began to doubt the accuracy of the Alexandrian
version (Justin, *dial.* 68 τολμῶσι λέγειν τὴν ἐξήγησιν ἣν ἐξηγήσαντο οἱ ἑβδομήκοντα ὑμῶν πρεσβύτεροι παρὰ Πτολεμαίῳ τῷ τῶν
Αἰγυπτίων βασιλεῖ γενόμενοι μὴ εἶναι ἔν τισιν ἀληθῆ). The
crucial instance was the rendering of עַלְמָה by παρθένος in Isa.
vii. 14, where νεᾶνις, it was contended, would have given the
true meaning of the Hebrew word (*ib.* 71, 84; Iren. iii. 21. 1).
But the dissatisfaction with which the LXX. was regarded by
the Jewish leaders of the second century was perhaps not
altogether due to polemical causes. The LXX. "did not suit
the newer school of [Jewish] interpretation, it did not correspond
with the received text[1]." An official text differing considerably from the text accepted in earlier times had received
the approval of the Rabbis, and the Alexandrian version,
which represented the older text, began to be suspected
and to pass into disuse. Attempts were made to provide
something better for Greek-speaking Israelites (Justin, *dial.* 71
αὐτοὶ ἐξηγεῖσθαι πειρῶνται). Of two such fresh translations
Irenaeus speaks in terms of reprehension (*l. c.* οὐχ ὡς ἔνιοί φασιν
τῶν νῦν μεθερμηνεύειν τολμώντων τὴν γραφήν...ὡς Θεοδοτίων...ὁ
Ἐφέσιος καὶ Ἀκύλας ὁ Ποντικός, ἀμφότεροι Ἰουδαῖοι προσήλυτοι).
Origen, who realised the importance of these translations, was
able to add to those of Aquila and Theodotion the version of
Symmachus and three others which were anonymous[2]. Of the
anonymous versions little remains, but Aquila, Theodotion, and
Symmachus are represented by numerous and in some cases
important fragments.

[1] Robertson Smith, *The O. T. in the J. Ch.*, p. 64; cf. *ib.* p. 87 f.;
Kirkpatrick, *Divine Library*, p. 63 ff.; cf. Buhl, p. 118 f.
[2] Eus. *H. E.* vi. 16.

3. AQUILA. The name had been borne in the Apostolic age by a native of Pontus who was of Jewish birth (Acts xviii. 2 Ἰουδαῖον ὀνόματι Ἀκύλαν, Ποντικὸν τῷ γένει). Aquila the translator was also of Pontus, from the famous sea-port[1] Sinope, which had been constituted by Julius Caesar a Roman colony; but he was of Gentile origin. He lived in the reign of Hadrian (A.D. 117—138), and was a connexion of the Emperor (πενθερίδης, Epiph., *Dial. of Timothy and Aquila;* πενθερός, Ps.-Ath., *Chron. Pasch.*). Hadrian employed his relative to superintend the building of Aelia Capitolina on the site of Jerusalem, and while there Aquila was converted to Christianity by Christians who had returned from Pella. Refusing, however, to abandon the pagan practice of astrology, he was excommunicated; upon which he shewed his resentment by submitting to circumcision and attaching himself to the teaching of the Jewish Rabbis. The purpose of his translation was to set aside the interpretation of the LXX., in so far as it appeared to support the views of the Christian Church.

This is the story of Epiphanius (*de mens. et pond.* 14 sq. : λαβὼν [sc. ὁ Ἀδριανὸς] τὸν Ἀκύλαν τοῦτον...Ἕλληνα ὄντα καὶ αὐτοῦ πενθερίδην, ἀπὸ Σινώπης δὲ τῆς Πόντου ὁρμώμενον, καθίστησιν αὐτὸν ἐκεῖσε ἐπιστατεῖν τοῖς ἔργοις κτλ....πικρανθεὶς δὲ...προσηλυτεύει καὶ περιτέμνεται Ἰουδαῖος· καὶ ἐπιπόνως φιλοτιμησάμενος ἐξέδωκεν ἑαυτὸν μαθεῖν τὴν Ἑβραίων διάλεκτον καὶ τὰ αὐτῶν στοιχεῖα. ταύτην δὲ ἀκρότατα παιδευθεὶς ἡρμήνευσεν οὐκ ὀρθῷ λογισμῷ χρησάμενος, ἀλλ᾽ ὅπως διαστρέψῃ τινὰ τῶν ῥητῶν, ἐνσκήψας τῇ τῶν οβ᾽ ἑρμηνείᾳ ἵνα τὰ περὶ Χριστοῦ ἐν ταῖς γραφαῖς μεμαρτυρημένα ἄλλως ἐκδώσει). The same tale is told in substance by the Pseudo-Athanasian author of *Synopsis script. sacr.*, c. 77, and in the *Dialogue between Timothy and Aquila* printed in *Anecdota Oxon.*, class. ser. pt viii. According to the writer of the *Dialogue* Aquila learned Hebrew in his 40th year, and there are other features peculiar to this form of the story which have led the editor, Mr F. C. Conybeare, to conjecture that it is independent of the Epiphanian narrative, though derived from the same source,

---

[1] Ramsay, *Hist. Geogr. of Asia Minor*, p. 27 f. ; cf. Hort, *Commentary on* 1 *Peter*, p. 172 ff.

which he believes to have been ultimately the history of Ariston of Pella (*op. cit.* p. xxvi. ff.). An Aquila figures in the Clementine romance (*hom.* ii. sqq., *recogn.* ii. sqq.) ; the name and character were perhaps suggested by some floating memories of the translator. Cf. Lagarde, *Clementina*, p. 12 f.

That Aquila was a proselyte to Judaism is attested by the Jewish tradition (Jer. Talm. *Meg.* 1. 11, *Kiddush.* 1. 1), in which he appears as הַגֵּר, ὁ προσήλυτος[1]. After his conversion to Judaism, Aquila became a pupil of R. Eliezer and R. Joshua (*Meg.* f. 71 *c*) or, according to another authority, of R. Akiba (*Kiddush.* f. 59 *a*). The latter statement seems to have been current among the Jews of Palestine in Jerome's time (Hieron. *in Isa.* viii. 14 "scribae et Pharisaei quorum suscepit scholam Akybas, quem magistrum Aquilae proselyti autumant"), and it derives some confirmation from the character of the version.

According to Epiphanius the *floruit* of Aquila is to be placed in the 12th year of Hadrian (Epiph. *de mens. et pond.* 13 Ἀδριανὸς ἔτη κα΄, οὗτινος τῷ δωδεκάτῳ ἔτει Ἀκύλας ἐγνωρίζετο...ὡς εἶναι ἀπὸ τοῦ χρόνου τῆς ἑρμηνείας τῶν οβ΄ ἑρμηνευτῶν ἕως Ἀκύλα τοῦ ἑρμηνευτοῦ, ἤγουν ἕως δωδεκάτου ἔτους Ἀδριανοῦ, ἔτη υλ΄ καὶ μῆνας δ΄. The 12th year of Hadrian was A.D. 128—9, the year in which the Emperor began to rebuild Aelia. This date is doubtless approximately correct, if Aquila was a pupil of R. Akiba, who taught from A.D. 95 to A.D. 135[2], or even of R. Eliezer and R. Joshua, who immediately preceded Akiba. It must have taken the Greek proselyte many years to acquire an adequate knowledge of Hebrew and of the Rabbinical methods of interpretation, and under these circumstances his great work could hardly have been completed before the fourth decade of the second century. When Irenaeus wrote his third book, in

---

[1] The name is written עֲקִילָס, אֲקִילָס, קִילָס, or עֲקִ־עָלַם, and in the Bab. Talmud, אֻנְקְלוֹס. On the identity of Aquila with Onkelos see Anger *de Onkelo Chaldaico* (before 1845), Friedmann *Onkelos u. Akylas* (Wien, 1896); or the brief statement in Buhl, p. 173.

[2] Field, *Hexapla*, prolegg. p. xviii.

the ninth decade, Aquila's translation might still be regarded as comparatively recent (τῶν νῦν μεθερμηνεύειν τολμώντων τὴν γραφήν...ὡς...Ἀκύλας).

4. It was natural that the version of Aquila should be received with acclamation by his co-religionists. His teachers congratulated him in the words of Ps. xlv. 3, יָפְיָפִ֫יתָ מִבְּנֵי אָדָם. The Talmud quotes or refers to his translation of not a few passages (Gen. xvii. 1; Lev. xix. 20, 23, 40; Esth. i. 6; Prov. xviii. 21, xxv. 11; Isa. iii. 20; Ezek. xvi. 10, xxiii. 43; Dan. v. 5, viii. 13). In Origen's time he was trusted implicitly in Jewish circles, and used by all Jews who did not understand Hebrew (*ep. ad African.* 2 φιλοτιμότερον πεπιστευμένος παρὰ Ἰουδαίοις...ᾧ μάλιστα εἰώθασιν οἱ ἀγνοοῦντες τὴν Ἑβραίων διά-λεκτον χρῆσθαι, ὡς πάντων μᾶλλον ἐπιτετευγμένῳ); and the same preference for Aquila seems to have been characteristic of the Jews in the fourth and fifth centuries (cf. Jerome on Ezek. iii. 5, and Augustine *de civ. Dei* xv. 23), and at a still later period, for even Justinian, when regulating the public reading of the Scriptures in the synagogues, thought it expedient to permit the use of Aquila (*novell.* 146: "at vero ii qui Graeca lingua legunt LXX. interpretum utentur translatione...verum...licentiam concedimus etiam Aquilae versione utendi"). It was equally natural that the proselyte's version should be regarded with distrust by Christians, who saw in it the work of a champion of Rabbinism as well as a bold attempt to displace the Septuagint[2]. Yet the few Christian writers who were students of the Hebrew Bible learnt to recognise the fidelity of Aquila's work. He was 'a slave to the letter' (δουλεύων τῇ Ἑβραικῇ λέξει); whatever was wanting in the Hebrew text was not to be

---

[1] *Megilla* 1. 9: in יפיפית there is a play upon יפת (cf. Gen. ix. 27).

[2] See Dr C. Taylor in the preface to Prof. Burkitt's *Fragments of Aquila*, p. vi.: "Aquila in a sense was not the sole or independent author of the version, its uncompromising literalism being the necessary outcome of his Jewish teachers' system of exegesis."

found in Aquila (οὐ κεῖται παρὰ τοῖς Ἐβραίοις, διόπερ οὐδὲ παρὰ τῷ Ἀκύλᾳ). So Origen confesses[1]; and Jerome, though when in a censorious mood he does not spare the proselyte (e.g. *praef. in Job, ep. ad. Pammach.*), elsewhere admits his honesty and diligence (*ep. ad Damas.* 12 "non contentiosius, ut quidam putant, sed studiosius verbum interpretatur ad verbum"; *ep. ad Marcell.* "iamdudum cum voluminibus Hebraeorum editionem Aquilae confero, ne quid forsitan propter odium Christi synagoga mutaverit, et—ut amicae menti fatear—quae ad nostram fidem pertineant roborandam plura reperio"). After these testimonies from the two most competent witnesses in the ancient Church, we need not stop to consider the invective of Epiphanius[2].

5. Until the summer of 1897 Aquila's version was known to students only from the description of ancient writers, chiefly Christian, and the fragments of the Hexapla (c. iii.), which when complete contained the entire work. These sources were used with admirable skill by Dr Field (*prolegomena in Hexapla*, p. xix. ff.) and Dr C. Taylor (*D. C. B.* art. *Hexapla*) to illustrate the purpose and style of Aquila's work. But an unexpected discovery has since placed at our disposal several larger fragments of the version, emanating from a Jewish source. Among the *débris* of the Genizah of the Cairo synagogue brought to Cambridge in 1897 through the efforts of Dr Taylor and Dr Schechter, Professor Burkitt was so fortunate as to discover some palimpsest scraps which under later Hebrew writing contain in a good uncial hand of the sixth century Aquila's translation of 1 Kings xx. 9—17 and 2 Kings xxiii. 12—27[3]. From the same treasure Dr Taylor recovered portions of Pss. xc.—ciii., and a Hexaplar fragment of Ps. xxii.[4]

---

[1] *Ep. ad Afric.* 3. Cf. Aug. *l.c.*   [2] See p. 31.
[3] *Fragments of the Books of Kings according to the translation of Aquila* (Cambridge, 1897).
[4] *Hebrew-Greek Cairo Genizah Palimpsests* (Camb. 1900). See also *Amherst Papyri*, i. p. 30 f. (London, 1900).

The student will find below specimens of these discoveries, placed for the purpose of comparison in parallel columns with the version of the LXX.

3 Regn. xxi. (1 Kings xx.) 10—13.

LXX. (Cod. B¹).   AQUILA.

¹⁰καὶ ἀπέστειλεν πρὸς αὐτὸν υἱὸς Ἀδὲρ λέγων Τάδε ποιήσαι μοι ὁ θεὸς καὶ τάδε προσθείη, εἰ ἐκποιήσει ὁ χοῦς Σαμαρείας ταῖς ἀλώπεξιν παντὶ τῷ λαῷ τοῖς πεζοῖς μου. ¹¹καὶ ἀπεκρίθη βασιλεὺς Ἰσραὴλ καὶ εἶπεν Ἱκανούσθω· μὴ καυχάσθω ὁ κυρτὸς ὡς ὁ ὀρθός. ¹²καὶ ἐγένετο ὅτε ἀπεκρίθη αὐτῷ τὸν λόγον τοῦτον, πίνων ἦν αὐτὸς καὶ πάντες βασιλεῖς μετ᾽ αὐτοῦ ἐν σκηναῖς· καὶ εἶπεν τοῖς παισὶν αὐτοῦ Οἰκοδομήσατε χάρακα· καὶ ἔθεντο χάρακα ἐπὶ τὴν πόλιν. ¹³καὶ ἰδοὺ προφήτης εἷς προσῆλθεν τῷ βασιλεῖ Ἰσραὴλ καὶ εἶπεν Τάδε λέγει Κύριος Εἰ ἑόρακας τὸν ὄχλον τὸν μέγαν τοῦτον; ἰδοὺ ἐγὼ δίδωμι αὐτὸν σήμερον εἰς χεῖρας σάς, καὶ γνώσῃ ὅτι ἐγὼ Κύριος.

¹⁰καὶ ἀπέστειλεν πρὸς αὐτὸν υἱὸς Ἀδὰδ καὶ εἶπεν Τάδε ποιήσαισάν μοι θεοὶ καὶ τάδε προσθείησαν, εἰ ἐξαρκέσει χοῦς Σαμαρίας τοῖς λιχάσιν² τοῦ παντὸς τοῦ λαοῦ ὃς ἐν ποσίν μου. ¹¹καὶ ἀπεκρίθη βασιλεὺς Ἰσραὴλ καὶ εἶπεν Λαλήσατε Μὴ καυχάσθω ζωννύμενος ὡς ὁ περιλυόμενος. ¹²καὶ ἐγένετο ὡς ἤκουσεν σὺν τὸ ῥῆμα τοῦτο, καὶ αὐτὸς ἔπιννεν αὐτὸς καὶ οἱ βασιλεῖς ἐν συσκιασμοῖς· καὶ εἶπεν πρὸς δούλους αὐτοῦ Θέτε· καὶ ἔθηκαν ἐπὶ τὴν πόλιν. ¹³καὶ ἰδοὺ προφήτης εἷς προσήγγισεν πρὸς Ἀὰβ βασιλέα Ἰσραὴλ καὶ εἶπεν Τάδε λέγει ЭЭЭЭ Εἶδες σὺν πάντα τὸν ὄχλον τὸν μέγαν τοῦτον; ἰδοὺ ἐγὼ δίδωμι αὐτὸν εἰς χεῖρά σου σήμερον, καὶ γνώσῃ ὅτι ἐγὼ ЭЭЭЭ.

---

¹ Cod. A is nearer to Aquila, as the following variants shew: 10 ποιησαισαν μοι οι θεοι και ταδε προσθεισαν A   12 οτε] ως A | παντες οι β. A 13 τω βασ.] pr τω Αχααβ A | τον οχλον] pr παντα A | εις χ. σας σημερον A.

² MS. χε[ιλι]ας[ιν]; see Burkitt, *op. cit.* p. 2.

4 Regn. (2 Kings) xxiii. 21—24.

LXX. (Cod. B[1]).

²¹καὶ ἐνετείλατο ὁ βασιλεὺς παντὶ τῷ λαῷ λέγων Ποιήσατε πάσχα τῷ κυρίῳ θεῷ ἡμῶν, καθὼς γέγραπται ἐπὶ βιβλίου τῆς διαθήκης ταύτης. ²²ὅτι οὐκ ἐγενήθη τὸ πάσχα τοῦτο ἀφ᾽ ἡμερῶν τῶν κριτῶν οἳ ἔκρινον τὸν Ἰσραήλ, καὶ πάσας τὰς ἡμέρας βασιλέων Ἰσραὴλ καὶ βασιλέων Ἰούδα· ²³ὅτι ἀλλ᾽ ἢ τῷ ὀκτωκαιδεκάτῳ ἔτει τοῦ βασιλέως Ἰωσεία ἐγενήθη τὸ πάσχα τῷ κυρίῳ ἐν Ἰερουσαλήμ. ²⁴καί γε τοὺς θελητὰς καὶ τοὺς γνωριστὰς καὶ τὰ θεραφεὶν καὶ τὰ εἴδωλα καὶ πάντα τὰ προσοχθίσματα τὰ γεγονότα ἐν γῇ Ἰούδα καὶ ἐν Ἰερουσαλὴμ ἐξῆρεν Ἰωσείας, ἵνα στήσῃ τοὺς λόγους τοῦ νόμου τοὺς γεγραμμένους ἐπὶ τῷ βιβλίῳ οὗ εὗρεν Χελκείας ὁ ἱερεὺς ἐν οἴκῳ Κυρίου.

AQUILA.

²¹καὶ ἐνετείλατο ὁ βασιλεὺς σὺν παντὶ τῷ λαῷ τῷ λέγειν Ποιήσατε φέσα τῷ ﬡﬡﬡﬡ θεῷ ὑμῶν κατὰ τὸ γεγραμμένον ἐπὶ βιβλίου τῆς συνθήκης ταύτης. ²²ὅτι οὐκ ἐποιήθη κατὰ τὸ φέσα τοῦτο ἀπὸ ἡμερῶν τῶν κριτῶν οἳ ἔκριναν τὸν Ἰσραὴλ καὶ πασῶν ἡμερῶν βασιλέων Ἰσραὴλ καὶ βασιλέων Ἰούδα· ²³ὅτι ἀλλὰ ἐν ὀκτωκαιδεκάτῳ ἔτει τοῦ βασιλέως Ἰωσιαοῦ ἐποιήθη τὸ φέσα τοῦτο τῷ ﬡﬡﬡﬡ ἐν Ἰερουσαλήμ. ²⁴καὶ καί γε σὺν τοὺς μάγους καὶ σὺν τοὺς γνωριστὰς καὶ σὺν τὰ μορφώματα καὶ σὺν τὰ καθάρματα καὶ σὺν πάντα προσοχθίσματα ἃ ὡράθησαν ἐν γῇ Ἰούδα καὶ ἐν Ἰερουσαλὴμ ἐπέλεξεν Ἰωσιαοῦ, ὅπως ἀναστήσῃ τὰ ῥήματα τοῦ νόμου τὰ γεγραμμένα ἐπὶ τοῦ βιβλίου [οὗ εὗρεν] Ἑλκιαοῦ ὁ ἱερεὺς οἴκῳ Κυρίου[2].

[1] The following variants in Cod. A agree with Aquila: 22 πασων ημερων A   23 το πασχα]+τουτο A

[2] MS. κγ, at the end of a line: see Burkitt, p. 16.

Ps. xc. (xci.) 6*b*—13.

LXX. (Cod. B).	AQUILA.

ἀπὸ συμπτώματος καὶ δαι-
μονίου μεσημβρινοῦ.
⁷πεσεῖται ἐκ τοῦ κλίτους σου
χιλιάς,
καὶ μυριὰς ἐκ δεξιῶν σου,
πρὸς σὲ δὲ οὐκ ἐγγιεῖ·
⁸πλὴν τοῖς ὀφθαλμοῖς σου κατα-
νοήσεις,
καὶ ἀνταπόδοσιν ἁμαρτωλῶν
ὄψῃ.
⁹ὅτι σύ, Κύριε, ἡ ἐλπίς μου·
τὸν ὕψιστον ἔθου καταφυγήν
σου.
¹⁰οὐ προσελεύσεται πρὸς σὲ κακά,
καὶ μάστιξ οὐκ ἐγγιεῖ τῷ σκη-
νώματί σου·
¹¹ὅτι τοῖς ἀγγέλοις αὐτοῦ ἐντε-
λεῖται περὶ σοῦ,
τοῦ διαφυλάξαι σε ἐν ταῖς
ὁδοῖς¹ σου.
¹²ἐπὶ χειρῶν ἀροῦσίν σε,
μή ποτε προσκόψῃς πρὸς λίθον
τὸν πόδα σου·
¹³ἐπ' ἀσπίδα καὶ βασιλίσκον
ἐπιβήσῃ.

ἀπὸ δηγμοῦ δαιμ[ονίζοντος με-
σημβρίας].
⁷πεσεῖται ἀπὸ πλαγίου σ[ου
χιλιάς],
καὶ μυριὰς ἀπὸ δεξι[ῶν σου]·
πρὸς σὲ οὐ προσεγγ[ίσει]·
⁸ἐκτὸς ἐν ὀφθαλμοῖς [σου ἐπι-
βλέ]ψεις,
καὶ ἀπότισιν ἀσεβῶν ὄψῃ.

⁹ὅτι σύ, ꜰꝪꝪꜰ, ἐλπίς μου·
ὕψιστον ἔθηκας οἰκητήριόν
σου.
¹⁰οὐ μεταχθήσεται πρὸς σὲ κακία,
καὶ ἀφὴ οὐκ ἐγγίσει ἐν σκέπῃ
σου·
¹¹ὅτι ἀγγέλοις αὐτοῦ ἐντελεῖταί
σε,
τοῦ φυλάξαι σε ἐν πάσαις
ὁδοῖς σου·
¹²ἐπὶ ταρσῶν ἀροῦσίν σε,
μήποτε προσκόψῃ ἐν λίθῳ
[πούς σου]·
¹³ἐπὶ λέαινα[ν]² καὶ ἀσπίδα πατή-
σεις.

---

¹ 11 ταις οδοις] pr πασαις A(R)T   ² MS. λεενα.

Ps. xci. (xcii.) 5—10.

LXX (Cod. B¹).	AQUILA.

LXX (Cod. B¹).

⁵ὅτι εὔφρανάς με, Κύριε, ἐν τῷ
  ποιήματί σου,
καὶ ἐν τοῖς ἔργοις τῶν χειρῶν
  σου ἀγαλλιάσομαι.
⁶ὡς ἐμεγαλύνθη τὰ ἔργα σου,
  Κύριε,
σφόδρα ἐβαρύνθησαν οἱ δια-
  λογισμοί σου.
⁷ἀνὴρ ἄφρων οὐ γνώσεται,
καὶ ἀσύνετος οὐ συνήσει ταῦτα.

⁸ἐν τῷ ἀνατεῖλαι τοὺς ἁμαρτωλοὺς
  ὡς χόρτον
καὶ διέκυψαν πάντες οἱ ἐργαζόμενοι τὴν ἀνομίαν,
ὅπως ἂν ἐξολεθρευθῶσιν εἰς
  τὸν αἰῶνα τοῦ αἰῶνος.
⁹σὺ δὲ Ὕψιστος εἰς τὸν αἰῶνα,
  Κύριε.
¹⁰ὅτι ἰδοὺ οἱ ἐχθροί σου ἀπο-
  λοῦνται,
καὶ διασκορπισθήσονται πάντες οἱ ἐργαζόμενοι τὴν
  ἀνομίαν.

AQUILA.

⁵[ὅτι ηὔφρανάς με, ᚱᚱ]ᚱᚱ, ἐν
  κατέργῳ σου,
[ἐν ποιήμασι] χειρῶν σου
  αἰνέσω.
⁶[ὡς ἐμεγαλύνθη] ποιήματά σου,
  ᚱᚱᚱᚱ,
σφόδρα [ἐβαθύνθ]ησαν λογισμοί σου.
⁷[ἀνὴρ] ἀσύνετος οὐ γνώσεται,
καὶ ἀνόητος οὐ συνήσει σὺι
  ταύτην.
⁸ἐν τῷ βλαστῆσαι ἀσεβεῖς ὁμοίως
  χλόῃ
καὶ ἤνθησαν πάντες κατεργαζόμενοι ἀνωφελές,
ἐκτριβῆναι αὐτοὺς ἕως ἔτι·

⁹καὶ σὺ Ὕψιστος εἰς αἰῶνα,
  ᚱᚱᚱᚱ.
¹⁰ἰδοὺ οἱ ἐχθροί σου, ᚱᚱᚱᚱ, ἰδοὺ
  οἱ ἐχθροί σου ἀπολοῦν-
  ται,
[σκορπι]σθήσονται πάντες κατ-
  εργαζό[μενοι ἀνωφελές].

6. If the student examines these specimens of Aquila's work and compares them with the Hebrew and LXX., the greater literalness of the later version and several of its most

---

¹ The following variants deserve attention: 6 εβαθυνθ. Bᵃᵇℵᶜ·ᵃRT
10 pr οτι ιδου οι εχθροι σου κε ℵAᵃRT

striking peculiarities will at once be apparent. He will notice especially the following. (1) There are frequent instances of an absolutely literal rendering of the original, e.g. 1 Kings xx. 10 ὃς ἐν ποσίν μου = אֲשֶׁר בְּרַגְלָי (LXX. τοῖς πεζοῖς μου); 12 θέτε· καὶ ἔθηκαν = שִׂימוּ וַיָּשִׂימוּ (LXX. οἰκοδομήσατε χάρακα, καὶ ἔθεντο χάρακα); 2 Kings xxiii. 21 τῷ λέγειν = לֵאמֹר (LXX. λέγων); 24 ἃ ὡράθησαν = אֲשֶׁר נִרְאוּ (LXX. τὰ γεγονότα). (2) Under certain circumstances[1] σύν is employed to represent the Hebrew אֶת, when it is the sign of the accusative[2]; e.g. 1 Kings xx. 12 σὺν τὸ ῥῆμα = אֶת־הַדָּבָר, 13 σὺν πάντα τὸν ὄχλον = אֶת־כָּל־הֶהָמוֹן, 2 Kings xxiii. 21 σὺν παντὶ τῷ λαῷ (where the dat. is governed by the preceding verb), 24 σὺν τοὺς μάγους κτλ. (3) The same Hebrew words are scrupulously rendered by the same Greek, e.g. καὶ καίγε = וְגַם occurs thrice in one context (2 Kings xxiii. 15, 19, 24); and in Ps. xcii. 8, 10 κατεργαζόμενοι ἀνωφελές twice represents פֹּעֲלֵי אָוֶן. (4) The transliterations adhere with greater closeness to the Hebrew than in the LXX.[3]; thus פֶּסַח becomes φέσα, יֹאשִׁיָּהוּ Ἰωσιαού, חִלְקִיָּהוּ Ἑλκιαού. (5) The Tetragrammaton is not transliterated, but written in Hebrew letters, and the characters are of the archaic type (𐤉𐤄𐤅𐤄, not יהוה); cf. Orig. *in Ps.* ii., καὶ ἐν τοῖς ἀκριβεστάτοις δὲ τῶν ἀντιγράφων Ἑβραίοις χαρακτῆρσιν κεῖται τὸ ὄνομα, Ἑβραϊκοῖς δὲ οὐ τοῖς νῦν ἀλλὰ τοῖς ἀρχαιοτάτοις—where the 'most exact copies' are doubtless those of Aquila's version, for there is no reason to suppose that any copyists of the Alexandrian version hesitated to write ο κ̄ς̄ or κ̄ε̄ for יהוה[4]. (6) That the crudities of Aquila's

---

[1] For these see Burkitt, *Aquila*, p. 12.

[2] This singular use of σύν appears also in the LXX., but only in Ecclesiastes and the Song of Songs, which Freudenthal is disposed to assign to Aquila (p. 65); cf. König, *Einleitung*, p. 108 n., and McNeile, *Introd. to Ecclesiastes.* [3] Aq. does not transliterate עַזְחַ‎אֵ‎ת (see Burkitt, p. 14).

[4] In a few Hexaplaric MSS. (e.g. Q, 86, 88, 243^mg, 264) the Greek letters ΠΙΠΙ are written for יהוה, but (with the exception of the Genizah Palimpsest, Taylor, p. 27) the Greek MSS. use it solely in their excerpts from the non-Septuagintal columns of the Hexapla, and only the Hexaplaric Syriac admits ΠΙΠΙ into the text of the LXX., using it freely for κύριος, even with a preposition (as ܠܗܝܐ). Oxyrh. Pap. 1007 (vol. VII.), late 3rd cent.,

style are not due to an insufficient vocabulary[1] is clear from
his ready use of words belonging to the classical or the literary
type when they appear to him to correspond to the Hebrew
more closely than the colloquialisms of the LXX. The following are specimens; 1 Kings xx. 10 LXX. ἐκποιήσει, Aq. ἐξαρκέσει; LXX. ἀλώπεξιν, Aq. λιχάσιν[2]; 12 LXX. σκηναῖς, Aq.
συσκιασμοῖς; 2 Kings xxiii. 21 LXX. διαθήκης, Aq. συνθήκης;
24 LXX. θεραφείν, Aq. μορφώματα; LXX. εἴδωλα, Aq. καθάρματα; Ps. xc. 8 LXX. ἀνταπόδοσιν, Aq. ἀπότισιν; *ib.* 10 LXX.
προσελεύσεται, Aq. μεταχθήσεται; LXX. μάστιξ, Aq. ἀφή; xci.
5 LXX. ποιήματι, Aq. κατέργῳ.

From the fragments which survive in the margins of
hexaplaric MSS. it is possible to illustrate certain other
characteristic features of Aquila which arise out of his extreme
loyalty to the letter of his Hebrew text. (1) Jerome remarks
upon his endeavour to represent even the etymological meaning of the Hebrew words (*ad Pammach.* 11 "non solum verba
sed etymologias quoque verborum transferre conatus est),"
and by way of example he cites the rendering of Deut. vii.
13, where Aquila substituted χεῦμα, ὀπωρισμόν, στιλπνότητα
for σῖτον, οἶνον, ἔλαιον in order to reflect more exactly the
Hebrew דְּגָן, תִּירֹשׁ, יִצְהָר.—as though, adds Jerome humorously,
we were to use in Latin *fusio, pomatio, splendentia.* Similarly,

has ZZ, representing doubled *yod*, in Gen. ii., iii. Ceriani expresses the
opinion that the use of ΠΙΙΙΙ is due either to Origen or Eusebius, i.e. one
of those fathers substituted ΠΙΙΙΙ for ﬧﬥﬣﬥ in the non-Septuagintal
columns, using the letters to represent the Hebrew characters which were
familiar to them. On the whole subject the student may consult Ceriani,
Monumenta sacra et profana, ii. p. 106 ff.; Schleusner, *s.v.* πίπι, Field,
Hexapla ad Esa. i. 2; Hatch and Redpath, *Concordance,* p. 1135; Driver
in *Studia Biblia,* i. p. 12, n. 3; *Z. D. M. G.* (1878), 465 ff., 501, 506.
Prof. Burkitt acutely points out (p. 16) that ﬧﬥﬣﬥ (and doubtless also
ΠΙΙΙΙ) was read as Κύριος, since in one place in the Aquila fragments where
there was no room to write the Hebrew characters "instead of οἴκῳ ﬧﬥﬣﬥ
we find οἴκῳ κ̄ῡ." On the orthography see Burkitt, p. 15, par. 4.

[1] Even Jerome speaks of Aquila as "eruditissimus linguae Graecae"
(in Isa. xlix. 5).　　　　[2] See Prof. Burkitt's note (p. 26).

Aquila represented עֶצֶם by ὀστεοῦν, and הִשְׂכִּיל by ἐπιστημο-
νίζειν or ἐπιστημονοῦν, and even coined the impossible form
ἀφημένος to correspond with נֶגוּעַ. (2) An attempt is made
to represent Hebrew particles, even such as defy translation;
thus ה local becomes the enclitic δε (e. g. νότονδε = הַנֶּגְבָּה,
Gen. xii. 9, Κυρήνηνδε = קִירָה, 2 Kings xvi. 9); and similarly
prepositions are accumulated in a manner quite alien from
Greek usage (e.g. εἰς ἀπὸ μακρόθεν = לְמֵרָחוֹק, 2 Kings xix. 25).
(3) Other devices are adopted for the purpose of bringing
the version into close conformity with the original; a word
of complex meaning or form is represented by two Greek
words (e.g. עֲזָאזֵל is converted into τράγος ἀπολυόμενος and
צְלָצַל into σκιὰ σκιά; a Hebrew word is replaced by a Greek
word somewhat similar in sound, e.g. for אֵלוֹן (Deut. xi. 30)
Aquila gives αὐλών, and for תְּרָפִים (1 Sam. xv. 23) θεραπεία[1].

Enough has been said to shew the absurdity of Aquila's
method when it is regarded from the standpoint of the modern
translator. Even in ancient times such a translation could
never have attained to the popularity which belonged to the
LXX.; that it was widely accepted by the Greek synagogues of
the Empire can only have been due to the prejudice created in
its favour by its known adherence to the standard text and the
traditional exegesis[2]. The version of Aquila emanated from
a famous school of Jewish teachers; it was issued with the full
approval of the Synagogue, and its affectation of preserving at
all costs the idiom of the original recommended it to orthodox
Jews whose loyalty to their faith was stronger than their sense
of the niceties of the Greek tongue. For ourselves the work of

---

[1] The student who wishes to pursue the subject may refer to Field,
Prolegg. p. xxi. sqq., and Dr Taylor's article *Hexapla* in Smith and Wace's
Dict. Chr. Biog. iii. p. 17 ff. Jerome speaks more than once of a second
edition of Aquila "quam Hebraei κατ᾽ ἀκρίβειαν nominant." The question
is discussed by Field (*prolegg.* xxiv. ff.).

[2] See Prof. Burkitt's article *Aquila* in the *Jewish Quarterly Review*,
Jan. 1898, p. 211 ff.

Aquila possesses a value which arises from another consideration. His " high standard of exactitude and rigid consistency give his translation, with all its imperfections, unique worth for the critic [1]." Its importance for the criticism of the Old Testament was fully recognised by the two greatest scholars of ancient Christendom, and there are few things more to be desired by the modern student of Scripture than the complete recovery of this monument of the text and methods of interpretation approved by the chief Jewish teachers of the generation which followed the close of the Apostolic age.

7. THEODOTION. With Aquila Irenaeus couples Theodotion of Ephesus, as another Jewish proselyte who translated the Old Testament into Greek (Θεοδοτίων ἡρμήνευσεν ὁ Ἐφέσιος καὶ Ἀκύλας...ἀμφότεροι Ἰουδαῖοι προσήλυτοι). Himself of Asiatic origin, and probably a junior contemporary of Theodotion, Irenaeus may be trusted when he assigns this translator to Ephesus, and describes him as a convert to Judaism. Later writers, however, depart more or less widely from this statement. According to Epiphanius, Theodotion was a native of Pontus, who had been a disciple of Marcion of Sinope before he espoused Judaism. According to Jerome, he was an Ebionite, probably a Jew who had embraced Ebionitic Christianity. His *floruit* is fixed by Epiphanius in the reign of the second Commodus, i.e. of the Emperor Commodus, so called to distinguish him from L. Ceionius Commodus, better known as L. Aurelius Verus.

Epiph. *de mens. et pond.* 17 περὶ τὴν τοῦ δευτέρου Κομόδου βασιλείαν τοῦ βασιλεύσαντος μετὰ τὸν προειρημένον Κόμοδον Λούκιον Αὐρήλιον ἔτη ιγ´, Θεοδοτίων τις Ποντικὸς ἀπὸ τῆς διαδοχῆς Μαρκίωνος τοῦ αἱρεσιάρχου τοῦ Σινωπίτου, μηνίων καὶ αὐτὸς τῇ αὐτοῦ αἱρέσει καὶ εἰς Ἰουδαισμὸν ἀποκλίνας καὶ περιτμηθεὶς καὶ τὴν τῶν Ἑβραίων φωνὴν καὶ τὰ αὐτῶν στοιχεῖα παιδευθείς, ἰδίως καὶ αὐτὸς ἐξέδωκε. Hieron. *ep. ad Augustin.:* "hominis Judaei atque blasphemi";

---

[1] Dr Taylor, pref. to *Fragments of Aquila*, p. vii.

praef. in Job: "Iudaeus Aquila, et Symmachus et Theodotio Judaizantes haeretici"; *de virr. ill.* 54 "editiones...Aquilae... Pontici proselyti et Theodotionis Hebionaei"; *praef. ad Daniel.:* "Theodotionem, qui utique post adventum Christi incredulus fuit, licet eum quidam dicant Hebionitam qui altero genere Iudaeus est[1]."

The date assigned to Theodotion by Epiphanius is obviously too late, in view of the statement of Irenaeus, and the whole account suspiciously resembles the story of Aquila. That within the same century two natives of Pontus learnt Hebrew as adults, and used their knowledge to produce independent translations of the Hebrew Bible, is scarcely credible. But it is not unlikely that Theodotion was an Ephesian Jew or Jewish Ebionite. The attitude of a Hellenist towards the Alexandrian version would naturally be one of respectful consideration, and his view of the office of a translator widely different from that of Aquila, who had been trained by the strictest Rabbis of the Palestinian school. And these expectations are justified by what we know of Theodotion's work. "Inter veteres medius incedit" (Hieron. *praef. ad evang.*); "simplicitate sermonis a LXX. interpretibus non discordat" (*praef. in Pss.*); "Septuaginta et Theodotio...in plurimis locis concordant" (*in Eccl.* ii.)—such is Jerome's judgement; and Epiphanius agrees with this estimate (*de mens. et pond.* 17: τὰ πλεῖστα τοῖς οβ´ συνᾳδόντως ἐξέδωκεν). Theodotion seems to have produced a free revision of the LXX. rather than an independent version. The revision was made on the whole upon the basis of the standard Hebrew text; thus the Job of Theodotion was longer than the Job of the LXX. by a sixth part of the whole (Orig. *ep. ad Afric.* 3 sqq., Hieron. *praef. ad Job*)[2], and in Daniel, on

---

[1] Marcion flourished c. A.D. 150; Commodus was Emperor from 180—192. The Paschal Chronicle, following Epiphanius, dates the work of Theodotion A.D. 184.

[2] See Field, *Hexapla*, p. xxxix.; Hatch, *Essays*, p. 215; Margoliouth, art. 'Job' in Smith's *Bible Dict.* (ed. 2).

the other hand, the Midrashic expansions which characterise the LXX. version disappear in Theodotion. His practice with regard to apocryphal books or additional matter appears not to have been uniform; he followed the LXX. in accepting the additions to Daniel and the supplementary verses in Job[1], but there is no evidence that he admitted the non-canonical books in general[2].

8. Specimens of Theodotion's style and manner may be obtained from the large and important fragments of his work which were used by Origen to fill up the *lacunae* in Jeremiah (LXX.). The following passage, preserved in the margin of Codex Marchalianus, will serve as an example[3].

Jeremiah xl. (xxxiii.) 14—26.

[14] Ἰδοὺ ἡμέραι ἔρχονται, φησὶ Κύριος, καὶ ἀναστήσω τὸν λόγον μου τὸν ἀγαθὸν ὃν ἐλάλησα ἐπὶ τὸν οἶκον Ἰσραὴλ καὶ ἐπὶ τὸν οἶκον Ἰούδα. [15] ἐν ταῖς ἡμέραις ἐκείναις καὶ ἐν τῷ καιρῷ ἐκείνῳ ἀνατελῶ τῷ Δαυὶδ ἀνατολὴν δικαίαν, ποιῶν κρίμα καὶ δικαιοσύνην ἐν τῇ γῇ. [16] ἐν ταῖς ἡμέραις ἐκείναις σωθήσεται ἡ Ἰουδαία καὶ Ἰερουσαλὴμ κατασκηνώσει πεποιθυῖα· καὶ τοῦτο τὸ ὄνομα ὃ καλέσει αὐτὴν Κύριος Δικαιοσύνη ἡμῶν. [17] ὅτι τάδε λέγει Κύριος, Οὐκ ἐξολοθρευθήσεται τῷ Δαυὶδ ἀνὴρ καθήμενος ἐπὶ θρόνον οἴκου Ἰσραήλ· [18] καὶ τοῖς ἱερεῦσι τοῖς Λευίταις οὐκ ἐξολοθρευθήσεται ἀνὴρ ἐκ προσώπου μου, ἀναφέρων ὁλοκαυτώματα καὶ θύων θυσίαν. [19] καὶ ἐγένετο λόγος Κυρίου πρὸς Ἰερεμίαν λέγων [20] Τάδε λέγει Κύριος Εἰ διασκεδάσετε τὴν διαθήκην μου τὴν ἡμέραν καὶ τὴν διαθήκην μου τὴν νύκτα, τοῦ μὴ εἶναι ἡμέραν καὶ νύκτα ἐν καιρῷ αὐτῶν· [21] καίγε ἡ διαθήκη μου διασκεδασθήσεται μετὰ Δαυὶδ τοῦ δούλου μου, τοῦ μὴ

---

[1] Orig. *ep. ad Afric.* 3.
[2] On Baruch see Nestle's remarks in Hastings' *D. B.* iv. (art. *Septuagint*).
[3] *O. T. in Greek*, iii. pp. vii. ff., 320 f.

εἶναι αὐτῷ υἱὸν βασιλεύοντα ἐπὶ τὸν θρόνον αὐτοῦ, καὶ ἡ πρὸς τοὺς Λευίτας τοὺς ἱερεῖς τοὺς λειτουργοῦντάς μοι. ²² ὡς οὐκ ἐξαριθμηθήσεται ἡ δύναμις τοῦ οὐρανοῦ, οὐδὲ ἐκμετρηθήσεται ἡ ἄμμος τῆς θαλάσσης, οὕτως πληθυνῶ τὸ σπέρμα Δαυὶδ τοῦ δούλου μου καὶ τοὺς Λευίτας τοὺς λειτουργοῦντάς μοι. ²³ καὶ ἐγένετο λόγος Κυρίου πρὸς Ἰερεμίαν λέγων ²⁴ Ἀρά γε οὐκ ἴδης τί ὁ λαὸς οὗτος ἐλάλησαν λέγοντες Αἱ δύο πατριαὶ ἃς ἐξελέξατο Κύριος ἐν αὐταῖς, καὶ ἰδοὺ ἀπώσατο αὐτούς; καὶ τὸν λαόν μου παρώξυναν τοῦ μὴ εἶναι ἔτι ἔθνος ἐνώπιόν μου. ²⁵ τάδε λέγει Κύριος Εἰ μὴ τὴν διαθήκην μου ἡμέρας καὶ νυκτός, ἀκριβάσματα οὐρανοῦ καὶ γῆς, οὐκ ἔταξα, ²⁶ καίγε τὸ σπέρμα Ἰακὼβ καὶ Δαυὶδ τοῦ δούλου μου ἀποδοκιμῶ, τοῦ μὴ λαβεῖν ἐκ τοῦ σπέρματος αὐτοῦ ἄρχοντα πρὸς τὸ σπέρμα Ἀβραὰμ καὶ Ἰσαὰκ καὶ Ἰακώβ· ὅτι ἐπιστρέψω τὴν ἐπιστροφὴν αὐτῶν, καὶ οἰκτειρήσω αὐτούς¹.

Unfortunately there is no other Greek version which can be compared with Theodotion in this passage, for the LXX. is wanting, and only a few shreds of Aquila and Symmachus have reached us. But the student will probably agree with Field that the style is on the whole not wanting in simple dignity, and that it is scarcely to be distinguished from the best manner of the LXX.[2] With his Hebrew Bible open at the place, he will observe that the rendering is faithful to the original, while it escapes the crudities and absurdities which beset the excessive fidelity of Aquila. Now and again we meet with a word unknown to the LXX. (e.g. ἀκριβάσματα = חֻקּוֹת)[3], or a reminiscence of Aquila ; on the other hand Theodotion agrees with the LXX. against Aquila in translating בְּרִית by διαθήκη. If in one place

---

[1] Another considerable fragment of Theodotion may be found in Jer. xlvi. (xxxix.) 4—13, see *O. T. in Greek*, p. 534 f.

[2] *Hexapla, prolegg.* p. xxxix. "Theodotionis stylus simplex et gravis est." LXX. of Jer. xxiii. 5, 6 may be set beside Θ of xl. 14, 15.

[3] Cod. A employs ἀκριβασμός in this sense (Jud. v. 15, 3 Regn. xi. 34, 4 Regn. xvii. 15), but under the influence of Theodotion, at least in the last two passages; see Field *ad loc.*

Theodotion is more obscure than Aquila (τὴν διαθήκην τὴν ἡμέραν...τὴν νύκτα, Aq. τῆς ἡμέρας...τῆς νυκτός), yet the passage as a whole is a singularly clear and unaffected rendering. His chief defect does not reveal itself in this context; it is a habit of transliterating Hebrew words which could have presented no difficulty to a person moderately acquainted with both languages. Field gives a list of 90 words which are treated by Theodotion in this way without any apparent cause[1]. When among these we find such a word as אֵל (which is represented by ἤλ in Mal. ii. 11), we are compelled to absolve him from the charge of incompetence, for, as has been pertinently asked, how could a man who was unacquainted with so ordinary a word or with its Greek equivalent have produced a version at all? Probably an explanation should be sought in the cautious and conservative temperament of this translator[2]. Field's judgement is here sounder than Montfaucon's; Theodotion is not to be pronounced *indoctior*, or *indiligentior*, but only "scrupulosior quam operis sui instituto fortasse conveniret[3]."

9.　The relation of the two extant Greek versions of Daniel is a perplexing problem which calls for further consideration. In his lost *Stromata* Origen, it appears[4], announced his intention of using Theodotion's version of Daniel; and an examination of Origen's extant works shews that his citations of Daniel "agree almost *verbatim* with the text of Theodotion now current[5]." The action of Origen in this matter was generally endorsed by the Church, as we learn from Jerome (*praef. in Dan.*: "Danielem prophetam iuxta LXX. interpretes ecclesiae

---

[1] *Op. cit.* p. xl. sq.

[2] *D. C. B.* art. *Hexapla* (iii. p. 22). Cf. *ib.* iv. p. 978.

[3] Thus in Mal. *l. c.* he was perhaps unwilling to use θεός in connexion with the phrase אֵל נֵכָר.

[4] Jerome on Dan. iv.: "Origenes in nono *Stromatum* volumine asserit se quae sequuntur ab hoc loco in propheta Daniele non iuxta LXX. interpretes...sed iuxta Theodotionis editionem disserere."

[5] Dr Gwynn in *D. C. B.* (iv. p. 974).

non legunt, utentes Theodotionis editione"; cf. *c. Rufin.* ii. 33). Jerome did not know how this happened, but his own words supply a sufficient explanation: "hoc unum affirmare possum quod multum a veritate discordet et recto iudicio repudiata sit." So universal was the rejection of the LXX. version of Daniel that, though Origen loyally gave it a place in his Hexapla, only one Greek copy has survived[1], Theodotion's version having been substituted in all other extant Greek MSS. of Daniel.

But the use of Theodotion's Daniel in preference to the version which was attributed to the LXX. did not begin with Origen. Clement of Alexandria (as edited) uses Theodotion, with a sprinkling of LXX. readings, in the few places where he quotes Daniel (*paed.* ii. 8, iii. 3, *strom.* i. 4, 21). In North Africa both versions seem to have influenced the Latin text of Daniel. The subject has been carefully investigated by Prof. F. C. Burkitt[2], who shews that Tertullian used "a form of the LXX. differing slightly from Origen's edition," whilst Cyprian quotes from a mixed text, in which Theodotion sometimes predominates. Irenaeus, notwithstanding his reverence for the LXX. and distrust of the later versions, cites Daniel after Theodotion's version[3]. Further, Theodotion's Daniel appears to be used by writers anterior to the date usually assigned to this translator. Thus Hermas (*vis.* iv. 2, 4) has a clear reference to Theodotion's rendering of Dan. vi. 22[4]. Justin (*dial.* 31) gives a long extract from Dan. vii. in which characteristic readings from the two versions occur in almost equal proportions[5]. Clement of Rome (1 Cor. 34) cites a part of the same context,

---

[1] The Chigi MS. known as Cod. 87 (H. P. 88); see *O. T. in Greek,* iii. pp. vi., xii., and cf. the subscription printed *ib.* p. 574.
[2] *Old Latin and Itala,* p. 18 ff.
[3] An exception in i. 19. 2 (Dan. xii. 9 f.) is due to a Marcosian source.
[4] See Salmon, *Intr. to the N. T.*[7] p. 639.
[5] On the trustworthiness of Justin's text here see Burkitt, *op. cit.* p. 25 n. (against Hatch, *Essays,* p. 190).

with a Theodotionic reading (ἐλειτούργουν, LXX. ἐθεράπευον). Barnabas (*ep.* iv. 5) also refers to Dan. vii., and, though his citation is too loose to be pressed, the words ἐξαναστήσονται ὄπισθεν αὐτῶν are more likely to be a reminiscence of ὀπίσω αὐτῶν ἀναστήσεται (Th.) than of μετὰ τούτους στήσεται (LXX.). The Greek version of Baruch (i. 15—18, ii. 11—19) undoubtedly supports Theodotion against the LXX. Still more remarkable is the appearance of Theodotionic renderings in the New Testament. A writer so faithful to the LXX. as the author of the Epistle to the Hebrews, in his only reference to Daniel (Heb. xi. 33 = Dan. vi. 23) agrees with Theodotion against the Chigi version[1]. The Apocalypse, which makes frequent use of Daniel, supports Theodotion on the whole; cf. Apoc. ix. 20 (Dan. v. 23), x. 6 (Dan. xii. 7), xii. 7 (Dan. x. 20), xiii. 7 (Dan. vii. 21), xix. 6 (Dan. x. 6), xx. 4 (Dan. vii. 9), xx. 11 (Dan. ii. 35)[2]. Even in the Synoptic Gospels Theodotion's rendering in Dan. vii. 13 (μετὰ τῶν νεφελῶν) occurs as well as the LXX. ἐπὶ τῶν ν.; comp. Mc. xiv. 62 with Mt. xxiv. 30, xxvi. 64[3].

From these premisses the inference has been drawn that there were two pre-Christian versions of Daniel, both passing as 'LXX.', one of which is preserved in the Chigi MS., whilst the other formed the basis of Theodotion's revision[4]. It has been urged by Dr Gwynn with much acuteness that the two Septuagintal Books of Esdras offer an analogy to the two versions of Daniel, and the appearance of the phrase ἀπηρείσατο αὐτὰ ἐν τῷ εἰδωλείῳ αὐτοῦ in 1 Esdr. ii. 9 and Dan. i. 2 (LXX.)

---

[1] Heb. *l. c.* ἔφραξαν στόματα λεόντων (Dan. Th., ἐνέφραξεν τὰ στόματα τῶν λεόντων : LXX., σέσωκέ με ἀπὸ τῶν λεόντων).

[2] The references are from Dr Salmon's *Intr.* p. 548 f. He adds: "I actually find in the Apocalypse no clear evidence that St John had ever seen the so-called LXX. version." See Bludau in *Th. Q.* 1897 (p. 1 ff.).

[3] The N. T. occasionally inclines to Theodotion in citations which are not from Daniel; cf. Jo. xix. 37 (Zech. xii. 10), 1 Cor. xv. 54 (Is. xxv. 8); see Schürer[3], iii. p. 324, "entweder Th. selbst ist älter als die Apostel, oder es hat einen 'Th.' vor Th. gegeben."

[4] *D. C. B.* art. *Theodotion* iv. p. 970 ff. Dr Salmon (*Intr.* p. 547) is disposed to accept this view.

has been regarded as an indication that the Greek Esdras and
the Chigi Daniel were the work of the same translator[1]. An
obvious objection to the hypothesis of two Septuagintal or
Alexandrian versions is the entire disappearance of the version
which was used *ex hypothesi* not only by the authors of the
Epistle to the Hebrews and the Apocalypse, but by Theodotion
and other writers of the second century. But Theodotion's
revision of Daniel may have differed so little from the stricter
Alexandrian version as to have taken its place without remark[2].

10. SYMMACHUS. Of this translator Irenaeus says nothing,
and it has been inferred, perhaps too hastily, that he was
unknown to the Bishop of Lyons, and of later date. Origen
knew and used Symmachus, and had received a copy of his
commentary on St Matthew from a wealthy Christian woman
named Juliana, to whom it had been given by the author.
According to Eusebius, Symmachus was an Ebionite, and this
is confirmed by Jerome; a less probable tradition in Epiphanius
represents him as a Samaritan who had become a convert to
Judaism[3].

Eus. *H. E.* vi. 17 τῶν γε μὴν ἑρμηνευτῶν αὐτῶν δὴ τούτων ἰστέον
Ἐβιωναῖον τὸν Σύμμαχον γεγονέναι...καὶ ὑπομνήματα δὲ τοῦ Συμμά-
χου εἰσέτι νῦν φέρεται ἐν οἷς δοκεῖ πρὸς τὸ κατὰ Ματθαῖον ἀποτεινό-
μενος εὐαγγέλιον τὴν δεδηλωμένην αἵρεσιν κρατύνειν. ταῦτα δὲ ὁ
Ὡριγένης μετὰ καὶ ἄλλων εἰς τὰς γραφὰς ἑρμηνειῶν τοῦ Συμμάχου
σημαίνει παρὰ Ἰουλιανῆς τινος εἰληφέναι, ἣν καί φησι παρ' αὐτοῦ
Συμμάχου τὰς βίβλους διαδέξασθαι. Hieron. *de virr. ill.* 54
"Theodotionis Hebionaei et Symmachi eiusdem dogmatis" (cf.
in Hab. iii. 13) ; *praef. in Job*: "Symmachus et Theodotion
Iudaizantes haeretici." Epiph. *de mens. et pond.* 15 ἐν τοῖς τοῦ
Σευήρου χρόνοις Σύμμαχός τις Σαμαρείτης τῶν παρ' αὐτοῖς σοφῶν μὴ
τιμηθεὶς ὑπὸ τοῦ οἰκείου ἔθνους...προσηλυτεύει καὶ περιτέμνεται
δευτέραν περιτομήν...οὗτος τοίνυν ὁ Σύμμαχος πρὸς διαστροφὴν τῶν

[1] *D. C. B.* iv. p. 977 n.; cf. Hastings' *D. B.*, i. p. 761.
[2] On the whole question of the date of Theodotion, see Schürer,
G. J. V.[3] iii. 323 f., where the literature of the subject is given.
[3] The name סומכוס occurs in the Talmud as that of a disciple of
R. Meir, who flourished towards the end of the second or beginning of the
third century. Geiger desires to identify our translator with this Symmachus; see Field, *prolegg. ad Hex.* p. xxix.

παρὰ Σαμαρείταις ἑρμηνειῶν ἑρμηνεύσας τὴν τρίτην ἐξέδωκεν
ἑρμηνείαν.

That Symmachus, even if of Jewish or Samaritan birth,
became an Ebionite leader is scarcely doubtful, since an
Ebionitic commentary on St Matthew bearing his name was
still extant in the fourth century[1]; the Symmachians, an Ebionite
sect probably named after him, are mentioned by Ambrosiaster
(*comm. in Gal., prolegg.*) and Augustine (*c. Faust.* xix. 4, *c. Crescon.*
i. 36)[2]. His *floruit* is open to some question. Dr Gwynn has
shewn[3] that Epiphanius, who makes Theodotion follow Symmachus, probably placed Symmachus in the reign of Verus,
i.e. Marcus Aurelius. Now in the *Historia Lausiaca*, c. 147,
Palladius says that Juliana sheltered Origen during a persecution,
i.e. probably during the persecution of the Emperor Maximius
(A.D. 238—241). If this was so, the literary activity of
Symmachus must have belonged, at the earliest, to the last
years of M. Aurelius, and it may be questioned whether
Epiphanius has not inverted the order of the two translators,
i.e. whether Theodotion ought not to be placed under M.
Aurelius and Symmachus under Commodus (A.D. 180—192)[4].
The version of Symmachus was in the hands of Origen when
he wrote his earliest commentaries, i.e. about A.D. 228[5]; but
the interval is long enough to admit of its having reached
Alexandria.

11. The aim of Symmachus, as Jerome perceived, was
to express the sense of his Hebrew text rather than to attempt

---

[1] Euseb. *l. c.*
[2] Philastrius, who represents the *Symmachiani* as holding other views,
says (c. 145): "sunt haeretici alii qui Theodotionis et Symmachi itidem
interpretationem diverso modo expositam sequuntur." See Harnack, *Gesch.
d. altchr. Litt.*, I. i. p. 212.
[3] *D. C. B.* iv. p. 971 ff. Σευήρου in *de pond. et mens.* 16 is on this
hypothesis a corruption of Οὐήρου. Cf. Lagarde's *Symmicta*, ii. p. 168.
[4] The Gospel of Peter, which cannot be much later than A.D. 170, and
may be fifteen or twenty years earlier, shews some verbal coincidences with
Symmachus (*Akhmîm fragment*, pp. xxxiv. 18, 20), but they are not
decisive.　　　　[5] Cf. *D. C. B.* iv. p. 103.

a verbal rendering: "non solet verborum κακοζηλίαν sed intel-
legentiae ordinem sequi" (*in Am.* iii. 11). While Aquila
endeavoured "verbum de verbo exprimere," Symmachus made
it his business "sensum potius sequi" (*praef. in Chron. Eus.*, cf.
praef. in Job). Epiphanius, who believed Symmachus to have
been a Samaritan proselyte to Judaism, jumped to the conclusion that his purpose was polemical (πρὸς διαστροφὴν τῶν
παρὰ Σαμαρείταις ἑρμηνειῶν ἑρμηνεύσας). But if Symmachus
had any antagonist in view, it was probably the literalism and
violation of the Greek idiom which made the work of Aquila
unacceptable to non-Jewish readers. So far as we can judge
from the fragments of his version which survive in Hexaplaric
MSS., he wrote with Aquila's version before him, and in his
efforts to recast it made free use of both the LXX. and Theodotion. The following extracts will serve to illustrate this view
of his relation to his predecessors.

MALACHI II. 13[1].

LXX.	AQ.
καὶ ταῦτα ἃ ἐμίσουν ἐποιεῖτε· ἐκαλύπτετε δάκρυσιν τὸ θυσια-στήριον Κυρίου καὶ κλαυθμῷ καὶ στεναγμῷ ἐκ κόπων. ἔτι ἄξιον ἐπιβλέψαι εἰς θυσίαν ἢ λαβεῖν δεκτὸν ἐκ τῶν χειρῶν ὑμῶν;	καὶ τοῦτο δεύτερον ἐποιεῖτε· ἐκαλύπτετε δακρύῳ τὸ θυσια-στήριον κλαυθμῷ καὶ οἰμωγῇ, ἀπὸ τοῦ μὴ εἶναι ἔτι νεῦσαι πρὸς τὸ δῶρον καὶ λαβεῖν εὐδοκίαν ἀπὸ χειρὸς ὑμῶν.

TH.	SYMM.
καὶ τοῦτο δεύτερον ἐποιήσατε· ἐκαλύπτετε δάκρυσιν τὸ θυσια-στήριον, κλαίοντες καὶ στένοντες, ἀπὸ τοῦ μὴ εἶναι ἔτι προσεγγίζοντα τὸ ὁλοκαύτωμα καὶ λαβεῖν τέλειον ἐκ χειρῶν ὑμῶν.	καὶ ταῦτα δεύτερον ἐποιεῖτε, καλύπτοντες ἐν δάκρυσιν τὸ θυσια-στήριον, κλαίοντες καὶ οἰμώσσοντες, ἀπὸ τοῦ μὴ εἶναι ἔτι νεύοντα πρὸς τὸ δῶρον καὶ δέξασθαι τὸ εὐδοκημένον ἀπὸ χειρὸς ὑμῶν.

[1] The Hexaplaric renderings are from Cod. 86 (Cod. Barberinus):
Field, *Hexapla*, ii. p. 1033.

But it must not be supposed that Symmachus is a mere reviser of earlier versions, or that he follows the lead of Aquila as Theodotion follows the LXX. Again and again he goes his own way in absolute independence of earlier versions, and sometimes at least, it must be confessed, of the original. This is due partly to his desire to produce a good Greek rendering, more or less after the current literary style; partly, as it seems, to dogmatic reasons. The following may serve as specimens of the Greek style of Symmachus when he breaks loose from the influence of his predecessors: Gen. xviii. 25 ὁ πάντα ἄνθρωπον ἀπαιτῶν δικαιοπραγεῖν, ἀκρίτως μὴ ποιήσῃς τοῦτο; Job xxvi. 14 τί δὲ ψιθύρισμα τῶν λόγων αὐτοῦ ἀκούσομεν, ὅπου βροντὴν δυναστείας αὐτοῦ οὐδεὶς ἐννοήσει; Ps. xliii. 16 δι' ὅλης ἡμέρας ἡ ἀσχημόνησίς μου ἄντικρύς μου, καὶ ὁ καταισχυμμὸς τοῦ προσώπου μου καλύπτει με. Ps. lxviii. 3 ἐβαπτίσθην εἰς ἀπεράντους καταδύσεις, καὶ οὐκ ἔστιν στάσις· εἰσῆλθον εἰς τὰ βάθη τῶν ὑδάτων, καὶ ῥεῖθρον ἐπέκλυσέν με. Eccl. iv. 9 εἰσὶν ἀμείνους δύο ἑνός· ἔχουσιν γὰρ κέρδος ἀγαθόν. Isa. xxix. 4 ὑπὸ γῆν ἐδαφισθήσεται ἡ λαλιά σου, καὶ ἔσται ὡς ἐγγαστρίμυθος ἡ φωνή σου καὶ ἀπὸ τῆς γῆς ἡ λαλιά σου ῥοίσεται.

It cannot be said that these renderings approach to excellence, but a comparison with the corresponding LXX. will shew that Symmachus has at least attempted to set himself free from the trammels of the Hebrew idiom and to clothe the thoughts of the Old Testament in the richer drapery of the Greek tongue. It is his custom to use compounds to represent ideas which in Hebrew can be expressed only by two or more words (e.g. בְּלִי־פָעַשׂ, Symm. ἀναιτίως, עֵין בְּעַיִן, Symm. ὀφθαλμοφανῶς, לְרֹאשׁ פִּנָּה, Symm. ἀκρογωνιαῖος); he converts into a participle the first of two finite verbs connected by a copula (Exod. v. 7 ἀπερχόμενοι καλαμάσθωσαν, 4 Regn. i. 2 σφαλέντες ἔπεσον); he has at his command a large supply of Greek particles (e.g. he renders אַךְ by ἄρα, ὄντως, ἴσως, δι' ὅλου, μόνον, οὕτως, ἀλλ'

ὅμως)[1]. More interesting and important is the tendency which
Symmachus manifests to soften the anthropomorphic expressions of the Old Testament; e.g. Gen. i. 27, ἔκτισεν ὁ θεὸς
τὸν ἄνθρωπον ἐν εἰκόνι διαφόρῳ[2]· ὄρθιον ὁ θεὸς ἔκτισεν αὐτόν.
Exod. xxiv. 10, εἶδον ὁράματι τὸν θεὸν Ἰσραήλ. Jud. ix.
13 τὸν οἶνον...τὴν εὐφροσύνην τῶν ἀνθρώπων. Ps. xliii. 24
ἵνα τί ὡς ὑπνῶν εἶ, Δέσποτα; In these and other instances Symmachus seems to shew a knowledge of current Jewish exegesis[3]
which agrees with the story of his Jewish origin or training.

> LITERATURE. On Aquila the student may consult R. Anger
> *de Onkelo Chaldaico*, 1845; art. in *D. C. B.* (W. J. Dickson);
> M. Friedmann, *Onkelos u. Akylas*, 1896; Lagarde, *Clementina*,
> p. 12 ff.; Krauss, *Akylas der Proselyt* (Festschrift), 1896; F. C.
> Burkitt, *Fragments of Aquila*, 1897; C. Taylor, *Sayings of the
> Jewish Fathers*[2], 1897 (p. viii.); Schürer[3], iii. p. 317 ff. On Sym-
> machus, C. H. Thieme, *pro puritate Symmachi dissert.*, 1755;
> art. in *D. C. B.* (J. Gwynn); Giov. Mercati, *l' età di Simmaco
> interprete*, 1892. On Theodotion, Credner, *Beiträge*, ii. p. 253 ff.;
> art. in *D. C. B.* (J. Gwynn); G. Salmon, *Intr. to the N. T.*[7], p.
> 538 ff.; Schürer[3], iii. p. 323 ff. Works which deal with the
> ancient non-Septuagintal versions in general will be mentioned
> in c. iii., under *Literature of the Hexapla*.

12. OTHER ANCIENT GREEK VERSIONS. The researches
of Origen (A.D. 185—253) brought to light three anonymous
versions besides those of Aquila, Theodotion and Symmachus;
from their relative position in the columns of his great collection (see c. iii.) they are known as the *Quinta* (ε΄), *Sexta* (ϛ΄),
and *Septima* (ζ΄) respectively. The following are the chief
authorities:

> Eus. *H. E.* vi. 16 τοσαύτη δὲ εἰσήγετο τῷ Ὠριγένει τῶν θείων
> λόγων ἀπηκριβωμένη ἐξέτασις ὡς...καί τινας ἑτέρας παρὰ τὰς καθη-
> μαξευμένας ἑρμηνείας ἐναλλαττούσας..., ἐφευρεῖν, ἃς οὐκ οἶδ' ὅθεν ἔκ
> τινων μυχῶν τὸν πάλαι λανθανούσας χρόνον εἰς φῶς ἀνιχνεύσας
> προήγαγεν...τίνος ἄρ' εἶεν οὐκ εἰδὼς αὐτὸ τοῦτο μόνον ἐπεσημήνατο

---

[1] For other examples see Field, *prolegg.* p. xxx. ff.; *D. C. B.* iv.
p. 19 f.
[2] Reading, perhaps, בצלם ובצלם אלהים; cf. Nestle, *Marginalien*,
pp. 3, 15.
[3] See *D. C. B.* iii. p. 20.

ὡς ἄρα τὴν μὲν εὕροι ἐν τῇ πρὸς ᾿Ακτίῳ Νικοπόλει...ἐπὶ μιᾶς αὖθις
σεσημείωται ὡς ἐν ᾿Ιεριχοῖ εὑρημένης ἐν πίθῳ κατὰ τοὺς χρόνους
᾿Αντωνίνου τοῦ υἱοῦ Σεβήρου.　　Epiph. *de mens. et pond.* 18 μετὰ
τὸν διωγμὸν τοῦ βασιλέως Σευήρου ηὑρέθη ἡ πέμπτη ἐν πίθοις ἐν
᾿Ιεριχῷ κεκρυμμένη ἐν χρόνοις τοῦ υἱοῦ Σευήρου τοῦ ἐπικληθέντος
Καρακάλλου τε καὶ Γέτα...ἐν δὲ τῷ ἑβδόμῳ αὐτοῦ ἔτει ηὑρέθησαν καὶ
βίβλοι τῆς πέμπτης ἐκδόσεως ἐν πίθοις ἐν ᾿Ιεριχῷ κεκρυμμένης μετὰ
ἄλλων βιβλίων ῾Εβραικῶν καὶ ῾Ελληνικῶν.　τὸν δὲ Καράκαλλον
διαδέχεται ᾿Αντωνῖνος ἕτερος...μετὰ τοῦτον ἐβασίλευσεν ᾿Αλέξανδρος...
ἔτη ιγ᾽· ἐν μέσῳ τῶν χρόνων τούτων ηὑρέθη ἕκτη ἔκδοσις, καὶ αὐτὴ
ἐν πίθοις κεκρυμμένη, ἐν Νικοπόλει τῇ πρὸς ᾿Ακτίῳ.　　Pseudo-Ath.
syn. scr. sacr. 77 πέμπτη ἑρμηνεία ἐστὶν ἡ ἐν πίθοις εὑρεθεῖσα κεκρυμμένη ἐπὶ ᾿Αντωνίνου βασιλέως τοῦ Καρακάλλα ἐν ᾿Ιεριχῷ παρά
τινος τῶν ἐν ᾿Ιεροσολύμοις σπουδαίων.　ἕκτη ἑρμηνεία ἐστὶν ἡ ἐν
πίθοις εὑρεθεῖσα, καὶ αὕτη κεκρυμμένη, ἐπὶ ᾿Αλεξάνδρου τοῦ Μαμαίας
παιδὸς ἐν Νικοπόλει τῇ πρὸς ῎Ακτιον ὑπὸ ᾿Ωριγένους γνωρίμων.
Hieron. *de virr. ill.* 54 "quintam et sextam et septimam editionem, quas etiam nos de eius bibliotheca habemus, miro labore
repperit et cum ceteris editionibus conparavit": *in ep. ad Tit.*
"nonnulli vero libri, et maxime hi qui apud Hebraeos versu
compositi sunt, tres alias editiones additas habent quam 'quintam' et 'sextam' et 'septimam' translationem vocant, auctoritatem sine nominibus interpretum consecutas." Cf. *in Hab.* ii. 11,
iii. 13.

It appears from the statement of Eusebius[1] that Origen found
the *Quinta* at Nicopolis near Actium, and that either the *Sexta*
or the *Septima* was discovered in the reign of Caracalla (A.D.
211—217) at Jericho; while Epiphanius, reversing this order,
says that the *Quinta* was found at Jericho c. A.D. 217, and the
Sexta at Nicopolis under Severus Alexander (A.D. 222—235)[2].
According to Epiphanius both the *Quinta* and the *Sexta*,
according to Eusebius the *Sexta* only, lay buried in a πίθος
(*dolium*), one of the earthenware jars, pitched internally, and
partly sunk in the ground, in which the *mustum* was usually
stored while it underwent the process of fermentation[3].　Since

---

[1] Jerome (*prol. in Orig. exp. Cant.*) confirms Eusebius, on whose words
see Dr Mercati, *Studi e Testi* 5, v. p. 47 (1901).

[2] The *Dialogue of Timothy and Aquila* identifies Nicopolis with
Emmaus Nicopolis in Palestine.

[3] *D. of Gk and Lat. Ant.* p. 1202. These πίθοι are said to have been
sometimes used instead of *cistae* or *capsae* for preserving books. In 1906
five Greek documents were found in an earthenware jar at Elephantine; see
Dr F. G. Kenyon in *Egypt Exploration Fund Archaeological Report* for
1907-8, p. 50.

Origen was in Palestine A.D. 217, and in Greece A.D. 231, it is natural to connect his discoveries with those years. How long the versions had been buried cannot be determined, for it is impossible to attach any importance to the vague statements of Eusebius (τὸν πάλαι λανθανούσας χρόνον). The version found at or near Nicopolis may have been a relic of the early Christianity of Epirus, to which there is an indirect allusion in the Pastoral Epistles[1]. The Jericho find, on the other hand, was very possibly a Palestinian work, deposited in the wine jar for the sake of safety during the persecution of Septimius Severus, who was in Palestine A.D. 202, and issued edicts against both the Synagogue and the Church[2]. Of *Septima* nothing is known, beyond what Eusebius tells us, and the very sparing use of it in the Psalter of some Hexaplaric MSS.; the few instances are so dubious that Field was disposed to conclude either that this version never existed, or that all traces of it have been lost[3].

There is no conclusive evidence to shew that any of these versions covered the whole of the Old Testament[4]. Renderings from *Quinta*[5] are more or less abundant in 2 Kings, Job, Psalms, Canticles, and the Minor Prophets, and a few traces have been observed in the Pentateuch. *Sexta* is well represented in the Psalms and in Canticles, and has left indications of its existence in Exodus, 1 Kings, and the Minor Prophets.

With regard to the literary character of *Quinta* and *Sexta*, the style of *Quinta* is characterised by Field as "omnium elegantissimus...cum optimis Graecis suae aetatis scriptoribus comparandus." *Sexta* also shews some command of Greek,

[1] Lightfoot, *Biblical Essays*, p. 432.
[2] Cf. Eus. *H. E.* vi. 7; Spartian. *in Sev.* 17.
[3] *Prolegg. ad Hexapla*, p. xlvi; see however R. Sinker, *Psalm of Habakkuk* (Camb. 1890), p. 42. Ps.-Athanasius calls Lucian the seventh version: ἑβδόμη πάλιν καὶ τελευταία ἑρμηνεία ἡ τοῦ ἁγίου Λουκιανοῦ.
[4] According to Harnack-Preuschen (i. p. 340) the opposite is implied by Eusebius' use of ἐναλλαττούσας in reference to these versions: "d. h. die eine war nur für diese, die andere nur für jene Bücher vorhanden."
[5] On *Quinta* see Mercati, *Studi e Testi* 5, IV. p. 28; and Burkitt in *Proc. Soc. Bibl. Archaeology*, June 1902.

but is said to be disposed to paraphrase; Field, while he
regards that charge as on the whole 'not proven,' cites a
remarkable example of the tendency from Ps. xxxvi. 35, which
ς' renders, Εἶδον ἀσεβῆ καὶ ἀναιδῆ ἀντιποιούμενον ἐν σκληρότητι
καὶ λέγοντα Εἰμὶ ὡς αὐτόχθων περιπατῶν ἐν δικαιοσύνῃ. Jerome[1]
attributes both versions to 'Jewish translators,' but the Christian origin of *Sexta* betrays itself[2] at Hab. iii. 13 ἐξῆλθες τοῦ
σῶσαι τὸν λαόν σου διὰ Ἰησοῦν τὸν χριστόν σου[3].

The Greek fathers of the fourth and fifth centuries quotes
non-Septuagintal renderings from an interpreter who is styled
ὁ Ἑβραῖος. Ὁ Σύρος is also cited, frequently as agreeing with
ὁ Ἑβραῖος. Nothing is known of these translators (if such they
were), but an elaborate discussion of all the facts may be seen
in Field[4].

13. The 'GRAECUS VENETUS.' This is a version of the
Pentateuch, together with the books of Ruth, Proverbs, Canticles, Ecclesiastes, Lamentations, and Daniel, preserved in
St Mark's Library at Venice in a single MS. of cent. xiv.—xv.
(*cod. Gr.* vii.)[5]. It was first given to the world by de Villoison
(Strassburg, 1784) and C. F. Ammon (Erlangen, 1790—1);
a new edition with valuable prolegomena by O. von Gebhardt
appeared at Leipzig in 1875[6]. This translation has been
made directly from the M. T., but the author appears to have
occasionally availed himself of earlier Greek versions (LXX.,

---

[1] *adv. Rufin.*

[2] "Prodens manifestissime sacramentum," as Jerome himself remarks.
No doubt the primary reference is to Joshua (Field), but the purport of the
gloss is unmistakable.

[3] *leg. fors.* Ἰησοῦ τοῦ χριστοῦ σου.

[4] *Prolegg.* pp. lxxv.—lxxxii. See also Lagarde, *Ueber den Hebräer
Ephraims von Edessa.* On τὸ Σαμαρειτικόν see Field, p. lxxii. ff., and
Nestle, *Urtext*, p. 206. For some ambiguous references to other(?) ver-
sions see Philostr. *haer.* cc. 143, 144.

[5] See Eichhorn, p. 421 ff.; De Wette-Schrader, p. 122 f.

[6] *Graecus Venetus Pentateuchi &c. versio Graeca. Ex unico biblioth.
S. Marci Venetae codice nunc primum uno volumine comprehensam atque
apparatu critico et philologico instructam edidit O. G. Praefatus est Fr.
Delitzsch.*

Aq., Symm., Theod.)[1]. His chief guide however appears to have been David Kimchi, whose interpretations are closely followed[2]. That he was a Jew is clear from incidental renderings (e.g. in Exod. xxiii. 20 he translates הַקֹּמִים τὸν ὀντωτήν[3], sc. יהוה). From the fact of his having undertaken a Greek version Gebhardt infers that he was a proselyte to Christianity, but the argument may be used to support an opposite conclusion; as a Jew he may have been moved by a desire to place before the dominant Orthodox Church a better rendering of the Old Testament than the LXX. Delitzsch wishes to identify him with Elissaeus, a Jewish scholar at the court of Murad I., who flourished in the second half of the 14th century.

The style of this remarkable version will be best illustrated by a few specimens :

Gen. vi. 2 f.

[2] τεθέανται γοῦν οἱ υἱεῖς τοῦ θεοῦ τὰς θυγατέρας τοῦ ἀνθρώπου ὅτι καλαὶ ἐτέλουν, καὶ ἔλαβον ἑαυτοῖς γυναῖκας ἀπὸ πασῶν ὧν εἴλοντο. [3] ἔφη τοίνυν ὁ ὀντωτής Οὐ κρινεῖ πνεῦμα τοὐμὸν ἐν τῷ ἀνθρώπῳ ἐς αἰῶνα, ἐφ᾽ οἷς ἔτι πέρ ἐστι σάρξ· τελέσουσι δ᾽ αἱ ἡμέραι αὐτοῦ ἑκατὸν καὶ εἴκοσιν ἔτη.

Prov. viii. 22 ff.

[22] ὁ ὀντωτὴς ἐκτίσατό με ἀρχὴν ὁδοῦ οἱ, πρὸ τῶν ἔργων αὐτοῦ ἐκ τότε. [23] ἀπ᾽ αἰῶνος κέχυμαι, ἀπὸ κρατός, ἀπὸ προλήμματος γῆς. [24] ἐν οὐκ ἀβύσσοις πέπλασμαι, ἐν οὐ πηγαῖς δεδοξασμένων ὑδάτων· [25] πρὶν ὄρη ἐμπαγῆναι, πρὸ τῶν βουνῶν ὠδίνημαι· [26] ἄχρις οὐκ ἐποίησε γῆν, διόδους καὶ κεφαλὴν κόνεων τῆς οἰκουμένης.

Daniel vii. 13.

[13] ὁράων ἐκύρησα ἐν ὁράσεσιν εὐφρόνας, αὐτίκα τε ξὺν ταῖς

---

[1] Gebhardt, p. lvii. ff.
[2] *Ib.* p. lxii.
[3] Ὀντωτής, ὀντουργός, οὐσιωτής are his usual renderings of יהוה.

νεφέλαις τῶν πόλων ὡς υἱεὺς ἀνθρώπω ἀφικνούμενος ἔην, μέχρι
τε τῷ παλαιῷ ταῖς ἀμέραις ἔφθασε κἀνώπιον τήνω προσήγαγόν
ἑ. ¹⁴ τήνῳ τ᾽ ἐδόθη ἀρχὰ τιμά τε καὶ βασιλεία, πάντες τε λαοὶ
ἔθνεα καὶ γλῶτται τήνῳ λατρευσείοντι· ἃ ἀρχά εὖ ἀρχὰ αἰῶνος
ὃς οὐ παρελευσείεται, ἅ τε βασιλεία εὖ ἅπερ οὐκ οἰχησείεται.

The student will not fail to notice the translator's desire to
render his text faithfully, and, on the other hand, his curiously
infelicitous attempt to reproduce it in Attic Greek ; and lastly
his use of the Doric dialect in Daniel to distinguish the
Aramaic passages from the rest of the book. The result
reminds us of a schoolboy's exercise, and the reader turns
from it with pleasure to the less ambitious diction of the LXX.,
which, with its many imperfections, is at least the natural
outgrowth of historical surroundings.

Klostermann (*Analecta* p. 30) mentions a MS. Psalter (Vat.
Gr. 343), bearing the date 22 April, 1450, which professes to be a
translation into the Greek of the fifteenth century (κατὰ τὴν νῦν
κοινὴν τῶν Γραικῶν φωνήν). A version of the Pentateuch into
modern Greek in Hebrew characters was printed at Constantinople in 1547, forming the left-hand column of a Polyglott
(Hebrew, Chaldee, Spanish, Greek). It is described in Wolf,
Bibliotheca Hebraea, ii. p. 355, and more fully in *La version
Neo-grecque du Pentateuche Polyglotte...remarques du Dr Lazare
Belléli* (Paris, 1897). This Greek version has recently been
transliterated and published in a separate form with an introduction and glossary by D. C. Hesseling (Leide, 1897). A Greek
version of Job (1576) is mentioned by Neubauer in *J. Q. R.* iv.
p. 18 f.

CHAPTER III.

The Hexapla, and the Hexaplaric and other Recensions of the Septuagint.

1. THE century which produced the versions of Aquila, Theodotion, and Symmachus saw also the birth of the great Christian scholar who conceived the idea of using them for the revision of the Alexandrian Greek Bible.

Origen was in his 17th year when his father suffered martyrdom (A.D. 202)[1]; at eighteen he was already head of the catechetical school of Alexandria[2]. The Old Testament from the first engaged his attention, and, rightly judging that it could not be fruitfully studied without a knowledge of the original, he applied himself at once to the study of Hebrew.

Eus. *H. E.* vi. 16 τοσαύτη δὲ εἰσήγετο τῷ Ὠριγένει τῶν θείων λόγων ἀπηκριβωμένη ἐξέτασις, ὡς καὶ τὴν Ἑβραΐδα γλῶτταν ἐκμαθεῖν τάς τε παρὰ τοῖς Ἰουδαίοις ἐμφερομένας πρωτοτύπους αὐτοῖς Ἑβραίων στοιχείοις γραφὰς κτῆμα ἴδιον ποιήσασθαι. Hieron. *de virr. ill.* 54 "quis autem ignorat quod tantum in scripturis divinis habuerit studii ut etiam Hebraeam linguam contra aetatis gentisque suae naturam edisceret[3]?"

The feat was perhaps without precedent, in the third century, among Christian scholars not of Jewish origin[4]; in one so

---

[1] Eus. *H. E.* vi. 2.
[2] Hieron. *de virr. ill.* 54.
[3] Cf. *ep. ad Paulam.*
[4] See *D. C. B.* art. *Hebrew Learning* (ii. p. 351 ff.).

young it seemed prodigious to a veteran like Jerome. These
studies, begun in Egypt, were continued in Palestine at Caesarea,
where Origen sought shelter during the storm of persecution
which burst upon Alexandria in the reign of Caracalla (A.D.
216—219). On his return to Egypt Origen's period of literary
productivity began, and between the years 220 and 250 he
gave to the world a succession of commentaries, homilies, or
notes on nearly all the books of the Old Testament[1]. In the
course of these labours, perhaps from the moment that he
began to read the Old Testament in the original, he was
impressed with the importance of providing the Church with
materials for ascertaining the true text and meaning of the
original. The method which he adopted is described by himself in his famous letter to Africanus (c. A.D. 240), and more
fully in his commentary on St Matthew (c. A.D. 245)[2].

> Orig. *ad Afric.* 5: καὶ ταῦτα δέ φημι οὐχὶ ὄκνῳ τοῦ ἐρευνᾶν καὶ
> τὰς κατὰ Ἰουδαίους γραφὰς καὶ πάσας τὰς ἡμετέρας ταῖς ἐκείνων
> συγκρίνειν καὶ ὁρᾶν τὰς ἐν αὐταῖς διαφοράς, εἰ μὴ φορτικὸν γοῦν
> εἰπεῖν, ἐπὶ πολὺ τοῦτο (ὅση δύναμις) πεποιήκαμεν, γυμνάζοντες
> αὐτῶν τὸν νοῦν ἐν πάσαις ταῖς ἐκδόσεσι καὶ ταῖς διαφοραῖς αὐτῶν
> μετὰ τοῦ πόσως μᾶλλον ἀσκεῖν τὴν ἑρμηνείαν τῶν ἑβδομήκοντα...
> ἀσκοῦμεν δὲ μὴ ἀγνοεῖν καὶ τὰς παρ᾽ ἐκείνοις, ἵνα πρὸς Ἰουδαίους
> διαλεγόμενοι μὴ προσφέρωμεν αὐτοῖς τὰ μὴ κείμενα ἐν τοῖς ἀντιγρά-
> φοις αὐτῶν, καὶ ἵνα συγχρησώμεθα τοῖς φερομένοις παρ᾽ ἐκείνοις, εἰ
> καὶ ἐν τοῖς ἡμετέροις οὐ κεῖται βιβλίοις. *In Matt.* xv. 14: τὴν μὲν
> οὖν ἐν τοῖς ἀντιγράφοις τῆς παλαιᾶς διαθήκης διαφωνίαν, θεοῦ
> διδόντος, εὕρομεν ἰάσασθαι, κριτηρίῳ χρησάμενοι ταῖς λοιπαῖς ἐκ-
> δόσεσιν· τῶν γὰρ ἀμφιβαλλομένων παρὰ τοῖς ο᾽ διὰ τὴν τῶν
> ἀντιγράφων διαφωνίαν, τὴν κρίσιν ποιησάμενοι ἀπὸ τῶν λοιπῶν
> ἐκδόσεων, τὸ συνᾷδον ἐκείναις ἐφυλάξαμεν· καί τινα μὲν ὠβελίσαμεν
> ἐν τῷ Ἑβραικῷ μὴ κείμενα, οὐ τολμῶντες αὐτὰ πάντῃ περιελεῖν, τινὰ
> δὲ μετ᾽ ἀστερίσκων προσεθήκαμεν· ἵνα δῆλον ᾖ ὅτι μὴ κείμενα παρὰ
> τοῖς ο᾽ ἐκ τῶν λοιπῶν ἐκδόσεων συμφώνως τῷ Ἑβραικῷ προσεθή-
> καμεν, καὶ ὁ μὲν βουλόμενος προῆται αὐτά· ᾧ δὲ προσκόπτει τὸ
> τοιοῦτον, ὃ βούλεται περὶ τῆς παραδοχῆς αὐτῶν ἢ μὴ ποιήσῃ.

[1] See *D. C. B.* art. *Origenes*, iv. p. 129 ff.
[2] Cf. Bp Westcott in *D. C. B.* iv. p. 99: "it was during this period
(i.e. before A.D. 215) in all probability that he formed and partly executed
his plan of a comparative view of the LXX. in connexion with the other
Greek versions."

2. To attempt a new version was impracticable. It may be doubted whether Origen possessed the requisite knowledge of Hebrew; it is certain that he would have regarded the task as almost impious. Writing to Africanus he defends the apocryphal additions to Daniel and other Septuagintal departures from the Hebrew text on the ground that the Alexandrian Bible had received the sanction of the Church, and that to reject its testimony would be to revolutionise her canon of the Old Testament, and to play into the hands of her Jewish adversaries (ἀθετεῖν τὰ ἐν ταῖς ἐκκλησίαις φερόμενα ἀντίγραφα καὶ νομοθετῆσαι τῇ ἀδελφότητι ἀποθέσθαι μὲν τὰς παρ' αὐτοῖς ἐπιφερομένας βίβλους, κολακεύειν δὲ Ἰουδαίοις καὶ πείθειν ἵνα μεταδῶσιν ἡμῖν τῶν καθαρῶν). In this matter it was well, he urged, to bear in mind the precept of Prov. xxii. 28, "Remove not the ancient landmark, which thy fathers have set." The same reasons prevented him from adopting any of the other versions in place of the Septuagint. On the other hand, Origen held that Christians must be taught frankly to recognise the divergences between the LXX. and the current Hebrew text, and the superiority of Aquila and the other later versions, in so far as they were more faithful to the original; it was unfair to the Jew to quote against him passages from the LXX. which were wanting in his own Bible, and injurious to the Church herself to withhold from her anything in the Hebrew Bible which the LXX. did not represent. Acting under these convictions Origen's first step was to collect all existing Greek versions of the Old Testament. He then proceeded to transcribe the versions in parallel columns, and to indicate in the column devoted to the Septuagint the relation in which the old Alexandrian version stood to the current Hebrew text.

3. The following specimen, taken from a fragment lately discovered at Milan, will assist the reader to understand the arrangement of the columns, and to realise the general appearance of the Hexapla.

Ps. xlv. (xlvi.) 1—3 [1].

HEBREW.	HEB. TRANSLITERATED.	AQUILA.
ולמנצח	λαμανασση	τῷ νικοποιῷ·
לבני קרח	[λ]αβνηκορ	τῶν υἱῶν Κόρε
על עלמות	αλ · αλμωθ	ἐπὶ νεανιοτήτων
שיר	σιρ	ᾆσμα.
אלהים לנו	ελωειμ · λανου*	[ὁ θεὸς ἡμῖν (?)]
מחסה ועז	μασε · ονοζ	ἐλπὶς καὶ κράτος,
עזרה	εζρ	βοήθεια
בצרות	βσαρωθ	ἐν θλίψεσιν
נמצא מאד	νεμσα μωδ	εὑρέθη* σφόδρα.
על כן	αλ · χεν·	ἐπὶ τούτῳ
לא נירא	λω · νιρα	οὐ φοβηθησόμεθα
בהמיר	βααμιρ	ἐν τῷ ἀνταλλάσσεσθαι
ארץ	ααρς	γῆν,
ובמוט	ουβαμωτ	καὶ ἐν τῷ σφάλλεσθαι
הרים	αριμ	ὄρη
בלב	βλεβ	ἐν καρδίᾳ
ימים[	ιαμιμ	θαλασσῶν.

* In the MS. λανου appears in the third column, where it has displaced Aquila's rendering.

* MS. εὑρέθης.

---

[1] Cf. *Un palimpsesto Ambrosiano dei Salmi Esapli* (Giov. Mercati) in *Atti d. R. Accademia d. Scienze di Torino*, 10 Apr. 1896; and E. Klostermann, *die Mailänder Fragmente der Hexapla*. The MS. does not supply the Hebrew column.

Ps. xlv. (xlvi.) 1—3.

SYMMACHUS.	LXX.	THEODOTION[1].
ἐπινίκιος·	εἰς τὸ τέλος·	τῷ νικοποιῷ*·
τῶν υἱῶν Κόρε	ὑπὲρ τῶν υἱῶν* Κόρε	τοῖς υἱοῖς Κόρε
ὑπὲρ τῶν αἰωνίων	ὑπὲρ τῶν κρυφίων	ὑπὲρ τῶν κρυφίων
ᾠδή.	ψαλμός.	ᾠδή*.
ὁ θεὸς ἡμῖν	ὁ θεὸς ἡμῶν†	ὁ θεὸς ἡμῶν
πεποίθησις καὶ ἰσχύς,	καταφυγὴ καὶ δύναμις,	καταφυγὴ καὶ δύναμις,
βοήθεια	βοηθὸς	βοηθὸς
ἐν θλίψεσιν	ἐν θλίψεσι	ἐν θλίψεσιν
εὑρισκόμενος σφόδρα.	ταῖς εὑρούσαις ἡμᾶς‡ σφόδρα.	εὑρέθη† σφόδρα.
διὰ τοῦτο	διὰ τοῦτο	διὰ τοῦτο
οὐ φοβηθησόμεθα	οὐ φοβηθησόμεθα	οὐ φοβηθησόμεθα
ἐν τῷ* συγχεῖσθαι	ἐν τῷ ταράσσεσθαι	ἐν τῷ ταράσσεσθαι
γῆν	τὴν γῆν	τὴν γῆν
καὶ κλίνεσθαι	καὶ μετατίθεσθαι	καὶ σαλεύεσθαι‡
ὄρη	ὄρη	ὄρη
ἐν καρδίᾳ	ἐν καρδίᾳ	ἐν καρδίᾳ
θαλασσῶν.	θαλασσῶν.	θαλασσῶν.
* MS. ταῖς.	* With interlinear variant τοῖς υἱοῖς (Th.). † MS. 1ᵃ manu ἡμῖν (? Aq. Sym.). ‡ With interlinear variant εὑρεθήσεται ἡμῖν.	* With marginal variants, εἰς τὸ τέλος, ψαλμός (LXX.). † With interlinear variant ταῖς εὑρούσαις ἡμᾶς (LXX.). ‡ With interlinear variant μετατίθεσθαι (LXX.).

[1] Or Quinta? Cf. H. Lietzmann in *G. G. A.* 1902, v., p. 332: "die letzte Columne ist nicht, wie man anfangs glaubte, Theodotion, sondern die Quinta mit Interlinearvarianten."

The process as a whole is minutely described by Eusebius and Jerome, who had seen the work, and by Epiphanius, whose account is still more explicit but less trustworthy.

Eus. *H. E.* vi. 16 : ταύτας δὲ ἁπάσας [sc. τὰς ἐκδόσεις] ἐπὶ ταὐτὸν συναγαγὼν διελών τε πρὸς κῶλον καὶ ἀντιπαραθεὶς ἀλλήλαις μετὰ καὶ αὐτῆς τῆς Ἑβραίων σημειώσεως τὰ τῶν λεγομένων Ἑξαπλῶν ἡμῖν ἀντίγραφα καταλέλοιπεν, ἰδίως τὴν Ἀκύλου καὶ Συμμάχου καὶ Θεοδοτίωνος ἔκδοσιν ἅμα τῇ τῶν ἑβδομήκοντα ἐν τοῖς Τετραπλοῖς ἐπικατασκευάσας. Hieron. *in ep. ad Tit.* iii. 9: "nobis curae fuit omnes veteris legis libros quos vir doctus Adamantius in Hexapla digesserat de Caesariensi bibliotheca descriptos ex ipsis authenticis emendare, in quibus et ipsa Hebraea propriis sunt characteribus verba descripta et Graecis literis tramite expressa vicino ; Aquila etiam et Symmachus, LXX. quoque et Theodotio suum ordinem tenent; nonnulli vero libri et maxime hi qui apud Hebraeos versu compositi sunt tres alias editiones additas habuit." Cf. his letter to Sunnias and Fretela (*ep.* 106) and to Augustine (*ep.* 112) and the preface to the Book of Chronicles. Epiph. *de mens. et pond.* 7 : τὰς γὰρ ἐξ ἑρμηνείας καὶ τὴν Ἑβραϊκὴν γραφὴν Ἑβραϊκοῖς στοιχείοις καὶ ῥήμασιν αὐτοῖς ἐν σελίδι¹ μιᾷ συντεθεικώς, ἄλλην σελίδα ἀντιπαράθετον δι᾿ Ἑλληνικῶν μὲν γραμμάτων Ἑβραϊκῶν δὲ λέξεων πρὸς κατάληψιν τῶν μὴ εἰδότων Ἑβραϊκὰ στοιχεῖα...καὶ οὕτως τοῖς λεγομένοις ὑπ᾿ αὐτοῦ ἐξαπλοῖς ἢ ὀκταπλοῖς τὰς μὲν δύο Ἑβραϊκὰς σελίδας καὶ τὰς ἐξ τῶν ἑρμηνευτῶν ἐκ παραλλήλου ἀντιπαραθεὶς μεγάλην ὠφέλειαν γνώσεως ἔδωκε τοῖς φιλοκάλοις. *Ib.* 19 τὰς δύο Ἑβραϊκὰς πρώτας κειμένας, μετὰ ταύτας δὲ τὴν τοῦ Ἀκύλα τεταγμένην, μεθ᾿ ἣν καὶ τὴν τοῦ Συμμάχου, ἔπειτα τὴν τῶν οβ᾿, μεθ᾿ ἃς ἡ τοῦ Θεοδοτίωνος συντέτακται, καὶ ἑξῆς ἡ πέμπτη τε καὶ ἕκτη².

It will be seen that the specimen corroborates ancient testimony in reference to the relative order of the four Greek versions (Aq., Symm., LXX., Theod.), and illustrates the method of division into corresponding κῶλα³ which made comparison easy. With regard to the order, it is clear that Origen did not mean it to be chronological. Epiphanius seeks to account for the position of the LXX. in the fifth column by the not less

---

¹ On σελίς, cf. Sir E. Maunde Thompson, *Handbook of Greek and Latin Palaeography*, p. 58.

² See also *ib.* 18 sq.; Hieron. *Praef. in Paral.*, and *in ep. ad Tit.*, c. iii.

³ Used here loosely as = κόμματα, the κῶλον being properly a line consisting of a complete clause, and of 8—17 syllables : cf. E. M. Thompson, *Gk and Lat. Palaeography*, p. 81 f.; J. R. Harris, *Stichometry*, p. 23 f.

untenable hypothesis that Origen regarded the LXX. as the standard of accuracy (*de mens. et pond.* 19: Ὠριγένης πυθόμενος τὴν τῶν οβ´ ἔκδοσιν ἀκριβῆ εἶναι μέσην ταύτην συνέθηκεν, ὅπως τὰς ἐντεῦθεν καὶ ἐντεῦθεν ἑρμηνείας διελέγχῃ). As we have learned from Origen himself, the fact was the reverse; the other Greek versions were intended to check and correct the LXX. But the remark, though futile in itself, suggests a probable explanation. Aquila is placed next to the Hebrew text because his translation is the most verbally exact, and Symmachus and Theodotion follow Aquila and the LXX. respectively, because Symmachus on the whole is a revision of Aquila, and Theodotion of the LXX. As to the κῶλα, it was of course necessary that the lines should be as short as possible when six or more columns had to be presented on each opening; and it will be seen that in the Psalms at least not more than two Hebrew words were included in a line, the corresponding Greek words being at the most three or four[1]. But the claims of the sense are not neglected; indeed it will appear upon inspection that the method adopted serves in a remarkable degree to accentuate the successive steps in the movement of the thought.

4. Besides the Hexapla, Origen compiled a Tetrapla, i.e. a minor edition from which he omitted the first two columns containing the Hebrew text in Hebrew and Greek characters; cf. Eus. *l.c.* ἰδίως τὴν Ἀκύλου καὶ Συμμάχου καὶ Θεοδοτίωνος ἔκδοσιν ἅμα τῇ τῶν ο´ ἐν τοῖς τετραπλοῖς ἐπικατασκευάσας[2]. Epiph. *de mens. et pond.* 19 τετραπλᾶ γάρ εἰσι τὰ Ἑλληνικὰ ὅταν αἱ τοῦ Ἀκύλου καὶ Συμμάχου καὶ τῶν οβ´ καὶ Θεοδοτίωνος ἑρμηνεῖαι συντεταγμέναι ὦσι. The Tetrapla is occasionally mentioned along with the Hexapla in scholia attached to MSS. of the LXX. Thus in the

---

[1] In the earlier Cairo palimpsest even such words as אֵל and μή had each a line to itself; see Nestle in Hastings' *D.B.* iv. 443.

[2] Ἐπικατασκευάζειν is *insuper vel postea concinnare* (Field, *prolegg.* p. xii.); cf. Dio Cass. l. 23 τὰ σκάφη κατεσκεύασε...καὶ ἐπ᾿ αὐτὰ πύργους ἐπεκατεσκεύασε. Oeconomus (iv. 873), who regards the Tetrapla as the earlier work, understands Eusebius to mean only that Origen added to the LXX. the three columns containing Α´Σ´Θ´.

Syro-Hexaplaric version at the end of Joshua it is stated that
the Greek codex on which the version was based had the note :
ἐγράφη ἐκ τοῦ ἑξαπλοῦ, ἐξ οὗ καὶ παρετέθη· ἀντεβλήθη δὲ καὶ
πρὸς τὸν τετραπλοῦν. Cod. Q still contains two similar
references to the Tetrapla (*O. T. in Greek*, iii., p. viii., notes).
Mention is also made in the MSS. of an Octapla (cf. the Syro-
Hexaplar in Job v. 23, vi. 28, and the Hexaplaric MSS. of the
Psalter in Ps. lxxv. 1, lxxxvi. 5, lxxxviii. 43, cxxxi. 4, cxxxvi. 1)[1].
The question arises whether the Octapla was a distinct work,
or merely another name for the Hexapla in books where the
columns were increased to eight by the addition of the *Quinta*
and *Sexta*. Eusebius appears to support the latter view, for
he speaks of the Hexapla of the Psalms as including the
Quinta and *Sexta* (*H. E.* vi. 16 ἔν γε μὴν τοῖς ἑξαπλοῖς τῶν
Ψαλμῶν μετὰ τὰς ἐπισήμους τέσσαρας ἐκδόσεις οὐ μόνον πέμπτην
ἀλλὰ καὶ ἕκτην καὶ ἑβδόμην παραθεὶς ἑρμηνείαν). Epiphanius,
on the other hand, seems to limit the Hexapla to the six
columns (*l. c.* τῶν τεσσάρων δὲ τούτων σελίδων ταῖς δυσὶ ταῖς
Ἑβραικαῖς συναφθεισῶν ἑξαπλᾶ καλεῖται· ἐὰν δὲ καὶ ἡ πέμπτη
καὶ ἡ ἕκτη ἑρμηνεία συναφθῶσιν...ὀκταπλᾶ καλεῖται)· But it
has been observed that when the scholia in Hexaplaric MSS.
mention the Octapla they are silent as to the Hexapla,
although the Octapla and the Tetrapla are mentioned together;
e.g. in Ps. lxxxvi. 5 we find the following note : ΜΗΤΗΡ ϹΙѠΝ·
τὸ ρ κατὰ προσθήκην ἔκειτο εἰς τὴν τῶν ο´ ἐν τῷ τετρασελίδῳ (the
Tetrapla), ἐν δὲ τῷ ὀκτασελίδῳ (the Octapla), ΜΗ ΤΗ ϹΙѠΝ, ἤγουν
δίχα τοῦ ρ. The inference is that the name 'Octapla' sometimes superseded that of 'Hexapla' in the Psalms, because in
the Psalter of the Hexapla there were two additional columns
which received the *Quinta* and *Sexta*. Similarly the term
'Heptapla' was occasionally used in reference to portions of the
Hexapla where a seventh column appeared, but not an eighth[2].

---

[1] Field, *Hexapla*, ii. *ad loc.* ; cf. Hieron. *in Psalmos* (ed. Morin.), p. 66.
[2] It occurs (e.g.) in the Hexaplaric Syriac at 2 Kings xvi. 2.

'Pentapla' is cited by J. Curterius from cod. Q at Isa. iii. 24, and Field's suspicion that Curterius had read his MS. incorrectly is not confirmed by a reference to the photograph, which exhibits ἐν τῷ πεντασελίδῳ. Origen's work, then, existed (as Eusebius implies) in two forms: (1) the Hexapla, which contained, as a rule, six columns, but sometimes five or seven or eight, when it was more accurately denominated the Pentapla, Heptapla, or Octapla; and (2) the Tetrapla, which contained only four columns answering to the four great Greek versions, excluding the Hebrew and Greek-Hebrew texts on the one hand, and the *Quinta* and *Sexta* on the other.

5. The Hebrew text of the Hexapla was of course that which was current among Origen's Jewish teachers in the third century, and which he took to be truly representative of the original. Portions of the second column, which have been preserved, are of interest as shewing the pronunciation of the Hebrew consonants and the vocalisation which was then in use. From the specimen already given it will be seen that כ = χ, ק = κ, and ס, צ, שׂ = σ, and that א ה ח ע are without equivalent[1]. The divergences of the vocalisation from that which is represented by the pointing of the M. T. are more important; see Dr Taylor's remarks in *D. C. B.* ii. p. 15 f.

In regard to Aquila, Symmachus, and Theodotion, and the minor Greek versions, Origen's task was limited to transcription under the conditions imposed by the plan of his work. But the fifth column, which contained the Hexaplaric LXX., called for the full exercise of his critical powers. If his first idea had been, as his own words almost suggest, merely to transcribe the LXX. in its proper place, without making material alterations in the text, a closer comparison of the LXX. with the current Hebrew text and the versions based upon it must soon have

[1] Cf. the practice of Aquila (Burkitt, *Fragments of the Books of Kings acc. to Aquila*, p. 14).

convinced him that this was impracticable. Let us suppose that there lay before him an Alexandrian or Palestinian MS., containing the 'common' text of the LXX. ($\dot{\eta}$ κοινή, or *vulgata editio*, as Jerome calls it[1]), i. e. the text of the Greek Bible as it was read by the Church of the third century. As the transcription proceeded, it would be seen that every column of the Greek contained clauses which were not in the Hebrew, and omitted clauses which the Hebrew contained. Further, in many places the order of the Greek would be found to depart from that of the Hebrew, the divergence being sometimes limited to a clause or a verse or two, but occasionally extending to several chapters. Lastly, in innumerable places the LXX. would be seen to yield a sense more or less at variance with the current Hebrew, either through misapprehension on the part of the translators or through a difference in the underlying text. These causes combined to render the co-ordination of the Alexandrian Greek with the existing Hebrew text a task of no ordinary difficulty, and the solution to which Origen was led appeared to him to be little short of an in-spiration (θεοῦ διδόντος εὕρομεν).

Origen began by assuming (1) the purity of the Hebrew text, and (2) the corruption of the κοινή where it departed from the Hebrew[2]. The problem before him was to restore the LXX. to its original purity, i.e. to the *Hebraica veritas* as he understood it, and thus to put the Church in possession of an adequate Greek version of the Old Testament without disturb-ing its general allegiance to the time-honoured work of the Alexandrian translators. Some of the elements in this complex process were comparatively simple. (1) Differences of order were met by transposition, the Greek order making way for the

---

[1] *Ep. ad Sunn. et Fret.*

[2] See Driver, *Samuel*, p. xlvi. : " he assumed that the original Septua-gint was that which agreed most closely with the Hebrew text as he knew it...a step in the wrong direction."

Hebrew. In this manner whole sections changed places in the
LXX. text of Exodus, 1 Kings, and Jeremiah; in Proverbs
only, for some reason not easy to determine, the two texts
were allowed to follow their respective courses, and the divergence of the Greek order from the Hebrew was indicated by
certain marks[1] prefixed to the *stichi* of the LXX. column.
(2) Corruptions in the κοινή, real or supposed, were tacitly
corrected in the Hexapla, whether from better MSS. of the
LXX., or from the renderings of other translators, or, in the
case of proper names, by a simple adaptation of the Alexandrian
Greek form to that which was found in the current Hebrew[2].
(3) The additions and omissions in the LXX. presented greater
difficulty. Origen was unwilling to remove the former, for
they belonged to the version which the Church had sanctioned,
and which many Christians regarded as inspired Scripture; but
he was equally unwilling to leave them without some mark of
editorial disapprobation. Omissions were readily supplied from
one of the other versions, namely Aquila or Theodotion; but
the new matter interpolated into the LXX. needed to be carefully
distinguished from the genuine work of the Alexandrian translators[3]. See Add. Notes.

6. Here the genius of Origen found an ally in the system
of critical signs which had its origin among the older scholars
of Alexandria, dating almost from the century which produced
the earlier books of the LXX. The Ἀριστάρχεια σήματα took
their name from the prince of Alexandrian grammarians,
Aristarchus, who flourished in the reign of Philopator (A.D.

---

[1] A combination of the asterisk and obelus; see below, p. 71.

[2] E.g. at Exod. vi. 16, Γηρσών was substituted by Origen for Γεδσών.
Whether his practice in this respect was uniform has not been definitely
ascertained.

[3] Hieron. *Praef. ad Chron.*: "quod maioris audaciae est, in editione
LXX. Theodotionis editionem miscuit, asteriscis designans quae minus ante
fuerant, et virgulis quae ex superfluo videbantur apposita." The Book
of Job offered the largest field for interpolation: a scholion in cod. 161
says, Ἰὼβ στίχοι ͵αχ´ χωρὶς ἀστερίσκων, μετὰ δὲ τῶν ἀστερίσκων ͵βϛ´.

222—205), and they appear to have been first employed in connexion with his great edition of Homer[1]. Origen selected two of these signs known as the obelus and the asterisk, and adapted them to the use of his edition of the Septuagint. In the Homeric poems, as edited by Aristarchus, the obelus marked passages which the critic wished to censure, while the asterisk was affixed to those which seemed to him to be worthy of special attention; cf. the *anecdoton* printed by Gardthausen : ὁ δὲ ὀβελὸς πρὸς τὰ ἀθετούμενα ἐπὶ τοῦ ποιητοῦ ἤγουν νενοθευμένα ἢ ὑποβεβλημένα· ὁ δὲ ἀστερίσκος...ὡς καλῶν εἰρημένων τῶν ἐπῶν. Similarly, in connexion with Platonic *dicta*, Diogenes Laertius (*platon.* iii. 657) used the obelus πρὸς τὴν ἀθέτησιν and the asterisk πρὸς τὴν συμφωνίαν τῶν δογμάτων. As employed by Origen in the fifth column of the Hexapla, the obelus was prefixed to words or lines which were wanting in the Hebrew, and therefore, from Origen's point of view, of doubtful authority[2], whilst the asterisk called attention to words or lines wanting in the LXX., but present in the Hebrew. The close of the context to which the obelus or asterisk was intended to apply was marked by another sign known as the *metobelus*. When the passage exceeded the length of a single line, the asterisk or obelus was repeated at the beginning of each subsequent line until the metobelus was reached.

Epiph. *de mens. et pond.* 2, 3 ὁ ἀστερίσκος...σημαίνει τὸ ἐμφερόμενον ῥῆμα ἐν τῷ Ἑβραικῷ κεῖσθαι...οἱ δὲ οβʹ ἑρμηνευταὶ παρῆκαν καὶ οὐχ ἡρμήνευκαν...ὀβελὸς δὲ...παρετίθη...ταῖς τῆς θείας γραφῆς λέξεσιν ταῖς παρὰ τοῖς οβʹ ἑρμηνευταῖς κειμέναις, παρὰ δὲ τοῖς περὶ Ἀκύλαν καὶ Σύμμαχον μὴ ἐμφερομέναις. Schol. ap. Tisch. *not. ed. cod, Sin.* p. 76 ὅσοις οἱ ὀβελοὶ πρόσκεινται ῥητοῖς, οὗτοι οὐκ ἔκειντο οὔτε παρὰ τοῖς λοιποῖς ἑρμηνευταῖς οὔτε ἐν τῷ Ἑβραικῷ, ἀλλὰ παρὰ μόνοις τοῖς οʹ· καὶ ὅσοις οἱ ἀστερίσκοι πρόσκεινται ῥητοῖς, οὗτοι ἐν μὲν τῷ Ἑβραικῷ καὶ τοῖς λοιποῖς ἑρμηνευταῖς ἐφέροντο, ἐν δὲ τοῖς οʹ οὐκέτι.

[1] See a complete list of these in Gardthausen, *Griech. Paläographie,* p. 288 f.

[2] On an exceptional case in which he obelised words which stood in the Hebrew text, see Cornill, *Ezechiel,* p. 386 (on xxxii. 17).

Occasionally Origen used asterisk and obelus together, as Aristarchus had done, to denote that the order of the Greek was at fault (*anecd.* ap. Gardthausen: ὁ δὲ ἀστερίσκος μετὰ ὀβελοῦ, ὡς ὄντα μὲν τὰ ἔπη τοῦ ποιητοῦ, μὴ καλῶς δὲ κείμενα: schol. ap. Tisch. *not. ed. Sin.* l. c. φέρονται μὲν παρὰ τοῖς ο΄, φέρονται δὲ ἐν τῷ Ἑβραικῷ καὶ παρὰ τοῖς λοιποῖς ἑρμηνευταῖς, τὴν θέσιν δὲ μόνην παραλλάσσουσιν οἱ λοιποὶ καὶ τὸ Ἑβραικὸν παρὰ τοὺς ο΄· ὅθεν ὠβέλισται ἐν ταὐτῷ καὶ ἠστέρισται, ὡς παρὰ πᾶσι μὲν φερόμενα, οὐκ ἐν τοῖς αὐτοῖς δὲ τόποις: also ap. *mon. sacr. ined.* iii. p. xvii. τὰ δὲ ἠστερισμένα ἐν ταὐτῷ καὶ ὠβελισμένα ῥητὰ...ὡς παρὰ πᾶσι μὲν φερόμενα, οὐκ ἐν τοῖς αὐτοῖς δὲ τόποις). The Aristarchian (or as they are usually called by students of the Old Testament, the Hexaplaric) signs are also used by Origen when he attempts to place before the reader of his LXX. column an exact version of the Hebrew without displacing the LXX. rendering. Where the LXX. and the current Hebrew are hopelessly at issue, he occasionally gives two versions, that of one of the later translators distinguished by an asterisk, and that of the LXX. under an obelus[1].

The form of the asterisk, obelus, and metobelus varies slightly. The first consists of the letter x, usually surrounded by four dots (※, the χῖ περιεστιγμένον); the form ⁜ occurs but seldom, and only, as it seems, in the Syro-Hexaplar. The ὀβελός, 'spit' or 'spear,' is represented in Epiphanius by ↘, but in the MSS. of the LXX. a horizontal straight line (—)[2] has taken the place of the original form, with or without occupying dot or dots (÷ ÷ ÷); the form ÷ was known as a *lemniscus,* and the form ÷ as a *hypolemniscus.* Epiphanius indeed (*op. cit.,* c. 8) fancies that each dot represents a pair of translators, so that the *lemniscus* means that the word or clause which the LXX. adds to the Hebrew had the support of two out of the thirty-six pairs which composed the whole body, whilst the *hypolemniscus*

---

[1] A somewhat different view of Origen's practice is suggested by H. Lietzmann (*Gött. gel. Anz.* 1902, 5) and G. Mercati (*Atti d. R. Acc. d. Sci. di Torino,* 10 Apr. 1896: vol. 31, p. 656 ff.

[2] This sometimes becomes a hook (᷼).

claims for it the support of only one pair. This explanation, it is scarcely necessary to say, is as baseless as the fiction of the cells on which, in the later Epiphanian form, it rests. Other attempts to assign distinct values to the various forms of the obelus have been shewn by Field to be untenable[1]. The *metobelus* is usually represented by two dots arranged perpendicularly (:), like a colon ; other forms are a sloping line with a dot before it or on either side (/., ·/.), and in the Syro-Hexaplar and other Syriac versions a mallet (✓). The latter form, as the least ambiguous, is used in Field's great edition of the Hexapla, and in the apparatus which is printed under the text of the LXX. version of Daniel in the Cambridge manual Septuagint.

Certain other signs found in Hexaplaric MSS. are mentioned in the following scholion (Εὐαγρίου σχ., one of the σχόλια εἰς τὰς παροιμίας printed in the *Notitia ed. cod. Sin.*, p. 76, from a Patmos MS.; see Robinson, *Philocalia*, pp. xiii., xvii. ff.): εἰσὶν[2] ὅσα προτεταγμένον ἔχουσι τὸν ἀριθμὸν ὧδε· ὅσα Ὠριγένην ἐπιγεγραμμένον ἔχει τούτῳ τῷ μονοσυλλάβῳ, φ...ὅσα δὲ περὶ διαφωνίας ῥητῶν τινῶν τῶν ἐν τῷ ἐδαφίῳ ἢ ἐκδόσεών ἐστιν σχόλια, ἅπερ καὶ κάτω νενευκυῖαν περιεστιγμένην ἔχει προτεταγμένην, τῶν ἀντιβεβληκότων τὸ βιβλίον ἐστίν· ὅσα δὲ ἀμφιβόλως ἔξω κείμενα ῥητὰ ἔξω νενευκυῖαν περιεστιγμένην ἔχει προτεταγμένην, διὰ τὰ σχόλια προσετέθησαν κατ᾽ αὐτὰ τοῦ μεγάλου εἰρηκότος διδασκάλου, ἵνα μὴ δόξῃ κατὰ κενοῦ τὸ σχόλιον φέρεσθαι, ἐν πολλοῖς μὲν τῶν ἀντιγράφων τῶν ῥητῶν οὕτως ἐχόντων, ἐν τούτῳ δὲ μὴ οὕτως κειμένων ἢ μηδ᾽ ὅλως φερομένων, καὶ διὰ τοῦτο προστεθέντων.

The following extract from the great Hexaplaric MS. known as G will enable the student, to whom the subject may be new, to practise himself in the interpretation of the signs. He will find it instructive to compare the extract with his Hebrew Bible on the one hand and the text of Cod. B (printed in the Cambridge LXX.) on the other[3].

[1] *Prolegg.* p. lix. sq.
[2] Lietzmann proposes to read: Εὐαγρίου σχόλια εἰσίν, ὅσα...ἀριθμόν, Ὠρ. δέ, ὅσα Ὠριγένην κ.τ.λ.
[3] The vertical bars denote, of course, the length of the lines of Cod. G. The lines of the LXX. column of the Hexapla, if we may judge by the specimen (p. 62 f.), varied in length according to the sense.

Joshua xi. 10—14 (Cod. Sarravianus).

και επεστρεψεν ι̅σ̅ εν | τω καιρω εκεινω κ | κατελαβετο ※ την
: ασωρ | και τον βασιλεα αυτης | ※ απεκτεινεν εν ρομ| ※ φαια :
ην δε ασωρ το προ|τερον αρχουσα πασω̅ | των βασιλειων του|των και
απεκτεινα̅ | παν ενπνεον ※ ο : εν | αυτη εν στοματι ξιφους | και
εξωλεθρευσαν : | —παντας : και ου κατελι|φθη εν αυτη ενπνε|ον και
την ασωρ ενε|πρησεν εν πυρι και πα|σας τας πόλεις των | βασιλειων ※
τουτω̅ : | και ※ παντας : τους βασι|λεις αυτων ελαβεν ι̅σ̅ | και
ανειλεν αυτους | εν στοματι ξιφους κ | εξωλεθρευσεν αυτους | ον
τροπον συνεταξε̅ | Μωσης ο παις κ̅υ̅· αλλα | πασας τας πολεις τας ||
κεχωματισμενας | ※ αυτων : ουκ ενεπρησεν ι̅η̅λ̅ πλην ※ την : α|σωρ
μονην ⸗ αυτην : ενεπρησεν ι̅σ̅ και πα̅|τα τα σκυλα αυτης ※ κ | ※ τα
κτηνη : επρονομευ|σαν εαυτοις οι υιοι ι̅η̅λ̅ | ※ κατα το ρημα κ̅υ̅ ο ενε|
※ τειλατο τω ι̅υ̅ : αυτους | δε παντας εξωλεθρευ|σεν εν στοματι ξιφους |
εως απωλεσεν αυτους | ου κατιλιπον ⸗ αυτω̅ : | ουδε εν ενπνεον ✱ ✱ ✱

7. The Hexapla was completed, as we have seen, by
A.D. 240 or 245; the Tetrapla, which was a copy of four
columns of the Hexapla, followed, perhaps during Origen's
last years at Tyre[1]. A large part of the labour of transcription may have been borne by the copyists who were in
constant attendance on the great scholar, but he was doubtless
his own διορθωτής, and the two Hebrew columns and the LXX.
column of the Hexapla were probably written by his own
hand.

Eusebius in a well-known passage describes the costly and
laborious process by which Origen's commentaries on Scripture
were given to the world: *H.E.* vi. 23 ταχυγράφοι γὰρ αὐτῷ πλείους
ἢ ἑπτὰ τὸν ἀριθμὸν παρῆσαν ὑπαγορεύοντι, χρόνοις τεταγμένοις ἀλλή-
λους ἀμείβοντες, βιβλιογράφοι τε οὐχ ἥττους ἅμα καὶ κόραις ἐπὶ τὸ
καλλιγραφεῖν ἠσκημέναις· ὧν ἁπάντων τὴν δέουσαν τῶν ἐπιτηδείων
ἄφθονον περιουσίαν ὁ Ἀμβρόσιος παρεστήσατο. Two of these
classes of workers, the βιβλιογράφοι and καλλιγράφοι (cf. Gardthausen, *Gr. Palaeographie*, p. 297), must have found ample
employment in the preparation of the Hexapla. The material
used was possibly papyrus. Although there are extant fragments
of writing on vellum which may be attributed to the second
century, "there is every reason to suppose that to the end of the
third century papyrus held its own, at any rate in Egypt, as the

[1] See the confused and inexact statement of Epiphanius, *de mens. et
pond.* 18.

material on which literary works were written" (Kenyon, *Palaeography of Gk papyri*, p. 113 f. ; on the size of existing papyrus rolls, see p. 16 ff.). This view receives some confirmation from Jerome's statement (*ep.* 141) that Acacius and Evagrius endeavoured to replace with copies on parchment some of the books in the library at Caesarea which were in a damaged condition ("bibliothecam...ex parte corruptam...in membranis instaurare conati sunt")[1]. According to Tischendorf (*prolegg. in cod. Frid. Aug.* § 1) cod. ℵ was written on skins of antelopes, each of which supplied only two leaves of the MS. The Hexapla, if copied in so costly a way, would have taxed the resources even of Origen's generous ἐργοδιώκτης.

It is difficult to conceive of a codex or series of codices so gigantic as the Hexapla. Like the great Vatican MS., it would have exhibited at each opening at least six columns, and in certain books, like the Sinaitic MS., eight. Its bulk, even when allowance has been made for the absence in it of the uncanonical books, would have been nearly five times as great as that of the Vatican or the Sinaitic Old Testament. The Vatican MS. contains 759 leaves, of which 617 belong to the Old Testament; when complete, the O. T. must have occupied 650 leaves, more or less. From these data it may be roughly calculated that the Hexapla, if written in the form of a codex, would have filled 3250 leaves or 6500 pages[2]; and these figures are exclusive of the *Quinta* and *Sexta*, which may have swelled the total considerably. Even the Tetrapla would have exceeded 2000 leaves. So immense a work must have been the despair of copyists, and it is improbable that any attempt was made to reproduce either of the editions as a whole. The originals, however, were long preserved at Caesarea in Palestine, where they were deposited, perhaps by Origen himself, in the library of Pamphilus. There they were studied by Jerome in the fourth century (*in Psalmos comm.* ed. Morin., p. 5 : " ἑξαπλοῦς Origenis in Caesariensi bibliotheca relegens"; *ib.* p. 12 : "cum vetustum Origenis hexaplum psalterium revolverem, quod ipsius manu

---

[1] See Birt, *das antike Buchwesen*, pp. 100, 107 ff.
[2] If the Hexapla was written in lines consisting of only one word like the Cairo palimpsest, this estimate is far too low ; see Nestle in Hastings, *D. B.* iv. p. 443.

fuerat emendatum"; *in ep. ad Tit.*: "nobis curae fuit omnes veteris legis libros quos v. d. Adamantius in Hexapla digesserat de Caesariensi bibliotheca descriptos ex ipsis authenticis emendare." There also they were consulted by the writers and owners of Biblical MSS.; compare the interesting note attached by a hand of the seventh century to the book of Esther in cod. ℵ: ἀντεβλήθη πρὸς παλαιότατον λίαν ἀντίγραφον δεδιορθωμένον χειρὶ τοῦ ἁγίου μάρτυρος Παμφίλου· πρὸς δὲ τῷ τέλει τοῦ αὐτοῦ παλαιοτάτου βιβλίου...ὑποσημείωσις τοῦ αὐτοῦ μάρτυρος ὑπέκειτο ἔχουσα οὕτως· ΜΕΤΕΛΗΜΦΘΗ ΚΑΙ ΔΙΟΡΘΩΘΗ ΠΡΟC ΤΑ ἙΖΑΠΛΑ Ὠριγενοῦс ὙΠ᾽ ΑΥΤΟΥ̂ ΔΙΟΡΘΩΜΕΝΑ (*O. T. in Greek*, ii. p. 780); and the notes prefixed to Isaiah and Ezekiel in Cod. Marchalianus (Q); the second of these notes claims that the copy from which Ezekiel was transcribed bore the subscription ΤΑΥ̂ΤΑ ΜΕΤΕΛΗΦΘΗ ἈΠΟ ΤΩ̂Ν ΚΑΤΑ ΤΑC ἘΚΔΟΣΕΙC ἙΖΑΠΛΩ̂Ν, ΚΑΙ ΔΙΟΡΘΩΘΗ ἈΠΟ ΤΩ̂Ν Ὠριγενοῦс ΑΥΤΟΥ̂ ΤΕΤΡΑΠΛΩ̂Ν ἌΤΙΝΑ ΚΑΙ ΑΥΤΟΥ̂ ΧΕΙΡΙ ΔΙΟΡΘΩΤΟ ΚΑΙ ἘCΚΟΛΙΟΓΡΑΦΗΤΟ (*ib.* iii. p. viii.)[1]. The library of Pamphilus was in existence in the 6th century, for Montfaucon (*biblioth. Coisl.* p. 262) quotes from *Coisl.* 202[2], a MS. of that century, a colophon which runs: ἀντεβλήθη δὲ ἡ βίβλος πρὸς τὸ ἐν Καισαρίᾳ ἀντίγραφον τῆς βιβλιοθήκης τοῦ ἁγίου Παμφίλου χειρὶ γεγραμμένον αὐτοῦ. But in 638 Caesarea fell into the hands of the Saracens, and from that time the Library was heard of no more. Even if not destroyed at the moment, it is probable that every vestige of the collection perished during the vicissitudes through which the town passed between the 7th century and the 12th[3]. Had the Hexapla been buried in Egypt, she might have preserved it in her sands; it can scarcely be hoped that the sea-washed and storm-beaten ruins of Kaisariyeh cover a single leaf.

[1] See also the note at the end of the Scholia on Proverbs printed in the *Notitia l. c.*: μετελήφθησαν ἀφ᾽ ὧν εὕρομεν ἐξαπλῶν, καὶ πάλιν αὐτοχειρὶ Πάμφιλος καὶ Εὐσέβιος διορθώσαντο.
[3] = H^paul, Gregory, p. 449, Scrivener-Miller, i. p. 183 f.
[3] See G. A. Smith, *Hist. Geogr. of Palestine*, p. 143 f.

LITERATURE. Fragments of the Hexapla were printed by Peter Morinus in his notes to the Roman edition of the Septuagint (1587). Separate collections have since been published by J. Drusius (*Vet. interpretum Graecorum...fragmenta collecta...a Jo. Drusio*, Arnheim, 1622), Bernard Montfaucon (*Origenis Hexaplorum quae supersunt*, Paris, 1713), and F. Field (Oxford, 1875), whose work has superseded all earlier attempts to recover the Hexapla. A fuller list may be seen in Fabricius-Harles, iii. 701 ff. Materials for an enlarged edition of Field are already beginning to accumulate; such may be found in Pitra, *Analecta sacra*, iii. (Venice, 1883), p. 551 ff.; E. Klostermann, *Analecta zur...Hexapla* (Leipzig, 1895), G. Morin, *Anecdota Maredsolana* iii. 1 (Mareds., 1895; cf. *Expositor*, June 1895, p. 424 ff.), and the Oxford Concordance. Among helps to the study of the Hexapla, besides the introductions already specified, the following may be mentioned: the Prolegomena in Field's *Hexapla*, the art. *Hexapla* in *D. C. B.* by Dr C. Taylor; the introduction to Dr Driver's *Notes on Samuel* (p. xliii. ff.), and Harnack-Preuschen, *Gesch. d. altchristt. Litt.* i. p. 339 ff. For the literature of the Syro-Hexaplaric version see c. iv.

8. The Hexapla as a whole was perhaps too vast to be copied[1], and copies even of particular books were rarely attempted; yet there was nothing to forbid the separate publication of the fifth column, which contained the revised Septuagint. This idea presented itself to Pamphilus and his friend Eusebius, and the result was the wide circulation in Palestine during the fourth century of the Hexaplaric LXX., detached from the Hebrew text and the other Greek versions, but retaining, more or less exactly, the corrections and additions adopted by Origen with the accompanying Hexaplaric signs. "Provinciae Palestinae," writes Jerome in his preface to Chronicles, "codices legunt quos ab Origene elaboratos Eusebius et Pamphilus vulgaverunt." Elsewhere[2] he warns his correspondents "aliam esse editionem quam Origenes et Caesariensis Eusebius omnesque Graeciae tractatores κοινήν (id est communem) appellant atque vulgatam..., aliam LXX. interpretum quae in ἑξαπλοῖς codicibus reperitur.. et Ierosoly-

---

[1] Hieron. *praef. in Jos.*: "et sumptu et labore maximo indigent."
[2] *Ep. ad Sunn. et Fret.* 2.

mae atque in orientis ecclesia decantatur." The Hexaplaric
text receives his unhesitating support: "ea autem quae
habetur in ἑξαπλοῖς...ipsa est quae in eruditorum libris incor-
rupta et immaculata LXX. interpretum translatio reservatur[1]."
This edition, sometimes described as τὸ Εὐσεβίου or τὸ Παλαι-
στιναῖον, or simply Ὠρ[ιγένης], is mentioned with great respect
in the scholia of MSS. which do not on the whole follow its
text. Specimens of such notes have already been given; they
usually quote the words in which Pamphilus describes the
part borne by himself and his friends respectively in the production of the book. Thus a note quoted by an early hand in
cod. ℵ at the end of 2 Esdras says, Ἀντωνῖνος ἀντέβαλεν,
Πάμφιλος διόρθωσα. The subscription to Esther ends Ἀντωνῖνος ὁμολογητὴς ἀντέβαλεν, Πάμφιλος διορθώσατο [τὸ] τεῦχος ἐν
τῇ φυλακῇ. The scholion prefixed to Ezekiel in Q introduces
the name of Eusebius, assigning him another function: Εὐσέβιος ἐγὼ τὰ σχόλια παρέθηκα· Πάμφιλος καὶ Εὐσέβιος διορθώσαντο. In its subscription to 1 Kings the Syro-Hexaplar quotes
a note which runs: Εὐσέβιος διορθωσάμην ὡς ἀκριβῶς ἠδυνάμην.
It would seem as though the work of comparing the copy with
the original was committed to the otherwise unknown[2] Antoninus, whilst the more responsible task of making corrections
was reserved for Pamphilus and Eusebius[3]. Part of the work
at least was done while Pamphilus lay in prison, i.e. between
A.D. 307 and 309, but it was probably continued and completed by Eusebius after the martyr's death.

The separate publication of the Hexaplaric LXX. was
undertaken in absolute good faith; Pamphilus and Eusebius
believed (as did even Jerome nearly a century afterwards) that
Origen had succeeded in restoring the old Greek version to its
primitive purity, and they were moved by the desire to com-
municate this treasure to the whole Church. It was impos-

---

[1] *Adv. Rufin.* ii. 27.
[2] Identified by some with an Antoninus martyred three months before
Pamphilus (Lake).
[3] On ἀντιβάλλειν and διορθοῦσθαι, see Scrivener-Miller, i. p. 55.

sible for them to foresee that the actual result of their labours would be to create a recension of the LXX. which was a mischievous mixture of the Alexandrian version with the versions of Aquila and Theodotion. The Hexaplaric signs, intended for the use of scholars, lost their meaning when copied into a text which was no longer confronted with the Hebrew or the later versions based upon it; and there was a natural tendency on the part of scribes to omit them, when their purpose was no longer manifest.

When we consider that the Hexaplaric Septuagint claimed to be the work of Origen, and was issued under the authority of the martyr Pamphilus and the yet greater Bishop of Caesarea, we can but wonder that its circulation was generally limited to Palestine[1]. Not one of our uncial Bibles gives the Hexaplaric text as a whole, and it is presented in a relatively pure form by very few MSS., the uncials G and M, which contain only the Pentateuch and some of the historical books, and the cursives 86 and 88 (Holmes and Parsons), which contain the Prophets. But a considerable number of so-called Hexaplaric codices exist, from which it is possible to collect fragments not only of the fifth column, but of all the Greek columns of the Hexapla; and a still larger number of our MSS. offer a mixed text in which the influence of the Hexaplaric LXX., or of the edition published by Pamphilus and Eusebius, has been more or less extensively at work[2]. The problems presented by this and other causes of mixture will come under consideration in the later chapters of this book.

9. While the Hexaplaric Septuagint was being copied at Caesarea for the use of Palestine, Hesychius was engaged in correcting the common Egyptian text.

---

[1] Jerome says indeed (*ep. ad Aug.* ii.): "quod si feceris (i.e. if you refuse Origen's recension) omnino ecclesiae bibliothecas damnare cogeris; vix enim unus vel alter inveniatur liber qui ista non habeat." But he is drawing a hasty inference from experiences gathered in Palestine.

[2] See c. v.

Hieron. *in praef. ad Paralipp.*: "Alexandria et Aegyptus in Septuaginta suis Hesychium laudat auctorem"; cf. *adv. Rufin.* ii. where the statement is repeated[1], and *praef. in Evangelia*, where the revision of Hesychius is represented as having included both Testaments, and his O. T. work is condemned as infelicitous ("nec in V.T. post LXX. interpretes emendare quod licuit"); the Hesychian revision of the Gospels is censured by the *Decretum Gelasii*, which even denounces them as apocryphal ("evangelia quae falsavit Hesychius, apocrypha").

It is not easy to ascertain who this Hesychius was. The most conspicuous person of that name is the lexicographer, and he has been identified with the reviser of the Greek Bible[2]. But later researches shew that Hesychius the lexicographer was a pagan who lived in the second half of the fourth century. The author of the Egyptian revision was more probably[3] the martyr Bishop who is mentioned by Eusebius in connexion with Phileas Bishop of Thmuis, Pachymius, and Theodorus (*H.E.* viii. 13 Φιλέας τε καὶ Ἡσύχιος καὶ Παχύμιος καὶ Θεόδωρος τῶν ἀμφὶ τὴν Αἴγυπτον ἐκκλησιῶν ἐπίσκοποι). The four names appear together again in a letter addressed to Meletius (Routh, *rell. sacr.* iv. p. 91 ff.); and Eusebius has preserved a pastoral written by Phileas in prison in view of his approaching martyrdom (*H. E.* viii. 10). Phileas was a distinguished scholar (*H. E.* viii. 9 διαπρέψας.. ἐν.. τοῖς κατὰ φιλοσοφίαν λόγοις, *ib.* 10 τῶν ἔξωθεν μαθημάτων ἕνεκα πολλοῦ λόγου ἄξιον...τοῦ ὡς ἀληθῶς φιλοσόφου.. μάρτυρος), and the association of his name with that of Hesychius suggests that he may have shared in the work of Biblical revision. It is pleasant to think of the two episcopal confessors employing their enforced leisure in their Egyptian prison by revising the Scriptures for the use of their flocks, nearly at the same time that Pamphilus and Eusebius

---

[1] Jerome speaks elsewhere (*in Esa.* lviii. 11) of "exemplaria Alexandrina."

[2] Fabricius-Harles, vii. p. 547 (cf. vi. p. 205).

[3] This is however mere conjecture; see Harnack-Preuschen, i. p. 442: "dass dieser Hesychius...identisch ist mit dem etwa gleichzeitigen Bibelkritiker gleichen Namens, ist nicht zu erweisen."

and Antoninus were working under similar conditions at Caesarea. It is easy to account for the acceptance of the Hesychian revision at Alexandria and in Egypt generally, if it was produced under such circumstances.

To what extent the Hesychian recension of the Old Testament is still accessible in MSS. and versions of the LXX. is uncertain. As far back as 1786 Münter threw out the very natural suggestion that the Egyptian recension might be found in the Egyptian versions. In his great monograph on the Codex Marchalianus Ceriani takes note that in the Prophets, with the exception perhaps of Ezekiel, the original text of that great Egyptian MS. agrees closely with the text presupposed by the Egyptian versions and in the works of Cyril of Alexandria, and that it is supported by the cursive MSS. 26, 106, 198, 306; other cursives of the same type are mentioned by Cornill[1] as yielding an Hesychian text in Ezekiel. For the remaining books of the LXX. we have as yet no published list of MSS. containing a probably Hesychian text, but the investigations now being pursued by the editors of the larger Cambridge LXX. may be expected to yield important help in this direction[2].

10. Meanwhile the rising school of Antioch was not inactive in the field of Biblical revision. An Antiochian recension of the κοινή had in Jerome's time come to be known by the name of its supposed author, the martyr Lucian[3].

Hieron. *praef. in Paralipp.*: "Constantinopolis usque Antiochiam Luciani martyris exemplaria probat." Cf. (Ep. cvi.) *ad Sunn. et Fret.* 2 "[ἡ κοινή]...a plerisque nunc Λουκιανός dicitur." Ps.-Athan. *syn. sacr. script.* ἑβδόμη πάλιν καὶ τελευταία ἑρμηνεία τοῦ ἁγίου Λουκιανοῦ τοῦ μεγάλου ἀσκητοῦ καὶ μάρτυρος, ὅστις καὶ αὐτὸς ταῖς προγεγραμμέναις ἐκδόσεσι καὶ τοῖς Ἐβραικοῖς ἐντυχὼν καὶ ἐποπτεύσας μετ' ἀκριβείας τὰ λείποντα ἢ καὶ περιττὰ τῆς ἀληθείας ῥήματα

---

[1] *Das Buch des Propheten Ezechiel*, p. 66 ff.; the Hesychian group in Ezekiel is βϛʹκλμφψ, i.e. codd. 49, 68, 87, 90, 91, 228, 238 (Parsons). See also Ceriani in *Rendiconti* (Feb. 18, 1886).

[2] For the Octateuch Mr McLean (*J. Th. St.* ii. 306) quotes as Hesychian or Egyptian MSS. H.-P. 44, 74, 76, 84, 106, 134, &c.

[3] Cf. the scholion in cod. M at 3 Regn. iii. 46 ἐντεῦθεν διαφόρως ἔχει τὰ ἀνατολικὰ βιβλία. The Lucianic text was also known as the ἐκκλησιαστικὴ ἔκδοσις (Oeconomus, iv. 548).

καὶ διορθωσάμενος ἐν τοῖς οἰκείοις τῶν γραφῶν τόποις ἐξέδοτο τοῖς χριστιανοῖς ἀδελφοῖς· ἥτις δὴ καὶ ἑρμηνεία μετὰ τὴν ἄθλησιν καὶ μαρτυρίαν τοῦ αὐτοῦ ἁγίου Λουκιανοῦ τὴν γεγονυῖαν ἐπὶ Διοκλητιανοῦ καὶ Μαξιμιανοῦ τῶν τυράννων, ἤγουν τὸ ἰδιόχειρον αὐτοῦ τῆς ἐκδόσεως βιβλίον, εὑρέθη ἐν Νικομηδείᾳ ἐπὶ Κωνσταντίνου βασιλέως τοῦ μεγάλου παρὰ Ἰουδαίοις ἐν τοίχῳ πυργίσκῳ περικεχρισμένῳ κονιάματι εἰς διαφύλαξιν (cf. the Acts of Lucian in Bolland. i. p. 363). Suidas *s.v.* οὗτος τὰς ἱερὰς βίβλους θεασάμενος πολὺ τὸ νόθον εἰσδεξαμένας, τοῦ γε χρόνου λυμηναμένου πολλὰ τῶν ἐν αὐταῖς καὶ τῆς συνεχοῦς ἀφ᾽ ἑτέρων εἰς ἕτερα μεταθέσεως...αὐτὸς ἁπάσας ἀναλαβὼν ἐκ τῆς Ἑβραΐδος ἐπανενεώσατο γλώσσης. Cf. also Cyr. Alex. *in Psalmos praef.*

Lucian, who was born at Samosata, began his studies at Edessa, whence he passed to Antioch at a time when Malchion was master of the Greek School (Eus. *H. E.* vii. 29, Hieron. *de virr. ill.* 71). At Antioch Lucian acquired a great reputation for Biblical learning (Eus. *H. E.* ix. 6 τοῖς ἱεροῖς μαθήμασι συγκεκροτημένος, Suid. *s.v.* αὐτὴν [sc. τὴν Ἑβραΐδα γλῶσσαν] ὡς τὰ μάλιστα ἦν ἠκριβωκώς). From some cause not clearly explained Lucian was under a cloud for several years between A.D. 270 and 299 (Theodoret[1], *H. E.* i. 3 ἀποσυναγωγὸς ἔμεινε τριῶν ἐπισκόπων πολυετοῦς χρόνου). On his restoration to communion he was associated with Dorotheus, who was a Hebrew scholar, as well as a student of Greek literature (Eus. *H. E.* vii. 32 φιλόκαλος δ᾽ οὗτος περὶ τὰ θεῖα γράμματα καὶ τῆς Ἑβραίων ἐπεμελήθη γλώττης, ὡς καὶ αὐταῖς ταῖς Ἑβραικαῖς γραφαῖς ἐπιστημόνως ἐντυγχάνειν· ἦν δὲ οὗτος τῶν μάλιστα ἐλευθερίων, προπαιδείας τε τῆς καθ᾽ Ἕλληνας οὐκ ἄμοιρος). As Pamphilus was assisted by Eusebius, as Phileas and others were probably associated with Hesychius, so (the conjecture may be hazarded) Dorotheus and Lucian worked together at the Antiochian revision of the Greek Bible. If, as Dr Hort thought, " of known names Lucian's has a better claim than any other to be associated with the early Syrian revision of the New Testament[2]," the

---

[1] Oeconomus refuses to identify this person with the martyr and saint (iv. p. 498 n.).
[2] *Introduction to the N. T. in Greek*, p. 138; c.. the *Oxford Debate on the Textual Criticism of the N. T.*, p. 29.

6

Syrian revision of the Old Testament, which called for a
knowledge of Hebrew, may have been due more especially
to the Hebraist Dorotheus. Lucian, however, has the exclusive credit of the latter, and possibly was the originator of
the entire work. If we may believe certain later writers, his
revision of the LXX. was on a great scale, and equivalent to a
new version of the Hebrew Bible; Pseudo-Athanasius goes so
far as to call it the ἑβδόμη ἑρμηνεία, placing it on a level with
the Greek versions of the Hexapla. But Jerome's identification
of 'Lucian' with the κοινή presents quite another view of its
character and one which is probably nearer to the truth. It
was doubtless an attempt to revise the κοινή in accordance
with the principles of criticism which were accepted at Antioch.
In the New Testament (to use the words of Dr Hort[1]) "the
qualities which the authors of the Syrian text seem to have
most desired to impress on it are lucidity and completeness...
both in matter and in diction the Syrian text is conspicuously
a full text." If the Lucianic revision of the LXX. was made
under the influences which guided the Antiochian revision of
the New Testament, we may expect to find the same general
principles at work[2], modified to some extent by the relation
of the LXX. to a Hebrew original, and by the circumstance
that the Hebrew text current in Syria in the third century
A.D. differed considerably from the text which lay before the
Alexandrian translators.

We are not left entirely to conjectures. During his work
upon the Hexapla[3] Field noticed that in an epistle prefixed
to the Arabic Syro-Hexaplar[4], the marginal letter ܠ (L) was said

---

[1] *Introduction*, p. 134 f.
[2] Cf. F. C. Burkitt, *Old Latin and Itala*, p. 91, "Lucian's recension
in fact corresponds in a way to the Antiochian text of the N. T. Both
are texts composed out of ancient elements welded together and polished
down."
[3] *Prolegg.* p. lxxxiv. f.
[4] See c. v.

to indicate Lucianic readings. Turning to the Syro-Hexaplar itself, he found this letter in the margin of 2 Kings (= 4 Regn.) at cc. ix. 9, 28, x. 24, 25, xi. 1, xxiii. 33, 35. But the readings thus marked as Lucianic occur also in the cursive Greek MSS. 19, 82, 93, 108; and further examination shewed that these four MSS. in the Books of Kings, Chronicles, and Ezra-Nehemiah agree with the text of the LXX. offered by the Antiochian fathers Chrysostom and Theodoret, who might have been expected to cite from 'Lucian.' Similar reasoning led Field to regard codd. 22, 36, 48, 51, 62, 90, 93, 144, 147, 233, 308 as presenting a more or less Lucianic text in the Prophets. Meanwhile, Lagarde had independently[1] reached nearly the same result, so far as regards the historical books. He satisfied himself that codd. 19, 82, 93, 108, 118[2], had sprung from a common archetype, the text of which was practically identical with that of the LXX. as quoted by Chrysostom, i.e., with the Antiochian text of the fourth century, which presumably was Lucianic. Lagarde proceeded to construct from these and other sources a provisional text of Lucian, but his lamented death intercepted the work, and only the first volume of his Lucianic LXX. has appeared (Genesis—2 Esdr., Esther).

The following specimen will serve to shew the character of Lucian's revision, as edited by Lagarde; an apparatus is added which exhibits the readings of codd. B and A.

3 Regn. xviii. 22—28.

[22] καὶ εἶπεν Ἡλίας πρὸς τὸν λαὸν Ἐγὼ ὑπολέλειμμαι προφήτης κυρίου, προφήτης μονώτατος, καὶ οἱ προφῆται τοῦ Βααλ τετρακόσιοι καὶ πεντήκοντα ἄνδρες, καὶ οἱ προφῆται τῶν ἀλσῶν τετρακόσιοι. [23] δότωσαν οὖν ἡμῖν δύο βόας, καὶ ἐκλεξάσθωσαν ἑαυτοῖς τὸν ἕνα καὶ μελισάτωσαν καὶ ἐπιθέτωσαν ἐπὶ ξύλα καὶ πῦρ μὴ ἐπιθέτωσαν· καὶ ἐγὼ ποιήσω τὸν βοῦν τὸν ἄλλον, καὶ πῦρ οὐ μὴ ἐπιθῶ. [24] καὶ βοᾶτε ἐν ὀνόματι θεῶν ὑμῶν, καὶ ἐγὼ ἐπικαλέσομαι ἐν ὀνόματι κυρίου τοῦ

---

[1] Cf. his *Prolegomena* to *Librorum V. T. Canon.* Pars prior graece (Gotting. 1883), p. xiv.
[2] Or, as he denotes them, *h, f, m, d, p.*

θεοῦ μου, καὶ ἔσται ὁ θεὸς ὃς ἂν ἐπακούσῃ σήμερον ἐν πυρί, οὗτός ἐστι
θεός. καὶ ἀπεκρίθη πᾶς ὁ λαὸς καὶ εἶπεν Ἀγαθὸς ὁ λόγος ὃν ἐλάλησας.
²⁵καὶ εἶπεν Ἡλίας τοῖς προφήταις τῆς αἰσχύνης Ἐκλέξασθε ἑαυτοῖς
τὸν βοῦν τὸν ἕνα, ὅτι ὑμεῖς πολλοί, καὶ ποιήσατε πρῶτοι, καὶ ἐπικαλεῖσθε ἐν ὀνόματι θεῶν ὑμῶν, καὶ πῦρ μὴ ἐπιθῆτε. ²⁶καὶ ἔλαβον τὸν
βοῦν καὶ ἐποίησαν, καὶ ἐπεκαλοῦντο ἐν ὀνόματι τοῦ Βααλ καὶ εἶπον
Ἐπάκουσον ἡμῶν, ὁ Βααλ, ἐπάκουσον ἡμῶν. καὶ οὐκ ἦν φωνὴ καὶ
οὐκ ἦν ἀκρόασις. καὶ διέτρεχον ἐπὶ τοῦ θυσιαστηρίου οὗ ἐποίησαν.
²⁷καὶ ἐγένετο μεσημβρία, καὶ ἐμυκτήρισεν αὐτοὺς Ἡλίας ὁ Θεσβίτης
καὶ προσέθετο λέγων Ἐπικαλεῖσθε ἐν φωνῇ μεγάλῃ ἅμα, μήποτε ἀδο-
λεσχία τις ἔστιν αὐτῷ, καὶ ἅμα μήποτε χρηματίζει αὐτὸς ἢ μήποτε
καθεύδει, καὶ ἐξαναστήσεται. ²⁸καὶ ἐπεκαλοῦντο ἐν φωνῇ μεγάλῃ καὶ
κατετέμνοντο κατὰ τὸν ἐθισμὸν αὐτῶν ἐν μαχαίραις καὶ ἐν σειρομάσ-
ταις ἕως ἐκχύσεως αἵματος ἐπ' αὐτούς.

22 Ηλειου ΒΑ | κυριου] pr του ΒΑ | om προφητης 2⁰ ΒΑ | οι
προφηται 2⁰] om οι Α | του αλσους ΒΑ | om τετρακοσιοι 2⁰ Α
23 om ουν ΒΑ | om και επιθ. επι ξυλα Α | ξυλα] των ξυλων Β | τον
αλλον]+και δωσω επι τα ξυλα Α 24 θεων] θεου Α | εαν ΒΑ | om
σημερον ΒΑ | om εστι ΒΑ | απεκριθησαν ΒΑ | ειπον Β ειπαν Α |
αγαθος ο λογος ον] καλον το ρημα ο ΒΑ 25 Ηλειου ΒΑ | βουν]
μοσχον ΒΑ | και ποι. πρωτοι οτι πολλοι υμεις ΒΑ | επικαλεσασθε
Β | θεων] θεου ΒΑ 26 ελαβεν Α | βουν] μοσχον ΒΑ+ον εδωκεν
αυτοις Α | Βααλ 1⁰]+εκ πρωιθεν εως μεσημβριας ΒΑ 27 Ηλειου
ΒΑ | προσεθετο λεγων] ειπεν ΒΑ | αμα] οτι θεος εστιν ΒΑ | μη-
ποτε 1⁰] οτι ΒΑ | τις εστιν αυτω] αυτω εστιν ΒΑ | καθευδει]+αυτος
ΒΑ 28 κατα τον εθισμον αυτων] om Β κατα το κριμα αυτων
Α | μαχαιρα Β | om εν 3⁰ Β

A comparison of 'Lucian' in this passage with the two great
uncials of the LXX. reveals two classes of variants in the former.
(1) Some of the changes appear to be due to a desire to render
the version smoother or fuller, e.g. Ἡλίας for Ἡλειού, the repeti-
tion of προφήτης before μονώτατος, the substitution of τῶν ἀλσῶν
for τοῦ ἄλσους, of ἀπεκρίθη for ἀπεκρίθησαν, and of ἀγαθὸς ὁ λόγος
for καλὸν τὸ ῥῆμα, and the addition of σήμερον. (2) Others seem
to indicate an attempt to get nearer to the Hebrew, e.g. δότωσαν
οὖν (וְיִתְּנוּ), βοῦν (פַּר); or an adherence to an older reading which
the Hexaplaric LXX. had set aside, e.g. the omission of ὃν ἔδωκεν
αὐτοῖς[1] and ἐκ πρωίθεν ἕως μεσημβρίας. On the other hand
Lucian follows the current Hebrew in κατὰ τὸν ἐθισμὸν αὐτῶν,
though he substitutes the easier ἐθισμός for Aquila's κρίμα, which
cod. A has taken over from the Hexapla.

Professor Driver, as the result of a wider examination, points
out[2] that the Lucianic recension is distinguished by (1) the sub-

[1] A Hexaplaric reading due to Aquila ; see Field *ad loc.*
[2] *Notes on the Heb. text of the Books of Samuel,* p. li. f.

stitution of synonyms for the words employed by the LXX.; (2) the occurrence of double renderings; (3) the occurrence of renderings "which presuppose a Hebrew original self-evidently superior in the passages concerned to the existing Massoretic text." The last of these peculiarities renders it of great importance for the criticism of the Hebrew Bible.

Lucian suffered martyrdom at Nicomedia under Maximin in the year 311 or 312[1]. According to the Pseudo-Athanasian Synopsis, his recension of the LXX. was subsequently discovered at Nicomedia, bricked up in a wall. The story may have arisen from a desire to invest the ἐβδόμη (as 'Lucian' is called by the author of the Synopsis) with the same air of romance that belonged to the *Quinta* and *Sexta*, both of which were found, as he asserts, ἐν πίθοις. It is more probable that copies were circulated from Antioch in the ordinary way, and that some of these after the persecution reached Nicomedia and Constantinople. The name of Lucian would be enough to guarantee the general acceptance of the work. He died in the peace of the Church, and a martyr; on the other hand his name was in high repute with the Arian leaders, who boasted of being συλλουκιανισταί[2]. Moreover, a revision which emanated from Antioch, the "ecclesiastical parent of Constantinople[3]," would naturally take root in the soil of the Greek East. In all dioceses which felt the influences of those two great sees, the Lucianic LXX. doubtless furnished during the fourth and fifth centuries the prevalent text of the Greek Old Testament[4].

11. The result of these multiplied labours of Christian scholars upon the text of the LXX. was not altogether satisfactory. Before the time of Jerome much of the original text of the Alexandrian Bible had disappeared. Men read their Old Testament in the recension of Lucian, if they lived in North Syria, Asia Minor, or Greece; in that of Hesychius, if they belonged

---

[1] Mason, *Persecution of Diocletian*, p. 324.
[2] Newman, *Arians*, p. 6 f.; Gwatkin, *Studies of Arianism*, p. 31 n.
[3] Hort, *Introd.* p. 143.
[4] On Lucian's work see the art. *Lucianic Recension of the LXX.* in *Ch. Q. R.* (Jan. 1901); E. Hautsch, *Der Lukiantext des Oktateuch* (in *Mitteilungen des Septuaginta Unternehmens*, Heft i., Berlin, 1910.

to the Delta or the valley of the Nile; in Origen's Hexaplaric edition, if they were residents at Jerusalem or Caesarea. Thus, as the scholar of Bethlehem complains, the Christian world was divided between three opposing texts ("totus...orbis hac inter se trifaria varietate compugnat[1]"). To Jerome, as a Palestinian and an admirer of Origen's critical principles, the remedy was simple; the Hexaplaric text, which had been assimilated to the *Hebraica veritas*, ought everywhere to take the place of the κοινή represented by Hesychius or Lucian. Fortunately the task was beyond his strength, and MSS. and versions still survive which represent more or less fully the three recensions of the fourth century. But the *trifaria varietas* did not continue to perplex the Church; a fusion of texts arose which affected the greater part of the copies in varying proportions. No one of the rival recensions became dominant and traditional, as in the case of the New Testament[2]; among the later MSS. groups may be discerned which answer more or less certainly to this recension or to that, but the greater number of the cursives present a text which appears to be the result of mixture rather than of any conscious attempt to decide between the contending types.

[1] *Praef. in Paralipp.*
[2] Cf. Hort, *Introd.* p. 142.

CHAPTER IV.

ANCIENT VERSIONS BASED UPON THE SEPTUAGINT.

THE Christian Churches of Greek-speaking countries throughout the Empire read the Old Testament in the Alexandrian Version. Few of the provinces were wholly non-Hellenic; Greek was spoken not only in Egypt and Cyrenaica, in Western Syria, Asia Minor, Macedonia, and Achaia, but to a great extent in the West, in Italy and at Rome. Roman satirists of the first century complained that the capital had become a Greek city; the upper classes acquired Greek; the freedmen and slaves in many cases spoke it as their mother tongue[1]. Official letters addressed to the Roman Church or proceeding from her during the first two centuries were written in Greek; only three or at the most four of the Bishops of Rome during the same period bear Latin names[1]. In Gaul the Greek tongue had spread up the valley of the Rhone from Marseilles to Vienne and Lyons; the Viennese confessors of A.D. 177 used it in their correspondence both with the Roman Bishops and with their brethren in Asia Minor; the Bishop of Lyons wrote in the same language his great work against the false *gnosis* of the age. The Old Testament as known to Clement of Rome and Irenaeus of Lyons is substantially the Greek version of

---

[1] The evidence is collected by Caspari, *Quellen zur Gesch. d. Taufsymbols*, iii. 267 f., and summarised by Sanday and Headlam, *Romans*, p. lii. ff.

the Seventy. To the Church of North Africa, on the other hand, the Greek Bible was a sealed book; for Carthage, colonised from Rome before the capital had been flooded by Greek residents, retained the Latin tongue as the language of common life. It was at Carthage, probably, that the earliest daughter-version of the Septuagint, the Old Latin Bible, first saw the light[1]; certainly it is there that the oldest form of the Old Latin Bible first meets us in the writings of Cyprian. Other versions followed as the result of missionary enterprise; and to this latter source we owe the translations of the Old Testament which were made between the second century and the ninth into Egyptian, Ethiopic, Arabic, Gothic, Armenian, Georgian, and Slavonic. All these versions rest either wholly or in part upon the Septuagint, and therefore possess a special interest for the student of the Greek Bible. One other group has a claim upon his consideration. The earliest of the Syriac versions of the Old Testament is on the whole a translation from the Hebrew, but it shews the influence of the Septuagint in certain books. The rest, which belong to post-Nicene times, are based directly upon the Alexandrian Greek, and one of them forms the most important of extant witnesses to the text of the Hexaplaric recension.

I. Latin Versions from the Septuagint.

(1) The Latin Bible before Jerome.

With the exception of Jerome himself, our earliest authority upon the origin of the Old Latin Bible is Augustine of Hippo, and it may be well to begin by collecting his statements upon the subject.

---

[1] On the other hand reasons have been produced for suspecting that the Latin version had its origin at Antioch; see *Guardian*, May 25, 1892, p. 786 ff., and Dr H. A. A. Kennedy in Hastings' *D. B.* iii p. 54 ff. [This chapter was already in type when Dr Kennedy's article came into my hands. I regret that for this reason I have been unable to make full use of his exhaustive treatment of the Latin versions.]

Aug. *de civ. Dei* xviii. 43 ex hac LXX. interpretatione etiam in Latinam linguam interpretatum est quod ecclesiae Latinae tenent. *De doctr. Christ.* ii. 16 [after a reference to the "Latinorum interpretum infinita varietas"] "qui enim scripturas ex Hebraea lingua in Graecam verterunt, numerari possunt, Latini interpretes nullo modo; ut enim cuique primis fidei temporibus in manus venit codex Graecus et aliquantulum facultatis sibi utriusque linguae habere videbatur ausus est interpretari." *Ib.* 22: "in ipsis autem interpretationibus Itala ceteris praeferatur." *Ep.* ii. 82 (*ad Hieronymum*): "ideo autem desidero interpretationem tuam de LXX. ut...tanta Latinorum interpretum qui qualescunque hoc ausi sunt quantum possumus imperitia careamus."

This is African testimony, but it belongs to the end of the fourth century, and needs to be verified before it can be unhesitatingly received. Many of the discrepancies to which Augustine refers may be due to the carelessness or officiousness of correctors or transcribers; if, as Jerome tells us, there were towards the end of the fourth century as many types of text as there were MSS. of the Latin Bible ("tot exemplaria quot codices"), it is clearly out of the question to ascribe each of these to a separate translator. A few specimens, taken from Cyprian and extant MSS. of the O. L., will enable the student to form some idea of the extent to which these differences are found in extant texts[1].

Genesis xlviii. 17 f.

CYPRIAN, *testimonia* i. 21[2].	LYONS MS.
[17]ubi vidit autem Ioseph quoniam superposuit pater suus manum dexteram super caput Effraim, grave illi visum est, et adprehendit Ioseph manum patris sui auferre eam a capite Effraim ad caput Manasse. [18]dixit autem Ioseph ad patrem suum Non sic, pater; hic est primitivus meus; superpone dexteram tuam super caput suum.	[17]videns autem Ioseph quod misisset pater ipsius dexteram suam super caput Ephrem, grave ei visum est, et adprehendit Ioseph manum patris sui ut auferret eam a capite Ephrem super caput Manassis. [18]dixit autem Ioseph patri suo Non sicut, pater; hic enim primitivus est; impone dextram tuam super caput huius.

[1] To facilitate comparison obvious errors of the MSS. and orthographical peculiarities have been removed.

[2] On the MSS. of the *Testimonia* cf. *O. L. Texts*, ii. p. 123 ff.

Exod. xxxii. 21—24.

LYONS MS

²¹et dixit Moyses ad Aron Quid fecit tibi populus hic quia induxisti super eos peccatum magnum? ²²et dixit Aron ad Moysen Noli irasci, domine; tu enim scis impetum populi huius. ²³dixerunt enim mihi Fac nobis deos qui praeeant nos; nam Moyses hic homo qui eduxit nos de Aegypto, nescimus quid factum sit ei. ²⁴et dixi eis Quicunque habet aurum demat sibi. et dederunt mihi, et misi illud in ignem, et exiit vitulus.

WÜRZBURG FRAGMENTS.

²¹et dixit Moyses ad Aron Quid fecit populus hic quia induxisti super eos peccatum magnum? ²²et dixit Aron ad Moysen Noli irasci, domine; tu enim scis impetum populi huius. ²³dixerunt enim mihi Fac nobis deos qui praeecedant nos; nam Moyses hic homo qui eduxit nos ex terra Aegypti, nescimus quid factum sit ei. ²⁴et dixi illis Quicunque habet aurum, demat; et dempserunt*, et dederunt mihi, et misi illud in ignem, et exiit vitulus.

* cod. *demiserunt*

MUNICH FRAGMENTS.

²¹ et dixit Moyses ad Aron Quid fecit tibi populus hic quoniam immisisti eis delictum maximum? ²²et dixit Aron ad Moysen Ne irascaris, domine; tu enim scis populi huius impetum. ²³dixerunt enim mihi Fac nobis deos qui praecedant nos; Moyses enim hic homo qui nos eiecit de terra Aegypti, nescimus quid acciderit ei. ²⁴et dixi eis Si qui habet aurum ....† tollat ad me; et dederunt mihi, et proieci in ignem, et exivit vitulus.

† hiat cod.

Leviticus iv. 27—29.

LYONS MS.

²⁷si autem anima deliquerit inprudenter de populo terrae in faciendo vel unum ex omnibus praeceptis Dei quod non faciet, et neglexerit, ²⁸et cognitum ei fuerit delictum in quo deliquit* in eo, et adferet† primitivum de ovibus feminum immaculatum quod deliquit; ²⁹et imponet manum supra caput eius et occident primitivum delicti in loco in quo occidunt holocausta.

* cod. *delinquit*   † cod. *adfert*

WÜRZBURG FRAGMENTS.

²⁷si autem anima una deliquerit invita de populo in terra eo quod fecit unum ab omnibus praeceptis Domini, quod fieri non debet, et neglexerit, ²⁸et cognitum fuerit peccatum eius quod peccavit in ipso, et adferet hedillam de capris feminam sine vitio propter delictum quod deliquit; ²⁹et superponet manum super caput delicti sui et victimabunt hedillam quae est delicti in loco ubi victimabunt holocausta.

Micah v. 2.

CYPRIAN, *testimonia* ii. 12.

et tu, Bethleem, domus illius
Ephratha, num exigua es ut
constituaris in milibus Iuda? ex
te mihi procedet ut sit princeps
apud Israel, et processiones eius
a principio, a diebus saeculi.

WEINGARTEN FRAGMENTS.

et tu, Be[thleem,] domus [ha-
bita]tioni[s¹ Efra]ta, nu[mquid]
mini[ma es] ut sis [in milibus]
Iuda? [ex te mi]hi pro[diet qui]
sit prin[ceps in] Istra[hel, et
eg]ressus ip[sius ab] initi[o, ex
diebus] saec[uli].

Isaiah xxix. 11, 18.

CYPRIAN, *testimonia* i. 4.

¹¹et erunt vobis hi omnes sermones sicut sermones libri qui
signatus est, quem si dederis
homini scienti litteras ad legendum dicet Non possum legere,
signatus est enim...¹⁸sed in illa
die audient surdi sermones libri,
et qui in tenebris et qui in
nebula sunt; oculi caecorum videbunt.

WÜRZBURG FRAGMENTS.

¹¹et erunt verba haec omnia
sicut verba libri huius signati,
quem si dederint homini scienti
litteras dicentes ex lege haec, et
dicet Non possum legere, signatum est enim...¹⁸et audient in
die illa surdi verba libri, et qui
in tenebris et qui in nebula;
oculi caecorum videbunt.

It is clearly unsafe to generalise from a few specimens, but
the student will not fail to observe that the variations in these
extracts may, perhaps without exception, be attributed either
to the ordinary accidents of transcription or to the recensions
of the original text. In the case of the New Testament
Dr Hort² held that there was "some justification for the
alternative view that Italy had an indigenous version of her
own, not less original than the African," and where both types
of text existed, he distinguished them by the designations
'African Latin' and 'European Latin,' applying the term
'Italian'³ to later revisions of the European text. The classification of the Old Latin authorities for the O. T. is less
advanced, and owing to the fragmentary character of most of

---

¹ Burkitt (*O. L. and Itala*, p. 93) proposes *rejectionis.*

² *Introduction*, p. 78 ff. Cf. Westcott, *Canon*, p. 252 ff.; Wordsworth,
O. L. Biblical Texts, i., p. xxx. ff.

³ On Augustine's use of this term see F. C. Burkitt, *O. L. and Itala*,
p. 55 ff.

the MSS. it is more difficult; but we may assume that it will proceed on the same general lines, and that the pre-Hieronymian types of text in the Old Testament as in the New will be found to be mainly two, i.e. the African, and the European, with a possible sub-division of the latter class[1]. In pursuing this enquiry use must be made not only of the surviving fragments of O. L. MSS., but of the numerous quotations of the Latin versions which occur in writings anterior to the final triumph of the Vulgate. As Dr Hort has pointed out[2], certain of the Latin fathers "constitute a not less important province of Old Latin evidence than the extant MSS., not only furnishing landmarks for the investigation of the history of the version, but preserving numerous verses and passages in texts belonging to various ages and in various stages of modification." These patristic materials were collected with great care and fulness by Sabatier (*Bibliorum sacrorum Latinae versiones antiquae... opera et studio D. Petri Sabatier O. S. B.*, Reims, 1743, '49, Paris, 1751; vols. i. ii. contain the O. T.); but after the lapse of a century and a half his quotations can no longer be accepted without being compared with more recent editions of the Latin fathers[3], and they often need to be supplemented from sources which were not at his command[4].

These researches are important to the student of the Septuagint in so far as they throw light on the condition of the Greek text in the second and third centuries after Christ. The Latin translation of the Old Testament which is largely quoted by Cyprian was probably made in the second century, and certainly represents the text of MSS. earlier than

---

[1] Cf. Berger, *Histoire de la Vulgate*, p. 6; Kennedy, in Hastings' *D. B.* p. 58 ff.
[2] *Introduction*, p. 83.
[3] For this purpose the Vienna *Corpus Scriptorum Ecclesiasticorum Latinorum* is the best collection available; but it is still far from complete.
[4] A revised Sabatier is promised by the Munich Academy (*Archiv*, viii. 2, p. 311 ff.).

the time of Origen. What Mr Burkitt has pointed out[1] in reference to the prophetic books is doubtless true in general; "no...passage [to which the asterisk is prefixed in Hexaplaric MSS.] is found in any form of the African Latin." Thus, as he remarks, "the Old Latin brings us the best independent proof we have that the Hexaplar signs introduced by Origen can be relied on for the reconstruction of the LXX." Again, M. Berger[2] has called attention to the prominence of Lucianic readings in certain Old Latin texts; and the fact that a Lucianic element is widely distributed in Old Latin MSS. and quotations has also been recognised by Vercellone[3] and Ceriani[4]. This element is found even in the African text[5], and its occurrence there suggests that the Antiochian recension, though it was made at the beginning of the fourth century, has preserved ancient readings which existed also in the African copies of the LXX., though they found no place in our oldest codices.

We proceed to give a list of the extant remains of the Old Latin Version of the LXX., and the editions in which they are accessible.

OLD LATIN FRAGMENTS OF THE OLD TESTAMENT.

i. PENTATEUCH.

Cod. Lugdunensis, vi. (Ulysse Robert, *Pentateuchi e Codice Lugdunensi versio Latina antiquissima*, Paris, 1881; *Librorum Levitici et Numerorum versio antiqua Itala e cod. perantiquo in bibliotheca Ashburnhamiensi conservato*, London, 1868; Delisle, *Découverte d'une très ancienne version latine de deux livres de la Bible* in the *Journal des Savants*, Nov. 1895, p. 702 ff.; U. Robert, *Heptateuchi partis post. versio Lat. antiquissima e cod. Lugd.*, Lyons, 1900[6].

[1] *Rules of Tyconius*, p. cxvi. f.
[2] *Histoire de la Vulgate*, p. 6. Cf. Driver, *Samuel*, p. lxxvii. f.
[3] *Variae lectiones*, ii., p. 426.
[4] *Monumenta sacra et profana*, I. i., p. xvi.; *Le recensioni dei LXX e la versione latina detta Itala* (*Rendiconti*, Feb. 18, 1886). See also Driver, *Notes on Samuel*, p. lxxviii. f.; Kennedy, in Hastings' *D.B.*, *l.c.*; Nestle, *Einführung*[2], pp. 148 note, 280 [E. Tr., p. 182 f.]; Wordsworth-White. p. 654.
[5] Burkitt, *Rules of Tyconius*, p. cxvii.
[6] Cf. N. McLean in *J. Th. St.* ii. 305 ff.

Containing Gen. xvi. 9—xvii. 18, xix. 5—29, xxvi. 33—xxxiii.
15, xxxvii. 7—xxxviii. 22, xlii. 36—l. 26; Exod. i. 1—vii. 19, xxi.
9—36, xxv. 25—xxvi. 13, xxvii. 6—xl. 32 ; Leviticus[1] i. 1—xviii.
30, xxv. 16—xxvii. 34; Numbers[1] ; Deuteronomy[2].

Fragmenta Wirceburgensia palimpsesta, ? vi. (E. Ranke, *Par palimpsestorum Wirceburgensium*[3], Vienna, 1871).

Containing Gen. xxxvi. 2—7, 14—24, xl. 12—20, xli. 4—5;
Exod. xxii. 7—28, xxv. 30—xxvi. 12, xxxii. 15—33, xxxiii. 13—27,
xxxv. 13—xxxvi. 1, xxxix. 2—xl. 30; Lev. iv. 23—vi. 1, vii. 2,
11, 16—17, 22—27, viii. 1—3, 6—13, xi. 7—9, 12—15, 22—25, 27—
47, xvii. 14—xviii. 21, xix. 31—xx. 3, xx. 12, 20—xxi. 2, xxii. 19—
29; Deut. xxviii. 42—53, xxxi. 11—26.

Fragmenta Monacensia, v.—vi. (L. Ziegler, *Bruchstücke einer vorhieronymianischen Übersetzung des Pentateuchs*, Munich, 1883).

Containing Exod. ix. 15—x. 24, xii. 28—xiv. 4, xvi. 10—xx. 5,
xxxi. 15—xxxiii. 7, xxxvi. 13—xl. 32; Lev. iii. 17—iv. 25, xi. 12—
xiii. 6, xiv. 17—xv. 10, xviii. 18—xx. 3; Num. iii. 34—iv. 8, iv. 31
—v. 8, vii. 37—73, xi. 20—xii. 14, xxix. 6—xxx. 3, xxxi. 14—xxxv.
6, xxxvi. 4—13; Deut. viii. 19—x. 12, xxii. 7—xxiii. 4, xxviii. 1—
31, xxx. 16—xxxii. 29.

Lectiones ap. Cod. Ottobonian., viii. (C. Vercellone, *variae lectiones*, Rome, 1860, i. p. 183 ff.).

Containing Gen. xxxvii. 27—35, xxxviii. 6—14, xli. 1—4, 14—
20, xlvi. 15—20, xlviii. 13, 20—22, xlix. 11—32, l. 1—25 ; Exod. x.
13—14, xi. 7—10, xvi. 16—36, xvii. 1—10, xxiii. 12—30, xxiv. 1—
18, xxv. 1—37, xxvi. 1—27, xxvii. 1—5.

Fragmenta Philonea (F. C. Conybeare, in *Expositor* IV. iv.
p. 63 ff.).

Consisting of Gen. xxv. 20—xxviii. 8 in a Latin version of
Philo, *quaest*.

Fragmenta Vindobonensia (J. Belsheim, *Palimpsestus Vindob.*,
1885).

Containing Gen. xii. 17—xiii. 14, xv. 2—12.

---

[1] Leviticus and Numbers formed until recently a separate codex, see
Robert, p. vi. f.
[2] Deut. xi. 4—xxxiv. 12 belongs to the fragment announced by Delisle
and published by Robert in 1900.
[3] Belonging to the Library of the University of Würzburg.

ii. HISTORICAL BOOKS.

Joshua, Judges i. 1—xx. 31.

    Cod. Lugdunensis (in the portion published by Robert in 1900).

Ruth.

    Cod. Complutensis, ix., Madrid, Univ. Libr. (S. Berger in *Notices et Extraits,* xxxiv. 2, p. 119 ff.).

1—4 Regn.

    Fragments of Corbie and St Germain MSS. (Sabatier); fragments from a Verona MS. and a Vatican MS. in Bianchini (*Vindiciae*, p. cccxli. ff.), from a Vienna MS. in Haupt's *vet. antehieron. vers. fragmenta Vindobonensia,* 1877, from an Einsiedeln MS. in *Notices et Extraits* xxxiv. 2, p. 127 ff., and from leaves found at Magdeburg and Quedlinburg[1] printed by W. Schum, 1876, Weissbrodt, 1887, and A. Düning, 1888. Fragments of 2 Regn. at Vienna published by J. Haupt, 1877. A Vienna palimpsest containing considerable fragments of 1—2 Regn. (J. Belsheim, *Palimpsestus Vind.*, 1885). Readings from the margin of Cod. Goth. Legionensis[2] printed by C. Vercellone, ii. p. 179 ff.; cf. *Archiv*, viii. 2. (The Verona and Vatican fragments should perhaps be classed as Vulgate.)

1 Esdras.

    An O. L. text is to be found in the Paris MS. Bibl. Nat. lat. 111, the Madrid MS. E. R. 8, and another in a Lucca MS. ap. Lagarde, *Septuagintastudien,* 1892.

Judith, Tobit.

    Cod. Complutensis.
    Cod. Goth. Legionensis.
    Cod. Vatic. regin. (Bianchini, *Vindiciae,* p. cccl. f.; Tobit only).
    O. L. texts are also to be found in the Paris MSS. Bibl. Nat. lat. 6, 93, 161 (Tobit), 11505, 11549 (Judith), 11553, in the Munich MS. 6239, the Milan MS. Amb. E 26 infr. (Tobit), and the Oxford MS. Bodl. auct. E. infr. 2 (Judith). See *Notices et Extraits* xxxiv. 2, p. 142 ff. Of these texts some were printed by Sabatier, and Munich 6239 is in Belsheim's *Libr. Tobiae,* &c. (1893).

Esther.

    Cod. Pechianus (Sabatier).
    Cod. Vallicellanus (Bianchini, *Vindiciae,* p. ccxciv. ff.).

---

[1] See V. Schultze, *die Quedlinburger Itala-Miniaturen der k. Bibliothek in Berlin* (Munich, 1898).

[2] On these see Berger, *Hist. de la Vulgate,* p. 18 f., and the caution in *O. L. and Itala,* p. 9 f.

Cod. Complutensis (see above under Ruth).

An O. L. text of Esther is found also in the Paris MS. Bibl. Nat. lat. 11549 (= Corb. 7), the Lyons MS. 356, the Munich MSS. 6225, 6239, the Monte Casino MS. 35 (*Biblioth. Casin.* i., 1873), the Milan MS. Amb. E. 26 infr. (see S. Berger *op. cit.*).

1, 2 Maccabees.

O. L. texts are to be found in the Paris MS. Bibl. Nat. lat. 11553 (Sabatier) and the Milan MS. Amb. E. 26 inf. (A. Peyron, *Cic. fragmm.* i. 70 ff. (1824).
(See Berger, *op. cit.*)

iii. POETICAL BOOKS.

Psalms.

Cod. Veronensis (in Bianchini).
Cod. Sangermanensis (in Sabatier).
A Reichenau palimpsest described by Mone, *l. u. gr. Messen,* p. 40.
Fragments of the ᾠδαί edited by F. F. Fleck (Leipzig, 1837), and L. F. Hamann (Jena, 1874).

Job.

Fragment. Floriacense (Sabatier).   Containing c. xl. 3—9.
Readings from the margin of Cod. Goth. Legionensis (*Notices et Extraits,* p. 111 ff.).

Proverbs, Ecclesiastes, Canticles.

Readings in a St Gallen MS., see *Notices et Extraits,* p. 137 ff.   Fragments published by Sabatier, Vogel, Mone, Berger (Hastings' *D. B.* iii. p. 50).

Wisdom, Sirach.

See Lagarde, *Mittheilungen* i. (Göttingen, 1884).   C. Donais, *Une ancienne Version latine de l'Ecclésiastique* (Paris, 1895).

iv. PROPHETS.

Fragmenta Wirceburgensia, vi. (?) (E. Ranke, *Par palimp. Wirceb.* p. 49 sqq.).
Containing Hos. i. 1—ii. 13, iv. 13—vii. 1; Jon. iii. 10—iv. 11; Isa. xxix. 1—xxx. 6, xlv. 20—xlvi. 11; Jer. xii. 12—xiii. 12, xiv. 15 —xvii. 10, xviii. 16—xxiii. 39, xxxv. 15—19, xxxvi. 2—xxxvii. 11, xxxviii. 23—xl. 5, xli. 1—17; Lam. ii. 16—iii. 40; Ezek. xxiv. 4—21, xxvi. 10—xxvii. 4, xxxiv. 16—xxxv. 5, xxxvii. 19—28, xxxviii. 8—20, xl. 3—xlii. 18, xlv. 1—xlvi. 9, xlviii. 28—35; Dan. i. 2—ii. 9, iii. 15—(26), viii. 5—ix. 10, x. 3—xi. 4, 20—42, and Bel.

Fragmenta Fuldensia, v. (E. Ranke, *Fragm. versionis ante-Hieronymianae,* Marburg, 1868).
Containing Hos. vii. 6 – ix. 1, Amos viii. 1—ix. 1, ix. 5—9, Mic. ii. 3—iii. 3.

Fragmenta Weingartensia, v. (E. Ranke, *Fragm. v. ante-H.*, Vienna, 1868; P. Corssen, *Zwei neue Fragmente d. Weingartener Prophetenhandschrift*, Berlin, 1899).

Containing Hos. iv. 13 f., v. 5, 7, vii. 16, viii. 1—6, 13 f., ix. 1—17, xii. 3, 7, 9, 12, xiii. 1, 3—xiv. 2; Amos v. 24—vi. 8; Mic. i. 5—iii. 3, iv. 3—vii. 20; Joel i. 1—14, ii. 3—5, iv. 2—4, 15—17; Jon. i. 14—iv. 8; Ezek. xvi. 52—xvii. 6, 19—xviii. 9, xxiv. 25— xxv. 14, xxvi. 10—xxvii. 7, 17—19, xxviii. 1—17, xxxiii. 7—11, xlii. 5, 6, 14, xliii. 22—xliv. 5, 19—xlv. 2, xlvi. 9—23, xlvii. 2—15, xlviii. 22—30; Dan. ii. 18—33, ix. 25—x. 11, xi. 18—23.

Fragmenta Stutgardiana (E. Ranke, *Antiquissima V. T. versionis Latinae fragmenta*, Marburg, 1888).

Containing Amos vii. 13—viii. 10; Ezek. xviii. 9—17, xx. 18— 21, xxvii. 7—17, xxxiii. 26—30, xxxiv. 6—12; Dan. xi. 35—39.

Fragmenta monast. S. Pauli Carinthiaci (A. Vogel, *Beiträge zur Herstellung der A. L. Bibelübersetzung*, Vienna, 1868).

Containing Ezek. xlii. 5, 6, 14, xliv. 19—xlv. 2, xlvi. 9—23, xlvii. 2—15.

Fragmenta palimpsesta Vaticana (F. Gustafsson, *Fragmenta V. T. in Latinum conversi a palimpsesto Vaticano eruta*, Helsingfors, 1881)[1].

Containing Hosea iv. 6, 7; Joel ii. 5—7; Amos v. 16—18, vii. 2—7, ix. 5—8; Jon. iii. 7—iv. 2; Hab. i. 16—ii. 3; Zeph. iii. 13—20; Zech. vii. 11—14, viii. 16—21.

Fragmenta palimpsesta Sangallensia (F. C. Burkitt, *O. L. and Itala*, Camb. 1896).

Containing Jer. xvii. 10—17, xxix. 13—19.

Codex Vallicellanus B. vii. (Bianchini, *Vindiciae*, p. ccxiii.).

Containing Baruch.
O. L. texts of Baruch are also to be found in the Paris MSS. Bibl. Nat. lat. 11, 161, 11951, and Arsenal. 65, 70; and in the Monte Casino MS. 35, and the Reims MS. 1.

Copious extracts from most of the books of the O. L. Bible are given in the anonymous *Liber de divinis scripturis sive Speculum*, wrongly attributed to St Augustine (ed. F. Weihrich in the Vienna *Corpus*, vol. xii.). Two other patristic collections of O. L. excerpts may also be mentioned here—the *Testimonia* of St Cyprian (ed. Hartel, *Corpus*, vol. iii. 1), and the *liber regularum Tyconii* (ed. F. C. Burkitt, in *Texts and Studies*, iii. 1). See also the *Collatio Carthaginiensis* printed in Dupin's *Optatus* (Paris, 1700), p. 379 ff.

[1] These fragments, as I am informed by Dr W. O. E. Oesterley, contain an almost purely Vulgate text, and should perhaps disappear from this list.

(2)   Latin versions of the LXX. revised or taken over by Jerome.

The great Pannonian scholar, Eusebius Hieronymus (A.D. 329—420), began his "useful labours[1]" upon the Old Testament at Rome about the year 383, probably (as in the case of his revision of the Gospels) at the suggestion of the Roman Bishop Damasus († 384).   His first attempt was limited to a revision of the Latin Psalter and conducted on lines which afterwards seemed to him inadequate.   A few years later—but before 390—1, when he began to translate from the Hebrew— a fresh revision of the Psalter from the LXX. was undertaken at the desire of Paula and Eustochium ; its immediate purpose was to remove errors which had already found their way into the copies of the earlier work, but the opportunity was seized of remodelling the Latin Psalter after the example of the Hexapla.

> *Praef. in libr. Psalmorum:* "psalterium Romae dudum positum emendaram et iuxta LXX. interpretes, licet cursim, magna illud ex parte correxeram.   quod quia rursum videtis, o Paula et Eustochium, scriptorum vitio depravatum, plusque antiquum errorem quam novam emendationem valere, cogitis ut...renascentes spinas eradicem.....notet sibi unusquisque vel iacentem lineam vel signa radiantia, id est vel obelos (÷) vel asteriscos (✳); et ubicunque viderit virgulam praecedentem (÷), ab ea usque ad duo puncta (:) quae impressimus, sciat in LXX. translatoribus plus haberi ; ubi autem stellae (✳) similitudinem perspexerit, de Hebraeis voluminibus additum noverit aeque usque ad duo puncta, iuxta Theodotionis dumtaxat editionem qui simplicitate sermonis a LXX. interpretibus non discordat."

These two revised Latin Psalters were afterwards known as *Psalterium Romanum* and *Psalterium Gallicanum* respectively. Both recensions established themselves in the use of the Latin Church[2], the former in the *cursus psallendi*, the latter in the *bibliotheca* or Church Bible.   At length Pius V. († 1572)

---

[1] Aug. *ep.* 82 (*ad Hieronymum*): "hi qui me invidere putant utilibus laboribus tuis."

[2] Cf. *adv. Rufin.* ii. 30 "psalterium...certe emendatissimum iuxta LXX. interpretes nostro labore dudum Roma suscepit" ; where, as Westcott says (Smith's *D. B.* iii. 1698 *n.*), he seems to include both revisions.

ordered the Gallican Psalter to be sung in the daily offices, an exception being made in favour of St Peter's at Rome, St Mark's at Venice, and the churches of the Archdiocese of Milan, which retained the 'Roman' Psalter[1]. In MSS. of the Vulgate a triple Psalter not infrequently appears, shewing Jerome's two Septuagintal revisions side by side with the *Psalterium Hebraicum*, his later translation from the Hebrew; but the 'Hebrew' Psalter never succeeded in displacing the Hieronymian revisions of the Old Latin, and the Latin Church still sings and reads a version of the Psalms which is based on the Septuagint. The liturgical Psalter of the Anglican Church "followeth…the Translation of the Great English Bible, set forth and used in the time of King *Henry* the Eighth, and *Edward* the Sixth"; i.e. it is based on Coverdale's version, which was "translated out of Douche and Latyn into Englishe"; and many of its peculiarities may be traced to the LXX. through the Gallican Psalter incorporated in the Vulgate[2].

The following specimen (Ps. lxvii.=lxviii. 12—14, 18—22) will enable the reader to form an idea of the relation between Jerome's two revisions of the Old Latin and his 'Hebrew'[3] Psalter.

ROMAN.	GALLICAN.	HEBREW.
[12] Dominus dabit verbum evangelizantibus virtute multa; [13] rex virtutum dilecti,et speciei domus dividere spolia. [14] si dormiatis in medios cleros, pennae columbae deargentatae,et posteriora dorsi eius in specie auri. [*diapsalma*]...... [18] currus Dei decem milium multiplex, milia laetantium. Dominus	[12] Dominus dabit verbum evangelizantibus virtute multa; [13] rex virtutum ✳ dilecti: et speciei domus dividere spolia. [14] si dormiatis inter medios cleros pennae columbae deargentatae et posteriora✳ dorsi eius in pallore auri. *diapsalma*........[18] currus Dei decem milibus multiplex, milia lae-	[12] Domine, dabis sermonem adnuntiatricibus fortitudinis plurimae, [13] reges exercituum foederabuntur, foederabuntur et pulcritudo domus dividet spolia. [14] si dormieritis inter medios terminos, pennae columbae deargentatae et posteriora eius in virore auri.......[18] currus Dei innumerabiles, milia

[1] Martène, *de ant. rit.* i. p. 18 f.
[2] Cf. Bp Westcott, *History of the English Bible*, pp. 206 ff., 351 ff. ; Kirkpatrick, *Psalms*, Intr. p. lxxiii f.
[3] Editions published in 1874 by Baer and Tischendorf (*Lib. Psalm. Heb. atque Lat.*) and by Lagarde (*Psalt. iuxta Hebraeos*).

ROMAN.	GALLICAN.	HEBREW.
in illis in Sina in sancto. [19] ascendens in altum captivam duxit captivitatem, dedit dona hominibus. etenim non credunt inhabitare. [20] Dominus Deus benedictus; benedictus Dominus de die in diem. prosperum iter faciet nobis Deus salutaris noster. *diapsalma.* [21] Deus noster deus salvos faciendi, et Domini exitus mortis. [22] verumtamen Deus conquassabit capita inimicorum suorum, verticem capilli perambulantium in delictis suis.	tantium: Dominus in eis ✳ in : Sina in sancto. [19] ascendisti in altum: cepisti captivitatem, accepisti dona in hominibus. etenim non credentes inhabitare Dominum Deum. [20] benedictus Dominus die quotidie; prosperum iter faciet nobis Deus salutarium nostrorum. *diapsalma.* [21] Deus noster, Deus salvos ÷ faciendi: et Domini ✳ Domini: exitus mortis. [22] verumtamen Deus confringet capita inimicorum suorum, verticem capilli ÷ perambulantium in delictis suis.	abundantium; Dominus in eis in Sina, in sancto. [19] ascendisti in excelsum, captivam duxisti captivitatem, accepisti dona in hominibus; insuper et non credentes habitare Dominum Deum. [20] benedictus Dominus per singulos dies; portabit nos Deus salutis nostrae. *semper.* [21] Deus noster deus salutis, et Domini Dei mortis egressus. [22] verumtamen Deus confringet capita inimicorum suorum, verticem crinis ambulantis in delictis suis.

The book of Job offered a still more promising field for the labours of the Hexaplarising reviser, for the Greek text as known to Origen fell greatly short of the current Hebrew, and it was this defective text which formed the basis of the Latin versions used by Cyprian and Lucifer and in the *Speculum*[1]. Jerome, who had access to the Hexapla at Caesarea, took advantage of Origen's revision, in which the lacunae of the Greek Job were filled up from Theodotion, and sent his friends, Paula and Eustochium, a Latin version of Job at once corrected and supplemented from the Hexaplaric LXX. The result gave him for the time profound satisfaction; he had lifted up Job from the dunghill[2], and restored him to his pristine state[3];

---

[1] Burkitt, *O. L. and Itala*, pp. 8, 32 f.

[2] *Praef. in libr. Job:* "qui adhuc apud Latinos iacebat in stercore et vermibus scatebat errorum."

[3] *ibid.* "integrum immaculatumque gaudete."

the difference between the Old Latin version and the new seemed to him to be nothing short of that which separates falsehood from truth[1]. The asterisks shewed that from 700 to 800 lines had been restored to this long mutilated book[2].

A few brief specimens from Lagarde's text[3] will suffice to shew the character of the work.

x. 4 aut sicut homo perspicit, perspicis? ※ aut sicut videt homo, videbis? ✓ aut humana est vita tua? aut anni tui sunt tanquam ※ dies ✓ hominis?

xix. 17 et rogabam uxorem meam ✓ invocabam ÷ blandiens filios ※ uteri mei ✓; at illi in perpetuum despexerunt me; cum surrexero, locuntur ad me.

xlii. 7 et defunctus est Job senex plenus dierum. ÷ scriptum est autem resurrecturum cum his quos Dominus suscitabit.

Jerome also revised from the Hexaplaric Septuagint, for the benefit of Paula and Eustochium, the 'books of Solomon' (Proverbs, Ecclesiastes, Canticles), treating the Greek text after the manner of Origen; but his work has perished, the preface alone surviving. A like fate has overtaken a translation of Chronicles, undertaken at the desire of Domnio and Rogatianus. This version of Chronicles appears from the preface to have been influenced by Jerome's Hebrew studies, which were now sufficiently matured to enable him to form an independent judgement in reference to the merits of his Greek text, though he still clung to his old belief in the inspiration of the original Septuagint.

Praef. in libros Salomonis: "tres libros Salomonis, id est, Proverbia, Ecclesiasten, Canticum canticorum, veteri LXX. auctoritati reddidi, vel antepositis lineis (÷) superflua quaeque

[1] *Ad Pammach.:* "veterem editionem nostrae translationi compara, et liquido providebitis quantum distet inter veritatem et mendacium." Jerome's satisfaction with his original revision of Job was continued even after he had produced a new version from the Hebrew; in the preface to the latter he leaves the student free to choose between the two ("eligat unusquisque quod vult").

[2] *Praef. in Job ed. Heb.* See below, pt II., c. ii.

[3] In *Mittheilungen*, ii.

designans, vel stellis (✳) titulo (?) praenotatis ea quae minus
habebantur interserens...et ubi praepostero ordine atque per-
verso sententiarum fuerat lumen ereptum suis locis restituens
feci intellegi quod latebat." *Praef. in libr. Paralipomenon*:
"cum a me nuper litteris flagitassetis ut vobis librum Paralipomenon Latino sermone transferrem, de Tiberiade legis quondam
doctorem qui apud Hebraeos admirationi habebatur assumpsi...
et sic confirmatus ausus sum facere quod iubebatis. libere enim
vobis loquor, ita et in Graecis et Latinis codicibus hic nominum
liber vitiosus est ut non tam Hebraea quam barbara quaedam...
arbitrandum sit. nec hoc LXX. interpretibus qui Spiritu sancto
pleni ea quae vera fuerant transtulerunt, sed scriptorum culpae
adscribendum....ubicunque ergo asteriscos...videritis ibi sciatis
de Hebraeo additum...ubi vero obelus, transversa scilicet virga,
praeposita est, illic signatur quid LXX. interpretes addiderint."

Whether Jerome dealt with the rest of the canonical books
of the Old Latin in the same manner must remain an open
question. No trace remains either of such revised versions or
of prefaces which once belonged to them, nor does he refer to
them in the prefaces of his translations from the Hebrew. On
the other hand his letters occasionally speak of his revision of
the Old Latin in terms which seem to imply that it was complete, and in one of them there is a passage which suggests that
the disappearance of the other books was due to the dishonesty
of some person whose name is not given.

Adv. Rufin. ii. 24: "egone contra LXX. interpretes aliquid
sum locutus quos ante annos plurimos diligentissime emendatos
meae linguae studiosis dedi?" *Ep.* 71 (*ad Lucinium*): "LXX.
editionem et te habere non dubito." *Ep.* 106 (*ad Sunn. et Fret.*):
"editionem LXX. interpretum quae et in ἐξαπλοῖς codicibus reperitur et a nobis in Latinum sermonem fideliter versa est." Cf.
Ep. Augustini ad Hieron. (116), (c. 405): "mittas obsecro interpretationem tuam de LXX. quam te edidisse nesciebam." At
a later time (c. 416) Jerome excuses himself from doing as
Augustine had desired, since "pleraque prioris laboris fraude
cuiusdam amisimus" (*Ep.* 134).

In any case Jerome's Hexaplarised version had little or
no influence on the text of the Latin Bible, except in the
Psalter. Even his translations from the Hebrew did not easily
supersede the Old Latin. The familiar version died hard and,

as the list of MSS. will have shewn, parts of it were copied as late as the seventh century. Even at Rome the old version long held its ground by the side of the new; in the last years of the sixth century, Gregory the Great, while basing his great commentary on Job upon the Vulgate, claimed a right to cite the Old Latin when it served his purpose, "quia sedes apostolica utrique nititur[1]."

The coexistence of the two versions naturally produced mixture in the MSS.[2], which was not altogether removed by the revisions of the sixth and ninth centuries. Moreover, the Old Latin version continued to hold its place in those books of the Church Bible which had no Semitic original, or of which the Semitic original was no longer current. In the preface to the Salomonic Books Jerome says explicitly: "porro in eo libro qui a plerisque *Sapientia Salomonis* inscribitur et in Ecclesiastico...calamo temperavi, tantummodo canonicas scripturas vobis emendare desiderans." The books of Tobit and Judith[3] were afterwards translated by him from the Aramaic (*praeff. in librum Tobiae, in librum Judith*), and these versions have been incorporated in the Vulgate, but the Vulgate Wisdom, Ecclesiasticus, Baruch, 1, 2 Maccabees are supplied from ante-Hieronymian sources. Thus to this day a considerable part of the Latin Bible is in greater or less degree an echo of the Septuagint.

LITERATURE. Besides the editions already mentioned the student may consult with advantage Eichhorn, *Einleitung*, i. 321; N. Wiseman, *Essays*, i. (London, 1853)—a reprint of his *Two letters on some parts of the controversy concerning* 1 *Joh. v.* 7; B. F. Westcott, art. *Vulgate* in Smith's *D. B.* iii.; H. Rönsch, *Itala u. Vulgata* (Marburg, 1869); F. Kaulen, *Handbuch zur Vulgata* (Mainz, 1870); Ziegler, *Die lat. Bibelübersetzungen vor*

---

[1] *Praef. ad Moralia in Job.*
[2] Cf. e.g. Berger, *op. cit.* p. xi.: "les textes des anciennes versions et de la nouvelle sont constamment mêlés et enchevêtrés dans les manuscrits."
[3] On the relation of Jerome's Latin Judith to the Septuagint see C. J. Ball in *Speaker's Commentary*, Apocrypha, p. 257 ff.

Hieronymus (Munich, 1879); Lagarde, *Probe einer neuen Ausgabe
der lat. Übersetzungen des A. T.* (1870); A. Ceriani, *Le recensioni
dei LXX e la versione latina detta Itala,* 1886; L. Salembier,
Une page inédite de l'histoire de la Vulgate, Amiens, 1890 ;
Bleek-Wellhausen (1893), p. 553 ff. ; Scrivener-Miller, ii. p.
191 ff.; Gregory, p. 949 ff.; F. C. Burkitt, *The Old Latin and
the Itala,* in *Texts and Studies* (Cambridge, 1896) ; E. Nestle,
Urtext, pp. 84 ff. [specially valuable for the bibliography of the
Latin versions] ; H. A. A. Kennedy, *The Old Latin Versions,*
in Hastings' *D. B.* iii. pp. 47—62; Corssen in *Jahresb. f. d. class.
Altertumswissensch* (1899); *Latin Versions of the O. T.,* art. in
Ch. Q. R. (Apr. 1901); W. O. Oesterley in *J. Th. Stud.* v. vi. (text
of Min. Proph.).

2. The Egyptian Versions.

The tradition of St Mark's episcopate at Alexandria[1] may
be taken as evidence, so far as it goes, of the early planting of
the Church in that city.   The first converts were doubtless, as
at Rome, Greek-speaking Jews, descendants of the old Jewish
settlers[2], and their Greek proselytes ; and the first extension of
the movement was probably amongst the Greek population
of the towns on the sea-coast of the Mediterranean.   As it
spread to the interior, to the villages of the Delta, to Memphis,
Oxyrhynchus, Panopolis, and eventually to Thebes, it en-
countered native Egyptians who spoke dialects of the Egyptian
tongue[3].   How soon they were evangelised there is no direct
evidence to shew, but the process may have begun shortly
after the Gospel reached Alexandria.   The native Church
retained its own tongue, and in the fourth and fifth centuries
Greek was still unknown to many of the monks and eccle-
siastics of Egypt.   Christianity however is probably responsible
for either introducing or spreading the use of a new system of

[1] See *Gospel acc. to St Mark,* p. xiv. f.   The Clementine Homilies (i.
8 ff.) attribute the foundation of the Alexandrian Church to Barnabas.   But
a yet earlier beginning is possible.   In Acts xviii. 24 cod. D reads Ἀλεξ-
ανδρεὺς...ὃς ἦν κατηχημένος ἐν τῇ πατρίδι τὸν λόγον τοῦ κυρίου, on which
Blass (*Acta app.* p. 201) remarks: "itaque iam tum (id quod sine testi-
monio suspicandum erat) in Aegyptum quoque nova religio permanaverat."
[2] Acts ii. 9 f. οἱ κατοικοῦντες...Αἴγυπτον.   *Ib.* vi. 9 τινὲς ἐκ τῆς συναγωγῆς τῆς λεγομένης...Ἀλεξανδρέων.   Cf. *Report of the Egypt Exploration
Fund,* 1899—1900, p. 54.
[3] Cf. what is said of St Anthony in the *Vita Antonii* (Migne, *P. G.*
xxvi. 944 sq.).

writing with characters which are chiefly of Greek origin[1]. This writing, known as Coptic—a corruption of Αἰγύπτιος—is found with some variations in all MS. fragments of the Egyptian versions of the Old and New Testaments.

The analogy of the Old Latin would lead us to suppose (as Bp Lightfoot remarks[2]) that no long interval passed between the acceptance of Christianity by any large number of native Egyptians, and the first attempts to translate the Scriptures into the Egyptian tongue. "We should probably not be exaggerating if we placed one or both of the principal Egyptian versions, the Bohairic and the Sahidic, or at least parts of them, before the close of the second century." The Bishop is writing with only the New Testament in view, but his argument applies equally to the Old. His view is on the whole supported by Dr Hort[3], Ciasca[4], and Mr A. C. Headlam[5]: but Mr Forbes Robinson, following Guidi, produces reasons for regarding it as 'not proven,' and prefers to say that "historical evidence...on the whole, points to the third century as the period when the first Coptic translation was made." "But this view," he adds, "can only be regarded as tentative. In the light of future discoveries it may have to be modified[6]."

The plurality of the Egyptian versions is well ascertained. Perhaps the geographical form of Egypt gave special opportunities for the growth of popular dialects; certain it is that increased knowledge of the language has added to the dialectic complications with which the Coptic scholar has to struggle[7].

---

[1] Of the 31 letters of the Coptic alphabet 7 only (ϣ, ϥ, ⳅ, ⳃ, ⳉ, ⳓ, ⳁ) are not from the Greek. On the pre-Christian systems see Clem. *strom.* v. 4 οἱ παρ' Αἰγυπτίοις παιδευόμενοι πρῶτον μὲν πάντων...ἐκμανθάνουσι τὴν ἐπιστολογραφικὴν καλουμένην (the Demotic), δευτέραν δὲ τὴν ἱερατικήν... ὑστάτην δὲ καὶ τελευταίαν τὴν ἱερογλυφικήν.

[2] Scrivener-Miller, ii. p. 97.

[3] *Intr. to N. T. in Greek*, p. 85.

[4] *Sacr. bibl. fragmenta Copto-Sahidica*, i. p. viii.

[5] Scrivener-Miller, ii. p. 105 f.

[6] Hastings' *D. B.* i. p. 672. Cf. Γ. E. Brightman in *J. Th. St.* i. 254.

[7] The Demotic, as it is known to us, appears to present no dialectic

It was in these popular dialects that the translations of the Bible were made. "Christianity...was in Egypt a great popular movement...the Scriptures were translated, not into the literary language, but into that of the people ; and the copies of these translations in each locality reflected the local peculiarities of speech." Fragments of Biblical versions have been found in the Bohairic[1], Sahidic, and Middle Egyptian dialects. The Bohairic dialect was spoken in Lower, the Sahidic in Upper, Egypt, and the Middle Egyptian in the intermediate province of Memphis. Some authorities speak of two other dialects, the Fayumic and Akhmimic, assigning to them certain Biblical fragments which are regarded by others as belonging to the Middle Egyptian.

Translations of books of the Old Testament into these Egyptian dialects were naturally made from the Alexandrian Greek version, and, if we may judge from the extensive use of the Old Testament in early Christian teaching, there is no reason to doubt that they were translated at as early a date as the Gospels and Epistles, if not indeed before them. Portions of the Old Testament exist in each of the Egyptian dialects. Hyvernat mentions fragments of Isaiah, Lamentations and Ep. of Jeremiah in Fayumic and Middle Egyptian, and of Exodus, Sirach, 2 Macc., and each of the Minor Prophets in Akhmimic[2]; in Bohairic he enumerates 6 MSS. of the Pentateuch, 14 of the Psalms, 5 of Proverbs, 3 of Job, 4 of the Minor Prophets, 5 of Isaiah, 3 of Jeremiah, 4 of Daniel, and

variation, perhaps because the specimens which have reached us were all the work of the single class—the scribes: see Hyvernat, *Étude sur les versions Coptes* in *Revue Biblique*, v. 3, p. 429; A. C. Headlam in Scrivener-Miller, p. 105.

[1] Formerly known as the Memphitic, a name which might be more appropriately applied to the form of Middle Egyptian current at Memphis. 'Bohairic' is derived from *el-Bohairah*, a district S. of Alexandria. 'Sahidic,' also called Thebaic, is from *es-sa'îd* = Upper Egypt. On some characteristics of the several dialects see Hyvernat, p. 431.

[2] Cf. Steindorff, *Die Apokalypse des Elias*, p. 2.

one MS. of Ezekiel; in Sahidic, though few complete MSS. of any Biblical book have survived, there is a large number of extant fragments representing most of the canonical books and certain of the non-canonical (the two Wisdoms, the Ep. of Jeremiah, and the Greek additions to Daniel).

The following list gives the more important publications which contain portions of the Old Testament in the Egyptian versions.

BOHAIRIC. D. Wilkins, *Quinque libri Moysis*, 1731; Fallet, *La version Cophte du pentateuque*, 1854; Lagarde, *Der Pentateuch koptisch*, 1867; *Bruchstücke der kopt. Übersetzungen des A. T.* in *Orientalia* i. 1879. The Psalter has been edited by R. Tuki, 1744, J. L. Ideler, 1837, Schwartze, 1848, Lagarde, *Psalterii versio Memphitica*, Göttingen, 1875, F. Rossi, *Cinque manoscritti* &c., 1894; Job by H. Tattam, 1846; the Prophets by Tattam (*Prophetae minores*, 1836, *Proph. maiores*, 1852).

SAHIDIC. Lagarde, *Aegyptiaca*, 1883; Ciasca, *Sacr. bibl. fragm. Coptosahidica Musei Borgiani*, 1885—9; Amélineau, *Fragments coptes* in *Recueil* v. (1884), and *Fragments de la version thébaine*, ib. vii.—x. (1886—9); the same scholar has edited Job in *Proceedings of the Soc. of Bibl. Arch.*, 1887; O. v. Lemm, *Bruchstücke*, 1885, *Sahidische Bibelfragmente*, 1890; Krall, *Mittheilungen*, 1887; F. Rossi, *Papiri Copti*, 1889, *Un nuovo codice*, 1893; Maspéro, *Fragments de l'Ancien Testament* in *Mémoires publiés par les membres de la mission arch. française au Caire*, vi., 1892; E. A. T. W. Budge, *The earliest known Coptic Psalter*, 1898[1]; *Coptic Biblical Texts in the Dialect of Upper Egypt*, 1912; N. Peters, *Die sahidisch-koptische Übersetzung d. Buches Ecclesiasticus...untersucht*, 1898; P. Lacau, *Textes de l'A. T. en copte sahidique*, 1901; Sir H. Thompson, *The Coptic Version of certain books of the O. T.*, 1908; *A Coptic Palimpsest*, 1911.

MIDDLE EGYPTIAN, &c. Tuki, *Rudimenta linguae Coptae*, 1778; Quatremère, *Recherches sur la langue et la littérature de l'Égypte*, 1808; Zoega, *Catal. codd. Copt.*, 1810; Engelbreth, *Fragmenta Basmurico-Coptica V. et N. T.*, 1811; Von Lemm, *Mittelägyptische Fragmente*, 1885; Krall, *Mittheilungen*, 1887; Bouriant in *Mémoires de l'Institut égyptien* ii., 1889, and in *Mémoires publiés par* &c. vi. 1; Steindorff, *die Apokalypse des Elias*, p. 2 ff. (Leipzig, 1899).

It may reasonably be expected that the Egyptian versions of the Old Testament, when they have been more fully recovered and submitted to examination by experts, will prove

[1] On the correspondence of this Psalter with cod. U see below, p. 143.

to be of much importance for the criticism of the text of the LXX. Ceriani[1] has shewn that the Greek text of Cod. Marchalianus agrees generally with that which underlies the Bohairic version of the Prophets, whilst both are in harmony with the text which is quoted by Cyril of Alexandria. A German scholar[2], starting with the Bohairic Prophets, finds that their text is similar to that of the Codex Alexandrinus, the Codex Marchalianus, a series of cursive Greek MSS., some of which had been recognised by Cornill[3] as Hesychian (22, 23, 26, 36, 40, 42, 49, 51, 62, 86, 91, 95, 97, 106, 114, 130, 147, 153, 185, 228, 233, 238, 240, 310, 311), and the Greek columns of the Complutensian Polyglott. Of the Sahidic fragments, Job is perhaps "a translation of Origen's revised text, *with the passages under asterisk omitted*[4]," whilst Isaiah is distinctly Hexaplaric, and traces of the influence of the Hexapla are also to be found in Proverbs, Ecclesiastes and Ezekiel, although in varying degrees. On the whole it is natural to expect the Hesychian recension to be specially reflected in Egyptian versions. But other influences may have been at work[5], and much remains to be done before these versions can be securely used in the work of reconstructing the text of the Greek Old Testament[6].

LITERATURE. Quatremère, *Recherches*; Zoega, *Catalogus*; L. Stern, *Koptische Grammatik*, 1880; *Kopten, Koptische Sprache u. Litteratur*, 1886; Scrivener-Miller, ii. p. 91 ff. (J. B. Lightfoot and A. C. Headlam); Gregory, *prolegg.*, p. 859 ff.; J. P. P. Martin, *Intr.*, partie théor., p. 310 ff.; H. Hyvernat, *Étude sur les versions coptes de la Bible* in *Revue biblique*, v. 3, 4, vi. 1; E. Nestle, *Urtext*, p. 144 ff.; W. E. Crum, *Coptic Studies*, 1897–8; *Catalogue of Coptic MSS. in Brit. Museum*, 1905; A. E. Brooke in *J. Th. St.* iii.

[1] See *O. T. in Greek*, iii. p. ix.
[2] A. Schulte in *Theol. Quartalschrift*, 1894–5; see Hyvernat, p. 69.
[3] *Ezechiel*, p. 66 ff.
[4] Burkitt in *Encycl. Brit.* iv. 5027; cf. Hatch, *Essays*, p. 215 ff.; Dillmann, *Textkritisches zum Buche Ijob*, p. 4; Burkitt, *O. L.* and *Itala*, p. 8; Kenyon, *Our Bible and the ancient MSS.*, p. 751.
[5] Hyvernat, p. 71.
[6] See the remarks of F. Robinson in Hastings' *Dict. of the Bible* i. 673 a.

3. THE ETHIOPIC VERSION.

Ethiopia is said to have been evangelised in the fourth century from Tyre. The Tyrian missionaries were probably of Greek speech[1], and brought with them the Greek Bible. But apart from this, the contiguity of Ethiopia to Egypt, and the circumstance that the first Bishop of Auxume received consecration at Alexandria, create an *a priori* probability that any early translations from the Old Testament into Ethiopic were based upon the Septuagint, whether immediately or through the Coptic versions.

Dillmann, who at one time had explained the numerous transliterations and other approaches to the Hebrew in the existing Ethiopic version by assuming that the translators worked upon a Hexaplaric text, ultimately found cause to classify the MSS. under three heads, (1) those which on the whole represent the text of the LXX. on which he supposed the version to have been based; (2) those of a later recension —the most numerous class—corrected by other MSS. of the LXX.; (3) those in which the original version has been revised from the Hebrew[2]. Lagarde, on the other hand, suggested that the version was translated from the Arabic, as late as the fourteenth century, and maintained that in any case the printed texts of the Ethiopic Old Testament depend upon MSS. which are too late and too bad to furnish a secure basis for the employment of this version in the reconstruction of the Septuagint[3]. "These suggestions are not however supported by a closer examination of the Ethiopic version of the Octateuch. The text as printed by Dillmann, and especially the readings of the oldest MS. he used, which is supported by a dated thirteenth century MS. brought from Abyssinia to Paris since

[1] Charles (art. *Ethiopic Version*, in Hastings' *D. B.* i. p. 792) states that "the Abyssinians first received Christianity through Aramaean missionaries." But Tyre in the fourth century was as Greek as Alexandria and Antioch.

[2] Nestle, *Urtext*, p. 148. Loisy, *Histoire critique*, I. ii. p. 231.

[3] *Ankündigung einer neuen Ausgabe der gr. Übersetzung d. A.T.*, p. 28; cf. *Materialen*, i. p. iii.

his edition was published, betray direct descent from a Septuagint text of a somewhat interesting type, which had apparently undergone less Hebrew or hexaplar revision than the Greek ancestors of the Armenian and Syro-hexaplar versions. We are safe in concluding with Charles, ' It is unquestionable that our version was made in the main from the Greek[1].' "

The Ethiopic version of the Old Testament contains all the books of the Alexandrian canon except 1—4 Maccabees, together with certain apocrypha which are not found in MSS. of the LXX. (Enoch, the Book of Jubilees, 4 Esdras, &c.). A considerable part of it has appeared in print. Dillmann edited the Octateuch and the four books of Kingdoms (1853–71), and the deuterocanonical books (1894); the book of Joel appeared in Merx, *Die Prophetie des Joels*, the book of Jonah in W. Wright's *Jonah in four Semitic versions* (London, 1857). The Psalms were printed by Ludolf (1701), Rödiger (1815), Dorn (1825), and Jeremiah, Lamentations and Malachi by Bachmann (1893); Bachmann also edited the Dodecapropheton, and part of Isaiah.

Lists of the MSS. may be seen in Wright, *Ethiopic MSS. of the British Museum* (London, 1878); Zotenberg, *Catalogue des MSS. éthiopiens de la Bibliothèque Nationale* (Paris, 1877); D'Abbadie, *Catalogue raisonné de MSS. éthiopiens* (Paris, 1859); Dillmann, *Catalogus MSS. Aethiop. in Bibliotheca Bodleiana* (Oxford, 1848), and *Abessinische Handschr. d. k. Biblioth. zu Berlin;* Müller, *Aethiop. Handschr. der k. Hofbiblioth. in Wien* (*ZDMG.* xvi. p. 554). For fuller information as to this Version see F. Prätorius, *Urtext*, p. 147 ff.

4. The Arabic Version.

The Arabic Old Testament printed in the Paris and London Polyglotts is a composite work, the Hexateuch being a translation from the Hebrew, and the books of Judges, Ruth, 1 Regn. i.—2 Regn. xii. 17, Nehemiah i.—ix. 27, and Job from the Peshitta; the Septuagint has supplied the basis for

---

[1] This criticism of Lagarde's view is due to Mr N. McLean, who has recently examined the Ethiopic Genesis for the larger Cambridge Septuagint.

the other poetical books and for the Prophets[1]. Some of the MSS. exhibit in certain books a translation which has come from the LXX. through the Coptic; the book of Job in this version has been published by Lagarde (*Psalterium Job Proverbia arabice*, Göttingen, 1876)[2].

The Arabic version directly derived from the LXX. is said to exhibit in the Prophets a text akin to that of Cod. A (Ryssel, in *ZAW.* 1885, p. 102 ff., 158). It shews traces of Hexaplaric influence (H. Hyvernat, in Vigouroux, *D. B.* i. p. 846).

EDITIONS of Arabic versions of the Septuagint. Besides the Polyglotts (Paris, 1645; London, 1652), mention may be made of the Psalters published at Genoa, 1516; Rome, 1614 and 1619; Aleppo, 1706; London (S.P.C.K.), 1725. In W. Wright's Book of Jonah the Arabic is from a MS. in the Bodleian (see p. vii.). Cf. H. Hyvernat, *op. cit.*

MSS. Lists of MSS. of the Arabic versions of the Old Testament will be found in the Preface to Holmes and Parsons, vol. i.; Slane's *Catalogue des MSS. Arabes de la Bibl. nat.*; Mrs M. D. Gibson's *Studia Sinaitica*, iii. (London, 1894), *Catalogue of Arabic MSS. at Sinai* (codd. 1—67). Cf. Hyvernat, *op. cit.*

LITERATURE. Schnurrer, *Bibliotheca Arabica*, 1780; H. E. G. Paulus, *Bodleiana specimina versionum Pent. Arab.*, 1789; Eichhorn, *Einleitung*, § 275 ff.; R. Holmes, *Praef. ad Pent.*; Rödiger, *De origine et indole Arab. libr. V. T. interpretationis* (Halle, 1829). Among more recent works reference may be made to Cornill, *Ezechiel*, p. 49 f.; Loisy, *Hist. crit.* I. ii. p. 238; Nestle in *Urtext*, p. 150 ff.; F. C. Burkitt, art. *Arabic Versions*, in Hastings' *D. B.* i. p. 136 ff.; H. Hyvernat, *op. cit.*

5. THE SYRIAC VERSIONS.

According to Moses bar-Cephas († 913), there are two Syriac versions of the Old Testament—the Peshitta, translated

---

[1] Loisy, *Hist. crit.*, I. ii. p. 239. Mr Burkitt in Hastings' *D. B.* (i. p. 137) writes "J(udges), S(amuel), K(ings), and Ch(ronicles), are all from the Peshitta."

[2] Lagarde gives for the Psalter four texts, viz. those published at Rome (1614), Paris (1645), Quzhayya (1612), Aleppo (1706); for Job, besides the versions mentioned in the text, that of the Paris Polyglott.

from the Hebrew in the time of King Abgar, and the version made from the Septuagint by Paul, Bishop of Tella. This statement is neither complete nor altogether to be trusted, but it may serve as a convenient point of departure for a summary of the subject.

(1) The origin of the Peshitta is still as obscure as when Theodore of Mopsuestia wrote : ἡρμήνευται δὲ ταῦτα εἰς μὲν τὴν τῶν Σύρων παρ' ὅτου δήποτε, οὐδὲ γὰρ ἔγνωσται μέχρι τῆς τήμερον ὅστις ποτὲ οὗτός ἐστιν[1]. That the translation on the whole was made from the Hebrew is the verdict of modern scholars as it was that of Moses bar-Cephas. Yet certain books display the influence of the LXX. While "the Pentateuch follows the Hebrew text and the Jewish exegesis, Isaiah and the twelve Minor Prophets contain much which is from the LXX., and the influence of the Greek version appears to have been felt also in the Psalter[2]." From the first the Peshitta seems to have included the non-canonical books of the Alexandrian Bible except 1 Esdras and Tobit, "and their diction agrees with that of the canonical books among which they are inserted[3]."

(2) The Syriac version ascribed to Paul, Bishop of Tella-dhe-Mauzelath (Constantine) in Mesopotamia, was a literal translation of the LXX. of the Hexapla, in which the Origenic signs were scrupulously retained. A note in one of the rolls of this version assigns it to the year 616—7 ; the work is said to have been produced at Alexandria under the auspices of Athanasius, Monophysite Patriarch of Antioch, who with five of his suffragans had gone thither to visit the Alexandrian Patriarch. Paul of Tella and Thomas of Harkel appear to have been of the party, and their visit in Alexandria led to

---

[1] Migne, *P. G.*, lxvi. 241; cf. *ib.* 252 f., 263, 466 ff., 492 ff.

[2] Nestle in *Urtext*, p. 230; cf. Bleek-Wellhausen, pp. 558—560; W. E. Barnes in *J. Th. St.* ii. 186 ff.

[3] Gwynn, *D. C. B.*, iv. p. 434.

the translation of the entire Greek Bible into Syriac, the New Testament having been undertaken by Thomas, while Paul worked upon the Old[1].

The version of Paul of Tella, usually called the Syro Hexaplar, was first made known to Europe by Andreas Masius (Andrew Du Maes, † 1573). In editing the Greek text of Joshua he used a Syriac MS. which contained part of Deuteronomy, Joshua, Judges, Kings, Chronicles, Ezra, Esther, Judith, and part of Tobit, in this translation. The codex which he employed has disappeared, but the Ambrosian library at Milan possesses another, possibly a second volume of the lost MS., which contains the poetical and prophetic books, in the order Psalms, Job, Proverbs, Ecclesiastes, Song of Solomon, the two Wisdoms, the twelve Prophets, Jeremiah (with Baruch, Lamentations, and the Epistle), Daniel (with Susanna and Bel), Ezekiel, Isaiah. Portions of the historical books of the Syro-Hexaplar[2] have been discovered among the Nitrian MSS. of the British Museum, and a catena, also at the Museum, contains fragments of Chronicles and the books of Esdras, while the Paris Library contributes 4 Kingdoms. Norberg edited Jeremiah and Ezekiel in 1787; Daniel was published by Bugati in 1788 and the Psalms in 1820; Middeldorpf completed the prophetical and poetical books in his edition of 1835, and in 1861 Ceriani added Baruch, Lamentations, and the Ep. of Jeremiah. Of the historical books Judges and Ruth were published by Skat Rördam in 1861, and Genesis and Exodus (i.—xxxiii. 2) by Ceriani (*Mon. sacr. et prof.* ii.), who has also given to the world the Milan fragments in *Mon.* vol. vii.

The Hexapla, Tetrapla, and occasionally the Heptapla, are

---

[1] Gwynn, *Paulus Tellensis* and *Thomas Harklensis*, in *D. C. B.*, iv. pp. 266 ff., 1014 ff.
[2] Viz., parts of Genesis and Joshua, half of Numbers, nearly the whole of Judges, Ruth, and 3 Kingdoms, and Exodus complete.

mentioned as the sources of the text in the subscriptions to the books of the Syro-Hexaplar. These subscriptions were doubtless translated with the rest of the Greek archetypes, but they shew the character of the copies employed by the translators. The version is servile to such an extent as sometimes to violate the Syriac idiom[1]. It is obvious that this extreme fidelity to the Greek, while it must have hindered the use of the version in the Monophysite churches of Syria, is of vast advantage to the Biblical critic. It places in his hands an exact reflexion of the Hexaplaric LXX. as it was read at Alexandria at the beginning of the 7th century, derived ultimately from the Hexapla and Tetrapla through the recension of Eusebius. Thus it supplements our scanty stock of Greek Hexaplaric MSS., and indeed forms our chief authority for the text of Origen's revision. In the case of one of the canonical books the version of Paul of Tella renders even greater service. One of the Greek texts of Daniel—that which Origen regarded as the true Septuagintal text—has survived only in a single and relatively late MS. The Syro-Hexaplar here supplies another and earlier authority, which enables us to check the testimony of the Chigi Greek.

(3) Other Syriac versions made from the Greek.

(*a*) Fragments of a Syriac version in the Palestinian dialect have been printed by Land, *Anecdota Syriaca*, iv. (Leyden, 1875), J. R. Harris, *Biblical Fragments from Mt Sinai* (London, 1890), G. H. Gwilliam, *Anecdota Oxoniensia*, Semitic Series, I. v., ix. (Oxford, 1893—6), G. Margoliouth, *Liturgy of the Nile* (London, 1897), and Mrs Lewis, *Studia Sinaitica*, vi. (London, 1897)[2]. This version has been made from the LXX.; in the Books of Kings the text is now known not to be Lucianic, as it was at first supposed to be (*Anecd.*

---

[1] Field, *Prolegg. in Hex.*, p. lxix., where many instances are produced.

[2] The fragments in *Studia Sinaitica* are accompanied by critical notes, the work of Dr Nestle, in which they are carefully compared with the Greek text (pp. xl.—lxxiv.).

Oxon. ix. p. 32); in the Greater Prophets, it is in part at least Origenic (*Studia Sinaitica*, pp. xvi., lxiii.); Job seems to have contained the interpolations from Theodotion which are found in the extant Greek texts of that book[1].

The following is a complete list of the Palestinian fragments included in the publications mentioned above : Gen. i. 1—iii. 24, vi. 9—ix. 19, xviii. 1—5, 18—xix. 30, xxii. 1—19; Ex. viii. 22ᵇ— xi. 10, xxviii. 1—12ᵃ; Num. iv. 46 f., 49—v. 2 f., 4, 6, 8; Deut. vi. 4 —16, vii. 25—26ᵃ, x. 12—xi. 28, xii. 28—xiv. 3; 2 Regn. ii. 19—22; 3 Regn. ii. 10ᵇ—15ᵃ, ix. 4—5ᵃ; Pss. viii. 2 f., xxi. 2, 19, xxii. 1, 5, xxiv. 1 f., xxix. 2, 4, xxx. 2, 6, xxxiv. 1, 11, xxxvii. 2, 18, xl. 2, 5, 7, xliii. 12—27, xliv.—xlvi., xlviii. 15 ff., xlix. 1—9, liv. 2, 22, lv. 7 ff., lvi. 1—7, lxiv. 2, 6, lxviii. 2, 3, 22, lxxvi. 2, 21, lxxvii. 52—65, lxxxi., lxxxii. 1—10, lxxxiv. 2, 8, lxxxv. 1, 15 f., lxxxvii. 2, 5—7, 18, lxxxix. 1—xc. 12, xcvii. 1, 8 f., ci. 2 f.; Prov. i. 1—19, ix. 1—11; Job xvi. 1—xvii. 16, xxi. 1—34, xxii. 3—12; Sap. ix. 8—11, 14—x. 2; Amos ix. 5—14ᵃ, viii. 9—12; Mic. v. 2—5; Joel i. 14—ii. 27, iii. 9—21; Jonah; Zech. ix. 9—15, xi. 11ᵇ—14; Isa. iii. 9ᵇ—15, vii. 10—16, viii. 8—xi. 16, xii. 1—6, xiv. 28—32, xv. 1—5, xxv. 1—3ᵃ, xxxv. 1—10, xl. 1—17, xlii. 5—10, 17—xliii. 21, xliv. 2—7, l. 4—9, lii. 13—liii. 12, lx. 1—22, lxi. 1—11, lxiii. 1—7; Jer. xi. 18—20[2].

(*b*) Mention is made[3] of a version of the Greek Old Testament attempted by the Nestorian Patriarch Mar Abbas (A.D. 552). But notwithstanding the declared preference of Theodore for the LXX., the Nestorians have always used the Peshitta, and there is no extant Nestorian version from the Greek.

(*c*) Of Jacobite versions from the LXX. there were several. (1) Polycarp the chorepiscopus, who in the fifth century laboured upon a translation of the New Testament under the auspices of Philoxenus, the Monophysite Bishop of Mabug, is known to have rendered the Greek Psalter into Syriac. The margin of the Syro-Hexaplar[4] mentions a Philoxenian 'edition' of Isaiah,

---

[1] Burkitt in *Anecd. Oxon.*, Semitic ser., I. ix. p. 44, and cf. Nestle's notes to *Studia Sinaitica*, vi.

[2] See *Studia Sin.*, vi. p. xiv. f. For recent additions see Nestle in Hastings' *D. B.* iv. 447.

[3] Bickell, *Conspectus rei Syr. lit.*, p. 9; cf. Ebedjesu in Assemani, iii. 71.

[4] Field, *Hexapla*, ii. p. 448.

to which two fragments printed by Ceriani[1] from the British Museum MS. Add. 17106 are believed to belong. The text of these fragments agrees on the whole with that of the Lucianic MSS. of the Prophets. (2) Another Monophysite, Jacob of Edessa, applied himself in 704—5 to the revision of the Syriac Old Testament, using for the purpose the Hexaplaric LXX.[2], and the fragments of the other Greek translations. Some books of this revised version exist in MS. at London and Paris[3], and a few specimens have been printed[4].

(*d*) From Melito downwards the Greek fathers refer occasionally to the Greek renderings of an interpreter who is called ὁ Σύρος. The student will find in Field's *prolegomena* a full and learned discussion of the question who this Syrian interpreter was. Field inclines to the opinion that he was a bilingual Syrian, of Greek origin, who translated into Greek from the Peshitta[5].

EDITIONS. PESHITTA. Lee, *V. T. Syriace* (London, 1823); *O. and N. T.*, 1826. A complete Syriac Bible has recently been published by the Dominicans of Mosul ((1)1887—91, (2)1888—92).

SYRO-HEXAPLAR. A. Masius, *Josuae-historia illustrata* (1574); M. Norberg, *Codex Syriaco-Hexaplaris* (1787); C. Bugati, *Daniel* (1788), *Psalmi* (1820); H. Middledorpf, *cod. Syrohexapl.*, lib. IV. Reg. e cod. Paris. Iesaias &c. e cod. Mediol. (1835): Skat Rördam, *libri Iudicum et Ruth sec. Syrohexapl.* (1861); P. de Lagarde, *V. T. ab Origene recensiti fragmenta ap. Syros servata v.* (1880), and *V. T. Graeci in sermonem Syrorum versi fragm. viii.* (in his last work *Bibliothecae Syriacae ...quae ad philologiam sacram pertinent*, 1892); G. Kerber, *Syrohexaplarische Fragmente* (*ZATW.*, 1896). Ceriani has published

---

[1] *Mon. sacr. et prof.* v.; cf. Gwynn in *D. C. B.* iv. p. 433.

[2] Gwynn, *D. C. B.* iii.

[3] 1 Regn. i. 1—3 Regn. ii. 11, and Isaiah are in the London MSS. lx., lxi. (Wright, *Catalogue*, p. 37 ff.), and the Pentateuch and Daniel are preserved at Paris.

[4] See Ladvocat, *Journal des savants*, for 1765; Eichhorn, *Bibliothek*, ii. p. 270; De Sacy, *Notices et extraits*, iv. p. 648 ff.; Ceriani, *Mon. sacr. et prof.* v. i. 1.

[5] On the other hand see Scrivener-Miller, ii. p. 7, note; and Bleek Wellhausen (1893), p. 560.

the contents of the London MS. in *Monumenta sacra et profana*, ii., and those of the Milan MS. in vol. vii. (1874) of the same series[1].

LITERATURE. G. Bickell, *Conspectus rei Syrorum literariae* (1871); Field, *Hexapla*, I. p. lxvii. sqq. (1875); W. Wright, *Syriac literature* in *Encycl. Britannica*, xxii. (1887); E. Nestle, *Littera-tura Syriaca* (1888), and *Urtext* (1897), p. 227 ff.; Scrivener-Miller, ii. p. 6 ff.; Gregory, p. 807 ff.; J. P. P. Martin, *Introduction* (p. théor.), p. 97 ff.; Loisy, *Histoire critique* I. ii. p. 234 f.; E. Nestle, *Syriac Versions* (in Hastings' *D. B.* iv.).

6. THE GOTHIC VERSION.

About the year 350 a translation of the Bible into the Gothic tongue was made by Ulfilas (Wulfila)[2], the descendant of a Cappadocian captive who had been brought up among the Goths in Dacia, and was in 341 consecrated Bishop of the Gothic nation, which was then beginning to embrace Arian Christianity. According to Philostorgius he translated the whole of the Old Testament except the books of Kingdoms, which he omitted as likely to inflame the military temper of the Gothic race by their records of wars and conquests (Philostorg. *loc. cit.*: μετέφρασεν εἰς τὴν αὐτῶν φωνὴν τὰς γραφὰς ἁπάσας πλήν γε δὴ τῶν Βασιλειῶν ἅτε τῶν μὲν πολέμων ἱστορίαν ἐχουσῶν, τοῦδε ἔθνους ὄντος φιλοπολέμου). Unfortunately only a few scanty fragments of the Gothic Old Testament have been preserved, i.e., some words from Gen. v. 3—30, Ps. lii. 2—3, 2 Esdr. xv. 13—16, xvi. 14—xvii. 3, xvii. 13—45. With the exception of the scrap from Genesis, they are derived from palimpsest fragments belonging to the Ambrosian Library which were discovered by Mai in 1817 and subsequently published at Milan by Mai and Castiglione; and they are printed in the great collection of Gabelentz and Loebe (*Ulfilas: V. et N. Testamenti...fragmenta*, Lipsiae, 1843) and in Migne *P. L.* xviii.; more recent editions are those of Uppstrom, Upsala, 1854—7; Massmann, Stuttgart 1855—7; Stamm, Paderborn, 1865; Bernhardt, Halle, 1875, 1884; G. H. Balg, *The First Germanic Bible*, Milwaukee, 1891; Stamm-Heyne, 1896.

---

[1] For the Apocryphal books see Lagarde, *Libri V. T. apocr. Syriace*, and Bensly-Barnes, *The fourth book of Maccabees in Syriac* (Camb. 1895).

[2] Socr. ii. 11, iv. 33, Theodoret iv. 37, Philostorg. ii. 5.

Lagarde (*Librorum V. T. canonicorum pars i.*, p. xiv., 1883) shews by an examination of the Esdras fragments that Ulfilas probably used MSS. of the Lucianic recension, and the same view is held by A. Kisch, *Der Septuaginta-Codex des Ulfilas* (*Monatschrift f. Gesch. u. W. des Judenthums*, 1873), and F. Kauffmann, *Beiträge zur Quellenkritik d. gothischen Bibel-übersetzung* (*Z. f. d. Phil.* 1896). Ulfilas was in Constantinople for some time about 340, and his MSS. of the LXX. were doubtless obtained in that city, which according to Jerome was one of the headquarters of the Lucianic LXX. ("Constantinopolis usque Antiochiam Luciani martyris exemplaria probat").

7.　THE ARMENIAN VERSION.

Armenian writers of the fifth century ascribe the inception of the Armenian Bible to Mesrop (354—441) and his associates. The book of Proverbs was the first translated, whether because it stood first in the volume[1] on which the translators worked, or because its gnomic character gave it a special importance in their eyes. The work is said to have been begun at Edessa, but MSS. were afterwards obtained from Constantinople; and Moses of Khoren, a nephew and pupil of Mesrop, was despatched to Alexandria to study Greek in order to secure "a more accurate articulation and division"[2] of the text. Moses indeed affirms that the earliest translations of the O.T. into Armenian were from the Syriac, and his statement receives some confirmation from the mention of Edessa as the place of origin, and from the circumstance that Syriac was the Church-language of Armenia before the introduction of the Armenian alphabet[3]. On the other hand the existing Armenian version

---

[1] So F. C. Conybeare (Hastings, i. p. 152). In Scrivener-Miller, ii. p. 151, he suggests that the earlier books had been rendered previously.

[2] On this see Conybeare, Scrivener-Miller, ii. p. 153.

[3] See Dr Salmon in *D. C. B.*, iii. p. 908.

is clearly Septuagintal. It fits the Greek of the LXX. "as a glove the hand that wears it"; keeping so close to the Greek that it "has almost the same value for us as the Greek text itself from which (the translator) worked would possess[1]." But, as Lagarde has pointed out[2], the printed text is untrustworthy, and the collation made for Holmes and Parsons cannot be regarded as satisfactory. A fresh collation will be made for the larger edition of the Cambridge Septuagint[3].

The order of the books of the O.T. in Armenian MSS., as given by Conybeare[4] (Octateuch, 1—4 Regn., 1—2 Paralipp., 1 and 2 Esdr., Esther, Judith, Tobit, 1—3 Macc., Psalms, Proverbs, Ecclesiastes, Canticles, Wisdom, Job[5], Isaiah, the Minor Prophets, Jeremiah, with Baruch and Lamentations, Daniel, Ezekiel) is on the whole consistent with the grouping found in the oldest Greek authorities[6], and seems to point to the use by the translators of good early codices.

MSS. Few codices of the entire Bible are earlier than the 13th century; one at Edschmiatzin belongs to the year 1151. Holmes assigns his Arm. 3 to A.D. 1063, but according to Conybeare it is a MS. of the eighteenth century.

EDITIONS. Venice (Psalter), 1565; Amsterdam, 1666; Constantinople, 1705; Venice, 1805 (the first edition which is of any critical value, by J. Zohrab); Venice, 1859—60 (by the Mechitarist fathers of San Lazzaro).

LITERATURE R. Holmes, *Praef. ad Pent.*; F. C. Conybeare in Scrivener-Miller, ii. 148 ff. and in Hastings' *D. B.*, *l.c.*;

[1] Conybeare, *op. cit.*, p. 151 f. He attributes the composite character of the Armenian text (of which he gives instances) to Hexaplaric influences.

[2] *Genesis Gr.*, p. 18.

[3] Mr McLean, who has collated the greater part of the Octateuch, informs me that "the Armenian shews a typical hexaplar text in Genesis and Exodus, agreeing closely with the Syriaco-hexaplar version, and in varying degrees with the MSS. that compose the hexaplar group." "The hexaplar element (he adds) is much less in evidence in Leviticus, Numbers, and Deuteronomy, but again appears strongly in Joshua, Judges, and Ruth."

[4] *Op. cit.*, p. 152 f.

[5] In some MSS. Job precedes the Psalter.

[6] See Part II. c. i.

H. Hyvernat, in Vigouroux' *D. B.*; C. R. Gregory, *Prolegg.* p. 912 ff.; J. P. P. Martin, *Introd.* (p. théor.), p. 323 ff.; E. Nestle in *Urtext*, p. 155, where fuller bibliographical information will be found.

8. THE GEORGIAN VERSION.

The origin of this version is obscure. According to Moses of Khoren, the Georgian as well as the Armenian version was the work of Mesrop. Iberia seems to have received the Gospel early in the fourth century, if not before; but it may have possessed no translation of the Scriptures until the movement initiated in Armenia by Mesrop had communicated itself to the neighbouring region. That the Georgian Old Testament was based upon the Greek is said to be manifest from the transliteration of Greek words which it contains.

MSS. A Psalter of cent. vii.—viii. is preserved at the monastery of St Catherine's, Mt Sinai, and at Athos there is a MS., dated 978, which originally contained the whole Bible, but has lost Lev. xii.—Joshua. Both the Sinai library and the Patriarchal library at Jerusalem are rich in Georgian MSS.

EDITIONS. The Georgian Bible was printed at Moscow in 1743 and at St Petersburg in 1816 and 1818; the Moscow edition is said to have been adapted to the Russian Church Bible.

LITERATURE. F. C. Alter, *über Georgianische Litteratur* (Vienna, 1798); A. A. Tsagarelli, *An account of the monuments of Georgian Literature* [in Russian], St Petersburg, 1886—94; A. Khakhanow, *Les MSS. Georgiens de la Bibliothèque Nationale à Paris* (without place or date, ? 1898).

9. THE SLAVONIC VERSION.

The Greek Bible was translated into Slavonic by the brothers Cyril and Methodius, from whom in the ninth century the Slavs received the faith. Of the Old Testament the Psalter alone was finished before the death of Cyril, but according to contemporary testimony Methodius brought the work to completion. As a whole this original version no longer exists, the codices having perished in the Tartar invasion of the thirteenth century; and the fragments of the Old Testament of Cyril and Methodius which are embedded in the present Slavonic Bible are "so mixed up with later versions as to be indistinguishable[1]." The existing version has not been made uniformly from the Greek. Esther was translated from the Hebrew, while Chronicles, Ezra and Nehemiah, and certain other books, were rendered from the Latin Vulgate in the fifteenth century. On the other hand the Octateuch, the books of Kingdoms, and the poetical books are from the Greek, and some of them, especially the Octateuch, contain old materials probably due, at least in part, to the work of Cyril and Methodius.

A Psalter in the Glagolitic script, preserved at Sinai, has been edited by Geitler (Agram, 1883); and there is a critical edition of the Slavonic Psalter by Amphilochius (Moscow, 1874—9).

So far as the Slavonic Old Testament is based on the LXX., its text is doubtless Lucianic; cf. Lagarde, *Praef. in Libr. V. T. can.* i. p. xv. "ni omnia fallunt Slavus nihil aliud vertit nisi Luciani recensionem," and Leskien in *Urtext*, p. 215, "dass im allgemeinen der Kirchenslavischen Übersetzung der griech. Text der Lucianischen (Antiochenisch-Konstantinopolita-nischen) Rezension zu Grunde liegt ist sicher."

LITERATURE. The Russian authorities are given by Mr Bebb in Scrivener-Miller, ii. p. 158. See also Gregory, *Prolegg.* p. 1112 ff.; Professor Leskien of Leipzig in *Urtext*, p. 211 ff.; the article in *Ch. Quarterly Review* cited above; and *Th. Literatur-zeitung*, 1901, col. 571.

[1] *The Russian Bible*, in *Ch. Quart. Review*, xli. 81 (Oct. 1895), p. 219.

CHAPTER V.

MANUSCRIPTS OF THE SEPTUAGINT.

THE great edition of the Septuagint published by Holmes and Parsons ends with a complete list of the MSS. employed (vol. v. ad fin., addenda). It enumerates 311 codices (I.—XIII., 14—311), of which I.—XIII., 23, 27, 39, 43, 156, 188, 190, 258, 262, are written in uncial letters, or partly so, while the rest are in minuscule or cursive hands. Since 1827, the date of the publication of the last volume of the Oxford edition, the list of available codices or fragments has been largely increased, owing partly to the researches and publications of Tischendorf, partly to the progress which has recently been made in the examination and cataloguing of Eastern libraries, and the discovery in Egypt of fragments of papyrus bearing Biblical texts. In this chapter an effort has been made to present the student with a complete list of all the MSS. which have been or are being used by editors of the LXX., and of the important fragments so far as they are known to us. It is, however, impossible to guarantee either the exhaustiveness or the correctness in regard to minor details of information which has been brought together from many sources and cannot be verified by enquiry at first hand.

SYSTEMS OF NOTATION. Two systems have been used to denote the uncial MSS. Holmes employed Roman numerals; Lagarde, the capitals of the Roman alphabet[1]. For the cursive MSS. Holmes used Arabic numerals, beginning with 14; but, as we have seen, several uncials were allowed to take rank among them. Later scholars have for the most part retained

[1] Lagarde's CEHKRSUYZ were unknown to the Oxford editors. Greek capitals have been used in the Cambridge manual LXX. for a few uncials not mentioned by Lagarde.

this method of notation for the cursives, excepting in the case of a few groups which are supposed to represent a particular recension; thus Lagarde adopted the symbols *f h m p z* for the Lucianic MSS. 82, 93, 118, 44[1], whilst Cornill with a similar object substituted the small letters of the Greek alphabet for the Arabic numerals[2]. Uniformity in this matter can scarcely be expected until the cursive codices have been thoroughly examined and catalogued; meanwhile it is sufficient to call attention to the variety of practice which exists.

Manuscripts of the LXX., whether uncial or cursive, rarely contain the whole of the Greek Old Testament. There are some notable exceptions to the general rule (e.g. A, B, C, S = א, 64, 68, 106, 122, 131), and the number of these exceptions may be increased by adding MSS. which have been broken up into two or more separate codices (e.g. G, N + V). But the majority of the copies seem never to have included more than a particular book (as Genesis, or the Psalms, with or without the liturgical ᾠδαί), or a particular group of books such as the Pentateuch (ἡ πεντάτευχος[3]) or the Octateuch (ἡ ὀκτάτευχος = Gen. —Ruth), the Historical Books (1 Regn.—2 Esdr., Esth., Judith, Tobit), the three or five books ascribed to Solomon, the Minor Prophets (τὸ δωδεκαπρόφητον), the Major Prophets (οἱ τέσσαρες), or the Prophets complete (τὸ ἑκκαιδεκαπρόφητον). Larger combinations are also found, e.g. Genesis—Tobit, the Poetical Books as a whole, or the Poetical Books with the Prophets.

In reference to the date of their execution, the uncial MSS. of the LXX. range from the third century to the tenth, and the cursives from the ninth to the sixteenth. Their present distribution may be seen from the descriptions; an analysis of the list of Holmes and Parsons gives the following general results: Italy, 129; Great Britain and Ireland, 54; France, 36; Austria, 26; Russia, 23; Germany, 13; Spain, 7; Holland, 6; Switzerland, 6; Denmark, 4. This summary conveys a general

---

[1] *Libr. V. T. can. pars i.,* p. v. sq.
[2] *Ezechiel,* p. 19 ff.
[3] Cf. Orig. *in Ioann.* t. xiii. 26, Epiph. *de mens. et pond.* 4. *Pentateuchus* occurs in Tertullian *adv. Marc.* i. 10.

idea of the proportion in which the MSS. of the LXX. were distributed among European countries, Greece excepted, at the beginning of the nineteenth century. But the balance will be considerably disturbed if we add the acquisitions of Tischendorf and other discoverers, and the treasures of the libraries at Athens, Athos, Patmos, Smyrna, Jerusalem, and Mount Sinai, which are now within the reach of the critical student.

I. UNCIAL MSS.

The following table of the Uncial MSS. may be found convenient. A detailed account of each will follow.

Symbols. H.-P.	Lagarde.	Name of Codex.	Century.	Present locality.
III	A	Alexandrinus	v	London
II	B	Vaticanus	iv	Rome
	C	Ephraemi	v	Paris
I	D	Cottonianus	v	London
	E	Bodleianus	ix—x	Oxford
VII	F	Ambrosianus	v	Milan
IV+V	G	Sarravianus	v	Leyden, Paris, St Petersburg
	H	Petropolitanus	vi	St Petersburg
XIII=13	I	Bodleianus	ix	Oxford
	K	Lipsiensis	vii	Leipzig
VI	L	Vindobonensis	v—vi	Vienna
X	M	Coislinianus	vii	Paris
XI	N	Basilianus	viii—ix	Rome
VIII	O¹	Dublinensis	vi	Dublin
XII	Q	Marchalianus	vi	Rome
	R	Veronensis	vi	Verona
	S=ℵ	Sinaiticus	iv	Leipzig, St Petersburg
262	T	Turicensis	vii	Zurich
	U	Londinensis	vii	London
23	V	Venetus	viii—ix	Venice
43	W	Parisiensis	ix	Paris
258	X	Vaticanus	ix	Rome
	Y²	Taurinensis	ix	Turin
	Zᵃ⁻ᵉ	Fragmenta Tischendorfiana		
	Γ	Cryptoferratensis	viii—ix	Grotta ferrata
	Δ	Bodleianus	iv—v	Oxford
	Θ	Washingtoniensis	v—vi	Detroit
	Π	Petropolitanus	viii—ix	St Petersburg

[1] For IX = P see under Cursive MSS. (H.-P. 294).
[2] This MS. ought to take rank among the cursives; see below, p. 145.

(A) Complete Bibles.

A (III). CODEX ALEXANDRINUS. British Museum, Royal, I. D. v.—viii.

A MS. of the O. and N. Testaments, with lacunae. The O. T. is defective in the following places : Gen. xiv. 14—17, xv. 1—5, 16—19, xvi. 6—9 (leaf torn across and the lower portion lost); 1 Regn. xii. 18—xiv. 9 (leaf missing); Ps. xlix. 19—lxxix. 10 (nine leaves missing). Slighter defects, due to the tearing of leaves, occur in Gen. i. 20—25, 29—ii. 3; Lev. viii. 6, 7, 16; Sirach l. 21, 22, li. 5.

The codex now consists of four volumes, of which the first three contain the O. T. in 639 leaves. The books are thus distributed : vol. i. Genesis—2 Chronicles; vol. ii. Hosea—4 Maccabees; vol. iii. Psalms—Sirach[1]. The first volume begins with a table of the Books, in a hand somewhat later than the body of the MS. The Psalter, which contains the ψαλμὸς ἰδιόγραφος (cli.) and the liturgical canticles, is preceded by the Epistle of Athanasius to Marcellinus, the ὑποθέσεις of Eusebius, a table, and the canons of the Morning and Evening Psalms. The books of vol. iii. are written στιχηρῶς.

The covers of the volumes bear the arms of Charles I. The codex had been sent to James I. by Cyril Lucar, patriarch successively of Alexandria and Constantinople, but did not reach England till after the succession of Charles. It had previously belonged to the Patriarchate of Alexandria, as we learn from an Arabic note at the beginning. Another but later Arabic note states that the MS. was the work of 'the martyr Thecla,' and Cyril Lucar has written on a leaf prefixed to vol. i.: " Liber iste ...prout ego traditione habebam, est scriptus manu Theclae nobilis faeminae Aegyptiae ante MCCC annos circiter, paulo post concilium Nicaenum." But, apart from palaeographical considerations[2], this date is discredited by the occurrence in the MS. of excerpts from the works of Athanasius and Eusebius, and the liturgical matter connected with the Psalter. It has been proposed to identify Thecla with a correspondent of Gregory of Nazianzus (see THECLA (10), *D. C. B.* iv., p. 897); but this later Thecla seems to have belonged to Cappadocia, not to Egypt. Portions of the text of cod. A were printed by Patrick Young, 1637 (Job), Ussher, 1655 (Judges vi., xviii.), Walton in the polyglott of 1657 (facsimile of Ps. i.), Gale, 1678 (Psalter); and the MS. was used by Grabe as the basis of his great edition

---

[1] For the order of the books see Part II. c. i.
[2] As to these see Kenyon, *Our Bible and the Ancient MSS.*, p. 129.

of the LXX. (1707—1720[1]). Baber in 1812 published the Psalter and in 1816—1821 the whole of the O. T. in facsimile type. Finally, an autotype facsimile, which, as Gregory well says, leaves nothing to be desired, was issued in 1881—3 by order of the Trustees of the British Museum under the editorship of Mr (now Sir) E. Maunde Thompson, who has added brief but valuable prolegomena.

The codex is written on leaves of fine vellum, arranged in quires usually of eight. The writing "varies in different parts of the MS., though sufficient uniformity is maintained to make it difficult to decide the exact place where a new hand begins...the style of writing in vol. iii. is for the most part different from that of the other volumes[2]." In a few of the superscriptions and colophons the occurrence of Egyptian forms of the Greek letters has been noted, "proving that the MS., if not absolutely written in Egypt, must have been immediately afterwards removed thither[3]." The leaves measure about 32 centimetres by 26.3; each leaf contains two columns of 49—51 lines, the lines usually consisting of 23—25 letters. Except in the third volume, the commencement of a new section or paragraph is marked by a large initial letter in the margin as well as by paragraph-marks. There are no breathings or accents by the first hand; an apostrophe occasionally separates words or consonants; here and there an asterisk is placed in the margin (e.g. Gen. xli. 19). Punctuation is limited to a single point, generally high. The abbreviations which occur are $\overline{\Theta C}$, $\overline{KC}$, $\overline{XC}$, $\overline{\Pi HP}$, $\overline{MHP}$, $\overline{YC}$, $\overline{ANOC}$, $\overline{OYNOC}$, $\overline{\Delta A\Delta}$, $\overline{IH\Lambda}$, $\overline{I\Lambda HM}$, $\overline{\Pi N A}$, and ϗ, ᷒, ᷓ, N,, τ, (καί, μου, σου, -ναι, -ται). There are numerous and lengthy erasures, over which a corrector has written the text which he preferred. The earliest corrector (A[1]) was contemporary with the scribe or nearly so; the second corrector (A[a]) may have lived a century later; a third and still later hand (A[b]) has also been at work. But the question of the 'hands' in this MS. remains to be worked out, and calls for the knowledge of an expert in palaeography.

B (II). CODEX VATICANUS (Vatican Library, Gr. 1209).

A MS. of the Old and New Testaments, defective at the beginning and in some other places. The O. T. has lost its first 31 leaves, the original hand beginning at Gen. xlvi. 28 (with the words πόλιν εἰς γῆν 'Ραμεσσή). Through the tearing of fol. 178 2 Regn. ii. 5—7, 10—13, has also disappeared, and the loss of

---

[1] See c. vi.
[2] *Prolegg.* i. p. 358.
[3] E. Maunde Thompson, *Cod. Alex.* i. p. 8 ff. *Ibid.*

10 leaves after fol. 348 involves a *lacuna* which extends from Ps. cv. (cvi.) 27 to Ps. cxxxvii. (cxxxviii.) 6^b. The longer gaps have been filled by a recent hand.

The present codex is a quarto volume containing 759 leaves, of which 617 belong to the O. T. Every book of the Greek O. T. is included, except 1—4 Maccabees, which never found a place in the MS. The order of the books differs from that which is followed in cod. A, the poetical books being placed between the canonical histories and the Prophets ; and there are variations also in the internal arrangement of the groups.

Of the history of this MS. before the sixteenth century nothing is certainly known. A Vatican collection of Greek MSS. was already in existence in the middle of the fifteenth century, and the greatest treasure in the present library was among its earliest acquisitions. It finds a place ·in the early catalogues of the Vatican[1]; reference is made to this MS. in letters addressed by the librarian of the Vatican to Erasmus in 1521 and 1533[2], and it formed the chief authority for the Roman edition of the LXX. in 1587. By this time its importance was already recognised, and it is amazing that an interval of nearly 300 years should have been allowed to pass before the actual text of the MS. was given to the world. A collation of B with the Aldine text was made by Bartolocci in 1669, and is still preserved at Paris in the Bibliothèque Nationale (*MS. gr. supplem.* 53). With other treasures of the Vatican the codex was carried to Paris by Napoleon, and there it was inspected in 1809 by Hug, whose book *De antiquitate codicis Vaticani* (Freiburg, 1810) aroused fresh interest in its text. On the restoration of the MS. to the Vatican it was guarded with a natural but unfortunate jealousy which for more than half a century baffled the efforts of Biblical scholars. Neither Tischendorf in 1843 and 1866 nor Tregelles in 1845 was permitted to make a full examination of the codex. Meanwhile the Roman authorities were not unmindful of the duty of publishing these treasures, but the process was slow, and the first results were disappointing. An edition printed by Mai in 1828 —38 did not see the light till 1857. It was followed in 1881 by Cozza's more accurate but far from satisfactory volumes in facsimile type. At length in 1890 under the auspices of Leo XIII. the Vatican Press issued a photographic reproduction worthy of this most important of Biblical MSS.[3]

---

[1] This has been proved by Nestle (*Academy*, May 30, 1891) against Batiffol (*La Vaticane de Paul III. à Paul V.*, Paris, 1890, p. 82. Cf. Nestle, *Septuagintastudien*, ii. p. 11, note i.

[2] *La Vaticane de Paul III. à Paul V.* (Paris, 1890). Gregory, *Prolegg.* p. 360.

[3] On this work see Nestle, *Septuagintast.* iii. p. 13 ff.

The codex is written on the finest vellum in a singularly beautiful hand[1] which "may be attributed to the fourth century," and probably to the middle of the century[2], and bears a resemblance to the hand which is found in papyri of the best Roman period[3]. The leaves are arranged in quinions (gatherings of ten pages); each page exhibits three columns of 42 lines with 16—18 letters in each line. There are no breathings or accents in the first hand; a point occurs but rarely; initial letters do not project into the margin. The text is written in two contemporary hands, the transition being made at p. 335. The MS. has been corrected more than once; besides the scribe or contemporary *diorthotes* (B[1]), we may mention an early corrector denoted as B[a], and a late *instaurator*, who has gone over the whole text, spoiling its original beauty, and preserving oftentimes the corrections of B[a] rather than the original text.

C. CODEX EPHRAEMI SYRI RESCRIPTUS PARISIENSIS. Bibliothèque Nationale, Gr. 9 (formerly Reg. 1905, Colbert. 3769).

A folio consisting at present of 209 leaves, of which 64 contain portions of the O. T. The fragments are as follows: Prov. i. 2 νοῆσαι—ii. 8, xv. 29 κρείσσων—xvii. 1, xviii. 11 ἡ δὲ δόξα—xix. 23, xxii. 17 τὴν δὲ σήν—xxiii. 25, xxiv. 22 e ὥστε ἄβρωτα—56 ἡ γῆ, xxvi. 23 χείλη λεῖα—xxviii. 2, xxix. 48—end of book; Eccl. i. 2 ματαιότης—14, ii. 18 ὑπὸ τὸν ἥλιον—end of book; Cant. i. 3—iii. 9 Σαλωμών; Job ii. 12 ῥήξαντες—iv. 12 ἐν λόγοις σου, v. 27 σὺ δὲ γνῶθι—vii. 7, x. 9—xii. 2 ἄνθρωποι, xiii. 18 οἶδα ἐγώ—xviii. 9 παγίδες, xix. 27 ἃ ὁ ὀφθαλμός—xxii. 14 νεφέλη, xxiv. 7 γυμνοὺς πολλούς—xxx. 1 ἐν μέρει, xxxi. 6—xxxv. 15 ὀργὴν αὐτοῦ, xxxvii. 5 —xxxviii. 17 θανάτου, xl. 20 περιθήσεις—end of book; Sap. viii. 5 ἐργαζόμενος—xii. 10 τόπον μετανοίας, xiv. 19—xvii. 18 εὐμελής, xviii. 24 ἐπὶ γάρ—end of book; Sir. prol. 1—vii. 14 πρεσβυτέρων, viii. 15 αὐτὸς γάρ—xi. 17 εὐσεβέσιν, xii. 16 καὶ ἐάν—xvi. 1 ἀχρήστων, xvii. 12—xx. 5 σοφός, xxi. 12—xxii. 19, xxvii. 19—xxviii. 25 σταθμόν, xxx. 8—xxxiv. 22 οὐ μή σοι, xxx. 25—xxxi. 6, xxxii. 22 καὶ ὁ κύριος—xxxiii. 13 Ἰακώβ, xxxvii. 11—xxxviii. 15, xxxix. 7—xliv. 27 ἀφικώμεθα, xlv. 24 ἵνα αὐτῷ—xlvii. 23 Ῥοβοάμ, xlviii. 11—xlix. 12 Ἰησοῦς υἱός. The distribution of the leaves is Proverbs 6, Ecclesiastes 8, Cant. 1, Job 19, Wisdom 7, Sirach 23.

[1] Specimens are given in Sir E. Maunde Thompson's *Greek and Latin Palæography*, p. 150; and F. G. Kenyon's *Our Bible &c.*, p. 136; E. Nestle, *Einführung*[2], *Tafel* 4.
[2] Sir E. M. Thompson, *op. cit.* p. 159; WH., Intr. p. 75.
[3] F. G. Kenyon, *Palæography of Greek papyri*, p. 120. See A. Rahlfs, *Alter u. Heimath der Vat. Bibelhandschrift*, in *G. G. N.*, 1899, i. p. 72 ff.

The copy of the Greek Bible of which these fragments have survived unfortunately fell during the middle ages into the hands of a scribe in want of writing materials.· Originally, as it seems, a complete Bible, written probably in the fifth century and, as Tischendorf believed, in Egypt, in the twelfth century it was taken to pieces, sponged, and used for other writings[1]. What became of the missing leaves we do not know; those of the Paris volume are covered with the Greek text of certain works of Ephrem the Syrian[2]. The book was probably brought to Florence early in the 16th century by Andreas Lascaris, the agent of Lorenzo de' Medici, and passing into the possession of Catharine de' Medici, accompanied her to France, where it found its way into the Royal Library. Here the value of the underlying text was recognised by Montfaucon, who called attention to it in his *Palaeographia Graeca*, and gave a specimen from the fragments of the N. T. (p. 213 f.). The O. T. fragments were partly examined by Wetstein and Thilo[3], but were not given to the world until in 1845 Tischendorf, who had published the N. T. portion in 1843, completed his task by printing the LXX. text.

This once noble MS. was written in single columns from 40 to 46 lines in length, each line containing about 40 letters[4]. The writing of the O. T. differs, according to Tischendorf, from that of the N. T.; it is more delicate, some of the letters (A, Δ, B, K, Ξ, X, Φ) assume different forms in the two portions of the codex, and there are other palaeographical indications that the hand which wrote the earlier books did not write the later. Nevertheless Tischendorf regarded the two hands as contemporary, and believed the codex to have been originally one. A seventh century corrector has left traces of his work, but his corrections are not numerous except in Sirach. As to the order of the books nothing can be ascertained, the scribe who converted the MS. into a palimpsest having used the leaves for his new text without regard to their original arrangement[5].

S = א. CODEX SINAITICUS. Leipzig and St Petersburg.

The remains of this great uncial Bible contain the following portions of the O. T.: Gen. xxiii. 19 αὕτη—xxiv. 4 πορεύσῃ, xxiv.

---

[1] On palimpsest MSS. see Sir E. M. Thompson, *Greek and Latin Palaeography*, p. 75 ff.
[2] For a list of these see Omont, *Inventaire sommaire des manuscrits grecs*, p. 2.
[3] Tischendorf, *Cod. Ephraemi rescriptus, prolegg.* p. 9.
[4] See a photographic facsimile in *Facsimilés des plus anciens manuscrits grecs de la Bibl. Nat.* (H. Omont, Paris, 1892).
[5] See Tischendorf, *op. cit., prolegg.* p. 5.

5 εἰς τὴν γῆν—8, 9 ῥήματος—14 καμήλους, 17 καὶ εἶπεν—19 ἕως ἄν, 25 αὐτῷ—27 τήν, 30 ἄνθρωπον—33 λαλῆσαι, 36 αὐτῷ(1°)—41 ἐκ τῆς, 41 ὁρκισμοῦ—46 ἀφ᾽; Num. v. 26 αὐτῆς—30 ποιήσει, vi. 5 ἅγιος—6 τετελευτηκυία, 11 κεφαλήν—12 αἱ (2°), 17 κανῷ—18 μαρτυρίου, 22, 23, 27 Κύριος, vii. 4 Μωυσῆν—5 Λευείταις, 12 Ναασσών—13 ἔν, 15 ἔνα (2°)—20 θυμιάματος, 1 Par. ix. 27 τὸ πρωΐ—xix. 17, 2 Esdr. ix. 9 Κύριος—end of book; Psalms—Sirach; Esther; Tobit; Judith; Joel, Obadiah, Jonah, Nahum, Habakkuk, Zephaniah, Haggai, Zechariah, Malachi; Isaiah, Jeremiah, Lam. i. 1—ii. 20; 1 and 4 Maccabees.

The forty-three leaves containing 1 Par. xi. 22—xix. 17, 2 Esdras ix. 9—end, Esther, Tobit i. 1—ii. 2, Jer. x. 25—end, and Lam. i. 1—ii. 20 were found by Tischendorf in a waste-paper basket at the Convent of St Catharine's, Mount Sinai, in 1844, and published by him in a lithographed facsimile under the name of *Codex Friderico-Augustanus*[1] (Leipzig, 1846); to these in *Mon. sacr. ined., nov. coll.* i. (1855) he was able to add Isa. lxvi. 12—Jer. i. 7 from a copy made during the same visit to Sinai. A second visit in 1853 enabled him to print in the next volume of the *Monumenta* (1857) two short fragments of Genesis (xxiv. 9, 10, 41—43). During a third visit to the Convent in 1859, he was permitted to see the rest of the codex, including 156 leaves of the Old Testament, and ultimately succeeded in carrying the whole to St Petersburg for presentation to the Czar Alexander II. This final success led to the publication in 1862 of the *Bibliorum Codex Sinaiticus Petropolitanus*, containing a facsimile of the St Petersburg portion of the Sinaitic MS. Lastly in 1867 Tisch-endorf completed his task by printing in his *Appendix Codicum* certain fragments of Genesis and Numbers which had been dis-covered by the Archimandrite Porfirius in the bindings of other Sinai MSS.[2]

This great Bible was written on leaves which originally measured 15 × 13½ inches, and were gathered, with two excep-tions, into quires of four. Each column contains 48 lines, with 12—14 letters in a line; and in all but the poetical books each page exhibits four columns, so that eight lie open at a time[3]; in the poetical books, where the lines are longer, two columns appear on each page, or four at an opening. The characters are assigned to the fourth century; they are well-formed and some-what square, written without break, except when an apostrophe or a single point intervenes; a breathing *prima manu* has been

---

[1] So called in honour of Frederick Augustus, King of Saxony.

[2] Cf. Tischendorf's remarks in *Litt. C.-Blatt*, 1867 (27).

[3] "They have much of the appearance of the successive columns in a papyrus roll, and it is not at all impossible that it [the MS.] was actually copied from such a roll." Kenyon, p. 124; cf. Scrivener-Miller, p. 95.

noticed at Tobit vi. 9, but with this exception neither breathings nor accents occur. Tischendorf distinguished four hands in the codex (A, B, C, D), and assigned to A the fragments of Chronicles, 1 Macc., and the last 4½ leaves of 4 Macc., as well as the whole of the N. T.; the fragments of Numbers and the Prophets are ascribed to B ; the poetical books to C; Tobit and Judith and the rest of 4 Macc. to D, who is identified with the scribe to whom we owe the N. T. of Codex Vaticanus. He also detected traces of five stages in the correction of the MS., which he represented by the symbols א^a, א^{c.a}, א^{c.b}, א^{c.c}, א^d. The first symbol covers the work of the diorthotes and other nearly contemporary correctors; א^{c.a, c.b, c.c} are three seventh century hands, of which the last appears chiefly in the Book of Job, whilst the later א^d has occupied itself with retracing faded writing in the Prophets.

After 1 Chron. xix. 17 cod. א (FA) passes without break to 2 Esdr. ix. 9, but the place is marked by the corrector א^{c.a} with three crosses and the note μέχρι τούτου [τοῦ] σημείου τῶν τριῶν σταυρῶν ἐστιν τὸ τέλος τῶν ἑπτὰ φύλλων τῶν περισσῶν καὶ μὴ ὄντων τοῦ Ἔσδρα. Five of these leaves remain, and the two which preceded them probably contained 1 Chron. vi. 50—ix. 27^a (H. St J. Thackeray in Hastings' *D.B.*, i. p. 762). Westcott (*Bible in the Church*, p. 307) supposes that the insertion of this fragment of 1 Chron. in the heart of 2 Esdras is due to a mistake in the binding of the copy from which the MS. was transcribed; comp. the similar error in the archetype of all our Greek copies of Sirach[1]. Whether 1 Esdras formed a part of cod. א is uncertain, the heading Ἔσδρας β' does not prove this, since cod. א contains 4 Maccabees under the heading Μακκαβαίων δ' although it certainly did not give the second and third books (Thackeray, *l. c.*).

No uniform edition or photographic reproduction of this most important MS. has yet appeared[2]. The student is still under the necessity of extracting the text of א from the five works of Tischendorf mentioned above. A homogeneous edition of the remains of the codex or a photographic reproduction of the text is one of our most urgent needs in the field of Biblical palaeography. (The N. T. has now appeared in collotype; H. and K. Lake, introd. by K. Lake, Oxford, 1911.)

N (XI). CODEX BASILIANO-VATICANUS. Vatican Library, Gr. 2106, formerly Basil. 145[3].

---

[1] Another explanation (suggested by Dr Gwynn) is given by Dr Lupton in Wace's Apocrypha, i., p. 2.

[2] A facsimile of 2 Esdr. xviii. 15—xix. 15 may be seen in Stade, *Gesch. d. Volkes Israel*, ii. p. 192.

[3] Cf. Wetstein, *N. T.* i. p. 133; Lagarde, *Septuagintastudien*, p. 48.

V (23). CODEX VENETUS. St Mark's Library, Venice, cod. Gr. 1[1].

Dr E. Klostermann (*Analecta*, pp. 9 f., 33 f.) has produced good reasons for believing that these two codices originally formed portions of a complete copy of the Greek Old Testament. The Vatican portion now contains Lev. xiii. 59—Num. xxi. 34, Num. xxii. 19—Deut. xxviii. 40, Deut. xxx. 16—Jud. xiv. 16, Jud. xviii. 2—1 Regn. xvii. 12, 1 Regn. xvii. 31—3 Regn. viii. 8, 3 Regn. xi. 17—end of 2 Paralip., 2 Esdr. v. 10—xvii. 3, Esther. The Venice MS. yields Job xxx. 8 to end, Prov., Eccl., Cant., Sap., Sirach, the Minor Prophets (in the order Hos., Am., Joel, Ob., Jon., Mic., Nah., Hab., Zeph., Hag., Zech., Mal.), Isa., Jer., Bar., Lam., Ezek., Daniel, Tobit, Judith, 1—4 Macc.

The Venice folio measures $16\frac{1}{2} \times 11\frac{2}{3}$ inches, the Vatican at present a little less, but the breadth and length of the columns is identical in the two codices; in both there are two columns of 60 lines. The Venice MS. contains 164 leaves, the Vatican 132. The first leaf of the Venice book begins the 27th quire of the original MS., and on computation it appears that, if to the Vatican leaves were added those which would be required to fill the lacunae of the earlier books and of Job, the entire number would make up 26 quires of the same size[2]. As regards the history of the separated portions, it appears that the Vatican MS. was originally brought to Rome from Calabria by a Basilian monk[3]; the Venice book was once the property of Cardinal Bessarion, by whom it was presented to St Mark's[4].

The handwriting of N and V is in the sloping uncials of cent. viii.—ix. Some use was made of V in the Roman edition of 1587, where it seems to have supplied the text of Maccabees; both codices were collated for Holmes and Parsons, who numbered V as a cursive.

(B) *Octateuch and Historical Books.*

D (I). CODEX COTTONIANUS. British Museum, Cotton MSS., Otho B. vi. 5—6.

A collection of fragments, the largest of which measures no more than $7 \times 5\frac{1}{2}$ inches, containing portions of the Book of Genesis with vestiges of pictures executed in a semi-classical style.

---

[1] Cf. *Deutsche Lit.-Zeit.* 1897, p. 1475 f.
[2] Klostermann, p. 9.
[3] Holmes, *Praef. ad Pentateuch.*
[4] It was the eighth of Bessarion's MSS.; see Schott in Eichhorn's *Repert.*, viii. 181.

No other uncial codex of the LXX., of which any portion remains, has suffered so lamentable a fate. Brought to England from Philippi[1] in the reign of Henry VIII. by two Orthodox Bishops[2], and presented to the English monarch, it remained in the Royal Library till the reign of Elizabeth, who gave it to her Greek tutor Sir John Fortescue, and from his hands after several vicissitudes it found its way into the Cotton collection. In 1731, while the codex was at Ashburnham House with the rest of that collection, it was reduced by fire to a heap of charred and shrivelled leaves. Even before the fire it had been imperfect[3]; the beginning and end of the book had disappeared, and other leaves were defective here and there; yet 165 or 166 leaves remained and 250 miniatures. The existing remains at the British Museum, though collected with the most scrupulous care, consist only of 150 mutilated fragments; to these must be added a smaller series preserved at the Baptist College, Bristol, to which institution they were bequeathed by Dr A. Gifford, formerly an Assistant Librarian at the Museum.

Most of the London fragments were deciphered and published by Tischendorf in 1857 (*Mon. sacr. ined., nov. coll.* ii.); the rest, together with the Bristol fragments, are now accessible in Dr F. W. Gotch's *Supplement to Tischendorf's Reliquiae cod. Cotton.* (London, 1881).

Happily we have means of ascertaining with some approach to completeness the text of this codex as it existed before the fire. Although no transcript had been made, the MS. was more than once collated—by Patrick Young and Ussher for Walton's Polyglott, and afterwards by Gale, Crusius, and Grabe; and Grabe's collation, which is preserved in the Bodleian, was published by Dr H. Owen (*Collatio cod. Cotton. Geneseos cum Editione Romana...*, Londini, 1778). Some assistance can also be obtained from the *Vetusta Monumenta* published by the London Society of Antiquaries (vol. i. 1747), where two plates are given depicting some of the miniatures, together with portions of the text of fragments which have since disappeared.

Lastly, among the Peiresc papers in the Bibliothèque Nationale, transcripts have been found of Gen. i. 13, 14, xviii. 24—26, xliii. 16, which were made from the MS. in 1606. They are printed in *Mémoires de la Société Nationale des Antiquaires de France*, liii. pp. 163—172[4]. As this discovery was overlooked

---

[1] Still an episcopal see in the time of Le Quien; see Lightfoot, *Philippians*, p. 64, note.

[2] They stated that it had once been the property of Origen.

[3] Walton's statement that Cod. D at one time contained the Pentateuch is however groundless; in the Cotton catalogue of 1621 it is described as "Genesis only."

[4] I owe the reference to Dr Nestle (*Urtext*, p. 71).

when the second edition of *The Old Testament in Greek*, vol. i., passed through the press in 1895, it may be convenient to the student to have the new fragments placed before him *in extenso.*

Gen. i. 13, 14...¹³ ἑσπέρα καὶ ἐγένετο πρωί, ἡμέρα τρίτη. ¹⁴ καὶ εἶπεν ὁ θεός Γενηθήτωσαν φωστῆρες ἐν τῷ στερεώματι τοῦ οὐρανοῦ εἰς φαῦσιν τῆς γῆς, καὶ ἀρχέτωσαν τῆς ἡμέρας καὶ τῆς νυκτὸς τοῦ δια-χω[ρίζειν]...

11. xviii. 24—26. ²⁴ ἐὰν ὦσιν πεντήκοντα δίκαιοι ἐν τῇ πόλει, ἀπολέσεις αὐτούς; οὐκ ἀνήσεις πάντα τὸν τόπον ἐκεῖνον ἕνεκα τῶν πεντήκοντα δικαίων, ἐὰν ὦσιν ἐν αὐτῇ ; ²⁵ μηδαμῶς σὺ ποιήσεις ὡς τὸ ῥῆμα τοῦτο, τοῦ ἀποκτεῖναι δίκαιον μετὰ ἀσεβοῦς, καὶ ἔσται ὁ δίκαιος ὡς ὁ ἀσεβής· μηδαμῶς. ὁ κρίνων πᾶσαν τὴν γῆν, οὐ ποιήσεις κρίσιν ; ²⁶ εἶπεν δὲ ὁ κύριος Ἐὰν εὕρω ἐν Σο[δόμοις]...

16. xliii. 16...θύματα καὶ ἑτοίμασον· μετ᾽ ἐμοῦ γὰ[ρ] φάγονται οἱ ἄνθρωποι οὗτοι ἄρτου[s] τὴν μεσημβρίαν...

The vellum of the MS. is fine, but not so thin as in some other early uncials. The leaves were arranged in quires of four. Each page, where the writing was not broken by an illustration, contained from 26 to 28 lines of 27 to 30 letters. The uncials are well formed, but vary to some extent in thickness and size. Initial letters are used, and the point is sometimes high, some-times middle or low. On the whole the codex may probably be assigned to cent. v.—vi. The hands of three scribes have been traced in the fragments, and there appear to have been two cor-rectors after the *diorthotes*; the earlier of the two, who seems to have lived in the eighth century, has retraced the faded letters.

E. CODEX BODLEIANUS. Bodleian Library, Oxford. Auct. T. infr. ii. 1.

The Bodleian volume contains the following fragments of Genesis: i. 1—xiv. 6, xviii. 24 δικαίων—xx. 14 καὶ ἀπέδωκεν, xxiv. 54 ἐκπέμψατε—xlii. 18 εἶπεν δὲ αὐ[τοῖς]. Another leaf, now at the Cambridge University Library, contains xlii. 18 [αὐ]τοῖς τῇ ἡμέρᾳ —xliv. 13 τὸν ἕνα καί, but the *verso*, to which xlii. 31—xliv. 13 belongs, is written in (?) contemporary minuscules. It is now known that this text is carried on by more than one cursive MS. The St Petersburg cod. lxii. begins where the Cambridge fragment leaves off (at Gen. xliv. 13 Βενιαμίν· ἐγὼ μὲν γάρ), and proceeds, with some lacunae, as far as 3 Regn. xvi. 28 (τὰ λοιπὰ τῶν συμπλοκῶν). The largest of the lacunae (Jos. xxiv. 27— Ruth, inclusive) is supplied by the British Museum MS. Add. 20002, which once belonged to the same codex as E, the Cam-bridge fragment, and St Petersburg cod. lxii.

The recent history of this MS. is both curious and instructive. The portions now at Oxford and London were brought from the East by Tischendorf in 1853; the Cambridge leaf and the St Petersburg portion followed in 1859. Tischendorf published the contents of the Bodleian volume in *Monumenta sacra inedita*, *n. c.* ii. (1857); the Cambridge leaf remained in his possession till his death in 1874, when it was purchased by the Syndics of the University Library. In 1891 it was recognised by the present writer and Mr H. A. Redpath as a continuation of the Bodleian Genesis[1]; and its contents were at once communicated to the *Academy* (June 6, 1891), and were afterwards incorporated in the apparatus of the Cambridge manual LXX. (vol. i., ed. 2, 1895). Finally, in 1898, Dr A. Rahlfs of Göttingen[2] proved that the Petersburg and London volumes originally formed a part of the codex to which the Oxford Genesis and the Cambridge leaf belonged. The entire MS. will be used for the apparatus of the larger Cambridge LXX.; a description by the Editors (Messrs Brooke and McLean) may be found in the *Classical Review* for May, 1899 (vol. xiii., pp. 209—11).

The Bodleian Genesis is written in large sloping uncials of a late form on 29 leaves of stout vellum ; each page carries two columns of 37—44 lines; in the earlier pages the letters are closely packed and there are sometimes as many as 28 in a line, but as the book advances the number seldom exceeds and sometimes fall below 20. Tischendorf was disposed to assign the writing to the 9th, or at the earliest the 8th century; but the debased character of the uncials, as well as the readiness of the scribe to pass from the uncial to the cursive script, point to a still later date[3]. According to the same authority the uncial leaves of the codex have passed through the hands of a nearly contemporary corrector, and also of another whose writing is more recent.

F (VII). CODEX AMBROSIANUS. Ambrosian Library, Milan. A. 147 infr.

The remains of this important Codex consist of the following

---

[1] Mr Bradshaw, I now learn, had previously noticed this, but he does not appear to have published the fact, or to have left any written statement about it.

[2] In his paper *über eine von Tischendorf aus dem Orient mit-gebrachte, in Oxford, Cambridge, London, u. Petersburg liegende Handschrift der Septuaginta*, reprinted from *Nachrichten der K. Gesellschaft der Wissenschaften zu Göttingen*, 1898; cf. *Th. L.-Z.*, Feb. 4, 1899, p. 74. See also E. Klostermann, *G. G. A.*, 1895, p. 257.

[3] "The date of the whole MS., including the uncial part, may very well be the tenth century" (*Class. Review, l.c.*).

fragments of the Octateuch: Gen. xxxi. 15 [ἀλλοτρί]αι—37 ἠραύνησας, xlii. 14 ὅτι κατάσκοποι—21 εἰσηκούσαμεν αὐτοῦ, 28 ἐταράχθησαν—xlvi. 6 τὴν κτῆσιν, xlvii. 16 εἰ ἐκλέλοιπεν—xlviii. 3 ὁ θεός μοι ὤφθη, xlviii. 21 τῶν πατέρων—li. 14 οἱ ἀδελφοί. Exod. i. 10 γῆς—viii. 19 τῷ [Φαραώ], xii. 31 οἱ υἱοί—xxx. 29 ὁ ἁπτ. αὐτῶν, xxxi. 18 ἐν τῷ ὄρει—xxxii. 6 θυσ[ίαν], xxxii. 13 [πολυπλη]θυνῶ—xxxvi. 3 προσ[εδέχοντο], xxxvii. 10 αἱ βάσεις—end of book. Lev. i. 1—ix. 18 κύκλῳ, x. 14 [ἀφαιρέμα]τος—end of book. Num. (without *lacuna*). Deut. i. 1—xxviii. 63 ηὐφράν[θη], xxix. 14 καὶ τὴν ἀράν —end of book. Jos. i. 1—ii. 9 ἐφ᾽ [ἡ]μᾶς, ii. 15 αὐτῆς ἐν τῷ τ[ε]ίχει —iv. 5 ἔμπροσθεν, iv. 10 [συ]νετέλεσεν—v. 1 Ἰορδάνην, v. 7 Ἰησοῦς —vi. 23 ἀδελφοὺς αὐτῆς, vii. 1 Ζαμβρί—ix. 27 τῆς σήμερον ἡμ[έρας], x. 37 ἦν ἐν αὐτῇ—xii. 12 βασ. Ἐγλών[1].

An inscription on a blank page states that the fragments were "ex Macedonia Corcyram advecta, ibique Ill. Card. Fed. Borromaei Bibliothecae Ambrosianae Fundatoris iussu empta eidemque Bibliothecae transmissa sunt." They attracted the notice of Montfaucon (*Diar. Ital.*, p. 11, *Pal. sacr.* pp. 27, 186), and were collated for Holmes, but in an unsatisfactory manner. Ceriani's transcript (*Mon. sacr. et prof.* iii., Mediol. 1864) supplies the text, for the accuracy of which the name of the Editor is a sufficient guarantee, and a learned preface, but the full prolegomena which were reserved for another volume have not appeared. A photograph is needed not only for palaeographical purposes, but to shew the marginal readings, many of which are Hexaplaric.

The MS. is written on the finest and whitest vellum, the leaves of which are gathered in fours[2]; three columns of writing stand on each page, and 35 lines in each column. The characters are those of cent. iv.—v.; initial letters are used, which project to half their breadth into the margin. Punctuation is frequent, and there is much variety in the use of the points; accents and breathings are freely added *prima manu*, a feature in which this MS. stands alone amongst early Uncials[3]. The colour of the ink changes after Deuteronomy, and the rest of the fragments seem to have been written by another scribe; but the work is contemporary, for the quire numbers have been added by the first scribe throughout. The MS. has passed through the hands of two early correctors, and the margins contain various readings, notes, and scholia.

---

[1] The fragments of Malachi and Isaiah, attributed to F in Holmes, followed by Tischendorf *V. T.*[2], and Kenyon (p. 62), belong to a MS. of cent. xi.; see Ceriani, *Mon. sacr. et prof., praef.* p. ix.

[2] See Sir E. Maunde Thompson, *Greek and Latin Pal.*, p. 62.

[3] Cf. Thompson, *op. cit.* p. 72, "they were not systematically applied to Greek texts before the 7th century."

G (IV, V). CODEX COLBERTO-SARRAVIANUS. (1) Leyden, University Library, Voss. Gr. Q. 8. (2) Paris, Bibliothèque Nationale, cod. Gr. 17, formerly Colbert. 3084. (3) St Petersburg, Imperial Library, v. 5.

Of this codex Leyden possesses 130 leaves and Paris 22, while one leaf has strayed to St Petersburg. When brought together the surviving leaves yield the following portions of the Octateuch: Gen. xxxi. 53 αὐτῶν—xxxvi. 18 ✳ θυγατρὸς 'Ανά. ¹*Exod. xxxvi. 8—29, *xxxvii. 3 ὑφαντοῦ—6, *xxxviii. 1—18, *xxxix. 1 [κατ]ειργάσθη—11, *16 σκεύη—19, xl. 2 ἐκεῖ τὴν κιβωτόν to end of book, *Lev. i. 1—iv. 26 ἐξ(ε)ιλάσεται περί, iv. 27 λαοῦ τῆς γῆς—xiii. 17 καὶ ἰδού, *xiii. 49 ἱματίῳ—xiv. 6 λήμψεται αὐτὸ καί, *xiv. 33—49 ἀφαγνί[σαι], *xv. 24 κοιμηθῇ—xvii. 10 προσ- [ηλύτων], *xviii. 28 [ἔ]θνεσιν—xix. 36 στάθμια δίκαια καί, xxiv. 9 καὶ τοῖς υἱοῖς—xxvii. 16 ἄνθρωπος τῷ. Num. i. 1—vii. 85 τῶν σκευῶν, xi. 18 τίς ψωμιεῖ—xviii. 2 φυλήν, xviii. 30 ἐρεῖς—xx. 22 παρεγένοντο οἱ, *xxv. 2 αὐτῶν καί—xxvi. 3, *xxix. 12 ἑορτάσετε— 33 σύγκρισιν, 34 καὶ χ(ε)ίμαρ(ρ)ον—end of book. Deut. iv. 11 ✳ [καρ]δίας: τοῦ οὐρανοῦ—26 ἐκεῖ κλη[ρονομῆσαι], vii. 13 τὸν σῖτον—xvii. 14 κατακληρονομή[σης], xviii. 8—xix. 4 τὸν πλη[σίον], xxviii. 12 [ἔθνε]σιν—xxxi. 11. Jos. ix. 33 [ἐκλέξη]ται—xix. 23 αὕτη ἡ κληρονομία. †Jud. ix. 48 αὐτὸς καὶ πᾶς—x. 6 'Ασσαρὼθ ✳ καὶ σὺν τοῖς, xv. 3 [Σαμ]ψών—xviii. 16 οἱ ἐκ τῶν υἱῶν, xix. 25 αὐτῇ ὅλην—xxi. 12 τετρακοσίοις.

The Leyden leaves of this MS. are known to have been in the possession of Claude Sarràve, of Paris, who died in 1651. After his death they passed into the hands successively of Jacques Mentel, a Paris physician, who has left his name on the first page, and of Isaac Voss († 1681), from whose heirs they were purchased by the University of Leyden. The Paris leaves had been separated from the rest of the MS. before the end of the 16th century, for they were once in the library of Henri Memme, who died in 1596. With a large part of that collection they were presented to J. B. Colbert in 1732, and thus found their way into the Royal Library at Paris. Among earlier owners of the St Petersburg leaf were F. Pithaeus, Desmarez, Montfaucon², and Dubrowsky. The text of the Leyden leaves and the St Petersburg leaf was printed in facsimile type by Tischendorf in the third volume of his *Monumenta sacra* (Leipzig, 1860); a splendid photographic reproduction of all the known leaves of the codex appeared at Leyden in 1897³.

---

¹ Fragments marked * are at Paris; that marked † is at St Petersburg.
² Montfaucon, *Pal. sacr.* p. 186 f.; Tischendorf, *Mon. sacr. ined. n. c.* iii. *prolegg.* p. xviii.
³ *V. T. gr. cod. Sarraviani-Colbertini quae supersunt in bibliothecis Leidensi Parisiensi Petropolitana phototypice edita. Praefatus est H. Omont.*

The leaves measure $9\frac{7}{8} \times 8\frac{7}{8}$ inches; the writing is in two columns of 27 lines, each line being made up of 13—15 letters. In Tischendorf's judgement the hand belongs to the end of the fourth or the first years of the fifth century. There are no initial letters ; the writing is continuous excepting where it is broken by a point or sign ; points, single or double, occur but rarely ; a breathing is occasionally added by the first hand, more frequently by an early corrector. Of the seven correctors noticed by Tischendorf three only need be mentioned here,—(A) a contemporary hand, (B) another fifth century hand which has revised Deuteronomy and Judges, and (C) a hand of the sixth century which has been busy in the text of Numbers.

In one respect this codex holds an unique position among uncial MSS. of the Octateuch. It exhibits an Origenic text which retains many of the Hexaplaric signs. Besides the asterisk (✳) and various forms of the obelus ($\div$, $\div$, $\div$, $\div$, and in the margin, ---), the metobelus frequently occurs (:, ·/, /·, ·/·). The importance of Cod. Sarravianus as a guide in the recovery of the Hexaplaric text has been recognised from the time of Montfaucon (comp. Field, *Hexapla*, i., p. 5); and it is a matter for no little congratulation that we now possess a complete and admirable photograph of the remains of this great MS.

H.   CODEX PETROPOLITANUS.   In the Imperial Library at St Petersburg.

This palimpsest consists at present of 88 leaves in octavo ; in its original form there were 44, arranged in quaternions. Under the patristic matter which is now in possession of the vellum, Tischendorf detected a large part of the Septuagint text of Numbers. The fragments recovered contain chh. i. 1—30, 40 —ii. 14, ii. 30—iii. 26, v. 13—23, vi. 6—vii. 7, vii. 41—78, viii. 2— 16, xi. 3·—xiii. 11, xiii. 28—xiv. 34, xv. 3—20, 22—28, 32—xvi. 31, xvi. 44—xviii. 4, xviii. 15—26, xxi. 15—22, xxii. 30—41, xxiii. 12— 27, xxvi. 54—xxvii. 15, xxviii. 7—xxix. 36, xxx. 9—xxxi. 48, xxxii. 7—xxxiv. 17, xxxvi. 1—end of book.   They are printed in *Monumenta sacr. ined., nov. coll.* i. (Leipzig, 1855).

In Tischendorf's judgement the upper writing is not later than the ninth century ; the lower writing he ascribes to the sixth ; for though the characters are generally such as are found in fifth century MSS., yet there are several indications of a later date, e.g. the numerous *compendia scribendi* and superscribed letters, and the occasional use of oblong forms.   Chapters and arguments are noted in the margin—the chapters of Numbers are 207—and at the end of the book the number of *stichi* is

specified (,γφλε' = 3535); the scribe appends his name—'Ιωάν-
νογ μοναχοῦ cεргίογ.

K. Fragmenta Lipsiensia. Leipzig, University Library (cod. Tisch. ii.).

Twenty-two leaves discovered by Tischendorf in 1844, of
which seventeen contain under Arabic writing of the ninth century fragments of Numbers, Deuteronomy, Joshua, and Judges
(Num. v. 17—18, 24—25; vii. 18—19, 30—31, 35—36, 37—40, 42
—43, 46—47; xv. 11—17, 19—24; xxvii. 1—xxviii. 5, xxviii. 10—
xxix. 2, xxxv. 19—22, 28—31. Deut. ii. 8—10, 15—19, ix. 1—10,
xviii. 21—xix. 1, xix. 6—9; xxi. 8—12, 17—19. Jos. x. 39—xi.
16, xii. 2—15, xxii. 7—9, 10—23; Jud. xi. 24—34, xviii. 2—20[1]).
The Greek writing is not later than cent. vii. The fragments
are printed in the first volume of *Monumenta sacra inedita, n. c.*

L (VI). Codex Purpureus Vindobonensis. Vienna, Imperial Library.

This MS. consists of 24 leaves of Genesis, with which are
bound up two leaves of St Luke belonging to Codex N of the
Gospels[2].
The Genesis leaves contain Gen. iii. 4—24, vii. 19—viii. 20,
ix. 8—15, 20—27; xiv. 17—20, xv. 1—5, xix. 12—26, 29—35;
xxii. 15—19, xxiv. 1—11, 15—20; xxiv. 22—31, xxv. 27—34, xxvi.
6—11, xxx. 30—37; xxxi. 25—34; xxxii. 1—18, 22—32; xxxv. 1
—4, 8, 16—20, 28—29, xxxvii. 1—19, xxxix. 9—18, xl. 14—xli. 2,
xli. 21—32, xlii. 21—38, xliii. 2—21, xlviii. 16—xlix. 3, xlix. 28—
33, l. 1—4.
Like the great Cotton MS. the Vienna purple Genesis is an
illustrated text, each page exhibiting a miniature painted in
water-colours. The writing belongs to the fifth or sixth century;
the provenance of the MS. is uncertain, but there are notes in
the codex which shew that it was at one time in North Italy.
Engravings of the miniatures with a description of the contents
may be found in P. Lambecii *Comm. de bibliotheca Vindobonensi,*
lib. iii. (ed. Kollar., 1776), and a transcript of the text in R.
Holmes's Letter to Shute Barrington, Bishop of Durham (Oxford,
1795); but both these earlier authorities have been superseded by
the splendid photographic edition lately published at Vienna (*die
Wiener Genesis herausgegeben von Wilhelm Ritter v. Hartel u.
Franz Wickhoff*, Wien, 1895).

---

[1] On the fragments of Judges see Moore, *Judges*, p. xlv.
[2] On the latter see H. S. Cronin, *Codex Purpureus Petropolitanus*,
p. xxiii.

M (X).   Codex Coislinianus.   Paris, Bibliothèque Nationale, Coisl. Gr. 1.

A MS. of the Octateuch and the Historical Books, with
lacunae; the 227 remaining leaves contain Gen. i. 1—xxxiv. 2,
xxxviii. 24—Num. xxix. 23, xxxi. 4—Jos. x. 6, Jos. xxii. 34—Ruth
iv. 19, 1 Regn. i. 1—iv. 19, x. 19—xiv. 26, xxv. 33—3 Regn. viii. 40.
This great codex was purchased in the East for M. Seguier,
and brought to Paris about the middle of the seventeenth century.   It was first described by Montfaucon, who devotes the
first 31½ pages of his *Bibliotheca Coisliniana* to a careful description of the contents, dealing specially with the capitulation and
the letters prefixed to the sentences.   Facsimiles were given by
Montfaucon, Bianchini (*Evangelium quadruplex*), Tischendorf
(*Monumenta sacr. ined.*, 1846), and Silvester, and a photograph
of f. 125 r., containing Num. xxxv. 33—xxxvi. 13, may be seen in
H. Omont's *Facsimilés*, planche vi.   Montfaucon gives a partial
collation of the codex with the Roman edition of the LXX., and
a collation of the whole was made for Holmes; an edition is
now being prepared by Mr H. S. Cronin.

The leaves, which measure 13 × 9 inches, exhibit on each page
two columns of 49 or 50 lines, each line containing 18—23 letters.
According to Montfaucon, the codex was written in the sixth or
at latest in the seventh century ("sexto vel cum tardissime sep-
timo saeculo exaratus"), but the later date is now usually accepted.   The margins contain a large number of notes *prima
manu*[1], among which are the excerpts from the N. T. printed by
Tischendorf in the *Monumenta* and now quoted as cod. F[a] of the
Gospels[2].   The MS. is said by Montfaucon to agree frequently
with the text of cod. A, and this is confirmed by Holmes as far
as regards the Pentateuch.   Lagarde (*Genesis graece*, p. 12)
styles it Hexaplaric; hexaplaric signs and matter abound in the
margins, and of these use has been made by Field so far as he
was able to collect them from Montfaucon and from Griesbach's
excerpts printed in Eichhorn's *Repertorium*.

Z[a, d].   Fragmenta Tischendorfiana.   Two of a series of
fragments of various MSS. discovered by Tischendorf and
printed in the first and second volumes of *Monumenta sacra
inedita, nov. coll.* i. ii. (1855, 1857).

Z[a].   Three palimpsest leaves containing fragments of 2—3
Regn. (2 Regn. xxii. 38—42, 46—49; xxiii. 2—5, 8—10; 3 Regn.

---

[1] Other notes occur in a hand of the ninth century and in a late cursive
hand.
[2] Gregory, i. p. 375; Scrivener-Miller, i. p. 134.

xiii. 4—6, 8—11, 13—17, 20—23, xvi. 31—33, xvii. 1—5, 9—12, 14—17). The upper writing is Armenian, the lower an Egyptian-Greek hand of the 7th century, resembling that of cod. Q (v. *infra*).

Z^d. Palimpsest fragment containing 3 Regn. viii. 58—ix. 1, also from the Nitrian MSS. There are two texts over the Greek of which the lower is Coptic, the upper Syriac ; the Greek hand belongs to cent. v.

Θ. CODEX WASHINGTONIENSIS. See Additional Notes.

II. FRAGMENTA TISCHENDORFIANA.

Four leaves taken from the binding of Cod. Porfirianus Chiovensis (P of the Acts and Catholic Epistles[1]), and published by Tischendorf in *Mon. sacr. ined.*, *nov. coll.* vi. p. 339 ff. They yield an interesting text of portions of 4 Maccabees (viii. 6, 12, 15, 29; ix. 28—30, 31—32). The writing appears to belong to cent. ix.

(C) *Poetical Books.*

I (13). CODEX BODLEIANUS. Oxford, Bodleian Library, Auct. D. 4. 1.

A Psalter, including the Old Testament Canticles and a *catena.* Described by Bruns in Eichhorn's *Repertorium*, xiii. p. 177; cf. Lagarde's *Genesis graece*, p. 11, and *Nov. Psalt. Gr. edit. Specimen*, p. 3. Parsons, who reckons it among the cursives, is content to say "de saeculo quo exaratus fuerit nihil dicitur"; according to Coxe (*Catalogus codd. Biblioth. Bodl.* i. 621), it belongs to the 9th century.

R. CODEX VERONENSIS. Verona, Chapter Library.

A MS. of the Psalter in Greek and Latin, both texts written in Roman characters. A few *lacunae* (Ps. i. 1—ii. 7, lxv. 20—lxviii. 3, lxviii. 26—33, cv. 43—cvi. 2) have been supplied by a later hand, which has also added the ψαλμὸς ἰδιόγραφος (Ps. cli.). The Psalms are followed *prima manu* by eight canticles (Exod. xv. 1—21, Deut. xxxii. 1—44, 1 Regn. ii. 1—10, Isa. v. 1—9, Jon. ii. 3—10, Hab. iii. 1—10, *Magnificat*, Dan. iii. 23 ff.).

Printed by Bianchini in his *Vindiciae canonicarum scripturarum*, i. (Rome, 1740), and used by Lagarde in the apparatus of his *Specimen* and *Psalterii Gr. quinquagena prima*, and in the Cambridge manual Septuagint (1891). A new collation was made in 1892 by H. A. Redpath, which has been employed in

---

[1] See Gregory, i. p. 447, Scrivener-Miller, i. p. 172 f.

the second edition of *The O. T. in Greek* (1896); but it is much to be wished that the Verona Chapter may find it possible to have this important Psalter photographed.

The codex consists of 405 leaves, measuring 10½ × 7½ inches; each page contains 26 lines. The Greek text appears at each opening on the left-hand page, and the Latin on the right.

T (262). CODEX TURICENSIS. Zurich, Municipal Library.

A purple MS. which contained originally 288 leaves; of these 223 remain. The text now begins at xxvi. (xxvii.) 1, and there are lacunae in the body of the MS. which involve the loss of Pss. xxx. 2—xxxvi. 20, xli. 6—xliii. 3, lviii. 24—lix. 3, lix. 9—10, 13—lx. 1, lxiv. 12—lxxi. 4, xcii. 3—xciii. 7, xcvi. 12—xcvii. 8. The first five Canticles and a part of the sixth have also disappeared; those which remain are 1 Regn. ii. 6—10 (the rest of the sixth), the *Magnificat*, Isa. xxxviii. 10—20, the Prayer of Manasses[1], Dan. iii. 23 ff., *Benedictus, Nunc Dimittis.*

Like Cod. R this MS. is of Western origin. It was intended for Western use, as appears from the renderings of the Latin (Gallican) version which have been copied into the margins by a contemporary hand, and also from the liturgical divisions of the Psalter. The archetype, however, was a Psalter written for use in the East—a fact which is revealed by the survival in the copy of occasional traces of the Greek στάσεις.

The characters are written in silver, gold, or vermilion, according as they belong to the body of the text, the headings and initial letters of the Psalms, or the marginal Latin readings. Tischendorf, who published the text in the fourth volume of his *nova collectio* (1869), ascribes the handwriting to the seventh century.

The text of T agrees generally with that of cod. A, and still more closely with the hand in cod. ℵ known as ℵ^{c.a}.

U. FRAGMENTA LONDINENSIA. London, British Museum, pap. xxxvii.

Thirty leaves of papyrus which contain Ps. x. (xi.) 2 [ε]ἰς φαρέτραν—xviii. (xix.) 6, xx. (xxi.) 14 ἐν ταῖς δυναστείαις σου—xxxiv. (xxxv.) 6 καταδιώκ[ω]ν.

These fragments of a papyrus Psalter were purchased in 1836 from a traveller who had bought them at Thebes in Egypt, where they had been found, it was said, among the ruins of a convent. Tischendorf assigned to them a high antiquity (*Pro-*

---

[1] Cf. Nestle, *Septuagintastudien*, iii. p. 17 ff.

legg. ad V. T. Gr., p. ix., "quo nullus codicum sacrorum antiquior videtur"), and he was followed by Lagarde, who as late as 1887 described the London codex as "bibliorum omnium quos noverim antiquissimus" (*Specimen*, p. 4). But a wider acquaintance with the palaeography of papyri has corrected their estimate, and the fragments are now ascribed by experts to cent. vi.—vii.[1]

The writing slopes, and the characters are irregularly formed; the scribe uses breathings and accents freely; on the other hand he writes continuously, not even breaking off at the end of a Psalm or distinguishing the title from the rest of the text. The hand is not that of a learned scribe or of the literary type[2].

It has been pointed out that the text of U corresponds closely with that of the Sahidic Psalter published by Dr Budge[3].

X (258). CODEX VATICANUS IOBI. Rome, Vatican Library, Gr. 749.

A MS. of Job with occasional lacunae; the remaining portions are i. 1—xvii. 13, xvii. 17—xxx. 9, xxx. 23—xxxi. 5, xxxi. 24 —xxxiv. 35. There are miniatures, and a catena in an uncial hand surrounding the text. At the beginning of the book Hexaplaric scholia are frequent[4].

The text is written in a hand of the ninth century. It was used by Parsons, and its Hexaplaric materials are borrowed by Field[5].

W (43). CODEX PARISIENSIS. Paris, Bibliothèque Nationale, Gr. 20.

A portion of an uncial Psalter containing in 40 leaves Ps. xci. 14—cxxxvi. 1, with *lacunae* extending from Ps. cx. 7 to cxii. 10, and from Ps. cxvii. 16—cxxvi. 4. So Omont (*Inventaire sommaire des mss. grecs*, p. 4); according to Parsons (*Praef. ad libr. Pss.*), followed generally by Lagarde (*Genesis gr.* 15), the omissions are Ps. c. 4—ci. 7, cx. 6—cxi. 10, cxvii. 16—cxviii. 4, cxviii. 176—cxxvi. 4.

The codex was written by a hand of the ninth or tenth century, and contains paintings which, as Parsons had been informed, are of some merit.

---

[1] See *Catalogue of Ancient MSS. in the British Museum*, i. (1881), where there is a photograph of Ps. xxiii. 10 ff., and Dr Kenyon's *Palaeography of papyri*, p. 116 f.
[2] Kenyon, *loc. cit.*
[3] Cf. F. E. Brightman in *J. Th. St.* ii. 275 f.
[4] See E. Klostermann, *Analecta zur Septuaginta*, &c., p. 63.
[5] *Hexapla*, ii. p. 2.

Z^e. See above under (B), p. 140.

Fragments of the fourth or fifth cent. (Tisch.), containing Pss. cxli. (cxlii.) 7—8, cxlii. (cxliii.) 1—3, cxliv. (cxlv.) 7—13.

(D)   *Prophets.*

O (VIII). FRAGMENTA DUBLINENSIA. Dublin, Trinity College Library, K. 3. 4.

Eight palimpsest leaves—in the original MS. folded as four—which are now bound up with Codex Z of the Gospels[1] and yield Isa. xxx. 2—xxxi. 7, xxxvi. 19—xxxviii. 2.

The original leaves of the Codex measured about 12×9 inches, and each contained 36 lines of 14—17 letters. The writing, which belongs to the early part of the sixth century, appears to be that of an Egyptian scribe, and Ceriani is disposed to connect the text of the fragments with the Hesychian recension[2]. They have been printed in facsimile type by Professor T. K. Abbott (*Par palimpsestorum Dublinensium*, Dublin, 1880), and are used in the apparatus of the Cambridge manual Septuagint.

Q (XII). CODEX MARCHALIANUS. Rome, Vatican Library, Gr. 2125.

A magnificent codex of the Prophets, complete, and in the order of cod. B (Hosea, Amos, Micah, Joel, Obadiah, Jonah, Nahum, Habakkuk, Zephaniah, Haggai, Zechariah, Malachi; Isaiah, Jeremiah with Baruch, Lamentations, Epistle, Ezekiel, Daniel (Theod.) with Susanna and Bel).

This MS. was written in Egypt not later than the sixth century. It seems to have remained there till the ninth, since the uncial corrections and annotations as well as the text exhibit letters of characteristically Egyptian form. From Egypt it was carried before the 12th century to South Italy, and thence into France, where it became the property of the Abbey of St Denys near Paris, and afterwards of René Marchal, from whom it has acquired its name. From the library of R. Marchal it passed into the hands of Cardinal F. Rochefoucauld, who in turn presented it to the Jesuits of Clermont. Finally, in 1785 it was purchased for the Vatican, where it now reposes.

The codex was used by J. Morinus, Wetstein and Montfaucon, collated for Parsons, and printed in part by Tischendorf in the

---

[1] See Gregory, i. p. 399 f.; Scrivener-Miller, i. p. 153.
[2] *Recensioni dei LXX.*, p. 6.

ninth volume of his *Nova Collectio* (1870). Field followed Montfaucon in making large use of the Hexaplaric matter with which the margins of the MS. abound, but was compelled to depend on earlier collations and a partial transcript. The liberality of the Vatican has now placed within the reach of all O.T. students a magnificent heliotype of the entire MS., accompanied (in a separate volume) by a commentary from the pen of Ceriani (1890). This gift is only second in importance to that of the photograph of Codex B, completed in the same year.

Codex Marchalianus at present consists of 416 leaves, but the first twelve contain patristic matter, and did not form a part of the original MS. The leaves measure $11\frac{3}{8} \times 7$ inches; the writing is in single columns of 29 lines, each line containing 24—30 letters. The text of the Prophets belongs, according to Ceriani, to the Hesychian recension; but Hexaplaric signs have been freely added, and the margins supply copious extracts from Aquila, Symmachus, Theodotion, and the LXX. of the Hexapla. These marginal annotations were added by a hand not much later than that which wrote the text, and to the same hand are due the patristic texts already mentioned, and two important notes[1] from which we learn the sources of the Hexaplaric matter in the margins. The result of its labours has been to render this codex a principal authority for the Hexapla in the Prophetic Books.

Y. CODEX TAURINENSIS. Turin, Royal -Library, cod. 9.

This codex consists of 135 leaves in quarto, and contains the δωδεκαπρόφητον. The MS. is difficult to read, and there are many lacunae. The text, written according to Stroth[2] in the ninth century, is surrounded by scholia, and prefaced by Theodoret's ὑποθέσεις to the various books.

The Turin MS. does not appear to have been used hitherto for any edition of the LXX., nor has any transcript or collation been published[3].

$Z^{b, c}$. See above, under (B), p. 140.

Z^b. Palimpsest fragments of Isaiah (iii. 8—14, v. 2—14, xxix. 11—23, xliv. 26—xlv. 5). As in Z^a, the upper writing is Armenian; the Greek hand belongs apparently to cent. viii.—ix.

Z^c. Palimpsest fragment of Ezekiel (iv. 16—v. 4) found among the Nitrian leaves at the British Museum. The Greek hand resembles that of Z^a, and is probably contemporary with it.

---

[1] Printed in *O. T. in Greek*, iii.[2], p. 8 f.
[2] In Eichhorn's *Repertorium*, viii. p. 202 f.
[3] The specimens and descriptions in the Turin catalogue (p. 74 ff.) seem to shew that the headings only are written in uncials.

S. S.

Γ. CODEX CRYPTOFERRATENSIS. Basilian Monastery of Grotta Ferrata, cod. E. β. vii.

This volume consists partly of palimpsest leaves which once belonged to a great codex of the Prophets. A scribe of the 13th century has written over the Biblical text liturgical matter accompanied by musical notation. Some portions of the book are doubly palimpsest, having been used by an earlier scribe for a work of St John of Damascus. About 130 leaves in the present liturgical codex were taken from the Biblical MS., and the Biblical text of 85 of these leaves has been transcribed and published (with many lacunae where the lower writing could not be deciphered) in Cozza-Luzi's *Sacrorum bibliorum vetustissima fragmenta*, vol. i (Rome 1867) and iii. (1877).

The original codex seems to have contained 432 leaves gathered in quires of eight; and the leaves appear to have measured about $10\frac{3}{4} \times 8\frac{1}{4}$ inches. The writing, which is in sloping uncials of the eighth or ninth century, was arranged in double columns, and each column contained 25—28 lines of 13—20 letters.

It cannot be said that Cozza's transcript, much as Biblical students are indebted to him for it, satisfies our needs. Uncial codices of the Prophets are so few that we desiderate a photographic edition, or at least a fresh examination and more complete collation of this interesting palimpsest.

Δ. FRAGMENTUM BODLEIANUM. Oxford, Bodleian Library, MS. Gr. bibl. d. 2 (P).

A fragment of Bel in the version of Theodotion (21 γυναικῶν— 41 Δανιήλ). A vellum leaf brought from Egypt and purchased for the Bodleian in 1888.

Written in an uncial hand of the fifth (?) century, partly over a portion of a homily in a hand perhaps a century earlier.

The following uncial fragments have not been used for any edition of the LXX., and remain for the present without a symbolical letter or number.

(1) A scrap of papyrus (B. M., *pap.* ccxii.) yielding the text of Gen. xiv. 17. See Catalogue of Additions to the MSS., 1888—93, p. 410. Cent. iii. (?).

(2) The vellum fragment containing Lev. xxii. 3—xxiii. 22, originally published by Brugsch (*Neue Bruchstücke des Cod. Sin.*, Leipzig, 1875), who believed it to be a portion of Codex Sinaiticus; a more accurate transcription is given by J. R. Harris, *Biblical Fragments*, no. 15 (cf. Mrs Lewis's *Studia Sin.* i. p. 97 f.). Cent. iv.

(3) Another Sinaitic fragment, containing Num. xxxii. 29, 30 (J. R. Harris, *op. cit.*, no. 1). Cent. vii.

(4) Another Sinaitic fragment, containing a few words of Jud. xx. 24—28 (J. R. Harris, *op. cit.*, no. 2). Cent. iv.

(5) Another Sinaitic fragment, containing Ruth ii. 19—iii. 1, iii. 4—7 (J. R. Harris, *op. cit.*, no. 3). Cent. iv.

(6) Part of a Psalter on papyrus (B. M., *pap.* ccxxx.), containing Ps. xii. 7—xv. 4; see *Athenaeum*, Sept. 8, 1894, and Kenyon, *Palaeography of Greek Papyri*, pp. 109, 131. Cent. iii.

(7) Part of a Psalter on a Berlin papyrus, containing Ps. xl. 26—xli. 4; see Blass in *Z. f. ägypt. Sprache*, 1881 (Kenyon, *op. cit.*, p. 131).

(8) Nine fragments of a MS. written in columns of about 25 lines, one on each page. The fragments give the text of Ps. ci. 3, 4, cii. 5—8, cv. 34—43, cvi. 17—34, cviii. 15—21, cxiii. 18—26, cxiv. 3—cxv. 2. J. R. Harris, *op. cit.*, no. 4. Cent. iv.

(9) A vellum MS. in the Royal Library at Berlin (MS. Gr. oct. 2), containing Ps. cxi.—cl., followed by the first four canticles and parts of Ps. cv. and cant. v. See E. Klostermann, *Z. f. A. T. W.*, 1897, p. 339 ff.

(10) Fragments discovered by H. A. Redpath at St Mark's, Venice, in the binding of cod. gr. 23, containing the text of Prov. xxiii. 21—xxiv. 35. Published in the *Academy*, Oct. 22, 1892. A fuller transcript is given by E. Klostermann, *Analecta*, pp. 34 ff.

(11) Portion of a leaf of a papyrus book, written in large uncials of cent. vii.—viii., exhibiting Cant. i. 6—9. This scrap came from the Fayûm and is now in the Bodleian, where it is numbered MS. Gr. bibl. g. 1 (P); see Grenfell, *Greek papyri* (Oxford, 1896), pp. 12 f.

(12) Palimpsest fragments of Wisdom and Sirach (cent. vi.—vii.), carried by Tischendorf to St Petersburg and intended for publication in the 8th volume of his *Monumenta*, which never appeared. See Nestle, *Urtext*, p. 74.

(13) Two palimpsest leaves of Sirach belonging to cod. 2 in the Patriarchal Library at Jerusalem: cf. Papadopulos, Ἱεροσ. Βιβλ., i. p. 14: τὰ ἀναπληρωτικὰ φύλλα 27 καὶ 56 εἰσὶ παλίμψηστα ὧν ἡ ἀρχικὴ γραφὴ ἀνῆκει εἰς τὸν ε´ αἰῶνα...τὸ παλαιὸν δὲ αὐτῶν κείμενόν ἐστι δίστηλον, καὶ ἐν φυλ. 56 διακρίνεται ἡ ἐπιγραφή coφία Ihcoγ γίογ cιράχ. The leaves contain Sir. prol. 1—i. 14, i. 29—iii. 11. Printed by J. R. Harris, *op. cit.*, no. 5.

(14) Part of a Papyrus book which seems to have contained the Minor Prophets. The discovery of this fragment was announced in 1892 by W. H. Hechler, who gave a facsimile of Zach. xii. 2, 3 ('Times,' Sept. 7, 1892; *Transactions of the Congress of Orientalists*, 1892, ii., p. 331 f.). Mr Hechler

claimed for this papyrus an extravagantly early date, but the
hand appears to belong to the seventh century; see Kenyon,
Palaeography of papyri, p. 118. This MS., which contains Zech.
iv.—xiv., Mal. i.—iv., is now the property of the University of
Heidelberg[1].

(15) Two leaves of a small vellum book, from the Fayûm,
now Bodl. MS. Gr. bibl. e. 4 (P); the handwriting, "in small,
fine uncials," yields the text of Zach. xii. 10—12, xiii. 3—5.
"About the fifth century" (Grenfell, *Greek papyri*, p. 11 f.).

(16) A Rainer papyrus, assigned to the third century and
containing Isa. xxxviii. 3—5, 13—16; see Nestle, *Urtext*, p. 74.

(17) A portion of a leaf of a papyrus book, bearing the
Greek text of Ezech. v. 12—vi. 3 (Bodl. MS. Gr. bibl. d. 4 (P));
see Grenfell, *Greek papyri*, pp. 9 ff. The text shews Hexaplaric
signs; the writing is said to belong to the third century (Kenyon,
Palaeography of papyri, p. 107).

(18) A fragment of a lead roll on which is engraved Ps.
lxxix (lxxx). 1—16, found at Rhodes in 1898. See *Sitzungsberichte
d. königl. Preuss. Akad. d. Wissenschaften zu Berlin*, 1898
(xxxvii.)[2].

II. CURSIVE MSS.

The following are the cursive MSS. used by Holmes and
Parsons, with the addition of others recently examined or
collated by the editors of the larger Cambridge Septuagint[3].

(A) *The Octateuch.*

14. Gen., Ex., *ep. Arist.*, *cat.* (xi)	Rome, Vat. Palat. Gr. 203	Klostermann, *Anal.* p. 11 n.
15. Octateuch (ix—x)	Paris, Nat. Coisl. Gr. 2	Hexaplaric in early books
16. Octateuch (xi)	Florence, Laur. v. 38	Batiffol, *Vat.*, p. 91
17. Genesis, *cat.* (x)	Moscow, Syn. 5, Vlad. 28	
18. Octateuch (x—xi)	Florence, Laur. Med. Pal. 242 (formerly at Fiesole)	

---

[1] Edited (1905) by Prof. G. Deissmann.

[2] The *Amherst Papyri*, pt. i. (1900), adds some small uncial fragments
from Gen. (i. 1—5) and Job (i. 21 f., ii. 3) and portions of Pss. v., lviii., lix.,
cviii., cxviii., cxxxv., cxxxviii.—cxl. Finally, Mrs Lewis (*Exp. Times*,
Nov. 1901) announces the discovery of a palimpsest from Mt Sinai containing Gen. xl. 3, 4, 7 in an uncial hand of the sixth or seventh century.

[3] The arabic numerals are the symbols employed by H. and P. For
descriptions of the unnumbered MSS., the writer is indebted to Messrs
Brooke and McLean, and Mr Brooke has also assisted him in verifying
and correcting the earlier lists.

19. Octateuch.......[1] Rome, Chigi R. vi. 38 Bianchini, *Vind.*, p.
    (? x)   279 ff.
                                                   Lucianic, Lagarde's *h*
20. Genesis (ix)   [Cod. Dorothei i.]
25. Gen., Ex., *ep.*   Munich, Staatsbibl. Field, ii. Auct. p. 3.
    Arist., cat. (xi) Gr. 9   Lag.'s *m* (*Gen. gr.*)
28. Num.,   Deut.,   Rome, Vat. Gr. 2122
    Jos., *imperf.*(xi) (formerly Basil.161)
29. Octateuch (inc.   Venice, St Mark's, Cf. Lagarde *Genesis*,
    Gen. xliii. 15)   Gr. 2   p. 6, *Septuagintast.*
    ...(x)   i. p. 11. Lag.'s *x*
30. Octateuch (inc.   Rome, Casan. 1444
    Gen. xxiv. 13)
    (xi)
31. Genesis, *cat.* (xvi) Vienna, Imp. Lib. ? Copied from Ald.
                        Theol. Gr. 4 (Lamb.) (Nestle.) Lag.'s *w*
32. Pentateuch (xii)   [Cod. Eugenii i.] Scrivener-Miller, i. p.
                                                   224
37. Lectionary (A.D.   Moscow,   Syn.   31,
    1116)   Vlad. 8
38. Octateuch...(xv)   Escurial, Y. 11. 5 Hexaplaric, cf. Field,
                                                   i. p. 398
44. Octateuch...(xv)   Zittau, A. 1. 1   Lagarde's *z*: see *Gene-*
                                                   sis gr., p. 7 ff. and
                                                   Libr. V. T. can. i.
                                                   p. vi. ; Scrivener-
                                                   Miller, i. p. 261 ;
                                                   Redpath, *Exp. T.*,
                                                   May 1897

45. Num. (*lect.*), (xi) Escurial
46. Octateuch...(xiv)   Paris, Nat. Coisl. Gr. 4 O.T. exc. Psalter
47. Fragment of lec-   Oxford, Bodl. Baron.
    tionary   201
50. Lectionary (xiii)   Oxford, Bodl. Seld. 30
52. Octateuch..., *ep.* Florence, Laur. Acq.
    Arist., cat. (x)   44
53. Octateuch (A.D.   Paris, **Nat.** Reg. Gr.
    1439)   17[A]
54. Octateuch, *ep. A-* Paris, Nat. Reg. Gr. Field, i. p. 223. La-
    rist. (xiii—xiv)   5   garde's *k*
55. Octateuch...(xi)   Rome, Vat. Regin. Part of a complete
                        Gr. 1   Bible, cf. Kloster-
                                                   mann, p. 12
56. Octateuch...(A.D.   Paris, **Nat.** Reg. Gr.
    1093)   3
57. Octateuch; *ep.*   Rome, Vat. Gr. 747 Field, i. pp. 5, 78
    Arist., cat. (xi)

[1] Dots in this position shew that the MS. extends beyond the Octateuch.

58. Pentateuch ...... (xiii)	Rome, Vat. Regin. Gr. 10	Hexaplaric. Field, i. p. 78
59. Octateuch (xv)	Glasgow, Univ. BE. 7^b. 10 (formerly at C.C.C., Oxford)	
61. Lectionary (xi)	Oxford, Bodl. Laud. 36	Scrivener-Miller, i. p. 329
63. Jos., Jud., Ruth (*imperf.*) (x)	Rome, Vat. 1252	Klostermann, p. 12
64. Octateuch ... (x —xi)	Paris, Nat. Reg. Gr. 2	Field, i. p. 5 O. and N.T.
68. Octateuch...(xv)	Venice, St Mark's, Gr. 5	O. and N.T. Scrivener-Miller, i. p. 219
70. Jos., Jud., Ruth ... (xi)	Munich, Gr. 372 (formerly at Augsburg)	
71. Octateuch...(xiii)	Paris, Nat. Reg. Gr. 1	
72. Octateuch (xiii)	Oxford, Bodl. Canon. Gr. 35 (formerly at Venice; see H. P.)	Hexaplaric. Tischendorf in *L. C.-Bl.*, 1867 (27)
73. Octateuch, *ep. Arist.* (part), *cat.* (xiii)	Rome, Vat. Gr. 746	Field, i. p. 78
74. Octateuch...(xiv)	Florence, Laur. Acq. 700 (49)	Hesychian
75. Octateuch (A.D. 1126)	Oxford, Univ. Coll. lii.	Lagarde's *o.* Hornemann, p. 41 ; Owen, *Enquiry*, p. 90
76. Octateuch...(xiii)	Paris, Nat. Reg. Gr. 4	Hesychian
77. Octateuch, *cat.* (xiii)	Rome, Vat. Gr. 748	
78. Gen., Ex., *cat.* (xiii)	Rome, Vat. Gr. 383	Field, i. p. 78
79. Gen., *ep. Arist.*, *cat.* (xiii)	Rome, Vat. Gr. 1668	
82. Octateuch...(xii)	Paris, Nat. Coisl. Gr. 3	Lucianic (in part). Rahlfs, *Sept.-St.* i. 5 ff. (Lagarde's *f*)
83. Pentateuch, *cat.* (xvi)	Lisbon, Archivio da Torre da Tombo 540 &c. (formerly at Evora)	? Copied from Ald. (Nestle)
84. Heptateuch (*imperf.*) (x)	Rome, Vat. Gr. 1901	Hesychian
85. Heptateuch (*imperf.* (xi)	Rome, Vat. Gr. 2058 (formerly Basil. 97)	Field, i. pp. 78, 397 (" praestantissimi codicis")
93. Ruth... (xiii)	London, B. M. Reg. i. D. 2	Lucianic (Lagarde's *m* in "Lucian")

94=131

105.	Exod. xiv. 6—26 &c. (xiii—xiv)	London, B. M. Burney	
106.	Octateuch..(xiv)	Ferrara, Bibl. Comm. Gr. 187	Hesychian. O. T., N. T. (582 Greg., 451 Scr.). Lagarde, *Ank.* p. 27
107.	Octateuch...(A.D. 1334)	Ferrara, Bibl. Comm. Gr. 188	Lagarde, *ib.*
108.	Octateuch...(xiv)	Rome, Vat. Gr. 330	Field, i. p. 5. Lucianic (Lagarde's *d*)
118.	Octateuch (*imperf.*) (xiii)	Paris, Nat. Reg. Gr. 6	Lucianic (Lagarde's *p*)
120.	Octateuch...(xi)	Venice, St Mark's, Gr. 4	
121.	Octateuch... (x)	Venice, St Mark's, Gr. 3	
122.	Octateuch...(xv)	Venice, St Mark's, Gr. 6	O. and N. T. (Ev. 206) in Latin order. Copy of 68. Lag.'s *y*
125.	Octateuch...(xv)	Moscow, Syn. 30, Vlad. 3	
126.	Heptateuch...... cat. *in Gen., Ex.* (A.D. 1475)	Moscow, Syn. 19, Vlad. 38	
127.	Octateuch... (x)	Moscow, Syn. 31 a, Vlad. 1	Field, i. p. 5. Lagarde, *Ank.* p. 3
128.	Octateuch (xii)	Rome, Vat. Gr. 1657, formerly Grotta ferrata	Field, i. pp. 168, 224
129.	Octateuch (xiii)	Rome, Vat. Gr. 1252	See note to 63
130.	Octateuch (?xiii)	Vienna, Th. **Gr. 3** (Nessel 57)	Field, i. p. 6. Lagarde's *t*: *Ank.* p. 26. See note to 131
131.	Octateuch ...... (x—xi)	Vienna, Th. **Gr. 1** (Nessel 23)	Field, i. p. 5: "in enumeratione Holmesiana [cod. 130] perverse designatur 131, et vice versa.' O. and N. T.
132.	Lectionary (palimpsest, xi—xii)	Oxford, Bodl. Selden. 9	
133.	Excerpts from MSS.byI.Voss	Leyden, Univ.	
134.	Octateuch... (xi)	Florence, Laur. v. 1	Hesychian

135. Gen., Ex. i. 1—xii. 4, *cat.* (xi)	Basle, A. N. iii. 13 (Omont 1)	Field, i. p. 6. Lagarde's *r* (*Genesis*, p. 6). Hexaplaric
136. Excerpts from Pentateuch (A.D. 1043)	Oxford, Bodl. Barocc. 196	
209. Jos., Jud., Ruth, *cat.* (xii)	[Cod. Dorothei iv]	
236. Jos., Jud., Ruth ... (xii)	Rome, Vat. Gr. 331	Klostermann, p. 78
237=73		
241. Jos., Jud., Ruth ... (xvii)	London, B. M. Harl. 7522	P. Young's copy of Cod. A
246. Octateuch ...... (xiii)	Rome, Vat. Gr. 1238	Cf. Batiffol, *d'un important MS. des Septante*, in *Bulletin Critique*, 1889, pp. 112 ff.
Josh.—Ruth (x—xi)	London, B.M. Add. 20002	Continuation of E (p. 134) with Petersburg lxii. See next page
Octateuch, *cat.* (xii—xiii)	London, B.M. Add. 35123	
Lev.—Ruth, *cat.* (A.D. 1104)	Lambeth, 1214	
Lev.—Ruth, *cat.* (A.D. 1264)	Paris, Nat. Coisl. Gr. 5	
Jos.—Ruth ...... *cat.* (xii)	Paris, Nat. Coisl. Gr. 7	
Octateuch ...... *schol.*	Paris, Arsenal 8415	Hexaplaric readings
Heptateuch (*imperf.*) (xiii)	Paris, Nat. Coisl. Gr. 184	Lucianic (?)
Lev.—Ruth, *cat.* (xiii)	Paris, Nat. Coisl. Gr. 6	
Octateuch...(xiv)	Paris, Nat. Suppl. Gr. 609	Hesychian (?)
Octateuch, *ep. Arist., cat.* (xii)	Paris, Nat. Reg. Gr. 128	
Ex.—Ruth, *cat.* (xv)	Paris, Nat. Reg. Gr. 132	Hexaplaric readings
Octateuch, *ep. Arist., cat.* (xiii)	Paris, Nat. Reg. Gr. 129	Hexaplaric readings
Gen.—Ex. (*imperf.*), *ep. Arist., cat.* (xv)	Paris, Nat. Reg. Gr. 130	

Ex.(*imperf.*),*cat.* (xvi)	Paris, Nat. Reg. Gr. 131	Hexaplaric readings (interlinear)
Gen. i.—iii. (?), *comm.* (palim.) (xiii)	Paris, Nat. Reg. Gr. 161	
Gen., Ex., *ep. Arist.,* *cat.* (A.D. 1586)	Escurial Σ. i. 16	Hexaplaric readings
Octateuch...(*imperf.*) (xi)	Escurial Ω. i. 13	
Octateuch, *cat.* (xiii)	Leyden, 13 (belongs to Voss collection)	
Exod. — Deut. (*imperf.*) (xi)...	Leipzig, Univ. Libr. Gr. 361	Hexaplaric readings. Published by Fischer in 1767 = Lips. (H. P.)
Gen., Ex., *ep. Arist.,cat.*(xvi)	Munich, Gr. 82	
Jos.—Ruth...(x)	Munich, Gr. 454 (formerly at Augsburg)	
Octateuch, *ep. Arist.,cat.*(xiii)	Zurich, Bibl. de la ville, c. 11	Hexaplaric matter
Gen. iv.—v., Ex. xii. — xxviii., *comm.* (xi)	Basle, O. ii. 17	
Octateuch, *cat.* (? xii)	Rome, Barb. Gr. iv. 56	
Gen., *cat.* (xvi)	Rome, Barb. Gr. vi. 8	
Num.—Ruth ... (xiv—xv)	Rome, Vat. Gr. 332	
Hexateuch... (x)	Grotta Ferrata Υ. γ. 1	
Gen.—Jos. (*imperf.*)... (x—xi)	St Petersburg,. Imp. Libr. lxii	Continuation of E (p. 134)
Gen., *comm. Chrys.*	Moscow, Syn. Vlad. 35	
Joshua—Ruth... *cat.* (xii)	Athos, Ivér. 15	
Octateuch (x)	Athos, Pantocr. 24	Hexaplaric readings
Octateuch... (x —xi)	Athos, Vatop. 511	
Octateuch ...... (A.D. 1021)	Athos, Vatop. 513	
Lev.—Ruth, *cat.* (xi—xii)	Athos, Vatop. 515	
Ex.—Ruth ...... (xiv)	Athos, Vatop. 516	Hexaplaric readings, much faded

Pentateuch (*im-perf.*), (A.D. 1327)	Athos, Protat. 53	Hexaplaric readings
Octateuch (A.D. 1013)	Athos, Laur. γ. 112	Hexaplaric readings (a few)
Genesis,*cat.*(?xi)	Constantinople, 224 (formerly 372)	
Octateuch... *cat.* (xi)	Athens, Bibl. Nat. 43	
Octateuch...(xiii)	Athens, Bibl. Nat. 44	Lucianic (?)
Octateuch, *cat. Niceph.* (xii)	Smyrna, σχολὴ εὐαγγ. I	
Pentateuch, *cat.* (xi)	Patmos, 216	
Num. — Ruth, *cat.* (xi)	Patmos, 217	
Heptateuch (*im-perf.*) (xiii)	Patmos, 410	
Pentateuch, *test. xii. patr.* (xv)	Patmos, 411	
Octateuch... (x —xi)	Sinai, 1	
Pentateuch, *cat.* (? x)	Sinai, 2	
Octateuch... (ix med.)	Jerusalem, H. Sepulchre 2	
Genesis, *cat.* (xii —xiii)	Jerusalem, H. Sepulchre 3	
Octateuch, *cat.* (xi)	Venice, Gr. 534 : see below, p. 508	

(B) *Historical Books.*

19[1]...1 Regn., 2 Esdr., Judith, Esth., 1—3 Macc.,&c. (x)	Rome, Chigi R. vi. 38	
29...1—4 Regn., 1— 3 Macc. (im-perf.), &c. (x)	Venice, St Mark's, Gr. 2	
38...1 Regn., 2 Regn. i. 1—xx. 18 (xv)	Escurial, Y. II. 5	
44...1 Regn., 2 Esdr., 1—4 Macc., Esth., Judith, Tob., (N. T.) &c. (xv)	Zittau, A. I. 1	

[1] Dots before the name of the first book quoted indicate that the MS. has already appeared under (A), where fuller information may be sought. This note applies *mutatis mutandis* to (C) and (D).

46...1 Regn.–2 Esdr., Esth., Judith, 1—4 Macc., Tob....	Paris, Nat. Coisl. Gr. 4	
52...1 Regn.–2 Esdr., Esth., Judith, 1—4 Macc., Tob., *schol.* (x)	Florence, Laur. Acq. 44	
55...1 Regn.–2 Esdr., Judith, Esth., Tob., 1—4 Macc. (xi)	Rome, Vat. Regin. Gr. 1	
56...1—4 Regn., 1— 2 Chron., 1—2 Macc. (xii)	Paris, Nat. Reg. Gr. 3	
58...1—4 Regn., 1— 2 Chron., 1—2 Esdr., Jud., Tob., Esth., &c. (xiii)	Rome, Vat. Regin. Gr. 10	
60. 1–2 Chron. (?xii)	Cambridge, Univ. Libr. Ff. i. 24	Walton, *Polygl.* vi. 121 ff.; J. R. Harris, *Origin of Leicester Cod.*, p. 21
64...1 Regn.–2 Esdr., Esth., Tob., 1—2 Macc. (x)	Paris, Nat. Reg. Gr. 2	
68...1 Regn.–2 Esdr., Esth., Judith, Tob., 1—3 Macc.... (xv)	Venice, St Mark's, Gr. 5	
70...1–4 Regn., parts of Chron., Tob. (xi)	Munich, Gr. 372 (formerly at Augsburg)	
71...2 Esdr., 1—3 Macc., Esth., Judith, Tob. (xiii)	Paris, Nat. Reg. Gr. 1	
74...1—2 Esdr., 1—4 Macc., Esth., Judith, Tob. (xiv)	Florence, St Mark's	
76...Esth., Judith, Tob. (xiii)	Paris, Nat. Reg. Gr. 4	
82...1—4 Regn. (xii —xiii)	Paris, Nat. Coisl. Gr. 3	
92. 1—4 Regn. (x)	Paris, Nat. Gr. 8	Field, i. p. 486

93...1–2 Esdr.,Esth., 1–3 Macc.(xiii)	London, B. M. Reg. i. D. 2	**Facsimile in Kenyon.** Two texts of Esther
98. 1—4 Regn., 1—2 Chron., *cat.*	Escurial, Σ. 2. 19	
106...1 Regn.–2 Esdr., Judith, Esth., 1—2 Macc.	Ferrara, Bibl. Comm. Gr. 187	
107...1 Regn.–2 Esdr., 1—3 Macc., Esth., Judith, Tob.(A.D.1334)	Ferrara, Bibl. Comm. Gr. 188	
108...1 Regn.–2 Esdr., Judith, Tob., Esth. (xiv)	Rome, Vat. Gr. 330	Cf. Field, i. p. 702
119. 1—4 Regn., 1—2 Chron., 1—2 Esdr. (x)	Paris, Nat. Gr. 7	
120...1 Regn.–2 Esdr., 1—4 Macc., Esth. (xi)	Venice, St Mark's, Gr. 4	
121...1 Regn.–2 Esdr. (x)	Venice, St Mark's, Gr. 3	
122...Historical Bks., ... (xv)	Venice, St Mark's, Gr. 6	
123. 1—4 Regn. (xi)	[Cod. Dorothei v.]	
125...Historical Bks., ... (xv)	Moscow, Syn. 30, Vlad. 3	
126...Judith,Tob.(xv)	Moscow, Syn. 19, Vlad. 38	
127...1—4 Regn., 1— 2 Chron. xxxvi. (x)	Moscow, Syn. 31 a, Vlad. 1	
131...Historical Bks. (exc. 4 Macc.) (? xii)	Vienna, Th. Gr. 1 (Nessel 23)	
134...1 Regn.–2 Esdr., 1 Macc. (x)	Florence, Laur. v. 1	
158. 1—4 Regn., 1—2 Chron.	Basle, B. 6. 22	Wetstein, *N. T.* i. p. 132
236...1 Regn.–2 Esdr., Esth., Judith, Tob., 1—4 Macc., *cat.* (xii)	Rome, Vat. Gr. 331	
241...1—4 Regn.,1—2 Chron.	London, B. M. Harl. 7522	
242. 1—4 Regn.	Vienna, Th. Gr. 5	
243. 1—4 Regn.,*cat.*	Paris, Nat. Coisl. 8	Field, i. p. 486

Missing? (marginal note, vertical, beside entry 107)

243*.1—4 Regn. (*cat.*),   Venice, St Mark's,   Field, i. p. 486
     1   Chron.—2   cod. 16
     Esdr.,   Esth.,
     Tob., Jud., 1—4
     Macc.

244. 1—4 Regn. (x)   Rome, Vat. Gr. 333
245. 1 Regn. (ix—x)   Rome, Vat. Gr. 334   Lucianic (Field)
246...1 Regn. (xiii)   Rome, Vat. Gr. 1238
247. 1—4   Regn.   (4   Rome, Vat. Gr. Urb. 1
     Regn. imperf.)
248...1—2 Esdr., Tob.,   Rome, Vat. Gr. 346   Nestle, *Marg.* p. 58
     Judith,   Esth.,
     &c. (xiv)

311...Historical Bks.   Moscow, Syn. 341
     (xi)

...1 Regn.–2 Esdr.,
     Esth., Tob.
...Judith,   1—3   Escurial, Ω. 1. 13
     Macc. (3 M.
     imperf.) (xi)
...1 Regn.–2 Chron.   Munich, Gr. 454 (? for-
     (x)   merly at Augsburg)
...1 Regn.–3 Regn.   St Petersburg, Imp.
     xvi. 28 (x or xi)   Libr. lxii.
...Tob.,   Judith,   Grotta Ferrata, A. γ. 1
     Esth., Ruth (x)   (catal., 29)
...Tobit (xiv or xv)   Rome, Vat. Gr. 332
...1 Esdr., Tobit   Leipzig, Univ. Libr.   Hexaplaric readings
     (fragments) (x   Gr. 361
     or xi)
...Esth.,   Judith,   Athos, Vatop. 511
     Tob., 1–4 Regn.
     (x or xi)
...Esth.,   Tob.,   Athos, Vatop. 513
     Judith   (A.D.
     1021)
...1–2 Chron. (xiv)   Athos, Vatop. 516
...1—4 Regn., *cat.*   Athens, Bibl. Nat. 43
     (xi)
...1 Regn.–2 Esdr.,   Athens, Bibl. Nat. 44
     Esth.,   Judith,
     Tob. (xiii)
...1—4 Regn., 1—   Paris, Arsenal 8415
     2 Chron. (xiv)
...1 Regn.–2 Esdr.,   Paris, Nat. Suppl. Gr.
     1—4   Macc.,   609
     Esth., Judith,
     Tob. (xiv)

...1—4 Regn. (xii)   Paris, Nat. Coisl. Gr.
7

(C) *Poetical Books.*

13. = I (see under
    Uncial MSS.)
21. Psalms, *schol.* [Cod. Eugenii iv.]
    (xiii—xiv)
27. Psalms i—lxx   Gotha, formerly Loth-   An uncial MS., La-
                   ringen   garde's M(ps) (*Spe-
                                           cimen*, p. 27)
39. Psalms (*imperf.*) [Cod. Dorothei ii.] An uncial MS., La-
    (ix)   garde's E(ps) (*Spe-
                                             cimen*, p. 2)
43. = W (see under   Lagarde's F(ps) (*Spe-*
    Uncial MSS.)   *cimen*, p. 2)
46...Prov., Eccl.,   Paris, Nat. Coisl. Gr.
    Cant.,   Job,   4
    Sap., Sir., ὕμ-
    νος τῶν πατ.
    ἡμῶν (xiv)
55...Job,   Psalms   Rome, Vat. Reg. Gr.
    (? xi)   I
65. Psalms, *cant.*, Leipzig
    Lat. (xii)
66. Psalms, *cant.* Eton Coll.
    (xiv)
67. Psalms, *cant.* Oxford, C.C.C. 19   Harris, *Leicester Co-*
    (xvi)   *dex*, p. 20
68...Poetical Books   Venice, St Mark's,
    (xv)   Gr. 5
69. Psalms, *cant.* Oxford, Magd. Coll. 9
    (? x)
80. Psalms, *cant.* Oxford, Christ Ch. A
    (xiii—xiv)
81. Psalms (xi)   Oxford, Christ Ch. 2
99. Psalms, *schol.*, Oxford, Trin. Coll. 78
    cat. (xii—xiii)
100. Psalms, *cant.* Oxford, Christ Ch. 3
    (xi—xii)
101. Psalms, *cant.* Oxford, Christ Ch. 20
    (xiii)
102. Psalms, *cant.* Oxford, Christ Ch. 1
    (xiii)
103. Prov.   i.—xix. Vienna, Th. Gr. 25   Klostermann, pp. 6,
    (xv)   18

104. Psalms i.–x. (xvi)	Vienna, Th. Gr. 27 (Nessel 229)	
106...Job, Prov.,Eccl., Cant.,Sap.,Sir. ...Psalms (xiv)	Ferrara, Bibl.Comm. Gr. 187	
109. Proverbs... (xiii)	Vienna, Th. Gr. 26	
110. Job, *schol.* (ix)	Vienna, Th. Gr. 9	Klostermann, p. 18
111. Psalms (ix)	Milan, Ambr. P. 65	
112. Psalms,*cat.* (A.D. 961)	Milan, Ambr. F. 12	
113. Psalms,*cat.* (A.D. 967)	Milan, Ambr. B. 106	
114...Psalms, *comm.*	Evora, Carthus. 2	
115. Psalms, *comm.*	Evora, Carthus. 3	
122...Poetical Books (xv)	Venice, St Mark's, Gr. 6	
124. Psalms, *cant.*	Vienna, Th. Gr. 21	
125...Proverbs(*comm. Chrys.*), Eccl., Cant., Sap. (xv)	Moscow, Syn. 30, Vlad. 3	
131...Poetical Books, &c. (? xii)	Vienna, Th. Gr. 23	
137. Job, *cat.* (xi—xii)	Milan, Ambr. B. 73	Field, ii. p. 2, and Auct. p. 5
138. Job (x)	Milan, Ambr. M. 65	Field, ii. p. 2
139. Proverbs — Job, *cat.* (x)	Milan, Ambr. A. 148	Field, ii. p. 2
140. Psalms	Basle, B. 10. 33	
141. Psalms (A.D. 1344)	Turin, B. 2. 42	
142. Psalms, *comm.*	Vienna, Th. Gr. 10 (Nessel 8)	
143. Psalms,*prooem.*	Vienna, Th. Gr. 19	
144=131		
145. Psalms, *cant.* (x)	Velletri, Borg.	
146. Psalms (x)	[Cod. Fr. Xavier]	In Capitular Lib. Toledo
147. Prov.—Job, *cat.* ... (xiii)	Oxford, Bodl. Laud. 30	Klostermann, p. 51
149. Job, Prov., Eccl., Cant., Sap., Pss.Sal.,*comm.* (xi)	Vienna, Th. Gr. 7	= 308*H. P. See Gebhardt, *Die Psalmen Salomo's*, p. 15
150. Psalms (? xiv)	Ferrara, Carmelit. 3	
151. Psalms (*imperf.*)	Venice, Bibl. Zen.	A Graeco-Latin MS.
152. Psalms (xi)	(Cod. Nan. 25)	Now in St Mark's Lib. Venice
154. Psalms, *cant.* (xiii)	(Cod. Meermanni I)	

155.	Psalms (xii–xiii)	(Cod. Meermanni II)	Now Bodl. Misc. Gr. 204
156.	Psalms, *interlin. Lat.*	Basle, A. 7. 3	An uncial MS. Lagarde's D(ps) (*Specimen*, p. 2, cf. *Ank.* p. 27)[1]
157.	Job, Prov., Eccl., Cant., Sap.	Basle, B. 6. 23	Wetstein, *N. T.* i. 132
159.	Eccl., Prov. (part), Cant., *schol.*(xi)	Dresden, 1	Klostermann, p. 39
160.	Job (xiv)	Dresden, 2	
161.	Job, Prov., Eccl., Cant. (xiv)	Dresden, 3	Field, ii. p. 2; cf. 6, 309, and Auct. 22. Cf. Klostermann, pp. 16, 39
	Job, *comm.* (xv)	Turin, Royal Library, 330	
162.	Psalms, *interlin. Latin* (xi)	Paris, Nat. Reg. Gr. 24	
163.	Psalms (xii)	Paris, Nat. Colbert. Gr. 26	
164.	Psalms (xiv)	London, B. M. Harl. 5533	
165.	Psalms (xiv)	London, B. M. Harl. 5534	
166.	Psalms, *cant.* (A.D. 1283)	London, B. M. Harl. 5535	
167.	Psalms, *cant.* (xiv)	London, B. M. Harl. 5553	
168.	Psalms (*imperf.*) (xi–xii)	London, B. M. Harl. 5570	
169.	Psalms (xii–xiii)	London, B. M. Harl. 5571	
170.	Psalms, *cant.* (xii)	London, B. M. Harl. 5582	
171.	Psalms, *cant.* (xiv)	London, B. M. Harl. 5653	
172.	Psalms, *cant.* (A.D. 1488)	London, B. M. Harl. 5737	
173.	Psalms, *cant.*	London, B. M. Harl. 5738	
174.	Psalms (*Latin, Arabic*) (A.D. 1153)	London, B. M. Harl. 5786	
175.	Psalms (xi)	London, B. M. 2. A. vi.	
176.	Psalms, *cant.*	London, B. M. Harl. 5563	

[1] The only Greek MS. which in Ps. xcv (xcvi) 10 adds απο τω ξυλω (sic); see below, p. 467.

177. Psalms (*imperf.*) cant. (xiii)	Paris, Nat. Gr. 27	
178. Psalms, cant. (A.D. 1059)	Paris, Nat. Gr. 40	
179. Psalms, cant. (xii)	Paris, Nat. Gr. 41	
180. Psalms, cant. (xii)	Paris, Nat. Gr. 42	
181. Psalms, cat. (xii)	Cod. Ducis Saxo-Goth.	
182. Psalms, cant. (xi)	Rome, Chigi 4	
183. Psalms, cant. (xii)	Rome, Chigi 5	
184. Psalms, comm. (ix—x)	Vienna, Th. Gr. 17	
185. Psalms, comm. (xi)	Vienna, Th. Gr. 18	
186. Psalms, comm. (xi)	Vienna, Th. Gr. 13	
187. Psalms (*imperf.*)	Paris, Nat. Coisl. Gr. 10	
188. Psalms (*imperf.*)	Paris, Nat. Coisl. Gr. 186	An uncial MS. Lagarde's H(ps)(*Specimen*, p. 3). Often agrees with 156
189. Psalms, cant.	Paris, Nat. Coisl. Gr. 13	
190. Psalms (*imperf.*) cant.	Paris, Nat. Coisl. Gr. 187	An uncial MS. Lagarde's K(ps) (*Specimen*, p. 3)
191. Psalms, cant.	Paris, Nat. Coisl. Gr. 188	
192. Psalms (*imperf.*) cant. (xiii)	Paris, Nat. Gr. 13	
193. Psalms, cant. (xii)	Paris, Nat. Gr. 21	
194. Psalms, cant. (xii)	Paris, Nat. Gr. 22	
195. Psalms, cant. (xii)	Paris, Nat. Gr. 23	
196. Psalms (inc. ii. 3), cant. (xii)	Paris, Nat. Gr. 25	
197. Psalms, cant. (xiv)	Paris, Nat. Gr. 29	
199. Psalms (xi)	Modena, Est. 37	
200. Psalms, cant.	Oxford, Bodl. Barocc. 15	Cf. Nestle, *Septuagintastud.* iii. p. 14
201. Psalms, cant.	Oxford, Bodl. Barocc. 107	
202. Psalms, cant., comm.	Oxford, Bodl. Cromw. 110	

S. S.

203. Psalms, *cant.*, Oxford, Bodl. Laud.
     prayers (A.D. C. 41
     1336)
204. Psalms (*imperf.*) Oxford, Bodl. Laud.
     schol., *prayers* C. 38
205. Psalms, *cant.* Cambridge, Trin.
     Coll.
206. Psalms, *cant.* Cambridge, Gonville Facsimile in Harris,
     (xiv) & Caius Coll. 348 *Leicester codex*
208. Psalms (*imperf.*), Tübingen, (cod.
     cant. Schnurrer)
210. Psalms (xiv) [Cod. Demetrii v.]
211. Psalms, *cant.* Rome, Vat. Gr. 1541
     (xiii)
212. Psalms (*imperf.*) Rome, Vat. Gr. 1542
     (xii)
213. Psalms (*imperf.*) Rome, Vat. Gr. 1848
     (xiii)
214. Psalms, *cant.* Rome, Vat. Gr. 1870
     (xiii)
215. Psalms, *cant.* Rome, Vat. Gr. 1873 Klostermann, p. 13
     (A.D. 1011)
216. Psalms, *cant.* (x) Rome, Vat. Gr. 1927
217. Psalms, *cant.* Rome, Vat. Gr. 341
     (A.D. 1029)
218. Psalms, li.—liii. ?
     (xiii—xiv)
219. Psalms, *cant.* Vienna, Th. Gr. 20
220 = 186 Vienna, Th. Gr. 13
221. Psalms, ix.—cl., Vienna, Th. Gr. 16
     comm.
222. Psalms, *cant.* Vienna, Th. Gr. 21
223. Psalms, *cant.* Vienna, Th. Gr. 22
225. Psalms, *cant.* Bologna, 720
     (xi)
226. Psalms, *cant.*, Rome, Barber. 1 (Gr.
     prayers (x) 372)
227. Psalms (*imperf.*) Rome, Barber. 2 (Gr.
     cant., *prayers* 322)
     (x)
228. Job, &c. (xiii) Rome, Vat. Gr. 1764
241...Prov., Eccl., London, B. M. Harl.
     Cant. 7522
248...Prov., Eccl., Rome, Vat. Gr. 346 Hexaplaric readings
     Cant., Job, Field, ii. p. 2
     Sap., Sir., &c.
     (xiv)

249. Job, Sap., Sir., &c.   Rome, Vat. Pius 1   Field, *l. c.*

250. Job   (xiv)   Munich, Elect. 148   Field, *l. c.*

251. Job, *cat.*, Psalms (xiv)   Florence, Laur. v. 27

252. Job, Prov., Eccl., Cant. (ix—x)   Florence, Laur. viii. 27   Field, *l. c.*; cf. p. 309 and Auct. p. 2

253. Job, Prov., Sir. (xi—xiv)   Rome, Vat. Gr. 336   Klostermann, p. 17 ff. Gebhardt, *Die Psalmen Salomo's* p. 25 ff.

254. Job, Prov. (xiii)   Rome, Vat. Gr. 337

255. Job   (ix)   Rome, Vat. Gr. 338   Field, ii. p. 2. Klostermann, p. 69 ff.

256. Job, *schol.* (xii)   Rome, Vat. Gr. 697   Field, *l. c.*

257. Job, *comm.* (x)   Rome, Vat. Gr. 743

258. Job, *cat., pict.* (ix)   Rome, Vat. Gr. 749   Field, *l. c.* Klostermann, p. 68

259. Job, *schol.* (x)   Rome, Vat. Pal. Gr. 230   Field, *l. c.* Klostermann, p. 11

260. Job, *cat.*, Prov.   Copenhagen, Royal Libr.

261. Job, Prov., Eccl., Sap. (xiv)   Florence, Laur. vii. 30

263. Psalms   Copenhagen, Royal Lib.

264. Psalms, *cat.*   Rome, Vat. Ottob. Gr. 398   Cf. Field, ii. p. 84 f., and Auct. p. 11

265. Psalms, *cant., pict.* (xiv)   Rome, Vat. Gr. 381

266. Psalms (imperf.) (xiii)   Rome, Vat. Gr. 2101

267. Psalms, *cant.* (xiv)   Rome, Vat. Ottob. Gr. 294

268. Psalms, *cat., cant.*   Rome, Vat. Gr. 2057   Cf. Field, ii. p. 84

269. Psalms, *comm. Athen.* (A.D. 897)   Rome, Vat. Pal. Gr. 44

270. Psalms, *cant.* (xii)   Rome, Vat. Gr. 1864

271. Psalms, *comm.* (xi)   Rome, Vat. Gr. 1747

272. Psalms (imperf.) *cat.* (xiii)   Rome, Vat. Pal. Gr. 247

273. Psalms, *cat.* (xiv)   Rome, Vat. Regin. Gr. 40   Cf. Field, ii. p. 84

274. Psalms (*imperf.*)   Rome, Vat.   Ottob.
     comm. (xiii)   Gr. 343
275. Psalms,*cant.*(xii)   Rome, Vat. **Gr.** 1874
276=221
277. Psalms, *cant.*   Vienna, Th. Gr. 24
278. Psalms   (xii—   Florence, Laur. v. 23
     xiii)
279. Psalms,   *cant.*   Florence, Laur. v. 35
     (xiii—xiv)
280. Psalms (xi)   Florence, Laur. v. 5
281. Psalms (xi)   Florence, Laur. v. 18
282. Psalms (xv)   Florence, Laur. v. 25
283. Psalms (xii)   Florence, Laur. vi. 36
284. Psalms,   *cant.*   Florence, Laur. v. 17
     (xiv)
285. Psalms,   *cant.*   Florence, Laur. v. 34
     (xiii)
286. Psalms,   *comm.*   Florence, Laur. v. 30
     (xii)
287. Psalms (*imperf.*)   Florence, Laur. v. 14
     comm. (xii)
288. Psalms,   *comm.*   Florence, Laur. xi. 5
     Thdt. (xii)
289. Psalms,   *comm.*   Florence, Laur. ix. 2
     Euth.-Zig.
     (xiii)
290. Psalms, *cant.*   Florence, Laur.
291. Psalms (xi—xii)   Florence, Laur. v. 39
292. Psalms, *cat.* (xi)   Florence, Laur. vi. 3
293. Psalms,   *metr.*   Florence, Laur. v. 37
     paraphr. (xv)
294. Psalms, lxxi. 14,   Cambridge, Emma-   Lagarde calls it P in
     –lxxxi. 7,cxxvii.   nuel College   *Genesis graece*, but
     3 — cxxix. 6,   N(ps) in the *Speci-*
     cxxxv. 11 —   *men.* Apparently a
     cxxxvi.   1,   copy in a Western
     cxxxvii. 4–cxli.   hand of an early
     21 (? xiii)   cursive Psalter; see
                                           M. R. James in
                                           Proceedings of the
                                           Cambridge Anti-
                                           quarian Society,
                                           1892—3, p. 168 ff.[1]

---

[1] Other Psalters used by Lagarde (*Specimen*, p. 3 f.) are St Gall 17 (ix) = G(ps); Munich 251 = L(ps); a Bamberg Graeco-Latin MS. and a Cologne MS. closely related to it, which he calls W and Z respectively. Cf. Rahlfs, *Sept.-St.* ii. pp. 7, 8.

295. Prov.,   *comm.*   Rome, Vat. Ottob.
     Procop. (xiv)   Gr. 56
296. Prov.—Sir. (xiii) Rome, Vat. Palat. Gr.
                    337
297. Prov., *cat.* (xii) Rome, Vat. Gr. 1802
298. Eccl.,*comm.*(xii) [Cod. Eugenii 3]
299. Eccl.,   *Comm.* Rome, Vat. Gr. 1694   Klostermann, p. 29 f.
     Greg. Nyss.,al.
     (xiii)
300. Cant.,   *comm.* [Cod. Eugenii 3]
     (xii)
302. Prov....(ix)=109
Psalms,A.D.1066 London, B. M. Add.
            19,352
Psalms   Rome, Vat. Gr. 754

(D) *Prophetical Books.*

22. Prophets (xi— London, B. M. Reg. Cod.   Pachomianus.
    xii)   i. B. 2   Lucianic ; Field, ii.
                               p. 428 f. Cornill's ξ

24. Isaiah, *cat.* (xii) [Cod. Demetrii i.]
26. Prophets (? xi)   Rome, Vat. Gr. 556   Hesychian (Cornill,
                                  Ceriani): cf. Klos-
                                  termann, p. 10 f.

33. Dan., Jer., *cat.* Rome, Vat. Gr. 1154 Originally belonged
    (x)   to same codex as
                                   Vat. gr. 1153: see
                                 Klostermann, p. 11.
                                 Cf. 87, 97, 238
34. Dan. (xii)   Rome, Vat. Gr. 803 Klostermann, p. 11 n.
35. Dan. (xii)   Rome, Vat. Gr. 866
36. Prophets (xiii)   Rome, Vat. Gr. 347   Lucianic   (Field).
                                   Cornill's *o*

40. Dodecaprophe-   [Cod. Dorothei iii.]
    ton (xii)
41. Isa., Jer. (ix—x) [Cod. Demetrii ii.]
42. Ezek.,Dan.,Min. [Cod. Demetrii iii.] Lucianic (Field)
    Proph.(xi—xii)
46...Isa., Jer., Bar., Paris, Nat. Coisl. Gr.
    Lam.,   Ep.   4
    Ezek.,   Dan.,
    Minor   Pro-
    phets... (xiv)
48. Prophets (xii)   Rome, Vat. Gr. 1794 Lucianic (Field), Cor-
                                   nill's *η*. Kloster-
                                   mann, pp. 11, 14
49. Prophets (xi)   Florence, Laur. xi. 4 Hesychius, Cornill's *κ*
51. Prophets (xi)   Florence, Laur. x. 8 Lucianic   (Field).
                                   Cornill's *θ*

58...Prophets (xiii)	Rome, Vat. Reg. **Gr.** 10	On the text of Daniel in this MS.see Klostermann, p. 12
62. Prophets (xiii)	Oxford, New Coll.	Lucianic (Field). Field, ii. p. 907; Burkitt, *Tyconius*, p. cviii; Klostermann, p. 51
68...Ezek.,Dodecapr. (xv)	Venice, St Mark's, Gr. 5	Hesychian. Cornill's ψ
70...Prophets(x—xi)	Munich, Gr. 372 (formerly at Augsburg)	
86. Isa., Jer., Ezek., Dodecapr.(?ix)	Rome, Barber. v. 45	Field, ii. p. 939. Walton, vi. 131 f.; Klostermann, p. 50
87. Prophets (?ix)	Rome, Chigi 2	Hesychian. Cornill's β. For the relation of 87 to 91 and 96 see Faulhaber *Die Propheten - catenen*. 33, 97, 238 are copied from 87
88. Isa., Jer., Ezek., Dan. (LXX.) (?xi)	Rome, Chigi 3	87 in Field (ii. p. 766). *O.T. in Greek* (iii. p. xiii.). Cf. Klostermann, p. 31
89. Daniel (xi)=239		
90. Isa., Jer., Ezek., Dan., *cat.* (xi)	Florence, Laur. v. 9	Lucianic (Field); in Ezekiel, Hesychian acc. to Cornill: Cornill's λ
91. Prophets, *cat.* (xi)	Rome, Vat. Ottob. Gr. 452	Hesychian (Cornill). Cornill's μ. See note on 87
93...Isa. (xiv)	London, B. M. Reg. i. D. 2	Lucianic (Field)
95. Dodecaproph., *comm. Theod. Mops.*	Vienna, Th. Gr. 163	Lucianic (Cornill)
96. Isa., Jer., Ezek., Dan.	Copenhagen	See note on 87
97. Dodecapr., Isa., *cat.* (x)	Rome, Vat. Gr. 1153	See notes on 33, 87
104...Isa. v.—lxii.	Vienna, Th. Bib. 27 (Nessel 229)	
105...Fragments of Prophets, &c. (xiii—xiv)	London, B. M. Burney	

106...Isa., Jer., Ezek., Dan., Minor Prophets to Micah (xiv)	Ferrara, Gr. 187	Hesychian
109...Isaiah, *cat.* = 302	Vienna, Th. Gr. 26	
114. Dodecaproph., *comm. Theod. Mops...*	Evora, Carthus. 2	
122...Prophets (xv)	Venice, St Mark's, · Gr. 6	
131...Prophets (? xii)	Vienna, Th. Gr. 1 (Nessel 23)	
147...Isa., Jer., Ezek., Dan. (imperf.), Dodecaproph.	Oxford, Bodl. Laud. 30	Lucianic (cf. Field, ii. p. 907)
148. Daniel (xii)	Rome, Vat. Gr. 2025	
153. Prophets (exc. Zech.), *comm.* (x)	Rome, Vat. Pal. Gr. 273	Lucianic (Cornill)
185...Dodecaproph. (xi)	Vienna, Th. Gr. 18	Lucianic (Cornill)
198. Prophets (imperf.) (ix)	Paris, Nat. Gr. 14	= Ev. 33. Burkitt, *Tyconius*, p. cviii
228...Prophets (xiii)	Rome, Vat. Gr. 1764	Hesychian (Cornill, but cf. Klostermann, p. 13f. Cornill's φ)
229. Jer., Dan., *comm.* (xiv)	Rome, Vat. Gr. 673	
230. Daniel (xiii)	Rome, Vat. Gr. 1641	
231. Jer. with Baruch &c. (xi)	Rome, Vat. Gr. 1670	From Grotta Ferrata. Lucianic, Cornill's ι. Cp. Klostermann. p. 14
232. Daniel (xii)	Rome, Vat. Gr. 2000	A Basilian MS., cp. Klostermann, p. 15
233. Prophets (xiii)	Rome, Vat. Gr. 2067	Lucianic (Field)
234. Susanna	Moscow, Syn. 341	
235. Susanna	Rome, Vat. Gr. 2048	
238. Ezekiel, *cat.* (x)	Rome, Vat. Gr. 1153	Hesychian (Cornill). Cornill's ς. See notes on 33, 87, 97
239. Prophets (A.D. 1046) = 89		
240. Dodecapr., *cat.* (A.D. 1286)	Florence, Laur. vi. 22	
301. Isaiah (ix)	Vienna, Th. Gr. 158	
302...Isaiah, *cat.* (xiii) = 109		

303. Isaiah,　　comm.　Vienna, Th. Gr. 100
　　　Cyril.
304. Isaiah　　i.—xxv.　Florence, Laur. iv. 2
　　　comm.　Basil.
　　　(xi)
305. Isaiah (imperf.),　Copenhagen, Reg.
　　　cat.
306. Isa., Ezek. (xi)　Paris, Nat. Gr. 16
307. Isaiah,　　comm.　Rome, Vat. Ottob.
　　　Basil. (xi)　　　Gr. 430
308. Isaiah,　　comm.　Rome, Vat. Gr. 1509　Lucianic (Field)
　　　Basil.　and
　　　Thdt. (xiii)
309. Isaiah, cat. (x)　Rome, Vat. Gr. 755　Cf. Klostermann, p.
　　　　　　　　　　　　　　　　　　　　　　11
310. Dodecapr.,schol.　Moscow, Syn. 209
　　　(xi)
311...Prophets (xi)=
　　　234
　　　...Prophets　　(ix,　Jerusalem, H. Sepul-
　　　med.)　　　　chre 2

III. Lectionaries.

From the second century the Greek-speaking Churches, following the example of the Hellenistic Synagogue, read the Greek Old Testament in their public assemblies.

Justin, *Apol.* i. 67 τὰ συγγράμματα τῶν προφητῶν ἀναγινώσκεται. *Const. ap.* ii. 57 μέσος δὲ ὁ ἀναγνώστης ἐφ᾽ ὑψηλοῦ τινος ἑστὼς ἀναγινωσκέτω τὰ Μωσέως καὶ Ἰησοῦ τοῦ Ναυή, τὰ τῶν Κριτῶν καὶ τῶν Βασιλειῶν κ.τ.λ. *Ibid.* viii. 5 μετὰ τὴν ἀνάγνωσιν τοῦ νόμου καὶ τῶν προφητῶν. Chrys. *in Rom.* xxiv. 3 ὁ μάτην ἐνταῦθα εἰσελθών, εἰπὲ τίς προφήτης, τίς ἀπόστολος σήμερον διελέχθη.

At a later time the ἀναγνώσεις or ἀναγνώσματα were copied consecutively for ecclesiastical use. The lectionaries or fragments of lectionaries which survive, although frequently written in large and showy uncials[1], are rarely earlier than the tenth or eleventh century; but a thorough investigation of their contents would doubtless be of interest, not only from a liturgical

---

[1] Specimens are given by H. Omont, *Facsimilés des plus anciens MSS. Grecs* (Paris, 1892), nos. xx.—xxii.

point of view, but for the light which it would throw on the ecclesiastical distribution of various types of text. Little has been done as yet in this direction, and our information, such as it is, relates chiefly to the N.T.

See Matthaei, *N. T. Gr.*, ad fin. vol. i.; Neale, *Holy Eastern Church*, General Intr., p. 369 ff.; Burgon, *Last twelve verses of St Mark*, p. 191 ff.; Scudamore, art. *Lectionary*, D. C. A. ii.; Nitzsch, art. *Lectionarium*, Herzog-Plitt, viii.; Gregory, *prolegg.* i. p. 161 ff., 687 ff.; Scrivener-Miller, i. p. 74 ff.; E. Nestle, *Urtext*, p. 76; M. Faulhaber, *Die Propheten-catenen nach röm. Handschriften* (Freiburg i. B., 1899).

The following list of MSS.[1] containing lections from the Old Testament has been drawn up from materials previously supplied by Dr E. Nestle. It will be seen that with few exceptions they are limited to those which are bound up with N.T. lections and have been catalogued under the head of N.T. lectionaries by Dr C. F. Gregory and Scrivener-Miller.

London, Sion College, Arc. i. 1 (vi or vii)	Gr. p. 720 (234, Scr. 227)
„ B. M. Add. 11841 (? xi)	Gr. p. 783 (79, Scr. 75)
„ B. M. Add. 18212 (xi)	Gr. p. 715 (191, Scr. 263)
„ B. M. Add. 22744 (xiii)	Gr. p. 731 (324, Scr. 272)
„ Burdett-Coutts, iii. 42 (xiv)	Gr. p. 730 (315, Scr. 253)
„ Burdett-Coutts, iii. 44 (xv)	Gr. p. 749 (476, Scr. 290)
„ Burdett-Coutts, iii. 46 (xiii)	Gr. p. 719 (226, Scr. 249)
„ Burdett-Coutts, iii. 53 (xv)	
Oxford, Christ Church, Wake 14 (xii)	Gr. p. 717 (207, Scr. 214)
„ Christ Church, Wake 15 (A.D. 1068)	Gr. p. 717 (208, Scr. 215)
Cambridge, Univ. Libr. Add. 1879 (? xi)	(Gen. xi. 4—9, Prov. xiii. 19—xiv. 6, Sir. xxxvii. 13—xxxviii. 6): a fragment purchased from the executors of Tischendorf
„ Christ's College, F. i. 8 (xi)	Gr. p. 714 (185, Scr. 222) = Z^scr, WH. 59
Ashburnham, 205 (xii)	Gr. p. 720 (237, Scr. 237-8)
Paris, Nat. Gr. 308 (xiii)	Gr. p. 779 (24)
„ Nat. Gr. 243 (A.D. 1133)	Omont, *MSS. Grecs datés*, no. xlvi.

----

[1] A few lectionaries have already been mentioned among the H.P. MSS. (37, 61, 132).

Paris, Nat. suppl. Gr. 32 (xiii)	Gr. p. 704 (84)
Rome, Vat. Reg. Gr. 59 (xii)	Gr. p. 757 (573, Scr. 395)
„　Vat. Gr. 168 (xiii or xiv)	Gr. p. 786 (188, Scr. 116)
„　Vat. Gr. 2012 (xv)	Gr. p. 756 (556, Scr. 387)
„　Barb. 18 (xiv)	Gr. p. 780 (40)
Grotta Ferrata, A΄ δ΄ 2 (x)	Gr. p. 748 (473, Scr. 323)
„　　A΄ δ΄ 4 (xiii)	Gr. p. 748 (475, Scr. 325)
„　　Δ΄ β΄ 22 (xviii)	Gr. p. 751 (506, Scr. 358)
Venice, St Mark's, i. 42 (xii)	Gr. p. 724 (268, Scr. 173)[1]
Trèves, Bibl. Cath. 143 F (x or xi)	Gr. p. 713 (179)
Athens, Nat. 86 (xiii)	Gr. D. 745 (443)
Salonica, Ἑλληνικοῦ γυμνασίου ιδ΄ (xv or xvi)	Gr. p. 771 (837)
Cairo, Patr. Alex. 927 (xv)	Gr. p. 776 (759, Scr. 140)
Sinai, 748 (xv or xvi)	Gr. p. 775 (900)
„　943 (A.D. 1697)	Gr. p. 775 (908)
St Saba, in tower, 16 (xii)	Gr. p. 770 (829, Scr. 364)
Jerusalem, H. Sepulchre (xiii)	Harris, p. 13

LITERATURE (on the general subject of this chapter). Stroth, in Eichhorn's *Repertorium* (vi., viii., xi.); the prolegomena to Grabe, Holmes and Parsons, Tischendorf, and *The Old Testament in Greek*; the prefaces to Lagarde's *Genesis graece, Libr. V. T. Canon.*, p. i., *Psalterii specimen*; Kenyon, *Our Bible and the Ancient MSS.*; Madan, *Summary*, p. 615 ff. (Holmes MSS., A.D. 1789—1805); Nestle, *Urtext*, p. 71 ff.; H. Omont, *Inventaire Summaire des MSS. Grecs de la Bibl. Nationale*; S. Berger, *Hist. de la Vulgate.*

The lists of MSS. given in this chapter must be regarded as tentative and incomplete. The student may supplement them to some extent by referring to recently published catalogues of MS. libraries, especially the following: V. Gardthausen, *Catalogus codd. Graecorum Sinaiticorum* (Oxford, 1886); Papadopulos Kerameus, Ἱεροσολυμιτικὴ Βιβλιοθήκη i.—iv. (St Petersburg, 1891 —1899); Sp. P. Lambros, *Catalogue of the Greek MSS. on Mount Athos* (Cambridge, vol. i., 1895; vol. ii., with index, 1900). He may also consult with advantage J. B. Pitra, *Analecta sacra*, iii. (1883), p. 551 ff.; H. A. Redpath, in *Academy*, Oct. 22, 1893; E. Klostermann's *Analecta zur Septuaginta* (1895); Mrs Lewis, in *Exp. Times*, xiii. 2, p. 55 ff.; H. Omont, in *Lit. C. Blatt*; A. Rahlfs, *Septuaginta-Studien*, ii. (1907).

---

[1] At Messina, as Mr Brightman informs me, there are six lectionaries of cents. xii, xiii. Mr T. W. Allen (*Notes on Greek MSS. in Italy*, 1890) mentions two at Bologna (xi) and one at Lucerne (xv).

CHAPTER VI.

PRINTED TEXTS OF THE SEPTUAGINT.

THE printed texts of the Septuagint fall naturally into two classes, viz. (1) those which contain or were intended to exhibit the whole of the Greek Old Testament; (2) those which are limited to a single book or to a group of books.

I. COMPLETE EDITIONS.

1. The first printed text of the whole Septuagint is that which forms the third column in the Old Testament of the great Complutensian Polyglott. This great Bible was printed at Alcalà (*Complutum*) in Spain under the auspices of Francisco Ximenes de Cisneros, Cardinal Archbishop of Toledo. Ximenes, who, in addition to his ecclesiastical offices, was Regent of Castile, began this undertaking in 1502 in honour of the birth of Charles V. (1500—1558), and lived to see the whole of the sheets pass through the press. He died Nov. 8, 1517, and the fourth volume, which completes the Old Testament and was the last to be printed, bears the date July 10, 1517. But the publication of the Polyglott was delayed for more than four years: the papal sanction attached to the N.T. volume is dated May 22, 1520, and the copy which was intended for the Pope seems not to have found its way into the Vatican Library until Dec. 5, 1521. The title of the complete work (6 vols. folio) is as follows: "Biblia sacra Polyglotta complectentia V.T.

Hebraico Graeco et Latino idiomate, N.T. Graecum et **Lati-**num, et vocabularium Hebraicum et Chaldaicum V.T. cum grammatica Hebraica necnon Dictionario Graeco. Studio opera et impensis Cardinalis Fr. Ximenes de Cisneros. Industria Arnoldi Gulielmi de Brocario artis impressorie magistri. Compluti, 1514[—15,—17]."

The O.T. volumes of the Complutensian Bible contain in three columns (1) the Hebrew text, with the Targum of Onkelos at the foot of the page, (2) the Latin Vulgate, (3) the Septuagint, with an interlinear Latin version—an order which is explained by the editors as intended to give the place of honour to the authorised version of the Western Church[1]. The prejudice which their words reveal does not augur well for the character of the Complutensian LXX. Nevertheless we have the assurance of Ximenes that the greatest care was taken in the selection of the MSS. on which his texts were based[2]. Of his own MSS. few remain, and among those which are preserved at Madrid there are only two which contain portions of the Greek Old Testament (Judges—Macc., and a Psalter). But he speaks of Greek MSS. of both Testaments which had been sent to him by the Pope from the Vatican Library[3], and it has been shewn that at least two MSS. now in that Library (cod. Vat. gr. 330 = H.P. 108, and cod. Vat. gr. 346 = H.P. 248) were used in the construction of the Complutensian text of the LXX.[4] There is

---

[1] Their words are: "mediam autem inter has Latinam B. Hieronymi translationem velut inter Synagogam et orientalem ecclesiam posuimus, tanquam duos hinc et inde latrones, medium autem Iesum, hoc est Romanam sive Latinam ecclesiam, collocantes."

[2] In the dedication to Leo X. he says: "testari possumus...maximi laboris nostri partum in eo praecipue fuisse versatum ut...castigatissima omni ex parte vetustissimaque exemplaria pro archetypis haberemus."

[3] "Ex ista apostolica bibliotheca antiquissimos tum V. tum N. Testamenti codices perquam humane ad nos misisti."

[4] See Vercellone, in *V. et N.T.* ed. Mai, i. p. v. n.; *Var. lectt.* ii. p. 436; *Dissertazioni Accademiche*, 1864, p. 407 ff.; Tregelles, *An account of the printed text of the Greek N.T.* (London, 1854), p. 2 ff.; Delitzsch, *Studien zur Entstehungsgeschichte der Polyglotten Bibel des Cardinals Ximenes*

reason to suppose that a Venice MS. (S. Marc. 5 = H.P. 68) was also employed; a copy of this MS. still exists at Madrid.

The editors of the Complutensian Polyglott were the Spaniard Antonio de Nebrija, Professor of Rhetoric at Alcalà, and his pupil Ferdinando Nūnez de Guzman (Pincianus); Diego Lopez de Zuñiga (Stunica); Juan de Vergara, Professor of Philosophy at Alcalà; a Greek from Crete, by name Demetrius; and three converts from Judaism, to whom the Hebrew text and the Targum were entrusted. The editing of the Greek LXX. text seems to have been left chiefly in the hands of Pincianus, Stunica and Demetrius.

The Complutensian text is followed on the whole in the Septuagint columns of the four great Polyglotts edited by Arias Montanus, Antwerp, 1569—72; B. C. Bertram, Heidelberg, 1586 —7, 1599, 1616; D. Wolder, Hamburg, 1596; Michael Le Jay, Paris, 1645.

2. In February 15$\frac{18}{19}$, after the printing of the Complutensian Polyglott but before its publication, Andreas Asolanus[1], father-in-law of the elder Aldus, issued from the Aldine press a complete edition of the Greek Bible bearing the title : Πάντα τὰ κατ᾽ ἐξοχὴν καλούμενα βιβλία, θείας δηλαδὴ γραφῆς παλαιᾶς τε καὶ νέας. Sacrae scripturae veteris novaeque omnia. *Colophon :* Venetiis in aedib[us] Aldi et Andreae soceri. mdxviii., mense Februario.

Like Ximenes, Andreas made it his business to examine the best MSS. within his reach. In the dedication he writes : "ego multis vetustissimis exemplaribus collatis biblia (ut vulgo appellant) graece cuncta descripsi." His words, however, do not suggest an extended search for MSS., such as was instituted by the Spanish Cardinal; and it is probable enough that he was content to use Bessarion's collection of codices, which is still preserved in St Mark's Library at Venice[2]. Traces have

(Leipzig, 1871); Lagarde, *Libr. V. T. can.* i., p. iii.; E. Nestle, *Septuagintastudien,* i., pp. 2, 13; E. Klostermann, *Analecta,* p. 15 f.

[1] On the orthography see Nestle, *Septuagintastudien,* ii., p. 11, note *b.*
[2] Cf. Lagarde, *Genesis graece,* p. 6; Cornill, *Ezechiel,* p. 79; Nestle,

been found in his text of three at least of those MSS. (cod. ii =
H.P. 29; cod. iii = H.P. 121; cod. v = H.P. 68).

The Aldine text of the LXX. was followed on the whole in
the editions of (1) Joh. Lonicerus, Strassburg, 1524, 1526; (2)?
with a preface by Philip Melanchthon, Basle, 1545; (3) H.
Guntius, Basle, 1550, 1582; (4) Draconites, in *Biblia Pentapla*,
Wittenburg, 1562—5; (5) Francis du Jon (Fr. Junius) or (?) Fr.
Sylburg, Frankfort, 1597; (6) Nic. Glykas, Venice, 1687.

3. In 1587 a third great edition of the Greek Old Testament was published at Rome under the auspices of Sixtus V.
(*editio Sixtina, Romana*). It bears the title: Η ΠΑΛΑΙΑ ΔΙΑΘΗΚΗ |
ΚΑΤΑ ΤΟΥΣ ΕΒΔΟΜΗΚΟΝΤΑ | ΔΙ ΑΥΘΕΝΤΙΑΣ | ΞΥΣΤΟΥ Ε′ ΑΚΡΟΥ ΑΡΧΙΕ-
ΡΕΩΣ | ΕΚΔΟΘΕΙΣΑ | VETVS TESTAMENTVM | IVXTA SEPTVAGINTA |
EX AVCTORITATE | SIXTI V. PONT. MAX. | EDITVM | ROMAE |
EX TYPOGRAPHIA FRANCISCI ZANETTI. M.D.LXXXVI(I)[1] | CVM
PRIVILEGIO GEORGIO FERRARIO CONCESSO.

The volume consists of 783 pages of text, followed by a
page of addenda and corrigenda, and preceded by three (unnumbered) leaves which contain (1) a dedicatory letter addressed
to Sixtus V. by Cardinal Antonio Carafa, (2) a preface to the
reader[2], and (3) the papal authorisation of the book. These
documents are so important for the history of the printed text
that they must be given in full.

(1) SIXTO QUINTO PONTIF. MAX. ANTONIUS CARAFA
CARDINALIS SANCTAE SEDIS APOSTOLICAE BIBLIOTHECARIUS

Annus agitur iam fere octavus ex quo Sanctitas vestra pro
singulari suo de sacris litteris benemerendi studio auctor fuit
beatae memoriae Gregorio XIII. Pont. Max. ut sacrosancta Sep-

Urtext, p. 65. On the source of the Psalms in this edition see Nestle,
Septuagintastudien, iii., p. 32.

[1] The second i has been added in many copies with the pen. The
impression was worked off in 1586, but the work was not published until
May 1587.

[2] "Elle n'est point signée, mais on sait qu'elle fut redigée par Fulvio
Orsini. Elle est d'ailleurs très inférieure à la lettre de Caraia." (P. Batiffol,
La Vaticane de Paul III. à Paul V., p. 89).

tuaginta Interpretum Biblia, quibus Ecclesia tum Graeca tum
Latina iam inde ab Apostolorum temporibus usa est, ad fidem
probatissimorum codicum emendarentur. Quod enim Sanctitas V.
pro accurata sua in perlegendis divinis scripturis diligentia anim-
advertisset, infinitos pene locos ex iis non eodem modo ab
antiquis sacris scriptoribus afferri quo in vulgatis Bibliorum
Graecis editionibus circumferrentur, existimassetque non aliunde
eam lectionum varietatem quam e multiplici eaque confusa veterum
interpretatione fluxisse; rectissime censuit ad optimae notae
exemplaria provocandum esse, ex quibus, quoad fieri posset, ea
quae vera et sincera esset Septuaginta Interpretum scriptura
eliceretur. Ex quo fit ut vestram non solum pietatem sed etiam
sapientiam magnopere admirer; cum videam S. V. de Graecis
Bibliis expoliendis idem multos post annos in mentem venisse
quod sanctos illos Patres Tridenti congregatos auctoritate ac
reverentia ductos verae ac purae Septuaginta interpretationis
olim cogitasse cognovi ex actis eius Concilii nondum pervulgatis.
Huius autem expolitionis constituendae munus cum mihi deman-
datum esset a Gregorio XIII., cuius cogitationes eo maxime
spectabant ut Christiana Religio quam latissime propagaretur,
operam dedi ut in celebrioribus Italiae bibliothecis optima quaeque exemplaria perquirerentur atque ex iis lectionum varietates
descriptae ad me mitterentur[1]. Quibus sane doctorum hominum
quos ad id delegeram industria et iudicio clarae memoriae
Gulielmi Cardinalis Sirleti (quem propter excellentem doctrinam et multiplicem linguarum peritiam in locis obscurioribus
mihi consulendum proposueram) persaepe examinatis et cum
vestro Vaticanae bibliothecae (cui me benignitas vestra nuper
praefecit) exemplari diligenter collatis; intelleximus cum ex ipsa
collatione tum e sacrorum veterum scriptorum consensione,
Vaticanum codicem non solum vetustate verum etiam bonitate
caeteris anteire; quodque caput est, ad ipsam quam quaere-
bamus Septuaginta interpretationem, si non toto libro, maiori
certe ex parte, quam proxime accedere. Quod mihi cum multis
aliis argumentis constaret, vel ipso etiam libri titulo, qui est κατὰ
τοὺς ἑβδομήκοντα, curavi de consilio et sententia eorum quos supra
nominavi, huius libri editionem ad Vaticanum exemplar emen-
dandam; vel potius exemplar ipsum, quod eius valde probaretur
auctoritas, de verbo ad verbum repraesentandum, accurate prius
sicubi opus fuit recognitum et notationibus etiam auctum. Factum
est autem providentia sane divina, ut quod Sanctitate vestra
suadente sui Cardinalatus tempore inchoatum est, id variis de
causis aliquoties intermissum per ipsa fere initia Pontificatus sui

[1] On the genesis of the Sixtine edition the curious reader may consult
Nestle, *Septuagintastudien,* i., ii., where the particulars are collected with
the utmost care and fulness.

fuerit absolutum; scilicet ut hoc praeclarum opus, vestro Sanctissimo nomini dicatum, quasi monumentum quoddam perpetuum esset futurum apud omnes bonos et vestrae erga Rempublicam Christianam voluntatis et meae erga Sanctitatem vestram observantiae.

(2) Praefatio ad Lectorem

Qui sunt in sacrosanctis scripturis accuratius versati, fatentur omnes Graecam Septuaginta Interpretum editionem longe aliis omnibus quibus Graeci usi sunt et antiquiorem esse et probatiorem. Constat enim eos Interpretes, natione quidem Iudaeos, doctos vero Graece, trecentis uno plus annis ante Christi adventum, cum in Aegypto regnaret Ptolemaeus Philadelphus, Spiritu sancto plenos sacra Biblia interpretatos esse, eamque interpretationem a primis Ecclesiae nascentis temporibus tum publice in Ecclesiis ad legendum propositam fuisse, tum privatim receptam et explanatam ab Ecclesiasticis scriptoribus qui vixerunt ante B. Hieronymum, Latinae vulgatae editionis auctorem. Nam Aquila quidem Sinopensis, qui secundus post Septuaginta eosdem libros ex Hebraeo in Graecum convertit et multo post tempore sub Hadriano principe floruit, et eius interpretatio, (quod ea quae de Christo in scripturis praedicta fuerant, ut a Iudaeis gratiam iniret aliter quam Septuaginta vertendo, subdola obscuritate involverit) iamdiu est cum a recte sentientibus, licet in hexaplis haberetur, aliquibus locis non est probata. Hunc vero qui subsequuti sunt, Symmachus et Theodotio, alter Samaritanus sub L. Vero, alter Ephesius sub Imp. Commodo, uterque (quamvis et ipsi in hexaplis circumferrentur) parum fidus interpres habitus est : Symmachus, quod Samaritanis offensus, ut placeret Iudaeis, non unum sanctae scripturae locum perturbato sensu corruperit ; Theodotio, quod Marcionis haeretici sectator nonnullis locis perverterit potius quam converterit sacros libros. Fuerunt praeter has apud Graecos aliae duae editiones incertae auctoritatis : altera Antonio Caracalla Imp. apud Hierichuntem, altera apud Nicopolim sub Alexandro Severo in doliis repertae. quae quod in octaplis inter Graecas editiones quintum et sextum locum obtinerent, quintae et sextae editionis nomen retinuerunt. Sed nec hae satis fidae interpretationes habitae sunt. His additur alia quaedam editio sancti Luciani martyris, qui vixit sub Diocletiano et Maximiano Impp., valde illa quidem probata, sed quae cum Septuaginta Interpretibus comparari nullo modo possit, vel ipsis etiam Graecis scriptoribus testantibus et Niceta confirmante his plane verbis in commentario Psalmorum : ἡμεῖς δὲ καὶ τὴν τοιαύτην ἔκδοσιν σεβαζόμενοι, τῇ τῶν ἑβδομήκοντα προσκείμεθα μάλιστα, ὅτι διῃρημένως τὴν τῆς

διαλέκτου μεταβολὴν ποιησάμενοι μίαν ἐν ἑκάστοις ἔννοιαν καὶ λέξιν
ἀποδεδώκασιν.

Adeo Septuaginta Interpretum editio magni nominis apud
omnes fuit; nimirum quae instinctu quodam divinitatis elabo-
rata bono generis humani prodierit in lucem. Sed haec etiam
ipsa, quod in hexaplis ita primum ab Origene collocata
fuerit ut eius e regione aliae editiones quo inter se comparari
commodius possent ad legendum propositae essent, deinde
vero varietates tantum ex iis ad illam sub obelis et asteriscis
notari essent coeptae, factum est ut vetustate notis obliteratis
insincera nimis et valde sui dissimilis ad nos pervenerit : quippe
quae insertis ubique aliorum interpretationibus, aliquibus autem
locis duplici atque etiam triplici eiusdem sententiae interpretatione intrusa, male praeterea a librariis accepta, suum ob id
nitorem integritatemque amiserit. Hinc illae lectionum penitus
inter se dissidentes varietates et, quod doctissimorum hominum
ingenia mentesque diu torsit, ipsae exemplarium non solum inter
se sed a veteribus etiam scriptoribus dissensiones. Quod malum
primo a multis ignoratum, ab aliis postea neglectum, quotidie
longius serpens, principem librum, et a quo tota lex divina et
Christiana pendent instituta, non levibus maculis inquinavit.
Quo nomine dici non potest quantum omnes boni debeant
Sixto V. Pont. Max. Is enim quod in sacris litteris, unde
sanctissimam hausit doctrinam, aetatem fere totam contriverit,
quodque in hoc libro cum veterum scriptis conferendo singu-
larem quandam diligentiam adhibuerit, vidit primus qua ratione
huic malo medendum esset; nec vidit solum, sed auctoritate
etiam sua effecit ut summus Pontifex Gregorius XIII. Graeca
Septuaginta Interpretum Biblia, adhibita diligenti castigatione,
in pristinum splendorem restituenda curaret. Quam rem exe-
quendam cum ille demandasset Antonio Carafae Cardinali, viro
veteris sanctitatis et omnium honestarum artium cultori, nulla
is interposita mora delectum habuit doctissimorum hominum
qui domi suae statis diebus exemplaria manuscripta, quae
permulta undique conquisierat, conferrent et ex iis optimas
quasque lectiones elicerent; quibus deinde cum codice Vaticanae bibliothecae saepe ac diligenter comparatis intellectum
est, eum codicem omnium qui extant longe optimum esse, ac
operae pretium fore si ad eius fidem nova haec editio para-
retur.

Sed emendationis consilio iam explicato, ipsa quoque ratio
quae in emendando adhibita est nunc erit aperienda, in primis-
que Vaticanus liber describendus, ad cuius praescriptum haec
editio expolita est. Codex is, quantum ex forma characterum
coniici potest, cum sit maioribus litteris quas vere antiquas
vocant exaratus, ante millesimum ducentesimum annum, hoc est
ante tempora B. Hieronymi et non infra, scriptus videtur. Ex

omnibus autem libris qui in manibus fuerunt unus hic prae aliis, quia ex editione Septuaginta si non toto libro certe maiorem partem constare visus est, mirum in modum institutam emendationem adiuvit; post eum vero alii duo qui ad eius vetustatem proximi quidem sed longo proximi intervallo accedunt, unus Venetus ex bibliotheca Bessarionis Cardinalis, et is quoque grandioribus litteris scriptus ; alter qui ex Magna Graecia advectus nunc est Carafae Cardinalis : qui liber cum Vaticano codice ita in omnibus consentit ut credi possit ex eodem archetypo descriptus esse. Praeter hos magno etiam usui fuerunt libri ex Medicea bibliotheca Florentiae collati, qui Vaticanas lectiones multis locis aut confirmarunt aut illustrarunt. Sed libri Vaticani bonitas non tam ex horum codicum miro consensu perspecta est, quam ex iis locis qui partim adducuntur partim explicantur ab antiquis sacris scriptoribus ; qui fere nusquam huius exemplaris lectiones non exhibent ac reponunt, nisi ubi aliorum Interpretum locum aliquem afferunt, non Septuaginta. quorum editio cum esset nova emendatione perpolienda, recte ad huius libri normam, qui longe omnium antiquissimus, solus iuxta Septuaginta inscribitur, perpolita est ; vel potius rectissime liber ipse ad litteram, quoad fieri potuit per antiquam orthographiam aut per librarii lapsus, est expressus. Nam vetus illa et iam obsoleta eius aetatis scriptura aliquibus locis repraesentata non est; cum tamen in aliis omnibus, nisi ubi manifestus apparebat librarii lapsus, ne latum quidem unguem, ut aiunt, ab huius libri auctoritate discessum sit, ne in iis quidem quae si minus mendo, certe suspicione mendi videbantur non carere. satius enim visum est locos vel aliquo modo suspectos (nec enim fieri potest ut in quantumvis expurgato exemplari non aliqua supersit macula) quemadmodum habentur in archetypo relinqui quam eos ex alicuius ingenio aut coniectura emendari : quod multa quae primo vel mendosa vel mutilata in hoc codice videbantur, ea postea cum aliis libris collata vera et sincera reperirentur. Nam in libris Prophetarum, qui maxime in hoc exemplari (uno excepto Daniele) puram Septuaginta editionem resipiunt, mirum quam multa non habeantur ; quae tamen recte abesse et eorum Interpretum non esse, intellectum est tum ex commentariis veterum scriptorum Graecis et Latinis, tum ex libris manuscriptis in quibus illa addita sunt sub asteriscis.

Atque haec ratio in notationibus quoque servata est, in quibus cum multa sint ex commentariis Graecis petita quae in codicibus manuscriptis partim mutilata partim varie scripta aliquibus locis circumferuntur, ea non aliter atque in archetypis exemplaribus reperiuntur descripta sunt, quo uniuscuiusque arbitratu adiuvantibus libris restitui possint. Nec vero illud omittendum, quod item pertinet ad notationes ; non omnia in iis repraesentata esse quae aut ad confirmandas lectiones Vaticanas e scriptoribus vulgatis, aut ad explenda quae in Septuaginta non habentur, ex aliorum editionibus afferri potuissent, quod in communibus libris cum legantur, inde sibi unusquisque nullo negotio ea parare possit. Quae vero in libris manuscriptis reperta, vel ad indicandas antiquarum tum lectionum tum interpretationum varietates (sub scholii illas nomine, quod ipsarum incerta esset auctoritas, nonnunquam relatas) vel ad stabiliendam scripturam Vaticanam et eius obscuriores locos illustrandos pertinere visa sunt, ea certe non sunt praetermissa.

Ordo autem librorum in Vaticano exemplari cum idem fere sit cum eo qui apud Graecos circumfertur, a vulgatis tamen editionibus variat in hoc quod primo habet duodecim Prophetas et hos ipsos aliter dispositos ; deinde reliquos quattuor, quemadmodum vulgo editi sunt. Atque hunc ordinem verum esse intelligimus ex eo quod illum agnoscunt et probant veteres Ecclesiastici scriptores. Et cum toto exemplari nulla capitum divisio sit, (nam in nova editione consultum est legentium commoditati) in libro tamen quattuor Prophetarum distinctio quaedam apparet subobscura, illi paene similis quam describit sanctus Dorotheus martyr, qui vixit sub Magno Constantino.

Maccabaeorum libri absunt ab hoc exemplari, atque item liber Genesis fere totus ; nam longo aevo consumptis membranis mutilatus est ab initio libri usque ad caput XLVII. et liber item Psalmorum, qui a Psalmo CV. usque ad CXXXVIII. nimia vetustate mancus est. Sed haec ex aliorum codicum collatione emendata sunt.

Quod si aliqua videbuntur in hac editione, ut ait B. Hieronymus, vel lacerata vel inversa, quod ea sub obelis et asteriscis ab Origene suppleta et distincta non sint ; vel obscura et perturbata, quod cum Latina vulgata non consentiant, et in aliquibus aliis editionibus apertius et expressius habeantur; eris lector admonendus, non eo spectasse huius expolitionis industriam ut haec editio ex permixtis eorum qui supra nominati sunt interpretationibus (instar eius quam scribit B. Hieronymus a Graecis κοινήν, a nostris appellatam Communem) concinnata, Latinae vulgatae editioni, hoc est Hebraeo, ad verbum respondeat ; sed ut ad eam quam Septuaginta Interpretes Spiritus sancti auctoritatem sequuti ediderunt, quantum per veteres libros fieri potest, quam proxime accedat. Quam nunc novis emendationibus illustratam et aliorum Interpretum reliquiis quae supersunt auctam, non parum profuturam ad Latinae vulgatae intelligentiam, dubitabit nemo qui hanc cum illa accurate comparaverit.

Quae si doctis viris et pie sentientibus, ut aequum est, probabuntur, reliquum erit ut Sixto V. Pont. Max. huius boni auctori gratias agant, et ab omnipotenti Deo publicis votis poscant,

optimum Principem nobis florentem quam diutissime servet.
qui cum omnes curas cogitationesque suas in amplificandam
ornandamque Ecclesiae dignitatem contulerit, dubitandum non
est quin Rep. Christiana optimis legibus et sanctissimis institutis
per eum reformata, religione ac pietate, revocatis antiquis ritibus,
in suum splendorem restituta, in hoc quoque publicam causam
sit adiuturus ut sacri veteres libri, hominum incuria vel improbi-
tate corrupti, pro sua eximia benignitate ab omni labe vindicati,
quam emendatissimi pervulgentur.

(3) Sixtus Papa V.

Ad perpetuam rei memoriam. Cupientes, quantum in nobis
est, commissi nobis gregis saluti quacunque ratione ac via pro-
spicere, ad pastoralem nostram curam pertinere vehementer
arbitramur Sacrae Scripturae libros, quibus salutaris doctrina
continetur, ab omnibus maculis expurgatos integros purosque
pervulgari. Id nos in inferiori gradu constituti, quantum potui-
mus, studio et diligentia nostra praestitimus, et in hac altissima
specula a Deo collocati assidue mentis nostrae oculis spectare
non desistimus. Cum itaque superioribus annis piae recorda-
tionis Gregorius Papa XIII. praedecessor noster, nobis sugge-
rentibus, Graecum Vetus Testamentum iuxta Septuaginta Interpretum editionem, qua ipsi etiam Apostoli nonnunquam usi
fuerunt, ad emendatissimorum codicum fidem expoliendum
mandaverit; eius rei cura dilecto filio nostro Antonio Sanctae
Romanae Ecclesiae Presbytero Cardinali Carafae, et ad id per
eum delectis eruditis aliquot viris demandata, et iam expolitio
huiusmodi, permultis exemplaribus ex diversis Italiae bibliothecis
et praecipue ex nostra Vaticana diligenter collatis matureque
examinatis, absoluta sit: Volumus et sancimus ad Dei gloriam
et Ecclesiae utilitatem, ut Vetus Graecum Testamentum iuxta
Septuaginta ita recognitum et expolitum ab omnibus recipiatur
ac retineatur, quo potissimum ad Latinae vulgatae editionis et
veterum Sanctorum Patrum intelligentiam utantur. Prohibentes
ne quis de hac nova Graeca editione audeat in posterum vel
addendo vel demendo quicquam immutare. Si quis autem
aliter fecerit quam hac nostra sanctione comprehensum est,
noverit se in Dei Omnipotentis beatorumque Apostolorum Petri
et Pauli indignationem incursurum.

Datum Romae apud Sanctum Marcum sub Anulo Piscatoris.
Die viii Octobris M.D.LXXXVI, Pontificatus nostri anno secundo.
Tho. Thom. Gualterutius.

The reader will not fail to note the intelligent appreciation
of the LXX., and the wide outlook over the history of the Greek

versions which are implied by these documents[1]. They shew
that the Vatican had already learnt the true value of the
Alexandrian Old Testament and, as a consequence, had re-
solved to place in the hands of the scholars of Europe as pure
a text as could be obtained of the version which was used by
the ancient Church, and was now felt to be essential to a right
understanding of the Fathers and of the Latin Vulgate. The
inception of the work was due to Pope Sixtus himself, who
had suggested it to his predecessor Gregory XIII. in 1578;
but the execution was entrusted to Cardinal Antonio Carafa
and a little band of Roman scholars including Cardinal Sirleto,
Antonio Agelli, and Petrus Morinus. Search was made in the
libraries of Italy as well as in the Vatican for MSS. of the LXX.,
but the result of these enquiries satisfied the editors of the
superiority of the great Vatican Codex (B = cod. Vat. gr. 1209)
over all other known codices, and it was accordingly taken as
the basis of the new edition. Use was made, however, of other
MSS., among which were a Venice MS. which has been identified with S. Marc. cod. gr. 1 (H. P. 23, Lag. V); a MS. belonging to Carafa, possibly cod. Vat. gr. 1252 (H. P. 63 + 129, cf.
Klostermann, p. 12 f., and Batiffol, *Bulletin critique*, 15 Mars
1889), and certain Laurentian MSS. of which collations are
still preserved in the Vatican Library (Vat. gr. 1241, 1242,
1244; see Batiffol, *La Vaticane*, p. 90 f.). From these and
other sources the editors supplied the large lacunae of Cod. B[2].
But they did not limit themselves to the filling up of gaps or
even to the correction of errors, as will appear from a
comparison of the Sixtine text with the photographic representation of the Vatican MS. The edition of 1587 is not an
exact reproduction of a single codex, even where the selected
MS. was available; but it is based as a whole on a great uncial

---

[1] Cf. Tregelles, *An account of the printed text, &c.*, p. 185.
[2] According to Nestle (*Septuagintastudien*, i. p. 9, ii. p. 12) Genesis i.
1—xlvi. 28 in cod. B are supplied from cod. Chis. R. vi. 38 (H.P. 19, Lag. *h*).

MS., and it is the first edition of the LXX. which possesses this character. Moreover, criticism has confirmed the judgement of the Roman editors in regard to the selection of their basal MS. It ·is a fortunate circumstance that the authority of the Vatican was given before the end of the sixteenth century to a text of the LXX. which is approximately pure.

Besides the text the Roman edition contained considerable materials for the criticism of the Greek Old Testament, collected by the labours of Morinus, Agelli, Nobilius, and others. These include readings and scholia from MSS. of the LXX., renderings from Aquila and the other non-Septuagintal Greek versions, and a large assortment of patristic citations.

Editions based upon the Sixtine are very numerous. The following list is abridged from Nestle's *Urtext* (p. 65 ff.):
1. Jo. Morinus, Paris, 1628, 1641. 2. R. Daniel, London, 4to and 8vo, 1653; Cambridge, 1653. 3. B. Walton, London, 1657 (the third column of his Polyglott). 4. Field, Cambridge, 1665 (with the *praefatio paraenetica* of J. Pearson[1], Lady Margaret Professor of Divinity, afterwards Bp of Chester). 5. J. Leusden, Amsterdam, 1683. 6. Leipzig, 1697 (with prolegomena by J. Frick). 7. L. Bos, Frankfort, 1709. 8. D. Mill, Amsterdam, 1725. 9. C. Reineccius, Leipzig, 1730. 10. Halle, 1759—62 (with a preface by J. G. Kirchner). 11. Holmes and Parsons, Oxford, 1798—1827. 12. Oxford, 1817 (with introduction by J. [G.][2] Carpzow). 13. F. Valpy, London, 1819. 14. London, 1821, 26, 31, 51, 69, 78 (the LXX. column of Bagster's Polyglott). 15. Venice, 1822. 16. Glasgow and London, 1822, 31, 43. 17. L. Van Ess, Leipzig, 1824, 35, 55, 68, 79, 87 (prolegomena and epilegomena separately in 1887). 18. London, 1837. 19. Didot, Paris, 1839, 40, 48, 55, 78, 82. 20. Oxford, 1848, 75. 21. A. F. C. von Tischendorf, Leipzig, 1850, 56, 60, 69, 75, 80, 87.
Of the above some are derived from the Sixtine indirectly, whilst others present a Sixtine text more or less modified, or accompanied by variants from other MSS.

4. The example of Rome was followed in the 18th century by England, which had meanwhile acquired an uncial Bible

---

[1] The *praefatio* was reprinted with Archd. Churton's notes by Prof. W. Selwyn (Cambridge, 1855). The 1665 edition was reissued by John Hayes, 1684.

[2] See Nestle, *Septuagintastudien*, iii.. p. 32, note *p*.

only less ancient, and in the view of some scholars textually more important than the great Vatican MS. The variants of Codex Alexandrinus had been given in Walton's Polyglott under the Sixtine text[1], but the honour of producing an edition on the basis of the English codex belongs to a Prussian scholar, John Ernest Grabe, an adopted son of the University of Oxford. This edition appeared ultimately in four folio volumes (1707—20), but only the first and fourth had been published when Grabe died (1712); the second and third were undertaken after his decease by Francis Lee, M.D., and William Wigan, D.D. respectively. Vol. i. (1707) contains the Octateuch, Vol. ii. (1719) the Historical Books, Vol. iii. (1720) the Prophets, Vol. iv. (1709) the Poetical Books. The title to the first volume runs: "Septuaginta | interpretum | tomus I | continens Octateuchum | quem | ex antiquissimo codice Alexandrino | accurate descriptum | et ope aliorum exemplarium, ac priscorum scriptorum | praesertim vero Hexaplaris editionis Origenianae | emendatum atque suppletum | additis saepe asteriscorum et obelorum signis | summa cura edidit | Joannes Ernestus Grabe S.T.P. | Oxonii, e theatro Sheldoniano | ...MDCCVII."

This title sufficiently indicates the general principles upon which this great undertaking was based. Like the Sixtine edition, Grabe's is in the main a presentation of the text exhibited in a single uncial codex; like the Sixtine, but to a greater extent, its text is in fact eclectic and mixed. On the other hand the mixture in Grabe's Alexandrian text is overt and can be checked at every point. He deals with his codex as Origen dealt with the κοινή, marking with an obelus the words, clauses, or paragraphs in the MS. for which he found no equivalent in the Massoretic Hebrew, and placing an aste-

---

[1] Patrick Young had projected a complete edition of cod. A (Walton's *Prolegomena*, ed. Wrangham, ii. p. 124). His transcript of the MS. is still preserved at the British Museum (Harl. 7522 = Holmes 241; see above, p. 152).

risk before such as he believed to have been derived from
Theodotion or some other non-Septuagintal source. If he
constantly adds to his MS. or relegates its readings to the
margin, such additions and substituted words are distinguished
from the text of cod. A by being printed in a smaller type.
So far as it professes to reproduce the text of the MS., his
edition is substantially accurate. The prolegomena by which
each volume is introduced are full and serviceable; and the
work as a whole, whatever may be thought of the method
adopted by the editors, is creditable to the Biblical scholarship
of the age.

Grabe's text was reproduced by Breitinger (Zurich, 1730—2),
and Reineccius (in his *Biblia sacra quadrilinguia*, Leipzig,
1750—1); also in a Greek Bible issued at Moscow in 1821 under
the authority of the Holy Synod. A more important work based
upon this edition is the Septuagint published by the Society for
Promoting Christian Knowledge under the care of Dr Field
(*Vetus Testamentum Graece iuxta LXX. interpretes. Recensionem Grabianam ad fidem codicis Alexandrini aliorumque
denuo recognovit...F. Field*, Oxonii, 1859). But the purpose
which the Society had in view forbade a critical treatment of the
materials, and whilst the learned editor has removed many of the
imperfections of Grabe's work, the text remains arbitrary and
mixed, and the arrangement is alien from that of all LXX. MSS.
the non-canonical books being relegated to an appendix as
ἀπόκρυφα.

5. Each of the four great editions of the Septuagint already
described (the Complutensian, Aldine, Sixtine, and Grabian)
endeavoured to supply a text approximately representing either
a group of MSS., or a single uncial of high antiquity. No
attempt had been made as yet to offer an exact reproduction
of a codex, or to provide a full *apparatus criticus*, the purpose
of the editors in each case being practical rather than critical.
This want was met in some degree in certain of the secondary
editions; thus the Basle reprint of the Aldine text (1545)
gave a short list of variants and conjectural emendations; in
the London Polyglott the readings of Codex Alexandrinus

were printed underneath the Sixtine text, and those of Codex Sarravianus were exhibited in the Septuagint of Lambert Bos. But the first comprehensive effort in this direction was made by Robert Holmes (1748—1805), Professor of Poetry at Oxford, and Canon of Christ Church, and, from 1804, Dean of Winchester. The preparations for his great work were begun in 1788. An appeal was made to the liberality of public bodies and private patrons of learning, and the task of collating MSS. was committed to a large number of scholars at home and on the continent, whose names are honourably mentioned in the opening pages of the first volume. From 1789 to 1805 an annual account was printed of the progress of the work[1], and the Bodleian Library contains 164 volumes of MS. collations (Holmes MSS. A.D. 1789—1805, nos. 16455—16617)[2] which were deposited there during those seventeen years. In 1795 a specimen of the forthcoming work was published together with a transcript of the Vienna Genesis in a letter to the Bishop of Durham (Shute Barrington). Genesis appeared separately in 1798, followed in the same year by the first volume bearing the title : *Vetus Testamentum Graecum cum variis lectionibus. Edidit Robertus Holmes, S.T.P., R.S.S., Aedis Christi Canonicus. Tomus primus. Oxonii : e typographeo Clarendoniano.* MDCCXCVIII. This volume, which contains the Pentateuch, with a preface and appendix, was the only one which Holmes lived to complete. He died Nov. 12, 1805, and two years later the editorship was entrusted to James Parsons[3], under whose care the remaining volumes were issued (Vol. ii., Joshua—2 Chronicles, 1810 ; Vol. iii., 2 Esdras—Canticles, 1823 ; Vol. iv., Prophets, 1827 ; Vol. v., the non-canonical books, 1 Esdras—3 Maccabees, 1827). At the end of Vol. v. there is a list of the Greek MSS. collated

---

[1] Cf. *Ch. Q. R.*, April 1899, p. 102.

[2] Cf. Madan's *Summary catalogue of MSS. in the Bodleian: Eighteenth century collections*, pp. 614—641.

[3] On Holmes' less distinguished coadjutor see *Ch. Q. R.* p. 104. Parsons died in 1847 at the age of 85.

for the work. Three hundred and eleven are enumerated (i.—
xiii., 14—311); a corrected estimate gives a total of 297 separate
codices, of which 20 are uncial. Besides the readings of this
large number of Greek MSS., the apparatus of Holmes and
Parsons exhibits the evidence of the Old Latin versions so far
as it had been collected by Sabatier, and of the Coptic (Memphitic and Sahidic), Arabic, Slavonic, Armenian and Georgian
versions, obtained partly from MSS., partly from printed texts.
Use was also made of patristic citations and of the four great
editions of the Septuagint, the Sixtine supplying the text, while
the Aldine, Complutensian and Alexandrine (Grabian) are cited
in the notes. In addition to these, Holmes employed the
printed text of the catena of Nicephorus (Leipzig, 1772—3),
and J. F. Fischer's edition of cod. Lips. 361 (Leipzig, 1767—8)[1].

The great work of Holmes and Parsons has been severely
criticised by later scholars, especially by Hatch[2] and Lagarde[3].
A vigorous defence of the Oxford editors will be found in a
recent article in the *Church Quarterly Review* (already quoted).
It appears to be certain that every effort was made by Holmes
to secure the services of the best scholars who were available
for the work of collation.

> Among the collators of Greek MSS. employed by the Oxford
> editors were Bandini (Florence), C. F. Matthäi (Moscow), F. C.
> Alter (Vienna), Schnurrer (Tübingen), Moldenhawer (Copen-
> hagen). "The Armenian Version was chiefly collated by Her-
> mannus Breden-Kemp (1793) and F. C. Alter (1795—1804), the
> latter also taking the Georgian..the Slavonic..Coptic..and
> Bohemian Versions. The Arabic Versions were undertaken
> by Paulus and Prof. Ford, and the Syriac quotations in the *Hor-*
> *reum mysteriorum* of Gregorius Bar-Hebraeus..by Dr Holmes"
> (F. C. Madan, *Summary catalogue*, p. 640).

But in so vast an accumulation of the labours of many
workers it was impossible to maintain an uniform standard of
merit; nor are the methods adopted by Holmes and his con-

---

[1] See above, p. 153.   [2] *Essays in Biblical Greek*, p. 132.
[3] *Libr. V. T. Canon. p. i.* p. xv.

tinuator altogether such as would commend themselves at the present day. The work is an almost unequalled monument of industry and learning, and will perhaps never be superseded as a storehouse of materials; but it left abundant room for investigations conducted on other lines and among materials which were not accessible to Holmes and his associates.

6. The next step was taken by A. F. C. von Tischendorf (1815—1874), who in the midst of his researches in Eastern libraries and his work upon the text of the New Testament found leisure to project and carry through four editions (1850, 1856, 1860, 1869) a manual text of the Septuagint. Its plan was simple, but suggestive. His text was a revised Sixtine; underneath it he placed an apparatus limited to the variants of a few great uncials: "eam viam ingressus sum (he writes[1]) ut textum per tria fere secula probatissimum repeterem, mutatis tantummodo quibus mutatione maxime opus esset, addita vero plena lectionis varietate ex tribus codicibus antiquissimis quos fere solos utpote editos confidenter adhibere licebat." The three MSS. employed by Tischendorf in his first edition (1850) were A (from Baber's facsimile), C (from his own facsimile), and FA, the portion of Cod. Sinaiticus which was published in 1846; in the third and fourth editions he was able to make further use of Cod. Sinaiticus, and to take into account Mai's edition of Cod. B.

Since Tischendorf's death three more editions of his Septuagint have appeared—a fifth in 1875, a sixth and a seventh in 1880 and 1887 respectively, the last two under the supervision of Dr Eberhard Nestle. Nestle added a *Supplementum editionum quae Sixtinam sequuntur omnium in primis Tischendorfianarum,* consisting of a collation of the Vatican and Sinaitic MSS. with the Sixtine text, the Vatican text being obtained from Vercellone and Cozza's facsimile, and the Sinaitic from Tischendorf's edition of א; an appendix contained a collation of Daniel (LXX.) from Cozza's edition of the Chigi MS. The *Supplementum* was reissued in 1887 with various enrichments, of which the most important

[1] *Prolegg.* § viii.

was a collation of cod. A from the London photograph which appeared in 1882—3. With these helps the reader of Tischendorf's Septuagint is able to correct and supplement the apparatus, and to compare the text with that of cod. B so far as it could be ascertained before the publication of the photograph.

7. Another of the great Biblical scholars of the nineteenth century, Paul de Lagarde, commenced an edition of the Greek Old Testament, which was intended to be a definite step towards the reconstruction of the text. Lagarde's general plan was announced in *Symmicta* ii. (1880), p. 137 ff., and in a modified and simpler form by a pamphlet published two years later (*Ankündigung einer neuen Ausgabe der griechischen übersetzung des A.T.*, Göttingen, 1882). A beginning was made by the appearance of the first half of the text of the Lucianic recension (*Librorum V.T. canonicorum pars prior Graece Pauli de Lagarde studio et sumptibus edita*, Göttingen, 1883). Lagarde's untimely death in 1891 left this work incomplete, and though his papers are preserved at Göttingen, it is understood that no steps will be taken to carry out the scheme, at least on the same lines. The published volume contains the Octateuch and the Historical Books as far as Esther. Of the last named book two texts are given, with an apparatus, but with this exception the text stands alone, and the reader knows only that it is an attempted reconstruction of Lucian, based upon six MSS. which are denoted *a f h m p z* (H. P. 108, 82, 19, 93, 118, 44). This is not the place to discuss Lagarde's critical principles, but it may be mentioned here that his attempt to reconstruct the text of Lucian's recension was but one of a series of projected reconstructions through which he hoped ultimately to arrive at a pure text of the Alexandrian version. The conception was a magnificent one, worthy of the great scholar who originated it; but it was beset with practical difficulties, and there is reason to hope that the desired end may be attained by means less complicated and more direct.

8. In the spring of 1883 the Syndics of the Cambridge

University Press issued a notice that they had undertaken
" [1] an edition of the Septuagint and Apocrypha with an ample
apparatus criticus intended to provide material for a critical
determination of the text," in which it was "proposed to give
the variations of all the Greek uncial MSS., of select Greek
cursive MSS., of the more important versions, and of the
quotations made by Philo and the earlier and more important
ecclesiastical writers." As a preliminary step they announced
the preparation of "a portable text...taken from the Vatican
MS., where this MS. is not defective, with the variations of two
or three other early uncial MSS." The suggestion was originally
due to Dr Scrivener, who submitted it to the Syndics of the
Press in the year 1875, but was ultimately prevented by many
preoccupations and failing health from carrying his project into
execution. After undergoing various modifications it was committed in 1883 to the present writer, instructed by a committee
consisting of Professors Westcott, Hort, Kirkpatrick, and Bensly;
to Dr Hort in particular the editor was largely indebted for
counsel in matters of detail. The first edition of the portable
text was completed in 1894 (*The Old Testament in Greek
according to the Septuagint*, vol. i., Genesis—4 Regn., 1887;
vol. ii., 1 Chron.—Tobit, 1891; vol. iii., Hosea—4 Macc.,
1894); the second and third revised editions [2] followed (vol. i.,
1895, 1901; vol. ii., 1896, 1907; vol. iii., 1899, 1905 [3]).
The larger Cambridge Septuagint has been entrusted to the
joint editorship of Dr A. E. Brooke, Fellow of King's College, and Mr N. McLean, Fellow of Christ's College; and
of the Octateuch, which will form the first volume, Genesis
appeared in 1906, Exod., Lev. 1909, Numb., Deut. 1911. It
reproduces the text of the manual Septuagint, but the apparatus
embraces, according to the original purpose of the Syndics,

---

[1] *Cambridge University Reporter*, March 13, 1883.
[2] Much of the labour of revision was generously undertaken by Dr Nestle,
and valuable assistance was also rendered by several English scholars; see
i. p. xxxiii., ii. p. xiv., iii. p. xviii. f.
[3] The fourth edition is in progress (i. 1909).

the evidence of all the uncial MSS., and of a considerable number of cursives "selected after careful investigation with the view of representing the different types of text"; the Old Latin, Egyptian, Syro-Hexaplar, and Armenian versions are also represented, whilst use is made of the quotations in Josephus as well as those in Philo and the more important Christian fathers. Such an apparatus falls far short of that presented by Holmes and Parsons, in regard to the quantity of evidence amassed; but efforts are being made to secure a relatively high degree of accuracy, and the materials are selected and arranged in such a manner as to enable the reader to study the grouping of the MSS. and other authorities. Thus the work proceeds upon the principle formulated by Lagarde : "editionem Veteris Testamenti Graeci...collatis integris codicum familiis esse curandam, nam familiis non accedere auctoritatem e codicibus, sed codicibus e familiis[1]."

A word may be added with regard to the text which will be common to the manual and the larger edition of the Cambridge Septuagint. It is that of the great Vatican MS., with its lacunae supplied from the uncial MS. which occupies the next place in point of age or importance. For a text formed in this way no more can be claimed than that it represents on the whole the oldest form of the Septuagint to be found in any one of our extant MSS. But it supplies at least an excellent standard of comparison, and until a critical text has been produced[2], it may fairly be regarded as the most trustworthy presentation of the Septuagint version regarded as a whole.

II. Editions of particular Books, or of Groups or Portions of Books.

The Pentateuch.

G. A. Schumann, 1829; *Pentateuchus hebraice et graece,* I (Genesis only published).

[1] *V. T. Libr. can.* praef. p. xvi.
[2] Cf. E. Nestle, *Zur Rekonstruktion der Septuaginta,* in *Philologus,* N. F. xii. (1899), p. 121 ff.

GENESIS.

P. A. de Lagarde, Leipzig, 1868 : *Genesis graece e fide editionis Sixtinae addita scripturae discrepantia e libris manu scriptis a se collatis et edd. Complutensi et Aldina adcuratissime enotata.* The MSS. employed are ADEFGS, 25, 29, 31, 44, 122, 130, 135. The text is preceded by useful lists of the available uncial MSS. and VSS. of the LXX.

DEUTERONOMY.

C. L. F. Hamann, Jena, 1874 : *Canticum Moysi ex Psalterio quadruplici...manu scripto quod Bambergae asservatur.*

JOSHUA.

A. Masius, Antwerp, 1574 : *Iosuae imperatoris historia.* Readings are given from the Codex Syro-hexaplaris Ambrosianus.

JUDGES.

J. Ussher, 1655 (in his *Syntagma*, Works, vol. vii.). Two texts in parallel columns (1) " ex codice Romano," (2) " ex codice Alexandrino."

O. F. Fritzsche, Zurich, 1867 : *liber Iudicum secundum lxx. interpretes.* A specimen had previously appeared (in 1866).

P. A. de Lagarde, 1891 (in his *Septuaginta-studien*, I. c. i.—v.). Two texts.

A. E. Brooke and N. McLean, Cambridge, 1897 : *The Book of Judges in Greek, acc. to the text of Codex Alexandrinus.*

[G. F. Moore, Andover, Mass. (in his *Critical and exegetical Commentary on Judges*, p. xlv.), promises an edition of the recension of the book exhibited by K, 54, 59, 75, 82, and Theodoret.]

RUTH.

Drusius, 1586, 1632.

L. Bos, Jena, 1788 : *Ruth ex versione lxx. interpretum secundum exemplar Vaticanum.*

O. F. Fritzsche, Zurich, 1867 : Ῥούθ κατὰ τοὺς ο'.

PSALMS.

Separate editions of the Greek Psalter were published at Milan, 1481; Venice, 1486; Venice, not later than 1498 (Aldus Manutius); Basle, 1516 (in *Hieronymi Opera*, t. viii., ed. Pellicanus); Genoa, 1516 (*Octaplum Psalterium Justiniani*); Cologne, 1518 (*Psalterium in iv. linguis cura Iohannis Potken*). Other known editions bear the dates 1524, 1530 (*Ps. sextuplex*),

1533, 1541, 1543, 1549, 1557, 1559, 1571, 1584, 1602, 1618, 1627, 1632, 1643, 1678 (the Psalter of cod. A), 1737, 1757, 1825, 1852, 1857, 1879 (*Ps. tetraglotton*, ed. Nestle), 1880, 1887 (Lagarde, *Novae psalterii gr. editionis specimen*), 1889 (Swete, *The Psalms in Greek acc. to the LXX., with the Canticles*; 2nd ed. 1896), 1892 (Lagarde, *Ps. gr. quinquagena prima*[1]).

JOB.

Patrick Young, 1637 (in the *Catena* of Nicetas).
J. Terrentius, Franeker, 1663.

ESTHER.

J. Ussher, 1655 (in his *Syntagma*, Works, vol. vii.). Two texts, one Hexaplaric from an Arundel MS. (H. P. 93). A second edition, Leipzig, 1696.
O. F. Fritzsche, Zurich, 1848 : Ἐσθήρ. *Duplicem libri textum ad opt. Codd. emendavit et cum selecta lectionis varietate edidit.* The Greek additions appear also in his *Libri apocryphi V. T.* (see below).

MINOR PROPHETS.

W. O. E. Oesterley, *Codex Taurinensis*, 1908 (with apparatus).

HOSEA.

J. Philippeaux, Paris, 1636; Hos. i.—iv., after Cod. Q.
D. Pareus, Heidelberg, 1605 : *Hoseas commentariis illustratus.*

AMOS.

Vater, Halle, 1810.
W. O. E. Oesterley, Cambridge, 1902 (parallel texts of Q, 22).

JONAH.

S. Münster, 1524, 1543.

ISAIAH.

S. Münster, 1540 (in Hebrew, Greek, and Latin).
J. Curter, Paris, 1580 (in *Procopii commentarii in Iesaiam*— text based on Cod. Q).
R. R. Ottley, Cambridge, 1906 (text of Cod. A).

JEREMIAH.

S. Münster, 1540.
G. L. Spohn, Leipzig, 1794: *Jeremias vates e vers. Judaeorum Alex. ac reliquorum interpretum Gr.* ; 2nd ed., 1824.

LAMENTATIONS.

Kyper, Basle, 1552 : *Libri tres de re gramm. Hebr. ling.* (Hebr Gr., Lat.).

[1] See also Nestle in Hastings, *D. B.* iv. 441.

EZEKIEL.

'Ιεζεκιὴλ κατὰ τοὺς ο', Rome, 1840.

DANIEL (Theod.).

Ph. Melanchthon, 1546.
Wells, 1716.

DANIEL (LXX.).

S. de Magistris (?), Rome, 1772 . *Daniel secundum lxx. ex tetraplis Origenis nunc primum editus e singulari Chisiano codice.* Reprinted at Göttingen, 1773, 1774 (Michaelis); at Utrecht, 1775 (Segaar); at Milan, 1788 (Bugati); and at Leipzig, 1845 (Hahn). Cozza, 1877. The LXX. text is also given in the editions of Holmes and Parsons, Oxf. ed. of 1848, 1875, Tischendorf, and Swete.

NON-CANONICAL BOOKS (in general)[1].

J. A. Fabricius, Frankfort and Leipzig, 1691 : *Liber Tobias, Judith, oratio Manasse, Sapientia, et Ecclesiasticus, gr. et lat., cum prolegomenis.* Other complete editions were published at Frankfort on the Main, 1694, and at Leipzig, 1804 and 1837 ; the best recent edition is that by

O. F. Fritzsche, Leipzig, 1871 : *Libri apocryphi V. T. gr.... accedunt libri V. T. pseudepigraphi selecti* [Psalmi Salomonis, 4—5 Esdras, Apocalypse of Baruch, Assumption of Moses]. This edition, besides the usual books, gives 4 Maccabees, and exhibits Esther in two texts, and Tobit in three ; there is a serviceable preface and an extensive apparatus criticus.

WISDOM OF SOLOMON.

Older editions : 1586, 1601, 1733, 1827.
Reusch, Freiburg, 1858; *Liber Sapientiae sec. exemplar Vaticanum.*
W. J. Deane, Oxford, 1881 : *The Book of Wisdom, the Greek text, the Latin Vulgate, and the A. V.; with an introduction, critical apparatus, and commentary.*

WISDOM OF SIRACH.

D. Hoeschel, Augsburg, 1604 : *Sapientia Sirachi s. Ecclesiasticus, collatis lectionibus var....cum notis.*
Linde, Dantzig, 1795 : *Sententiae Iesu Siracidae ad fidem codd. et versionum.*
Bretschneider, Regensburg, 1806 : *Liber Iesu Siracidae.*
Cowley-Neubauer, *Original Hebrew of a portion of Ecclesiasticus*, &c. (Oxford, 1897); Schechter-Taylor, *Wisdom of Ben Sira* (Cambridge, 1899)[2].
J. H. A. Hart, Cambridge, 1910 (text of Cod. 248).

[1] A fuller list is given by Nestle in Hastings, *D.B.* iv. 441.
[2] See Nestle's art. *Sirach* in Hastings, iv.

TOBIT.

Reusch, Bonn, 1870 : *Libellus Tobit e cod. Sinaitico.*

BARUCH.

Kneucker, Leipzig, 1879.

1 MACCABEES.

Drusius, Frankfort, 1600; Bruns, Helmstadt, 1784.

PSALMS OF SOLOMON.

J. L. de la Cerda, in an appendix to his *Adversaria Sacra,* Lyons, 1626.

J. A. Fabricius, in *Codex pseudepigraphus V. T.,* Hamburg and Leipzig, 1715.

A. Hilgenfeld, in *Zeitschrift für wissensch. Th.* xi., and in *Messias Iudaeorum,* Leipzig, 1869.

E. E. Geiger, Augsburg, 1871 : *Der Psalter Salomo's herausgegeben.*

O. F. Fritzsche in *Libri apocryphi V. T. gr.*

B. Pick, Alleghany, Pens., in the *Presbyterian Review,* 1883.

H. E. Ryle and M. R. James, Cambridge, 1891 : *Psalms of the Pharisees commonly called the Psalms of Solomon;* the Greek text with an apparatus, notes, indices, and an introduction.

H. B. Swete in *O. T. in Greek,* vol. iii., Cambridge, 1894; 2nd ed. 1899.

O. von Gebhardt, Leipzig, 1895 : *Die Psalmen Salomo's.*

ENOCH (the Greek version of).

The fragments [in Ep. Jud. 14, 15 ; the Chronography of G. Syncellus (ed. W. Dindorf, in *Corpus hist. Byzant.,* Bonn, 1829); *ZDMG.* ix. p. 621 ff. (a scrap printed by Gildemeister); the *Mémoires publiés par les membres de la mission archéologique française au Caire,* ix., Paris, 1892] have been collected by Dillmann, *über den neufundenen gr. Text des Henoch-buches* (1893); Lods, *Livre d'Henoch* (1893); Charles, *Book of Enoch,* (1893), and are printed with an apparatus in the *O. T. in Greek,* vol. iii., 2nd ed. (Cambridge, 1899).

LITERATURE (upon the general subject of this chapter).

Le Long-Masch, ii. p. 262 ff., Fabricius-Harles, p. 673 ff., Rosenmüller, *Handbuch,* i. p. 47 ff., Frankel, *Vorstudien zu der Septuaginta,* p. 242 ff., Tischendorf, *V. T. Gr., prolegomena* § vii. sqq., Van Ess [Nestle], *epilegomena* § 1 sqq., Loisy, *Histoire critique,* I. ii. p. 65 ff., Nestle, *Septuaginta-studien,* i. 1886, ii. 1896, iii. 1899; *Urtext,* p. 64 ff.

PART II.

THE CONTENTS OF THE ALEXANDRIAN
OLD TESTAMENT.

PART II.

CHAPTER I.

TITLES, GROUPING, NUMBER, AND ORDER OF THE BOOKS.

THE Greek Old Testament, as known to us through the few codices which contain it as a whole, and from the lists which appear in the Biblical MSS. or in ancient ecclesiastical writings, differs from the Hebrew Bible in regard to the titles of the books which are common to both, and the principle upon which the books are grouped. The two collections differ yet more materially in the number of the books, the Greek Bible containing several entire writings of which there is no vestige in the Hebrew canon, besides large additions to the contents of more than one of the Hebrew books. These differences are of much interest to the Biblical student, since they express a tradition which, inherited by the Church from the Alexandrian synagogue, has widely influenced Christian opinion upon the extent of the Old Testament Canon, and the character and purpose of the several books.

1.   The following tables shew (A) the Hebrew, Greek, and Latin titles of the canonical books of the Old Testament; (B) the order and grouping of the books in (1) lists of Jewish origin, (2) the great uncial MSS. of the Greek Bible, (3) patristic and synodical lists of the (*a*) Eastern, (*b*) Western Church.

A. Titles of the Books.

Hebrew	Transliteration [1]	Septuagint	Vulgate Latin
בְּרֵאשִׁית	Βρησίθ	Γένεσις	Genesis
וְאֵלֶּה שְׁמוֹת	Οὐέλε σμώθ	Ἔξοδος	Exodus
וַיִּקְרָא	Οὐικρά	Λευ[ε]ιτικόν	Leviticus
וַיְדַבֵּר	Ἄμμες φεκωδείμ [2]	Ἀριθμοί	Numeri
אֵלֶּה הַדְּבָרִים	Ἔλε ἀδδεβαρείμ	Δευτερονόμιον	Deuteronomium
יְהוֹשֻׁעַ	Ἰωσούε βὲν Νούν	Ἰησοῦς	Iosue
שׁוֹפְטִים	Σαφατείμ	Κριταί	Iudices
שְׁמוּאֵל	Σαμουήλ	Βασιλειῶν $\begin{cases} α', β' \\ γ', δ' \end{cases}$	Regum $\begin{cases} 1, 2 \\ 3, 4 \end{cases}$
מְלָכִים	Οὐαμμὲλχ Δαβίδ [3]		
יְשַׁעְיָה, יְשַׁעְיָהוּ	Ἰεσσιά	Ἡσαίας	Isaias
יִרְמְיָה, יִרְמְיָהוּ	Ἰερεμιά	Ἰερεμίας	Ieremias
יְחֶזְקֵאל	Ἰεζεκιήλ	Ἰεζεκιήλ	Ezechiel
הוֹשֵׁעַ		Ὡσῆε	Osee
יוֹאֵל		Ἰωήλ	Ioel
עָמוֹס		Ἀμώς	Amos
עֹבַדְיָה		Ὀβδειού, Ἀβδ[ε]ιού	Abdias

---

[1] As given by Origen ap. Eus. *H. E.* vi. 25.

[2] I.e. חֹמֶשׁ פִּקּוּדִים 'fifth of the precepts'; cf. the Mishnic title סֵפֶר פִּקּוּדִים (Ryle, *Canon of the O. T.*, p. 294). Jerome transliterates the initial word, *vayedabber*; cf. Epiph. (Lagarde, *Symmicta* ii. 178), οὐαϊδαβήρ, ἥ ἐστιν Ἀ ιθμῶν. The book is also known as בְּמִדְבַּר.

[3] I.e. וְהַמֶּלֶךְ דָּוִד (first two words of 1 Kings i.), *Malachim*, Jerome; ὀμαλαχείμ, Epiphanius.

Hebrew	Transliteration	Septuagint	Vulgate Latin
יוֹנָה		Ἰωνᾶς	Ionas
מִיכָה		Μ[ε]ιχαίας	Michaeas
נָחוּם, נַחוּם		Ναούμ	Nahum
חֲבַקּוּק		Ἀμβακούμ	Habacuc
צְפַנְיָה		Σοφονίας	Sophonias
חַגַּי		Ἀγγαῖος	Aggaeus
זְכַרְיָה		Ζαχαρίας	Zacharias
מַלְאָכִי		Μαλαχίας	Malachias
תְּהִלִּים	Σφὰρ θελλείμ	Ψαλμοί, Ψαλτή-ριον	Psalmi
מִשְׁלֵי	Μελώθ[1]	Παροιμίαι	Proverbia
אִיּוֹב	Ἰώβ	Ἰώβ	Iob
שִׁיר הַשִּׁירִים	Σὶρ ἀσσιρίμ	Ἆσμα, ᾆσματα [ᾀσμάτων]	Canticum canticorum
רוּת [2]		Ῥούθ	Ruth
אֵיכָה [3]		Θρῆνοι	Threni, Lamentationes
קֹהָלֶת	Κωέλθ	Ἐκκλησιαστής	Ecclesiastes
אֶסְתֵּר	Ἐσθήρ	Ἐσθήρ	Esther
דָּנִיֵּאל	Δανιήλ	Δανιήλ	Daniel
עֶזְרָא	Ἐζρά	Ἔσδρας	Esdras 1, 2
דִּבְרֵי-הַיָּמִים	Δαβρὴ ἰαμείν	Παραλειπομένων α′, β′	Paralipomenon 1, 2

---

[1] With variants Μεσλώθ, Μισλώθ (leg. for. Μσλώθ). *Masaloth,* Jerome; δμεθαλώθ, Epiphanius.

[2] Origen includes Ruth with Judges under Σαφατείμ.

[3] Epiph. *l.c.*: ἔστι δὲ καὶ ἄλλη μικρὰ βίβλος ἣ καλεῖται Κινώθ [Mishn. קִינוֹת], ἥτις ἑρμηνεύεται Θρῆνος Ἰερεμίου.

B (1). ORDER OF THE BOOKS IN JEWISH LISTS[1].

TALMUDIC	SPANISH MSS.	GERMAN & FRENCH MSS.	MASSORETIC MSS.	PRINTED BIBLES
I *Torah*	,,	,,	,,	,,
II *Nebiim*	,,	,,	,,	,,
Joshua	Joshua	Joshua	Joshua	Joshua
Judges	Judges	Judges	Judges	Judges
Samuel	Samuel	Samuel	Samuel	1, 2 Samuel
Kings	Kings	Kings	Kings	1, 2 Kings
Jeremiah	Isaiah	Jeremiah	Isaiah	Isaiah
Ezekiel	Jeremiah	Isaiah	Jeremiah	Jeremiah
Isaiah	Ezekiel	Ezekiel	Ezekiel	Ezekiel
xii Prophets	xii Prophets	xii Prophets	xii Prophets	Hosea
				Joel
				Amos
				Obadiah
				Jonah
				Micah
				Nahum
				Habakkuk
				Zephaniah
				Haggai
				Zachariah
				Malachi
III *Kethubim*	,,	,,	,,	,,
Ruth	Chronicles	Psalms	Chronicles	Psalms
Psalms	Psalms	Proverbs	Psalms	Proverbs
Job	Job	Job	Job	Job
Proverbs	Proverbs	Song of Songs	Proverbs	Song of Songs
Ecclesiastes	Ruth	Ruth	Ruth	Ruth
Song of Songs	Song of Songs	Lamentations	Song of Songs	Lamentations
Lamentations	Ecclesiastes	Ecclesiastes	Ecclesiastes	Ecclesiastes
Daniel	Lamentations	Esther	Lamentations	Esther
Esther	Esther	Daniel	Esther	Daniel
Ezra-Neh.	Daniel	Ezra-Neh.	Daniel	Ezra-Neh.
Chronicles	Ezra-Neh.	Chronicles	Ezra-Neh.	1, 2 Chronicles

[1] This list has been adapted from Ryle, *Canon of the O.T.* (table following p. 280).

B (2). ORDER OF THE BOOKS IN UNCIAL MS. BIBLES.

Codex Vaticanus (B)	Codex Sinaiticus (א)
Γένεσις	Γένεσις
Ἔξοδος	*
Λευειτικόν	*
Ἀριθμοί	Ἀριθμοί
Δευτερονόμιον	*
Ἰησοῦς	*
Κριταί	*
Ῥούθ	*
Βασιλειῶν α΄—δ΄	*
Παραλειπομένων α΄, β΄	Παραλειπομένων α΄, [β΄]
Ἔσδρας α΄, β΄	Ἔσδρας [α΄], β΄
Ψαλμοί	Ἐσθήρ
Παροιμίαι	Τωβείθ
Ἐκκλησιαστής	Ἰουδείθ
Ἆσμα	Μακκαβαίων α΄, δ΄
Ἰώβ	Ἡσαίας
Σοφία Σαλωμῶνος	Ἰερεμίας
Σοφία Σειράχ	Θρῆνοι Ἰερεμίου
Ἐσθήρ	*
Ἰουδείθ	*
Τωβείτ	*
Ὡσῆε	*
Ἀμώς	*
Μειχαίας	*
Ἰωήλ	Ἰωήλ
Ὀβδειού	Ἀβδειού
Ἰωνᾶς	Ἰωνᾶς
Ναούμ	Ναούμ
Ἀμβακούμ	Ἀμβακούμ
Σοφονίας	Σοφονίας
Ἀγγαῖος	Ἀγγαῖος
Ζαχαρίας	Ζαχαρίας
Μαλαχίας	Μαλαχίας
Ἡσαίας	Ψαλμοὶ Δᾱδ ρνα΄ (*subscr.*)
Ἰερεμίας	Παροιμίαι [+ Σολομῶντος *subscr.*]
Βαρούχ	Ἐκκλησιαστής
Θρῆνοι	Ἆσμα ἀσμάτων
Ἐπιστολὴ Ἰερεμίου	Σοφία Σαλομῶντος
Ἰεζεκιήλ	Σοφία Ἰησοῦ υἱοῦ Σειράχ
Δανιήλ	Ἰώβ

Codex Alexandrinus (A)

Γένεσις κόσμου
Ἔξοδος Αἰγύπτου
Λευειτικόν
Ἀριθμοί
Δευτερονόμιον
Ἰησοῦς υἱὸς Ναυή
Κριταί
Ῥούθ [ὁμοῦ βιβλία η']
Βασιλειῶν α'—δ'
Παραλειπομένων α', β' [ὁμοῦ βιβλία ϛ']
Προφῆται ιϛ'
 Ὡσῆε α
 Ἀμώς β'
 Μιχαίας γ'
 Ἰωήλ δ'
 Ἀβδειού ε'
 Ἰωνᾶς ϛ'
 Ναούμ ζ'
 Ἀμβακούμ η'
 Σοφονίας θ'
 Ἀγγαῖος ι'
 Ζαχαρίας ια'
 Μαλαχίας ιβ'
Ἡσαίας προφήτης ιγ'
Ἰερεμίας προφήτης ιδ'
 Βαρούχ
 Θρῆνος [+ Ἰερεμίου, *subscr.*]
 Ἐπιστολὴ Ἰερεμίου
Ἰεζεκιὴλ προφήτης ιε'
Δανιήλ [+ προφήτης ιϛ', *catal.*]
Ἐσθήρ
Τωβίτ (Τωβείτ, *subscr.*)
Ἰουδείθ
Ἔζρας α' ὁ ἱερεύς (Ἔσζρας α' ἱερεύς, *catal.*)
Ἔζρας β' ἱερεύς (Ἔσζρας β' ἱερεύς *catal.*)
Μακκαβαίων α'—δ'
Ψαλτήριον (Ψαλμοὶ ρν' καὶ ἰδιόγραφος α' *subscr.*, *seq.* ᾠδαὶ ιδ'. Ψαλτήριον μετ' ᾠδῶν *catal.*)
Ἰώβ
Παροιμίαι Σολομῶντος
Ἐκκλησιαστής
Ἄσματα (Ἆσμα *subscr.*) ᾀσμάτων
Σοφία Σολομῶντος (Σ. Σολομῶνος *subscr.*; + ἢ Πανάρετος, *catal.*)
Σοφία Ἰησοῦ υἱοῦ Σιράχ (Σειράχ, *subscr.*)
Ψαλμοὶ Σολομῶντος, *catal.*

Codex Basiliano-Venetus (N+V)

*

*

(N) Λευιτικόν
Ἀριθμοί
Δευτερονόμιον
Ἰησοῦς
Ῥούθ
Κριταί
Βασιλειῶν α'—δ'
Παραλειπομένων α', β'
Ἔσδρας [α'], β'
Ἐσθήρ
*
*
*
(V) Ἰώβ (*subscr.*)
Παροιμίαι
Ἐκκλησιαστής
Ἄσμα ᾀσμάτων
Σοφία Σολομῶντος
Σοφία Ἰησοῦ υἱοῦ Σιράχ
Ὡσῆε
Ἀμώς
Ἰωήλ
Ἀβδιού
Ἰωνᾶς
Μιχαίας
Ναούμ
Ἀμβακούμ
Σοφονίας
Ἀγγαῖος
Ζαχαρίας
Μαλαχίας
Ἡσαίας
Ἰερεμίας
Βαρούχ
Θρῆνοι
Ἰεζεκιήλ
Δανιήλ
Τωβίτ
Ἰουδίθ
Μακκαβαίων α'—δ'

B (3) (*a*). ORDER OF THE BOOKS IN PATRISTIC AND
SYNODICAL LISTS OF THE EASTERN CHURCH.

1. Melito (*ap.* Eus. *H.E.* iv. 26).

Μωυσέως πέντε
Γένεσις
Ἔξοδος
Ἀριθμοί
Λευιτικόν
Δευτερονόμιον
Ἰησοῦς Ναυή
Κριταί
Ῥούθ
Βασιλειῶν τέσσαρα
Παραλειπομένων δύο
Ψαλμῶν Δαβίδ
Σαλομῶνος Παροιμίαι, ἣ καὶ Σοφία[1]
Ἐκκλησιαστής
Ἆσμα ᾀσμάτων
Ἰώβ
Προφητῶν
Ἠσαίου
Ἰερεμίου
Τῶν δώδεκα ἐν μονοβίβλῳ
Δανιήλ
Ἰεζεκιήλ
Ἔσδρας

2. Origen (*ap.* Eus. *H.E.* vi. 25).

Γένεσις
Ἔξοδος
Λευιτικόν
Ἀριθμοί
Δευτερονόμιον
Ἰησοῦς υἱὸς Ναυή
Κριταί
Ῥούθ
Βασιλειῶν α΄—δ΄
Παραλειπομένων α΄, β΄
Ἔσδρας α΄, β΄
Βίβλος Ψαλμῶν
Σολομῶντος Παροιμίαι
Ἐκκλησιαστής
Ἆσμα ᾀσμάτων
Ἠσαίας
Ἰερεμίας σὺν Θρήνοις καὶ τῇ Ἐπι-
στολῇ ἐν ἑνί
Δανιήλ
Ἰεζεκιήλ
Ἰώβ
Ἐσθήρ
Ἔξω δὲ τούτων ἐστὶ
Τὰ Μακκαβαϊκά

3. Athanasius (*ep. fest.* 39,
Migne, *P.G.* xxvi. 1436).

Γένεσις
Ἔξοδος
Λευιτικόν
Ἀριθμοί
Δευτερονόμιον
Ἰησοῦς ὁ τοῦ Ναυή
Κριταί
Ῥούθ
Βασιλειῶν τέσσαρα βιβλία
Παραλειπομένων α΄, β΄
Ἔσδρας, α΄, β΄
Βίβλος Ψαλμῶν
Παροιμίαι
Ἐκκλησιαστής

4. Cyril of Jerusalem (*Catech.* iv. 35).

Αἱ Μωσέως πρῶται πέντε βίβλοι
Γένεσις
Ἔξοδος
Λευιτικόν
Ἀριθμοί
Δευτερονόμιον
Ἑξῆς δέ
Ἰησοῦ υἱοῦ Ναυή
Τῶν Κριτῶν βιβλίον μετὰ τῆς Ῥούθ
Τῶν δὲ λοιπῶν ἱστορικῶν βιβλίων
Βασιλειῶν α΄—δ΄
Παραλειπομένων α΄, β΄
Τοῦ Ἔσδρα α΄, β΄
Ἐσθήρ (δωδεκάτη)

[1] Cf. Eus. *H. E.* iv. 22 ὁ πᾶς τῶν ἀρχαίων χορὸς Πανάρετον Σοφίαν τὰς
Σολομῶνος παροιμίας ἐκάλουν.

Ἄσμα ἀσμάτων
Ἰώβ
Προφῆται
  Οἱ δώδεκα
  Ἡσαΐας
  Ἰερεμίας καὶ σὺν **αὐτῷ** Βαρούχ,
    Θρῆνοι, Ἐπιστολή
  Ἰεζεκιήλ
  Δανιήλ
Ἔστι καὶ ἕτερα βιβλία τούτων ἔξωθεν,
  οὐ κανονιζόμενα μὲν τετυπωμένα δὲ
  παρὰ τῶν πατέρων ἀναγινώσκεσθαι
  τοῖς ἄρτι προσερχομένοις...
    Σοφία Σολομῶντος
    Σοφία Σιράχ
    Ἐσθήρ
    Ἰουδίθ
    Τωβίας

Τὰ δὲ στιχηρὰ τύγχανει πέντε
  Ἰώβ
  Βίβλος Ψαλμῶν
  Παροιμίαι
  Ἐκκλησιαστής
  Ἄσμα ἀσμάτων (ἑπτακαιδέκατον
    βιβλίον)
Ἐπὶ δὲ τούτοις τὰ προφητικὰ πέντε
  Τῶν δώδεκα προφητῶν μία βίβλος
  Ἡσαΐου μία
  Ἰερεμίου [μία] μετὰ Βαρούχ καὶ
    Θρήνων καὶ Ἐπιστολῆς
  Ἰεζεκιήλ
  Δανιήλ (εἰκοστὴ δευτέρα βίβλος)
Τὰ δὲ λοιπὰ πάντα ἔξω κείσθω ἐν δευ-
  τέρῳ

5ᵃ. Epiphanius (*haer.* I. i. 6).

α΄. Γένεσις
β΄. Ἔξοδος
γ΄. Λευιτικόν
δ΄. Ἀριθμοί
ε΄. Δευτερονόμιον
ϛ΄. Ἰησοῦ τοῦ Ναυή
ζ΄. Τῶν Κριτῶν
η΄. Τῆς Ῥούθ
θ΄. Τοῦ Ἰώβ
ι΄. Τὸ Ψαλτήριον
ια΄. Παροιμίαι Σολομῶντος
ιβ΄. Ἐκκλησιαστής
ιγ΄. Τὸ Ἄσμα τῶν ἀσμάτων
ιδ΄–ιζ΄. Βασιλειῶν α΄—δ΄
ιη΄, ιθ΄. Παραλειπομένων α΄, β΄
κ΄. Τὸ Δωδεκαπρόφητον
κα΄. Ἡσαΐας ὁ προφήτης
κβ΄. Ἰερεμίας ὁ προφήτης, μετὰ τῶν
    Θρήνων καὶ Ἐπιστολῶν αὐτοῦ
    τε καὶ Βαρούχ
κγ΄. Ἰεζεκιὴλ ὁ προφήτης
κδ΄. Δανιὴλ ὁ προφήτης
κε΄, κϛ΄. Ἔσδρα α΄, β΄
κζ΄. Ἐσθήρ

  Ἡ Σοφία τοῦ Σιράχ
  Ἡ [Σοφία] τοῦ Σολομῶντος

5ᵇ. Epiphanius (*de mens. et pond.* 4).

Πέντε νομικαί (ἡ πεντάτευχος ἢ καὶ
  νομοθεσία)
  (Γένεσις—Δευτερονόμιον)
Πέντε στιχήρεις
  (Ἰώβ, Ψαλτήριον, Παροιμίαι Σα-
    λομῶντος, Ἐκκλησιαστής, Ἄσμα
    ἀσμάτων)
Ἄλλη πεντάτευχος, τὰ καλούμενα Γρα-
  φεῖα, παρά τισι δὲ Ἁγιόγραφα λε-
  γόμενα (Ἰησοῦ τοῦ Ναυή, βίβλος
  Κριτῶν μετὰ τῆς Ῥούθ, Παραλει-
  πομένων α΄, β΄, Βασιλειῶν α΄, β΄,
  Βασιλειῶν γ΄, δ΄)
Ἡ προφητικὴ πεντάτευχος (τὸ δωδεκα-
  πρόφητον, Ἡσαΐας, Ἰερεμίας, Ἰεζε-
  κιήλ, Δανιήλ)
Ἄλλαι δύο (τοῦ Ἔσδρα δύο, μία λογι-
  ζομένη, τῆς Ἐσθήρ)

  Ἡ τοῦ Σολομῶντος ἡ Πανάρετος
  λεγομένη
  Ἡ τοῦ Ἰησοῦ τοῦ υἱοῦ Σειράχ

5ᶜ. Epiphanius (*de mens. et pond.* 23).

Γένεσις κόσμου
Ἔξοδος τῶν υἱῶν Ἰσραὴλ ἐξ Αἰγύπτου
Λευιτικόν
Ἀριθμῶν
Τὸ Δευτερονόμιον
Ἡ τοῦ Ἰησοῦ τοῦ Ναυή
Ἡ τοῦ Ἰώβ
Ἡ τῶν Κριτῶν
Ἡ τῆς Ῥούθ
Τὸ Ψαλτήριον
Τῶν Παραλειπομένων α΄, β΄
Βασιλειῶν α΄—δ΄
Ἡ Παροιμιῶν
Ὁ Ἐκκλησιαστής
Τὸ Ἄσμα τῶν ἀσμάτων
Τὸ Δωδεκαπρόφητον
Τοῦ προφήτου Ἡσαίου
Τοῦ Ἰερεμίου
Τοῦ Ἰεζεκιήλ
Τοῦ Δανιήλ
Τοῦ Ἔσδρα α΄, β΄
Τῆς Ἐσθήρ

6. Gregory of Nazianzus (*carm.* I. xii. 5 ff.).

Βίβλοι ἱστορικαὶ ιβ΄
(Γένεσις, Ἔξοδος, Λευιτικόν, Ἀριθ-
μοί, Δεύτερος νόμος, Ἰησοῦς, Κρι-
ταί, Ῥούθ, Πράξεις βασιλήων,
Παραλειπόμεναι, Ἔσδρας)
Βίβλοι στιχηραὶ ε΄
(Ἰώβ, Δαυίδ, τρεῖς Σολομωντίαι,
Ἐκκλησιαστής, Ἄσμα. Παροι-
μίαι)
Βίβλοι προφητικαὶ ε΄
(Οἱ δώδεκα—Ὠσῆε, Ἀμώς, Μιχαίας,
Ἰωήλ, Ἰωνᾶς, Ἀβδίας, Ναούμ,
Ἀββακούμ, Σοφονίας, Ἀγγαῖος,
Ζαχαρίας, Μαλαχίας—Ἡσαίας,
Ἰερεμίας, Ἐζεκιήλ, Δανιῆλος)

7. Amphilochius (*ad Seleuc.* ap. Greg. Naz.
carm. II. vii., Migne, *P.G.* xxxvii. 1593).

Ἡ πεντάτευχος
(Κτίσις, Ἔξοδος, Λευιτικόν, Ἀριθ-
μοί, Δευτερονόμιον)
Ἰησοῦς
Οἱ Κριταί
Ἡ Ῥούθ
Βασιλειῶν α΄—δ΄
Παραλειπομένων α΄, β΄
Ἔσδρας α΄, β΄
Στιχηραὶ βίβλοι ε΄
(Ἰώβ, Ψαλμοί, τρεῖς Σολομῶντος—
Παροιμίαι, Ἐκκλησιαστής, Ἄσμα
ἀσμάτων)
Προφῆται οἱ δώδεκα
(Ὠσῆε, Ἀμώς, Μιχαίας, Ἰωήλ,
Ἀβδίας, Ἰωνᾶς, Ναούμ, Ἀμβα-
κούμ, Σοφονίας, Ἀγγαῖος, Ζαχα-
ρίας, Μαλαχίας)
Προφῆται οἱ τέσσαρες
(Ἡσαίας, Ἰερεμίας, Ἐζεκιήλ, Δα-
νιήλ)
Τούτοις προσεγκρίνουσι τὴν Ἐσθήρ
τινες

8. Pseudo-Chrysostom (*syn. script. sacr.*
praef.). Migne, *P.G.* lvi. 513 sqq.

Τὸ ἱστορικόν, ὡς
Ἡ Γένεσις
Ἡ Ἔξοδος
Τὸ Λευιτικόν
Οἱ Ἀριθμοί
Τὸ Δευτερονόμιον (ἡ ὀκτάτευχος)
Ἰησοῦς ὁ τοῦ Ναυή
Οἱ Κριταί
Ῥούθ
Αἱ Βασιλεῖαι α΄—δ΄
Ἔσδρας
Τὸ συμβουλευτικόν, ὡς
Αἱ Παροιμίαι
Ἡ τοῦ Σιρὰχ Σοφία
Ὁ Ἐκκλησιαστής
Τὰ Ἄσματα τῶν ἀσμάτων
Τὸ προφητικόν, ὡς
Οἱ δεκαὲξ προφηταί
Ῥούθ (?)
Δαυείδ

9. Σύνοψις ἐν ἐπιτόμῳ *ap.* Lagarde,
  Septuagintast., ii. p. 60 f.[1]

Τὰ Μωσαϊκά
  α΄. Γένεσις
  β΄. Ἔξοδος
  γ΄. Λευιτικόν
  δ΄. Ἀριθμοί
  ε΄. Δευτερονόμιον
Τὰ ἕτερα
  ϛ΄. Ἰησοῦς ὁ τοῦ Ναυή
  ζ΄. Κριταί
  η΄. Ῥούθ
    Τέλος τῆς ὀκτατεύχου
Τὸ τετραβασίλειον
  θ΄. Βασιλειῶν α΄
  ι΄. Βασιλειῶν β΄
  ια΄. Βασιλειῶν γ΄
  ιβ΄. Βασιλειῶν δ΄
  ιγ΄. Παραλειπόμενα α΄
  ιδ΄. Παραλειπόμενα β΄
  ιε΄. Ἔσδρα α΄
  ιϛ΄. Ἔσδρα β΄
  ιζ΄. Ἐσθήρ
  ιη΄. Τωβίτ
  ιθ΄. Ἰουδήθ
  κ΄. Ἰώβ
Τοῦ Σολομῶντος
  κα΄. Σοφία
  κβ΄. Παροιμίαι
  κγ΄. Ἐκκλησιαστής
  κδ΄. Ἄσμα ᾀσμάτων
Οἱ ιβ΄ προφῆται
  κε΄. Ὡσηέ
  κϛ΄. Ἀμώς
  κζ΄. Μιχαίας
  κη΄. Ἰωήλ
  κθ΄. Ἀβδιού
  λ΄. Ἰωνᾶς
  λα΄. Ναούμ
  λβ΄. Ἀββακούμ
  λγ΄. Σοφονίας
  λδ΄. Ἀγγαῖος
  λε΄. Ζαχαρίας
  λϛ΄. Μαλαχίας
Οἱ δ΄ μεγάλοι προφῆται
  λζ΄. Ἡσαίας
  λη΄. Ἱερεμίας
  λθ΄. Ἰεζεκιήλ
  μ΄. Δανιήλ
    Τέλος τῶν ἑξ καὶ δέκα προφητῶν
  μα΄. Σοφία Ἰησοῦ τοῦ Σιράχ

10. Anonymi *dial. Timothei et Aquilae.*
  α΄. Γένεσις
  β΄. Ἔξοδος
  γ΄. Τὸ Λευιτικόν ⎫ Ἡ Μωσαικὴ
  δ΄. Οἱ Ἀριθμοί ⎬ πεντάτευχος
  ε΄. Τὸ Δευτερονόμιον ⎭
  ϛ΄. Ὁ τοῦ Ναυή
  ζ΄. Οἱ Κριταί, μετὰ τῆς Ῥούθ
  η΄. Τὰ Παραλειπόμενα α΄, β΄
  θ΄. Τῶν βασιλειῶν α΄, β΄
  ι΄. Τῶν βασιλειῶν γ΄, δ΄
  ια΄. Ἰώβ
  ιβ΄. Τὸ Ψαλτήριον τοῦ Δαυίδ
  ιγ΄. Αἱ Παροιμίαι Σολομῶντος
  ιδ΄. Ὁ Ἐκκλησιαστής, σὺν τοῖς Ἄ-
      σμασιν
  ιε΄. Τὸ δωδεκαπρόφητον· Ἡσαίας,
      Ἰερεμίας, Ἰεζεκιήλ, Δανιήλ,
      Ἔσδρας
  κα΄. Ἰουδίθ
  κβ΄. Ἐσθήρ
    Ἀπόκρυφα
    Τοβίας
    Ἡ Σοφία Σολομῶντος
    Ἡ Σοφία Ἰησοῦ υἱοῦ Σιράχ

[1] Lagarde, *l.c.*: "ich wiederhole sie, von mir redigiert."

11. Junilius *de inst. reg. div. legis* i. 3 ff.
(ed. Kihn).

Historia (xvii)
Genesis
Exodus
Leviticus
Numeri
Deuteronomium
Iesu Nave
Iudicum
Ruth
Regnn. i—iv
[Adiungunt plures Paralipome-
non ii, Iob i, Tobiae i, Es-
drae ii, Iudith i, Hester i,
Macchabaeorum ii]
Prophetia (xvii)
Psalmorum cl
Osee
Esaiae
Ioel
Amos
Abdiae
Ionae
Michaeae
Naum
Habacuc
Sophoniae
Hieremiae
Ezechiel
Daniel
Aggaei
Zachariae
Malachiae
Proverbia (ii)
Salomonis Proverbiorum
Iesu filii Sirach
[Adiungunt quidam libr. Sapi-
entiae et Cantica Cantico-
rum]
Dogmatica (i)
Ecclesiastes

12. Pseudo-Athanasii *syn. scr. sacr.*
(Migne, *P.G.* xxviii. 283 ff.).

Γένεσις
Ἔξοδος
Λευιτικόν
Ἀριθμοί
Δευτερονόμιον
Ἰησοῦς ὁ τοῦ Ναυή
Κριταί
Ῥούθ
Βασιλειῶν α', β'
Βασιλειῶν γ', δ'
Παραλειπομένων α', β'
Ἔσδρας α', β'
Ψαλτήριον Δαβιτικόν
Παροιμίαι Σολομῶντος
Ἐκκλησιαστὴς τοῦ αὐτοῦ
Ἆσμα ἀσμάτων
Ἰώβ
Προφῆται δώδεκα εἰς ἓν ἀριθμούμενοι
Ὡσῆε, Ἀμώς, Μιχαίας, Ἰωήλ, Ἀβ-
διού, Ἰωνᾶς, Ναούμ, Ἀμβακούμ,
Σοφωνίας, Ἀγγαῖος, Ζαχαρίας,
Μαλαχίας
Ἑξῆς δὲ ἕτεροι τέσσαρες
Ἡσαίας
Ἰερεμίας
Ἐζεκιήλ
Δανιήλ
Ἐκτὸς δὲ τούτων εἰσὶ πάλιν ἕτερα
βιβλία κ.τ.λ. (as in Athanasius,
but adding
Μακκαβάϊκα βιβλία δ'
Πτολεμαϊκά
Ψαλμοὶ καὶ ᾠδὴ Σολομῶντος
Σωσάννα)

13. Leontius (*de Sectis* ii.).

Τὰ ἱστορικὰ βιβλία (ιβ')
(Γένεσις, Ἔξοδος, Ἀριθμοί, Λευιτικόν, Δευτερονόμιον· Ἰησοῦς τοῦ
Ναυή, Κριταί, Ῥούθ, Λόγοι τῶν
βασιλειῶν α'—δ', Παραλειπόμεναι, Ἔσδρας)

14. John of Damascus (*de fide orthod.*
iv. 17).

Πρώτη πεντάτευχος, ἣ καὶ νομοθεσία
(Γένεσις, Ἔξοδος, Λευιτικόν, Ἀριθ-
μοί, Δευτερονόμιον)
Δευτέρα πεντάτευχος, τὰ καλούμενα
Γραφεῖα, παρά τισι δὲ Ἁγιόγραφα
(Ἰησοῦς ὁ τοῦ Ναυή, Κριταὶ μετὰ

Τὰ προφητικά (ε')
('Ησαίας, 'Ιερεμίας, 'Ιεζεκιήλ, Δανιήλ, τὸ Δωδεκαπρόφητον)
Τὰ παραινετικά (δ')
('Ιώβ, Παροιμίαι Σολομῶντος, 'Εκκλησιαστής, τὸ ᾶσμα τῶν ᾀσμάτων, τὸ Ψαλτήριον)

τῆς 'Ρούθ, Βασιλειῶν α', β', Βασιλειῶν γ', δ', τῶν Παραλειπομένων
α', β')
Τρίτη πεντάτευχος, αἱ στιχηραὶ βίβλοι
(τοῦ 'Ιώβ, τὸ Ψαλτήριον, Παροιμίαι Σολομῶντος, 'Εκκλησιαστής,
τοῦ αὐτοῦ, τὰ ᾶσματα τῶν 'Ασμά-
των τοῦ αὐτοῦ)
Τετάρτη πεντάτευχος ἡ προφητική
(τὸ Δωδεκαπρόφητον, 'Ησαίας, 'Ιερεμίας, 'Ιεζεκιήλ, Δανιήλ)
Ἄλλαι δύο
(τοῦ Ἔσδρα α', β', ἡ 'Εσθήρ)

'Η Πανάρετος τ. ἐ. ἡ Σοφία τοῦ Σολομῶντος
'Η Σοφία τοῦ 'Ιησοῦ

---

15. Nicephorus, *Stichometria*.

Α. Ὅσαι εἰσὶ γραφαὶ ἐκκλησιαζόμεναι
        καὶ κεκανονισμέναι
α'. Γένεσις στίχ. ,δτ'
β'. Ἔξοδος στίχ. ,βω'
γ'. Λευιτικόν στίχ. ,βψ'
δ'. 'Αριθμοί στίχ. ,γφλ'
ε'. Δευτερονόμιον στίχ. ,γρ'
ς'. 'Ιησοῦς στίχ. ,βρ'
ζ'. Κριταὶ καὶ 'Ρούθ στίχ. ,βυν'
η'. Βασιλειῶν α', β' στίχ. ,βσμ'
θ'. Βασιλειῶν γ', δ' στίχ. ,βσγ'
ι'. Παραλειπόμενα α', β' στίχ. ,εφ'
ια'. Ἔσδρας α', β' στίχ. ,εφ'
ιβ'. Βίβλος Ψαλμῶν στίχ. ,ερ'
ιγ'. Παροιμίαι Σολομῶντος στίχ.
        ,αψ'
ιδ'. 'Εκκλησιαστής στίχ. ψν'
ιε'. Ἄσμα ᾀσμάτων στίχ. σπ'
ις'. 'Ιώβ στίχ. ,αω'
ιζ'. 'Ησαίας προφήτης στίχ. ,γω'
ιη'. 'Ιερεμίας προφήτης στίχ. ,δ'
ιθ'. Βαρούχ στίχ. ψ'
κ'. 'Ιεζεκιήλ στίχ. ,δ'
κα'. Δανιήλ στίχ. ,β'
κβ'. Οἱ δώδεκα προφῆται στίχ. ,γ'
        Ὁμοῦ τῆς παλαιᾶς διαθήκης
        βίβλοι κβ'.

---

16. Ebedjesu (*catal. libr. Eccl.*, Assemani,
        Bibl. Or. iii. 5 f.).

Genesis
Exodus
Liber sacerdotum
Numeri
Deuteronomii
Josue filii Nun
Iudicum
Samuel
Regum
Liber Dabariamin
Ruth
Psalmi David Regis
Proverbia Salomonis
Cohelet
Sirat Sirin
Bar-Sira
Sapientia Magna
Iob
Isaias
Hosee
Ioel
Amos
Abdias
Ionas
Michaeas
Nahum
Habacuc
Sophonias

B. ῞Οσαι ἀντιλέγονται καὶ οὐκ ἐκκλη-
σιάζονται

α'. Μακκαβαϊκὰ γ' στίχ. ͵ϛτ'
β'. Σοφία Σολομῶντος στίχ. ͵αρ'
γ'. Σοφία υἱοῦ τοῦ Σιρὰχ στίχ.
 ͵βω'
δ'. Ψαλμοὶ καὶ ᾠδαὶ Σολομῶντος
 στίχ. ͵βρ'
ε'. Ἐσθὴρ στίχ. τν'
ϛ'. Ἰουδὶθ στίχ. ͵αψ'
ζ'. Σωσάννα στίχ. φ'
η'. Τωβίτ, ὁ καὶ Τωβίας στίχ. ψ'

Aggaeus
Zacharias
Malachias
Hieremias
Ezechiel
Daniel
Iudith
Esther
Susanna
Esdras
Daniel Minor ·
Epistola Baruch
Liber traditionis Seniorum
Josephi proverbia
Historia filiorum Samonae [i. e.
 Maccab. iv]
Liber Maccabaeorum (i—iii)

17. Laodicene Canons (lx.).

α'. Γένεσις κόσμου
β'. ῎Εξοδος ἐξ Αἰγύπτου
γ'. Λευιτικόν
δ'. Ἀριθμοί
ε'. Δευτερονόμιον
ϛ'. Ἰησοῦς Ναυή
ζ'. Κριταί, Ῥούθ
η'. Ἐσθήρ
θ'. Βασιλειῶν α', β'
ι'. Βασιλειῶν γ', δ'
ια'. Παραλειπομένων α', β'
ιβ'. ῎Εσδρας α', β'
ιγ'. Βίβλος Ψαλμῶν ρν'
ιδ'. Παροιμίαι Σολομῶντος
ιε'. Ἐκκλησιαστης
ιϛ'. Ἄσμα ᾀσμάτων
ιζ'. Ἰώβ
ιη'. Δώδεκα προφῆται
ιθ'. Ἡσαίας
κ'. Ἰερεμίας καὶ Βαρούχ, Θρῆνοι καὶ
 Ἐπιστολαί
κα'. Ἰεζεκιήλ
κβ'. Δανιήλ

18. Apostolic Canons (lxxxiv.).

Μωυσέως πέντε
 (Γένεσις, ῎Εξοδος, Λευιτικόν, Ἀ-
 ριθμοί, Δευτερονόμιον)
Ἰησοῦς Ναυή
Ῥούθ
Βασιλειῶν τέσσαρα
Παραλειπομένων δύο
῎Εσδρα δύο
Ἐσθήρ
Μακκαβαίων τρία
Ἰώβ
Ψαλτήριον
Σολομῶντος τρία
 (Παροιμίαι, Ἐκκλησιαστής,
 Ἄσμα ᾀσμάτων)
Προφητῶν δεκάδυο ἔν
Ἡσαίου ἔν
Ἰερεμίου ἔν
Ἰεζεκιήλ ἔν
Δανιήλ ἔν
῎Εξωθεν δὲ προσιστορείσθω μανθά-
 νειν ὑμῶν τοὺς νέους τὴν Σοφίαν
 τοῦ πολυμαθοῦς Σιράχ

19. List in *Codd. Barocc.* 206; *B.M. Add.* 17469; *Coisl.* 120.

Περὶ τῶν ξ' βιβλίων, καὶ ὅσα τούτων
 ἐκτός
α'. Γένεσις
β'. ῎Εξοδος
γ'. Λευιτικόν
δ'. Ἀριθμοί

ε'. Δευτερονόμιον
ϛ'. Ἰησοῦς
ζ'. Κριταὶ καὶ Ῥούθ
η'–ια'. Βασιλειῶν α'—δ'
ιβ'. Παραλειπόμενα α', β'
ιγ'. Ἰώβ

S. S.

14

ιδ'. Ψαλτήριον
ιε'. Παροιμίαι
ιϛ'. Ἐκκλησιαστής
ιζ'. Ἄσμα ᾀσμάτων
ιη'. Ἔσδρας
ιθ'. Ὡσῆε
κ'. Ἀμώς
κα'. Μιχαίας
κβ'. Ἰωήλ
κγ'. Ἰωνᾶς
κδ'. Ἀβδιού
κε'. Ναούμ
κϛ'. Ἀμβακούμ
κζ'. Σοφονίας
κη'. Ἀγγαῖος

κθ'. Ζαχαρίας
λ'. Μαλαχίας
λα'. Ἡσαίας
λβ'. Ἰερεμίας
λγ'. Ἰεζεκιήλ
λδ'. Δανιήλ[1]

* *
* *

Καὶ ὅσα ἔξω τῶν ξ'
α'. Σοφία Σολομῶντος
β'. Σοφία Σιράχ
γ'–ϛ'. Μακκαβαίων [α'—δ']
ζ'. Ἐσθήρ
η'. Ἰουδήθ
θ'. Τωβίτ

B (3) (*b*). ORDER OF THE BOOKS IN PATRISTIC AND SYNODICAL LISTS OF THE WESTERN CHURCH.

1. Hilary, *prol. in libr. Psalm.*

i—v. Moysi[s] libri quinque
vi. Iesu Naue
vii. Iudicum et Ruth
viii. Regnorum i, ii
ix. Regnorum iii, iv
x. Paralipomenon i, ii
xi. Sermones dierum Esdrae
xii. Liber Psalmorum
xiii—xv. Salomonis Proverbia, Ecclesiastes, Canticum Canticorum
xvi. Duodecim Prophetae
xvii—xxii. Esaias, Jeremias cum Lamentatione et Epistola, Daniel, Ezekiel, Job, Hester

[xxiii—xxiv. Tobias, Judith][2]

2. Ruffinus (*Comm. in symb.* 36).

Moysi[s] quinque libri
(Genesis, Exodus, Leviticus, Numeri, Deuteronomium)
Iesus Naue
Iudicum, simul cum Ruth
Regnorum iv
Paralipomenon (=Dierum liber)
Esdrae ii
Hester
Prophetarum
(Esaias, Ieremias, Ezechiel, Daniel, xii Prophetarum liber i)
Iob
Psalmi David
Salomon[is] iii
(Proverbia, Ecclesiastes, Cantica Canticorum)

Sapientia Salomonis
Sapientia Sirach (=Ecclesiasticus)
Tobias
Iudith
Maccabaeorum libri

---

[1] The B.M. MS. counts Ruth as a separate book and after Daniel places the numeral λε'.

[2] "Quibusdam autem visum est additis Tobia et Judith xxiv libros secundum numerum Graecarum literarum connumerare."

3. Augustine (*de doctr. Chr.* ii. 13).

[Historiae:]
Quinque Moyseos [libri]
(Genesis, Exodus, Leviticus,
Numeri, Deuteronomium)
Iesu Naue
Iudicum
Ruth
Regnorum libri iv
Paralipomenon libri ii
Iob
Tobias
Esther
Iudith
Machabaeorum libri ii
Esdrae libri ii
Prophetae:
David liber Psalmorum
Salamonis libri iii
(Proverbiorum, Canticum Can-
ticorum, Ecclesiastes)
Sapientia, Ecclesiasticus [1]
Prophetarum xii
(Osee, Ioel, Amos, Ab-
dias, Ionas, Michaeas,
Nahum, Habacuc, So-
phonias, Aggaeus, Za-
charias, Malachias)
Prophetae iv maiorum volu-
minum
(Isaias, Ieremias, Daniel,
Ezechiel)

} proprie prophetae

4. Innocent I. (*ep. ad Exsuperium*).

Moysi[s] libri quinque
(Genesis, Exodi, Levitici, Nu-
meri, Deuteronomii)
Iesu Naue
Iudicum
Regnorum libri iv
Ruth
Prophetarum libri xvi
Salomonis libri v
Psalterium
Historiarum:
Job
Tobias
Hester
Iudith
Machabaeorum libri ii
Esdrae libri ii
Paralipomenon libri ii

5. Pseudo-Gelasius *decret. de libr.*

Moysis v libri:
Genesis
Exodus
Leviticus
Numeri
Deuteronomium
Iesu Naue
Iudicum
Ruth
Regum i—iv

6. Cassiodorius (*de inst. Div. litt.* 14).

Genesis
Exodus
Leviticus
Numeri
Deuteronomium
Iesu Nave
Regum i—iv
Paralipomenon i, ii
Psalterium

---

[1] Of the canonicity of these two books Augustine speaks with some
reserve: "de quadam similitudine Salomonis esse dicuntur...qui tamen
quoniam in auctoritatem recipi meruerunt inter propheticos numerandi
sunt."

Item libri prophetarum numero xvi:
(Isaias, Ieremias, Ezechiel, Daniel,
Osee, Amos, Michas, Iohel,
Abdias, Ionas, Naum, Abacu,
Sofonias, Agaeus, Zacharias,
Maleachias)
Paralipomena i, ii
Psalmorum cl
Salamonis libri iii
(Proverbiorum, Ecclesiastes,
Canticum Canticorum)
Liber Sapientiae filii Siracis
Alius subsequens liber Sapientiae
Item historiarum:
Iob
Tobias
Hester
Iudith
Macchabaeorum libri ii

Salomonis libri v
(Proverbia, Sapientia, Ecclesias-
ticus, Ecclesiastes, Canticum
canticorum)
Prophetae
(Isaias, Hieremias, Ezechiel, Da-
niel, Osee, Amos, Michaeas,
Joel, Abdias, Jonas, Naum,
Abbacuc, Sofonias, Aggaeus,
Zacharias, Malachias, qui et
Angelus)
Job
Tobi[as]
Esther
Iudith
Esdrae [libri] ii
Machabaeorum libri ii

7. Isidorus (*de ord. libr. s. scr.*).

1. Quinque libri Moyseos
2. Iesu Nave, Iudicum, Ruth
3. Regum i—iv, Paralipomenon i,
   ii, Tobiae, Esther, Iudith,
   Esdrae, Machabaeorum libri
   duo

4. Prophetae: Psalmorum liber i,
   Salomonis libri iii (Proverbiorum, Ecclesiastes, Cantica
   Canticorum), Sapientia, Ecclesiasticus, libri xvi Prophetarum

8. Mommsen's List, cited by Zahn, *Gesch. d. N. T. Kanons*, ii. p. 143 f.; Sanday, *Studia Biblica*, iii. p. 222 f.; Preuschen, *Analecta*, p. 138 [1].

Libri canonici
Genesis versus $\overline{III}$DCC
Exodus $\overline{ver}$ $\overline{III}$
Numeri $\overline{ver}$ $\overline{III}$
Leviticus $\overline{ver}$ $\overline{IICCC}$
Deuteronomium $\overline{ver}$ $\overline{IIDCC}$
Hiesu Nave $\overline{ver}$ MDCCL
Iudicum $\overline{ver}$ MDCCL
Fiunt libri vii $\overline{ver}$ $\overline{XVIIIC}$
Rut $\overline{ver}$ CCL
Regnorum liber i $\overline{ver}$ $\overline{IICCC}$

Regnorum liber ii $\overline{ver}$ $\overline{IICC}$
Regnorum liber iii $\overline{ver}$ $\overline{IIDL}$
Regnorum liber iv $\overline{ver}$ $\overline{IICCL}$
Fiunt versus $\overline{VIIIID}$
Paralipomenon liber i $\overline{ver}$ $\overline{IIXL}$
liber ii $\overline{ver}$ $\overline{IIC}$
Machabeorum liber i $\overline{ver}$ $\overline{IICCC}$
liber ii $\overline{ver}$ MDCCC
Iob $\overline{ver}$ MDCC
Tobias $\overline{ver}$ DCCCC
Hester $\overline{ver}$ DCC

---

[1] The text of Preuschen has been followed; it is based on a St Gall
MS. which appears to be less corrupt than the Cheltenham MS. used by
Mommsen and others.

Iudit v̄e̅r̅ MC
Psalmi Davitici cli v̄e̅r̅ V
Salomonis v̄e̅r̅ V̅ID
Prophetae maiores v̄e̅r̅ X̅VCCCLXX
  numero IIII
Esaias v̄e̅r̅ IIIDLXXX

Ieremias v̄e̅r̅ I̅I̅I̅I̅CCCCL
Daniel v̄e̅r̅ MCCCL
Ezechiel v̄e̅r̅ I̅I̅I̅CCCXL
Prophetae xii v̄e̅r̅ IIIDCCC
Erunt omnes versus numero
  LXVIIIID

9. List in *Cod. Claromontanus.*

Versus scribturarum sanctarum
  ita Genesis versus IIIID
Exodus versus I̅I̅I̅DCC
Leviticum versus I̅I̅DCCC
Numeri versus I̅I̅I̅DCL
Deuteronomium ver. I̅I̅I̅CCC
Iesu Nauve ver. I̅I̅
Iudicum ver. I̅I̅
Rud ver. CCL
Regnorum ver.
  primus liber ver. I̅I̅D
  secundus lib. ver. I̅I̅
  tertius lib. ver. I̅I̅DC
  quartus lib. ver. I̅I̅CCCC
Psalmi Davitici ver. V̅
Proverbia ver. I̅DC
Aeclesiastes DC
Cantica canticorum CCC
Sapientia vers. I̅
Sapientia I̅H̅U̅ ver. I̅I̅D
XII Profetae ver. I̅I̅I̅CX
  Ossee ver. DXXX
  Amos ver. CCCCX
  Micheas ver. CCCX
  Ioel ver. XC
  Abdias ver. LXX
  Ionas ver. CL
  Naum ver. CXL
  Ambacum ver. CLX
  Sophonias ver. CXL
  Aggeus vers. CX
  Zacharias ver. DCLX
  Malachiel ver. CC
Eseias ver. IIIDC
Ieremias ver. I̅I̅I̅I̅LXX

10. *Liber sacramentorum* (Bobbio, cent. vi, vii).

Liber Genesis
Exodum
Leviticum
Numeri
Deuteronomium
Josue
Judicum
Libri mulierum
  Ruth
  Hester
  Judith
Maccabeorum libri duo
Job
Thobias
Regum quattuor
Prophetarum libri xvi
Daviticum v
Solomonis iii
Esdra i
  Fiunt libri Veteris numero
  xliiii

11. Council of Carthage, A.D. 397 (can. 47 = 39).

Ezechiel ver. $\overline{\text{IIIDC}}$
Daniel ver. $\overline{\text{IDC}}$
Maccabeorum sic.
   lib. primus ver. $\overline{\text{IICCC}}$
   lib. secundus ver. $\overline{\text{IICCC}}$
   lib. quartus ver. $\overline{\text{I}}$
Iudit ver. $\overline{\text{ICCC}}$
Hesdra $\overline{\text{ID}}$
Ester ver. $\overline{\text{I}}$
Iob ver. $\overline{\text{IDC}}$
Tobias ver. $\overline{\text{I}}$

Genesis
Exodus
Leviticus
Numeri
Deuteronomium
Iesu Naue
Iudicum
Ruth
Regnorum libri iv
Paralipomenon libri ii
Job
Psalterium Davidicum
Salomonis libri v
xii libri Prophetarum
Iesaias
Ieremias
Ezechiel
Daniel
Tobias
Iudith
Hester
Hesdrae libri ii
Machabaeorum libri ii[1]

2. We may now proceed to consider the chief points which these tables illustrate.

(1) THE TITLES OF THE BOOKS. It will be seen that the Hebrew titles fall into three classes. They consist of either (1) the first word or words of the book (Genesis—Deuteronomy, Proverbs, Lamentations); or (2) the name of the hero or supposed author (Joshua, Judges, Samuel, Kings, Isaiah and the other Prophets, Job, Ruth, Esther, Daniel, Ezra); or (3) a description of the contents (Psalms, Song of Songs, Chronicles). Titles of the second and third class are generally reproduced in the Greek; there are some variations, as when Samuel and Kings become 'Kingdoms,' and 'Diaries' (דִּבְרֵי־הַיָּמִים) is changed into 'Omissions' (Παραλειπόμενα[2]), but the system of nomenclature is the same. But titles of the first class disappear in the Greek, and in their place we find descriptive names, suggested in almost every case by words in the ver-

---

[1] See also the Latin list printed by Mr C. H. Turner in *J. Th. St.* i. 557 ff.
[2] Or less correctly Παραλειπόμενοι, 'omitted books,' as in some lists.

sion itself. Thus *Genesis* appears to come from Gen. ii. 4 αὕτη ἡ βίβλος γενέσεως οὐρανοῦ καὶ γῆς, *Exodus* from Ex. xix. 1 τῆς ἐξόδου τῶν υἱῶν Ἰσραὴλ ἐκ γῆς Αἰγύπτου, *Numbers* from Num. i. 2 κατὰ ἀριθμὸν ἐξ ὀνόματος, *Deuteronomy* from Deut. xvii. 18 γράψει αὐτῷ τὸ δευτερονόμιον τοῦτο εἰς βιβλίον[1], *Ecclesiastes* from Eccl. i. 1 ῥήματα ἐκκλησιαστοῦ.

The Greek titles are probably of Alexandrian origin and pre-Christian use. Not only were they familiar to Origen (Eus. *H. E.* vi. 25), but they are used in Melito's list, although it came from Palestine. Some of them at least appear to have been known to the writers of the New Testament; cf. Acts ii. 30 ἐν βίβλῳ ψαλμῶν, xiii. 33 ἐν τῷ ψαλμῷ τῷ δευτέρῳ, Rom. ix. 25 ἐν τῷ Ὡσῆε λέγει[2]. Philo[3] uses Γένεσις, Λευιτικὸν or Λευιτικὴ βίβλος, Δευτερονόμιον, Βασιλεῖαι, Παροιμίαι, but his practice is not quite constant; e.g. he calls Exodus ἡ Ἐξαγωγή[4]; Deuteronomy is sometimes ἡ Ἐπινομίς, and Judges ἡ τῶν Κριμάτων[5] βίβλος. Similar titles occur in the Mishna[6], whether suggested by the Alexandrian Greek, or independently coined by the Palestinian Jews; thus Genesis is סֵפֶר יְצִירָה, Numbers ס׳ מִסְפָּרִים, Proverbs ס׳ חָכְמָה, Lamentations קִינוֹת.

Through the Old Latin version the Greek titles passed into the Latin Bible[7], and from the Latin Bible into the later versions of Western Christendom. In three instances, however, the influence of Jerome restored the Hebrew titles; 1, 2 King-

---

[1] On this rendering see Driver, *Deuteronomy*, p. i. The Massora calls the book מִשְׁנֵה הַתּוֹרָה.

[2] See also Acts xiii. 20, 33, Rom. x. 16, xv. 11, Heb. xi. 22.

[3] See Prof. Ryle's *Philo and Holy Scripture*, p. xx. ff.

[4] So in Cohn-Wendland's edition (iii. 4, 57, 230); in ii. 271 this title is ascribed to Moses, although ἐξαγωγή does not like ἔξοδος occur in the Alexandrian version of the book. Ἡ Ἐξαγωγή was also the title of the Hellenist Ezekiel's poem on the Exodus (see below, p. 371).

[5] Cf. the change from מְלָכִים to Βασιλεῖαι.

[6] See Ryle, *Canon of the O.T.*, p. 294.

[7] Sometimes in a simple transliteration, as *Genesis* &c. Tertullian has *Arithmi*, but in Cyprian the Latin *Numeri* is already used; see Burkitt, *O. L. and Itala*, p. 4.

doms have become 1, 2 Samuel, and 3, 4 Kingdoms, 1, 2
Kings, whilst 'Chronicles,' representing the Hebrew הַיָּמִים־דִּבְרֵי,
has taken the place of *Paralipomenon.*

> Cf. Hieron. *Prol. Gal.*: "tertius sequitur *Samuel,* quem nos
> *Regnorum* primum et secundum dicimus; quartus *Malachim,* id
> est *Regum,* qui tertio et quarto *Regnorum* volumine continetur...
> septimus *Dabre aiamim,* id est 'Verba dierum,' quod significan-
> tius *Chronicon* totius divinae historiae possumus appellare."
> The Greek titles vary slightly in different codices and lists.
> Besides the variations of cod. A which appear in Table B (2),
> the following are mentioned in the apparatus of Holmes and
> Parsons. *Joshua*: Ἰησοῦς ὁ Ναυή, ὁ τοῦ Ναυή, *Judges*: Κριταὶ
> τοῦ Ἰσραήλ, αἱ τῶν κριτῶν πράξεις. *Chronicles*: Παραλειπομένων
> τῶν βασιλειῶν Ἰούδα. *Psalms*: Δαυὶδ προφήτου καὶ βασιλέως
> μέλος. When Nehemiah is separated from Ezra its title is:
> τὰ περὶ Νεεμίου or λόγοι Ν. υἱοῦ Ἀχαλία. A few further forms
> may be gleaned from the patristic lists. As an alternative for
> Παραλειπομένων the Apostolic Canons give τοῦ βιβλίου τῶν ἡμε-
> ρῶν, while Ezra is known to Hilary as *sermones dierum Esdrae.*
> The Psalter is sometimes βίβλος Ψαλμῶν, *liber Psalmorum,* or
> Ψαλτήριον Δαβιτικόν, *Psalmi David regis, Psalterium Daviti-
> cum.* For Ἀσμα ἀσμάτων we have occasionally ᾄσματα ἀσμάτων
> —a form rejected by Origen (*ap.* Eus. *H.E.* vi. 25 οὐ γάρ, ὡς
> ὑπολαμβάνουσί τινες, Ἄσματα ἀσμάτων), but used by Pseudo-
> Chrysostom and John of Damascus, and found in cod. A
> and in several of the Latin lists[1]; cf. the English Article vi.
> "*Cantica, or Songs of Solomon.*" The lesser Prophets are οἱ
> δώδεκα or δεκαδύο, τῶν δώδεκα προφητῶν μία βίβλος, τὸ δωδεκα-
> πρόφητον, *prophetae xii*; the greater, οἱ τέσσαρες, *prophetae iv,
> prophetae iv maiorum voluminum,* or simply *maiores*; when
> the two collections are merged into one they become οἱ δεκαέξ
> or οἱ ἑκκαίδεκα, τὸ ἑκκαιδεκαπρόφητον, *prophetae xvi.*

(2) THE GROUPING OF THE BOOKS. The methods of
grouping adopted in the Hebrew and Alexandrian Greek
Bibles differ not less widely than the nomenclature of the
books. The Hebrew canon is uniformly tripartite, and "the
books belonging to one division are never (by the Jews) transferred to another[2]." Its three groups are known as the Law

---

[1] The official Vulgate had *Canticum,* until the plural was adopted by
Sixtus V. ; see Nestle, *ein Jubiläum der Lat. Bibel,* p. 18.

[2] Driver, *Introd.,* p. xxvii.

(תּוֹרָה), the Prophets (נְבִיאִים), and the Writings (כְּתוּבִים).
The Massora recognised, however, certain subdivisions within
the second and third groups; the Prophets were classed
as *Former* (רִאשׁוֹנִים), i.e. Joshua, Judges, Samuel, Kings;
and *Latter* (אַחֲרוֹנִים), and among the 'Latter' the Twelve
minor Prophets formed a single collection[1]. Similarly 'the five
Rolls' (מְגִלּוֹת), i.e. Ruth, Canticles, Ecclesiastes, Lamentations, Esther, made a subsection among the Kethubim. The tripartite division of the canon was known at
Alexandria in the second century B.C., for the writer of the
prologue to Sirach refers to it more than once (1 f. τοῦ νόμου
καὶ τῶν προφητῶν καὶ τῶν ἄλλων τῶν κατ᾽ αὐτοὺς ἠκολουθηκότων:
6 f. τοῦ νόμου καὶ τῶν προφητῶν καὶ τῶν ἄλλων πατρίων βιβλίων:
14 f. ὁ νόμος καὶ αἱ προφητεῖαι καὶ τὰ λοιπὰ τῶν βιβλίων). It is
also recognised in the New Testament, where the Law and the
Prophets are mentioned as authoritative collections, and in one
passage the 'Writings' are represented by the Psalter (Lc.
xxiv. 44 πάντα τὰ γεγραμμένα ἐν τῷ νόμῳ Μωυσέως καὶ τοῖς
προφήταις καὶ ψαλμοῖς). But the New Testament has no
comprehensive name for the third group, and even Josephus
(*c. Ap.* i. 8) speaks of four poetical books (probably Psalms,
Job, Proverbs and Ecclesiastes) as forming with the Law and
the Prophets the entire series of sacred books; the rest of
the Hagiographa seem to have been counted by him among
the Prophets[2]. At Alexandria the later books were probably
attached to the canon by a looser bond. The writer of the
De vita contemplativa appears to recognise four groups[3] (§ 3
νόμους, καὶ λόγια θεσπισθέντα διὰ προφητῶν, καὶ ὕμνους, καὶ τὰ
ἄλλα οἷς ἐπιστήμη καὶ εὐσέβεια συναύξονται καὶ τελειοῦνται).

Only the first of the three Palestinian groups remains undis-

---

[1] So already in Sir. xlix. 10 τῶν ιβʹ προφητῶν.
[2] See Ryle, *Canon of the O.T.*, p. 165 f.
[3] Unless we omit the comma after ὕμνους and regard ϑ. καὶ τὰ ἄλλα as
= the Hagiographa; cf. Joseph. *c. Ap.* as quoted below, p. 220.

turbed[1] in the Alexandrian Greek Bible, as it is preserved to us
in MSS. and described in Christian lists.   When the Law was
translated into Greek, it was already a complete collection,
hedged round with special sanctions, and in all forms of the
Greek Bible it retains its precedence and has resisted any extensive intrusion of foreign matter.   It is otherwise with the
Prophets and the Hagiographa.   Neither of these groups
escaped decomposition when it passed into the Greek Bible.
The Former Prophets are usually separated from the Latter,
the poetical books coming between.   The Hagiographa are
entirely broken up, the non-poetical books being divided
between the histories and the prophets.   This distribution is
clearly due to the characteristically Alexandrian desire to
arrange the books according to their literary character or
contents, or their supposed authorship.   Histories were made
to consort with histories, prophetic and poetical writings with
others of their respective kinds.   On this principle Daniel
is in all Greek codices and catalogues one of the Greater
Prophets, while Ruth attaches itself to Judges, and Canticles
to Ecclesiastes.

In many of the Greek patristic lists the Alexandrian
principle of grouping receives express recognition.   Thus
Cyril of Jerusalem, Gregory of Nazianzus, and Leontius,
divide the books of the Old Testament into (1) historical
—12, including the Mosaic Pentateuch; (2) poetical—5;
(3) prophetical—5.   Epiphanius, followed by John of Damascus, endeavours to combine this grouping with a system of
pentateuchs[2]—(1) legal, (2) poetical, (3) historical[3], (4) pro-

---

[1] Yet even the Torah was not always kept apart in the Greek Bible, as
the names Octateuch and Heptateuch witness.

[2] Dr Sanday (in *Studia Biblica*, iii. p. 240) regards this as Palestinian,
identifying it with Cyril's method.   But Cyril begins with a dodecad
(δωδεκάτη ἡ Ἐσθήρ· καὶ τὰ μὲν Ἱστορικὰ ταῦτα).

[3] The term γραφεῖα (כְּתוּבִים) or ἁγιόγραφα is transferred to this group.

phetical—an end which he attains by relegating Ezra and Esther to an appendix. Pseudo-Chrysostom's arrangement is similar, though slightly different in some of its details; according to his view the Bible began with an Octateuch, and the στιχηρά are broken up, the Psalter being placed with the Prophets, and the Salomonic books described as 'hortatory'[1] (τὸ συμβουλευτικόν). Even in the eccentric arrangement of Junilius[2] the Greek method of grouping is clearly dominant.

The relative order of the groups in the Greek Bible, being of literary and not historical origin, is to some extent liable to variation. The 'five books of Moses' always claim precedence, and the 'rest of the histories' follow, but the position of the poetical and prophetical books is less certain. Codex B places the poetical books first, whilst in Codd. א and A the prophets precede. But the order of cod. B is supported by the great majority of authorities both Eastern and Western (Melito, Origen, Athanasius, Cyril, Epiphanius (1, 3), Gregory, Amphilochius, the Laodicene and 'Apostolic' canons, Nicephorus, Pseudo-Chrysostom, the Cheltenham list, the African canons of 397, and Augustine). Two reasons may have combined to favour this arrangement. 'David' and 'Solomon' were higher up the stream of time than Hosea and Isaiah. Moreover, it may have seemed fitting that the Prophets should immediately precede the Evangelists.

(3) THE NUMBER OF THE BOOKS. In our printed Hebrew Bibles the books of the Old Testament are 39 (Law, 5; Former Prophets (Joshua—2 Kings), 6; Latter Prophets, 15; Hagiographa, 13). But Samuel, Kings, Ezra-Nehemiah, and

---

[1] So Leontius (τὰ παραινετικά), but he classed the Psalter among them.
[2] See Kihn, *Theodor v. Mopsuestia u. Junilius*, p. 356 f.

Chronicles[1], were originally single books[2], and the Minor Prophets were also counted as a single book. Thus the number is reduced to 24 (Law, 5; Former Prophets, 4; Latter Prophets, 4; Hagiographa, 11), and this answers to the prevalent Jewish tradition. On the other hand Josephus expressly limits the books to 22 (Law, 5; Prophets, 13; Hymns and moral pieces, 4). He has probably included the historical Hagiographa among the Prophets, and treated Ruth and Lamentations as appendices to Judges and Jeremiah respectively.

Both traditions were inherited by the Church, but the latter was predominant, especially in the East. In some lists indeed the twenty-two books became twenty-seven, the 'double books' being broken up into their parts (Epiph. 1)[3]; in some a similar treatment of the Dodecapropheton raised the number to 34 (the 'Sixty Books'), and there are other eccentricities of numeration which need not be mentioned here.

Josephus, *c. Ap.* i. 8 : οὐ μυριάδες βιβλίων εἰσὶ παρ' ἡμῖν ἀσυμφώνων καὶ μαχομένων, δύο δὲ μόνα πρὸς τοῖς εἴκοσι βιβλία...καὶ τούτων πέντε μέν ἐστι Μωυσέως...οἱ μετὰ Μωυσῆν προφῆται...συνέγραψαν ἐν τρισὶ καὶ δέκα βιβλίοις· αἱ δὲ λοιπαὶ τέσσαρες ὕμνους εἰς τὸν θεὸν καὶ τοῖς ἀνθρώποις ὑποθήκας τοῦ βίου περιέχουσιν. He is followed by Origen *ap.* Eus. *l.c.* οὐκ ἀγνοητέον δ' εἶναι τὰς ἐνδιαθήκους βίβλους ὡς Ἑβραῖοι παραδιδόασιν, ὅσος ὁ ἀριθμὸς τῶν παρ' αὐτοῖς στοιχείων ἐστίν· and Cyril. Hier. *catech.* iv. 33 ἀναγίνωσκε τὰς θείας γραφάς, τὰς εἴκοσι δύο βίβλους τῆς παλαιᾶς διαθήκης. Similarly Athanasius, *ep. fest.* 39 (Migne, *P.G.* xxvi. col. 1437). When another numeration was adopted, efforts were

---

[1] Chronicles-Ezra-Nehemiah appears to have been originally a single book. But while Ezra and Nehemiah are still joined in the Greek Bible, Chronicles stands by itself both in 𝕸 and 𝕲, and in 𝕸 it follows Nehemiah and forms the last book of the Canon (cf. Mt. xxiii. 35, and see Barnes, *Chronicles*, in the *Cambridge Bible*, pp. x.—xiii.).

[2] The division probably began in the LXX.

[3] Jerome, *Prol. Gal.*: "quinque a plerisque libri duplices aestimantur." As the twenty-two books answered to the twenty-two letters of the Hebrew alphabet, so these 'double books' were thought to correspond to the 'double letters,' i.e. those which had two forms (צ, פ, נ, מ, כ). The 'double books' were not always identical in different lists; see Sanday, *op. cit.* p. 239.

made to shew that it did not involve a real departure from the canon of twenty-two; cf. Epiph. *haer.* i. 1. 8, αὗταί εἰσιν αἱ εἴκοσι ἑπτὰ βίβλοι αἱ ἐκ θεοῦ δοθεῖσαι τοῖς Ἰουδαίοις, εἴκοσι δύο δὲ ὡς τὰ παρ᾽ αὐτοῖς στοιχεῖα τῶν Ἑβραικῶν γραμμάτων ἀριθμούμεναι διὰ τὸ διπλοῦσθαι δέκα βίβλους εἰς πέντε λεγομένας· *dial. Tim. et Aq.* (ed. Conybeare, p. 66), αὗται αἱ βίβλοι αἱ θεόπνευστοι καὶ ἐνδιάθετοι, κϚ´ μὲν οὖσαι, κβ´ δὲ ἀριθμούμεναι διὰ τὸ...ἐξ αὐτῶν διπλοῦσθαι.

On the other hand the numeration in 4 Esdr. xiv. 44 rests, if *nongenti quatuor* be the true reading, on a tradition which makes the Hebrew books 24. This tradition is supported by the testimony of the Talmud and the Rabbinical literature[1], and the Canon is known in Jewish writings by the name כ״ד ספרים, "the Twenty-Four Books." It finds a place in certain Western Christian writers, e.g. Victorinus of Petau *comm. in Apoc.*: "sunt autem libri V.T. qui accipiuntur viginti quatuor quos in epitome Theodori invenies[2]." Victorinus compares the 24 books to the 24 Elders of Apoc. iv., and the same fancy finds a place in the Cheltenham list ("ut in apocalypsi Iohannis dictum est *Vidi XXIIII seniores mittentes coronas suas ante thronum*, maiores nostri probant hoc libros esse canonicos"). Jerome knows both traditions, though he favours the former (*Prol. Gal.* "quomodo igitur viginti duo elementa sunt...ita viginti duo volumina supputantur...quamquam nonnulli Ruth et Cinoth inter Hagiographa scriptitent et libros hos in suo putent numero supputandos et per hoc esse priscae legis libros viginti quatuor").

Let us now turn to the ecclesiastical lists and see how far the Hebrew Canon was maintained.

Our earliest Christian list was obtained from Palestine[3], and probably represents the contents of the Palestinian Greek Bible. It is an attempt to answer the question, What is the true number and order of the books of the Old Testament? Both the titles and the grouping are obviously Greek, but the books are exclusively those of the Hebrew canon. Esther does not appear, but the number of the books is twenty-two, if we are intended to count 1—4 Regn. as two.

---

[1] Cf. Ryle, *Canon*, pp. 157 f., 222, 292; Sanday, *op. cit.* p. 236 ff.

[2] Zahn offers a suggestion, to which Sanday inclines, that the writer refers to the *Excerpta ex Theodoto* which are partly preserved in the works of Clement of Alexandria.

[3] Melito *ap.* Eus. *H. E.* iv. 26 ἐπειδὴ μαθεῖν τὴν τῶν παλαιῶν βιβλίων ἐβουλήθης ἀκρίβειαν, πόσα τὸν ἀριθμὸν καὶ ὁποῖα τὴν τάξιν εἶεν...ἀνελθὼν εἰς τὴν ἀνατολὴν καὶ ἕως τοῦ τόπου ἔνθα ἐκηρύχθη καὶ ἐπράχθη...ἔπεμψά σοι.

The next list comes from Origen. It belongs to his commentary on the first Psalm, which was written at Alexandria[1], i.e. before A.D. 231. The books included in it are expressly said to be the twenty-two of the Hebrew canon (εἰσὶ δὲ αἱ εἴκοσι δύο βίβλοι καθ᾽ Ἑβραίους αἵδε). Yet among them are the first book of Esdras[2] and the Epistle of Jeremiah, which the Jews never recognised. With the addition of Baruch, Origen's list is repeated by Athanasius, Cyril, Epiphanius (1), and in the Laodicean canon; Amphilochius mentions two books of Esdras, and it is at least possible that the Esdras of Gregory of Nazianzus is intended to include both books, and that the Epistle, or Baruch and the Epistle, are to be understood as forming part of Jeremiah in the lists both of Gregory and Amphilochius. Thus it appears that an expansion of the Hebrew canon, which involved no addition to the number of the books, was predominant in the East during the fourth century.

The Eastern lists contain other books, but they are definitely placed outside the Canon. This practice seems to have begun with Origen, who after enumerating the twenty-two books adds, ἔξω δὲ τούτων ἐστὶ τὰ Μακκαβαϊκά. Athanasius takes up the expression, but names other books—the two Wisdoms, Esther[3], Judith, and Tobit[4]. Palestine was perhaps naturally conservative in this matter; Cyril will not allow his catechumens to go beyond the Canon, and Epiphanius mentions only, and that with some hesitation, the two books of Wisdom (εἰσὶ δὲ καὶ ἄλλαι παρ᾽ αὐτοῖς βίβλοι ἐν ἀμφιλέκτῳ[5]...

---

[1] Eus. *H.E.* vi. 24.

[2] Already cited freely by Josephus as an authority for the history of the period. Origen, it should be added, regards 1, 2 Esdras as a single volume (Ἔσδρας πρώτη, δευτέρα ἐν ἑνί).

[3] Cf. Melito's omission of Esther, and the note appended to the list of Amphilochius.

[4] The N.T. members of the same class are the *Teaching* and the *Shepherd*.

[5] *Haer.* I. i. 1.

αὗται χρήσιμοι μέν εἰσι καὶ ὠφέλιμοι, ἀλλ᾽ εἰς ἀριθμὸν ῥητῶν οὐκ ἀναφέρονται)[1]. And this was the prevalent attitude of the East even at a later time. There are exceptions; Pseudo-Chrysostom places Sirach among the Hortatory books of the canon; the Apostolic canons, while excluding Sirach, include three books of Maccabees. But John of Damascus reflects the general opinion of the Greek fathers when, while reckoning both books of Esdras[2] as canonical, he repeats the verdict of Epiphanius upon the two Wisdoms, Ἐνάρετοι μὲν καὶ καλαί, ἀλλ᾽ οὐκ ἀριθμοῦνται[3].

On the other hand the West, further from the home of the Hebrew canon, and knowing the Old Testament chiefly through the Latin version of the LXX., did not scruple to mingle non-canonical books with the canonical. Hilary and Ruffinus[4] were doubtless checked, the one by the influence of Eastern theologians, the other by the scholarship of Jerome; but Hilary mentions that there were those who wished to raise the number of the canonical books to twenty-four by including Tobit and Judith in the canon. From the end of the fourth century the inclusion of the non-canonical books in Western lists is a matter of course. Even Augustine has no scruples on the subject; he makes the books of the Old Testament forty-four (*de doctr. Chr.* ii. 13 "his xliv libris Testamenti Veteris terminatur auctoritas[5]"), and among them Tobit, Judith, and two books of Maccabees take rank with the histories; and the two Wisdoms, although he confesses that they were not the work of Solomon, are classed with the

---

[1] *De mens. et pond.* 4.

[2] Like Origen, he explains that they form together but a single book (τοῦ Ἔσδρα αἱ δύο εἰς μίαν συναπτόμεναι βίβλον).

[3] The non-canonical books (τὰ ἔξω) are however carefully distinguished from real *apocrypha* when the latter are mentioned; e.g. in the stichometry of Nicephorus, and in the list of the 'Sixty Books.'

[4] *In symb.* 38 "alii libri sunt qui non canonici sed ecclesiastici a maioribus appellati sunt."

[5] Cf. *Retract.* ii. 4.

Prophets. His judgement was that of his Church (Conc. Carth. iii. *can.* xlvii. "sunt canonicae scripturae Salomonis libri quinque...Tobias, Judith...Machabaeorum libri duo"). The African Church had probably never known any other canon, and its belief prevailed wherever the Latin Bible was read.

There can be little doubt that, notwithstanding the strict adherence of the Eastern lists to the number of the Hebrew books, the Old Latin canon truly represents the collection of Greek sacred books which came into the hands of the early Christian communities at Antioch, Alexandria, and Rome. When Origen and the Greek fathers who follow him fix the number of the books at twenty-two or twenty-four, they follow, not the earlier tradition of the Church, but the corrected estimate of Christian scholars who had learned it from Jewish teachers. An earlier tradition is represented by the line of Christian writers, beginning with Clement of Rome, who quoted the 'Apocryphal' books apparently without suspecting that they were not part of the Canon. Thus Clement of Rome[1] places the story of Judith side by side with that of Esther; the Wisdom of Sirach is cited by Barnabas[2] and the *Didache*[3], and Tobit by Polycarp[4]; Clement of Alexandria[5] and Origen appeal to Tobit and both the Wisdoms, to which Origen adds Judith[6]. Our earliest MSS. of the Greek Bible confirm the impression derived from the quotations of the earliest Christian writers. Their canon corresponds not with that of the great writers of the age when they were written, but with that of the Old Latin version of the LXX. Codd. B ℵ A contain the two Wisdoms, Tobit, and Judith; 1—2 Maccabees are added in ℵ, and 1—4 Maccabees in A; cod. C still exhibits the two Wisdoms, and when complete may have contained other books of the same class.

---

[1] 1 *Cor.* 55.   [2] c. 19. 9.   [3] c. 4.
[4] *Philipp.* 10.   [5] *Strom.* i. 10, v. 14.
[6] Cf. Westcott in *D.C.B.* iv. p. 130.

Moreover, the position of the books shews that the scribes of these MSS. or of their archetypes lacked either the power or the will to distinguish them from the books of the Hebrew canon. In the light of the facts already produced, it is clear that the presence of the non-canonical books in Greek Bibles cannot be attributed to the skilled writers of the fourth and fifth centuries. They have but perpetuated an older tradition —a tradition probably inherited from the Alexandrian Jews.

An explanation of the early mixture of non-canonical books with canonical may be found in the form under which the Greek Bible passed into the keeping of the Church. In the first century the material used for literary purposes was still almost exclusively papyrus, and the form was that of the roll[1]. But rolls of papyrus seldom contained more than a single work, and writings of any length, especially if divided into books, were often transcribed into two or more separate rolls[2]. The rolls were kept in boxes (κιβωτοί, κίσται, *capsae, cistae*)[3], which served not only to preserve them, but to collect them in sets. Now while the sanctity of the five books of Moses would protect the *cistae* which contained them from the intrusion of foreign rolls, no scruple of this kind would deter the owner of a roll of Esther from placing it in the same box with Judith and Tobit; the Wisdoms in like manner naturally found their way into a Salomonic collection; while in a still larger number of instances the two Greek recensions of Esdras consorted together, and Baruch and the Epistle seemed rightly to claim a place with the roll of Jeremiah. More rarely such a writing as the Psalms of Solomon may have found its way into the company of kindred books of the canon. It is not a serious objection to this hypothesis

[1] See Kenyon, *Palaeography of Greek papyri*, pp. 24, 113 ff.
[2] *Ib.* p. 122: "no papyrus roll of Homer hitherto discovered contains more than two books of the Iliad. Three short orations fill the largest roll of Hyperides."
[3] E. M. Thompson, *Greek and Latin Palaeography*, p. 57.

that Philo does not quote the Apocrypha, and has no certain allusion to it[1]. A great scholar would not be deceived by the mixture of heterogeneous rolls, which might nevertheless seriously mislead ordinary readers, and start a false tradition in an unlettered community such as the Christian society of the first century.

(4) THE INTERNAL ORDER OF THE GROUPS. Even in Jewish lists of the Hebrew Canon there are variations in the internal order of the Prophets and the Hagiographa. The 'Great Prophets' occur in each of the three orders (1) Isaiah, Jeremiah, Ezekiel; (2) Jeremiah, Ezekiel, Isaiah; (3) Jeremiah, Isaiah, Ezekiel[2]. The order of the Hagiographa varies more extensively. In the printed Bibles they are arranged in three subdivisions: (1) Psalms, Proverbs, Job; (2) Canticles, Ruth, Ecclesiastes, Lamentations, Esther (the five Megilloth); (3) Daniel, Ezra, Chronicles. The Talmudic order is as follows: Ruth, Psalms, Job, Proverbs, Ecclesiastes, Canticles, Lamentations, Daniel, Esther, Chronicles. The MSS. vary, many agreeing with the printed Bibles; others, especially those of Spanish *provenance*, following the order: Chronicles, Psalms, Job, Proverbs, Ruth, Canticles, Ecclesiastes, Lamentations, Esther, Daniel, Ezra[3].

In the lists of the Greek Bible and the sequence of its MSS. the Law and the 'Former Prophets' generally retain their Hebrew order, with the noteworthy exception that Ruth is always attached to Judges. But there are also minor exceptions which are of some interest. Even in the Pentateuch Melito, Leontius, and the Cheltenham list reverse the common order of Leviticus and Numbers[4]. The sequence is broken in some lists after Ruth (Laod., Epiph. 1), or even after Joshua

[1] Ryle, *Philo and Holy Scripture*, p. xxxiii.
[2] See Ryle, *Canon*, p. 225 ff.
[3] Ryle, *ib.*, pp. 229 ff., 281 f.
[4] On this see Sanday, *Studia Biblica*, iii. p. 241.

(Epiph. 3¹) or Deuteronomy (Epiph. 2). Occasionally Chronicles, which is an intruder from the Hagiographa, precedes 1—4 Regn. (Epiph. 2, *Dial. Tim. et Aq.*), or drops out altogether (Ps.-Chrys., Junilius, Cod. Clarom.). All these disturbances of the normal order may be ascribed to local or individual influences, and find no support in the uncial MSS. of the Greek Bible. But it is otherwise when we come to the 'Latter Prophets' and the Hagiographa. With regard to the Prophets, three questions of order arise. (1) There is the relative order of the Twelve and the Four. In the majority of patristic lists the Twelve precede (Ath., Cyr., Epiph., Greg., Amph., &c.), and this is also the order of Codd. A, B, N-V. But Cod. ℵ begins with the Four, and it is supported by other authorities, chiefly Western (Ruff., Chelt., Ps.-Gelasius, Cassiodorius, Nicephorus); whilst in a few the subdivisions are mixed (Melito, Junilius, Ebedjesu²). (2) The internal order of the δωδεκαπρόφητον in most of the MSS. and catalogues³ where it is stated differs from the Hebrew order in regard to the relative positions of the prophets in the first half of the group; the Hebrew order being Hosea, Joel, Amos, Obadiah, Jonah, Micah, but the Greek, Hosea, Amos, Micah, Joel, Obadiah, Jonah. The dominant Greek order may perhaps be due to "an attempt to secure greater accuracy in the chronological arrangement⁴." (3) The

---

[1] Ruth is attached to 1 Regn. in the Cheltenham list, and Augustine inclines to this arrangement (see Sanday, *l.c.*, p. 242). The result was to create a *Heptateuch*; for the word cf. J. E. B. Mayor, *The Latin Heptateuch*, p. xxxvi. R. Peiper's text of the *Heptateuchos*, to which Prof. Mayor refers (p. xxxiv.), appeared in the Vienna *Corpus scr. eccl. lat.* vol. xxiii. (1895).

[2] For statements by early Mohammedan writers as to the extent of the Jewish and Christian Canons see Margoliouth in *Exp. Times*, Nov. 1899, p. 91.

[3] The chief exceptions are: Cod. v, Hosea, Amos, Joel, Obadiah, Jonah, Micah; Greg. Naz. and Cod. Barocc., Hosea, Amos, Micah, Joel, Jonah, Obadiah; Junilius, Ebedjesu, Augustine, the Hebrew order.

[4] Ryle, *Canon*, p. 229.

Greek order of the Greater Prophets follows the oldest Hebrew tradition (Isaiah, Jeremiah, Ezekiel), but it appends Lamentations to Jeremiah, and enlarges the group by placing Daniel either before (Melito, Origen, Hilary, Chelt., Augustine), or, more usually, after Ezekiel.

The relative order of the Hagiographa in the LXX. is more perplexing. For Ruth, Lamentations, and Daniel we have already accounted; there remain Chronicles, Job, Psalms, Proverbs, Ecclesiastes, Canticles, Esther, and Ezra. Chronicles, in accordance with the theory enshrined in its Greek name, usually follows Kings. Psalms, Proverbs, Ecclesiastes, Canticles, for the most part hold together in that order, as a group of poetical books; but there are many exceptions. 'David' sometimes goes with the Prophets (Ps.-Chrys., Junilius, Augustine, Isidorus), and the group is then regarded as 'Salomonic,' or 'hortatory.' Lists which admit the two books of Wisdom usually join them to this subdivision (Ebedjesu, Carth., Augustine, Innocent, Cod. Clarom., Ps.-Gelasius, Cassiodorius, Isidorus). The internal order of the Salomonic books varies (Proverbs, Ecclesiastes, Canticles ; Ecclesiastes, Canticles, Proverbs ; Proverbs, Canticles, Ecclesiastes) ; the Wisdoms usually follow, but sometimes break the sequence of the three canonical books. Much difficulty seems to have been felt as to the place of Job ; the book normally appears in connexion with the poetical books, either last or first, but it is sometimes placed among the histories (Augustine, Innocent, Cod. Clarom., Ps.-Gelasius, Cassiodorius), or after the Prophets (Origen). The position of Esdras is not less uncertain ; its normal place is after Chronicles, but it is also found before or after the Prophets (Melito, Epiph., John of Damascus, Cod. Barocc.), or in connexion with a group of the apocryphal histories (cod. A, Carth., Augustine, &c.). Esther is still more erratic; sometimes it follows the poetical books, sometimes the Prophets, sometimes the histories ; not a few lists place it among the antilegomena, or omit it altogether. When admitted to a place in the Canon, it is usually to be found at or near the end (Origen, Epiphanius, Amphilochius, John of Damascus, Hilary, Carth., Cod. Clarom., Ps.-Gelasius, Cassiodorius), and in company with apocryphal books, especially Judith[1] and Tobit (codd. BℵA, Chelt., Carth., Augustine, and the later Latin lists[2]). It seems as if the doubt which the Jewish authorities felt with regard to this book was inherited by many Christians. On the other hand Cyril, who represents the tradition of the Church of Jerusalem, makes it the twelfth of the canonical books, and in the Laodicene list it stands eighth.

Except in cases where an old or well-defined tradition fixed the internal order of groups of books, there was clearly room for every possible variation so long as the books were written on separate rolls. The *cista* might serve to keep a group together, but it offered no means of fixing the relative order of its contents. In the codex, on the other hand, when it contained more than one writing, the order was necessarily fixed[3], and the scribe unconsciously created a tradition which was followed by later copyists. The 'transition to vellum,' and the consequent transition from the roll to the codex, does not seem to have been general before the fourth century, although in the case of Biblical MSS. it may have begun a century earlier[4]; and thus we may regard our earliest uncial codices as prototypes of the variations in order which mark the mass of later MSS. A single instance may suffice. It has been stated that Esther is frequently found in company

[1] The proximity of Esther to Judith in many lists is perhaps due to the circumstance that in both books the central figure is a woman; cf. p. 213 (right-hand column).

[2] Cf. Ryle, *Canon*, p. 199 ff.

[3] Cf. Sanday, *Studia Biblica*, iii. p. 233 ff.

[4] See Kenyon, *Palaeography of papyri*, p. 119 f.; Sanday, *l.c.* Papyrus was freely used for codices in Egypt during the third century; cf. Grenfell and Hunt, *Oxyrhynchus Papyri*, ii. p. 2.

with Judith and Tobit.   But these books occur in varying
order in the oldest MSS.; in B we have Esther, Judith, Tobit,
but in א A, Esther, Tobit, Judith; a favourite Western order
is Tobit, Esther, Judith (Chelt., Augustine, Innocent, Gelasius,
Cassiodorius, Isidorus); another, sanctioned at Carthage in
397, is apparently more common in MSS. of the Vulgate, viz.,
Tobit, Judith, Esther[1].   Such variations, resting on no obvious
principle, are doubtless ultimately due to the judgement or
caprice of a few scribes, whose copies supplied the archetypes
of the later Greek MSS. and the daughter-versions of the
Septuagint.

LITERATURE.   On the general subject of this chapter the
student may consult C. A. Credner, *Gesch. d. N.T. Kanons* (ed.
Volkmar, Berlin, 1860); Th. Zahn, *Gesch. d. N.T. Kanons*, ii.,
p. 143 ff. (Erlangen, 1890); B. F. Westcott, *Hist. of the Canon of
the N.T.*[6] (Cambridge, 1891); W. Sanday, *The Cheltenham List*,
in *Studia Biblica*, iii., pp. 226—243 (Oxford, 1891); Buhl,
Kanon u. Text des A.T. (Leipzig, 1891); H. E. Ryle, *Canon of
the O.T.* (London, 1892); E. Preuschen, *Analecta* (Leipzig, 1893);
H. L. Strack, art. *Kanon des Alten Testamentes* in *P.R.E.*[3] ix.
741—767.

---

[1] For the order of the books in Latin MS. Bibles see S. Berger, *Histoire de la Vulgate*, pp. 301-6, 331-9.

CHAPTER II.

BOOKS OF THE HEBREW CANON.

THE books which are common to the Hebrew Bible and the Alexandrian Version[1] differ in regard to their contents as well as in their titles and order. Differences of contents may conveniently be considered under two heads, as they affect the sequence or the subject-matter.

(A) DIFFERENCES OF SEQUENCE.

1. The following table shews the principal instances in which the Greek and the Hebrew books are at variance in reference to the order of the contents. The chapters and verses in the left-hand column are those of the Cambridge Septuagint; the right-hand column follows the numeration of the printed Hebrew Bibles.

GREEK.	HEBREW.
Gen. xxxi. 46^b—52	Gen. xxxi. 48^a, 47, 51, 52^a, 48^b, 49, 50^a, 52^b
„ xxxv. 16—21	„ xxxv. 16+21, 17—20, 22^a
Exod. xx. 13—15	Exod. xx. 14, 15, 13
„ xxxv. 8—11, 12, 15—16, 17, 18, 19^b	„ xxxv. 9—12, 17, 13—14, 16, 19, 15

[1] Following the order of *The Old Testament in Greek*, these are Genesis, Exodus, Leviticus, Numbers, Deuteronomy, Joshua, Judges, Ruth, 1—4 Kingdoms (vol. i.), 1—2 Paralipomena, 2 Esdras, Psalms, Proverbs, Ecclesiastes, Canticles, Job, Esther (vol. ii.), the Twelve Minor Prophets, the Four Greater Prophets (vol. iii.)—37 in all.

GREEK.	HEBREW.
Exod. xxxvi. 8ᵇ—40	Exod. xxxix. 1—31
„ xxxvii. 1—2	„ xxxvi. 8—9
„ „ 8—6	„ „ 35—38
„ „ 7—21	„ xxxviii. 9—23
„ xxxviii. 1—17	„ xxxvii. 1—24
„ „ 18—20	„ xxxvi. 20—34
21—24	„ xxxviii. 1—7
„ „ 25	„ xxxvii. 29
„ „ 26	„ xxxviii. 8
„ „ 27	„ xl. 30—32
„ xxxix. 1—10	„ xxxviii. 24—31
„ „ 11	„ xxxix. 32
„ „ 13—23	„ „ 33—43
„ xl. 6ᵇ—8, 10—25, 26, 27 —32	„ xl. 8—10, 12—27, 29, 33, 38
Num. i. 24—37	Num. i. 26—37, 24—25
„ vi. 22—26	„ vi. 22, 23, 27, 24, 25, 26
„ xxvi. 15—47	„ xxvi. 19—27, 15—18, 44— 47, 28—43
Josh. ix. 3—33	Josh. viii. 30—33, ix. 3—27
„ xix. 47—48	„ xix. 48, 47
3 Regn. iv. 17, 18, 19	1 Kings iv. 18, 19, 17
„ „ 20—21, 22—24 25—30	„ „ 7—8, 2—4, 9—14
„ v. 1—16, 17	„ v. 15—30, 32ᵇ
„ vi. 2—3	„ v. 31—32ᵃ
„ vi. 4—5, 6—7, 8, 9—15, 16—34	„ vi. 37—38, 2—3, 14, 4 —10, 15—36
„ vii. 1—6, 7, 8—9, 10— 11, 12—13	„ vii. 13—18, 21, 19—20, 23—24, 26, 25
„ vii. 14—37, 38—50	„ vii. 27—51, 1—12
„ x. 23—24ᵃ, 24ᵇ, 25	„ ix. 15, 17—19, 20—22
„ „ 26—29 30	„ x. 23—26
	„ v. 1ᵃ
„ „ 31—33	„ x. 27—29
„ xi. 3—8	„ xi. 4, 3, 7, 5, 8, 6
„ xx. xxi	„ xxi. xx
Psalms ix. 22—39	Psalms x. 1—18
„ x.—cxii	„ xi.—cxiii
„ cxiii. 1—8	„ cxiv. 1—8
„ cxiii. 9—12	„ cxv. 1—4
„ cxiv	„ cxvi. 1—9
„ cxv	„ cxvi. 10—19
„ cxvi.—cxlvi	„ cxvii.—cxlvii. 11
„ cxlvii. 1—9	„ cxlvii. 12—20

GREEK.	HEBREW.
Prov. xv. 27ᵇ—xvi. 4, 6, 9	Prov. xvi. 6, xv. 28, xvi. 7, xv 29
	„ xvi. 8—9, xv. 30—33ᵃ
	„ xvi. 5, 4ᵃ
„ xx. 10ᵃ—12, 13ᵇ—16, 17 —24	„ xx. 20—22, 10—13, 23— 30
„ xxiv. 24—37, 38—49, 50— 68, 69—77, xxix. 28— 49	„ xxx. 1—14, xxiv. 23—34, xxx. 15—33, xxxi. 1—9, 10 —31
Jer. xxv. 14—19	Jer. xlix. 34ᵃ—39
„ xxvi. 1	„ „ 36ᵇ
„ „ 2—28	„ xlvi. 2—28
„ xxvii	„ l
„ xxviii	„ li
„ xxix. 1—7	„ xlvii. 1—7
„ „ 8—23	„ xlix. 7—22
„ xxx. 1—5, 6—11, 12—27	„ „ 1—5, 28—33, 23—27
„ xxxi	„ xlviii
„ xxxii. 1—24	„ xxv. 15—38
„ xxxiii	„ xxvi
„ xxxiv. 1—18	„ xxvii. 2—22
„ xxxv	„ xxviii
„ xxxvi	„ xxix
„ xxxvii	„ xxx
„ xxxviii. 1—34, 35—37, 38— 40	„ xxxi. 1—34, 37, 35, 36, 38— 40
„ xxxix	„ xxxii
„ xl	„ xxxiii
„ xli	„ xxxiv
„ xlii	„ xxxv
„ xliii	„ xxxvi
„ xliv	„ xxxvii
„ xlv	„ xxxviii
„ xlvi	„ xxxix
„ xlvii	„ xl
„ xlviii	„ xli
„ xlix	„ xlii
„ l	„ xliii
„ li. 1—30, 31—35	„ xliv. 1—30, xlv. 1—5
Ezech. vii. 3—9	Ezek. vii. 6—9, 3—5

2. Each of these contexts must be separately examined with the view of discovering the extent and the cause of the divergence. This can be done but briefly here; for further

particulars the student is referred to the commentaries which deal with the several books.

In the following pages 𝕲 = the Greek text, and 𝕲ᴬ·ᴮ·ᵉᵗᶜ· = the Greek text as given in cod. A, cod. B, or as the case may be; 𝕸 = the Massoretic text as printed in the Hebrew Bibles.

GEN. xxxi. 46 ff. The passage is in some confusion; "*vv.* 45, 47, 51—54 appear to embody E's account...*vv.* 46, 48—50 the account given by J¹." 𝕸 is loosely put together, and *v.* 50ᵇ, which 𝕲 omits, is hardly consistent with *vv.* 48, 52. In 𝕲 the materials seem to have been re-arranged with the view of giving greater consistency to the narrative.

GEN. xxxv. 16 ff. The transposition in 𝕲 appears to be due to a desire to locate Eder (Γάδερ) between Bethel and Bethlehem ; see art. EDER in Hastings' *D. B.* (i. p. 644).

EXOD. xx. 13—15. 𝕲ᴮ and 𝕸 represent here two distinct traditions with regard to the order of the Decalogue. For the order followed by 𝕲ᴮ see Lc. xviii. 20, Rom. xiii. 9, Jas. ii. 11, Philo *de x. orac.* 10, *de spec. legg.* iii. 2 ; that of 𝕲ᴬᶠ𝕸 is supported by Mt., Mc., and Josephus. In Deut. v. 17—19 cod. B wavers between the two, but cod. A consistently agrees with 𝕸².

EXOD. xxxv.—xl. is "the sequel to c. xxv.—xxxi., relating the execution of the instructions there communicated to Moses," the correspondence being so close that "in the main, the narrative is repeated *verbatim*—with the single substitution of past tenses for future³." But whilst in c. xxv. ff. the LXX. generally follows the Massoretic order, in the corresponding sections at the end of the book "extraordinary variations occur in the Greek, some verses being omitted altogether, while others are transposed and knocked about with a freedom very unlike the usual manner of the translators of the Pentateuch⁴."

---

¹ Driver, *Intr.* p. 15.

² The Nash (Heb.) Papyrus agrees generally with 𝕲 ; see S. A. Cook, *A Unique Biblical Papyrus, Exp. T.* xiv. 200; Burkitt, in *J.Q.R.* xvi. 559.

³ Driver, *Intr.* pp. 37, 38.

⁴ Robertson Smith, *O. T. in the J. Ch.* p. 124 f.

The passage deals with the building and furniture of the Tabernacle, and the attire of the Priesthood. The following rough table will enable the student to see how the details are arranged in the LXX. and Heb. severally.

𝕲

Ornaments of the Ministers.
Ephod (xxxvi. 9—12).
Onyx stones (xxxvi. 13—14).
Breastplate (xxxvi. 15—29).
Robe of Ephod (xxxvi. 30—34).
Linen vestments (xxxvi. 35—37).
Crown plate (xxxvi. 38—40).

Structure of the Tabernacle and Court.
Hangings (xxxvii. 1—2).
Veils (xxxvii. 3—6).
Court (xxxvii. 7—18).

Furniture of the Tabernacle, &c.
Ark (xxxviii. 1—8).
Table (xxxviii. 9—12).
Candlestick (xxxviii. 13—17).
Altar of Burnt-offering (xxxviii. 22—24).
Oil and Incense (xxxviii. 25—26).
Laver (xxxviii. 27).

𝕸

Structure of the Tabernacle.
Hangings (xxxvi. 8—19).
Boards (xxxvi. 20—34).
Veils (xxxvi. 35—38).

Furniture of the Tabernacle and its Court.
Ark (xxxvii. 1—9).
Table (xxxvii. 10—16).
Candlestick (xxxvii. 17—24).
Altar of incense (xxxvii. 25—29).
Altar of Burnt-offering (xxxviii. 1—7).
Laver (xxxviii. 8).
Court (xxxviii. 9—20).

Ornaments of the Ministers.
Ephod (xxxix. 2—5).
Onyx stones (xxxix. 6—7).
Breastplate (xxxix. 8—21).
Robe of the Ephod (xxxix. 22—26).
Linen vestments (xxxix. 27—29).
Crown plate (xxxix. 30—31).

It is clear from this comparison that both 𝕲 and 𝕸 follow a system, i.e. that the difference of sequence is due to a deliberate rearrangement of the groups. Either the Alexandrian translator has purposely changed their relative order, giving precedence to the ornaments of the priesthood which are subordinated in the M. T. of cc. xxxv.—xl., as well as in both texts of cc. xxv.—xxx.; or he had before him in c. xxxv. ff. another Hebrew text in which the present Greek order was observed. Many O. T. scholars (e.g. Kuenen, Wellhausen, Dillmann) regard cc. xxxv.—xl. as belonging to a "secondary and posterior stratum of P[1]." Thus it is permissible to suppose that the Hebrew text before the original translators of Exodus did not contain this section, and that it was supplied afterwards from a longer Hebrew recension of the book in which the last six chapters had not yet reached their final form. That the translation of these chapters was not made by the same hand as the rest of Exodus has been gathered from the fact that the Hebrew technical terms which are common to xxv.—xxx. and xxxv.—xl. are in certain cases differently rendered in the two contexts[2].

NUMBERS i. 24 ff., xxvi. 15 ff. Each of these passages contains a census of the tribes, and in each the order of the tribes is slightly different in 𝔊 and 𝔐. In both lists 𝔐 places Gad third, and Asher eleventh; whereas according to 𝔊 Gad is ninth in the first of the two lists, and sixth in the second, and in the second Asher is seventh. The effect of the sequence presented by 𝔊 is to bring Gad into close proximity to Asher, a position which this tribe occupies in i. 5—15 (𝔊 and 𝔐). For this there may have been genealogical reasons; see Gen. xxx. 10 ff., xlix. 19.

C. vi. 22 ff. Here 𝔐 obviously has the simpler and more natural order, and λέγοντες αὐτοῖς at the end of *v.* 23 seems to shew that the Greek order, though supported by BAℵ*, is the result of an early accidental displacement in the Greek text.

JOSHUA ix. 3 ff. In the present Hebrew text the ceremony at Ebal and Gerizim follows immediately upon the taking of Ai, but in 𝔊 it is separated from the latter incident by the hostile gathering of the western kings (ix. 1, 2) and placed immediately before the story of the Gibeonites. 𝔐 "involves a geographical difficulty, for Ebal lies considerably to the north

---

[1] See Driver, *Intr.* pp. 35, 39; Addis, *Documents of the Hexateuch*, ii. p. 276 f.

[2] Robertson Smith, *O. T. in the J. Ch.* p. 125. Mr H. St J. Thackeray notes, however, that "the same technical terms are sometimes differently rendered in adjacent verses."

of Ai, and until the intervening territory was conquered...it is difficult to understand how Joshua could have advanced thither[1]." The situation however is scarcely improved if we adopt the order of 𝔊, unless the gathering of the kings is taken to imply a further victory on the Israelite side which opened the way to central Palestine. Dillmann suggests that ix. 2 was once followed by the details of a battle. If so, it is possible that 𝔊 still preserves the original order, though in common with 𝔐 it has lost this record.

C. xix. 47—48. On these verses, which exchange places in the Greek, see under (B)[2].

3 REGN. iv. 17 ff.

The change of order in *vv.* 17—19 needs no discussion; the transposition may be due to an accident of transcription in the archetype of Cod. B, or, like the variations in Num. i., xxvi., to some consideration connected with the placing of the tribes. The real problem of the passage begins at iv. 20. Its nature may best be understood from a table of the contents. These consist of the details of Solomon's personal greatness and public works; the facts are arranged by 𝔊[B] and 𝔐 respectively as follows :

𝔊[B]	𝔐
Provision for the royal table (iv. 20—23).	Solomon's marriage (iii. 1).
Solomon's power (iv. 24).	Provision for the royal table (v. 2 f., 7 f.).
His wisdom (iv. 25—30).	The King's power (v. 4).
His marriage (iv. 31).	His wisdom (v. 9—14).
His wife's dowry (iv. 32 ff.).	His negociations with King Hiram (v. 15—25).
His negociations with King Hiram (v. 1—12).	His corvée of workmen (v. 27—32).
His corvée of workmen (v. 13—17).	Foundations of the Temple laid (vi. 1).
Foundations of the Temple laid (vi. 1—5).	Dimensions of the Temple (vi. 6).
Dimensions of the Temple (vi. 6 f.).	Details of the building (vi. 2, 7, 36).

[1] Driver, *Intr.* p. 100.　　　　[2] Cf. *infra*, p. 244.

𝔊ᴮ	𝔐
Details of the building (vi. 8—34).	Building of the royal palaces (vii. 1—12).
Work of Hiram the artist (vii. 1—37).	Work of Hiram the artist (vii. 12—51).
Building of the royal palaces (vii. 38—50).	Solomon's wife's dowry (ix. 16 f.).

As in the disturbed section at the end of Exodus, it is easy to see that each order follows a system : (1) Whilst 𝔐 places the marriage of Solomon to Pharaoh's daughter, and the use made by the king of his wife's marriage portion, in their historical settings, 𝔊ᴮ brings the two incidents together, as the finishing strokes to the picture of Solomon's power. Again, whilst 𝔐 deals with the whole of Solomon's public works before it describes the skill of Hiram, 𝔊ᴮ completes the history of the building of the Temple with the account of Hiram's labours before it describes the construction of the royal palaces.

The above comparison is necessarily rough; it does not shew the minor differences of order, or the omissions and additions of the Greek text. A closer examination leaves little doubt that 𝔊ᴮ has been translated from a recension of the book earlier than that which is preserved in the Massoretic text[1].

C. x. 23—33. The text of 𝔊ᴮ, ᴸᵘᶜ· here admits two passages which it had passed over in the earlier contexts, where they stand in 𝔐 (c. ix. 15, 17—22, v. 1). Of ix. 10—28 Prof. Driver remarks that it "consists of a series of notices imperfectly connected together," and that its "literary form ...is, for some reason, less complete than that of any other portion of the Books of Kings[2]." Under these circumstances it is not surprising that some of these notices occupied another

---

[1] Cf. Driver, *Intr.* p. 182, and note ;. C. F. Burney, in Hastings' *D. B.* p. 862 ff.

[2] *Intr.* p. 181.

place in the text which was before the Alexandrian translator. C. v. 1ᵃ, which in the Greek order is x. 30, belongs in 𝕳 to another similar collection of loosely-connected paragraphs. The arrangement followed by 𝕲ᴮ is perhaps not materially better, but it probably represents an earlier stage in the formation of the book.

C. xi. 3—8. Here 𝕲ᴮ, ᴸᵘᶜ· presents a text which differs from 𝕲ᴬ and 𝕳 both in order and in form. A comparison of 𝕲ᴮ with 𝕲ᴬ and 𝕳 will be found to be instructive ; the latter is diffuse and repeats itself unnecessarily (3 ἔκλιναν γυναῖκες αὐτοῦ τὴν καρδίαν αὐτοῦ...4 αἱ γυναῖκες αὐτοῦ ἐξέκλιναν τὴν καρδίαν αὐτοῦ...5 ἐπορεύθη Σαλωμὼν ὀπίσω τῆς Ἀστάρτης...7 τότε ᾠκοδόμησεν Σ. ὑψηλὸν...τῇ Ἀστάρτῃ) ; the former presents the facts[1] briefly and in a logical sequence. Here as elsewhere in this book Cod. A represents the Hexaplaric Greek, and not the original LXX.[2]

Cc. xx., xxi. The relative order of these chapters is reversed in 𝕳, which justifies the change by prefacing the story of Naboth with the words וַיְהִי אַחַר הַדְּבָרִים הָאֵלֶּה. "The dislocation may have been due to the desire to bring the prophecy of Ahab's death nearer to the account of its occurrence[3]." Obviously wrong as the present Hebrew order is, Cod. A has adopted it, interpolating the inapposite ἐγένετο μετὰ τὰ ῥήματα ταῦτα, which Origen had borrowed from Aquila ; and even Lucian (if he is here rightly represented by Lagarde) has been led into the same error, though he seems to retain the true sequence of the chapters.

PSALMS ix.—cxlvii.

Throughout the greater part of the Psalter 𝕲 and 𝕳

---

[1] B however omits the important statement of *v.* 3ᵃ, which comes "from the older narrative" (Driver).

[2] See Field *ad loc.*, and cf. Silberstein, *über den Ursprung der im cod. Alex. u. Vat. des dritten Königsbuches...überlieferten Textgestalt* (Giessen, 1893).

[3] C. F. Burney, *l.c.*

follow different systems of numeration. This is due to certain consecutive Psalms in the Hebrew Psalter being counted as one in the Greek (ix. + x. Heb. = ix. LXX.; cxiv. + cxv. Heb. = cxiii. LXX.), and certain of the Hebrew Psalms being *vice versa* divided in the Greek into two (cxvi. Heb. = cxiv. + cxv. LXX.; cxlvii. Heb. = cxlvi. + cxlvii. LXX.).

In the Heb. Psalms ix. and x. there are traces of an acrostic system which have been taken to indicate that the two Psalms were originally one[1]. Many Hebrew MSS. join Psalms cxiv., cxv.[2], as in the LXX. For the division of Psalms cxvi. and cxlvii. it is less easy to account, but it may have been due to a desire to make up the number of the Psalms to 150[3].

PROVERBS xxiv.—xxxi.

In the first great section of this book (cc. i.—ix.) there is no important difference of order, nor does the second section (x.—xxii. 1[b]) or the third (xxii. 17—xxiv. 22) offer more than an occasional variation in the grouping of proverbs, combined with omissions and additions on either side. But at c. xxiv. 23 we enter upon a series of collections which seem at one time to have formed distinct books or cycles of proverbial teaching, and here 𝕲 and 𝕸 differ widely, as a comparison of the contents will shew.

𝕲	𝕸
Words of Agur (xxiv. 24—37).	Sayings of the Wise (xxiv. 23—34).
Sayings of the Wise (xxiv. 38—49).	Proverbs of Solomon (xxv. 1—xxix. 21).
Rest of the Words of Agur (xxiv. 50—68).	Words of Agur (xxx. 1—33).

[1] See Cheyne, *Book of Psalms*, p. 228; Bleek-Wellhausen, p. 471. Prof. Kirkpatrick (*Psalms*, 1. p. 41) speaks with less confidence.

[2] See Kennicott, ii. p. 410. It should be added that in the MSS. Pss. cxvi., cxvii., cxviii. are also often written continuously.

[3] "Both in Palestine and in Alexandria great importance seems to have been attached to this number. In Palestine, however, there were some who counted only 147 Psalms" (Cheyne *op. cit.* p. xiv.). See also Lagarde, *nov. Ps. gr. spec.*, p. 8.

               ረ   ስ

&#4648;	&#4661;
Words of Lemuel (xxiv. 69—77).	Words of Lemuel (xxxi. 1—9).
Proverbs of Solomon (xxv. 1— xxix. 27).	Praise of the Virtuous Woman (xxxi. 10—31).
Praise of the Virtuous Woman (xxix. 28—49).	

Evidently the order of this portion of the book had not been finally settled when the Alexandrian translator did his work[1]. Moreover he has failed to understand ·the headings of the two sections attributed to Agur and Lemuel[2], and has broken up Agur's collection, the unity of which he seems not to have recognised, placing the Sayings of the Wise between the fragments; unless, indeed, he found them divided in his Hebrew archetype.

JEREMIAH xxv.—li. A glance at the table which stands near the beginning of this chapter will shew that the section c. xxv. 15—xlv. 5 (ስ) answers in a general way to c. xxxii. 1—li. 35 (ረ), whilst c. xlvi. 1—li. 64 (ስ) is represented, though not without considerable interruptions of the present Hebrew order, by c. xxv. 14—xxxi. 44 (ረ). Speaking roughly these two sections have exchanged places in the Greek text[3]. In ረ the prophecies against the nations precede˙the parable of the intoxicating cup (xxv. 15 ff. = xxxii. 1 ff.); in ስ they form the final section of the book, coming immediately before the historical appendix (c. lii.). If these prophecies were circulated in a separate form, the words of c. xxv. 13 might naturally have led an Alexandrian collector to place them where they stand in the LXX., whereas in Palestine they were treated as a postscript to the earlier collections and placed

---

[1] Cf. Robertson Smith, *O. T. in J. Ch.* p. 111; Toy, *Proverbs*, p. xxxiii.

[2] See Lagarde, *Anmerkungen zur griech. Übersetzung d. Proverbien*, pp. 90, 91.

[3] Cf. Origen *ad Afric.* 4 πολλὰ δὲ τοιαῦτα καὶ ἐν τῷ ᾿Ιερεμίᾳ κατενοήσαμεν, ἐν ᾧ καὶ πολλὴν μετάθεσιν καὶ ἐναλλαγὴν τῆς λέξεως τῶν προφητευομένων εὕρομεν.

after xlv. 5. The two texts differ however not only in regard to the place which they assign to the section as a whole, but in the relative order of the prophecies. The order of the nations denounced is in ᚷ Elam, Egypt, Babylon, Philistia, Edom, Ammon, Kedar, Damascus, Moab; but in ﬡ, Egypt, Philistia, Moab, Ammon, Edom, Damascus, Kedar, Elam, Babylon. The prophecies had apparently been grouped in the Alexandrian ·collection after one manner, and after another in the collection which was current in Palestine.

EZEKIEL vii. 3—9. Here the divergence of the LXX. from the Hebrew text was noticed by Jerome, who writes: " in hoc capitulo iuxta LXX. interpretes ordo mutatus est et confusus, ita ut prima novissima sint et novissima vel prima vel media, ipsaque media nunc ad extrema nunc ad principia transferantur." The transposition, to whichever side it is to be ascribed, may be explained by the genius of the passage which is in " a lyric strain such as is unwonted in Ezekiel[1]." A full examination of the context may be seen in Cornill[2], who justly describes it as " eine stark verderbte Stelle," and finds a solution in the hypothesis of a doublet (cf. *vv.* 3—4, 7—8).

(B) DIFFERENCES OF SUBJECT-MATTER.

1. A further comparison of the LXX. with the Massoretic Hebrew reveals the presence in each text of a considerable number of passages which are not to be found in the other. This fact was known to Origen, and frankly recognised by him (*ep. ad African.* § 3 καὶ ἐν ἄλλοις δὲ πολλοῖς ἁγίοις βιβλίοις εὕρομεν πῆ μὲν πλείονα παρ' ἡμῖν κείμενα ἢ παρ' Ἑβραίοις, πῆ δὲ λείποντα); and the Hexapla, as we have seen[3], was the result of a mistaken endeavour to assimilate the LXX. to the current

---

[1] Driver, *Intr.* p. 263.　　[2] *Ezechiel*, p. 212.
[3] Pt. I. c. iii.

Hebrew text. Its remains are still invaluable as bearing witness to the condition of both texts in the second and third centuries after Christ. The student who would grasp the nature and extent of the problem must examine them in Field's great edition; in this place we will content ourselves with some notice of additions and omissions which extend to entire verses or paragraphs.

PENTATEUCH. As a whole, the Law has escaped material changes in either direction. But there are a few important exceptions In Gen. iv 8 the LXX. supplies the words of Cain (διέλθωμεν εἰς τὸ πεδίον), which are wanting in the Hebrew Bible. The supplementary chapters of Exodus are on the whole shorter in 𝔊 than in 𝕳; the former has nothing to answer to c. xxxv. 8, xxxvii. 25—28, xl. 6—8, 11, and exhibits c. xxxvi. 8—34 in an abridged form. In the Song of Moses the last four distichs are expanded in 𝔊 into eight, thus:

> [εὐφράνθητε, οὐρανοί, ἅμα αὐτῷ,
>   καὶ προσκυνησάτωσαν αὐτῷ υἱοὶ θεοῦ·]
> εὐφράνθητε, ἔθνη, μετὰ τοῦ λαοῦ αὐτοῦ,
>   [καὶ ἐνισχυσάτωσαν αὐτῷ πάντες ἄγγελοι θεοῦ.]
> ὅτι τὸ αἷμα τῶν υἱῶν αὐτοῦ ἐκδικᾶται,
>   [καὶ ἐκδικήσει] καὶ ἀνταποδώσει δίκην τοῖς ἐχθροῖς,
> [καὶ τοῖς μισοῦσιν ἀνταποδώσει,]
>   καὶ ἐκκαθαριεῖ [Κύριος] τὴν γῆν τοῦ λαοῦ.

There is nothing in 𝕳 which corresponds with the bracketed words of the version. Yet they are present in all uncial MSS. of the LXX., and were probably in the earlier copies of Deuteronomy which passed into the possession of the Christian Church. Possibly the Song was circulated in a separate form in more than one translation. The present Greek text seems to be the result of conflation, lines 1 and 3, 2 and 4, 6 and 7, being doublets; line 2 = 4 appears to be an adaptation of Ps. xcvi. (xcvii.) 7.

JOSHUA. Besides innumerable smaller variations in this book which shew that it was not regarded by the translators as sharing the peculiar sanctity of the Torah[1], there are in the last four chapters several important contexts in which 𝕲 and 𝕸 differ by defect or excess[2].

C. xix. 47—48 (𝕸). The order of these verses is reversed in 𝕲, so as to bring the words αὕτη ἡ κληρονομία κτλ. into juxtaposition with the list of the Danite towns (*vv.* 41—46); and to each of the verses which have thus exchanged places the LXX. attaches a rider, based apparently upon Judges ii. 34 f., and describing the relations between the new settlers and the Amorites.

C. xx. 4—6. Omitted in 𝕲. "It is probable that the ch. in its original form (P) has been enlarged by additions from the law of homicide in Dt. (c. 19) at a comparatively late date, so that they were still wanting in the MSS. used by the LXX. translators[3]."

C. xxi. 36—37, 42 a—d. The printed Hebrew Bibles omit *vv.* 36—37, which contain the names of the Levitical cities in the territory of Reuben, and they seem to have been obelised in the Greek by Origen. They are found, however, in the majority of Hebrew MSS.[4], and are necessary to the completeness of the narrative. *Vv.* 42 a—c are little more than a doublet of c. xix. 50, 51 b; 42 d appears to be based upon c. v. 3.

C. xxiv. 30 a—33 b. *V.* 30 a continues the story of the flint knives (v. 7, xxi. 42 d). 𝕲, which omits *v.* 31, a doublet of Judges ii. 7, adds to the book a postscript, *v.* 33 a—b, based on *v.* 33, 1 Sam. iv. 3 ff., Judges ii. 6, 11 ff., iii. 14[5].

---

[1] See G. A. Smith in Hastings' *D. B.* ii. p. 784.
[2] *Op. cit.*, p. 781 ff.   [3] Driver, *Intr.* p. 105.
[4] See Kennicott, i. p. 474, De Rossi, i. p. 96 ff.; and cf. Field, *Hexapla*, i. p. 387, Addis, *Documents of the Hexateuch*, ii. p. 472 ff.
[5] See Knobel in *Kurzgef. exeg. Handbuch zum A.T.*, p. 488.

1 SAMUEL (1 REGN.).

C. ii. 9, 10. The closing stanza òf this hymn, like that of the Song of Moses, is presented by 𝕲 in a modified and expanded form. *Vv.* 8 c, 9 a are omitted in 𝕲, which substitutes διδοὺς εὐχήν…δικαίου ("apparently an attempt to accommodate the Song more closely to Hannah's position[1]"), and inserts in the heart of *v.* 10 a passage from Jerem. ix. 23, 24, taken from the Greek version, but with variations which form an instructive study:—

1 Regn. ii.	Jer. ix.
ὁ φρόνιμος ἐν τῇ φρονήσει…ὁ δυνατὸς ἐν τῇ δυνάμει…τὸν Κύριον, καὶ ποιεῖν κρίμα καὶ δικαιοσύνην ἐν μέσῳ τῆς γῆς.	ὁ σοφὸς ἐν τῇ σοφίᾳ…ὁ ἰσχυρὸς ἐν τῇ ἰσχύι…ὅτι ἐγώ εἰμι Κύριος ὁ ποιῶν ἔλεος καὶ κρίμα καὶ δικαιοσύνην ἐπὶ τῆς γῆς.

It has been noticed that 1 Regn. ii. 11 a (καὶ κατέλιπεν αὐτὸν ἐκεῖ ἐνώπιον Κυρίου) probably corresponds to 1 Sam. i. 28 b (וַיִּשְׁתַּחוּ שָׁם לַיהוָה). If so, the Song has been inserted in 𝕲 and 𝕸 at different points in the narrative[2]; and it seems to be a reasonable inference that it was not in the original draft of the book. Such a hypothesis will account for the freedom with which it has been treated in 𝕲.

Cc. xvii—xviii. This is the most important of the contexts in which 𝕲ᴮ differs from 𝕲ᴬ 𝕸 in the way of defect. The omitted verses contain the story of David's visit to the camp of Israel (xvii. 12—31); David's interview with Saul and Jonathan (xvii. 55—xviii. 5); Saul's attempts upon David's life (xviii. 10—11, 17—19); besides occasional details of less importance (xvii. 41, 50; xviii. 30).

These omissions have been variously explained. According to Wellhausen and Kuenen[3], the Greek translator, or the scribe of the archetype followed by Cod. B, has deliberately

---

[1] Driver, *Samuel,* p. 20.
[2] See Wellhausen, *der Text d. B. Samuelis,* p. 42; Driver, *op. cit.,* pp. 17, 18, 21; H. P. Smith, *Samuel,* p. 13.
[3] Driver, *Intr.,* p. 170; *Samuel,* p. 116 f.

removed the missing verses, from a desire to harmonise. Certainly the result of their absence is to reduce, if not altogether to remove, the conflict between c. xvi. 14 ff., which represents David as an experienced warrior with whose reputation Saul is already acquainted, and cc. xvii., xviii., where on a later occasion he appears as a shepherd lad of whom the king has as yet heard nothing. But, as Robertson Smith has pointed out, it is difficult to believe that simple omissions made without changing a word of what was left could produce a complete and consecutive narrative such as we find in 𝔊. He concludes that the verses omitted by 𝔊 are "interpolations in the Hebrew text, extracts from a lost biography of David...not found in the text which lay before the LXX. translators[1]." Driver[2] doubts whether the verses can have been interpolated in a strict sense, "for an interpolation would not insert anything at variance with the narrative interpolated." "We seem therefore (he adds) shut up to the conclusion that the verses omitted in the Vat. MS. belong to an independent narrative, which was in parts incorporated with the older account, but not in all MSS. existing when the LXX. translated the book."

The omissions are supplied in 𝔊^A, ^Luc., but probably from a non-Septuagintal source; the passages are marked with an asterisk in the Hexaplaric MSS. 64, 92[3].

C. xxiii. 11—12. Here 𝔊^B omits by homoeoteleuton the Heb. from יֵרֶד (v. 11) to יַסְגִּירוּ (v. 12). But it also omits בַּעֲלֵי קְעִילָה בְיָדוֹ (v. 11), and Wellhausen conjectures with probability that εἰ ἀποκλεισθήσεται was wanting in the original form of the LXX.[4]

1 KINGS (3 REGN.).

In this book 𝔊^B contains a large quantity of additional matter, of varying character and worth[5].

---

[1] *O. T. in J. Ch.*, pp. 121, 431 ff.; cf. Kirkpatrick, 1 *Samuel*, p. 241 ff.
[2] 1 *Samuel*, p. 117.
[3] Cf. Field *ad loc.*   [4] See H. P. Smith, *Samuel*, p. 212.
[5] See C. F. Burney, *Notes on Heb. Text of Books of Kings*, esp. pp. xix–xxx.

C. ii. 35 a—n, 46 a—l, are summaries of Solomon's personal history, which have been attached, probably by the accidents of transcription, to the verses which they severally follow. On examination each of these passages proves to be made up partly of translations from verses which are not represented in the true LXX., partly of fragments of the LXX. which occur elsewhere in their true order, partly of brief descriptions gathered from other parts of the book.

Thus ii. 35 a—b=iv. 25—26, c=iv. 31, d=v. 15, e=vii. 10 ff., f—g=ix. 24—25 (𝕸), h=v. 16, i—k=x. 23 ff., l—o=ii. 8—9. Similarly, ii. 46 a=iv. 20 (𝕸), b=v. 2 (𝕸), c=iii. 1 (𝕸), d=ix. 18 (𝕸), e=iv. 22—23, f=iv. 24, g=v. 5 (𝕸), h=2 ff., i—k=x. 29—30.

C. viii. 53a is an addition of quite another character and of the highest interest. The true LXX. (𝕲ᴮ) omits viii. 12, 13, which in cod. A are thus supplied from Aquila[1]: τότε εἶπεν Σαλωμών Κύριος εἶπεν τοῦ σκηνῶσαι ἐν γνόφῳ. οἰκοδόμησα οἶκον κατοικητηρίου σοι, ἔδρασμα τῆς καθέδρας σου αἰῶνος. But after v. 53 𝕲 gives the substance of these words in a poetical form which is expressly attributed to an older source :

τότε ἐλάλησεν Σ. ὑπὲρ τοῦ οἴκου ὡς συνετέλεσεν τοῦ οἰκοδομῆσαι αὐτόν Ἥλιον ἐγνώρισεν (Luc., ἔστησεν) ἐν οὐρανῷ Κύριος· | εἶπεν τοῦ κατοικεῖν ἐκ γνόφου (A, ἐν γνόφῳ) | οἰκοδόμησον οἶκόν μου, οἶκον ἐκπρεπῆ (A, εὐπρεπῆ) σαυτῷ, | τοῦ κατοικεῖν ἐπὶ καινότητος. | οὐκ ἰδοὺ αὕτη γέγραπται ἐν βιβλίῳ τῆς ᾠδῆς;

Though this occurs in cod. A and Lucian, it was wanting in the Hebrew text which was before the translators of the second century A.D., for in the Hexapla it appeared only in the LXX. column[2]. But (as its very errors shew) it is a translation of a Hebrew original, and the βιβλίον τῆς ᾠδῆς from which it came is doubtless none other than the Book of Jashar (סֵפֶר הַיָּשָׁר, read as הַשִּׁיר 'ס)[3]. Here 𝕲 has preserved

---

[1] Cf. Field *ad loc.*

[2] See Field *ad loc.*, who quotes from cod. 243, ταῦτα ἐν τῷ ἐξαπλῷ παρὰ μόνοις φέρεται τοῖς ο'.

[3] Cf. Driver, *Intr.*, p. 182. See Appendix on Thackeray's examination of this passage in *J. Th. St.* xi. 44.

for us a precious relic, which in 𝕸 has been first misplaced and then partly lost[1].

C. xii. 24 a—z. The longest interpolation in the book, partly similar to the Greek additions in c. ii., but presenting greater difficulties. After rehearsing the facts connected with the death of Solomon, and summarising the reign of Rehoboam, the interpolator tells the story of the rise of Jeroboam and the revolt of Israel, going over the ground already covered in cc. xi—xii., and anticipating c. xiv. (𝕸).

The parallels are xii. 24 a=xi. 43, xiv. 21—22; b=xi. 26—28; c=xi. 40; d—f=xi. 43[b]; xii. 2—5 (𝕸); g—n[a]=xiv. 1—20 (𝕸); n[b]—z=xii. 3—24.

But the passage is no mere cento of verses to be found elsewhere either in 𝕲 or 𝕸; it is a second and distinct recension of the story, resting equally with the first upon a Hebrew original. So different and indeed in some respects contradictory are the accounts that they "cannot possibly have stood from the first in the same volume." The same action is ascribed in the one "to Shemaiah, at Shechem, in the days of Rehoboam"; and in the other "to Ahijah, at Jerusalem, in the days of Solomon[2]." In fact, the present Greek version of 1 Kings has preserved two ancient accounts of the dismemberment of the Kingdom of David and Solomon, and though one of these survives also in 𝕸 there is no *a priori* ground for deciding which of the two is the more trustworthy. It is worthy of notice that cod. B omits the reference to Jeroboam's residence in Egypt in xii. 2, and the visit of Jeroboam's wife to Ahijah as it is told in c. xiv. 1—20, though it gives the two irreconcilable accounts of the meeting of Jeroboam with the prophet (xi. 29 ff., xii. 24 o). The whole of the narrative, so far as it exists only in the Greek, is omitted by A and

---

[1] See the passage discussed in Robertson Smith, *O. T. in J. Ch.*, p. 433.

[2] Robertson Smith, *op. cit.*, p. 118.

the Syro-hexaplar, but it seems to have been retained by Lucian[1].

C. xvi. 28 a—h consists of another recension of the summary of Jehoshaphat's reign which occurs in c. xxii. 41—44, 47—50, where the last four verses are omitted altogether in 𝕲ᴮ. Lucian, who agrees with 𝕲ᴮ in the interpolation at xvi. 28, omits xxii. 40 b—52.

2 KINGS (4 REGN.).

C. i. 18 a—d. An addition similar in character to that which follows 3 Regn. xvi. 28. The summary of Joram's reign has attached itself to the beginning as well as to the end of the story of Elijah's ascension, whilst in 𝕸 it finds a place only at the end (iii. 1—3). In this instance, however, 𝕲ᴬ, ᴸᵘᶜ· agrees with 𝕲ᴮ in repeating the summary, though with some variations. The student will find a comparison instructive.

1 CHRONICLES i. 10—16, 17 b—23 are wanting in 𝕲ᴮ, which thus shortens the genealogy by omitting (1) the posterity of Ham, except the Cushites, (2) the longer of two lists of the posterity of Shem. Both passages are supplied (from Gen. x. 13—18, 22—29) by cod. A, in a version which came from Hexaplaric sources (see Field, i. p. 704).

2 CHRONICLES xxxv. 19 a—d, xxxvi. 2 a—c, 5 a—d, are versions of 2 Kings xxiii. 24—27, 31 b—33, xxiv. 1—4, based apparently upon a recension of the Hebrew which differs from 𝕸, and only in part assimilated to 𝕲.

2 ESDRAS xxi, xxii. (Neh. xi, xii.). The lists of princes and Levites are much shortened in 𝕲ᴮ, which omits altogether xxi. 16, 20, 21, 28, 29, 32—35 ; xxii. 4—6, 9, 15—21, 38, 40, 41.

---

[1] Lagarde, *V.T. Gr.* i. *ad loc.* For a careful treatment of the differences between 𝕲 and 𝕸 in 3 Regn. see Herzfeld, *Gesch. d. Volkes Israel,* ii.

PSALMS.

In 𝕲 many of the Psalms receive titles, or additions to their titles, which are wanting in 𝔐. The following is a list of those which occur in the uncial MSS.

x. (xi.) + ψαλμός.   So xiii. (xiv.), xxiv. (xxv.), xliii. (xliv.), lxxx. (lxxxi.).

xxiii. (xxiv.) + τῆς μιᾶς σαββάτου.
xxvi. (xxvii.) + πρὸ τοῦ χρισθῆναι.
xxviii. (xxix.) + ἐξοδίου σκηνῆς.
xxix. (xxx.) pr. εἰς τὸ τέλος.
xxx. (xxxi.) + ἐκστάσεως.
xxxii. (xxxiii.).   Τῷ Δαυείδ.
xxxvii. (xxxviii.) + περὶ σαββάτου.
xli. (xlii.) + ψαλμὸς τῷ Δαυείδ (cod. A.).
xlii. (xliii.).   Ψαλμὸς τῷ Δαυείδ.
xlvii. (xlviii.) + δευτέρᾳ σαββάτου.
lxv. (lxvi.) + ἀναστάσεως.
lxvi. (lxvii.) + τῷ Δαυείδ (om. ᾠδῆς).
lxix. (lxx.) + εἰς τό Σῶσαί με Κύριον.
lxx. (lxxi.).   Τῷ Δαυείδ, υἱῶν Ἰωναδὰβ καὶ τῶν πρώτων αἰχμαλωτισθέντων.
lxxv. (lxxvi.) + πρὸς τὸν Ἀσσύριον.
lxxix. (lxxx.) + ὑπὲρ τοῦ Ἀσσυρίου.
xc. (xci.).   Αἶνος ᾠδῆς τῷ Δαυείδ.
xcii. (xciii.).   Εἰς τὴν ἡμέραν τοῦ προσαββάτου, ὅτι κατῴκισται ἡ γῆ· αἶνος ᾠδῆς τῷ Δαυείδ.
xciii. (xciv.).   Ψαλμὸς τῷ Δαυείδ, τετράδι σαββάτου.
xciv. (xcv.).   Αἶνος ᾠδῆς τῷ Δαυείδ.
xcv. (xcvi.).   Ὅτι ὁ οἶκος οἰκοδομεῖται μετὰ τὴν αἰχμαλωσίαν· ᾠδὴ τῷ Δαυείδ.
xcvi. (xcvii.).   Τῷ Δαυείδ, ὅτε ἡ γῆ αὐτοῦ καθίσταται.
xcvii. (xcviii.) + τῷ Δαυείδ.
xcviii. (xcix.).   Ψαλμὸς τῷ Δαυείδ.
ciii. (civ.).   Τῷ Δαυείδ.
civ. (cv.).   Ἀλληλουιά: so cv., cvi. (cvi., cvii.), cxiii. (cxiv., cxv.), cxiv. (cxvi.) 1—9, cxvi. (cxvii.), cxvii. (cxviii.), cxxxv. (cxxxvi.), [but in each of these cases the Greek title is the equivalent of a final הַלְלוּיָהּ in the M.T. of the preceding Psalm].
cx. (cxi.).   Ἀλληλουιά: so cxi., cxii. (cxii., cxiii.), cxxxiv. (cxxxv.), [but in each of these cases the Greek title is the equivalent of an opening הַלְלוּיָהּ in the M.T. of the Psalm].
cxv. (cxvi. 10—19).   Ἀλληλουιά.   So cxviii. (cxix.).
cxxxvi. (cxxxvii.).   Τῷ Δαυείδ.

cxxxvii. (cxxxviii.)+Ζαχαρίου A (-ρίας T).

cxxxviii. (cxxxix.)+Ζαχαρίου (cod. A.)+ἐν τῇ διασπορᾷ (A^a T).

cxlii. (cxliii.)+ὅτε αὐτὸν ὁ υἱὸς καταδιώκει (κατεδίωξεν A).

cxliii. (cxliv.)+πρὸς τὸν Γολιάδ.

cxlv. (cxlvi.). Ἀλληλουιά· Ἀγγαίου καὶ Ζαχαρίου Heb. תְּהִלָּה לְדָוִיד).

cxlvi. (cxlvii. 1—11). Ἀλληλουιά· Ἀγγαίου καὶ Ζαχαρίου (where Ἀλλ. answers to the first word of the Psalm in 𝔐 as in cx. (cxi.)).

cxlvii. (cxlvii. 10—20). As cxlvi., except that Ἀλλ. is not in 𝔐.

cxlviii. As cxlvi. but Ἀλλ. is here represented in 𝔐 both at the end of the preceding Psalm and at the beginning of Ps. cxlviii.

cxlix. Ἀλληλουιά. In 𝔐 at the end of cxlviii. and the beginning of cxlix.

cl. Ἀλληλουιά. As in cxlix.

On the questions raised by the Greek titles see Neubauer in *Studia Bibl.* ii. p. 1 ff., Driver, *Intr.* p. 348 ff., the commentaries, e.g. those of Perowne, Kirkpatrick, and Cheyne, and the last-named author's *Origin of the Psalter.* Valuable traditions are probably embodied in the liturgical notes which assign certain Psalms to particular days of the week (τῇ μιᾷ σαββάτου, δευτέρᾳ σ., τετράδι σ.[1], εἰς τὴν ἡμέραν τοῦ προσαββάτου (cf. Mc. xv. 42)), and in those which attribute others to the time of the Return (Ζαχαρίου, Ἀγγαίου) or to the Dispersion (ἐν τῇ διασπορᾷ). On the other hand some of the Greek titles appear to be fanciful (πρὸ τοῦ χρισθῆναι, πρὸς τὸν Γολιάδ), whilst others are obscure (ἐκστάσεως, ἀναστάσεως).

For the Christian (mystical) interpretation of the Greek titles see Athan. *de titulis Psalmorum* (Migne, *P. G.* xxvii. 591 sqq.), the *variorum prolegomena* in Pitra's *Analecta sacra* ii. p. 411 sqq., and Corderii *exp. patr. Gr. in Psalmos*, passim.

Ps. xiii. (xiv.) 3 a—c. This, the only long interpolation in the Greek Psalter, is found upon examination to be made up of Pss. v. 10 b, cxxxix. (cxl.) 4 b, ix. (x.) 17 a, Isa. lix. 7, 8, Ps. xxxv. (xxxvi.) 1 a, all taken or abridged from the LXX. version with slight variations. That it never formed a part of the

---

[1] Cf. πέμπτῃ σαββάτου prefixed to Ps. lxxxi. in the cursive MS. 156 (*Urtext*, p. 75).

Hebrew Psalm may be safely affirmed, yet it is quoted continuously in Rom. iii. 13—18, where it follows without break upon an abridgement of Ps. xiii. (xiv.) 1—3.

The Greek addition had a place in the κοινή, according to Jerome *praef. in Isa.*; cf. Field, *ad loc.* Whether it was brought into the text of the LXX. from the Epistle[1], or was already in the Greek Psalm as known to St Paul, cannot perhaps now be ascertained. But it doubtless had its origin in the Rabbinical practice of stringing together passages excerpted from various books of the Old Testament (Sanday and Headlam on Romans, *l. c.*), and it may have existed under this form in a collection of *testimonia* used by the Apostle (on such collections see Hatch, *Essays*, p. 203, Westcott, *Hebrews*, p. 476 ff.).

Ps. cli. (ψαλμὸς ἰδιόγραφος)[2]. The MSS. of the LXX. contain after Ps. cl. a Psalm which bears the title Οὗτος ὁ ψαλμὸς ἰδιόγραφος εἰς Δαυεὶδ καὶ ἔξωθεν τοῦ ἀριθμοῦ, ὅτε ἐμονομάχησεν τῷ Γολιάδ, O. L., *hic psalmus sibi proprie scriptus est David, extra numerum, cum pugnavit cum Golia[th]*. The letter of Athanasius to Marcellinus, which is incorporated in cod. A, speaks freely of this Psalm as the work of David, and as Ps. cli. (§ 14 οἱ μὲν καυχήσεως τῆς ἐν Κυρίῳ ἀπαγγέλλοντες λόγους εἰσὶ κβ´ καὶ κϛ´, λη´...ρνα´ : § 25 τῷ ἐκλεξαμένῳ κυρίῳ διδοὺς δόξαν ψάλλε καὶ σὺ τὸν ρνα´ ἴδιον ὄντα τοῦ Δαυείδ) ; and it is quoted as a Psalm of David by the author of the pseudonymous letter of Mary to Ignatius (cent. iv. ; Lightfoot, *Ignatius*, iii. 144, φησὶν γάρ που αὐτὸς ὅτι Μικρὸς ἤμην, κτλ.). Moreover the scribe of Cod. ℵ regarded it as a part of the Psalter, for his subscription runs ΨΑΛΜΟΙ ΔΑΔ ΡΝΑ. In cod. A, however, it is carefully excluded from the Psalter proper (subscr. ΨΑΛΜΟΙ ΡΝ ΚΑΙ ΙΔΙΟΓΡΑΦΟΣ ᾱ), and the judgement of the Laodicene canon (βίβλος ψαλμῶν ἑκατὸν πεντήκοντα) is upheld by the title which in all the MSS.

---

[1] Cf. Hatch, *Essays*, p. 209 ff.
[2] Cf. Oeconomus, iii. p. 634 f.

pronounces this 'autograph' (ἰδιόγραφος) work of David to be
ἔξωθεν or ἐκτὸς τοῦ ἀριθμοῦ, *i.e.* τῶν ρν΄ ψαλμῶν.

This Psalm is clearly based on 1 Kings xvi. 7, 11, 26, 43,
51; 2 Kings vi. 5; 2 Chron. xxix. 26; Ps. lxxviii. 70, lxxxix.
20. Its resemblance to the LXX. of those passages is not so
close as to suggest a Greek original, but on the other hand
there is no evidence that it ever existed in Hebrew. Whether
it had a Hebrew or a Greek original, it was probably added to
the Greek Psalter after the translation of the fifth book was
complete.

For the literature of Ps. cli. see Fabricius-Harles, iii. p. 749,
and Fabricius, *Cod. pseudepigr.* v. 7², p. 905 ff.

THE ECCLESIASTICAL CANTICLES.

In certain uncial MSS. and a large proportion of the cursives the Psalms are followed by a collection of liturgical ᾠδαί
(*cantica*). The following table shews the sources and order of
those which are given by codd. A, R, T.

A	R	T
1. Exod. xv. 1—19.	Exod. xv. 1—21.	
2. Deut. xxxii. 1—43.	Deut. xxxii. 1—44.	
3. 1 Regn. ii. 1—10.	1 Regn. ii. 1—10.	
4. Isa. xxvi. 9—20.	Isa. v. 1—9.	
5. Ion. ii. 3—10.	Ion. ii. 3—10.	
6. Hab. iii. 1—19.	Hab. iii. 1—19.	[6] 1 Regn. ii. [1]—10.
7. Isa. xxxviii. 10—20.	*Magnificat.*	7. *Magnificat.*
8. *Prayer of Manas-*	Dan. iii. 52—90.	8. Isa. xxxviii. 10—20.
seh[1].		9. *Prayer of Manas-*
9. Dan. iii. 26—45.		*seh*[1].
10. „ „ 52—88.		10. Dan. iii. 26—45.
11. *Magnificat.*		11. „ „ 52—56.
12. *Nunc dimittis.*		12. „ „ 57—90.
13. *Benedictus.*		13. *Benedictus.*
14. *Morning Hymn.*		14. *Nunc dimittis.*
		15. *Morning Hymn.*

[1] The προσευχὴ Μανασσῆ (so Cod. A; Cod. T. πρ. Μανασσῆ υἱοῦ
Ἐζεκίου) is usually regarded as an attempt by a Hellenistic Jew to reconstruct the prayer mentioned in 2 Chron. xxxiii. 18; see, however Ball

The nine Odes now sung at Lauds in the Orthodox Church are (following the order of cod. A) nos. 1, 2, 3, 6, 4, 5, 9, 10, 11+13; the Roman Church uses at Lauds on successive days of the week 10, Isa. xii., Isa. xxxviii. 10—20, 3, 1, 6, 2, whilst 13, 11, 12 are recited daily at Lauds, Vespers, and Compline respectively[1]. The Mozarabic Breviary, as printed, provides no fewer than 76 scriptural canticles. Little has been done as yet to examine either the Greek or the Latin Psalters with the view of determining the local distribution of these canticles; but the student may refer to art. *Canticles* in *DCA.*, and also to Martene, *de ant. rit. eccl.*, p. 25, Neale, *Hist. of the H. Eastern Church*, ii. p. 834 f., Freeman, *Principles of Divine Service*, i. p. 124 f.; on the Canticles of the Latin Church he may consult with advantage Thomasius, *opp.* ii. pp. xv. sqq., 295 sqq.

The text of the O. T. canticles in the Psalter of cod. A differs in places from that which is given by the same MS. where the canticles appear with their context in the books to which they severally belong. Thus we find the following variants: Exod. xv. 14 ὠργίσθησαν, *cant.* ἐφοβήθησαν: Deut. xxxii. 7 γενεῶν γενεαῖς, *cant.* γενεᾶς γενεῶν: 18 γεννήσαντα, *cant.* ποιήσαντα: 1 Regn. ii. 10ᵃ φρονήσει, *cant.* σοφίᾳ: 10ᵇ ἄκρα γῆς, *cant.*+δίκαιος ὤν. But the deviations are not numerous, and the text of the canticles appears on the whole to belong to the same family as that of the body of the MS.

The division of the Psalter into books[2] seems to have been already made when it was translated into Greek, for though the Greek codices have nothing to answer to the headings ספר ראשון, etc., which appear in the printed Hebrew Bible, the Doxologies at the end of the first four books appear in the

in *Speaker's Comm.* (Apocr. ii. 362 ff.). The Greek text appears in *Const. Apost.* ii. 22 and in the *Didascalia*, where it follows a reference to Chron. *l. c.*; in MSS. of the LXX. it finds a place only among the canticles. See Fabricius-Harles, iii. 732, Westcott in Smith's *D. B.* ii. 226, Schürer[3], iii. 337 f.: and for the text with an *apparatus*, Fritzsche, *V. T. Gr. libr. Apocr.*, pp. xiv. sq., 92 sq. A detailed account of the editions, MSS., and versions and a discussion of the origin of the Prayer will be found in Dr Nestle's *Septuagintastudien* iii. (Stuttgart, 1899), p. 6 ff.; see also Ryssel in Kautzsch's *Apokryphen u. Pseudepigraphen.*

[1] For some other orders see Dom Morin in *Revue Bénédictine* (cited by A. E. Burn, *Creeds*, p. 262).

[2] A pre-Christian arrangement, as Hippolytus already knew (*hypoth. in Psalmos*, τὸ ψαλτήριον εἰς πέντε διεῖλον βιβλία οἱ Ἑβραῖοι). Cf. Robertson Smith, *O. T. in Jewish Ch.*, p. 194 n. In the lists of the Canon "the mention of five Books of Psalms is peculiar to Codex Amiatinus" (Sanday, in *Studia Biblica* iii. p. 242 ff.).

Greek as well as in the M. T. (Ps. xl. (xli.) 14, lxxi. (lxxii.) 18—20, lxxxviii. (lxxxix.) 5, cv. (cvi.) 48).

PROVERBS. The variations of 𝕲 and 𝕸 in this book are treated by Lagarde in his early book *Anmerkungen zur griech. Übersetzung der Proverbien.* There is a considerable number of Greek verses for which 𝕸 offers no Hebrew equivalent, and there are some Hebrew verses or half-verses for which there is no Greek. Of the Greek verses not in 𝕸 some (e.g. iv. 27 a—b, vi. 8 a—c) appear to be of Greek, perhaps early Christian, origin; others have been collected from various contexts (e.g. iii. 16 = Isa. xlv. 23 a + Prov. xxxi. 26; xxvi. 11 = Sir. iv. 21), or are fragments of the book which have been accidentally inserted twice (iii. 22 a = iii. 8, 28 c = xxvii. 1); others, again, seem to have arisen from the fusion of two renderings (xv. 18 a, xvi. 17); but there remain not a few which probably represent genuine portions of the original collections, though wanting in the present Hebrew text, e.g. vii. 1 a, viii. 21 a, ix. 12 a—c, 18 a—c, xii. 11 a, 13 a, xvii. 6 a, xviii. 22 a, xxii. 8 a (cited in 2 Cor. ix. 7), xxiv. 22 a—e, xxvii. 20 a, 21 a.

JOB. The LXX. text of Job current in Origen's time is known to have been very much shorter than the Greek text preserved in extant MSS. and the M.T.

> *Ad African.* 4 πλεῖστά τε ὅσα διὰ μέσου ὅλου τοῦ Ἰὼβ παρ᾽ Ἐβραίοις μὲν κεῖται παρ᾽ ἡμῖν δὲ οὐχί, καὶ πολλάκις μὲν ἔπη τέσσαρα ἢ τρία· ἔσθ᾽ ὅτε δὲ καὶ δεκατέσσαρα καὶ δεκαεννέα καὶ δεκαέξ (*for. leg. ἐννέα καὶ ἕξ*[1]). Cf. Hieron. *praef. in Hiob*: "cui [sc. libro Iob], si ea quae sub asteriscis addita sunt subtraxeris, pars maxima voluminis detruncabitur, et hoc duntaxat apud Graecos. ceterum apud Latinos...septingenti ferme aut octingenti versus desunt."

The asterisks are preserved in certain cursive MSS. of the

---

[1] For this correction see a note by Dr Nestle in *Exp. Times*, Aug. 1899 (p. 523).

Greek Job[1] and in MSS. of Jerome's version, while the shorter form is represented by the earliest form of the O.L. and in the Sahidic version. Most of the extant Greek MSS., including the best uncials, offer a text in which the lacunae are supplied (chiefly from Theodotion), but which still falls short of the fulness of the Hexaplaric LXX. and of 𝕸[2].

Dr Hatch[3] in his Essay *On Origen's revision of the LXX. text of Job* advocates the theory that the LXX. represents a shorter Hebrew text which was afterwards expanded into the longer form. Bickell, in his early book *De indole ac ratione versionis Alexandrinae* (p. 42), maintained that the omissions were chiefly due to the translator, and this view is supported by recent critics. The evident desire of the translator to follow classical models suggests that he was an Alexandrian Hellenist[4] who intended his version for general reading, rather than for use in the synagogue[5]. Under such circumstances he may have been tempted to reduce the length of his original, especially in passages where it did not lend itself readily to his treatment. On the other hand he has not scrupled here and there to add to the original. Thus in c. ii. 9 he seeks to heighten the effect and at the same time to soften the harshness of the words uttered by Job's wife (χρόνου ...πολλοῦ προβεβηκότος...λέγων Ἰδοὺ ἀναμένω κτλ.)[6].

The two notes at the end of the Greek Job (xlii. 17a, b—e) scarcely profess to belong to the book. The first (γέγραπται δὲ αὐτὸν πάλιν ἀναστήσεσθαι μεθ᾽ ὧν ὁ κύριος ἀνίστησιν) may be either a Pharisaic or a Christian gloss, intended to balance the ἐτελεύτησεν Ἰώβ of the previous hemistich, and arising out of

---

[1] Cf. Hatch, *Essays*, p. 216; Field, *Hexapla*, ii. p. 1 f.; E. Klostermann, *Analecta*, p. 63 f.

[2] Burkitt, *O. L. and Itala*, p. 8.   [3] *Essays*, p. 214 ff.

[4] On the translator's date cf. Schürer[3], iii. pp. 311, 356 f.

[5] Cf. Hatch, *op. cit.*, p. 219: "It was made after Judaism had come into contact with Greek philosophy. It may be presumed to have been intended not only for Greek-speaking Jews, but also for aliens." The version shews some knowledge of Homer and Aeschylus (cf. Smith, *D. B.*[2], vol. I. pt. ii. p. 1723).

[6] Cf. *Testament of Job* (ed. M. R. James, *Apocr. anecd.* ii. p. 117).

xix. 26 ἐπὶ γῆς ἀναστῆσαι (*v. l.* ἀναστήσει) τὸ δέρμα μου, to which passage γέγραπται seems to refer. The second note, which professes to come from an Aramaic source (οὗτος ἑρμηνεύεται ἐκ τῆς Συριακῆς βίβλου¹), confuses Job (אִיּוֹב) with the Edomite king Jobab (יוֹבָב) (Gen. xxxvi. 33 f. = 1 Chron. i. 44 f.), and bases on this identification a pedigree of the patriarch, according to which he was 'fifth from Abraham,' and a descendant of Esau. Similar statements occur in a fragment of the Hellenistic writer Aristeas quoted by Polyhistor, and from Polyhistor by Eusebius (*praep. ev.* ix. 25). From a comparison of this extract with the note attached to Job, Freudenthal was led to ascribe the note to Aristeas². Beyond the geographical description of Uz (ἐπὶ τοῖς ὁρίοις τῆς Ἰδουμαίας καὶ Ἀραβίας), and the statements that Job's wife was an Arab woman and that her son's name was Ennon or Enon (*v. l.*), the note contains nothing new: 17 *c*—*d* rests upon Gen. xxxvi. 32—35 (LXX.), and 17 *e* on Job ii. 11 (LXX.).

ESTHER. In the Greek Esther we reach the maximum of interpolation. Of 270 verses, 107 are wanting in the present Hebrew text, and probably at no time formed a part of the Hebrew book³. The Greek additions are distributed through the book in contexts as long as average chapters⁴. In the Latin Bible they are collected at the end of the canonical book, where they fill several consecutive chapters (x. 4—xi. 5 = F, xi. 2—xii. 6 = A, xiii. 1—7 = B, xiii. 8—xiv. 19 = C, xv. 4—19 = D, xvi. 1—24 = E). This arrangement is due to Jerome, who relegated the Greek interpolations to the end of the canonical book; but it has had the effect of making them unintelligible. In their Greek sequence they form part of a consecutive history; A, which precedes c. i., introduces the story by describing the events which led to the first advancement of Mordecai at the court of Artaxerxes; B and E, which

¹ "Ἐκ τῆς Σ. β. weist doch auf einen Midrasch oder ein Targum hin" (Dillmann, *Hiob*, p. 361).
² Schürer³, iii. p. 311.
³ Cf. Origen, *ad Afric.* 3 ἐκ τῆς Ἐσθὴρ οὔτε ἡ τοῦ Μαρδοχαίου εὐχὴ οὔτε ἡ τῆς Ἐσθήρ...παρ᾽ Ἐβραίοις φέρονται· ἀλλ᾽ οὐδὲ αἱ ἐπιστολαί· ἀλλ᾽ οὐδὲ ἡ τῷ Ἀμμὰν ἐπὶ καθαιρέσει τοῦ τῶν Ἰουδαίων ἔθνους γεγραμμένη, οὐδὲ ἡ τοῦ Μαρδοχαίου.
⁴ In the Cambridge LXX. they are distinguished by the Roman capitals A—F, a notation suggested by Dr Hort.

follow iii. 13 and viii. 12, profess to give copies of the letters
of Artaxerxes referred to in those verses; c and d, which come
between c. iv. and c. v., contain the prayers of Mordecai and
Esther, and a description of Esther's approach to the King;
f is an epilogue, which completes the story by relating the
institution of the feast of Purim. Such Haggadic accretions
will not create surprise if it be remembered that Esther was
among the latest of the Kethubim, and that its canonicity was
matter of dispute in Jewish circles even in the last years of the
first century A.D.[1]

A note attached to the last of the Greek additions professes
to relate the circumstances under which the book was brought
to Egypt: "in the fourth year of the reign of Ptolemy and
Cleopatra, Dositheus, who said that he was a priest and Levite,
and his son Ptolemy, brought the above Letter of Purim[2], as
they called it, which had been translated (so they said) by
one Lysimachus, son of Ptolemy, a resident at Jerusalem."
As Fritzsche remarks[3], no fewer than four Ptolemies married a
Cleopatra (Epiphanes, Philometor, Physcon, and Lathyrus), so
that the date intended by the fourth year of Ptolemy and
Cleopatra is by no means certain, though it is perhaps most
naturally interpreted as = B.C. 178–7 (? 166–5), the fourth year
of Philometor[4]. But the historical value of the note is more
than doubtful[5].

The Greek text of Esther exists in two recensions (1) that of
אABN 55, 93 *b*, 108 *a*, 249 al., (2) that of 19, 93 *a*, 108 *b*; both are
exhibited by Ussher (*Syntagma*), Fritzsche (Ἐσθήρ, 1848; *libri
apocryphi*, 1871), and Lagarde (*libr. canon. V. T.* i., 1883). The

---

[1] See Ryle, *Canon*, p. 139 f., 203 ff.; and cf. *supra*, p. 228 f.

[2] Φρουραί (Φρουραια א*, Φρουριμ א^{c.a}), cf. c. ix. 26, and Jos. *ant.* vi. 13
οἱ Ἰουδαῖοι τὰς προειρημένας ἡμέρας ἑορτάζουσιν προσαγορεύσαντες αὐτὰς
φρουρέας (v. l. φρουραίας, Lat. *conservatores*). The 'Letter of Purim'
seems to be the book of Esther as a whole; cf. c. ix. 20.

[3] *Handbuch zu d. Apocrypha*, i. p. 73.

[4] Ryssel (in Kautzsch, *Apokr.*, p. 212) inclines to B.C. 114, the fourth
year of Soter ii (Lathyrus), and Willrich to B.C. 48–7, that of Ptolemy xiv.

[5] See above, p. 25.

recensions differ considerably in the Greek additions as well as in the version. On the date of the Greek Esther the student may consult Jacob, *Das Buch Esther bei dem LXX.* in *ZATW.*, 1890 (p. 241 ff.).

JEREMIAH. Besides the extensive transpositions already noticed, the LXX. text of Jeremiah differs widely from M.T. in the way of excess and defect. The subject has received careful treatment from Dr A. W. Streane (*Double Text of Jeremiah*, Cambridge, 1896), whose verdict is on the whole in favour of the LXX. text, especially with regard to its omissions. He points out that "the tendency to diffuseness, characteristic of later Judaism...[and] likely specially to affect the writing of Jeremiah, as a prophet whose memory was of marked interest to the post-exilic Jews...operated much more slightly among Egyptian Jews than with their brethren elsewhere[1]"; and concludes that "the 'omissions' to be observed in the LXX. of Jeremiah, speaking generally, exist only in consequence of its nearer approximation to the original form of the Hebrew text."

The Greek additions, in Jeremiah, rarely exceed a few words in a verse (see the list in Streane, p. 19). Omissions are more numerous, and sometimes extend over several consecutive verses of 𝕸; the following are the most noteworthy: viii. 10[b]—12, x. 6, 8, 10, xvii. 1—5[a], xxix. (xxxvi., LXX.) 16—20, xxxiii. (xl., LXX.) 14—26, xxxix. (=xlvi., LXX.) 4—13, lii. 28—30. Of these passages viii. 10[b]—12 seems to be based on vi. 12—15, and xxix. 16—20 on xxiv. 8—10; x. 6, 8, 10, xxxix. 4—13 and lii. 28—30 are probably interpolations in the M.T. On the other hand it is possible that the omission of xvii. 1—5[a] was due to homœoteleuton, the eye of the translator or the scribe of his archetype having passed from יהוה (xvi. 21) to יהוה (xvii. 5[a]). It is more difficult to account for the absence from 𝕲 of the Messianic passage xxxiii. 14—26. Dr Streane thinks that it must have been wanting in the Hebrew text which lay before the translators. Possibly the Messianic hope which it emphasises had less interest for a subject of the Ptolemies than for the Jews of Palestine.

LAMENTATIONS. The Greek translator has prefixed a heading which connects the book with Jeremiah (καὶ ἐγένετο...ἐκάθισεν Ἰερεμίας κλαίων κτλ.),

---

[1] P. 24 f. Cf. A. B. Davidson in Hastings' *D.B.* ii. 573 ff. Thackeray, on the other hand, instances the large Alexandrian additions to Esther and Daniel.

DANIEL. Like Esther the Book of Daniel in both its Greek forms[1] contains large contexts which have no equivalent in 𝕲. There are three such passages in the Greek Daniel: (1) the story of Susanna (Σουσάννα, Σωσάννα), which in the version of Theodotion[2] as given by the great uncials precedes Dan. i. 1; (2) the story of Bel and the Dragon (Βὴλ καὶ Δράκων) which follows Dan. xii. 13; (3) after Dan. iii. 23 a digression of 67 verses (iii. 24—90, LXX., Th.), consisting of (a) the prayer of Azarias (24—45), (b) details as to the heating of the furnace and the preservation of Azarias and his friends (46—51), (c) the Song of the Three (52—90). In the Greek MSS. no break or separate title divides these Greek additions from the rest of the text, except that when Daniel is divided into "visions," the first vision is made to begin at i. 1, Susanna being thus excluded from the number; Bel, on the other hand, is treated as the last of the visions (ὅρασις ιβ´ AQ). Internal evidence appears to shew that both these stories originally had a separate circulation; Susanna does not form a suitable prologue to Dan. i.[3], for v. 6 introduces Daniel as a person hitherto unknown to the reader; and the position of Bel as an epilogue to the prophetic portion of the book is still less appropriate. From the Fathers, however, it is clear that in the earliest Christian copies of the LXX. both Susanna and Bel formed a part of Daniel, to which they are ascribed by Irenaeus and Tertullian, and implicitly by Hippolytus. The remarkable letter of Julius Africanus to Origen which throws doubt on the genuineness of Susanna, calling attention to indications of its Greek origin, forms a solitary exception to the general view; even Origen labours to maintain their canonicity.

Iren. iv. 26. 3 "et audient eas quae sunt a Daniele propheta voces" (*Sus.* 56, 52 f.), iv. 5. 2 "quem et Daniel propheta...annuntiavit" (*Bel* 4 f., 25). Tert. *de idololatria*, 18 (*Bel* 4 f.). Hippol. *in*

[1] Vide *supra*, p. 46 ff.

[2] On Theodotion's Bel, see Gaster in *J. of Bibl. Archaeology*, xvi. 289, 290, 312 ff., xvii. 71 ff.

[3] Susanna is perhaps made to precede Daniel because it describes events which belong to his early life; cf. *v.* 44 ff. and *v.* 62 in a, b (LXX.).

Sus. (Lagarde, p. 145) αὕτη μὲν οὖν ἡ ἱστορία γεγένηται ὕστερον, προεγράφη δὲ τῆς βίβλου πρώτης. Africanus, *ep. ad Orig.* θαυμάζω δὲ πῶς ἔλαθέ σε τὸ μέρος τοῦ βιβλίου τοῦτο κίβδηλον ὄν κτλ. *Orig. ad African.* παρ' ἀμφοτέροις (LXX. and Theodotion) ἔκειτο τὸ περὶ τὴν Σωσάνναν (ὡς σὺ φῇς) πλάσμα, καὶ αἱ τελευταῖαι ἐν τῷ Δανιὴλ περικοπαί. It will be noticed that the extracts from Hippolytus and Origen shew that Susanna and Bel occupied in MSS. of the second and third centuries the same relative positions which they occupy in extant MSS. of the fourth and fifth.

Notwithstanding the objection shrewdly based by Africanus on the paronomasia (σχῖνος, σχίζειν) in *Sus.* 54 f., Ball (*Speaker's Comm.*, Apocrypha, ii. p. 330 f.) has given reasons for believing that both Susanna and Bel once existed in an Aramaic or a new-Hebrew original[1]. The LXX. version represents Bel as a fragment of Habakkuk (cod. 87, Syro-Hex., tit. ἐκ προφητείας Ἀμβακοὺμ υἱοῦ Ἰησοῦ ἐκ τῆς φυλῆς Λευί), an attribution evidently due to *v.* 33 ff., but inconsistent with the place of the story in the Gk. MSS.

The addition to Dan. iii. 23 is clearly Midrashic and probably had a Semitic original[2]. The two hymns contained in it found a place, as we have seen, among the Greek ecclesiastical Canticles, where they appear as the προσευχὴ Ἀζαρίου and the ὕμνος τῶν πατέρων ἡμῶν (cod. A) or *ὕ.* τῶν τριῶν παίδων (cod. T).

Besides these additions, which are common to both texts of Daniel, the text of the LXX. contains a large number of shorter interpolations, especially in c. iii.—vi. where "the original thread of the narrative is often lost in a chaos of accretions, alterations, and displacements[3]." The student can easily test this statement by comparing the two versions as they stand face to face in the Cambridge LXX., especially in c. iii. 1—3, 46, iv. 14 (17), 19 (22), 29—34 (32—37), v. 13—23, vi. 2—5

---

[1] Cf. J. T. Marshall in Hastings, *D. B.* iv. 632; on the other hand, see Kamphausen in *Encycl. Biblica*, i. 1013, and comp. Rothstein, *Apokr.*, p. 173 ff. On the Aramaic version of the additions from Theodotion's Greek cf. Schürer[3], iii. p. 333.

[2] Ball, *l. c.*, p. 308. See Nestle, *Exp. T.* xii. 527, and Daubney, *Exp. T.* xviii. 287.   [3] Bevan, *Daniel*, p. 46.

(3—6), 12—14 (13—15), 22 (23). But the whole of this section of the book in the LXX. may be regarded as a paraphrase rather than a translation of a Hebrew text. In Susanna Theodotion has here and there a much longer text than the LXX. (cf. Sus. 14—27, 42—50), and both in Susanna and Bel the two Greek versions sometimes diverge so widely as to exhibit the story in distinct forms which appear to represent different traditions.

LITERATURE upon the canonical books (considered separately or in groups).

PENTATEUCH. Amersfoordt, *Dissert. philol. de variis lectionibus Holmes. Pentateuchi* (1815). Hug, *de Pentateuchi vers. Alexandrina commentatio* (1818). Töpler, *de Pentateuchi interpretationis Alexandrinae indole* (1830). Thiersch, *de Pentateuchi versione Alexandrina,* libri iii (1841). Frankel, *über den Einfluss der paläst. Exegese auf die alex. Hermeneutik* (1851). Howorth, *the LXX. and Samaritan v. the Hebrew text of the Pentateuch* (*Academy,* 1894).

GENESIS. Lagarde, *Genesis Graece* (1868). Deutsch, *exeg. Analecten zur Genesisübersetzung der LXX.* (in *Jüd. Litt. Blatt,* 1879). Spurrell, *Genesis,* ed. 2 (1898).

EXODUS. Selwyn, *Notae criticae in Versionem LXXviralem, Exod. i—xxiv* (1856).

NUMBERS. Selwyn, *Notae,* &c., *Liber Numerorum* (1857). Howard, *Numbers and Deuteronomy acc. to the LXX. translated into English* (1887).

DEUTERONOMY. Selwyn, *Notae,* &c., *Liber Deuteronomii* (1858). Howard, *op. cit.* (1887). Driver, *critical and Exegetical Commentary on Deut.* (1895).

JOSHUA. Hollenberg, *Der Charakter der alex. Übersetzung des Buches Josua* (1876).

JUDGES. Fritzsche, *Liber Iudicum sec. LXX. interpretes* (1867). Schulte, *de restitutione atque indole genuinae versionis graece Iudicum* (1889). Lagarde, *Septuagintast.* i. (1891), (Jud. i—v., texts of A and B). Moore, *critical and Exegetical Comm. on Judges* (1895).

RUTH. Fritzsche, 'Ρούθ κατὰ τοὺς ο' (1867).

1, 2 KINGDOMS. Wellhausen, *Der Text der Bücher Samuelis untersucht* (1871). Woods, *the light thrown by the LXX. on the Books of Samuel* (in *Studia Biblica*, i. 21, 1885). Driver, *Notes on the Hebrew Text of the Books of Samuel* (1890). Steinthal, *zur Geschichte Sauls u. Davids* (1891). Kerber, *Syrohex. Fragmente zu den beiden Samuelis-büchern* (*ZATW.*, 1898). J. Méritan, *la Version Grecque des livres de Samuel, précédée d'une introduction sur la critique textuelle* (1898). H. P. Smith, *Critical and exeg. comm. on the Books of Samuel* (1899).

3, 4 KINGDOMS. Silberstein, *Über den Ursprung der im Codex Alex. u. Vat. des dritten Königsbuches der Alex. Übersetzung überlieferten Textgestalt* (in *ZATW.*, 1893). C. F. Burney, *Notes on the Heb. Text of the Books of Kings* (1903).

1, 2 CHRONICLES, EZRA-NEHEMIAH. Howorth, *The true LXX. version of Chr.-Ezra-Neh.* (in *Academy*, 1893). Nestle, *Marginalien* (1893), p. 29 ff.

PSALMS. Sinker, *Some remarks on the LXX. version of the Psalms* (1879). Baethgen, *der text-kritisches Werth des alten Übersetz. zu d. Psalmen* (1882). Lagarde, *psalteri graeci specimen* (1887); *psalmorum quinquagena prima* (1892). Mercati, *un palimpsesto Ambrosiano dei Salmi Esapli* (1896). Jacob, *Beiträge zu einer Einleitung in die Psalmen* (I. Exc. v.), (1896).

PROVERBS. Lagarde, *Anmerkungen zur griech. Übersetz. der Proverbien* (1863). Pinkuss, *die syr. Übersetzung des Proverbien...in ihrem Verhältniss zu dem Mass. Text, den LXX. u. dem Targ. untersucht* (*ZATW.*, 1894).

ECCLESIASTES. Wright, *The book of Koheleth* (1883). Grätz, *Koheleth* (1884). Klostermann (E.), *de libri Coheleth versione Alexandrina* (1892). Dillmann, *über die Gr. Übersetzung des Koheleth* (1892). Köhl, *observ. ad interpr. Gr. et Lat. vet. libri Job* (1834).

JOB. Bickell, *De indole ac ratione versionis Alexandrinae Jobi* (1862); *der ursprüngliche Septuaginta-text des Buches Hiob* (1886). Hatch, *on Origen's revision of the Book of Job* (in *Essays*, 1889). Dillmann, *Text-kritisches zum B. Ijob* (1890). Maude, *die Peschittha zu Hiob nebst einem Anhang über ihr Verhältniss zu LXX. u. Targ.* (1892). Beer, *der Text des B. Hiob* (1895). Driver, in *Cont. Review* (Feb. 1896). Cheyne, in *Enc. Bibl.*, 2489 f. (1901).

ESTHER. Jacob, *Esther bei dem LXX.* (*ZATW.*, 1890). On the Greek additions see Ryssel in Kautzsch, *Apokr.*, p. 193 ff.

DODECAPROPHETON.   Vollers, *Das Dod. der Alexandriner* (1880), continued in *ZATW.*, 1883-4.   Stekhoven, *de alex. Vertaling van het Dod.* (1887).

HOSEA.   Treitel, *Die alex. Übersetzung des Buches Hosea* (1888).

MICAH.   Ryssel, *Untersuchungen über die Textgestalt des B. Micha* (1887).   Taylor, *the Mass. text and the ancient versions of Micah* (1891).

OBADIAH.   Seydel, *Vaticinium Obadiae......ratione habita transl. Alex.* (1869).

NAHUM.   Reinke, *Zur Kritik der ält. Vers. d. Proph. Nahum* (1867).

HABAKKUK.   Sinker, *Psalm of Habakkuk* (1890).

ZECHARIAH.   Lowe, *Comm. on Zech.* (1882).

ISAIAH.   Scholz, *Die Masor. Text u. alex. Übersetzung des B. Jesaias* (1880).   Weiss, *Peschitta zu Deuterojesaia u. ihr Verhältniss zu M.T., LXX. u. Targ.* (1893).

JEREMIAH.   Movers, *De utriusque recens. Jeremiae indole et origine* (1837).   Wichelhaus, *de Jeremiae vers. Alexandr. indole* (1847).   Schulz, *de Ieremiae textus Hebr. et Gr. discrepantia* (1861).   Scholz, *der Masor. Text u. die LXX. Übersetz. des B. Jeremias* (1875).   Kühl, *das Verhältniss der Massora zur Septuaginta in Jeremia* (1882).   Workman, *the text of Jeremiah* (1889).   Coste, *die Weissagungen der Propheten Ieremias* (1895).   Streane, *the double text of Jeremiah* (1896).   The question of the two recensions is dealt with at length in Bleek-Wellhausen, *Einleitung*, § 158 ff.

LAMENTATIONS.   Goldwitzer, *Übersetzung mit Vergleichung d. LXX.* (1828).

EZEKIEL.   Merx, *Der Werth der LXX. für die Textkritik der AT am Ezechiel aufgezeigt* (*Jb. pr. Th.*, 1883).   Cornill, *das Buch des Proph. Ezechiel* (1886); cf. Lagarde in *Gött. gelehrte Anzeigen* (1 June, 1886).

DANIEL.   Bludau, *De alex. interprete libri Daniel indole* (1891); *die alex. Übersetzung des B. Daniel* (1897).   Bevan, *the Book of Daniel* (1892).   Löhr, *textkrit. Vorarbeiten zu einer Erklärung des Buches Daniel* (*ZATW.*, 1895).   On the Greek additions see Rothstein in Kautzsch, *Apokr.*, p. 172 ff.

CHAPTER III.

Books not included in the Hebrew Canon.

The MSS. and many of the lists of the Greek Old Testament include certain books which find no place in the Hebrew Canon. The number of these books varies, as we have seen; but the fullest collections contain the following: 1 Esdras, Wisdom of Solomon, Wisdom of Sirach, Judith, Tobit, Baruch and the Epistle of Jeremiah, i.—iv. Maccabees. We may add the Psalms of Solomon, a book which was sometimes included in MSS. of the Salomonic books, or, in complete Bibles, at the end of the Canon; and the Greek version of Enoch, although by some accident it has been excluded from the Greek Bible, on other grounds claims the attention of every Biblical student. There is also a long list of *pseudepigrapha* and other *apocrypha* which lie outside both the Hebrew and the Greek Canons, and of which in many cases only the titles have survived. The present chapter will be occupied by a brief examination of these non-canonical writings of the Greek Old Testament.

1. 1 Esdras. In MSS. of the lxx. the canonical book Ezra-Nehemiah appears under the title Ἔσδρας βʹ, Ἔσδρας αʹ being appropriated by another recension of the history of the Captivity and Return. The 'Greek Esdras' consists of an

independent and somewhat free version of portions of 2
Chronicles and Ezra-Nehemiah, broken by a long context
which has no parallel in the Hebrew Bible.

> Thus 1 Esdr. i. = 2 Chron. xxxv. 1—xxxvi. 21 ; ii. 1—14 = Ezra
> i. ; ii. 15—25 = Ezra iv. 7—24; iii. 1—v. 6 is original; v. 7—70
> = Ezra ii. 1—iv. 5; vi., vii. = Ezra v., vi.; viii. 1—ix. 36 = Ezra vii.
> 1—x. 44; ix. 37—55 = Neh. vii. 73ᵇ—viii. 13ª. The Greek book
> ends abruptly, in a manner which suggests that something has
> been lost ; cf. ix. 55 καὶ ἐπισυνήχθησαν with 2 Esdr. xviii. 13
> συνήχθησαν οἱ ἄρχοντες κτλ. The student may compare the
> ending of the Second Gospel (Mc. xvi. 8).

The context 1 Esdr. iii. 1—v. 6 is perhaps the most interesting of the contributions made by the Greek Bible to
the legendary history of the Captivity and Return. We owe to
it the immortal proverb *Magna est veritas et praevalet* (iv. 41[1]),
and the story which forms the setting of the proverb is worthy
of the occasion. But in its present form it is certainly unhistorical; Zerubbabel (iv. 13) belonged to the age of Cyrus,
and it was Cyrus and not Darius (iv. 47 f.) who decreed the
rebuilding of Jerusalem. It has been suggested that "this
story is perhaps the nucleus of the whole (book), round which
the rest is grouped[2]." In the grouping chronological order
has been to some extent set aside; the displacement of Ezra
iv. 7—24 (= 1 Esdr. ii. 15—25) has thrown the sequence of
events into confusion, and the scene is shifted from the court
of Artaxerxes to that of Darius, and from Darius back again
to Cyrus, with whose reign the history had started. Yet
Josephus[3], attracted perhaps by the superiority of the Greek
style, uses 1 Esdras in preference to the Greek version of
the canonical Ezra-Nehemiah, even embodying in his narrative the legend of Zerubbabel[4]. He evades the difficulty

---

[1] The future (*praevalebit*) is without authority. In *v.* 38 Cod. A gives
ἰσχύσει, but in *v.* 41 ὑπερισχύει is unchallenged. The Latin texts have the
present in both verses.

[2] H. St J. Thackeray, in Hastings' *D. B.* i. p. 76.

[3] *ant.* x. 4. 4—xi.   [4] *ant.* xi. 3. 2 sqq.

arising out of the premature reference to Artaxerxes by substituting Cambyses[1]. In the early Church the Greek Esdras
was accepted without suspicion; cf. e.g. Clem. Alex. *strom.*
i. 21; Origen, *in Joann.* t. vi. 1, in Jos. *hom.* ix. 10;
Cyprian, *ep.* 74. 9. Jerome, however (*praef. in Ezr.*), dis-
carded the book, and modern editions of the Vulgate
relegate it to an appendix where it appears as 3 Esdras, the
titles 1 Esdras and 2 Esdras being given to the two parts
of the canonical book Ezra-Nehemiah[2].

The relation of the two Greek recensions of **Ezra** to
one another is a problem analogous to that which is presented
by the two 'versions' of Daniel, and scarcely less perplexing.
It has been stated with great care in Hastings' *Dictionary
of the Bible* (i. p. 759 ff.), by Mr H. St J. Thackeray. He
distinguishes three views, (1) that 1 Esdras is a compilation
from the LXX. version of 2 Chronicles and Ezra-Nehemiah,
(2) that it is based on an earlier Greek version of those books,
and (3) that it is an independent translation of an earlier
Hebrew text; and while refusing to regard any solution as
final, he inclines to the second. The third has recently
found a champion in Sir H. H. Howorth[3], who adds to it the
suggestion that 1 Esdras is the true Septuagintal (i.e. the
Alexandrian) version, whilst 2 Esdras is later, and probably
that of Theodotion. Mr Thackeray is disposed to regard this
contention as "so far correct that [1 Esdras] represents the
first attempt to present the story of the Return in a Gr[eek]
dress," 2 Esdras being "a more accurate rendering of the
Heb[rew]" which was "subsequently...required and...supplied
by what is now called the LXX. version[4]."

2. WISDOM OF SOLOMON. The Greek title is Σοφία
Σαλωμῶνος (Σαλομῶντος, Σολομῶντος, Σαλωμών). But the book

---

[1] *ant.* xi. 2. 1 sqq.   [2] The English Article (vi) follows this numeration.
[3] In the *Academy* for 1893.
[4] And possibly the work of Theod. (*Gramm. of O. T. in Gk*, p. 13.
(In Cod. ℵ, 1 Chron. xi. 22—xix. 17 goes on without a break to Esd. β.
ix. 9, the whole being headed Εσδ. β.)

was often cited as ἡ Σοφία, ἡ πανάρετος Σοφία, a name which it shared with Proverbs and Ecclesiasticus; see Lightfoot on Clem. 1 *Cor.* 55. In the Muratorian fragment it is described as " Sapientia ab amicis Salomonis in honorem ipsius scripta." The Latin versions and fathers called the book *Sapientia* or *Sophia Salomonis* (Cyprian, *O. L.*), but also simply *liber Sapientiae* (Lactantius, Vulg.).

No other book in the Greek Bible is so manifestly Alexandrian in tone and style. Some early Christian writers attributed it to Philo (Hieron. *praef. in libros Salomonis:* "nonnulli scriptorum veterum hunc esse Iudaei Philonis affirmant"), and it has been ingeniously conjectured that this view found a place in the Greek archetype of the Muratorian fragment[1]. But though Wisdom has strong points of likeness to the works of Philo, it is free from the allegorizing spirit of that writer, and its conception of the Logos is less developed than his[2]. On the other hand it clearly belongs to a period when the Jewish scholars of Alexandria were abreast of the philosophic doctrines and the literary standards of their Greek contemporaries. The author is acquainted with the Platonic doctrine of the four cardinal virtues[3] (c. viii. 7 εἰ δικαιοσύνην ἀγαπᾷ τις, οἱ πόνοι ταύτης εἰσὶν ἀρεταί· σωφροσύνην γὰρ καὶ φρόνησιν ἐκδιδάσκει, δικαιοσύνην καὶ ἀνδρείαν), and with the Platonic sense of ὕλη (c. xi. 17 κτίσασα τὸν κόσμον ἐξ ἀμόρφου ὕλης· cf. Philo, *de victim.* 13, *de mund. opif.* 12). His ideas on the subject of preexistence (c. viii. 20), of the relation of the body to the spirit (c. ix. 15), of Wisdom as the soul of the world (vii. 24), are doubtless due to the same source. His language is no less distinctly shaped upon Greek models; " no existing work represents perhaps more completely the style of compo-

---

[1] *Ab amicis* suggests ὑπὸ φίλων, and ὑπὸ φίλων has been thought to be a corruption of ὑπὸ Φίλωνος. See Tregelles *can. Mur.*, p. 53, and cf. Zahn, *Gesch. d. N. T. Kanons*, ii. p. 100.

[2] See this worked out by W. J. Deane, *Book of Wisdom*, p. 33 f.; C. J. Bigg, *Christian Platonists*, p. 14 ff.

[3] See *Rep.* 427—439, 442, &c.

sition which would be produced by the sophistic school of rhetoric[1]," as it existed under the conditions of Greek life at Alexandria. This remark may be illustrated by the peculiar vocabulary of the book. Unusual words abound, e.g. ἀκηλί-δωτος, ἀμβρόσιος, ἔξαλλος, ζωτικός, ἰοβόλος, κακόμοχθος, κινητικός, κρυσταλλοειδής, ὁμοιοπαθής, παντεπίσκοπος, πολυμερής, πρωτό-πλαστος· ἀγερωχία, ἀπαύγασμα, ἀπόρροια, εἰδέχθεια, ἐνέργεια, εὐδράνεια, ῥεμβασμός, συλλογισμός· μετακιρνᾶν, μεταλλεύειν, προυφεστάναι[2]. In some of these we can trace the influence of philosophical thought, in others the laboured effort of the writer to use words in harmony with the literary instincts of the age and place to which he belonged.

The object of the book is to protect Hellenistic Jews from the insidious influences of surrounding ungodliness and idolatry, but while its tone is apologetic and even polemical, the point of view is one which would commend itself to non-Jewish readers. The philosophical tendencies and the literary style of *Wisdom* favour the view that it is earlier than Philo, but not earlier than the middle of the second century B.C. As to the author, the words in which Origen dismissed the question of the authorship of the Epistle to the Hebrews may be applied to this pre-Christian writing—τίς δὲ ὁ γράψας...τὸ μὲν ἀληθὲς θεὸς οἶδεν. It is the solitary survival from the wreck of the earlier works of the philosophical school of Alexandria which culminated in Philo, the contemporary of our Lord.

3. WISDOM OF JESUS, SON OF SIRACH. In cod. B the title of this book is simply Σοφία Σειράχ[3], but codd. AC give the fuller and more accurate form Σοφία Ἰησοῦ υἱοῦ Σειράχ (cf. c. L. 27 παιδείαν...ἐχάραξα ἐν τῷ βιβλίῳ τούτῳ Ἰησοῦς υἱὸς

---

[1] Westcott in Smith's *B. D.* iii. 1780. Cf. Jerome, *l. c.* "ipse stylus Graecam eloquentiam redolet."

[2] See Deane, p. 27, Westcott, p. 178, Ryle, Smith's *B. D*[2]. i. p. 185.

[3] Σειράχ = סירא. "In the Hebrew Josippon (Pseudo-Josephus) the form שירך is a transliteration from the Latin" (Cowley and Neubauer, *Original Hebrew of a portion of Ecclesiasticus*, p. ix. n.).

Σειράχ[1]). Jerome had seen a Hebrew Sirach which shared
with the canonical book the title of Proverbs (*praef. in libros
Salom.*: "Hebraicum reperi...Parabolas (משלים) praenotatum").
The later name, *Ecclesiasticus*, which appears in Cyprian (e.g.
testim. ii. 1 "apud Salomonem...in Ecclesiastico"), marks the
book as the most important or the most popular of the *libri
ecclesiastici*—the books which the Church used for the purpose of
instruction, although they were not included in the Jewish canon.

> Cf. Rufin. *in symb.* 38: "alii libri sunt qui non canonici sed
> ecclesiastici a maioribus appellati sunt, id est, Sapientia quae
> dicitur Salomonis, et alia Sapientia quae dicitur filii Sirach, qui
> liber apud Latinos hoc ipso generali vocabulo *Ecclesiasticus*
> appellatur, quo vocabulo non auctor libelli sed scripturae qua-
> litas cognominata est."

The Wisdom of the Son of Sirach was the work of
a Palestinian (c. L. 27 Ἰησοῦς ὁ Ἰεροσολυμείτης), and written
in Hebrew; the Greek version was made by the grandson
of the writer during a visit to Alexandria (*prolog.*, *ll.* 5, 18 ff.).
This visit is said to have begun ἐν τῷ ὀγδόῳ καὶ τριακοστῷ
ἔτει ἐπὶ τοῦ Εὐεργέτου βασιλέως—words which, simple as they
seem, are involved in a double ambiguity, since there
were two Ptolemies who bore the name Euergetes, and
it is not clear whether the 38th year is to be reckoned
from the commencement of the reign of Euergetes or from
some other point of departure. But, assuming that the
Euergetes intended is Euergetes II., i.e. Physcon[2], and that
the translator is counting from the time when Physcon was
associated in the government with his brother and predecessor Philometor, we arrive at B.C. 132 as the *terminus a quo*
of the Greek version, and the original may have been composed some fifty years earlier.

Fragments of the original are preserved in Rabbinic

[1] On Ἐλεαζάρ (which follows Σειράχ in the Greek) see Ryssel in
Kautzsch, *Apokr.*, p. 253. The newly-discovered Hebrew reads שמעון
בן ישוע בן אלעזר בן סירא, on which see Schechter, *Wisdom of Ben
Sira*, p. 65; Nestle in Hastings' *D. B.* iv. p. 541 f.

[2] Cf. Deissmann, *Bible Studies* (E. Tr.), p. 339 ff.

literature. These are in the dialect of the Talmud; but recent discoveries have brought to light a large part of the book in classical Hebrew. A comparison of the Greek version with the Hebrew text, so far as it has been printed, reveals considerable differences, especially when the Greek text employed is that of cod. B, which was unfortunately chosen for the purpose by the Oxford editors of the Hebrew fragments. It must be remembered that these fragments come from a MS. of the 11th or 12th century, which may present a corrupt form of the Hebrew text; and on the other hand, that there are considerable variations in the Greek text of Sirach, cod. B differing widely from the majority of the MSS.[1] Much remains to be done before the text of Sirach can be settled with any confidence. Meanwhile Professor Margoliouth has thrown doubt upon the originality of the Hebrew fragments, which he regards as belonging to an eleventh century version made from the Syriac with the help of a Persian translation from the Greek[2]. At present few experts accept this theory, but the question must perhaps be regarded as *sub iudice.*

In all the known MSS. of the Greek Sirach[3], there is a remarkable disturbance of the sequence. They pass from c. xxx. 34 to c. xxxiii. 13 b, returning to the omitted passage after xxxvi. 16 a. The error seems to have arisen from a transposition in the common archetype of the pairs of leaves on which these two nearly equal sections were severally written[4]—a fact which is specially instructive in view of the large divergences in the Greek MSS. to which reference has

---

[1] Cf. Hatch, *Essays*, p. 281. A group of MSS. headed by V = 23 contains a considerable number of verses or stichi omitted by the rest of our Greek authorities; see Smith, *D. B²*. I. i. p. 842.

[2] *Origin of the original Hebrew of Ecclesiasticus*, 1899. See on this a letter by Prof. Driver in the *Guardian*, June 28, 1899, and Dr Taylor's remarks in *Ben Sira*, p. lxx ff.

[3] It now appears that even H-P. 248 is no exception, so that Fritzsche's "uno fortasse cod. 248 excepto" (*Libri apocr.* p. 462) must be deleted. On this MS. see Fritzsche, p. xxiii; Zenner in *Z. K. Th.*, 1895. The text of Sirach after 248 has been edited by J. H. A. Hart, for the Cambridge University Press (1909).

[4] See Fritzsche in *exeg. Handbuch*, v. p. 169 f.

been made. The true order is preserved in the Old Latin[1], Syriac, and Armenian versions.

4. JUDITH ('Ἰουδείθ, -δίθ, -δήθ, = יְהוּדִית, cf. Gen. xxvi. 34, where the same spellings are found in the cursives, though the uncials exhibit Ἰουδείν, Ἰουδίν), an historical romance, of which the scene is laid in the days of Nebuchadnezzar (c. i. 2). The date of its composition is uncertain. A *terminus ad quem* is provided by the fact that Clement of Rome knew the story (1 *Cor.* 55 Ἰουδὶθ ἡ μακαρία…παρέδωκεν Κύριος Ὀλοφέρνην ἐν χειρὶ θηλείας)[2]; and the name of Judith's enemy has suggested a *terminus a quo*, for Olophernes[3] appears to be a softened form of Orophernes, the name of a Cappadocian king, c. B.C. 158, who may have been regarded as an enemy of the Jews[4]. The religious attitude of the author of *Judith* is that of the devout Pharisee (cf. e.g. viii. 6, x. 2 ff., xi. 13, xii. 7), and the work may have been a fruit of the patriotic feeling called forth by the Maccabean wars.

Origen's Jewish teachers knew nothing of a Semitic original (cf. *ad African.* 13 : Ἑβραῖοι τῷ Τωβίᾳ οὐ χρῶνται οὐδὲ τῇ Ἰουδήθ, οὐδὲ γὰρ ἔχουσιν αὐτὰ καὶ ἐν ἀποκρύφοις Ἑβραιστί, ὡς ἀπ' αὐτῶν μαθόντες ἐγνώκαμεν). Jerome, on the other hand, not only says expressly (*praef. in Iudith*) : "apud Hebraeos liber Iudith inter apocrypha (*v.l.* hagiographa) legitur," but he produced a version or paraphrase from an Aramaic source ("ea quae intellegentia integra ex verbis Chaldaeis invenire potui, Latinis expressi")[5]. The relation of this Aramaic text to the original of the Greek book remains uncertain.

---

[1] On the O.L. of the Wisdoms see above, pt. i. c. IV (pp. 96, 103).
[2] See Lightfoot's note *ad loc.* and his remarks in *Clement* i. p. 313 ff.
[3] Not Ὀλοφέρνης, as is presupposed by the Latin.
[4] Cf. art. *Holofernes* in Hastings' *D. B.* ii. p. 402. There were, however, earlier kings of the same name (*op. cit.* p. 823; cf. Schürer[3], iii. p. 169 f., n. 19).
[5] See however Ball in *Speaker's Comm.* Apocr. i. pp. 243, 259 ff.; and F. C. Porter in Hastings' *B. D.* ii. p. 822[b].

The Greek Judith is said by Fritzsche[1] to exist in three recensions: (1) that of the Uncials and the majority of the cursives, (2) that of codd. 19, 108, and (3) that which is represented by cod. 58, and is in general agreement with the Old Latin and Syriac versions, which are based upon a Greek text.

5. Tobit (Τωβείτ (-βίτ, -βήτ), Τωβείθ, *Tobias, liber Tobiae, utriusque Tobiae*), a tale of family life, the scene of which is laid at Nineveh and Ecbatana, the hero being an Israelite of the tribe of Naphtali, who had been carried into captivity by Shalmanezer. The book appears to have been written for Jewish readers, and in Hebrew or Aramaic. The Jews of Origen's time, however, refused to recognise its authority (Orig. *de orat.* 14 τῇ δὲ τοῦ Τωβῆτ βίβλῳ ἀντιλέγουσιν οἱ ἐκ περιτομῆς, ὡς μὴ ἐνδιαθήκῳ), or even to include it among their apocrypha (see above, under Judith); but it was accepted by the Church (*ep. ad African. l. c.* χρῶνται τῷ Τωβίᾳ αἱ ἐκκλησίαι), and there is abundant evidence of its popularity among Christians (cf. Ps. Clem. 2 *Cor.* 16. 4, Polyc. *ad Smyrn.* 10. 2, Clem. Alex. *strom.* ii. 23, vi. 12, Orig. *de orat.* 11, *in Rom.* viii. 11, *c. Cels.* v. 19, Cypr. *testim.* iii. 1, 6, 62). Gnostics shared this feeling with Catholics; the Ophites placed Tobit among their prophetical books (Iren. i. 30. 11).

Jerome translated Tobit as he translated Judith, from a 'Chaldee,' i.e. Aramaic, copy, but with such haste that the whole was completed in a single day (*praef. in Tob.* "exigitis ut librum Chaldaeo sermone conscriptum ad latinum stylum tradam...feci satis desiderio vestro...et quia vicina est Chaldaeorum lingua sermoni Hebraico, utriusque linguae peritissimum loquacem reperiens unius diei laborem arripui, et quidquid ille mihi Hebraicis verbis expressit, hoc ego

---

[1] Fritzsche, *libri apocr.* p. xviii sq.; Schürer[3], iii. p. 172. The text in codd. 19, 108, is said to be Lucianic (Max Löhr in Kautzsch, *Apokr.*, p. 147).

accito notario sermonibus Latinis exposui[1]"). Thus, as in
the case of Judith, we have two Latin versions, the Old
Latin, based upon the Greek, and Jerome's rough and ready
version of the Aramaic.

The Greek text itself exists in two principal recensions,
represented by the two great uncials B and א. In c. vi. 9—
xiii. 18 Fritzsche adds a third text supplied by the cursives
44, 106, 107[2]. The relation of the two principal texts to each
other has recently been discussed by Nestle (*Septuagintastudien*, iii.) and by J. Rendel Harris (in the *American Journal
of Theology*, iii. p. 541 ff.). Both, though on different grounds,
give preference to the text of א. Harris, however, points out
that while א is probably nearer to the original Hebrew, B
may exhibit the more trustworthy text of the Alexandrian
version of the book.

6. BARUCH and THE EPISTLE OF JEREMIAH (Βαρούχ, Ἐπιστολὴ Ἰερεμίου, [*prophetia*] *Baruch*) were regarded by the Church
as adjuncts of Jeremiah, much in the same way as Susanna and
Bel were attached to Daniel. Baruch and the Epistle occur
in lists which rigorously exclude the non-canonical books;
they are cited as 'Jeremiah' (Iren. v. 35. 1, Tert. *scorp.* 8,
Clem. Alex. *paed.* i. 10, Cypr. *testim.* ii. 6); with Lamentations
they form a kind of trilogy supplementary to the prophecy
(Athan. *ep.* 39 Ἰερεμίας καὶ σὺν αὐτῷ Βαρούχ, Θρῆνοι, Ἐπιστολή,
Cyril. Hier. *catech.* iv. 33 Ἰερεμίου μετὰ Βαρούχ καὶ Θρήνων καὶ
Ἐπιστολῆς[3]). In some Greek MSS. the Epistle follows Baruch
without break, and in the Latin and English Bibles it forms
the sixth and last chapter of that book.

---

[1] A Chaldee text, corresponding in some respects to Jerome's Latin, is
preserved in the Bodleian, and has been edited by Neubauer (Oxford, 1878).

[2] An Oxyrh. Pap. 1076 (vol. viii) gives a new recension of c. ii. 2, 3,
4, 8.

[3] Origen, while omitting Baruch, includes the Epistle in a formal list
of the Hebrew canon (Eus. *H. E.* vi. 25 Ἰερεμίας σὺν Θρήνοις καὶ τῇ
Ἐπιστολῇ ἐν ἑνί).

The Epistle (ἀντίγραφον ἐπιστολῆς ἧς ἀπέστειλεν 'Ιερεμίας πρὸς τοὺς ἀχθησομένους [*v. l.* ἀπαχθέντας] αἰχμαλώτους εἰς Βαβυλῶνα) seems to have been suggested by Jer. xxxvi. (xxix.) 1 (cf. 2 Kings xxv. 20 ff.). It is generally recognised that this little work was written in Greek by a Hellenist who was perhaps anterior to the writer of 2 Maccabees (cf. 2 Macc. ii. 1 ff.)[1].

The problem presented by Baruch is less simple. This book is evidently a complex work consisting of two main sections (i. i.—iii. 8, iii. 9—v. 9)[2], each of which may be subdivided (i. 1—14, historical preface; i. 15—iii. 8, confession and prayer; iii. 9—iv. 4, exhortation; iv. 5—v. 9, encouragement). Of these subsections the first two shew traces of a Hebrew original; cf. e.g. i. 10 μάννα = מִנְחָה, ii. 3 ἄνθρωπον = אִישׁ, iii. 4 τῶν τεθνηκότων = מֵתֵי (for מְתֵי)[3]; the third has been held[4] to rest on an Aramaic document, whilst the fourth is manifestly Hellenistic.

An investigation by Professor Ryle and Dr James[5] into the relation between the Greek version of the Psalms of Solomon and the Greek Baruch, led them to the conclusion that Baruch was reduced to its present form after the destruction of Jerusalem by Titus; and the tone of Bar. iv. 30 seems certainly to point to that period. On the other hand it is difficult to understand the unhesitating acceptance of the book by Christian writers from Athenagoras (*suppl.* 9) until the time of

---

[1] On the first point see J. T. Marshall in Hastings' *D. B.* ii. p. 579, and on the other hand Schürer[3], iii. p. 344. Cf. Nestle, *Marginalien*, p. 42 f.

[2] In the first section the Divine Name is Κύριος or K. ὁ θεός, while in the second it is either [ὁ] θεός or ὁ αἰώνιος, ὁ ἅγιος. See Dr Gifford in *Speaker's Comm., Apoc.*, ii. f. 253. Thackeray holds that "the first half of Baruch is, beyond a doubt, the production of the translator of Jer. β." *Gramm. of O. T. in Gk.* i. pp. 12, 13; *J. Th. St.* iv. 261 ff.

[3] "On the margin of the Syro-hexaplar text of Baruch there are three notes by a scribe stating that certain words in i. 17 and ii. 3 are 'not found in the Hebrew.'" (A. A. Bevan in *Encycl. Biblica*, i. 494.)

[4] E.g. by J. T. Marshall in Hastings' *D. B.* i. p. 251.

[5] *Psalms of the Pharisees*, pref., esp. p. lxxvii.

Jerome, and its practical inclusion in the canon, if the Greek version in its present form proceeded from a Palestinian Jew, and was the work of the last quarter of the first century A.D.[1] As to its use by the Jews there are contradictory statements in early Christian writers, for while the *Apostolical Constitutions*[2] inform us that the Jews read Baruch publicly on the Day of Atonement, Jerome says expressly that they neither read it nor had it in their possession, and his statement is confirmed by Epiphanius.

Const. Ap. v. 20 καὶ γὰρ καὶ νῦν δεκάτῃ τοῦ μηνὸς Γαρπιαίου συναθροιζόμενοι τοὺς Θρήνους Ἰερεμίου ἀναγινώσκουσιν...καὶ τὸν Βαρούχ. Hieron. *praef. comm. in Ierem.* "vulgo editioni Septuaginta copulatur, nec habetur apud Hebraeos"; *praef. vers. Ierem.* "apud Hebraeos nec legitur nec habetur." Epiph. *de mens. et pond.* 5 οὐ κεῖνται αἱ ἐπιστολαὶ [Βαροὺχ καὶ Ἰερεμίου] παρ' Ἑβραίοις.

7. BOOKS OF MACCABEES (Μακκαβαίων α΄, β΄, γ΄, δ΄, *Machabaeorum libri;* τὰ Μακκαβαϊκά, Hippol. *in Dan.* iv. 3; Orig. ap. Eus. *H. E.* vi. 25). The four books differ widely in origin, character, and literary value; the bond which unites them is merely their common connexion with the events of the age which produced the heroes of the Hasmonaean or Maccabean[3] family.

1 MACCABEES. This book seems to have been used by Josephus (*ant.* xii. 6. 1 sqq.), but it is doubtful whether he was acquainted with its Greek form. On the other hand, the Greek 1 Macc. was undoubtedly known to the Christian school of Alexandria; cf. Clem. Alex. *strom.* i. § 123 τὸ τῶν

---

[1] Dr Nestle points out that Baruch and Jeremiah seem to have been translated by the same hand, unless the translator of Baruch deliberately copied the translator of Jeremiah. Certain unusual words are common to the two books in similar contexts, e.g. ἄβατος, ἀποστολή, δεσμώτης, πεινῶσα. Cf. Thackeray, *l. c.*

[2] v. 20. But the reference to Baruch is wanting in the Syriac Didascalia (Smith, *D. B.*[2] i. p. 359).

[3] For the name Μακκαβαῖος see Schürer, *E. T.* i. p. 212 f. n.; it belonged primarily to Judas, cf. 1 Macc. i. 4 ἀνέστη Ἰούδας ὁ καλούμενος M.; Joseph. *ant.* xii. 6 Ἰούδας ὁ καλ. M.

Μακκαβαϊκῶν, Origen ap. Eus. *l.c.* τὰ Μακκαβαϊκὰ ἅπερ ἐπιγέγραπται Σαρβὴθ σαβαναιέλ (*v.l.* Σ. σαβανὲ ἔλ). Whatever may be the meaning of this title[1], it is clearly Semitic, and may be taken as evidence that the book was circulated in a Semitic original. Jerome appears to have seen a copy of this Hebrew or Aramaic text (*prol. gal.* "Maccabaeorum primum librum Hebraicum repperi"), but it has long disappeared[2], and the book is now extant only in versions. The Latin and Syriac versions are based upon the Greek; the Old Latin exists in two recensions, one of which has taken its place in the Latin Bible, whilst the other is preserved in a St Germain's and a Madrid MS.; a Lyons MS. gives a text in which the two are mixed[3].

The history of 1 Macc. covers about 40 years (B.C. 175 —132). There are indications that the writer was removed by at least a generation from the end of his period (cf. c. xiii. 30, xvi. 23 f.). He was doubtless a Palestinian Jew, but his work would soon have found its way to Alexandria, and if it had not already been translated into Greek, it doubtless received its Greek dress there shortly after its arrival.

2 MACCABEES. The existence of a book bearing this title is implied by Hippolytus, who quotes 1 Macc. with the formula ἐν τῇ πρώτῃ βίβλῳ τῶν Μακκαβαϊκῶν ἀναγέγραπται, and by Origen, if we may trust the Latin interpretation (*in ep. ad Rom.*, t. viii. 1 "in primo libro Machabaeorum scriptum est"); the title itself occurs in Eus. *praef. ev.* viii. 9 (ἡ δευτέρα τῶν Μακκαβαίων). But the evidence goes further back. Philo shews some knowledge of the book in *Quod omnis probus liber*, § 13, and the author of the Ep. to the Hebrews has a clear reminiscence of its Greek (Heb. xi. 31 ἄλλοι δὲ ἐτυμπανίσθησαν κτλ., cf. 2 Macc. vi. 19, 30).

[1] For various attempts to interpret it see Ryle, *Canon*, p. 185; R. Kraetzschmar, in *Exp. T.*, xii. p. 93 ff.

[2] A Hebrew text is printed by A. Schweizer, *Über die Reste eines heb. Textes vom ersten Makkabäerbuch* (Berlin, 1901); but see Th. Nöldeke in *Lit. Centralblatt*, March 30, 1901.

[3] Berger, *Histoire de la Vulgate*, pp. 62, 68.

The writer is described by Clement of Alexandria (*strom.* v. 14) as ὁ συνταξάμενος τὴν τῶν Μακκαβαϊκῶν ἐπιτομήν. This is precisely what he claims to do (c. ii. 23 ὑπὸ Ἰάσωνος τοῦ Κυρηναίου δεδηλωμένα διὰ πέντε βιβλίων, πειρασόμεθα δι᾽ ἑνὸς συντάγματος ἐπιτεμεῖν). The work of the Cyrenian has perished, whilst the Alexandrian epitome survives. For Alexandrian the epitomist probably was; "the characteristics of the style and language are essentially Alexandrian...the form of the allusion to Jason shews clearly that the compiler was not his fellow countryman[1]." "The style is extremely uneven; at times it is elaborately ornate (iii. 15—39, v. 20, vi. 12—16, 23—28, vii. &c.); and again, it is so rude and broken as to seem more like notes for an epitome than a finished composition" (xiii. 19—26); indeed it is difficult to believe that such a passage as the one last cited can have been intended to go forth in its present form. That the work never had a Semitic original was apparent to Jerome (*prol. gal.* "secundus Graecus est, quod ex ipsa quoque φράσει probari potest"). The vocabulary is extraordinarily rich in words of the later literary Greek, and the book betrays scarcely any disposition to Hebraise[2].

The second book of Maccabees presents a striking contrast to the first. Covering a part of the same period (B.C. 175 —160), it deals with the events in a manner wholly different. In 1 Maccabees we have a plain and usually trustworthy history; in 2 Maccabees a partly independent but rhetorical and inaccurate and to some extent mythical panegyric of the patriotic revolt[3].

3 MACCABEES. A third book of Μακκαβαικά finds a place

---

[1] Westcott in Smith's *D. B.*[1] ii. p. 175.

[2] See the list of words given by Westcott, *l. c.* i. and in Smith's *D. B.*[2] i. and *Apocrypha*.

[3] So Luther, in his preface to 2 Macc.: "so billig das erste Buch sollte in die Zahl der heiligen Schrift genommen sein, so billig ist dies andere Buch herausgeworfen, obwohl etwas Gutes darinner steht."

in some Eastern lists (*can. Apost., Niceph. stichom.*). A Greek book under that title is found in codd. AV and a few cursives[1]. There is a Syriac version, but no Latin, nor is the book mentioned in any Western list, although the stichometry of Cod. Claromontanus implies a knowledge of its existence, for it mentions a fourth book. Similarly cod. ℵ passes from the first book to the fourth, whether the omission of the second and third is due to the deliberate judgement of the scribe or to his want of an archetype.

A more exact description of 3 Maccabees would be that which it seems to have borne in some circles—the Ptolemaica[2]. The story belongs to the reign of Ptolemy Philopator (B.C. 222 —205), and the scene is laid at Alexandria. The king, infuriated by the refusal of the Jerusalem priesthood to admit him to the Holy of Holies, returns to Egypt with the intention of avenging himself on the Alexandrian Jews; but by the interposition of Providence his plans are defeated, and he becomes, like Darius in Daniel and Artaxerxes in Esther, the patron of the people he had purposed to destroy.

There are reasons for believing that this romance rests upon some historical basis. "The author...evidently has good knowledge of the king and his history...the feast kept by the Egyptian Jews at a fixed date [c. vii. 11] cannot be an invention...that Philopator in some way injured the condition of the Jews, and that they were concerned in the insurrection of the nation, seems very probable[3]." Moreover Josephus has a somewhat similar tale drawn from another source, and con-

---

[1] Fritzsche has used codd. 19, 44, 55, 62, 64, 71, 74, 93.

[2] In the Pseudo-Athanasian *synopsis* where the MSS. give Μακκαβαικὰ δ', Πτολεμαικά. Credner proposed to read M. καὶ (ϛ) Πτολ. An explanation of the existing reading attempted by Fabricius, *cod. pseud. epigr. V. T.* i. p. 1164, is hardly to be considered satisfactory. Zahn (*Gesch. d. NTlichen Kanons*, ii. p. 317) suggests πολεμικά, but this is more ingenious than convincing. But Wendland (*Aristeas*, p. 133) and Thackeray consider that Πτολεμαϊκὰ means the letter of Aristeas.

[3] Mahaffy, *Empire of the Ptolemies*, p. 267 ff.

nected with another reign[1] (*c. Ap.* ii. 5). The presĕnt book
is doubtless Alexandrian, and of relatively late origin, as its
inflated style, "loaded with rhetorical ornament[2]," sufficiently
testifies. Some critics (Ewald, Hausrath, Reuss[3]) would place
it in the reign of Caligula, but the knowledge of earlier
Alexandrian life which it displays points to an earlier date,
perhaps the first century B.C.[4]

4 MACCABEES. According to Eusebius and Jerome this
book was the work of Josephus[5].

> Eus. *H. E.*, iii. 10 πεπόνηται δὲ καὶ ἄλλο οὐκ ἀγεννὲς σπού-
> δασμα τῷ ἀνδρὶ (SC. Ἰωσήπῳ) περὶ αὐτοκράτορος λογισμοῦ, ὅ τινες
> Μακκαβαϊκὸν ἐπέγραψαν τῷ τοὺς ἀγῶνας τῶν ἐν τοῖς οὕτω καλου-
> μένοις Μακκαβαϊκοῖς συγγράμμασιν ὑπὲρ τῆς εἰς τὸ θεῖον εὐσεβείας
> ἀνδρισαμένων Ἑβραίων περιέχειν. Hieron. *de virr. ill.* 13 "alius
> quoque libro eius qui inscribitur περὶ αὐτοκράτορος λογισμοῦ
> valde elegans habetur, in quo et Maccabeorum digesta martyria"
> (cf. *c. Pelag.* ii. 5).

The book is a philosophical treatise upon the question,
εἰ αὐτοδέσποτός ἐστιν τῶν παθῶν ὁ εὐσεβὴς λογισμός. But the
greater part of it[6] is occupied by a rhetorical panegyric upon
the Jewish martyrs, Eleazar, and the seven brothers and their
mother, who perished in the Maccabean troubles. This
portion appears to be based on 2 Macc. vi. 18—vii. 42,
which it amplifies with an extraordinary wealth of language
and a terribly realistic picture of the martyrs' sufferings.
The rhetoric of the writer, however, is subordinated to his
passion for religious philosophy. In philosophy he is a pupil
of the Stoics; like the author of the Wisdom of Solomon
he holds fast by the doctrine of the four cardinal Virtues
(i. 18 τῆς δὲ σοφίας εἰδέαι καθιστᾶσιν φρόνησις καὶ δικαιοσύνη

---

[1] That of Euergetes II. (Physcon); cf. Mahaffy, p. 381.
[2] Westcott in Smith's *D. B.* ii. p. 179.   [3] Schürer[3], iii. p. 365.
[4] "The date is probably c. 80 B.C.," Thackeray thinks, "as shown by
epistolary formulae and papyrus evidence."
[5] The same belief is expressed by the fact that the book is found in
some MSS. of Josephus. See Fabricius-Harles, v. 26 f.
[6] Viz. c. iii. 19, to the end.

καὶ ἀνδρία καὶ σωφροσύνη), and he sternly demands that the πάθη shall be kept under restraint by the power of Reason. In religion he is a legalist with Pharisaic tendencies; he believes in future punishment (ix. 9, xiii. 15), in the eternal life which awaits the righteous (xv. 3, xvii. 5, xviii. 23), and in the atonement for sin which is made by voluntary sacrifice (vi. 29, xxii. 22).

The style of 4 Macc. abounds in false ornament and laboured periods. But on the whole it is "truly Greek[1]," and approaches nearer than that of any other book in the Greek Bible to the models of Hellenic philosophy and rhetoric. It does not, however, resemble the style of Josephus, and is more probably a product of Alexandrian Judaism during the century before the fall of Jerusalem.

8. To the books of the Hebrew canon (τὰ ἐνδιάθηκα, τὰ εἰκοσιδύο) and the 'external' books (τὰ ἔξω), which on the authority of Jerome the reformed Churches of the West have been accustomed to call the Apocrypha, some of the ancient lists add certain *apocrypha* properly so named. Thus the catalogue of the 'Sixty Books,' after reciting the canonical books of the O. and N. Testaments, and τὰ περὶ (*leg.* πέρα) τούτων ἔξω (the two Wisdoms, 1—4 Maccabees, Esther, Judith, Tobit), continues : Καὶ ὅσα ἀπόκρυφα· Ἀδάμ, Ἐνώχ, Λάμεχ, Πατριάρχαι, Προσευχὴ Ἰωσήφ, Ἐλδάδ, Διαθήκη Μωυσέως, Ἀνάληψις Μωυσέως, Ψαλμοὶ Σολομῶντος, Ἡλίου ἀποκάλυψις, Ἡσαίου ὅρασις, Σοφονίου ἀποκάλυψις, Ζαχαρίου ἀποκάλυψις, Ἔσδρα ἀποκάλυψις. The Pseudo-Athanasian *Synopsis* and the *Stichometry* of Nicephorus count among the ἀπόκρυφα τῆς παλαιᾶς, together with certain of the above, Ἀβραάμ...Βαρούχ, Ἀββακούμ, Ἐζεκιήλ, καὶ Δανιήλ, ψευδεπίγραφα[2]. Ebed Jesu mentions also a book called *Traditions of the Elders*, the *History of Asenath*, and

---

[1] Westcott in Smith's *D. B.*[1] ii. p. 181.
[2] On this list see Zahn, *Gesch. d. NTlichen Kanons*, ii. p. 289 ff. and M. R. James, *Testament of Abraham*, p. 7 ff. (in *Texts and Studies*, ii. 2).

even the Fables of Aesop disguised under the title *Proverbs of Josephus*. Besides these writings the following are censured in the Gelasian *notitia librorum apocryphorum : Liber de filiabus Adae Leptogenesis, Poenitentia Adae, Liber de Vegia nomine gigante, qui post diluvium cum dracone...pugnasse perhibetur, Testamentum Iob, Poenitentia Iambre et Mambre, Solomonis interdictio*.

Though the great majority of these writings at one time existed in Greek, they were not admitted into collections of canonical books. A partial exception was made in favour of the PSALMS OF SOLOMON. This book is mentioned among the ἀντιλεγόμενα of the O.T. in the Stichometry of Nicephorus and in the Pseudo-Athanasian *Synopsis*. An earlier authority, the compiler of the catalogue at the beginning of Codex Alexandrinus, allows it a place in his list, although after the final summary of the books of the Old and New Testaments[1]. If the Codex itself contained these Psalms, they have perished together with a portion of Ps. Clem. *ad Cor. ii.*, the book which in the list immediately precedes them. It has been conjectured[2] that they once had a place in Cod. Sinaiticus, which like Cod. A has lost some leaves at the end of the N.T. Their absence from the other great uncials and from the earlier cursives may be due to the influence of the Laodicean canon (lix.), ὅτι οὐ δεῖ ἰδιωτικοὺς ψαλμοὺς[3] λέγεσθαι ἐν τῇ ἐκκλησίᾳ οὐδὲ ἀκανόνιστα βιβλία, ἀλλὰ μόνα τὰ κανονικὰ τῆς παλαιᾶς καὶ καινῆς διαθήκης. Happily the Psalms survived in private collections, and find a place in a few relatively

---

[1] The catalogue ends ΟΜΟΥ ΒΙΒΛΙΑ . . | and below, ΨΑΛΜΟΙ ϹΟΛΟ-ΜΩΝΤΟϹ | ΙΗ.

[2] By Dr J. R. Harris, who points out (*Johns Hopkins Univ. Circular*, March 1884) that the six missing leaves in ℵ between Barnabas and Hermas correspond with fair accuracy to the space which would be required for the Psalms of Solomon. Dr Harris has since discovered a Syriac version of sixteen of these Psalms (out of eighty contained in the MS.).

[3] Cf. Bals. *ap.* Beveregii *Synod.* p. 480 εὑρίσκονταί τινες ψαλμοὶ πέρα τοὺς ρν´ ψαλμοὺς τοῦ Δαβὶδ λεγόμενοι τοῦ Σολομῶντος...τούτους οὖν ὀνομάσαντες οἱ πατέρες ἰδιωτικούς.

late cursives of the poetical and the Sapiential books of the
O.T., where they follow the Davidic Psalter or take their place
among the writings attributed to Solomon[1].

The Psalms of Solomon are shewn by their teaching and
spirit to be the work of the Pharisaic school, and internal
evidence connects them with the age of Pompey, whose death
appears to be described in Ps. ii. 30 ff.[2] The question of the
date of the Greek version turns upon the nature of the relation
which exists between the Greek Psalms and the Greek Book
of Baruch. Bishop Ryle and Dr James, who regard Baruch
iv. 36—v. 9 (Greek) as based on the Greek of Ps. Sol. xi.,
are disposed to assign the version of the Psalms to the last
decade of the first century B.C.[3]. They observe that the Messianic passages contain "no trace of Christian influence at
work."[4] On the other hand there are interesting coincidences
between the Greek phraseology of the Psalter and that of
the *Magnificat* and other Lucan canticles[4].

One other *apocryphon* of the Greek Old Testament claims
attention here. The BOOK OF ENOCH has since 1838 been
in the hands of scholars in the form of an Ethiopic version
based upon the Greek. But until 1892 the Greek version
was known only through a few fragments—the verse quoted
by St Jude (*cf.* 14 f.), a brief tachygraphic extract in cod.
Vat. gr. 1809, published in facsimile by Mai (*patr. nov.
biblioth.* ii.), and deciphered by Gildemeister (*ZDMG.*, 1855,
p. 622 ff.), and the excerpts in the *Chronographia* of Georgius
Syncellus[5]. But in 1886 a small vellum book was found in

[1] In the latter case they go with the two Wisdoms in the order Sap.,
Ps. Sol., Sir. or (in one instance) Sap., Sir., Ps. Sol.
[2] Ryle and James, *Psalms of the Pharisees*, p. xl ff., xliv ff. Schürer[3],
iii. p. 152 f.
[3] Ryle and James, p. lxxii ff. On the date see W. Frankenberg, *die
Datierung der Psalmen Salomos* (Giessen, 1896).
[4] Ryle and James, p. xc ff.
[5] These may be conveniently consulted in the *Corpus historiae By-
zantinae*, t. 1, where they are edited by W. Dindorf.

a Christian grave in Akhmîm (Panopolis), in Upper Egypt, which contained *inter alia* the first thirty-two chapters of Enoch in Greek—nearly the whole of the first section of the book. This large fragment was published by M. Bouriant in the ninth volume of *Mémoires publiés par les membres de la mission archéologique Française au Caire* (Paris, 1er fasc. 1892; 3e fasc. 1893).

The newly recovered Greek belongs to the oldest part of Enoch, which may be regarded as in the main a Palestinian work of the second century B.C.[1]. The Greek version is the parent of the Ethiopic, and of pre-Christian date, since it was in the hands of St Jude. Thus it possesses a strong claim upon the attention of the student of Biblical Greek, while the book itself possesses an almost unique value as an exposition of Jewish eschatology.

The Greek version of Enoch seems to have been circulated in the ancient Church; cf. Barn. 4. 16; Clem. Alex. *ecl. proph.* 2; Orig. *de princ.* i. 3. 3, iv. 35, *hom. in Num.* 28. 2. The book was not accepted by authority (Orig. *c. Cels.* v. 54 ἐν ταῖς ἐκκλησίαις οὐ πάνυ φέρεται ὡς θεῖα τὰ ἐπιγεγραμμένα τοῦ Ἐνὼχ βιβλία: in Ioann. t. vi. 25 εἰ τῳ φίλον παραδέχεσθαι ὡς ἅγιον τὸ βιβλίον. Hieron. *de virr. ill.* 4 "apocryphus est"), but opinion was divided, and Tertullian was prepared to admit the claims of a writing which had been quoted in a Catholic Epistle (*de cult. faem.* i. 3 "scio scripturam Enoch ...non recipi a quibusdam quia nec in armarium Iudaicum admittitur...a nobis quidem nihil omnino reiciendum est quod pertineat ad nos...eo accedit quod E. apud Iudam apostolum testimonium possidet)." In the end, however, it appears to have been discredited both in East and West, and, if we may judge by the almost total disappearance of the Greek version, it was rarely copied by Catholics even for private

---

[1] See Schürer[3], iii. p. 196 ff.

study. A mere chance has thrown into our hands an excerpt made in the eighth or ninth century, and it is significant that in the Akhmîm book Enoch is found in company with fragments of a pseudonymous Gospel and Apocalypse[1].

LITERATURE of the non-canonical Books. *The Variorum Apocrypha*, edited by C. J. Ball (London, 1892).

1 ESDRAS. De Wette-Schrader, *Lehrbuch*, §§ 363—4; König, *Einleitung*, p. 146; Dähne, *Gesch. Darstellung*, iii. p. 116 ff.; Nestle, *Marginalien*, p. 23 f.; Bissell, *Apocrypha of the O. T.*, p. 62 ff.; H. St J. Thackeray, *art.* 1 Esdras in Hastings' *D. B.*, i.; Schürer[3], iii. p. 326 ff.; Büchler, *das apokr. Ezra-Buchs* (*MGWJ.*, 1897). Text and apparatus: Holmes and Parsons, t. v.; Fritzsche, *libri apocr. V. T. Gr.*, pp. viii.—x., 1—30; Lagarde, *libr. V. T. canon.*, p. i. (Lucianic); *O. T. in Greek*, ii. (text of B, with variants of A); W. J. Moulton, *über die Überlieferung u. d. textkrit. Werth des dritten Ezra-Buchs, ZATW.*, 1899, 2, 1900, 1. Commentaries: Fritzsche, *exeg. Handbuch z. d. Apokr.*, i.; Lupton, in *Speaker's Comm., Apocrypha*, i.; Guthe, in Kautzsch, *Apokryphen*, p. 1 ff.

WISDOM OF SOLOMON. Fabricius-Harles, iii. 727. De Wette-Schrader, *Lehrbuch*, §§ 378—382; König, *Einleitung*, p. 146; Dähne, *Darstellung*, ii. p. 152 ff.; Westcott, in Smith's *D. B.* iii. p. 1778 ff.; Drummond, *Philo Judaeus*, i. p. 177 ff. Text and apparatus: Holmes and Parsons, v.; Fritzsche, *libr. apocr. V. T. Gr.*, pp. xxiv. f., 522 ff.; *O. T. in Greek*, ii. p. 604 ff. (text of B, variants of אAC). Commentaries: Bauermeister, *comm. in Sap. Sol.* (1828); Grimm, *exeg. Handbuch*, vi.; Reusch, *observationes Criticae in libr. Sapientiae* (Friburg, 1858); Deane, *the Book of Wisdom* (Oxf., 1881); Farrar, in *Speaker's Comm., Apocr.*, i.; Siegfried, in Kautzsch, *Apokryphen*, p. 476 ff. On the Latin version see Thielmann, *die lateinische Übersetzung des Buches der Weisheit* (Leipzig, 1872).

[1] A collection of Greek O. T. apocrypha might perhaps include, amongst other remains of this literature, the *Rest of the Words of Baruch* (*ed.* J. Rendel Harris), the *Apocalypse of Baruch* (*ed.* M. R. James), the *Testament of Abraham* (*ed.* M. R. James), parts of the *Oracula Sibyllina* (*ed.* A. Rzach), the *Testaments of the XII Patriarchs* (*ed.* Sinker), the Latin *Ascension of Isaiah* (*ed.* O. von Gebhardt, with the new Greek fragments), and perhaps also the Latin versions of certain important books which no longer survive in the Greek, e.g. 4 Esdras (*ed.* R. L. Bensly), the *Assumption of Moses* (*ed.* R. H. Charles), the *Book of Jubilees, ἡ λεπτὴ Γένεσις* (*ed.* R. H. Charles).

WISDOM OF THE SON OF SIRACH. Fabricius-Harles, iii. 718;
De Wette-Schrader, § 383 ff.; König, p. 145. Westcott and
Margoliouth, *Ecclesiasticus,* in Smith's *D. B.*[2] i. 841; Schürer[3],
iii. p. 157 ff. (where a full list of recent monographs will be
found). Text with apparatus: Holmes and Parsons, v.; Fritzsche;
O. T. in Greek, ii. (text of B, variants of אAC); cf. J. K. Zenner,
Ecclesiasticus nach cod. Vat. 346 (*Z. K. Th.,* 1895). Bretschnei-
der, *liber Iesu Siracidae Gr.,* Ratisbon, 1806. Cf. Hatch, *Essays,*
p. 296 ff. Nestle, *Marginalien* (1893), p. 48 ff. Klostermann,
Analecta, p. 26 f. Commentaries: Bretschneider (*ut supra*);
Fritzsche, *exeg. Handbuch,* v.; Edersheim in *Speaker's Comm.,*
Apocr. ii.; Ryssel, in Kautzsch, *Apokryphen,* p. 230 ff.

On the newly discovered Hebrew text with relation to the
versions see Cowley and Neubauer, *The original Hebrew of a
portion of Ecclesiasticus,* Oxford, 1897; Smend, *das hebr. Fragment der Weisheit des Jesus Sirach,* 1897; Halévy, *Étude sur la
partie du texte hébreu de l'Ecclésiastique* (Paris, 1897); Schlatter,
das neu gefundene hebr. Stück des Sirach (Güterslob, 1897),
I. Lévi, *L'Ecclésiastique,* Paris, 1898, 1901; C. Taylor, in *JQR.,*
1898; D. S. Margoliouth, *The origin of the 'Original Hebrew'
of Ecclesiasticus,* Oxford, 1899; S. Schechter and C. Taylor, *The
Wisdom of Ben Sira,* Cambridge, 1899; S. Schechter, in *JQR.*
and *Cr. R.,* Oct. 1899; various articles in *Exp. Times,* 1899;
A. A. Bevan in *JThSt.,* Oct. 1899; H. Herkenne, *De Veteris
Latinae Ecclesiastici capp.* i—xliii (Leipzig, 1899); E. Nestle in
Hastings, *D. B.* iv. 539 ff.

JUDITH. Fabricius-Harles, iii. p. 736; De Wette-Schrader,
§ 373 ff.; König, p. 145 f.; Nestle, *Marginalien,* p. 43 ff.; West-
cott-Fuller in Smith's *D. B.*[2] I. ii. p. 1850 ff.; F. C. Porter in
Hastings' *D. B.* ii. p. 822 ff.; Schürer[3], iii. p. 167. Text and
apparatus: Holmes and Parsons, v.; Fritzsche, p. xviii f.,
165 ff.; *Old Testament in Greek,* ii. (text of B, variants of אA).
Commentaries: Fritzsche, *exeg. Handbuch,* ii.; Wolff, *das Buch
Judith...erklärt* (Leipzig, 1861); Scholz, *Commentar zum B.
Judith* (1887, 1896); cf. Ball in *Speaker's Comm., Apocr.,* i.;
Löhr, in Kautzsch, *Apokryphen,* p. 147 ff.

TOBIT. Fabricius-Harles, iii. 738; De Wette-Schrader, § 375 ff.;
König, p. 145 f.; Westcott in Smith's *D. B.* iii. p. 1523;
Schürer[3], iii. p. 174. Text and apparatus: Holmes and Parsons,
v.: Fritzsche, pp. xvi ff., 108 ff.; *Old Testament in Greek,* ii.
(texts of B and א, with variants of A); Reusch, *libellus Tobit e
cod. Sin. editus* (Bonn, 1870); Neubauer, *the Book of Tobit:* a
Chaldee text (Oxford, 1878). Commentaries: Fritzsche, *exeg
Handbuch, Apokr.,* ii.; Reusch, *das Buch Tobias übersetzt u.
erklärt* (Friburg, 1857); Sengelmann, *das Buch Tobits erklärt*
(Hamburg, 1857); Gutberlet, *das Buch Tobias übersetzt u. erklärt*

(Munster, 1877); Scholz, *Commentar z. Buche Tobias* (1889); Rosenmann, *Studien z. Buche Tobit* (Berlin, 1894); J. M. Fuller in *Speaker's Comm., Apocr.,* i.; Löhr, in Kautzsch, *Apokryphen,* p. 135 ff. Cf. E. Nestle, *Septuagintastudien,* iii. (Stuttgart, 1899); J. R. Harris in *American Journal of Theology,* July, 1899.

BARUCH and EPISTLE. Fabricius-Harles, iii. p. 734 f.; De Wette-Schrader, § 389 ff.; König, p. 485 f.; Westcott-Ryle, in Smith's *D. B.*[2] i. p. 359 ff.; J. T. Marshall, in Hastings' *D. B.* i. p. 249 ff. ii. p. 579 ff.; Schürer[3], iii. p. 338 ff.; A. A. Bevan, in *Encycl. Biblica,* i. 492 ff. Text and apparatus: Holmes and Parsons, v.; Fritzsche, pp. xv f., 93 ff.; *Old Testament in Greek,* iii. (text of B, with variants of AΩΓ). Commentaries: Fritzsche, *exeg. Handbuch, Apokr.,* i.; Reusch, *Erklärung des Buchs Baruch* (Freiburg, 1853); Hävernick, *de libro Baruch* (Königsberg, 1861); Kneucker, *das Buch Baruch* (Leipzig, 1879); E. H. Gifford in *Speaker's Comm., Apocr.,* ii.; Rothstein, in Kautzsch, *Apokryphen,* p. 213 ff.

1—4 MACCABEES. Fabricius-Harles, iii. p. 745 ff.; De Wette-Schrader, § 365 ff.; König, p. 482 ff.; Westcott in Smith's *D. B.*[1] ii. p. 170 ff.; Schürer[3], iii. pp. 139 ff., 359 ff., 393 ff.; Rosenthal, *das erste Makkabäerbuch* (Leipzig, 1867); Willrich, *Juden u. Griechen vor der makkab. Erhebung* (1895); Freudenthal, *die Fl. Josephus beigelegte Schrift.* (Breslau, 1869); Wolscht, *de Ps. Josephi oratione...*(Marburg, 1881). Text and apparatus: Holmes and Parsons, v. (books i.—iii.); Fritzsche, pp. xix ff., 203 ff.; *Old Testament in Greek,* iii. (text of A with variants of אV in books i. and iv. and V in ii., iii.). Commentaries: Keil, *Komm. über die Bücher der Makk.* (Leipzig, 1875); Bensly-Barnes, 4 *Maccabees in Syriac* (Cambridge, 1895)[1]; Grimm in Fritzsche's *exeg. Handbuch, Apokr.,* iii., iv.; Bissell, in Lange-Schaff's *Comm.*; G. Rawlinson in *Speaker's Comm., Apocr.,* ii. (books i.—ii.); Fairweather and Black, 1 *Maccabees* (Cambridge, 1897); Kautzsch and Kamphausen, in Kautzsch, *Apokryphen,* p. 24 ff.

PSEUDEPIGRAPHA. The student will find fuller information on this subject in Fabricius, *Codex pseudepigraphus V. T.* (Hamburg, 1722): Herzog-Plitt, xii. p. 341 ff. (art. by Dillmann on *Pseudepigrapha des A. T.*); Deane, *Pseudepigrapha* (Edinburgh, 1891); J. E. H. Thomson, *Books which influenced our Lord and His Apostles* (Edinburgh, 1891); Smith's and Hastings' *Bible Dictionaries*; Schürer[3], iii. pp. 150 ff., 190 ff.; the works of Credner and Zahn; M. R. James, *Testament of Abraham* in *Texts and Studies* (II. ii. p. 7 ff.); *Encyclopaedia Biblica,* artt. *Apo-*

---

[1] A collation of the Syriac 4 Macc. with the Greek has been contributed by Dr Barnes to *O. T. in Greek*[2], vol. iii. (p. 900 ff.).

calyptic Literature and *Apocrypha* (i. 213–58). For the literature of the several writings he may refer to Strack, *Einleitung*,
p. 230 ff. In Kautzsch's *Apokr. u. Pseudepigraphen* the following O. T. *pseudepigrapha* are included: *Martyrdom of Isaiah*
(Beer), *Sibylline Oracles*, iii.—v., and *prooem.* (Blass), *Ascension
of Moses* (Clemen), *Apocalypse of Moses* (Fuchs), *Apocalypse of
Esdras* (Gunkel), *Testament of Naphtali*, Heb. (Kautzsch), *Book
of Jubilees* (Littmann), *Apocalypse of Baruch* (Ryssel), *Testaments of XII Patriarchs* (Schnapp). On the eschatology of this
literature see Charles, *Eschatology, Hebrew, Jewish and Christian* (London, 1899).

PSALMS OF SOLOMON. Fabricius, *Cod. pseudepigr. V.T.*, i. p. 914 ff.;
Fritzsche, *libr. apocr. V. T. gr.*, pp. xxv ff., 569 ff.; Ryle and
James, *Psalms of the Pharisees* (Cambridge, 1891); O. v. Geb-
hardt, *die Psalmen Salomo's* (Leipzig, 1895); *Old Testament in
Greek*[2] (Cambridge, 1899[1]). Ryle and James' edition is specially
valuable for its full Introduction, and Gebhardt's for its inves-
tigation into the pedigree and relative value of the MSS. On
the date see Frankenberg, *die Datierung der Psalmen Salomos*
(Giessen, 1896). An introduction and German version by Dr R.
Kittel will be found in Kautzsch, *Pseudepigraphen*, p. 127 ff.

BOOK OF ENOCH. Laurence, *Libri Enoch versio aethiopica* (Ox-
ford, 1838); Dillmann, *Liber Henoch aethiopice* (Leipzig, 1851);
Bouriant, *Fragments du texte grec du livre d'Énoch*...in *Mé-
moires*, &c. (see above); Lods, *le livre d'Énoch* (Paris, 1892);
Dillmann, *über den neugefundenen gr. Text des Henoch-Buches*
(Berlin, 1892); Charles, *The Book of Enoch* (Oxford, 1893), *The
Ethiopic Version of the Book of Enoch* (Oxford, 1906), and art. in
Hastings' *D. B.* i. p. 705 ff.; *Old Testament in Greek*, iii.[2]
(Cambridge, 1899). For a fragment of a Latin version see James,
Apocr. anecdota in *Texts and Studies*, ii. 3, p. 146 ff. An intro-
duction and German version by Dr G. Beer will be found in
Kautzsch, *Pseudepigraphen*, p. 217 ff.

---

[1] The text in the Cambridge manual LXX., which is that of cod. Vat.
gr. 336, and is accompanied by an apparatus and a brief description of the
MSS., can be had, together with the text of Enoch, in a separate form.

CHAPTER IV.

THE GREEK OF THE SEPTUAGINT.

1. No thorough treatment of the Greek idiom of the LXX. is known to exist. Two ancient treatises upon the dialect of Alexandria, by Irenaeus (Minutius Pacatus) and Demetrius Ixion[1], have unhappily disappeared. In modern times the ground has been broken by Sturz and Thiersch[2], and within the last few years Deissmann[3] has used the recently discovered papyri of Egypt to illustrate the connotation or the form of a number of Septuagint nouns and verbs. Much has also been done by Dr H. A. A. Kennedy[4] and the Abbé J. Viteau[5] in the way of determining the relation of Septuagint Greek to the classical and later usage, and to the Greek of the N.T.; and the N.T. grammars of Winer-Moulton, Winer-Schmiedel, and Blass contain incidental references to the linguistic characteristics of the Alexandrian version. But a separate grammar of the Greek Old Testament was long a real want, and the time has now come for attempting to supply it. Biblical scholars have now at

---

[1] See Fabricius-Harles, vi. p. 193 f. Both writers lived in the time of Augustus.

[2] Sturz's treatment of the dialect of Alexandria and Egypt needs to be checked by more recent researches, but it is still the most complete work upon the subject. Thiersch deals directly with the Greek of the LXX., but he limits himself to the Pentateuch.

[3] *Bibelstudien* (1895), and *Neue Bibelstudien* (1897).

[4] *Sources of N.T. Greek* (1895).

[5] *Étude sur le Grec du N.T.* (1896).

their disposal a store of trustworthy materials in the Oxford Concordance, and the larger Cambridge Septuagint will supply an accurate and sufficient textual guide. On the basis of these two works it ought to be possible for the workers of the twentieth century to prepare a satisfactory grammar and lexicon[1]. Meanwhile in this chapter nothing more can be attempted than to set before the beginner some of the linguistic problems presented by the Greek of the Septuagint, and to point out the chief features which distinguish it from other forms of the language.

2. The student who enters upon this subject with some knowledge of the Greek New Testament must begin by reminding himself of the different conditions under which the two parts of the Greek Bible were produced. The Greek Old Testament was not like the New Testament the work of a single generation, nor are its books as homogeneous in their general character. The Septuagint is a collection of translations interspersed with original Greek works, the translations belonging partly to the third century B.C., partly to the second and first, and the original works chiefly to the end of this period. Even in the case of the Pentateuch we are not at liberty to assume that the translators worked at the same time or under the same circumstances. These considerations complicate our enquiry, and lead us to expect in the LXX. great varieties of manner and language. In the earlier work we shall meet with the colloquial Greek which the Jews learnt to speak shortly after their settlement in Egypt. Later translations will approximate to the literary style of the second century, except in cases where this tendency has been kept in check by a desire to follow the manner of the older

---

[1] A lexicon was planned in 1895 by a Cambridge Committee, but the work is suspended for the present. There have now appeared, dealing with the Accidence, R. Helbing's *Grammatik der Septuaginta*, i. *Laut- und Wortlehre*, Göttingen, 1907; and H. St J. Thackeray's *Grammar of the O. T. in Greek*, vol. I. *Introd. Orthography and Accidence*, Cambridge, 1909.

books. Lastly, in the original writings, many of which are relatively late, and in which the writers were free from the limitations that beset the translator, the Greek will be nearly identical with that which was written by the Jewish-Alexandrian historians and philosophers of the time.

3. We begin by investigating the literary conditions under which both the translators and the writers lived at Alexandria.

In the middle of the second century B.C. Polybius[1] found Alexandria inhabited by three races, the native Egyptians, who occupied the site of the old seaport Rhacôtis, the mercenary class (τὸ μισθοφορικόν), who may be roughly identified with the Jews, and the Greeks of the Brucheion, a mixed multitude claiming Hellenic descent and wedded to Hellenic traditions (εἰ μιγάδες, Ἕλληνες ὁμοῦ ἀνέκαθεν ἦσαν, καὶ ἐμέμνηντο τοῦ κοινοῦ τῶν Ἑλλήνων ἔθους). This fusion of various elements in the Greek population of the city must have existed from the first. The original colony was largely made up of the veterans of Alexander's Macedonian army, volunteers from every part of Greece, and mercenaries from the Greek colonies of Asia Minor, and from Syria. Even in the villages of the Fayûm, as we now know, by the side of the Macedonians there were settlers from Libya, Caria, Thrace, Illyria, and even Italy[2], and Alexandria presented without doubt a similar medley of Hellenic types. Each class brought with it a dialect or idiom of its own. The Macedonian dialect, e.g., is said to have been marked by certain phonetic changes[3], and the use of barbarous terms such as

---

[1] *ap.* Strab. 797.
[2] Mahaffy in *Flinders Petrie Papyri*, i. p. 42. Cf. *Empire of the Ptolemies*, p. 178 f.
[3] As the change of φ into β (Βερενίκη for Φερενίκη, &c.), cf. Sturz, *de dial. Mac.*, p. 51, n.

ἀδή = οὐρανός, βεθύ[1] = ἀήρ, δανός = θάνατος, and of Greek words in unusual senses, as παρεμβολή, ‘camp,’ ῥύμη, street[2]. Some of these passed into the speech of Alexandria, and with them were echoes of the older dialects—Doric, Ionic, Aeolic—and other less known local varieties of Greek. A mongrel *patois*, ἡ ’Αλεξανδρέων διάλεκτος, as it was called in the title of the treatise of Demetrius Ixion, arose out of this confusion of tongues.

No monument of the Alexandrian ‘dialect’ remains, unless we may seek it in the earlier books of the Alexandrian Greek Bible. We have indeed another source from which light is thrown on the popular Greek of Egypt under the earlier Ptolemies. A series of epistolary and testamentary papyri has recently been recovered from the Fayûm, and given to the world under the auspices of the Royal Irish Academy[3]; similar collections have been published by Drs Grenfell and Hunt[4]. The Greek of these documents is singularly free from dialectic forms, owing perhaps to local circumstances, as Professor Mahaffy suggests; but the vocabulary has, in common with the LXX., many striking words and forms, some of which are rare elsewhere.

The following list has been formed from the indices to the Flinders Petrie collection : ἀναδενδράς, ἀναφάλακρος, ἀναφάλαντος, ἀρχισωματοφύλαξ, ἀρχιτεκτονεῖν, ἄχυρον, βασίλισσα, γένημα, διῶρυξ, ἐπιγονή, ἐργοδιώκτης, εὐίλατος, ἐφιδεῖν, ἐφιορκεῖν, θέριστρον, ὀλιγο-ψυχεῖν, ὀχύρωμα, ὀψώνιον, παιδίον, παραδεῖξαι, παρεπίδημος, περι-δέξιον, περιοδεύειν, πράκτωρ, πρεσβύτεροι, στενοχωρεῖν, χῶμα. The Berlin papyri yield many other such words, e.g. ἀναμέτρησις, γλύμμα, δικαίωμα, ἱεροψάλτης, ἱματισμός, καταλοχισμός, κτηνοτρόφος, μισοπονηρία, ὁλοσχερής, συμπλήρωσις, ὑπομνηματισμός.

---

[1] A list of these words, collected from Hesychius and other lexicographers, may be seen in Sturz, p. 34 ff.

[2] From Q. Curtius (*De rebus gestis Alexandri M.*, vi. 9. 36) it appears that the Macedonian and the native Greeks understood one another with difficulty.

[3] In the *Cunningham Memoirs* for 1891, ’93, edited by Prof. Mahaffy.

[4] In *Fayûm Towns and their Papyri* (London, 1900), pp. 100—112. Further contemporary illustrations of Alexandrian Greek may be found in Wilcken's *Griechische Ostraka* (1899).

The following letter of the time of Philadelphus will serve to shew the style of these documents, and at the same time the use in them of certain Septuagint words. It is addressed by the foremen (δεκάταρχοι) of a gang engaged in a stone quarry to the engineer of the works (ἀρχιτέκτων):

Κλέωνι χαίρειν. οἱ δεκάταρχοι τῶν ἐλευθέρ[ων] λατόμων ἀδικούμεθα·· τὰ γὰρ ὁμολογηθέντα ὑπὸ 'Απολλωνίου τοῦ διοικητοῦ οὐθὲν γίνεται ἡμῖν, ἔχει δὲ τὴν γραφὴν Διότιμος. σπούδασον οὖν ἵνα καθὰ ἐξειλήφαμεν ἤδη, ὑπὸ Διονυσίου καὶ Διοτίμου χρηματισθῇ ἡμῖν, καὶ μὴ τὰ ἔργα ἐνλειφθῇ, καθὰ καὶ ἔμπροσθεν ἐγένετο. ἐὰν γὰρ αἴσθωνται οἱ ἐργαζόμενοι οὐθὲν ἡμᾶς εἰληφότας τὸν σίδηρον ἐνέχυρα θήσουσιν[1].

4. Simultaneously with the growth of the colloquial mixed dialect, a deliberate attempt was made at Alexandria to revive the glories of classical Greek. The first Ptolemy, who had been the companion of Alexander's early days, retained throughout his life a passion for literature and learning. Prompted, perhaps, by Demetrius of Phalerum, Soter founded at Alexandria the famous Museum, with its cloisters and. lecture rooms and dining hall where scholars lived a common life under a warden appointed by the King[2]. To Soter is also attributed the establishment of the great library which is said to have contained 400,000 MSS[3]. Under his successor the Museum and Library became a centre of literary activity, and the age to which the inception of the Greek Bible is usually ascribed produced Aratus, Callimachus, Herondas, Lycophron, and Theocritus. There is however no reason to suppose that the Jewish translators were officially connected with the Museum, or that the classical revival under Soter and Philadelphus affected them directly. Such traces of a literary style as we find in the Greek Pentateuch are probably

[1] *Flinders Petrie Papyri*, II. xiii. (p. 33). The reader will notice several LXX. words (δεκάταρχος=LXX. δεκάδ., διοικητής, χρηματίζεσθαι, ἐνέχυρον). Sometimes these papyri afford illustrations of the LXX. which are not merely verbal; cf. II. xiv. 2 ἐς τὰ ἄχυρα πρὸς τὴν πλίνθον.

[2] Strabo, 794; cf. Mahaffy, *Empire of the Ptolemies*, p. 91 ff.

[3] Joseph., *ant.* xii. 2. Seneca, *de tranquil. animae* 9. Cf. Susemihl, *Gesch. d. griech. Litteratur in d. Alexandrinerzeit*, i. 336.

due not to the influence of the scholars of the Royal Library, but to the traditions of Greek writing which had floated down from the classical period and were already shaping themselves under altered conditions into a type of Greek which became the common property of the new Hellenism.

5. The later Greek, the κοινή or Ἑλληνικὴ διάλεκτος—the dialect in general use among Greek-speaking peoples from the fourth century onwards[1]—was based on Attic Greek, but embraced elements drawn from all Hellenic dialects. It was the literary language of the cosmopolitan Hellas created by the genius of Alexander. The change had begun indeed before Alexander. Even Xenophon allows himself to make free use of words of provincial origin, and to employ Attic words with a new connotation; and the writings of Aristotle mark the opening of a new era in the history of the Greek language[2]. But the golden age of the κοινή begins in the second century with Polybius (c. B.C. 145), and extends a century or two beyond the Christian era, producing such writers as Diodorus Siculus (B.C. 40), Strabo (A.D. 10), Plutarch (A.D. 90), and Pausanias (A.D. 160). The language used by the writers of the Greek Diaspora may be regarded as belonging to a subsection of an early stage of the κοινή, although, since the time of Scaliger, it has been distinguished from the latter by the term 'Hellenistic[3].' A 'Hellenist[4]' is properly a foreigner who affects Greek manners and speaks the Greek tongue. Thus the Jewish Greek spoken in Palestine was 'Hellenistic' in the strictest sense. The word is often used to describe the Greek of such thoroughly Hellen-

---

[1] See Professor Jebb in Vincent and Dickson's *Handbook to modern Greek*, p. 290.

[2] Mullach, *Gramm. d. Vulgarsprache*, p. 48. H. A. A. Kennedy, *Sources of N. T. Greek*, p. 11 ff.

[3] See Winer-Moulton, p. 29.

[4] Acts vi. 1, xi. 20.

ised writers as Philo and Josephus, and the post-apostolic teachers of the ancient Church; but it is applied with special appropriateness to the Alexandrian Bible and the writings of the New Testament, which approach most nearly to the colloquial Greek of Alexandria and Palestine.

6. Such were the local types of Greek upon which the Jewish translators of the O.T. would naturally mould their work. While the colloquial Greek of Alexandria was their chief resource, they were also influenced, in a less degree, by the rise of the later literary style which was afterwards known as the κοινή.

We are now prepared to begin our examination of the vocabulary and grammar of the Alexandrian Bible, and we may commence by testing the vocabulary in the translated books. Let us select for this purpose the first three chapters of Exodus, 1 Kingdoms, 2 Chronicles, Proverbs, and Jeremiah, books which are, perhaps, fairly representative of the translation as a whole. Reading these contexts in the Cambridge manual edition, and underlining words which are not to be found in the Greek prose of the best period, we obtain the following results. In Exod. i.—iii. there are 19 such words; in 1 Regn. i.—iii., 39; in 2 Chron. i.—iii., 27; in Prov. i.—iii., 16; in Jer. i.—iii., 34; making a total of 135 later words in 15 chapters, or nine to a chapter. Of these words 52—considerably more than a third—appear to be peculiar to the LXX., or to have been used there for the first time in extant literature.

The following are the Septuagintal words observed in the above-named passages. *Verbs:* ἀνδριοῦν, δευτεροῦν, διοδεύειν, ἐνευλογεῖσθαι, ἐξολεθρεύειν, ἐξουθενεῖ[1], εὐοδοῦν, κατακληρονομεῖν, κατασκοπεύειν, κατεμβλέπειν, κατοδυνᾶν, ὀλεθρεύειν, ὀρθοτομεῖν, ὀρθρίζειν, πνευματοφορεῖσθαι, πτωχίζειν, σκοπεύειν, συνεδριάζειν, τριετίζειν, τροφεύειν, φιλεχθρᾶν. *Nouns:* ἀγάπη, ἀσυνθεσία, ἀσφαλτόπισσα, βδέλυγμα, γένημα, δόμα, ἐργοδιώκτης, θλιμμός, καταπέτασμα, κρίμα, λατόμος, μέθυσμα, ὁλοκαύτωμα, ὁλοκαύτωσις, ὁρόφωμα, παντοκράτωρ,

[1] Or ἐξουδενοῦν, other forms being due to mixture; Thackeray, *Gr. O. T.* p. 105.

προσήλυτος, πρόσκομμα, ῥοίσκος, σύντριμμα. *Foreign words* (a) with Greek terminations : ἄβρα, θῖβις, σίκλος· (b) transliterated : αἰλάμ, δαβείρ, ἐφοὺδ βάρ, νέβελ, ἐλωὲ σαβαώθ, οἰφι, σερσέρεθ, χερουβείμ.

A similar experiment has been made by Dr H. A. A. Kennedy in reference to one of the books of the Pentateuch. Of 110 late words and forms observed in Deut. i.—x. he found that 66 belonged to Biblical Greek, 16 of these being peculiar to the LXX. ; of 313 such words in the entire book, 152 proved to be Biblical, and 36 peculiar to the Old Testament; nearly half belonged to the κοινή, and more than a fourth had been used by the writers of tragedy and comedy.

A complete list of the late words in the LXX. is still a *desideratum.* Lists which have been made for the N.T. shew that out of 950 post-Aristotelian words about 314—just under one third—occur also in the Greek O.T.[1] But the writers of the N.T. have taken over only a part—perhaps a relatively small part—of the vocabulary of the LXX. As Dr T. K. Abbott has pointed out[2], Psalm l. (li.) alone yields four important words (ἀγαθύνειν, ἀκουτίζειν, ἀνόμημα, ἀνταναιρεῖν) which find no place in the N.T. This fact is suggestive, for the Psalm is doctrinally important, and the words are such as would have lent themselves readily to N.T. use.

The following LXX. words are condemned by Phrynichus as non-Attic : αἰχμαλωτίζεσθαι, ἀποτάσσεσθαι, βασίλισσα, βουνός, βρέχειν (in the sense of ὕειν), γρηγορεῖν, ἐλεύσεσθαι, ἐξάδελφος, κατόρθωμα, μεγιστάν, μέθυσος, οἰκοδομή, παιδίσκη, πάπυρος, παρεμβολή, πεποίθησις, πλῆξαι, ῥάπισμα, ῥύμη, σκορπίζεσθαι, σύσσημον. Some of these words are said to be provincialisms ; e.g. βουνός is Sicilian, σκορπίζεσθαι is Ionic, παρεμβολή and ῥύμη are Macedonian[3].

As our knowledge of Alexandrian Greek increases, it may be that the greater part of the words which have been regarded as peculiar to the LXX. will prove to belong to the usage of Egyptian Greek. Deissmann has already shewn that many well-known

---

[1] Kennedy, *op. cit.*, p. 62. Cf. the lists in the appendix to Grimm-Thayer's *Lexicon of N. T. Greek* (p. 691 ff.).

[2] *Essays*, p. 69.   [3] See above, p. 292.

Septuagintal words find a place in the Greek papyri of the Ptolemaic period, and therefore presumably belonged to the language of business and conversation at Alexandria. Thus γογγύζειν occurs in a papyrus of 241—239 B.C.; ἐργοδιώκτης, 255 B.C.; παρεπίδημος, 225 B.C.; forms such as ἦλθα, ἐπήλθοσαν, γέγοναν, οἶδες, can be quoted from the papyri *passim*; ἀναστρέφεσθαι and ἀναστροφή in an ethical sense, λειτουργεῖν in reference to the service of a deity, περιτέμνεσθαι of circumcision, πρεσβύτερος of an official, are shewn to have been in use in Egypt under the Ptolemies. In many cases however words receive a new connotation, when they pass into Biblical Greek and come into contact with Hebrew associations. As examples the following may suffice : ἄγγελος, γραμματεύς, διάβολος, εἴδωλον, ἔθνη, ἐκκλησία, παντοκράτωρ, πεντηκοστή, προσήλυτος, χριστός.

The forms of many words have undergone a change since the age of classical Greek. A few specimens may be given from the pages of Phrynichus :

Attic Greek.	Greek of the LXX.	Attic Greek.	Greek of the LXX.
ἀποκρίνασθαι	ἀποκριθῆναι	μιαρός	μιερός
ἀφείλετο	ἀφείλατο	μόχλος	μόκλος (MSS.)
ἄχρι, μέχρι	ἄχρις, μέχρις	νεοσσός, -σία	νοσσός, -σία
γενέσθαι	γενηθῆναι	νουμηνία	νεομηνία
γλωσσοκομεῖον	γλωσσόκομον	ὄρθριος	ὀρθρινός
διψῆν	διψᾶν	οὐδείς	οὐθείς[1]
δυοῖν	δυσί	πεινῆν	πεινᾶν
ἐδεῖτο	ἐδέετο	πήχεων	πηχῶν
εὕρημα	εὕρεμα	ποδαπός	ποταπός
καθά	καθώς	ταχύτερον	τάχιον
καταμύειν	καμμύειν		

7. But the vocabulary of the LXX. is not its most characteristic feature. With no other vocabulary than that of the Alexandrian translators, it might be possible to produce a fairly good piece of Greek prose in the style of the later prose writers. It is in its manner, in the construction of the sentences and the disposition of the words, that the Greek of the LXX. is unique, and not only or chiefly in its lexical eccentricities. This may perhaps be brought home to the student most effectually by a comparison of the Greek Bible with two great Hellenistic writers of the first century A.D. (*a*) In the

---

[1] οὐθείς began to yield again to οὐδείς before the end of the second century B.C., and was obsolete at the date when the earliest extant MSS. of the LXX. were written. It is hence an archaism in them (Thackeray, *Gr. O. T.* pp. 58 ff.).

works of Philo we have a cultured Hellenist's commentary on the earlier books of the LXX., and as he quotes his text *verbatim*, the student can discern at a glance the gulf which divides its simple manner, half Semitic, half colloquial, from the easy command of idiomatic Greek manifested by the Alexandrian exegete. We will give two brief specimens.

Philo *de opif. mundi* 7 : φησὶ δ' ὡς ἐν ἀρχῇ ἐποίησεν ὁ θεὸς τὸν οὐρανὸν καὶ τὴν γῆν, τὴν ἀρχὴν παραλαμβάνων, οὐχ ὡς οἴονταί τινες τὴν κατὰ χρόνον· χρόνος γὰρ οὐκ ἦν πρὸ κόσμου, ἀλλ' ἢ σὺν αὐτῷ γέγονεν ἢ μετ' αὐτόν· ἐπεὶ γὰρ διάστημα τῆς τοῦ κόσμου κινήσεώς ἐστιν ὁ χρόνος, προτέρα δὲ τοῦ κινουμένου κίνησις οὐκ ἂν γένοιτο, ἀλλ' ἀναγκαῖον αὐτὴν ἢ ὕστερον ἢ ἅμα συνίστασθαι, ἀναγκαῖον ἄρα καὶ τὸν χρόνον ἢ ἰσήλικα κόσμου γεγονέναι ἢ νεώτερον ἐκείνου· πρεσβύτερον δ' ἀποφαίνεσθαι τολμᾶν ἀφιλόσοφον. *De migr. Abrahami* 39: ἐὰν μέντοι σκοπούμενος μὴ ῥᾳδίως καταλαμβάνῃς ἃ ζητεῖς, ἐπίμενε μὴ κάμνων.. οὗ χάριν ὁ φιλομαθὴς τοῦ τόπου Συχὲμ ἐνείληπται, μεταληφθὲν δὲ τοὔνομα Συχὲμ ὠμίασις καλεῖται, πόνου σύμβολον, ἐπειδὴ τοῖς μέρεσι τούτοις ἀχθοφορεῖν ἔθος, ὡς καὶ αὐτὸς ἑτέρωθι μέμνηται λέγων ἐπί τινος ἀθλητοῦ τοῦτον τὸν τρόπον Ὑπέθηκε τὸν ὦμον εἰς τὸ πονεῖν, καὶ ἐγένετο ἀνὴρ γεωργός. ὥστε μηδέποτε, ὦ διάνοια, μαλακισθεῖσα ὀκλάσῃς, ἀλλὰ κἄν τι δοκῇ δυσθεώρητον εἶναι, τὸ ἐν σαυτῇ βλέπον διανοίξασα διάκυψον εἴσω.

(*b*) Josephus is not a commentator, but a historian who uses the LXX. as an authority, and states the facts in his own words. We will contrast a few passages of the Greek Bible with the corresponding contexts in the *Antiquities*.

Exod. ii. 2—4.	Joseph. *ant.* ii. 9. 4.
ἐσκέπασαν αὐτὸ μῆνας τρεῖς ...ἔλαβεν αὐτῷ ἡ μήτηρ αὐτοῦ θῖβιν, καὶ κατέχρισεν αὐτὴν ἀσφαλτοπίσσῃ καὶ ἐνέβαλεν τὸ παιδίον εἰς αὐτήν...καὶ κατεσκόπευεν ἡ ἀδελφὴ αὐτοῦ μακρόθεν μαθεῖν τί τὸ ἀποβησόμενον αὐτῷ.	τρεῖς μὲν μῆνας παρ' αὐτοῖς τρέφουσι λανθάνοντες...μηχανῶνται πλέγμα βίβλινον..ἔπειτα χρίσαντες ἀσφάλτῳ..ἐντιθέασι τὸ παιδίον...Μαριάμη δὲ τοῦ παιδὸς ἀδελφὴ..ἀντιπαρεξήει φερόμενον ὅποι χωρήσει ὀψομένη τὸ πλέγμα.

1 Regn. i. 1—4.	Joseph. *ant.* v. 10. 2.
ἄνθρωπος ἦν ἐξ Ἀρμαθάιμ.. ἐξ ὄρους Ἐφράιμ.. καὶ τούτῳ δύο γυναῖκες· ὄνομα τῇ μιᾷ Ἄννα καὶ τῇ μιᾷ Φεννάνα. καὶ ἦν τῇ Φεννάνᾳ παιδία, καὶ τῇ Ἄννᾳ οὐκ ἦν παιδίον .. πλὴν ὅτι τὴν Ἄνναν ἠγάπα Ἑλκανὰ ὑπὲρ ταύτην.	ἀνὴρ τῶν ἐν μέσῳ πολιτῶν τῆς Ἐφράμου κληρουχίας Ῥαμαθὰν πόλιν κατοικῶν ἐγάμει δύο γυναῖκας Ἄνναν τε καὶ Φεννάναν. ἐκ δὲ ταύτης καὶ παῖδες αὐτῷ γίνονται, τὴν δὲ ἑτέραν ἄτεκνον οὖσαν ἀγαπῶν διετέλει.

2 Chron. iii. 1—2.

καὶ ἤρξατο Σαλωμὼν τοῦ
οἰκοδομεῖν τὸν οἶκον Κυρίου..
καὶ ἤρξατο οἰκοδομὴ ἐν τῷ μηνὶ
τῷ δευτέρῳ ἐν τῷ ἔτει τῷ τετάρ-
τῳ τῆς βασιλείας αὐτοῦ.

Joseph. *ant.* viii. 3. 1.

τῆς δὲ οἰκοδομίας τοῦ ναοῦ
Σολομὼν ἤρξατο τέταρτον ἔτος ἤδη
τῆς βασιλείας ἔχων μηνὶ δευτέρῳ.

Isa. xxxix. 6—7.

ἰδοὺ ἡμέραι ἔρχονται καὶ
λήμψονται πάντα τὰ ἐν τῷ οἴκῳ
σου καὶ...εἰς Βαβυλῶνα ἥξει...
καὶ ἀπὸ τῶν τέκνων σου ὧν
γεννήσεις λήμψονται, καὶ ποιή-
σουσιν σπάδοντας ἐν τῷ οἴκῳ
τοῦ βασιλέως τῶν Βαβυλωνίων.

Joseph. *ant.* x. 2. 2.

ἴσθι οὐ μετ᾽ ὀλίγον χρόνον εἰς
Βαβυλῶνά σου τοῦτον μετατεθησό-
μενον τὸν πλοῦτον καὶ τοὺς ἐκ-
γόνους εὐνουχισθησομένους καὶ
ἀπολέσαντας τὸ ἄνδρας εἶναι, τῷ
Βαβυλωνίῳ δουλεύσοντας βασιλεῖ.

Josephus, it will be seen, has rewritten each passage, and in doing so, has not only modified the vocabulary, but revolutionised the style. On turning from the left hand to the right hand column we pass from a literal translation of Semitic texts to an imitation of classical Greek. But the contrast is not entirely due to the circumstance that the passages taken from the Septuagint are translations, while the *Antiquities* is an original work. Translations, however faithful, may be in the manner of the language into which they render their original. But the manner of the LXX. is not Greek, and does not even aim at being so. It is that of a book written by men of Semitic descent, who have carried their habits of thought into their adopted tongue. The translators write Greek largely as they doubtless spoke it; they possess a plentiful vocabulary and are at no loss for a word, but they are almost indifferent to idiom, and seem to have no sense of rhythm. Hebrew constructions and Semitic arrangements of the words are at times employed, even when not directly suggested by the original. These remarks apply especially to the earlier books, but they are true to a great extent in regard to the translations of the second century; the manner of the older translations naturally became a standard to which later translators thought it right to conform themselves. Thus the grandson of Jesus son of Sirach writes his prologue in the literary style of the Alexandrian Jews of the time of Euergetes, but in the body of the work he drops into the Biblical manner, and his translation differs little in general character from that of the Greek version of Proverbs.

8. From the general view of the subject we proceed to a detailed account of some of the more characteristic features of the language of the LXX. They fall under three heads— orthography, accidence, syntax. Under the second head a full list of examples from the Pentateuch will be given, with the view of familiarising the beginner with the vocabulary of the earlier books.

I. ORTHOGRAPHY.

In the best MSS. of the LXX. as of the N.T. a large number of peculiar spellings occur, of which only a part can be assigned to itacism and other forms of clerical error. In many of the instances where the great uncial MSS. of the Greek Bible persistently depart from the ordinary orthography they have the support of inscriptions contemporary with the translators, and it is manifest that we have before us specimens of a system which was prevalent at Alexandria[1] and other centres of Greek life[2] during the third and second centuries before Christ.

To a considerable extent the orthography of the MSS. is the same in the LXX. and the N.T. The student may find ample information with regard to the N.T. in the *Notes on Orthography* appended to Westcott and Hort's Introduction, and in the best N. T. grammars (Ph. Buttmann, Winer-

---

[1] Cf. Sturz, *de dial. Maced.*, p. 111 ff.
[2] See (e.g.) K. Meisterhans, *Grammatik der Attischen Inschriften* (Berlin, 1885); Deissmann, *Neue Bibelstudien*, Marburg, 1897. E. Mayser, *Grammatik der griechischen Papyri aus der Ptolemäerzeit*, 1. Teil, Leipzig, 1898 (Progr. des Gymn. Heilbronn).

Moulton, Winer-Schmiedel, Blass). But even in MSS. which like אBAC originally contained the whole of the Greek Scriptures, the Greek Old Testament possesses an orthography which is in part peculiar to itself, and certain features which are common to both Old and New Testaments are found with greater frequency and with a wider application in the LXX. than in the N.T. The reader of the Cambridge manual LXX. who is interested in this question, can readily work out the details from the apparatus criticus, and more especially from the appendix, where he will find all the spellings of the uncial MSS. employed which were not thought worthy of a place in the footnotes to the text. For those to whom orthography is of little interest the specimens given below will probably suffice.

Consonants. Assimilation neglected in compounds: ἐνγασ-τρίμυθος, συνκατακληρονομεῖν, συνσεισμός, ἐνκαίνια, ἐνχειρίδιον. Assimilation where there is no composition: ἐμ μέσῳ, ἐγ γαστρί. Use of ν ἐφελκυστικόν before consonants (omission is rare, except in a few cases such as πᾶσι before the art.); use of the final s in ἄχρις, μέχρις, οὕτως, ἄντικρυς. Retention of the μ in fut. and aor. pass. of λαμβάνειν (λήμψομαι, ἐλήμφθην), and in words formed from it, e.g. πρόσλημψις. Οὐθείς, μηθείς (see p. 297, note) for οὐδείς, μηδείς. Γ dropped in the middle of a word between vowels, as κραυή, ὀλίος, φεύειν (especially in cod. א). Ῥ not doubled in compounds, e.g. ἐπιραντίζειν, κολοβόρις, κατάρακτος, and reduplicated in the augment (ῥεραντισμένος); σσ for ττ in ἐλάσσων, ἥσσων, and ρσ for ρρ in ἄρσην, θαρσεῖν. In some verbal forms consonants are doubled, e.g. βέννειν, κτέννειν, χύννειν. Rough and smooth consonants are occasionally exchanged, e.g. κύθρα (1 Regn. ii. 14, B) for χύτρα.

Vowels. Ει for ι in syllables where ι is long, e.g. Semitic words such as Λευεί, Λευείτης, Δανείδ, Σειών, and Greek words as τραπεζείτης, γείνεσθαι, γεινώσκειν. Also (perhaps by itacism) in innumerable instances of ῑ[1]: e.g. ὄρειον, ἀληθεινός, ἀδικεία, κρεινεῖν. Ι for ει, e.g. τίχος, λιτουργεῖν, ἀλίφειν, ἄλιμμα, κατελίφθην, παράδιγμα, δανίζειν, ὀφιλέτης, ἅγιος, and esp. in nouns in -εία, -εια, e.g. ἀπωλία, ἐνδία, παιδία, Σαμαρία, στρατία, and those in εἰον, as δάνιον, εἰδώλιον. Α for ε, as ἐραυνᾶν; ε for α, as ἐκαθερίσθην, μιερός, τεσσεράκοντα.

[1] Especially in cod. B (*O.T. in Greek*, I. p. xiii.).

Omission of a syllable consisting of ι, as in πεῖν, ταμεῖον. Pre-
fixing of a vowel, as in ἐχθές.

Breathings. Rough breathing for smooth : e.g. οὐχ ὀλίγος,
ἐφ’ ἐλπίδι, ἔφιδε, οὐχ εἰσακούσομαι (Jer. vii. 16), καθ’ ὀφθαλμούς
(Ezech. xx. 14). Similarly we find ἄλσος, ἀλώπηξ, ἐνιαυτός Dt.
xiv. 20 (Nestle, *Septuagintastudien* i. p. 19, ii. pp. 12, 13, 20 f.).
Smooth breathing for rough: οὐκ ἔνεκεν (2 Regn. vii. 12), οὐκ
ὑπάρχει (Job xxxviii. 26, A).

Abnormal spellings such as these occur on every page of
an uncial MS. of the LXX. and sometimes cause great per-
plexity to an editor of the text. So far as they correctly
represent the written or spoken Greek of the period, their
retention is, generally speaking, desirable. In some cases the
MSS. are unanimous, or each MS. is fairly persistent in its
practice ; in others, the spelling fluctuates considerably. The
Cambridge manual LXX. usually adopts a spelling which is
persistently given by the MS. whose text it prints, and on
the same principle follows the fluctuations of its MS. where
they are of any special interest. But the whole question of
orthography is far from having reached a settlement.

II. ACCIDENCE. We will deal with (i.) the formation
of words, (ii.) the declension of nouns, (iii.) the conjugation
of verbs.

(i.) Formation of words.

(*a*) Words formed by termination :

Verbs. In -οῦν from nouns in -ος : ἀμαυροῦν, ἀποδεκατοῦν, ἀπο-
λυτροῦν, ἀποτυφλοῦν, ἀσφαλτοῦν, διαβιοῦν, ἐκτυποῦν, ἐλαττονοῦν, ἐπι-
διπλοῦν, ἐπιπεμπτοῦν, ἐρυθροδανοῦν, εὐοδοῦν, θανατοῦν, καταχρυσοῦν,
κυροῦν, παλαιοῦν, παραζηλοῦν, περικυκλοῦν, συγκυροῦν. In -ίζειν,
-άζειν, -ιάζειν, -ύζειν : ἁγιάζειν, αἱρετίζειν, ἀκουτίζειν, ἀναβιβάζειν,
ἀναθεματίζειν, ἀπογαλακτίζειν, αὐγάζειν, ἀφαγνίζειν, ἀφανίζειν, ἀφορίζειν, βαδίζειν, γελοιάζειν, γρύζειν, δανίζειν, διαγογγύζειν, διασκεδάζειν,
διασκορπίζειν, διαχωρίζειν, ἐκθερίζειν, ἐκκλησιάζειν, ἐκμυελίζειν,
ἐκσπερματίζειν, ἐκτοκίζειν, ἐνταφιάζειν, ἐνυπνιάζειν, ἐνωτίζεσθαι,
ἐξεικονίζειν, ἐξετάζειν, ἐξοπλίζειν, ἐξορκίζειν, ἐπικλύζειν, ἐπιραντίζειν,
ἐπισκιάζειν, ἐπιστοιβάζειν, ἐπιφημίζειν, θυσιάζειν, καταβιάζειν, κατα-
σκιάζειν, κατασοφίζειν, κληδονίζειν, κομίζειν, κουφίζειν, λεπίζειν,
λευκαθίζειν, μακαρίζειν, μελίζειν, οἰωνίζειν, ὀνυχίζειν, ὀπτάζειν,
ὀρθρίζειν, παραδειγματίζειν, παραδοξάζειν, παραλογίζειν, περιασπί-

ζειν, περιονυχίζειν, περιραντίζειν, πλεονάζειν, πολυχρονίζειν, προσεγγίζειν, προσοχθίζειν, σαββατίζειν, σκεπάζειν, σπερματίζειν, στηρίζειν, στοχάζειν, συμποδίζειν, συναθροίζειν, συνοικίζειν, σφακελίζειν, σχολάζειν, τειχίζειν, φαυλίζειν, φλογίζειν, χλωρίζειν, χρονίζειν, ψωμίζειν.

In -εύειν : ἀγχιστεύειν, διοδεύειν, ἐξολεθρεύειν, ἱερατεύειν, καταδυναστεύειν, κατακυριεύειν, καταφυτεύειν, κατοχεύειν, μεταλλεύειν, προφητεύειν, πρωτοκεύειν, στρατοπεδεύειν, τροφεύειν, ὑδρεύειν.

Nouns. In -μα, from verbs : ἀγίασμα, ἄγνισμα, ἀδίκημα, αἴνιγμα, ἄλλαγμα, ἀνάστεμα, ἀνόμημα, ἀνταπόδομα, ἀπόδομα, ἀσέβημα, αὔγασμα, ἀφαίρεμα, βδέλυγμα, διήγημα, δικαίωμα, διόρυγμα, διχοτόμημα, δόμα, ἐγκατάλιμμα, ἔδεσμα, ἐκκόλαμμα, ἐκτύπωμα, ἐπίθεμα, ἐπικάλυμμα, ἐπιτήδευμα, ἔψεμα, ἡμίσευμα, θήρευμα, θυμίαμα, θυσίασμα, ἱεράτευμα, κάρπωμα, κατάκαυμα, καταπέτασμα, καύχημα, κλέμμα, λέπισμα, ὁλοκαύτωμα, ὅραμα, ὀφείλημα, ὀχύρωμα, παράδειγμα, παράθεμα, παράρυμα, περίθεμα, περίψωμα, προσόχθισμα, πρόσταγμα, πρωτογένημα, στερέωμα, συνάντημα, συνκάλυμμα, σύστεμα, τάγμα, τίμημα, τόξευμα, φαλάκρωμα, φύλαγμα, φύραμα, χόρτασμα, χώνευμα.

In -μός, from verbs : ἀφανισμός, γογγυσμός, ἐνδελεχισμός, ἐνπορισμός, ἐξιλασμός, ἐπισιτισμός, ἱματισμός, καθαρισμός, μηρυκισμός, οἰωνισμός, ὁρισμός, ὁρκισμός, παροξυσμός, πειρασμός, σταθμός, στεναγμός, φραγμός, χωρισμός.

In -σις, from verbs : ἀναίρεσις, ἀνάμνησις, ἀποκιδάρωσις, ἄφεσις, βεβαίωσις, γόγγυσις, γύμνωσις, δήλωσις, διάβασις, διασάφησις, ἐκδίκησις, ἔκστασις, ἔκχυσις, ἐπερώτησις, κατακάρπωσις, κατάλειψις, κατάσχεσις, κατοίκησις, ὁλοκάρπωσις, ὁλοκαύτωσις, ὁμοίωσις, πλήρωσις, πόρευσις, πρᾶσις, σύγκρασις, συνάντησις, συντίμησις, σύστασις, ταπείνωσις, ὑπερόρασις, ὑπέροψις, ὑπόστασις, φαῦσις, χαράκωσις, χήρευσις.

In -ή, from verbs : ἀλοιφή, ἀναζυγή, ἀποσκευή, ἀποστολή, ἀποστροφή, ἀφή, διασκευή, δοχή, ἐκτριβή, ἐντολή, ἐπαγωγή, ἐπισκοπή, καταφυγή, ὁλκή, παραβολή, προνομή, προφυλακή, συναγωγή, τροπή.

In -τής, from verbs (m.) : αἰνιγματιστής, ἐνταφιαστής, ἐξηγητής, ἐπιθυμητής, ἑρμηνευτής, πολεμιστής, ῥαφιδευτής, σκιπαστής, σχολαστής.

Adjectives. In -ινος : δειλινός, δερμάτινος, καρύινος, ὀστράκινος, πράσινος, στυράκινος, φλόγινος.

In -ιος : ἐνιαύσιος, ὁμομήτριος, πολυχρόνιος, ὑποχείριος.

In -ικός : ἀρσενικός, εἰρηνικός, λαμπηνικός, λειτουργικός, λιθουργικός, μυρεψικός, πατρικός, ποικιλτικός, πολεμικός, προφασιστικός.

In -τος : ἀκατασκεύαστος, ἀλυσιδωτός, ἀόρατος, ἀπερικάθαρτος, ἐπικατάρατος, εὐλογητός, λαξευτός, μισθωτός, ὀνομαστός, πλεοναστός, φορολογιστός.

(b) Words formed by composition :

Verbs compounded with two prepositions : ἀνθυφαιρεῖν, ἀνταποδοῦναι, ἀποκαθιστᾶν, ἐνκαταλείπειν, ἐνπεριπατεῖν, ἐξαναστέλλειν, ἐπισυνιστᾶν, κατεμβλέπειν, παρεμβάλλειν, συναναλαμβάνειν, συνανα-

στρέφεσθαι,συναπολλύειν, συνεκπολεμοῦν, συνεπακολουθεῖν, συνεπι-
σκέπτειν, συνκατακληρονομεῖν, συνπαραλαμβάνειν, συνπροπέμπειν.
Nouns. Compounded with nouns : ἀσφαλτόπισσα, δασύπους,
ἑτερόζυγος, καμηλοπάρδαλις, κολοβόρις, μακροήμερος, μακροχρόνιος,
μικρόθυμος, ὁλόκληρος, ὁλοπόρφυρος, πολυέλεος, πολυχρόνιος, σκληροτράχηλος, χοιρογρύλλιον.

Compounded with a prefix or preposition : ἀντιπρόσωπος,
Ἀντιλίβανος, ἀρχιδεσμοφύλαξ, ἀρχιδεσμώτης, ἀρχιερεύς, ἀρχιμάγειρος,
ἀρχιοινοχόος, ἀρχισιτοποιός, ἐπίπεμπτος, εὐπρόσωπος, κατάλοιπος,
κατάξηρος, παράλιος, παρεπίδημος, περιδέξιον, περίλυπος, περίοικος,
περίχωρος, ὕπανδρος, ὑπερμήκης.

Compounded with a verb stem, and forming a fresh noun or
a verb : ἀνεμοφθόρος, γλωσσότμητος, ἐργοδιώκτης, θανατηφόρος,
θηριάλωτος, θηρόβρωτος, ἱπποδρόμος, ἰσχνόφωνος, κτηνοτρόφος,
νυμφαγωγός, σιτοποιός, σφυροκόπος, τελεσφόρος, χαροποιός, δι-
χοτομεῖν, ζωογονεῖν, κλοποφορεῖν, κρεανομεῖν, λιθοβολεῖν, λιμαγ-
χονεῖν, νευροκοπεῖν, ὀρνιθοσκοπεῖν, συμβολοκοπεῖν, τεκνοποιεῖν,
ψωραγριᾶν.

(ii.)   Declension of nouns :

Declension 1.   Nouns in -ρᾰ, -υῖα, form gen. in ης, dat. ῃ, μαχαίρῃ,
μαχαίρης Gen. xxvii. 40, Exod. xv. 9 ("vielfach bei A, bes. in Jerem.,"
W.-Schm.), κυνομυίης Exod. viii. 17, ἐπιβεβηκυίης 1 Regn. xxv. 20.

Declension 2.   Certain nouns in -ους end also in -ος, e.g.
χείμαρρος, ἀδελφιδός.   The Attic form in -εώς disappears ; e.g. λαός
and ναός are written for λεώς and νεώς—the latter however occurs
in 2 Macc. (A).   Nouns in -αρχος pass occasionally into the first
declension, e.g. τοπάρχης Gen. xli. 34, κωμάρχης Esth. ii. 3, γενε-
σιάρχης Sap. xiii. 3   ὀστέον usu. contr. in nom. acc., uncontr. in
gen. dat.

Declension 3.   Uncontracted forms are frequent, as βαθέα
Job xii. 22, πήχεων, χειλέων, and in the plural nom. and acc.
of neuters in -ας, as κέρατα, πέρατα.   Γῆρας makes gen. γήρους
dat. γήρει.   Metaplasmus occurs in some words, e.g. δύο, δυσί, πᾶν
with masc. noun, πύλη, πύλεσιν (3 Regn. xxii. 11, A), σάββατα,
σάββασιν, τέσσαρες, τεσσάροις, χείρ, χείραν.   Acc. in -αν for -α,
νύκταν Exod. xiii. 21, τίναν Nah. iii. 19, and freq. in א and A[1].

Proper nouns.   Many are mere transliterations and indeclinable, e.g. Ἀδάμ, Ἀβραάμ, Ἰωσήφ, Σαμουήλ, Δανείδ, Ἀχαάβ, Ἡλειού,
Ἐλεισαῖε, Δανιήλ.   On the other hand some well-known names
receive Greek terminations and are declined, as Μωυσῆς or Μωσῆς,
Ἰησοῦς, Ἐζεκίας, Ἡσαίας, Ἱερεμίας ; while some are found in both
forms, e.g. we have both Ἡλειού and Ἡλ(ε)ίας, Μανασσή and
Μανασσῆς, Σολομών indecl. and Σολομών gen. -μῶνος or -μῶντος.
But in the translated books the indeclinable forms prevail, and
there is no appearance of the forms Ἄβραμος, Ἰσράηλος, Ἰώσηπος,

<hr>

[1] See Thackeray, *Gr. O. T.* pp. 146, 147, "always a vulgarism"; also
J. Psichari, *Essai sur le grec de la Septante*, in *Revue des Études Juives*, LV.
No. 110, p. 164 ff.

which are familiar to the reader of Josephus. In the case of local names transliteration is usual, e.g. Ἰερουσαλήμ, Βηθλέεμ, Βαιθήλ, Σειών. A few however have Greek terminations, as Σαμάρεια or Σαμαρία, Ἰόρδανος, and some names of foreign localities are Hellenised, as Βαβυλών, Συρία, ἡ ἐρυθρὰ θάλασσα, Ἰδουμαία, Αἴγυπτος, and the two Egyptian towns Ἡρώων πόλις (Gen. xlvi. 28), Ἡλίου πόλις (Exod. i. 11). The declension of the Hellenised names presents some irregularities; thus we find Μωυσῆς, -σῆ, -σεῖ, -σῆν· Ἰησοῦς, -σοῦ, -σοῖ, -σοῦν· Μανασσῆς, -σῆ.

(iii.) Conjugation of verbs

Augments. Doubled, as in κεκατήρανται Num. xxii. 6, xxiv. 9, ἀπεκατέστησεν Gen. xxiii. 16, παρεσυνεβλήθη Ps. xlviii. 13, 21 (A). Prefixed to prepositions, e.g. ἐπρονόμευσαν Num. xxi. 1, Deut. ii. 35, ἐπροφήτευσαν Num. xi. 25 f., ἠνωτίσαντο 2 Esdr. xix. 30 (B). Lengthened, as ἤμελλον Sap. xviii. 4, ἠβουλόμην Isa. i. 29, xiii. 9, ἠδυνήθην, ἠδυνάσθην, 2 Chr. xx. 37, Jer. v. 4. Omitted, as in ἀνέθη Jud. viii. 3, ἀφέθη Isa. xxxiii. 24, αὐτάρκησεν Deut. xxxii. 10, ἐξολόθρευεν 1 Chr. xxi. 15, ἴδεν Gen. i. 4, κατορθώθη 2 Chr. xxxv. 10.

Tenses and Persons. (1) Verbs in -ω. New presents, as ἀμφιάζω, γρηγορῶ, βέννω, κτέννω. Futures and aorists[1] with reduplication: κεκράξομαι (Job vi. 5), ἐκέκραξα (Num. xi. 2), ἐπεποίθησα (Jud. ix. 26 A); cf. ἐκέκραγον, Isa. vi. 3. Contracted futures in -ῶ from -άσω: ἐργᾷ Gen. iv. 2, ἁρπᾷ Lev. xix. 13, ἐκδικᾶται Deut. xxxii. 43, ἐγκαυχᾷ Ps. li. 3, συμβιβᾷ Isa. xl. 13, ἀποδοκιμῶ Jer. xxxviii. (xxxi.) 37. Futures (and aor.) with short vowels, πονέσω, Isa. xix. 10. Irregular futures: ἔδομαι, φάγομαι, χεῶ (Exod. iv. 9). Second aor. forms with termination in -α: εἴδαμεν 1 Regn. x. 14, ἔφυγαν 2 Regn. x. 14, ἐφάγαμεν 2 Regn. xix. 42, ἐλθάτω Esth. v. 4. Person endings: 2nd p. s. pres. pass. or middle in -σαι: πίεσαι, φάγεσαι (Ezech. xiii. 18, Ruth ii. 9, 14), ἀπεξενοῦσαι 3 Regn. xiv. 6. 3rd p. pl. imperf. and aor. act. in -οσαν: ἐγεννῶσαν Gen. vi. 4, ἤλθοσαν Exod. xv. 27, κατελίποσαν Exod. xvi. 24, κατενοοῦσαν Exod. xxxiii. 8, ἠνομοῦσαν Ezech. xxii. 11; cf. the opt. αἰνέσαισαν Gen. xlix. 8, ἔλθοισαν Deut. xxxiii. 16. 3rd p. pl. aor. mid. in -εντο: ἐπελάθεντο Jud. iii. 7 (A), Hos. xiii. 6 (B), Jer. xviii. 15 (B*A), &c. 3rd p. pl. perf. act. in -αν: ἑώρακαν Deut. xi. 7; πέποιθαν, Judith vii. 10. 2nd p. s. 1st aor. and perf. act. in -ες: ἀπέσταλκες Exod. v. 22; ἔδωκες, 2 Esdr. xix. 10, Ezech. xvi. 21. (2) Verbs in -μι. From εἰμί we have ἤμην, ἦσθα. From κάθημαι, κάθου Ps. cix. (cx.) 1. From ἵστημι, ἑστηκέναι, ἑστηκώς. From δίδωμι, ἐδίδετο Exod. v. 13 (A), Jer. xii. 34; δοῖ, Ps. xli. 3 (B), 2 Regn. iii. 39 (A).

III. Syntax.

Many of the irregularities which fall under this head are

[1] See, however, Lightfoot on Clem. Rom. i. 34; Thackeray, *Gr. O. T.*, p. 235.

due to the influence of the Hebrew text or of Semitic habits
of thought. These will be treated in the next section. In
this place we shall limit ourselves to constructions whicĥ
appear to be characteristic of the Greek idiom used by the
translators.

Cases and Numbers. Nom. for voc., e.g. ὁ θεός for θεέ, Ps.
xxi. 2, esp. in the phrase Κύριε ὁ θεός; θυγάτηρ=θύγατερ, Ruth ii.
2, 22, iii. 1, &c. Disuse of the Dual.

Comparison. Use of a preposition with the positive for the
comparative, e.g. μέγας παρὰ πάντας, Exod. xviii. 11; ἀγαθὸς
ὑπὲρ δέκα, 1 Regn. i. 8.

Numerals. Ἑπτά=ἑπτάκις, Gen. iv. 24. Omission of καί
when numbers are coupled, e.g. δέκα δύο, δέκα ἕξ, δέκα πέντε, &c.

Verbs. Relative rarity of the optative mood[1], and disappearance of that mood in dependent clauses. Periphrasis with εἰμί,
e.g. πεποιθὼς ἔσομαι, 2 Regn. xxii. 3; ἴσθι πεποιθώς, Prov. iii. 5.
Indicative with ἄν : imperf. and aor., ὅταν εἰσήρχετο, Gen. xxxviii.
9; ὅταν ἐπῆρεν, Exod. xvii. 11; ὅταν κατέβη, Num. xi. 9; ἡνίκα ἂν
εἰσεπορεύετο, Jud. vi. 3; ἐὰν ἔσπειραν, Jud. vi. 2. Coordination
of indicative with conjunctive : Exod. viii. 8 ἐξαποστελῶ αὐτούς,
καὶ θύσωσι, Lev. vi. 2 ψυχὴ ἐὰν ἁμάρτῃ καὶ...παρίδῃ...καὶ ψεύσηται,
ἢ ἠδίκησεν...ἢ εὗρεν...καὶ ψεύσηται...καὶ ὀμόσῃ κτλ. Use of infinitive, with or without the article, to express object, purpose, subject, or result[1]; e.g. (*a*) ἐζήτει ἀνελεῖν, Exod. ii. 15 : ἤρξατο τοῦ
οἰκοδομεῖν, 2 Chr. iii. 1; (*b*) παραγίνεται βοηθῆναι, 2 Regn. viii. 5;
ἀπέστειλεν τοῦ ἰδεῖν, Gen. viii. 7; (*c*) συνέβη κρεμασθῆναι, Gen. xli.
13; τὸ προσκολλᾶσθαι ἀγαθόν Ps. lxxii. 28; (*d*) ὁ θεὸς ἐγὼ τοῦ
θανατῶσαι καὶ ζωοποιῆσαι, 4 Regn. v. 7.

Connexion of the sentence. Use of gen. abs. in reference to
the subject of the verb: e.g. πορευομένου σου...ὅρα, Exod. iv. 21.
Anacoluthon : ἰδὼν δὲ Φαραὼ...ἐβαρύνθη ἡ καρδία Φαραώ, Exod.
ix. 7. Use of the finite verb where the classical language prefers
to employ a participle.

9.   Besides the non-classical forms and constructions which
may fairly be placed to the credit of Alexandrian Greek, the
translated books of the Greek Bible naturally exhibit a large

---

[1] Yet see Job iii. 3 ff., xxiv. 18 f., Ps. cviii. (cix.) 14, Isai. xlix. 15,
Ps. lxii. (lxiii.) 6, Prov. xxv. 26, and the exx. quoted on p. 305.

[2] I follow mainly the classification of C. W. Votaw in his excellent
thesis on the subject (Chicago, 1896). Votaw has shewn that in the translated books of the O. T. there is almost an equal number of cases of the
anarthrous and the articular inf., whereas in the N. T. the articular inf. is
seldom found except in St Luke.

number of irregularities which are of Semitic origin. The
following are examples.

(*a*) *Lexical.*

1. Transliterations, and Greek words formed from the
Hebrew or Aramaic.

2. Words coined or adopted to express Semitic ideas, as
ἀκροβυστία, ἀναθεματίζειν, ὁλοκαύτωμα, σκανδαλίζειν, σπλαγχνίζειν.

3. Phrases answering to the Hebrew idiom: e.g. ἄρτον φαγεῖν
= אָכַל לֶחֶם, ἔλεος ποιεῖν μετά τινος = עָשָׂה חֶסֶד עַם, ἐνώπιον τοῦ
κυρίου = לִפְנֵי־יְהוָֹה, ζητεῖν ψυχήν = בִּקֵּשׁ נֶפֶשׁ, θυσία σωτηρίου = זֶבַח
שְׁלָמִים, λαμβάνειν πρόσωπον = נָשָׂא פָנִים, πᾶσα σάρξ = כָּל־בָּשָׂר,
υἱὸς τεσσεράκοντα καὶ ἑνὸς ἐνιαυτῶν = בֶּן־אַרְבָּעִים וְאַחַת שָׁנָה.

4. Words with a new connotation: ἅγιος, ἁμαρτωλός, ἀρετή,
ἀφόρισμα, ἄφρων, διάβολος, διαθήκη, δικαιοσύνη, ἐκκλησία, ἐλεημοσύνη, ἐξιλασμός, καρδία, Κύριος or ὁ κύριος, λειτουργεῖν, ματαιότης,
ὁσιότης, πειράζειν, προφήτης, πτωχός, σάρξ, φυγαδευτήριον.

(*b*) *Grammatical*[1].

Nouns. Repeated to express distribution, e.g. ἄνθρωπος
ἄνθρωπος = אִישׁ אִישׁ, Num. ix. 10; ἔθνη ἔθνη = גּוֹי גּוֹי, 4 Regn.
xvii. 29. Similarly δύο δύο, Gen. vi. 19; κατὰ μικρὸν μικρόν (AF),
Exod. xxiii. 30. Emphatic adverbs also are occasionally doubled
after the Hebrew manner, as σφόδρα σφόδρα, Exod. i. 12, Ezech.
ix. 9; cf. σφόδρα σφοδρῶς, Gen. vii. 19 (A).
Pronouns. Otiose use, e.g. Gen. xxx. 1 τελευτήσω ἐγώ (מֵתָה
אָנֹכִי); Exod. ii. 14 σὺ θέλεις (אַתָּה אֹמֵר); Exod. xxxvi. 4 αὐτός,
αὐτοί. To Semitic influence is also due the wearisome iteration
of the oblique cases of personal pronouns answering to the
Hebrew suffixes, e.g. Jer. ii. 26 αὐτοὶ καὶ οἱ βασιλεῖς αὐτῶν καὶ οἱ
ἄρχοντες αὐτῶν καὶ οἱ ἱερεῖς αὐτῶν καὶ οἱ προφῆται αὐτῶν. The
fem. αὕτη is occasionally used for τοῦτο after the manner of the
Heb. זֹאת, as in Gen. xxxv. 17, 27, xxxvi. 1, Ps. cxvii. (cxviii.) 23;
see Driver on 1 Sam. iv. 7. To the circumstance that the
Hebrew relative is indeclinable we owe the pleonastic use of the
pronoun after the Greek relative in such passages as Gen. xxviii.
13, ἐφ᾽ ἧς...ἐπ᾽ αὐτῆς (אֲשֶׁר...עָלֶיהָ); Deut. i. 22 δι᾽ ἧς...ἐν αὐτῇ

---

[1] On this head see esp. Frankel, *Vorstudien,* p. 132 ff.; Thiersch, *de
Pentat. vers. Alex.,* p. 111 ff.; Thumb, *Die griech. Spr....des Hellenismus,*
pp. 128 ff., 171 ff.: Thackeray, *Gr. O. T.* p. 25 ff.; Psichari, *op. cit.,* p. 183 ff.

(בָּהּ...אֲשֶׁר); Prov. iii. 15 ὧν...αὐτῶν. A similar redundancy occurs with relative adverbs: Deut. ix. 28, ὅθεν...ἐκεῖθεν (אֲשֶׁר...מִשָּׁם); 2 Chr. i. 3, οὗ...ἐκεῖ.

Verbs. The following Hebraisms may be specially noted. Various phrases used to represent the Heb. inf. abs. when prefixed to a finite verb, e.g. Exod. iii. 7, ἰδὼν ἴδον (רָאֹה רָאִיתִי); Deut. xxxi. 18, ἀποστροφῇ ἀποστρέψω (הַסְתֵּר אַסְתִּיר); also the Heb. idiom וַיֹּסֶף לְ: e.g. Exod. xiv. 13, οὐ προσθήσεσθε ἔτι ἰδεῖν, 1 Regn. iii. 6 προσέθετο καὶ ἐκάλεσεν (cf. *v.* 8 προσέθ. καλέσαι, Job xxix. 1 προσθεὶς εἶπεν (וַיֹּסֶף...וַיֹּאמֶר). Constructions with prepositions contrary to the Greek idiom: βδελύσσεσθαι ἀπό (מִפְּנֵי), Exod. i. 12; φείδεσθαι ἐπί, Deut. vii. 16; ἐπερωτᾶν ἐν Κυρίῳ (שָׁאַל בַּיהוָה), 1 Regn. x. 22; εὐδοκεῖν ἐν or ἐπί (חָפֵץ בְּ). Hebrew forms of adjuration as 1 Regn. iii. 14 εἰ (אִם) ἐξιλασθήσεται, ib. 17 τάδε ποιήσει σοι ὁ θεός, ἐάν... A question standing for the expression of a wish: Num. xi. 29 καὶ τίς δῴη πάντα τὸν λαὸν Κυρίου... ; Ps. lii. (liii.) 6 τίς δώσει ἐκ Σειὼν τὸ σωτήριον τοῦ Ἰσραήλ; Ἐγώ εἰμι followed by an ind. (Jud. vi. 18 ἐγώ εἰμι καθίσομαι, 2 Regn. ii. 2 ἐγώ εἰμι πορεύσομαι)—a construction limited in B to Judges, Ruth, 2—4 Regn. Periphrases such as ἔσομαι διδόναι (Tob. v. 15, BA). Pleonastic use of λέγων = לֵאמֹר, often solœcistically: e.g. Gen. xv. 1 ἐγενήθη ῥῆμα Κυρίου...λέγων, xlv. 16 διεβοήθη ἡ φωνὴ...λέγοντες.

Particles. Pleonastic use of καί and δέ, (1) in an apodosis, e.g. Num. xv. 14, ἐὰν...προσγένηται, ..., καὶ ποιήσει κάρπωμα; Prov. i. 28, ἔσται ὅταν...ἐγὼ δέ...; (2) after a participle: Num. xxi. 11, καὶ ἐξάραντες...καὶ παρενέβαλον. Use of καί in a coordinated clause, where a dependent clause might have been expected; e.g. Num. xxxv. 2, συντάξεις τοῖς υἱοῖς Ἰσραήλ, κ α ὶ δώσουσιν κτλ.

Prepositions. See under *Verbs.* Peculiar uses of the Heb. prepositions are often reflected in the Greek; e.g. 1 Regn. i. 24, ἀνέβη ἐ ν μόσχῳ (בְּפָרִים); Lev. xxi. 10, ὁ μέγας ἀπὸ τῶν ἀδελφῶν αὐτοῦ (הַגָּדוֹל מֵאֶחָיו). A number of new prepositions or prepositional phrases are used to express the Hebrew לִפְנֵי, e.g. ἔναντι, ἀπέναντι, κατέναντι, ἐνώπιον, κατενώπιον, ἀπό, ἐπί, πρό, προσώπου. Similarly ὀπίσω represents אַחֲרֵי; ἐν μέσῳ, ἀνὰ μέσον, διὰ μέσου = בְּתוֹךְ, ἀπὸ (ἐκ) μέσου = מִתּוֹךְ; διὰ χειρός, εἰς χεῖρας, ἐκ χειρός = מִיַּד, בְּיַד; ὁδόν = דֶּרֶךְ. The use of σύν to express the prefix אֵת, which is characteristic of Aquila, occurs in codex A six times in 3 Regn., once in Esther (where it probably came from the Hexapla), and frequently in Ecclesiastes, where even cod. B shews this peculiarity, e.g. Eccl. ii. 17 ἐμίσησα σὺν τὴν ζωήν (אֶת־הַחַיִּים)[1].

10. Both the vocabulary and the syntax of the LXX. exhibit remarkable affinities with the modern language. Mr Geldart (*Modern Greek Language*, p. 101 f.) urges the study of modern Greek upon Biblical students on the ground that "the Greek of the present day affords a better commentary on the language of the LXX. and of the N.T. than the writings of contemporary historians, rhetoricians, grammarians and philosophers[2]." He adds: "The phraseology of the LXX. is modern to an extent which is quite marvellous...let me mention a few well-known words common to the LXX. and modern Greek : ἐπισκέπτομαι, ἀποκρίνομαι, ἐπιστρέφω, προσκυνῶ, ἐνώπιον, πρόσκομμα, πειράζω, ἀκολουθῶ, κοιμῶμαι, ὅλος, κατοικῶ, καθέζομαι, καθίζω, τὰ ἱμάτια, ὑπάγω... The Greek of the N.T....is by no means so vulgar, so merely a vernacular, as that of the LXX." This estimate is perhaps overdone ; certainly there are considerations which suggest caution in the use of modern Greek usage as a key to the meaning of the LXX. But the general similarity of the Alexandrian vocabulary and, to a less extent, of the Alexandrian syntax to those of the spoken language indicates a common affinity to the old colloquial Greek, which ultimately triumphed over the classical standards[3]. That the resemblance is less marked in the case of the New Testament is due to the different circumstances under which it was written. Bilingual Palestinian writers of the first century naturally possessed a more limited vocabulary and employed a more chastened style than Alexandrian translators of the time of Philadelphus and Euergetes, who had been born in the heart of a great Greek city teeming with a cosmopolitan population.

[1] See above, p. 39, n. 2.
[2] See Psichari, *op. cit.*, p. 179 ff.; S. Menardos, *The Value of Byzantine and Modern Greek*, Oxford, 1909.
[3] Cf. Prof. Jebb in Vincent and Dickson, p. 289 : "modern Greek has inherited, not only the ancient literature, but also an oral tradition which preceded that literature, which co-existed with it, and which has survived it."

11. Some of the non-canonical books of the Greek Old Testament, which were either (*a*) loosely translated or paraphrased from a Hebrew original, or (*b*) originally written in Greek, need separate treatment in regard to their lexical and grammatical character. Such are (*a*) 1 Esdras, Daniel (LXX.), (*b*) Wisdom, 2—4 Maccabees.

The *lexicography* of the ' Apocrypha' has been separately treated by C. A. Wahl (*Clavis libr. V. T. apocryphorum philologica*, Leipzig, 1853), and with the help of the Oxford Concordance it may be studied independently. But, for the sake of the student who has not the necessary leisure to examine the subject in detail, it is desirable to notice here the more conspicuous words in each of the books referred to above.

1 ESDRAS.

ἀκολούθως = κατά, dat. (2 Esdr., 2 Macc.)
ἀναγνώστης = γραμματεύς, 2 Esdr.
ἀναμφισβητήτως
ἀναπλήρωσις (Dan.)
ἀνιεροῦν (3 Macc.)
ἀντίγραφον (Esth., Ep.-Jer., 1, 2 Macc.)
ἀντιπαρατάσσειν
ἀπονοεῖσθαι (2 Macc.)
ἀποσημαίνειν
ἀποστατίς (2 Esdr.)
βιβλιοφυλάκιον
δημαγωγεῖν, -γία
διάδημα (Esth., Sap., Isa., 2, 4 Macc.)
δογματίζειν (Esth., Dan., 2, 3 Macc.)
δυσσέβεια, -βημα (2 Macc.)
εἰδωλεῖον (Dan., 1 Macc.)
ἐμφυσιοῦν
ἐπακουστός
ἐπιδόξως
ἐπισπεύδειν (Esth.[1], Prov.[1])
ἐρωμένη, ἡ (cod. B)
εὐθαρσής (1, 2 Macc.)
εὐπρεπῶς (Sap.)

εὐφυής (Sap., 2 Macc.)
ἱερόδουλος
ἱεροψάλτης
ἱστορεῖν
καταλοχισμός (1, 2 Chr.)
κολακεύειν (Job[1], Sap.[1])
ληστεύειν
λωποδυτεῖν
μανιάκη (Dan.)
μεγαλειότης
μεριδαρχία
μεταγενέστερος
ὀνοματογραφία
ὁρκωμοσία (Ez.)
πειθαρχεῖν (Jer., Dan.)
προκαθηγεῖσθαι (cod. B)
προπομπή
προσκεφάλαιον (Ez.)
συνβραβεύειν
σωματοφύλαξ (Judith, 2 Macc.)
ὑπομνηματίζειν
φορολογία (1 Macc.)
χαμαιπετής
χάσκειν
χρηματιστήριον
χρυσοχάλινος (2 Macc.)

DANIEL.

ἀποθαυμάζειν (Sir.)
ἀποτυμπανίζειν (3 Macc.)
ἀρχιεύνουχος
ἀρχιπατριώτης (Jos.[1])
δαμάζειν
δημεύειν
διαμελίζειν
διάπυρος (3 Macc.)
διοικητής (2 Esdr., Tob.)
ἐγκύκλιος
ἐποργίζεσθαι (2 Macc.)
ἑστιατορία (4 Regn.)
εὐκαταφρόνητος
εὐσήμως
θερμασία (Jer.[1])
κηλιδοῦσθαι (Jer.)
κονίαμα

κοπανίζειν (3 Regn.)
μανιάκης (1 Esdr.[1])
μεγαλειότης (1 Esdr., Jer.[1])
πρόσοψις (2 Macc.)
σαμβύκη
σοφιστής (Exod.[1])
συναλοᾶν
συνμολύνεσθαι
σύριγξ
ὕπατος
ὑπεραινετός
ὑπερένδοξος
ὑπερμεγεθής (1 Chr.)
ὑπερυψοῦν (Ps.[2])
ὑπερφερής
φιλόσοφος (4 Macc.)

WISDOM.

This book contains an unusually large vocabulary, consisting in great part of compound words. The following list, taken from c. i.—vi., will suffice to shew its lexical character*.

ἀγερωχία (2, 3 Macc.)
ἀδιάπτωτος
ἀθανασία (4 Macc.)
ἀκαταμάχητος
ἀκηλίδωτος (Ps.[1])
ἀκοίμητος
ἀλαζονεύεσθαι (Ps.[1])
ἀμάραντος
ἀμόλυντος
ἀναποδισμός
ἀνεκλιπής
ἀνεξικακία
ἀνυπόκριτος
ἀπήμαντος
ἀπολογία
ἀπότομος, ἀποτόμως
ἀτέλεστος
ἀτίμητος (3 Macc.)

αὐτοσχεδίως
ἀφθόνως
βασκανία (4 Macc.)
δεκαμηνιαῖος
διορθωτής
δύσχρηστος (Isa.[1])
ἐπισφαλῶς
ἐπιτήδειος (1 Chr., 1—3 Macc.)
ἐπιφημίζειν (Deut.[1])
ἐργατεία
εὐκλεής (Jer.[1])
εὔκυκλος
εὐμορφία (3 Macc.)
εὔστοχος
θυμήρης
ἰδιότης (3 Macc.)
κακοπραγία
κακότεχνος

* Cf. *supra*, p. 268 f., for some interesting examples from other parts of the book.

καταδαπανᾶν
κατάλυπος
κατάχρεως
μακρόβιος (Isa.¹)
μονοήμερος
ὁμοιοπαθής (4 Macc.)
ὁπλοποιεῖν
παράδοξος (Judith, Sir., 2, 4
  Macc.)
παραμύθιον

πολύγονος (4 Macc.)
πομπεύειν
πρωτόπλαστος
στεφανηφορεῖν
συγγνωστός
συλλογισμός (Ex.¹)
τεκμήριον (3 Macc.)
φιλάνθρωπος
χρησιμεύειν (Sir.)

In 2—4 Maccabees the reader finds himself at length face to face with the full richness of the Alexandrian literary style, as it was written by cultured Hellenists of the second and first centuries B.C. The writers, especially the writer of 4 Maccabees, may be said to revel in the use of compound words, many of which may have been of their own coinage. Specimens follow.

2 MACCABEES.

ἀγορανομία
ἀκαριαῖος
ἀκρόπολις
ἀκρωτηριάζειν
ἀλλοφυλισμός
ἀναλημπτέος
ἀπευθανατίζειν
ἀρχηγενέτης
ἀσυλία
αὐθαίρετος
βαρβαροῦν
δειλανδριᾶν
δευτερολογεῖν
διάσταλσις
δοξικός
δυσπέτημα
ἐπευλαβεῖσθαι

εὐαπάντητος
θεομαχεῖν
θωρακισμός
κατευθεκτεῖν
λεληθότως
λιτανεία
ὁπλολογεῖν
πατρῷος
πολεμοτροφεῖν
πολυπραγμονεῖν
προσαναλέγεσθαι
προσυπομιμνήσκειν
σπλαγχνισμός
συμμισοπονηρεῖν
συνεκκεντεῖν
τερατοποιός
ψυχαγωγία

3 MACCABEES.

ἀλογιστία
ἀμνησικακία
ἀνείκαστος
ἀνεπίστρεπτος

ἀνέφικτος
ἀσινής
βαρυηχής
βυθοτρεφής

γραφικός
δημοτελής
δικαιοκρίτης
δυσαίακτος
εὐκατάλλακτος
κισσόφυλλον
λαογραφία
λιβανοῦν
μεγαλοκράτωρ
μεγαλομερής
μιεροφαγία
μίσυβρις

νεανικός
πανόδυρτος
παραναγινώσκειν
πολύδακρυς
προκατασκιροῦν
σιδηρόδεσμος
ὑπομαστιαῖος
ὑπόφρικος
φοβεροειδής
χαρτηρία
χειρονομία
ψυχουλκεῖν

4 MACCABEES.

αἱμοβόρος
ἀναμοχλεύειν
ἀποσκυθίζειν
ἀρθρεμβόλος
ἀσθενόψυχος
ἀσυρής
αὐτοδέσποτος
γαλακτοποιεῖν
γαλακτοτροφία
εἰδωλόθυτος
ἐναγκάλισμα
ἐναποσφραγίζειν
ἐπιρωγολογεῖσθαι
ἑπταμήτωρ
εὐλογιστία
θανατηφόρος

ἱεροπρεπής
ἰσόπαλις
καλλίπαις
κηρογονία
μαλακοψυχεῖν
ξιφηφόρος
ὀροφοιτεῖν
παθοκρατεῖσθαι, -τία
παιδοχαρακτήρ
πηδαλιουχεῖν
προσεπικατατείνειν
συμπάθεια
συναγελάζειν
φιλομήτωρ
φιλοστοργία
φωταγωγεῖν

In the *style* of the originally Greek books there is little to remind us of the Semitic origin of the writers. The Wisdom of Solomon follows generally the parallelisms of Hebrew poetry, and its language is moulded to some extent by the LXX. of the Psalms and of Proverbs. In 2—4 Maccabees the influence of the canonical books appears in the retention of transliterated names such as Ἀβραάμ, Ἰσραήλ, Δανιήλ. But Ἰερουσαλήμ has become Ἰεροσόλυμα, and Eleazar is usually Ἐλεάζαρος. Of Hebrew constructions or modes of thought there is only an occasional instance, whilst it is obvious that the writers lose no opportunity of exhibiting their skill in the literary style of contemporary Alexandrian Greek.

LITERATURE. F. W. Sturz, *De dialecto Macedonica et Alexandrina* (1808); H. W. J. Thiersch, *De Pentateuchi versione Alexandrina*, libri iii. (1841); Z. Frankel, *Vorstudien zu der Septuaginta* (1841); F. W. A. Mullach, *Gramm. d. Vulgarsprache in historischer Entwicklung* (1856); G. v. Zezschwitz, *Profangräcität u. hellenist. Sprachgeist* (1859); E. Reuss, art. *Hellenistisches Idiom* (in Herzog-Plitt, vi., 1880); W. Schmid, *Der Atticismus...von Dionysius v. Halikarnass bis auf d. zw. Philostratus* (Stuttgart, 1889—97); K. Meisterhans, *Gramm. d. Attischen Inschriften* (1881); R. C. Jebb, App. to Vincent and Dickson's *Handbook to modern Greek* (1881); E. Hatch, *Essays in Biblical Greek* (1889), pp. 1—130; H. A. A. Kennedy, *Sources of N. T. Greek* (1895); G. A. Deissmann, *Bibelstudien* (1895), and *Neue Bibelstudien* (1897),—also his art., *Hellenistisches Griechisch*, in Hauck, vii. p. 627 ff. (Leipzig, 1899), where a full bibliography will be found. Phrynichus, ed. Lobeck (1820); W. G. Rutherford, *The new Phrynichus* (1881); Du Cange, *Glossarium ad scriptores mediae et infimae Graecitatis* (Lyons, 1688); J. C. Biel, *Novus thesaurus philologicus, sive lexicon in LXX.* (The Hague, 1779); J. F. Schleusner, *Novus thesaurus philologico-criticus...V. T.* (Leipzig, 1820); E. A. Sophocles, *Greek Lexicon for the Roman and Byzantine periods*[2] (1888); H. Anz, *Subsidia...e Pentateuchi vers. Alex. repetita* (in *Diss. philolog. Hal.* xii. Halle, 1894); J. Viteau, *Étude sur le Grec du N.T. comparé avec celui des Septante* (Paris, 1896); E. Hatch and H. A. Redpath, *Concordance to the Septuagint* (1897); Th. Zahn, *Einleitung in das N. T.*, i., pp. 24 ff. (1897); *Byzantinische Zeitschrift* (1892 ff.); *Archiv für Papyrusforschung* (Leipzig, 1899 ff.); G. A. Deissmann, *Die sprachl. Erforschung der griech. Bibel*, and *Die Sprache der griech. Bibel* (*Th. Rundschau* i., p. 463 ff.); A. Thumb, *Die griechische Sprache im Zeitalter des Hellenismus* (Strassburg, 1901).

Much information on points of grammar and orthography may also be gleaned from the N.T. grammars—A. Buttmann, *Grammatik d. NTlichen Sprachgebrauchs* (Berlin, 1859); Winer-Moulton, *Treatise on the Greek of the N.T.*[8] (1877); Winer-Schmiedel, *Grammatik d. NTlichen Sprachidioms*, Theil i.—ii. (1894—8); F. Blass, *Grammatik d. NTlichen Griechisch* (1896, or the same translated by H. St J. Thackeray, 1898); A. R. Jannaris, *Historical Greek Grammar* (1897); and from the Introduction and Appendix to Westcott and Hort's *N. T. in Greek* (*Intr.*, pp. 302—313, *App.*, pp. 148—180). The *Gramm. Untersuchungen über die biblische Gräcität* of K. H. A. Lipsius is limited to such matters as accentuation, punctuation, and the abbreviations used in Biblical Greek MSS.; but within its own scope it is a serviceable book.

CHAPTER V.

THE SEPTUAGINT AS A VERSION.

THE purpose of this chapter is to prepare the beginner for grappling with the problems presented by the Septuagint when it is regarded as a translation of the Hebrew Bible. Almost at the outset of his study of the Alexandrian version he will find himself confronted by difficulties which can only be met by a study of the general purpose and character of the work, the limitations by which the translators were beset, and the principles which guided them in the performance of their task.

I. The reader of the Septuagint must begin by placing before his mind the conditions under which it was produced, and the relation of the original work to our present texts, Hebrew and Greek.

1. (a) Strictly speaking the Alexandrian Bible is not a single version, but a series of versions produced at various times and by translators whose ideals were not altogether alike. Internal evidence[1] of this fact may be found in the varying standards of excellence which appear in different books or groups of books. The Pentateuch is on the whole a close and serviceable translation; the Psalms[2] and more especially

---

[1] The external evidence has been briefly stated in Part i. c. i. (p. 23 ff.).
[2] Cf. R. Sinker, *Some remarks on the LXX. Version of the Psalms*, p. 9 ff.

the Book of Isaiah shew obvious signs of incompetence. The translator of Job was perhaps more familiar with Greek pagan literature[1] than with Semitic poetry; the translator of Daniel indulges at times in a Midrashic paraphrase. The version of Judges which appears in our oldest Greek uncial MS. has been suspected by a recent critic[2] of being a work of the 4th century A.D.; the Greek Ecclesiastes savours of the school of Aquila[3]. When we come to details, the evidence in favour of a plurality of translators is no less decisive. A comparison of certain passages which occur in separate contexts distinctly reveals the presence of different hands. The reader can readily form a judgement upon this point if he will place side by side in the Hebrew and the Greek 2 Regn. xxii. 2 ff. and Ps. xvii. (xviii.) 3 ff., 4 Regn. xviii. 17—xx. 19 and Isa. xxxvi. 1—xxxix. 8, or Mic. iv. and Isa. ii.

A single specimen may be given from Ps. xvii. compared with 2 Regn. xxiii.

Ps. xvii. 3—6.

³Κύριος στερέωμά μου καὶ καταφυγή μου καὶ ῥύστης μου· ὁ θεός μου βοηθὸς καὶ ἐλπιῶ ἐπ᾽ αὐτόν................... ⁴αἰνῶν ἐπικαλέσομαι Κύριον, καὶ ἐκ τῶν ἐχθρῶν μου σωθήσομαι. ⁵περιέσχον με ὠδῖνες θανάτου, καὶ χείμαρροι ἀνομίας ἐξετάραξάν με· ⁶ὠδῖνες ᾅδου περιεκύκλωσάν με, προέφθασάν με παγίδες θανάτου. ⁷καὶ ἐν τῷ θλίβεσθαί με ἐπεκαλεσάμην τὸν κύριον, καὶ πρὸς τὸν θεόν μου ἐκέκραξα· ἤκουσεν ἐκ ναοῦ ἁγίου αὐτοῦ φωνῆς μου, καὶ ἡ κραυγή μου [ἐνώπιον αὐτοῦ εἰσελεύσεται] εἰς τὰ ὦτα αὐτοῦ.

2 Regn. xxii. 2—6.

²Κύριε πέτρα μου καὶ ὀχύρωμά μου καὶ ἐξαιρούμενός με ἐμοί· ³ὁ θεός μου φύλαξ ἔσται μου, πεποιθὼς ἔσομαι ἐπ᾽ αὐτῷ .... ⁴αἰνετὸν ἐπικαλέσομαι Κύριον, καὶ ἐκ τῶν ἐχθρῶν μου σωθήσομαι. ⁵ὅτι περιέσχον με συντριμμοὶ θανάτου, χείμαρροι ἀνομίας ἐθάμβησάν με· ⁶ὠδῖνες θανάτου ἐκύκλωσάν με, προέφθασάν με σκληρότητες θανάτου. ⁷ἐν τῷ θλίβεσθαί με ἐπικαλέσομαι Κύριον, καὶ πρὸς τὸν θεόν μου βοήσομαι, καὶ ἐπακούσεται ἐκ ναοῦ αὐτοῦ φωνῆς μου, καὶ ἡ κραυγή μου ἐν τοῖς ὠσὶν αὐτοῦ.

---

[1] Cf. e.g. Job ix. 9, xlii. 14; from the latter passage Theodore of Mopsuestia argued the pagan origin of the book (*D. C. B.* iv. p. 939).

[2] Moore, *Judges*, p. xlvi.

[3] According to McNeile (*Introd. to Ecclesiastes*) it is the earlier edition of Aquila's version; cf. Thackeray, *Gr. O. T.* pp. 13, 60.

One of these versions has doubtless influenced the other, but that they are the work of separate hands seems to be clear from the differences of method which appear e.g. in the renderings of סֶלַע, מְצוּדָה in the first verse, and the use of the aorist and the future in vv. 6, 7.

If further proof is needed it may be found in the diverse renderings of the same Hebrew words in different parts of the Canon. This argument must be used with caution, for (as we shall presently see) such diversities are to be found not only in the same book but in the same context. But after making allowance for variations of this kind, there remain abundant instances in which the diversity can only be attributed to a change of hand. Thus פְּלִשְׁתִּים is uniformly represented in the Hexateuch by Φυλιστιείμ, but in Judges and the later books by ἀλλόφυλοι; פֶּסַח is φάσεκ or φάσεχ in Chronicles[18] and Jeremiah[1], but πάσχα in all other books; אוּרִים is δήλωσις or δῆλοι in the Pentateuch, but in Ezra-Nehemiah φωτίζοντες, φωτίσων; תֻּמִּים is ἀλήθεια in Exodus, but in Ezra τέλειον; in Isaiah צְבָאֹת is σαβαώθ more than 50 times, whilst παντοκράτωρ, which in other books is the almost uniform rendering of the word when it is used as a title of Deity, does not once occur; קָהָל is συναγωγή in Gen., Exod., Lev., Num., and again in the Prophets, but ἐκκλησία in Deuteronomy (with one exception) and onwards to the end of the historical books. The singular[1] phrase ἐγώ εἰμι = אָנֹכִי is limited to Judges, Ruth, and 2—4 Regn.; σύν = אֵת of the object occurs in the true LXX. only in Ecclesiastes; ἀμήν is peculiar to Chronicles and Ezra, other books which contain the Heb. word (Num., Deut., 1 Regn., Psalms, Jer.) preferring γένοιτο. Similar results may be obtained from a comparison of the forms assumed by the same proper names in different books. Elijah (אֵלִיָּהוּ) is Ἠλειού in the Books of Kings, but Ἠλίας in Malachi and Sirach. The lists in Chronicles use the Hebrew form of Gentile names (Θεκωεί, Ἀναθωθεί, &c.), where other books adopt the Greek (Θεκωείτης,

---

[1] On Job xxxiii. 31 see Thackeray, *Gramm. O. T.* p. 55.

Ἀναθωθείτης, &c.). In Ezra אֲחַשְׁוֵרוֹשׁ becomes Ἀσσούηρος, but Ἀρταξέρξης is substituted by the translator of Esther, and Ξέρξης by the LXX. translator of Daniel (ix. 1)[1]. It is difficult to resist the force of this cumulative evidence in support of a plurality of translators, especially when it is confirmed by what we know of the external history of the Septuagint.

(*b*) Further it is clear that the purpose of the version in the later books is not altogether that which the translators of the Pentateuch had in view. The Greek Pentateuch, as we have seen, was intended to supply the wants of the Alexandrian Synagogue. The Book of the Twelve Prophets, and the three major Prophets, were probably translated with the same general purpose, but under a diminished sense of responsibility, since the Prophets, even after their admission to the Canon, were not regarded as sharing the peculiar sanctity of the Law. But the Hagiographa, excepting perhaps the Psalter, stood on a much lower level, and such books as Job, Esther, and Daniel were perhaps viewed by the Alexandrians as national literature[2] which was not yet classical and might be treated with the freedom allowed by custom in such cases to the interpreter and the scribe. Our estimate of the translator's work must clearly take account of his attitude towards the book upon which he is engaged.

(*c*) It is important also to bear in mind the peculiar difficulties which beset the translators in their attempts to render the Hebrew Scriptures into Greek. To translate a Semitic book into the language of the West was a new venture when it was undertaken at Alexandria; the Greek Pentateuch "was the work of pioneers and necessarily had the defects of such work[3]." No wonder if even in the later books the Hebrew

---

[1] Theod. has Ἀσσουήρου in Daniel.
[2] Cf. prol. to Sirach: τῶν ἄλλων πατρίων βιβλίων.
[3] A. F. Kirkpatrick in *Expositor*, v. iii. p. 268. Cf. W. R. Smith, *O.T. in Jewish Ch.*, pp. 75 f.

idiom refused to lend itself to the forms even of Hellenistic Greek without losing to some extent its identity, as the translator of Sirach complains[1]. Moreover the majority of the translators had probably learnt the sacred language in Egypt from imperfectly instructed teachers, and had few opportunities of making themselves acquainted with the traditional interpretation of obscure words and contexts which guided the Palestinian Jew[2]. The want of a sound tradition is especially manifest in poetical passages and books, and it makes itself felt in the numerous transliterations, and in faulty readings and renderings of the text[3]. Such things may well make the reader smile at the claim of inspiration which was set up for the LXX., but they ought neither to mislead his judgement, nor to lessen his admiration for the courage and the general success of the Alexandrian translators.

2. The student must also endeavour to realise the condition of the Hebrew text which lay before the Alexandrian translators.

(*a*) The text of the Hebrew Bible has undergone no material change since the beginning of the second century A.D. A vast store of various readings has been collected from the MSS. by the diligence of Kennicott and De Rossi, but few among them appear to be more than the omissions or corruptions which spring from the accidents of transcription. All existing MSS. belong to one type of text, and it is, in the main, the type which was known to Jerome, to Origen, and to Aquila, and which is reflected in the Targums and the Talmud.

---

[1] *Prol.* οὐ γὰρ ἰσοδυναμεῖ κτλ.

[2] Even in Palestine "before the Christian era...the exegetical tradition was still in a rudimentary stage" (Kirkpatrick, *Divine Library*, p. 69).

[3] Dr Nestle points out that the mistakes of the LXX. are sometimes due to Aramaic or Arabic colloquialisms, and gives the following examples: Aramaic: Num. xxiv. 7 ἐξελεύσεται. Ps. cxl. 4 προφασίζεσθαι. Hos. ii. 23 (25) ἠγαπημένην, vi. 5 ἀπεθέρισα. Isa. iv. 2 ἐπιλάμψει, liii. 10 καθαρίσαι. Jer. xxxviii. (xxxi.) 13 χαρήσονται. Arabic: Ps. lxxxiii. 7 δώσει. Dan. vii. 22 (LXX.) ἐδόθη.

But it is not that which was possessed by the Alexandrians of the third and second centuries, B.C. At some time between the age of the LXX. and that of Aquila a thorough revision of the Hebrew Bible must have taken place, probably under official direction ; and the evidence seems to point to the Rabbinical school which had its centre at Jamnia in the years that followed the fall of Jerusalem as the source from which this revision proceeded[1]. The subject, as a whole, will be treated in a later chapter; meanwhile it is sufficient to warn the beginner that in the LXX. he has before him the version of an early text which often differed materially from the text of the printed Hebrew Bible and of all existing Hebrew MSS.

(*b*) The palaeographical character of the MSS. employed by the translators requires consideration. It will be remembered that the newly discovered fragments of Aquila present the Tetragrammaton in archaic letters[2]. These letters belong to the old Semitic alphabet which was common to the Hebrew, Moabite, Aramaic, and Phoenician languages, and which appears on the Moabite stone and in the Siloam inscription and, with some modifications, in MSS. of the Samaritan Pentateuch, and on coins of the Maccabean period. The transition from this ancient character to the square letters[3] which are used in existing Hebrew MSS. and in the printed Bibles must have been practically complete in our Lord's time, since He refers to the *yodh* as the smallest letter, and to the κεραι which are peculiar to the square alphabet (Mt. v. 18). That the change had begun

---

[1] See W. R. Smith, *O. T. in J. Church*, pp. 56 f.; Driver, *Samuel*, p. xxxix.; Kirkpatrick, *Divine Library of the O. T.*, p. 64. Among the Rabbis of Jamnia were Eleazar, Joshua, and Akiba, the reputed teachers of Aquila; see Edersheim-White, *History of the Jewish Nation*, pp. 132 ff., 174 f.

[2] See pp. 39 f.

[3] כְּתָב מְרֻבָּע, or, as the Talmud calls it, כ' אַשּׁוּרִית ; see Driver, *Samuel*, pp. ix. ff.

in the MSS. employed by the Alexandrian translators[1] may be gathered from the fact that they repeatedly confuse letters which are similar in the square character but not in the archaic. Professor Driver holds that the alphabet of their MSS. was a transitional one, in which ו and י, ב and מ, ה ח and ס, as well as ב and כ, ד and ר, were more or less difficult to distinguish[2].

A few examples may be given from Driver's list. (1) 1 Regn. ii. 29 ὀφθαλμῷ (עין, for עון); xii. 3 ἀποκρίθητε κατ᾽ ἐμοῦ (ענו בי, for עיני בו); Ps. xxi. (xxii.) 17 ὤρυξαν (כארו, for כארי); Isa. xxix. 13 μάτην δὲ σέβονταί με (ותהו יראתם אתי, for ותהי יראתם אתי). (2) 1 Regn. vi. 20 διελθεῖν (לעבר, for לעמד); Jer. xxvi. (xlvi.) 25 τὸν υἱὸν αὐτῆς (בנה for מנא)[3]; 1 Regn. iv. 10 ταγμάτων (רגלי, for רגלי), xxi. 7 Δωὴκ ὁ Σύρος (דאג הארמי, for ד׳ האדמי).

Another cause of confusion was the *scriptio defectiva* in the case of ו and י where they represent long vowels, e.g. 1 Regn. xii. 8 καὶ κατῴκισεν αὐτούς (וישבם, for וישיבם); Ps. v. tit. ὑπὲρ τῆς κληρονομούσης (אל הנחלת, for אל הנחילות); Job xix. 18 εἰς τὸν αἰῶνα (עלם, for עוילים); Jer. vi. 23 ὡς πῦρ (כאש, for כאיש). Abbreviations, also, probably gave rise to misunderstandings; see the instances in Driver, *op. cit.*, pp. lxiii. f., lxx. note 2, and others collected from Jeremiah by Streane, *Double Text*, p. 20.

In the case of numerals errors appear to have arisen from the use of similar letters as numerical signs: e.g. 2 Regn. xxiv. 13 τρία ἔτη, 𝕸 'seven years,' where ז has been read for ג. Here 𝕲 has the support of the Chronicler (1 Chron. xxi. 12): see König in Hastings' *D.B.*, iii. p. 562.

Further, in the MSS. used by the LXX. the words seem not to have been separated by any system of punctuation or spacing. On the Moabite stone[4] and in the Siloam inscription[5] a point has been used for this purpose, but the Phoeni-

---

[1] Except perhaps those which lay before the translators of the Pentateuch; see Driver, *l.c.*

[2] A specimen of such a script, but of much later date, may be seen in Driver, *op. cit.*, p. lxv.

[3] Cf. Streane *ad loc.* and on Jer. xx. 17.

[4] See Driver, *op. cit.*, p. lxxxvi., or Hastings' *D.B.* iii. art. *Moab.*

[5] Driver, *op. cit.*, p. xv.

cian inscriptions are without punctuation, and so were probably
the early Biblical rolls. The division adopted by the LXX. is
frequently at variance with that of the Massoretic text, and
is sometimes preferable to the latter, sometimes inferior; but
the differences witness to the absence of divisions in the
Hebrew MSS. and the non-employment of the final letters
ךםןףץ.

Thus Gen. xlix. 19, 20 αὐτῶν κατὰ πόδας. Ἀσήρ...=אשר : עקבם
(𝔐, מאשר : עקב); Deut. xxvi. 5 Συρίαν ἀπέβαλεν=יאבד ארם
(𝔐, ארמי אבד); 1 Regn. i. 1 ἐν Νασείβ=בנציב (𝔐, בן צוף);
Ps. xliii. (xliv.) 5 ὁ θεός μου ὁ ἐντελλόμενος=מצוה אלהי (𝔐, אלהים
צוה); Jer. xxvi. (xlvi.) 15 διὰ τί ἔφυγεν ἀπὸ σοῦ ὁ Ἆπις;=נס מדוע
חף (𝔐, נסחף מדוע); Zech. xi. 7 εἰς τὴν Χαναανίτην=לכנעני (𝔐 לכן
עניי).

Lastly, almost every page of the LXX. yields evidence that
the Hebrew text was as yet unpointed. Vocalisation was in
fact only traditional until the days of the Massora, and the
tradition which is enshrined in the Massoretic points differs,
often very widely, from that which was inherited or originated
by the Alexandrian translators[1].

A few examples may suffice: Gen. xv. 11 καὶ συνεκάθισεν
αὐτοῖς = אֹתָם וַיֵּשֶׁב (𝔐, אֹתָם וַיַּשֵּׁב); Num. xvi. 5 ἐπέσκεπται=בֹּקֶר
(𝔐, בֹּקֶר); 1 Regn. xii. 2 καθήσομαι=יָשַׁבְתִּי (𝔐, וְשַׂבְתִּי); Nah. iii. 8
μερίδα Ἀμμών=אָמוֹן מְנַת (𝔐, אָמוֹן מִנֹּא); Isa. ix. 8 θάνατον (דָּבָר,
𝔐, דָּבָר) ἀπέστειλεν Κύριος ἐπὶ Ἰακώβ. In proper names the
differences of the vocalisation are still more frequent and apparent, e.g. Μαδιάμ (מִדְיָן); Βαλαάμ (בִּלְעָם), Γόμορρα (עֲמֹרָה), Χοδολ-
λογόμορ (כְּדָרְלָעֹמֶר), Φασγά (פִּסְגָּה), Σαμψών (שִׁמְשׁוֹן).

(*c*) One other preliminary consideration remains. The
student must not leave out of sight the present state of the
Greek text. A homogeneous text is not to be found even in the

---

[1] Jerome in the last years of the 4th century knows nothing of a system of
vowel points; see Nowack, *Die Bedeutung des Hieronymus für die ATliche
Textkritik* (Göttingen, 1875).

oldest of our uncial MSS., and the greater number of Greek codices are more or less influenced by the Hexapla. The Lucianic text is subject to another vice, the Antiochian passion for fulness, which encouraged the blending or the accumulation of various renderings and thus created doublets[1]. Besides these recensional errors there are the mistakes, itacistic or other, which are incident to the transmission of ancient books. The state of the Greek text has been touched upon already, and will form the subject of a chapter in the third part of this book. Here it is sufficient to notice the presence of mixture and corruption as a factor in the problem which the student of the LXX. must keep in view.

II. We are now prepared to deal with those features of the version which are not incidental but characteristic of the translators' principles and methods.

1. The reader of the Alexandrian Greek Bible is continually reminded that he has before him a translation of a Semitic writing.

(*a*) As a whole the version aims at fidelity, and often pursues this aim to the extent of sacrificing the Greek idiom. The first chapter of Genesis will supply instances of extreme literalness, e.g. *v.* 4 ἀνὰ μέσον τοῦ φωτὸς καὶ ἀνὰ μέσον τοῦ σκότους· *v.* 5 ἐγένετο ἑσπέρα καὶ ἐγένετο πρωί, ἡμέρα μία· *v.* 20 ἑρπετὰ ψυχῶν ζωσῶν. As we proceed, we are still conscious of moving in an atmosphere which is Hebrew and not Greek. Hebrew constructions meet us everywhere; such phrases as ἀφικέσθαι ἕως πρός τινα, παρασιωπᾶν ἀπό τινος, προστιθέναι (τοῦ) ποιεῖν, λαλεῖν ἐν χειρί τινος, ἐχθὲς καὶ τρίτην, ἀπὸ γενεῶν εἰς γενεάς (ἕως γενεᾶς καὶ γενεᾶς, εἰς γενεὰν καὶ γενεάν), may be found in the Prophets and Hagiographa as well as in the Pentateuch. Occasionally the translators set the sense at defiance in their

---

[1] Cf. Driver, *op. cit.*, p. lviii.

desire to be true to what they conceive to be the meaning of the Hebrew, as when in 1 Regn. i. 26 they render 'בִּ (δέομαι) by ἐν ἐμοί. In some books, especially perhaps in the Psalms and in Isaiah, entire sentences are unintelligible from this cause. Even when the Alexandrians have rightly understood their original they have generally been content to render it into Greek with little regard for rhythm or style, or the requirements of the Greek tongue.

(*b*)　To the same spirit of loyalty may be ascribed in part the disposition to transliterate words which present unusual difficulty. The number of transliterations other than those of proper names is considerable[1], and they are to be found in nearly all the translated books. In some cases they are due to misunderstanding, as in Jud. i. 19 Ῥῆχαβ διεστείλατο αὐτοῖς where (ה)ברזל seems to have been read as הבדיל, and רכב consequently treated as a proper name; in others, the Hebrew form is purposely maintained (e.g. ἀλληλουιά, ἀμήν). But in the majority of instances transliteration may be taken for a frank confession of ignorance or doubt; it is clearly such, for example, in Jud. viii. 7 ἐν ταῖς ἀβαρκηνείν, 4 Regn. ii. 14 ἀφφώ (אַף הוא), Jer. xxxviii. (xxxi.) 40 πάντες ἀσαρημὼθ ἕως νάχαλ Κεδρών. As in the first and third of these specimens, the article is often included; and when a proper name is transliterated, the name is sometimes for this reason not easily recognised; thus Ramathaim (1 Regn. i. 1) becomes Ἀρμαθάιμ (הרמתים)[2]. Similarly the ה local is taken over in the transliteration, as in Gen. xxxv. 6 εἰς Λοῦζα = לוּזָה. Sometimes two words are rolled into one, as in Οὐλαμμαύς = אוּלָם לוּז (Gen.

---

[1] Thus Hatch and Redpath take note of 39 transliterations, exclusive of proper names, under A alone. They are thus distributed: Pentateuch, 4; Histories, 26; Psalms &c., 3; Prophets, 6. The principles by which the LXX. appear to have been guided in these transliterations of Hebrew consonants and vowel-sounds are expounded by Frankel, *Vorstudien*, p. 107 ff.

[2] Unless the α is here prothetic, which is however less probable.

xxviii. 19)[1]. A doublet is occasionally created by adding a translation to the transliterated Hebrew, e.g. in 1 Regn. vi. 11, 15 τὸ θέμα ἐργάβ, vii. 4 τὰ ἄλση Ἀσταρώθ, xxiii. 14 ἐν Μασερὲμ ἐν τοῖς στενοῖς. In the case of a significant proper name, where it is necessary for the reader to be made aware of its meaning, the LXX. sometimes translate without transliterating, e.g. Gen. iii. 20 ἐκάλεσεν Ἀδὰμ τὸ ὄνομα τῆς γυναικὸς Ζωή (חַוָּה); xi. 9 ἐκλήθη τὸ ὄνομα αὐτοῦ Σύγχυσις (בָּבֶל); xiv. 13 ἀπήγγειλεν Ἀβρὰμ τῷ περάτῃ (הָעִבְרִי).

2. The Alexandrian translators, however, while loyal to their original, sometimes even to a fault, manifest nothing like the slavish adherence to the letter with which Aquila has been charged. They often amplify and occasionally omit; they interpret, qualify or refine; they render the same Hebrew words by more than one Greek equivalent, even in the same context; they introduce metaphors or grammatical constructions which have no place in the Hebrew text and probably at no time had a place there, or they abandon figures of speech where they exist in the original.

(*a*) Slight amplifications, which are probably not to be ascribed to a fuller text, occur frequently in all parts of the LXX.; e.g. the insertion of λέγων before a quotation, or of pronouns which are not expressed in the Hebrew, or of single words added in order to bring out the sense, as in Gen. xxxiv. 10 ἰδοὺ ἡ γῆ πλατεῖα ἐναντίον ὑμῶν, xl. 17 ἀπὸ πάντων τῶν γενημάτων ὧν ὁ βασιλεὺς Φαραὼ ἐσθίει, Deut. vii. 16 φάγῃ πάντα τὰ σκῦλα τῶν ἐθνῶν (Heb. 'thou shalt eat all the nations'). The translators frequently manifest a desire to supply what the original had omitted or to clear up what was ambiguous: they name the subject or object when the Hebrew leaves it

---

[1] Cf. Hieron. *Quaest. hebr.* p. 44 (ed. Lagarde), *De situ et nom.* pp. 106, 158. Pearson (*Praef. paraen.* p. 6) endeavours to defend the LXX. even here.

to be understood (Gen. xxix. 9 αὐτὴ γὰρ ἔβοσκεν τὰ πρόβατα
τοῦ πατρὸς αὐτῆς, Heb. 'fed them'; xxxiv. 14 καὶ εἶπαν αὐτοῖς
Συμεὼν καὶ Λευὶ οἱ ἀδελφοὶ Δείνας υἱοὶ δὲ Λείας, Heb.
'and they said unto them'), or they add a clause which seems
to follow as a necessary consequence (2 Regn. xii. 21 ἀνέστης
καὶ ἔφαγες ἄρτον καὶ πέπωκας: xvi. 10 καὶ ἄφετε αὐτὸν καὶ
οὕτως καταράσθω = לְקַלֵּל (כֹּה קֹ) כִּי), or they make good an apo-
siopesis (Exod. xxxii. 32 εἰ μὲν ἀφεῖς αὐτοῖς τὴν ἁμαρτίαν αὐτῶν
ἄφες). Less frequently they insert a whole sentence which is
of the nature of a gloss, as in Gen. i. 9 καὶ συνήχθη τὸ ὕδωρ τὸ
ὑποκάτω τοῦ οὐρανοῦ εἰς τὰς συναγωγὰς αὐτῶν καὶ ὤφθη ἡ ξηρά,
which is merely an expansion of καὶ ἐγένετο οὕτως in the terms
of the preceding command συναχθήτω κτλ.; or 1 Regn. i. 5 ὅτι
οὐκ ἦν αὐτῇ παιδίον, a reminiscence of *v.* 2 τῇ Ἅννᾳ οὐκ ἦν
παιδίον. On the other hand the LXX. not uncommonly present
a shorter text, as compared with M.T., e.g. Gen. xxxi. 21 καὶ
διέβη τὸν ποταμόν (Heb. 'he rose up and passed over'), ib. 31
εἶπα γάρ Μή ποτε κτλ. (Heb. 'Because I was afraid, for I
said...'); 1 Regn. i. 9 μετὰ τὸ φαγεῖν αὐτοὺς ἐν Σηλώ (Heb.
'after they had eaten in Shiloh and after they had drunk').

(*b*) The translators frequently interpret words which call
for explanation. Hebraisms are converted into Greek phraseology, e.g. בֶּן־נֵכָר becomes ἀλλογενής (Exod. xii. 43), and בֶּן־שָׁנָה
ἐνιαύσιος (Num. vii. 15); וַאֲנִי עֲרַל שְׂפָתָיִם is rendered by ἐγὼ δὲ
ἄλογός εἰμι (Exod. vi. 12). A difficult word or phrase is exchanged for one more intelligible to a Greek reader; thus
ἡ ἔρημος is used for הַנֶּגֶב (Gen. xii. 9); 'Urim and Thummim'
become ἡ δήλωσις καὶ ἡ ἀλήθεια (Exod. xxviii. 26); in the Psalms
ἀντιλήμπτωρ is written for מָגֵן (Ps. iii. 4), βοηθός for צוּר (xvii. = xviii.
3), and γλῶσσα for כָּבוֹד (Ps. xv. = xvi. 9); similarly in Jer. ii. 23
τὸ πολυάνδριον 'the cemetery' stands for הַגַּיְא, i.e. the valley of
Hinnom[1]. An effort is made to represent Hebrew money by its
nearest Greek equivalent; thus for שֶׁקֶל we have δίδραχμον (Gen.

---

[1] Similarly in Prov. xxii. 10, where the LXX. read וישב בת דין, the
last two words are rendered ἐν συνεδρίῳ.

xxiii. 15, Deut. xxii. 29, 2 Esdr. xv. 15) as well as σίκλος, and for גֵּרָה ὀβολός. Occasionally a whole clause is interpreted rather than translated; e.g. Gen. i. 2 ἡ δὲ γῆ ἦν ἀόρατος καὶ ἀκατασκεύαστος, Exod. iii. 14 ἐγώ εἰμι ὁ ὤν, Ps. xl. (xxxix.) 7 σῶμα δὲ κατηρτίσω μοι. A dogmatic interest has been detected in some of these paraphrastic renderings, chiefly where the LXX. have endeavoured to avoid the anthropomorphisms of the original; examples are most frequent in the Pentateuch, e.g. Gen. xviii. 25 μηδαμῶς σὺ ποιήσεις (Heb. 'that be far from thee'); Exod. iv. 16 σὺ δὲ αὐτῷ ἔσῃ τὰ πρὸς τὸν θεόν (לֵאלֹהִים); xxiv. 10 εἶδον τὸν τόπον οὗ εἱστήκει ὁ θεὸς τοῦ Ἰσραήλ (Heb. 'they saw the God of Israel,' Aq. εἶδον τὸν θεὸν Ἰσραήλ); ib. 11 τῶν ἐπιλέκτων τοῦ Ἰσραὴλ οὐ διεφώνησεν οὐδὲ εἷς; Num. xii. 8 τὴν δόξαν (תְּמֻנַת) Κυρίου εἶδεν; Exod. xv. 3 Κύριος συντρίβων πολέμους (אִישׁ מִלְחָמָה); Deut. xiv. 23 ὁ τόπος ὃν ἂν ἐκλέξηται Κύριος ὁ θεός σου ἐπικληθῆναι (לְשַׁבֵּן) τὸ ὄνομα αὐτοῦ ἐκεῖ; Jos. iv. 24 ἡ δύναμις τοῦ κυρίου (יַד־יְהֹוָה). Such renderings manifest the same spirit of reverence which led the LXX. to write ὁ κύριος or the anarthrous Κύριος, or not infrequently ὁ θεός, for the Tetragrammaton, just as their Palestinian brethren read for it אֲדֹנָי or אֱלֹהִים[1]. In other places the LXX. appear to be guided by the Jewish *Halacha*, e.g. Gen. ii. 2 συνετέλεσεν ὁ θεὸς ἐν τῇ ἡμέρᾳ τῇ ἕκτῃ (הַשְּׁבִיעִי, Aq. τῇ ἑβδόμῃ); Lev. xxiv. 7 ἐπιθήσετε ἐπὶ τὸ θέμα λίβανον καθαρὸν καὶ ἅλα[2]; xix. 7 ἐὰν δὲ βρώσει βρωθῇ τῇ ἡμέρᾳ τῇ τρίτῃ, ἄθυτόν ἐστιν (Heb. 'an abomination')[3]. Of *Haggada* also there are clear traces, as in Exod. xii. 40 ἐν γῇ Αἰγύπτῳ καὶ ἐν γῇ Χανάαν, 1 Regn. i. 14 εἶπεν αὐτῇ τὸ παιδάριον Ἠλεί[4]; v. 6

---

[1] See W. R. Smith, *O. T. in J. Church*, p. 77. Aquila, as we gather from Origen and now know from his published fragments (p. 39 f.), wrote the word in archaic Hebrew characters, which however were read as Κύριος.

[2] "Because salt as well as frankincense was used in the actual ritual of their period" (W. R. Smith, *op. cit.*, p. 77).

[3] On xxiii. 11 see p. 17.

[4] "An evident attempt to shield the priest from the charge of harshness" (II. P. Smith, *Samuel*, p. 10).

καὶ μέσον τῆς χώρας αὐτῆς ἀνεφύησαν μύες, καὶ ἐγένετο σύγχυσις
θανάτου μεγάλη ἐν τῇ πόλει.

(c) The LXX. render the same Hebrew word by more than
one Greek equivalent, sometimes even in the same context. In
some cases the change appears to be either arbitrary, or due
to the desire of avoiding monotony; e.g. in Ps. xxxvi. (xxxvii.)
רָשָׁע is translated by ἁμαρτωλός in vv. 10, 12, 14, 16, 17, 20, 21,
32, 40, but by ἀσεβής in vv. 28, 35, 38. In many others it may
be ascribed to the circumstance that certain common Hebrew
words take a special colouring from the contexts in which they
occur, and must be rendered accordingly. Thus נתן, 'give[1],'
which belongs to this class has received in the LXX. more than
30 different renderings; sometimes it is translated by a paraphrase, e.g. Jos. xiv. 12 αἰτοῦμαί σε (לִ נָתַן), Deut. xxi. 8 ἵνα μὴ
γένηται (אַל תִּתֵּן); when it is rendered directly, the following
Greek verbs (besides διδόναι and its compounds) are used to
represent it: ἄγειν, ἀποστέλλειν, ἀποτίνειν, ἀφιέναι, δεικνύναι,
δωρεῖσθαι, ἐᾶν, ἐκτιθέναι, ἐκτίνειν, ἐκχέειν, ἐλεᾶν, ἐμβάλλειν, ἐγκα-
ταλείπειν, ἐπαίρειν, ἐπιβάλλειν, ἐπιτιθέναι, ἐπιχέειν, ἐφιστάναι,
ἱστάναι, καταβάλλειν, καθιστάναι, κατατάσσειν, κρεμάζειν, παρα-
τιθέναι, περιτιθέναι, ποιεῖν, προεκφέρειν, προσιέναι, προστιθέναι,
στηρίζειν, συνάγειν, φέρειν. This is a somewhat extreme instance, but a glance at Hatch and Redpath will shew that
there are many which do not fall far behind it, and that in the
majority of cases the ordinary words of the Hebrew Bible
have more than one equivalent in the Greek of the LXX.
The Alexandrian translators have evidently made an honest
endeavour to distinguish between the several connotations of
the Hebrew words. Thus, to take a few examples: קֵץ is
variously rendered by ἄκρον, ἀρχή, κλίτος, μέρος, πέρας, τάξις,

---

[1] The example is suggested by Dr Hatch (*Essays*, p. 18), who gives
many of the passages at length. The *index Hebraeus* at the end of Trom-
mius will enable the student to add other instances (besides διδόναι and its
compounds).

χρόνος; among the equivalents of דָּבָר are ἀπόκρισις, ἐπερώτησις, κρίμα, πρᾶγμα, τρόπος, φωνή; for לֵב we have not only
καρδία, ψυχή, φρήν, νοῦς, διάνοια, στόμα, φρόνησις, but στῆθος
and even σάρξ; for פָּקַד, ἀριθμεῖν, ἐπισκέπτεσθαι, ἐτάζειν, ἐκδι-
κεῖν; for צְדָקָה, δικαιοσύνη, ἐλεημοσύνη, εὐφροσύνη. Conversely,
the same Greek word often serves for several Hebrew words.
Thus διαθήκη, which is generally the LXX. rendering of בְּרִית,
stands also for עֵדוּת (Exod. xxvii. 21, xxxi. 7), תּוֹרָה (Dan.
ix. 13, LXX.) and even דָּבָר (Deut. ix. 5); ἐξαιρεῖν, λυτροῦν,
ῥύεσθαι are all used to represent גָּאַל; εἴδωλον appears in different
contexts for צֶלֶם, פֶּסֶל, עֹצֶב, בָּמָה, חַמָּן, חֶבֶל, בַּעַל, אֱלִיל, אֱלוֹהַּ, אֵל,
תְּרָפִים, שִׁקֻּץ. Even in the same context or verse this some-
times occurs. Thus in Gen. i.—iii. γῆ translates אֲדָמָה, אֶרֶץ,
עָפָר, שָׂדֶה; in Exod. xii. 23 עָבַר and פֶּסַח are both represented
by παρέρχεσθαι; in Num. xv. 4 f. θυσία is used both for מִנְחָה
and זֶבַח. In such cases it is difficult to acquit the translators
of carelessness; but they are far less frequent than instances
of the opposite kind. On the whole the LXX. even in the
Pentateuch shews no poverty of words, and considerable skill
in the handling of synonyms.

(*d*) In reference to metaphors the Alexandrians allow
themselves some discretion. Thus in Gen. vi. 2 'the sons of
God' become οἱ ἄγγελοι τοῦ θεοῦ; in Num. xxiv. 17 'a sceptre
(שֵׁבֶט) shall rise' is rendered by ἀναστήσεται ἄνθρωπος; in Deut.
x. 16 'the foreskin of your heart' is turned euphemistically into
τὴν σκληροκαρδίαν ὑμῶν; in Isa. ix. 14 μέγαν καὶ μικρόν represents
Heb. 'both branch and rush.' Occasionally the translators
indulge in *paronomasia*, without authority from the Heb., e.g.
Gen. xxv. 27 οἰκῶν οἰκίαν = יֹשֵׁב אֹהָלִים; xxvi. 18 καὶ ἐπωνόμασεν αὐτοῖς ὀνόματα שֵׁמוֹת לָהֶן וַיִּקְרָא; Job xxvii. 12 κενὰ κενοῖς;
xxx. 13 ἐξετρίβησαν τρίβοι μου.

(*e*) Lastly, the reader of the Septuagint must expect to
find a large number of actual blunders, due in part perhaps to

a faulty archetype, but chiefly to the misreading or misunderstanding of the archetype by the translators. Letters or clauses have often been transposed; omissions occur which may be explained by homoioteleuton; still' more frequently the translation has suffered through an insufficient knowledge of Hebrew or a failure to grasp the sense of the context. It follows that the student must be constantly on his guard against errors which may easily result from too ready an acceptance of the evidence offered by the Alexandrian version. Taken as a whole, and judged in the light of the circumstances under which it was produced, it is a monument of the piety, the skill, and the knowledge of the Egyptian Jews who lived under the Ptolemies, and it is an invaluable witness to the pre-Christian text of the Old Testament. But whether for textual or for hermeneutical purposes it must be used with caution and reserve, as the experience of the Ancient Church shews. With this subject we shall deal in a future chapter; it is sufficient to note the fact here.

III. The beginner, for whose use this chapter is chiefly intended, will now be prepared to open his Septuagint and his Hebrew Bible, and to compare the two in some familiar contexts. The following notes may assist him in a first effort to grapple with the problems which present themselves.

GEN. xv. 1—6.

1. Τὰ ῥήματα...ῥῆμα, Heb. דָּבָר...דְּבָרִים. Λέγων = לֵאמֹר; cf. *v.* 4, where, as elsewhere, Aq. renders, τῷ λέγειν. Ὑπερασπίζω σου, Heb. '*am* a shield to thee'; cf. Deut. xxxiii. 29, Prov. ii. 7, al. Ὁ μισθός σου πολύς. Vulg., A.V., R.V. connect Heb. with the foregoing, supplying וֹ. 2. Δεσπότης = אֲדֹנָי, as in *v.* 8, and not infrequently in Jer. and Dan. (LXX.). Ἀπολύομαι ἄτεκνος—an interpretation rather than a literal rendering of הוֹלֵךְ עֲרִירִי¹. Υἱὸς Μάσεκ τῆς οἰκογενοῦς μου = בֶּן מֶשֶׁק בֵּת בֵּיתִי: cf. Hieron. *quaest.*

---

¹ Philo has ἀπελεύσομαι (see below).

in Gen. "ubi nos habemus *Et filius Masec vernaculae meae*, in Hebraeo scriptum est וּבֶן מֶשֶׁק בֵּיתִי, quod Aquila transtulit ὁ υἱὸς τοῦ ποτίζοντος οἰκίαν μου...Theodotio vero καὶ υἱὸς τοῦ ἐπὶ τῆς οἰκίας μου." Δαμασκὸς Ἐλιέζερ, a literal rendering of the Heb., leaving the difficulty unsolved. 3. Ἐπειδή = הֵן, and so in xviii. 31, xix. 19; did LXX. read אִם? Οἰκογενής here = בֶּן־הַבָּיִת. Κληρονομήσει με—a Hebraism, = κληρονόμος μου ἔσται. 4. Καὶ εὐθὺς ...ἐγένετο = וְהִנֵּה. Φωνή = דָּבָר, as in xi. 1, but apparently not elsewhere. Ὅς...οὗτος, הוּא...אֲשֶׁר. Ἐκ σοῦ, euphemism for Heb. מִמֵּעֶיךָ, unless the LXX. read מִמְּךָ. 5. Πρὸς αὐτόν, ∧ Heb. 6. Καὶ ἐπίστευσεν = וַיֹּאמֶן (cf. Haupt *ad loc.*). Ἀβράμ, ∧ Heb. Τῷ θεῷ = בַּיהוָה. Ἐλογίσθη...εἰς δικ., Heb. 'he counted it...for righteousness'; possibly the LXX. read as in Ps. cvi. 31 (M.T.), where they have the same rendering. The N.T. follows LXX. here (Jas. ii. 23, Rom. iv. 3, Gal. iii. 6).

EXOD. xix. 16—24.

16. Ἐγένετο δὲ...καὶ ἐγένοντο = וַיְהִי...וַיְהִי. Γενηθέντος πρὸς ὄρθρον = בִּהְיֹת הַבֹּקֶר. Ἐπ᾿ ὄρους Σεινά, Heb. 'on the mountain.' Φωνή, cod. F with 𝕸 pr. καί. 17. Ὑπὸ τὸ ὄρος Σ. (om. Σ. AF), Heb. 'at the nether part (בְּתַחְתִּית) of the mountain.' 18. Διὰ τὸ καταβεβηκέναι, an idiomatic rendering of מִפְּנֵי־אֲשֶׁר יָרַד. Τὸν θεόν = יהוה, cf. 21. Ὁ καπνός, Heb. 'the smoke of it.' Ἐξέστη, Heb. as *v.* 16 where LXX. renders ἐπτοήθη. Ὁ λαός = הָעָם; M.T., הָהָר. 19. Προβαίνουσαι ἰσχυρότεραι = הֹולֵךְ וְחָזֵק. 20. Ἐκάλεσεν ...Μωϋσῆν, Heb. לְמֹשֶׁה; the ל after קרא is dropt in accordance with Greek idiom[1]. 21. Λέγων, ∧ Heb. Ἐγγίσωσιν, a softening of the Heb. 'break forth' (הֲרֹס); in the next verse ἐγγίζειν = נגשׁ *ni.* 22. καί, Heb. 'and also' (וְגַם), usually καί γε, Aq. καὶ καίγε (Burkitt, *Aquila*, p. 13). Κυρίῳ τῷ θεῷ, a double rendering of אֶל יְהוָה. Ἀπαλλάξῃ ἀπ᾿ αὐτῶν: another instance of euphemism: Heb. 'break forth upon them' (Aq. διακόψῃ ἐν αὐτοῖς). 23. Προσαναβῆναι: the double compound occurs six times in Jos. xi.—xix. Ἀφόρισαι: the verb is here as in *v.* 12 the equivalent of גבל *hi.* 'enclose,' but with the added thought of consecration which is latent in ἀφορίζειν, ἀφόρισμα, ἀφορισμός (cf. Exod. xxix.

---

[1] Or, as Dr Nestle suggests, it may have been taken as introducing the acc., as in later Hebrew or in Aramaic.

26, Ezech. xx. 40). 24. Ἀπολέσῃ, euphemistic, as ἀπαλλάξῃ in
v. 22; Aq. again, διακόψῃ.

NUM. xxiii. 7—10.

7. Παραβολήν: here for the first time =מָשָׁל. Lyons Pent.,
parabula. Μεσοποταμίας, i.e. אֲרַם נַהֲרַיִם (Gen. xxiv. 10), or פַּדֶּן
אֲרָם (Gen. xxv. 20): here an interpretation of the simple אֲרָם.
Ἀπ᾽, λέγων, ʌ Heb. Ἐπικατάρασαί μοι, and καταράσωμαι in *v.* 8,
represent זֹעַם, whilst ἄρασαι answers to ארר, and ἀράσωμαι (*v.* 8)
to נקב, an unusual instance of carelessness or poverty of
language on the part of the translator; ὀρέων (*v.* 9) is equally
unfortunate as a rendering of צֻרִים, while on the other hand
ὄψομαι, προσνοήσω fairly represent the Heb. Προσνοεῖν renders
שׁוּר again in Job xx. 9, xxiv. 15. 10. Ἐξακριβάζεσθαι (Num.[1], Job[1],
Dan. LXX.[1]), a late form for ἐξακριβοῦν in LXX. and Jos. Τὸ
σπέρμα, Heb. 'the dust': did LXX. read זרע, or have they glossed
עפר? Καὶ τίς ἐξαριθμήσεται, reading וּמִי יִסְפֹּר. Δήμους Ἰσραήλ,
Heb. 'the fourth part of Israel' (Aq. τοῦ τετάρτου Ἰ.). Ἡ ψυχή
μου, as Heb., whilst the next word is sacrificed to an alliteration
(ψυχή, ψυχαῖς). Τὸ σπέρμα μου is a gloss on אַחֲרִיתִי (cf. Brown,
Heb. and Eng. Lex., p. 31); ὡς τὸ σπέρμα τούτων, Heb. 'as he.'

This passage illustrates both the greater freedom which the
Greek translators allowed themselves in poetical contexts, and
their comparative incompetence to deal with them.

DEUT. vi. 1—9.

1. Αὗται αἱ ἐντολαί, Heb. 'this is the commandment.' Ὁ
θεὸς ἡμῶν, Heb. 'your God.' Οὕτως, ʌ Heb. Εἰσπορεύεσθε,
Heb. 'go over'; the Greek has lost the local reference, as in
iv. 14, 4 Regn. iv. 8. 2. Ἵνα φοβῆσθε...ὑμῶν, Heb. 2nd pers.
sing. Σήμερον, ʌ ﬦ. Οἱ υἱοὶ κτλ., Heb. 'thy son and thy
son's son.' Ἵνα μακροημερεύσητε, Heb. 'and that thy days may
be prolonged'; μακροημερεύειν (μακροήμερος γίνεσθαι) represents
this or a similar phrase in iv. 40, v. 30, xi. 9, 21, xxxii. 47; μακροχρόνιος, μακροχρονίζειν also occur in iv. 40, v. 16, xvii. 20,
xxxii. 27. The group is not found elsewhere in the LXX. except
in Exod.[1], Jud.[1], and in Sirach. 3. Δοῦναι ʌ M.T.; perhaps
added to complete the sense of the Greek; yet see *v.* 10 (לָתֶת לָךְ).
4. Καὶ ταῦτα...Αἰγύπτου ʌ Heb; perhaps repeated from iv. 45
to form an introduction to Ἄκουε κτλ. 5. Διανοίας...ψυχῆς...δυνά-
μεως. The readings vary; for διανοίας AF Luc. read καρδίας, and
the text of B is here *super rasuram*; for δυνάμεως some texts
give ἰσχύος. The N.T. citations (Mt. xxii. 37 = Mc. xii. 29 ff.,

Lc. x. 27) present much diversity, giving both renderings of לְבָבְךָ and both of מְאֹדֶךָ; cf. Dittmar, *V. T. in Novo*, p. 50 f. 6. καὶ ἐν τῇ ψυχῇ σου, ‸ Heb.; for 'in thy heart' Heb. has 'upon,' "as it were imprinted there (Jer. xxxi. 33)[1]." 7. Προβιβάσεις, Heb. 'shalt impress them upon'; Aq. δευτερώσεις, as if the root were שׁנה. 'Εν αὐτοῖς = בָּם. Καθήμενος κτλ., Heb. 'in thy sitting &c.'; ἐν οἴκῳ, ἐν ὁδῷ are inexact, Heb. 'in thy house,' 'in the way.' 8. 'Ασάλευτον (F, ἀσάλευτα) = לְטֹטָפֹת, 'for frontlets,' circlets or tires for the head: Lyons Pent. (reading σαλευτά), *mobilia*. 'Ασάλευτον occurs in the same phrase in Exod. xiii. 16, Deut. xi. 18. Aq. seems to have rendered the Heb. here and in Exod. by νακτά, i.e. 'compressed,' 'tight,' which Field (*Hexapla*, i. 103) explains as the "thecas in quas schedulae membraneae ...inferciebantur." The LXX. rendering may be an Alexandrian name for the φυλακτήριον, but the whole subject is obscure. 9. Φλιάς = מְזוּזֹת, as in Exod. xii. 7 ff.

JOS. x. 12—14.

12. Ἦ ἡμέρᾳ παρέδωκεν...ὑποχείριον—idiomatic rendering of בְּיוֹם תֵּת...לִפְנֵי. The words that follow (ἡνίκα...'Ισραήλ) seem to be a gloss derived from *v.* 10. Καὶ εἶπεν 'Ιησοῦς, Heb. 'and he said in the eyes of Israel.' Στήτω, Heb. 'be still.' Γαβαών, 𝕸 'Gibeon.' Αἰλών, 𝕸 'Aijalon' (אַיָּלוֹן); cf. 2 Chron. xi. 10 A, Αἰαλών. 13. 'Εν στάσει = עָמַד, which is thus distinguished from the verb represented by ἔστη. 'Ο θεός, Heb. גּוֹי, Aq. τὸ ἔθνος. Unless a primary error is to be suspected here, the LXX. has glossed its original, from motives of piety. After the stanza 𝕸 inserts a reference to the Book of Jashar, which is wanting in non-Hexaplaric texts of the LXX.; cod. G adds, ※ οὐχὶ τοῦτο γεγραμμένον ἐπὶ βιβλίου τοῦ εὐθοῦς ✢. Οὐ προεπορεύετο κτλ., a loose rendering of Heb. לֹא אָץ לָבוֹא כְּיוֹם תָּמִים. 14. 'Ημέρα τοιαύτη οὐδὲ τὸ πρότερον οὐδὲ τὸ ἔσχατον, a good example of a conscientious compromise between idiomatic and literal modes of rendering (cf. Heb.). 'Ανθρώπου, בְּקוֹל אִישׁ. Συνεπολέμησεν τῷ 'Ι., Heb. 'fought for Israel.'

JUD. v. 28—30[2].

28. 𝕲ᴮ here omits the difficult word ותיבב (𝕲ᴬ, καὶ κατεμάν-

---

[1] Driver, *ad loc.*
[2] In this passage the text of B in *O.T. in Greek*, i. 489, should be compared with that of A (ed. Brooke and McLean)

θανεν). Ἐκτὸς τοῦ τοξικοῦ, 'forth from the loophole'; cf. Symm. in Ezek. xl. 16 θυρίδες τοξικαί: ᏻᴬ διὰ τῆς δικτυωτῆς, 'through the lattice' (cf. 4 Regn. i. 2, Ezek. xli. 16). Ἐπιβλέπουσα...Σισαρά in A appears to be a supplementary gloss. Ἡσχύνθη (B) confuses בֹּשֵׁשׁ *pōlēl* with בּוֹשׁ *kal*; the general sense of the former is given by ἠσχάτισεν A. For ἐσχατίζειν cf. 1 Macc. v. 53; has it been suggested here by its similarity to the word used in B? Πόδες: A more literally ἴχνη, but πούς represents פַּעַם elsewhere, e.g. Ps. lvi. (lvii.) 6, Prov. xxix. 5. 29. Αἱ σοφαὶ ἄρχουσαι: A, again aiming at a literal rendering, σοφαὶ ἀρχουσῶν. On the other hand B's ἀπέστρεψεν λόγους αὐτῆς ἑαυτῇ is close and yet idiomatic, while A's ἀπεκρίνατο ἐν ῥήμασιν αὐτῆς goes too far afield; the latter appears to be a Hexaplaric correction (Field, *ad loc.*). 30. Οὐχ εὑρήσουσιν αὐτὸν διαμερίζοντα σκύλα; so ᏻᴮᴬ; Heb. 'are they not finding, [are they not] dividing booty?' LXX. seem to have read מחלק for יחלקו. Οἰκτείρμων οἰκτειρήσει B, φιλιάζων φίλοις A; both, while labouring to keep up the alliteration of the Heb., miss its point through ignorance of a rare use of רַחַם[1]; for φιλιάζειν cf. xiv. 20 B, 2 Chron. xix. 2. Ποικιλτῶν (A, ποικίλων) misses the dual 'embroidery on both sides' (R. V.), or 'a couple of pieces,' "precisely as רחמתים above" (Moore). Βάθη in A seems to be an error for βαφή, which is found in several cursives; see Field, *ad loc.*, and Lagarde's Lucian. Τῷ τραχήλῳ αὐτοῦ σκύλα = apparently לצואריו שלל; M.T. 'for the necks of the spoil.' ᏻᴬ substitutes the usual ἀνατολή for the spirited and literal rendering of B (cf. Ps. xviii.=xix. 7), and appears to have read בגברתי; cf. Ps. xix. (xx.) 7.

This passage is a severe test of the translator's knowledge and skill, and shews him perhaps at his worst.

1 REGN. xvii. 37—43.

37. 𝕸 begins וַיֹּאמֶר דָּוִד, A, Luc. καὶ εἶπεν Δ. Ἐκ χειρὸς τοῦ λέοντος...τῆς ἄρκου, an exact rendering; cf. Gen. ix. 5 ἐκ χειρὸς πάντων τῶν θηρίων. Luc., Th., ἐκ στόματος τοῦ λ. καὶ ἐκ χειρὸς τῆς ἄρκου. Τοῦ ἀπεριτμήτου, repeated from *v.* 36 (Λ 𝕸). 38. μανδύαν (Jud. iii. 16, 2 Regn. x. 4): +αὐτοῦ, A, with 𝕸. Περικεφαλαίαν χ. περὶ τὴν κεφαλὴν αὐτοῦ: Luc. (A), with 𝕸, π. χ. ἐπέθηκεν ἐπί κτλ., adding, καὶ ἐνέδυσεν αὐτῷ θώρακα. 39. Ἔζωσεν τὸν Δαυείδ, sc. Σαούλ (cf. *v.* 38); Luc., A, follow Heb. in making David the object of the verb (ἐζώσατο Δαυείδ). Ἐκοπίασεν περιπατήσας (A, περιπατῆσαι) ἅπαξ καὶ δίς, 'more than once he wearied

---

1 "Of the versions only [Vulg.] comes near the true sense" (Moore). Jerome renders *pulcherrima feminarum.*

himself with walking (strove to walk) in them,' reading וַיֵּלֶא, as in Gen. xix. 11 וַיִּלְאוּ, LXX. παρελύθησαν (Wellhausen, Driver, H. P. Smith). Ἅπαξ καὶ δίς occurs also in Deut. ix. 13 (where, as here, there is nothing in the Heb. to correspond), and in Neh. xiii. 20, where it represents פַּעַם וּשְׁתָּיִם. Ἀφαιροῦσιν αὐτὰ ἀπ' αὐτοῦ, reading the verb probably as וַיְסִרֵם, and omitting דּוּד. 40. Λίθους τελείους in B is obviously wrong, and A scarcely mends matters by omitting the adjective. Correct, with Lucian, λίθους λείους. Ἐν τῷ καδίῳ ποιμενικῷ : καδίον = καδίσκος, here only in LXX., and perhaps unknown elsewhere : ποιμενικός (הָרֹעִים) again in Zach. xi. 15. Εἰς συλλογήν, apparently for לִילְקוּט (בִגְבִלְקוֹט, Aq. καὶ ἐν ἀναλεκτηρίῳ). 41 is wanting in 𝔊B, and probably belongs to the same recension of the story which has supplied the great gaps vv. 12—31, 55—xviii. 5. 42. Heb. 'looked and saw'; so A, Luc. Πυρράκης· cf. xvi. 12, Gen. xxv. 25. 43. Ὡσεί, added by the translators to soften the opprobrious κύων. Ἐν ῥάβδῳ καὶ λίθοις, 𝔐 'in (with) staves'; καὶ λίθοις is probably intended to make the question correspond to the statement of *v.* 40. The next words in the LXX. καὶ εἶπεν Δαυείδ Οὐχί, ἀλλ' ἢ χείρω[ν] κυνός are evidently of the same character—a "singularly vapid reply" (Driver).

4 REGN. ii. 11—18.

11. Αὐτῶν πορευομένων ἐπορεύοντο καὶ ἐλάλουν—an interesting attempt to combine Greek idiom with some reminiscence of the Heb. phrase; Lucian abandons the Heb., and corrects, αὐτῶν πορευομένων καὶ λαλούντων. Ἵππος πυρός, Heb. 'horses of fire'; cf. ἱππεύς, Heb. 'horsemen,' *v.* 12. Ἀνὰ μέσον (בֵּין), cf. Gen. i. 7 διεχώρισεν...ἀνὰ μέσον. Ἀνελήμφθη, Heb. 'went up'; the Greek verb is apparently repeated from vv. 9, 10, where it = לקה. From this passage it has been borrowed by the translator of Sirach (xlviii. 9, 14, xlix. 14, B), and by two writers in the N.T. ('Mc.' xvi. 19, Acts i. 2, 11); on its symbolical use see the writer's *Apostles' Creed*, p. 70 f. Ὡς, ₐ Heb.; cf. 1 Regn. xvii. 43 (above). 12. Πάτερ πάτερ, Heb. 'my father' *bis*. Διέρρηξεν...ῥήγματα, after the Heb.: Lucian omits the noun, probably because of the harshness of the assonance. 13. Καὶ ὕψωσεν = וירם ; Luc., καὶ ἀνείλατο. Μηλωτήν, 'sheepskin,' an interpretation of אַדֶּרֶת (Vulg. *pallium*) wherever it is used of Elijah's characteristic raiment (3 Regn. xix. 13, 19, 4 Regn. ii. 8 ff.); cf. Heb. xi. 37 περιῆλθον ἐν μηλωταῖς. Ἐπάνωθεν, sc. αὐτοῦ (Heb., Luc.). Ἐλεισαῖε, ₐ Heb.; καὶ ἐπέστρεψεν Ἐλεισαῖε is Hexaplaric, and wanting in B*, but

supplied by B^(ab) A Luc. 14. ʹΟ θεός, 𝕸 יְהוָֹה אֱלֹהָי. ʹΑφφώ, a transliteration answering to אַף הוּא (𝕸.); in x. 10 the same form = אֱפוֹא, which was perhaps the reading before the LXX. in this place. Aq. καίπερ αὐτός, but Symm. καὶ νῦν, whence Jerome *etiam nunc.* 15. καὶ οἱ ἐν ʹΙερειχώ: ʌ καί A Luc. with 𝕸. 16. יֵשׁ is not represented by 𝕲^(AB); Luc. adds εἰσί. Υἱοὶ δυνάμεως, בְּנֵי־חַיִל. ʹΕν τῷ ʹΙορδάνῃ, ʹΕλεισαῖε, ʌ Heb., Luc. 18. In A Luc. Aq. Th. 𝕸 the verse begins 'And they returned to him'; cf. *v.* 13.

Ps. cix. (cx.) 1—4.

1. [ʹΟ] κύριος τῷ κυρίῳ μου, יְהוָֹה לַאדֹנִי. ʹΕκ δεξιῶν, לִימִינִי; in *v.* 5 the same Gr. is used for עַל יְמִינִי. Υποπόδιον τῶν ποδῶν σου: ὑποκάτω is the reading of the best authorities in Mt. xxii. 44, Mc. xii. 36, but ὑποπ. keeps its place in Lc.^(ev. act.), Hebrews. 2. καὶ κατακυρίευε = ורדה apparently. 3. Μετὰ σοῦ, עִמְּךָ (𝕸, עַמְּךָ). ʹΗ ἀρχή seems to point to a reading נדיבה or נדיבת (cf. Job xxx. 15, Isa. xxxii. 8); τῶν ἁγίων (σου) = קדשים (קדשיך); Symm. ἐν ὄρεσιν (בהררי) for בהדרי (ἁγίοις. ʹΕκ γαστρὸς πρὸ ἑωσφόρου ἐγέννησά σε, though not quoted in the N.T., had an important place in post-apostolic Christian teaching from Justin onwards (cf. Justin, *Tryph.* cc. 63, 76, 83; Tert. *adv. Marc.* v. 9; Cypr. *test.* 17, *ep.* 63); in the Arian age it was commonly cited on the Catholic side —see e.g. Cyril. Hierus., *catech.* vii. 2, xi. 5; Athan. *or. c. Arian.* iv. 27 sq.; *de decr.* 3, &c.; Hilar. *de trin.* vi. 16, xii. 8. The O.L. seems to have rendered uniformly *ex utero ante luciferum genui te,* with the variant *generavi* in Tert. *l.c.*; Jerome's 'Hebrew' Psalter reads with 𝕸 *quasi de vulva orietur tibi ros adolescentiae.* The LXX. appear to have read their Heb. text as מרחם מִשְׁחָר יַלְדֻתֶּיךָ, perhaps dropping לכטל as unintelligible. 4. Κατὰ τὴν τάξιν, עַל דִּבְרָתִי, Aq. Symm. κατὰ λόγον. Cf. Heb. v. 6 ff., vii. 11, 15 (κατὰ τὴν ὁμοιότητα). The translator probably had before him the LXX. of Gen. xiv. 18; he transliterates the unique name מלכי־צדק in the same way.

PROV. viii. 22—25, 30—31.

22. ʺΕκτισέν με. So 𝕲^(אBA etc.) O.L. (*condidit, creavit*); codd. 23 = V, 252, with Aq. Symm. Th. Vulg. (*possedit*), give ἐκτήσατο—both possible meanings of קנה. The former rendering supplied the Arians with one of their stock arguments (cf. Athan. *or. c. Arian.* ii. 44 sqq.). Εἰς ἔργα αὐτοῦ, a loose and partial translation, probably a confession of inability to understand the Heb.; Th.

πρὸ τῆς ἐργασίας ἀπὸ τότε. 23. Ἐθεμελίωσέν με, reading apparently יסדני where 𝕸 has נָסַכְתִּי; cf. Ps. lxxvii. (lxxviii.) 69. Πρὸ τοῦ τὴν γῆν ποιῆσαι, a poor rendering of Heb., probably adopted to bring this clause into line with *v.* 24 with which the LXX. seem to have connected it. 24. LXX. overlook חוללתי and נכבדי, unless they intend to convey the general sense by ποιῆσαι and προελθεῖν. 25. Πάντων, ∧ 𝕸. Γεννᾷ με, 𝕸 'I was brought forth.' 30. ἁρμόζουσα = אָמוֹן, the word being referred by the translator to אמן; similarly Symm. Th., ἐστηριγμένη. Ἡ προσέχαιρεν implies the reading שעשועיו; יום יום is connected by LXX. with the next clause. 31. Ὅτε...συντελέσας : Heb. 'rejoicing in the world of his earth.' LXX. seem to have read משחק בתכלית, as Lagarde suggests; had תבל stood in their text, οἰκουμένη would have been ready at hand as a rendering (cf. 2 Regn. xxii. 16, Ps. ix. 9, &c.). Εὐφραίνετο, reading שעשעיו. Υἱοὶ ἀνθρώπων = בְּנֵי אָדָם ; cf. υἱοὺς Ἀδάμ, Deut. xxxii. 8; ב' אָדָם is translated by this phrase in Ps. x. (xi.) 4, and repeatedly in the poetical books.

JOB xix. 23—27.

23. Τίς γὰρ ἂν δῴη ; See above p. 308 ; the phrase is repeated in the Hebrew, but the translator contents himself with using it once. אֵפוֹ is ignored ; its usual equivalent in the LXX. is νῦν or οὖν, unless it is transliterated (p. 324). Εἰς τὸν αἰῶνα seems to represent לָעַד, which in 𝕸 belongs to the next verse ; Th. translates it εἰς μαρτύριον, reading the word as לְעֵד. 24. B* omits ἐν πέτραις ἐγγλυφῆναι which appears to be necessary to the sense ; in supplying it BᵃᵇאA prefix ἤ, a manifest gloss. 25. Ἀέναός ἐστιν ὁ ἐκλύειν με μέλλων, a paraphrase of Heb. 'my *Goel* lives' ; ἀέναος in the LXX. elsewhere = עֹלָם, and גֹּאֵל is ἀγχιστεύς (Ruth iii. 9, etc.), or λυτρωτής (Ps. xviii. 14, lxxvii. 35). 25—26. Ἐπὶ γῆς ἀναστῆσαι or ἀναστήσει appears to correspond with עַל עָפָר יָקוּם (קים), and τὸ δέρμα μου τὸ ἀναντλοῦν ταῦτα with עוֹרִי נִקְּפוּ זֹאת. 𝕲ᴬ points to לְחָיוֹת עוֹרִי מְכַלְכֵּל זֹאת (Siegfried in Haupt *ad loc.*). But the translator perhaps interprets his text in the light of the doctrine of the Resurrection, which was accepted from Maccabean times (cf. Job xlii. 17ᵃ, and see Dan. xii. 2, 2 Macc. vii. 14, xii. 43) ; as cited by Clem. R. 1 Cor. 26 (ἀναστήσεις τὴν σάρκα μου ταύτην τὴν ἀναντλήσασαν ταῦτα πάντα), the words are brought into still nearer agreement with the faith of the

Church; see *Apostles' Creed*, p. 89 f. Παρὰ γὰρ Κυρίου...συνετε-
λέσθη corresponds in position with words which 𝔐 divides and
points as וּמִבְּשָׂרִי אֶחֱזֶה אֱלוֹהַּ, but seems to be partly borrowed
from the next verse. 𝔊ᴬ suggests וּמֵאֱלוֹהַּ נֶעֱשׂוּ לִי אֵלֶּה (Siegfried).   27. Πάντα δέ μοι συντετέλεσται· 𝔐, כָּלוּ כִלְיֹתַי.

MICAH v. 1 (iv. 14)—4 (3).

1. Ἐμφραχθήσεται θυγάτηρ ἐμφραγμῷ, i.e. תתגדרי בת גדר.
Τὰς φυλὰς τοῦ Ἰσραήλ : LXX. read שִׁבְטֵי יִשְׂרָאֵל for 'י שֹׁפֵט.   2. Βηθλέεμ οἶκος Ἐφράθα : did LXX. read בֵּית־לֶחֶם בֵּית אֶפְרָתָה? 'Ολιγο-
στὸς εἶ τοῦ εἶναι 'art little to be,' as Heb.   The passage is quoted
in Mt. ii. 6 in a Greek paraphrase[1] which substitutes οὐδαμῶς
ἐλαχίστη for 'little to be,' and τοῖς ἡγεμόσιν (אַלֻּפֵי) for 'thousands'
(אַלְפֵי).   3. Ἕως καιροῦ τικτούσης τέξεται, apparently for ἕως καιροῦ
οὗ τίκτουσα τέξεται or ἕ. κ. τικτούσης ὅτε τέξεται.   4. Καὶ ὄψεται,
τὸ ποίμνιον αὐτοῦ were obelised in Hex. and find no place in 𝔐;
the former has perhaps originated in a misreading of ורעה as
וראה, so that καὶ ὄψ. καὶ ποιμανεῖ is in fact a doublet. Κύριος,
subject; Heb. 'in the strength of J.,' the subject being the same
as in *v.* 1. Ὑπάρξουσιν, וְיָשְׁבוּ; the LXX. read ישבו, connecting
the verb with the previous words; for ישב=ὑπάρχειν cf. Ps.
liv. (lv.) 20 ὁ ὑπάρχων πρὸ τῶν αἰώνων.

JEREM. xxxviii. 31—37 (xxxi. 30—36).

Vv. 31—34 are cited in Heb. viii. 8—12, q.v.   31. Διαθήσομαι,
in Hebrews συντελέσω, cf. Jer. xli. (xxxiv.) 8 συντελέσαι (כרת)
διαθήκην, and ib. 15. Τῷ οἴκῳ *bis*, in Hebrews ἐπὶ τὸν οἶκον.
32. Διεθέμην, in Hebrews ἐποίησα : the writer appears to dislike
the repeated alliteration in διατίθεσθαι διαθήκην. Ἐν ἡμέρᾳ ἐπι-
λαβομένου μου, for the more usual τοῦ ἐπιλαβέσθαι με or ὅτε (ᾗ)
ἐπελαβόμην. Ὅτι οὐκ ἐνέμειναν ἐν...Heb. 'which...they broke';
ἠμέλησα αὐτῶν, reading גָּעַלְתִּי for בָּעַלְתִּי.   33. ἡ διαθήκη μου, Heb.
'the covenant.' Διδοὺς δώσω, a Hebraism not represented in 𝔐; in
Hebrews διδούς appears without δώσω, and so AQ in Jer. Εἰς τὴν
διάνοιαν αὐτῶν, Heb. 'in their inward parts.'   34. עוֹד 1° has no
equivalent in the Greek; τὸν πολίτην αὐτοῦ, Heb. 'his neighbours'
(cf. Prov. xi. 9. 12, xxiv. 43=28), reminds us that we are dealing

---

[1] The paraphrastic character of the reference appears more distinctly in
the second stanza ἐκ σοῦ...Ἰσραήλ, which blends Mic. v. 1ᵇ, 3ᵃ. It will
be observed that cod. A reads ἡγούμενος with Mt.

with an Alexandrian version. 'Aπό...ἕως, וְעַד ...לְ; ἀδικίαις... ἁμαρτιῶν, ℳ, 'iniquity,' 'sin.' 35—37. In ℳ 36, 37 precede 35. 35. Φησὶν Κύριος, Heb. 'thus saith J.' (at the beg. of the verse). Ὑψωθῇ, reading יָרוּמוּ for יָמֻדּוּ; ταπεινωθῇ, Heb. 'be searched.' Οὐκ ἀποδοκιμῶ : ἀποδ. is a contracted future (cf. p. 305); οὐκ is inserted, because the drift of the verse has been misunderstood (cf. Streane, p. 156 f.). Τὸ γένος Ἰσραήλ, Heb. 'all the seed of I.'; γένος = זֶרַע again in *v.* 37. 36. Σελήνην, ℳ, 'the ordinances of the moon' (but cf. הַחֻקִּים in *v.* 35, Heb.). Κραυγήν, reading perhaps רגש or רגן for רגע. 37. Κύριος Παντοκράτωρ = יְהוָה צְבָאוֹת, as almost invariably in the Prophets[1] from Hosea xii. 5 (6) onwards, with the exception of Isaiah, who transliterates צְבָאוֹת (Κύριος σαβαώθ, Isa. i. 9, al.). See Thackeray, *J. Th. St.* IV. p. 245 ff.; this passage is from his " Jer. β."

DAN. xii. 1—4.

1. Χώραν (LXX.), probably a corruption for ὥραν (cf. Bevan, p. 48); παρελεύσεται (LXX.), reading יעבר for יעמד (ἀναστήσεται, Th.). Ὁ ἄγγελος (LXX.), a gloss; Th. literally, ὁ ἄρχων. Ἐπὶ τοὺς υἱούς (LXX., Th.), ...עַל בְּנֵי. Ἐκείνη ἡ ἡμέρα, LXX., ἔσται καιρός Th.; Th. is again more literal than LXX. Θλίψις οἵα οὐ γέγονεν (cf. Mt. xxiv. 21, Mc. xiii. 19). Th. repeats the subject with the view of preventing ambiguity; in the sequel LXX. (as handed down to us) overlook וּ, while Th. adds ἐν τῇ γῇ or ἐπὶ τῆς γῆς. Ὑψωθήσεται LXX.; Bevan suggests a corruption for ἐκσωθήσεται or some other compound of σωθήσεται; but ὑψ. may be a gloss upon the tamer word which stood in the original. Th. rightly, σωθήσεται. Ὃς ἂν εὑρεθῇ, הַנִּמְצָא—overlooked by Th., unless we accept the reading of AQ, ὁ εὑρεθεὶς [ὁ] γεγραμμένος. 2. Ἐν τῷ πλάτει τῆς γῆς, LXX.; ἐν γῆς χώματι Th., Heb. 'in the ground of dust' (but see Bevan, p. 201 f.). Διασπορὰν καὶ αἰσχύνην, LXX.; διασπ. is perhaps a gloss on αἰσχ.; for the word see Deut. xxviii. 25. 3. Οἱ φωστῆρες τοῦ οὐρανοῦ, LXX., a reminiscence of Gen. i. 14 (LXX.); cf. Sap. xiii. 2. Οἱ κατισχύοντες τοὺς λόγους LXX., reading מַהֲדִיקִים הָרַבִּים for מַצְדִּיקֵי־הָרַבִּים; Th. translates מַצְדִּיקִים הָרַבִּים. Τὰ ἄστρα τοῦ οὐρανοῦ (LXX.), the ordinary Biblical phrase, used in iii. 36, 63; Heb., Th. have 'the stars.' 4. Ἀπομανῶσιν (LXX.), διδαχθῶσιν (Th.). Both senses have been found in the Heb.; cf. Bevan, *ad loc.* Πλησθῇ ἡ γῆ ἀδικίας, LXX., reading רעה or רעת for דעת.

---

[1] Zech. xiii. 2, Jer. xxvi. (xlvi.) 10 are the only exceptions, and in both cases the MSS. are divided.

The student who has gone through these extracts, or who is able to dispense with help of this kind, is recommended to begin the careful study of some one book or group of books. For several reasons the Books of Samuel (1—2 Regn.) offer a promising field for work of this kind. They are on the whole the part of the Old Testament in which the value of the Septuagint is most manifest and most generally recognised[1], and invaluable help in the study of both the Hebrew text and the versions is at hand in the commentaries of Wellhausen, Driver, and H. P. Smith[2]. But whatever book may be selected, the method and the aims of the reader will be the same. He will read the Greek in the first place as a version, and he will use all the means at his disposal for ascertaining the original text which lay behind it. But he will read. it also as a monument of early Hellenistic Greek, and mark with growing interest its use of words and phrases which, originating at Alexandria in connexion with the work of translating the Hebrew Scriptures, eventually became the vehicle of a fuller revelation in the writings of the Apostolic age.

LITERATURE on the general subject of this chapter : *Pearsoni praefatio paraenetica* (Cambridge, 1665; *cum notulis E. Churton*, 1865); Hody, *De Bibl. textibus originalibus* (Oxford, 1705); Dr T. Brett, *A Letter showing why our English Bibles differ from the Septuagint*, London, 1743 (dated Oct. 17, 1729); *A Dissertation on the Ancient Versions of the Bible*, London, 1760; Thiersch, *De Pent. vers. Alexandrina* (Erlangen, 1841); Frankel, *Vorstudien zu der Septuaginta* (Leipzig, 1841); *Ueber den Einfluss der palästinischen Exegese auf die alex. Hermeneutik*, 1857 ; Geiger, *Nachgelassene Schriften*, iv. 73 ff. (Berlin, 1875—8); Selwyn, art. *Septuagint* in Smith's *D. B.* ii. (London, 1863); Wellhausen, do. in *Encyclopaedia Britannica* (London, 1886);

---

[1] W. R. Smith, *O. T. in J. Church*, p. 83.
[2] If the student prefers to begin with Genesis, he will learn much as to the LXX. version from Spurrell's *Notes* (ed. 2, 1898). For more advanced study Proverbs will form a suitable subject, and here he may seek help from Lagarde's *Anmerkungen*, and Professor Toy's commentary in the ' International Critical ' series.

W. R. Smith, *Old Testament in Jewish Church* (1881, ed. 2, 1892); Hatch, *Essays in Biblical Greek* (Oxford, 1889); Driver, *Notes on the Books of Samuel*, Intr. (Oxford, 1890; second ed., 1913); Buhl, *Kanon u. Text des O. T.* (Leipzig, 1891); Nestle, *Marginalien* (Tübingen, 1893); Streane, *Double Text of Jeremiah* (Cambridge, 1896); Kirkpatrick in *Expositor*, April 1896: Redpath in *A. J. Th.* VII. (1903); the various Introductions to the Old Testament; Commentaries on particular books, esp. those of Dillmann and Spurrell (Genesis), Driver (Deuteronomy), Moore (Judges), Wellhausen, Driver, and H. P. Smith (Samuel), Burney (Kings), Mozley (Psalter), Toy (Proverbs), Ryssel (Micah), Oesterley (Amos), Ottley (Isaiah), Cornill (Ezekiel). A complete commentary on the LXX., or on any of the groups of books which compose it, is still a *desideratum*.

On the Semitic style of the LXX. the reader may consult the Εἰσαγωγή of Adrianus (Migne, *P. G.* xcviii. or ed. F. Gössling).

CHAPTER VI.

TEXT-DIVISIONS: *STICHI*, CHAPTERS, LECTIONS, *CATENAE.*

THE Greek Old Testament, as it appears in the editions of the last three centuries, is divided into chapters and verses which correspond generally with those of the printed Hebrew Bible.

The traditional text-divisions of the Hebrew and the Greek Bible are not absolutely identical. Besides the more serious differences described in Part II. c. i., it not unfrequently happens that a Greek chapter is longer or shorter than the corresponding chapter of the Hebrew by a verse or more, and that as a consequence there are two systems of verse-numeration throughout the succeeding chapter[1].

A system of verse-division[2] is mentioned in the Mishnah (*Meg.* 4. 4, *Kidd.* 30. 1). The Massorets noted the number of verses (פְּסוּקִים) at the end of each book and portion of the canon; thus Deuteronomy is stated to consist of 955 *pesukim*, and the entire Torah of 5888. Of chapter-divisions in the Hebrew Bible there are three kinds. (*a*) There is a pre-Talmudic division of the canon into sections known as פרשיות. The parashahs are of two kinds, open and closed, i.e. para-

---

[1] In such cases both systems are represented in the Cambridge edition of the LXX. (see *O. T. in Greek*, i. p. xiv.).

[2] For a full account of the divisions of the Hebrew text see Buhl, *Kanon u. Text*, p. 222; Bleek-Wellhausen, p. 574 f.; Ryle, *Canon of the O. T.*, p. 235. Blau, *Massoretic Studies*, iii., in *J.Q.R.*, Oct. 1896.

graphs, which begin a new line, and sub-paragraphs[1], which are preceded only by a space. They are still registered in the printed Bibles by the פ (for פְּתוּחָה, 'open') and ס (for סְתוּמָה, 'closed') which occur at intervals throughout the Torah[2]. (*b*) A second system of parashahs breaks up the text into longer sections for the use of the synagogue. The Law was divided into 54 Sabbath lessons according to the Babylonian tradition, but into 154 according to the tradition of Palestine. With few exceptions[3] the beginning of a lesson coincides with that of an open or closed parashah; the coincidence is marked in the Torah by a thrice repeated פ or ס. The Prophets were similarly divided for synagogue reading, but the prophetic lections were known as *haphtaroth* (הַפְטָרוֹת) and were not, like the liturgical parashahs, distinguished by signs inserted in the text. (*c*) Lastly, the printed Hebrew Bibles are divided into chapters nearly identical with those of the English versions. This system of capitulation is relatively modern, and was applied first to the Latin Vulgate in the thirteenth century, probably by Stephen Langton, Archbishop of Canterbury († 1228)[4]. It was adapted to the Hebrew Bible in R. Isaac Nathan's Concordance, a work of the fifteenth century, in which use was also made of the older division into verses or *pesukim*.

Of printed editions the Bomberg Hebrew Bible of 1521 was the first to employ the mediaeval system of chapters; the verse-division found a place in the Latin version of Pagnini (1528), and the Latin Vulgate of Robert Stephen (1555), and finally in the Hebrew Bible of Athias (1661). Both chapters

---

[1] A similar system of paragraphing has been adopted in the English Revised Version, and in the Cambridge LXX.; see R.V. *Preface*, and *O.T. in Greek*, i. p. xv.

[2] In Baer's edition they are given throughout the Bible.

[3] In the Pentateuch there is only one, the lesson (12) which begins at Gen. xlvii. 28 (Ryle, p. 236).

[4] See Gregory, *prolegg.* p. 167 ff.

and verses were applied to the text of the Septuagint before the sixteenth century; the capitulation appeared in the Complutensian Polyglott and in the Aldine edition of 1518, and the verse-numeration in the Frankfort edition of the Aldine text[1].

Neither the verses nor the chapters of the existing text-division occur in MSS. of the Greek Old Testament, except in relatively later copies[2], or in older MSS. where the numerals have been supplied by a recent hand. But the student who examines MSS. of the LXX. or their facsimiles finds himself confronted by other systems which are both interesting and in some respects important. To these the present chapter will be devoted.

1.   We begin with the shorter divisions, known as στίχοι, κῶλα, or κόμματα.

(*a*) Στίχος, Lat. *versus*, is properly a series of objects placed in a row. The word is used in the LXX. of the stones in the High Priest's breastplate (στίχος λίθων, Exod. xxviii. 17 ff.), the pomegranates wrought upon the capitals of the pillars in the Temple (στίχοι ῥοῶν, 3 Regn. vii. 6), and the rows of cedar-wood shafts (τριῶν στίχων στύλων κεδρίνων, *ib.* 9). When applied to the art of writing, the word signifies a continuous line of letters or syllables. The extent of an author's literary work was measured by the *stichi* he had written; cf. e.g. Diogenes Laertius iv. 24, Κράντωρ κατέλιπεν ὑπομνήματα εἰς μυριάδας στίχων τρεῖς : Dionysius Halicarn. vi. 1126 πέντε ἢ ἐξ μυριάδας στίχων τοῦ ἀνδρὸς (sc. Δημοσθένους) καταλελοιπότος. The 'line' might be measured in various ways, as by the limits imposed upon the scribe by the breadth of his papyrus, or in the case of poetry by the number of feet in the metre; or again it might be fixed in each instance by the requirements of

---

[1] It prints the verse-numbers in the margin, and begins every verse with a capital letter.
[2] E.g. H.-P. 38 (xv.), 122 (xv.), where the modern chapters are marked.

the sense; or it might depend upon a purely conventional standard. Evidence has been produced[1] to shew that the last of these methods was adopted in the copying of Greek prose writings, and that the length of the prose *stichus* was determined by that of the Homeric hexameter, i.e. it was normally a line of sixteen syllables; in some instances the Iambic trimeter seems to have been the standard preferred, and the line consisted of twelve syllables[2]. The number of letters in the *stichus* was on the average 37—38 in the one case, and 28—29 in the other. Such a system served more than one useful purpose. Besides facilitating reference, it regulated the pay of the scribe, and consequently the price of the book. The number of the lines in a book once determined, it might be written in any form without affecting the cost[3]. The compiler of the Cheltenham list explains that dishonest scribes at Rome and elsewhere purposely suppressed or mutilated the stichometry[4]. Thus the careful entry of the στίχοι in the margins of ancient books, or the computation at the end of the number of στίχοι contained in them, was not due to mere custom or sentiment, but served an important practical end.

(*b*) Besides this conventional measurement there existed another system which regulated the length of the line by the sense. Sense-divisions were commonly known as κῶλα or κόμματα. The *colon*, according to Suidas, is a line which forms a complete clause (ὁ ἀπηρτισμένην ἔννοιαν ἔχων στίχος); the *comma* is a shorter *colon*[5].

This arrangement was originally used in transcribing poetry, but before Jerome's time it had been applied to the great prose

---

[1] By Ch. Graux, *Revue de philologie*, II. (1878), p. 97 ff.
[2] J. R. Harris, *Stichometry*, pp. 8, 15.
[3] See E. Maunde-Thompson, *Gr. and Lat. Palaeography*, i. p. 80 ; Prof. Sanday, in *Studia Biblica*, iii. p. 263 f.; J. R. Harris, *op. cit.* p. 26.
[4] "Indiculum versuum in urbe Roma non ad liquidum, sed et alibi avariciae causa non habent integrum."
[5] See Wordsworth-White, *Epilogus*, p. 733, nn. 1, 2.

authors; cf. Hieron. *praef. ad Isa.*[1]: "nemo cum prophetas versibus viderit esse descriptos, metro eos aestimet apud Hebraeos ligari, et aliquid simile habere de Psalmis vel operibus Salomonis; sed quod in Demosthene et Tullio solet fieri, ut per cola scribantur et commata, qui utique prosa et non versibus conscripserunt, nos quoque, utilitati legentium providentes, interpretationem novam scribendi genere distinximus"; *praef. in Ezech.*[2]: "legite igitur et hunc iuxta translationem nostram, quoniam per cola scriptus et commata manifestiorem legentibus sensum tribuit." Cf. Cassiod. *de inst. div. litt.*, praef. Hesychius of Jerusalem (†c. 433) treated the Greek text of the Dodecapropheton in the same way[3]: ἔστι μὲν ἀρχαῖον τοῦτο τοῖς θεοφόροις τὸ σπούδασμα στιχηδόν, ὡς τὰ πολλά, πρὸς τὴν τῶν μελετωμένων σαφήνειαν τὰς προφητείας ἐκτίθεσθαι. οὕτω τοιγαροῦν ὄψει μὲν τὸν Δαβὶδ κιθαρίζοντα, τὸν Παροιμιαστὴν δὲ τὰς παραβολὰς καὶ τὸν Ἐκκλησιαστὴν τὰς προφητείας ἐκθέμενον· οὕτω συγγραφεῖσαν τὴν ἐπὶ τῷ Ἰὼβ βίβλον, οὕτω μερισθέντα τοῖς στίχοις τὰ τῶν Ἀσμάτων ᾄσματα...οὐ μάτην ἐν ταῖς δώδεκα βίβλοις τῶν προφητῶν καὶ αὐτὸς ἠκολούθησα.

Specimens of colometry may be seen in Codd. א B, where the poetical books are written in *cola* of such length that the scribe has been compelled to limit himself in this part of his work to two columns instead of dividing his page into three or four.

Among the lists of the books of the O.T. canon printed in an earlier chapter of this book (Part II. c. i.) there are three which are accompanied by a stichometry. We will now collect their measurements and exhibit them in a tabular form.

Book.	Stichometry of Nicephorus.	Stichometry of Cod. Clarom.	Stichometry of Mommsen's list.
Genesis	4300	4500	3700
Exodus	2800	3700	3000
Leviticus	2700	2800	2300
Numbers	3530	3650	3000
Deuteronomy	3100	3300	2700
Joshua	2100	2000	1750
Judges	} 2450 {	2000	1750[4]
Ruth		250	250

---

[1] Migne, *P. L.* xxviii. 771.
[2] Migne, *P. L.* xxviii. 938.
[3] Migne, *P. G.* xxiii. 1339 sq.
[4] Total of first 7 books, ' 18000.'

Book.	Stichometry of Nicephorus.	Stichometry of Cod. Clarom.	Stichometry of Mommsen's list.
1 Kingdoms	} 2240 {	2500	2300
2 Kingdoms		2000	2200
3 Kingdoms	} 2203 {	2600	2550
4 Kingdoms		2400	2250[1]
1 Paralip.	} 5500 {		2040
2 Paralip.			2100
1 Esdras	} 5500 {		
2 Esdras		1500	
Psalms	5100	5000	5000
Proverbs	1700	1600	
Ecclesiastes	750	600	
Song	280	300	
Job	1800	1600	1700
Wisdom	1100	1000	
Sirach	2800	2500	
Esther	350	1000	700
Judith	1700	1300	1100
Tobit	700	1000	900
Hosea		530	
Amos		410	
Micah		310	
Joel		90	
Obadiah		70	
Jonah		150	
Nahum		140	
Habakkuk		160	
Zephaniah		140	
Haggai		110	
Zechariah		660	
Malachi		200	
(Dodecapropheton	3000	[2970]	3800)
Isaiah	3800	3600	3580
Jeremiah	4000	4070	4450
Baruch	700		
Ezekiel	4000	3600	3340
Daniel	2000[2]	1600	1350
1 Maccabees	} 7300 {	2300	2300
2 Maccabees		2300	1800
3 Maccabees			
4 Maccabees		1000	

[1] In Mommsen's list the following totals are also given: Ruth and 1—4 Kingdoms, 9500; Salomonic books, 6500; Major Prophets, 15370; the whole canon, 69500.

[2] Susanna is calculated separately (500).

The figures given above correspond to those in the lists printed in c. i., which follow the text of Preuschen (*Analecta,* pp. 156f., 142ff., 138f.). Some variants and suggested rectifications may be seen in Zahn, *Gesch. d. NTlichen Kanons,* ii., pp. 295 ff., 143 ff., and Sanday, *Studia Biblica,* iii., pp. 266 ff.

Many MSS. of the Greek Bible contain more or less complete stichometries of the several books of the canon. Either the total number of *stichi* is registered at the end of the book, or a record is kept throughout the book by placing a figure or figures in the margin at the end of each centenary of lines. Some of our oldest MSS. reproduce in this form the stichometry of their archetypes; in other cases, a stichometry which has been copied into the margin by a second or later hand. Thus in Cod. B, the margins of 1—4 Regn. and Isaiah present a nearly complete record[1] of *stichi* written *prima manu,* and doubtless transcribed from the MSS. to which the scribe owed his copy of those books. A marginal register of *stichi* is also found in part of Cod. F, beginning with Deuteronomy, and in Cod. Q, where it is due to the hand which has added the Hexaplaric matter. The entries in B and Q agree generally in Isaiah; in both MSS. the last entry occurs at Isa. lxv. 19, where the number of *stichi* reaches 3500. But the famous Chigi MS. of the Prophets (Cod. 87) counts 3820 *stichi* in Isaiah[2]. This approaches the number given by Nicephorus, whilst the total number of *stichi* in BQ, 3600, agrees with the computation of the Claromontane list. The addition of 200 *stichi* in Nicephorus and Cod. 87 is due, Ceriani suggests, to the greater length of the Hexaplaric and Lucianic texts[3]. There is a similar disparity between the stichometry of Nicephorus and the reckoning of Cod. F in Deuteronomy,

---

[1] It is printed by Harris, *Stichometry,* p. 59 ff. Cf. Nestle, *Introd. to the Textual Criticism of the N.T.* (E. tr.), p. 4.

[2] ωκ, or as Allatius read the MS., ΓωΗ (3808); see Cozza, *Sacr. bibl. vet. fragm.* iii. p. xv.

[3] *De cod. March.,* p. 23 f.

where in F the *stichi* are 3000[1], but in Nicephorus 3100. On the other hand the later uncial K makes the *stichi* of Numbers to be 3535, which comes very near to the reckoning of Nicephorus[2].

Stichometrical variation is doubtless chiefly or largely due to divergent types of text. But other causes of disparity were at work. It was easy for scribes to misread the letters which represented the number of the lines, especially when they were mechanically copied from an archetype. The older signs may have been sometimes misunderstood[3], or those which were intelligible may have been confused by careless copying. A glance at the comparative table on p. 346 f. will shew that several of the larger discrepancies can only be explained in some such way.

The following stichometry is derived chiefly from Dr E. Klostermann's *Analecta*[4], giving the result of his researches among cursive MSS., with some additions supplied by the Editors of the larger LXX.

Genesis	4308[5]	H.-P. 30, 52, 85; Barb. iii. 36; Vat. gr. 746; Pal. gr. 203; Athos, Pantocr. 24, Laur. γ. 112; Athens, Nat. 44
Exodus	3400	H.-P. 30, 52, 85; Barb. iii. 36; Athens, Nat. 44
Leviticus	2700	H.-P. 30, 52, 54, 85; Barb. iii. 36; Paris, Reg. gr. 2; 2000, Athens, Nat. 44
Numbers	3535[6]	H.-P. 30, 52, 85; Barb. iii. 36; Vat. gr. 2122; Athens, Nat. 44; Paris, Reg. gr. 2
Deuteronomy	3100	H.-P. 30, 52, 54, 85; Barb. iii. 36; Vat. gr. 2122; Paris, Reg. gr. 2
Joshua	2100	H.-P. 30, 54, 85; Barb. iii. 36; Paris, Reg. gr. 2

[1] The symbol used is Ϟ, which occurs also in B. On this symbol, see J. Woisin, *De Graecorum notis numeralibus*, n. 67 (Kiel, 1886).

[2] The numeration of the *stichi* in the poetical books ascribed to the greater uncials in the Cambridge manual LXX. is derived from Dr Nestle's *Supplementum*[2] (Leipzig, 1887), and rests on an actual counting of the lines, and not on statements in the MSS. themselves.

[3] Cf. J. R. Harris, *Stichometry*, p. 31.

[4] See p. 44 ff. Cf. *J. Th. St.*, ii. p. 238 ff.

[5] 4400 in H.-P. 54.

[6] 3530 in H.-P. 54.

Judges	2100[1]	Barb. iii. 36; 2156, Paris, Reg. gr. 2; Athos, Pantocr. 24
Ruth	300	Barb. iii. 36; Paris, Reg. gr. 2
1 Kingdoms	2500	Barb. iii. 36 (500, Ven. Marc. gr. xvi)
2 Kingdoms	2343	Barb. iii. 36; 2042, Ven. Marc. gr. xvi
3 Kingdoms	2400	Barb. iii. 36; Ven. Marc. gr. xvi
4 Kingdoms	2600	Barb. iii. 36; Ven. Marc. gr. xvi
1 Paralip.	2000	Barb. iii. 36 ⎫ 5000, Ven. Marc. gr. xvi
2 Paralip.	3000	Barb. iii. 36 ⎭
1 Esdras	1300	Barb. iii. 36 ⎫ 3100, Ven. Marc. gr. xvi
2 Esdras	1800	Barb. iii. 36 ⎭
Psalms	5100	Barb. iii. 36[2]
Proverbs	1750	H.-P. 161, 248; Barb. iii. 36
Ecclesiastes	750	H.-P. 161, 248; Barb. iii. 36; 753, H.-P. 253
Song	286	H.-P. 161, 248; Barb. iii. 36; 353, H.-P. 253
Job	2200	(including asterisked lines, 1600 without them) H.-P. 161(?), 248; Barb. iii. 36
Wisdom	1250	Barb. iii. 36; Ven. gr. i. 13
Sirach	2650	Barb. iii. 36; Ven. gr. i. 13
Esther	750	Barb. iii. 36; Ven. Marc. gr. xvi, Ven. gr. i. 13
Judith	1300	Barb. iii. 36; Ven. Marc. gr. xvi
Tobit	750	Barb. iii. 36; Ven. Marc. gr. xvi, Ven. gr. i. 13
Hosea	750	H.-P. 86
Joel	210	H.-P. 86
Habakkuk	150	H.-P. 86
Zephaniah	160	H.-P. 86
Haggai	120	H.-P. 86
Zechariah	670	H.-P. 86; 776, H.-P. 231
Malachi	190	H.-P. 86; 204, H.-P. 231[3]
Isaiah	3700	H.-P. 231; 3820, Barb. iii. 36
Jeremiah	4500	H.-P. 231; 3800, Barb. iii. 36
Baruch	514	H.-P. 231; 350, Barb. iii. 36
Lamentations[4]	ΗΦ(?)	H.-P. 86; $\overline{\mu}$(?) H.-P. 231; 860, Barb. iii. 36
Ep. of Jeremiah	200	Barb. iii. 36
Ezekiel	4500	H.-P. 231; 4000, Barb. iii. 36
Daniel	1800	H.-P. 231; 1720, Barb. iii. 36
Susanna	224	H.-P. 231

[1] 2450 in H. P. 54.
[2] Ecclesiastical Canticles, 600, Barb. iii. 36.
[3] Total of Minor Prophets variously calculated at 3750, 3500, 3300 (Barb. iii. 36).
[4] Possibly a corruption of πε (see next page).

2. No complete system of capitulation is found in any of our existing uncial MSS. of the Greek Old Testament. Yet even the Vatican MS., which is written continuously except in the poetical books, bears traces of a system of chapter-divisions which is older than itself[1]. It begins with Proverbs, and from that book onwards chapter-numbers appear in the margin of the canonical writings, whilst in some instances there is a double capitulation, as the following table will shew.

Proverbs	61	16	Zephaniah		5
Ecclesiastes	25	7	Haggai		3
Song	40	5	Zechariah		18
Job		33	Malachi		6
Hosea		11	Isaiah		74
Amos		6	Jeremiah	100	98
Micah		7	Baruch		9
Joel		3	Lamentations	85[2]	
Obadiah		1	Ep. of Jeremiah	6	
Jonah		3	Ezekiel	56	
Nahum		3	Daniel	[21]	21[3]
Habakkuk		4			

The figures in the left-hand column are *prima manu*; those on the right are in a hand of perhaps the eleventh century (? that of 'Clement the Monk,' the industrious *instaurator* who has left his name on pp. 238 and 264 of the MS.[4]). In Proverbs, Ecclesiastes, and Song the capitulation of the later hand differs widely, as will be observed, from the system which the original scribe reproduced from his archetype. But in the Prophets the corrector seems simply to have followed the numbers inscribed in the margin by B*; the latter can be detected here and there under the large coarse characters of the later hand, and towards the end of Jeremiah and throughout

---

[1] Tischendorf (*Mon. sacr. ined. n. c.*, i. prolegg., p. xxvii.) points out that Tertullian recognises a system of chapters in Numbers.

[2] In this book the chapter-numbers correspond to the divisions indicated in the original by the letters of the Hebrew alphabet, and in the recension by transliteration of the Hebrew alphabetic names.

[3] This number includes the Greek additions.

[4] See the pref. to Fabiani and Cozza's facsimile, p. xvii. sqq.

Daniel the two sets of numbers are distinctly visible. In Jeremiah the *instaurator* here and there breaks away from the guidance of the first hand, and the totals are slightly different. But the difference is probably accidental, and it is certainly slight; whereas in the Salomonic books another system is followed, in which the chapters are three or four times as long as those of the older capitulation.

Cod. A is broken into paragraphs throughout the prose books, the beginning of each paragraph being indicated not only by paragraph-marks, but by the use of a capital letter which projects into the margin. Besides the paragraphing certain books—Deuteronomy, Joshua, 3—4 Kingdoms, Isaiah —retain traces of a capitulation imperfectly copied from the archetype. In Deuteronomy chapter-marks occur at cc. i. 1, 9, 19, 40; ii. 1, 7, 14; in Joshua they begin at ix. 1 ($\overline{\iota\beta}$) and proceed regularly (x. 1, 16, 29, 31, 34, 36, 38; xi. 1, &c.) down to xix. 17 ($\overline{\lambda\eta}$); in 3 Regn. the first numeral occurs at c. viii. 22 ($\overline{\kappa\beta}$), and the last at xxi. 17 ($\overline{\nu\theta}$); 4 Regn. returns only one or two numbers (e.g. $\overline{\theta}$ stands opposite to c. iii. 20). In Isaiah, again, the entries are few and irregular; $\overline{\beta}$ appears at c. ii. 1, and $\overline{\theta}$ at xxi. 1.

Cod. א seems to have no chapter-marks *prima manu*, but in Isaiah they have been added by א[c.a] throughout the book[1].

Jeremiah, the Epistle of Jeremiah, and Ezekiel are capitulated in cod. Q, and in the two last-named books the capitulation of Q agrees with that of B. In Jeremiah, where the agreement is less complete, the chapters in Q do not proceed beyond c. xxiv., a circumstance which suggests a Hexaplaric origin[2].

Cod. M like cod. B exhibits two systems of capitulation[3],

---

[1] Tischendorf, notes to facsimile, p. v.
[2] Ceriani, *de cod. March.*, p. 24 ff.
[3] See Montfaucon, *Biblioth. Coisliniana*, p. 4 sqq.

one of which is accompanied by brief headings corresponding
in general character to the τίτλοι of the Gospels. The two
capitulations, which are represented with more or less of completeness in the Hexateuch and in 1–3 Kingdoms[1], differ
considerably, as the following table will shew:

	Marginal Capitulation.	Capitulation accompanied by titles.
Genesis	106	99
Exodus	84	110
Leviticus	54	61
Numbers	53	51
Deuteronomy	65[2]	94[3]

Cod. Sin. I. (x.) is divided into κεφάλαια which number as
follows: Genesis, 150; Exodus, 88; Leviticus, 63; Deuteronomy, 69; Joshua, 30; 1 Regn., 66; 2 Regn., 63[4].

A list of sections quoted by Dr Klostermann[5] from the
cursive MS. cod. Barberini iii. 36 (cent. x. or xi.) exhibits
another widely different scheme[6]:

Genesis	26	3 Kingdoms	16	Habakkuk	2
Exodus	8	4 Kingdoms	17	Zephaniah	3
Leviticus	12	Hosea	5	Haggai	3
Numbers	21	Amos	6	Zechariah	13
Deuteronomy	35	Micah	6	Malachi	2
Joshua	8	Joel	4	Isaiah	43
Judges	4	Obadiah	2	Jeremiah	41
1 Kingdoms	15	Jonah	3	Ezekiel	21
2 Kingdoms	11	Nahum	2	Daniel	9

[1] Another Coislin MS. (Coisl. gr. 8) gives the following capitulation
for some of the later histories: 1 Chron. 83, 2 Chron. 86, Tobit 21, Judith
34, 1 Esdr. 109, 2 Esdr. 80, Esther 55.
[2] Beginning at c. iv. 41.
[3] In Judges there is no capitulation, but the periods of bondage are
distinguished as Δογλεία ᾱ, B̄, &c., and the exploits of the successive
judges by κριτhc ᾱ, B̄ and so forth.
[4] Cf. the numbers in B. M. Add. MS. 35123: Gen., 148; Exod., 84;
Lev., 62; Num., 61; Deut., 69; Josh., 30; Jud., 33.
[5] *Analecta*, p. 80 ff. This division into sections, however, refers not to
the text of the books, but to that of the synopsis contained in the MS.
Cf. also the κεφάλαια in Hab. iii. found in Barb. v. 45 (86, H.-P.).
[6] Interesting traces of another old capitulation are to be found in the
ἐκλογὴ τοῦ νόμου printed in Cotelerii *Eccl. Gr. Mon.* i. p. 1. The chapters

It is clear that no induction can be drawn from the facts which are at present within our reach; nor can the various systems of capitulation be safely classified until some scholar has collected and tabulated the chapter-divisions of a large number of MSS. of varying ages and provenance[1]. It is probable, however, that the systems, which at present seem to be nearly as numerous as the capitulated copies of the LXX., will prove to be reducible to a few types reproduced by the scribes with many variations in detail.

The 'titles' deserve separate consideration. In the few instances where we are able to institute a comparison these headings seem to be independent. In Numbers, e.g., the following table shews little correspondence between those in codd. K, M, even when the chapters coincide.

Num.	Cod. K.	Cod. M.
vii. 10.	Τὰ δῶρα τῶν ἀρχόντων.	Περὶ τῶν δώρων ὧν προσήνεγκαν οἱ [ι]β΄ ἄρχοντες.
viii. 5.	Περὶ τοῦ ἁγνισμοῦ τῶν Λευ[ιτῶν].	Ἀφορισμὸς τῶν Λευειτῶν εἰς τὸ λειτουργεῖν Κυρίῳ.
xi. 16.	Περὶ τῶν πρεσβυτέρων ληψομένων[2] τὸ πνεῦμα.	Περὶ ο΄ πρεσβυτέρων τῶν προφητευσάντων.

here are shorter and therefore more numerous than in any of the lists given above, e.g. Exod. xxii. 1—27 forms part of the 68th chapter and Deut. xxv. 11 ff. of the 93rd in their several books, while Leviticus apparently contains 150 chapters and Numbers 140.

[1] Paragraphs or sections marked by capitals protruding into the margin or written in red ink, or (less frequently) distinguished by numbers, occur perhaps in the majority of cursives; the following list of cursives thus divided is taken from descriptions of MSS. made for the use of the Editors of the larger LXX.: H.-P. x. xi., 16, 17, 18, 29, 38, 46, 53, 54, 56, 57, 59, 64 (double system of capitulation), 68, 70, 73, 74, 76, 78, 79 (in Gen. χπβ΄), 83, 84, 93, 108, 118, 120, 121, 123, 126, 127, 128 (contemporary numbers), 130, 131, 134; B. M. Add. 35123, Lambeth 1214; Paris Ars. 8415; Esc. Ω. i. 13, Σ. i. 16; Munich gr. 454; Grotta Ferrata A. γ. 1; Leipzig gr. 361; Athos, Pantocr. 24 (double system of capitulation, τίτλοι), Vatop. 513, 516; Laur. γ. 112 (both chapters and στίχοι numbered); Athens, nat. gr. 44; Sinai 1, Jerusalem, H. Sep. 2.

[2] Tischendorf (*Mon. sacr. ined. n. c.* i. p. 78) prints ΔΨΟΜΕΝωΝ.

	Cod. K.	Cod. M.
Num.		
xii. 1.	Ἀαρὼν καὶ Μαρία κατὰ Μωυσῆν.	Περὶ τῆς λέπρας Μαριὰμ ἣν ἔσχεν ὑβρίσασα τὴν γυναῖκα Μωσῆ.
xiii. 1.	Περὶ τῶν κατασκεψαμένων τὴν γῆν.	Περὶ τῶν ἀποσταλέντων κατασκοπῆσαι τὴν γῆν.
xiv. 23.	Περὶ Χά[λεβ] υἱοῦ ['Ιεφοννή].	
xiv. 34.	"Οτι ὅσας ἡμέρας κατεσκέψαντο τὴν γῆν, τοσαῦτα ἔτη ἐποίησαν ἐν τῇ ἐρήμῳ.	
xvi. 1.	Περὶ Κόρε καὶ Δαθὰν καὶ Ἀβιρὼν καὶ Αὐνάν.	Περὶ τῆς ἐπαναστάσεως τῆς κατὰ Μωσῆν παρὰ τοῦ Κόρε συναγωγῆς.
xvii. 1.	Περὶ τῆς ῥάβδου Ἀαρὼν τῆς βλαστησάσης.	
xxi. 21.	Περὶ Σηὼν βασιλέως Ἀμορραίων.	Περὶ τῶν ἀποσταλέντων πρὸς Σηών, καὶ πῶς ἐνίκησεν αὐτὸν ὁ Ἰσραήλ.
xxxiii. 1.	"Επαρσις καὶ σταθμοὶ τῶν υἱῶν Ἰσραήλ.	Πῶς διώδευσαν οἱ υἱοὶ Ἰσραήλ.
xxxiii. 3.	Περὶ τοῦ νυχθήμερον.	
xxxv. 9.	Περὶ τῶν πόλεων τῶν φυγαδευτηρίων.	Περὶ φονέως.

The following τίτλοι for Exod. ii.—viii. are taken from a Vienna MS. (Th. gr. 3):

α. περὶ τῆς γεννήσεως Μωυσέως.
β. πρώτη ὀπτασία πρὸς Μωυσῆν ἐν τῇ βάτῳ.
γ. περὶ τῆς συναντήσεως μετ᾽ (?) Ἀαρών.
δ. εἴσοδος (?) Μωυσέως καὶ Ἀαρὼν πρὸς Φαραώ.
ε. περὶ τῶν μαστιγωθέντων γραμματέων.
ϛ. περὶ τῆς ῥάβδου τῆς στραφείσης εἰς ὄφιν.
ζ. πρώτη πληγή· μεταστροφὴ τοῦ ὕδατος εἰς αἷμα.
η. δευτέρα πληγή, τῶν βατράχων.
θ. τρίτη πληγή, τῶν σκνιπῶν. Κτλ.

Examples occur of longer headings, which aim at giving a comprehensive summary or a brief interpretation. (*a*) The preface to Hesychius's colometrical arrangement of the Minor Prophets is followed by a complete set of τίτλοι for the Twelve Prophets and Isaiah[1]. The numbers are as follows: Hosea

---

[1] Migne, *P. G.* xciii., 1345 sqq. The titles for Isaiah with a collection

20, Joel 10, Amos 17, Obadiah 3, Jonah 4, Micah 13, Nahum 5, Habakkuk 4, Zephaniah 7, Haggai 5, Zechariah 32, Malachi 10, Isaiah 88. The titles are with scarcely an exception polemical or dogmatic in character, e.g. Hosea : ā. Εἰκὼν τῆς τῶν Ἰουδαίων συναγωγῆς, ἐξ ἧς ὁ Χριστὸς τὸ κατὰ σάρκα τίκτεται, καὶ λαοῦ τὸ μὲν ἐν ἀπιστίᾳ ἔμεινεν, τὸ δὲ ὕστερον ἐπιστρέφει καὶ σώζεται. (*b*) The Syro-hexaplaric Daniel is divided into ten chapters, each headed by a full summary of its contents[1].

3. One class of sections calls for separate treatment. In Part I. c. v. (p. 168 f.) some account has been given of MSS. which consist of lessons taken from the Old Testament. Few of these lectionaries are older than the eleventh century, and only one goes back to the sixth or seventh. But the choice of passages for public reading in the services of the Church must have begun at a much earlier period. The public reading of the O. T. Scriptures was an institution inherited by the Church from the Synagogue (Lc. iv. 16 ff., Acts xiii. 15, xv. 21; cf. 1 Tim. iv. 13), and there is evidence that it was prevalent in Christian communities of the second and third centuries[2]. At one great Christian centre provision was made for the liturgical reading of the Bible on certain week-days as well as on Sunday. "At Alexandria (writes Socrates) on Wednesdays and Fridays the Scriptures are read and the clergy expound them...and this is at Alexandria a practice of long standing, for it was on these occasions that Origen appears to have given most of his instructions in the Church[3]." Turning to Origen's homilies on the Old Testament

---

of glosses, apparently by the same author, have been edited by M. Faulhaber from cod. Vat. Gr. 347 (*Hesychii Hieros. interpretatio Isaiae*, Freiburg i. Breisgau, 1900).

[1] Bugati, *Daniel*, p. 1. See also the περιοχαὶ (or ὑποθέσεις) εἰς τοὺς ψαλμούς ascribed to Eusebius of Caesarea, which precede the Psalter in Cod. A (printed in Migne, *P. G.* xxiii. 67 sqq.).

[2] See above, p. 168, and cf. Gregory, *Textkritik*, i. p. 337.

[3] *H. S.* v. 22 ἐν Ἀλεξανδρείᾳ τῇ τετράδι καὶ τῇ λεγομένῃ παρασκευῇ γραφαί

we find allusions which shew that they were usually based on the lesson for the day, and we get light upon the length of the selected passages.

In *Hom. in Num.* xv. Origen apologises to his hearers for not keeping strictly to the lesson for the day : "licet non ordo lectionum quae recitantur de illis dicere magis exigat quae lector explicuit, tamen quoniam nonnulli fratrum deposcunt ea potius quae de prophetia Balaam scripta sunt ad sermonem disputationis adduci, non ita ordini lectionum satisfacere aequum credidi ut desideriis auditorum." This homily probably belongs to Origen's life at Caesarea[1], and if so, it is clear that at Caesarea as well as at Alexandria there was a well-defined order of Church lessons before the middle of the third century. In another homily, on the Witch of Endor (*in* 1 *Sam.* hom. iii.), Origen complains that the O.T. lesson for the day was too long to be expounded at a single sitting : τὰ ἀναγνωσθέντα πλείονά ἐστι· καὶ ἐπεὶ χρὴ ἐπιτεμνόμενον εἰπεῖν, δυσὶ περικοπαῖς ἀνεγνώσθη τὰ περὶ Ναβάλ...εἶτα μετὰ τοῦτο ἡ ἱστορία ἡ περὶ τοῦ κεκρύφθαι τὸν Δαυίδ... εἶτα τὰ ἑξῆς ἡ ἱστορία ἦν τρίτη, ὅτε κατέφυγεν πρὸς Ἀχάρ...ἑξῆς τούτοις ἦν ἡ ἱστορία ἡ διαβόητος ὑπὲρ τῆς ἐγγαστριμύθου...τεσσάρων οὐσῶν περικοπῶν...ὅτι ποτὲ βούλεται ὁ ἐπίσκοπος προτεινάτω. On this occasion the O.T. lesson seems to have extended from 1 Regn. xxv. 1 to xxviii. 25, including four περικοπαί or shorter sections, which, judging from the description, corresponded in length very nearly to our own chapters[2].

The lections to which Origen refers were doubtless those which were read in the pre-anaphoral portion of the Liturgy in the hearing of the catechumens as well as the faithful. In the liturgy of Apost. Const. ii., the Pentateuch, Joshua, Judges, the Kingdoms, the Chronicles, Ezra, Nehemiah, Job, the Salomonic books, and the sixteen Prophets, are all mentioned as books from which the Old Testament lection might be taken; i.e. all the books of the Hebrew Canon, with the exception of the

τε ἀναγινώσκονται, καὶ οἱ διδάσκαλοι ταύτας ἑρμηνεύουσι...καὶ τοῦτό ἐστιν ἐν Ἀλεξανδρείᾳ ἔθος ἀρχαῖον· καὶ γὰρ Ὠριγένης τὰ πολλὰ ἐν ταύταις ταῖς ἡμέραις φαίνεται ἐπὶ τῆς ἐκκλησίας διδάξας.

[1] *D. C. B.* iv. p. 104.

[2] Cf. the τίτλοι in the Coislin MS. (M), where μη', μθ', ν' are nearly identical with cc. xxxi., xxxii., xxxiii. respectively (Montfaucon, *Bibl. Coisl.,* p. 28).

Psalter and perhaps the Book of Esther, were employed for
this purpose. The order in Book viii. names only the Law
and the Prophets, but probably the scope is the same. The
'Prophet,' i.e. the Old Testament lesson, preceded the
'Apostle' (the Epistle) in the liturgy of Antioch as known to
St Chrysostom at the end of the fourth century, and it held its
place in the East generally till the seventh[1]. In the West the
'prophecy' was read by the North African Church of St Augustine's time, and it still holds its ground in the Mozarabic
and Ambrosian rites[2]. In Egypt, as John Cassian tells us,
the monastic communities read two lessons from Scripture
both at Nocturns and Vespers, and (Saturdays and Sundays
excepted) one of the two lessons was from the Old Testament[3];
and the West generally adopted the custom of reading both
the Old and the New Testament in the daily offices.

Before the formation of Lectionaries the liturgical lessons
were marked in the margins of Church Bibles by the words
ἀρχή, τέλος, written opposite to the beginning and end of the
περικοπή[4]. Such traces of adaptation to liturgical use are found
even in cod. B, though not *prima manu*[5]. Whether any of
the larger chapters which appear in certain MSS. (e.g. the
later system in cod. B) are of the nature of lections, must
remain doubtful until the whole subject has received the
fuller treatment which it demands.

The Psalter obviously needed no capitulation, nor was it
ever read by the ἀναγνώστης in the lessons for the day. But
special Psalms were recited or sung in the Church, as they had

---

[1] Brightman, *Eastern Liturgies*, pp. 470, 476, 527, 580. See Chrys.
in Rom. xxiv. 3 (cited above, p. 168).

[2] *D. C. A.*, *Prophecy, Liturgical* (ii. 173ᵇ ff.).

[3] *De inst. coenob.* ii. 6.

[4] On this word see Suicer, *Thesaurus*, ii. 673 sqq. It is used by Justin,
Dial. 78 and Clem. Al., *Strom.* iii. 38. In Origen (quoted above) the περικοπή is merely a section; at a later time it was used for the ἀνάγνωσμα.

[5] Fabiani and Cozza, *prolegg.*, p. xix.

been in the Synagogue[1], and in some early monastic communities arrangements were made for a regular recitation of the Psalter both in public and private[2]. The scribe of cod. A has copied into his MS. a list of Psalms for daily use, in which three are appointed to be said at each of the two public services, and one is selected for private use at each hour of the day and night. It is as follows:

Κανόνες ἡμερινῶν ψαλμῶν.					Κ. νυκτερινοὶ τῶν ψαλμῶν.				
'Ορθρινοὶ³	γ'	ξβ'	αμ'	ρμα'	Λυχνικοὶ⁴	γ'	ρκθ'	ρκ'	ιβ'
"Ωρ[α]	α'	ψαλμὸς		η'	"Ωρ[α]	α'	ψαλμὸς		οδ'
,,	β'	,,		κθ'	,,	β'	,,		κθ'
,,	γ'	,,		α'	,,	γ'	,,		νδ'
,,	δ'	,,		μα'	,,	δ'	,,		ς'
,,	ε'	,,		ν'	,,	ε'	,,		δ'
,,	ς'	,,		ο'	,,	ς'	,,		μ'
,,	ζ'	,,		ξθ'	,,	ζ'	,,		να'
,,	η'	,,		δ'	,,	η'	,,		π'
,,	θ'	,,		ρια'	,,	θ'	,,		πζ'
,,	ι'	,,		ρμ	,,	ι'	,,		ζο'
,,	ια'	,,		ρη'	,,	ια'	,,		κα'
,,	ιβ'	,,		ρκ'	,,	ιβ'	,,		νς'

The existing order of the Orthodox Eastern Church divides the Psalter into 20 sections known as καθίσματα, each of which is broken by the recitation of a *Gloria* into three στάσεις. The larger sections are i.—viii., ix.—xvi., xvii.—xxiii., xxiv.—xxxi., xxxii.—xxxvi., xxxvii.—xlv., xlvi.—liv., lv.—lxiii., lxiv.—lxix., lxx.—lxxvi., lxxvii.—lxxxiv., lxxxv.—xc., xci.—c., ci.—civ., cv.—cviii., cix.—cxvii., cxviii., cxix.—cxxxi., cxxxii.—cxlii., cxliii.—cl. In the later liturgical Greek Psalter the *cathismata* are divided by an ornamental band or some other mark of separation, and the *staseis* by a marginal $\overset{z}{\lambda o}$ (δόξα, i.e. the Doxology, which was repeated at the end of each)[5].

---

[1] See p. 251.
[2] Cf. Cassian, *Inst.* iii. 289.
[3] Cf. *Const.* viii. 37, μετὰ τὸ ῥηθῆναι τὸν ὀρθρινόν.
[4] Cf. *Const.* viii. 34, τὸν ἐπιλυχνικὸν ψαλμόν.
[5] Cf. *O. T. in Gr.*, ii. p. xi.

(1) A few other text-divisions, peculiar to certain contexts or books, may be specified here. In Isaiah it was not unusual to mark in the margin the place where each of the books of Origen's commentary ended (τόμος α'—λϛ', cf. Eus. *H.E.* vi. 36). Both in Isaiah and in Daniel certain prophetic ὁράσεις were distinguished. Thus cod. Qᵐᵍ places ὅΡΑCιC λ̄ opposite to Isa. vii. 1, and οΡΑCιC Η' at c. xvii. 1. In Daniel cod. A marks 12 ὁράσεις, which begin respectively at Sus. 1, Dan. i. 1, ii. 1, iii. 1, iii. 98, v. 1, v. 30, vii. 1, viii. 1, ix. 1, xi. 1, Bel 1, and the same method of division is used in codd. QΓ. In Lamentations each stanza is preceded by a representation of the Hebrew letter with which it begins, e.g. ἀλέφ (ἄλφ, ἀλφά[1]), βήθ, γίμελ (γίμλ), δάλεθ (δέλεθ, δέλτ, δέλθ), and so forth[2]. In the analogous case of Psalm cxviii. (cxix.), there are no signs of this treatment, except in the Graeco-Latin Psalters RT[3].

In the Song a marginal enumeration distinguishes the speeches of the interlocutors, and some MSS. (e.g. א and V) add marginal notes after the manner of stage-directions, such as ἡ νύμφη πρὸς τὸν νυμφίον, ταῖς νεανίσιν ἡ νύμφη, αἱ νεανίδες τῷ νυμφίῳ[4].

Small departures from the continuous or slightly paragraphed writing of the oldest MSS. are found in a few contexts which lend themselves to division. Thus even in cod. B the blessings of the tribes in Gen. xlix. 3—27 are separated and numbered ᾱ—ῑΒ. A similar treatment but without marginal enumeration is accorded to Deut. xiv. 12—18 and 1 Paral. i. 51—54, Eccl. iii. 1—8. The ten words of the Decalogue are numbered in the margins of codd. BA, but not *prima manu*; and the systems of numeration differ to some extent. Thus according to Bᵃ, α' = prologue, β' = i + ii, γ' = iii, δ' = iv, ε' = v, ϛ' = vii, ζ' = viii, η' = vi, θ' = ix, ι' = x, while A¹ makes γ' = iv, δ' = v, ε' = vi; the other numbers in A are effaced, or were never appended.

(2) It would be interesting, if sufficient materials were available, to pursue the subject of text-division with reference to the daughter-versions of the LXX. On the stichometry and capitulation of the Latin Bible much information has been brought together by M. Berger (*Histoire de la Vulgate*, p. 307 ff.) and Wordsworth-White (*Epilogus*, p. 733 ff.); for the stichometry see also Dr Sanday in *Studia Biblica*, iii. p. 264 f. But it remains

---

[1] The variations in the MSS. are interesting and instructive.
[2] Greek numerals are sometimes added in the margin; see above, p. 351.
[3] R gives the Heb. letters in Greek; T the corresponding Greek numerals.
[4] In cod. V = 23 these become sometimes lengthy τίτλοι, e.g. at v. 7 ἐξῆλθεν μὴ εὑροῦσα τὸν νυμφίον ἡ νύμφη καὶ ὡς ἐν νυκτὶ εὑρεθεῖσα ἀπὸ τῶν φυλακῶν τῆς πόλεως τραυματίζεται, καὶ αἴρουσιν αὐτῆς τὸ θέριστρον οἱ τειχοφυλακοῦντες.

doubtful whether these divisions of the Latin Bible belonged
originally to Jerome's version or were transferred to it from the
Old Latin[1]; or, supposing the latter view to be correct, whether
they came from the MSS. of the LXX. which were used by the
early African or Italian translators. In referring to the N.T.
Tertullian speaks of *capitula* not seldom (*ad uxor.* ii. 2, *de
monog.* 11, *de virg. vel.* 4, *de praescr.* 5, *adv. Prax.* 20); but it
is not clear that he uses the word to connote definitely marked
sections.

On the capitulation of the Coptic versions the student will
find something in Wilkins, *Pentat. praef., ad fin.,* and Lagarde,
Orientalia, p. 125 ff.; on the Egyptian lectionary, he may consult the list of authorities collected by Brightman, *Ancient
Liturgies,* p. lxix. For the Ethiopic version, cf. Dillmann's *Ethiopic Pentateuch,* 1. ii., pp. 163 f., 173. The stichometry of the
Syro-Hexaplaric is discussed by Lagarde, *Mittheilungen,* iv.
(1891), p. 205 f. A list of Church lessons, taken from the Pales-
tinian-Syriac lectionary recently discovered by Mrs Lewis and
Mrs Gibson, is given by Nestle in *Studia Sinaitica,* vi. p.
xxix. ff.

4. In connexion with the subject of text-division it will be
convenient to mention the expositions which accompany and
often break up the text in MSS. of the Greek Bible. The
student will have observed that many of the codices enumerated in Part 1. c. v. (pp. 148—168) contain commentaries,
either original (*comm.*), or compiled (*cat.*). Of the Greek
commentators something will be said when we come to consider the use of the LXX. by the Greek fathers; in this place
we will limit ourselves to the relatively late compilations which
are based on the exegetical works of earlier writers[2].

Such expositions were formerly described as ἐκλογαί or
παραγραφαί, or as ἐπιτομαὶ ἑρμηνειῶν, or ἐξηγήσεις ἐρανισθεῖσαι
ἀπὸ διαφόρων πατέρων, or συνόψεις σχολικαὶ ἐκ διαφόρων ὑπο-
μνημάτων συλλεχθεῖσαι, or by some similar periphrasis. The
use of the technical term *catena* (σειρά) is of comparatively
modern date. *Catena aurea* is a secondary title of the great

---

[1] Cf. Sanday, *op. cit.,* p. 272.
[2] *Ch. Q. R.* i. 99, p. 34: "the process of drawing up Catenae goes on
from the fifth to the fourteenth or fifteenth century."

compendium of comments on the Four Gospels brought together by Thomas Aquinas, and a Greek MS. Psalter of the 16th century (Vat. Gr. 2240) adopts the phrase, translating it by χρυσῆ ἄλυσις. Σειρά is used in this sense by the editor of the Greek catena of Nicephorus, which bears the title Σειρὰ ἑνὸς καὶ πεντήκοντα ὑπομνηματιστῶν εἰς τὴν Ὀκτάτευχον καὶ τὰ τῶν Βασιλειῶν. The metaphor so happily expresses the principle on which such commentaries are constructed, that books of this description are now universally known as catenae or σειραί. They are 'chains' in which each link is supplied by some ancient author, scraps of exegesis threaded together by the ingenuity or industry of a collector who usually elects to be anonymous.

The catenists drew their materials from all sources within their reach. They laid under contribution Jewish writers such as Philo and Josephus, heretics like Basileides, Valentinus, and Marcion, suspects like Origen, Eusebius of Caesarea, Apollinarius, and Theodore of Mopsuestia, as well as the accepted teachers and Saints of the Catholic Church. Their range extended from the first century to the fifth or sixth, and they had access to a number of writers whose works have since disappeared. Hence their value in the eyes of patristic scholars and editors. But they are not without importance for the purposes of the biblical student. The text embedded in the commentary may be late[1], but the commentary itself often preserves the witness of early writers to an old and valuable type.

The catena is usually written in the broad margins which surround the text, or it embodies the text, which in that case is usually distinguished from it by being written in uncials or in coloured ink, or enclosed within marks of quotation. The names of the authors who have been pressed into the service of the catenist are commonly inserted in the margin at the

---

[1] See, however, the facts collected in *Ch. Q. R.* i. 99, p. 46 f.

place where their contributions begin : thus χργc[οcτόμογ],
ὠρ[ιгένογc], εγc[εβίογ], θεολ[ώρογ] ἀντ[ιοχέοc], гρнг[ορίογ],
κγρ[ίλλογ]. If a second passage from the same author occurs
in the same context it is introduced as τοῦ ἀγτοῦ ; an anonymous writer is ἄλλοc. Unfortunately in the copying of catenae
such attributions have often been omitted or misplaced, or even
erroneously inserted, and as to this particular the student
must be on his guard against a too unsuspecting acquiescence
in the witness of his MS. Nor can he place implicit confidence in the verbal accuracy of the excerpts. The catenists
evidently regarded themselves as free, while retaining the
substance, to abbreviate and otherwise modify the language
of their authors.

The following is a list of the chief Greek catenae of the Old
Testament which have appeared in type. *Octateuch, Historical
books:* the Catena of Nicephorus, 2 vols., Leipzig, 1772—3;
Psalms: B. Corderii *expositio Graecorum patrum,* 3 vols., Antwerp, 1643; *Proverbs:* Commentary of Procopius first printed
by Mai, and in Migne, *P. G.* lxxxvii.; *Song:* Commentary ascribed
to Eusebius and Polychronius (Meursius, Leyden, 1617); *Job:*
Catena of Nicetas of Serrae (P. Junius, i.e. Patrick Young,
London, 1636); *Isaiah:* Commentary of Procopius (J. Curterius,
Paris, 1580); *Jeremiah,* with Lamentations and Baruch: Catena
published by M. Ghisler, 3 vols., Leyden, 1623; *Daniel:* Catena
published by A. Mai in *Script. vet. nov. coll.* I. On these see
Ch. Q. R. i. 99, pp. 36—42.

The nineteenth century has added little to our collection
of printed Greek catenae on the Old Testament, and the
earlier editions do not always adequately represent the witness
of the best MSS. Meanwhile a great store of MS. catenae
awaits the examination of Biblical scholars. Some of these
are at Athos, Athens, Smyrna and Jerusalem, but there is an
abundant supply in libraries more accessible to Western
students, at St Petersburg, Rome, Paris, and London. Perhaps
no corner of the field of Biblical and patristic research offers so
much virgin soil, with so good a prospect of securing useful if
not brilliant results.

The following LXX. MSS. amongst others contain catenae on one or more of the books which form their text: H.-P. 14, 17, 24, 25, 31, 33, 52, 57, 73, 77, 78, 79, 83, 87, 90, 91, 97, 98, 99, 109, 112, 128, 135, 147, 181, 209, 238, 240, 243, 264, 272, 292, 302, 309; London B.M. Add. 35123, Lambeth 1214; Paris, Coisl. gr. 5, 7, Reg. gr. 128, 129, 130, 131, 132, 161; Zurich c. 11 ; Basle gr. iv. 56, vi. 8; Esc. Σ. i. 16; Leyden, 13; Munich gr. 82; Athos Vatop. 15, Ivér. 15 ; Athens, nat. 43; Constantinople 224; Smyrna, Ev. sch. 1 ; Patmos, 216, 217; Sinai 2; Jerusalem H. Sep. 3. Scholia are to be found in H.-P. 14, 16, 38, 52, 56, 64, 70, 77, 79, 93, 128, 130, 131, 135, 159, 256, 310; Paris Ars. 8415, Coisl. gr. 184.

On the Paris O. T. catenae see H. Lietzmann, *Catenen*, p. 37 ff. Some of the Vatican catenae are handled by Pitra, *analecta sacra* 11, Klostermann, *analecta*, passim ; a full and valuable account of Roman MS. catenae on the Prophets is given by Faulhaber (*die Propheten-Catenen*). For lists of the catenae in the great libraries of Europe and the East, the student must consult the published catalogues, e.g. Montfaucon, Omont (Paris), Stephenson (Vatican), Lambeccius (Vienna), Lambros (Athos), Papadopulos (Jerusalem). The more important MSS. are enumerated by Harnack-Preuschen, and Heinrici, and in the older work of Fabricius-Harles. A *Catenarum graecarum catalogus* by G. Karo and H. Lietzmann is in progress (*Nachrichten der K. Gesellschaft der Wissenschaften zu Göttingen* (Philologisch-hist. Klasse), 1902 ff.

5. Besides catenae and detached scholia the margins of LXX. MSS. frequently contain notes of various kinds, written oftentimes in perplexing abbreviations. Lists of abbreviations are given by the principal palaeographical authorities, such as Montfaucon's *Palaeographia Graeca*, Gardthausen's *Griechische Paläographie*, and Sir E. Maunde Thompson's *Handbook of Greek and Latin Palaeography*; but the subject can only be mastered by working upon the MSS. themselves or their facsimiles. It may be useful, however, to print here a few of the abbreviated notes and symbols which occur in the *apparatus* of the Cambridge manual LXX., or are of frequent occurrence in the principal codices.

ά = Ἀκύλας.　ϲ΄, ϲγ΄ = Σύμμαχος.　θ΄, θε΄ = Θεοδοτίων.

ού κ΄ π΄ εβρ΄ = οὐ κεῖται παρ᾽ Ἑβραίοις.　οἱ ωβ΄ ου κ΄ π΄ εβρ΄ = οἱ ὠβελισμένοι (στίχοι) οὐ κεῖνται παρ᾽ Ἑβραίοις.　ομˢ τοιϲ ο΄ = ὁμοίως τοῖς ἐβδομήκοντα.　οι γ̄ = οἱ τρεῖς, i.e. Aquila, Sym-

machus, Theodotion. π´ = πάντες. λ = Λουκιανός (Field,
$\overset{0}{}$

Hexapla, I. lxxxv.). οι λ = οἱ λοιποί. μο$\overset{0}{}$^{N} = μόνος. ϕ = ὡραῖον,
ϕ or ϕ = Ὠριγένης. For πιπι see above, p. 39 f.

Θ = σημείωσαι, σημειωτέον, σημεῖον. ΓΡ = γράψον or γράφεται.
αρ^{Χ} = ἀρχή. τε´ = τέλος. cτι^{Χ} = στίχος. κε´ = κεφάλαιον. κα^{Θ} = κά-
θισμα. αν^{Δ} = ἀνάγνωσμα. ϕ = διώρθωται (i.e. 'corrected thus
far'), a mark inserted by the διορθωτής usually at the end of a
book. For further particulars see Field, *op. cit.,* p. xciv. sqq[1].

LITERATURE.

Stichometry, colometry, &c.

Kitto, *Cyclopaedia of Biblical Literature,* art. *Verse*; Herzog-
Plitt, art. *Stichometrie*; Gregory, i. p. 112 f.; Scrivener-Miller,
i., p. 52 ff.; Gardthausen, *Paläographie,* p. 127 ff.; E. M. Thompson, *Handbook,* p. 78 ff.; Zahn, *Gesch. d. Kanons,* ii. p. 295 ff.;
Sanday in *Studia Biblica,* iii. p. 261 ff.; J. R. Harris, *Stichometry,*
passim; Wordsworth-White, *Epilogus,* p. 733 ff. (Oxford, 1898).

Capitulation.

Schürer, II. ii. 79 ff.; Buhl, *Kanon u. Text d. A. T.,* p. 222;
Ryle, *Canon of the O.T.,* p. 235; Morinus, *Exerc. Bibl.* xvii. 3;
Dathius, *De ordine pericoparum* (opusc. iv.); Zacagni, *Collectanea,*
praef., pp. lxvii., lxxxi.; Montfaucon, *Biblioth. Coisl.,* p. 1 ff.;
the Benedictine *Prolegomena in div. S. Hieron. biblioth.* iv.
(reprinted in Migne, *P. L.* xxviii. 101 sqq.); Suicer, *Thes. eccl.*
s.vv. κεφάλαιον, περικοπή; Herzog-Plitt, art. *Perikopen*; Gregory,
i. p. 120 ff.; Scrivener-Miller, i. p. 56 ff.; Thomasii *opp.* i.;
Berger, *Histoire de la Vulgate,* p. 323 ff.

Lections.

Suicer, *Thes. eccl.* s.vv. ἀνάγνωσμα, ἀνάγνωσις, γραφή; Brill, *De
lectionariis or. et occ. eccl.* (Helmstadt, 1703); Neale, *Hist. of the
H. Eastern Church,* i. p. 369; Herzog-Plitt, artt. *Lectionen,
Perikopen*; *D.C.A.,* art. *Lections*; Burgon, *Last twelve verses of
St Mark,* p. 191 ff.; E. Ranke, *Das kirchl. Perikopen-system der
röm. Liturgie* (Berlin, 1847).

Acrostics.

P. A. de Lagarde, *Symmicta* i. 107; C. Taylor in Hastings'
Encycl. of Religion and Ethics, i. p. 75; G. Bickell, art. *Acrostic*
in Oxford *New English Dict.*; I. Abrahams, art. *Acrostics* in
Jewish Encycl.; Driver, *Introd. to Lit. of O. T.,* ch. vii.

---

[1] For terms connected with writing and reading which occur in the text
of the LXX. see Nestle, *Introd. to the Textual Criticism of the N. T.,* p. 46 f.

Catenae.

T. Ittig, *De bibliothecis et catenis patrum* (Leipzig, 1707); J. C. Wolf, *De catenis Gr. patrum* (Wittenberg, 1742); Fabricius-Harles, viii. p. 637 ff.; J. G. Dowling, *Notitia scriptorum ss. patrum* (Oxford, 1839); Walch-Danz, *Biblioth. patristica* (Jena, 1834), p. 247 ff.; Harnack-Preuschen, *Gesch. d. altchr. Litteratur,* i. p. 835 ff.; G. Heinrici, in Hauck, *Real-Encyklop.* iii., art. *Catenen*; L. Eisenhofer, *Procopius von Gaza,* Freiburg, 1897; P. Batiffol, in Vigouroux' *D. B.* ii., p. 482 ff., art. *Chaînes Bibliques*; Lietzmann, *Catenen* (Freiburg i. B., 1897); M. Faulhaber, *Die Propheten-Catenen nach römischen Handschriften,* in *Biblische Studien,* iv. 2, 3 (Freiburg i. Breisgau, 1899). The two last-named works are indispensable to students who desire to prosecute research in this field. The whole subject is summarised with admirable clearness and precision in the *Church Quarterly Review* for Apr. 1900, pp. 29—48.

PART III.

LITERARY USE, VALUE, AND TEXTUAL CONDITION OF THE GREEK OLD TESTAMENT.

PART III.

CHAPTER I.

LITERARY USE OF THE LXX. BY NON-CHRISTIAN HELLENISTS.

1. A HAPPY accident has preserved fragments of the lost literature produced by the Hellenised Jews of Alexandria between the inception of the Alexandrian Version and the Christian era. The Greek historiographer, Alexander Cornelius—better known as Polyhistor (ὁ πολυΐστωρ), from his encyclopaedic learning—wrote a treatise *On the Jews* which contained extracts from Jewish and Samaritan Hellenistic writings[1]. Of these a few were copied from Polyhistor's book by Clement of Alexandria and Eusebius of Caesarea, in whose pages they may still be read. They consist of fragments of the historians Demetrius, Eupolemus, Artapanus, and Aristeas, the poets Philo, Theodotus, and Ezekiel, the philosopher Aristobulus, and Cleodemus or Malchas. There is reason to believe that Demetrius flourished c. B.C. 200; for the other writers the date of Polyhistor (c. B.C. 50) supplies a *terminus ad quem*, if we may assume[2] that he wrote the work attributed to him by Clement and Eusebius.

---

[1] Cf. Joseph., *ant.* i. 15, Clem. Al. *strom.* i. 130, Eus. *pr. ev.* ix. 17.
[2] See Schürer[3], iii. p. 347 f.

The following references will enable the student to find the fragments: (1) Demetrius: Clem. Al. *strom.* i. 141. Eus. *pr. ev.* ix. 19(?), 21, 29. (2) Eupolemus: Clem. Al. *strom.* i. 141. Eus. *pr. ev.* ix. 17, 26 (= Clem. Al. *strom.* i. 153), 30—34, 39. (3) Artapanus: Eus. *pr. ev.* ix. 18, 23, 27. (4) Aristeas: Eus. *pr. ev.* ix. 25. (5) Philo the poet: Eus. *pr. ev.* ix. 20, 24, 37 (cf. Clem. Al. *strom.* i. 154). (6) Theodotus: Eus. *pr. ev.* ix. 22. (7) Ezekiel the poet: Eus. *pr. ev.* ix. 28 (=Clem. Al. *strom.* i. 155), 29. (8) Aristobulus: Eus. *pr. ev.* viii. 10; ix. 6 (= Clem. Al. *strom.* i. 22); xiii. 12. (9) Cleodemus or Malchas: Eus. *pr. ev.* ix. 20.

Several of these fragments bear traces of a knowledge and use of the Greek Bible, and this evidence is not the less convincing because, with one exception, the purpose of the writers has kept them from actual quotation. They wished to represent their national history in a form more acceptable to their pagan neighbours; but while avoiding the uncouth phraseology of the Greek Bible they frequently betray its influence. A few extracts will make this plain.

Demetrius: (*a*) τὸν θεὸν τῷ Ἀβραὰμ προστάξαι Ἰϲⲁⲁⲕ ⲧⲟ̀ⲛ γⲓ̀ⲟⲛ ὁλοⲕⲁⲣⲡⲱ̄ⲥⲁⲓ αὐτῷ· τὸν δὲ ἀναγαγόντα τὸν παῖδα ἐπὶ τὸ ὄρος πυρὰν νῆσαι καὶ ἐⲡⲓθⲉ͂ⲓⲛⲁⲓ τὸν Ἰσαάκ· ⲥⲫⲁ́ⲍⲉⲓⲛ δὲ μέλλοντα κωλυθῆναι ὑπὸ ἀⲅⲅⲉ́ⲗⲟⲩ ⲕⲣⲓⲟ̀ⲛ αὐτῷ πρὸς τὴν ⲕⲁ́ⲣⲡⲱⲥⲓⲛ παραστήσαντος[1]. (*b*) ἐκεῖθεν δὲ ἐⲗθⲉ͂ⲓⲛ ⲉⲓⲥ Χⲁⲫⲣⲁθⲁ́, ἔνθεν παραγενέσθαι ⲉⲓⲥ Ἐⲫⲣⲁ́θⲁ, ⲏ̀ⲛ ⲉ͂ⲓⲛⲁⲓ Βⲏθⲗⲉ́ⲉⲙ...καὶ τελευτῆσαι Ῥαχὴλ ⲧⲉⲕⲟ̀ⲩⲥⲁⲛ τὸν Βενιαμίν[2]. (*c*) φησὶ γὰρ τὸν Ἀβραὰμ παῖδας ⲡⲣⲟ̀ⲥ ⲁⲛⲁⲧⲟⲗⲁ̀ⲥ ἐπὶ κατοικίαν πέμψαι· διὰ τοῦτο δὲ καὶ Ἀⲁⲣⲱ̀ⲛ ⲕⲁ̀ⲓ Μⲁⲣⲓⲁ̀ⲙ εἰπεῖν ⲉ̀ⲛ Ἀⲥⲏⲣⲱ̀θ Μωσῆν Ⲁⲓθⲓⲟⲡⲓ́ⲇⲁ γῆμαι ⲅⲩⲛⲁ͂ⲓⲕⲁ[3] (*d*) μὴ ἔχοντα δὲ ⲩ̈́ⲇⲱⲣ ἐκεῖ γλυκὺ ἀλλὰ ⲡⲓⲕⲣⲟ́ⲛ, τοῦ θεοῦ εἰπόντος, ⲍⲩ́ⲗⲟⲛ τι ἐⲙⲃⲁⲗⲉ͂ⲓⲛ εἰς τὴν πηγήν, καὶ γενέσθαι γλυκὺ τὸ ⲩ̈́ⲇⲱⲣ. ἐκεῖθεν δὲ ⲉⲓⲥ Ἐⲗⲉⲓ̀ⲙ ἐⲗθⲉ͂ⲓⲛ, καὶ εὑρεῖν ἐκεῖ Ⲇⲱ́ⲇⲉⲕⲁ μὲν ⲡⲏⲅⲁ̀ⲥ ⲩ̈ⲇⲁ́ⲧⲱⲛ, ἒⲃⲇⲟⲙⲏ́ⲕⲟⲛⲧⲁ δὲ ⲥⲧⲉⲗⲉ́ⲭⲏ ⲫⲟⲓⲛⲓ́ⲕⲱⲛ[4]. (For other coincidences, see above, p. 18.)

Eupolemus: ⲉⲩ̀ⲗⲟⲅⲏⲧⲟ̀ⲥ ὁ θⲉⲟ̀ⲥ ⲟ̀ⲥ ⲧⲟ̀ⲛ ⲟⲩ̀ⲣⲁⲛⲟ̀ⲛ ⲕⲁ̀ⲓ ⲧⲏ̀ⲛ ⲅⲏ̀ⲛ ἔⲕⲧⲓⲥⲉⲛ, ὃς εἵλετο ἄνθρωπον χρηστὸν ἐκ χρηστοῦ ἀνδρός...καὶ ἀρχιτέκτονά ⲥⲟⲓ ἀⲡⲉ́ⲥⲧⲁⲗⲕⲁ ἄνθρωπον Τύριον ἐκ μητρὸς Ἰουδαίας ἐκ τῆς φυλῆς Δάν[5].

[1] Cf. Gen. xxii. 1 ff.
[2] Cf. Gen. xxxv. 16.
[3] Cf. Gen. xxv. 6; Num. xi. 34—xii. 1.
[4] Cf. Exod. xv. 23 ff.
[5] Cf. 2 Chron. ii. 12 ff.

Aristeas: τὸν Ἠσαὺ γήμαντα Βασσάραν ἐν Ἐδὼм γεννῆσαι Ἰώβ· катоιкеῖν δὲ τοῦτον ἐν τῇ ΑγсíтιΔι χώρᾳ ἐπὶ τοῖс ὁρίοιс τῆс Ἰδογмаíас каì Ἀραβíас· γενέσθαι δὲ αὐτὸν Δίκαιον καὶ πολύκτηνον, κτήσασθαι γὰρ αὐτὸν πρόβата μὲν ἑπτакιсχίλια, камήλογс δὲ тριсχιλίас, ζεγгη Βοων πεντако̀сιа, ὅνογс θηλεíас νομάδας πεντακοсíας[1].

Ezekiel (in his tragedy ἡ Ἐξαγωγή):

Μαριὰμ δ᾽ ἀδελφή μου κατώπτευεν πέλας·
κἄπειτα θυγάτηρ βασιλέως ἅβραις ὁμοῦ
κατῆλθε λουτροῖς, χρῶτα φαιδρῦναι νέον.
Ἰδοῦса δ᾽ εὐθὺς καὶ λαβοῦσ᾽ ἀνείλετο,
ἔγνω δ᾽ Ἑβραῖον ὄντα· καὶ λέγει τάδε
Μαριὰμ ἀδελφὴ προσδραμοῦσα βασιλίδι·
Θέλεις τροφόν σοι παιδὶ τῷδ᾽ εὕρω ταχὺ
ἐκ τῶν Ἑβραίων; ἡ δ᾽ ἐπέσπευσεν κόρην·
μολοῦσα δ᾽ εἶπε μητρί, καὶ παρῆν ταχὺ
αὐτή τε μήτηρ κἄλαβέν μ᾽ ἐς ἀγκάλας.
εἶπεν δὲ θυγάτηρ βασιλέως Τοῦτον, γύναι,
τρόφεγε, κἀгὼ мιсθὸν ἀποΔώсω σέθεν.

*　　*　　*　　*　　*

οὐκ εὔλογος πέφυκα, γλῶσσα δ᾽ ἐστί μου
δύσφραστος, ἰсχνόφωνος, ὥστε μὴ λόγους
ἐμοὺς γενέσθαι βασιλέως ἐναντίον[2].

Aristobulus: (a) ἐν χειρὶ κρατаιᾷ ἐзήгаген ὁ θεός cε ἐз Αἰгýπτου[3]. (b) ἰδὸγ χεὶρ Κγρίογ ἔcтаι[4] ἐν τοῖс κτήνεсí coγ καὶ ἐν πᾶσι τοῖс ἐν τοῖс πεΔίοιс θάνατος мέгас.

2.   Besides these fragments, some complete books have survived the wreck of the pre-Christian literature of the Jewish colony at Alexandria.   They are included in the Alexandrian Greek Bible, but may be employed as separate witnesses of the literary use of the canonical translations.   And the evidence supplied by them is ample.   Thus the writer of Wisdom knows and uses not only Exodus (Sap. xvi. 22 = Exod. ix. 24,

---

[1] Cf. Job xlii. 17 b, c, i. 1 ff.   Pseudo-Aristeas *ad Philocratem* makes abundant use of the Greek Pentateuch, as the reader may see by referring to the Appendix, where LXX. words and phrases are indicated by the use of small uncials.

[2] Cf. Exod. ii. 4 ff.; iv. 10, where οὐκ εὔλογος is read by cod. F.

[3] Exod. xiii. 9.

[4] Exod. ix. 3.   Ἔσται A, ἐπέσται B.   Καὶ ἐν πᾶσι, which is wanting in our MSS., may be due to a slip of memory, or it is a short way of expressing what follows in the text (ἔν τε τοῖς ἵπποις κτλ.).

and perhaps also Sap. xii. 8 = Exod. xxiii. 28) and Deuteronomy (Sap. vi. 7 = Deut. i. 17, Sap. xi. 4 = Deut. viii. 15), but Isaiah (Sap. ii. 12 = Isa. iii. 10, Sap. xv. 10 = Isa. xliv. 20). The translator of Sirach not only recognises the existence of the Greek Pentateuch and Prophets and 'the other books,' but shews everywhere the influence of the Greek phraseology of the LXX.[1] In 2 Maccabees vii. 6 we have a *verbatim* quotation from Deut. xxxii. 36, and in 4 Maccabees xviii. 14 ff. a catena of references to the Greek Bible, including direct citations of Isa. xliii. 2, Ps. xxxiii. 19, Prov. iii. 18, Ezek. xxxvii. 4, Deut. xxxii. 39, xxx. 20—all from the LXX. The picture which the last-named passage draws of a Jewish father reading and teaching his children out of the Greek Bible (cf. 2 Tim. iii. 15) is a suggestive one, but the book, it must be remembered, is of uncertain date, possibly as late as the time of Josephus, to whom it was at one time ascribed[2].

3. The Jewish portions of the Sibyllines, notwithstanding the epic form in which they are cast, exhibit clear signs of the influence of the LXX. Thus in Sibyll. iii. 312 ἐξέχεας is a reminiscence of Ps. lxxviii. 3, LXX.; *ib.* 606 χειροποίητα...ἐν σχισμαῖς πετρῶν κατακρύψαντες is borrowed from Isa. ii. 19 ff., LXX.; *ib.* 708 ff. is probably modelled on the Greek of Isa. xi. 6 ff.

4. There remains one Alexandrian Jewish writer, the greatest of the succession, whose extant works happily are numerous and throw abundant light on the literary use of the Septuagint at Alexandria.

Philo's literary life probably coincided as nearly as possible with the first forty or five and forty years of the first century

---

[1] See Edersheim in Wace's *Apocr.* ii. p. 26.

[2] Cf. A. Deissmann in Kautzsch, *Pseudepigraphen*, p. 150: "als Abfassungszeit wird man den Zeitraum von Pompejus bis Vespasian annehmen dürfen."

A.D.; in 40 A.D. he could speak of himself as already an old man[1], but his literary activity was not yet at an end, as appears from his account of the embassy to Rome in that year. Thus the evidence of his writings belongs to a period just antecedent to the rise of the earliest Christian literature, and his numerous quotations enable us to form a fair idea of the condition of the text of the LXX. in Alexandrian copies shortly before it passed into the hands of the Church.

The following list of Philo's works may be useful for reference. Cohn and Wendland's order is followed so far as their edition has been published.

A. Exegetical works. *De opificio mundi* (Gen. i.). *Legum allegoriae* (ii. 1—iii. 19). *De Cherubim etc.* (iii. 24—iv. 1). *De sacrificiis Abelis et Caini* (iv. 2 f.). *Quod deterius potiori insidiari soleat* (iv. 3—15). *De posteritate Caini* (iv. 16—26). *De gigantibus* (vi. 1—4). *Quod Deus sit immutabilis* (vi. 4—12). *De agricultura* (ix. 20). *De plantatione Noe* (ix. 20). *De ebrietate* (ix. 21—23). *De sobrietate* (ix. 24). *De confusione linguarum* (xi. 1—9). *De migratione Abrahami* (xii. 1—6). *Quis rerum divinarum heres* (xv.). *De congressu eruditionis gratia* (xvi. 1—6). *De fuga et inventione* (xvi. 6—14). *De mutatione nominum* (xvii. 1—22). *De somniis* i., ii. (xxviii. 12 ff., xxxi. 11—13, xxxvii., xl., xli.). *De Abrahamo. De Josepho. De vita Moysis. De decalogo. De circumcisione. De monarchia. De praemiis sacerdotum. De victimis. De sacrificantibus. De mercede meretricis. De specialibus legibus* (3rd—10th commandments of the Decalogue). *De iudice. De iustitia. De fortitudine. De humanitate. De creatione principum. De tribus virtutibus. De poenitentia. De nobilitate. De praemiis et poenis. De execrationibus. Quaestiones et solutiones* (1) *in Genesim,* (2) *in Exodum*[2]. B. Philosophical works. *De nobilitate. Quod omnis probus liber sit. De vita contemplativa. De incorruptibilitate mundi. De providentia. De ratione animalium. De mundo.* C. Political works. *In Flaccum. De legatione ad Caium.*

In his exegetical writings Philo quotes the LXX. directly, announcing each citation by a formula such as φησί, εἶπεν,

---

[1] *Leg. ad Cai.* i. 28.
[2] On these see J. R. Harris, *Fragments of Philo,* p. 11 ff., and F. C. Conybeare, *Expositor,* IV. iv. p. 456 ff.

λέγει, λέγεται, γέγραπται, or some more elaborate phrase[1]. In this way he reproduces a considerable portion of the Greek text of the Pentateuch, as well as a few passages from Joshua, Judges, 1, 3 Kingdoms, 1 Chronicles, Psalms, Proverbs, Isaiah, Jeremiah, and some of the minor Prophets. His Greek is, on the whole, clearly that of the Alexandrian version, which he regarded as the work of men divinely qualified for their task[2]. Nevertheless his quotations often differ from the Greek of the LXX., as it is found in our extant MSS., or in the oldest and best of them.

5. The task of comparing Philo's quotations with the LXX. has been undertaken in Germany by C. F. Hornemann and C. Siegfried, and in England more recently by Professor Ryle; and from these investigations the student may derive a general acquaintance with the subject, although even the latest of them will need revision when the critical edition of Philo's works, now in course of being published, has reached completion. The following specimens will shew the extent to which Philo departs from the LXX.

Gen. ii. 7 εἰς ψυχὴν ζωῆς (LXX. εἰς ψ. ζῶσαν)[3]. iv. 21 οὗτος ἐστὶ πατὴρ ὁ καταδείξας ψαλτήριον καὶ κιθάραν (LXX., ἦν ὁ κ.). vi. 7 ἐθυμώθην (LXX. ἐνεθυμήθην). vi. 14 νοσσιὰς νοσσιὰς ποιήσεις τὴν κιβωτόν (νοσσιάς *semel* LXX.). ix. 25 παῖς οἰκέτης δοῦλος δούλων ἔσται (LXX. π. οἰκέτης ἔσται, and so Philo, ii. 225. 20). xv. 18 ἕως τοῦ ποταμοῦ, τοῦ μεγάλου ποταμοῦ Εὐφράτου (LXX. om. ποταμοῦ 2⁰)[4]. xviii. 12 οὔπω μοι γέγονε τὸ εὐδαιμονεῖν ἕως τοῦ νῦν (LXX. omit τὸ εὐδ. and so Philo once, iii. 184. 28). Exod. iv. 10 οὐκ εἰμὶ εὔλογος (so Philo, apparently[5]: LXX. οὐκ ἱκανός εἰμι). xv. 17 ἕδρασμα εἰς καθέδραν σου κατειργάσω (LXX. εἰς ἕτοιμον κατοικητήριόν σου ὃ κατ.). xx. 23 μετ᾽ ἐμοῦ (LXX., ὑμῖν αὐτοῖς). xxiii. 2 μετὰ πολλῶν (LXX., μετὰ πλειόνων). Lev. xix. 23 ξύλον βρώσεως (LXX., ξ. βρώσιμον, and so Philo ii. 152. 8). Deut. viii. 18 ἀλλὰ μνείᾳ μνησθήσῃ (LXX. καὶ μνησθ.). xxi. 16 κληροδοτῇ (LXX., κατακληρονομῇ B, κατακληροδοτῇ AF, and these readings are found as variants in Phil. i. 209. 4).

[1] Cf. Ryle, *Philo*, p. xlv. f. [2] Cf. *vit. Moys.* 6, 7.
[3] On this see Nestle, *Zur neuen Philo-Ausgabe* in *Philologus*, 1900, p. 259. Dr Nestle informs me that cod. 75 often agrees with Philo.
[4] See Nestle, *op. cit.*, p. 270. [5] See above, p. 371.

The student who is at the pains to examine the readings
given above, will find that while some of them may be merely
recensional, or even due to slips of memory, the greater part
imply a different rendering of the Hebrew, or even in some
cases a different Hebrew text from that which is presupposed
by the LXX. (Gen. vi. 14, Deut. viii. 18), whilst in others we
seem to have a conflation of two renderings (Gen. iv. 21, ix.
25), one of which is preserved in all extant MSS. of the LXX.,
while the other agrees more nearly with the Hebrew. When
the MSS. of the LXX. are at variance, Philo inclines on the
whole to Cod. B[1], but the preponderance is not strongly
marked. Thus in Exodus—Deuteronomy, he agrees with B
against one or more of the other uncials sixty times, while in
fifty-two places he takes sides against B. It has been observed
that in several instances where Philo opposes the combined
witness of the uncials, he goes with Lucian; e.g. Lev. xviii. 5
ὁ ποιήσας; Deut. xii. 8 ὅσα, xxxii. 4 + ἐν αὐτῷ.

Besides substantial variants, Philo's quotations shew many
departures from the LXX. which may be ascribed to inaccuracy,
defects of memory, or the writer's method of citing. Thus
(*a*) he omits certain words with the view of abbreviating;
(*b*) he substitutes for a portion of his text a gloss or other
explanatory matter of his own; (*c*) he exchanges Hebraisms
and words or phrases which offend him for others in accordance with a correct literary style; (*d*) he forms a fresh sentence
out of two or more different contexts.

E.g. (*a*) Gen. xxiv. 20 καὶ δραμοῦσα ἐπὶ τὸ φρέαρ ὑδρεύσατο
ταῖς καμήλοις (LXX., καὶ ἔδραμεν ἐπὶ τὸ φρέαρ ἀντλῆσαι ὕδωρ καὶ
ὑδρ. πάσαις ταῖς καμήλοις). (*b*) Num. v. 2 ἐξαποστειλάτωσαν ἐκ
τῆς ἁγίου ψυχῆς (LXX. ἐκ τῆς παρεμβολῆς) πάντα λεπρόν. (*c*) Gen.
xxviii. 13 ἡ γῆ (v. l. τὴν γῆν) ἐφ᾽ ἧς σὺ καθεύδεις (+ ἐπ᾽ αὐτῆς LXX.)

---

[1] In Genesis i.—xlvi. 27, where B is wanting, Philo shews on the
whole a similar preference for the text represented by D. The figures,
which are Dr Ryle's, are based on Mangey's text, but the new edition, so
far as examined, gives very similar results.

σοὶ δώσω αὐτήν. (*d*) Gen. xvii. 1+xxxv. 11 ἐγώ εἰμι θεὸς σός· ἐγὼ
ὁ θεός σου· αὐξάνου καὶ πληθύνου (Phil. iii. 161. 4 f.).

The majority of Philo's quotations from the LXX. are
modified in one or other of these ways. Philo entertained
the highest veneration for the Jewish canon, especially for
the law, which he regarded as a body of Divine oracles[1]; and
his respect for the Alexandrian Version was at least as great
as that with which the Authorised Version is regarded in
England, and Luther's Version in Germany. Nevertheless he
did not scruple to quote his text freely, changing words at
pleasure, and sometimes mingling interpretation with citation.
This method of dealing with a source, however high its
authority, was probably not peculiar to Philo, but a literary
habit which he shared with other Jewish writers of his age[2].
We shall have occasion to observe it again when we consider
the use of the LXX. by the writers of the New Testament.

6.   The Alexandrian Version was also used by the Palestinian Jew, Flavius Josephus, who represents Jewish Hellenistic literature in the generation which followed Philo. He was
born at Jerusalem within the lifetime of the great Alexandrian
(A.D. 37—8). He was descended from a priestly family[3];
his early education familiarised him with the learning of the
Rabbis, and the opinions of the great schools of Jewish
thought; in his nineteenth year he was enrolled a member
of the sect of the Pharisees[4]. His earliest work, on the
Jewish War, was written in Aramaic[5], and when he desired to
translate it into Greek, he was constrained to seek assistance
(*c. Ap.* i. 9 χρησάμενός τισι πρὸς τὴν Ἑλληνίδα φωνὴν συνεργοῖς
οὕτως ἐποιησάμην τῶν πράξεων τὴν παράδοσιν). But the *Antiquities of the Jews* (αἱ Ἰωσήπου ἱστορίαι τῆς Ἰουδαϊκῆς ἀρχαιολογίας),

---

[1] See Ryle, p. xvi. ff.
[2] Cf. *D. C. B.* iv. p. 387ᵃ.
[3] *Vit.* 1.   [4] *Ib.* 2.
[5] *B. J. prooem.* 1 τῇ πατρίῳ [sc. γλώσσῃ] συντάξας.

which appear to have been completed in A.D. 93—4, form an original Greek work which, so far as we know, was composed without material help. In it Josephus professes to interpret the Hebrew records for the benefit of Hellenic readers: *Ant.* i. *proem.* 1 ταύτην δὲ τὴν ἐνεστῶσαν ἐγκεχείρισμαι πραγματείαν, νομίζων ἅπασι φανεῖσθαι τοῖς Ἕλλησιν ἀξίαν σπουδῆς· μέλλει γὰρ περιέξειν ἅπασαν τὴν παρ' ἡμῖν ἀρχαιολογίαν καὶ διάταξιν τοῦ πολιτεύματος ἐκ τῶν Ἑβραϊκῶν μεθηρμηνευμένην γραμμάτων. His chief source, therefore, was the Hebrew Bible, with which he was doubtless acquainted from boyhood[1]. Nevertheless, there is ample evidence in the *Antiquities* that the writer knew and, for the purpose of his work, used the Alexandrian Greek version. He does not, indeed, like Philo, quote formally either from the Hebrew or from the Greek, but he shews a knowledge of both.

His indebtedness to the LXX. appears in a variety of ways. (*a*) He interprets proper names as they are interpreted by the LXX. e.g. *Ant.* I. 1. 2 Εὖα...σημαίνει...πάντων μητέρα (Gen. iii. 20); I. 2. 1 Κάϊς...κτίσιν (v. l. κτῆσιν) σημαίνει (Gen. iv. 1); iii. 1. 6 καλοῦσι δὲ Ἑβραῖοι τὸ βρῶμα τοῦτο μάννα· τὸ γὰρ μὰν ἐπερώτησις...'τί τοῦτ' ἔστιν' ἀνακρίνουσα (Exod. xvi. 15); v. 10. 3 Σαμουῆλον...θεαίτητον ἄν τις εἴποι (1 Regn. i. 20). (*b*) His narrative frequently follows a Heb. text different from the M.T., but represented by the LXX.; e.g. *Ant.* vi. 4. 1 ἦσαν ἑβδομήκοντα τὸν ἀριθμόν (1 Regn. ix. 22, 𝕸 בִּשְׁלֹשִׁים); vi. 11. 4 ὑποθεῖσα τοῖς ἐπιβολιαίοις ἧπαρ (כבד) αἰγός (1 Regn. xix. 13, 𝕸 כְּבִיר); vi. 12. 4 Δώηγος δ' ὁ Σύρος ὁ τὰς ἡμιόνους αὐτοῦ βόσκων (1 Regn. xxii. 9, 𝕸 וְהוּא נִצָּב עַל־עַבְדֵי־שָׁאוּל הָאֲדֹמִי דֹּאֵג); vii. 2. 1 μόνον εὑρόντες...τὸν Ἰέσβωθον καὶ μήτε τοὺς φύλακας παρόντας μήτε τὴν θυρωρὸν ἐγρηγορυῖαν (cf. 2 Regn. iv. 6 LXX. καὶ ἰδοὺ ἡ θυρωρὸς ἐνύσταξεν καὶ ἐκάθευδεν); vii. 5. 3 ὕστερον ὁ τῶν

---

[1] He possessed a copy of the sacred books which Titus granted him from the spoils of the Temple: *Vit.* 75 τὴν αἴτησιν ἐποιούμην Τίτον...βιβλίων ἱερῶν [καὶ] ἔλαβον χαρισαμένου Τίτου.

Αἰγυπτίων βασιλεὺς Σούσακος...ἔλαβε (2 Regn. viii. 7, LXX.;Λℳ).
(c) Whilst retailing in his own words the story of the Hebrew
records, he falls from time to time into the peculiar phraseology of the Alexandrian version. A few examples will make
this evident. *Ant.* i. 1 (Gen. i. 1 ff.), ἐν ἀρχῇ ἔκτισεν ὁ θεὸς
τὸν οὐρανὸν καὶ τὴν γῆν...γενέσθαι φῶς ἐκέλευσεν ὁ θεός...
διεχώρισε τό τε φῶς καὶ τὸ σκότος...καὶ αὕτη μὲν ἂν εἴη
πρώτη ἡμέρα, Μωυσῆς δ᾽ αὐτὴν μίαν εἶπε...τὸ τῶν τετραπόδων
γένος ἄρρεν καὶ θῆλυ ποιήσας. i. 10. 3 (Gen. xv. 9 f.) δάμα-
λιν τριετίζουσαν καὶ αἶγα τριετίζουσαν καὶ κριὸν ὁμοίως
τριετῆ καὶ τρυγόνα καὶ περιστερὰν κελεύσαντος διεῖλε, τῶν
ὀρνέων οὐδὲν διελών. i. 18. 7 (Gen. xxvii. 30) παρῆν Ἡσαῦς
ἀπὸ τῆς θήρας. i. 20. 2 (Gen. xxxii. 23 f.) χειμάρρουν τινὰ
Ἰάβακχον λεγόμενον διαβεβηκότων Ἰάκωβος ὑπολελειμμένος
...διεπάλαιεν. ii. 4. 1 (Gen. xxxix. 1) Ἰώσηφον δὲ πωλούμενον
ὑπὸ τῶν ἐμπόρων ὠνησάμενος Πετεφρῆς ἀνὴρ Αἰγύπτιος ἐπὶ
τῶν Φαραώθου μαγείρων. ii. 6. 1 (Gen. xli. 45) προσηγόρευσεν
αὐτὸν Ψονθονφάνηχον...ἄγεται γὰρ καὶ Πετεφροῦ θυγατέρα τῶν
ἐν τῇ Ἡλιουπόλει ἱερέων...Ἀσέννηθιν ὀνόματι. ii. 7. 5 (Gen.
xlvi. 28) ἀπαντησόμενος ἔξεισι καὶ καθ᾽ Ἡρώων πόλιν αὐτῷ
συνέβαλεν[1]. (d) There is evidence to shew that Josephus used
1 Esdras, which is known only in a Greek form, and the Book
of Esther with the Greek additions. 1 *Esdras.* *Ant.* xi. 1. 1
(1 Esdr. ii. 3 f.) Κῦρος ὁ βασιλεὺς λέγει Ἐπεί με ὁ θεὸς ὁ
μέγιστος τῆς οἰκουμένης ἀπέδειξε βασιλέα, τὸν ναὸν αὐτοῦ
οἰκοδομήσω ἐν Ἱεροσολύμοις ἐν τῇ Ἰουδαίᾳ χώρᾳ. xi. 2. 2
(1 Esdr. ii. 21, cf. 2 Esdr. iv. 17) βασιλεὺς Καμβύσης
Ῥαθύμῳ τῷ γράφοντι τὰ προσπίπτοντα καὶ Βεελζέμῳ καὶ
Σεμελίῳ γραμματεῖ καὶ τοῖς λοιποῖς τοῖς συντασσομένοις
καὶ οἰκοῦσιν ἐν Σαμαρείᾳ καὶ Φοινίκῃ τάδε λέγει. xi. 3.
2—8 = 1 Esdr. iii.—iv. *Esther.* *Ant.* xi. 6. 6 = Esth. B; xi.
6. 8 ff. = C, D; xi. 6. 12 f. = E. The first Book of Maccabees

---

[1] For some of these instances I am indebted to a collation made by
Mr C. G. Wright for the Editors of the larger LXX.

was also known to Josephus in its Greek form[1], which underlies his account of the Maccabean wars, just as the Greek
translation of the canonical books is used in the earlier books
of the *Antiquities*.

A recent examination, by A. Mez, of Basle[2], into the
Biblical text presupposed by Josephus' history in *Ant.* v.—vii.
has led to the following results, which are important for the
criticism of the LXX. (1) The Josephus text of the LXX. has
no affinity with the characteristic text of cod. B. (2) In Joshua
it generally approximates to the text of 𝕳. (3) In Judges
it is frequently, but not constantly, Lucianic; in 1, 2 Kingdoms
it agrees with Lucian so closely as to fall into the same omissions and misconceptions; only in four instances, other than
proper names, does it contravene a Lucianic reading, and
three of these are numerical differences, whilst in the fourth
'Lucian' appears to have undergone correction, and the reading of Josephus survives in cod. A. These investigations, so
far as they go, point to a probability that in these books the
Greek Bible of Palestine during the second half of the first
century presented a text not very remote from that of the recension which emanated from Antioch early in the fourth.
While Philo the Alexandrian supports on the whole the text
of our oldest uncial cod. B, Josephus the Palestinian seems
to have followed that of an 'Urlucian.'

LITERATURE. Hellenistic writers before Philo: Text: C.
Müller, *Fragmenta historica Graeca* iii. J. Freudenthal, *Hellenistische Studien* i., ii. (Breslau, 1875). Cf. Susemihl, *Geschichte
der griech. Litteratur in der Alexandrinerzeit*, ii. p. 356 ff.; E.
Schürer, *Geschichte des jüdischen Volkes*[3], iii. p. 345 ff.; Oeconomus,
ii. 76.

Philo: Text: L. Cohn and P. Wendland, *Philonis Alexandini
opera quae supersunt* (Berlin, vol. i. 1896; vol. ii. 1897; vol. iii.
1898; vol. iv. 1902; vol. v. 1906—in progress). Cf. C. F.
Hornemann, *Specimen exercitationum criticarum in versionem*

---

[1] Bloch, *Die Quellen d. Fl. Josephus*, p. 8 ff.
[2] *Die Bibel des Josephus*, p. 79 ff.

LXX. interpretum ex Philone (Göttingen, 1773); C. Siegfried, *Philo und der überlieferte Text der LXX.* (in *Z. f. wiss. Theologie*, 1873, pp. 217 ff., 411 ff., 522 ff.); A. Edersheim in *D. C. B.* iv. p. 357 ff.; E. Hatch, *Essays in Biblical Greek* (Oxford, 1889), p. 140 ff.; F. C. Conybeare, in *Expositor*, 1891, p. 456 ff.; and *Jewish Q. R.*, 1893, p. 246 ff., 1896, p. 88 ff.; H. E. Ryle, *Philo and Holy Scripture* (London, 1895); P. Wendland, in *Philologus* 1898, p. 283 ff., 521 ff., 1899, 274 ff.; L. Massebieau, *Le classement des œuvres de Philon* (in *Bibliothèque de l'école des hautes études* I. pp. 1—91); J. Drummond, in Hastings' *D. B.* suppl. 197; J. H. A. Hart, in *J. Q. R.* xvii. p. 78 ff.; Aug. Schröder, *De Philonis Alexandrini Vet. Test.*, Greifswald, 1907.

Sibyllines. Text: A. Rzach, *Oracula Sibyllina*, Vienna, 1891. Cf. F. Blass in Kautzsch, *Pseudepigraphen*, p. 177 ff.

Josephus. Text: B. Niese, *Fl. Josephi opera* (Berlin, 1887—1895). Cf. Spittler, 1779, J. G. Scharfenberg, 1780; E. Schürer², E. T. I. i. p. 77 ff.; A. Edersheim in *D. C. B.* iii. p. 441 ff.; C. Siegfried in Stade's *Z. f. d. A Tliche Wissenschaft*, 1883, p. 32 ff.; H. Bloch, *Die Quellen des Fl. Josephus in seiner Archäologia* (Leipzig, 1879); A. Mez, *Die Bibel des Josephus untersucht für Buch v.—vii. der Archäologia* (Basle, 1895).

CHAPTER II.

Quotations from the LXX. in the New Testament.

1. The writings of the New Testament were the work of some nine authors, of different nationalities and antecedents. Six of them, according to the traditional belief, were Palestinian Jews; a seventh, though 'a Hebrew of Hebrew parentage,' belonged by birth to the Dispersion of Asia Minor; of the remaining two, one was possibly a Gentile from Antioch, and the other a 'Hellenist with Alexandrian proclivities.' Some diversity of practice as to the literary use of the Greek Old Testament may reasonably be expected in a collection of books having so complex an origin.

With few exceptions, the books of the New Testament abound in references to the Old Testament and in quotations from it. An exhaustive list of these may be seen at the end of Westcott and Hort's *New Testament in Greek* (Text, p. 581 ff.), and in their text the corresponding passages are distinguished by the use of a small uncial type. But this device, though otherwise admirable[1], does not enable the student to distinguish direct citations from mere allusions and reminiscences; and as the distinction is important for our present purpose, we will begin by placing before him a table of passages in the Old Testament which are formally quoted by New Testament writers.

[1] See below, p. 403.

By passages formally cited we understand (1) those which are cited with an introductory formula, such as τοῦτο γέγονεν ἵνα πληρωθῇ τὸ ῥηθέν (Mt.), οὕτως or καθὼς γέγραπται, or γέγραπται simply (Mt., Mc., Lc., Paul), γεγραμμένον ἐστίν (Jo.), Μωυσῆς (Δαυείδ) λέγει or εἶπεν, λέγει or εἶπεν ἡ γραφή (Jo., Paul), or τὸ ἅγιον πνεῦμα (Hebrews); (2) those which, though not announced by a formula, appear from the context to be intended as quotations, or agree verbatim with some context in the O. T.

Table of O.T. passages quoted in the N.T.

Gen.	i. 27 (v. 2)	Mt.	xix. 4, Mc. x. 6
	ii. 2	Heb.	iv. 4
	7	1 Cor.	xv. 45
	24	Mt.	xix. 5 f., Mc. x. 7 f., 1 Cor. vi. 16, Eph. v. 31
	v. 24	Heb.	xi. 5
	xii. 1	Acts	vii. 3
	3ᵇ (xxii. 18)		iii. 25, Gal. iii. 8
	xv. 5	Rom.	iv. 18
	6	Jas.	ii. 23, Rom. iv. 3, Gal. iii. 6
	13 f.	Acts	vii. 6 f.
	xvii. 5	Rom.	iv. 17
	xviii. 10, 14		ix. 9
	xxi. 10	Gal.	iv. 30
	12	Rom.	ix. 7, Heb. xi. 18
	xxii. 16 f.	Heb.	vi. 13 f.
	xxv. 23	Rom.	ix. 12
	xlvii. 31	Heb.	xi. 21
Exod.	ii. 14	Acts	vii. 27 f.
	iii. 5 ff.	Mt.	xxii. 32, Mc. xii. 26, Lc. xx. 37, Acts vii. 32 ff.
	ix. 16	Rom.	ix. 17
	xii. 46 (Num. ix. 12, Ps. xxxiii. 20)	John	xix. 36
	xiii. 12	Lc.	ii. 23
	xvi. 4, 15 (Ps. lxxvii. 24)	John	vi. 31 ff.
	18	2 Cor.	viii. 15
	xix. 13	Heb.	xii. 20
	xx. 12—17 (Deut. v. 16 ff.)	Mt.	v. 21, 27, xv. 4—6, xix. 18 f., Mc. vii. 10, x. 19, Lc. xviii. 20, James ii. 11, Rom. vii. 7, xiii. 9, Eph. vi. 2 f.
	xxi. 16 (17)		xv. 4, Mc. vii. 10

Exod.	xxi. 24 (Lev. xxiv. 20, Deut. xix. 21)	Mt.	v. 38
	xxii. 28	Acts	xxiii. 5
	xxiv. 8	Heb.	ix. 19 f.
	xxv. 40		viii. 5
	xxxii. 1	Acts	vii. 40
	6	1 Cor.	x. 7
	xxxiii. 19	Rom.	ix. 15
Lev.	xi. 44 f. (xix. 2, xx. 7, 26)	1 Pet.	i. 16
	xii. 6, 8	Lc.	ii. 22 ff.
	xviii. 5 (2 Esdr. xix. 29)	Rom.	x. 5, Gal. iii. 12
	xix. 18	Mt.	v. 43, xix. 19, xxii. 39, Mc. xii. 31, Lc. x. 27, James ii. 8, Rom. xiii. 9, Gal. v. 14
	xxvi.11f.(Ezek. xxxvii.27)	2 Cor.	vi. 16
Num.	xvi. 5	2 Tim.	ii. 19
Deut.	iv. 35	Mc.	xii. 32
	vi. 4 f.	Mt.	xxii. 37 f., Mc. xii. 29—33, Lc. x. 27
	13, 16		iv. 7, 10, Lc. iv. 8, 12
	viii. 3		iv. 4, Lc. iv. 4
	ix. 19	Heb.	xii. 21 (?)
	xviii. 15, 18 f.	Acts	iii. 22 f., vii. 37
	xix. 15	Mt.	xviii. 16, Jo. viii. 17, 2 Cor. xiii. 1
	xxi. 23	Gal.	iii. 13
	xxiv. 1	Mt.	v. 31, xix. 7, Mc. x. 4
	xxv. 4	1 Cor.	ix. 9, 1 Tim. v. 18
	xxvii. 26	Gal.	iii. 10
	xxix. 4	Rom.	xi. 8
	18	Heb.	xii. 15
	xxx. 12—14	Rom.	x. 6—8
	xxxi. 6, 8 (Jos. i. 5)	Heb.	xiii. 5
	xxxii. 21	Rom.	x. 19
	35		xii. 19, Heb. x. 30
	36 (Ps. cxxxiv. 14)	Heb.	x. 30
	43 (Ps. xcvi. 7)		i. 6
2 Regn.	vii. 8, 14	2 Cor.	vi. 18, Heb. i. 5
3 Regn.	xix. 10, 14, 18	Rom.	xi. 3 f.
Psalm	ii. 1 f.	Acts	iv. 25 f.
	7		xiii. 33, Heb. i. 5, v. 5
	viii. 2	Mt.	xxi. 16
	5—7	1 Cor.	xv. 27, Heb. ii. 6—8
	xiii. 3 (v. 10, ix. 28, xxxv. 2, lii. 1—3, cxxxix. 4, Isa. lix. 7 f.)	Rom.	iii. 10—18

Psalm	xv. 8—11	Acts	ii. 25—28
	xvii. 50	Rom.	xv. 9
	xviii. 5		x. 18
	xxi. 2	Mt.	xxvii. 46, Mc. xv. 34
	9		xxvii. 43
	19	Jo.	xix. 24
	23	Heb.	ii. 12
	xxiii. 1	1 Cor.	x. 26
	xxxi. 1 f.	Rom.	iv. 6—8
	xxxiii. 13—17	1 Pet.	iii. 10—12
	xxxiv. 19 (lxviii. 5)	Jo.	xv. 25
	xxxix. 7—9	Heb.	x. 5—7
	xl. 10	Jo.	xiii. 18
	xliii. 22	Rom.	viii. 36
	xliv. 7 f.	Heb.	i. 8 f.
	l. 6	Rom.	iii. 4
	liv. 23	1 Pet.	v. 7
	lxvii. 19	Eph.	iv. 8
	lxviii. 10	Jo.	ii. 17, Rom. xv. 3
	23 f.	Rom.	xi. 9 f.
	26	Acts	i. 20
	lxxvii. 2	Mt.	xiii. 35
	lxxxi. 6	Jo.	x. 34
	lxxxviii. 21	Acts	xiii. 22
	xc. 11 f.	Mt.	iv. 6, Lc. iv. 10 f.
	xciii. 11	1 Cor.	iii. 20
	xciv. 8—11	Heb.	iii. 7—11
	ci. 26—28		i. 10—12
	ciii. 4		i. 7
	cviii. 8	Acts	i. 20
	cix. 1	Mt.	xxii. 44, Mc. xii. 36, Lc. xx. 42 f., Acts ii. 34 f., Heb. i. 13
	4	Heb.	v. 6 (vii. 17, 21)
	cxi. 9	2 Cor.	ix. 9
	cxv. 1		iv. 13
	cxvi. 1	Rom.	xv. 11
	cxvii. 6	Heb.	xiii. 6
	22 f.	Mt.	xxi. 42, Mc. xii. 10 f., Lc. xx. 17, 1 Pet. ii. 7
Prov.	iii. 11 f.	Heb.	xii. 5 f.
	34	Jas.	iv. 6, 1 Pet. v. 5
	xi. 31	1 Pet.	iv. 18
	xxv. 21 f.	Rom.	xii. 20
	xxvi. 11	2 Pet.	ii. 22
Job	v. 13	1 Cor.	iii. 19
Hos.	i. 10	Rom.	ix. 26

Hos.	ii. 23	Rom.	ix. 25
	vi. 6	Mt.	ix. 13, xii. 7
	xi. 1		ii. 15
	xiii. 14	1 Cor.	xv. 55 f.
Amos	v. 25, 27	Acts	vii. 42 f.
	ix. 11 f.		xv. 15—17
Mic.	v. 2	Mt.	ii. 5 f. (Jo. vii. 42)
Joel	ii. 28—32	Acts	ii. 17—21
Hab.	i. 5		xiii. 41
	ii. 3 f.	Rom.	i. 17, Gal. iii. 11, Heb. x. 37 f.
Zech.	iii. 2	Jude	9
	ix. 9	Mt.	xxi. 5, Jo. xii. 15
	xi. 13		xxvii. 9 f.
	xii. 10	Jo.	xix. 37
	xiii. 7	Mt.	xxvi. 31, Mc. xiv. 27
Mal.	i. 2 f.	Rom.	ix. 13
	iii. 1	Mt.	xi. 10, Mc. i. 2, Lc. vii. 27
Isa.	i. 9	Rom.	ix. 29
	vi. 9 f.	Mt.	xiii. 14 f., Mc. iv. 12, Lc. viii. 10, Jo. xii. 40 f., Acts xxviii. 26 f.
			i. 23
	vii. 14		
	viii. 14	Rom.	ix. 33, 1 Pet. ii. 8
	17	Heb.	ii. 13
	ix. 1 f.	Mt.	iv. 15 f.
	x. 22 f.	Rom.	ix. 27 f.
	xi. 10		xv. 12
	xxii. 13	1 Cor.	xv. 32
	xxv. 8		54
	xxviii. 11 f.		xiv. 21
	16	Rom.	ix. 33, x. 11, 1 Pet. ii. 6
	xxix. 10		xi. 8
	13	Mt.	xv. 8 f., Mc. vii. 6 f.
	14	1 Cor.	i. 19
	xl. 3—5	Mt.	iii. 3, Mc. i. 3, Lc. iii. 4—6, Jo. i. 23
	6—8	1 Pet.	i. 24 f.
	13 f.	Rom.	xi. 34 f., 1 Cor. ii. 16
	xlii. 1—4	Mt.	xii. 18—21
	xlv. 23	Rom.	xiv. 11
	xlix. 6	Acts	xiii. 47
	8	2 Cor.	vi. 2
	lii. 5	Rom.	ii. 24
	7 (Nah. i. 15)		x. 15
	11	2 Cor.	vi. 17

S. S.

25

Isa.	lii. 15	Rom.	xv. 21
	liii. 1	Jo.	xii. 38, Rom. x. 16
	4	Mt.	viii. 17
	5 f.	1 Pet.	ii. 24 f.
	7 f.	Acts	viii. 32 f.
	12	Mc.	xv. 28, Lc. xxii. 37
	liv. 1	Gal.	iv. 27
	13	Jo.	vi. 45
	lv. 3	Acts	xiii. 34
	lvi. 7	Mt.	xxi. 13, Mc. xi. 17, Lc. xix. 46
	lix. 20 f.	Rom.	xi. 26 f.
	lxi. 1 f.	Lc.	iv. 18 f.
	lxiv. 4	1 Cor.	ii. 9 (?)
	lxv. 1 f.	Rom.	x. 20 f.
	lxvi. 1 f.	Acts	vii. 49 f.
	24	Mc.	ix. 48
Jer.	vii. 11	Mt.	xxi. 13, Mc. xi. 17, Lc. xix. 46
	ix. 23 f. (1 Regn. ii. 10)	1 Cor.	i. 31, 2 Cor. x. 17
	xxxviii. 15	Mt.	ii. 18
	31—34	Heb.	viii. 8—12
Dan.	xii. 11 (ix. 27, xi. 31)	Mt.	xxiv. 15, Mc. xiii. 14

Thus upon a rough estimate the passages directly quoted from the Old Testament by writers of the New Testament are 160. Of these 51 belong to the Pentateuch, 46 to the Poetical Books, and 61 to the Prophets. Among single books the Psalter supplies 40 and Isaiah 38; i.e. nearly half of the passages expressly cited in the N.T. come from one or other of these two sources.

2. The table already given shews the extent to which the Old Testament is directly cited in the New. In that which follows the comparison is inverted, and the student will be able to see at a glance how the quotations are distributed among the several groups of writings of which the New Testament is made up.

(1) *Quotations in the Synoptic Gospels.*

Mt.	Mc.	Lc.	O. T.
i. 23			Isa. vii. 14
	—	ii. 23	Exod. xiii. 12

Mt.		Mc.	Lc.	O. T.
ii.	6			Mic. v. 2
	15			Hos. xi. 1
	18			Jer. xxxviii. 15
iii.	3	i. 3	iii. 4—6	Isa. xl. 3—5
iv.	4		iv. 4	Deut. viii. 3
	6		10 f.	Ps. xc. 11 f.
	7		12	Deut. vi. 16
	10		8	13
	15 f.			Isa. ix. 1 f.
v.	21			Exod. xx. 13
	27			14
	31			Deut. xxiv. 1
	33			Num. xxx. 3 (cf. Deut. xxiii. 21)
	38			Exod. xxi. 24
	43			Lev. xix. 18
viii.	17			Isa. liii. 4
ix.	13 (xii. 7)			Hos. vi. 6
xi.	10	i. 2	vii. 27	Mal. iii. 1
xii.	7			Hos. vi. 6
	18—21			Isa. xlii. 1
xiii.	14 f.			vi. 9 f.
	35			Ps. lxxvii. 2
			iv. 18 f.	Isa. lxi. 1 ff. + lviii. 6
xv.	4	vii. 10		Exod. xx. 12, xxi. 17
	8 f.	6		Isa. xxix. 13
		ix. 48		lxvi. 24
xix.	5 f.	x. 6—8		Gen. i. 27 + ii. 24
	18 f.	x. 19	xviii. 20 f.	Exod. xx. 12—17
xxi.	4 f.			Zech. ix. 9 + Isa. lxii. 11
	13	xi. 17	xix. 46	Isa. lvi. 7 + Jer. vii. 11
	16			Ps. viii. 2
	42	xii. 10	xx. 17	cxvii. 22 f.
xxii.	24	19	28	Deut. xxv. 5 (cf. Gen. xxxviii. 8)
	32	26	37	Exod. iii. 6
	37	29 f.	x. 27ᵃ	Deut. vi. 4 f.
	39	31	27ᵇ	Lev. xix. 18
		32		Deut. iv. 35
	44	36	xx. 42 f.	Ps. cix. 1
xxiv.	15	xiii. 14		Dan. xii. 11
			xxii. 37	Isa. liii. 12
xxvi.	31	xiv. 27		Zech. xiii. 7
xxvii.	9 f.			xi. 13
	46	xv. 34		Ps. xxi. 1

25—2

(2) Quotations in the Fourth Gospel.

Jo.	i. 23	Isa.	xl. 3
	ii. 17	Ps.	lxviii. 10
	vi. 31	Exod.	xvi. 4, 15 (Ps. lxxvii. 24f.)
	45	Isa.	liv. 13
	x. 34	Ps.	lxxxi. 6
	xii. 15	Zech.	ix. 9
	38	Isa.	liii. 1
	40		vi. 10
	xiii. 16	Ps.	xl. (xli.) 10
	xv. 25		xxxiv. 19 (lxviii. 5)
	xix. 24		xxi. 19
	36	Exod.	xii. 46 (Num. ix. 12, Ps. xxxiii. 21)
	37	Zech.	xii. 10

(3) Quotations in the Acts.

Acts	i. 20	Ps.	lxviii. 26 + cviii. 8
	ii. 17—21	Joel	ii. 28—32
	25—28	Ps.	xv. 8—11
	34 f.		cix. 1
	iii. 22 f. (vii. 27)	Deut.	xviii. 15, 18 f.
	25	Gen.	xii. 3 + xxii. 18
	iv. 25 f.	Ps.	ii. 1 f.
	vii. 3	Gen.	xii. 1
	6 f.		xv. 13 f.
	27 f., 35	Exod.	ii. 14
	33 f.		iii. 6—8
	40		xxxii. 23
	42 f.	Amos	v. 25—27
	49 f.	Isa.	lxvi. 1 f.
	viii. 32 f		liii. 7 f.
	xiii. 22	Ps.	lxxxviii. 21 etc.
	33		ii. 7
	34	Isa.	lv. 3
	35	Ps.	xv. 10
	41	Hab.	i. 5
	47	Isa.	xlix. 6
	xv. 16—18	Jer.	xii. 15 + Amos ix. 11 f. + Isa. xlv. 21
	xxviii. 26 f.	Isa.	vi. 9 f.

(4) *Quotations in the Catholic Epistles.*

James	ii. 8	Lev.	xix. 18
	11	Exod.	xx. 13 f.
	23	Gen.	xv. 6
	iv. 6	Prov.	iii. 34
1 Peter	i. 24 f.	Isa.	xl. 6—9
	ii. 6		xxviii. 16
	iii. 10—12	Ps.	xxxiii. 12—17
	iv. 18	Prov.	xi. 31
	v. 7	Ps.	liv. 23
2 Peter	ii. 22	Prov.	xxvi. 11
Jude	9	Zech.	iii. 2

(5) *Quotations in the Epistles of St Paul.*

Rom.	i. 17	Hab.	ii. 4
	ii. 24	Isa.	lii. 5
	iii. 4	Ps.	l. 6
	10—18		xiii. 1—3[1]
	20		cxlii. 2
	iv. 3, 22	Gen.	xv. 6
	7 f.	Ps.	xxxi. 1 f.
	17	Gen.	xvii. 5
	18		xv. 5
	vii. 7	Exod.	xx. 14, 17
	viii. 36	Ps.	xliii. 23
	ix. 7	Gen.	xxi. 12
	9		xviii. 10
	12		xxv. 23
	13	Mal.	i. 2 f.
	15	Exod.	xxxiii. 19
	17		ix. 16
	26	Hos.	i. 10
	27	Isa.	x. 22 f.
	29		i. 9
	33		viii. 14 + xxviii. ·16
	x. 6—9	Deut.	xxx. 11—14
	15	Isa.	lii. 7 (Nah. i. 15)
	16		liii. 1
	18	Ps.	xviii. 5
	19	Deut.	xxxii. 21
	20 f.	Isa.	lxv. 1 f.

---

[1] See above, p. 251 f.

Rom.	xi. 1 f.	Ps.	xciii. 14
	3 f.	3 Regn.	xix. 10, 14, 18
	8	Isa.	xxix. 10 + Deut. xxix. 4
	9	Ps.	lxviii. 23 f. + xxxiv. 8
	26 f.	Isa.	lix. 20 + xxvii. 9
	34 f.		xl. 13
	xii. 20 f.	Prov.	xxv. 21 f.
	xiii. 9	Exod.	xx. 13 ff., Lev. xix. 18
	xiv. 11	Isa.	xlv. 23
	xv. 3	Ps.	lxviii. 10
	9		xvii. 50 (2 Regn. xxii. 50)
	10	Deut.	xxxii. 43
	11	Ps.	cxvi. 1
	12	Isa.	xi. 10
	21		lii. 15
1 Cor.	i. 19		xxix. 14
	31	Jer.	ix. 24
	ii. 9	Isa.	lxiv. 4 + lxv. 17 (?)
	20	Ps.	xciii. 11
	vi. 16	Gen.	ii. 24
	ix. 9	Deut.	xxv. 4
	x. 7	Exod.	xxxii. 6
	26	Ps.	xxiii. 1
	xiv. 21	Isa.	xxviii. 11 f.
	xv. 32		xxii. 13
	45	Gen.	ii. 7
	54 f.	Isa.	xxv. 8 + Hos. xiii. 14
2 Cor.	iv. 13	Ps.	cxv. 1
	vi. 2	Isa.	xlix. 8
	16 ff.	Ezek.	xxxvii. 27 + Isa. lii. 11
	viii. 15	Exod.	xvi. 18
	ix. 9	Ps.	cxi. 9
	x. 17	Jer.	ix. 24
Gal.	ii. 16	Ps.	cxlii. 2
	iii. 6	Gen.	xv. 6
	8		xii. 3
	10	Deut.	xxvii. 26
	11	Hab.	ii. 4
	12	Lev.	xviii. 5
	13	Deut.	xxi. 23
	iv. 27	Isa.	liv. 1
	30	Gen.	xxi. 10
	v. 14	Lev.	xix. 18
Eph.	iv. 8	Ps.	lxviii. 19
	25	Zech.	viii. 16

Eph.	iv. 26	Ps.	iv. 5
	v. 31	Gen.	ii. 24
	vi. 2	Exod.	xx. 12
1 Tim.	v. 18	Deut.	xxv. 4
2 Tim.	ii. 19	Num.	xvi. 5

(6) *Quotations in the Epistle to the Hebrews.*

Heb.	i. 5	Ps.	ii. 7 (2 Regn. vii. 14)
	6		xcvi. 7 (Deut. xxxii. 43)
	7		ciii. 4
	8 f.		xliv. 7 f.
	10—12		ci. 26—28
	13		cix. 1
	ii. 6—8		viii. 5—7
	12		xxi. 23
	13	Isa.	viii. 17 f.
	iii. 7—12	Ps.	xciv. 8—11
	iv. 4	Gen.	ii. 2
	v. 6 (vii. 17, 21)	Ps.	cix. 4
	vi. 13 f.	Gen.	xxii. 16 f.
	viii. 5	Exod.	xxv. 40
	8—13, x. 16 f.	Jer.	xxxviii. 31—34
	ix. 20	Exod.	xxiv. 8
	x. 5—10	Ps.	xxxix. 7—9
	30	Deut.	xxxii. 35 f.
	37 f.	Hab.	ii. 3 f.
	xi. 5	Gen.	v. 24
	18		xxi. 12
	21		xlvii. 31
	xii. 5 f.	Prov.	iii. 11 f.
	15	Deut.	xxix. 18
	20	Exod.	xix. 12 f.
	26	Hagg.	ii. 6
	xiii. 5	Deut.	xxxi. 6, 8
	6	Ps.	cxvii. 6

Some interesting results follow from an inspection of these lists. (1) The Synoptic Gospels have 46 distinct quotations (Mt. 40, Mc. 19, Lc. 17), of which 18 are peculiar to Mt., 3 to Mc., 3 to Lc. There are 10 which are common to the three, 3 common to Mt. and Mc., 4 to Mt. and Lc., but none which are shared by Mc. and Lc. to the exclusion of Mt. (2) Of the 12 quotations in the Fourth Gospel, 3 only are also in the Synoptists. (3) The 23 quotations in the Acts occur almost exclusively in the speeches. (4) The Johannine Epistles do not quote the O. T. at all, and the other Catholic Epistles contain few direct citations. (5) Of 78 quotations in St Paul, 71 are in the four first Epistles (Romans 42, 1—2 Corinthians 19, Galatians 10); there are none in the Epistles of the Roman captivity, with the exception of Ephesians, which has five. (6) The Epistle to the Hebrews quotes 28 passages, of which 21 are not cited in any other N. T. writing[1]. (7) The Apocalypse does not quote, but its language is full of O. T. phraseology to an extent unparalleled in the other books.

3. Hitherto no account has been taken of the relation which the N. T. quotations bear to the Alexandrian version, although for the sake of convenience the references to the O. T. have been given according to the order and numeration of the Greek Bible. We may now address ourselves to this further question; and it may at once be said that every part of the N. T. affords evidence of a knowledge of the LXX., and that a great majority of the passages cited from the O. T. are in general agreement with the Greek version. It is calculated by one writer on the subject that, while the N. T. differs from the Massoretic text in 212 citations, it departs from the LXX. in 185[2]; and by another that "not more than fifty" of the citations "materially differ from the LXX.[3]" On either estimate the LXX. is the principal source from which the writers of the N. T. derived their O. T. quotations.

More may be learnt by patiently examining the details of the evidence. This cannot be done here in full, but we may

[1] Westcott, *Hebrews*, p. 473.
[2] Turpie, *O.T. in the N.*, p. 267.
[3] Grinfield, *Apology for the LXX.*, p. 37.

point out the method to be pursued in such an investigation, and its chief results.

Each group of the N. T. writings must be interrogated separately. (*a*) Beginning with the Synoptic Gospels, we observe that the quotations partly occur in narratives or dialogue which are common to the Synoptists or to two of them, and are partly due to the individual writer. Between these two classes of quotations there is a marked contrast. Citations belonging to the common narrative, or to sayings reported by all the Synoptists, or to two of them, with few exceptions adhere closely to the LXX., the differences being only textual or in the way of omission.

Some examples will make this clear. (1) *Citations common to Mt., Mc., Lc.* Mt. xxi. 13 = Mc. xi. 17 = Lc. xix. 46 = LXX., Mc. alone completing the verse. Mt. xxi. 42 = Mc. xii. 10 = Lc. xx. 17 = LXX., Lc. omitting παρὰ Κυρίου κτλ. Mt. xxii. 37 = Mc. xii. 29 f. = Lc. x. 27ᵃ = LXX., with variants[1]. Mt. xxii. 39 = Mc. xii. 31 = Lc. x. 27ᵇ = LXX. Mt. xxii. 44 = Mc. xii. 36 = Lc. xx. 42 f., = LXX. with the variant ὑποκάτω in Mt., Mc. (2) *Citations common to Mt., Mc.* Mt. xv. 4 = Mc. vii. 10 = LXX., cod. A. Mt. xv. 8 f. = Mc. vii. 6 = LXX., with variants[2]. Mt. xix.5 f. = Mc. x. 6 ff. = LXX., Mc. omitting προσκολληθήσεται κτλ. Mt. xxiv. 15 = Mc. xiii. 14 = LXX. and Th. Mt. xxvi. 31 = Mc. xiv. 27 (omitting τῆς ποίμνης) = LXX., cod. A, with one important variant not found in any MS. of the LXX.; cod. B has quite a different text[3]. (3) *Citations common to Mt., Lc.* Mt. iv. 4 = Lc. iv. 4 = LXX., Lc. omitting the second half of the quotation. Mt. iv. 6 = Lc. iv. 10 f. = LXX., except that the clause τοῦ διαφυλάξαι is omitted by Mt. and in part by Lc. Mt. iv. 7 = Lc. iv. 12 = LXX. Mt. iv. 10 = Lc. iv. 8 = LXX., cod. A.

Thus it appears that of 14 quotations which belong to this class only two (Mt. xv. 8 f., xxvi. 31) depart widely from the LXX. But when we turn from the quotations which belong to the common narrative to those which are peculiar to one of the Synoptists, the results are very different.

[1] On these see Hatch, *Essays*, p. 104, and the writer's *St Mark*, p. 255.
[2] Hatch, *op. cit.*, p. 177 f.
[3] *St Mark*, p. 318 f.

In Mt. there are 16 quotations which are not to be found in Mc. or Lc. (Mt. i. 23, ii. 6, 15, 18, iv. 15 f., v. 33, 38, 43, viii. 17, ix. 13=xii. 7, xii. 18 ff., xiii. 14 f., 35, xxi. 4 f., 16, xxvii. 9 f.). Of these 4 (v. 38, ix. 13, xiii. 14 f., xxi. 16) are in the words of the LXX. with slight variants; 4 exhibit important variants, and the remaining 7 bear little or no resemblance to the Alexandrian Greek[1]. Neither Mc. nor Lc. has any series of independent quotations; Mc. ix. 48, xii. 32 are from the LXX., but shew affinities to the text of cod. A; Lc. iv. 18 f. differs from the LXX. in important particulars.

It may be asked whether the quotations in the Synoptists which do not agree with our present text of the LXX., or with its relatively oldest type, imply the use of another Greek version. Before an answer to this question can be attempted, it is necessary to distinguish carefully between the causes which have produced variation. It may be due to (*a*) loose citation, or to (*b*) the substitution of a gloss for the precise words which the writer professes to quote, or to (*c*) a desire to adapt a prophetic context to the circumstances under which it was thought to have been fulfilled, or to (*d*) the fusing together of passages drawn from different contexts. Of the variations which cannot be ascribed to one or other of these causes, some are (*e*) recensional, whilst others are (*f*) translational, and imply an independent use of the original, whether by the Evangelist, or by the author of some collection of excerpts which he employed.

The following may be taken as specimens of these types of variation. (*a*) Mt. ii. 18, xxi. 4 f.; (*b*) Mt. ii. 6, xxvii. 9 f.; (*c*) Mt. ii. 15; (*d*) Lc. iv. 18 f.; (*e*) Mt. xii. 18 ff., Mc. xii. 29 f.; (*f*) Mt. xiii. 35[b]. But more than one cause of divergence may have been at work in the same quotation, and it is not always easy to decide which is paramount; e.g. in Mt. ii. 15 the substitution of τὸν υἱόν μου for τὰ τέκνα αὐτῆς may be due either to the Evangelist's desire to adapt the prophecy to the event, or to a correction of the LXX. from the Heb. (לִבְנִי?).

The three last-named causes of variation need to be considered at some length.

---

[1] Cf. Sir J. C. Hawkins, *Hor. Syn.*, p. 123 ff.

(1) A few of the Synoptic quotations are manifestly composite. E.g. Mt. xxi. 4 f., which is mainly from Zech. ix. 9, opens with a clause from Isa. lxii. 11 (εἴπατε τῇ θυγατρὶ Σιών Ἰδού κτλ.). Lc. iv. 18 f., which is professedly an extract from a synagogue lesson Isa. lxi. 1 ff., inserts in the heart of that context a clause from Isa. lviii. 6 (ἀποστεῖλαι τεθραυσμένους ἐν ἀφέσει). Still more remarkable is the fusion in Mc. i. 2 f., where, under the heading καθὼς γέγραπται ἐν τῷ Ἡσαίᾳ τῷ προφήτῃ, we find Mal. iii. 1 + Isa. xl. 3[1]. Here the parallel passages in Mt., Lc., quote Isaiah only, using Malachi in another context (Mt. xi. 10, Lc. vii. 27).

(2) There is a considerable weight of evidence in favour of the belief that the Evangelists employed a recension of the LXX. which came nearer to the text of cod. A than to that of our oldest uncial B. This point has been recently handled in Hilgenfeld's *Zeitschrift f. Wissenschaftliche Theologie*[2], by Dr W. Staerk, who shews that the witness of the N. T. almost invariably goes with codd. ℵAF and Lucian against the Vatican MS., and that its agreement with cod. A is especially close[3]. It may of course be argued that the text of these authorities has been influenced by the N. T.[4]; but the fact that a similar tendency is noticeable in Josephus, and to a less extent in Philo, goes far to discount this objection. Still more remarkable is the occasional tendency in N. T. quotations to support Theodotion against the LXX.[5] Some instances have been given already; we may add here Mt. xii. 18 = Isa. xlii. i:

Mt.	LXX.	Th.
ἰδοὺ ὁ παῖς μου ὃν ἡρέτισα, ὁ ἀγαπητός μου ὃν εὐδόκησεν ἡ ψυχή μου.	Ἰακὼβ ὁ παῖς μου ἀντιλήμψομαι αὐτοῦ· Ἰσραὴλ ὁ ἐκλεκτός μου, προσεδέξατο αὐτὸν ἡ ψυχή μου.	ἰδοὺ ὁ παῖς μου, ἀντιλήψομαι αὐτοῦ· ὁ ἐκλεκτός μου ὃν εὐδόκησεν ἡ ψυχή μου.

---

[1] *St Mark*, p. 2.
[3] xxxvi., p. 97 f.
[5] Cf. p. 48.

[2] In nos. xxxv., xxxvi., xxxviii., xl.
[4] Cf. Zahn, *Einleitung*, ii. p. 314 ff.

Such coincidences lend some probability to the supposition that Theodotion's version bears a relation to the recension of the Alexandrian Greek which was in the hands of the early Palestinian Church.

(3) Certain quotations in the First Gospel are either independent of the LXX., or have been but slightly influenced by it. These require to be studied separately, and, as they are but few, they are printed below and confronted with the LXX.

<table>
<tr><td align="center">Mt. ii. 6</td><td align="center">Mic. v. 2, 4</td></tr>
<tr><td>

καὶ σύ, Βηθλέεμ, γῆ ᾿Ιούδα,
οὐδαμῶς ἐλαχίστη εἶ ἐν τοῖς
ἡγεμόσιν ᾿Ιούδα· ἐκ σοῦ γὰρ
ἐξελεύσεται ἡγούμενος, ὅστις
ποιμανεῖ τὸν λαόν μου ᾿Ισραήλ.

</td><td>

καὶ σύ, Βηθλέεμ, οἶκος
᾿Εφράθα, ὀλιγοστὸς εἶ τοῦ εἶναι
ἐν χιλιάσιν ᾿Ιούδα· ἐξ οὗ μοι
ἐξελεύσεται τοῦ εἶναι εἰς ἄρχοντα
τοῦ ᾿Ισραήλ...καὶ ποιμανεῖ...

</td></tr>
<tr><td>

ουδαμως] μη D | εκ σου] εξ
ου (B*)אC(D) | om γαρ א*.

</td><td>

εξ ου] εκ σου Bᵇ˙ᶜAQ | εξε-
λευσεται]+ηγουμενος A

</td></tr>
</table>

On the relation of the LXX. in this passage to the M. T. see above p. 338. Χιλιάσιν, ἡγεμόσιν answer to different vocalisations of אלפי, but οὐδαμῶς ἐλαχίστη εἶ and ἡγούμενος ὅστις π. τὸν λ. μου are paraphrastic. The Evangelist has put into the mouth of the Scribes an interpretation rather than a version of the prophecy.

<table>
<tr><td align="center">Mt. iv. 15 f.</td><td align="center">Isa. ix. 1 f.</td></tr>
<tr><td>

γῆ Ζαβουλὼν καὶ γῆ Νεφ-
θαλείμ, ὁδὸν θαλάσσης, πέραν
τοῦ ᾿Ιορδάνου, Γαλειλαία τῶν
ἐθνῶν, ὁ λαὸς ὁ καθήμενος ἐν
σκοτίᾳ φῶς εἶδεν μέγα· καὶ τοῖς
καθημένοις ἐν χώρᾳ καὶ σκιᾷ
θανάτου φῶς ἀνέτειλεν αὐτοῖς.

</td><td>

χώρα Ζαβουλών, ἡ γῆ Νεφ-
θαλείμ, καὶ οἱ λοιποὶ οἱ τὴν
παραλίαν καὶ πέραν τοῦ ᾿Ιορ-
δάνου, Γαλειλαία τῶν ἐθνῶν. ὁ
λαὸς ὁ πορευόμενος ἐν σκότει,
ἴδετε φῶς μέγα· οἱ κατοικοῦντες
ἐν χώρᾳ σκιᾷ θανάτου, φῶς
λάμψει ἐφ᾿ ὑμᾶς.

</td></tr>
<tr><td>

οι καθημενοι D | και σκια]
om και D*

</td><td>

Νεφθαλειμ]+οδον θαλασσης
אᶜ˙ᵃAQ(Aq. Th.) | παραλιαν]+
κατοικουντες אᶜ˙ᵃAQ | πορευ-
ομενος] καθημενος A | σκια] pr
και אᶜ˙ᵃAQΓ

</td></tr>
</table>

Here Mt. differs widely both from LXX. and M. T., yet he has points of agreement with both. The influence of LXX. is seen in γῆ Z., Γ. τῶν ἐθνῶν, χώρᾳ [καὶ] σκιᾷ. On the other hand ὁδὸν θαλάσσης, εἶδεν, αὐτοῖς agree with M.T. The writer quotes from memory, or from a collection of loosely cited *testimonia*.

Mt. viii. 17	Isa. liii. 4
αὐτὸς τὰς ἀσθενείας ἡμῶν ἔλαβεν καὶ τὰς νόσους ἐβάστασεν.	οὗτος τὰς ἁμαρτίας ἡμῶν φέρει καὶ περὶ ἡμῶν ὀδυνᾶται.

Mt.'s version is based upon Heb., from which the LXX. departs. Cf. Symm.: τὰς ἁμαρτίας ἡμῶν αὐτὸς ἀνέλαβεν καὶ τοὺς πόνους ὑπέμεινεν.

Mt. xiii. 35	Ps. lxxvii. 2
ἀνοίξω ἐν παραβολαῖς τὸ στόμα μου· ἐρεύξομαι κεκρυμμένα ἀπὸ καταβολῆς.	ἀνοίξω ἐν παραβολαῖς τὸ στόμα μου· φθέγξομαι προβλήματα ἀπ᾽ ἀρχῆς.

καταβολῆς]+κοσμου ℵ*CD

V. 35ᵃ in Mt. follows the LXX. *verbatim*, while 35ᵇ is an independent rendering of the Heb. The departure from the LXX. in the second half of the text is not altogether for the sake of exactness; if ἐρεύξομαι is nearer to אַבִּיעָה than φθέγξομαι, ἀπὸ καταβολῆς introduces a conception which has no place in מִנִּי־קֶדֶם, and in this sense the Greek phrase is practically limited to the N. T. (see Hort on 1 Pet. i. 20).

Mt. xxvii. 9 f.[1]	Zach. xi. 13
καὶ ἔλαβον...τὴν τιμὴν τοῦ τετιμημένου ὃν ἐτιμήσαντο ἀπὸ υἱῶν Ἰσραήλ, καὶ ἔδωκαν αὐτὰ εἰς τὸν ἀγρὸν τοῦ κεραμέως, καθὰ συνέταξέν μοι Κύριος.	καὶ εἶπεν Κύριος πρὸς μέ Κάθες αὐτοὺς εἰς τὸ χωνευτήριον καὶ σκέψομαι εἰ δόκιμόν ἐστιν, ὃν τρόπον ἐδοκιμάσθη ὑπὲρ αὐτῶν. καὶ ἔλαβον...καὶ ἐνέβαλον αὐτοὺς εἰς τὸν οἶκον Κυρίου εἰς τὸ χωνευτήριον.

εδωκεν A*ᵛⁱᵈ εδωκα ℵ   εδοκιμασθην B*ᶠᵒʳᵗℵAQ

Mt. has re-arranged this passage, and given its sense, without regard to the order or construction of the original. In doing this he has abandoned the LXX. altogether, and approximates to the Heb.; cf. Aq. ἡ τιμὴ ἣν ἐτιμήθην ὑπὲρ αὐτῶν.

---

[1] Mt. ascribes this prophecy to Jeremiah: τότε ἐπληρώθη τὸ ῥηθὲν διὰ Ἰερεμίου τοῦ προφήτου. The slip is probably due to a confusion between Zach. l. c. and Jer. xviii. 2.

In these five passages the compiler of the first Gospel has more or less distinctly thrown off the yoke of the Alexandrian version and substituted for it a paraphrase, or an independent rendering from the Hebrew. But our evidence does not encourage the belief that the Evangelist used or knew another complete Greek version of the Old Testament, or of any particular book. It is to be observed that he uses this liberty only in quotations which proceed from himself, if we except the references to the O. T. in the Sermon on the Mount (Mt. v. 21, 27, 31, 33, 38, 43) which are hardly of the nature of strict citations; the formula ἐρρέθη τοῖς ἀρχαίοις distinguishes them from that class, and suggests that they purport only to give the general sense.

(b) The Fourth Gospel quotes the LXX. *verbatim*, or with slight variants, in cc. ii. 17, x. 34, xii. 38, xix. 24, 36; and more freely in vi. 31, 45, xv. 25. In other places the author takes a more or less independent course: e.g. in i. 23, quoting Isa. xl. 3 he writes εὐθύνατε τὴν ὁδὸν Κυρίου for ἑτοιμάσατε τ. ὁ. Κ., εὐθείας ποιεῖτε τὰς τρίβους τοῦ θεοῦ ἡμῶν (cf. Mt. iii. 3, Mc. i. 3, Lc. iii. 4); in xii. 40, Isa. vi. 9, 10 is paraphrased τετύφλωκεν αὐτῶν τοὺς ὀφθαλμοὺς καὶ ἐπώρωσεν αὐτῶν τὴν καρδίαν, which agrees neither with the LXX. nor with M.T.; in xix. 37 ὄψονται εἰς ὃν ἐξεκέντησαν is a non-Septuagintal rendering of Zach. xii. 10, which was perhaps current in Palestine, since εἰς ὃν ἐξεκέντησαν appears also in Theodotion (cf. Aq., Symm., and Apoc. i. 7)[1].

(c) The quotations from the O. T. in the Acts are taken from the LXX. exclusively. With the exception of the περιοχή in c. viii. 32[2], they occur only in the speeches. A few points deserve special notice. In vii. 43 (= Amos v. 26) the LXX. is followed against M.T. (Ῥαμφά(ν) or Ῥαιφάν, מ״א כִּיּוּן). Similarly in xiii. 34 (= Isa. lv. 3) τὰ ὅσια Δαυείδ is read with the LXX. for חַסְדֵי דָוִד. C. xiii. 22 is a conflation of Ps. lxxxviii.

---

[1] See against this Nestle, *Textual Criticism of the N. T.*, p. 291.
[2] An exact citation, with one or two variants of the A type.

21 + lxxi. 20 + 1 Regn. xiii. 14 + Isa. xliv. 28. C. xv. 16 ff., which is introduced by the formula τούτῳ συμφωνοῦσιν οἱ λόγοι τῶν προφητῶν, καθὼς γέγραπται, presents a remarkable instance of free citation accompanied by conflation, which calls for separate study.

Acts xv. 16 ff.

μετὰ ταῦτα ἀναστρέψω καὶ
ἀνοικοδομήσω τὴν σκηνὴν Δαυεὶδ
τὴν πεπτωκυῖαν, καὶ τὰ κατε-
στραμμένα αὐτῆς ἀνοικοδομήσω
καὶ ἀνορθώσω αὐτήν, ὅπως ἂν
ἐκζητήσωσιν οἱ κατάλοιποι τῶν
ἀνθρώπων τὸν κύριον καὶ πάντα
τὰ ἔθνη ἐφ᾽ οὓς ἐπικέκληται τὸ
ὄνομά μου ἐπ᾽ αὐτούς, λέγει
Κύριος ὁ ποιῶν ταῦτα * *
* 1.

κατεστραμμενα] κατεσκαμ-
μενα ACD

Jer. xii. 15 + Amos ix. 11 f.

μετὰ τὸ ἐκβαλεῖν με αὐτοὺς
ἐπιστρέψω ... ἀναστήσω τὴν
σκηνὴν Δαυεὶδ τὴν πεπτωκυῖαν..
καὶ τὰ κατεσκαμμένα αὐτῆς ἀναστήσω καὶ ἀνοικοδομήσω αὐτὴν
καθὼς αἱ ἡμέραι τοῦ αἰῶνος,
ὅπως ἐκζητήσωσιν οἱ κατά-
λοιποι τῶν ἀνθρώπων, καὶ
πάντα τὰ ἔθνη ἐφ᾽ οὓς ἐπικέκληται τὸ ὄνομά μου ἐπ᾽
αὐτούς, λέγει Κύριος ὁ ποιῶν
ταῦτα.

κατεσκαμμενα] κατεστραμ-
μενα A^bQ*
οπως]+αν A | ανθρωπων]+
τον κυριον A

The combination in this quotation of looseness with close adherence to the LXX. even where it is furthest from the Heb. (e.g. in ὅπως ἐκζητήσωσιν κτλ.) is significant, especially when it is remembered that the speaker is St James of Jerusalem.

(*d*) The Catholic Epistles use the LXX. when they quote the O.T. expressly, and with some exceptions keep fairly close to the Alexandrian Greek. Thus Jas. ii. 8, 11[2], 23, iv. 6, 1 Pet. i. 24[3], iv. 18, v. 5, are substantially exact. 1 Pet. ii. 6 differs from the LXX. of Isa. xxviii. 16. 1 Pet. iii. 10 ff., an unacknowledged extract from Ps. xxxiii. 12 ff., is adapted to the context by a slight change in the construction, but otherwise generally follows the LXX.: θέλων ζωὴν ἀγαπᾶν καὶ ἰδεῖν ἡμέρας ἀγαθάς for θέλων ζ., ἀγαπῶν ἰδ. ἡμ. ἀγαθάς is probably

---

[1] On this reading see W. H.[2], *Notes on select readings*, p. 96.
[2] Cf. Mc. x. 19, Lc. xviii. 20. Jas. ii. 23, v. 20, 1 Pet. iv. 8, differ from LXX.
[3] On the few variants in this passage see Hort, *St Peter*, p. 93.

a slip, shewing that the writer was quoting from memory. In 2 Pet. ii. 22 (= Prov. xxvi. 11) κύων ἐπιστρέψας ἐπὶ τὸ ἴδιον ἐξέραμα is nearer to the Heb. than κ. ὅταν ἐπέλθῃ ἐπὶ τὸν ἑαυτοῦ ἐμετόν, and appears to be an independent rendering.

(e) More than half of the direct quotations from the O.T. in the Epistles of St Paul are taken from the LXX. without material change (Rom. i. 17, ii. 24, iii. 4, iv. 7 f., 18, vii. 7, viii. 36, ix. 7, 12, 13, 15, 26, x. 6 ff., 16, 18, 19, 20 f., xi. 26 f., 34 f., xii. 20 f., xiii. 9, xv. 3, 9, 10, 11, 12, 21; 1 Cor. iii. 20, vi. 16, x. 7, 26, xv. 32; 2 Cor. iv. 13, vi. 2, viii. 15, ix. 9; Gal. iii. 6, 10, 11, 12, iv. 27, v. 14; Eph. iv. 26; 2 Tim. ii. 19). A smaller proportion shew important variants (Rom. iii. 20 = Gal. ii. 16 πᾶσα σάρξ for πᾶς ζῶν LXX.; ix. 9 κατὰ τὸν καιρὸν τοῦτον ἐλεύσομαι, καὶ ἔσται τῇ Σάρρᾳ υἱός for ἥξω...κατὰ τὸν καιρὸν τοῦτον...καὶ ἔξει υἱὸν Σάρρα LXX.; ix. 17 εἰς αὐτὸ τοῦτο ἐξήγειρά σε for ἕνεκεν τούτου διετηρήθης, and δύναμιν for ἰσχύν LXX.[1]; ix. 27 ὁ ἀριθμὸς τῶν υἱῶν Ἰ., ἐπὶ τῆς γῆς; xiv. 11 ζῶ ἐγώ for κατ' ἐμαυτοῦ ὀμνύω, ἐξομολογήσεται τῷ θεῷ for ὀμεῖται τὸν θεόν LXX.; 1 Cor. i. 19 ἀθετήσω for κρύψω LXX.; Gal. iii. 8 πάντα τὰ ἔθνη for πᾶσαι αἱ φυλαὶ τῆς γῆς LXX.; iii. 13 ἐπικατάρατος (cf. v. 20) for κεκαταραμένος LXX.; Eph. iv. 8 ἔδωκεν δόματα τοῖς ἀνθρώποις for ἔλαβες δ. ἐν ἀνθρώπῳ[2] LXX.; iv. 25 μετὰ τοῦ πλησίον for πρὸς τὸν πλ. LXX.; v. 31 ἀντὶ τούτου for ἕνεκεν τ., om. αὐτοῦ 1°, 2°; cf. Mt. xix. 5 f., Mc. x. 7 f.; vi. 3 καὶ ἔσῃ μακροχρόνιος for κ. ἵνα μακροχρ. γένῃ).

In other passages St Paul departs still further from the LXX., quoting freely, or paraphrasing, or fusing two distinct passages into a single citation, or occasionally deserting the Alexandrian version altogether. Examples of loose quotations or of paraphrases will be found in Rom. ix. 27, xi. 3, 4, 1 Cor. xv. 45, Gal. iv. 30; conflation occurs in Rom. iii. 10 ff.[3], ix. 33, xi. 8, 9, 26 f.; 1 Cor. xv. 54 f., 2 Cor. vi. 16 ff.

---

[1] B^A reads δύναμιν.   [2] ἀνοῖς B^aℵR^a.
[3] On this passage, see above, p. 251 f.

The following instances will shew how far reconstruction is carried in cases of conflation.

Rom. ix. 33 ἰδοὺ τίθημι ἐν Σιὼν λίθον προσκόμματος καὶ πέτραν σκανδάλου· καὶ ὁ πιστεύων ἐπ᾽ αὐτῷ οὐ καταισχυνθήσεται[2].

Isa. viii. 14 οὐχ ὡς λίθου προσκόμματι συναντήσεσθε οὐδὲ ὡς πέτρας πτώματι[1]. xxviii. 16 ἰδοὺ ἐγὼ ἐμβάλλω εἰς τὰ θεμέλια Σειὼν λίθον πολυτελῆ, ἐκλεκτὸν ἀκρογωνιαῖον, ἔντιμον...καὶ ὁ πιστεύων οὐ μὴ καταισχυνθῇ.

Rom. xi. 8 ἔδωκεν αὐτοῖς ὁ θεὸς πνεῦμα κατανύξεως, ὀφθαλμοὺς τοῦ μὴ βλέπειν καὶ ὦτα τοῦ μὴ ἀκούειν, ἕως τῆς σήμερον ἡμέρας.

Isa. xxix. 10 πεπότικεν ὑμᾶς Κύριος πνεύματι κατανύξεως. Deut. xxix. 4 καὶ οὐκ ἔδωκεν Κύριος ὁ θεὸς ὑμῖν καρδίαν εἰδέναι καὶ ὀφθαλμοὺς [τοῦ] βλέπειν καὶ ὦτα ἀκούειν ἕως τῆς ἡμέρας ταύτης.

1 Cor. ii. 9 ἃ ὀφθαλμὸς οὐκ εἶδεν καὶ οὖς οὐκ ἤκουσεν καὶ ἐπὶ καρδίαν ἀνθρώπου οὐκ ἀνέβη, ὅσα ἡτοίμασεν ὁ θεὸς τοῖς ἀγαπῶσιν αὐτόν[3].
αγαπωσιν] υπομενουσιν Clem. R. i. 34, 8.

Isa. lxiv. 3 οὐκ ἠκούσαμεν οὐδὲ οἱ ὀφθαλμοὶ ἡμῶν εἶδον θεὸν πλὴν σοῦ, καὶ τὰ ἔργα σου ἃ ποιήσεις τοῖς ὑπομένουσιν ἔλεον. lxv. 17 οὐδ᾽ οὐ μὴ ἐπέλθῃ αὐτῶν ἐπὶ καρδίαν.

1 Cor. xv. 54 f. κατεπόθη ὁ θάνατος εἰς νῖκος[4]. ποῦ σου, θάνατε, τὸ νῖκος; ποῦ σου, θάνατε, τὸ κέντρον;

Isa. xxv. 8 κατέπιεν ὁ θάνατος ἰσχύσας. Hos. xiii. 14 ποῦ ἡ δίκη σου, θάνατε; ποῦ τὸ κέντρον σου, ᾅδη;

In some cases a wide departure from the LXX. is probably to be explained by the supposition that the Apostle quotes from memory; e.g.:

Rom. xi. 2 ff.
οὐκ οἴδατε ἐν Ἠλείᾳ τί λέγει ἡ γραφή...Κύριε, τοὺς προφήτας σου ἀπέκτειναν, τὰ θυσιαστήριά σου κατέσκαψαν, κἀγὼ ὑπελείφθην μόνος, καὶ ζητοῦσιν τὴν ψυχήν μου. ἀλλὰ τί λέγει αὐτῷ ὁ χρηματισμός; Κατέλιπον ἐμαυτῷ ἑπτακισχιλίους ἄνδρας, οἵτινες οὐκ ἔκαμψαν γόνυ τῇ Βάαλ.

3 Regn. xix. 14 ff.
καὶ εἶπεν Ἠλειού...τὰ θυσιαστήριά σου καθεῖλαν καὶ τοὺς προφήτας σου ἀπέκτειναν ...καὶ ὑπολέλιμμαι ἐγὼ μονώτατος καὶ ζητοῦσι τὴν ψυχήν μου...καὶ εἶπεν Κύριος πρὸς αὐτόν...καταλείψεις ἐν Ἰσραὴλ ἑπτὰ χιλιάδας ἀνδρῶν, πάντα γόνατα ἃ οὐκ ὤκλασαν γόνυ τῷ Βάαλ.

---

[1] Aq. καὶ εἰς στερεὸν σκανδάλου.
[2] Cf. 1 Pet. ii. 8 (Hort).
[3] On this passage see Resch, *Agrapha*, p. 154 ff.
[4] So Theodotion.

The following quotation also is probably from memory[1], but the Apostle's knowledge of the original has enabled him to improve upon the faulty rendering of the LXX.

<table>
<tr><td>1 Cor. xiv. 21</td><td>Isa. xxviii. 11 f.</td></tr>
<tr><td>ἐν τῷ νόμῳ γέγραπται ὅτι Ἐν ἑτερογλώσσοις καὶ ἐν χείλεσιν ἑτέρων λαλήσω τῷ λαῷ τούτῳ, καὶ οὐδ' οὕτως εἰσακούσονταί μου, λέγει Κύριος.</td><td>διὰ φαυλισμὸν χειλέων, διὰ γλώσσης ἑτέρας· ὅτι λαλήσουσιν τῷ λαῷ τούτῳ...καὶ οὐκ ἠθέλησαν ἀκούειν.</td></tr>
</table>

Jerome, quoting these words from St Paul, rightly adds, "Quod mihi videtur iuxta Hebraicum de praesenti sumptum capitulo." Aquila's rendering is remarkably similar, ὅτι ἐν ἑτερογλώσσοις καὶ ἐν χείλεσιν ἑτέροις λαλήσω τῷ λαῷ τούτῳ. Theodotion unfortunately is wanting.

(*f*) The Ep. to the Hebrews is in great part a catena of quotations from the LXX. "The text of the quotations agrees in the main with some form of the present text of the LXX.[2]" A considerable number of the passages are cited exactly, or with only slight variation (i. 5, 8 f., 13; ii. 6 ff., 13; iv. 4, v. 6, vi. 13 f., viii. 5, xi. 5, 18, 21; xii. 5 f., xiii. 6). The writer usually follows the LXX. even when they differ materially from the Heb. (viii. 8 ff.[3], x. 5 ff., σῶμα δὲ κατηρτίσω μοι, 37 ἐὰν ὑποστείληται, xi. 21 ῥάβδου, xii. 5 μαστιγοῖ[4]). But he sometimes deserts both version and original, substituting a free paraphrase, or apparently citing from memory (i. 6, ix. 20 ἐνετείλατο, x. 30[5], xii. 19 f., 26). Some of his readings are interesting: in i. 7 we have πυρὸς φλόγα for πῦρ φλέγον[6]; in i. 12 ὡς ἱμάτιον seems to be a doublet of ὡσεὶ περιβόλαιον. Notice also ii. 12 ἀπαγγελῶ for διηγήσομαι (perhaps after Ps. xxi. 31 f.); iii. 9 ἐν δοκιμασίᾳ for ἐδοκίμασαν (ΕΔΟΚΙΜΑϹΙΑ for ΕΔΟΚΙΜΑϹΑ), and iii. 10 τεσσεράκοντα ἔτη· διὸ προσώχθισα for

---

[1] As ἐν τῷ νόμῳ seems to indicate.
[2] Westcott, *Hebrews*, p. 476.
[3] Cf. p. 338.
[4] Yet "he nowhere shews any immediate knowledge of the Hebrew text" (Westcott, *op. cit.*, p. 479).
[5] Cf. Rom. xii. 19. Apparently a stock quotation, current in this form.
[6] Aᵃ has πυρὸς φλέγα (sic) in Ps. ciii. 4.

τεσσ. ἔτη προσώχθ.; x. 6 εὐδόκησας for ἤτησας B, ἐζήτησας ℵART; xii. 15 ἐνοχλῇ for ἐν χολῇ, a corruption supported even in the LXX. by B*AF*.

In the Epistles, as in the Gospels, the text of the LXX. which is employed inclines to cod. A rather than to cod. B. But its agreement with the A text is not without exception; and there are other elements in the problem which must not be overlooked. As in the Gospels, again, we notice from time to time a preference for Lucianic readings, or for the readings of Theodotion. It has been reasonably conjectured that the writers of the N.T. used a recension which was current in Palestine, possibly also in Asia Minor, and which afterwards supplied materials to Theodotion, and left traces in the Antiochian Bible, and in the text represented by cod. A. We shall revert to this subject in a later chapter; for the present it is enough to notice the direction to which the evidence of the N.T. seems to point.

4. We have dealt so far with direct quotations. But in estimating the influence of the LXX. upon the N.T. it must not be forgotten that it contains almost innumerable references of a less formal character. These are in many cases likely to escape notice, and it is not the least of the debts which we owe to the Westcott and Hort text, that attention is called to them by the use of uncial type. They will be found chiefly (*a*) in the words of our Lord (e.g. Mt. vii. 23 = Lc. xiii. 27, Mc. x. 21, 35 f. = Lc. xii. 52 f., xi. 5 = Lc. vii. 22, xi. 21, 23 = Lc. x. 15, 28 f., xiii. 32 = Mc. iv. 32 = Lc. xiii. 19, xvii. 17 = Lc. ix. 41, xviii. 16, xxi. 33 = Mc. xii. 1 = Lc. xx. 9, xxiv. 29 ff. = Mc. xiii. 24 ff. = Lc. xxi. 25 ff., xxiv. 39 = Lc. xvii. 27, xxvi. 64 = Mc. xiv. 62 = Lc. xxii. 69; Mc. iv. 29, vi. 23, ix. 48, xvi. 19; Lc. xii. 53, xxi. 22, 24, xxiii. 30, 46); (*b*) in the canticles oi Lc. i.—ii.; (*c*) in St Stephen's speech, and, though more sparsely, in the other speeches of the Acts; (*d*) in the Epistle

of St James[1] and the First Epistle of St Peter; (*e*) in the Epistles of St Paul; where, though not so numerous as the citations, the allusions to the LXX. are more widely distributed, occurring in 1, 2 Thessalonians, Philippians and Colossians, as well as in the great dogmatic Epistles; ·(*f*) in the Epistle to the Hebrews (ii. 16, iii. 5 f., vi. 7 f., 19 f., vii. 1 ff., x. 29 f., xi. 12 f., 17 f., 28, xii. 12—21, xiii. 11, 20); and especially (*g*) in the Apocalypse, where references to the Greek Old Testament abound in every chapter.

5. This summary by no means represents the extent of the influence exerted upon the N.T. by the Alexandrian Version. The careful student of the Gospels and of St Paul is met at every turn by words and phrases which cannot be fully understood without reference to their earlier use in the Greek Old Testament. Books which are not quoted in the N.T., e.g. the non-canonical books of Wisdom, Ecclesiasticus and Maccabees, find echoes there, and not a few of the great theological words which meet us in the Apostolic writings seem to have been prepared for their Christian connotation by employment in the Alexandrian appendix to the Canon[2]. Not the Old Testament only, but the Alexandrian version of the Old Testament, has left its mark on every part of the New Testament, even in chapters and books where it is not directly cited[3]. It is not too much to say that in its literary form and expression the New Testament would have been a widely different book had it been written by authors who knew the Old Testament only in the original, or who knew it in a Greek version other than that of the LXX.

LITERATURE. F. Junius, *Sacrorum Parallelorum libri iii.* (Heidelberg, 1588); J. Drusius, *Parallela Sacra* (Franeker,

[1] See Mayor, *St James*, pp. lxviii.ff., cxxxix.
[2] The facts are collected by Dr Ryle in Smith's D.B.[2] art. *Apocrypha* (i. pp. 183, 185).
[3] See below, c. iv.

1594); H. Hody, *De Bibl. textibus*, p. 243 ff. (Oxford, 1705); W. Surenhusius, ספר המשיח sive βίβλος καταλλαγῆς (Amsterdam, 1713); H. Owen, *Modes of quotation used by the Evangelical writers explained and vindicated* (London, 1789); H. Gough, *N. T. Quotations* (London, 1855); A. Tholuck, *Das A. T. in N.T.—erste Beilage* (Gotha, 1836); D. McC. Turpie, *The Old Testament in the New* (London, 1868); *The New Testament view of the Old* (London, 1872); Kautzsch, *De Veteris Testamenti locis a Paulo ap. allegatis* (Leipzig, 1869); C. Taylor, *The Gospel in the Law* (Cambridge, 1869); H. Monnet, *Les citations de l'Ancien Testament dans les Épîtres de Saint Paul* (Lausanne, 1874); Böhl, *Die ATlichen Citate im N.T.* (Vienna, 1878); C. H. Toy, *Quotations in the New Testament* (New York, 1884); E. Hatch, *Essays in Biblical Greek*, p. 131 ff. (Oxford, 1889); W. Staerk, in Hilgenfeld's *Zeitschrift für Wissenschaftliche Theologie*, xxxv.—xl.; Bp Lightfoot's *Biblical Essays*, p. 136 ff. (London, 1893); A. Clemen, *Der Gebrauch des A.T. in den NTlichen Schriften* (Gütersloh, 1895); H. Vollmer, *Die ATlichen Citate bei Paulus* (Freiburg in B., 1895); J. C. Hawkins, *Horae Synopticae*, pp. 123 ff. (Oxford, 1889); W. Dittmar, *Vetus Testamentum in Novo* i. (Göttingen, 1899); Th. Zahn, *Einleitung in das N.T.*, ii. p. 313 ff., and elsewhere (see *Sachregister s. ATliche Citate* (Leipzig, 1899); E. Hühn, *Die ATlichen Citate und Reminiscenzen im N.T.* (Tübingen, 1900). See also the commentaries on particular books of the N.T., e.g. Bp Westcott, *Hebrews*, p. 469 ff.; J. B. Mayor, *St James*, p. lxviii. ff.; H. B. Swete, *St Mark*, p. lxx. ff.; *Apocalypse*, p. cxxxix. ff.; G. Milligan, *Thessalonians*, pp. liv., lviii. f.

CHAPTER III.

QUOTATIONS FROM THE LXX. IN EARLY CHRISTIAN WRITINGS.

"THE quotations from the LXX. in the Greek Fathers are an almost unworked field[1]." So wrote Dr Hatch in 1889, and the remark is still true. Indeed, this field can hardly be worked with satisfactory results until the editor has gone before, or a competent collator has employed himself upon the MSS. of the author whose quotations are to be examined. The 'Apostolic Fathers' can already be used with confidence in the editions of Lightfoot and Gebhardt-Harnack; the minor Greek Apologists have been well edited in *Texte und Untersuchungen*, and it may be hoped that the Berlin edition of the earlier Greek Fathers[2] will eventually supply the investigator with trustworthy materials for the Ante-Nicene period as a whole. But for the present the evidence of many Ante-Nicene and of nearly all later Greek Church-writers must be employed with some reserve. In this chapter we shall limit ourselves to the more representative Christian writers before Origen.

1. The earliest of non-canonical Christian writings, the letter addressed c. A.D. 96 by the Church of Rome to the Church of Corinth, abounds in quotations from the O.T.; and more than half of these are given substantially in the words of the LXX. with or without variants.

[1] *Biblical Essays*, p. 133.
[2] *Die Griechischen Christlichen Schriftsteller der ersten drei Jahrhunderte* (Hinrichs, Leipzig). The volumes already published contain part of Hippolytus and an instalment of Origen.

The following is a list of the exact or nearly exact quotations of the LXX. in Clem. R. *ad Cor.* Gen. ii. 23 (vi. 3), iv. 3 ff. (iv. 1 ff.), xii. 1 ff. (x. 3), xiii. 14 ff. (x. 4 f.), xv. 5 (x. 6), xviii. 27 (xvii. 2); Exod. ii. 14 (iv. 9); Deut.. xxxii. 8 f. (xxix. 2); Ps. ii. 7 f. (xxxvi. 4), xi. 5 f. (xv. 5), xvii. 26 f. (xlvi. 2), xviii. 2 ff. (xxvii. 7), xxi. 7 ff. (xvi. 15 f.), xxiii. 1 (liv. 3), xxx. 19 (xv. 5), xxxi. 1 f. (l. 6), 10 (xxii. 8), xxxiii. 12—20 (xxii. 1 ff.), xxxvi. 35 f. (xiv. 5), xlix. 16 ff. (xxxv. 7 ff.), l. 3 ff. (xviii. 2 ff.), lxi. 5 (xv. 3), lxxvii. 36 (xv. 4), lxxxviii. 21 (xviii. 1), ciii. 4 (xxxvi. 3), cix. 1 (xxxvi. 5), cxvii. 18 (lvi. 3), 19 f. (xlviii. 2), cxxxviii. 7 f. (xxviii. 3), cxl. 5 (lvi. 5); Prov. i. 23 ff. (lvii. 3 ff.), ii. 21 f. (xiv. 4), iii. 12 (lvi. 3 f.), 34 (xxx. 2), xx. 21 (xxi. 2); Job iv. 16 ff. (xxxix. 3 ff.), v. 17 ff. (lvi. 6 ff.), xi. 2 f. (xxx. 4), xix. 26 (xxvi. 2); Sap. xii. 12+xi. 22 (xxvii. 3); Mal. iii. 1 (xxiii. 5); Isa. i. 16 ff. (viii. 4), vi. 3 (xxxiv. 6), xiii. 22 (xxiii. 5), xxix. 13 (xv. 2), liii. 1 ff. (xvi. 3 ff.), lx. 17 (xlii. 5), lxvi. 2 (xiii. 3); Jer. ix. 23 f. (xiii. 1); Ezech. xxxiii. 11 (viii. 2); Dan. vii. 10, Th. (xxxiv. 6).

The variants are often of much interest, as shewing affinities to certain types of LXX. text. The following are specially worthy of notice: Ps. xxi. 7 ἐξουθένημα, אAR; xxxi. 1 f. οὗ, א*BA (ag. אᶜ·ᵃ ᾧ); xxxiii. 14 χείλη τοῦ, אᶜ·ᵃAR; 16 om. ὅτι, אᶜ·ᵃAR; xxxvi. 36 ἐξεζήτησα (H.P. 99, 183); xlix. 21 ἄνομε, א*; 22 ἅρπ. ὡς λέων, R; l. 17 τὸ στόμα...τὰ χείλη; lxxxviii. 21 ἐλέει, B*; Prov. ii. 21 χρηστοὶ ἔσονται οἰκήτορες γῆς, ἄκακοι δὲ ὑπολειφθήσονται ἐπ' αὐτῆς, cf. א*ᶜ·ᵃA—a doublet wanting in B, whose reading "appears to shew the hand of an Alexandrian reviser" (Toy, cf. Lagarde); iii. 12 παιδεύει, אA; xx. 21 (27) λύχνος, a reading found in A as a doublet (φῶς... ἢ λύχνος); Job iv. 21 ἐτελεύτησαν (for ἐξηράνθησαν), A; v. 17 ff. is without the additions of the A text, and nearly as in B; Isa. i. 17 χήρᾳ, B*, ag. BᵃᵇאA, δεῦτε καὶ διελεγχθ. (διαλεχθ. Cᶜˡᵉᵐ), אAQ; liii. 5 ἁμαρτίας...ἀνομίας tr., אAQ; 6 ὑπὲρ τῶν ἁμαρτιῶν ἡμῶν; 8 ἥκει for ἤχθη, Qᵐᵍ, 62, 90 al., Syrohex.ᵐᵍ; 9 εὑρέθη δόλος, אᶜ·ᵃAQ (see Lightfoot's note); τῆς πληγῆς, B (A, ἀπὸ τ. πλ.); lx. 17 ἄρχοντας] ἐπισκόπους | ἐπισκόπους] διακόνους; Ezech. xxxiii. 11 ἁμαρτωλοῦ, A (B, ἀσεβοῦς); Dan. vii. 10 ἐλειτούργουν, Th. (LXX. ἐθεράπευον)[1].

[1] On Clement's quotations from the Psalms and Isaiah, see Hatch, *Essays*, pp. 175—9.

(*a*) A few readings imply correction from the Hebrew, or rather perhaps a Greek text with affinities to the translations of the second century; e.g. Ps. cxxxviii. 8 ἐὰν καταστρώσω, ᾽Α. Σ. ἐὰν στρώσω (LXX. ἐὰν καταβῶ); Isa. lxvi. 2 πρᾷον, ᾽Α. (LXX. ταπεινόν). Others seem to be due to the imperfect memory of the writer, who has not verified his quotations by referring to his papyrus, e.g. Ps. lxxxviii. 21 ἐν ἐλέει αἰωνίῳ: Mal. iii. 1 ὁ ἅγιος[1] for ὁ ἄγγελος.

(*b*) A large proportion of Clement's quotations are composite[2]; sixteen passages may be thus described. Some of these consist of citations accurately given from the LXX. and strung together, with or without a *formula citandi* (e.g. lvi. 3—14 = Ps. cxvii. 18 + Prov. iii. 12 + Ps. cxl. 5 (φησίν) + Job v. 17—26 (καὶ πάλιν λέγει)). In other cases one of the citations is correctly given, and another quoted loosely (e.g. xiv. 4 = Prov. ii. 21 f. (A) + Ps. xxxvi. 38, confused with 21[b]). But more commonly in Clement's conflate quotations, texts are fused together without regard to verbal accuracy; cf. e.g. xxvi. 20 λέγει γάρ που Καὶ ἐξαναστήσεις με καὶ ἐξομολογήσομαί σοι· καὶ ἐκοιμήθη καὶ ὑπνώσα· ἐξηγέρθην, ὅτι σὺ μετ᾽ ἐμοῦ εἶ, where fragments of Pss. xxvii. 7, iii. 5, xxii. 4 are blended into an arabesque. Except in this class of quotations Clement is not often guilty of citing loosely; see however xx. 7 (Job xxxviii. 11), xxviii. 3 (Ps. cxxxviii. 7), xxxii. 3 (Gen. xv. 5), xlii. 5 (Isa. lx. 17).

(*c*) Special interest attaches to Clement's quotations of passages which are also quoted in the N.T. The following are the most instructive instances: (1) Gen. xii. 1 = Acts vii. 3 = Clem. x. 3: Clem. reads ἄπελθε for ἔξελθε (LXX. and Acts), but rejects καὶ δεῦρο with A*D* against Acts and cod. E.

---

[1] The Latin version supports the MSS. of the Greek text of Clement in both cases, so that with our present knowledge we are not at liberty to assume a transcriptional error.

[2] On 'composite' quotations from the LXX. see Hatch, *op. cit.* p. 203 ff.

(2) Exod. ii. 14 = Acts vii. 27 = Clem. iv. 11: Clem. reads κριτήν for ἄρχοντα—"perhaps from confusion with Lc. xii. 14" (Lightfoot). (3) Jer. ix. 23 f. (1 Regn. ii. 10) = 1 Cor. i. 31, (2 Cor. x. 17) = Clem. xiii. 1; here the relation of Clement to the Biblical texts is best shewn by juxtaposition:

Jer. *l.c.*	1 Regn. *l.c.**	Clem. *l.c.*
μὴ καυχάσθω ὁ σο-φὸς ἐν τῇ σοφίᾳ αὐτοῦ, καὶ μὴ καυχάσθω ὁ ἰσχυρὸς ἐν τῇ ἰσχύι αὐτοῦ, καὶ μὴ καυχάσθω ὁ πλούσιος ἐν τῷ πλού-τῳ αὐτοῦ· ἀλλ᾽ ἢ ἐν τούτῳ καυχάσθω ὁ καυ-χώμενος, συνίειν καὶ γινώσκειν ὅτι ἐγώ εἰμι Κύριος ὁ ποιῶν ἔλεος καὶ κρίμα καὶ δικαι-οσύνην ἐπὶ τῆς γῆς.	μὴ καυχάσθω ὁ φρό-νιμος ἐν τῇ φρονήσει αὐτοῦ, καὶ μὴ καυχά-σθω ὁ δυνατὸς ἐν τῇ δυνάμει αὐτοῦ, καὶ μὴ καυχάσθω ὁ πλούσιος ἐν τῷ πλούτῳ αὐτοῦ· ἀλλ᾽ ἢ ἐν τούτῳ καυ-χάσθω ὁ καυχώμενος, συνίειν καὶ γινώσκειν τὸν κύριον, καὶ ποιεῖν κρίμα καὶ δικαιοσύνην ἐν μέσῳ τῆς γῆς. * Cf. p. 245.	μὴ καυχάσθω ὁ σο-φὸς ἐν τῇ σοφίᾳ αὐτοῦ, μηδὲ ὁ ἰσχυρὸς ἐν τῇ ἰσχύι αὐτοῦ, μηδὲ ὁ πλούσιος ἐν τῷ πλού-τῳ αὐτοῦ· ἀλλ᾽ ἢ †ὁ καυχώμενος ἐν Κυρίῳ καυχάσθω†, τοῦ ἐκζη-τεῖν αὐτὸν καὶ ποιεῖν κρίμα καὶ δικαιοσύνην. † 1 Cor. i. 31, 2 Cor. x. 17: see Lightfoot's note *ad loc.*

(4) Ps. xxi. 9 = Matt. xxvii. 43 = Clem. xvi. 15; Clem. agrees with LXX., Mt. substitutes πέποιθεν for ἤλπισεν, τὸν θεόν for Κύριον, and εἰ for ὅτι. (5) Ps. xxxiii. 12 ff. = 1 Pet. iii. 10 ff. = Clem. xxii. 1 ff.; Clem. agrees with LXX. against St Peter, who changes the construction (ὁ θέλων...παυσάτω κτλ.). (6) Ps. cix. 1 = Mt. xxii. 44 (Mc., Lc.), Acts ii. 34 f., Heb. i. 13 = Clem. xxxvi. 5: Clem. reads ὑποπόδιον with Lc., Acts, Hebr., against ὑποκάτω Mt., Mc. (BD). (7) Prov. iii. 12 = Heb. xii. 6 = Clem. lvi. 4: see above, p. 402. (8) Prov. iii. 34 = Jas. iv. 6, 1 Pet. v. 5 = Clem. xxx. 2: Θεός (ὁ θ. Jas., Pet.) against Κύριος LXX.; M.T. יהוה‎, but with reference to יְהֹוָ֑ה‎ in *v.* 33. (9) Isa. xxix. 13[1] = Mt. xv. 8, Mc. vii. 6 = Clem. xv. 1: again the passages must be printed in full:

---

[1] See Hatch, *op. cit.*, p. 177 f.

Isa. *l.c.*	Mt., Mc. *ll.cc.*	Clem. *l.c.*
ἐγγίζει μοι ὁ λαὸς οὗτος ἐν τῷ στόματι αὐτοῦ, καὶ ἐν τοῖς χείλεσιν αὐτῶν τιμῶσίν με, ἡ δὲ καρδία αὐτῶν πόρρω ἀπέχει ἀπ᾿ ἐμοῦ.	ὁ λαὸς οὗτος (οὗτος ὁ λαὸς Mc.) τοῖς χείλεσίν με τιμᾷ, ἡ δὲ καρδία αὐτῶν πόρρω ἀπέχει ἀπ᾿ ἐμοῦ.	Οὗτος ὁ λαὸς τοῖς χείλεσίν με τιμᾷ, ἡ δὲ καρδία αὐτῶν πόρρω ἄπεστιν ἀπ᾿ ἐμοῦ.
om ἐν τῷ στόμ. αὐτοῦ καὶ ἐν אAQ.	ἀπέχει] Mc. ἀφέστηκεν D ἄπεστιν L 2ᵖᵉ	τοῖς χείλεσιν] τῷ στοματι Cᶜˡᵉᵐ. ἄπεστιν] ἀπέχει Cᶜˡᵉᵐ.

Through constant citation, the context has taken more than one type; Clement's is close to that of the Evangelists, but has not been borrowed from them in their present form, as ἄπεστιν shews. (10) Isa. liii. 1—12 = Clem. xvi. 3—14; cf. Jo. xii. 38 (Rom. x. 16), Mt. viii. 17, Acts viii. 32 f., 1 Pet. ii. 22, Mc. xv. 28.

The general result of this examination is to shew (*a*) that Clement's text of the LXX. inclines in places to that which appears in the N.T., and yet presents sufficient evidence of independence; (*b*) that as between the texts of the LXX. represented by B and A, while often supporting A, it is less constantly opposed to B than is the New Testament; and (*c*) that it displays an occasional tendency to agree with Theodotion and even with Aquila against the LXX. It seems in fact to be a more mixed text than that which was in the hands of the Palestinian writers of the N.T. These conclusions harmonise on the whole with what we know of the circumstances under which Clement wrote. The early Roman Church was largely composed of Greek-speaking Jews, the freedmen of Roman families; and Clement himself, as Lightfoot has suggested[1], was probably of Jewish descent and a freedman or the son of a freedman of Flavius Clemens, the cousin of Domitian. Under these circumstances it was natural that the text of Clement's copies of Old Testament books,

---

[1] *Clement of Rome*, p. 61. Dr Nestle (*Z. f. die NTliche Wissenschaft*, i. 2) points out the Semitic style which reveals itself in Clement, e.g. v. 6 ἑπτάκις, xii. 5 γινώσκουσα γινώσκω.

while derived from Palestinian archetypes, should contain readings brought to the capital by Jewish-Greek visitors from other lands.

2. Whatever the history of the so-called Second Epistle of Clement to the Corinthians, whether it is of Roman or of Corinthian origin, like the genuine Epistle it makes extensive use of the Greek Old Testament. The following quotations occur: Gen. i. 27 (xiv. 2); Mal. iv. 1 (xvi. 3); Isa. xxix. 13 (iii. 5), xxxiv. 4 (xvi. 3), lii. 5 (xiii. 2), liv. 1 (ii. 1), lviii. 9 (xv. 3), lxvi. 18 (xvii. 4 f.), 24 (vii. 6, xvii. 24); Jer. vii. 11 (xiv. 1), Ezech. xiv. 14, 18, 20 (vi. 8). The last of these passages is cited very freely or rather summarised, although introduced by the words λέγει ἡ γραφὴ ἐν τῷ Ἐζεκιήλ. The writer follows Clement in the form of several of his quotations (iii. 5 = Clem. 1 Cor. xv. 2, xiv. 2 = Clem. 1 Cor. xxxiii. 5; in xiii. 2 he quotes Isa. lii. 5 as it is quoted by Polycarp (see below)).

3. Another second century document, indisputably Roman, the Shepherd of Hermas, contains no quotation from the LXX. But Ps. ciii. 15 LXX. has supplied the writer with a phrase in *Mand.* xii. 3. 4, and *Vis.* iv. 2. 4 supplies evidence that he knew and read a version of Daniel which was akin to Theodotion's. The passage runs: ὁ κύριος ἀπέστειλεν τὸν ἄγγελον αὐτοῦ τὸν ἐπὶ τῶν θηρίων ὄντα, οὗ τὸ ὄνομά ἐστιν †Σεγρί†[1], καὶ ἐνέφραξεν τὸ στόμα αὐτοῦ ἵνα μή σε λυμάνῃ. Compare Dan. vi. 22 (23) Th., ὁ θεός μου ἀπέστειλεν τὸν ἄγγελον αὐτοῦ καὶ ἐνέφραξεν τὰ στόματα τῶν λεόντων (LXX. σέσωκέ με ὁ θεὸς ἀπὸ τῶν λεόντων), καὶ οὐκ ἐλυμήναντό με[2].

4. The Old Testament is quoted in the Epistle of Barnabas even more profusely than in the Epistle of Clement,

---

[1] The acute conjecture of Dr J. Rendel Harris, who saw that the name, which appears in the MS. as Θεγρί or the like, must be an attempt to reproduce the verb סגר (Dan. *l. c.*).

[2] See above, p. 47, n. 4.

but with less precision. The writer is fairly exact in well-known contexts belonging to the Psalter or the Book of Isaiah[1], but elsewhere he appears to trust to memory, and not to concern himself greatly about the words of his author. Even when preceded by a *formula citandi* his citations often wander far from the LXX., although they are clearly based upon it; e.g. Exod. xxxiii. 1—3 is quoted in Barn. vi. 8 after this manner: τί λέγει ὁ ἄλλος προφήτης Μωυσῆς αὐτοῖς; Ἰδοὺ τάδε λέγει Κύριος ὁ θεός Εἰσέλθατε εἰς τὴν γῆν τὴν ἀγαθήν, ἣν ὤμοσεν Κύριος τῷ Ἀβραὰμ καὶ Ἰσαὰκ καὶ Ἰακώβ, καὶ κατακληρονομήσατε αὐτήν, γῆν ῥέουσαν γάλα καὶ μέλι. Similar liberties are taken even when the writer mentions the book which he is quoting: x. 2 Μωυσῆς…λέγει αὐτοῖς ἐν τῷ Δευτερονομίῳ Καὶ διαθήσομαι πρὸς τὸν λαὸν τοῦτον τὰ δικαιώματά μου—a sentence which, though it has all the notes of a strict quotation, proves to be a mere summary of Deut. iv. 1—23.

The following analysis of the quotations in Barnabas may be found useful. (*a*) Exact or nearly exact: Gen. i. 28 (Barn. vi. 12), Exod. xx. 14 (xix. 4), Deut. x. 16 (ix. 5), Ps. i. 1, 3—6 (x. 1, xi. 6 f.), xvii. 45 (ix. 1), xxi. 17, 19 (vi. 6), cix. 1 (xii. 10), cxvii. 12, 22 (vi. 4, 6), Prov. i. 17 (v. 4), Isa. i. 2, 10 ff. (ii. 5, ix. 3, xv. 8), iii. 9 f. (vi. 7), v. 21 (iv. 11), xxviii. 16 (vi. 2 f.), xxxiii. 13 (ix. 1), 16 (xi. 4 f.), xl. 12 (xvi. 2), xlii. 6 ff. (xiv. 7), xlv. 2 f. (xi. 4), xlix. 6 f. (xiv. 8), liii. 5, 7 (v. 2), lxi. 1 f. (xiv. 9), lxvi. 1 f. (xvi. 2). (*b*) Partly exact, partly free: Gen. xxv. 21 ff. (xiii. 2), xlviii. 9—11, 14 ff. (xiii. 4 f.), Isa. xxviii. 16 (vi. 2), lviii. 4 ff. (iii. 1 f.), Jer. ii. 12 f. (xi. 2). (*c*) Free: Gen. i. 26 (vi. 12), 28 (vi. 18), Lev. xxiii. 29 (vii. 3), Deut. ix. 12 (iv. 8), x. 16 (ix. 5), Ps. xxi. 21, cxviii. 120, xxi. 17 (v. 13), Zech. xiii. 7 (v. 12), xvi. 1 f. (xi. 3), xl. 3 (ix. 3), Isa. l. 6 ff. (v. 14, vi. 1), lxv. 2 (xii. 4), Jer. iv. 3 (ix. 5), vii. 2 (ix. 2), ix. 26 (ix. 5), Ezech. xi. 19, xxxvi. 26 (vi. 14). (*d*) Free, with fusion: Gen. xvii. 23 + xiv. 14 (ix. 8), Exod. xx. 8 + Ps. xxiii. 4 (xv. 1), Exod. xxxii. 7 + Deut. ix. 12 (iv. 8), xxxiv. 28 + xxxi. 18 (iv. 7), Ps. xli. 3 + xxi. 23 (vi. 15), l. 19 + apocryphon (ii. 10), Jer. vii. 22 f. + Zech. vii. 10, viii. 17 (ii. 7 f.). (*e*) Free summary: Lev. xi., Deut. xiv. (x. 1), Deut. iv. 10 ff. (x. 2), Ezech. xlvii. (xi. 10). (*f*) Very loose citation: Gen. ii. 2 (xv. 3), xvii. 5 (xiii. 6), Exod. xvii. 14 (xii. 9), xxiv. 18 + xxxi. 18 (xiv. 2), xxxiii. 1 ff. (vi. 8), Lev. xvi. 7 ff.

---

[1] See Hatch, *Essays*, p. 180 ff.

(vii. 6), Deut. xxvii. 15 (xii. 6), Ps. xxxiii. 13 (ix. 2), Sir. iv. 31 (xix. 9), Isa. xlix. 17 (xvi. 3), Dan. vii. 7 f., 24 (iv. 4), ix. 24 (xvi. 6).

As the Epistle of Barnabas is not improbably a relic of the earliest Alexandrian Christianity, it is important to interrogate its witness to the text of the LXX. This can best be done, as we have seen, by examining its quotations from the Psalms and Isaiah.

Ps. i. 1 ἐπὶ καθέδραν, Bℵ (ag. ἐ. καθέδρᾳ AR), 5 οἱ ἀσεβεῖς, ἁμαρτωλοί, B (ag. ἀσεβεῖς, οἱ ἁμ. A). xvii. 45 ὑπήκουσαν, ℵ* | μου, ℵ^{c.a} RU (ag. μοι 1° Bℵ*A). xxi. 17 περιέσχεν, H.-P. 81, 206. cix. 1 Κύριος, R | ὑποπόδιον (ag. ὑποκάτω, Mc. xii. 36, BD). Isa. iii. 9 ὅτι, ΑΓ; v. 21 ἑαυτῶν, AQ; xxviii. 16 ἐμβαλῶ, ℵAQ; xlii. 7 καὶ ἐξαγαγεῖν | δεδεμένους] πεπεδημένους (as Justin, *Dial.* 26, 65, 122). xlix. 6 τέθεικα, ℵAQ* (ag. δέδωκα BQ^{mg}), 7 λυτρωσάμενος (for ῥυσά-μενος); liii. 5 ἀνομίας, ἁμαρτίας, ℵAQ, 7 τοῦ κείραντος αὐτόν, ℵ^{c.a} AQ; lviii. 5 λέγει Κύριος, Q, 6 ἰδοὺ αὕτη ἡ νηστεία ἥν; lxi. 1 τα-πεινοῖς, ℵ*; lxvi. 1 ἡ δὲ γῆ, ℵAQ | ἡ (for καὶ 2°), ℵA.

The leaning in Isaiah towards the text of Q, especially when found in company with A or ℵA, is noteworthy, and it is worth mentioning that in Zech. xiii. 7, where the text of Barnabas does not seem to have been influenced by the Gospels, it agrees with A in adding τῆς ποίμνης. Occasionally the text used by Barnabas seems to have been revised from the Heb.; e.g. in Jer. ii. 12 ἐξέστη, ἔφριξεν become ἔκστηθι, φριξάτω in accordance with M.T.; in Gen. ii. 2 Barnabas has with M.T. ἐν τῇ ἡμέρᾳ τῇ ἑβδόμῃ where the LXX. read ἐ. τ. ἡ. τῇ ἕκτῃ[1].

5. The Asiatic Christian writers of the second century, Ignatius of Antioch and Polycarp of Smyrna, afford a striking contrast to Clement of Rome and Barnabas of Alexandria, in the rarity of their appeals to the Old Testament. (a) The genuine Epistles of Ignatius quote it only twice with a *formula citandi* (Prov. iii. 34 = Eph. v. 3, xviii. 17 = Magn. xii. 1);

[1] For further details see Hatch, *op. cit.* p. 180 ff.

two or three allusions (Ps. xxxii. 9 = Eph. xv. 1, Isa. v. 26 =
Smyrn. i. 2, lii. 5 = Trall. viii. 2) complete the instances of a
direct use of the LXX. by this writer. When he quotes or
alludes, he is fairly close to the LXX., unless we may except
the last instance, where δι᾽ ὑμᾶς διὰ παντὸς τὸ ὄνομά μου
βλασφημεῖται ἐν τοῖς ἔθνεσιν appears to be changed into οὐαὶ
δι᾽ οὗ ἐπὶ ματαιότητι τὸ ὄνομά μου ἐπί τινων βλασφημεῖται—a
form which occurs also in Pseudo-Clement (2 Cor. xiii. 2) and
Polycarp (Phil. x. 3)[1]. (*b*) Polycarp is no less sparing in his
references to the O. T. than Ignatius. He quotes only Isa.
lii. 5[1] (x. 3), Tob. iv. 10 = xii. 9 (x. 2), Ps. iv. 5 (xii. 1)—the
last-named passage perhaps indirectly, from Eph. iv. 26—and
Prov. iii. 4 (vi. 1). In Phil. vi. 1 there is an allusion to Ezech.
xxxiv. 4, from which it may be gathered that Polycarp read
there ἐπιστρέψατε, with cod. A.

6. Irenaeus may be taken next, for though he belonged
to the next generation and his literary activity was connected
with the West, his copies of the Old Testament writings were
doubtless of Asiatic *provenance*. His method of quotation
however differs widely from that of the earlier writers. He
is a theologian and a controversialist, and he quotes the
Scriptures to refute an antagonist or to support the traditional
faith. Accordingly his citations are, with few exceptions,
either exact extracts, or but slightly abridged and adapted,
and he is almost wholly free from the habit of loose paraphrase. How copiously he cites, especially in *Adv. haereses*
iii. iv., will appear from the following list[2].

Gen. i. 3 (iv. 32. 1), 5 (v. 23. 2), 26 (iii. 23. 2, iv. 20. 1, v. 1. 3);
ii. 1 f. (v. 28. 3), 5 (iii. 21. 10), 7 (ii. 34. 4, iv. 20. 1, v. 7. 1, v. 15.
2), 8 (iv. 5. 1), 16 f. (v. 23. 1), 23 (iii. 22. 4); iii. 1 ff. (v. 23. 1), 8
(v. 17. 1), 9 (v. 15. 4), 13 (iii. 23. 5), 14 (iii. 23. 3), 15 (iv. 40. 3,
v. 21. 1), 19 (v. 16. 1); iv. 7 (iv. 18. 3), 9 (iii. 23. 4), 10 (v. 14. 1);

[1] On this quotation, however, see Nestle in *Exp. Times*, ix., p. 14 f.
[2] The chapters and sections are those of Stieren.

ix. 5 f. (v. 14. 1); xiii. 14 f., 27 (v. 32. 2); xiv. 22 (iv. 5. 5); xv. 18
(v. 32. 2); xvii. 9 ff. (iv. 16. 1); xix. 24 (iii. 6. 1), 31 ff. (iv. 31. 1);
xxvii. 27 ff. (v. 33. 3); xlix. 10 ff. (iv. 10. 2), 18 (iii. 10. 3). Exod.
i. 13 f. (iv. 30. 2); iii. 7 f. (iv. 7. 4), 8, 14 (iii. 6. 2), 19 (iv. 29. 2);
xiii. 2 (i. 3. 4); xx. 3, 5 (i. 29. 4), 12 (iv. 9. 3); xxiii. 20 (iv. 20. 5):
xxv. 40 (iv. 14. 3); xxvi. 16 (ii. 24. 3); xxxi. 13 (iv. 16. 1); xxxiii.
2 f. (iv. 15. 1), 20 (i. 19. 1), 21 ff. (iv. 20. 9); xxxiv. 6 f. (iv. 20. 8).
Num. xvi. 15 (iv. 26. 4); xviii. 20 (iv. 8. 3); xxiv. 17 (iii. 9. 2).
Deut. iv. 14 (iv. 16. 5), 19 (iii. 6. 5); v. 2 f. (iv. 16. 2), 8 (iii. 6. 5),
22 (iv. 15. 1, 4); vi. 4 ff. (iv. 2. 2, v. 22. 1); viii. 3 (iv. 16. 3); x.
12 (iv. 16. 4), 16 (iv. 16. 1); xvi. 5 f. (iv. 10. 1), 16 (iv. 18. 1);
xviii. 1 (iv. 8. 3); xxviii. 66 (iv. 10. 2, v. 18. 3); xxx. 19 f. (iv. 16.
4); xxxii. 1 (iv. 2. 1), 4 (iii. 18. 7), 6 (iv. 10. 2 ; 31. 2), 8 f. (iii. 12.
9); xxxiii. 9 (iv. 8. 3). 1 Regn. xii. 2 f. (iv. 26. 4); xv. 22 (iv. 17.
1). 2 Regn. xi. 27, xii. 1 ff. (iv. 27. 1). 3 Regn. viii. 27 (iv. 27. 1);
xi. 1 ff. (iv. 27. 1); xviii. 21, 24, 36 (iii. 6. 3); xix. 11 f. (iv. 20. 10).
Ps. ii. 8 (iv. 21. 3); iii. 6 (iv. 31. 1); vii. 11 (iii. 10. 4); viii. 3 (i.
14. 8); xiii. 3 (i. 19. 1); xviii. 2 (i. 14. 8), 7 (iv. 33. 13); xx. 5 (ii.
34. 3); xxii. 4 f. (v. 31. 2); xxiii. 1 (iv. 36. 6); xxxi. 1 f. (v. 17. 3);
xxxii. 6 (i. 22. 1; iii. 8. 2), 9 (ii. 2. 5, iii. 8. 2); xxxiii. 13 ff. (iv.
17. 3, 36. 2), 17 (iv. 28. 1); xxxiv. 9 (iv. 11. 3); xxxix. 7 (iv. 17.
1); xliv. 3 ff. (iv. 33. 11), 7 (iii. 6. 1); xlviii. 13 (iv. 4. 3), 21 (iv.
41. 3), 23 (v. 7. 2); xlix. 1 (iii. 6. 1), 3 f. (v. 18. 3), 9 ff. (iv. 17. 1);
l. 14 (iii. 17. 2), 18 ff. (iv. 17. 1); lvii. 4 f. (iii. 10. 1, iv. 41. 3);
lxviii. 27 (iii. 22. 2); lxxv. 2 (iii. 9. 2), 3 (iv. 33. 11); lxxvii. 5 ff.
(iii. 16. 3); lxxix. 1 (iii. 11. 8); lxxxi. 1, 6 f. (iii. 6. 1, iii. 19. 1);
lxxxiv. 12 (iii. 5. 1); lxxxv. 13 (v. 31. 1); xc. 13 (iii. 23. 7); xciv.
4 ff. (iii. 10. 4); xcv. 1 (iv. 9. 1), 5 (iii. 6. 3); xcvii. 2 (iii. 10. 3);
xcviii. 1 (iv. 33. 13); ci. 26 ff. (iv. 3. 1); ciii. 30 (v. 33. 1); cix. 1
(ii. 28. 7, iii. 6. 1); cx. 10 (iii. 23. 5); cxiii. 11 (iii. 8. 3); cxxxi.
10 f. (iii. 9. 2); cxlv. 6 (i. 10. 1); cxlviii. 5 f. (ii. 34. 2, iv. 41. 1).
Prov. i. 20 f. (v. 20. 1); iii. 19 f. (iv. 20. 3); v. 22 (iii. 9. 3); viii.
15 (v. 24. 1), 22 ff., 27 (iv. 20. 3); xix. 17 (iv. 18. 6); xxi. 1 (v.
24. 1). Sap. vi. 19 (iv. 38. 3). Hos. iv. 1 (i. 19. 1); xii. 10 (iii.
12, 13, iv. 20. 6). Amos i. 2 (iii. 20. 4); viii. 9 f. (iv. 33. 12). Mic.
vii. 19 (iii. 20. 4). Joel iii. 16 (iv. 33. 11). Jon. i. 9, ii. 3, iii. 8 f.
(iii. 20. 1). Hab. iii. 2 (iii. 16. 7), 3 ff. (iii. 20. 4, iv. 33. 11). Zech.
vii. 9 ff. (iv. 17. 3, iv. 36. 2); viii. 16 f. (iv. 17. 3), 17 (iv. 36. 2); xii.
10 (iv. 33. 11). Mal. i. 10 f. (iv. 17. 5), ii. 10 (iv. 20. 2); iv. 1 (iv.
4. 3). Isa. i. 2 (iv. 2. 1, iv. 41. 2), 3 (i. 19. 1), 8 f. (iv. 4. 2, iv. 33.
13), 11 (iv. 17. 1), 16 (iv. 17. 1, iv. 36. 2, iv. 41. 3), 22 (iv. 12. 1),
23 (iv. 2. 6); ii. 3 f. (iv. 34. 4), 17 (iv. 33. 13); v. 6 (iii. 17. 3), 12
(ii. 22. 2, iv. 2. 4); vi. 5 (iv. 20. 8), 11 f. (v. 34. 2, v. 35. 1); vii.
10 ff. (iii. 21. 4); viii. 3 f. (iii. 16. 4, iv. 33. 11); ix. 6 (iii. 16. 3, iv.
33. 11); xi. 1 ff. (iii. 9. 3), 6 ff. (v. 33. 4); xii. 2 (iii. 10. 3); xiii. 9
(v. 35. 1); xxv. 8 (v. 12. 1), 9 (iv. 9. 2); xxvi. 10 (v. 35. 1), 19 (iv.
33. 11, v. 15. 1, v. 34. 1); xxvii. 6 (iv. 4. 1); xxviii. 16 (iii. 21. 7);

xxix. 13 (iv. 12. 4); xxx. 1 (iv. 18. 3), 25 f. (v. 34. 2); xxxi. 9 (v. 34. 4); xxxii. 1 (v. 34. 4): xxxiii. 20 (iii. 20. 4); xxxv. 3 f. (iii. 20. 3, iv. 33. 11); xl. 15, 17 (v. 29. 1); xli. 4 (iv. 5. 1); xlii. 5 (iv. 2. 1, v. 12. 2), 10 ff. (iv. 9. 1); xliii. 5 ff. (iv. 14. 1), 10 (iii. 6. 2, iv. 5. 1), 18 (iv. 33. 14), 23 (iv. 17. 3), xlv. 7 (iv. 40. 1); xlvi. 9 (i. 5. 4), xlviii. 22 (i. 16. 3); xlix. 16 (v. 35. 2); li. 6 (iv. 3. 1), liii. 4 (iv. 33. 11), 8 (ii. 28. 5); liv. 11 ff. (v. 34. 4); lvii. (iv. 34. 4), 16 (v. 12. 2); lviii. 6 ff. (iv. 17. 3), 14 (v. 34. 2); lx. 17; lxi. 1 ff. (iii. 9. 3); lxiii. 9 (iii. 20. 4); lxv. 1 (iii. 6. 1), 17 ff. (iv. 26. 4, v. 35. 2, 34. 4), 21 (v. 35. 1), 22 (v. 15. 1), 25 (v. 33. 4), lxvi. 1 (iv. 2. 5), 2 (iv. 17. 3), 3 (iv. 18. 3), 22 (v. 36. 1). Jer. i. 5 (v. 15. 3); ii. 29 (iv. 37. 7); iv. 22 (iv. 2. 1); v. 8 (iv. 41. 3, v. 7. 2); vi. 17 ff. (iv. 36. 2), 20 (iv. 17. 2); vii. 2 f. (iv. 17. 2), 3 (iv. 36. 2), 21 (iv. 17. 3), 25 (iv. 36. 5), 29 f. (iv. 36. 2); viii. 16 (v. 30. 2); ix. 2 (iv. 25. 3), 24 f. (iv. 17. 3); x. 11 (iii. 6. 3); xi. 15 (iv. 17. 3); xiv. 9 (iv. 33. 12), xvii. 9 (iii. 18. 3, iv. 33. 11); xxii. 17 (iv. 18. 3, iii. 21. 9); xxiii. 7 f. (v. 34. 1), 20 (iv. 26. 1), 23 (iv. 19. 2), 29 (v. 17. 4); xxxi. 10 ff. (v. 34. 3), 26 (iv. 31. 1); xxxv. 15 (iv. 36. 5); xxxvi. 30 f. (iii. 21. 9); xxxviii. 11 (iii. 8. 21). Lam. iv. 20 (iii. 20. 3). Bar. iv. 36—v. fin. (v. 35. 1). Ezech. ii. 1 (iv. 20. 10); xx. 12 (iv. 16. 1), 23 f. (iv. 15. 1), xxviii. 25 f. (v. 34. 1); xxxvi. 26 (iv. 23. 4); xxxvii. 1 ff. (v. 15. 1), 12 (v. 34. 1). Dan. ii. 23 f., 41 ff. (v. 26. 1); iii. 24 ff. (v. 5. 2); vii. 8 (v. 25. 33), 10 (ii. 7. 4), 14 (iv. 20. 11), 20 ff. (v. 25. 3), 27 (v. 34. 2); viii. 11 f., 23 ff. (v. 25. 4); ix. 7 (v. 25. 4); xii. 3 f., 7 (iv. 26. 1), 9 f. (i. 19. 2), xii. 13 (v. 34. 2). Sus. 52 f., 56 (iv. 26. 3). Bel 3 f., 24 (iv. 5. 2).

The Latin version, in which the greater part of these quotations are clothed, appears to be exact where it can be tested (cf. e.g. Isa. xlvi. 9 (i. 5. 4), xlviii. 22 (i. 16. 3), Dan. xii. 9 (i. 19. 2)). Assuming that it is so throughout, it is obvious that in Irenaeus we have an important witness to the LXX. text of the second century. The following variants taken from Books iii., iv., will shew the general tendencies of his text:

Gen. xlix. 10 *cui repositum est* (M^mg ᾧ ἀπόκειται[1]); 18 *in salutem tuam sustinui te, Domine* (cf. F^corr mg ap. Field). Exod. xxv. 40 *facies omnia* (F ποιήσεις πάντα, Luc.) *secundum typum eorum quae vidisti.* Num. xxiv. 17 *surget dux in Israel* (cf. Heb. טבֶשֵׁ, Σ. σκῆπτρον; LXX. ἄνθρωπος ἐξ 'I.). Deut. v. 22 (19) *scripsit ea in duabus tabulis lapideis* (+λιθίνας B^abA Luc.); xxxii. 6

---

[1] Cf. Justin, *Dial.* 120.

et fecit te et creavit te (+καὶ ἔκτισέν σε AF, +καὶ ἔπλασέν σε Luc.). 1 Regn. xv. 22 *auditus bonus super sacrificium* (ἀγαθή Luc.). Ps. xxxix. 7 *aures autem perfecisti mihi* (possibly a correction from the Gallican Psalter, but a few cursives read after the Heb. ὠτία or ὦτα); xliv. 17 *facti sunt tibi filii* (B^bART ἐγενήθησαν, ag. B*א ἐγενν.); xlix. 10 *bestiae terrae* (ἀγροῦ א^{c.a}A, δρυμοῦ Bא*), 15 *in die tribulationis tuae* (θλίψεώς σου א^{c.a}AR); ci. 27 *mutabis eos* (ἀλλάξεις א*, ἑλίξεις B(א^{c.a})AR(T)); cix. 1 *suppedaneum pedum tuorum* (ὑποπόδιον, not ὑποκάτω); cxiii. 11 om. ἐν τοῖς οὐρανοῖς (with א^{c.a}AT). Mic. vii. 19 *ipse* (αὐτός AQ)...*proiciet* (ἀπορρίψει A(Q), ἀποριφήσονται B), om. πάσας. Hab. iii. 3 *pedes eius* (οἱ πόδες AQ, κατὰ πόδας B). Isa. i. 17 *iustificate viduam* (χήραν B^{a.b}אΑΓ ag. χήρᾳ B*Q*); xi. 4 *arguet gloriosos terrae* (τοὺς ἐνδόξους אQ^{cor}, ag. τ. ταπεινούς BAQ*); xxv. 9 om. καὶ σώσει ἡμᾶς...ὑπεμείναμεν αὐτῷ (with אAQ*, a hexaplaric addition, cf. Field, *ad loc.*); xxix. 13 *populus hic labiis me honorat* (om. with אAQ ἐν τῷ στόματι αὐτοῦ καὶ ἐν); xliii. 23 *non servisti mihi in sacrificiis*=οὐ[δὲ] ἐδούλευσάς μοι ἐν ταῖς θυσίαις [σου] א^{c.a} (ΑΓ), *fecisti in* (cf. A* ΕΠΟΙΗϹΑΕΕΝ); lxv. 1 *qui me non quaerunt* (ζητοῦσιν אAQ, ag. ἐπερωτῶσιν B). Jer. xliii. 31 *inferam super eos* (αὐτούς אAQ*, ag. αὐτόν BQ^{corr}), *locutus sum super eos* (ἐπ᾽ αὐτούς AQ, πρὸς αὐτ. Bא). Bar. v. 2 *laetitiae* (LXX. δικαιοσύνης).

A special interest attaches to Irenaeus' extracts from Daniel[1]. For the most part they follow the version of Theodotion quite closely, even in the Greek additions. Two exceptions are worth noting: Dan. vii. 10 is quoted by Irenaeus as it is by Clement of Rome, in a form which agrees with neither LXX. nor Th.; Dan. xii. 9 is cited in the form Ἀπότρεχε, Δανιήλ· οὗτοι γὰρ οἱ λόγοι ἐμπεφραγμένοι εἰσίν, ἕως οἱ συνιέντες συνιῶσι καὶ οἱ λευκοὶ λευκανθῶσι, where ἀπότρεχε is a LXX. reading, whilst ἐμπεφραγμένοι is from Th. and the rest of the sentence seems to be suggested by his version (cf. ἕως...ἐκλευκανθῶσιν, Th.). This quotation however is professedly taken from a Valentinian source, which may account for its freedom.

7. Like Irenaeus, Justin quotes profusely, and his aim as an apologist and a controversialist compels him to cite his documents with some regard to verbal accuracy. For the criticism of the LXX his writings afford even richer materials

---

[1] See above, p. 47.

than those of Irenaeus, since his subject leads him, especially in the Dialogue with Trypho the Jew, to quote long extracts without break or interpolated matter; more than once an entire Psalm, or a passage exceeding in length one of our modern chapters, is copied into his pages, presumably as it stood in his text of the Greek Old Testament.

In the following list of Justin's quotations from the LXX. account has been taken only of his undoubted writings. *A.*=the First Apology, *D.*=the Dialogue; the Second Apology contains nothing to our purpose.

Gen. i. 1 ff. (*A.* 59, 64), 26 ff. (*D.* 62); iii. 15 (*D.* 102), 22 (*D.* 62); ix. 24—27 (*D.* 139); xi. 6 (*D.* 102); xv. 6 (*D.* 92); xvii. 14 (*D.* 23); xviii. 2 ff. (*D.* 126), 13 ff. (*D.* 56); xix. 1 ff. (*D.* 56), 23—25 (*D.* 56), 27 f. (*D.* 56) ; xxvi. 4 (*D.* 120); xxviii. 10—19 (*D.* 58, 120); xxxi. 10—13 (*D.* 58); xxxii. 22—30 (*D.* 58, 126); xxxv. 6—10 (*D.* 58); xlix. 8—12 (*A.* 32, 54; *D.* 52, 120). Exod. ii. 23 (*D.* 59); iii. 2—4 (*D.* 60), 3 ff. (*A.* 63); vi. 2—4 (*D.* 126); xvii. 16 (*D.* 49); xx. 22 (*D.* 75); xxiii. 20 f. (*D.* 75); xxxii. 6 (*D.* 20). Lev. xxvi. 40 f. (*D.* 16). Num. xi. 23 (*D.* 126); xxi. 8 f. (*A.* 60); xxiv. 17 (*A.* 32, *D.* 106). Deut. x. 16 f. (*D.* 16); xxi. 23 (*D.* 96); xxvii. 26 (*D.* 95); xxxi. 2 f. (*D.* 126), 16—18 (*D.* 74); xxxii. 7—9 (*D.* 131), 15 (*D.* 20), 16—23 (*D.* 119), 20 (*D.* 27, 123), 22 (*A.* 60), 43 (*D.* 130); xxxiii. 13—17 (*D.* 91). Jos. v. 2 (*D.* 24); v. 13—vi. 2 (*D.* 62). 2 Regn. vii. 14—16 (*D.* 118). 3 Regn. xix. 10, 18 (*D.* 39). Ps. i. (*A.* 40); ii. (*A.* 40); ii. 7 f. (*D.* 122); iii. 5 f. (*A.* 38, *D.* 97); viii. 3 (*D.* 114); xiii. 2 ff. (*D.* 27); xvii. 44 f. (*D.* 28); xviii. 3 ff. (*A.* 40, *D.* 64); xxi. 1—24 (*D.* 18), 8 f. (*A.* 38), 17 ff. (*A.* 35, 38, *D.* 97); xxiii. (*D.* 36); xxiii. 7 (*A.* 51, *D.* 85); xxxi. 2 (*D.* 141); xliv. (*D.* 38); xliv. 7 ff. (*D.* 56, 63); xlvi. 6—9 (*D.* 37); xlix. (*D.* 22); lxvii. 19 (*D.* 39); lxxi. 1—19 (*D.* 34, 64, 121); lxxi. 17—19 (*D.* 64); lxxxi. (*D.* 124); xcv. 1 ff. (*A.* 41), 5 (*D.* 79), 10 (*D.* 73); xcviii. (*D.* 37); xcviii. 1—7 (*D.* 64); cix. (*D.* 32); cix. 1 ff. (*A.* 45, *D.* 56), 3 ff. (*D.* 63), 4 (*D.* 118); cxxvii. 3 (*D.* 110); cxlviii. 1 f. (*D.* 85). Prov. viii. 21—29 (*D.* 129), 24—36 (*D.* 61). Job i. 6 (*D.* 79). Hos. x. 6 (*D.* 103). Amos v. 18—vi. 7 (*D.* 22). Mic. iv. 1—7 (*D.* 109); v. 2 (*A.* 34). Joel ii. 28 f. (*D.* 87). Jon. iv. 4 ff. (*D.* 107). Zech. ii. 6 (*A.* 52), 11 (*D.* 119), 10—iii. 2 (*D.* 115); iii. 1 ff. (*D.* 79); vi. 12 (*D.* 121); ix. 9 (*A.* 35, *D.* 53); xii. 10—12 (*A.* 52), 12 (*D.* 121); xiii. 7 (*D.* 53). Mal. i. 10—12 (*D.* 28, 41). Isa. i. 3 (*A.* 63), 7 (*A.* 47), 9 (*A.* 53, *D.* 140), 11 f. (*A.* 37), 16 ff. (*A.* 44, 61), 23 ff. (*D.* 27, 82); ii. 3 f. (*A.* 39), 5 ff. (*D.* 24, 135); iii. 9 (*D.* 136), 9—11 (*D.* 17), 9—15 (*D.* 133), 16 (*D.* 27); v. 18—25 (*D.* 17, 133), 20 (*A.* 49); vi. 10 (*D.* 12); vii. 10—16

(*D.* 42, 66), 14 (*A.* 33); viii. 4 (*D.* 77); ix. 6 (*A.* 35); xi. 1—3 (*D.* 87); xiv. 1 (*D.* 123); xvi. 1 (*D.* 114); xix. 24 f. (*D.* 123); xxvi. 2 ff. (*D.* 24); xxix. 13 f. (*D.* 27, 32, 78, 123); xxx. 1—5 (*D.* 79); xxxiii. 13—19 (*D.* 70); xxxv. 1—7 (*D.* 69), 4 ff. (*A.* 48); xxxix. 3 (*D.* 50); xl. 1—17 (*D.* 50); xlii. 1—4 (*D.* 123, 135), 5—13 (*D.* 65), 6 f. (*D.* 26), 16 (*D.* 122), 19 f. (*D.* 123); xliii. 10 (*D.* 122), 15 (*D.* 135); xlv. 23 (*A.* 52); xlix. 6 (*D.* 121), 8 (*D.* 122); l. 4 (*D.* 102), 6 ff. (*A.* 38); li. 4 f. (*D.* 11); lii. 10 f. (*D.* 13), 13—liii. 8 (*A.* 50), lii. 15—liii. 1 (*D.* 118); liii. 1 ff. (*D.* 42); liii. 8—12 (*A.* 51), 9 (*D.* 97); liv. 1 (*A.* 53); lv. 3 f. (*D.* 12), 3—13 (*D.* 14); lvii. 1 ff. (*A.* 48), 1—4 (*D.* 16), 1 (*D.* 110), 2 (*D.* 97, 118), 5 f. (*D.* 27); lviii. 1—11 (*D.* 15), 2 (*A.* 35), 6 f. (*A.* 37), 13 ff. (*D.* 27); lxii. 10—lxiii. 6 (*D.* 26); lxii. 12 (*D.* 119); lxiii. 15—lxiv. 12 (*D.* 25); lxiii. 17 (*A.* 52); lxiv. 10 ff. (*A.* 47, 52); lxv. 1 ff. (*A.* 49, *D.* 24), 1 (*D.* 119), 2 (*A.* 35, 38, *D.* 97), 8 ff. (*D.* 136), 9—12 (*D.* 135), 17—25 (*D.* 81); lxvi. 1 (*A.* 37, *D.* 22), 5—11 (*D.* 85), 23 f. (*D.* 44), 24 (*A.* 52, *D.* 140). Jer. ii. 12 (*D.* 114), 13 (*D.* 19); iv. 3 (*D.* 28); vii. 21 ff. (*D.* 22); ix. 25 ff. (*D.* 28), 26 (*A.* 53); xxxviii. 15 (*D.* 78), 27 (*D.* 123), 31 f. (*D.* 11). Thren. iv. 20 (*A.* 55). Ezech. iii. 17—19 (*D.* 82); xiv. 20 (*D.* 44, 140); xvi. 3 (*D.* 77); xx. 19—26 (*D.* 21); xxxvi. 12 (*D.* 123); xxxvii. 7 ff. (*A.* 53). Dan. vii. 9—28 (*D.* 31), 13 (*A.* 51).

From the circumstances of Justin's life we are prepared to find in his writings an eclectic text of the LXX. Of Palestinian birth but of Greek parentage, he seems to have divided his maturer life between Ephesus and Rome; and each of these associations may have supplied textual peculiarities. The general result may be gathered from a few specimens of the readings exhibited by Justin's longer extracts from the O.T.

Gen. xxviii. 10—19. 11 ἔθηκε, *D*sil E   13 ἐστήρικτο ἐπ᾿ αὐτήν· ὁ δὲ εἶπεν | ὁ θεός 1°] pr Κύριος | om ὁ θεός 2°   14 γῆς, DE | ἐπί 1°] εἰς | om ἐπί 2°, 3°, 4° (ἐπ᾿) | λίβα] νότον   15 ἐν ὁδῷ πάσῃ ᾗ ἄν   18 ὑπέθηκεν, *D*sil   19 om ἐκείνου | Οὐλαμμαούς, DE* | τὸ ὄνομα. xxxii. 22—30. 24 ἄγγελος μετ᾿ αὐτοῦ, *D* 26 με εὐλογήσῃς, *D*sil E   28 om ἔτι, E | ἔσται τὸ ὄνομά σου, D | τοῦ θεοῦ, E | δυνατός] + ἔσῃ, *D*sil E   29 om σύ, D 30 ἐσώθη] ἐχάρη (but ἐσώθη, *infr. D.* 126). Deut. xxxii. 16—23. 16 ἐξεπίκραναν, AF   17 om καὶ οὐ θεῷ, θεοῖς | ᾔδεισαν] οἴδασιν | πρόσφατοι] pr καί, A   20 om ἡμερῶν, AF   21 παρώξυναν] παρώργισαν, A   22 κανθήσεται] pr καί | om κάτω. Deut. xxxiii. 13—17. 13 ἐπ᾿] ἀπό (cf. ἀπ᾿ AF) | οὐρανῶν, δρόσων | ἀβύσσου   14 καθ᾿ ὥραν] καθαρῶν   15 ἀπό] pr καί, AF |

ἀενάων] pr καὶ ποταμῶν   16 καθ' ὥραν] καρπῶν | τῇ βάτῳ | ἐπ']
ἐν, AF   17 τῆς γῆς, AF   Jos. v. 13—vi. 2.   13 om καὶ 2° |
ἴδεν] ὁρᾷ | ἐναντίον] κατέναντι | om καὶ ἡ ῥομφαία...αὐτοῦ | ὁ Ἰησοῦς
14 ὁ δέ] καί   15 τὸ ὑπόδημα ἐκ] τὰ ὑποδήματα | ἐφ' ᾧ | om νῦν
(so A, but adding σύ) | ἅγιος] γῆ ἁγία.   vi. 1 ἐξ αὐτῆς ἐξεπορ. | om
οὐδὲ εἰσεπορεύετο   2 om ἐγώ   Ps. xxi. 1—24.   4 τοῦ Ἰσραήλ
ℵ^{c.a}U   7 ἀνθρώπων, ℵRU | ἐξουθένημα, ℵAR   8 καὶ (ℵU)
ἐλάλησαν χείλεσιν   11 ἀπὸ γαστρός, ℵ^{c.a}   12 βοηθῶν]+μοι,
ℵ^{c.a}R*   14 ὁ ἁρπάζων] om ὁ, RU   15 ἐξεχύθη, ℵ^{c.a}R
16 ὡσεὶ] ὡς, ℵARU   17 πόδας]+μου, ℵ^{c.a}ARU   Ps. xlix.
1 om καί 2°, ℵ^{c.a}RT   3 ἐναντίον] ἐνώπιον, RT   4 διακρῖναι]
pr τοῦ, ℵ^{c.a}ART   6 ὁ θεός, ℵRT   7 διαμαρτυροῦμαι, ℵ^{c.a}T
10 δρυμοῦ] ἀγροῦ, ℵ^{c.a}A   16 ἐκδιηγῇ, ℵ^{c.a}AT   19 δολιότητας,
ℵ^{c.a}Rª   21 +τὰς ἁμαρτίας σου, B^cℵ^{c.a}T   22 οὐ μή, ℵ^{c.a}RT
23 τοῦ θεοῦ] μου, ℵ^{c.a}T.   Prov. viii. 21ª—36.   24 τὰς
πηγὰς προελθεῖν (but in D. 129 πρ. τ. πηγάς)   25 τῶν
βουνῶν (but D. 129 omits art.)   26 ὁ θεός   28 καὶ ὡς (1°)]
ἡνίκα, ℵA   29 καὶ ὡς] ἡνίκα   35 ἡτοίμασται   36 ἀσεβοῦσιν]
+εἰς, ℵ^{c.a}A.   Amos v. 18—vi. 7.   18 τοῦ κυρίου   19 ἐὰν φύγῃ]
ὅταν ἐκφύγῃ, A | ἄρκτος | ὁ ὄφις   20 αὕτη] αὐτοῖς   22 τὰ ὁλο-
καυτώματα, A | τὰς θυσίας | προσδέξομαι]+αὐτά, AQ^{mg} | σωτηρίου,
A   23 ἀπόστησον | ἦχον] πλῆθος | ψαλμῶν· ὄργανον   25 om
μ' ἔτη | +λέγει Κύριος, AQ   26 'Ραφάν | om αὐτῶν, AQ*.   vi. 1
ἀπετρύγησαν] pr οἱ ὠνομασμένοι ἐπὶ τοῖς ἀρχηγοῖς (a doublet for
the Greek which follows, ascribed to Symmachus by SH) | om
καί 2° | αὐτοί] ἑαυτοῖς, Qª | τοῦ Ἰσρ.] om τοῦ   2 +εἰς Χαλάνην,
22, 36, 42; Heb. | διέλθατε] πορεύθητε | Ἐμὰθ 'Ραββά] Ἀμὰθ τὴν
μεγάλην (τὴν μεγ., Symm. "20, 36, 51 al.") | ἀλλοφύλων] pr τῶν |
πλείονι, A | om. ἐστίν | ὑμετέρων ὁρίων] ὁρ. ὑμῶν   3 κα-
κήν] πονηράν   4 καθεύδοντες] κοιμώμενοι | ἐρίφους] ἄρνας
5 ἑστῶτα, AQ   6 τὸν διυλισμένον (a doublet)] ἐν φιάλαις (Heb.)
7 δυναστῶν]+τῶν ἀποικιζομένων | καὶ μεταστραφήσεται οἴκημα
κακουργῶν (a doublet of καὶ ἐξαρθ. κτλ.).   Zach. ii. 10—iii. 2.
10 τέρπου] χαῖρε (cf. Eus. d.e., p. 252) | ὅτι, ℵ   11 καταφεύ-
ξονται] προστεθήσονται | κατασκηνώσω | ἐπιγνώσῃ] γνώσονται |
Παντοκράτωρ] τῶν δυνάμεων | ἀπέσταλκε   12 τῇ μερίδι] καὶ
τὴν μερίδα, ℵ^{c.a}A, and, without καί, ℵ*Qͬ | αἱρετιεῖ] ἐκλέξεται "86
in textu ex alio videlicet interprete" (Field).   iii. 1 om Κύριος,
Κυρίου | τὸν Ἰησοῦν] om τόν, AQͬ | ὁ διάβολος] om ὁ   2 om
ἐπιτίμησαι (1°)...διάβολε | om ὡς (Heb.).   Mal. i. 10—12.
10 θέλημά μου | τὰς θυσίας ὑμῶν   11 ἀπό, AΓ | om καί 1°,
AQ | προσάγεται] προσφέρεται | διότι μέγα] ὅτι τιμᾶται (ὅτι μέγα
D. 41) | om Παντοκράτωρ.   Isa. i. 16—20.   17 χήραν,
B^{ab}ℵAΓ   18 δεῦτε]+ καί, ℵAQͬ | διαλεχθῶμεν [1] | χιόνα,
ἔρεον] ἔρεον, χιόνα   19 (A. 61 omits καὶ ἐὰν θέλητε...φάγεσθε.)

---

[1] See above, p. 407.

Isa. lii. 13—liii. 12. lii. 13 ἰδοὺ] ἴδε γὰρ *A*. 14 πολλοὶ ἐπί σε
A.D. 15 θαυμασθήσονται *D*. | om ἐπ᾿ αὐτῷ *A*. 16 om
ὄψονται *A*. liii. 2 ἐναντίον] ἐνώπιον *A*. | ἐν. αὐτοῦ ὡς παιδ.
A.D. 3 τοὺς υἱοὺς τῶν ἀνθρώπων] τοὺς ἀνθρώπους *A*. (cf. πάντας
ἀνθρώπους, AQ*) 5 αὐτός | ἀνομίας, ἁμαρτίας *A*., אAQ | om
ἡμῶν 3° *A*. 6 om Κύριος *A*. 7 κείροντος *A.D.*, B +αὐτόν
A., א^{c.a}AQ 8 τοῦ λαοῦ μου] αὐτῶν *A*. | ἤχθη] ἥκει *A.D.*, Q^{mg}
9 θανάτου]+αὐτοῦ *A*., B^{a.b}אAQ 10 τοῦ πόνου] om τοῦ *A*.
11 αὐτῶν] ἡμῶν *A.D.* 12 παρεδόθη] pr αὐτός *A*. Isa. lxii. 10
—lxiii. 6. 11 ταῖς θυγατράσιν | σοὶ ὁ σωτήρ, אAQ | om αὐτοῦ 1°,
AQ* 12 οὐ καταλελειμμένη, (א). lxiii. 1 ἐρύθημα, B | ἱματίων]
+αὐτοῦ | βίᾳ] pr ἀναβαίνων (cf. Symm. βαίνων, Heb.) 3 +ληνὸν
ἐπάτησα μονώτατος, Symm., Heb. (a doublet of πλ. καταπεπ.) |
om μου, אAQ | +εἰς γῆν, B^{a.b}אAQ 5 οὐδείς, אAQ | ἀντελάβετο,
א | om αὐτούς | om μου 1°

To shew Justin's relation to the two recensions of Daniel,
it is necessary to place some verses side by side with the
corresponding contexts of the LXX. and Theodotion[1].

Justin, *Dial.* 31.	Dan. vii. 9—14, LXX.	Ibid., Th.
ἐθεώρουν ἕως ὅτου θρόνοι ἐτέθησαν, καὶ ὁ παλαιὸς ἡμερῶν ἐκάθητο ἔχων ΠΕΡΙΒΟΛΗΝ ὡσεὶ χιόνα λευκήν, καὶ τὸ ΤΡΙΧΩΜΑ τῆς κεφαλῆς αὐτοῦ ὡσεὶ ἔριον καθαρόν, ὁ θρόνος αὐτοῦ ὡσεὶ φλὸξ πυρός, οἱ τροχοὶ αὐτοῦ πῦρ φλέγον. ποταμὸς πυρὸς εἷλκεν ἐκπορεγόμενος ἐκ προσώπου αὐτοῦ· χίλιαι χιλιάδες ἐλειτούργουν αὐτῷ καὶ μύριαι μυριάδες παρεισστήκεισαν αὐτῷ· βίβλοι ἀνεῴχθησαν καὶ κριτήριον ἐκάθισεν. ἐθεώρουν τότε ΤΗΝ ΦΩΝΗΝ	ἐθεώρουν ἕως ὅτε θρόνοι ἐτέθησαν, καὶ παλαιὸς ἡμερῶν ἐκάθητο ἔχων ΠΕΡΙΒΟΛΗΝ ὡσεὶ χιόνα, καὶ τὸ ΤΡΙΧΩΜΑ τῆς κεφαλῆς αὐτοῦ ὡσεὶ ἔριον λευκὸν καθαρόν· ὁ θρόνος ὡσεὶ φλὸξ πυρός, τροχοὶ αὐτοῦ πῦρ καιόμενον. ποταμὸς πυρὸς ἕλκων, καὶ ἐξεπορεύετο ΚΑΤΑ ΠΡΟΣΩΠΟΝ αὐτοῦ ποταμὸς πυρός· χίλιαι χιλιάδες ἐθεράπευον αὐτὸν καὶ μύριαι μυριάδες παρεισστήκεισαν αὐτῷ· καὶ κριτήριον ἐκάθισε καὶ βίβλοι ἠνεῴχθησαν. ἐθεώρουν	ἐθεώρουν ἕως ὅτου θρόνοι ἐτέθησαν, καὶ παλαιὸς ἡμερῶν ἐκάθητο, καὶ τὸ ἔνδυμα αὐτοῦ ὡσεὶ χιὼν λευκόν, καὶ ἡ θρὶξ τῆς κεφαλῆς αὐτοῦ ὡσεὶ ἔριον καθαρόν· ὁ θρόνος αὐτοῦ φλὸξ πυρός, οἱ τροχοὶ αὐτοῦ πῦρ φλέγον. ποταμὸς πυρὸς εἷλκεν ἔμπροσθεν αὐτοῦ· χίλιαι χιλιάδες ἐλειτούργουν αὐτῷ, καὶ μύριαι μυριάδες παρειστήκεισαν αὐτῷ· κριτήριον ἐκάθισεν, καὶ βίβλοι ἠνεῴχθησαν. ἐθεώρουν τότε ἀπὸ φωνῆς τῶν λόγων τῶν μεγάλων ὧν τὸ

[1] Words common to Justin and LXX. but not in Th. are printed in
small uncials; those common to Justin and Th. but not to LXX., in
thick cursives. Most of the remaining words are to be found in the
three texts.

Justin, *Dial.* 31.	Dan. vii. 9—14, LXX.	Ibid., Th.
τῶν μεγάλων λόγων ὧν τὸ κέρας λαλεῖ, καὶ ἀπετυμπανίσθη τὸ θηρίον, καὶ ἀπώλετο τὸ σῶμα αὐτοῦ καὶ ἐδόθη εἰς καῦσιν πυρός· καὶ τὰ λοιπὰ θηρία μετεστάθη τῆς ἀρχῆς αὐτῶν, καὶ χρόνος ζωῆς τοῖς θηρίοις ἐδόθη ἕως καιροῦ καὶ χρόνου. ἐθεώρουν ἐν ὁράματι τῆς νυκτός, καὶ ἰδοὺ μετὰ τῶν νεφελῶν τοῦ οὐρανοῦ ὡς υἱὸς ἀνθρώπου ἐρχόμενος, καὶ ἦλθεν ἕως τοῦ παλαιοῦ τῶν ἡμερῶν, καὶ παρῆν ἐνώπιον αὐτοῦ· καὶ οἱ παρεστηκότες προσήγαγον αὐτόν. καὶ ἐδόθη αὐτῷ ἐξουσία καὶ τιμὴ βασιλική, καὶ πάντα τὰ ἔθνη τῆς γῆς κατὰ γένη καὶ πᾶσα δόξα λατρεύουσα· καὶ ἡ ἐξουσία αὐτοῦ ἐξουσία αἰώνιος ἥτις οὐ μὴ ἀρθῇ, καὶ ἡ βασιλεία αὐτοῦ οὐ μὴ φθαρῇ.	τότε τὴν φωνὴν τῶν λόγων τῶν μεγάλων ὧν τὸ κέρας ἐλάλει· θεωρῶν ἤμην, καὶ ἀπετυμπανίσθη τὸ θηρίον, καὶ ἀπώλετο τὸ σῶμα αὐτοῦ καὶ ἐδόθη εἰς καῦσιν πυρός. καὶ τοὺς κύκλῳ αὐτοῦ ἀπέστησε τῆς ἐξουσίας αὐτῶν, καὶ χρόνος ζωῆς ἐδόθη αὐτοῖς ἕως χρόνου καὶ καιροῦ. ἐθεώρουν ἐν ὁράματι τῆς νυκτός, καὶ ἰδοὺ ἐπὶ τῶν νεφελῶν τοῦ οὐρανοῦ ὡς υἱὸς ἀνθρώπου ἤρχετο, καὶ ὡς παλαιὸς ἡμερῶν παρῆν· καὶ οἱ παρεστηκότες παρῆσαν αὐτῷ. καὶ ἐδόθη αὐτῷ ἐξουσία καὶ τιμὴ βασιλική, καὶ πάντα τὰ ἔθνη τῆς γῆς κατὰ γένη καὶ πᾶσα δόξα αὐτῷ λατρεύουσα· καὶ ἡ ἐξουσία αὐτοῦ ἐξουσία αἰώνιος ἥτις οὐ μὴ ἀρθῇ, καὶ ἡ βασιλεία αὐτοῦ ἥτις οὐ μὴ φθαρῇ.	κέρας ἐκεῖνο ἐλάλει, ἕως ἀνῃρέθη τὸ θηρίον καὶ ἀπώλετο, καὶ τὸ σῶμα αὐτοῦ ἐδόθη εἰς καῦσιν πυρός. καὶ τῶν λοιπῶν θηρίων ἡ ἀρχὴ μετεστάθη, καὶ μακρότης ζωῆς ἐδόθη αὐτοῖς ἕως καιροῦ καὶ καιροῦ. ἐθεώρουν ἐν ὁράματι τῆς νυκτός, καὶ ἰδοὺ μετὰ τῶν νεφελῶν τοῦ οὐρανοῦ ὡς υἱὸς ἀνθρώπου ἐρχόμενος, καὶ ἕως τοῦ παλαιοῦ τῶν ἡμερῶν ἔφθασεν· καὶ προσήχθη αὐτῷ. καὶ αὐτῷ ἐδόθη ἡ ἀρχὴ καὶ ἡ τιμὴ καὶ ἡ βασιλεία, καὶ πάντες οἱ λαοί, φυλαί, καὶ γλῶσσαι δουλεύουσιν αὐτῷ· ἡ ἐξουσία αὐτοῦ ἐξουσία αἰώνιος ἥτις οὐ παρελεύσεται, καὶ ἡ βασιλεία αὐτοῦ οὐ διαφθαρήσεται.

The student will notice that Justin's O.T. text is a mixed one. (*a*) In Genesis it contains many readings of D or DE where those later uncials depart from A; (*b*) in Deuteronomy it occasionally supports A or AF against B, and (*c*) in the Psalms the group ART, with the concurrence sometimes of ℵ*, sometimes of ℵc.a; (*d*) in the Prophets it not seldom agrees with Q (AQ, ℵAQ). In the Minor Prophets it is startling to find in Justin more than one rendering which is attributed to Symmachus; and as it is in the highest degree improbable that

his text has been altered from the text of Symmachus, or at
a later time from a Hexaplaric copy of the LXX., we are led
to the conclusion that these readings belong to an older
version or recension from which both Justin and Symmachus
drew. It is at least possible that many of the readings in
which Justin appears to stand alone may be attributable to the
same origin.

Justin's Daniel text requires separate notice. It will be
seen to be in fundamental agreement with the LXX., but not
without a fair number of Theodotion's readings. Ἐλειτούργουν
meets us here, as in Clement of Rome, and the phrases τὰ
λοιπὰ θηρία μετεστάθη τῆς ἀρχῆς, μετὰ τῶν νεφελῶν ἐρχόμενος,
ἕως τοῦ παλαιοῦ, προσήγαγον αὐτόν, are undoubtedly due to
Theodotion, or rather to the version on which he worked. On
the other hand ἔχων περιβολήν, τὸ τρίχωμα, πῦρ φλέγον, ἀπετυμ-
πανίσθη, χρόνος ζωῆς, οἱ παρεστηκότες, and the whole of *v.* 14
as clearly belong to the Chigi text. That this mixture is not
due to an eclectic taste or a fickle memory is clear from the
fact that the same text meets us in the Latin version of the
passage as given by Tertullian[1].

In a few instances Justin shews a disposition to criticise
the LXX. reading. E.g. in Ps. lxxxi. (lxxxii.) 7, he probably
proposed to read ὡς ἄνθρωπος (כְּאָדָם) for ὡς ἄνθρωποι[2].
Similarly in Deut. xxxii. 8 he realises that the LXX. has substituted ἀγγέλων θεοῦ for בְּנֵי־יִשְׂרָאֵל[3]. He maintains that in
Gen. xlix. 10 the reading of the LXX. is ἕως ἂν ἔλθῃ ᾧ ἀπόκειται,
though according to the Jewish interpreters of his time the
words should rather be rendered ἕως ἂν ἔ. τὰ ἀποκείμενα αὐτῷ.
His text of the LXX. contained some remarkable interpolations; thus he quotes Ps. xcv. (xcvi.) 10[a] in the form ὁ κύριος

---

[1] Burkitt, *Old Latin and Itala*, p. 23 ff.
[2] *Dial.* 124. In the editions ἄνθρωποι occurs twice, but the context
appears to shew that the singular should stand in the quotation.
[3] *Dial.* 13 f.

ἐβασίλευσεν ἀπὸ τοῦ ξύλου[1], and ascribes to Jeremiah the words
ἐμνήσθη δὲ κύριος ὁ θεὸς ἀπὸ Ἰσραὴλ τῶν νεκρῶν αὐτοῦ τῶν
κεκοιμημένων εἰς γῆν χώματος, καὶ κατέβη πρὸς αὐτοὺς εὐαγγελί-
σασθαι αὐτοῖς τὸ σωτήριον αὐτοῦ[2]. He cites also some words
which appear to have found a place in his copy after 2 Esdr.
vi. 21: καὶ εἶπεν Ἔσδρας τῷ λαῷ Τοῦτο τὸ πάσχα ὁ σωτὴρ ἡμῶν
καὶ ἡ καταφυγὴ ἡμῶν· καὶ ἐὰν διανοηθῆτε καὶ ἀναβῇ ὑμῶν
ἐπὶ τὴν καρδίαν ὅτι Μέλλομεν αὐτὸν ταπεινοῦν ἐν σημείῳ, καὶ
μετὰ ταῦτα ἐλπίσωμεν (? ἐλπίσητε) ἐπ᾽ αὐτόν, οὐ μὴ ἐρημωθῇ ὁ
τόπος οὗτος εἰς ἅπαντα χρόνον, λέγει ὁ θεὸς τῶν δυνάμεων· ἐὰν δὲ
μὴ πιστεύσητε αὐτῷ μηδὲ εἰσακούσητε τοῦ κηρύγματος αὐτοῦ,
ἔσεσθε ἐπίχαρμα τοῖς ἔθνεσι[3]. These passages appear to be of
Christian origin, yet Justin is so sure of their genuineness that
he accuses the Jews of having removed them from their copies.

8. Hippolytus of Portus, as we learn from the inscription on the chair of his statue and from other ancient
sources, was the author of a large number of Biblical
commentaries[4]. These included works on the Hexaemeron
and its sequel (τὰ μετὰ τὴν ἑξαήμερον); on Exodus, and
portions of Numbers and Samuel; on the Psalms, Proverbs,
Ecclesiastes, and Song of Songs; on Zechariah, Isaiah, Jeremiah, parts of Ezekiel, and the Book of Daniel. Of these
exegetical works there remains only the commentary on Daniel[5],

---

[1] *Ap.* i. 41, *Dial.* 73. Cf. Tert. *c. Marc.* iii. 19, *adv. Jud.* 10. No
existing Greek MS. of the Psalter is known to contain the words except
cod. 156 (see p. 160), which gives them in the suspicious form ἀπὸ τῷ ξύλῳ.
A ligno is found in the Sahidic and in the Latin of R and in some other
O. L. texts. Cf. the hymn *Vexilla regis*: "impleta sunt quae concinit |
David fideli carmine | dicendo nationibus | Regnavit a ligno Deus" (for
the literature see Julian, *Dict. of Hymnology*, p. 1220).

[2] *Dial.* 72. The same Apocryphon is quoted by Irenaeus (iii. 20. 4, iv.
22. 1, 33. 1, 12, v. 31. 1) and attributed by him to Jeremiah (iv. 31. 1) or
to Isaiah (iii. 20. 4). Cf. Lightfoot, *Clement*, ii. p. 40, and the writer's
Apostles' Creed[3], p. 58 f.

[3] *Dial. ib.*

[4] On his works see Lightfoot, *Clement of Rome*, ii. pp. 388 ff., 419 ff.

[5] Edited by G. W. Bonwetsch and H. Achelis in the new Berlin Corpus
(*Hippolytus' Werke*, i., Leipzig, 1897).

with fragments of most of the rest. The great treatise *Adversus omnes haereses* yields but little in the way of Scriptural quotations[1], but the minor theological works collected by Lagarde[2] supply a considerable number of fairly long extracts from the Pentateuch, the Psalms, and the Prophets. The text of the LXX. which is exhibited in these passages is often of much interest, as a few specimens will shew.

Gen. i. 7 ἐπάνω] ὑπεράνω 28 κατακυριεύσατε] κατακληρονομήσατε. xlix. 8 ff. (Lag. 5 (1), 102 (2)) 8 αἰνεσάτωσαν (1) αἰνέσουσιν (2) 9 ἐκ βλαστοῦ μου υἱέ (2) 10 ᾧ ἀπόκειται (1), τὰ ἀποκείμενα αὐτῷ (2) | αὐτός] + ἔσται (1) 12 χαροποί (cf. Field, *ad loc.*) | ὡς ἀπὸ οἴνου: cf. ἀπὸ οἴνου, ADF. Exod. xx. 13 ff. οὐ μοιχεύσεις, οὐ φονεύσεις, οὐ κλέψεις. Deut. xxxii. 34 f. 34 παρ' ἐμοῦ 35 ὅταν] pr ἐν καιρῷ, AF. xxxiii. 22 ἐκπηδήσεται, B. Ruth ii. 9 ὑδρεύονται, A 14 ἐν τῷ ὄξει, BᵃˑᵇA. Ps. lxviii. 1 ff. 4 ἐγγίζειν] ἐλπίζειν (BᵃˑᵇℵR) με (R) 5 ἥρπαζον 6 ἔγνως] οἶδας | ἀπεκρύβησαν, ℵᶜˑᵃ 8 ἐκάλυψαν ἐντροπῇ 10 κατέφαγε. Prov. vi. 27 ἀποδήσει] ἀποδεσμεύει. xxiii. 29 f. 29 ἀηδίαι, ℵA | πελιδνοί, Bᵇ 30 ἐν οἴνῳ | ἰχνευόντων] κατασκοπούντων. Job ii. 9ᵈ πλανῆτις, ℵᶜˑᵃA. Am. v. 12 καταπατοῦντες, AQ*. Mic. ii. 7 f. 7 πορεύονται 8 κατέναντι] κατὰ πρόσωπον | δοράν] δόξαν (sic). iii. 5 ἤγειραν] ἡγίασαν, Qᵐᵍ. v. 5 ἔσται αὕτη ἡ παρ' ἐμοῦ εἰρήνη ὅταν ὁ Ἀσσύριος (cf. AQ) ἐπέλθῃ. Mal. iv. 4 ἀποστέλλω] πέμψω | πρίν] + ἤ | ἡμέραν] pr τήν, Γ 5 πατέρων ἐπὶ τέκνα | ἐλθὼν πατάξω, ℵᶜˑᵇ. Isa. x. 12 ff. 13 om. ἐν bis, ℵAQΓ 14 τῇ χειρί] + μου, AQ 16 Κύριος σαβαώθ] ἀδωναὶ Κύριος 17 πυρὶ καιομένῳ] φλογί (cf. Symm.). xiv. 4 ff. 11 εἰς ᾅδου] εἰς γῆν | κατακάλυμμα] κατάλειμμα 12 πρός] εἰς, ℵ* 14 νεφελῶν, ℵAQΓ 16 θαυμάσουσιν, ℵAQΓ 19 τεθνηκότων] πεπτωκότων 20 καθαρός] κομψός | χρόνον] χρόνιος 21 σφαγῆναι] εἰς σφαγήν. xlv. 11 + καὶ τῶν θυγατέρων μου (cf. ℵAQ) 13 om βασιλέα, ℵᶜˑᵇAQ 14 ἐν σοὶ προσκυνήσουσιν. lxvi. 24 τελευτήσει, BℵQ (ag. A, τελευτᾷ). Ezech. xxviii. 5 ἐμπορίᾳ] ἐμπειρία. Dan. ii. 1 ff. 1 βασιλεία] + Ναβουχοδονοσόρ, A 5 ἐάν] + οὖν, AQ | σύγκρισιν] + αὐτοῦ, Q

The text of Hippolytus, it will be seen, like most of the patristic texts, leans slightly to AF in the Pentateuch, ℵ* or ℵᶜˑᵃ in the poetical books, and AQ in the Prophets. At the

[1] The references in the *Index locorum* of Duncker and Schneidewin's edition (Göttingen, 1859) direct the reader for the most part to mere allusions, or citations of only a few consecutive words.

[2] In *Hippolyti Romani quae feruntur omnia Graece* (Leipzig, 1858).

same time it is full of surprises, and often stands quite alone among existing witnesses.

9. Our last witness is Clement of Alexandria. Clement had learnt the Christian faith during his early travels in Asia Minor and Magna Graecia, and he may have received copies of O.T. writings from his first Christian masters. Hence it must not be too hastily assumed that the text of his O.T. quotations is purely Alexandrian. On the other hand it is reasonable to suppose that during the period of his literary activity he was familiar with the Alexandrian text and used it when he quoted from his MS. On the whole therefore we may expect his quotations to be fairly representative of the Biblical text current at Alexandria during the generation preceding the compilation of the Hexapla.

Clement quotes both the Jewish and the Christian scriptures profusely, but his extracts seldom extend beyond two or three verses, and are often broken by comments or copied with considerable freedom. His purpose was didactic and not polemical; even in the λόγος προτρεπτικός he aims to persuade rather than to compel assent, whilst the *Paedagogus* and the *Stromateis* are addressed exclusively to persons under instruction, to whom the Scriptures were a familiar text-book. Hence he is exact only when verbal precision is necessary; often it is sufficient for his purpose to work into his argument a few words from a Scriptural context, giving the sense of the rest in his own words. Still it is possible even in these broken references to catch glimpses of the text which lay before him, and in the dearth of early Christian literature emanating from Alexandria, these are of no little value to the student of the Greek Bible[1]. A generally full and accurate index of Clement's

---

[1] Clement's text of the Gospels has been examined by Mr P. M. Barnard (*Biblical texts of Clement of Alexandria in the Four Gospels and the Acts*, Cambridge, 1899) with some interesting and important results. His text

Biblical quotations will be found in the edition of Potter; here it must suffice to give some specimens of the text which they exhibit in the Pentateuch, the poetical books, and the Prophets.

(*a*) Gen. i. 26 (*strom.* v. 29) κατ᾿ εἰκόνα καὶ ὁμοίωσιν ἡμετέραν (elsewhere Cl. reads ὁμ. ἡμῶν, or omits the pronoun). xxxvii. 24 (*strom.* v. 54) ὁ δὲ λάκκος κενός, DE. Exod. xx. 13 ff. (*protrept.* 108, *strom.* ii. 33) οὐ φονεύσεις οὐ μοιχεύσεις...οὐ κλέψεις οὐ ψευδομαρτυρήσεις, AF. Lev. xviii. 1 ff. (*strom.* ii. 46). 3 ἐν αὐτῇ (ἐπ᾿ αὐτῇ B*, ἐπ᾿ αὐτῆς BᵃᵇAF) οὐ ποιήσετε (ποιηθήσεται B*) 4 πορεύεσθε A 5 ὁ ποιήσας αὐτά. Deut. xxxii. 23 ff. (*paed.* i. 68) 23 συντελέσει (συντελέσω AF, συνπολεμήσω, B) 24 ἐπαποστελῶ, A | τῆς γῆς, A (F) 41 ff. ἀνταποδώσω, AF 42 + καὶ ἡ μάχαιρά μου φάγεται κρέα ἀπὸ αἵματος τραυματιῶν, AF (*b*) Ps. xxxiii. 12 ff. (*strom.* iv. 111). 13 ἡμέρας ἰδεῖν, אAR 14 χείλη σου, אᶜ·ᵃAR. xcv. 5 (*protrept.* 62) δαιμονίων εἰσὶν εἴδωλα (cf. Iren.). cii. 14 (*paed.* i. 62) μνήσθητι, א* Th. cxl. 5 (*paed.* i. 79) ἐλεγχέτω με δίκαιος καὶ παιδευσάτω. cl. 4 ὀργάνῳ, אᴿT. Prov. i. 25 (*paed.* i. 85) ὑπηκούετε, אA | οὐ προσείχετε, אAC (ἠπειθήσατε, B). iii. 5 ff. (*strom.* ii. 4). 6 ἐν πάσαις, A | τὰς ὁδούς σου]+ὁ δὲ πούς σου οὐ μὴ προσκόπτῃ (cf. אᶜ·ᵃ: SH pr ÷) 12 παιδεύει, אA (ἐλέγχει, B). xxiii. 13 μὴ ἀπόσχου (ἀπόσχῃ LXX.) νήπιον παιδεύων (A; παιδεύειν, B). Sir. i. 18 (*paed.* i. 68)+φόβος γὰρ Κυρίου ἀπωθεῖται ἁμαρτήματα (so far 248), ἄφηβος δ᾿ οὐ δυνήσεται δικαιωθῆναι, O.L. ix. 9 (*paed.* ii. 54) μὴ συμβολοκοπήσῃς] μὴ συμματακλιθῇς ἐπ᾿ ἀγκῶνα, O.L. xxxiv. 25 (*paed.* ii. 31) ἀπώλεσεν] ἠχρείωσε. xxxvi. 6 (*paed.* i. 42) ὡς φίλος μῶκος] ὁ φιλήδονος καὶ μοῖχος (cf. ὡς φιλόμοιχος, 55, 254). xxxviii. 1 (*paed.* ii. 68) om. τιμαῖς, 106, 296, O.L. xxxix. 13 (*paed.* ii. 76) ἀγροῦ (ὑγροῦ אAC)] ὑδάτων. 18 (*paed.* ii. 44) ὃς ἐλαττώσει] ἐλάττωσις εἰς, Heb. (*c*) Am. iv. 13 (*protrept.* 79) ἰδοὺ ἐγώ, Bᵃ·ᵇAQ (om B*). Nah. iii. 4 (*paed.* i. 81) ἐπίχαρις, Bᵃ·ᵇQ. Mal. i. 10 ff. (*strom.* v. 137). 11 om. καί 1°, AQ | θυμίαμα] θυσία | προσάγεται] προσφέρεται (cf. Justin). Isa. ix. 6 (*paed.* i. 24) υἱὸς καὶ ἐδόθη, אAQΓ | om ἐγενήθη, Γ | ἐκλήθη (καλεῖται, BאQΓ, καλέσει, A) | +θαυμαστὸς σύμβουλος (אᶜ·ᵃA) θεὸς δυναστὴς πατὴρ αἰώνιος ἄρχων εἰρήνης (אᶜ·ᵃA). 7 μεγάλη ἡ ἀρχὴ αὐτοῦ] +τῷ πληθύνειν τὴν παιδείαν, Th. | ὅριον] πέρας, Th., Symm. xi. 1 ff. (*paed.* i. 61). xi. 4 ἐλέγξει τοὺς ἁμαρτωλοὺς τῆς γῆς (cf. Iren.). xxix. 13 (*paed.* i. 76) ὁ λαὸς οὗτος τοῖς χείλεσιν αὐτῶν τιμῶσί με, ἡ δὲ καρδία αὐτῶν πόρρω ἐστὶν ἀπ᾿ ἐμοῦ· μάτην δὲ σέβονταί με διδάσ-

of the LXX. is not likely to be equally instructive, but it ought to reward a patient investigator. [Since this note was written an examination of Clement's LXX. text has been made by Dr O. Stählin (*Clemens Alex. u. die Septuaginta*, Nürnberg, 1901).]

κοντες διδασκαλίας ἐντάλματα ἀνθρώπων (cf. Mt. xv., Mc. vii.).
lxvi. 13 (*paed.* i. 21) ὑμᾶς παρακαλέσω, א.   Jer. ix. 23 f. (*paed.*
i. 37): *v.* 24 abbreviated as in 1 Cor. i. 31.   xiii. 24 ff. (*strom.*
iv. 165 f.).   24 διέσπειρα, Bאֿ{Q} (διεφθειρα A) | ὑπό, אAQ (ἀπό,
B) | φερόμενα] πετώμενα   25 ἀπειθεῖν ὑμᾶς ἐμοί   27 μοιχεία
anarthr., Q | χρεμετισμός anarthr., B.   xxiii. 23 f. (*protrept.* 78).
24 εἰ ποιήσει τι ἄνθρωπος (εἰ κρυβήσεταί τις, B, εἰ κρ. ἄνθρωπος,
AQ).   Bar. iii. 13 (*paed.* i. 92) om χρόνον, B.   Thren. i. 1
(*paed.* i. 80) ἄρχοντα χωρῶν ἐγενήθη εἰς φόρους.   Dan. ix. 24 ff.
(*strom.* i. 125) as in Th. (B*), with the addition καὶ ἥμισυ τῆς
ἑβδομάδος καταπαύσει θυμίαμα θυσίας καὶ πτερυγίου ἀφανισμοῦ ἕως
συντελείας καὶ σπουδῆς τάξιν ἀφανισμοῦ (cf. BᵃᵇAQ).

10.   This examination has been but partial, even within
the narrow field to which it was limited.   It has dealt only
with direct quotations, and in the case of Hippolytus and
Clement of Alexandria, only with a few of these.   Moreover,
the student who wishes to examine the whole of the evidence
must not limit himself to the few great writers who have been
named.   Even if he adds the writings of Aristides, Tatian,
Athenagoras, Theophilus, and the anonymous *Teaching* and
Epistle to Diognetus, there will still remain the fragments
collected in the *Relliquiae Sacrae* and by the researches of
Pitra, and the Pseudo-Clementine, apocryphal, and Gnostic
literature of the second century.   Still more important help
may be obtained from Latin Christian writers who quote the
O.T. in the Old Latin version, e.g. Cyprian, Lucifer, Vigilius
of Thapsus, the Donatist Tyconius, and the author of the
Speculum[1].   This part of the evidence was collected for
Holmes and Parsons, and will be presented in a more permanent form, if not at so much length, in the apparatus of the
larger Septuagint.

Much useful and interesting work might be done by following the lines of Dr Hatch's attempt to collect and compare
the early evidence in reference to particular texts and con-

---

[1] See above, p. 97, and the art. *Old Latin Versions* in Hastings' *D. B.*
iii. (already mentioned, p. 88).

stantly recurring extracts from the LXX.[1] Perhaps however it would be expedient to limit such an investigation to post-apostolic Christian writers, and to carry it beyond Justin. Moreover, Dr Hatch's proposal to estimate the value of MSS., "according as they do or do not agree with such early quotations," seems to be at least precarious. It is conceivable and even probable that the peculiarities of early patristic quotations may be partly due to corruption incident upon the process of citing, whether from memory or from a MS.; and for various other reasons the text of a fourth century MS. may on the whole present a purer text than that which appears in a second century writing. This point, however, must be reserved for fuller consideration in a later chapter[2].

11. With Origen the science of Christian Biblical criticism and hermeneutics may be said to have begun. In the Old Testament his interest was peculiarly strong; it supplied him with the amplest opportunities of exercising his skill in allegorical interpretation; and his knowledge both of the original and of the Greek versions prepared him to deal with the difficulties of his text. Unhappily there is no class of his writings which has suffered so severely. Of his great commentaries on the Old Testament, only fragments have survived; and the Homilies, with the exception of one on the Witch of Endor, and nineteen on the book of Jeremiah, have reached us only in the Latin translations of Rufinus and Jerome. But even fragments and versions of Origen are precious, and the following list of his O.T. remains[3] may be of service to the student of the LXX.

Genesis. Fragments of Commentary (t. i., iii.), and notes from catenae. Homilies (17) in Latin, tr. by Rufinus. *Exodus.* Fragments of Commentary, and notes. Homilies (13) in Latin,

---

[1] *Essays*, i. p. 129 ff. ("On Early Quotations from the Septuagint.")
[2] See Part III. c. vi.
[3] They are collected in Migne, *P. G.* xi.—xvii.

tr. by Rufinus. *Leviticus.* Fragments and notes from catenae. Homilies (16) in Latin, tr. by Rufinus. *Numbers.* Notes from catenae. Homilies (28) in Latin, tr. by Rufinus. *Deuteronomy.* Notes from catenae, &c. *Joshua.* Fragments and notes from catenae, &c. Homilies (26) in Latin, tr. by Rufinus. *Judges.* Notes from catenae. Homilies (9) in Latin, tr. by Rufinus. *Ruth.* A note on Ruth i. 4. 1—4 *Kingdoms.* Homily ὑπὲρ τῆς ἐγγαστριμύθου. Fragments. Homily in Latin on 1 Regn. i. ff. *Psalms.* Fragments of the Commentaries and Homilies; notes from catenae. Homilies (9) in Latin, tr. by Rufinus [on Pss. xxxvi.—xxxviii.]. *Proverbs.* Fragments and notes, Greek and Latin. *Ecclesiastes.* Notes from catenae. *Canticles.* Fragments and notes. Homilies (2) in Latin, tr. by Jerome. Commentary (prol., tt. i.—iv.) in Latin, tr. by Rufinus. *Job.* Notes from catenae. Fragment of a Homily, in Latin. *The xii. Prophets.* Fragment on Hosea xii. (in *Philocal.* 8). *Isaiah.* Fragments (2) of the Commentaries, in Latin. Homilies (9) in Latin, tr. by Jerome. *Jeremiah.* Homilies (19) in Greek, and notes from catenae. Homilies (2) in Latin, tr. by Jerome. *Lamentations.* Notes from catenae. *Ezekiel.* Fragments, and notes from catenae. Homilies (14) in Latin, tr. by Jerome.

12.   It is impossible within the limits of an Introduction to enumerate all the ecclesiastical writers who during the golden age of patristic literature quoted or commented upon the Greek Old Testament. But the student who is not a specialist in this field may be glad to have before him the names and dates of the principal Greek Fathers, with some notice of such of their extant works as are concerned with O.T. exegesis. The Roman numerals in brackets direct him to the volumes of Migne's *Patrologia Graeca,* in which the authors are to be found; in the case of a few writings which are not included in the *Patrologia* and some others, references are given to other editions.

Acacius of Caesarea, † 366.   Fragments in catenae.
Ammonius of Alexandria, c. 460.   Fragments on Genesis and Daniel.   (lxxxv.)
Anastasius of Antioch, † 598.   (lxxxix.)
Anastasius of Sinai, cent. vi.—vii.   (lxxxix.)
Apollinarius of Laodicea (the younger), † c. 393.   (xxxiii., cf. Dräseke's edition in *Texte u. Unters.* vii.)

Apostolical Constitutions, cent. iii.—iv. (ed. Lagarde).
Asterius of Amasea, c. 400. (xl.)
Athanasius of Alexandria, †373. On the Psalms; Titles of the
Psalms¹,fragments in the catenae. (xxv.—xxviii.)
Basil of Caesarea, †379. Homilies on the Hexaemeron, the
Psalms and Isaiah i.—xvi. (xxix.—xxxii.)
Basil of Seleucia, c. 450. Homilies on the O.T. (lxxxv.)
Cosmas Indicopleustes, c. 550. (lxxxviii.)
Cyril of Alexandria, †444. Works on the Pentateuch (περὶ τῆς
ἐν πνεύματι καὶ ἀληθείᾳ προσκυνήσεως, and γλαφυρά), comm. on
saiah, comm. on the xii. Prophets; fragments on Kingdoms,
Psalms, Proverbs, Canticles, and the minor Prophets. (lxviii.
—lxxvii.)
Cyril of Jerusalem, †386. (xxxiii.)
Didymus of Alexandria, †395. Fragments on the Psalms and
in the catenae. (xxxix.)
Diodorus of Tarsus, †c. 390. Fragments from the catenae.
(xxxiii.)
Dionysius the Pseudo-Areopagite, cent. v. (iii.—iv.)
Dorotheus the Archimandrite, cent. vi.—vii. (lxxxviii.)
Ephraem the Syrian, †373. Fragments of Commentaries on the
Pentateuch, the historical and the poetical books. (Rome,
1732 ff.)
Epiphanius of Salamis, †403. (xli.—xliii.)
Eusebius of Caesarea, †339. Commentary on the Psalms; notes
on Isaiah; fragments of other O.T. commentaries; books περὶ
τῶν τοπικῶν ὀνομάτων τῶν ἐν τῇ θείᾳ γραφῇ and περὶ τῆς τοῦ
βιβλίου τῶν προφητῶν ὀνομασίας.
Eusebius of Emesa, †359. Fragments in the catenae of a comm.
on Genesis. (lxxxvi.)
Eustathius of Antioch, †337. On the Witch of Endor, ag.
Origen. (xviii.)
Evagrius of Pontus, †398. Fragments in catenae.
Gennadius of Constantinople, †471. Fragments on Genesis,
Exodus, the Psalms &c. (lxxxv.)
Gregory of Nazianzus, †389. (xxxv.—xxxviii.)
Gregory of Neocaesarea, †c. 270. (x.)
Gregory of Nyssa, †395. (xliv.—xlvi.)
Hesychius of Jerusalem, †c. 438. (xciii.)
Isidore of Pelusium, †c. 450. (lxxviii.)
John Chrysostom, †407. Homilies on 1 Regn., Psalms (iii.—
xii., xlviii.—xlix., cviii.—cxl.); a commentary on Isa. i.—viii.
11; various hands. (xlvii.—lxiv.)
John of Damascus, †c. 760. (xciv.—xcvi.)
Julianus of Halicarnassus, †536. Fragments in catenae.
Macarius Magnes, cent. iv. (ed. Blondel).
Maximus Confessor, †662. (xc.—xci.)

---

¹ See, however, H. M. Gwatkin, *Arianism*, p. 69 n.

Methodius of Olympus, cent. iii.—iv. (xviii.)
Nilus of Sinai, †c. 430. (lxxix.)
Olympiodorus of Alexandria, †cent. vi. (xciii.)
Peter of Alexandria, †311. (xviii.)
Philo of Carpasia, c. 380. Commentary on Canticles. (xl.)
Photius of Constantinople, †c. 891. (ci.—civ.)
Polychronius of Apamea, †430. Fragments on the Pentateuch,
    Job, Proverbs, Canticles, and Daniel; comm. on Ezekiel.
Procopius of Gaza, cent. vi. Commentaries on Genesis—Judges,
    1 Regn.—2 Chr., Prov., Cant., Isaiah. (lxxxvii.)
Severianus of Gabala, †c. 420. Fragments of commentaries in
    the catenae. (lxv.)
Severus of Antioch, †c. 539. Fragments in the catenae.
Theodore of Heraclea, †c. 355. Fragments of comm. on Isaiah.
    (xviii.)
Theodore of Mopsuestia, †428. Fragments of commentaries on
    Genesis (Syriac and Latin), the rest of the Pentateuch and
    the historical books: comm. on the Psalms in Syriac and
    large fragments in Greek: a commentary on the xii. Prophets.
    (lxvi.)
Theodoret of Cyrrhus, †c. 458. Εἰς τὰ ἄπορα τῆς θείας γραφῆς,
    questions on the Pentateuch and historical books. Commen-
    taries on the Psalms, Canticles, the xii. Prophets, Isaiah, Jere-
    miah (including Baruch and Lam.), Ezekiel, Daniel. (lxxx.—
    lxxxiv.)
Titus of Bostra, †c. 370. (xviii.)
Victor of Antioch, cent. v.—vi. (?).

LITERATURE. T. Ittig, *De bibliothecis et catenis patrum*
(Leipzig, 1707). J. G. Walch, *Bibliotheca patristica*, ed. J. T. L.
Danz (Jena, 1834). J. G. Dowling, *Notitia Scriptorum ss.
Patrum* (Oxford, 1839). Oeconomus, vol. iv. (Athens, 1849).
J. Nirschl, *Lehrbuch der Patrologia u. Patristik* (Mainz, 1881).
O. Bardenhewer, *Patrologie* (Freiburg i. B., 1894). Fessler-
Jungmann, *Institutiones Patrologiae* (1890). H. Hody, *De
textibus Bibliorum*, p. 277 ff. Schleusner, *Opuscula critica ad
versionem Graecam V.T. pertinentia* (Leipzig, 1812). Credner,
Beiträge zur Einleitung in die biblischen Schriften, vol. ii. (Halle,
1834). R. Gregory, Prolegomena (*de scriptoribus ecclesiasticis*,
p. 1131 ff.). Scrivener-Miller, ii. p. 167 ff. Hatch, *Biblical
Essays*, p. 131 ff.

CHAPTER IV.

THE GREEK VERSIONS AS AIDS TO BIBLICAL STUDY.

I. No question can arise as to the greatness of the place occupied by the Alexandrian Version in the religious life of the first six centuries of its history. The Septuagint was the Bible of the Hellenistic Jew, not only in Egypt and Palestine, but throughout Western Asia and Europe. It created a language of religion which lent itself readily to the service of Christianity and became one of the most important allies of the Gospel. It provided the Greek-speaking Church with an authorised translation of the Old Testament, and when Christian missions advanced beyond the limits of Hellenism, it served as a basis for fresh translations into the vernacular[1].

The Septuagint has long ceased to fulfil these or any similar functions. In the West, after the fourth century, its influence receded before the spread of the Latin Vulgate; in the East, where it is still recited by the Orthodox Church in the ecclesiastical offices, it lost much of its influence over the thought and life of the people. On the other hand, this most ancient of Biblical versions possesses a new and increasing importance in the field of Biblical study. It is seen to be valuable alike to the textual critic and to the expositor, and its services are welcomed by students both of the Old Testament and of the New.

[1] See Part I., c. iv.

A. As the oldest version of the Hebrew Bible, the Septuagint claims especial attention from Old Testament scholars. It represents a text and, to some extent, an interpretation earlier than any which can be obtained from other sources.

1. (*a*) The printed Hebrew Bibles give on the whole the Massoretic text, i.e. a text which has passed through the hands of the Massorets, a succession of Jewish scholars who endeavoured to give permanence to the traditional type.

Massora (מָסוֹרָה, מַסּוֹרֶת, *traditio*) is already mentioned in the saying of R. Akiba, *Pirqe Aboth*, iii. 20 מסורה סייג לתורה, 'tradition is a fence to the Law'[1]; but the word is used there in reference to halachic rather than to textual tradition. It is probable, however, that Akiba and his contemporaries were concerned with the settling of the text which later generations protected by the 'Massora' technically so called. The work of the Massorets (בעלי־המסרת), who flourished from the sixth century to the tenth, consisted chiefly in reducing to a system of rules the pronunciation of the text which had been fixed by their predecessors. The Massora[2] embodies the readings which tradition substituted for the written text (כְּתִיב, קְרִי), the corrections known as the תִּקּוּן סוֹפְרִים[3], and observations on the text tending to stereotype its interpretation in minute points. To the Massorets we also owe the perfecting of the system of vowel-points and accents. The labours of the Massorets culminated in the Western text of R. Ben Asher (cent. x.), and that which appeared about the same time in the East under the auspices of R. Ben Naphtali. The former has been repeated with minor variations in all Western MSS.

The attitude of Christian scholars towards the Jewish traditional text has varied with the progress of Biblical learning.

---

[1] See Schürer, *E. T.* ii. i. p. 329 n.; Dr C. Taylor, *Sayings of the Jewish Fathers*, p. 54 f.

[2] For the text see the great work of C. D. Ginsburg, *The Massorah, compiled from MSS., alphabetically and lexically arranged*, 3 vols. (London, 1880–5), or the Bible of S. Baer; and for the Massorets and their work, cf. Buxtorf, *Tiberias*, Ginsburg's *Introduction* (London, 1897), and his edition of the *Massoreth ha-massoreth* of Elias Levita, or the brief statements in Buhl, *Kanon u. Text* (p. 96 ff.), and in *Urtext* (p. 20 ff.); or Strack, art. *Text of the O.T.*, in Hastings, *D.B.* iv.

[3] On these see Dr W. E. Barnes in *J. Th. St.*, April 1900.

The question of its relation to the text presupposed by the Septuagint was scarcely present to the minds of Christian writers before the time of Origen[1]. Origen, when the problem forced itself upon him, adopted, as we have seen[2], a middle course between the alternatives of rejecting the LXX. and refusing to accept the testimony of his Jewish teachers. Jerome took a bolder line; his new Latin version was based on the 'original Hebrew,' and on textual questions he appealed with confidence to the verdict of contemporary Jewish opinion : *prol. gal.* "quanquam mihi omnino conscius non sim mutasse me quidpiam de Hebraica veritate ...interroga quemlibet Hebraeorum cui magis accommodare debeas fidem." Like Origen he indignantly, and on the whole doubtless with justice, repudiated the charge which was laid by some Christians against the Jews of having falsified their MSS.[3] But neither Origen nor Jerome entertained a suspicion that the Jewish official text had, whether by accident or design, departed from the archetype.

Mediaeval Europe knew the Old Testament almost exclusively through Jerome's Latin, as the Ancient Church had known it through the LXX.[4] When at length the long reign of the Vulgate in Western Europe was broken by the forces of the Renaissance and the Reformation, the attention of scholars was once more drawn to that which purported to be the original text of the Old Testament. The printing of the Hebrew text commenced among the Jews with the Psalter of 1477; the *editio princeps* of the Hebrew Bible as a whole appeared in

---

[1] See C. J. Elliott's art. *Hebrew Learning*, in *D. C. B.* ii., esp. the summary on p. 872 b.

[2] Above, p. 60 ff.

[3] See his comm. on Isaiah vi. 9 (Migne, *P. L.* xxiv. 99).

[4] A few mediaeval scholars had access to the Hebrew, e.g. the Englishmen Stephen Harding (†1134), Robert Grosseteste (†1253), Roger Bacon (†c. 1292), the Spaniard Raymundus Martini (†c. 1286), and especially the Norman Jew, Nicolas de Lyra (†1340). On Lyra see Siegfried in Merx, *Archiv*, i. p. 428, ii. p. 28.

1488, and three editions followed before the end of the fifteenth century[1]. Meanwhile Christian scholars had once more begun to learn the Hebrew language from Jewish teachers, and in 1506 the publication of John Reuchlin's *Rudiments* placed the elements of Hebrew learning within the reach of the theologians of Europe. Under the circumstances it was not strange that the earlier Reformers, who owed their Hebrew Bible and their knowledge of the language to the Rabbis, should have, like Jerome, regarded the traditional text as a faithful reproduction of the inspired original. In the next century a beginning was made in the criticism of the Hebrew text by the Protestant divine Louis Cappelle (L. Cappellus, †1658), and the Oratorian Jean Morin (J. Morinus, †1659), who pressed the claims of the LXX. and the Samaritan Pentateuch. A furious controversy ensued, in the course of which the Swiss Reformed Churches committed themselves to an absolute acceptance not only of the consonantal text, but of the vowel points. This extreme position was occupied not only by theologians, but by experts such as the two Buxtorfs of Basle (††1629, 1664), who maintained that the Massoretic text in its present state had come down unchanged from the days of Ezra and the 'Great Synagogue.'

The views of Louis Cappelle were set forth in *Arcanum punctuationis revelatum*, Amsterdam, 1624; *Critica sacra*, Paris, 1650; those of J. Morin in *Exercitationes ecclesiasticae in utrumque Samaritanorum Pentateuchum* (Paris, 1631), and *Exercitationes de hebraici graecique textus sinceritate* (Paris, 1633). The younger Buxtorf answered Cappelle in his treatises *De punctorum origine* (1648) and *Anticritica* (1653): see Schnedemann, *Die Controverse des L. Cappellus mit den Buxtorfen* (Leipzig, 1879), Loisy, *Histoire critique*, p. 167 ff. The *formula consensus ecclesiarum Helveticarum* (1675) declared (*can.* ii., iii.): "Hebraicus Veteris Testamenti codex quem ex traditione ecclesiae Iudaicae, cui olim *oracula Dei commissa sunt*, accepimus hodieque retinemus, tum quoad consonas tum quoad vocalia, sive puncta ipsa sive punctorum saltem potestatem, et tum quoad res tum quoad

---

[1] See De Wette-Schrader, *Lehrbuch*, p. 217 f.

verba θεόπνευστος...ad cuius normam...universae quae extant
versiones...exigendae et, sicubi deflectunt, revocandae sunt.
Eorum proinde sententiam probare neutiquam possumus, qui
lectionem quam Hebraicus codex exhibet humano tantum arbitrio
constitutam esse definiunt, quique lectionem Hebraicam quam
minus commodam iudicant configere eamque ex LXX. seniorum
aliorumque versionibus Graecis...emendare religioni neutiquam
ducunt[1]."

Reference has been made to the place occupied by the
Samaritan Pentateuch in this controversy. A Samaritan
recension of the Law was known to Origen, who quoted it in
the Hexapla (Num. xiii. 1 ἃ καὶ αὐτὰ ἐκ τοῦ τῶν Σαμαρειτῶν
Ἑβραικοῦ μετεβάλομεν, xxi. 13 ἃ ἐν μόνοις τῶν Σαμαρειτῶν
εὕρομεν: see Field, *Hex.* I. p. lxxxii. f.), and Jerome (*prol. gal.*,
comm. in Gal. iii. 10); reference is made to it also by Eusebius
(*Chron.* I. xvi. 7 ff.), and by so late a writer as Georgius
Syncellus (cent. viii.), who attaches a high value to its testimony
(*Chronogr.* p. 83 διαφωνοῦσι τὰ Ἑβραικὰ ἀντίγραφα πρὸς τὸ
Σαμαρειτῶν ἀρχαιότατον καὶ χαρακτῆρσι διαλλάττον· ὃ καὶ ἀληθὲς
εἶναι καὶ πρῶτον Ἑβραῖοι καθομολογοῦσιν). In the seventeenth
century, after a long oblivion, this recension was recovered by
a traveller in the East and published in the Paris Polyglott of
1645. The rising school of textual criticism represented by
Morin at once recognised its importance as concurring with
the Septuagint in its witness against the originality of the
Massoretic text. Few questions, however, have been more
hotly discussed than the relation of the Samaritan to the
Alexandrian Pentateuch. Scholars such as Selden, Hottinger,
and Eichhorn contended that the Greek Pentateuch was based
upon Samaritan MSS. Samaritans were undoubtedly to be
found among the early Palestinian settlers in Egypt. Of the
first Ptolemy Josephus writes: πολλοὺς αἰχμαλώτους λαβὼν
ἀπὸ τῆς Σαμαρείτιδος καὶ τῶν ἐν Γαριζείν, κατῴκισεν ἅπαντας εἰς
Αἴγυπτον ἀγαγών. It is significant that Σαμάρεια occurs among

---

[1] Niemeyer, *Collectio Confessionum* (Leipzig, 1840), p. 731.

the names of villages in the Fayûm[1], and a letter ascribed to
Hadrian, and certainly not earlier than his reign, mentions
Samaritans as resident at Alexandria. On the other hand the
traditional account of the origin of the LXX. directly con-
tradicts this hypothesis, nor is it probable that the Jews of
Alexandria would have had recourse to the Samaritans for
MSS. of the Law, or that they would have accepted a version
which had originated in this manner. Moreover the agreement
of the Greek and Samaritan Pentateuchs is very far from
being complete. A careful analysis of the Samaritan text led
Gesenius to the conclusion, which is now generally accepted,
that the fact of the two Pentateuchs often making common
cause against the printed Hebrew Bibles indicates a common
origin earlier than the fixing of the Massoretic text, whilst their
dissensions shew that the text of the Law existed in more
than one recension before it had been reduced to a rigid uniformity.

On the Samaritan Pentateuch the reader may consult J. Morinus, *Exercitationes ecclesiasticae in utrumque Samaritanorum
Pentateuchum*; L. Cappellus, *Critica sacra*, iii. c. 20; Walton,
prolegg. (ed. Wrangham, Camb. 1828), ii. p. 280 ff.; R. Simon,
Histoire critique du Vieux Testament, i. c. 12; Eichhorn, *Einleitung*, ii. § 383 ff.; Gesenius, *De Pentateuchi Samaritani origine
indole et auctoritate comm.* (Halle, 1815); S. Kohn, *De Penta-
teucho Samaritano eiusque cum versionibus antiquis nexu* (Leipzig, 1865); *Samareitikon u. Septuaginta*, in *MGJS.*, 1893;
E. Deutsch, *Samaritan Pentateuch*, in Smith's *D. B.* iii. 1106 ff.;
E. König, art. *Sam. Pentateuch*, Hastings' *D. B.* suppl. vol. p. 71;
J. W. Nutt, *Introduction to Fragments of a Sam. Targum*
(London, 1872); J. Skinner in *J. Q. R.* xiv. 26; P. Glaue and
A. Rahlfs, *Mitteilungen des Sept. Unternehmens*, ii. (Berlin, 1911),
for fragments of Gr. transl. of Sam. Pentateuch.

The prevalent belief in the originality of the Massoretic
text appeared to receive confirmation from the researches of
Kennicott[2] and De Rossi[3], which revealed an extraordinary
agreement in all existing MSS. of the Hebrew Bible. But as

[1] As early as 255 B.C. (Thackeray); *Petrie Pap.* Series II. iv. (11).
[2] *Vetus T. Hebraicum cum variis lectionibus* (Oxford, 1776—80).
[3] *Variae lectiones V. T.* (Parma 1784—8): *Supplementum* (1798).

no MS. of the Hebrew Bible has come down to us which is earlier than the beginning of the tenth century[1], this evidence merely shews the complete success of the Massorets and the Sopherim who preceded them in preserving the traditional text, and the question remains to be answered at what period the tradition was created. It may be traced in the fourth century, when Jerome received substantially the same text from his Jewish teachers in Palestine; and in the third, for Origen's Hebrew text did not differ materially from that of Jerome or of the Massorets. We can go yet another step further back; the version of Aquila, of which considerable fragments have now been recovered, reveals very few points in which the consonantal text of the second century differed from that of our printed Bibles[2]. Other witnesses can be produced to shew that, even if Hebrew MSS. of a much earlier date had been preserved, they would have thrown but little light on textual questions[3]. On the whole, modern research has left no room for doubting that the printed Hebrew Bible represents a *textus receptus* which was already practically fixed before the middle of the second century. But it is equally clear that no official text held undisputed possession in the first century, or was recognised by the writers of the New Testament. Thus we are driven to the conclusion that the transition from a fluctuating to a relatively fixed text took effect during the interval between the Fall of Jerusalem and the completion of Aquila's version. The time was one of great activity in Palestinian Jewish circles. In the last days of Jerusalem a school had been founded at Jamnia (Jabneh, *Yebna*)[4], near the Philistine seaboard, by R. Jochanan ben Zaccai. To this

[1] "The earliest MS. of which the age is certainly known bears date A.D. 916" (Pref. to the R.V. of the O.T. p. ix. 2).

[2] Cf. F. C. Burkitt, *Aquila*, p. 16 f.

[3] Cf. S. R. Driver, *Samuel*, p. xxxix.: "Quotations in the Mishnah and Gemara exhibit no material variants...the Targums also pre-suppose a text which deviates from (the M.T.) but slightly."

[4] Neubauer, *Géographie du Talmud*, p. 73 f.

centre the representatives of Judaism flocked after the destruction of the city, and here, until the fresh troubles of the war of Bar-Cochba (A.D. 132—5), Biblical studies were prosecuted with new ardour under a succession of eminent Rabbis. At Jamnia about A.D. 90 a synod was held which discussed various questions connected with the settlement of the Canon. At Jamnia also traditionalism reached its zenith under the teaching of R. Eliezer ben Hyrcanus, R. Joshua ben Chananya, and their more famous pupil R. Akiba ben Joseph, the author of the dogma that every word, particle and letter in the Hebrew Bible has a meaning, and serves some purpose which can be expressed by hermeneutical methods. From this canon of interpretation to the establishment of an official text is but a single step; a book of which the very letters possess a divine authority cannot be left to the unauthorised revision of scribes or editors. Whether the result was reached by a selection of approved readings, or by the suppression of MSS. which were not in agreement with an official copy, or whether it was due to an individual Rabbi or the work of a generation, is matter of conjecture. But it seems to be clear that in one way or another the age which followed the fall of Jerusalem witnessed the creation of a standard text not materially different from that which the Massorets stereotyped and which all MSS. and editions have reproduced[1].

(*b*) It is the business of the textual critic to get behind this official text, and to recover so far as he can the various recensions which it has displaced. In this work he is aided by the Ancient Versions, but especially by the Septuagint. Of the Versions the Septuagint alone is actually earlier than the fixing of the Hebrew text. In point of age, indeed, it must yield to the Samaritan Pentateuch, the archetype of

---

[1] See W. Robertson-Smith, *O.T. in Jewish Ch.*, p. 62 f.; A. F. Kirkpatrick, *Divine Library of the O.T.*, p. 63 ff.

which may have been in the hands of the Samaritans in the days of Nehemiah (c. B.C. 432)[1]; but the polemical bias of that people, and the relatively late date of the MSS. on which the printed text depends, detract largely from the value of its evidence, which is moreover limited to the Torah.

Some of the difficulties which beset the use of the LXX. as a guide to the criticism of the text have been stated already when its character as a version was discussed[2]; others, arising out of the present condition of the version, will be noticed in the last chapter of this book. "The use of the Ancient Versions (as Prof. Driver writes[3]) is not...always such a simple matter as might be inferred.... In the use of an Ancient Version for the purposes of textual criticism, there are three precautions which must always be observed : we must reasonably assure ourselves that we possess the Version itself in its original integrity : we must eliminate such variants as have the appearance of originating merely with the translator; the remainder, which will be those that are due to a difference of text in the MS. (or MSS.) used by the translator, we must then compare carefully, in the light of the considerations just stated, with the existing Hebrew text, in order to determine on which side the superiority lies." "In dealing with the LXX. (Prof. Kirkpatrick reminds us) we have to remember...that the LXX. is not a homogeneous work, but differs very considerably in its character in different books, if not in parts of books[4]." Moreover in the case of the LXX. the task of the textual critic is complicated by the existence of more than one distinct recension of the Greek. He has before him in many contexts a choice of readings which represent a plurality of Hebrew archetypes[5].

---

[1] See Ryle, *Canon*, p. 91 f.
[2] Pt. II., c. v., p. 315 ff.
[3] *Samuel*, p. xxxix. f.
[4] *Expositor* v. iii., p. 273.
[5] See H. P. Smith, *Samuel*, p. 397 f., and the remarks that follow.

The following list of passages in which the LXX. reflects a Hebrew text different from ‫מ‬ will enable the student to practise himself in the critical use of the Version.

Gen. iv. 8 ‫מ‬ does not give the words of Cain, though ‫וַיֹּאמֶר‬ leads the reader to expect them. 𝔊 supplies Διέλθωμεν εἰς τὸ πεδίον (‫נֵלְכָה הַשָּׂדֶה‬), and this is supported by Sam., Targ. Jer., Pesh., Vulg. **xxxi.** 29 ‫אֲבִיכֶם‬, 𝔊 ‫אביך‬ (τοῦ πατρός σου); so Sam., cf. v. 30. **xli.** 56 ‫אֶת־כָּל־אֲשֶׁר בָּהֶם‬, 𝔊 πάντας τοὺς σιτοβολῶνας (‫אֹצְרֹת בָּר‬)[1], cf. Sam., ‫את כל אשר בהם בר‬). **xlix.** 10 𝔊 ἕως ἂν ἔλθῃ τὰ ἀποκείμενα αὐτῷ, perhaps reading ‫שֶׁלּוֹ‬ (=‫אֲשֶׁר לוֹ‬) for ‫מ‬ ‫שִׁילֹה‬: but see Ball in Haupt, *Sacred Books*, ad loc., and cf. the Greek variant ᾧ ἀπόκειται. **Exod. v.** 9 ‫וְיַעֲשׂוּ...יִשְׁעוּ‬, 𝔊 μεριμνάτωσαν...μεριμνάτωσαν (‫וישעו...ישעו‬). **xiv.** 25 ‫וַיָּסַר‬, 𝔊 καὶ συνέδησεν (‫ויאסר‬). **xxx.** 6 ‫לִפְנֵי הַפָּרֹכֶת...לִפְנֵי הַכַּפֹּרֶת‬. 𝔊 omits the second clause: so Sam. **Lev. xiii.** 31 ‫שֵׂעָר שָׁחֹר‬, 𝔊 θρὶξ ξανθίζουσα (‫ש' צָהֹב‬). **Num. xxiv.** 23 𝔊 prefixes καὶ ἰδὼν τὸν Ὤγ (‫וַיַּרְא‬) ‫אֶת־עוֹג‬); cf. vv. 20, 21. **Deut. iv.** 37 ‫בְּזַרְעוֹ אַחֲרָיו‬, i.e. Abraham's posterity (Driver, *ad loc.*); 𝔊 τὸ σπέρμα αὐτῶν μετ᾽ αὐτοὺς ὑμᾶς, i.e. ‫בזרעם אחריכם‬; so Sam. **Josh. xv.** 59 𝔊 +Θεκὼ...πόλεις ἕνδεκα καὶ αἱ κῶμαι αὐτῶν. The omission of these names in ‫מ‬ is doubtless due to homoioteleuton. **Jud. xiv.** 15 ‫בַּיּוֹם הַשְּׁבִיעִי‬. 𝔊, as the context seems to require, ἐν τῇ ἡμέρᾳ τῇ τετάρτῃ (‫הרביעי‬); but see Moore in Haupt, *Sacred Books*, ad loc. **xvi.** 13 f. 𝔊 supplies a long lacuna in ‫מ‬ (καὶ ἐνκρούσῃς...τῆς κεφαλῆς αὐτοῦ) caused by homoioteleuton; on the two Greek renderings of the passage see Moore in Haupt, *ad loc.* **xix.** 18 𝔊 εἰς τὸν οἶκόν μου ἐγὼ πορεύομαι (‫מ‬ ‫אֶת־בֵּית יְהֹוָה אֲנִי הֹלֵךְ‬). The final letter of ‫ביתי‬ has probably been taken by ‫מ‬ for an abbreviation of ‫יהוה‬. **1 Sam. i.** 24 ‫בְּפָרִים שְׁלֹשָׁה‬, 𝔊 ἐν μόσχῳ τριετίζοντι, dividing and pronouncing ‫בְּפַר מְשֻׁלָּשׁ‬. **ii.** 33 𝔊 supplies ‫בחרב‬ (ἐν ῥομφαίᾳ) which ‫מ‬ seems to have lost. **iii.** 13 𝔊 ὅτι κακολογοῦντες θεὸν υἱοὶ αὐτοῦ, reading ‫אלהים‬ for ‫להם‬. **iv.** 1. The first clause in ‫מ‬ is irrelevant in this place, and must either be connected with iii. 21 or struck out altogether. In place of it 𝔊 has the appropriate introduction, καὶ ἐγενήθη...εἰς πόλεμον (‫ויהי בימים‬

_____

[1] Lagarde (*Symmicta* i., p. 57) suggests a form ‫אישבורא‬.

אֶת־אַשְׁדּוֹד וְאֶת v. 6. For (הֲהֵם וַיִּקְבְּצוּ פְלִשְׁתִּים לְמִלְחָמָה עַל יִשְׂרָאֵל. 𝔊 has καὶ μέσον τῆς χώρας αὐτῆς ἀνεφύησαν μύες. Cf. vi. 4 f., גְּבוּלֶיהָ and see Driver and Budde (in Haupt's *Sacred Books*) *ad loc.* H. P. Smith would strike out the reference to mice in both contexts. **vi. 19** וַיַּךְ בְּאַנְשֵׁי בֵית־שֶׁמֶשׁ. 𝔊 καὶ οὐκ ἠσμένισαν οἱ υἱοὶ Ἰεχονίου ἐν τοῖς ἀνδράσιν Βαιθσάμυς, where the first six words represent an original of which 𝔐 preserves only three letters. Restoration is complicated by the fact that ἀσμενίζειν is ἅπ. λεγ. in the LXX. Klostermann suggests וְלֹא חָדוּ בְנֵי יְכָנְיָהוּ. **ix. 25 f.** וַיְדַבֵּר עִם שָׁאוּל עַל־הַגָּג וַיִּשְׁכָּמוּ. 𝔊, more in harmony with the context, καὶ διέστρωσαν τῷ Σαοὺλ (וַיִּרְבְּדוּ לְשָׁאוּל) ἐπὶ τῷ δώματι, καὶ ἐκοιμήθη (וַיִּשְׁכָּב). **x. 21** 𝔊 +καὶ προσάγουσιν τὴν φυλὴν Ματταρεὶ εἰς ἄνδρας, a clause necessary to the sense. **xii. 3** וְאַעְלִים עֵינַי בּוֹ. 𝔊 καὶ ὑπόδημα (cf. Gen. xiv. 23, Am. ii. 6, viii. 6); ἀποκρίθητε κατ' ἐμοῦ (וְנַעֲלַיִם עָנוּ בִי). With 𝔊 compare Sir. xlvi. 19 χρήματα καὶ ἕως ὑποδημάτων...οὐκ εἴληφα, where for ὑποδ. the newly recovered Hebrew has נֶעְלָם 'a secret gift,' leg. fort. נַעֲלַיִם 'a pair of sandals'; see, however, *Wisdom of Ben Sira*, p. lxvii. **xii. 8** 𝔊 supplies καὶ ἐταπείνωσεν αὐτοὺς Αἴγυπτος, omitted by 𝔐 through homoio-teleuton. **xiv. 18** הַגִּישָׁה אֲרוֹן הָאֱלֹהִים, 𝔊 προσάγαγε τὸ ἐφούδ. "The Ephod, not the ark, was the organ of divination" (Driver). **xiv. 41 f.** 𝔐 הָבָה תָמִים. 𝔊ᴸᵘᶜ, supplying the lacuna, Τί ὅτι οὐκ ἀπεκρίθης τῷ δούλῳ σου σήμερον; εἰ ἐν ἐμοὶ ἢ ἐν Ἰωναθὰν τῷ υἱῷ μου ἡ ἀδικία; Κύριε ὁ θεὸς Ἰσραήλ, δὸς δήλους (אוּרִים)· καὶ εἰ τάδε εἴποις Ἐν τῷ λαῷ ἡ ἀδικία, δὸς ὁσιότητα (תֻּמִּים). Similarly in *v.* 42 𝔊 preserves the words ὃν ἂν κατακληρώσηται...τοῦ υἱοῦ αὐτοῦ, which 𝔐 has lost through homoioteleuton. See the note in Field, *Hexapla*, i. p. 510. **xx. 19** אֵצֶל הָאֶבֶן הָאָזֶל, 𝔊 παρὰ τὸ ἐργὰβ ἐκεῖνο=הַלָּז אֵצֶל הָאַרְגָּב, 'beside yonder cairn.' Similarly *v.* 41 ἀπὸ τοῦ ἀργάβ=מֵאֵצֶל הָאַרְגָּב. **2 Sam. iv. 6.** For the somewhat incoherent sentence in 𝔐, 𝔊 substitutes καὶ ἰδοὺ ἡ θυρωρὸς τοῦ οἴκου ἐκάθαιρεν πυρούς, καὶ ἐνύσταξεν καὶ ἐκάθευδεν—words which explain the incident that follows. **xvii. 3** 𝔊 ὃν τρόπον ἐπιστρέφει ἡ νύμφη πρὸς τὸν ἄνδρα αὐτῆς· πλὴν ψυχὴν ἑνὸς ἀνδρὸς σὺ ζητεῖς. In the archetype of 𝔐 the eye of the scribe has passed from אִישׁ to אִשָּׁה, and the sentence thus mutilated has been re-arranged. **xxiv. 6** וְאֶל־אֶרֶץ תַּחְתִּים חׇדְשִׁי. No 'land of Tahtim Hodshi' is known. 𝔊ᴸᵘᶜ here preserves the true text, εἰς γῆν Χεττιεὶμ Καδής

=קדשה אל ארץ החתים, 'to the land of the Hittites, even to Kadesh.' For the last word Ewald, followed by H. P. Smith, preferred חֶרְמֹנָה, 'to Hermon.' 1 **Kings** xvii. 1 הַתִּשְׁבִּי מִתֹּשָׁבֵי גִלְעָד. 𝕲 ὁ Θεσβείτης ἐκ Θεσβὼν τῆς Γαλαάδ ('ג מִתֹּשָׁבֹּן?). 2 **Chron.** xxxiii. 19 עַל דִּבְרֵי חוֹזָי. 𝕲 ἐπὶ τῶν λόγων τῶν ὁρώντων (החוזים). **Neh.** ix. 17 בְּמִרְיָם. 𝕲 ἐν Αἰγύπτῳ (במצרים). **Ps.** xvi. (xv.) 2 אָמַרְתְּ sc. נַפְשִׁי. 𝕲 εἶπα (אָמַרְתִּי) is manifestly right, and has been admitted into the text by the English Revisers. **xxii. 16** (xxi. 17) כָּאֲרִי, Aq. ὡς λέων. 𝕲 ὥρυξαν (כרו=כארו). **xxvii.** (xxvi.) 13 לוּלֵא (so 𝕸) is apparently read by 𝕲 as לוֹ, and then connected with the previous verse. See Cheyne, *Book of Psalms*, p. 379, and Abbott, *Essays*, p. 25. Wellhausen (Haupt, *ad loc.*) would retain 𝕸 without the *puncta extraordinaria.* **xlii. 5** (xli. 6) 𝕲 +[καὶ] ὁ θεός μου, as 𝕸 in *v.* 12. **xlix. 11 (xlviii. 12)** קִרְבָּם בָּתֵּימוֹ לְעוֹלָם. 𝕲 οἱ τάφοι αὐτῶν οἰκίαι αὐτῶν εἰς τὸν αἰῶνα. **lxix. 26 (lxviii. 27)** יְסַפֵּרוּ, 𝕲 προσέθηκαν (יוֹסִיפוּ). **lxxii. (lxxi.) 5** יִירָאוּךָ עִם שָׁמֶשׁ. 𝕲 καὶ συνπαραμενεῖ (ויאריך) τῷ ἡλίῳ. **ci. (c.) 5** אֹתוֹ לֹא אוּכָל. 𝕲 τούτῳ οὐ συνήσθιον (אִתּוֹ לֹא אֹכֵל). **Prov. x. 10ᵇ** in 𝕸 is repeated from *v.* 8ᵇ which has displaced the true ending of *v.* 10. 𝕲 restores the latter (ὁ δὲ ἐλέγχων μετὰ παρρησίας εἰρηνοποιεῖ), and thus supplies the contrast to 10ᵃ which is required to complete the couplet. **Jer. vi. 29** וּרְעִים לֹא נִתָּקוּ. 𝕲 πονηρία[ι] αὐτῶν οὐκ ἐτάκη[σαν] (ורעם לא נמק). **xi. 15** הָרַבִּים. 𝕲 μὴ εὐχαί...; (הַנְּדָרִים); see however Streane, *Double text*, p. 133. **xxiii. 33** אֶת־מַה מַשָּׂא. 𝕲 ὑμεῖς ἐστε τὸ λῆμμα (dividing and pronouncing אַתֶּם הַמַּשָּׂא). **Ezek. xlv. 20** בְּשִׁבְעָה בַחֹדֶשׁ. 𝕲 ἐν τῷ ἑβδόμῳ μηνί, μιᾷ τοῦ μηνός (הַשְׁבִיעִי בְּאֶחָד לַחֹדֶשׁ). **Mal. ii. 3** הַזֶּרַע. 𝕲 τὸν ὦμον =הַזְּרֹעַ.

(*c*) In dealing with such differences between the Greek version and the traditional Hebrew text the student will not start with the assumption that the version has preserved the true reading. It may have been preserved by the official Hebrew or its archetype, and lost in the MSS. which were followed by the translators : or it may have been lost by both. Nor will he assume that the Greek, when it differs from the

Hebrew, represents in all cases another Hebrew text; for the difference may be due to the failure of the translators to understand their Hebrew, or to interpret it aright. His first business is to decide whether the Greek variant involves a different Hebrew text, or is simply another expression for the text which lies before him in the printed Hebrew Bible. If the former of these alternatives is accepted, he has still to consider whether the text represented by the LXX. is preferable to that of the Hebrew Bible and probably original. There is a presumption in favour of readings in which 𝕲 and 𝔐 agree, but, as we have said, not an absolute certainty that they are correct, since they may both be affected by a deep-seated corruption which goes back to the age of the Ptolemies. When they differ, 𝕲 will usually deserve to be preferred when it (*a*) fills up a lacuna which can be traced to homoioteleuton in the Hebrew, or (*b*) removes an apparent interpolation, or (*c*) appears to represent a *bona fide* variant in the original, which makes better sense than the existing text. Its claims in these cases are strengthened if it has the support of other early and probably independent witnesses such as the Samaritan Pentateuch and the Targum, or of Hebrew variants which survive in existing MSS. of the Massoretic text, or in the Q'ri[1].

For guidance as to the principles on which the LXX. may be employed in the criticism of the Hebrew Text the student may consult Lagarde, *Anmerkungen zur griech. Übersetzung der Proverbien*, p. 1 ff.; Wellhausen, *Der Text der Bücher Samuelis*, p. 1 ff.; Robertson Smith, *O. T. in the Jewish Church*[2], p. 76 ff.; Driver, *Notes on the Hebrew Text of the Books of Samuel*, p. xlviii. f.; H. P. Smith, *Comm. on Samuel*, pp. xxix. ff., 395 ff.; Toy, *Comm. on Proverbs*, p. xxxii. f. See also below, c. vi.

2. In the field of O.T. interpretation the witness of the LXX. must be received with even greater caution. It is evident that Greek-speaking Jews, whose knowledge of Hebrew

---

[1] On the relation of the LXX. to the Q'ri, see Frankel, *Vorstudien*, p. 219 ff.

was probably acquired at Alexandria from teachers of very moderate attainments, possess no prescriptive right to act as guides to the meaning of obscure Hebrew words or sentences. Transliterations, doublets, confused and scarcely intelligible renderings, reveal the fact that in difficult passages they were often reduced to mere conjecture. But their guesses may at times be right; and in much that seems to be guesswork they may have been led by gleams of a true tradition. Thus it is never safe to neglect their interpretation, even if in the harder contexts it is seldom to be trusted. Indirectly at least much may be learned from them; and their wildest exegesis belongs to the history of hermeneutics, and has influenced thought and language to a remarkable degree.

(*a*) The following specimens will serve to illustrate the exegesis of the LXX. in the historical books.

Gen. iv. 1 ἐκτησάμην ἄνθρωπον διὰ τοῦ θεοῦ. iv. 7 οὐκ ἐὰν ὀρθῶς προσενέγκῃς ὀρθῶς δὲ μὴ διέλῃς, ἥμαρτες; ἡσύχασον. vi. 3 οὐ μὴ καταμείνῃ τὸ πνεῦμά μου ἐν τοῖς ἀνθρώποις τούτοις εἰς τὸν αἰῶνα διὰ τὸ εἶναι αὐτοὺς σάρκας. xxx. 11 καὶ εἶπεν Λεία Ἐν τύχῃ· καὶ ἐπωνόμασεν τὸ ὄνομα αὐτοῦ Γάδ. xxxvii. 3 ἐποίησεν δὲ αὐτῷ χιτῶνα ποικίλον (cf. 2 Regn. xiii. 18). xli. 43 ἐκήρυξεν ἔμπροσθεν αὐτοῦ κήρυξ. xlvii. 31 προσεκύνησεν Ἰσραὴλ ἐπὶ τὸ ἄκρον τῆς ῥάβδου αὐτοῦ. xlviii. 14 ἐναλλὰξ [*D* ἐναλλάξας] τὰς χεῖρας. xlix. 6 ἐνευροκόπησαν ταῦρον. 19 Γάδ, πειρατήριον πειρατεύσει αὐτόν· αὐτὸς δὲ πειρατεύσει αὐτῶν κατὰ πόδας. Exod. i. 16 καὶ ὦσιν πρὸς τῷ τίκτειν. iii. 14 ἐγώ εἰμι ὁ ὤν. xvi. 15 εἶπαν ἕτερος τῷ ἑτέρῳ Τί ἐστιν τοῦτο; xvii. 15 ἐπωνόμασεν τὸ ὄνομα αὐτοῦ Κύριος καταφυγή μου. xxi. 6 πρὸς τὸ κριτήριον τοῦ θεοῦ. xxxii. 32 καὶ νῦν εἰ μὲν ἀφεῖς αὐτοῖς τὴν ἁμαρτίαν αὐτῶν, ἄφες. Lev. xxiii. 3 τῇ ἡμέρᾳ τῇ ἑβδόμῃ σάββατα ἀνάπαυσις κλητὴ ἁγία τῷ κυρίῳ. Num. xxiii. 10ᵇ ἀποθάνοι ἡ ψυχή μου ἐν ψυχαῖς δικαίων, καὶ γένοιτο τὸ σπέρμα μου ὡς τὸ σπέρμα τούτων. xxiv. 24 καὶ κακώσουσιν Ἑβραίους. Deut. xx. 19 μὴ ἄνθρωπος τὸ ξύλον τὸ ἐν τῷ ἀγρῷ, εἰσελθεῖν...εἰς τὸν χάρακα; xxxii. 8 ἔστησεν ὅρια ἐθνῶν κατὰ ἀριθμὸν ἀγγέλων θεοῦ. 15 ἀπελάκτισεν ὁ ἠγαπημένος. Jos. v. 2 ποίησον σεαυτῷ μαχαίρας πετρίνας ἐκ πέτρας ἀκροτόμου. Jud. i. 35 ἤρξατο ὁ Ἀμορραῖος κατοικεῖν ἐν τῷ ὄρει τῷ ὀστρακώδει (Α τοῦ μυρσινῶνος), ἐν ᾧ αἱ ἄρκοι καὶ ἐν ᾧ αἱ ἀλώπεκες, ἐν τῷ μυρσινῶνι καὶ ἐν Θαλαβείν (Α om. ἐν τῷ μ. κ. ἐν Θ.). viii. 13 ἐπέστρεψεν Γεδεὼν...ἀπὸ ἐπάνωθεν τῆς παρατάξεως Ἄρες (Α ἐκ τοῦ πολέμου ἀπὸ ἀναβάσεως Ἄρες). xii. 6 καὶ εἶπαν αὐτῷ Εἶπον δὴ Στάχυς (Α Σύνθημα). xv. 14 ff. ἦλθον ἕως Σιαγόνος...καὶ εὗρεν σιαγόνα ὄνου...καὶ ἔρρηξεν ὁ θεὸς τὸν λάκκον τὸν ἐν τῇ Σιαγόνι...διὰ τοῦτο ἐκλήθη τὸ ὄνομα αὐτῆς Πηγὴ τοῦ ἐπικαλουμένου, ἥ ἐστιν ἐν Σιαγόνι. xviii. 30 υἱὸς Γηρσὸμ υἱὸς (A υἱοῦ) Μανασσή (בֶּן־מֹשֶׁה : on the נ *suspensum* see Moore in comm. on *Sacred Books, ad loc.*). 1 Regn. x. 5 οὗ ἐστιν ἐκεῖ τὸ ἀνάστεμα τῶν ἀλλοφύλων· ἐκεῖ Νασείβ ὁ ἀλλόφυλος. xiii. 21 καὶ ἦν ὁ τρυγητὸς ἔτοιμος τοῦ θερίζειν· τὰ δὲ σκεύη ἦν τρεῖς σίκλοι εἰς τὸν ὀδόντα, καὶ τῇ ἀξίνῃ, καὶ τῷ δρεπάνῳ ὑπόστασις ἦν ἡ αὐτή. xx. 30 υἱὲ κορασίων αὐτομολούντων (Luc.+ γυναικοτραφῆ). xxvii. 10 κατὰ νότον τῆς Ἰουδαίας. xxxi. 10 ἀνέθηκαν τὰ σκεύη αὐτοῦ εἰς τὸ Ἀσταρτεῖον. 2 Regn. i. 21 θυρεὸς Σαοὺλ οὐκ ἐχρίσθη ἐν ἐλαίῳ. xii. 31 διήγαγεν (A ἀπήγαγεν) αὐτοὺς διὰ τοῦ πλινθείου (Luc. περιήγαγεν αὐτοὺς ἐν μαδεββά). xx. 6 μή ποτε...σκιάσει τοὺς ὀφθαλμοὺς ἡμῶν. xxiv. 15 ἀπὸ πρωίθεν [καὶ] ἕως ὥρας ἀρίστου. 3 Regn. xiii. 12 καὶ δεικνύουσιν αὐτῷ οἱ υἱοὶ αὐτοῦ τὴν ὁδόν. 4 Regn. i. 2 f. ἐπιζητήσατε ἐν τῷ Βάαλ μυῖαν θεὸν Ἀκκαρών (Luc. ἐπερωτήσατε διὰ τοῦ Βάαλ μυῖαν προσόχθισμα θεὸν Ἀκκαρών). viii. 13 τίς ἐστιν ὁ δοῦλός σου, ὁ κύων ὁ τεθνηκώς, ὅτι ποιήσει τὸ ῥῆμα τοῦτο; xxiii. 22 f. οὐκ ἐγενήθη [κατὰ] τὸ πάσχα τοῦτο ἀφ᾽ ἡμερῶν τῶν κριτῶν...ὅτι ἀλλ᾽ ἢ τῷ ὀκτωκαιδεκάτῳ ἔτει τοῦ βασιλέως Ἰωσεία ἐγενήθη τὸ πάσχα [τοῦτο] (cf. 2 Chr. xxxv. 18).

(*b*) The translated titles of the Psalms form a special and interesting study. The details are collected below, and can be studied with the help of the commentaries, or of Neubauer's article in *Studia Biblica* ii. p. 1 ff.[1]

Ψαλμός, מִזְמוֹר *passim* (שִׁגָּיוֹן in Ps. vii., שִׁיר in Ps. xlv. (xlvi.)).

Ὠδή, שִׁיר *passim* (מִזְמוֹר in Ps. iv., הִגָּיוֹן in Ps. ix. 17).

Ψαλμὸς ᾠδῆς, שִׁיר מִזְמוֹר Pss. xxix., xlvii., lxvii., lxxiv., lxxxii., lxxxvi., xci., xciii. (A); ᾠδὴ ψαλμοῦ, מִזְמוֹר שִׁיר מ׳ or שׁ׳ מִזְמוֹר (lxv., lxxxii., lxxxvii., cvii.).

Προσευχή, תְּפִלָּה (Pss. xvi., lxxxv., lxxxix., ci., cxli.).

Ἀλληλουιά, הַלְלוּ־יָהּ (Pss. civ.—cvi., cx.—cxiv., cxvi., cxvii., cxxxiv., cxxxv., cxlv., cxlvi., cxlviii.—cl.).

Αἴνεσις, תְּהִלָּה (Ps. cxliv.).

Στηλογραφία, εἰς στηλογραφίαν, מִכְתָּם (Pss. xv., lv.—lix.). Aq. τοῦ ταπεινόφρονος καὶ ἁπλοῦ, Th. τοῦ ταπ. καὶ ἀμώμου.

Εἰς τὸ τέλος, לַמְנַצֵּחַ (Pss. iv.—xiii., xvii., xviii., xxi., xxix., xxx., xxxv.—lxi., lxiii.—lxix., lxxiv.—lxxvi., lxxix., lxxx., lxxxiii.,

[1] The titles which are given in the LXX. but are wanting in 𝔐, have been enumerated in Pt. II. c. ii. (p. 250 ff.).

lxxxiv., lxxxvii., cii., cviii., cxxxviii., cxxxix.). Cf. Aq. τῷ νικοποιῷ, Symm. ἐπινίκιος, Th. εἰς τὸ νῖκος.

'Εν ὕμνοις, בִּנְגִינוֹת (Pss. vi., liii., liv., lx., lxvi., lxxv.).

'Εν ψαλμοῖς, בִּנְגִינוֹת (Ps. iv.).

'Υπὲρ τῆς κληρονομούσης, (?) אֶל־הַנְּחִילוֹת (Ps. v.). Aq. ἀπὸ κληρο-δοσιῶν, Symm. ὑπὲρ κληρουχιῶν.

'Υπὲρ τῆς ὀγδόης, עַל־הַשְּׁמִינִית (Pss. vi., xi.).

'Υπὲρ τῶν λόγων Χουσεὶ υἱοῦ 'Ιεμενεί, עַל־דִּבְרֵי־כוּשׁ בֶּן־יְמִינִי (Ps. vii.). Aq., Symm., Th. περί, κτλ.

'Υπὲρ τῶν ληνῶν, עַל־הַגִּתִּית (Pss. viii., lxxx., lxxxiii.). Aq., Th. ὑπὲρ τῆς γετθίδος.

'Υπὲρ τῶν κρυφίων τοῦ υἱοῦ, עַל־מוּת לַבֵּן (Ps. ix.; cf. xlv.). Aq. ὑπὲρ νεανιότητος τοῦ υἱοῦ, Th. ὑπὲρ ἀκμῆς τοῦ υἱοῦ, Symm. περὶ τοῦ θανάτου τοῦ υἱοῦ.

'Υπὲρ τοῦ ἀντιλήμψεως τῆς ἑωθινῆς, עַל־אַיֶּלֶת הַשַּׁחַר (Ps. xxi.). Aq. ὑπὲρ τῆς ἐλάφου τῆς ὀρθρινῆς. Symm. ὑπὲρ τῆς βοηθείας τῆς ὀρθρ.

'Υπὲρ τῶν ἀλλοιωθησομένων, עַל־שֹׁשַׁנִּים (Pss. xliv., lix., lxviii., lxxix.). Aq. ἐπὶ τοῖς κρίνοις, Symm. ὑπὲρ τῶν ἀνθῶν, Th. ὑπὲρ τῶν κρίνων.

'Υπὲρ τοῦ ἀγαπητοῦ (ᾠδή), יְדִידֹת (שִׁיר) (Ps. xliv.). Aq. ᾆσμα προσφιλίας, Symm. ᾆσμα εἰς τὸν ἀγαπητόν, Th. τοῖς ἠγαπη-μένοις.

'Υπὲρ τοῦ λαοῦ τοῦ ἀπὸ τῶν ἁγίων μεμακρυμμένου, עַל־יוֹנַת אֵלֶם רְחֹקִים (Ps. lv.). Aq. ὑπὲρ περιστερᾶς ἀλάλου μακρυσμῶν. Symm. ὑπὲρ τῆς περιστερᾶς ὑπὸ τοῦ φίλου αὐτοῦ ἀπωσμένου. Ε'. ὑπὲρ τῆς π. τῆς μογγιλάλου κεκρυμμένων.

'Υπὲρ 'Ιδιθούν, עַל־יְדוּתוּי (Pss. xxxviii., lxi., lxxvi.).

'Υπὲρ μαελὲθ (τοῦ ἀποκριθῆναι), עַל־מַחֲלַת (לְעַנּוֹת) (Pss. lii., lxxxvii.). Aq. ἐπὶ χορείᾳ (Symm. διὰ χοροῦ) τοῦ ἐξάρχειν.

Εἰς ἀνάμνησιν, לְהַזְכִּיר (Pss. xxxvii., lxix.).

Εἰς ἐξομολόγησιν, לְתוֹדָה (Ps. xcix.). Aq. εἰς εὐχαριστίαν.

Εἰς σύνεσιν, συνέσεως, מַשְׂכִּיל (Pss. xxxi., xli.—xliv., li.—liii., lxxiii., lxxxvii., lxxxviii., cxli.). Aq. ἐπιστήμονος, ἐπιστήμης, ἐπιστη-μοσύνης.

Μὴ διαφθείρῃς, אַל־תַּשְׁחֵת (Pss. lvi.—lviii., lxxiv.). Symm. (Ps. lxxiv.) περὶ ἀφθαρσίας.

Τοῦ ἐνκαινισμοῦ τοῦ οἴκου, חֲנֻכַּת־הַבַּיִת (Ps. xxix.).

Τῶν ἀναβαθμῶν, הַמַּעֲלוֹת (Pss. cxix.—cxxxiii.). Aq., Symm., Th.
τῶν ἀναβάσεων, εἰς τὰς ἀναβάσεις.

It may be added that סֶלָה[1] (Pss. iii. 3, 5, iv. 3, 5, vii. 6, &c., &c.)
is uniformly διάψαλμα in the LXX.; Aq. renders it ἀεί, Symm.
and Th. agree with the LXX. except that in Ps. ix. 17 ἀεί is
attributed to Th. In the Psalm of Habakkuk (Hab. iii. 3) Symm.
renders εἰς τὸν αἰῶνα, Th. εἰς τέλος, and in *v.* 13 εἰς τέλος has found
its way into copies of the LXX. (cf. א[c.a], and Jerome: "ipsi LXX.
rerum necessitate compulsi...nunc transtulerunt *in finem*").

(*c*) Exegetical help is sometimes to be obtained from a
guarded use of the interpretation affixed by the LXX. (1) to
obscure words, especially ἅπαξ λεγόμενα, and (2) to certain
proper names. Some examples of both are given below.

(1) Gen. i. 2 ἀόρατος καὶ ἀκατασκεύαστος. 6 στερέωμα.
iii. 8 τὸ δειλινόν. 15 τηρήσει...τηρήσεις. vi. 2 οἱ ἄγγελοι τοῦ
θεοῦ (cf. Deut. xxxii. 8, Job i. 6, ii. 1). 4 οἱ γίγαντες. viii. 21
διανοηθείς. xxii. 2 τὸν ἀγαπητόν. xlix. 10 ἡγούμενος.
Exod. vi. 12 ἄλογος. viii. 21 κυνόμυια. xii. 22 ὕσσωπος.
xxv. 29 ἄρτοι ἐνώπιοι (cf. ἄ. προκείμενοι xxxix. 18=36, ἄ. τοῦ
προσώπου 1 Regn. xxi. 6). xxviii. 15 λόγιον, Vulg. *rationale*.
Exod. xxxiv. 13 τὰ ἄλση Vulg. *luci*, A.V. *groves*. Lev. xvi. 8 ff. ὁ
ἀποπομπαῖος, ἡ ἀποπομπή. Deut. x. 16 σκληροκαρδία. Jud.
xix. 22 υἱοὶ παρανόμων (cf. υἱοὶ λοιμοί 1 Regn. ii. 12, and other
renderings, which employ ἀνομία, ἀνόμημα, ἀποστασία, ἀσεβής,
ἄφρων). 2 Regn. i. 18 τὸ βιβλίον τοῦ εὐθοῦς. 3 Regn. x. 11 ξύλα
πελεκητά (cf. 2 Chr. ii. 8, ix. 10 f. ξ. πεύκινα). Ps. viii. 6 παρ'
ἀγγέλους. xv. 9 ἡ γλῶσσά μου. xvi. 8 κόρα ὀφθαλμοῦ. l. 14
πνεῦμα ἡγεμονικόν. cxxxviii. 15 ἡ ὑπόστασίς μου. 16 τὸ ἀκατέρ-
γαστόν σου. Prov. ii. 18 παρὰ τῷ ᾅδῃ μετὰ τῶν γηγενῶν
(a doublet). Job ix. 9 Πλειάδα καὶ Ἕσπερον καὶ Ἀρκτοῦρον
(cf. xxxviii. 31). Zeph. i. 10 ἀπὸ τῆς δευτέρας (cf. 4 Regn. xxii. 14).
Isa. xxxviii. 8 (4 Regn. xxii.) τοὺς δέκα ἀναβαθμούς. Ezech.
xiii. 18 προσκεφάλαια, ἐπιβόλαια.

(2) *Abarim, mountains of,* הַר־הָעֲבָרִים, τὸ ὄρος τὸ ἐν τῷ πέραν,
Num. xxvii. 12 (cf. xxi. 11, xxxiii. 44). *Agagite,* Βουγαῖος, Esth.
iii. 1, A 17 (xii. 6); Μακεδών, E (xvi.) 10. *Ararat, land of,*
אֶרֶץ־אֲרָרָט, Ἀρμενία, Isa. xxxvii. 38. *Ashtoreth* עַשְׁתֹּרֶת, Ἀστάρτη

---

[1] On this word see an article by C. A. Briggs, in the *Journal of Biblical
Literature,* 1899, p. 132 ff., and art. *Selah,* in Hastings, *D.B.* iv.

(the Phoenician 'Ashtart), Jud. ii. 13, 4 Regn. xxiii. 13. *Baca,*
valley of, עֵמֶק הַבָּכָא, ἡ κοιλὰς τοῦ κλαυθμῶνος, Ps. lxxxiii. 7 (cf.
Jud. ii. 5, 2 Regn. v. 24, 1 Chr. xiv. 14). *Caphtor, Caphtorim,*
Καππαδοκία, Καππάδοκες, Deut. ii. 23, Am. ix. 7. *Cherethites,*
כְּרֵתִים, Κρῆτες, Zeph. ii. 5, Ezech. xxv. 16. *Dodanim,* דֹּדָנִים,
Ῥόδιοι (רדנים), Gen. x. 4. *Enhakkore* עֵין־הַקּוֹרֵא, Πηγὴ τοῦ
ἐπικαλουμένου, Jud. xv. 19. *Ichabod,* אִיכָבוֹד, οὐαὶ βαρχαβώθ
(?=אוֹי בָרְחֹבוּת, Wellh.), 1 Regn. iv. 21. *Javan,* ἡ Ἑλλάς, Isa.
lxvi. 19 (cf. Joel iii. 6). *Jehovah-nissi,* Κύριος καταφυγή μου,
Exod. xvii. 15. *Keren-happuch,* קֶרֶן הַפּוּךְ, Ἀμαλθείας κέρας, Job
xlii. 14. *Kiriath-sepher,* קִרְיַת סֵפֶר, πόλις γραμμάτων, Jos. xv. 15 f.,
Macpelah, הַמַּכְפֵּלָה, τὸ σπήλαιον τὸ διπλοῦν, Gen. xxiii. 17, 19
(xxv. 9, xlix. 30, l. 13). *Moriah, land of,* אֶרֶץ הַמֹּרִיָּה, ἡ γῆ ἡ
ὑψηλή, Gen. xxii. 2. *Pisgah,* הַפִּסְגָּה, τὸ λελαξευμένον, Num.
xxi. 20, xxiii. 14, Deut. iii. 27 (cf. Deut. iv. 49). *Zaanaim,*
plain of, אֵלוֹן בְּצַעֲנַנִּים, δρῦς πλεονεκτούντων (B), δρ. ἀναπαυομένων
(A), Jud. iv. 11 (cf. Moore, *ad loc.*). *Zaphnath-paaneah,* צָפְנַת
פַּעְנֵחַ, Ψονθομφανήχ, Gen. xli. 45 (Ball, *ad loc.* compares Egypt.
suṭʼ a en pa-ānχ). *Pharaoh-Hophra,* פַּ' חָפְרַע, ὁ Οὐαφρή, Jer. li.
(xliv.) 30 (cf. W. E. Crum in Hastings, *D. B.* ii. p. 413).

B. The Septuagint is not less indispensable to the study
of the New Testament than to that of the Old. But its
importance in the former field is more often overlooked, since
its connexion with the N.T. is less direct and obvious, except
in the case of express quotations from the Alexandrian
version[1]. These, as we have seen, are so numerous that in
the Synoptic Gospels and in some of the Pauline Epistles they
form a considerable part of the text. But the New Testament
has been yet more widely and more deeply influenced by the
version through the subtler forces which shew themselves in
countless allusions, lying oftentimes below the surface of the
words, and in the use of a vocabulary derived from it, and in
many cases prepared by it for the higher service of the Gospel.

---

[1] On the quotations see above p. 392 ff.

1. The influence of the LXX. over the writings of the N.T. is continually shewn in combinations of words or in trains of thought which point to the presence of the version in the background of the writer's mind, even when he may not consciously allude to it.

This occurs frequently (*a*) in the sayings of our Lord, where, if He spoke in Aramaic, the reference to the LXX. is due to the translator: e.g. Mt. v. 3 ff. μακάριοι οἱ πτωχοί...οἱ πενθοῦντες... οἱ πραεῖς (Isa. lxi. 1 ff., Ps. xxxvi. 11). vi. 6 εἴσελθε εἰς τὸ ταμεῖόν σου (Isa. xxvi. 20). x. 21, 35 ἐπαναστήσονται τέκνα ἐπὶ γονεῖς...ἦλθον γὰρ διχάσαι...θυγατέρα κατὰ τῆς μητρὸς αὐτῆς καὶ νύμφην κτλ. (Mic. vii. 6). xxi. 33 ἄνθρωπος ἐφύτευσεν ἀμπελῶνα καὶ φραγμὸν αὐτῷ περιέθηκεν κτλ. (Isa. v. 2). Mc. ix. 48 βληθῆναι εἰς γέενναν ὅπου ὁ σκώληξ αὐτῶν οὐ τελευτᾷ καὶ τὸ πῦρ οὐ σβέννυται (Isa. lxvi. 24). Jo. i. 51 ὄψεσθε τὸν οὐρανὸν ἀνεῳγότα καὶ τοὺς ἀγγέλους τοῦ θεοῦ ἀναβαίνοντας καὶ καταβαίνοντας (Gen. xxviii. 12); (*b*) in the translated evangelical record: Mc. vii. 32 φέρουσιν αὐτῷ κωφὸν καὶ μογιλάλον...καὶ ἐλύθη ὁ δεσμός κτλ. (Isa. xxxv. 5 f., xlii. 7). xv. 29 οἱ παραπορευόμενοι ἐβλασφήμουν αὐτὸν κινοῦντες τὰς κεφαλάς: cf. Lc. xxiii. 35 ἱστήκει ὁ λαὸς θεωρῶν· ἐξεμυκτήριζον δέ κτλ. (Ps. xxi. 8, Isa. li. 23, Lam. ii. 15); (*c*) in the original Greek writings of the N.T., where allusions of this kind are even more abundant; 1 Pet. ii. 9 ὑμεῖς δὲ γένος ἐκλεκτόν, βασίλειον ἱεράτευμα, ἔθνος ἅγιον, λαὸς εἰς περιποίησιν, ὅπως τὰς ἀρετὰς ἐξαγγείλητε κτλ. (Exod. xix. 5 f., xxiii. 22 f., Isa. xliii. 20). iii. 14 τὸν δὲ φόβον αὐτῶν μὴ φοβηθῆτε μηδὲ ταραχθῆτε, κύριον δὲ τὸν χριστὸν ἁγιάσατε ἐν ταῖς καρδίαις ὑμῶν (Isa. viii. 12 f.). Rom. xii. 17 προνοούμενοι καλὰ ἐνώπιον πάντων ἀνθρώπων: cf. 2 Cor. viii. 21 προνοοῦμεν γὰρ καλὰ οὐ μόνον ἐνώπιον Κυρίου ἀλλὰ καὶ ἐνώπιον ἀνθρώπων (Prov. iii. 4; in Rom. *l. c.* this allusion is preceded by another to Prov. iii. 7). 2 Cor. iii. 3 ff.: Exod. xxxi., xxxiv. (LXX.) are in view throughout this context. Eph. ii. 17 εὐηγγελίσατο εἰρήνην ὑμῖν τοῖς μακρὰν καὶ εἰρήνην τοῖς ἐγγύς (Isa. lvii. 19, cf. lii. 7, lxi. 1). Phil. i. 19 οἶδα γὰρ ὅτι τοῦτό μοι ἀποβήσεται εἰς σωτηρίαν (Job xiii. 16). Heb. vi. 8 γῆ... ἐκφέρουσα...ἀκάνθας καὶ τριβόλους...κατάρας ἐγγύς (Gen. iii. 17).

These are but a few illustrations of a mental habit everywhere to be observed in the writers of the N.T., which shews them to have been not only familiar with the LXX., but saturated with its language. They used it as Englishmen use the Authorised Version of the Bible, working it into the texture of their thoughts and utterances. It is impossible to do justice to their writings unless this fact is recognised, i.e., unless the reader is on the watch for unsuspected references to the Greek O.T., and able to appreciate its influence upon his author's mind.

2. To what extent the vocabulary of the N.T. has been influenced by the LXX. is matter of keen controversy. In a weighty essay *On the Value and Use of the Septuagint* Dr Hatch has maintained that "the great majority of N.T. words are words which, though for the most part common to Biblical and to contemporary secular Greek, express in their Biblical use the conceptions of a Semitic race, and which must consequently be examined by the light of the cognate documents which form the LXX.[1]" This statement, which has been hotly contested, may conveniently form the basis of our discussion of the subject.

(*a*) "The great majority of N.T. words are...common to Biblical and contemporary secular Greek." This is certainly true. Thus Dr H. A. A. Kennedy[2] enumerates about 150 words out of over 4800 in the N.T. which are "strictly peculiar to the LXX. and N.T." The list is as follows:

ἀγαθοποιεῖν, ἀγαθωσύνη, ἀγαλλιᾶσθαι, ἀγαλλίασις, ἁγιάζειν, ἁγιασμός, ἁγιωσύνη, αἴνεσις, ἀκρογωνιαῖος, αἰχμαλωτεύειν, ἀλίσγημα, ἀλληλουιά, ἀλλογενής, ἀμέθυστος, ἀμήν, ἀμφιάζειν, ἀναζωννύειν, ἀναθεματίζειν, ἀνεξιχνίαστος, ἀνθρωπάρεσκος, ἀνταπόδομα, ἀποδεκατοῦν, ἀποκάλυψις, ἀποκεφαλίζειν, ἀποφθέγγεσθαι, βάτος, βδέλυγμα, βεβηλοῦν, βροχή, γέεννα, γνώστης, γογγύζειν, γυμνότης, δεκατοῦν, δεκτός, διαγογγύζειν, δολιοῦν, δότης, δυναμοῦν, ἑβδομηκοντάκις, εἰρηνοποιεῖν, ἐκζητεῖν, ἐκμυκτηρίζειν, ἐκπειράζειν, ἐκπορνεύειν, ἐκριζοῦν, ἐλεγμός, ἔλεγξις, ἐμπαιγμός, ἐμπαίκτης, ἔναντι, ἐνδιδύσκειν, ἐνδοξάζειν, ἐνδυναμοῦν, ἐνευλογεῖν, ἐνκαινίζειν, ἔνταλμα, ἐνταφιάζειν, ἐνώπιον, ἐνωτίζεσθαι, ἐξάπινα, ἐξαστράπτειν, ἐξολεθρεύειν, ἐξουδενοῦν, ἐξυπνίζειν, ἐπαύριον, ἐπισκοπή, ἐπαναπαύειν, ἐπιγαμβρεύειν, ἐπιφαύσκειν, ἐρήμωσις, εὐδοκία, ἐφημερία, ἥττημα,

---

[1] *Essays*, p. 34.   [2] *Sources of N.T. Greek*, p. 88.

θέλησις, ἱερατεύειν, ἱεράτευμα, καθαρίζειν, καθαρισμός, κατακαυχᾶ-
σθαι, κατακληρονομεῖν, κατάνυξις, κατανύσσειν, κατενώπιον, κατοι-
κητήριον, καύσων, καύχησις, κλυδωνίζεσθαι, κόρος, κραταιοῦν, λαξευτός,
λειτουργικός, λύτρωσις, μακροθυμεῖν, μάννα, ματαιότης, ματαιοῦν,
μεγαλειότης, μεγαλωσύνη, μετοικεῖν, μίσθιος, μογιλάλος, μοιχαλίς,
νῖκος, ὀλεθρεύειν, ὀλιγόψυχος, ὁλοκληρία, ὀπτάνειν, ὀπτασία, ὀρθοτομεῖν, ὀρθρίζειν, ὁρκωμοσία, οὐαί, παγιδεύειν, παραζηλοῦν, παρα-
πικρασμός, παροικία, παροργισμός, πατριάρχης, πειρασμός, περι-
κάθαρμα, περιούσιος, περισσεία, πληροφορεῖν, πρόσκομμα, προσοχθίζειν, πρωινός, ῥαντίζειν, ῥαντισμός, σαβαώθ, σάββατον, σαγήνη,
σατανᾶς, σάτον, σητόβρωτος, σίκερα, σκάνδαλον, σκληροκαρδία,
σκληροτράχηλος, στήκειν, στυγνάζειν, συνεγείρειν, ταπεινόφρων,
ὑπακοή, ὑπάντησις, ὑπολήνιον, ὑπεροψοῦν, ὑστέρημα, φωστήρ,
χερουβείμ, ψιθυρισμός, ὠτίον.

Since the publication of Dr Kennedy's book some of these
words (e.g. γογγύζειν, λειτουργικός[1]) have been detected in early
papyri, and as fresh documents are discovered and examined,
the number of 'Biblical' Greek words will doubtless be still
further diminished. Indeed the existence of such a class of
words may be almost entirely due to accidental causes, such as
the loss of contemporary Hellenistic literature.

(*b*) On the other hand it must not be forgotten that the
Greek vocabulary of Palestinian Greek-speaking Jews in the
first century A.D. was probably derived in great part from their
use of the Greek Old Testament. Even in the case of
writers such as St Luke, St Paul, and the author of the
Epistle to the Hebrews, the LXX. has no doubt largely regulated the choice of words. A very considerable number of
the words of the N.T. seem to have been suggested by that
version, or in any case may be elucidated from it.

E.g.: ἀγαθωσύνη, ἀγαλλιᾶσθαι, ἁγνίζειν, ἀγρυπνεῖν, αἴνιγμα,
αἱρετίζειν, ἀλαζονεύεσθαι, ἀλλογενής, ἀδιαλείπτως, ἀμάραντος, ἀμέ-
ριμνος, ἀμφίβληστρον, ἄμφοδον, ἀπελπίζειν, ἀπερίτμητος, ἁπλότης,
ἀπόκρυφος, βδέλυγμα, γλωσσόκομον, γνωρίζειν, διάδημα, δίδραχμα,
δίστομος, διυλίζειν, δωρεάν, ἐναγκαλίζεσθαι, ἐνταφιάζειν, ἐνωτίζεσθαι,
ἑορτάζειν, ἐξέφνης, ἐξουδενοῦν, εὔκολος, εὐοδοῦν, θεοσέβεια, ἱκανοῦ-
σθαι, ἱκανός, ἰκμάς, ἱστορεῖν, καμμύειν, κατάγελως, καταδυναστεύειν,
κατακλυσμός, κατακυριεύειν, καταποντίζειν, καταφιλεῖν, καυχᾶσθαι,
κλάσμα, κοράσιον, κόφινος, λιθόστρωτος, λικμᾶν, μεσονύκτιον, μογιλάλος, μυκτηρίζειν, νεομηνία, νῖκος, νυστάζειν, οἰκουμένη (ἡ), ὁμοθυμα-

---

[1] Deissmann, *Bibelstudien*, pp. 106, 138.

δόν, ὀστράκινος, παγιδεύειν, παιδάριον, παραδειγματίζειν, παρακούειν, παρεπίδημος, πάροικος, περικεφαλαία, περίλυπος, περίχωρος, περί-ψημα, πήρα, πλεονάζειν, πολυλογία, πολυπραγμονεῖν, προσήλυτος, προσκεφάλαιον, ῥάπισμα, ῥύμη, σαγήνη, σίκερα, σίνδων, σκόλοψ, στενοχωρία, συλλογίζεσθαι, συμβιβάζειν, σύμφυτος, ταμ(ι)εῖον, τετρά-δραχμον, τρυμαλία, τυμπανίζειν, ὑπογραμμός, φιμοῦν, χορτάζειν, χρηματίζειν, ψευδοπροφήτης. To these may be added a consider-able class of words which are based on LXX. words though they do not occur in the LXX.; e.g.: ἀπροσωπολήμπτως, βάπτισμα (-μός), δαιμονίζεσθαι, πνευματικός, σαρκικός, ψευδόχριστος.

(*c*) The influence of the LXX. is still more clearly seen in the N.T. employment of religious words and phrases which occur in the LXX. at an earlier stage in the history of their use. The following list will supply illustrations of these :

ἀγάπη, ἀγαπητός, ἁγιάζειν, ἁγιασμός, ἀδελφός, ἀδόκιμος, αἵρεσις, αἰσθητήριον, ἀκρογωνιαῖος, ἀνάθεμα, ἀναζωπυρεῖν, ἀνακαινίζειν, ἀνα-στροφή, ἀνατολή, ἀνεξιχνίαστος, ἀπαρχή, ἀπαύγασμα, ἄφεσις, ἀφο-ρίζειν, βαπτίζειν, βεβαίωσις, βλασφημεῖν, γαζοφυλάκιον, γέεννα γραμματεύς, γρηγορεῖν, δαιμόνιον, διαθήκη, δόγμα, ἔθνη, εἰρηνικός εἰρηνοποιεῖν, ἐκκλησία, ἔκστασις, ἐλεημοσύνη, ἐνέργεια, ἐξομολο γεῖσθαι, ἐξουσία, ἐπερώτημα, ἐπίσκοπος, ἐπισυνάγειν, ἐπιφάνεια ἐπιχορηγεῖν, ἑτοιμασία, εὐαγγελίζεσθαι, εὐαρεστεῖν, εὐδοκία, εὐλάβεια ζηλωτής, ζωγρεῖν, ζωογονεῖν, θέλημα, θρησκεία, ἱλασμός, ἱλαστήριον Ἰουδαισμός, καταλλαγή, κατάνυξις, κήρυγμα, κυβέρνησις, Κύριος λειτουργεῖν, λόγος, λοιμός, λυτροῦσθαι, μεγαλειότης, μεγαλωσύνη μεταμέλεια, μετεωρίζεσθαι, μονογενής, μορφή, μυστήριον, νεόφυτος ὁλόκληρος, ὀρθοτομεῖν, ὁσιότης, παραβολή, παράδεισος, πάροικος, πει-ρασμός, περιούσιος, περιοχή, περιποιεῖσθαι, πίστις, πληροφορεῖσθαι, πλήρωμα, πνεῦμα, πρεσβύτερος, προσάγειν, ῥύεσθαι, σάρξ, σκάν-δαλον, σκληροτράχηλος, σεμνός, συνείδησις, σφραγίζειν, σωτηρία, τάρταρος, ὑπόστασις, ὑστέρημα, Ὕψιστος, φιλάνθρωπος, φῶς, χα-ρακτήρ, χειρόγραφον, χριστός. Many of the characteristic phrases of the N.T. also have their roots in the LXX., e.g. εἰκὼν θεοῦ (Gen. i. 26), ὀσμὴ εὐωδίας (viii. 21), πάροικος καὶ παρεπίδημος (xxiii. 4), πρόσωπον πρὸς πρόσωπον (xxxii. 30), λαὸς περιούσιος (Exod. xix. 5), δόξα Κυρίου (xl. 29), θυσία αἰνέσεως (Lev. vii. 2), λαμβάνειν πρόσωπον (xix. 15), ἡ διασπορά (Deut. xxx. 4), γενεὰ διεστραμμένη, σκολιά (xxxii. 5), μὴ γένοιτο (Jos. xxii. 29), ἵλεώς σοι (2 Regn. xx. 20), μικρὸν ὅσον ὅσον (xxvi. 20), διάβολος (1 Chron. xxi. 1), τὸ σωτήριον τοῦ θεοῦ (Ps. xcvii. 3), ᾠδὴ καινή, ὄνομα καινόν, and the like (Ps. cxliii. 9, Isa. lxii. 2, &c.), Κύριος ὁ παν-τοκράτωρ (Am. ix. 5), δοῦλος Κυρίου (Jon. i. 9), τράπεζα Κυρίου (Mal. i. 7), ἡμέρα ἐπισκοπῆς (Isa. x. 3), ἡμέρα Κυρίου (xiii. 6, 9), ὁ παῖς [τοῦ θεοῦ] (xli. 8, &c.), ἐγώ εἰμι (xliii. 10), ἐκ κοιλίας μητρός (xlix. 1), τὰ πετεινὰ τοῦ οὐρανοῦ (Ezech. xxxi. 6), ὁ Γὼγ καὶ Μαγώγ (xxxviii. 2).

The non-canonical books have their full share in the contribution which the Septuagint makes to the vocabulary of the N.T. Many Biblical words either occur for the first time in the O.T. 'Apocrypha,' or reach there a further stage in the history of their use, or appear in new combinations. The following examples will repay examination : αἰών, ἀπαύγασμα, ἀποκάλυψις, ἀποστολή, ἀσύνετος, ἄφεσις, βαπτίζειν, βασιλεία (τοῦ θεοῦ), δαιμόνιον, διακονία, διαπονεῖσθαι, δικαιοῦν, ἔκβασις, ἐκλεκτός, ἐμβατεύειν, ἐπίσκοπος, ἐπιστροφή, ἐπιτιμία, ἐπιφάνεια, εὔσπλαγχνος, εὐχαριστία, ἴδιος, ἱλασμός, ἱλαστήριον, κανών, κλῆρος, κληροῦν, κοινός, κοινοῦν, κόσμος, κτίσις, λειτουργία, λειτουργός, μυστήριον (τοῦ θεοῦ), νόμος, παρουσία, πεντηκοστή, σημεῖα καὶ τέρατα, σκανδαλίζειν, συμπάθεια, συμπαθεῖν, σωτήρ, χάρις καὶ ἔλεος, χριστός.

(*d*) "The great majority of N.T. words and phrases express...the conceptions of a Semitic race, and...must consequently be examined by the light of...the LXX." But the connotation will usually be found to have undergone considerable changes, both in ordinary words and in those which are used in a religious sense. In order to trace the process by which the transition has been effected the N.T. student must begin with an investigation into the practice of the LXX. Such an enquiry may be of service in determining the precise meaning which is to be given to the word in the N.T., but it will more frequently illustrate the growth of religious thought or of social life which has led to a change of signification. Dr Hatch indeed laid down as "almost self-evident" canons the two propositions (1) that "a word which is used uniformly, or with few and intelligible exceptions, as the translation of the same Hebrew word, must be held to have in Biblical Greek the same meaning as that Hebrew word"; and (2) that "words which are used interchangeably as translations of the same Hebrew word, or group of cognate words, must be held to have in Biblical Greek an allied or virtually identical meaning[1]." These principles led him to

[1] *Essays*, p. 35.

some remarkable departures from the traditional interpretation of N.T. words (e.g. ἀρετή = הוֹד or תְּהִלָּה = δόξα, ἔπαινος; διάβολος = שָׂטָן = 'enemy'; ὁμοθυμαδόν = יַחְדָּו, יַחַד = 'together'; πτωχοί = πένητες = πραεῖς = ταπεινοί = 'fellahin'; πονηρός, malicious, mischievous; ὑποκριτής, the equivalent of πονηρός, πανοῦργος, and the like). A searching examination of these views will be found in Dr T. K. Abbott's essay *On N.T. Lexicography*[1]. The πρῶτον ψεῦδος of Dr Hatch's canons lies in his use of the term 'Biblical Greek' as inclusive of the pre-Christian Greek of the Alexandrian translators, and the Palestinian Greek of the Apostolic age. While it is evident that the writers of the N.T. were largely indebted to the Alexandrian version for their Greek vocabulary, we cannot safely assume that they attached to the Greek words and phrases which they borrowed from it the precise significance that belonged to them in the older book. Allowance must be made for altered circumstances, and in particular for the influence of the Gospel, which threw new meaning into the speech as well as the life of men. One or two instances will shew the truth of this remark. Ἀγάπη in the LXX. rarely rises above the lower sense of the sexual passion, or at best the affection of human friendship; the exceptions are limited to the Greek Book of Wisdom (Sap. iii. 9, vi. 18[2]). But in the N.T., where the word is far more frequent, it is used only of the love of God for men, or of men for God or Christ, or for the children of God as such. Ἐκκλησία in the LXX. is the congregation of Israel; in the N.T., except perhaps in Mt. xviii. 17, it is the new community founded by Christ[3], viewed in different aspects and with many shades of meaning. Εὐαγγέλιον in the LXX. occurs only in the plural, and perhaps only

---

[1] *Essays*, p. 65 ff.
[2] Ἀγάπησις occurs in the sense of Divine love (Hos. xi. 4, Zeph. iii. 17, Jer. xxxi. 3).
[3] See Hort, *The Christian Ecclesia*, p. 9 f.

in the classical sense of 'a reward for good tidings' (2 Regn. iv. 10); in the N.T. it is from the first appropriated to the Messianic good tidings (Mc. i. 1, 14), probably deriving this new meaning from the use of εὐαγγελίζεσθαι in Isa. xl. 9, lii. 7, lx. 6, lxi. 1.

Thus on the whole it is clear that caution must be used in employing the practice of the LXX. to determine the connotation of N.T. words. On the one hand the interpreter ought not to be led astray by visions of the solidarity of 'Biblical Greek,' for the Greek of the N.T., though in fact largely derived from the Greek of the LXX., has in not a few instances cast off the traditions of its source under the inspiration of another age. On the other hand, the student of the N.T. will make the LXX. his starting-point in examining the sense of all words and phrases which, though they may have been used in classical Greek or by the κοινή, passed into Palestinian use through the Greek Old Testament, and in their passage received the impress of Semitic thought and life. Bishop Pearson's judgement on this point is still fully justified: "LXXviralis versio...ad Novum Instrumentum recte intelligendum et accurate explicandum perquam necessaria est...in illam enim omnes idiotismi veteris linguae Hebraicae erant transfusi...multa itaque Graeca sunt in Novo Foedere vocabula quae ex usu Graecae linguae intelligi non possunt, ex collatione autem Hebraea et ex usu LXX. interpretum facile intelliguntur[1]."

II. The Greek versions of the second century A.D. are in many respects of less importance to the Biblical student than the Septuagint. Not only are they later by two to four centuries, but they exist only in a fragmentary state, and the text of the fragments is often insecure. But there are services which they can render when rightly employed, and which the careful student will not forget to demand.

---

[1] *Praef. paraen.*, ed. E. Churton, p. 22 f.

1. Each of these versions has characteristics of its own, which must be taken into account in estimating its value.

(*a*) Aquila represents the official Hebrew text in its earliest stage, and his extreme literalness and habit of translating ἐτυμολογικῶς[1] render it easy to recover the text which lay before him. In the large fragments of 3 and 4 Regn. published by Mr Burkitt, Aquila's Hebrew text differs from that of the printed Bibles only in thirteen readings[2], an average of one variant in every second verse. Still more important is Aquila's reflexion of the exegetical tradition of the school of Jamnia. Here as in his text he is often in direct opposition to the LXX., and serves as a useful makeweight against the influence of the Alexandrian interpretation. Especially is this the case in regard to the meaning of obscure words, which Aquila translates with a full knowledge of both languages and of other Semitic tongues[3], whilst the LXX. too often depended upon guess-work. This merit of Aquila was recognised by Jerome, who makes use of his interpretations in the Vulgate[4]. Moreover the influence which his work has exercised over the text of the LXX. renders it important to the textual critic of the older Greek version[5]. (*b*) The paraphrasing manner of Symmachus hinders the free use of his version either for textual or hermeneutical purposes. But it is often interesting as revealing the exegetical tendencies of his school, and its fulness serves to correct the extreme literalness of Aquila. Jerome used it for his Vulgate even more freely than he used Aquila; cf. Field, *Hexapla* i., p. xxxiv. "quem tam presse secutus est magnus ille interpres Latinus...ut aliquando nobis successerit ex Hieronymi Latinis Symmachi Graeca...satis probabiliter extricare."
(*c*) Theodotion, besides contributing a whole book to the *textus*

---

[1] See above, p. 40.
[2] Cf. *Aquila*, p. 16 f.
[3] Field, *Hexapla*, I. p. xxiv.
[4] *Ibidem.*
[5] See Burkitt, *Aquila*, p. 18 ff.

receptus of the Greek Old Testament, preserves in his text of
the other books traces of a recension of the LXX. which seems
at one time to have had a wide circulation, since Theodotionic
readings occur in the LXX. quotations of the N.T. and in those
of other Christian writers before A.D. 150[1].

2. All the post-Christian translators of the O.T., but especially Aquila, Symmachus, and the author of the Quinta[2], appear
to have been not only competent Hebraists, but possessed of a
more or less extensive knowledge of Greek literature. These
qualifications render them valuable allies to the interpreter
whether of the New or of the Old Testament. (*a*) In the
case of the O.T. they serve to confirm or correct the LXX.
renderings, or to illustrate their meaning. The renderings of
the earlier version are not infrequently retained, e.g. Gen. i. 2
מְרַחֶפֶת Oʹ ἐπεφέρετο, ʼΑ.Σ.Θ. ἐπιφερόμενον. 6 רָקִיעַ, OʹʼΑ.Σ.Θ.
στερέωμα. 10 מִקְוֵה־הַמַּיִם, Oʹ Σ.Θ. τὰ συστέματα (συστήματα) τῶν
ὑδάτων. More often they are set aside in favour of other words
which do not materially differ in signification, but seem to have
been preferred as more exact, or as better Greek, e.g. Gen. xlix. 19
גְּדוּד Oʹ πειρατήριον, ʼΑ. εὔζωνος, Σ. λόχος. Exod. v. 13 הַנֹּגְשִׂים
Oʹ οἱ ἐργοδιῶκται, ʼΑ. οἱ εἰσπράκται. Jud. v. 16 חִקְרֵי־לֵב Oʹ
ἐξετασμοὶ καρδίας, ʼΑ. ἀκριβολογίαι κ., Σ. ἐξιχνιασμοὶ κ. Ps.
lxxxviii. 8 אֵל נַעֲרָץ בְּסוֹד קְדֹשִׁים Oʹ ὁ θεὸς δοξαζόμενος ἐν βουλῇ
ἁγίων, ʼΑ. Ἰσχυρὸς κατισχυρευόμενος ἐν ἀπορρήτῳ ἁ., Σ. θεὲ
ἀήττητε ἐν ὁμιλίᾳ ἁ. At other times their rendering lies far
apart from that of the LXX., manifesting complete dissent from
the Alexandrian version, e.g. Gen. xlvii. 31 המטה Oʹ τῆς
ῥάβδου, ʼΑ.Σ. τῆς κλίνης. Num. xxiii. 21 תְּרוּעַת (מֶלֶךְ) Oʹ τὰ
ἔνδοξα, ʼΑ. ἀλαλαγμός, Σ. σημασία, Θ. σαλπισμός. 1 Regn. xiii.
20 מַחֲרַשְׁתּוֹ, Oʹ τὸ θέριστρον (ʼΑ.Θ. ἄροτρον, Σ. ὕνιν) αὐτοῦ. Ps.
ii. 12, נַשְּׁקוּ־בַר Oʹ δράξασθε παιδείας, Α. καταφιλήσατε ἐκλεκτῶς,

---

[1] See pp. 47 ff., 395 f., 403, 417 etc.
[2] On the excellence of his Greek scholarship see Field, *op. cit.* p. xliv.

Σ. προσκυνήσατε καθαρῶς. To these instances may be added others where the later translators substitute a literal rendering for a paraphrase or a gloss; e.g. in Deut. x. 16 'A. has ἀκρο-βυστίαν καρδίας for the euphemistic σκληροκαρδίαν of the LXX.; in Ps. xv. 9 'A.Σ.Θ. restore δόξα for the interpretative γλῶσσα.

(*b*) Dr Hatch points out[1] that "in a large number of instances the word which one or other of the translators substitutes for the LXX. word is itself used in other passages of the LXX. as the translation of the same Hebrew word"; and he draws the conclusion that "the words which are so inter-changed are practically synonymous." But his inference must be received with reserve, for the interchange may not be so free as appears at first sight; so careful a translator as Aquila (e.g.) has probably regulated his use of words which are generally synonymous with a view to the requirements of the particular context.

(*c*) Many of the words of the N.T. which are not to be found in the LXX. occur in the fragments of the later Greek versions, and receive important illustration from their use of them. Indeed, in not a few instances these versions supply the only or the best explanation of rarer words or connotations. The following are examples. Ἀδημονεῖν, 'A. Job xviii. 20, Σ. Ps. lx. 3, cxv. 2, Eccl. vii. 17, Ezech. iii. 15; ἀποκαραδοκία, cf. 'A. Ps. xxxvi. 7 (ἀποκαραδόκει); δαιμονίζειν, 'A. Ps. xc. 6. ἐνκακεῖν, 'to faint,' Σ. Gen. xxvii. 46; ἐμβριμᾶσθαι, 'A. Ps. vii. 12, Σ. Isa. xvii. 13; ἐνθύμησις, 'thought,' Σ. Job xxi. 27, Ezech. xi. 21; ἐπίβλημα, 'patch,' Σ. Jos. ix. 5; θεομάχος, Σ. Prov. ix. 18, xxi. 16, Job xxvi. 5; καταφέρεσθαι, 'to drop asleep,' 'A. Ps. lxxv. 7; μορφοῦν, 'A. Isa. xliv. 13[2]. Even where the unusual word and meaning occur in the LXX., it will often

---

[1] *Essays*, p. 28.

[2] These instances are chiefly from Hatch (*Essays*, p. 25). They might easily be multiplied by an inspection of the Oxford Concordance or of the Lexicon and Hexapla at the end of Trom.

be found that the later versions supply more abundant or more appropriate illustrations. Thus after the Septuagint these fragments, which are happily receiving continual additions from Hexaplaric MSS., offer the most promising field for the investigation of N.T. lexicography and one, moreover, which has been little worked.

On the whole, perhaps, no sounder advice could be given to a student of the language of the N.T., than to keep continually at hand the Septuagint, the remains of the Hexapla as edited by Field, and the Oxford Concordance which forms a complete index to both. It is only when he has made some way with the evidence of the Greek versions of the Old Testament that he will be in a position to extend his researches to non-Biblical literature, such as the papyri, the remains of the Hellenistic writers, and the great monuments of the later Greek.

LITERATURE (on the general subject of the chapter). J. Pearson, *Praefatio Paraenetica* (ed. E. Churton), p. 16 sqq.; H. Hody, *de Bibl. textibus orig.*, III. c. ii., p. 293; J. F. Fischer, *Prolusiones de versionibus Graecis librorum V. T.* (Leipzig, 1772); Z. Frankel, *Vorstudien zur Septuaginta* (Leipzig, 1841), p. 263 ff.; E. W. Grinfield, *N. T. Gr., editio Hellenistica* (London, 1843); *Scholia Hellenistica in N. T.* (London, 1848); *An Apology for the Septuagint* (London, 1850); W. R. Churton, *The Influence of the LXX. Version of the O. T. upon the progress of Christianity* (Cambridge, 1861); W. Selwyn, art. *Septuagint*, in Smith's *D.B.*, iii. (London, 1863); W. H. Guillemard, *The Greek Testament, Hebraistic edition* [St Matthew] (Cambridge, 1875); E. Hatch, *Essays on Biblical Greek*, i.—iii. (Oxford, 1889); S. R. Driver, *Notes on the Hebrew Text of Samuel*, Intr., p. xxxvi. ff. (Oxford, 1890); A. F. Kirkpatrick, *The Divine Library of the O. T.*, p. 63 ff. (London, 1891); *The Septuagint Version*, in *Expositor*, v. iii., p. 263 ff. (London, 1896); T. K. Abbott, *Essays chiefly on the original texts of the O. and N. Testaments* (London, 1891); A. Loisy, *Histoire critique du texte et des versions de la Bible* (Amiens, 1892); H. A. A. Kennedy, *Sources of N. T. Greek, or the Influence of the LXX. on the vocabulary of the N. T.* (Edinburgh, 1895); H. L. Strack, in Hastings, *D. B.* iv. p. 731.

CHAPTER V.

INFLUENCE OF THE LXX. ON CHRISTIAN LITERATURE.

1. THE Church inherited from the Hellenistic Synagogue an entire confidence in the work of the Alexandrian translators. It was a treasure common to Jew and Christian, the authorised Greek Bible to which at first both appealed. When after the beginning of the second century a distrust of the LXX. sprang up among the Jews[1], Christian teachers and writers not unnaturally clung to the old version with a growing devotion. They pleaded its venerable age and its use by the Evangelists and Apostles; they accepted and often embellished the legend of its birth[2], and, following in the steps of Philo, claimed for it an inspiration not inferior to that of the original. When the divergences of the Septuagint from the current Hebrew text became apparent, it was argued that the errors of the Greek text were due to accidents of transmission, or that they were not actual errors, but Divine adaptations of the original to the use of the future Church.

Iren. iii. 21. 3 f. "quum...Deus...servavit nobis simplices scripturas in Aegypto...in qua et Dominus noster servatus est... et haec earum scripturarum interpretatio priusquam Dominus noster descenderet facta sit et antequam Christiani ostenderentur interpretata sit...vere impudorati et audaces ostenduntur qui nunc volunt aliter interpretationes facere, quando ex ipsis

[1] See above, p. 30 f.
[2] See above, p. 13 f.

scripturis arguantur a nobis...etenim apostoli quum sint his omnibus vetustiores, consonant praedictae interpretationi, et interpretatio consonat apostolicae traditioni. etenim Petrus et Ioannes et Matthaeus et Paulus et reliqui deinceps et horum sectatores prophetica omnia ita annuntiaverunt quemadmodum Seniorum interpretatio continet. unus enim et idem Spiritus Dei qui in prophetis quidem praeconavit...in Senioribus autem interpretatus est bene quae bene prophetata fuerant. Cyril. Hieros. *cat.* iv. 33 f. : ἀναγίνωσκε τὰς θείας γραφάς, τὰς εἴκοσι δύο¹ βίβλους τῆς παλαιᾶς διαθήκης ταύτας, τὰς ὑπὸ τῶν ἑβδομήκοντα δύο ἑρμηνευ. τῶν ἑρμηνευθείσας...οὐ γὰρ εὑρεσιλογία καὶ κατασκευὴ σοφισμάτων ἀνθρωπίνων ἦν τὸ γινόμενον, ἀλλ᾽ ἐκ πνεύματος ἁγίου ἡ τῶν ἁγίῳ πνεύματι λαληθεισῶν θείων γραφῶν ἑρμηνεία συνετελεῖτο. Chrys. *in Matt. hom.* v. τῶν ἄλλων μᾶλλον ἁπάντων τὸ ἀξιόπιστον οἱ ἑβδομήκοντα ἔχοιεν ἂν δικαίως. οἱ μὲν γὰρ μετὰ τὴν τοῦ Χριστοῦ παρουσίαν ἡρμήνευσαν, Ἰουδαῖοι μείναντες, καὶ δικαίως ἂν ὑποπτεύοιντο ἅτε ἀπεχθείᾳ μᾶλλον εἰρηκότες, καὶ τὰς προφητείας συσκιάζοντες ἐπίτηδες· οἱ δὲ ἑβδομήκοντα πρὸ ἑκατὸν ἢ καὶ πλειόνων ἐτῶν τῆς τοῦ Χριστοῦ παρουσίας ἐπὶ τοῦτο ἐλθόντες καὶ τοσοῦτοι ὄντες πάσης τοιαύτης εἰσὶν ὑποψίας ἀπηλλαγμένοι. καὶ διὰ τὸν χρόνον καὶ διὰ τὸ πλῆθος καὶ διὰ τὴν συμφωνίαν μᾶλλον ἂν εἶεν πιστεύεσθαι δίκαιοι. Hieron. *ep.* xxxiii. (*ad Pammach.*) : "iure LXX. editio obtinuit in ecclesiis vel quia prima fuit et ante Christi facta adventum, vel quia ab Apostolis...usurpata"; *praef. in Paralip.* "si LXX. interpretum pura et ut ab eis in Graecum versa est editio permaneret, superflue me...impelleres ut Hebraea volumina Latino sermone transferrem." Aug. *de doctr. Chr.* 22 " qui (LXX. interpretes) iam per omnes peritiores ecclesias tanta praesentia Sancti Spiritus interpretati esse dicuntur ut os unum tot hominum fuisse...quamobrem, etiamsi aliquid aliter in Hebraeis exemplaribus invenitur quam isti posuerunt, cedendum esse arbitror divinae dispositioni quae per eos facta est...itaque fieri potest ut sic illi interpretati sint quemadmodum congruere Gentibus ille qui eos agebat...Spiritus S. indicavit." (Cf. *quaest. in Hept.* i. 169, vi. 19; *in Ps.* cxxxv. ; *de civ. Dei* viii. 44.)

2.   Under these circumstances the Septuagint Version of the Old Testament necessarily influenced the literature and thought of the Ancient Church in no ordinary degree. How largely it is quoted by Greek Christian writers of the first four centuries has already been shewn[2]. But they were not content to cite it as the best available version of the Old

---

[1] See above, p. 219 ff.
[2] Part III. c. 3.

Testament; they adopted without suspicion and with tenacity its least defensible renderings, and pressed them into the service of controversy, dogma, and devotion. This remark applies also in effect to the Latin Christian writers before Jerome, who were generally dependent on a literal translation based upon the Greek Bible[1]. To Tertullian and Cyprian, as well as to Clement and Barnabas, Justin[2] and Irenaeus, the Septuagint was the Old Testament authorised by the Church, and no appeal lay either to any other version or to the original. Nor was this tradition readily abandoned by the few who attained to some knowledge of Hebrew. Origen, while recognising the divergence of the LXX. from the Hebrew, and endeavouring to reconcile the two by means of the Hexapla[3], was accustomed to preach and comment upon the ordinary Greek text[4]. He even builds his system of interpretation on the LXX. rendering of Prov. xxii. 20[5]. Jerome was long in reaching his resolve to adopt the Hebrew text as the basis of his new Latin version, and when at length he did so, his decision exposed him to obloquy[6]. Augustine, while sympathising with Jerome's purpose, thought it a doubtful policy to unsettle the laity by lowering the authority of the LXX.[7]

The following examples of Christian interpretation based upon the LXX. will shew how largely that version influenced the

[1] See above, p. 87 ff.

[2] Justin occasionally adopts a rendering preferred by his Jewish antagonists, or does not press the rendering of the LXX. But he makes this concession only where the alternative does not affect his argument; see *Dial.* 124, 131.

[3] See above, p. 60 ff.

[4] *Comm. in Cant.* i. 344, "tamen nos LXX. interpretum scripta per omnia custodimus, certi quod Spiritus Sanctus mysteriorum formas obtectas inesse voluit in scripturis divinis."

[5] See below, p. 468.

[6] See his Preface to the Gospels, addressed to Damasus.

[7] Aug. *Ep.* ii. 82, § 35. He deprecates the change of *cucurbita* into *hedera* in Jon. iii. 6 ff. on the ground that the LXX. doubtless had good reasons for translating the Hebrew word by κολόκυνθα: "non enim frustra hoc puto LXX. posuisse, nisi quia et huic simile sciebant."

hermeneutics of the Ancient Church. The exegesis is often obviously wrong, and sometimes it is even grotesque ; but it illustrates the extent to which the authority of the LXX. became a factor in the thought and life of the Church both in ante-Nicene and early post-Nicene times. A careful study of these passages will place in the hands of the young student of patristic literature a key which may unlock many of his difficulties.

Gen. i. 2 ἡ δὲ γῆ ἦν ἀόρατος καὶ ἀκατασκεύαστος. Iren. i. 18. 1 τὸν ἀόρατον δὲ καὶ τὸν ἀπόκρυφον αὐτῆς μηνύοντα εἰπεῖν Ἡ δὲ γῆ κτλ. Tert. *bapt.* 3 "(aqua) plurima suppetit, et quidem a primordio... terra autem erat invisibilis et incomposita...solus liquor dignum vectaculum Deo subiciebat." **ii. 2** τῇ ἡμέρᾳ τῇ ἕκτῃ. Iren. v. 28. 3 φανερὸν οὖν ὅτι ἡ συντέλεια αὐτῶν τὸ ‚ϛ ἔτος ἐστί. **iv. 7** οὐκ ἐὰν ὀρθῶς προσενέγκῃς κτλ. Iren. iii. 23. 4 "Cain quum accepisset consilium a Deo uti quiesceret in eo quod non recte divisisset eam quae erga fratrem erat communicationem...non solum non acquievit, sed adiecit peccatum super peccatum" ; cf. iv. 18. 3. **xiv. 14** ἠρίθμησεν...δέκα καὶ ὀκτὼ καὶ τριακοσίους (cod. D). Barn. 9. 8 μάθετε ὅτι τοὺς δεκαοκτὼ πρώτους, καὶ διάστημα ποιήσας λέγει τριακοσίους· τὸ δεκαοκτὼ (ΙΗ) ἔχεις Ἰησοῦν· ὅτι δὲ ὁ σταυρὸς ἐν τῷ Τ ἤμελλεν ἔχειν τὴν χάριν λέγει καὶ τριακοσίους (Τ). Cf. Clem. Al. *strom.* vi. 11. Hil. *syn.* 86. Ambr. *de fide* i. *prol.* **xxxi. 13** ἐγώ εἰμι ὁ θεὸς ὁ ὀφθείς σοι ἐν τόπῳ θεοῦ (D^{sil}E). Just. *Dial.* 58 (cf. 60). **xlviii. 14** ἐπέβαλεν...ἐναλλὰξ τὰς χεῖρας. Tert. *bapt.* 8 " sed est hoc quoque de vetere sacramento quo nepotes suos...intermutatis manibus benedixerit et quidem ita transversim obliquatis in se, ut Christum deformantes iam tunc portenderent benedictionem in Christum futuram." **xlix. 10** οὐκ ἐκλείψει ἄρχων ἐξ Ἰούδα καὶ ἡγούμενος κτλ. Justin *Dial.* 52 οὐδέποτε ἐν τῷ γένει ὑμῶν ἐπαύσατο οὔτε προφήτης οὔτε ἄρχων...μέχρις οὗ οὗτος Ἰησοῦς Χριστὸς καὶ γέγονε καὶ ἔπαθεν (cf. *ib.* 120). Iren. iv. 10. 2 "inquirant enim... id tempus in quo defecit *princeps et dux* ex Iuda et qui est *gentium spes*...et invenient non alium nisi Dominum nostrum Iesum Christum annuntiatum." Cypr. *test.* i. 21. Eus. *dem. ev.* i. 4. Cyril. H. xii. 17 σημεῖον οὖν ἔδωκε τῆς Χριστοῦ παρουσίας τὸ παύσασθαι τὴν ἀρχὴν τῶν Ἰουδαίων. εἰ μὴ νῦν ὑπὸ Ῥωμαίους εἰσίν, οὔπω ἦλθεν ὁ Χριστός· εἰ ἔχουσι τὸν ἐκ γένους Ἰούδα καὶ τοῦ Δαβίδ, οὔπω ἦλθεν ὁ προσδοκώμενος.

Exod. xvi. 36 τὸ δὲ γόμορ τὸ δέκατον τῶν τριῶν μέτρων ἦν. Clem. Al. *strom.* ii. 11 ἐν ἡμῖν γὰρ αὐτοῖς τρία μέτρα, τρία κριτήρια μηνύεται, αἴσθησις...λόγος...νοῦς. **xvii. 16** ἐν χειρὶ κρυφαίᾳ πολεμεῖ Κύριος ἐπὶ Ἀμαλὴκ ἀπὸ γενεῶν εἰς γενεάς. Just. *Dial.* 49 νοῆσαι δύνασθε ὅτι κρυφία δύναμις τοῦ θεοῦ γέγονε τῷ σταυρωθέντι Χριστῷ. Iren. iii. 16. 4 "occulte quidem sed potenter manifestans, quoniam absconsa manu expugnabat Dominus Amalech." **xxxiii. 19** καλέσω ἐπὶ τῷ ὀνόματι Κυρίου ἐναντίον σου (AF). Amb.

de Sp. s. **i.** 13 "Dominus ergo dixit quia in nomine suo vocabit Dominum ; Dominus ergo et Patris est nomen et Filii." **Lev. iv.** 5 ὁ ἱερεὺς ὁ χριστός. Tert. *bapt.* 7 "Aaron a Moyse unctus est, unde Christus dicitur a chrismate, quod est unctio, quae Domino nomen accommodavit." **Num. xxiii.** 19 οὐχ ὡς ἄνθρωπος ὁ θεὸς διαρτηθῆναι οὐδὲ ὡς υἱὸς ἀνθρώπου ἀπειληθῆναι. Cypr. *test.* ii. 20 [under the heading "Quod cruci illum fixuri essent Iudaei"]. **xxiv.** 17 ἀνατελεῖ ἄστρον ἐξ Ἰακώβ, καὶ ἀναστήσεται ἄνθρωπος ἐξ Ἰσραήλ. Eus. *dem. ev.* i. 3, 6. Cypr. *test.* ii. 10 [under the heading, "Quod et homo et Deus Christus," &c.].

Deut. xxviii. 66 ἔσται ἡ ζωή σου κρεμαμένη ἀπέναντι τῶν ὀφθαλμῶν σου...καὶ οὐ πιστεύσεις τῇ ζωῇ σου. Tert. (*Jud.* 11) quotes this as "*Erit vita tua pendens*" in ligno *ante oculos tuos; et non credes vitae tuae*," explaining the words of the "signi sacramentum...in quo vita hominibus praestruebatur, in quo Judaei non essent credituri." Cf. Cyril H. xiii. 19 ὅτι ἡ ζωὴ ἦν ἡ ἐπὶ τοῦ ξύλου κρεμασθεῖσα Μωσῆς ἀποκλαιόμενός φησι κτλ. **xxxii.** 8 ἔστησεν ὅρια ἐθνῶν κατὰ ἀριθμὸν ἀγγέλων θεοῦ. Justin (*dial.* 131) cites the last three words as κ. ἀριθμοὺς υἱῶν Ἰσραήλ, adding οἱ ἑβδομήκοντα ἐξηγήσαντο ὅτι Ἕστησεν ὅ. ἐθνῶν κ. ἀριθμὸν ἀγγ. θεοῦ· ἀλλ᾽ ἐπεὶ καὶ ἐκ τούτου πάλιν οὐδέν μοι ἐλαττοῦται ὁ λόγος, τὴν ὑμετέραν ἐξήγησιν εἶπον. Iren. iii. 12. 9, quoting the LXX., comments : "populum autem qui credit Deo iam non esse sub angelorum potestate."

Jos. v. 3 ἐποίησεν Ἰησοῦς μαχαίρας πετρίνας ἀκροτόμους καὶ περιέτεμεν τοὺς υἱοὺς Ἰσραήλ. Tert. *Jud.* 9 "circumcisis nobis petrina acie, id est, Christi praeceptis (petra enim Christus multis modis et figuris praedicatus est)."

3 Regn. xxii. 38 ἀπένιψαν τὸ αἷμα ἐπὶ τὴν κρήνην Σαμαρείας... καὶ αἱ πόρναι ἐλούσαντο ἐν τῷ αἵματι : Amb. *de Sp. s.* 1.16 "fidelis ad puteum (Gen. xxiv. 62), infidelis ad lacum (Jer. ii. 13)...meretrices in lacu Jezabel se cruore laverunt."

Ps. ii. 12 δράξασθε παιδείας. Cyp. *test.* iii. 66 "*continete[1] disciplinam*" [under the heading "Disciplinam Dei in ecclesiasticis praceptis observandam"]. **iv.** 7 ἐσημειώθη ἐφ᾽ ἡμᾶς τὸ φῶς τοῦ προσώπου σου. Amb. *de Sp.* 1. 14 "quod est ergo *lumen signatum* nisi illius signaculi spiritalis *in quo credentes signati* (inquit) *estis Spiritu promissionis sancto[2]*." **vi.** 6 ἐν δὲ τῷ ᾅδῃ τίς ἐξομολογήσεταί σοι; Cypr. *test.* iii. 114 [under the heading "Dum in carne est quis, exhomologesin (cf. *Stud. Bibl.* iv. 282, 290 n.) facere debere"]. **ix. tit.** εἰς τὸ τέλος. Hil. *ad loc.* "intellegendum quotiens qui titulos habent *in fine*, non praesentia in his sed ultima contineri." **Ib.** ὑπὲρ τῶν κρυφίων τοῦ υἱοῦ. Orig. *ad loc.* κρύφιά ἐστι γνῶσις ἀπόρρητος τῶν περὶ Χριστοῦ τοῦ ἀλη-

---

[1] v.l. *adprehendite*.　　　　　　　　[2] *Eph.* i. 13.

θινοῦ θεοῦ μυστηρίων. Athan. *ad loc.* λέγει Ὑπὲρ τῶν ἀκαταλήπτων μυστηρίων τοῦ υἱοῦ. **xxi. 7.** See under Hab. ii. 11. **30** καὶ ἡ ψυχή μου αὐτῷ ζῇ. Iren. v. 7. 1 "tamquam immortali substantia eius existente." **xxxii. 6** τῷ λόγῳ τοῦ κυρίου...τῷ πνεύματι τοῦ στόματος αὐτοῦ. See Iren. iii. 8. 3, Tert. *Prax.* 7, Cypr. *test.* ii. 3, Ambr. *de Sp. s.* iii. 11, Hil. *trin.* xii. 39. **xliv. 1** ἐξηρεύξατο ἡ καρδία μου λόγον ἀγαθόν. Tert. *Prax.* 7 "solus ex Deo genitus, proprie de vulva cordis ipsius secundum quod et Pater ipse testatur Eructavit cor meum sermonem optimum." *Marc.* ii. 4 "adhibet operi bono optimum etiam ministrum, sermonem suum." Cf. Cypr. *test.* ii. 3. **lxxxvi. 4** μνησθήσομαι Ῥαάβ. Cyril. H. ii. 9 ὦ μεγάλης τοῦ θεοῦ φιλανθρωπίας καὶ πορνῶν μνημονευούσης ἐν γραφαῖς (the LXX. having transliterated רחב and רהב alike). Cf. Hieron. *comm. in Ps.* ad loc. **Ib. 5** Μήτηρ Σειὼν ἐρεῖ ἄνθρωπος, καί Ἄνθρωπος ἐγενήθη ἐν αὐτῇ, καί Αὐτὸς ἐθεμελίωσεν αὐτὴν ὁ ὕψιστος. Tert. *Prax.* 27 "invenimus illum directo et Deum et hominem expositum, ipso hoc psalmo suggerente quoniam Deus homo natus est in illa, aedificavit eam voluntate Patris"; cf. *Marc.* iv. 13 "'Mater Sion' dicet homo, et 'homo factus est in illa' (quoniam Deus homo natus est)...aedificaturus ecclesiam ex voluntate patris." Hieron. *comm. in Pss.* (ed. G. Morin) *ad loc.*: "pro 'mater Sion' LXX. interpretes transtulerunt: 'numquid Sion (μὴ τῇ Σ.) dicat homo?'...sed vitiose P litera graeca addita fecit errorem[1]." Jerome however retains the interpretation 'homo Christus,' which depends on the LXX. reading ἄνθρωπος. **lxxxvii. 6** ἐν νεκροῖς ἐλεύθερος. Cyril. H. x. 4 οὐκ ἀπομείνας ἐν νεκροῖς, ὡς πάντες ἐν ᾅδῃ, ἀλλὰ μόνος ἐν νεκροῖς ἐλεύθερος. **xci. 13** δίκαιος ὡς φοίνιξ ἀνθήσει. Tert. *res. carn.* 13 "id est de morte, de funere, uti credas de ignibus quoque substantiam corporis exigi posse" (cf. Clem. R. 1 Cor. 25, Lightfoot, p. 85 n.). **xcv. 5** πάντες οἱ θεοὶ τῶν ἐθνῶν δαιμόνια. Just. *dial.* 55 οἱ θεοὶ τῶν ἐθνῶν...εἴδωλα δαμονίων εἰσίν, ἀλλ' οὐ θεοί (cf. ib. 79, 83). Iren. iii. 6. 3. Tert. *idololatr.* 20. Cypr. *test.* iii. 59. **Ib. 10** ὁ κύριος ἐβασίλευσε [ἀπὸ τοῦ ξύλου]. Just. *apol.* i. 41, *Dial.* 73 f.[2] Tert. *Marc.* iii. 19; *Jud.* 10 "age nunc, si legisti penes prophetam in psalmis: *Deus regnavit a ligno*, expecto quid intelligas, ne forte lignarium aliquem regem significari putetis et non Christum." *ib.* 13 "unde et ipse David regnaturum ex ligno dominum dicebat." Auctor *de montibus Sina et Sion* 9 "Christus autem in montem sanctum ascendit lignum regni sui." Cf. Barn. 8 ἡ βασιλεία Ἰησοῦ ἐπὶ ξύλου. **xcviii. 5** προσκυνεῖτε τῷ ὑποποδίῳ τῶν ποδῶν αὐτοῦ. Ambr. *de Sp. s.* iii. 11 "per *scabellum* terra intelligitur, per terram autem caro Christi quam hodieque in mysteriis adoramus, et quam Apostoli in Domino Jesu...adorarunt." Cf. Aug. *ad loc.* **cvi. 20** ἀπέστει-

---

[1] Cf. the *Tractatus in Psalmos*, p. 402.
[2] See above, p. 424, n., and cf. Deut. xxviii. 66.

λεν τὸν λόγον αὐτοῦ καὶ ἰάσατο αὐτους. Cypr. *test.* ii. 3 [under
the heading "Quod Christus idem sit sermo Dei"]. **cix.** 3ᵇ ἐκ
γαστρὸς πρὸ ἑωσφόρου ἐξεγέννησά σε. Just. *apol.* i. 45, *dial.* 32.
Tert. *Marc.* v. 9 "nos edimus evangelia...nocturna nativitate
declarantia Dominum ut hoc sit *ante luciferum*...nec *generavi
te* edixisset Deus nisi filio vero...cur autem adiecit *ex utero*...
nisi quia curiosius voluit intellegi in Christum *ex utero generavi
te*, id est, ex solo utero sine viri semine?" Cypr. *test.* i. 17.
Cyril. H. vii. 2 ἅπερ ἐπὶ ἄνθρωπων ἀναφέρειν πάσης ἀγνωμοσύνης
ἀνάπλεων. xi. 5 τὸ 'σήμερον' (Ps. ii. 7) ἄχρονον, πρὸ πάντων τῶν
αἰώνων· ἐκ γαστρὸς πρὸ ἑωσφόρου κτλ. Cf. Athan. *or. c. Ar.* iv.
27 f.

Prov. viii. 22 Κύριος ἔκτισέν με ἀρχὴν ὁδῶν αὐτοῦ. Just. *dial.*
61. Iren. iv. 20. 3. Tert. *Prax.* 7. Cypr. *test.* ii. 1 [under the
heading *Christum...esse sapientiam Dei, per quam omnia facta
sunt*]. Hil. *trin.* xii. 45 "quaerendum est quid sit natum ante
saecula Deum rursum in initium viarum Dei et in opera
creari." Cf. Athan. *or. in Ar.* ii. 16 ff. **xxii.** 20 καὶ σὺ δὲ
ἀπόγραψαι αὐτὰ σεαυτῷ τρισσῶς. Orig. *Philoc.* 1. 11 (*de princ.* iv.)
οὐκοῦν τριχῶς ἀπογράφεσθαι δεῖ εἰς τὴν ἑαυτοῦ ψυχὴν τὰ τῶν ἁγίων
γραμμάτων νοήματα.

Job xl. 14 πεποιημένον ἐνκαταπαίζεσθαι ὑπὸ τῶν ἀγγέλων αὐτοῦ.
Applied to the Devil by Cyr. H. *cat.* viii. 4.

Hos. xii. 4 (A) ἐν τῷ οἴκῳ μου εὕροσάν με. Tert. *Marc.* iv. 39
"per diem in templo docebat ut qui per Osee praedixerat," &c.
(For the reading of B, cf. Orig. *Philoc.* viii. 1.)

Amos ix. 6 ὁ οἰκοδομῶν εἰς τὸν οὐρανὸν ἀνάβασιν αὐτοῦ. Tert.
Marc. iv. 34 "aedificantem illis ascensum suum in caelum."

Hab. ii. 11 λίθος ἐκ τοίχου βοήσεται καὶ κάνθαρος ἐκ ξύλου
φθέγξεται αὐτά. Ambr. *in Luc.* xxiii. "bonus vermis qui haesit
in ligno (Ps. xxi. 7), bonus scarabaeus qui clamavit e ligno...
clamavit quasi scarabaeus *Deus Deus meus*"; *or. de obitu Theo-
dosii* 46 "[Helena] adoravit illum qui pependit in ligno...illum
(inquam) qui sicut scarabaeus clamavit ut persecutoribus suis
Pater peccata donaret." Hieron. *in Abac., ad loc.* "quidam e
nostris vermem in ligno loquentem illum esse aiunt qui dicit in
Psalmo (xxi. 7) *Ego natus sum vermis et non homo.*" **iii. 2** ἐν
μέσῳ δύο ζῴων γνωσθήσῃ. Tert. *Marc.* iv. 22 "in medio duo
animalium cognosceris, Moysi et Eliae." Eus. *dem. ev.* vi. 15
δύο ζωὰς (reading ζωῶν in text) τοῦ προφητευομένου δηλοῦσθαι
ἔφαμεν, μίαν μὲν τὴν ἔνθεον, θατέραν δὲ τὴν ἀνθρωπίνην.

Zach. vi. 12 ἰδοὺ ἀνήρ, Ἀνατολὴ ὄνομα αὐτῷ. Just. *dial.* 106,
121. Tert. *Valent.* 3 "amat figura Spiritus sancti orientem,
Christi figuram."

Isa. i. 22 οἱ κάπηλοί σου μίσγουσι τὸν οἶνον ὕδατι. Iren. iv.
12. 1 "ostendens quod austero Dei praecepto miscerent seniores
aquatam traditionem." **iii. 9 f.** οὐαὶ τῇ ψυχῇ αὐτῶν, διότι βεβού-

λευνται βουλὴν πονηρὰν καθ' ἑαυτῶν εἰπόντες Δήσωμεν (v.l. ap. Justin., al. ἄρωμεν) τὸν δίκαιον, ὅτι δύσχρηστος ἡμῖν ἐστιν. Barn. vi. 7, Just. *dial.* 17, 133, 136 f. Tert. *Marc.* iii. 22. Cyril H. xiii. 12. **vii. 14** ἡ παρθένος. Just. *dial.* 43, 67, 71, 84. Iren. iii. 21. 1 ff. Tert. *Marc.* iii. 13, iv. 10. Cypr. *test.* ii. 9. Eus. *dem. ev.* vii. 1. Cyr. H. xii. 21. **ix. 6** μεγάλης βουλῆς ἄγγελος. Hil. *trin.* iv. 23 "qui Angelus Dei dictus est, idem Dominus et Deus est ; est autem secundum prophetam Filius Dei *magni consilii angelus.*" **x. 23** λόγον συντετμημένον ποιήσει Κύριος. Tert. *Marc.* iv. 4 "compendiatum est enim novum testamentum et a legis laciniosis oneribus expeditum" (cf. iv. 16). **xxx. 4** ὅτι εἰσὶν ἐν Τάνει ἀρχηγοὶ ἄγγελοι πονηροί. Just. *dial.* 79 πονηροὺς ἀγγέλους κατῳκηκέναι καὶ κατοικεῖν λέγει καὶ ἐν Τάνει, τῇ Αἰγυπτίᾳ χώρᾳ. **xlv. 1** οὕτως λέγει Κύριος ὁ θεὸς τῷ χριστῷ μου Κύρῳ [read as κυρίῳ]. Barn. xii. 11, Tert. *Prax.* 28, *Jud.* 7, Cypr. *test.* 1. 21. **Ib. 14** καὶ ἐν σοὶ προσεύξονται. Ambr. *de Sp. s.* ii. 8 "in Christo orare nos debere Deus Pater dicit." **liii. 3** ἄνθρωπος ἐν πληγῇ ὤν. Tert. *de carne Chr.* 15. **Ib. 8** τὴν γενεὰν αὐτοῦ τίς διηγήσεται; Eus. *h. e.* i. 2. **liv. 15** προσήλυτοι προσελεύσονταί σοι δι' ἐμοῦ. Ambr. *de Sp. s.* ii. 9 "Deus Pater ad Filium dicit: *Ecce proselyti venient ad te per me.*" **lx. 17** δώσω τοὺς ἄρχοντάς σου ἐν εἰρήνῃ καὶ τοὺς ἐπισκόπους σου ἐν δικαιοσύνῃ. Iren. iv. 26. 5 τοιούτους πρεσβυτέρους ἀνατρέφει ἡ ἐκκλησία, περὶ ὧν καὶ προφήτης φησίν Δώσω κτλ. Cf. Clem. R. 1 Cor. 42. **lxiii. 1** ἐρύθημα ἱματίων ἐκ Βόσορ. Hieron. *comm. in Isa.* ad loc. "quod multi pro errore lapsi putant de carne (בשר) Domini intellegi." **Ib. 9** οὐ πρέσβυς οὐδὲ ἄγγελος, ἀλλ' αὐτὸς ἔσωσεν αὐτούς. Iren. iii. 20. 4 "quoniam neque homo tantum erit qui salvat nos neque sine carne (sine carne enim angeli sunt)." Tert. *Marc.* iv. 22 "*non legatus,* inquit Esaias, *nec nuncius, sed ipse* Deus *salvos eos faciet,* ipse iam praedicans et implens legem et prophetas."

Jer. xi. 19 δεῦτε καὶ ἐμβάλωμεν ξύλον εἰς τὸν ἄρτον αὐτοῦ. Tert. *Marc.* iii. 19 "utique 'in corpus'...sic enim Deus in evangelio... revelavit, panem corpus suum appellans." Cypr. *test.* ii. 20. **xvii. 9** ἄνθρωπός ἐστιν, καὶ τίς γνώσεται αὐτόν; Iren. iii. 18. 3, 19. 2, iv. 33. 11; Tert. *carn. Chr.* 15, *Jud.* 14.

Bar. iii. 38 μετὰ τοῦτο ἐπὶ τῆς γῆς ὤφθη καὶ ἐν τοῖς ἀνθρώποις συνανεστράφη. Cyril. H. xi. 15 βλέπεις θεὸν μετὰ τὴν Μωσέως νομοθεσίαν ἐνανθρωπήσαντα;

Lam. iv. 20 πνεῦμα προσώπου ἡμῶν χριστὸς Κύριος συνελήμφθη ἐν ταῖς διαφθοραῖς αὐτῶν. Just. *apol.* i. 55. Iren. iii. 10. 11. Tert. *Marc.* iii. 6 "Christum, spiritum scilicet creatoris, sicut propheta testatur" &c. *Prax.* 14 "ergo si Christus personae paternae spiritus est, merito spiritus cuius persona erat (id est Patris) eum faciem suam ex unitate scilicet pronuntiavit." Cyril. H. xiii. 7. Ambr. *de Sp. s.* 1. 9 "et Christus spiritus dicitur quia Ieremias dixit," &c.

From these specimens it is clear that the Ancient Church was profoundly influenced by the Greek Old Testament in a variety of ways. Two may be mentioned here. (1) The Alexandrian Greek with its daughter-version, the Old Latin, supplied the basis of a practical interpretation which, notwithstanding numerous errors of text and of treatment, ministered to the religious life of the Christian Society. It was from the LXX. version and not from the official Hebrew of the Synagogue that the pre-Hieronymian Church derived her devotional use of the Old Testament, as it is on the whole the Greek and not the Hebrew Bible which still supplies the Roman Breviary and the Anglican Prayer-book with the substance of their liturgical Psalters. The Alexandrian School based its exegetical work upon the LXX., and the errors and obscurities of the version often yielded materials peculiarly adapted to the requirements of the allegorists; whilst the School of Antioch was no less whole-hearted in its devotion to the old Alexandrian version[1]. This spirit of loyalty to the LXX. continued to the age of the later Greek expositors; it is reflected in the *catenae*, and it fundamentally affects the traditional interpretation of the Old Testament throughout the orthodox East. Even in the West, through the spread of the Greek exegesis, and the use of the Old Latin version by the earlier Latin fathers, it has acquired a predominant influence. Thus, for good or for evil, the popular interpretation of the O. T. has been moulded by the LXX. rather than by the Hebrew text. (2) The LXX. supplied the Ancient Church with controversial weapons at two great crises in her history—during the early struggle with the rival forces of Monotheism, Judaism, Marcionism, and the various schools of Gnosticism, and in the long conflict with Arianism. Arians

---

[1] For Chrysostom's use of the LXX. see F. H. Chase, *Chrysostom: a study in the history of Biblical Interpretation*, p. 28 ff. (Cambridge, 1887); and for Theodore of Mopsuestia, cf. H. Kihn, *Th. v. Mops.*, p. 87 ff. (Freiburg i. B., 1880).

as well as Catholics appealed to the Alexandrian version.
Thus Arius did not hesitate to argue from Joel ii. 25, LXX.
(ἡ ἀκρὶς καὶ...ἡ κάμπη ἡ δύναμίς μου ἡ μεγάλη) that the Son
is the Power of God in no higher sense than any other agency
by which great effects are wrought upon the face of nature[1].
Both parties had recourse to Prov. viii. 22, where the LXX.
rendering of קָנָנִי by ἔκτισέν με seemed to Arius to justify the
statement that the Logos Himself had a beginning of existence,
like the created universe[2]. Unconvincing as such arguments
are now, they had an overwhelming weight in the fourth
century, and Hilary speaks as if the cause of orthodoxy might
be saved by wresting this crucial passage out of the hands of
the Arians (*de Trin.* xii. "hic hiemis eorum maximus fluctus
est, haec tortuosa turbinis gravis unda est, quae excepta a
nobis et securo navigio infracta, usque ad ipsum nos tutis-
simum portum optati litoris prosequetur"). Neither the con-
troversies of the second nor those of the fourth century can
be fully understood without an appreciation of the place which
the Greek Old Testament occupied in the thought and language of the Ancient Church.

3. Familiarity with the LXX. is not less essential to the
student of the devotional life of the Early Church. The Greek
Liturgies, especially perhaps in the oldest parts, are steeped
in the language of the Greek Old Testament. (*a*) The prayers
of the Psalter are worked into their text, often with little or
no change; e.g. *St Clement* (B. 5)[3] δὸς αὐτοῖς καρδίαν καινὴν
καὶ πνεῦμα εὐθὲς ἐγκαίνισον ἐν τοῖς ἐγκάτοις αὐτῶν (Ps. l. 12);
ib. (B. 8) καὶ ἀποδώσῃ αὐτοῖς τὴν ἀγαλλίασιν τοῦ σωτηρίου καὶ
πνεύματι ἡγεμονικῷ στηρίσῃ αὐτούς (Ps. l. 14); *St James* (B. 37)
σῶσον ὁ θεὸς τὸν λαόν σου καὶ εὐλόγησον τὴν κληρονομίαν σου

---

[1] Fragment of the *Thalia*, in Athan. *or. c. Ar.* i. 6.
[2] *Ib.* ἀρχὴν τοῦ κτίζεσθαι ἔσχε καὶ αὐτός.
[3] The references are to the pages of Mr Brightman's *Liturgies, Eastern
and Western,* i. (Oxford, 1896).

(Ps. xxvii. 9)[1]; *ib.* (B. 55) ἐπιλαβοῦ ὅπλου καὶ θυρεοῦ καὶ
ἀνάστηθι εἰς τὴν βοήθειάν μου (Ps. xxxiv. 2); *St Mark* (B. 117)
ἐξαπόστειλον τὸ φῶς σου καὶ τὴν ἀλήθειάν σου (Ps. xlii. 3)...καὶ
ταχὺ προκαταλαβέτωσαν ἡμᾶς οἱ οἰκτειρμοί σου, Κύριε (Ps.
lxxviii. 8). (*b*) Many of their magnificent addresses to God
and to Christ are from the LXX. e.g. *St Clement* (B. 12)
Κύριε παντοκράτωρ, ὕψιστε, ἐν ὑψηλοῖς κατοικῶν, ἅγιε ἐν ἁγίοις
ἀναπαυόμενε, ἄναρχε, μόναρχε (Isa. lvii. 15 + 3 Macc. ii. 2);
ib. (B. 24) ὁ μέγας, ὁ μεγαλώνυμος (Jer. xxxix. 19); *St James*
(B. 44) ὁ ἐν ὑψηλοῖς κατοικῶν καὶ τὰ ταπεινὰ ἐφορῶν (Ps.
cxii. 5 f.); *St Mark* (B. 137) ὁ καθήμενος ἐπὶ τῶν χερουβίμ
(Ps. lxxix. 2); *Sarapion* (J. Th. St. i.) θεὲ τῆς ἀληθείας (Ps.
xxx. 6); τῶν δυνάμεων (Ps. lviii. 6); τῶν πνευμάτων (Num.
xvi. 22). (*c*) Passing allusions are made to the LXX., sometimes difficult to explain without its aid, e.g. *St Clement*
(B. 6) ὁ τὸν ἀνθρωποκτόνον ὄφιν δεσμώτην παραδοὺς ἡμῖν ὡς
στρουθίον παιδίοις (cf. Job xl. 14); *ib.* (B. 15) λόγον θεὸν
...ἄγγελον τῆς μεγάλης βουλῆς σου (Isa. ix. 6); *St James*
(B. 55) τῶν τὸ ἅγιόν σου θυσιαστήριον κυκλούντων διακόνων
(Ps. xxv. 6); *ib.* (B. 57) ἐν χώρᾳ ζώντων (Ps. cxiv. 9); *St Mark*
(B. 126) εἰσόδους καὶ ἐξόδους ἡμῶν ἐν πάσῃ εἰρήνῃ κατακόσμησον
(1 Regn. xxix. 6: Ps. cxx. 8); *ib.* (B. 133) ἐξ ἑτοίμου κατοικητηρίου σου (Exod. xv. 17; 3 Regn. viii. 39 ff.); *St Basil*
(B. 335) ἡ ἐλπὶς τῶν ἀπηλπισμένων (Judith ix. 11); *Sarapion:*
ὁ θανατῶν καὶ ζωογονῶν (1 Regn. ii. 6). (*d*) Much of the
technical phraseology of the Liturgies is from the LXX.: e.g.
τὰ ἅγια (Lev. xxii. 2), ἀναφορά (Num. iv. 19), δῶρα (Gen. iv. 4),
θυσία (Gen. iv. 3), λειτουργία (Exod. xxxvii. 19), θυσία αἰνέσεως
(Lev. vii. 3 f., Ps. xlix. 14, 23), πρόθεσις (Exod. xxxix. 18),
προκείμενα (Lev. xxiv. 7), προσφορά (3 Regn. vii. 34), τελειοῦν
(Exod. xxix. 9). (*e*) The same is true with regard to some of
the oldest Eucharistic formulae, e.g. the *Preface* and *Sanctus*[2]

---

[1] Cf. *St Basil* (B. 311).
[2] The composite quotation in Clem. R. 1 Cor. xxxiv. (Dan. vii. 10 +

which are based on Isa. vi. 2—3, the *Kyrie eleison* (Psalms, *passim*), the *Gustate* (Cyril H. *myst.* v. 20)[1].

4. The Greek terminology of Christian Doctrine is largely indebted to the Alexandrian translators. It is true that in this case most of the technical language of theology has passed through the New Testament and received there a fuller preparation for the use of the Church : and the influence of Greek philosophy and of Gnostic speculation must also be borne in mind by the student of the language of dogma. But it is perhaps even more important that he should trace it back to its source in the Greek Old Testament, which was far more familiar to Christian teachers of the first three centuries than the writings of Plato or of the schools of Basileides and Valentinus. The patristic use of such terms as ᾅδης, ἀνάστασις, εἰκών, ἐκκλησία, ἐφόδιον, θυσία, θυσιαστήριον, Κύριος, λόγος, μονογενής, ξύλον, οὐσία, παντοκράτωρ, παντοδύναμος, παράδεισος, πνεῦμα ἅγιον, πίστις, προσφορά, σάρξ, σοφία, ὑπόστασις, φύσις, φῶς, χάρις, can best be understood by the student who begins by investigating their use in the Septuagint.

Indirectly, but not less extensively, the earliest Latin theology drew a store of theological language from the LXX. Such words as *aeternalis, altare, benedictio, congregatio, converti, daemonium, eleemosyna, exomologesis, glorificare, hostia, iustitia, misericordia, oblatio, propitiatio, sacerdos, sacrificium, salvare, testamentum, unicus, viaticum,* are examples which might easily be multiplied. In the case of some of these terms (e. g. *sacerdos = episcopus, sacrificium = eucharistia*) the choice contributed largely to the development of doctrine, and it is reasonable to suppose that they entered the vocabulary

Isa. vi. 3) is probably an echo of an early Roman Preface. A reference to Dan. *l.c.* in the same connexion is not uncommon; cf. *St Clement* (B. 18), *St Mark* (B. 131), Sarapion (*J. Th. St.* i. 1, p. 105).

[1] To these may perhaps be added the ῍Α ὀφθαλμὸς οὐκ εἶδε (cf. Clem. R. *l.c.*). On *Kyrie eleison* see a paper by Mr Edm. Bishop, in the *Downside Review,* 1899—1900 (published separately by Walters, Weston-super-mare).

of the Western Church through the Latin version of the Septuagint, and not directly from Pagan use. It is noteworthy that Cyprian, whose own style has been said to shew "small respect for the language of the Latin Bible[1]," persistently used these O. T. words in reference to the Christian ministry and the Eucharistic offering.

5. One great monument of ancient Christianity, which still exercises a direct influence over the vast Latin communion, seemed at one time likely to serve as a counteracting force to the Septuagint. It was the deliberate purpose of Jerome to set aside in the West the authority of a daughter-version of the LXX., and to establish in its place, by means of his new Latin Bible, that of the official Hebrew text. Nevertheless, through a variety of causes, the Vulgate, as it is now read by the Latin Church, perpetuates many of the characteristic features of the LXX. (*a*) The Psalter of the Vulgate, as we have seen, is taken from Jerome's second revision of the Old Latin, and not from his *Psalterium Hebraicum*, or translation of the Hebrew text; and the books of Wisdom, Sirach, Baruch, and 1, 2 Maccabees, are given in the Old Latin forms[2]. (*b*) The rest of the Old Testament retains, in the Clementine Vulgate, numerous traces of Septuagint readings and renderings. A few examples may be given: Gen. iii. 15 "tu insidiaberis (τηρήσεις) calcaneo eius"; iv. 8 "dixitque Cain ad Abel fratrem eius Egrediamur foras" (διέλθωμεν εἰς τὸ πεδίον); vi. 5 "non permanebit (οὐ μὴ καταμείνῃ) Spiritus meus in homine"; xlix. 10 "ipse erit expectatio (προσδοκία) gentium"; Num. xxiv. 24 "vastabuntque Hebraeos"; Isa. vii. 14 "ecce virgo concipiet"; Lam. iv. 20 "Spiritus oris nostri Christus dominus"; Zech. iii. 8 "adducam servum meum Orientem" (Ἀνατολήν). It must indeed

---

[1] E. W. Watson, in *Studia Biblica*, p. 194 f.
[2] See above, pp. 98 f., 103.

be remembered that loans from the LXX. are not always of Jerome's borrowing; some of them have made their way into the text of the Vulgate during the course of its transmission (see Vercellone, *Variae lectiones vulgatae Latinae bibliorum editionum*, II. p. viii sqq.). But they hold their place in the authorised Latin Bible of the West, and represent there to this day the influence of the Alexandrian Greek version. (*c*) Many of the words of the Vulgate are more or less complete transliterations of the Greek words used by the LXX. in the same contexts, survivals in great part from the O. L., where they had familiarised themselves to Latin ears[1]. Thus we have *arceuthinus* (2 Chr. ii. 8), *azyma, azymi* (Gen. xix. 3, Exod. xii. 8), *blasphemare* (Lev. xxiv. 11), *cartallus* (Deut. xxvi. 2), *cataplasmare* (Isa. xxxviii. 21), *cauma* (Job xxx. 30), *choerogryllus* (Lev. xi. 5), *christus* (1 Regn. ii. 10), *chytropus* (Lev. xi. 35), *cidaris* (Lev. xvi. 4), *creagra* (2 Chr. iv. 11), *doma* (Jer. xix. 13), *ecclesia* (1 Regn. xvii. 47), *gazophylarium* (Ezech. xl. 17), *holocaustum* (Lev. i. 3), *laganum* (Exod. xxix. 23), *latomus* (3 Regn. v. 15), *luter* (3 Regn. vii. 17 = 30), *naulum* (Jon. i. 3), *nycticorax* (Deut. xiv. 17), *sabbatum* (Exod. xvi. 23), *synagoga* (Num. xxvii. 21), *theristrum* (Gen. xxxviii. 14), *thymiama* (Exod. xxx. 1), *zelotes* (Exod. xx. 5), *zelotypia* (Num. v. 15). If we turn to the books which are directly derived from the O. L., such forms are of course even more numerous; it is enough to specify *acediari* (Sir. vi. 26), *acharis* (Sir. xx. 19 = 21), *allophyli* (Ps. lv. 1), *artaba* (Bel 2), *decachordus* (Ps. xci. 4), *diplois* (Ps. cviii. 29), *eleemosyna* (Tob. xi. 14 = 22), *Iudaismus* (2 Macc. viii. 1), *neomenia* (Ps. lxxx. 4), *palatha* (Judith x. 5), *pentapolis* (Sap. x. 6), *poderis* (Sap. xviii. 24), *rhomphaea* (Sir. xxi. 4), *tympanistria* (Ps. lxvii. 26), *zelare* (Ps. lxxii. 3). Several of these words belong to ordinary post-Augustan Latin, but their use in the Vulgate may fairly be

---

[1] Cf. Kaulen, *Handbuch zur Vulgata* (Mainz, 1870), pp. 83 ff., 130 f., 189 ff.

ascribed to the influence of the LXX., usually through the O. L. The same may be said of many Vulgate reproductions of Hebrew names, e.g. *Moyses, Balaam, Gomorrha, Gabaon, Ierusalem, Pharao,* where the LXX. spelling or pronunciation has been retained, no doubt because of its familiarity.

The influence of the other Greek versions over Jerome's great work, if less subtle and widely diffused, has been more direct, and in the matter of interpretation more important. Thus it was from Aquila that Jerome borrowed the following readings[1]: Exod. ii. 5 *in papyreone* ('A. ἐν μέσῳ τοῦ παπυρεῶνος); Deut. xxxiii. 12 *quasi in thalamo morabitur* ('A. παστώσει); Job xiv. 12 *donec atteratur caelum* ('A. ἕως ἂν κατατριβῇ ὁ οὐρανός); Amos ii. 13 *ego stridebo subter vos, sicut stridet plaustrum* ('A. τριζήσω...τρίζει); Jer. xlix. (xxix.) 19 *ad pulcritudinem robustam* ('A. πρὸς εὐπρέπειαν στερεάν). His debts to Symmachus are still more numerous, and only a few can be given here[2]; Num. xxv. 8 *in lupanar* (Σ. εἰς τὸ πορνεῖον); Jos. x. 42 *uno cepit impetu* (Σ. ἠχμαλώτευσεν μιᾷ ὁρμῇ); Jud. xv. 19 *molarem dentem* (Σ. τὴν μύλην); 1 Regn. ix. 24 *quia de industria servatum est tibi* (Σ. ὅτι ἐπίτηδες τετήρηταί σοι); 4 Regn. ii. 14 *ubi est Dominus deus Eliae etiam nunc?* (Σ. καὶ νῦν); Isa. liv. 8 *in momento indignationis* (Σ. ἐν ἀτόμῳ ὀργῆς); Ezek. viii. 10 *in circuitu per totum* (Σ. κύκλῳ διόλου). It may be added that not a few of the Greek words retained in the Vulgate are from the later versions and not from the LXX. ; e.g. *grabatus* (Amos iii. 12, 'A.), *laicus* (1 Regn. xxi. 4, 'A. Σ. Θ.), *lecythus* (3 Regn. xvii. 12 ff.), *tristegum* (Gen. vi. 16, Σ.).

The subject is too large to be adequately handled in a single chapter. But enough has been said to indicate the nature and extent of the influence which the Greek versions and the Septuagint in particular have exercised over Christian thought and letters, both in East and West, and the conse-

---

[1] Field, *Hexapla*, i., p. xxiv.
[2] For other exx. see Field, *op. cit.*, p. xxxiv.

quent importance of these translations for the student of ecclesiastical history and literature. Bishop Pearson's judgement as to the serviceableness of the LXX. to patristic students will always remain true : " si Graecos patres consulueris, quis eos de rebus divinis disserentes intelliget, qui normam quam semper in animo dum scriberent habuere non ante cognitam atque perspectam habeat?...sed ad Latinos patres non minus quam Graecos recte intelligendos LXX. viralis versio frequens utilis est, imo necessaria[1]." He might have added that in the Latin Christendom of to-day the influence of the Greek versions is not extinct; the echoes of their text, their renderings, and their interpretations are still to be heard in the Bible, the worship, and the theology of the Western Church.

LITERATURE (on the general subject of the chapter). J. Pearson, *Praefatio paraenetica ad V. T. Graecum* (ed. E. Churton, Cambridge, 1855), H. Hody, *de Bibliorum textibus*, III. iii. sqq. J. G. Rosenmüller, *Historia interpretationis librorum sacr. in ecclesia Christiana* (1795—1814). W. R. Churton, *The influence of the Septuagint version upon the progress of Christianity* (Cambridge, 1861). F. W. Farrar, *History of Interpretations* (London, 1886). A. F. Kirkpatrick, *The Septuagint Version* (in *Expositor*, V. vi. 1896).

---

[1] *Praef. paraen.*, ed. E. Churton, p. 25 f.

CHAPTER VI.

TEXTUAL CONDITION OF THE LXX., AND PROBLEMS ARISING OUT OF IT.

1. WHEN the work of the Seventy-two had been accomplished, the Jews of Alexandria (so the legend goes) were bidden to invoke curses, after their manner, upon any who should dare to add to the version or take from it, or alter it in other ways (Aristeas *ad fin.*: ἐκέλευσαν διαράσασθαι, καθὼς ἔθος αὐτοῖς ἐστιν, εἴ τις διασκευάσει προστιθεὶς ἢ μεταφέρων τι τὸ σύνολον τῶν γεγραμμένων ἢ ποιούμενος ἀφαίρεσιν). The imprecation, it has been acutely observed, may point to an early deterioration of the text of the Greek Pentateuch, which the Pseudo-Aristeas desired to check. This inference is insecure, for the story is sufficiently explained by a reference to such passages as Deut. iv. 2, xii. 32[1]; but it is certain that textual corruption began before the Christian era. There are traces of it in the writings of Philo, which cannot be due to blunders in Philo's own text.

E.g. in *quis rer. div. her.* 56 Philo quotes Gen. xv. 15 in the form now universal in MSS. of the LXX. (μετ᾽ εἰρήνης τραφεὶς ἐν γήρει καλῷ), adding the comment: οὐκοῦν...τὸ τέλειον γένος... εἰρήνη καὶ ἐλευθερίᾳ βεβαιοτάτῃ ἐντρεφόμενον κτλ. This is perhaps the most convincing example, but we may add Gen. xvi. 14 Βαράδ = ἐν κακοῖς (*de fug.* 38), i.e. Βαράκ (Luc.); xxi. 6 οὐ χαριεῖταί μοι (*de mut. nom.* 24, where however, as in *legg. all.* ii. 21, iii. 78, *quod det. pot. insid. sol.* 33, Cohn and Wendland read συγχ. μοι with cod. A[phil]); Exod. xvii. 6 ἔστηκα πρὸ τοῦ σε ἐπὶ τῆς πέτρας ἐγχωρεῖν (*de somn.* ii. 32, cf. B πρὸ τοῦ σε[2]...ἐν

[1] Cf. Apoc. xxii. 18 f.
[2] Thackeray, however, points out that this may not be textual corruption; cf. Lev. xviii. 30 πρὸ τοῦ ὑμᾶς, Numb. xiii. 23 πρὸ τοῦ Τάνιν Αἰγύπτου.

Χωρήβ, AF πρὸ τοῦ σε ἐλθεῖν...ἐν X.). Similar corruptions probably exist in some of the N.T. citations, e.g. σῶμα[1] in Heb. x. 5 (Ps. xxxix.=xl. 7), and ἐνοχλῇ[2] for ἐν χολῇ in Heb. xii. 15 (Deut. xxix. 18 (17)). It may be added that double renderings already appear in Philo. E.g. in citing Deut. xix. 14 his MSS. give οἱ πατέρες σου (B) in *de post. Caini* 25, but οἱ πρότεροί σου (A) in *de justitia* 3.

Justin, as we have seen[3], charges his Jewish contemporaries with the deliberate excision of numerous passages in the LXX. which were favourable to their Christian antagonists (*dial.* 71 πολλὰς γραφὰς τέλεον περιεῖλον ἀπὸ τῶν ἐξηγήσεων τῶν γεγενη-μένων ὑπὸ τῶν παρὰ Πτολεμαίῳ γεγενημένων πρεσβυτέρων)[4]. But of the four passages produced in proof of his assertion three are mere glosses, probably of Christian origin; while the fourth, a genuine part of the book of Jeremiah (xi. 19), is now found in all MSS. of the LXX. The charge, though made in good faith, seems to have rested on no better foundation than a natural distrust of the Jews, who in Justin's time were active and bitter opponents of the Church. It is equally improbable that the Greek O. T. was wilfully interpolated by Christians, or that, if they attempted this, the existing text has been affected by it to any appreciable extent. A few traces may be found of the accidental influence of N. T. citations, e.g. the interpolation in Ps. xiii. 3, and perhaps also the reading σῶμα in Ps. xxxix.; but apart from these, the Septuagint, during the first two centuries after Christ, suffered little from Christian hands beyond errors of transcription. What Dr Hort has written in reference to the N.T. is doubtless true also of the LXX.: "accusations of wilful tampering with the text are...

---

[1] As in all our MSS. of Ps. xxxix.
[2] See codd. B*AF* in Deut. *l.c.*
[3] Above, p. 424.
[4] Cf. *dial.* 120; Iren. iii. 21. 1, 5; Eus. *dem. ev.* vi. p. 257 c, d.

not unfrequent in Christian antiquity...but with a single exception, wherever they can be verified they prove to be groundless, being in fact hasty and unjust inferences from mere diversities of inherited text[1]."

Accidental corruptions[2], however, and variations of reading and rendering grew apace, and in the third century Origen complains of the uncertainty of the Biblical text in both its parts[3] (*comm. in Matt.* t. xv. 14 δηλονότι πολλὴ γέγονεν ἡ τῶν ἀντιγράφων διαφορά, εἴτε ἀπὸ ῥαθυμίας τινῶν γραφέων εἴτε ἀπὸ τόλμης τινῶν μοχθηρᾶς τῆς διορθώσεως τῶν γραφομένων εἴτε καὶ ἀπὸ τῶν τὰ ἑαυτοῖς δοκοῦντα ἐν τῇ διορθώσει προστιθέντων ἢ ἀφαιρούντων[4]). Besides intentional changes he notices elsewhere (1) double renderings: *hom. in* 1 *Regn.*, i. 4 "non me latet...quod in aliquibus exemplaribus habetur *erat vir quidam* (ἄνθρωπός τις ἦν, codd. M, 44, &c.), sed in his exemplaribus quae emendatiora probavimus ita habetur, *erat vir unus* (A, ἐγένετο ἄνθρωπος εἷς)"; (2) transpositions: on Jer. xlvii. 4 he has the note ἡ τῶν ο´ ἔν τισι τόποις μετατεθεῖσα ὥστε τὰ πρῶτα ὕστερα καὶ τὰ ὕστερα πρῶτα γενέσθαι; (3) errors of transcription: in Jer. xv. 10, where most of his copies read, as ours do now, ὠφέλησα, ὠφέλησεν, he maintains that this reading is a γραφικὸν

---

[1] *Intr. to N.T. in Greek*, p. 283. The one exception which Dr Hort mentions in connexion with the N.T., the excision practised by Marcion, finds no parallel in the Christian history of the Greek O.T.

[2] A good example of corruption in the Greek is to be found in Num. iii. 24, where all Greek MSS. and the O.L. (Lyons Pentateuch) read Δαήλ *Dael* for Λαήλ (לאל). The name of Joshua's father in the LXX. is Ναυή (O. L. *Nave*), probably in the first instance an error for Ναύν (ΝΑΥΗ for ΝΑΥΝ) = נון. Another well-known instance is the A text of Jud. v. 8 σκέπη νεανίδων σιρομαστῶν ἀνήφθη καὶ σιρομάστης, which, as Ewald pointed out, conceals the doublet (1) σκέπην ἐὰν ἴδω καὶ σιρομάστην, (2) σκέπη ἐὰν ὀφθῇ καὶ σιρομάστης. In 1 Esdr. v. 34 Σαφάγ B is an orthographical error (cf. A).

[3] Though he is referring especially to MSS. of the N.T. his next words shew that the remark is meant to include the LXX.: τὴν μὲν οὖν ἐν τοῖς ἀντιγράφοις τῆς παλαιᾶς διαθήκης διαφωνίαν κτλ. (see, for the rest, above, p. 60).

[4] The gravest instance of ἀφαίρεσις was found in the book of Job; see bove, p. 255.

ἁμάρτημα for ὠφείλησα ὠφείλησεν. Such faults were specially common in the case of proper names : *in Joann.* t. vi. 41 τὸ δ' ὅμοιον[1] περὶ τὰ ὀνόματα σφάλμα πολλαχοῦ τοῦ νόμου καὶ τῶν προφητῶν ἔστιν ἰδεῖν, ὡς ἠκριβώσαμεν ἀπὸ 'Εβραίων μαθόντες, καὶ τοῖς ἀντιγράφοις αὐτῶν τὰ ἡμέτερα συγκρίναντες.

In these criticisms Origen makes no attempt to distinguish between supposed errors which are properly textual, and those which belong to the translation itself. His sole criterion of error was divergence from the official Hebrew, and he assumed that all divergences were textual only, the translation having been originally exact. Nevertheless there can be little doubt that in the course of four centuries many actual corruptions such as he describes must have accumulated in the MSS. of the LXX. The κοινὴ ἔκδοσις[2], as the uncorrected MSS. were called, needed revision, and the literary activity of the third century endeavoured to supply it. At Caesarea in Palestine, at Antioch, in Egypt, independent attempts were made to restore the Septuagint to its primitive purity. But the remedies which were adopted unhappily increased the disease. "The Hexapla, from its very nature, encouraged the formation of mixed texts[3]"; the Hexaplaric recension, divorced from the rest of the work, accentuated this tendency, and the other recensions had a similar effect, although they aimed at the simpler task of correcting the errors of the κοινή.

2. Of the Hexaplaric, Lucianic, and Hesychian recensions some account has been given already[4]. In this place we have only to consider how far it is possible to employ them in the criticism of the text. Their importance to the critic of the LXX. lies in the fact that they were based upon copies of the κοινή, as it was read in Palestine, Syria, and Egypt during the

---

[1] In the context Origen refers to the apparent confusion of Γάδαρα and Γέργεσα in the Gospels.
[2] 'Η κοινὴ ἔκδοσις was also used of the LXX. as compared with the Hebrew text and the other Greek versions: see Nestle in Hastings, *D.B.* iv. 438.   [3] Driver, *Samuel*, p. xlvii.   [4] See above, Part I. c. iii.

third century. But in order to recover from them this un-revised text, two preliminary tasks have to be undertaken. The recensions themselves must first, as far as possible, be restored from existing materials, and we must then proceed to eliminate from them such elements as are recensional, or are due to the reviser's hand.

As to the first of these processes, the materials from which it is proposed to recover the recensions are fairly abundant and varied, but there is much uncertainty as to the attribution of some of them, whilst others present a particular recension only in certain books or portions of books, or with more or less of mixture. The principal authorities for each recension have already been mentioned, but it may be well to collect them here in a compact form.

Hexaplaric[1]. Codd. G, M, Q; 15, 22, 38, 58, 72, 86, 88, 135, 137, 138, 139, 161, 248, 249, 250, 252, 255, 256, 258, 259, 264, 268, 273; Paris Nat. Reg. gr. 129, 131, 132, Ars. 8415, Escurial Σ. 1. 16, Leipzig gr. 361, Zurich c. 11, Athos Vatop. 516, Pantocr. 24, Protaton. 53, Laur. γ. 112. Versions: Sahidic (in part), Armenian (in part), Syro-hexaplar.

Lucianic[2]. Codd. 19, 22, 36, 48, 51, 62, 82, 90, 93, 95, 108, 118, 144, 147, 153, 185, 231, 233, 245, 308; Paris Coisl. gr. 184, Athens bibl. nat. 44. Versions: Old Latin, Philoxenian Syriac, Gothic, Armenian (in part), Slavonic. Fathers: Chrysostom, and other writers of the School of Antioch[3].

Hesychian[4]. Codd. Q, 26, 44, 49, 68, 74, 76, 84, 87, 90, 91, 106, 107, 134, 198, 228[5], 238, 306. Paris suppl. gr. 609. Versions: Bohairic, Armenian (in part). Cyril of Alexandria; other Egyptian writers.

The fragments of the Hexapla have been collected by the labours of a succession of scholars such as P. Morinus, Drusius, Montfaucon, and especially Field, in whose *Origenis Hexaplorum quae supersunt* may be found all the remains of

---

[1] For fuller information see pp. 78, 112 ff., 118 ff., 137 f., 140, 148 ff.

[2] See pp. 82 ff., 93, 116 ff., 148 ff.

[3] Lagarde would add (*Ankündigung*, p. 27) the writings of the Emperor Julian.

[4] See pp. 80, 107 ff., 145, 148 ff., and on the recensions generally cf. Ceriani in *Rendiconti d. R. Ist. Lomb.* (18 Feb. 1886).

[5] 228, and 238 to some extent, fluctuate between Luc. and Hes.; see Oesterley, *Amos*, p. 19 f.

Origen's works which were available in 1875. These editions do not aim at restoring the text of the Hexaplaric LXX. in a connected form. Such a restoration, however, has been attempted in the case of Lucian's recension by Lagarde[1], who desired to see a similar work accomplished for the recension of Hesychius, and an edition in which the two texts should appear facing one another on opposite pages. When this had been done, he proposed (1) to eliminate from these any Hexa plaric matter, by comparing them with the fragments of Aquila, Symmachus, and Theodotion; and (2) to collect the readings which departed most widely from the M. T. By this process he hoped that a point of departure would be reached from which the reconstruction of the LXX. might begin[2].

This scheme is worthy of the great scholar who initiated it, and it was the first serious effort to grasp the problem of scientific reconstruction. But its progress has been checked and perhaps finally stopped by its author's premature death, and its successful accomplishment under any circumstances was at least problematical. So long as no MS. or version presents an unmixed text of either Lucian or Hesychius, and much uncertainty remains as to the exact sources from which they are to be recovered, restorations of this kind cannot be regarded as more than tentative or provisional. Meanwhile, such attempts are not free from danger. Since the publication of Lagarde's edition, there has been a tendency on the part of Biblical students to cite it as 'Lucian,' without reserve. Lagarde himself is careful not to claim finality for his work; he describes it as "editionem...in gravioribus omnibus satis fidam," and looks forward to a more exact

[1] See above, p. 83 f.
[2] An earlier scheme is set forth in *Genesis Graece*, p. 21: "primum molior librum e codicum uncialium qui hexaplares non sunt...consensu haud raro certa coniectura emendando edendum...deinceps propositum est ...editionem hexaplarem curare...tertio loco...adparatum criticum integrum adiungere cogito."

representation of Lucian's text : "conlatis codicibus versioni-
busque eam praebentibus et patrum ea utentibus excussis
efficiendum erit ut etiam in minutioribus adcurate edita
dici merito possit[1]." But this hope has not been fulfilled,
and an edition of Lucian which falls short of exactness in
smaller details cannot be directly used for the critical editing
of the LXX. It has rendered valuable services in other depart-
ments of Biblical study, exhibiting sufficiently the characteristics of this recension, and repeatedly offering, especially in
the four books of Kingdoms, renderings of a Hebrew text
distinct from 𝕸[2]. But in the delicate task of reconstructing
the Greek text, recourse must be had to the actual evidence
which lies behind Lagarde's work. For this purpose it would
seem to be more important to provide texts based upon groups
of MSS., somewhat after the manner of the *Collection of four
important MSS.* (the Ferrar-group) published by Dr T. K. Abbott.
Doubtless such groups would mainly follow the lines of the
ancient recensions, but the identification would not be
complete, and the student would have before him not only the
general result, but the whole of the evidence upon which it
was based.

3. Perhaps a more lasting service was rendered to the
textual criticism of the Septuagint by the axioms and principles
which Lagarde's long study of the problem enabled him to lay
down for the guidance of the student and the future editors.
His early book *Anmerkungen zur griechischen Übersetzung der
Proverbien* (1863) starts with the following axioms : (1) Since
the MSS. of the LXX. are all directly or indirectly the result of
an eclectic process, any attempt to restore the original text
must also proceed on eclectic principles ; and the critic must
chiefly depend upon (*a*) his acquaintance with the style of the

[1] *Praef.* xv.
[2] See Driver, *Samuel,* pp. lii. f., lviii. : I. Hooykas, *Iets over de grieksche
vertaling van het O. T.,* p. 12 ff.

several translators and (*b*) his faculty of referring readings to a Semitic original or, when they are not of Semitic origin, recognising them as corruptions of the Greek archetype. (2) Where the critic has to make choice between two readings, he will do well to prefer (*a*) a free translation to one which is slavishly exact, and (*b*) a translation based upon another Hebrew text to one which represents the M. T. In the preface to his Lucianic Septuagint, published twenty years later, three principles are asserted : (1) A critical text of the Greek O. T. cannot be based on the authority of any one MS. or without regard to the grouping of MSS. ; (2) the restoration of the text common to any one family must not be regarded as more than a step forward in the right direction ; (3) even a critical text, when reached by these or other means, will not be free from the element of uncertainty.

Lagarde's own words are as follows : *Anmerkungen*, p. 3 : "nur drei axiome schicke ich voraus : I. die manuscripte der griechischen übersetzung des alten testaments sind alle entweder unmittelbar oder mittelbar das resultat eines eklektischen verfahrens : darum muss, wer den echten text wiederfinden will, ebenfalls eklektiker sein. Sein maasstab kann nur die kenntniss des styles der einzelnen übersetzer, sein haupthilfsmittel muss die fähigkeit sein, die ihm vorkommenden lesarten auf ihr semitisches original zurückzuführen oder aber als originalgriechische verderbnisse zu erkennen. II. wenn ein vers oder verstheil in einer freien und in einer sklavisch treuen übertragung vorliegt, gilt die erstere als die echte. III. wenn sich zwei lesarten nebeneinander finden, von denen die eine den masoretischen text ausdrückt, die andre nur aus einer von ihm abweichenden urschrift erklärt werden kann, so ist die letztere für ursprünglich zu halten." *Libr. V.T. can.* i. p. xvi. : "tenenda tria esse aio : [1] editionem veteris testamenti graeci curari non posse ad unius alicuius codicis auctoritatem, sed conlatis integris codicum familiis esse curandam : nam familiis non accedere auctoritatem a codicibus, sed codicibus a familiis : [2] unius alicuius familiae editionem nihil esse nisi procedendi ulterius adminiculum : [3] errare qui si quando ipsa manus veterum interpretum inventa sit, in ea legenda adquiesci debere perhibeant, quum conlatis vetera emendandi periculis omnibus indagandum sit quae explicationis veteris testamenti per quatuor saecula fata

fuerint, ut tandem aliquando pateat quam incerta in hoc literarum genere omnia sint, et quam multa nulla alia re nisi coniectura nitantur sciolorum, superstitiosorum, desperantium."

4. These principles have been stated at length, because
they are fruitful in themselves, and they mark an important step
in the progress of LXX. textual criticism. But it is obvious that
they do not form a complete and coherent code of critical
canons. Indeed, Lagarde's later axioms to some extent limit
and correct the earlier, for the recognition of the principle of
grouping the MSS. and taking their evidence according to families
evidently serves as a check upon the extreme eclecticism
recommended in the first axiom of 1863. Nevertheless the
series forms an excellent starting-point for a brief discussion of
the problems which lie before the future critical editor of the
LXX. and the principles by which he must be guided.

By a singular accident the first two printed editions
of the Greek Old Testament exhibit on the whole the
Lucianic and Hesychian texts respectively', whilst the Roman
edition of 1587 and the Oxford edition of 1707—20 are
roughly representative of the two great uncial codices, B and
A. Thus the earlier editors anticipated, though imperfectly and
(in the case of the Complutensian and Aldine Septuagints)
unwittingly, the two methods of editing the Greek O. T.
which are still in use. Of the advantages and disadvantages
of the recensional method, enough has been said. The other,
which consists of printing the text of a single MS., with or
without an *apparatus criticus*, is clearly desirable only in the
case of a MS. which sufficiently represents an important type
of text, and may thus be profitably used as a standard of comparison. Such are the two great uncials already mentioned.

Cod. B, as was pointed out by Dr Hort[2], "on the whole

---

[1] Cornill, *Ezechiel*, p. 79 : "ein wunderbar glücklicher Zufall hätte uns
somit in der Aldine im Grossen und Ganzen den Hesych gegeben, wie die
Complutensis im Grossen und Ganzen den Lucian darstellt."
[2] See *O.T. in Greek*, p. xi. f.

presents the version of the Septuagint in its relatively oldest form." Taken as a whole, it is neutral in its relation to the recensions of the third and fourth centuries; its text is neither predominantly Lucianic nor Hesychian[1] nor Hexaplaric. Cornill, indeed, was at one time led by certain appearances in the B text of Ezekiel to believe that in that prophet at least the scribe of B had extracted his text from the fifth column of the Hexapla, or rather, from the edition of Eusebius and Pamphilus[2]. Lagarde, however, at once pointed out the difficulties which beset Cornill's theory[3], and Hort, in a letter to the *Academy* (Dec. 24, 1887), dismissed it with the remark, "What Cornill does seem to me to have proved is that in Ezekiel B and the LXX. text of the Hexapla have an element in common at variance with most other texts"; adding, "The facts suggest that B in the Septuagint was copied from a MS. or MSS. partially akin in text to the MS. or MSS. from which Origen took the fundamental text for the LXX. column of his Hexapla[4]." Eventually Cornill withdrew his suggestion, observing that the forms of the proper names in B shew no sign of having been influenced by Origen's corrections[5].

If we accept Dr Hort's view, which at present holds the field, the Vatican MS. in the O. T. as a whole carries us back to the third century text known to Origen, and possibly to one much earlier. In other words, not only is the Vatican MS. our oldest MS. of the Greek Bible, but it contains, speaking quite generally, the oldest text. But it would be an error to suppose that this is true in regard to every context or even every book,

[1] This however has been doubted; see Nestle, *Introd. to the Textual Criticism of the N. T.*, pp. 61 f., 183 f.
[2] See his *Ezechiel*, pp. 84, 95. The theory was suggested by an early hypothesis of Lagarde (*Anmerkungen*, p. 3) that the text of B was extracted from a glossed codex.
[3] In *Gött. gelehrte Anzeigen*, 1886 (reprinted in *Mittheilungen*, ii. p. 49 ff.).
[4] On the *provenance* of B and א see Hort, *Intr.*[2], p. 264 ff., Harris, *Stichometry*, p. 71 ff., Robinson, *Euthaliana*, p. 42 ff., and the summary in Kenyon, *Our Bible and the Ancient MSS.*, p. 128.
[5] *Gött. gelehrte Nachrichten*, xxx. (1888, 8, p. 194 ff.).

and a still graver error to treat the text of B as necessarily representing everywhere the original Septuagint. As Mr Burkitt has pointed out[1], "the O. L. and the Hexaplar text convict B here and there of interpolation, especially in Isaiah." "Certainly (he writes in another place[2]) in the books of Kings it is free from some of the gross interpolations which have befallen most other MSS. But it cannot claim to transmit to us an *unrevised* text of the κοινὴ ἔκδοσις. Many of its readings shew marks of irregular revision and the hand of an editor. As a result of this critical process, B sometimes tends to agree with the Massoretic text where other LXX. authorities represent a widely different underlying Hebrew. B also contains a certain number of widely spread corruptions that are of purely Greek origin, which are absent from earlier forms of the LXX. such as the Old Latin[3]." In certain books the general character of B breaks down altogether, i.e. the archetype of B in those books was of another kind. Thus in Judges B was formerly suspected of representing the Hesychian recension[4], whilst a living scholar has hinted that it may give the text of a translation not earlier than the fourth century A.D.[5] The Cambridge editors of the A text of Judges wisely content themselves with " the surmise that [as regards B and A in this book] the true text of the Septuagint is probably contained neither in the one nor in the other exclusively, but must be sought for by comparing in detail, verse by verse, and word by word, the two recensions, in the light of all other available evidence,

---

[1] *Tyconius*, p. cxvii.

[2] *Aquila*, p. 19.

[3] An interesting and plausible specimen of this class of errors occurs in 4 Regn. iii. 21 B, καὶ εἶπον Ὦ (A, with 𝔐, καὶ ἐπάνω). The process of corruption is evident (ΕΠΑΝѠ, ΕΙΠΑΝѠ, ΕΙΠΟΝѠ). In Sirach instances are especially abundant, e.g. xliii. 17 ὠνείδισεν (A, ὠδίνησεν); 23 ἐφύτευσεν αὐτὴν Ἰησοῦς (H. P. 248 ἐφ᾽ ἐν αὐτῇ νήσους); 26 εὐωδία τέλος (248 εὐοδοῖ ὁ ἄγγελος).

[4] Grabe, *ep. ad Millium* (1705).

[5] Moore, *Judges*, p. xlvi.

and especially of the extant remains of the Hexapla[1] "—a remark which is capable of a much wider application[2].

Cod. A, the great rival of cod. B, "exhibits a text which has been systematically corrected so as to agree more closely with the Hebrew[3]." "In all four books of Kings and in some other parts A has been conformed to the Hexaplar text...In fact A is often little more than a transcript of the fourth column of the Hexapla, but without the critical signs by which Origen's additions were marked off from the rest[4]." In other words, adaptation to the Hebrew has been effected not by direct use of the official Hebrew text, but through the medium of Origen's work. Thus, if B represents in part the text which lay before Origen when he began his task, A, at least in the historical books, answers roughly to the result at which he arrived.

Yet A is very far from being, even in the earlier books, a mere reproduction of the Eusebian recension. It has been extensively hexaplarised, but it possesses a large element of ancient readings which are not Hexaplaric, and which it shares, to a great extent, with the Lucianic family. Moreover, as we have already seen, the citations of the LXX. in the N. T. and by Christian writers of the first three centuries, often support the readings of A with a remarkable unanimity[5]. These phenomena point to the presence in A of an underlying text of great antiquity, possibly a pre-Christian recension made in Syria[6]. It must be observed, however, that the text of this MS. is not

---

[1] A. E. Brooke and N. M꜀Lean, *The Book of Judges in Greek acc. to the text of Cod. Alexandrinus* (Cambridge, 1897), p. v.

[2] On the B text of Sirach and Tobit see above, pp. 271, 274.

[3] Driver, *Samuel*, p. l.

[4] Burkitt, *Aquila*, p. 19; cf. p. 53 f. Cf. Silberstein, *Über den Ursprung der im cod. Alex. u. Vaticanus des dritten Königsbuches...überlieferten Textgestalt* (Giessen, 1893).

[5] Above, pp. 395 f., 403, 413, 422.

[6] It is, however, possible that the readings in B, which have no such support and are indeed almost unique, belong to a still earlier text of the LXX., which had not received Palestinian revision. Cf. p. 429.

homogeneous throughout. The Psalms are evidently copied from a Psalter written for ecclesiastical use, and it is interesting to notice how constantly A here appears in company with the later liturgical Psalters R and T, and with the seventh century corrector of א known as א^{c.a}. In the Prophets אAQ are in frequent coalition against B, and in agreement with the group which is believed to be representative of the Hesychian recension.

As to cod. א it is more difficult to form a judgement. We are still dependent for its text on Tischendorf's facsimiles. Moreover, with the exception of a few fragments of Genesis and Numbers, larger portions of 1 Chronicles and 2 Esdras, and the Books of Esther, Judith and Tobit, 1 and 4 Maccabees, this MS. is known to us only in the poetical and prophetical books. Notes at the end of 2 Esdras and Esther claim for the MS. that in those books it was corrected by the aid of a copy of the Hexaplaric text written under the supervision of Pamphilus[1]. But the first hand of א often agrees with A against B, and the combinations אART in the Psalms, אAC in the other poetical books, and אAQ in the Prophets, are not uncommon. In Tobit, as we have seen, א follows a recension which differs widely from B. On the whole, however, it comes nearer to B than any of the other uncials, often confirming its characteristic or otherwise unique readings. Cod. C is yet more fragmentary and its fragments are limited to the poetical books which follow the Psalter.

Thus if a single uncial MS. is to be adopted as a standard of comparison, it is obvious that either A or B must be chosen for the purpose, and B is to be preferred as being freer from Hexaplaric interpolations and offering generally a more neutral text. The latter MS. has therefore been employed by recent editors, and this course is probably the best that can be

---

[1] See above, p. 75. The N. T. has now appeared in collotype, with introduction by Prof. K. Lake (Oxford, 1911).

followed. But the method of editing the text of a single MS. leaves much to be desired, for, as Lagarde rightly insists, no single MS. and no single family of MSS. can be regarded as a trustworthy or sufficient representative of the original LXX.

5. There remains the alternative of constructing a critical text. This can only be done by the scientific use of all existing materials[1]. The task which lies before the critical editor of the LXX. is partly similar to that of the N. T. editor, and partly *sui generis*. The general principles which will guide him are those which have been expounded by Dr Hort in the second part of *Introduction to the N. T. in Greek*[2]. The documents moreover fall into the same three classes : (1) MSS., (2) versions, (3) literary citations; although in the case of the LXX., the versions are 'daughter-versions' and not based upon an original text, and the citations are not limited to post-apostolic Christian writers, but may be gathered also from Philo, Josephus, and the New Testament. But in the application of the principles of criticism to these documents the critic of the LXX. must strike out a path for himself. Here his course will partly be shaped by the fact that he is dealing with a version and not with an original text[3], and by the history of the transmission of the version, which is only to a limited extent identical with that of the transmission of the Greek New Testament.

(*a*) The first business of the critic of the LXX. is to review the documentary evidence which is available for his use. This has been already described at some length (MSS., pp. 122—170; Versions, pp. 87—121; Citations, pp. 369—432). The preliminary work of preparing these materials for use is still in progress. We now have access to photographic reproductions

---

[1] Cf. Nestle, *Zur Rekonstruction der Septuaginta* (in *Philologus*, 1899).
[2] Ed. 2 (1896), pp. 19—72.
[3] The original text may be regarded as the primary document for the text of the version.

of codd. ABGLQ⊕, facsimiles or printed texts of אCDEFHKO RTUYZΓΠ, and collations of the remaining uncials, and of a large number of the cursives. But the facsimiles are more or less inadequate, and the older collations of unpublished MSS. need careful verification. To turn to the versions, the fragments of the Old Latin are now for the most part accessible in carefully edited but scattered texts, and the more important of the Egyptian and Syriac versions have received much attention; but the Armenian, Ethiopic, Arabic, Georgian and Slavonic are still but partially explored. Good progress is being made in the editing of Philo, Josephus, and the Christian fathers, both Greek and Latin. Thus, while much remains to be done in the way of perfecting the *apparatus criticus* of the Greek O. T., there is an abundance of materials ready for immediate use, and every prospect that in a few years the store will be largely increased.

(*b*) When an editor has been found who is competent to undertake reconstruction, he will probably desire to limit himself to that one task, after the example of the editors of the *New Testament in Greek*[1], and his resources, if not as abundant as those of the N. T. editors, will be both sufficient and trustworthy. But with the materials thus ready to his hand, how is he to proceed? As in the case of the New Testament, he will begin by interrogating the history of his text. Here there are certain landmarks to guide him at starting. As we have seen, the three recensions which in the fourth century had a well-defined local distribution, have been connected with groups of extant documents—two of them quite definitely, the third with some probability. Other groups representing less clearly recognised families have emerged from recent enquiries, such as that which yields the text characteristic of the catenae (H. P. 14, 16, 28, 52, 57, 73,

---

[1] Cf. Hort, *Intr.*[2], p. 90.

77, Paris Reg. Gr. 128, and many others), the pair H. P. 54, 75, with which ⊕ and 59 may also to some extent be classed, and the codices which correspond more or less closely with cod. A and cod. B respectively.   It is probable that as the collation and examination of MSS., versions, and fathers proceed, other groups, or other members of the groups already mentioned, will come to light, leaving an ever diminishing number of documents which present a text either too mixed or too peculiar to be classified.

(c) In operating upon the groups thus obtained the critical editor will possess two chief aids towards the discrimination of ancient elements from those which are later or recensional. (1) While the East in Jerome's time was divided between the Lucianic, Hesychian, and Hexaplaric texts, the great Western dioceses, Carthage, Milan, and Rome, read the LXX. under the guise of a Latin version, beneath which originally lay a Greek text anterior to the Hexapla itself.   Consequently, the Old Latin, in its purest types, carries us behind all our existing MSS., and is sometimes nearer to the Septuagint, as the Church received that version from the Synagogue, than the oldest of our uncial MSS.   Readings which have disappeared from every known Greek MS. are here and there preserved by the daughter-version, and in such cases the O. L. becomes a primary authority for the Greek text[1].   But besides these occasional contributions of a direct nature, this version is of the highest value as enabling the critical editor to detect pre-Origenic readings and to distinguish them from those which are later or recensional.   In regard to the latter point the test is not an absolute one, because it is always possible that the reading on which an O.L. rendering is based was one of two or more that were both current in the κοινή before Origen's time.   (2) But the O. L. is not our only witness to the read-

---

[1] Burkitt, *Tyconius*, p. cxvii. f.

ings of the κοινή. Its evidence may often be checked and confirmed by that of the Syro-Hexaplar and the fragments of the Hexaplaric Greek, where the obeli and asterisks distinguish readings which existed in Origen's MSS. from those which were interpolated from other sources, or rewritten with their aid[1].

(*d*) By such means the critic may often satisfy himself that he has reached the text of the Septuagint as it was found in Christian MSS. of the third, perhaps even of the second century. It is another question how far the κοινὴ ἔκδοσις of the Christian Church was identical with the pre-Christian text or texts of Alexandria and Jerusalem. Early citations from the LXX. suggest a diversity of readings and possibly the existence of two or more recensions in the first century, and lead us to believe that many of the variations of our MSS. have come down from sources older than the Christian era.

Here our documentary evidence fails us, and we have to fall back upon the 'internal evidence of readings.' The variants which remain after eliminating Hexaplaric matter, and recensional changes later than the Hexapla, resolve themselves into two classes; viz. (1) readings which affect merely the Greek text, such as (*a*) corruptions obvious or possible, or (*b*) doublets, whether brought together in a conflate text, or existing in different MSS.; and (2) readings which presuppose a difference in the original. In dealing with both classes much help may be obtained from Lagarde's earlier axioms[2]. In detecting corruptions the student must chiefly depend on his faculty of recognising a Semitic original under Greek which does not directly suggest it; in deciding between double renderings, he will set aside that which bears marks of correction or of assimilation to the official Hebrew or to later Greek versions based

---

[1] On this point see Burkitt, *Aquila*, p. 33 f.
[2] Above, p. 484 f.

upon it, choosing that which is freer, less exact, and perhaps less grammatical, as being probably nearer to the work of the original translator. Lastly, when the variants imply divergent Hebrew texts, he will prefer, *ceteris paribus*, that which departs from the Massoretic text. The application of these rules, however, calls for knowledge and judgement of no ordinary kind[1].

6. It cannot be doubted that the future will produce a school of critics competent to deal with the whole question of Septuagint reconstruction, and that a critical edition of the Old Testament in Greek will hereafter take its place on the shelves of the scholar's library by the side of the present *New Testament in Greek* or its successor. Meanwhile some immediate wants may be mentioned here. (1) Several important uncial MSS. still need to be reproduced by photography, particularly codd. א, F, R, V, T; and the process might well be extended to some of the weightier cursives. (2) Texts of which photographs have been published, or of which verified transcripts or collations exist, deserve in some cases detailed examination, with the view of determining their precise character in the several books or groups of books, and their relation to one another and to a common standard, such as the text of B. (3) The stores of fresh Hexaplaric matter which have accumulated during the interval of years since the publication of Field's great book[2], will soon be sufficient to form a supplementary volume, which might also contain the corrections supplied by photography and by the more exact collation of Hexaplaric MSS. (4) Is it too much to hope that the University which has the honour of having issued from its Press the Septuagint of Holmes and Parsons

---

[1] On the scope for conjecture where evidence fails, see Hatch, *Essays*, p. 281, where some other remarks are to be found which deserve attention but need sifting and safeguarding.

[2] See the second *fasciculus* of Dr Redpath's Supplement to the Oxford Concordance.

may see fit to reprint at least the apparatus of that monumental work with such emendations and abbreviations as it may be possible to adopt without seriously interfering with the scope and method of the edition? It is improbable that a collection of all the evidence on so vast a scale will ever be attempted again, and until this has been done, Holmes and Parsons cannot be superseded as a storehouse of facts. (5) A proposal was made by Dr Nestle at the London Oriental Congress of 1892 to compile a '*Variorum* Septuagint,' giving the text of B with marginal variants sufficient to correct the errors of that MS. There can be little doubt that such an edition would be serviceable, especially if the scheme could be so far extended as to include a selection from all the variants, after the manner of the English '*Variorum* Bible.' (6) Every student of the Old Testament will wish success to the undertaking which is now in progress at the Cambridge Press. Although the text of the Larger Septuagint will be simply that of the standard MS. employed in the manual edition, its *apparatus* will for the first time present to the critical scholar the essential documentary evidence, verified with scrupulous care, and arranged in a form at once compendious and helpful to research.

LITERATURE. W. Selwyn, art. *Septuagint*, in Smith's D. B. iii. (London, 1863). P. de Lagarde, *Anmerkungen zur gr. Übersetzung der Proverbien* (Leipzig, 1863); *Genesis Graece* (Leipzig, 1868); *Ankündigung einer neuen Ausgabe der gr. Übersetzung des A. T.* (Göttingen, 1882); *Librorum V. T. canonicorum pars prior* (Göttingen, 1883); review of Cornill's *Ezechiel* in *Gött. gelehrte Anzeigen*, June 1, 1886 (reprinted in *Mittheilungen*, ii. 49 ff., Göttingen, 1887). J. Wellhausen, *Der Text der Bücher Samuelis* (Göttingen, 1871); art. *Septuagint* in *Encycl. Brit.*[9] (London, 1886). C. H. Cornill, *Das Buch des Propheten Ezechiel* (Leipzig, 1886); in *Gött. gelehrte Nachrichten* xxx. (1888, 8, p. 194 ff.). A. Ceriani, *Le recensioni dei LXX. e la versione latina detta Itala* in *Rendiconti del R. Istituto Lombardo* II. xix., xxi. (1883—4); review of the *O. T. in Greek* in *Rendiconti*

ii. xxi., xii. (1888); *De codice Marchaliano* (Rome, 1890). W.
Sanday and F. J. A. Hort, letters in *Academy*, Dec. 10 and 24,
1887. V. Ryssel, *Untersuchungen über die Textgestalt...des
Buches Micha*, p. 175 ff. (Leipzig, 1887). I. Hooykas, *Iets over
de grieksche vertaling van het Oude Testament* (Rotterdam,
1888). H. Oort, *De Lagarde's plan van eene vitgaaf der Septua-
ginta* (? 1882). E. Hatch, *Essays on Biblical Greek*, iv.—vii.
(Oxford, 1889). S. Driver, *Notes on the Hebrew Text of the
Books of Samuel*, Intr. p. xlvii. ff. (Oxford, 1890). A. Dillmann,
Textkritisches zum Buche Ijob (in *Sitzungsberichte d. k. P.
Akademie d. Wiss. zu Berlin*, 1890, liii.). E. Nestle, *The
Variorum Septuagint*, in *Proceedings of Oriental Congress held
at London*, 1892 ; *Urtext* p. 77 f. (1897); *Zur Rekonstruktion
der Septuaginta*, in *Philologus*, N. F., xii. 1 (1899) p. 121 ff.
E. Klostermann, *De libro Coheleth versione Alexandrina* (Kiel,
1892); review of *The O. T. in Greek* in *Gött. gelehrte Anzeigen*
(1895. 4). S. Silberstein, *Über den Ursprung der im Cod. Alex.
u. Vat. des dritten Königsbuches überlieferten Textgestalt* (Giessen,
1893). Bleek-Wellhausen, *Einleitung in das A. T.*, p. 549 ff.
(Berlin, 1893). F. C. Burkitt, *The Rules of Tyconius*, p. cxlii. ff.
(Cambridge, 1894); *The Old Latin and Itala* (Cambridge, 1896);
*Fragments of the Books of Kings according to the translation of
Aquila* (Cambridge, 1897). G. Moore, *Commentary on the Book
of Judges*, p. xliv. ff. H. P. Smith, *Commentary on the Books of
Samuel*, pp. xxx. ff., 402 ff. (Edinburgh, 1899). A. Rahlfs, *Septua-
ginta-Studien*, i.—iii., Göttingen, 1904, 1907, 1911 ; C. F. Burney,
Notes on the Heb. Text of the Books of Kings, Oxford, 1903;
W. O. E. Oesterley, *Studies in...Amos*, Cambridge, 1902 ;
C. C. Torrey, *Apparatus for the criticism of Chronicles, Ezra,
Nehemiah*, in *O. T. and Semitic Studies* (Chicago), xi. ; H. St J.
Thackeray in *J. Th. St.*, xii. 46 ; and many of the works named
on pp. 27, 28 ; 104; 191—4; 262—4; 285—8.

ADDITIONAL NOTES.

P. 10 ff. The 'Letter of Aristeas' can now be read in Mr H. St J. Thackeray's English translation (*J.Q.R.* xv. April 1903, and separately reprinted by Macmillan, 1904), which is furnished with a short introduction and notes, taking account of Wendland's edition and translation. The *ostensible* date of the writing is about 250 B.C.; or earlier, for Philadelphus is apparently spoken of as still living, and the references to his father (§§ 12, 22) would suggest that his reign was not very far advanced. Nor is anything said to imply the death of Eleazar, whose high priesthood is usually dated 292—277 B.C. (see §§ 125, 321). The writer professes, as a Greek at Philadelphus' court (§ 40, cf. 173), to regard the Jews, their country, and their customs, from an outsider's point of view (§§ 3, 6, 112, etc.). But it remains generally agreed, that he betrays himself to be in reality a Jew, writing at a later time. There is, however, some difference of opinion as to the actual date of writing. Schürer, placing it as early as 200 B.C., is supported by Herriot (*Philon le Juif*); Wendland from 96 to 63, rather towards the earlier date; Willrich (in *Judaica*, 1900) as late as A.D. 33; but this view is not generally accepted. Hart (*Ecclesiasticus in Greek*, 243 ff., 263 ff.) finds evidence that the author knew and used the Prologue to the Greek Sirach; which, however, he dates early, some little time after 247 B.C. Wendland also sees some connexion, but accepts the more usual date of the years following 132 B.C. for Ecclesiasticus. Thackeray, who thinks that Hart makes too much of some identities of language, pronounces, on the strength of some linguistic details, as well as on internal grounds, for a date not earlier than the middle of the second century B.C., and perhaps between 140 or 130 B.C. for the earlier, and 80 B.C. for the later limit. Probably 100—80 B.C. fairly represents the resultant of his view and Wendland's.

On the other hand, Mr I. Abrahams (*J.Q.R.* xiv. p. 321 ff., Jan. 1902) defends a date practically the same as Schürer's. He points out that the writer, though a Jew, draws his historical information, and his description of Palestine, from non-Jewish sources, and his 'Table-discourses,' §§ 187—292, from Greek learning and not from Jewish gnomic wisdom. (On this latter point, however, opinions will still differ, as in the case, e.g., of Ecclesiastes.) He adds further, that, though there may be error, if not fraud, in the part assigned to Demetrius Phalereus, yet the 'Letter' has been exposed, through the additions made to the story by Christian writers, to some unfair suspicion; and that the story, as Josephus read it, appears to have presented nothing incredible to his mind. This is, perhaps, as far as anyone can now go in rehabilitating the credit of the 'Letter,' in which, however, a considerable substratum of fact is usually allowed to exist. The view of Wendland and Thackeray probably now commands the most general assent; though some adhere to the position of Schürer and Abrahams.

P. 23. That Aristeas speaks only of the Law may be seen in §§ 3, 10, 46, 171, 176; while the statement of Epiphanius is implicitly contradicted by § 302.

P. 24. If the usual dates for Ecclesiasticus and its Prologue are accepted, a little time must be allowed *after* B.C. 132, the date of the writer's arrival in Egypt, before he could produce his work. Nor need the collections of the Prophets and Hagiographa, though in existence, have been finally completed when he wrote. See Thackeray, *Grammar of O.T. in Greek*, pp. 13, 15 ff. ; also in *J. Th. Stud.* VIII. 262 ff.

P. 34 f. Besides these portions of Aquila, the Amherst Papyrus, I. iii. c., contains Gen. i. 1—5, Aquila as well as LXX. The Rainer fragments of Ps. lxviii. 13, 14, 30—33, lxxx. 11—15 (C. Wessely in *Mélanges Chatelain*, 1910) have been shown by P. Capelle (*Revue Benedictine*, 1911, p. 64 ff.) to be certainly not Aquila, and most probably Symmachus. Dr Nestle (*Exp. Times*, May 1911) also pronounced for Symmachus.

P. 39, note 4. On the possible connexion of abbreviations in MSS. with these methods of writing the Divine Name, see L. Traube, *Nomina Sacra* (Munich, 1907) : Bd 2 of *Quellen und Untersuchungen zur lateinischen Philologie des Mittelalters*.

P. 47 f. The appearance of Theodotion's renderings before his reputed time (as in the N.T. quotations) is not yet satisfactorily explained ; see Thackeray, *Gramm. O.T. in Greek*, p. 15 : 'Critics have...been forced to the conclusion that there must have been, in addition to the loose Alexandrian paraphrase, a third version, re-sembling that of Θ, but made before his time and in use in Palestine in the first century B.C.' Nestle, in *ZNTW*, Nov. 1907, remarks on Schürer's Dilemma, p. 48, note 3 : ' " entweder...vor Theodotion gegeben " muss dahin ergänzt werden " oder ist das Dilemma falsch gestellt, und hat Theodotion das N.T. benützt, nicht umgekehrt." '

P. 55, cf. p. 63. Prof. Burkitt, on 'The so-called Quinta of 4 Kings' (*Proc. Soc. Bibl. Archaeology*, June 1902), says : 'I venture therefore to make the conjecture that the *Quinta* in 4 Kings is... a collection of variants set in the margin of the Hexapla, and that this collection contained, among other things, some notable readings of the genuine LXX.' And above: '...the fragments of the Hexapla in the Ambrosian Library at Milan preserve just such a collection of detached readings in a *fifth column.*'

P. 66. On Eusebius, and the *Quinta* and *Sexta*, see Mercati, *Studi e Testi* 5, v. p. 51 ff.; on the Hexapla see also Kenyon, *Our Bible and the Ancient MSS.*, p. 54 ff., and appendix, p. x, in third edition.

P. 69 ff. For twenty years after Field's great work on the Hexapla appeared, the question of the existence of critical marks in the Hexapla itself remained as he left it. With this is bound up the further question of Origen's actual method; whether the LXX. text in the Hexapla was a revised one, or unrevised. Field pronounced for the former alternative, and for the presence of the critical marks in the Hexapla. His words are (vol. I. p. lii):

'Non desunt quidem qui existiment Origenem priorem viam iniisse: videlicet, ut distinctiones praedictas non in editionem hexaplarem introduceret, sed in aliam seorsim adornatam, qualem hodieque exhibent codex Graecus Sarravianus, et versio P. Telensis Syrohexaplaris. Sed, ut Hieronymi declarationem taceamus, in scholiis Graecis innumera exstant loca, quae contrarium aperte probant; nempe ed. τῶν Ο' hexaplarem non diversam fuisse ab ea quam in exemplaribus modo memoratis hodie manu terimus.'

(Jerome's words are to be found on page 69, note 3, of this book.)

Of late, however, fresh doubts have arisen, perhaps stimulated by the discovery of the Cairo and Milan fragments of copies of the Hexapla itself. The work was so huge (see p. 74) that it had scarcely been suspected that copies had been made; but it is not proved that the fragments represent more than portions, or single books.

Mercati, the discoverer of the Milan palimpsest, gives the first hint of doubt (1896, *Atti d. Accad. d. Scienze*, Torino, XXXI. p. 656):

'Aggiungasi che Origene l' aveva arrichitta di prolegomeni e di scolii, per non dire degli obeli e degli asterischi, coi quali s' ingegnò di rendere anche più visibili le singole parole e particelli crescenti o mancanti nei LXX., rispetto all' Ebraico, se pure questa operazione non fu ristretta alle Tetraple od al testo dei LXX., estratto dall' una delle due collezioni mentovate, secondo che altri ha voluto,' with a note ' E veramente distribuito il testo, come lo è nel palimpsesto Ambrosiano delle Esaple non rimane più tanto necessaria questa aggiunta d' obeli e di asterischi per quanto riguarda l' Esaple, cfr. i prol. dal Field.'

Lietzmann, in his review of the first edition of this work (*G.G.A.* May 1902), raises some similar points; the following is an English rendering of some of his remarks :

'Had the *Urhexapla*, in its LXX. column, the κοινή without corrections or additions, or a text already revised, [and] provided with obeli and asterisks; that is, with the additions from Theodotion? One inclines to take the former view as correct, reflecting that the Hexapla was meant to be the foundation for [future] critical work. Swete depends on Field....Field refers to "innumera loca," but quotes none expressly; and to the difficulty in regard to the transpositions,...which he does not thresh out....Eusebius and Jerome say nothing about critical marks in the fifth column'; Jerome, indeed, says something which points the other way (*praef. Dan.*, ep. 57, 11, and ep. 106). Still the other view may be right...but caution is still imperatively needed.'

The arguments, then, appear to run much as follows:

(1) No critical marks have been found in the fragments discovered ; and this though Jerome has them in the 'Gallican' Psalter, and the 'codices hexapl.' have them. (2) Eusebius and Jerome do not mention them. (3) Field gives practically no examples to support his view. (4, Mercati) The marks were less needed in the Hexapla, where the texts could be seen side by side. (5, Lietzmann) The Hexapla, as a foundation for critical labour, should preferably have had the pure text. (6) The variety of numbers named, Tetrapla, Quintupla, etc., up to eight, indicates a variety of works and copies at any rate in *Psalms*. (7) The Milan fragment is not an exact copy; its last column is not Theod., but Quinta. It had, however, notes and a *catena*, descending from Origen himself.

To these arguments it may be replied (1) that critical marks may have disappeared in the copies as they notoriously did in other cases, in course of transmission. But as Jerome certainly knew of them, he might well use them. (2) The passages referred to by Field may be taken as mentioning them. (3) In default of specific quotations, Field's long work at the Hexapla gives great weight to his impressions. As the question was not specially prominent in his day, he may have thought he had said enough ; but he can hardly have used a phrase such as 'innumera loca' at random. Lietzmann says he finds only one passage—in the margin of the MS. Vat. 754 on Ps. cxxxi. 4...ἐν δὲ τῷ ὀκτασελίδῳ παρὰ μόνοις τοῖς ο′ ἔκειτο ὠβελισμένον—which appears to support Field ; but it would be scarcely safe to assert that no more are forthcoming. (4) Origen's motives, and his judgement, can scarcely be determined. Collection of information was then thought more of than a pure text as we should now consider it, and he may have aimed at massing all the facts he could in his great work. The suggestion that the Tetrapla, or an extracted LXX. text, should have received Origen's critical treatment, and not the Hexapla, whether right or not, appears arbitrary. (6) The varying number of columns mentioned can be simply explained as on pp. 66, 67: 'Hexapla' was the standing number, and the normal name; the others might be applied when more, or fewer, columns were used. The Psalms can hardly be taken, in any case, as a normal specimen of the O.T. (7) If the Milan fragment is not an exact copy, it affords less certain ground for argument.

On the whole, the arguments against Field's view are not yet completely convincing, even if he based it on impressions rather than definite proof. It may however be well to keep the other possibility in mind, and to suspend judgement, at least until the Milan fragments have been published in full and duly considered.

Perhaps it is worth while to add, that Professor K. Lake, in his Introduction to the photograph of the Sinaitic N.T., suggests that there may have been only one MS., that of Pamphilus, between a corrector of Cod. F—A = Sin and the original Hexapla; in which case the texts of ℵ and B do not bear witness to a purely pre-Hexaplar text in the Hexapla generally.

P. 76. An enlarged edition of the collection of Nobilius was embodied in the Latin translation of the Editio Sixtina (1588), reprinted by P. Morinus, 1624. Montfaucon's work was abridged by Bahrdt (2 vols., Leipzig, 1769). The Oxford concordance, suppl. fasc. ii., takes account of fresh matter available since the appearance of Field's work, which however is not likely, so far as it extends, to be superseded for years to come.

P. 82. On 'Lucian' as the κοινή see A. Rahlfs, *Septuaginta-Studien*, II. pp. 134, 170 f. Jerome's words (Ep. cvi. 2) are:

'In quo illud breviter admoneo ut sciatis aliam esse editionem quam Origenes et Caesariensis Eusebius omnesque Graeciae tractatores κοινήν, id est communem appellant, atque vulgatam, et a plerisque nunc Λουκιανὸς dicitur; aliam Septuaginta interpretum quae in Ἑξαπλοῖς codicibus reperitur et a nobis in Latinum sermonem fideliter versa est, et Jerosolymae atque in Orientis ecclesiis decantatur.'

P. 85. Since the publication of Lagarde's work (see page 188) the Lucianic Text has received much attention. See A. Rahlfs, *Sept.-Studien*, II. III., Göttingen, 1907, 1911; F. C. Burkitt, *Rules of Tyconius*, pp. cviii., cxvi f.; *The O.L. and the Itala*, p. 9; art. *Text and Versions in Encycl. Bibl.* vol. IV.; W. O. E. Oesterley, *Studies in...the Book of Amos*; C. F. Burney, *Notes on Heb. Text of Books of Kings*, 1903.

P. 93, also 104, 107, etc. For references to the symbols used in the larger Cambridge LXX. for materials in the Old Latin and other versions, see below, on p. 170. Some of these materials may be mentioned under the particular books of the Bible they contain.

P. 96. *L'ancienne Version Latine du Cantique* I—III. 4 is treated by D. A. Wilmart in *Revue Benedictine* XXVIII. 11—36.

P. 97. There has now appeared *Die Konstanz-Weingartener Propheten fragmenta in phototypischen Reproduction* (W. N. Du Rieu ; introd. Paul Lehman), 1912.

P. 100. A discovery of much interest has lately been made at Monte Cassino, where Dom Amelli has found a revised Latin Psalter, of a kind hitherto unknown, and edited it (*Collectanea Biblica Latina cura et studio Monachorum S. Benedicti. Vol.* I. *Liber Psalmorum iuxta antiquissimam latinam Versionem...ex Casinensi Cod.* 557 *curante D. Ambrosio M. Amelli O.S.B. Rome,* 1912).

The MS., of the twelfth century, contains the Psalter in four versions (cf. the fourfold Psalters noted below, on p. 165); (i) Jerome's 'Hebrew' Psalter, (ii) the 'Gallican,' and (iv) the 'Roman'; (iii) is the newly discovered revision. It appears to have been made upon an Old Latin or non-Vulgate foundation, with renderings apparently from the Hebrew, and even some transliterations. Professor Burkitt (in *J. Th. St.* XIV. 55) thinks that the various renderings, following in turn Aq., Symm., and especially Theodotion, are best accounted for if the reviser worked from a copy of the Hexapla. In this case the transliterations, if not due to Theodotion, may have been taken from the column containing the Hebrew in Greek characters ; and similarly can be explained a few places where the reviser follows the LXX. against the three later versions. Professor Burkitt, indeed, thinks it possible that the work might have been done by one ignorant of the actual Hebrew letters. Perhaps this is rather far to go ; but it is pointed out that among the 'readings derived from the Hebrew text' no case of confusion between ד and ר is recorded : certainly an unusual circumstance. It is possible, however, that the reviser may not have been exactly ignorant of Hebrew or the Hebrew script, even though when at work he 'only used the Greek transliteration found in MSS. of the Hexapla.'

P. 107. The store of available Coptic material for the O.T. has been much enriched of late years. *The Coptic Version of certain O.T. books from a Papyrus,* edited by Sir Herbert Thompson (Oxford, 1908), gives a fragment of Job xxxix, and large portions of Proverbs, Ecclesiastes, Canticles, Wisdom and Sirach. The papyrus (Pap. Or. 5984) was acquired by the British Museum in 1901. The leaves, preserved in 62 frames between glass, are of large size for papyri in codex form. Slight verbal differences from Lagarde's Turin MS. are found ; the British Museum text being considered inferior to it in Wisdom, but superior in Sirach. It is dated sixth to seventh century (or seventh to eighth, according to W. E. Crum in *J. Th. Stud.* April 1910).

A *Coptic Palimpsest*, by the same transcriber and editor (1911), is dated by him in the earlier half of the seventh century. [B.M. Add. 17183, obtained from the Nitrian valley in 1847.] The upper writing is Syriac. This MS., a parchment, was noticed by Lagarde, *Orientalia*, 1879 ; and small portions had previously appeared. It contains Josh., Judg., Ruth, Judith, Esther ; originally 228 leaves, of which 42 are missing. The writing is a plain square uncial. The text in Joshua shows independence : in Judg. and Ruth the text is akin to B.

Dr E. A. Budge has edited and transcribed Pap. Or. 7594 (*Coptic Biblical Texts in the Dialect of Upper Egypt*, 1912) containing Deuteronomy, with gaps, Jonah all but complete, as well as the Acts of the Apostles. There are papyrus fragments in the cover, one of which contains Dan. i. 17, 18, in Theod.'s version. The leaves have been rubbed, making the text illegible in places. The editor considers that Deuteronomy is a copy made for private use ; the text of Jonah, apparently by the same hand, agrees in some small points with AQ. Dr Budge assigns the papyrus to the fourth century ; but it is possibly a century later than this. Out of 133 leaves, 24 are missing. The papyrus was acquired by the British Museum in April 1911, and published barely a twelvemonth after.

In the *Catalogue of Coptic MSS. in the British Museum*, by W. E. Crum, Nos. 1—59 and 932—955 contain portions of the O.T. in Sahidic ; 59 is Habak. iii, 940 is a complete volume, containing 151 Psalms. Nos. 493—496 are Middle Egyptian O.T., and 712—731 Bohairic. 712 gives 364 leaves of the Pentateuch.

Other works are : P. J. Balestri, *Sacrorum Bibliorum fragmenta Copto-Sahidica Musei Borgiani*, Rome, 1904 : J. Goettsberger, *Die Syro-Koptischen Bibel-citate...aus den Scholien des Barhebräus* in *ZATW*. XXI. (1901) p. 128 ff. ; F. E. Brightman in *J. Th. Stud.* II. p. 275 f., and S. Gaselee in *J. Th. Stud.* XI. p. 246 ff. Fragments in Coptic, chiefly of Pss., have also been found on ostraca : see W. E. Crum, *Coptic Ostraca from the collections of the Egypt Exploration Fund*, etc. (London, 1902).

P. 108. The earlier editions of this book stated that 'of the Sahidic fragments, those that belong to the book of Job yield a pre-Origenic text': but Professor Burkitt, in the article referred to in note 4, has come to the conclusion that the facts require this to be modified, as it now appears. L. Dieu, however, in *Muséon*, 1912,

p. 147 ff. (*Nouveaux Fragments préhexaplaires du livre de Job en copte sahidique*) supports the previous view, in opposition to Professor Burkitt and Mr Crum (on No. 939 in his *Catalogue*).

P. 110. To list of books add : F. O. Kramer, *Die aethiopische Übersetzung des Zacharias: Text zum ersten Male herausgegeben, Prolegomena, Kommentar : eine Vorstudie zur Geschichte und Kritik des Septuaginta-textes*, Heft I. Leipzig, 1908.

P. 116. Add : P. A. de Lagarde, *Libri V. T. Apocryphi Syr.*, Leipzig, 1861 ; A. M. Ceriani, *Trans. Syra Pescitto V. T. ex Cod. Ambros.*, Milan, 1876—79.

P. 119. Add : J. Goettsberger, *Die Syro-armenischen...Bibelcitate...des Barhebräus, ZATW.* XXI. 1901, pp. 101—127.

P. 125. CODEX ALEXANDRINUS. Professor Burkitt, in *J. Th. Stud.* XI. (p. 603), suggests that there is no reason for identifying the Athanasius who signs the Arabic note at the beginning of the MS. with the Patriarch (III.) of that name, since he does not sign in Patriarchal style. He concludes that the MS. was not necessarily in Egypt before 1616; that it came from Athos, and is therefore Constantinopolitan, not Alexandrian. The question must probably be regarded as an open one, until more general attention has been paid to it ; but Professor Burkitt's suggestion is apparently regarded with favour by Professor Souter (see his note in the *Novum Test. Graece*, Oxford, 1910, p. vii.).

P. 130. CODEX SINAITICUS. The N.T. of this MS. has now been issued in collotype reproduction (by H. and K. Lake, Oxford, 1911). Professor K. Lake's Introduction draws attention to several interesting details. According to him, the MS. was at Caesarea between the beginning of the fifth and that of the seventh century A.D. He quotes Harnack's remark on the resemblance of its Psalter to the Psalms in the (Coptic) text of the *Pistis Sophia* : 'Dieser Text steht dem Cod. Sin. wie ein Zwillingsbruder nahe.' With regard to the four hands distinguished by Tischendorf in the MS., Professor Lake considers that the corrector A¹ is probably, and A² almost certainly, identical with the scribe D, and that Cod. Vaticanus was not written by this scribe. The corrector, C, of the FA portion of the MS. used, he thinks, a copy corrected by Pamphilus himself, which alone 'intervenes between [him] and the original Hexapla.' See above, on p. 69 ff.

P. 132. CODEX ZUQNINENSIS. Two Syriac MSS., Vat. Syr. 162, at Rome, 122 leaves, and B.M. Add. 14665 foll. 1—7, five leaves, contain, under a valuable chronicle, including that of 'Joshua the

Stylite,' palimpsest fragments which are assigned to six Greek uncial MSS., distinguished by the editor as under:

Z¹, cent. vi, portions of Judges xvi—xxi. The text is Lucianic, to be compared with K 54 59 75 82.

Z², cent. vi, portions of 3 Reg. ii—viii. and xxi. Lucianic, akin to 82 93 rather than 19 108. (Part in Brit. Mus.)

Z³, cent. v, a single leaf, in Brit. Museum, containing 3 Reg. viii. 58—ix. 1. Egyptian, not Lucianic, in text. This is referred to on p. 141 as Z^d. Doubly palimpsest; the liturgical writing above the biblical text and below the Syriac, is, according to Tisserant, not, as was thought, Coptic but Greek.

Z⁴, cent. vi, large portions of Pss. viii—xxxvii. Lucianic? the text is said to be of a character between A and $\aleph$^{c.a.}.

Z⁵, sloping uncials of cent. vii—viii. Large fragments of Ezek. i, iii—ix, xxii—xxvi, xxviii, xxxv—xlviii. Lucianic. (Part in Brit. Mus.)

Z⁶, cent. vi—vii. Fragments of later chapters of Ezek., and Dan. iii. 2—15. Lucianic.

The MSS. are named from Zuknīn, a village near Amid. The Biblical fragments have been transcribed and edited with great care by Eugène Tisserant in *Studi e Testi* 23 (*Cod. Zuqninensis rescriptus Veteris Test.*, Rome, 1911).

P. 141. Θ. WASHINGTON CODEX. For full information, see the Introduction by Professor H. A. Sanders, to the reproduction of the MS. (*University of Michigan Studies*, Humanistic Series, vol. 8).

This is an uncial MS. containing Deuteronomy and Joshua, almost entire. It was bought, on Dec. 19, 1906, by Mr C. L. Freer, at Gizeh, from a dealer named Ali. (Three other MSS. were bought at the same time, containing the Psalms, the Gospels —Gregory's and Souter's W—and the Pauline Epistles.) It is intended that it shall find a home in the Smithsonian Institute at Washington; meantime it remains at Detroit, Michigan. Professor Sanders remarks that many stories have been told of it, which are untrue; that it had not been often shown before the purchase was made. When first examined in America, the desert sand was still in the folds. The vellum is 'moderate'; the hand an upright, square uncial. The size of the leaves varies, from 30 to 31·9 × 25·5 to 26·1 centimetres : average, 30·6 × 25·8, or about 12 × 10¼ inches. There is a lacuna in Deuteronomy from v. 16 ὁ θεός σου to vi. 18 τὴν γῆν τὴν ἀγαθήν, and in Joshua from iii. 3 τῷ λαῷ λέγοντες to iv. 10—λατο Κύριος. Deut. i. 3–5, 17 are fragmentary. There are 102 leaves, with 3 blank pages : two columns on the page, with 31 lines, of 13 to 14 letters in each. The text of Deuteronomy seems to resemble that of the cursives 54 and 75 (see p. 493); in Joshua it is somewhat akin to A. There is a small Hexaplaric element. Professor Sanders assigns the MS. to the fifth century, probably the first half; Mr Brooke (in *J. Th. Stud.* XIII. 458 ff.) perhaps to the sixth century, at any rate not later. Professor Sanders suggests that this and the three companion MSS. 'perhaps originated in a Greek monastery, were united in a Coptic one, and found in the ruins of one.' Dr A. S. Hunt (*The Year's Work in Class. Studies*, 1908) says that ' in all probability they belong to a group of Greek and Coptic MSS., proceeding eventually from the White Monastery near Sohag, of which another portion has been obtained for Berlin by C. Schmidt. Of the Berlin section the most valuable item seems to be an early copy on papyrus of part of the Book of Genesis....'

P. 141. C. Poetical Books.

Here may be noticed the Leipzig papyrus (Univ. Lib. Pap. 39), called λ by Heinrici (*Beiträge zur Geschichte und Erklärung des N.T.*, IV. Leipzig, 1913), and L by Rahlfs, *Sept.-Studien*, II. p. 5. It comes from Ashmunên, in Middle Egypt, and contains Ps. xxx. 5—xxxi. 1, xxxii. 18—lv., with gaps in the earlier part. Rahlfs dates it later than A.D. 338, but within the fourth century. It may be compared with U [B.M. Pap. 37], see p. 142. It must not be confused with the Munich MS., Gr. 251, of the Psalter, called L by Lagarde, in his *Novae Psalt. gr. editionis specimen*, which is assigned to the tenth century: Rahlfs, *op. cit.* p. 14 ; see p. 164, note. Rahlfs mentions some other uncial Psalters, still awaiting complete collation : Paris, Arsenal 8407 ; Jerusalem, Patr. Lib. 96, containing Ps. xx. 10—cxlviii. 6, six leaves at St Petersburg ; Berlin, Royal Lib. Harn. 552 (Graeco-Latin) ; one at Moscow (Rumjant-zowski Museum), see Tischendorf *V. T. Gr.* proleg. 45 ; and one at Uspenskoe, dated A.D. 862, described by Amphilochius (Am-filokhy, Archimandrite) in his critical edition of the Slavonic Psalter. All these are of the ninth century ; later are Trier 7, a Latin text with interlinear Greek version of Ps. i.—liv. ; and incomplete Graeco-Latin MSS. at Würzburg, Cues, St Gall, and Essen.

P. 144. In 1904, at Turin, there was destroyed by fire an uncial MS. of the Psalms ; which is now represented only by a few photographs, fortunately taken a few weeks before, and now in the possession of Professor Swete and Dr Oesterley (who writes of this 'Lost Uncial Codex' in *Exp. Times*, vol. XVII. p. 353 ff., May 1906). It was a well-written MS. of the eighth or ninth century, with a *catena*, which included passages from Modestus and Cosmas Indicopleustes, but not Cyr., Epiph., Greg. Nyss., Greg. Naz. Its text bore some resemblance to that of Cod. R. A brief description was contained in Pasini's *Codices Manuscripti Bibliothecae Regii Taurinensis Athenaei* (Turin, 1749).

P. 145. Y. CODEX TAURINENSIS.

This MS. has been transcribed by Dr Oesterley, and published with select apparatus (*J. Th. Stud.* VI.—VIII., reprinted by H. Frowde, 1908). It is not an uncial, only the headings being in uncial letters. The body of the MS. is written in a fairly upright cursive hand, many letters not joined ; the writing is continuous, with capitals sometimes at the beginning, sometimes in the middle of lines or words. The MS. was damaged in a fire in 1666, but escaped with slight damage in 1904 (see above) ; it is now said to consist of 93 leaves of fine vellum, with a polished surface. The date is given as the ninth or tenth century.

P. 146. A portion of the same MS. as Γ is at Rome (Vat. Gr. 1658). From this (not palimpsest) come the readings for Zach. iv. 3 —viii. 16 in *The O.T. in Greek*, vol. iii.

P. 146 ff. Among the fragments more recently discovered, the following may be noticed : several have been used for the apparatus of the larger Cambridge LXX., see below, on p. 170 :

Gen. i. 1—5, LXX. and Aquila : Amh. Pap. I. iii *c*. U_2. See p. 148, note 2.

Gen. ii. iii. (fragm.). Late third century, fragment of vellum leaf. Oxyrh. 1007. See p. 39, note 4.

Old Latin of Gen. v. 4—13, v. 29—vi. 2. Fourth century, uncial, portion of vellum leaf, with interesting text. Oxyrh. 1073.

Gen. xiv. xv. xix. xx. xxiv. xxvii. About forty-five verses, mostly fragmentary. Parts of four leaves from a papyrus codex. Late second or early third century. Oxyrh. 656. U_4.

Gen. xvi. 8—12. Part of a column of a roll. Third cent. Oxyrh. 1166.

Gen. xxi. xxii. xxiv. Vellum fragments from the binding of Paris, Bibl. Nat. 1397. Δ_2.

Gen. xxv. 19—22, xxvi. 3, 4. Vellum fragments. Strassburg, Pap. 748. Δ_3. An early papyrus, of the time of Constantine, containing parts of the Book of Genesis, in an early cursive hand. Berlin, Royal Library. See C. Schmidt in *Theol. Literaturzeitung*, 1908, No. 12, col. 360; also above, p. 507.

Gen. xxxi. 42—46, 48—54. Papyrus leaf of book. Fourth cent. Oxyrh. 1167.

Gen. xxxvii. 3, 4, 9. Geneva, 99. See *Archiv* II. p. 224 ff. Δ_4. Exod. xv. Heidelberg.

Exod. xix. 1, 2, 5, 6. Large round uncials, a fragment of a handsome MS. Sixth century? Amh. Pap. 191 (see below). U_5.

Exod. xxxi. 13, 14, xxxii. 7, 8. Fragments, third century. Oxyrh. 1074.

Exod. xl. 26—32. Third century. Oxyrh. 1075.

Deut. ii. 37—iii. 1, iii. 3, 4, 5, 8—10, 12, 13. Lower part of leaf of papyrus book, large rough round uncials, fourth century. Text generally with B against AF. Rylands Pap. 1.

Deut. xxxii. 3—10. Amh. Pap. 192. U₆.

Josh. iv. 23—v. 1. Vellum leaf, fourth century. Oxyrh. 1168.

1 Sam. (1 Regn.) ii. Heidelberg.

2 Sam. (2 Regn.) xv. xvi., fragm. Strassburg. See Deissmann, *Licht vom Osten*....

Psalms (LXX. numbering) : information largely derived from A. Rahlfs, *Septuaginta-Studien*, II.

Ps. xiv. White marble slab. Lapethus, in Cyprus. See Rahlfs, *Sept.-Studien*, II. p. 16. Perdrizet, *Bulletin de correspondance hellénique* 20, 1896. Fourth century.

Ps. xxvi. Parchment roll. Rahlfs, p. 18. Wessely, *Wiener Studien* 4 (1882), p. 214 ff. Vienna.

Ps. lxxvii. 20—31, 51—61. Greek text with Arabic translation. Eighth or ninth century. Rahlfs, p. 19. Damascus.

Ps. lxviii. 30—37, lxx. 3—8. Cursive, late fourth or fifth century. Oxyrh. 845.

Ps. lxviii., lxxx. fragm. Wessely's fragments, see above, on p. 34. Vienna, Rainer Pap.

P. xc. 1, 2. Papyrus, amulet. Fourth century. Rahlfs, p. 17. Heinrici, *Beiträge zur Gesch. u. Erkl. d. N. T.* IV. p. 31. Vienna, Rainer Pap. 8032.

Ps. xc. 5—16. Fifth or early sixth century. Irregular semi-cursive hand. Amulet? Rylands Pap. 3.

Ps. xc. 1—13. Wax tablet, amulet? J. Nicole, Geneva.

Ps. cv. 38—45, cvi. 2—10. Parchment. Rahlfs, p. 17. Fifth century. Berlin, Egypt. Museum.

Ps. cxviii. 27—58, fragm. Rahlfs, p. 14. Heinrici, p. 35 f. Leipzig, Univ. Lib. Pap. 170.

Ps. cxliii. 1—cxliv. 6, fragmentary. Two tattered vellum leaves, palimpsest, uncial, sixth century. *J. Th. Stud.* IV. C. Taylor, p. 130, J. H. A. Hart, p. 215 ff. From the Taylor-Schechter collection.

Prov. x. 11—19. Amh. Pap. 193.

Job i. 15—21, v. 24—vi. 9. Remains of two leaves of a papyrus book, large upright uncial. Sixth or seventh century. There seems no doubt that Amh. Pap. iv. (see page 148, note 2) is the continuation from the first leaf. Rylands Pap. 2.

Tobit ii. 2, 3, 4, 8. Oxyrh. Pap. 1076.

Isai. vi. 10 as quoted in N.T. (Matt. xiii. 15, Acts xxviii. 27). Oxyrh. 405, 406.

Isai. lviii. 11—14. The under side of Amh. Pap. 191 (see above). *Archiv* II. p. 382.

Amos ii. 6—8, 9—12. Sixth century, large heavy uncial. Oxyrh. 846.

P. 154. To (A) add : London, B. M. Curzon 66. Octateuch, *cat.* Petersburg, Imp. Lib. cxxii. Gen. (part), *cat.* and *cant.* Rome, Vat. Reg. Gr. 7. Octateuch, *cat.* Venice, Gr. 15. Octateuch, *cat.* London, Burney 34. Pentateuch, Rome, Reg. Pii II. 20.

P. 158. The cursive 67, Mr Thackeray points out, is a near

relative of 206 (Gonv. and Caius Coll. 348 ; cf. M. R. James, *Descriptive Catalogue*, I. p. 392). Another MS. by the scribe of 206 is Trin. Coll. Camb. O. 3. 14. See J. Rendel Harris, *Origin of Ferrar group of MSS.*, p. 24. The Trin. Coll. MS. has no titles ; 206 has none after Ps. lxxvii. See Holmes and Parsons on Ps. lxxviii.

P. 162. The Barberini MSS. have apparently been renumbered since the time of Holmes and Parsons, who gave their 226 and 227 as Barber. 1 and 2. The present Barber. 1 and 2 are not Psalters ; this information comes from Dr Mercati to the Rev. J. Mearns, who suggests that when the collations were received at Oxford, the MSS. were without numbers, and were simply distinguished as 1 and 2 by the editor. He thinks the present Barberini catalogue may date from 1830 or somewhat earlier, but not from as early as 1790.

P. 163. Mr Thackeray notes that 272 ends with Ps. lxxvi. (H.-P. give readings to verse 17), and 287 begins with the following Psalm.

P. 165. To list (C) add Psalms, Rome, Vat. Gr. 754, from Rahlfs, II. p. 23. Also :

Leipzig, Univ. Lib. Tisch. v, complete from Ps. xvii. 35 onward : and five Psalters with Greek text in Roman letters : viz.,

Paris, Bibl. Nat. N. acq. Lat. 2195.
This and the following are akin to W and Z on p. 164, note 1. W contains four texts, viz., Jerome's 'Gallican,' 'Roman,' and 'Hebrew' Psalters, and the Greek ; this MS. has them in the same order.

Valenciennes, no. 14. Another fourfold Psalter. Paris, Bibl. Nat. Lat. 15198. Threefold, 'Heb.' 'Rom.' Greek. Paris, Bibl. Nat. Suppl. Gr. 188. Latin interlinear version. Camb., C.C.C. 468. Also a Latin text.

P. 166. 62 and 147 have something in common ; they form, in fact, a sub-group, akin to, but distinct from, the Lucianic MSS. of the Prophets generally. See Burkitt, *Tyconius*, p. cviii, and Oesterley, *Studies in...Amos*, pp. 9 ff., 17 ff. They are also among the four MSS. which give a peculiar version of Habak. iii. ; see on p. 247, below.

P. 170. The symbols used by the editors of the larger Cambridge LXX. are here brought together, so far as they are yet published :

I. Uncial MSS. :

(*a*) Bibles originally complete, or believed to have been so : AB[C]S, as on p. 124.

(*b*) Containing the Octateuch, or parts of it : DEFGHKLMθ.

II. Cursives, quoted by small letters:

a	= Holmes and Parsons' 15.		n	= H.-P.	75.
b' =	,,	,, 19.	o =	,,	82.
b =	,,	,, 108.	p =	,,	106.
[b = agreement of b' + b].			q =	,,	120.
c	= H.-P. 38.		r =	,,	129.
d =	,,	44.	s =	,,	131.
e =	,,	52.	t =	,,	134.

u = Jerusalem, Holy Sepulchre, 2 (p. 154).

f =	,,	53.	
g =	,,	54.	
h =	,,	55.	

v = Athos, Pantocrator. 24 (p. 153).

i =	,,	56.	
j =	,,	57.	
k =	,,	58.	

w = Athens, Bibl. Nat. 44 (p. 154).

x = London, B. M. Curzon 66.

l =	,,	59.	

y = H.-P. 121.

m =	,,	72.	

z = ,, 85.

$a_2 = \begin{cases} \text{St Petersburg, Imp. Library, 62 (p. 153)} \\ \text{London, B.M. Add. 20002 (p. 152)} \end{cases}$ continuation of E.

b_2 = H.-P. 29.
c_2 = ,, 135.
d_2 = ,, 61.

III. Cursives, quoted occasionally on the authority of H.-P., and by their numbers:

14, 16, 18, 20, 25, 30—32, 37, 64, 68, 71, 73, 74, 76, 77—79, 83, 84, 105, 107, 118, 125—128, 130, 132, 133, 136.

IV. Fragments: generally papyrus, unless otherwise stated:

U_2 = Amh. Pap. I. iii c. Gen. 1—5, LXX. and Aq.: p. 148, note 2.
U_3 = Brit. Mus. Pap. ccxii. Gen. xiv. 17: p. 146 (1).
U_4 = Oxyrh. Pap. 656. Gen. xiv. xv. xix. xx. xxiv. fragm.: parts of four leaves of a codex.
U_5 = Amh. Pap. cxci. Exod. xix. 1, 2, 5, 6.
U_6 = Amh. Pap. cxcii. Deut. xxxii. 3—6, 8—10.
Δ_2 = Vellum fragments in binding of Paris, Bibl. Nat. Gr. 1397. Gen. xxi. xxii. xxiv.
Δ_3 = Strassburg, Pap. Gr. 748: vellum fragm. of Gen. xxv. xxvi.
Δ_4 = Geneva, 99 vellum fragm. of Gen. xxxvii.
Δ_5 = Palimpsest fragm. Gen. xl. 3, 4, 7: p. 148, note 2.
Δ_6 = Vellum fragm. Levit. xxii. 3—xxiii. 22: p. 146 (2).
Δ_7 = Vellum fragm. from Sinai, Numb. xxxii. 29 : p. 147 (3).

V. Versions:

𝔄 = Armenian: Zohrab's edition, Venice, 1805: p. 119.

𝔄-ed. = Z.'s text, 𝔄-cod or -codd variants in his notes.

𝕭 = Bohairic : p. 107.

𝕭¹ = Lagarde's edition, Leipzig, 1867.

𝕭ʷ = Wilkins' ed., London, 1731.

𝕭ᵖ = Paris, Bibl. Nat. Copt. 1 (for Genesis).

𝕭ᵛ = Rome, Vat. Copt. 1 (for Deut.).

ℭ = Sahidic : p. 107.

ℭᶜ　　 = Ciasca's edition, Rome, 1885.

ℭᵐ　　 = Maspéro's ed., Paris, 1892.

ℭ-cod = Ciasca's Bodleian MS.

ℭᵖ　　 = Paris, Bibl. Nat. Copt. 1296 (fragm.).

ℭᵇ　　 = B.M. Or. 5287 (fragm.).

ℭᵗ　　 = B.M. Add. 17183 (Thompson, *A Coptic Palimpsest*).

𝔈 = Ethiopic : p. 110.

𝔈ᶜ = Dillmann's Codex C.

𝔈ᶠ =　　 ,,　　 ,,　 F.

𝔈ᵖ = Paris, Bibl. Nat. Eth. 3 (Zotenberg).

𝕷 = Old Latin : pp. 88, 93 ff.

𝕷ᵇ = Vienna palimpsest, ed. I. Belsheim, 1885.

𝕷ʳ = Lyons octateuch, ed. U. Robert, 1881, 1900.

𝕷ᵛ = *Variae Lectiones*, C. Vercellone, Rome, 1860.

𝕷ʷ = Würzburg Palimpsest (fragm.), ed. E. Ranke, Vienna, 1871.

𝕷ᶻ = Munich Palimpsest (fragm.), ed. L. Ziegler, 1883.

𝕻 = Palestinian Aramaic : p. 114.

𝕻¹ = *a Palestinian Syriac Lectionary*, ed. Mrs A. S. Lewis, *Stud. Sin.* vi.

𝕻ᶜ = *Cod. Clinaei Rescriptus*, ed. Mrs Lewis, *Hor. Sem.* viii.

𝕻ᵈ = Christlich-palästinisch-aramaische Texte, ed. H. Duensing.

𝕻ᵍ = fragm. in *Anecdota Oxoniensia* (Sem. Series, I. v, ix.), ed. G. H. Gwilliam and J. F. Stenning.

𝕻ᵖ = St Petersburg fragm. in *Anecdota Syriaca*, ed. J. P. N. Land, 1875.

𝕻ᵗ = *Palestinian Syriac Texts*, from Palimpsest Fragments in the Taylor-Schechter collection : ed. Mrs A. S. Lewis and Mrs M. D. Gibson.

𝕻ˢ = Christlich-palästinische fragmenta, ed. F. Schulthess.

𝕾　 = Syro-hexaplar : pp. 113, 116.

𝕾 ap-Barh = quotations in the Auṣar Rāzē (Horreum Mysteriorum) of Bar-hebraeus.

𝕾ᵐ　　　 = readings supplied by A. Masius from his MS.

P. 173. See J. Dahse, *Zur Herkunft des alttestamentlichen Textes der Aldina*, in *ZATW*. XXIX. p. 177 ff. (1909).

P. 182. Field's Cambridge edition of 1665 was reissued by John Hayes in 1684, still under Field's name : ' page for page, and

I suppose line for line,' as Dr Brett says in his *Letter* (see p. 340) quoted by Dr Nestle in *Exp. Times*, vol. 17, p. 380. 'By which he put a Cheat upon the World,' Dr Brett continues; but from inquiries made by Dr Bethune-Baker (*J. Th. Stud.* VI. 612 ff.) it would seem that Field's remaining sheets may have been issued without intending 'a Cheat.'

P. 186. The *text* of Holmes and Parsons seems to have been based to some extent on that of Bos; as Nestle in Hastings' *D.B.* (IV. 449) says, 'The text in the work is a reprint of *b* [the Sixtine]; but as it seems, after a copy of Bos, corrected, but not everywhere, according to an original copy.' H. Lietzmann, reviewing the first edition of this *Introduction* in *G.G.A.* May 1902, pleads for a 'friendly word' on Lambert Bos's edition, with its variants from the Aldine and Complutensian, and collection of the Hexaplaric material then known; as useful even now, and 'nicht antiquiert.'

P. 192. Professor Meinhold and Professor Lietzmann have issued *Amos* in Hebrew, a corrected text, side by side with the text of Q (*Materials for Theological Lecturers and Students*, Nos. 15, 16, Cambridge, 1906).

P. 200. Professor A. R. S. Kennedy, in *Exp. Times*, XXII. 9, p. 321 ff. June 1911, points out that a Heb. MS. at Edinburgh, which he regards as important, has the order Jer. Ezek. Isa.

P. 239. Mr Thackeray thinks that 3 Regn. xxii. may have originally been joined to 4 Regn. Thus xx. and xxi. would have been at the end of the book, where transposition might have more easily taken place than in the middle.

P. 242. With regard to the order of Jeremiah's prophecies in 𝔐 and 𝔊, Mr Thackeray has investigated the Greek text, and finds evidence that the book was divided between two translators (*J. Th. Stud.* IV. 14, p. 253 ff., *Gramm. of O.T. in Gr.*, p. 11 ff.). He places the division between Jer. *a* and *β* at the end of chap. xxviii.; and L. Köhler (*Beobachtungen am hebräischen und griech. Text von Jeremia*, Leipzig, 1908) substantially agrees, but places the division about a chapter later. Thackeray also finds signs of division in Ezekiel, and—so far as concerns *transcription*—in Exodus and Leviticus. In the Books of Kingdoms he distinguishes translators of different dates. In Isaiah, on the contrary, he finds no clear trace of division, though Mr Gray (*J. Th. Stud.* XII. 46, p. 286) thinks otherwise. On these questions see also Schäfer in *Theologie und Glaube*, 1909, 3, *Ist das Buch Ezekiel in der Septuaginta von einem oder mehreren Dolmetscher übersetzt?* and Mr Thackeray's other articles in *J. Th. Stud.*, IV. p. 398 ff., 578 ff., VIII. p. 262 ff., IX. p. 88 ff.

P. 247.	Mr H. St J. Thackeray (in *J. Th. Stud.* XI. 44, July
1910) has closely examined the passage 3 Regn. viii. 53*a*, and has
reconstructed the underlying Hebrew text.	Professor Burkitt had
already (*J. Th. Stud.* X. 39, April 1909) surveyed it with a like
object in view, and decided that Luc. ἔστησεν was an attempt to
correct LXX. ἐγνώρισεν, not, as had generally been said, reading
הכין for הבין, but without reference to the Hebrew, which must
almost certainly be הודיע.	Mr Thackeray, taking this evidence to
the letters of the original Hebrew, proposes to divide them differently, and instead of

שמש הודיע בשמים

to read	שמש הוד יעב שמים.

The Lucianic alteration may have been caused by the awkward-
ness of the preposition which now disappears.	Reading ἐκ γνόφου,
he takes ἐκ as =מ, preferably meaning 'without,' 'away from';
and the result is a fairly consistent stanza, of a character which
modern critics would accept as older in form than that of the
M.T. in *vv.* 12, 13, and as better placed here:

> 'Sun, glory beclouds the heaven:
> Jahve hath promised to dwell without the thick darkness.
> Build Thou my house,
> A celestial Palace for Thyself.'

Possibly, according to Mr Thackeray, this represents a development
from an original 'popular incantation in times of eclipse,' as
Josh. x. 12 from a sun-staying incantation.	Further links of
connexion appear between these passages, as in the reference in
each to the Book of Jashar; referred to also in the lament of
David over Saul and Jonathan, 2 Regn. i. 19 ff., where 'nature
allusions' again appear.	These references, however, are differently
attested; in Joshua it is a Hexaplar addition to the Greek; probably also in 2 Regn., where it is read by AB, etc. but not, according
to H.-P., by N, 64, 71, 92, 106, 119, 242.	In 3 Regn. it stands in
LXX., but not in M.T. (probably excised, Mr Thackeray thinks).

There remains the difficult line τοῦ κατοικεῖν ἐπὶ καινότητος.
The link between καινότης and what might be expected to correspond from the M.T. in *v.* 13 (cf. 2 Chron. vi. 2), namely עולמים
'for ever,' is found in עלומים, 'youth'; ἐπί is על; τοῦ κατοικεῖν is
לשבת, which can better be rendered 'for the Sabbath'; and emending
עלומים to עלמות, in the light of such titles to the Psalms as those
of ix. and xlvi. (cf. also the end of xlviii. and 1 Chron. vi. 20), and
taking account of renderings by Aquila and other versions, we
get, instead of the puzzling close to the stanza, a liturgical or
musical direction, לשבת על־עלמות; i.e.:

For the Sabbath.	On Alamoth ('for soprano voices').

Mr Thackeray is inclined to connect 'Jashar' with שׁיר 'sing' rather than with ישׁר 'upright'; in which case the LXX. βιβλίον τῆς ᾠδῆς here is more right than had been supposed. He points to the opening words, 'Then sang...' of Exod. xv., Numb. xxi. 17; this, however, is not material to his general argument.

Another illuminating discovery, by the same writer, on a kindred matter, concerns the difficult 'Psalm of Habakkuk' (Hab. iii.), and appeared in *J. Th. Stud.* XII. 46, Jan. 1911. This is the chapter where alone, outside the Psalter, the word 'Selah,' LXX. διάψαλμα, occurs. Four MSS., namely V(=H.-P. 23), 86 (Rome, Barber. v. 45), and the Oxford MSS. 62 and 147, have in this single chapter a widely different Greek version from that contained in the other MSS. (On 62 and 147 see above, on p. 166.) This text has been commented on by Dr Sinker (*The Psalm of Habakkuk*, Cambridge, 1890) and by Dr E. Klostermann, who prints the texts of the Barberini MS. with variants in his *Analecta* (Leipzig, 1895), p. 50 ff.

In *v.* 9 of the 'Psalm' occurs a clause so difficult that, it is commonly said, more than a hundred renderings have been proposed: שבעות מטות אמר, A.V. '*According to* the oaths of the tribes, *even* thy word,' R.V. 'The oaths to the tribes were a sure word,' Sinker, Gesenius and others, 'Sworn were the chastisements (rods) of thy word,' etc. The difficulty lies in the shortness of the clause, the absence of construction, and the variety of possible renderings of the three *unpointed* words. The first word may be 'oaths,' 'seven,' 'weeks,' etc.; the second, 'tribes' or 'rods' (not, properly, 'shafts' or 'arrows'); and the third 'saith' (verb) or 'word' (noun). The ordinary text of the LXX. has ἐπὶ [τὰ] σκῆπτρα λέγει [κύριος, a gloss]: Sinker, and Nestle (*ZATW.* 1900, p. 167 f.), suggested ἑπτά for ἐπὶ τά. But the Barberini text, which Mr Thackeray believes to be the oldest Greek version, has ἐχόρτασας [τὰς] βολίδας τῆς φαρέτρας αὐτοῦ.

The details must be sought in his paper; here it can only be pointed out that he shows how ἐχόρτασας (=שָׂבַעְתָּ) and βολίδας (=מטות) support the consonants of M.T., while LXX. λέγει suggests אמר. (Κύριος is obelized in Syro-hex.) He deduces that we have here a lectionary note, which has been merged in the text: WEEKS (or SEVEN)—RODS—SAITH. 'Weeks' is the key or catchword for the lesson from the Law, to be read when Hab. iii. was the Haphtarah or Prophetical lesson, namely, Deut. xvi. 9 ff.; 'Rods' similarly directs to Numb. xvii. or 'Tribes' to Numb. xxx. 2; and 'saith' to Gen. xii. Again, τῆς φαρέτρας αὐτοῦ stands for יתרו, Job xxx. 11; but it should be *Jethro*, indicating Exod. xviii.-xx. For the Primitive Lessons from the Law, the Triennial Cycle, and the later, Babylonian, annual Cycle of Lessons, see the paper by Dr Adolf Büchler in *J. Q. R.*, v. 424, and *Jewish Encycl.*, vol. XII.

The variety of lessons provided by the catchwords, and the varying length of the lesson from Habakkuk, are thus explained. Having dealt with other readings, and with the Selahs, *v.* 3, 13, 19, Mr Thackeray arrives at the conclusion that Hab. iii., or part of it, besides being used as a canticle, was read from very early times as a lesson at Pentecost, being an integral part of the book perhaps by the third century B.C. The Babylonian cycle had it for a lesson on the second day of the extended Pentecost festival (see the note in printed Hebrew Bibles at Hab. ii. 20). The 'Director of Music,' whose date must be about 250 B.C., adopted it as a canticle, adding the Selahs. In something like this state the text found its way to Egypt, about 200 B.C., and the Barberini version was made from it not long after; but the lectionary notes were not understood by the translator, whose version was intended for use as a lesson at Alexandria. Later, when Ezekiel and the minor Prophets as a whole were translated, the Barberini version was ignored; but as a short lesson, ending *v.* 3, continued to be read in some districts, a conflate text of these verses arose for synagogue interpretation. The result, among other things, is to show that here, at any rate, the consonantal text has come down almost uncorrupted.

P. 251. On the titles of the Psalms, see also F. W. Mozley, *The Psalter of the Church*, p. 46 ff.

P. 256. See Professor Burkitt in *Encycl. Bibl.* on the Sahidic Job, as above, on p. 108. A passage worthy of special attention is xxviii. 21 ff.; cf. Clem. Alex. *Strom.* vi. 6 (673).

P. 258. Willrich would assign the final note to Esther in the LXX. (xi. 1 in A.V.) to B.C. 48—7.

P. 261. See Nestle on *The Song of the Three Holy Children in Greek Bibles* (*Exp. Times,* XII. p. 527 f.); and W. H. Daubney, *The Song of the Three,* ibid. 287.

P. 262 ff. The more recent volumes of the 'Westminster Commentaries' and the *International Critical Commentary* are usually worth consulting, but they vary considerably in the amount of attention bestowed on the LXX. Many of the small volumes in the *Century Bible* series deal here and there with the readings of the LXX.; e.g. Professor Bennett's *Genesis* and Professor Skinner's 1 *and* 2 *Kings.* To these should be added:

Joshua. M. Gasten, *Das Buch Josh. in Heb.-Samaritan Rezension. Entdeckt u. zum ersten Male herausgegeben S. A.* (*aus ZDMG.*) 62, p. 109 ff. *The Samaritan Book of Joshua and the Septuagint,* in *Proc. Soc. Bibl. Arch.* XXXI., April 1909.

Judges and Ruth. J. S. Black and A. W. Streane, in *Smaller Cambridge Bible for Schools.*

3, 4 Kingdoms. A. Rahlfs, *Septuaginta-Studien,* I. and III.

1, 2 Chronicles, Ezra-Nehemiah. C. C. Torrey, *Apparatus for the Criticism of Chronicles-Ezra-Nehemiah,* in *O. T. and Semitic Studies,* XI. p. 55 ff. *Ezra Studies,* Chicago, 1910.

Psalms. F. W. Mozley, *The Psalter of the Church,* Cambridge, 1905.

Ecclesiastes. A. H. McNeile, *An Introduction to Ecclesiastes,* Cambridge, 1904; L. Levy, *Das Buch Qoheleth, ein Beitrag zur Geschichte des Sadduzäismus, krit. untersucht, übers. u. erklärt,* Leipzig, 1912.

Canticles. W. Riedel, *Ausliegung des Hohenlieder,* 1898; W. W. Cannon, *The Song of Songs,* Cambridge, 1913.

Esther. G. Jahn, *Das Buch Ester nach LXX. hergestellt, übers. u. krit. erklärt,* 1901; L. B. Paton, *A Text-crit. Apparatus to the Book of Esther* (*O. T. and Semitic Studies,* XI. p. 3 ff.).

Dodecapropheton. P. Riessler, *Die Kleinen Propheten oder das Zwölfprophetenbuch,* Rottenburg, 1911; W. O. E. Oesterley, *Codex Taurinensis,* 1908.

Amos. W. O. E. Oesterley, *Studies in the Greek and Latin Versions of the Book of Amos,* Cambridge, 1902; J. Meinhold and H. Lietzmann, *Amos the Prophet* (Heb. and Greek texts), 1906.

Nahum. A. B. Davidson in *Camb. Bibl. for Schools.*

Habakkuk. W. R. Betteridge, *The Interpretation of Prophecy in Habakkuk,* in *A. J. Th.* VIII. Oct., 1904; H. St J. Thackeray, in *J. Th. Stud.* XII. 46, Jan. 1911; M. L. Margolis, *The Character of the Anonymous Version of Hab. iii.,* in *A. J. Sem. Lit.,* 24, p. 76 ff.

Zephaniah. S. Zandstra, *The Witness of the Vulgate, Peshitta, and Septuagint to the Text of Zephaniah,* New York, 1909.

Isaiah. R. R. Ottley, *Isaiah according to the Septuagint,* 2 vols., Cambridge, 1904, 1906.

Ezekiel. G. Jahn, *Das Buch Ezechiel nach LXX.,* 1905.

Daniel. G. Jahn, *Das Buch Daniel nach LXX.,* 1904; W. H. Daubney, *The Three Additions to Daniel,* Cambridge, 1906.

P. 267. Sir H. Howorth has expressed his views further in *Proc. Soc. Bibl. Arch.* 23, 24, and *J. Th. Stud.* v. 19, and holds that Chronicles also is the work of Theodotion. Thackeray is now (*Gramm. of O.T. in Greek,* p. xx) inclined to agree with regard to 2 Esdras, but has his doubts about Chronicles. See, however, Torrey, *Ezra Studies,* p. 66 ff., and *Apparatus for Text. Crit. of Chronicles-Ezra-Nehemiah.* Thackeray is also of opinion that the hand of the writer of 1 Esdras may 'be traced in the earlier chapters of the Chisian text of Daniel' (*Gramm. O.T.G.* p. 12). Sir H. Howorth's views were to some extent anticipated by Pohlmann in the Tübingen *Quartalschrift*, 1859.

P. 268. On the style of Wisdom, see Thackeray on *Rhythm in Wisdom, J. Th. Stud.* VI. p. 232 ff. ; with which may be coupled his article on *The Poetry of the Greek Book of Proverbs*, ibid. XIII. 49, p. 46 ff. He dates Wisdom, on grounds of spelling, between 132 and 100 B.C. (*Gramm. O.T.G.* p. 62).

P. 270. Mr J. H. A. Hart (*Ecclesiasticus in Greek*, p. 259 ff.) fixes the date of the grandson's arrival in Egypt as 247 B.C., interpreting the Greek phrase as 'in the eight-and-thirtieth year, under King Euergetes'; i.e. in the thirty-eighth year of Philadelphus, in which he had been succeeded by Euergetes I. He urges that no Jew could have worked in Egypt under Euergetes II. (See above, on p. 10 ff.) Dr Oesterley combats this view in his Introduction to the book in *Camb. Bible for Schools*; but it deserves careful examination. It is curious that the names, which might have been expected to fix the date of composition of the book, admit of alternative explanations.

P. 271. Professor Margoliouth's theory concerning the extant Hebrew of Ecclesiasticus cannot be said to be gaining ground. Yet, on the other hand, there is a tendency to agree that the Hebrew text, as we possess it, is not the original of the Greek, which, assuming it to be translated from Hebrew, must have followed two other recensions. The A.V. follows mainly the text of 248 and the cursives resembling it ; the R.V. that of the uncials, which is considerably shorter. The Hebrew now extant comes from four MSS. dating about the eleventh century. They include the greater part of the book, from iii. 6 onward, except xxvii. 6— xxx. 11. Some verses occur in two MSS., a few even in three; there is some variety, and considerable corruption in some places.

P. 273. Mozley, *Psalter of the Church*, p. xii, remarks on Jerome's method: 'So that neither his eyes saw the page of the original, nor his fingers held the pen.' Oxyrh. Pap. 1076, containing Tobit ii. 2, 3, 4, 8, appears to give a third recension. Dr J. Rendel Harris points out a connexion between Tobit and the Book of Jubilees; he holds that whichever borrowed from the other did so in Hebrew or Aramaic. The ℵ text seems to show traces of Aramaic influence in the forms of proper names.

P. 275. Baruch *a* (i. 1—iii. 8) is 'beyond a doubt,' Thackeray thinks, 'the production of the translator of Jeremiah β' (*J. Th. Stud.* IV. p. 261 ff. ; *Gramm. of O.T.G.* p. 12 ; cf. p. 276, note 1). Schürer thinks this part was composed in Hebrew, and later translated, and the second part added. Thus he dates iii. 9—iv. 4 about 70 A.D., while Marshall places it, in its original form, nearly 400 years earlier.

P. 279, note 2. Wendland (*Aristeas*, p. 133) says: 'equidem censeo Πτολεμαϊκά esse Aristeae, qui ex Ptolemaei ephemeridibus se hausisse testatur.'

P. 283. It is possible that the *Odes of Solomon*, of which the Syriac text was discovered by Dr Rendel Harris, and published in 1910 (ed. 2, 1911), have no real title to be mentioned here, as they may be Christian productions of a time which would remove them from any list of O.T. apocryphal writings. In view, however, of their possibly close connexion with the *Psalms of Solomon*, they may receive a passing notice. The Syriac text contained 17 (or 18) Psalms and 42 Odes. These latter have been variously estimated and explained; some, at first, thinking them to be the work of a Jewish Christian, others to be Jewish, but with Christian interpolations. The question turns mainly on the fourth and sixth Odes. The latest published theory is that of the Bishop of Ossory, who holds them to be hymns sung by (Eastern) Christians on the occasion of their public baptism. In this case, the date would be about the end of the first century A.D., while the view that their origin was Jewish admits a date as early, perhaps, as 100 B.C. Dr Bernard's view, which has already gained some adherents, is published in the Cambridge *Texts and Studies*, vol. VIII. no. 3; and the Syriac text of the Odes has also been published separately.

P. 285. To the list in the iootnote may be added the *Story of Ahikar* (*from the Syriac, Arabic, Armenian, Ethiopic, Greek, and Slavonic Versions*, edited by F. C. Conybeare, J. Rendel Harris, and Agnes Smith Lewis, Cambridge, 1898), and *The Book of the Secrets of Enoch* (or 2 Enoch), though extant only in a Slavonic version. It may be convenient also to refer here to the *Pistis Sophia*, a Gnostic work known from a Coptic MS. in the British Museum (ed. J. H. Petermann, Berlin, 1851; and examined by A. Harnack, in O. von Gebhardt's and A. Harnack's *Texte und Untersuchungen*, Band VII. 2, Leipzig, 1892); the canonical Psalter is freely quoted in it, with a text bearing marked resemblances to that of Cod. ℵ; and until Dr Rendel Harris's recent discovery, the *Odes of Solomon* were chiefly known from its quotation of them.

LITERATURE of the non-Canonical Books, add:

1 Esdras. P. Riefster, *D. text-krit. Wert des 3 Ezra-buches*, in *Bibl. Zeitung*, 5, p. 146.

Wisdom of Solomon. J. A. F. Gregg, in *Camb. Bible for Schools*.

Wisdom of the Son of Sirach. J. H. A. Hart, *Ecclesiasticus in Greek*, Cambridge, 1909; W. O. E. Oesterley in *Camb. Bible for Schools*, 1912. N. Schmidt in *Temple Bible*; R. Smend, *Griechisch-syrisch-hebräischer Index zur Weisheit d. Jes. Sirach*, 1907. On the Heb. text: J. Knabenbauer, *Comm. in Ecclesiasticum*, Paris, 1902; R. Smend, *Die Weisheit d. Jes. Sir. erklärt*, Berlin, 1906, also a Germ. translation, 1906; H. L. Strack, *Die Sprüche Jesus d. S. Sirachs*, Leipzig, 1903; A. Fuchs, *Textkr. Untersuchungen zum Heb. Ekkl.*, in *Bibl. Studien*, 1907; *Ecclesiasticus Hebraice...*, Freiburg, 1905; articles in *Encycl. Bibl.* and *Jewish Encycl.*

Facsimiles of the Fragments hitherto recovered of the Book of Ecclesiasticus in Hebrew have been published jointly by the Universities of Oxf. and Camb.

Judith. H. Willrich in *Judaica*, 1900, pp. 1—39.

Tobit. Zunz, *Die gottesdienstlichen Vorträge der Juden*, 1832; M. Löhr, *Alexandrinus und Sinaiticus zum Buche Tobit*, in *ZATW.* XX. p. 243 ff. (1900); J. H. Moulton, *The Iranian background of Tobit*, in *Exp. Times*, XI. p. 257 ff.; E. Cosquin in *D. B.* IV. p. 785 ff.; also articles in *Revue Biblique*, Jan. 1899, in *Jewish Encycl.* XII. p. 171 (C. H. Toy) and *Encycl. Bibl.* (W. Erbt).

Baruch. A. M. Amelli, *De libri Baruch vetustissima latina versione*, Montecassino, 1902.

1—4 Maccabees. W. Fairweather and J. S. Black, 1 *Maccabees*, in *Camb. Bible for Schools*; B. Niese, *Kritik der beiden Makkabäerbücher*, Berlin, 1900; R. Laqueur, *Kritische Untersuchungen zum zweiten Makkabäerbuch*, Strassburg, 1904; G. Mercati, *Frammenti Urbinati d' un' antica versione latina del libro II. de' Maccabei*, in *Revue Biblique*, II. p. 184 ff.; I. Abrahams in *J. Q. R.* 1896, p. 39, 1897, p. 39; H. Willrich, *Jason von Kyrene und das ii Makkabäerbuch*, in *Judaica*, 1900, pp. 131 ff.; A. Schlatter, *Jason von Cyrene*, Munich, 1891; A. Büchler, *Die Tobiaden und die Oniaden im II Makkabäerbuch*, Vienna, 1899.

Pseudepigrapha. R. H. Charles and A. Cowley, *An early source of the Testaments of the Twelve Patriarchs, J. Q. R.* XIX. p. 566 ff.

General. L. E. T. André, *Les Apocryphes de l'Ancien Testament*, Florence, 1903; A. Bertholet, *Apocryphen*, in K. Budde's *Geschichte der alt-hebräischen Literatur*, Leipzig, 1906; arts. in *Encycl. Bibl.* and Schaff-Herzog *Encycl.*

In 1913 appeared the two great volumes of the Oxford *Apocrypha and Pseudepigrapha*, edited by Prof. R. H. Charles. This contains translations, with critical and explanatory notes and full Introductions, of all the books of the Apocrypha, 3 and 4 Maccabees, 1 and 2 Enoch, 2 and 3 Baruch, The Book of Jubilees, The Testaments of the XII. Patriarchs, The Letter of Aristeas, The Sibylline Oracles, The Story of Aḥiḳar, and a few other works. The editor has had the assistance of various eminent scholars, including the producers of the original edition of the Story of Aḥiḳar ; and the work, from its comprehensive and complete character, promises to be indispensable to students for years to come. It is only possible here to indicate its great importance.

P. 289. During the last ten to twenty years, students have devoted great and increasing attention to the Greek language of those centuries during which the books of the Greek Bible, translated or original, appeared. Large quantities of papyri, literary and familiar, have been discovered and examined ; including many Biblical fragments. The Oxyrhynchus, Tebtunis, Amherst, Rylands, and other collections—many of them edited with admirable skill by Drs Grenfell and Hunt—form a rich store, which will doubtless continue to grow. The study of these materials has brought about a certain shifting in the estimate formed of the language of the Greek Bible, to which Professor Deissmann and Professor Moulton have given a strong impulse. They urge that the difference between the language of the Greek Old and New Testaments, and other contemporary Greek, is shown by the study of the papyri to be, lexically and grammatically, almost non-existent ; they bring forward parallels from the papyri to almost every construction and phrase formerly termed a 'Hebraism' ; and account for them as colloquial, ordinary, or illiterate Greek of the period, rather than as Semiticised, or as specially Egyptian or Alexandrian. They make an exception as regards what they call 'translation Greek' ; but the student whose interest lies mainly in the Septuagint may think that so large a portion of it comes under this head, that the exception may carry them further from their main position than they are in fact prepared to go. Against their view Wellhausen (in his *Einleitung in die drei erste Evangelien*, 1905) speaks strongly for Aramaism in the N.T. itself ; and others (e.g. G. C. Richards in his review of Moulton's prolegomena to his *Grammar of the New Test. in Greek*, in *J. Th. Stud.* X. 38, p. 283 ff. Jan. 1909) feel the Semitic tone or cast of much of the Greek Bible, and of particular expressions in it, to be so marked, that even the appearance of parallel or identical expressions in the papyri does not entirely convince them that Semitic influence is out of the question as the cause that produces them where they stand, and in the quantity that is present. On the whole, there is a natural tendency for those who are mainly New Testament scholars and Greek philologists to favour what may be called the purely Greek theory, while the Semitic influence is more prominent in the minds of those whose life's study has been chiefly concerned with Hebrew and Aramaic. But a general survey of the question suggests that the difference is rather a matter of terms and of aspect than of real divergence as to the main mass of facts. The balance is very fairly held by the author of the *Grammar of the*

Old Testament in Greek : see pp. 25 ff., 31 ff. He speaks of...
'a general recognition that the basis of the language of the Greek
Bible is the vernacular employed throughout the whole Greek-
speaking world since the time of Alexander the Great. The
number of " Hebraisms" formerly so called has been reduced by
phenomena in the papyri, the importance of which Deissmann was
the first to recognise': but follows this with a caution: 'the
emphasis which has been laid upon the occurrence of certain
words and usages in the Egyptian papyri which are exactly equivalent to, or bear a fairly close resemblance to, phrases in the Greek
Bible hitherto regarded as " Hebraic" is likely to create a false impression, especially as regards the nature of the Semitic element
in the LXX.' He points out the slightness of dialect-differences in
the κοινή, and dismisses the theory of a '"Jewish-Greek" jargon, in
use in the Ghettos of Alexandria'; but adds, 'Notwithstanding
that certain so-called " Hebraisms" have been removed from that
category...it is impossible to deny the existence of a strong Semitic
influence in the Greek of the LXX.' He agrees in the main with
Dr J. H. Moulton as to 'the *overworking* of...certain correct,
though unidiomatic, modes of speech, because they happen to
coincide with Hebrew idioms.' Once more: 'The Hebraic character of these books [the Pentateuch and some other of the earlier
versions] consists in the *accumulation* of a number of just tolerable
Greek phrases, which nearly correspond to what is normal and
idiomatic in Hebrew.'

The present writer must content himself with a reference to his
Isaiah according to the Septuagint, vol. I. p. 35 ff., 'Methods of
Rendering,' for a slightly different view of the subject. But it
may be of interest to quote a passage from a book published so
long ago as 1875 (A. Carr, *Notes on St Luke*, Introduction, p. 9 ff.)
to show how far it was possible even then, before the discovery and
study of the papyri had made much progress, to estimate the
nature of the Greek of the Alexandrian and New Testament
periods. Most of the following passages might have been written
yesterday.

'When the books of the New Testament were written, Greek
had become the literary language of the world.... The Greek
dialect which the Evangelists and Apostles adopted or found is
a far less exact representative of thought than the Greek that was
handled by Thucydides or Euripides—the middle voice is rapidly
disappearing, the dual number is never employed, the tenses of
verbs are losing their distinctive force, and the aorist is beginning
to be used...to the exclusion of the synthetic perfect.... The Attic
dialect...was in a sense limited and peculiar. Its fastidious nature
made it impatient of foreign intrusion. Hellenistic Greek, on the
contrary, was all-embracing in its sympathies.... The purest Attic
appears on the same page with an antiquated Aeolic form or a

modern barbarism. The campaigns of Alexander...the luxury of eastern satraps, the schools of Alexandria,...the Homeric enthusiasm of the grammarians,...have contributed to store the rich though barbarous magazine of Hellenistic Greek.

' It will be seen that Hellenistic Greek did not grow degenerate in the lips of natives, but was corrupted by foreigners; and, just as the waters of a stream are coloured by the soil over which they flow, so the Greek language in the New Testament is strongly influenced by Aramaic forms of expression. It is, indeed, often simply Aramaic thinly disguised by a Greek dress. But, on the other hand, there has been, perhaps, too great a tendency to set down every idiom that offends the scholar's ear as a Hebrew mode of expression. This strangeness of idiom is frequently to be referred to other causes. Sometimes it is the influence of Latin; sometimes the idiom will be found to be Greek as well as Hebrew, but Greek of a kind that had been heretofore confined to the speech of the vulgar.'

P 314. Literature. Add:

G. A. Deissmann, *Licht vom Osten*, 1907; English trans. by L. R. M. Strachan, London, 1910; *Bible Studies* (including *Bibel-Studien* and *Neue Bibel-Studien*), trans. A. Grieve, Edinburgh, 1901; *Philology of the Greek Bible*, 1908; R. Helbing, *Grammatik der Septuaginta*, i. *Laut- und Wortlehre*, 1907; H. St J. Thackeray, *Grammar of the Old Test. in Greek*, vol. i. Introd., *Orthography and Accidence*, Cambridge, 1909; J. Psichari, *Essai sur le Grec de la Septante*, in *Revue des Études Juives*, Tome LV. No. 110, Paris, 1908; R. Meister, *Prolegomena zu einer Grammatik der Septuaginta*, in *Wiener-Studien*, XXVII. 2; *Beiträge zur Lautlehre der LXX.*, Vienna, 1909; G. N. Hatzidakis, *Einleitung in die neugriechische Grammatik*, Leipzig, 1892; A. Thumb, *Handbook of the Modern Greek Vernacular*, trans. S. Angus, Edinburgh, 1912; art. *Hellenistic Greek* in Funk and Wagnall's *American Standard Bible Dictionary*; J. Wackernagel, *Hellenistica*, Göttingen, 1907; U. von Wilamowitz-Moellendorff, *Ueber die Entstehung der griechischen Schriftsprache*, Leipzig, 1879.

On the grammar of the New Testament: J. H. Moulton, *A Grammar of N. T. Greek*, Prolegomena, ed. 3, 1908; *N. T. Greek in the Light of Modern Discovery*, in *Camb. Biblical Essays*, 1909; F. Blass, *Philology of the Gospels*, 1898; J. de Zwaan, *Syntaxis der Wijzen en Tijden in het Grieksche Nieuwe Testament*, Haarlem, 1906.

In connexion with Semitism in N.T. Greek: J. Wellhausen, *Einleitung in die drei ersten Evangelien*, Berlin, 1905; G. C. Richard's review of Moulton's Prolegomena, *Gramm. of N. T. Greek*, in *J. Th. Stud.* x. 38, pp. 283 ff. Monographs and articles on special points extend over a wide range: e.g. H. F. Allen, *The Infinitive in Polybius compared with the Infin. in Biblical Greek*, Chicago, 1907; H. A. Redpath on *The Present Position of the Study of the LXX.* and on *The Geography of the LXX.*, in *A. J. Th.* VII. (Jan., Apr. 1903).

The Oxford *Concordance to the Septuagint* was completed in 1906.

Introductory: *Selections from the Septuagint according to the text of Swete*, by F. C. Conybeare and St G. Stock, Boston, 1905.

The publications of papyri have become very numerous; among them are:

British Museum Papyri, ed. F. G. Kenyon, 1893.
Paris Papyri (in *Notices et Extraits*), ed. Brunet de Presle, 1858, 1865.
Berlin, *Griechische Urkunden*, ed. U. Wilcken, 1895, 1898, 1903, ed. W. Schubart, 1911.
Flinders Petrie Papyri, ed. J. P. Mahaffy (in *Proc. R.I.A.*), 1891, etc.
Papyri Graeci Regii Taurinensis Musei Aegyptii, ed. Peyrow, Turin, 1826.
Geneva Papyri, ed. J. Nicole, 1896, 1900.
Corpus Papyrorum Raineri, ed. C. Wessely, Vienna, 1895.
Florence Papyri, ed. Vitelli, Milan, 1905.
Die Septuaginta Papyri...der Heidelberger Papyrus Sammlung, ed. G. A. Deissmann, 1905.
Papyri Graeci Musei antiquarii publici, ed. C. Leemans, Leyden, 1843.
Papyrus Grecs de l'Université de Lille, ed. P. Collart and J. Lesquier, Paris, 1908.
Karanis Papyri, ed. E. J. Goodspeed, Chicago, 1900.
Eine Mithras-Liturgie, ed. A. Dieterich, Leipzig, 1903.
Pathyris Papyri, ed. de Ricci (*Archiv* II. p. 514).
Griech. Pap. der k. Bibl. zu Strassburg, ed. F. Preisigke, 1907, 1912.
Griech. Papyri zu Giessen, ed. E. Kornemann and P. M. Meyer, Leipzig and Berlin, 1912.
And the various publications of the Egypt Exploration Fund, chiefly edited by B. P. Grenfell and A. S. Hunt:
The Oxyrhynchus Papyri, edited with translations and notes. Nine parts up to 1912.
Fayûm Towns and their Papyri, 1900; *The Amherst Papyri*, 1900, 1901; *The Tebtunis Papyri* (Univ. of California Publications), two parts; the *Hibeh Papyri*, 1906.

Also *Catalogue of the Greek Papyri in the John Rylands Library*, Manchester, ed. A. S. Hunt, 1911.

Here may be mentioned also ΛΟΓΙΑ ΙΗΣΟΥ, *from an early Greek Papyrus; New Sayings of Jesus, and Fragment of a lost Gospel; Fragment of an uncanonical Gospel from Oxyrhynchus; An Alexandrian erotic Fragment, and other Greek Papyri, chiefly Ptolemaic; New Classical Fragments and other Papyri.*

Coptic Ostraca, from the collections of the E. E. Fund, etc.... texts edited...by W. E. Crum, London, 1902.

In connexion with the study of these papyri, various selections and aids have appeared.

S. Witkowski, *Epistulae privatae Graecae quae in papyris aetatis Lagidarum servantur*, Leipzig, 1905; H. Lietzmann, *Greek Papyri (Materials for Theol. Lect. and Students*, No. 14), Cambridge, 1905; G. Milligan, *Selections from the Greek Papyri*, Cambridge, 1910.

F. G. Kenyon, *Palaeography of Greek Papyri*, 1899; E. Mayser, *Grammatik der griechischen Papyri aus der Ptolemäerzeit*, Leipzig, 1906; W. Crönert, *Memoria Graeca Herculanensis*, Leipzig, 1903; L. Mitteis and U. Wilcken, *Grundzüge und Chrestomathie der Papyruskunde*, 4 vols., Leipzig and Berlin, 1912.

The publications on the kindred study of Inscriptions are widely scattered, largely in periodicals, and so numerous that only a small selection can be mentioned here :

E. S. Roberts and E. A. Gardner, *Introduction to Greek Epigraphy*, vol. 1 (out of print), vol. 2, 1905; W. Larfeld, *Handbuch der Griechischen Epigraphik*, Leipzig, vol. 1, 1908, vol. 2, 1902; E. Schwyzer (formerly Schweizer), *Grammatik der pergamenischen Inschriften*, Berlin, 1898, and a new edition of K. Meisterhans' *Grammatik der attischen Inschriften*, Berlin, 1900; E. Nachmanson, *Laute und Formen der magnetischen Inschriften*, Upsala, 1903; O. Kern, *Die Inschriften von Magnesia am Maeander*, Berlin, 1900; F. Hiller von Gaertringen, *Inschriften von Priene*, 1906.

The Berlin *Inscriptiones Graecae* now extend to twelve volumes; there are also four vols. of *Inscr. Gr. ad res Romanas pertinentes*, Paris; and the *Recueil d'Inscriptions grecques*, ed. C. Michel (Brussels, 1900, suppl. i. 1911).

(The study of the Inscriptions is important, because they range over the whole of the Greek-speaking territory, while papyri are chiefly confined to Egypt. Hence they are used to establish the position that the κοινή was, in the main, homogeneous and free from dialectical differences. Their style is, naturally, more elevated than that of letters and local documents, but they belong to the κοινή, and are not altogether remote from the more 'vulgar' Greek which is found in the bulk of papyri.)

P. 317. γένοιτο also occurs in Isa. xxv. 1, where the Hebrew word has presumably been taken for אָמֵן by LXX., though M.T. points it differently.

P. 319. The spelling of the Hebrew Bible is perhaps based on that of a MS., no longer extant, of about A.D. 135.

P. 321. Other cases of possible confusions are between :

כ and ר, see 4 Regn. v. 19, where כִּבְרַת is transliterated δεβραθά.

ר and ו, Isai. xxviii. 10, 13, θλίψις (צַר) for צָו.

ר and ה, Isai. viii. 12, σκληρόν = קָשֶׁה for קֶשֶׁר 'conspiracy.'

ס and מ, Isai. iii. 10, δήσωμεν, root אסר for אמר.

Cf. the strong remarks in Driver's *Hebrew Tenses* (p. xiii. in first ed.) on the worthlessness of LXX.'s evidence as between ۱ and ٫ with numerous instances.

P. 324. With ἐν ἐμοί of 1 Regn. i. 26, cf. ἐπ' ἐμοί, Isai. xxi. 2, for 'עֲלֵ‎, "Go up.'

(*b*). On transliteration, Thackeray (*Gramm. O.T.G.* p. 31) points out that it is rare in the Pentateuch, Isaiah, Jerem. *a*, and the Minor Prophets; and absent altogether from Ezek. *β*, Proverbs, Psalms (except in titles, and ἀλληλουιά), and from Job, apart from the Hexaplar additions from Theodotion. In Isaiah, moreover, only two instances occur, of which σωρήχ, v. 2, is *possibly* a proper name; while νεχωθά, xxxix. 2, is in a passage that runs parallel with 4 Kingdoms; the transliteration occurs in both places in the Greek, and in Isaiah is not impossibly a doublet.

P. 327. The LXX. appear to avoid the familiar metaphor of a 'Rock' in nearly all cases;

See Deut. xxxii. 5, 15, 18, 30, 31, 37; 2 Regn. xxiii. 3; Ps. xvii. 2, 32 (= 2 Regn. xxii. 2, 32), xxx. 3, lx. 2, lxi. 6; Habak. i. 12; Isai. xvii. 10, xxx. 29, xxxii. 2, xliv. 8; but not xxxi. 9. Gen. xlix. 24 is hardly a certain instance, Heb. being different.

P. 330. Gen. xv. 1—6.

1. πολὺς ἔσται. Heb. has here Hiphil inf. abs., used predicatively.
2. ἀπολύομαι. For this sense of the verb, cf. Soph. *Antig.* 1265, 1314; also in Polybius. Can הֹלֵךְ have the sense of 'depart this life'? See xxv. 32; Eccles. v. 15; Isai. xxxviii. 10; Ps. xxxviii. 14.
3. κληρονομήσει. This sense is found also in the later literary Greek.
4. Ἐκ σοῦ. Cf. Exod. i. 5.

P. 333. Josh. x. 13. H.-P. give G.'s reading wrongly as ἔθνους.

P. 336. 4 Regn. ii. 14. καὶ διερράγησαν, Luc. καὶ οὐ διῃρέθη, Vulg. *et non sunt divisae.*
Consult throughout this passage Burney's *Notes on the Hebrew Text of the Books of Kings.*

Ps. cix. (cx.) 1—4. See Mozley, *Psalter of the Church,* p. 164.

P. 340. Literature.

Add: M. L. Margolis, *Studien in griech. A.T., ZATW.,* 27, p. 212; H. A. Redpath, *Mytholog. Terms in the LXX.,* in *A.J. Th.* 9, 1. p. 34 (Jan. 1905).

P. 360. It was pointed out by the late Dr C. Taylor that in Lam. ii.—iv., whereas in the Hebrew פ precedes ע, the Greek uncials (except Q^mg and sometimes Q*), while preserving the order of the verses, prefix αιν and φη in the order now usual. Conversely, in Prov. xxix. 43, 44 (= Heb. xxxi. 26, 25) אB have the פ verse before the ע verse.

P. 366. Add : E. Lindl, *Die Octateuch-Catene des Prokop von Gaza und die Septuagintaforschung*, Munich, 1902.

P. 380. Add : J. Herriot, *Philon le Juif*, Paris, 1898.

P. 387. The phrase χλωρὸς χόρτος, Mark vi. 39, is curious. It is not given by Westcott and Hort as a reference to the Old Testament ; but, whereas it is peculiar to Mark's account, it is found in the LXX., Gen. i. 30, Isa. xv. 6, xxxvii. 27 A.

P. 398. In Zech. xii. 10 the LXX. verb is κατωρχήσαντο, i.e. רקדו for דקרו (see Bp Lightfoot, *Biblical Essays*, p. 136).

P. 418. Rahlfs (*Sept.-Studien*, II. p. 206) regards Justin's quotations as having been corrected by scribes from texts of the LXX.; as also those of the Fathers, e.g. Theodoret (p. 175) and Clem. Rom. (p. 201). He refers to Hilgenfeld, in Baur and Zeller's *Theolog. Jahrbücher*, 1850, and Bousset, *Die Evangeliencitate Justins d. Märtyrers*, p. 19 ff. : also Hatch, *Essays in Bibl. Greek*, p. 186 ff.

P. 424. The question has been raised (in correspondence, by Mr R. B. Girdlestone) whether there are to be found any distinctively Jewish, as opposed to Christian, MSS. of the LXX. It is not easy to answer categorically. But, in view of the dates when the translation appears to have been made, and the fact that the latest books to be translated offer, in general, the smallest opportunities for changes to be made by Christian hands, it would seem that the translation, originally purely Jewish, can have suffered very little in this way. (See p. 30 ff.) For instance, the famous addition in Ps. xcv. 10, though widely current in Christian literature, has practically almost no support in MSS. of the LXX.; and the reading ἄρωμεν in Isa. iii. 10 has actually none, occurring as it does in Justin, *D.* 136, 137. Clem. Alex. *Strom.* v. 14, *auferamus* Tert. *adv. Marc.* III. 22. All existing MSS. give what Justin calls the Jewish reading, δήσωμεν ; while, as Hatch, *Essays*, p. 197, points out, neither reading corresponds with the Hebrew as we have it. In Josh. xv. again, the LXX. text after *v.* 59 appears to represent an accidental, and very natural, omission in the Hebrew ; cf. xxi. 36, 37. It is not even necessary to suppose that the words αὕτη ἐστὶν Βαιθλεέμ are a Greek interpolation.

The just conclusion seems to be that, previous to Origen, the text was scarcely affected, if at all; and Origen's intentions were certainly not such as to impair the *Hebraica veritas* ; so that if any Christian additions have slipped here or there into the text, they are probably few and slight ; there is no trace of anything that approaches to deliberate Christianising of the text. The times when such a thing might have been possible were not those when the LXX. text passed through its main vicissitudes. See Kenyon, *Our Bible and the Ancient Manuscripts*, p. 89 ff., and his conclusion that ' the vast majority of the differences between the Hebrew and the Greek throughout the Old Testament could have had no possible partisan motive whatever.'

See also page 479.

P. 427. Mr Thackeray (*J. Th. Stud.* XIII. 49), writing on *The Poetry of the Greek Book of Proverbs*, finds an astonishing number of metrical and quasi-metrical passages. He now adds that 'Clem. Alex.'s text of Proverbs...occasionally preserves the metrical and probably original forms which have disappeared from other texts, e.g. :

Prov. ii. 21. ὅτι εὐθεῖς κατασκηνώσουσι γῆν]
Clem. Al. *Strom.* II. 19, 483ᴾ
χρηστοὶ δὲ ἔσονται οἰκήτορες γῆς,
?orig. text χρηστοὶ δ' ἔσονται τῆσδε γῆς οἰκήτορες.
Cf. Cod. V, Arm. and Clem. Rom. ; also the readings of ℵA.
vi. 23 b. καὶ ἔλεγχος καὶ παιδεία]
Strom. I. 29, 247ᴾ
ὁδοὺς γὰρ βιότητος ἐλέγχει παιδεία,
?orig. παιδεία γὰρ ὁδοὺς βιότητος ἐλέγχει.
βιότης = βιὸς is else a ἅπαξ λεγ. in Prov. v. 23.

Similarly Chrysostom is possibly right in reading, in Prov. xv. 17b :

ἢ παράθεσις μόσχων μετὰ ἔχθρας
ἢ βοῦς ἀπὸ φάτνης.'

P. 432. Literature: add Constantinus Oikonomus, vol. IV.

P. 442. There is an excursus on Gen. xlix. 10 in the earlier editions (previous to the fourth) of Cheyne's *Prophecies of Isaiah*.

P. 448. Ὑπὲρ τῶν κρυφίων τοῦ υἱοῦ. See Mr Thackeray's paper in *J. Th. Stud.* XI. 44, referred to above, on p. 247.

P. 486. In 1907 Professor Rahlfs developed a provisional plan for a scientific edition of the LXX. : the Academy of Berlin, the Royal Society of Göttingen, and the Prussian Ministerium of Instruction to cooperate. MSS. were to be collated, in Greek, Coptic, Ethiopic, Syriac, Armenian, Georgian and Slavonic. The

Latin MSS. to be left to the Pontifical Commission for the revision of the Vulgate. The Fathers to be examined by various scholars; Dr E. Hautsch taking Theodoret. See *Erster Bericht über das Septuaginta-Unternehmen,* 1908 (*Nachrichten d. k. G. d. W. zu Göttingen*); Geschäftliche Mitteilungen, 1909, Heft 1.

See also a brief account by Dr Nestle in *A. J. Th.* XIV. 2 (April 1910); as well as his *Die grosse Cambridger Septuaginta* (Verhandlungen der XIII. Internationalen Orientalistenkongresses, 1902).

P. 490. Both A and B, as has been seen, show here and there signs of considerable Hexaplaric addition. It is therefore fortunate that, owing to the varying character of the books in our great Greek Bibles, this influence seldom affects both MSS. equally in the same passages. On Job, see Burkitt, *O. L. and Itala,* pp. 6 ff., 32 ff. Even within the same book, Rahlfs finds the character of A different in what remains of Psalms xxx.—ciii. and at the beginning and end of the book. On Cod. ℵ see Professor Kirsopp Lake's Introduction to the photograph of the N.T. (cf. above, on p. 130). On the text of the Prophets see O. Procksch, *Stud. z. Geschichte der Sept.* (below). His verdict is in favour of A's text, with Q near to it; ℵ he places next, and B akin to it. This latter text, though inferior to AQ, he considers to be that on which Origen worked. The text underlying the hexaplaric cursives comes, he thinks, between AQ and ℵB, but nearer to the latter. The pre-hexaplar cursives approximate to A. The history of the Septuagint is 'the story of its removal from the maximum to the minimum distance from the M.T.' This account is mainly based on an excellent survey in *A. J. Th.* XIV. p. 493.

L. Dieu (*Muséon,* 1912, p. 223 f.) who has investigated the text of Job from various points of view—see above, on p. 108—considers that A in that book is mainly Lucianic. This he deduces from the intrinsic character of its text ('corrections d'après l'hébreu, doublets, remaniements d'après des passages parallèles, corrections destinées à éclaircir le sens ou compléter la phrase, tendances à l'atticisme': cf, Rahlfs, *Sept. Stud.* II. p. 230, 236, III. p. 158, 172, 281 ff.), as well as from its associates, which are here rather curious; an anonymous Arian commentary on ch. i.—iii., known only in a Latin translation; a commentary formerly attributed to Origen, but assigned by Dr H. Usener to Julian of Halicarnassus; and another, in the Laurentian Library at Florence, attributed, though somewhat doubtfully, to Chrysostom. To these are to be added V, in the first, the cursives 249 and 254, in the second, and 55, 68, 106, 261 in the third degree of closeness. Some of these, especially 68 and 106, are held to give a Hesychian text in other books; and in Isaiah, for instance, 106 goes very closely with A, and is, perhaps, the more markedly Hesychian. For 55, see Rahlfs, II. p. 235.

S. S.

M. Dieu considers that A's text in Job is nearer to the original than that of אB; he calls the Sahidic to witness; but see above, on pp. 85, 108. He also adduces in support the marginal readings of Cod. Gothicus Legionensis: see Rahlfs, III. 158, and *Notices et Extraits*, XXXIV. pp. 134 ff.

P. 497. Add:

O. Procksch, *Studien zur Geschichte der Septuaginta*, in Kittel's *Beiträge zur Wissenschaft vom A.T.* Heft 7, Leipzig, 1910; G. Jahn, *Beiträge z. Beurteilung der Septuaginta. Ein Wurdigung Wellhausencher Textkritik*, 1902; *Ester* (1901), *Daniel* (1904), *Ezechiel* (1905); J. Dahse, *Textkritische Studien*, in *ZATW.* 1908, pp. 18 ff., 161 ff.

APPENDIX.

THE LETTER OF ARISTEAS

INTRODUCTION.

The so-called letter of Aristeas to Philocrates appeared first in print in a Latin translation by Matthias Palmerius of Pisa (Rome, 1471). The editio princeps of the Greek text was not published until 1561, when Simon Schard brought out at Basle a text based on a MS. hitherto supposed to be lost, with a few readings taken from a second (Vatican) MS. Wendland in his recent edition (1900) has made it practically certain that Schard's principal MS. was Codex Monacensis 9, which at that time was at Tübingen and easily accessible to him. As to his second MS., there exists in the Library at Basle (MS. O. IV. 10, no. 21 in Omont's *Catalogue of Swiss MSS.*) a MS. presented to it by Schard, which is beyond a doubt a copy of the Vatican MS. denoted by K in the present text; and a list of readings appended to Schard's edition under the heading 'castigationes in Aristeam juxta exemplar Vaticanae' appears to be a scanty selection of the readings of K. Schard's edition was followed by others in the seventeenth century based upon his work; but it does not appear that any fresh collation of MSS. was undertaken[1]. Until 1870 the latest edition of the text was that which Hody prefixed to his work *De Bibliorum Textibus*, published at Oxford in 1705. This was merely a reprint of the text of Schard, Hody naïvely confessing in his preface that he did not consider the work of collating MSS. of a work of such doubtful authenticity to be worth the trouble. 'Non me fugit servari in Bibliotheca Regia Parisina, aliisque quibusdam, exemplaria istius MSS. Sed de tali opusculo, quod tanquam foetum supposititium penitus rejicio, Amicos solicitare, et in Partes longinquas mittere, vix operae pretium existimavi. Eas curas relinquo illis, quibus tanti esse res videbitur.'

The first step towards a critical edition of the text was taken by Moriz Schmidt, who in 1870 brought out in Merx's *Archiv* (Band I.) a text based on a complete collation of two Paris MSS., which he denoted by B and C, and a partial collation of a third, A, which was used to supply the opening of the letter which was missing in B and C. Schmidt's edition, though a valuable beginning, is far from satisfactory. A full use was not made of the evidence for the text afforded by the paraphrase of Josephus and the extracts of Eusebius. Moreover a large number of MSS. of the letter is now known to exist; and fresh light has been thrown on the language by the papyri of the Ptolemaic period which have at various times been discovered in Egypt.

The valuable help which these papyri offer as an illustration of the letter, shewing that the writer possessed an accurate knowledge

---

[1] The earlier editions are enumerated by Schmidt in his preface to the text (Merx, *Archiv*, Bd. I. 1870).

of the official titles and phraseology of the Ptolemaic court, was first pointed out by Prof. Lumbroso. He says[1], 'Depuis quarante ans, un rayon de lumière inattendu a jailli des inscriptions et des papyrus, qui jette sur elle un jour nouveau ; chose frappante : il n'est pas un titre de cour, une institution, une loi, une magistrature, une charge, un terme technique, une formule, un tour de langue remarquable dans cette lettre, il n'est pas un témoignage d'Aristée concernant l'histoire civile de l'époque, qui ne se trouve enregistré dans les papyrus ou les inscriptions et confirmé par eux'[2]. A close examination of the larger evidence from the papyri now available will probably corroborate the opinion, to which other evidence seems to point, that the letter was written under some one of the later Ptolemies. In any case the evidence of the papyri is an important factor to be taken into account in establishing a text.

Another illustration of the text is afforded by a kindred work, also dealing with the history of the Jews of Egypt under the Ptolemaic rule, the third Book of Maccabees[3].

Prof. Lumbroso further supplemented Schmidt's work upon the text by collating the Paris MS. A throughout, and also a MS. in the British Museum (F), and one at Venice (G) ; he also indicated the existence of five MSS. in the Vatican, but it does not appear that he has published any collations of these Roman MSS.

In 1893 the want of an edition of the letter was represented to the present writer, and in a journey to Italy in the autumn of that year he collated the five Vatican MSS. mentioned by Lumbroso (HKLIM), and one in the library of the Barberini palace (P), and revised the collations which had already been made of the MSS. at Venice (G) and Paris (ABC); at Paris he also collated the fragment Q and the MS. D, so far as was necessary to establish the fact that it was a copy of A. He has since collated a MS. at Florence (T) and another at Zurich (Z). On his learning subsequently that Prof. Mendelssohn of Dorpat had for many years been preparing an edition of the letter, which was nearly ready, the work which he had begun was put aside. Prof. Mendelssohn's death postponed the appearance of the expected German edition ; a fragment only, consisting of the text of about

---

[1] *Recherches sur l'économie politique de l'Égypte sous les Lagides,* par G. Lumbroso (Turin, 1870), p. xiii.

[2] Some instances are the titles ἀρχισωματοφύλακες, οἱ ἐπὶ τῶν χρειῶν, χρηματισταί, οἱ ὑπηρέται τῶν ταγμάτων (cf. ταγματικοῖς ὑπηρέταις Wilcken, *Actenstücke Pap.* VIII.), the phrase ἐὰν φαίνηται, the correct use of εὐτύχει at the close of a petition from a subordinate to a higher official, the words ἑκατοντάρουρος and παρεύρεσις, the phrase παραγενέσθαι εἰς τοὺς τόπους.

[3] Cf. especially 3 Maccabees iii. 25—28 (προστετάχαμεν—διειλήφαμεν—μηνύειν δὲ τὸν βουλόμενον) with Ar. p. 523. 23 ff. (προστετάχαμεν—διειλήφαμεν—τὸν δὲ βουλόμενον προσαγγέλλειν).

a fifth of the letter with commentary but without introduction, was published soon after his death[1]. The remainder of his work was placed in the hands of Prof. Wendland, who has now brought out a text on which no pains have been spared, followed by the *testimonia* critically edited, and full and valuable indices[2]. The present writer had, before the appearance of the German edition, been entrusted by Dr Swete with the preparation of a text of the letter from such materials as he had at hand. In this second edition he has made free use of Wendland's work, as also of his translation of the letter in Kautzsch's *Apokryphen und Pseudepigraphen des Alten Testaments.* The apparatus criticus will show how many obscurities have been cleared up by the acute conjectures of Mendelssohn, Wendland, and their collaborateurs. For one happy emendation (§ 105, p. 538) the writer is indebted to the Rev. H. A. Redpath. For convenience of reference Wendland's sections have been inserted in the margin. It must be added that one early MS. (Cod. Monacensis 9), which stands by itself, and is probably the parent of Schard's edition, is unrepresented in the present text.

The following genealogical table will show approximately how the MSS. which have been used are related to each other.

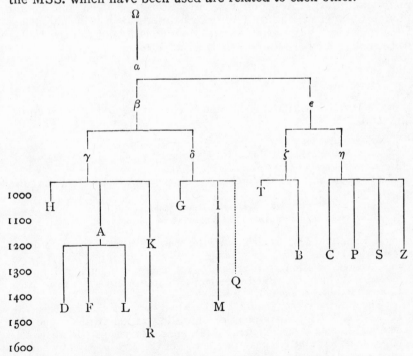

---

[1] *Aristeae quae fertur ad Philocratem epistulae initium*, ed. L. Mendelssohn et M. Krascheninnikov (Dorpat, 1897).

[2] *Aristeae ad Philocratem Epistola* etc. Ludovici Mendelssohn schedis usus edidit Paulus Wendland (Leipzig, Teubner, 1900).

The MSS. denoted in the above table are as follows:

H	Vat. 747.	M	Ottobon. 32.
A	Paris 128.	Q	Paris 950.
D	Paris 130.	T	Florence Laur. Acquisti 44.
F	Brit. Mus. Burney 34.	B	Paris 129.
L	Vat. 746.	C	Paris 5.
K	Vat. 383.	P	Barberini IV. 56.
R	Basle O. IV. 10 (Omont 21).	S	Vat. 1668.
G	Venice 534.	Z	Zurich Bibl. de la Ville C. 11
I	Palat. 203.		(Omont 169).

It will be seen that the MSS. fall into two main groups, which may for convenience be described as the A and B groups, the A group again falling into two smaller groups HKA and GIM, and the B group into two smaller groups TB and CPSZ. The real problem in fixing the text is to determine the relative value of the A and B groups. An examination of the readings shows, in the opinion of the present writer, that the B group, which was followed by Schmidt, while presenting a specious text, is in reality based on a recension, although in a few passages it has kept the original readings ; in the A group no correction has taken place, and though the text which has here been handed down is by no means free from corruption, yet the true reading is in most cases rather to be looked for here than in the revised B text.

The group HA(DFL)K(R).

H, CODEX VATICANUS. Rome. Vat. Gr. 747, saec. xi. membr. foll. 260.

fol. 1. Aristeas.

12. Letter of Theodoret to Hypatius. καὶ ἄλλοι μὲν φιλομαθεῖς ἄνδρες—εἰς προοίμιον τῆς θεοπνεύστου γραφῆς.

13. Catena of Theodoret and other patristic writers on the Octateuch.

259. πόσαι παραδόσεις εἰσὶ τῆς θείας γραφῆς.

260. ποσάκις καί ποτε ἐπορθήθησαν οἱ ἐξ Ἰσραήλ.

A beautiful MS., in clearly written cursive characters, which hang from ruled lines, containing coloured illustrations throughout (five in the Aristeas portion), ornamental red head-pieces and red initial letters in the margin. Single column, 48 lines in a page : size of page 14 × 10½ in., of writing 11¼ × 7¾ in.

The Catena is apparently by the same hand as the Aristeas, the LXX. text being in the same size of writing as the Aristeas, and the marginal Catena in smaller writing (80 lines in a page). There is one large omission in the Aristeas, two leaves of the MS. apparently having been lost. The verso of fol. 3 ends with τὴν τράπεζαν (p. 530. 8), and λείπει is written in an early hand at the foot of the page ; fol. 4 begins with μὲν πεδινῶν (538. 11) and ÷ is written in the margin.

K, CODEX VATICANUS. Rome. Vat. Gr. 383, saec. xii.—-xiii.
membr. 319 foll.

fol. 1. Aristeas.
29. Theodoret to Hypatius.
19vo. Catena on Genesis.
187. Catena on Exodus.

Size of page 12¾ × 9 in., of writing 10½ × 7¼ in.: 38 lines in a page.
The leaves at the beginning are soiled and worm-eaten. The words
hang from ruled lines : the right-hand margin is irregular, the writing
going beyond the perpendicular line in places. The writing is upright
with very thick strokes, clear, but rather untidy.

R, CODEX BASILEENSIS. Basle. Codd. Gr. O. IV. 10 (Omont[1]
21). This MS., written in the sixteenth century, apparently for
Schard's edition, but only very sparingly used by him in an
appendix of readings, is clearly a direct transcript of the preceding
MS. This may be shown by the following instances out of many :
ου KR (ων cett.) p. 519. 4, διαθεσις καθαρα KR (καθ. διαθεσις cett.)
p. 519. 8, κυριωτερον KR (κυριωτατον cett.) p. 519. 9, οι ανδρες
ασφαλως KR (ασφ. οι ανδρες cett.) p. 528. 10, σαλισγουμενοι KR
(συναλισγ. cett.) p. 543. 23, χρωμεθα KR (χρωμενα cett.) p. 544. 10,
om. και περι τουτων—σεμνοτητα KR p. 548. 16 f. The MS. has the
inscription at the end, 'donum Simonis Schardii Magdiburgiensis.'

A, CODEX REGIUS. Paris. Bibl. Nat. Gr. 128, saec. xii.
membr. 610 pagg.

p. 1. Aristeas.
26. Theodoret to Hypatius.
27. Preface to Genesis from Gregory of Nyssa, inc. ἐπειδήπερ εἰσα-
γώγιμον πρὸς θεογνωσίαν...
28. Catena on the Octateuch.
608. On the versions of Holy Scripture, the names of God, etc.

Single column : words hang from ruled lines, 47 lines in a page :
a neat writing in brown ink, initial letters in crimson : size of page
14½ × 10¾ in., of writing 11 × 7 in. A hand of the fourteenth century
(Lumbroso[2]) has added some marginal notes (on Theopompus and
Theodectes, a saying of Alexander the Great, etc.), many of which are
rubbed and almost illegible, but they may be read in D which has
copied them. Montfaucon (*Bibl. Bibliothecarum*, II. 725) mentions this
MS., and describes it as written 'manu XII. circiter saeculi.' On p. 610
is written a note, +ισιν εν (?) ταυτα εις δοξαν | θ͞υ και της αγιας τριαδος
φι|λα [? φυλλα] τριακοσια γ ητοι (?) τ͞ γ͞ +.

---

[1] *Catalogue des Manuscrits Grecs des Bibliothèques de Suisse* (Leipzig,
1886).
[2] *Atti della R. Accad. di Torino*, vol. IV. 1869.

Descendants of A(DFL).
D, CODEX REGIUS. Paris. Bibl. Nat. Gr. 130, saec. xv. chart.
288 foll.

    fol. 1. Aristeas.
    26vo. Theodoret to Hypatius.
    27.   Gregory of Nyssa's Preface.
    28.   Catena on Genesis and Exodus, 1—12.

The rest of the Catena and the remaining matter contained in A
are to be found in MS. Paris 132, written by the same hand as D.
Omont's Catalogue describes the MS. as 'copied by George Gregoro-
poulus'; Omont takes this apparently from the 1740 catalogue which
says '*videtur* a Gregoropulo exaratus'; the name of the scribe does not
seem to occur in the MS. A clearly written MS. in a hand similar
to that of M (of the same century). Page 13¾ × 9½ in. : writing 9 × 5½ in.
Another hand has underlined in red ink passages where there are
clerical errors and has corrected the text to that of A. This MS. was
not collated throughout, as it appeared certain from an examination of a
few passages that it was a copy of A (see below).

F, CODEX BURNEIENSIS. British Museum. Burney MS. 34,
saec. xv. chart. 645 pagg.

    Same contents as A, viz.
    p. 1. Aristeas.
    21.   Theodoret to Hypatius.
    22.   Passages from Gregory of Nyssa's book on the six days of
creation.
    25.   Catena on the Octateuch.
    643. πόσαι παραδόσεις κ.τ.λ.
    644. ποσάκις καὶ ποτε ἐπορθήθησαν οἱ ἐξ Ἰσραήλ.
    644. Evagrius Scitensis on the ten names of God.
    645. Three chronological notes.
    645. On the works of God in the six days.

L, CODEX VATICANUS. Rome. Vat. Gr. 746, pt. 1., saec. xv.
(partim saec. xi.—xii.?) membr. 251 foll.

    fol. 1. Aristeas.
    12.   Theodoret to Hypatius.
    13.   Catena on Genesis and Exodus.

The portion of the MS. containing the Catena is certainly old
(eleventh or twelfth century) and possibly a copy of H or of an ancestor
of H. There are the same illustrations of O.T. history as in H, better
preserved but not so beautifully painted. The writing too is rougher,
not so neat as in H, but in the same style. The Aristeas (together with
the letter to Hypatius and the first page of the Catena) is supplied
by a much later hand on white shiny unruled parchment, the Catena
being on a browner parchment, and the letters there hanging from
ruled lines. The Aristeas is written in a single column: size of page

13 × 11 in., of writing 11¾ × 8¾ in., the number of lines in a page varying from 21 to 43. It is written apparently in two different hands; pp. 1—3 are written rather diffusely; from εἰσὶ δὲ πρώτης φυλῆς (p. 528. 10) the writing becomes more compact and neat, with more lines in a page : with the words τὰ συμβαίνοντα τοῖς φίλοις (p. 565. 14) the diffuse writing comes in again. The beginning of the Aristeas is lost ; the MS. begins with -ματων ω βασιλευ (p. 521. 24). It ends with ριστεας ιλοκρατει (sic). This ending marks a peculiarity of the MS. ; the rubricator has omitted to fill in the initial capital letters, hence we find αι for και, ρος for προς, αμβανειν for λαμβανειν, etc.

HKA. It is clear from their general agreement in readings that these MSS. form one group. Notice the omissions which they have in common :

(1) p. 564. 1. προς τουτ—ποιησεσιν επιτελοι (50 letters) om HKA(DFL) ins GIM and B group.

(2) p. 566. 10. εστιν επιτελεια—διατηρεις την (53 letters) om HKA(DFL) ins GIM and B group.

(3) p. 559. 19. καθως υπο—διοικειται κατα (51 letters) om HKA(DFL)GIM ins B group.

From the first two of these omissions it appears that HKA must be derived from an original (γ) which omitted these lines, an ancestor of γ having probably had lines of the length of 50 letters ; from the evidence of GIM we deduce that this group, while connected with the HKA group, is not derived from γ. H and A are more closely connected than H and K ; notice 551. 18 αναπτω (σιν sup lin) H αναπτω A* ; 562. 20 απαν H (τ suprascr H^corr) απαν A.

ADFL. That these MSS. form a united group within the HKA group is shown by their almost universal agreement. Notice e.g. the readings 536. 1 χρωμενοι ADFL (συγχρωμενοι cett.), 537. 4 εισεληλυθεναι ADFL (εληλυθεναι cett.), 547. 3 ευλογιας ADFL (λογιας cett.), 569. 21 επανεπαυσατο (sic) ADFL, and the omissions which they have in common :

539. 27. ουτος δε εξεισιν—Αζωτιων χωραν ⎫
550. 21. γαρ ων ανθρωπος—συνεστρωσε δε παντα ⎬ om ADFL.
554. 8.   προς ευφροσυνην—ελυθη τη δε ⎭

That D is a direct transcript of A is proved by its omitting exactly a line of A, so that on p. 558. 9 it reads μεταδορημενα (sic) σοι διαμενη, where the lines in A were divided thus : μεταδο|τικος ων και μεγαλομερης ουδεποτ αν απολιποι δοξης ινα δε τα προει|ρημενα σοι διαμενη. Moreover, certain marginal notes in A, which are there almost illegible, have been copied by D, where they are all clear: e.g. on 553. 25 ὁ καὶ Ἀλέξανδρος εἶπεν ἐρωτηθεὶς πῶς ἐν ὀλίγῳ μεγάλα κατώρθωσεν, ὅτι, φησίν, οὐδέποτε πράγματα ἐπιβαλὼν ἠμελήθη. At 541. II συμβουλευοντῶ of A (the stroke over the ω being very faint) has become συμβουλευοντα in D. That F is a direct transcript of A is proved by its repeating a line of A twice over, reading at 550. 16 a μεν ετι και νυν εκαστον αποτελειν· ην γαρ ουτω διατεταγμενον υπο του βασιλεως a μεν ετι και νυν ορας· οσαι γαρ κ.τ.λ. The lines in A are arranged thus: εκελευσε την ετοιμασιαν εις | εκαστον αποτελειν· ην γαρ ουτω διατεταγμενον υπο του βασιλεως a μεν ετι και νυν | ορας· οσαι γαρ κ.τ.λ. Lastly, that L is a direct transcript of A is made practically certain[1] by 529. 21, where L omits the words συνιδειν πραγματων—καλλονην εκελευσε which form exactly a line in A. Just below (530. 1) L negligently inserts in the text (where it is quite unsuitable) after του χρυσου a gloss which occurs in the margin of A, and which is quoted in the apparatus criticus.

These cases appear to put the parentage of these three MSS. beyond a doubt, and their evidence has therefore not been recorded in the apparatus. The few deviations from their parent MS. which they exhibit may be neglected.

The group GIM(Q).

This group presents few substantial variants from the HKA text. It differs chiefly from that text in matters of orthography, the frequent use of itacisms, etc. Its retention of two lines which are omitted by HKA (see above) proves that it is not derived from the immediate parent of those MSS., while its omission of another line in common with HKA is proof that both groups go back to a common ancestor rather higher up in the line.

G, CODEX VENETUS. Venice. Bibl. Marciana, Gr. 534, saec. xi. (circa, Zanetti's catalogue) membr. 296 foll.

fol. 1.　　Aristeas.
　6vo.　　Theodoret to Hypatius.
　7.　　Catena on the Octateuch.
　296.　　πόσαι παραδόσεις εἰσὶ τῆς θείας γραφῆς.

Size of page $12\frac{1}{4} \times 9\frac{1}{2}$ in., of writing $9\frac{3}{4} \times 7$ in. It is written in minuscules hanging from ruled lines in one column containing 67 closely packed and closely written lines, the whole of the Aristeas being compressed into $5\frac{1}{4}$ leaves. The Aristeas with the Theodoret seems to have been tacked on to the MS. later, as there is a second numbering of pages (α, β, γ, etc.) beginning on fol. 7, but it is by the same hand as that which wrote, at any rate, the first few lines of the Catena; the text of the Septuagint appears to have been the work of several hands. The Aristeas is very much stained and blotted, especially the first leaf, which has been in parts rewritten, but in places the writing is utterly illegible. In the Venice Catalogue it is placed first in an 'Appendix Graecorum Codicum ex legato Jacobi Contareni, Jo. Bapt.

[1] It should be noted, however, that in 572. 20 L reads ποιητικως with HK as against A.

Recanati Aliorumque'; a note in the catalogue adds 'catenam hanc in Bibliotheca Julii Justiniani D. M. Procuratoris vidit Montfauconius et descripsit in Diario Italico[1].'

I, CODEX PALATINUS. Rome. Bibl. Vatic. Pal. Gr. 203, saec. xi. membr. 304 foll.

fol. 1.   Aristeas.
22.   Theodoret to Hypatius.
23vo.   Catena on Genesis and Exodus.
304vo. ends in the middle of Exodus. At the end is written 'deest unum et alterum folium.'

It is written in double columns, the words hanging from ruled lines: the size of page being $14\frac{1}{4} \times 10\frac{1}{2}$ in., of writing $11\frac{1}{2} \times 3\frac{1}{2}$ in. The Aristeas and the Catena are by the same hand. The bookplate (apparently common to all the Palatine collection) has the words 'Sum de bibliotheca, quam Heidelberga capta spolium fecit et P. M. Gregorio XV trophaeum misit Maximilianus utriusque Bavariae Dux etc. S. R. I. Archidapifer et Princeps Elector, anno Christi MDCXXIII.'

M, CODEX OTTOBONIANUS. Rome. Bibl. Vatic. Ottobon. Gr. 32, saec. xv. chart. 70 foll.

fol. 1—14.   Παλλαδίου περὶ τῶν τῆς Ἰνδίας ἐθνῶν καὶ τῶν Βραγμάνων.
15, 16.   blank.
17—27.   τοῦ φιλοπόνου Ἰωάννου εἰς τὸ ἐπίλοιπον τῆς φυσικῆς ἀκροάσεως.
28.   blank.
29—44.   τοῦ φιλοσοφωτάτου καὶ ῥητορικωτάτου Κύρου Θεοδωρούτου προδρόμου.
45—70vo.   Ἀριστέας Φιλοκράτῃ.

Size of page $14\frac{1}{2} \times 9\frac{1}{2}$ in., of writing $9\frac{1}{4} \times 5$ in.; the writing is in single column, bounded by two vertical lines, but no horizontal lines are visible. The contents are all written by the same neat hand in which the tall τ is the chief characteristic; the Aristeas sheets are rather broader than the rest. On the first leaf is written a list of the contents and the name of a former owner of the MS.: 'Anonymi Geographia, Philosophia anonym., Palladius de rebus et moribus Indicis, Aristeas. Ex codicibus Ioannis Angeli Ducis ab Altaemps[2].'

---

[1] See Montfaucon, *Diar. Ital.* (Paris, 1702), 433 ff., where a list of the MSS. in Justinian's library is given, including a Catena on the Octateuch of the eleventh century. This is apparently the MS. referred to in the Venice Catalogue; but Montfaucon does not appear to mention that it contained Aristeas.

[2] The library of Colonna was bought by Jean Ange duc d'Altemps in 1611; in 1689 part of the collection was transferred to the Ottobonian palace. See Batiffol, *La Vaticane de Paul III. à Paul V.* (Paris, 1890), pp. 57—59.

GIM agree in almost all cases, including omissions such as
528. 10 om ασφαλως GIM, mistakes such as 529. 14 καταθηκουσας
GIM (καθηκ. cett.), 534. 1 μεγαλοις GIM (μεγαλοι cett.), 552. 26
δυναμενων GIM (δυναμεων cett.), and ·peculiarities of spelling and
vocalization. They almost always insert ν εφελκυστικόν before
consonants, write iota adscript, interchange ο and ω (προτευουσα,
πασχωμεν [= πασχομεν], μεταφερον [= -ων]) and ι and η (φιλικοος,
δαψηλως, τινικαυτα, προδιλως), and use itacisms such as βουλεσθε
for βουλεσθαι, αιρειν for εριν.

It appears that G and I are copied from one and the same
MS. ; their contemporary date and a few cases where they are
at variance (e.g. 520. 12 η παιδεια αυτη G, η παιδειας διαγωγη I) make
it improbable that either is a transcript of the other.

M is undoubtedly a direct copy of I. With the exception of
some slight corrections or blunders on the part of M, they are in
entire agreement. Notice e.g. 531. 5 προς την χρησιν την τραπεζαν
IM (την τραπ. προς την χρ. cett.), 540. 7 μετα IM (μεταλλα cett.),
541. 3 γεγραπται IM (γεγραφεναι cett.), 543. 25 βροτων IM (βρωτων
cett.), 571. 24 γραφης IM (μεταγραφης cett.). At 573. 21 M omits
the words και τα ακολουθα παντα, which form exactly a line in the
double-column MS. I. The readings of M have therefore not been
recorded in the apparatus.

We may mention here:

Q, CODEX REGIUS. Paris. Bibl. Nat. Gr. 950, saec. xiv.
bombycinus, 576 pagg.

This MS. contains a very miscellaneous collection of fragments
beginning with (p. 1) an anonymous fragment on the resurrection, (p. 2)
a fragment of Athanasius on the heresy of Paul of Samosata, and including (p. 111) a fragment on the ten feasts of the Jews, and (p. 217)
an anonymous work on the measurement of the earth. On p. 341 occur
the letters of Abgarus and Christ, on p. 343 a fragment of Photius,
'de termino vitae et de Spiritus Sancti processione,' on pp. 351—371
the fragments of Aristeas, followed on p. 371 by the treatise already
included περὶ τῶν δέκα ἑορτῶν (here given at greater length), and other
fragments which need not be enumerated. The Aristeas fragments
are not a sixth part of the letter ; they are (p. 351) 520. 15 inc. κατα-
σταθεις επι της—521. 9 υποχειρια ποιουμενος, and (p. 353) 529. 24 inc.
δυο πηχεων το μηκος—537. 21 προκαθημενου προς θεωριαν. They are
introduced by the heading επιστολης Αριστεως προς Φιλοκρατην εκφρασις.
χρυσης τραπεζης ην εποιησεν ο βασιλευς Πτωλομαιος και απεστειλεν εις
Ιερουσαλημ προς τον τοτε αρχιερεα Ελεαζαρον. Omont's catalogue merely
calls the fragments 'De Ptolemaeo rege et lege mosaica '; the folio catalogue of 1740 more correctly describes them as 'fragmenta ex Aristea.'

There are 24 lines in a page ; the writing is rough and untidy with
thick strokes, and very rough red initial capitals. Some of its readings
and spellings connect it with the GIM group, e.g. 532. 28 (λιαν for λειαν),
534. 8 αναστασιν (for ανατασιν), 535. 4 σμιξιν (for σμηξιν), but its text
bears a closer relation to that of the otherwise solitary Codex Monacensis. Its evidence has not been recorded in this edition.

The group TBCPSZ.

We now come to a group which presents considerable variations from those which we have considered. The readings of this group are at first sight attractive and have the appearance of representing a purer text. A closer .examination will however, show that a certain amount of revision must have gone on here, not only in some common ancestor of the group, but also in the individual members of it. We find that various members of the group have sometimes corrected the text in different ways, that even where they are consistent in their readings, they seldom have the support of Eusebius, who has introduced other slight alterations of his own into the text, and again we find that in places the reading of the HKA and GI groups, which the B text has rejected, is corroborated by the usage of Alexandrian papyri which are contemporary or nearly contemporary with the pseudo-Aristeas. While, then, in some places it is possible that the B text has retained or has successfully restored the right reading, the text of this group is usually to be regarded with suspicion, as an ingenious attempt to remove the obscurities of a Greek which had become unintelligible. The group is here spoken of as the B group, because the MS. B is that on which Schmidt's text was based, and it is also the MS. which exhibits the greatest number of variants ; but a far older member of the group and one which exhibits the Aristeas text entire has now come to light, namely the Florence MS. T, which we will describe first.

T, Codex Laurentianus. Florence. Bibl. Mediceo-Laurent. Acquisti 44.

According to the Catalogue of Rostagno the date of the Aristeas, Pentateuch and Catena is the tenth century, of Joshua and the remaining books about the thirteenth. It seems doubtful whether the former part is earlier than the eleventh century. The material is parchment: number of leaves 384: size of page $14\frac{1}{2} \times 12$ in. There are quires of 8 leaves with signatures of the (?) thirteenth century. To the end of the Pentateuch the writing is in single column with 46 lines in a page; in the latter part there are two columns with 65 lines to a page. The writing hangs from ruled lines.

fol. 1.   Aristeas to Philocrates.
11vo.   Introduction to O.T. books: τὰ ἐν τῇ παρούσῃ βίβλῳ ἀναγεγραμμένα τεύχη......διατί ἔκαστον τούτων οὕτως καλεῖται καὶ ἀπὸ μέρους τί περιέχει ἔκαστον...
14vo.   Theodoret, εἰς τὰ ἄπορα τῆς θείας γραφῆς.
15.   Pentateuch with Catena.
311.   Joshua—Chronicles, Esdras 1—3, Esther, Judith, Maccabees 1—4, Tobit (to 3. 15).

It contains the inscription, 'Codicem e Liguria advectum propo-
nente A. M. Bandinio comparavit Ferdinandus III magnus dux Etruriae
et Bibl. Laurent. donavit die 3 Aug. MDCCXCVIII.'

B, CODEX REGIUS. Paris. Bibl. Nat. Gr. 129, saec. xiii.
bombycinus, 539 foll.

fol. 2. Aristeas inc. (522. 12) $\overline{a\nu\omega\nu}$ $\overset{\pi\rho o\sigma}{}$ $\upsilon\pi o\tau\iota\theta\epsilon\mu\epsilon\nu o\varsigma$ $\lambda o\gamma o\nu$.
    15. Catena on the Octateuch.

It is written in double columns: size of page $13\frac{1}{4} \times 9\frac{1}{4}$ in., of writing
$10\frac{1}{2} \times 3\frac{1}{4}$ in.; the writing is enclosed by vertical lines, but there are no
horizontal lines except at the top and bottom of the page. The Aristeas
is in bad condition, being torn and stained. There are a few plain red
initial letters. The writing is rather sloping, and fairly large and clear.
Schmidt says, 'This MS. has been subsequently collated most carefully
with its original by the rubricator, when the writer himself had already
performed this duty quite conscientiously. Hence all corrections of the
rubricator and of the first hand are equivalent to the authority of the
original MS.' A later hand has added a few headings in the margin
($\pi\epsilon\rho\iota$ $\tau o\hat{\upsilon}$ 'Iopδávov, etc.). The Catena is apparently by the same hand
as the Aristeas, but has more ornamentation and red initials. In some
places part of a leaf has been cut or torn away.

C, CODEX REGIUS. Paris. Bibl. Nat. Gr. 5, saec. xiii.—xiv.
chart. et bombyc., 402 foll.

fol. 1. Aristeas fragments.
    14. Anonymous introduction to the books of the O.T. (inc. τo $\mu\epsilon\nu$
        $o\upsilon\nu$ $\beta\iota\beta\lambda\iota o\nu$).
    45. Catena on the Octateuch.

The Aristeas is written in a single column: the size of page being
$12\frac{1}{2} \times 9$ in., of writing varying from 9×7 in. to $7\frac{3}{4} \times 5\frac{3}{4}$ in. The Aristeas
and the introduction to O.T. are by the same hand, a large square
upright writing with thick strokes and red initials in the margin: the
page is unruled. In the latter part of the MS., foll. 45—60 are written
in double columns in a rougher hand; at fol. 61 the first hand begins
again, and the remainder is sometimes in single, sometimes in double
columns, text and commentary coming alternately and the order of
books being confused (Judges, Joshua, Deuteronomy, Numbers). The
fragments of Aristeas contained are less than half the letter; they are
528. 17 $\Sigma a\beta\beta a\tau a\iota o\varsigma$—532. 17 $\delta\upsilon o$ $\mu\epsilon\nu$ $\eta\sigma a\nu$ $\tau\eta$, 553. 10 o $\delta\epsilon$ $\epsilon\iota\pi\epsilon\nu$ $\epsilon\upsilon\chi o\mu\epsilon$-
$\nu o\varsigma$—563. 16 $\eta\rho\omega\tau a$, 567. 7 $-\sigma\iota\lambda\epsilon\nu$ $\kappa\rho o\tau\omega$ $\delta\epsilon$—end.

P, CODEX BARBERINUS. Rome. Bibl. Barberina Gr. IV. 56,
saec.? xiii. membr., 229 foll.

fol. 1. Pseudo-Athanasian Synopsis (frag.).
    inc. $\pi a\sigma a$ $\gamma\rho a\phi\eta$ $\eta\mu\omega\nu$ $\tau\omega\nu$ $X\rho\iota\sigma\tau\iota a\nu\omega\nu$ $\theta\epsilon o\pi\nu\epsilon\upsilon\sigma\tau o\varsigma$ $\epsilon\sigma\tau\iota$, at
end $\lambda\epsilon\iota\pi\epsilon\iota$.

2.   Fragment of Aristeas inc. (538. 10) πινοησαντες· της γαρ χωρας expl. (568. 1) περιβαλλοντας το ζην· ως (note λειπει).

10.   Catena on the Octateuch.

224.   Catena on the Apocalypse inc. δηλει (sic) τον της συντελειας καιρον.

It is written in double columns in a very minute upright and neat hand, with about 60 lines packed into a column, the words hanging from ruled lines; the size of page is 9¾ × 7 in., of writing 8¼ × 3¾ in. At the bottom of fol. 1 is written 'Caroli Strozzae Thomae filii 1635.'

S, CODEX VATICANUS. Rome. Vat. Gr. 1668, saec. ? xiii. membr., 358 foll.

It is written in single column, with 29 lines in a page, the size of page being 12¼ × 8½ in., and the writing hanging from ruled lines; there are quires of 8 leaves.

fol. 1—37vo.   Aristeas (complete).

37vo.—358.   Catena on Genesis.

On the recto of the first leaf is the note ' Emptus ex libris ill^{ml} Lelii Ruini ep^i Balneoregien. 1622.'

This MS. escaped notice when the other Roman MSS. were examined and has consequently not been collated in full; but some collations of selected passages kindly made by Mr N. McLean, Fellow of Christ's College, are sufficient to show that it belongs to this group.

Z, CODEX TURICENSIS. Zurich. Stadtbibliothek C. 11 (169 Omont's catalogue), saec. xiii. bombyc., 736 pagg.[1]

p. 1.   Aristeas.

p. 1 (= 21).   Catena on the Octateuch.

p. 669.   Ιερωνυμου επιστολη προς Δεξτρον επαρχον πραιτωρι απο ρωμαικ εις ελληνικα μεταβληθεισα ('S. Hieronymi liber de viris illustribus a Sophronio graece versus,' Omont). It is written in single column, the size of page being 13½ × 9 in., and the writing hangs from ruled lines. The Aristeas portion is badly preserved; a hole passes through the twenty pages which contain it, causing lacunae. There are several marginal readings, some of which are obviously conjectural (e.g. ισως φιλοφρονησεσι, ισως μαλλον). The Jerome is not by the hand which has written the remainder of the MS.

That the above MSS. form a single group appears primarily from their omissions. The following lines are omitted by all[2] the

---

[1] The greater part of this MS. was collated from the original. The collation of the last few pages has been made from photographs, for which the writer is indebted to the courtesy of the Librarian, Dr Hermann Escher.

[2] S omits (1), (3), and (7). It has not been tested for the other passages.

members of the group which are extant at the several passages referred to.

(1) 523. 9. εγκρατεις εγενοντο—και την χωραν (78 letters) om BTZ.

(2) 529. 11. βουλεσθαι και—διστα ζειν δε (51 letters) om BCTZ.

(3) 532. 17. απο της βασεως—τορεια και (48 letters) om BTZ.

(4) 533. 13. θεσιν ηθελεν—ως αν τις (41 letters) om BTZ.

(5) 547. 12. και κακοποιουσι—τροφην αλλα (48 letters) om BPTZ.

(6) 548. 13. -τας ημερα θυσιαζειν—οι προσφερον- (46 letters) om BPTZ.

(7) 552. 13. γενοιο—τη περι σεαυτον (47 letters) om BPTZ.

(8) 564. 25. θεου δε—τοις αξιοις (45 letters) om BPTZ.

(9) 566. 24. ησαν γαρ ικανοι πρεσβεις (20 letters) om BPTZ.

Also at 533. 4 the words προς την της αληθειας—τεθεντων (48 letters) are omitted by T^{txt}SZ (C and P do not contain the passage); but they are inserted in the margin of T, apparently by the first hand, and are found in B. These omissions show that an ancestor of the group was written by a careless scribe who dropped several lines (averaging 48 letters) of his archetype. From the last instance quoted, and from numerous other passages, it appears that B and T bear a specially close relationship; indeed it is conceivable that B is a copy of T, but in that case it has introduced several corrections of its own, not found in the parent MS.[1]

As to the value of the readings of this group, it appears that the 'singular' readings of B are in nearly all cases due to a correction of the text. Instances of these are 522. 18 the insertion of εν λογω before βραχει, 525. 12 εαν ουν φανηται σοι εννομον B (εαν ουν φανηται cett., εαν ουν φαινηται Eus.). The phrases εαν φαινηται σοι and εαν φαινηται are abundantly attested by the Alexandrian papyri in petitions of subordinates to high officials, but the insertion of εννομον receives no support. Again we have 526. 13 χαριστηριον B (χαριστικον cett. Eus.), 527. 18 ανδρες των τετιμημενων παρα σοι Ανδρεας και Αριστεας B (Ανδρεας των τετ. παρα σοι και Αρ. cett.: B has misunderstood the genitive), 529. 18 οιδα γαρ ως δαψιλους της υλης αυτοις ουσης B (ετι γαρ επι τα της ουσης cett. Eus.), 538. 1 σχημα B (χυμα='size' cett.: B has removed a characteristic word of Aristeas, cf. 521. 17, 567. 11). The readings of BT, where the other members of the group are opposed to them, are also generally to be rejected: e.g. 525.25 νομισματα BT (νομισματος cett. Eus. Jos.), 526.25 δυναμενους BT (δυνατους cett. Eus.): they have occasionally corrected the order of words, 551. 19 διατελοιη εχων BT (εχ. διατ. cett.),

---

[1] The divergence of the two subdivisions of the B group is seen in the difficult passage (531. 6) where BT omit the words ωστε και την των κυματων θεσιν, while CSZ retain them and add πεποιησθαι καθ ο αν μερος.

569. 5 τῶν ἰδιωτῶν τινες BT (τινες τ. ιδ. cett.). Where however the members of the group unite as against the HKA and GI groups, the reading gains in probability, and more especially is this the case where the group has the support of either Eusebius or the GI group. Thus in 526. 2 ανασπαστους BTZGI Eus¹ (αναρπαστους HKA), 526. 6 προοντας BᶜᵒʳʳTZ Eus. (παροντας cett.), 547. 7 ins και ποτων PZGI Eus¹ (om cett.), the B reading is right. But in some places the whole group has been affected by correction. Thus in 519. 11 TSZ (the only extant members at this point) read εαυτους προεδωκαμεν εις τον προειρημενον ανδρα πρεσβειαν, but the reading εαυτους επεδωκαμεν κ.τ.λ. of the other MSS. is corroborated by the usage of the papyri of the second century B.C. (Paris Pap. 49 καταπεπειραμαι...εις παν το σοι χρησιμον εμαυτον επιδιδοναι, Par. Pap. 63 col. 6 προθυμως εαυτους επιδιδοντων, Grenfell, *Erotic Fragment*, etc. XLII. 6 εις τε παν το παραγγελλομενον | προθυμ]ως εαυτους επιδεδωκοτων).

A few instances where correction is seen at work may be quoted. At 550. 10 HKAGI read παντα δυναμιν ειπε παρεσται καθηκοντως, οις συγχρησησθε (-σεσθε), καμοι μεθ υμων. Παντα δυναμιν, which is clearly wrong, is corrected by BTZ to πασαν δυναμιν, by P to παντ(=πανθ)α δυναιμην; παρεσται is further corrected by BT to παρεσταναι and καμοι to καμε, corrections which give a grammatical but hardly an intelligible sentence. The slight alteration of δ᾽ υμιν for δυναμιν (a correction of Mendelssohn, which had also suggested itself to the present writer) restores sense to the passage, and the B text is seen to be due to conjecture. Similarly at 555. 1 B and P have corrected in different ways the characteristic word απεφηνατο ('answer'), B reading ειπε and P απεκρινατο: a little before (553. 21) B reads αποκρινεσθαι where the remaining MSS. have αποφαινεσθαι. At 527. 1 BTZ read τον αρχισωματοφυλακα (B at first wrote σωματοφυλακα: των αρχισωματοφυλακων cett.), thus removing an idiomatic use of the genitive, frequently attested by the papyri. The above instances will afford sufficient proof that a good deal of recension has gone on in this group. At the same time it is clear that in other places it has escaped the corruptions which the other groups have undergone, though it is sometimes difficult to say whether a reading of this group is primitive or due to correction. The agreement of the group with Eusebius (where his evidence exists) is, as was said, sometimes a test; but in the majority of cases the B text is not corroborated by Eusebius, and in a few instances where one or two members only of the group agree with Eusebius, this appears to be due to a fortuitous coincidence in emendation. Such a passage is 527. 4 γραφε BT Eus. (γραφων cett.). In this instance Eusebius altered the form of the sentence by reading γραφε and inserting γαρ after κεχαρισμενος; in BT the change to γραφε was due to κεχαρισμενος εση having become

corrupted to και χαρισαμενος εση ; the participle γραφων is corroborated by Josephus (ἐπιστέλλων περὶ ὧν ἂν θέλῃς ποιήσεις κεχα-
ρισμένα).

The extracts of Eusebius, consisting of about a quarter of the
letter, are contained in the eighth and ninth books of the *Praepa-
ratio Evangelica* (VIII. 2—5, 9, IX. 38). The Eusebian MSS. which
are to be followed in these books are, as Heikel[1] has shown, I
(Codex Venetus Marcianus 341) and O (Codex Bononiensis 3643).
The extracts from Aristeas in these two MSS. have been collated
for the present text, and their evidence is quoted as Eus[i] and Eus°.
For the other Eusebian MSS. the text of Gaisford (Oxford, 1843)
has been used ; O was unknown to Gaisford, and his collation of
I was incomplete. The Venice MS. by its general agreement
with the Aristeas MSS. shows itself to be far the best text of
Eusebius ; the Bologna MS. or one of its ancestors has been very
carelessly copied, and there are numerous omissions which did
not always appear worthy of record in the apparatus to the present
text. With regard to the value of the Eusebian text, it may be
well to quote the verdict of Freudenthal[2] on the general character
of his extracts from earlier writers. He says, 'Eusebius shows
himself more reliable in the text (Wortlaute) of his originals than
in the names and writings of the excerpted authors. It is true
that he occasionally allows himself small alterations in the text,
most frequently in the opening words of the extracts. He often
abbreviates his originals, drops repetitions (beseitigt Doppel-
glieder), omits individual words and whole sentences, and no small
number of inaccuracies of other kinds are also to be met with.
On the other hand it is only in extremely rare cases that he inserts
additions of his own, and the cases in which we meet with fundamental alterations of the text are still more uncommon.' This
estimate is quite borne out by the Eusebian extracts from Aristeas,
where there are frequent instances of slighter alterations and
omissions, which the paraphrase of Josephus often helps us to
detect. Among omissions we have 520. 16 ει δυνατον om Eus. (ins
Jos. Ar. codd.), 525. 10 και πολιτευομενων om Eus. (ins Ar. codd. :
Jos. however omits the words in his paraphrase, and they may
be a gloss). Of alterations we may note out of numerous instances
525. 24 where the strange word ρισκοφυλακας is altered to χρημα-
τοφυλακας (Jos. paraphrases τοὺς φύλακας τῶν κιβωτῶν, ἐν αἷς ἐτύγ-
χανον οἱ λίθοι), 526. 17 επικρινων κατεστησα (a bad correction, because

---

[1] *De Praeparationis Evangelicae Eusebii edendae ratione* (Helsing-
forsiae, 1888).
[2] *Hellenistische Studien,* Alexander Polyhistor (Breslau, 1875) p. 7 f.
See also the note on p. 203 on Eusebius and Pseudo-Aristeas.

the royal plural used throughout the rest of the letter of Ptolemy is dropped), 572. 9 ακριβως (ηκριβωμενως Ar. codd.), 573. 2 κατα δε την αιτησιν (κατα δε την ανεσιν Jos. Ar. codd.). In a few cases a rather longer addition is made; at 544. 22 before των συγγενικων the words ουτε των υποβεβηκοτων ουτε are possibly, and at 546. 14 the words επι των πολεων και οικησεων δια το σκεπαζεσθαι are certainly to be attributed to the hand of Eusebius; just before the last passage (546. 11) συντηρουντας τας αρχας και μεσοτητας και τελευτας is an unintelligible[1] alteration of the correct reading και συντηρουντος. Among passages where Eusebius is certainly right may be mentioned 526. 2 ανασπαστους Eus[i] GIBTZ (αναρπαστους cett.), 542. 10 ενδεικτικως (ενδικως Ar. codd.), 547. 7 the insertion of και ποτων Eus[i] GIPZ, and lastly 541. 21. The readings in this passage are instructive:

(1) προς τα δι ημων επιζητηθεντα Eus.
(2) προς δι ημων επιζητηθεντα GIMZ*.
(3) προς ημων επιζητηθεντα HKADFL.
(4) προς δε ημων επιζητηθεντων BPTZ[corr].

Eusebius preserves the true text; the τα then dropped out, and while in the HKA group the reading was still further corrupted, in the B group sense was restored to the passage by a conjectural emendation. Passages where Eusebius and Josephus unite as against the Aristeas MSS. are 524. 18 αναγραφης (αντιγραφης Ar.), 525. 5 τετυχηκε (τετευχε Ar.), 526. 8 omission of the negative, ? 528. 7 the perfect απεσταλκαμεν (Jos. has the perfect πεπομφαμεν : απεστειλαμεν Ar.), 572. 20 ποιητων Jos. Eus. B (ποιητικων or ποιητικως Ar. cett.) ; in such cases the patristic reading should generally be followed. On the whole the Eusebian evidence is of the greatest importance ; it tends to show that the GI group, especially if supported by any member of the B group, is nearest to the primitive text.

Lastly, with regard to the evidence of Josephus, he gives in the twelfth book of the *Jewish Antiquities* a paraphrase of about two-fifths of the letter, omitting the central portion, namely the visit to Palestine, the discourse with Eleazar and the seventy-two questions and answers. He has taken the trouble to reshape nearly every sentence, while retaining many of the characteristic words of Aristeas. Under the circumstances it is not always possible to reconstruct his text, and at some of the most difficult passages his evidence is uncertain ; in some cases the text was certainly unintelligible to him. He is however often useful in enabling us to detect the alterations which have been introduced into the text

---

[1] Wendland suggests that the words are an interpolation from Plato, *Legg.* 715 E, ὁ μὲν δὴ θεός, ὥσπερ καὶ ὁ παλαιὸς λόγος, ἀρχήν τε καὶ τελευτὴν καὶ μέσα τῶν ὄντων ἁπάντων ἔχων κ.τ.λ.

by Eusebius or the B group. It is needless to add that Niese's text of Josephus has been followed.

Beside the MSS. of Aristeas above mentioned the following are known to the present writer, which he has not had the opportunity of collating : Codex Monacensis 9 (saec. xi.), quoted in Wendland's edition, Codex Atheniensis 389 (circa saec. xv., chart., foll. 328, Aristeas and Catena)[1], Codex Scorialensis Σ. I. 6 (dated 1586, and written χειρὶ Νικολάου Τουρριανοῦ καὶ βασιλικοῦ ἀντιγραφέως, Aristeas and Catena on Genesis and Exodus)[2].

The collations here given are not absolutely complete. Itacisms and other orthographical details have not been generally recorded, neither have all the slight omissions of the Codex O of Eusebius; but apart from these no substantial variants have, it is hoped, been omitted. The dates of the various correctors' hands have not been accurately ascertained ; the symbol B[1], T[1] has been used to denote a correction probably by the first hand or a hand nearly contemporary with the date of the MSS. B and T. Words are enclosed within daggers † † where the MS. reading is left in the text, although possibly corrupt: angular brackets < > denote emendations of, or insertions introduced into, the reading of the MSS.; square brackets [ ] signify that words found in the MSS. are probably to be omitted.

---

[1] Κατάλογος τῶν χειρογράφων τῆς ἐθν. βιβλ. τῆς Ἑλλάδος ὑπὸ Ἰωάννου Σακκελίωνος καὶ Ἀλκ. Ι. Σακκελίωνος (Athens, 1892).

[2] E. Miller, *Catalogue des Manuscrits Grecs de la Bibl. de l'Éscurial* (Paris, 1848). An examination of a few pages of this MS. which the Rev. P. M. Barnard, B.D., kindly made for the writer in 1894 shows that it agrees most often with the GI group. Passages where it stands alone are 548. 15 om του, 549. 8 ποσεων, 549. 21 μια φωνη (for υπο μ. φ.), 550. 14 προσκελευσαμενος, 572. 20 om των ιστορικων, 573. 19 κυλινδιον.

ΑΡΙΣΤΕΑΣ ΦΙΛΟΚΡΑΤΕΙ

Ἀξιολόγου διηγήσεως, ὦ Φιλόκρατες, περὶ τῆς γενηθείσης ἡμῖν 1
ἐντυχίας πρὸς Ἐλεάζαρον τὸν τῶν Ἰουδαίων ἀρχιερέα συνεσταμένης,
διὰ τὸ σὲ περὶ πολλοῦ πεποιῆσθαι, παρ' ἕκαστα †ὑπομιμνήσκων†,
συνακοῦσαι περὶ ὧν ἀπεστάλημεν καὶ διὰ τί, πεπείραμαι σαφῶς
5 ἐκθέσθαι σοι, κατειληφὼς ἣν ἔχεις φιλομαθῆ διάθεσιν, ὅπερ μέ- 2
γιστόν ἐστιν ἀνθρώπῳ, προσμανθάνειν ἀεί τι καὶ προσλαμβάνειν,
ἤτοι κατὰ τὰς ἱστορίας, ἢ καὶ κατ' αὐτὸ τὸ πρᾶγμα πεπειραμένῳ.
οὕτω γὰρ κατασκευάζεται ψυχῆς καθαρὰ διάθεσις, ἀναλαβοῦσα τὰ
κάλλιστα· καὶ πρὸς τὸ πάντων κυριώτατον νενευκυῖα τὴν εὐσέ-
10 βειαν ἀπλανεῖ κεχρημένη κανόνι διοικεῖ. Τὴν προαίρεσιν ἔχοντες 3
ἡμεῖς πρὸς τὸ περιέργως τὰ θεῖα κατανοεῖν, ἑαυτοὺς ἐπεδώκαμεν εἰς
τὸν προειρημένον ἄνδρα πρεσβείαν, καλοκαγαθίᾳ καὶ δόξῃ προτε-
τιμημένον ὑπό τε τῶν πολιτῶν καὶ τῶν ἄλλων, καὶ κατακεκτημένον
μεγίστην ὠφέλειαν τοῖς σὺν ἑαυτῷ καὶ τοῖς κατὰ τοὺς ἄλλους
15 τόπους πολίταις, πρὸς τὴν ἑρμηνείαν τοῦ θείου νόμου, διὰ τὸ γεγρά-
φθαι παρ' αὐτοῖς ἐν διφθέραις ἑβραϊκοῖς γράμμασιν. ἣν δὴ καὶ 4
ἐποιησάμεθα ἡμεῖς σπουδῇ, λαβόντες καιρὸν πρὸς τὸν βασιλέα περὶ
τῶν μετοικισθέντων εἰς Αἴγυπτον ἐκ τῆς Ἰουδαίας ὑπὸ τοῦ πατρὸς
τοῦ βασιλέως, πρώτως κεκτημένου τήν τε πόλιν καὶ τὰ κατὰ τὴν
20 Αἴγυπτον παρειληφότος. Ἄξιόν ἐστι καὶ ταῦτά σοι δηλῶσαι.
πέπεισμαι γάρ σε μᾶλλον ἔχοντα πρόσκλισιν πρὸς τὴν σεμνότητα 5
καὶ τὴν τῶν ἀνθρώπων διάθεσιν τῶν κατὰ τὴν σεμνὴν νομοθεσίαν διεξαγόντων, περὶ ὧν προαιρούμεθα <δηλοῦν, ἀσμένως σε>

---

2 ευτυχιας GZ | συνισταμενης T   3 υπομιμνησκειν Wend. (-σκων codd HKAGITZ
omn)   4 ων] ου Κ   6 προσμανθανοντι Ζ   7 om και I | κατ αυτο] κατα
ταυτο HKAGI | πεπειραμενων HKGIT   8 διαθεσις καθ. Κ   9 κυριω-
τερον Κ   10 διοικ. την προαιρεσιν. Εχοντες codd corr Wend.   11 προε-
δωκ. TZ | εις] εις την προς Wend.   12 τετιμ. TZ   13 κατεκτημ. ΗΑΙ
κατακτ. G txt ΚΤΖ   16 αυτου T   17 post σπουδη lacunam statuit
Wend.   19 om τα TZ   21 προσκλησιν codd   23 δηλουντες μεν ως
σε codd, txt ex conj Schmidt

ἀκούσεσθαι, προσφάτως παραγεγενημένον ἐκ τῆς νήσου πρὸς
ἡμᾶς, καὶ βουλόμενον συνακούειν ὅσα πρὸς ἐπισκευὴν ψυχῆς
6 ὑπάρχει. καὶ πρότερον δὲ διεπεμψάμην σοι περὶ ὧν ἐνόμιζον
ἀξιομνημονεύτων εἶναι τὴν ἀναγραφήν, ἣν μετελάβομεν παρὰ τῶν
κατὰ τὴν λογιωτάτην Αἴγυπτον λογιωτάτων ἀρχιερέων περὶ τοῦ 5
7 γένους τῶν Ἰουδαίων. φιλομαθῶς γὰρ ἔχοντί σοι περὶ τῶν δυναμένων ὠφελῆσαι διάνοιαν δέον ἐστὶ μεταδιδόναι, μάλιστα μὲν πᾶσι
τοῖς ὁμοίοις, πολλῷ δὲ μᾶλλον σοὶ γνησίαν ἔχοντι τὴν αἵρεσιν, οὐ
μόνον κατὰ τὸ συγγενὲς ἀδελφῷ καθεστῶτι τὸν τρόπον, ἀλλὰ καὶ τῇ
8 πρὸς τὸ καλὸν ὁρμῇ τὸν αὐτὸν ὄντα ἡμῖν. χρυσοῦ γὰρ χάρις ἢ 10
κατασκευή τις ἄλλη τῶν τετιμημένων παρὰ τοῖς κενοδόξοις ὠφέλειαν
οὐκ ἔχει τὴν αὐτήν, ὅσον ἡ παιδείας ἀγωγὴ καὶ ἡ περὶ τούτων
• φροντίς. ἵνα δὲ μὴ περὶ τῶν προλεγομένων μηκύνοντες ἀδόλεσχόν
τι ποιῶμεν, ἐπὶ τὸ συνεχὲς τῆς διηγήσεως ἐπανήξομεν.

§ Jos Eus 9 ⁵Κατασταθεὶς ἐπὶ τῆς τοῦ βασιλέως βιβλιοθήκης Δημήτριος ὁ 15
Φαληρεὺς ἐχρηματίσθη πολλὰ διάφορα πρὸς τὸ συναγαγεῖν, εἰ
δυνατόν, ἅπαντα τὰ κατὰ τὴν οἰκουμένην βιβλία· καὶ ποιούμενος
ἀγορασμοὺς καὶ μεταγραφὰς ἐπὶ τέλος ἤγαγεν, ὅσον ἐφ᾽ ἑαυτῷ, τὴν
10 τοῦ βασιλέως πρόθεσιν. παρόντων οὖν ἡμῶν ἐρωτηθεὶς Πόσαι
τινὲς μυριάδες τυγχάνουσι βιβλίων; εἶπεν Ὑπὲρ τὰς εἴκοσι, 20
βασιλεῦ· σπουδάσω δ᾽ ἐν ὀλίγῳ χρόνῳ πρὸς τὸ πληρωθῆναι πεντήκοντα μυριάδας τὰ λοιπά. προσήγγελται δέ μοι καὶ τῶν Ἰουδαίων
νόμιμα μεταγραφῆς ἄξια καὶ τῆς παρὰ σοὶ βιβλιοθήκης εἶναι.
11 Τί τὸ κωλῦον οὖν, εἶπεν, ἐστί σε τοῦτο ποιῆσαι; πάντα γὰρ ὑπο-
τέτακταί σοι τὰ πρὸς τὴν χρείαν. ὁ δὲ Δημήτριος εἶπεν 25
Ἑρμηνείας προσδεῖται· χαρακτῆρσι γὰρ ἰδίοις κατὰ τὴν Ἰουδαίων
χρῶνται, καθάπερ Αἰγύπτιοι τῇ τῶν γραμμάτων θέσει, καθὸ καὶ
φωνὴν ἰδίαν ἔχουσιν. ὑπολαμβάνονται Συριακῇ χρῆσθαι· τὸ δ᾽

HKAGITZ   3 διεπεμψ. σοι] διεπεμψαμεθα G   6 σοι] μοι conj Schmidt   7 μα-
Jos Eus
λιστα] μαλλον G   8 γνησιως G   9 αλλα και τον τροπον Wend.
12 παιδεια αυτη G παιδειας διαγ. I   14 ποιουμεν Ζ παθωμεν Gᵛⁱᵈ | επανη-
ξωμεν Κ   16 om ει δυνατον Eus   19 ουν ins Eus om Ar codd
21 σπουδασω Eus πληρωσω Ar   22 προσηγγελται Eus (cf Jos μεμηνυσθαι)]
προσαγγελλεται codd | των] pr τα Eus   24 εστι σε] αυτοι G | αποτετακται
Eus   28 υπολαμβανονται]+ δε Eus

οὐκ ἔστιν, ἀλλ' ἕτερος τρόπος. Μεταλαβὼν δὲ ἕκαστα ὁ βασιλεὺς
εἶπε γραφῆναι πρὸς τὸν ἀρχιερέα τῶν Ἰουδαίων, ὅπως τὰ προειρημένα
τελείωσιν λάβῃ.¶   Νομίσας δὲ ἐγὼ καιρὸν εἶναι περὶ ὧν πολ- 12 ¶ Eus
λάκις ἠξιώκειν Σωσίβιόν τε τὸν Ταραντῖνον καὶ Ἀνδρέαν, τοὺς
5 ἀρχισωματοφύλακας, περὶ τῆς ἀπολυτρώσεως τῶν μετηγμένων ἐκ
τῆς Ἰουδαίας ὑπὸ τοῦ πατρὸς τοῦ βασιλέως—ἐκεῖνος γὰρ ἐπελθὼν
τὰ κατὰ κοίλην Συρίαν καὶ Φοινίκην ἅπαντα, συγχρώμενος εὐημερίᾳ
μετὰ ἀνδρείας, τοὺς μὲν μετῴκιζεν, οὓς δὲ ᾐχμαλώτιζε, φόβῳ πάντα
ὑποχείρια ποιούμενος· ἐν ὅσῳ καὶ πρὸς δέκα μυριάδας ἐκ τῆς τῶν
10 Ἰουδαίων χώρας εἰς Αἴγυπτον μετήγαγεν, ἀφ' ὧν ὡσεὶ τρεῖς μυριάδας 13
καθοπλίσας ἀνδρῶν ἐκλεκτῶν εἰς τὴν χώραν κατῴκισεν ἐν τοῖς
φρουρίοις (ἤδη μὲν καὶ πρότερον ἱκανῶν εἰσεληλυθότων σὺν τῷ
Πέρσῃ, καὶ πρὸ τούτων ἑτέρων συμμαχιῶν ἐξαπεσταλμένων πρὸς
τὸν τῶν Αἰθιόπων βασιλέα μάχεσθαι σὺν Ψαμμιτίχῳ· ἀλλ' οὐ
15 τοσοῦτοι τῷ πλήθει παρεγενήθησαν, ὅσους Πτολεμαῖος ὁ τοῦ
Λάγου μετήγαγε)· καθὼς δὲ προείπομεν, ἐπιλέξας τοὺς ἀρίστους 14
ταῖς ἡλικίαις καὶ ῥώμῃ διαφέροντας καθώπλισε, τὸ δὲ λοιπὸν χύμα
πρεσβυτέρων καὶ νεωτέρων, ἔτι δὲ γυναικῶν, εἴασεν εἰς τὴν οἰκετίαν,
οὐχ οὕτως τῇ προαιρέσει κατὰ ψυχὴν ἔχων, ὡς κατακρατούμενος
20 ὑπὸ τῶν στρατιωτῶν, δι' ἃς ἐπεποίηντο χρείας ἐν τοῖς πολεμικοῖς
ἀγῶσιν—ἡμεῖς δὲ ἐπεί τινα παρεύρεσιν εἰς τὴν ἀπόλυσιν αὐτῶν
ἀπελάβομεν, καθὼς προδεδήλωται, τοιούτοις ἐχρησάμεθα λόγοις
πρὸς τὸν βασιλέα   Μήποτε ἄλογον ᾖ ἐλέγχεσθαι ὑπ' αὐτῶν 15
τῶν πραγμάτων, ὦ βασιλεῦ. τῆς γὰρ νομοθεσίας κειμένης πᾶσι
25 τοῖς Ἰουδαίοις, ἣν ἡμεῖς οὐ μόνον μεταγράψαι ἐπινοοῦμεν, ἀλλὰ καὶ
διερμηνεῦσαι, τίνα λόγον ἕξομεν πρὸς ἀποστολήν, ἐν οἰκετίαις
ὑπαρχόντων ἐν τῇ σῇ βασιλείᾳ πληθῶν ἱκανῶν; ἀλλὰ τελείᾳ καὶ
πλουσίᾳ ψυχῇ ἀπόλυσον τοὺς συνεχομένους ἐν ταλαιπωρίαις,
κατευθύνοντός σου τὴν βασιλείαν τοῦ τεθεικότος αὐτοῖς θεοῦ τὸν
30 νόμον, καθὼς περιείργασμαι. τὸν γὰρ πάντων ἐπόπτην καὶ κτίστην 16

4 ηξιωσα συνεχως τους περι τον Ταρ. G   5 σωματοφυλακας A | εκ] απο HKAGI
TZ   8 μετοικ. Z | ους] τους Gvid   11 εκλελεγμενων T | κατελιπεν G TZ Jos
12 μεν]+ουν I | ικανως H | συνεληλ. Z | om συν T   14 Αιθ.] Αιγυπτιων T
15 τω πληθ. om TZ   18 νεωτ. και πρεσβ. I | δε]+και K   21 επει] επι
GI   26 ικετειαις K   28 απολυσας G   29 σου] σοι TZ

θεὸν οὗτοι σέβονται, ὃν καὶ πάντες, ἡμεῖς δέ, βασιλεῦ, προσονομά-
ζοντες ἑτέρως Ζῆνα καὶ Δία· τοῦτο δ᾽ οὐκ ἀνοικείως οἱ πρῶτοι
διεσήμαναν, δι᾽ ὃν ζωοποιοῦνται τὰ πάντα καὶ γίνεται, τοῦτον
ἁπάντων ἡγεῖσθαί τε καὶ κυριεύειν. ὑπερηρκὼς δὲ σύμπαντας ἀνθρώπους τῇ λαμπρότητι τῆς ψυχῆς ἀπόλυσιν ποιῆσαι τῶν ἐνεχομένων 5
17 ταῖς οἰκετίαις.   Οὐδὲ πολὺν χρόνον ἐπισχών, καὶ ἡμῶν κατὰ
ψυχὴν πρὸς τὸν θεὸν εὐχομένων, τὴν διάνοιαν αὐτοῦ κατασκευάσαι
πρὸς τὸ τοὺς ἅπαντας ἀπολυθῆναι (κτίσμα γὰρ ὃν θεοῦ τὸ γένος
τῶν ἀνθρώπων καὶ μεταλλοιοῦται καὶ τρέπεται πάλιν ὑπ᾽ αὐτοῦ·
διὸ πολλαχῶς καὶ ποικίλως ἐπεκαλούμην τὸν κυριεύοντα κατὰ 10
18 καρδίαν, ἵνα συναναγκασθῇ, καθὼς ἠξίουν, ἐπιτελέσαι· μεγάλην
§ B γὰρ εἶχον ἐλπίδα, περὶ σωτηρίας ᵃ ἀνθρώπων προτιθέμενος λόγον, ὅτι
τὴν ἐπιτέλειαν ὁ θεὸς ποιήσει τῶν ἀξιουμένων· ὃ γὰρ πρὸς δικαιοσύνην καὶ καλῶν ἔργων ἐπιμέλειαν ἐν ὁσιότητι νομίζουσιν ἄνθρωποι
ποιεῖν, κατευθύνει τὰς πράξεις καὶ τὰς ἐπιβολὰς ὁ κυριεύων ἁπάντων 15
19 θεός), ὁ δὲ διανακύψας καὶ προσβλέψας ἱλαρῷ τῷ προσώπῳ Πόσας
ὑπολαμβάνεις μυριάδας ἔσεσθαι; ἔφη.   παρεστὼς δὲ Ἀνδρέας
ἀπεφήνατο Βραχεῖ πλεῖον μυριάδων δέκα.   ὁ δέ, Μικρόν γε, εἶπεν,
Ἀριστέας ἡμᾶς ἀξιοῖ πρᾶγμα.   Σωσίβιος δὲ καὶ τῶν παρόντων
τινὲς τοῦτ᾽ εἶπον Καὶ γὰρ ἄξιόν ἐστι τῆς σῆς μεγαλοψυχίας, ὅπως 20
χαριστήριον ἀναθῇ τῷ μεγίστῳ θεῷ τὴν τούτων ἀπόλυσιν. μεγίστως
γὰρ τετιμημένος ὑπὸ τοῦ κρατοῦντος τὰ πάντα καὶ δεδοξασμένος
ὑπὲρ τοὺς προγόνους, εἰ καὶ μέγιστα ποιήσεις χαριστήρια, καθῆκόν
20 ἐστί σοι.   Διαχυθεὶς δὲ εὖ μάλα τοῖς ὀψωνίοις εἶπε προσθεῖναι,
καὶ σώματος ἑκάστου κομίζεσθαι δραχμὰς εἴκοσι, καὶ περὶ τούτων 25
ἐκθεῖναι πρόσταγμα, τὰς δὲ ἀπογραφὰς ποιεῖσθαι παρ᾽ αὐτά,
μεγαλείως χρησάμενος τῇ προθυμίᾳ, τοῦ θεοῦ τὴν πᾶσαν ἐπιτελέ-
σαντος ἡμῶν προαίρεσιν, καὶ συναναγκάσαντος αὐτὸν ἀπολυτρῶσαι
μὴ μόνον τοὺς συνεληλυθότας τῷ στρατοπέδῳ τοῦ πατρός, ἀλλὰ καὶ

HKAGIBT   1 ω βασιλευ TZ   2 ετερως Ar codd] ετυμως hic hab Jos sed fort pro
Z Jos   ουκ ανοικειως | ζηνα· (al ζην· a) και δια τουτο δ codd (δ om T)   3 τουτων Z
5 απολ. ποι.] αποποιησαι I   6 ικεταις I   8 ον] ων Z   12 om γαρ
TZ | υποτιθεμενος B* (προστιθ. Bᶜᵒʳʳ) | οτε Z   13 δικαιοσ.] ελεημοσυνην G
15 βουλας B επιβουλ. T   16 διακυψας A ανακυψας G   18 Βραχει] pr
εν λογω B βραχυ K | ενδεκα Jos   19 αξιω G   24 εφη B   25 δραγμας I

εἴ τινες προῆσαν, ἢ μετὰ ταῦτα παρεισήχθησαν εἰς τὴν βασιλείαν.
ὑπὲρ τὰ τετρακόσια τάλαντα τὴν δόσιν ἀπέφαινον εἶναι. καὶ τοῦ 21
προστάγματος δὲ τὸ ἀντίγραφον οὐκ ἄχρηστον οἴομαι κατακε-
χωρίσθαι. πολλῷ γὰρ ἡ μεγαλομοιρία φανερωτέρα καὶ εὔδηλος
5 ἔσται τοῦ βασιλέως, τοῦ θεοῦ κατισχύοντος αὐτὸν εἰς τὸ σωτηρίαν
γενέσθαι πλήθεσιν ἱκανοῖς. ἣν δὲ τοιοῦτο   Τοῦ βασιλέως προσ- 22
τάξαντος—Ὅσοι τῶν συνεστρατευμένων τῷ πατρὶ ἡμῶν εἰς τοὺς κατὰ
Συρίαν καὶ Φοινίκην τόπους ἐπελθόντες τὴν τῶν Ἰουδαίων χώραν
ἐγκρατεῖς ἐγένοντο σωμάτων Ἰουδαϊκῶν καὶ ταῦτα διακεκομίκασιν εἰς
10 τε τὴν πόλιν καὶ τὴν χώραν ἢ καὶ πεπράκασιν ἑτέροις, ὁμοίως δὲ καὶ
εἴ τινες προῆσαν ἢ καὶ μετὰ ταῦτά εἰσιν εἰσηγμένοι τῶν τοιούτων,
ἀπολύειν παρὰ χρῆμα τοὺς ἔχοντας, κομιζομένους αὐτίκα ἑκάστου
σώματος δραχμὰς εἴκοσι, τοὺς μὲν στρατιώτας τῇ τῶν ὀψωνίων
δόσει, τοὺς δὲ λοιποὺς ἀπὸ τῆς βασιλικῆς τραπέζης. νομίζομεν 23
15 γὰρ καὶ παρὰ τὴν τοῦ πατρὸς ἡμῶν βούλησιν καὶ παρὰ τὸ καλῶς
ἔχον ἠχμαλωτεῦσθαι τούτους, διὰ δὲ τὴν στρατιωτικὴν προπέτειαν
τήν τε χώραν αὐτῶν κατεφθάρθαι καὶ τὴν τῶν Ἰουδαίων μεταγωγὴν
εἰς τὴν Αἴγυπτον γεγονέναι· ἱκανὴ γὰρ ἦν ἡ παρὰ τὸ πεδίον
γεγονυῖα ἐκ τῶν στρατιωτῶν ὠφέλεια· διὸ παντελῶς ἀνεπιεικής
ἐστι καὶ ἡ τῶν ἀνθρώπων καταδυναστεία. πᾶσιν οὖν ἀνθρώποις τὸ 24
δίκαιον ἀπονέμειν ὁμολογούμενοι, πολλῷ δὲ μᾶλλον τοῖς ἀλόγως
καταδυναστευομένοις, καὶ κατὰ πᾶν ἐκζητοῦντες τὸ καλῶς ἔχον πρός
τε τὸ δίκαιον καὶ τὴν κατὰ πάντων εὐσέβειαν, προστετάχαμεν ὅσα
τῶν Ἰουδαϊκῶν ἐστι σωμάτων ἐν οἰκετίαις <πανταχῆ> καθ᾽ ὁντινοῦν
25 τρόπον ἐν τῇ βασιλείᾳ, κομιζομένους ᾽τοὺς ἔχοντας τὸ προκείμενον
κεφάλαιον ἀπολύειν, καὶ μηδένα κακοσχόλως περὶ τούτων μηδὲν
οἰκονομεῖν· τὰς δ᾽ ἀπογραφὰς ἐν ἡμέραις τρισίν, ἀφ᾽ ἧς ἡμέρας
ἔκκειται τὸ πρόσταγμα, ποιεῖσθαι πρὸς τοὺς καθεσταμένους περὶ

2 υπερ] Fort deperiit aliquid ante hoc verbum | τριακοσια TB (τ) HKAGIBT
3 κατακεχωρισθ..ι ΒΤ* vid Ζ (-ησθαι)] κατακεχωρισται cett   6 Του βασ. Z Jos
προστ. (cum praeced conj codd) ad decretum refert Wend. quasi titulum
habet Nestle   9 εγκρατεις—την χωραν 10 om ΒΤΖ   12 κομιζομενου Τ
13 δραγμας ΒΤΖ | τους]+εχοντας ΒΤΖ   17 om των ΒΤΖ   21 ομολο-
γουμενως HKAGIT* vid -μενοις ZTcorr vid txt ex corr Schmidt   23 παντα Β
24 εστι]+των HAGI | οικεταις ΤΖ | πανταχη ex conj] παντι μη HKAITZ
παντα μη G παντι Β παντι και We. | οντινα ουν ΚΒΤ   28 κατεσταμενους
HKATZ κατεσταλ..ι. GI

25 τούτων, καταδεικνύντας εὐθὺ καὶ τὰ σώματα. διειλήφαμεν γὰρ καὶ
ἡμῖν συμφέρειν καὶ τοῖς πράγμασι τοῦτ᾽ ἐπιτελεσθῆναι. τὸν δὲ
βουλόμενον προσαγγέλλειν περὶ τῶν ἀπειθησάντων, ἐφ᾽ ᾧ τοῦ φανέντος ἐνόχου τὴν κυρίαν ἕξειν· τὰ δὲ ὑπάρχοντα τῶν τοιούτων εἰς
26 τὸ βασιλικὸν ἀναληφθήσεται. Εἰσδοθέντος τοῦ προστάγ- 5
ματος, ὅπως ἐπαναγνωσθῇ τῷ βασιλεῖ, τὰ ἄλλα πάντ᾽ ἔχοντος
πλὴν τοῦ Καὶ εἴ τινες προῆσαν ἢ καὶ μετὰ ταῦτα εἰσηγμένοι εἰσι
τῶν τοιούτων, αὐτὸς τοῦτο ὁ βασιλεὺς προσέθηκε, μεγαλομοιρίᾳ
καὶ μεγαλοψυχίᾳ χρησάμενος, ἐκέλευσέ τε τῶν διαφόρων δόσιν
ἀθρόαν οὖσαν ἀπομερίσαι τοῖς ὑπηρέταις τῶν ταγμάτων καὶ βασι- 10
27 λικοῖς τραπεζίταις. οὕτω δοχθὲν ἐκεκύρωτο ἐν ἡμέραις ἑπτά· πλεῖον
δὲ ταλάντων ἑξακοσίων ἑξήκοντα ἡ δόσις ἐγεγόνει. πολλὰ γὰρ καὶ
τῶν ἐπιμαστιδίων τέκνων σὺν ταῖς μητράσιν ἐλευθεροῦντο. προσαν-
ενεχθέντος εἰ καὶ περὶ τούτων εἰκοσαδραχμία δοθήσεται, καὶ τοῦτ᾽
ἐκέλευσεν ὁ βασιλεὺς ποιεῖν, ὁλοσχερῶς περὶ τοῦ δόξαντος ἅπαντ᾽ 15
ἐπιτελῶν.

§ Eus 28 ⁵Ὡς δὲ κατεπράχθη ταῦτα, τὸν Δημήτριον ἐκέλευσεν εἰσδοῦναι
περὶ τῆς. τῶν Ἰουδαϊκῶν βιβλίων ἀναγραφῆς. πάντα γὰρ διὰ
προσταγμάτων καὶ μεγάλης ἀσφαλείας τοῖς βασιλεῦσι τούτοις
διῳκεῖτο, καὶ οὐδὲν ἀπερριμμένως οὐδ᾽ εἰκῆ. διόπερ καὶ τὸ τῆς 20
εἰσδόσεως καὶ τὰ τῶν ἐπιστολῶν ἀντίγραφα κατακεχώρικα, καὶ τὸ
τῶν ἀπεσταλμένων πλῆθος καὶ τὴν ἑκάστου κατασκευήν, διὰ τὸ
μεγαλομοιρίᾳ καὶ τέχνῃ διαφέρειν ἕκαστον αὐτῶν. τῆς δὲ εἰσδό-
29 σεώς ἐστιν ἀντίγραφον τόδε   Βασιλεῖ μεγάλῳ παρὰ Δημητρίου.
προστάξαντός σου, βασιλεῦ, περὶ τῶν ἀπολιπόντων εἰς τὴν συμπλή- 25
ρωσιν τῆς βιβλιοθήκης βιβλίων, ὅπως ἐπισυναχθῇ, καὶ τὰ διαπεπ-
τωκότα τύχῃ τῆς προσηκούσης ἐπισκευῆς, πεποιημένος οὐ παρέργως

HKAGIBT   3 εφ ω ex conj (cf 3 Macc 3²⁸)] εφη codd εφην Iᵛⁱᵈ   5 εισδοθεντος]
Z Jos Eus   +ουν B +δε Wend. cum cod Mon (Jos)   7 ει και K | η] ει GIZ | εισιν
εισηγ. Wend. cum cod Mon   8 αυτος Wend. cum Jos] αυτο codd
10 ουσαν]+δοσιν B   11 πλειων TZ ⌣   12 εξηκ. και τετρακοσ. Jos
13 ηλευθ. B   14 προσανεν.]+δε We. (cod Mon)   15 ολοσχ. ποι. ο β. B
17 τω Δημητριω BT | εκδουναι Eusⁱ et Joscodd aliq   18 αναγραφης Jos et
Eus] αντιγραφης Ar codd omn   19 ασφαλ.] ακριβειας Eus   20 διωκητο
Ar codd txt Eus (διωκειται Eusᵒ) | και 1°] ins Eus om Ar | το Eus] τα Ar
21 εκδοσεως BTZ Euscodd aliq   24 αντιγραφον (-φα B) εστιν ουτως BT
25 προστεταχοτος Eusᵒ | απολειφθεντων Eus   26 της]+δια Eusᵒ

τὴν ἐν τούτοις ἐπιμέλειαν, προσαναφέρω σοι τάδε. τοῦ νόμου 30
τῶν Ἰουδαίων βιβλία σὺν ἑτέροις ὀλίγοις τισὶν ἀπολείπει· τυγχάνει
γὰρ Ἑβραϊκοῖς γράμμασι καὶ φωνῇ λεγόμενα, ἀμελέστερον δέ, καὶ
οὐχ ὡς ὑπάρχει, σεσήμανται, καθὼς ὑπὸ τῶν εἰδότων προσανα-
5 φέρεται· προνοίας γὰρ βασιλικῆς οὐ τέτευχε. δέον δέ ἐστι καὶ 31
ταῦθ᾽ ὑπάρχειν παρά σοι διηκριβωμένα, διὰ τὸ καὶ φιλοσοφωτέραν
εἶναι καὶ ἀκέραιον τὴν νομοθεσίαν ταύτην, ὡς ἂν οὖσαν θείαν. διὸ
πόρρω γεγόνασιν οἵ τε συγγραφεῖς καὶ ποιηταὶ καὶ τὸ τῶν ἱστορικῶν
πλῆθος τῆς ἐπιμνήσεως τῶν προειρημένων βιβλίων, καὶ τῶν κατ᾽
10 αὐτὰ πεπολιτευμένων[καὶ πολιτευομένων]ἀνδρῶν, διὰ τὸ ἁγνήν τινα
καὶ σεμνὴν εἶναι τὴν ἐν αὐτοῖς θεωρίαν, ὥς φησιν Ἑκαταῖος ὁ
Ἀβδηρίτης. ἐὰν οὖν φαίνηται, βασιλεῦ, γραφήσεται πρὸς τὸν 32
ἀρχιερέα τὸν ἐν Ἱεροσολύμοις, ἀποστεῖλαι τοὺς μάλιστα καλῶς
βεβιωκότας καὶ πρεσβυτέρους ὄντας ἄνδρας, ἐμπείρους τῶν κατὰ
15 τὸν νόμον τὸν ἑαυτῶν, ἀφ᾽ ἑκάστης φυλῆς ἕξ, ὅπως τὸ σύμφωνον ἐκ
τῶν πλειόνων ἐξετάσαντες καὶ λαβόντες τὸ κατὰ τὴν ἑρμηνείαν
ἀκριβές, ἀξίως καὶ τῶν πραγμάτων καὶ τῆς σῆς προαιρέσεως, θῶμεν
εὐσήμως. εὐτύχει διὰ παντός. Τῆς δὲ εἰσδόσεως ταύτης γενο- 33
μένης, ἐκέλευσεν ὁ βασιλεὺς γραφῆναι πρὸς τὸν Ἐλεάζαρον περὶ
20 τούτων, σημάναντας καὶ τὴν γενομένην ἀπολύτρωσιν τῶν αἰχμαλώτων. ἔδωκε δὲ καὶ εἰς κατασκευὴν κρατήρων τε καὶ φιαλῶν καὶ
τραπέζης καὶ σπονδείων χρυσίου μὲν ὁλκῆς τάλαντα πεντήκοντα
καὶ ἀργυρίου τάλαντα ἑβδομήκοντα καὶ λίθων ἱκανόν τι πλῆθος—
ἐκέλευσε δὲ τοὺς ῥισκοφύλακας τοῖς τεχνίταις, ὧν ἂν προαιρῶνται,
25 τὴν ἐκλογὴν διδόναι—καὶ νομίσματος εἰς θυσίας καὶ ἄλλα πρὸς
τάλαντα ἑκατόν. δηλώσομεν δέ σοι περὶ τῆς κατασκευῆς, ὡς ἂν 34
τὰ τῶν ἐπιστολῶν ἀντίγραφα διέλθωμεν. ἦν δὲ ἡ τοῦ βασιλέως
ἐπιστολὴ τὸν τύπον ἔχουσα τοῦτον Βασιλεὺς Πτολεμαῖος 35

---

1 εν] επι H | ταδε] τα δε cum seqq conj Ar Eus   5 τετυχηκε Jos HKAGIBT
Eus | ετι Eus   10 αυτας Ar et Eus^{io}.   Fort βιβλων supra legendum | και Z Jos Eus
πολιτευομενων om Eus et Jos^{vid} 11 om φησιν Eus^i 12 om ουν Eus^o |
φαιν. Eus] φανηται Ar codd φανηται σοι εννομον B   14 om οντας Eus
15 αφ Jos Eus] εφ HAGIBT   18 εκδοσεως Eus^i 20 σημαναντα Ar
txt Eus et Jos^{vid} (δηλουντας) | γεναμενην GB^{vid}TZ   23 ικανων I καλον
Eus^i 24 χρηματοφυλ. Eus | om τοις Eus^i | om αν BTZ | προαιρουνται B
25 νομισματα BT txt codd cett Eus Jos

Ἐλεαζάρῳ ἀρχιερεῖ χαίρειν καὶ ἐρρῶσθαι. ἐπεὶ συμβαίνει πλείονας τῶν Ἰουδαίων εἰς τὴν ἡμετέραν χώραν κατῳκίσθαι γενηθέντας ἀνασπάστους ἐκ τῶν Ἱεροσολύμων ὑπὸ Περσῶν, καθ᾽ ὃν ἐπεκράτουν χρόνον, ἔτι δὲ καὶ συνεληλυθέναι τῷ πατρὶ ἡμῶν εἰς τὴν Αἴγυπτον
36 αἰχμαλώτους,—ἀφ᾽ ὧν πλείονας εἰς τὸ στρατιωτικὸν σύνταγμα 5 κατεχώρισεν ἐπὶ μείζοσι μισθοφορίαις, ὁμοίως δὲ καὶ τοὺς προόντας κρίνας πιστοὺς φρούρια κτίσας ἀπέδωκεν αὐτοῖς, ὅπως τὸ τῶν Αἰγυπτίων ἔθνος φόβον [μὴ] ἔχῃ διὰ τούτων· καὶ ἡμεῖς δὲ παραλαβόντες τὴν βασιλείαν φιλανθρωπότερον ἀπαντῶμεν τοῖς πᾶσι, πολὺ δὲ
37 μᾶλλον τοῖς σοῖς πολίταις—ὑπὲρ δέκα μυριάδας αἰχμαλώτων ἠλευ- 10 θερώκαμεν, ἀποδόντες τοῖς κρατοῦσι τὴν κατ᾽ ἀξίαν ἀργυρικὴν τιμήν, διορθούμενοι καὶ εἴ τι κακῶς ἐπράχθη διὰ τὰς τῶν ὄχλων ὁρμάς, διειληφότες εὐσεβῶς τοῦτο πρᾶξαι, καὶ τῷ μεγίστῳ θεῷ χαριστικὸν ἀνατιθέντες, ὃς ἡμῖν τὴν βασιλείαν ἐν εἰρήνῃ καὶ δόξῃ κρατίστῃ παρ᾽ ὅλην τὴν οἰκουμένην διατετήρηκεν· εἴς τε τὸ στράτευμα τοὺς 15 ἀκμαιοτάτους ταῖς ἡλικίαις τετάχαμεν, τοὺς δὲ δυναμένους καὶ περὶ ἡμᾶς εἶναι, τῆς περὶ τὴν αὐλὴν πίστεως ἀξίους, ἐπὶ χρειῶν καθεστά-
38 καμεν. βουλομένων δ᾽ ἡμῶν καὶ τούτοις χαρίζεσθαι καὶ πᾶσι τοῖς κατὰ τὴν οἰκουμένην Ἰουδαίοις καὶ τοῖς μετέπειτα, προῃρήμεθα τὸν νόμον ὑμῶν μεθερμηνευθῆναι γράμμασιν Ἑλληνικοῖς ἐκ τῶν παρ᾽ 20 ὑμῶν λεγομένων Ἑβραϊκῶν γραμμάτων, ἵν᾽ ὑπάρχῃ καὶ ταῦτα παρ᾽
39 ἡμῖν ἐν βιβλιοθήκῃ σὺν τοῖς ἄλλοις βασιλικοῖς βιβλίοις. καλῶς οὖν ποιήσεις καὶ τῆς ἡμετέρας σπουδῆς ἀξίως ἐπιλεξάμενος ἄνδρας καλῶς βεβιωκότας πρεσβυτέρους, ἐμπειρίαν ἔχοντας τοῦ νόμου, καὶ δυνατοὺς ἑρμηνεῦσαι, ἀφ᾽ ἑκάστης φυλῆς ἕξ, ὅπως ἐκ τῶν πλείονων 25 τὸ σύμφωνον εὑρεθῇ, διὰ τὸ περὶ μειζόνων εἶναι τὴν σκέψιν. οἰόμεθα γὰρ ἐπιτελεσθέντος τούτου μεγάλην ἀποίσεσθαι δόξαν.

HKAGIBT
Z Jos Eus

1 επει συμβ. KZ Eus] επισυμβαινει codd cett   2 κατοικεισθαι Ar codd κατωκεισθαι Eus txt Jos^vid | αναρπαστους HKA Eus^edd txt GIBTZ Eus^i
4 συνεισελ. G^vid I Eus^i   5 ων]+και Eus   6 προοντας B^corr TZ Eus] παροντας HKAGIB* vid   8 μη hab Ar codd omn om Jos Eus recte ut videtur | εχει GI   11 αργυρ. κατ. αξ. Z   13 πρασσειν Eus | χαριστηριον B txt codd cett Eus   14 δοξη]+τη Eus   16 και om GI   17 της] pr και Eus | αξιως ZT² | επι χειρων κατεστακαμεν (-ησαμεν B) Ar codd επικρινων κατεστησα Eus txt emend Schmidt   21 υμιν (-ων^i) εβρ. λεγ. Eus
23 επιλεξας Eus txt Ar Jos   25 δυναμενους BT

ἀπεστάλκαμεν δὲ περὶ τούτων Ἀνδρέαν τῶν ἀρχισωματοφυλάκων 40
καὶ Ἀριστέαν, τιμωμένους παρ᾽ ἡμῖν, διαλεξομένους σοι καὶ κομί-
ζοντας ἀπαρχὰς εἰς τὸ ἱερὸν ἀναθημάτων καὶ εἰς θυσίας καὶ τὰ ἄλλα
ἀργυρίου τάλαντα ἑκατόν. γράφων δὲ καὶ σὺ πρὸς ἡμᾶς περὶ ὧν ἐὰν
5 βούλῃ κεχαρισμένος ἔσῃ, καὶ φιλίας ἄξιόν τι πράξεις, ὡς ἐπιτελεσ-
θησομένων τὴν ταχίστην περὶ ὧν ἂν αἱρῇ. ἔρρωσο. Πρὸς 41
ταύτην τὴν ἐπιστολὴν ἀντέγραψεν ἐνδεχομένως ὁ Ἐλεάζαρος
ταῦτα Ἐλεάζαρος ἀρχιερεὺς βασιλεῖ Πτολεμαίῳ φίλῳ
γνησίῳ χαίρειν. αὐτός τε ἔρρωσο καὶ ἡ βασίλισσα Ἀρσινόη,
10 ἡ ἀδελφή, καὶ τὰ τέκνα, καλῶς ἂν ἔχοι καὶ ὡς βουλόμεθα, καὶ
αὐτοὶ δὲ ὑγιαίνομεν. λαβόντες τὴν παρὰ σοῦ ἐπιστολὴν μεγάλως 42
ἐχάρημεν διὰ τὴν προαίρεσίν σου καὶ τὴν καλὴν βουλήν, καὶ συνα-
γαγόντες τὸ πᾶν πλῆθος παρανέγνωμεν αὐτοῖς, ἵνα εἰδῶσιν ἣν ἔχεις
πρὸς τὸν θεὸν ἡμῶν εὐσέβειαν. ἐπεδείξαμεν δὲ καὶ τὰς φιάλας ἃς
15 ἀπέστειλας, χρυσᾶς εἴκοσι καὶ ἀργυρᾶς τριάκοντα, κρατῆρας πέντε,
καὶ τράπεζαν εἰς ἀνάθεσιν, καὶ εἰς προσαγωγὴν θυσιῶν καὶ εἰς
ἐπισκευὰς ὧν ἂν δέηται τὸ ἱερὸν ἀργυρίου τάλαντα ἑκατόν, ἅπερ 43
ἐκόμισεν Ἀνδρέας τῶν τετιμημένων παρὰ σοὶ καὶ Ἀριστέας, ἄνδρες
καλοὶ καὶ ἀγαθοὶ καὶ παιδείᾳ διαφέροντες καὶ τῆς σῆς ἀγωγῆς καὶ
20 δικαιοσύνης ἄξιοι κατὰ πάντα· οἳ καὶ μετέδωκαν ἡμῖν τὰ παρὰ σοῦ,
πρὸς ἃ καὶ παρ᾽ ἡμῶν ἀκηκόασιν ἁρμόζοντα τοῖς σοῖς γράμμασι.
πάντα γὰρ ὅσα σοι συμφέρει, καὶ εἰ παρὰ φύσιν ἐστίν, ὑπακουσό- 44
μεθα· τοῦτο γὰρ φιλίας καὶ ἀγαπήσεως σημεῖόν ἐστι. μεγάλα γὰρ
καὶ σὺ καὶ ἀνεπίληστα τοὺς πολίτας ἡμῶν κατὰ πολλοὺς τρόπους

1 τουτων Jos Eus] τουτου Ar | τον αρχισωματοφυλακα B (αρχι sup lin HKAGIBT
prima manu) TZ Jos txt Ar codd cett Eus^i (των σωμ.^ο)   2 Αρισταιον Jos ^Z Jos Eus
Eus^ο (-εαν Eus^i cum Ar codd) | κομιζοντες Z   4 γραφε BT Eus txt codd
cett et Jos^vid | αν B Eus^ο (εαν Eus^i cum codd cett)   5 κεχαρ.] και χαρι-
σαμενος Ar codd κεχαρισμενος γαρ Eus   7 ταυτ. την επ.] ταυτα Eus^ο
8 ταδε Eus^i (ουτως^ο)   9 ει αυτος τε ερρωσαι Eus txt (cf 2 Macc 9^20, 11^28)
Ar codd (-σαι Z)   12 συναγοντες K   13 ανεγνωμεν G^corr vid Jos παρεγν.
IG*? B* +αυτην Eus^ο Jos   16 προαγωγην Z   17 προσδεηται Eus txt
Ar codd Jos   18 εκομιζον Ar codd -σεν Eus^i (-ζεν cett) -σαν Jos | Ανδρεας]
ανδρες B | και] pr Ανδρεας B | Αρισταιος Jos Eus^ο (-εας ^i)   20 παρεδωκαν
B   21 γραμμασι] πραγμασι Eus   24 και συ BT (σοι G και σοι IZ cf
Jos τας σας ευεργεσιας)] om codd cett Eus | ανεπιληπτα A | πολλους τροπους
Eus (cf Jos πολυμερως)] πολλοις HA πολυ K πολλους cett

45 εὐηργέτηκας. εὐθέως οὖν προσηγάγομεν ὑπὲρ σοῦ θυσίας καὶ τῆς
ἀδελφῆς καὶ τῶν τέκνων καὶ τῶν φίλων· καὶ ηὔξατο πᾶν τὸ πλῆθος,
ἵνα σοι γένηται καθὼς προαιρῇ διὰ παντός, καὶ διασώζῃ σοι τὴν
βασιλείαν ἐν εἰρήνῃ μετὰ δόξης ὁ κυριεύων ἀπάντων θεός, καὶ ὅπως
γένηταί σοι συμφερόντως καὶ μετὰ ἀσφαλείας ἡ τοῦ ἁγίου νόμου 5
46 μεταγραφή. παρόντων δὲ πάντων ἐπελέξαμεν ἄνδρας καλοὺς καὶ
ἀγαθοὺς πρεσβυτέρους, ἀφ' ἑκάστης φυλῆς ἕξ, οὓς καὶ ἀπεστείλαμεν
ἔχοντας τὸν νόμον. καλῶς οὖν ποιήσεις, βασιλεῦ δίκαιε, προστάξας,
ὡς ἂν ἡ μεταγραφὴ γένηται τῶν βιβλίων, ἵνα πάλιν ἀποκαταστα-
¶JosEus 47 θῶσι πρὸς ἡμᾶς ἀσφαλῶς οἱ ἄνδρες. ἔρρωσο.¶   Εἰσὶ δὲ πρώτης 10
φυλῆς· Ἰώσηφος Ἐζεκίας Ζαχαρίας Ἰωάννης Ἐζεκίας Ἐλισσαῖος.
δευτέρας· Ἰούδας Σίμων Σομόηλος Ἀδαῖος Ματταθίας Ἐσχλεμίας.
τρίτης· Νεεμίας Ἰώσηφος Θεοδόσιος Βασέας Ὀρνίας Δάκις.
48 τετάρτης· Ἰωνάθας Ἀβραῖος Ἐλισσαῖος Ἀνανίας Χαβρίας...
πέμπτης· Ἴσακος Ἰάκωβος Ἰησοῦς Σαββαταῖος Σίμων Λευίς. 15
ἕκτης· Ἰούδας Ἰώσηφος Σίμων Ζαχαρίας Σομόηλος Σελεμίας.
§ C 49 ἑβδόμης· Σαββαταῖος Σεδεκίας Ἰάκωβος Ἴσαχος Ἰησίας Ναθαῖος.
ὀγδόης· Θεοδόσιος Ἰάσων Ἰησοῦς Θεόδοτος Ἰωάννης Ἰωνάθας.
ἐνάτης· Θεόφιλος Ἀβραμος Ἀρσαμος Ἰάσων Ἐνδεμίας Δανίηλος.
50 δεκάτης· Ἱερεμίας Ἐλεάζαρος Ζαχαρίας Βανέας Ἐλισσαῖος Δαθαῖος. 20
ἑνδεκάτης· Σαμούηλος Ἰώσηφος Ἰούδας Ἰωνάθης Χαβεῦ Δοσίθεος.
δωδεκάτης· Ἰσάηλος Ἰωάννης Θεοδόσιος Ἀρσαμος Ἀβιήτης Ἐζε-
51 κῆλος. οἱ πάντες ἑβδομήκοντα δύο.   Καὶ τὰ μὲν πρὸς τὴν
τοῦ βασιλέως ἐπιστολὴν τοιαύτης ἐτύγχανεν ἀντιγραφῆς <ὑπὸ>
τῶν περὶ τὸν Ἐλεάζαρον. 25

HKAGIBC   **4** om εν BT | κυριευοντων απαντων BT   **5** om σοι Eus   **6** om δε
TZ Jos Eus Eus | επελεξαμεν Jos] επιλεξαμην (sic) Eus¹ εξελεξαμην Eus⁰ επελεξαμεθα
(απελ. BT om Z) Ar codd   **7** απεσταλκαμεν Eus Josᵛⁱᵈ (πεπομφαμεν)
10 οι ανδρ. ασφ. Κ om ασφ. GI   **11** Ιωσηπος Ιεζεκιας Β   **12** Ματ-
θιας ΚΑ | Σεχλεμιας Βᵛⁱᵈ   **13** Ιωσηπος Β* ᵛⁱᵈ | Βασαιας Τ Βασβιας Ζ
14 Αβραιος Β | post Χαβριας nomen excidit fort Χελκιας (Epiphan. *De
mens. et pond.* 9 vers. Syr.) Wend.   **15** Σαβατταιος Ι   **16** Σιμων
Ιωσηφος ΗΚΑ   **17, 18** om Σεδεκ.—Θεοδοσιος Ι om Σεδεκ.—Ιησους Αᵗˣᵗ
ins Αᵐᵍ om Ισαχος—Ναθαιος C   **17** Ιεισιας GZ | Ματθαιος ΗΚΑ
18 Ιωναθαν Β   **19** Δανιηλ TZ om C   **20** Βαναιας BCTZ | Θαδδαιος Ζ
22 δωδεκατος C   **24** επιβολην AGICT* (-βουλ. T¹) | υπο] υπερ codd

⁵Ὡς δὲ ἐπηγγειλάμην καὶ τὰ τῶν κατασκευασμάτων διασαφῆσαι, § Jos
ποιήσω. πολυτεχνίᾳ γὰρ διαφέροντα συνετελέσθη, τοῦ βασιλέως
πολλὴν ἐπίδοσιν ποιουμένου καὶ παρ' ἕκαστον ἐπιθεωροῦντος τοὺς
τεχνίτας. διὸ παριδεῖν οὐδὲν ἠδύναντο οὐδὲ εἰκῇ συντελέσαι.
5 πρῶτον δέ σοι τὰ περὶ τῆς τραπέζης ἐξηγήσομαι. Προεθυ- 52
μεῖτο μὲν οὖν ὁ βασιλεὺς ὑπέροπλόν τι ποιῆσαι τοῖς μέτροις τὸ
κατασκεύασμα. προσέταξε δὲ πυθέσθαι τῶν ἀνὰ τὸν τόπον, πηλίκη
τίς ἐστιν ἡ προοῦσα καὶ κειμένη κατὰ τὸ ἱερὸν ἐν Ἱεροσολύμοις.
ὡς δὲ ἀπεφήναντο τὰ μέτρα, προσεπηρώτησεν, εἰ κατασκευάσει 53
10 μείζονα. τινὲς μὲν οὖν καὶ τῶν ἱερέων καὶ τῶν ἄλλων ἔλεγον μηδὲν
ἐπικωλύειν. ὁ δὲ εἶπε βούλεσθαι καὶ πενταπλῆν τοῖς μεγέθεσι
ποιῆσαι, διστάζειν δὲ μήποτε ἄχρηστος γένηται πρὸς τὰς λειτουργίας. οὐ γὰρ αἱρεῖσθαι τὸ κεῖσθαι μόνον ἐν τῷ τόπῳ <τὰ> παρ' 54
αὑτοῦ, πολὺ δὲ μᾶλλον χάριν ἕξειν, ἐὰν τὰς καθηκούσας λειτουργίας
15 ἐπὶ τῶν ὑπ' αὑτοῦ κατεσκευασμένων οἷς καθῆκε ποιῶνται δεόντως.
οὐ γὰρ ἕνεκεν σπάνεως χρυσοῦ τὰ προσυντετελεσμένα βραχύμετρα 55
καθέστηκεν, ἀλλὰ φαίνεται πρός τινα λόγον, εἶπεν, οὕτως συνεστη-
κέναι τοῖς μέτροις. ἔτι γὰρ ἐπιταγῆς οὔσης οὐθὲν ἂν ἐσπάνιζε·
διόπερ οὐ παραβατέον οὐδὲ ὑπερθετέον τὰ καλῶς ἔχοντα. τῇ μὲν 56
20 οὖν ποικιλίᾳ τῶν τεχνῶν ἐκέλευσεν ὅτι μάλιστα χρήσασθαι, σεμνῶς
ἅπαντα διανοούμενος καὶ φύσιν ἔχων ἀγαθὴν εἰς τὸ συνιδεῖν πραγμάτων ἔμφασιν. ὅσα δ' ἂν ᾖ ἄγραφα, πρὸς καλλονὴν ἐκέλευσε
ποιεῖν· ὅσα δὲ διὰ γραπτῶν, μέτρα αὐτοῖς κατακολουθῆσαι.
ΔΥΟ γὰρ ΠΗΧΕΩΝ τὸ ΜΗΚΟΣ, τὸ δὲ ΥΨΟΣ ΠΗΧΕΟΣ ΚΑΙ ΗΜΙΣΟΥΣ 57
25 συνετέλουν, χρυσίου δοκίμου στερεὰν πάντοθεν τὴν ποίησιν ἐργα-

24 Ex 25²² ff

1 των] pr κατα GIC | επισκευασματων Β σκευασμ. C   2 om ποιησω HKAGIB
ΒΤ   3 επιθεωρουντας CTZ   4 ουδεν] ουδε Β   6 om ουν C   7 om   CTZ Jos
δε Z   11 κωλυειν BCTZ Jos | βουλεσθαι—δε 12 om BCTZ   12 μη-
ποτε] μητε GI   13 τα ins Schmidt   14 καταθηκουσας GI   16 ενεκα
Β | προσσυν. Α* (προσυν. Αᶜᵒʳʳ) προτετ. Β (συν suprascr pr man)   18 ετι
γαρ επιταγης bene conj Mend. cf § 103] οιδα γαρ ως δαψιλους της υλης αυτοις
Β ετι γαρ επι τα (τας CT*Z) της codd cett | αν om H supra lin Z   22 εγ-
γραφα Κ   24 πηχεων] pr και ημισους Jos qui et post μηκος add (ex LXX
vid) ενος δε το ευρος

S. S.   36

σάμενοι, λέγω δὲ οὐ περί τι περιεπτυγμένου τοῦ χρυσοῦ, τὸν δὲ
58 ἐλασμὸν αὐτὸν ἐπιδεδέσθαι. cτεφάνην δὲ ἐποίησαν παλαιcτιαίαν
κυκλόθεν· τὰ δὲ κυμάτια cτρεπτά, τὴν ἀναγλυφὴν ἔχοντα σχοινί-
δων ἔκτυπον, τῇ τορείᾳ θαυμαστῶς ἔχουσαν ἐκ τῶν τριῶν μερῶν·
59 ἦν γὰρ τριγωνία. καὶ καθ᾽ ἕκαστον μέρος ἡ διατύπωσις τῆς ἐνεργείας 5
τὴν αὐτὴν διάθεσιν εἶχεν, ὥστε, καθ᾽ ὃ ἂν μέρος στρέφοιτο, τὴν
πρόσοψιν εἶναι τὴν αὐτήν, κειμένου δὲ κατὰ τῆς στεφάνης τὸ μὲν
¶ Η εἰς αὐτὴν τὴν τράπεζαν ¶ ἀπόκλιμα τὴν διατύπωσιν ἔχειν τῆς ὡραιό-
τητος, τὸ δὲ ἐκτὸς κλίμα πρὸς τὴν τοῦ προσάγοντος εἶναι θεωρίαν.
60 διὸ τὴν ὑπεροχὴν ὀξεῖαν εἶναι τῶν δύο κλιμάτων συνέβαινε, μετέωρον 10
ἐπικειμένην, ὡς προειρήκαμεν, τριγώνου κατεσκευασμένου, καθ᾽ ὃ ἂν
μέρος στρέφοιτο. λίθων τε πολυτελῶν ἐν αὐτῷ διαθέσεις ὑπῆρχον
ἀνὰ μέσον τῶν σχοινίδων· ἕτερος παρὰ ἕτερον πλοκὴν εἶχον ἀμί-
61 μητον τῇ ποιήσει. πάντες δ᾽ ἦσαν διὰ τρημάτων κατειλημμένοι
χρυσαῖς περόναις πρὸς τὴν ἀσφάλειαν. ἐπὶ δὲ τῶν γωνιῶν αἱ 15
62 κατακλεῖδες συνέσφιγγον πρὸς τὴν συνοχήν. ἐκ πλαγίων δὲ κατὰ
τὴν στεφάνην κυκλόθεν τὰ πρὸς τὴν ἄνω πρόσοψιν ᾠθεσία κατεσκεύαστο διάλιθος, †ἐκτύπωσιν ἔχουσα προσοχῆς† συνεχέσιν ἀνα-
γλυφαῖς ῥαβδωταῖς, πυκνὴν ἐχούσαις τὴν πρὸς ἄλληλα θέσιν περὶ
63 ὅλην τὴν τράπεζαν. ὑπὸ δὲ τὴν ἐκτύπωσιν τῶν λίθων τῆς 20
ᾠθεσίας, στέφανον ἐποίησαν οἱ τεχνῖται πάγκαρπον, ἐν ὑπεροχῇ
προδήλως ἔχοντα βοτρύων καὶ σταχύων, ἔτι δὲ φοινίκων καὶ μήλων
ἐλαίας τε καὶ ῥοῶν καὶ τῶν παραπλησίων. τοὺς δὲ λίθους ἐργασά-
μενοι πρὸς τὴν τῶν προειρημένων καρπῶν διατύπωσιν, ἔχοντας

HKAGIB   1 χρυσου] ad hoc A^corr in mg add ου κατα τι μερος της τραπεζης συνε-
CTZ Jos   σταλμενου του χρυσου και ουχ ορωμενου· αλλα δια παντων επιλαμποντος· και
κατα τας σωματικας διαστασεις ητοι κατα βαθος και κατα μηκος και κατα
πλατος ομοιως εχοντος· στερεα γαρ ην δι ολου του σχηματος. το δε ειδος ως
φησιν Θεοδωριτος (-ρητ. L) τριγωνος κατα λογον αναγωγης υψηλοτερας και
θειοτερας. Haec verba L textui inseruit   3, 4 σχοινιδων GIBT*¹] σχοι-
νιδον HKAC -ηδον T¹¹Z (σχοινοειδη Jos)   4 εκτυπον T¹² εκτοπον cett
5 τριγωνα Wend. (cf Jos)   7 κειμενου δε κατα] κειμενης δε και B   11 κει-
μενην BCTZ   12 εν αυτω] εν εαυτω GICZ εαυτω T   13 σχοινιδων (-ηδ.
Z) codd   16 κατακλειδαι C | συνεσφιγγον KA]+δε cett   18 εκτυπωσιν B]
εκτυπων (εκ τυπων GI) cett | Fort legendum προοχης (conj Schmidt) | συν-
οχεσιν GIBC   19 εχουσας CZ   22 δε]+και A

ἑκάστου γένους τὴν χρόαν, ἀνέδησαν τῷ χρυσίῳ κύκλῳ περὶ ὅλην
τὴν τῆς τραπέζης κατασκευὴν κατὰ κρόταφον. μετὰ δὲ τὴν τοῦ 64
στεφάνου διάθεσιν, ὁμοίως κατὰ τὴν τῆς ᾠοθεσίας διασκευὴν κατεσκεύαστο, καὶ τὰ λοιπὰ τῆς ῥαβδώσεως καὶ διαγλυφῆς, <διὰ τὸ>
5 κατ᾽ ἀμφότερα τὰ μέρη τὴν τράπεζαν πρὸς τὴν χρῆσιν πεποιῆσθαι,
καθ᾽ ὃ ἂν μέρος αἴρωνται, ὥστε καὶ τὴν τῶν κυμάτων θέσιν καὶ τὴν
τῆς στεφάνης εἶναι κατὰ τὸ τῶν ποδῶν μέρος. ἔλασμα γὰρ ἐποίη- 65
σαν καθ᾽ ὅλου τοῦ πλάτους τῆς τραπέζης στερεὸν δακτύλων τεσσάρων,
ὥστε τοὺς πόδας ἐνίεσθαι εἰς τοῦτο, περόνας <σὺν> κατακλεῖσιν
10 ἔχοντας ἐσφίγχθαι κατὰ τὴν στεφάνην, ἵνα, καθ᾽ ὃ ἂν αἴρωνται
μέρος, ἡ χρῆσις ᾖ· τοῦτο δὲ κατὰ ἐπιφάνειαν θεωρεῖται ἀμφοτε-
ροδεξίου τῆς κατασκευῆς οὔσης. ἐπ᾽ αὐτῆς δὲ τῆς τραπέζης 66
μαίανδρον ἔκτυπον ἐποίησαν, ἐν ὑπεροχῇ λίθους ἔχοντα κατὰ μέσον
πολυτελεῖς τῶν <πολυειδῶν>, ἀνθράκων τε καὶ σμαράγδων, ἔτι δὲ
15 ὄνυχος καὶ τῶν ἄλλων γενῶν τῶν διαφερόντων ἐν ὡραιότητι.
μετὰ δὲ τὴν τοῦ μαιάνδρου διάθεσιν ἐπέκειτο σχιστὴ πλοκή, 67
θαυμασίως ἔχουσα, ῥομβωτὴν ἀποτελοῦσα τὴν ἀνὰ μέσον θεωρίαν·
ἐφ᾽ ᾗ κρυστάλλου λίθος καὶ τὸ λεγόμενον ἤλεκτρον ἐντετύπωτο,
ἀμίμητον θεωρίαν ἀποτελοῦν τοῖς θεωροῦσι. τοὺς δὲ πόδας ἐποίησαν 68
20 τὰς κεφαλίδας ἔχοντας κρινωτάς, ἀνάκλασιν κρίνων ὑπὸ τὴν τράπεζαν
λαμβανόντων, τὰ δὲ τῆς ἐντὸς προσόψεως ὀρθὴν ἔχοντα τὴν πετά-
λωσιν. ἡ δὲ ἐπ᾽ ἐδάφους ἔρεισις τοῦ ποδὸς ἄνθρακος λίθου πάν- 69
τοθεν παλιστιαία, κρηπῖδος ἔχουσα τάξιν κατὰ τὴν πρόσοψιν, ὀκτὼ
δὲ δακτύλων τὸ πλάτος ἔχουσα· ἐφ᾽ ὃν ἐπίκειται τὸ πᾶν ἔλασμα
25 τοῦ ποδός. κατεσκεύασαν δὲ ἐκφύοντα κισσὸν ἀκάνθῳ πλεκόμενον 70
ἐκ τοῦ λίθου, σὺν ἀμπέλῳ περιειλούμενον κυκλόθεν τῷ ποδὶ σὺν

1, 2 ολην την] ολην T την ολην C   3 κατα] pr <κατω τα> Wend. | KAGIBC
διασκευην] κατασκευην ΚBCTZ +η codd omn   4 δια το] και codd ωστε   TZ Jos
Wend. et om in lin 6   5 προς την χρ. την τρ. I   6 ωστε—θεσιν om
BT | θεσιν]+πεποιησθαι καθ ο αν μερος CZ   8 στερεων T   9 περονας
κατα κλεισιν codd περονας <δε εν> κ. Wend.   11 θεωρηται GI
14 πολυειδων ex Jos (λιθους...αξιολογους ωσπερ αστερας ποικιλης ιδεας) conj
Lumbroso] πυλιαδων codd   16 σχιστη] κτιστη B   18 om ηλεκτρον C |
εντετυπωτο Jos B¹] ενετυπ. KAGIB* ενετετυπ. Z ετετυπωτο C   21 ορθην]
αρκουντως T   23 παλαισταιου BCTZ   24 ον] ων C   25 κατεσκευασαν
corr Wend.] -σεν GIC -σε cett | ακανθη BT   26 περιειλημενον G

τοῖς βότρυσιν, οἳ λιθουργεῖς ἦσαν, μέχρι τῆς κεφαλῆς. ἡ δ᾽
αὐτὴ διάθεσις ἦν τῶν τεσσάρων ποδῶν, πάντα ἐνεργῶς πεποιη-
μένα καὶ προσηγμένα, τῆς ἐμπειρίας καὶ τέχνης τὰς ὑπεροχὰς
ἀπαραλλάκτως ἔχοντα πρὸς τὴν ἀλήθειαν, ὥστε καὶ ῥιπίζοντος τοῦ
κατὰ τὸν ἀέρα πνεύματος κίνησιν ἐπιδέχεσθαι τὴν τῶν φύλλων 5
θέσιν, πρὸς τὴν τῆς ἀληθείας διάθεσιν τετυπωμένων ἁπάντων.
71 ἐποίησαν δὲ τριμερὲς τὸ στόμα τῆς τραπέζης, οἱονεὶ τρίπτυχον,
πελεκίνοις συναρμοζόμενα γομφωτοῖς πρὸς ἑαυτὰ κατὰ τὸ πάχος τῆς
κατασκευῆς, ἀθέατον καὶ ἀνεύρετον τὴν τῶν ἁρμῶν κατασκευάσαντες
συμβολήν. ἡμιπηχίου δὲ οὐκ ἐλάσσονος ἦν τὸ πάχος τῆς ὅλης 10
72 τραπέζης, ὥστε πολλῶν εἶναι ταλάντων τὴν ὅλην διασκευήν. ἐπεὶ
γὰρ οὐ προῄρητο τοῖς μεγέθεσιν οὐδὲν προσθεῖναι ὁ βασιλεύς, ὅσον
ἔδει δαπανηθῆναι κατασκευαζομένων μειζόνων, ταῦτα ἀποδέδωκε
πλείονα· καὶ κατὰ τὴν προαίρεσιν αὐτοῦ πάντα ἐπετελέσθη
θαυμασίως καὶ ἀξιολόγως ἔχοντα, καὶ ταῖς τέχναις ἀμίμητα, καὶ τῇ 15
73 καλλονῇ διαπρεπῆ. Τῶν δὲ κρατήρων δύο μὲν ἦσαν ‹χρυσοῖ›
¶C τῇ ˥κατασκευῇ, φολιδωτὴν ἔχοντες ἀπὸ τῆς βάσεως μέχρι τοῦ μέσου
τὴν διασκευὴν τῇ τορείᾳ, καὶ τὴν τῶν λίθων ἀνὰ μέσον τῶν φολίδων
74 σύνδεσιν πολυτέχνως ἔχοντες. εἶτα μαίανδρος ἐπέκειτο πηχυαῖος
ὕψει, τὴν δ᾽ ἐκτύπωσιν ἐνυπῆρχε διὰ λιθώσεως ποικίλης, ἐμφαίνων 20
σὺν ὡραιότητι τὸ τῆς τέχνης φιλόπονον. ἐπὶ δὲ τούτου ῥάβδωσις,
ἐφ᾽ ᾗ διαπλοκὴ ῥόμβων, δικτυωτὴν ἔχουσα τὴν πρόσοψιν ἕως ἐπὶ τὸ
75 στόμα. τὸ δ᾽ ἀνὰ μέσον ἀσπιδίσκοι λίθων ἑτέρων παρ᾽ ἑτέροις, τοῖς
γένεσι παραλλαγὴν ἐχόντων, τετραδακτύλων οὐκ ἔλαττον, ἀνεπλή-
ρουν τὸ τῆς καλλονῆς ἐναργές. ἐπὶ δὲ τῆς στεφάνης τοῦ στόματος 25
κρίνων τύπωσις σὺν ἀνθεμίσι καὶ βοτρύων σχοινιαὶ διάπλοκοι
76 διετυποῦντο κυκλόθεν. οἱ μὲν οὖν διὰ τοῦ χρυσοῦ τοιαύτην εἶχον
τὴν κατασκευήν, χωροῦντες ὑπὲρ δύο μετρητάς· οἱ δ᾽ ἀργυροῖ λείαν

KAGIBC
TZ Jos
1 οἱ] ο GI   2 εναργως BZ   3 προηγμενα Wend.   7 στομα]
σχημα Jos   8 συναρμοζομενον ΚΑ   9 αθετον codd txt ex Jos (αορατον)
10 ημιπηχυαιου B | ην ΚΒ] η cett   12 προειρητο GCTZ | οσων CTZ
13 om μειζονων C | απεδωκε Wend. cf autem § 173   14 απετελεσθη BCT
15 την τεχνην C   16 χρυσοι (om codd) ex Jos (χρυσεοι) supplevi
17, 18 απο της βασ.—τορεια·και om BTZ   18 πορεια G   19 συνθεσιν
GI   25 ? ενεργες   26 σχοινιω codd txt ex Jos conj Schmidt   28 λιαν
GIZT* fort

εἶχον τὴν διασκευήν, ἔνοπτρον δὴ γεγονυῖαν πρὸς αὐτὸ τοῦτο θαυμασίως ἔχουσαν, ὥστε πᾶν τὸ προσαχθὲν ἀπαυγάζεσθαι σαφέστερον
μᾶλλον ἢ ἐν τοῖς κατόπτροις. οὐκ ἐφικτὸν δ᾽ ἐστὶν ἐξηγήσασθαι 77
τὰ προσυντελεσθέντα πρὸς τὴν τῆς ἀληθείας ἔμφασιν. ὡς γὰρ
5 ἐπετελέσθη, τεθέντων τῶν κατασκευασμάτων ἑτέρου παρ᾽ ἕτερον—
λέγω δὲ πρῶτον ἀργυροῦ κρατῆρος, εἶτα χρυσοῦ, πάλιν ἀργυροῦ καὶ
χρυσοῦ—παντελῶς ἀνεξήγητος ἐγένετο τῆς προσόψεως ἡ διάθεσις,
καὶ τῶν πρὸς τὴν θεωρίαν προσιόντων οὐ δυναμένων ἀφίστασθαι διὰ
τὴν περιαύγειαν καὶ τὸ τῆς ὄψεως τερπνόν. ποικίλη γὰρ ἦν ἡ τῆς 78
10 ἐπιφανείας ἐνέργεια. προσορώντων γὰρ πρὸς αὐτὴν τὴν τοῦ χρυσίου
κατασκευήν, ψυχαγωγία τις ἦν μετὰ θαυμασμοῦ, συνεχῶς ἐφ᾽ ἕκαστον
ἐπιβαλλούσης τῆς διανοίας τεχνίτευμα. καὶ πάλιν ὅτε πρὸς τὴν·
τῶν ἀργυρῶν προσβλέψαι τις θέσιν ἤθελεν, ἀπέλαμπε τὰ πάντα
κυκλόθεν, ὡς ἄν τις ἔστηκε, καὶ διάχυσιν ἐποίει μείζονα τοῖς θεω-
15 μένοις· ὥστε παντελῶς ἀνεξήγητον εἶναι τῶν ἐνηργημένων τὴν
πολυτεχνίαν. Τὰς δὲ χρυσᾶς φιάλας διετόρευσαν στεφάνοις 79
ἀμπέλου κατὰ μέσον, περὶ δὲ τὰ χείλη κισσοῦ τε καὶ μυρσίνης ἔτι
δ᾽ ἐλαίας ἀνέπλεξαν στέφανον ἔκτυπον, πολυτελεῖς ἐνέντες λίθους·
καὶ τὰς λοιπὰς δὲ τορείας διηλλαγμένως ἐπετέλεσαν, ἅπαντα φιλοτι-
20 μηθέντες εἰς ὑπεροχὴν δόξης τοῦ βασιλέως ποιῆσαι. καθόλου γὰρ 80
οὔτ᾽ ἐν τοῖς βασιλικοῖς ὑπῆρχε ρισκοφυλακίοις τοιαύτη κατασκευὴ
τῇ πολυτελείᾳ καὶ τεχνουργίᾳ, οὔτ᾽ ἔν τινι ἄλλῳ. πρόνοιαν γὰρ οὐ
μικρὰν ἐποιεῖτο ὁ βασιλεύς, φιλοδοξῶν εἰς τὰ καλῶς ἔχοντα.
πολλάκις γὰρ τὸν δημόσιον χρηματισμὸν παρίει, τοῖς δὲ τεχνίταις 81
25 παρήδρευεν ἐπιμελῶς, ἵνα καθηκόντως τῷ τόπῳ συντελέσωσιν, εἰς
ὃν ἀπεστέλλετο τὰ τῶν ἔργων.¶ διὸ πάντα σεμνῶς ἐγεγόνει, καὶ ¶ Jos
καταξίως τοῦ τε ἀποστέλλοντος βασιλέως καὶ τοῦ προστατοῦντος
ἀρχιερέως τοῦ τόπου. καὶ γὰρ τὸ τῶν λίθων πλῆθος ἄφθονον, καὶ 82

---

1 δη] δε TZ om BC   **2** προσαχεν GI προσταχθεν Z   **4** προσσυντ. B KAGIBTZ
4, 5 προς την—τεθεντων om Tᵗˣᵗ (insᵐᵍ) Z   **6** προτερον Z   **13** προσ-   Jos
βλεψεται Τ επιβλεψεται Β   **13, 14** θεσιν—ως αν τις om BTZ
14 εστηκη Wend.   **18** ενιεντες ΒΤΖ   **19** τορειας ΚΑᶜᵒʳʳ] πορειας cett |
διηλλαγμενας Β   **22** και τεχν.] της τεχνουργιας Β   **23** εποιει ΚΑGI
24 παριει TZ] παρηει cett   **25** επιτελεσωσιν Β*

μεγάλοι τοῖς μεγέθεσιν, οὐκ ἔλαττον πεντακισχιλίων· καὶ ταῖς τέχναις
κρατιστεύοντα πάντα, ὥστε πενταπλασίως τοῦ χρυσοῦ τιμιωτέραν
εἶναι τὴν τῶν λίθων δόσιν καὶ τὴν τῶν τεχνῶν ἐνέργειαν.

83   Ὑπολαμβάνων οὖν καὶ τούτων τὴν ἀναγραφὴν ἀναγκαίαν εἶναι,
δεδήλωκά σοι.   τὰ δ᾽ ἑξῆς περιέχει τὴν πρὸς τὸν Ἐλεάζαρον ὁδὸν 5
ἡμῖν γενομένην· τὴν δὲ θέσιν τῆς ὅλης χώρας πρῶτον δηλώσω.
Ὡς γὰρ παρεγενήθημεν ἐπὶ τοὺς τόπους, ἐθεωροῦμεν τὴν πόλιν μέσην
κειμένην τῆς ὅλης Ἰουδαίων ἐπ᾽ ὄρους ὑψηλὴν ἔχοντος τὴν ἀνάτασιν.
84 ἐπὶ δὲ τῆς κορυφῆς κατεσκεύαστο τὸ ἱερὸν ἐκπρεπῶς ἔχον· καὶ οἱ
περίβολοι τρεῖς, ὑπὲρ ἑβδομήκοντα δὲ πήχεις τῷ μεγέθει, καὶ τὸ 10
πλάτος ἀκόλουθον καὶ τὸ μῆκος τῆς κατὰ τὸν οἶκον διασκευῆς
ὑπῆρχε, μεγαλομοιρίᾳ καὶ χορηγίᾳ κατὰ πάντα ὑπερβαλλούσῃ
85 διῳκοδομημένων ἁπάντων.   καὶ τοῦ θυρώματος δὲ καὶ τῶν περὶ αὐτὸ
συνδέσμων κατὰ τὰς φλιὰς καὶ τῆς τῶν ὑπερθύρων ἀσφαλείας
86 ἔκδηλος ἦν ἡ τῶν χρημάτων γεγονυῖα ἀφειδὴς δαπάνη.   τοῦ τε 15
καταπετάσματος ἡ διατύπωσις θυρώσει κατὰ πᾶν ὁμοιοτάτη ὑπῆρχε·
καὶ μάλιστα διὰ τὴν τοῦ πνεύματος ὑποδρομὴν ἀδιάλειπτον κίνησιν
λαμβανούσης τῆς διυφῆς, διὰ τὸ ἀπ᾽ ἐδάφους γινομένης τῆς ὑποδρο-
μῆς <κατατείνειν> τὴν κόλπωσιν μέχρι τῆς ἄνω διατάσεως, ἡδεῖάν
τινα καὶ δυσαπάλλακτον τὴν θεωρίαν ἔχοντος τοῦ πράγματος.   20
87 Ἥ τε τοῦ θυσιαστηρίου κατασκευὴ <συμμέτρως ἔχουσαν> πρὸς τὸν
τόπον καὶ τὰ θύματα διὰ τοῦ πυρὸς ἐξαναλούμενα τὴν διοικοδομὴν
εἶχε, τῆς δ᾽ ἀναβάσεως τῆς πρὸς αὐτό, πρὸς τὴν εὐκοσμίαν ἔχοντος
τοῦ τόπου καθηκόντως τὸ κλίμα τῶν λειτουργούντων ἱερέων κεκα-

KAGIBTZ   1 μεγαλοις GI | ελαττον]+των ΚΑ   5 ημιν οδον Β   6 δηλωσον GIZ
-σαι Κ   7 επι του τοπου ΒΤ¹ επι του και τοπους GI et sic cett sed cum
lacuna post του et ᾽ς pro και posito, επι του...ς (+τους LD) τοπους.   Txt ex
papyris confirmatur   8 Ιουδαιων KAGI] Ιουδαιας cett | ψιλην Κ | ανα-
στασιν GI   9 ευπρεπως ΒΤ   12 υπερβαλλ. Β] υπερβαλουση Α^corr περι-
βαλουση cett   13 και 1°] κακ conj Schmidt   16 θυρωσι GI -σιν Z
17 αδιαληπτον KGIZ   18 απ] επ Β | γενομ. ΒΤΖ   19 κατα codd κατα-
τεινειν conj Schmidt   20 εχειν ex εχοντος Τ*^vid   21 om κατασκευη Τ*
(ins Τ¹) Z | συμμετρον εχουσα codd txt ex corr Mend.   24 λειτουργουντων
corr Mend.] λειτουργων (-γιων ΒΤ) των codd

λυμμένων μέχρι τῶν σφυρῶν ΒΥϹϹΙΝΟΙϹ ΧΙΤѠϹΙΝ. ⁸Ὁ δὲ οἶκος βλέ- 88 § Eus
πει πρὸς ἔω, τὰ δ' ὀπίσθια αὐτοῦ πρὸς ἑσπέραν· τὸ δὲ πᾶν ἔδαφος
λιθόστρωτον καθέστηκε καὶ κλίματα πρὸς τοὺς καθήκοντας τόπους
ἔχει τῆς τῶν ὑδάτων ἐπιφορᾶς ἕνεκεν, ἢ γίνεται διὰ τὴν σμῆξιν τῶν
5 ἀπὸ τῶν θυσιῶν αἱμάτων. πολλαὶ γὰρ μυριάδες κτηνῶν προσά-
γονται κατὰ τὰς τῶν ἑορτῶν ἡμέρας. ὕδατος δὲ ἀνέκλειπτός ἐστι 89
σύστασις, ὡς ἂν καὶ πηγῆς ἔσωθεν πολυρρύτου φυσικῶς ἐπιρρεούσης,
ἔτι δὲ θαυμασίων καὶ ἀδιηγήτων ὑποδοχείων ὑπαρχόντων ὑπὸ γῆν,
καθὼς ἀπέφαινον πέντε σταδίων κυκλόθεν τῆς κατὰ τὸ ἱερὸν κατα-
10 βολῆς καὶ ἑκάστου τούτων σύριγγας ἀναρίθμους, καθ' ἕκαστον
μέρος ἑαυτὰ συναπτόντων τῶν ῥευμάτων· καὶ πάντα ταῦτα μεμο- 90
λιβῶσθαι κατ' ἐδάφους καὶ τοῦ τοίχου· ἐπὶ δὲ τούτων κεχύσθαι
πολύ τι πλῆθος κονιάσεως, ἐνεργῶς γεγενημένων ἁπάντων·¶ εἶναι ¶ Eus
δὲ πυκνὰ τὰ στόματα πρὸς τὴν βάσιν, ἀοράτως ἔχοντα τοῖς πᾶσι
15 πλὴν αὐτοῖς οἷς ἐστιν ἡ λειτουργία, ὡς ῥοπῇ καὶ νεύματι πάντα
καθαρίζεσθαι τὰ συναγόμενα παμπληθῆ τῶν θυμάτων αἵματα.
πεπεισμένος δὲ καὶ αὐτὸς τὴν τῶν ὑποδοχείων κατασκευὴν δηλώσω 91
καθὼς ἐπιστώθην. προήγαγον γὰρ πλέον σταδίων τεσσάρων ἐκ τῆς
πόλεως, καὶ πρός τινα τόπον ἐκέλευσαν κατακύψαντα συνακοῦσαι
20 τοῦ γινομένου ψόφου τῆς ἀπαντήσεως τῶν ὑδάτων· ὥστε συμφανές
μοι γεγονέναι τὸ μέγεθος τῶν ἀγγείων, καθὼς δεδήλωται.
Τῶν δὲ ἱερέων ἡ λειτουργία κατὰ πᾶν ἀνυπέρβλητός ἐστι τῇ ῥώμῃ 92
καὶ τῇ τῆς εὐκοσμίας καὶ σιγῆς διαθέσει. πάντες γὰρ αὐτοκελεύ-
στως διαπονοῦσι πολλῆς γινομένης κακοπαθείας, καὶ ἑκάστῳ τὸ
25 διατεταγμένον μέλει. καὶ ἀδιαλείπτως ὑπηρετοῦσιν, οἱ μὲν τὴν
ξυλείαν, οἱ δὲ ἔλαιον, οἱ δὲ σεμίδαλιν, οἱ δὲ τὰ τῶν ἀρωμάτων, ἕτεροι

1 Ex 36³⁵ (cf 28³⁹)

1 αποβλεπει Eus   2 ηω Eus   4 επιφορας] επιρροης Eus   6 αν- KAGIBTZ
επιληπτος B txt Eus (-λιπ.ᵒ) KT ανεκληπτος cett   9 επεφαινον Eus Eus
10 εκαστου] εκ Eus   11 εαυτας Ar codd Eusⁱᵒ (-ταις Eusᵃˡ) txt Schmidt |
ταυτα παντα Eus | μεμολιβουσθαι Ar codd txt Eusⁱᵒ B¹   12 τους τοιχους
Eusᵒ (των -ων Eusⁱ) | πολυ τι πληθ. κεχ. K   13 om τι Eus | κονιας εως
Ar codd Eusᵒ | ενεργων Z   15 ριπη Tᶜᵒʳʳ | ρευματι B   16 παμπληθει
KABᶜᵒʳʳ   17 πεπεισμενοις (-νως A) et αυτοις codd corr Schmidt   19 εκε-
λευσαν B] εκελευσε (-σεν GI) cett   25 μελλει GIBTZ   26 ετερος G

τὰ τῆς σαρκὸς ὁλοκαυτοῦντες, ἰσχύι διαφερόντως συγχρώμενοι·
93 διαλαβόντες γὰρ ἀμφοτέραις τῶν μόσχων τὰ σκέλη, πλεῖον ὄντα
ταλάντων δύο σχεδὸν ἑκάστου, ἀναρρίπτουσιν ἑκατέραις θαυμασίως
ὕψος ἱκανὸν καὶ οὐχ ἁμαρτάνουσι τῆς ἐπιθέσεως. ὁμοίως δὲ καὶ τὰ
τῶν προβάτων ἔτι δ᾽ αἰγῶν τοῖς βάρεσι καὶ πιμελῇ θαυμασίως ἔχει. 5
κατὰ πᾶν γὰρ ἐκλεγομένων οἷς ἐπιμελές ἐστιν ἀμώμητα καὶ τῇ
94 παχύτητι διαφέροντα, τὸ προειρημένον ἐπιτελεῖται. πρὸς δὲ τὴν
ἀνάπαυσιν τόπος αὐτοῖς ἐστὶν ἀποτεταγμένος, οὗ καθίζουσιν οἱ
διαναπαυόμενοι. τούτου δὲ γινομένου, τῶν διαλελοιπότων ἐγείρονται
95 πρόθυμοι, οὐδενὸς ἐπιτάσσοντος τὰ τῆς λειτουργίας. ἥ τε πᾶσα 10
σιγὴ καθέστηκεν, ὥστε ὑπολαμβάνειν, μηθ᾽ ἕνα ἄνθρωπον ἐν τῷ
τόπῳ παρεῖναι, πρὸς τοὺς ἑπτακοσίους παρόντων τῶν λειτουργῶν—
καὶ τῶν προσαγόντων δὲ τὰ θύματα πολύ τι πλῆθος—ἀλλὰ φόβῳ
96 καὶ καταξίως μεγάλης θειότητος ἅπαντ᾽ ἐπιτελεῖται. Μεγάλην
δὲ ἔκπληξιν ἡμῖν παρέσχεν, ὡς ἐθεασάμεθα τὸν Ἐλεάζαρον ἐν τῇ 15
λειτουργίᾳ, τά τε τοῦ στολισμοῦ καὶ τῆς δόξης, ᾗ συνίσταται διὰ
τὴν ἔνδυσιν οὗ φορεῖ χιτῶνος καὶ τῶν περὶ αὐτὸν λίθων· χρυσοῖ
γὰρ κώδωνες περὶ τὸν ποΔΉΡΗ εἰσὶν αὐτοῦ, μέλους ἦχον ἀνιέντες
ἰδιάζοντα· παρ᾽ ἑκάτερον δὲ τούτων ἄνθεσι πεποικιλμένοι ῥοΐσκοι,
97 τῇ χρόᾳ θαυμασίως ἔχοντες. κατέζωστο δὲ διαφόρῳ ζώνΗ δια- 20
πρεπεῖ, διυφασμένῃ καλλίστοις χρώμασιν. ἐπὶ δὲ τοῦ στήθους
φορεῖ τὸ λεγόμενον λόΓΙΟΝ, ἐν ᾧ συνεσφιγμένοι λίθοι Δεκαδύο,
διαλλάσσοντες τοῖς γένεσι, χρυσῷ κεκολλημένοι, τὰ τῶν φυλάρ-
χων ὀΝΌΜΑτα κατὰ τὴν ἐξ ἀρχῆς διάταξιν γενηθεῖσαν, ἀπαυγά-
98 ζοντες ἕκαστος ἀνεξήγητον τῆς ἰδιότητος τὴν φυσικὴν χρόαν. ἐπὶ 25
δὲ τῆς κεφαλῆς ἔχει τὴν λεγομένην κίΔΑΡΙΝ, ἐπὶ δὲ ταύτης τὴν
ἀμίμητον μίτρΑΝ, τὸ καθηγιασμένον βασίλειον ἐκτυποῦν ἐπὶ

17 ff Ex 28⁴·²⁷⁻³¹   20 ib³⁵   21 ff ib¹⁵⁻²³
26 ff ib³²ᶠᶠ

KAGIBTZ   1 χρωμενοι A   2 πλειων BT   3 ταλ. δυο] ταλαντου B   4 υψος]
pr εις BT | επιθεσ.] επιθυμιας Z (-εσεως sup ras in T)   5 προβ.] πραγμα-
των Zᵗˣᵗ (προβ.· Zᵐᵍ) | βαρεσι codd   6 οις τι πιμελες εστιν B   8 om
αυτοις BT   11 ωστε υπολαμβανειν conj Schmidt] ως τυπον λαμβανειν
codd | εν] επι A   12 τας επτακοσιας Z   16 η] ης BTZ | συνιστατο KA
19 τουτον K   21 διυφασμενοι K   27 εκτυπον GI (-πων Z)

πετάλω χρυσῷ γράμμασιν ἁγίοις ὄνομα τοῦ θεοῦ, κατὰ μέσον τῶν
ὀφρύων, δόξῃ πεπληρωμένον, ὁ κριθεὶς ἄξιος τούτων ἐν ταῖς λει-
τουργίαις. ἡ δὲ συμφάνεια τούτων ἐμποιεῖ φόβον καὶ ταραχήν, 99
ὥστε νομίζειν εἰς ἕτερον ἐληλυθέναι ἐκτὸς τοῦ κόσμου· καὶ διαβε-
5 βαιοῦμαι, πάντα ἄνθρωπον προσελθόντα τῇ θεωρίᾳ τῶν προειρημένων εἰς ἔκπληξιν ἥξειν καὶ θαυμασμὸν ἀδιήγητον, μετατραπέντα
τῇ διανοίᾳ διὰ τὴν περὶ ἕκαστον ἁγίαν κατασκευήν. Πρὸς 100
γὰρ τὴν ἐπίγνωσιν ἁπάντων ἐπὶ τὴν παρακειμένην ἄκραν τῆς πόλεως
ἀναβάντες ἐθεωροῦμεν· ἣ κεῖται μὲν ἐν ὑψηλοτάτῳ τόπῳ, πύργοις
10 ἐξησφαλισμένη πλείοσι, μέχρι κορυφῆς εὐμήκεσι λίθοις ἀνῳκοδομη-
μένων αὐτῶν, ὡς μεταλαμβάνομεν, πρὸς φυλακὴν τῶν περὶ τὸ ἱερὸν
τόπων· ἵνα, ἐὰν ἐπίθεσίς τις ἢ νεωτερισμὸς ἢ πολεμίων ἔφοδος 101
γένηται, μηθεὶς δύνηται ὁδὸν εἰς τοὺς περιβόλους ποιήσασθαι τοὺς
περὶ τὸν οἶκον· ἐπικειμένων καὶ ὀξυβελῶν ἐπὶ τῶν πύργων τῆς
15 ἄκρας καὶ ὀργάνων ποικίλων, καὶ τοῦ τόπου κατὰ κορυφὴν ὄντος τῶν
προειρημένων περιβόλων, ὡσανεὶ φυλασσομένων τῶν πύργων ὑπὸ 102
τῶν πιστοτάτων ἀνδρῶν καὶ τῇ πατρίδι μεγάλας ἀποδείξεις δεδωκό-
των· οἵτινες οὐκ εἶχον ἐξουσίαν ἐξιέναι τῆς ἄκρας, εἰ μὴ ταῖς
ἑορταῖς, καὶ τοῦτο ἐκ μέρους, οὐδὲ εἰσοδεύειν εἴων οὐδένα. μετὰ 103
20 ἀκριβείας δὲ πολλῆς εἶχον, εἰ καί τις ἐπιταγὴ γένοιτο διὰ τοῦ
προκαθηγουμένου πρὸς θεωρίαν ¶ εἰσδέξασθαί τινας· οἷον καὶ καθ᾽
ἡμᾶς ἐγεγόνει. μόλις γὰρ ἀνόπλους ὄντας ἡμᾶς δύο παρεδέξαντο
πρὸς τὸ κατανοῆσαι τὰ τῶν θυσιῶν. ἔλεγον δὲ καὶ δι᾽ ὅρκων πεπι- 104
στῶσθαι τὸ τοιοῦτον· τοὺς γὰρ πάντας ὀμωμοκέναι, κατ᾽ ἀνάγκην
25 <ἐπιτελουμένους> θείως τὸ κατὰ τὸν ὁρισμὸν πρᾶγμα, ὄντας πεντα-
κοσίους μὴ παραδέξασθαι πλεῖον ἀνθρώπων πέντε κατὰ τὸ αὐτό·
τοῦ γὰρ ἱεροῦ τὴν πᾶσαν εἶναι φυλακὴν τὴν ἄκραν· καὶ τὸν κατα-
βαλλόμενον αὐτὴν τὴν προφυλακὴν τῶν εἰρημένων οὕτως ἠσφαλί-

---

1 κατα]+το BTZ   2 δοξης BT | post πεπληρ. fort excidit aliquid KAGIBTZ
3 εμφανεια IZ | ποιει B | φοβον] φημην Z   4 εισελ. A | διαβεβαιουται B
6 ηκειν BT | ανεκδιηγ. BT   11 ως μεταλαμβανωσι προφυλακης B
12 τις η η και νεωτ. BT (τις η και ν. Z)   13 δυνηται B] δυναται cett
19 εις μερος BT εις μερους Z^vid   21 προκαθημενου B*T* txt B¹T¹ cett
25 επιτελουμενου codd (τελουμενους Z^mg) | του B | ορκισμον conj Mend. |
πραγματος B

105 σθαι. Τῆς δὲ πόλεώς ἐστι τὸ χύμα συμμέτρως ἔχον, οἷον τεσσαράκοντα σταδίων ὄντος τοῦ περιβόλου, καθόσον εἰκάσαι δυνατόν. ἔχει δὲ τὴν τῶν πύργων θέσιν θεατροειδῆ, καὶ φαινομένων διόδων—τῶν ὑποκειμένων, τῶν δ᾽ ἐπάνωθεν—<εἰθισμένως>, καὶ τὰς διὰ τούτων διεξόδους. ἀνάκλασιν γὰρ ἔχει τὰ τῶν τόπων, ὡς ἂν ἐπ᾽ ὄρους τῆς 5
106 πόλεως ᾠκοδομημένης. εἰσὶ δὲ καὶ διαβάθραι πρὸς τὰς διόδους. οἱ μὲν γὰρ μετέωροι τὴν ὁδείαν, οἱ δ᾽ ὑπ᾽ αὐτὰς ποιοῦνται, καὶ μάλιστα διεστηκότες τῆς ὁδείας, διὰ τοὺς ἐν ταῖς ἁγνείαις ὄντας, ὅπως μηδενὸς
107 θιγγάνωσιν ὧν οὐ δέον ἐστίν. Οὐκ ἀλόγως δὲ τὴν πόλιν
§ P συμμετρίᾳ καθηκούσῃ κατεσκεύασαν οἱ πρῶτοι, σοφῶς δὲ ⁵ἐπινοή- 10
§ II σαντες. τῆς γὰρ χώρας πολλῆς οὔσης καὶ καλῆς, καί τινων ⁸μὲν πεδινῶν, τῶν κατὰ τὴν Σαμαρεῖτιν λεγομένην, καὶ τῶν συναπτόντων τῇ τῶν Ἰδουμαίων χώρᾳ, τινῶν δὲ ὀρεινῶν, τῶν <συναπτόντων τῇ τῶν Ἰουδαίων χώρᾳ, χρῇ> πρὸς τὴν γεωργίαν καὶ τὴν ἐπιμέλειαν τῆς γῆς γίνεσθαι συνεχῶς, ἵνα καὶ διὰ τοῦτο οὗτοι τὴν εὐ- 15 καρπίαν ἔχωσιν· οὗ καὶ γινομένου γεωργεῖται <πάντα μετὰ> δαψιλείας
108 πολλῆς ἐν πάσῃ τῇ προειρημένῃ χώρᾳ. τῶν δὲ πόλεων ὅσαι μέγεθος ἔχουσι καὶ τὴν ἀκόλουθον εὐδαιμονίαν, ταύταις συμβέβηκεν εὐανδρεῖν, ἀμελεῖσθαι δὲ τῆς χώρας, πάντων ἐπὶ τὸ κατὰ ψυχὴν ἱλαροῦσθαι νενευκότων, καὶ τῇ κατασκευῇ πάντας ἀνθρώπους 20
109 ἐπὶ τὰς ἡδονὰς εὐκαταφόρους εἶναι. τοῦτο δὲ ἐγίνετο περὶ τὴν Ἀλεξάνδρειαν ὑπερβάλλουσαν πάσας τῷ μεγέθει καὶ εὐδαιμονίᾳ τὰς πόλεις. οἱ γὰρ ἀπὸ τῆς χώρας εἰς αὐτὴν ἀποξενούμενοι κατα-
110 μένοντες ἐφ᾽ ἱκανὸν εἰς ἐλάττωσιν ἦγον τὰ τῆς ἐργασίας. ὅθεν ὁ βασιλεύς, ἵνα μὴ καταμένωσι, προσέταξε μὴ πλέον εἴκοσιν ἡμερῶν 25 παρεπιδημεῖν· καὶ τοῖς ἐπὶ τῶν χρειῶν ὁμοίως δι᾽ ἐγγράπτων διαστολὰς ἔδωκεν, ἐὰν ἀναγκαῖον ᾖ κατακαλέσαι, διακρίνειν ἐν
111 ἡμέραις πέντε. πρὸ πολλοῦ δὲ ποιούμενος καὶ χρηματιστὰς καὶ

HKAGIBP 1 χυμα] σχημα B 2 οντος] εντος Z 4 ειθισμενως conj Redpath
TZ (usitato more theatri)] ηθισμενων KGIT*ᵛⁱᵈZ ειθισμενων cett 5 εξοδους B
8 διεστηκοτας KGITZ (-κυιας edd) | της] τας K | μηδενι BZ 11 πεδινων
μεν P 12 λεγομενων codd omn 13, 14 των—γεωργιαν] τω προς τη
γεωργια B των πρ. την γεωργιαν cett verba ex conj addidi 15 om
και P 16 παντα μετα Mend.] μεν παντα codd 19 ευανδρειν] ευ
(sequente lacuna) B 20 και] και τω vel δια το conj Schmidt 22 υπερ-
βαλλουσα HA*GIT*Z 23 επιξενουμενοι BP

τοὺς τούτων ὑπηρέτας ἐπέταξε κατὰ νομούς, ὅπως μὴ πορισμὸν
λαμβάνοντες οἱ γεωργοὶ καὶ προστάται τῆς πόλεως ἐλαττῶσι τὰ
ταμιεῖα, λέγω δὲ τὰ τῆς γεωργίας πρόσφορα. Παρεξέβημεν 112
δὲ ταῦτα διὰ τὸ καλῶς ἡμῖν τὸν Ἐλεάζαρον ὑποδεδειχέναι τὰ
5 προειρημένα. μεγάλη γὰρ ἐστὶν ἡ τῶν γεωργουμένων φιλοπονία.
καὶ γὰρ ἐλαϊκοῖς πλήθεσι σύνδενδρός ἐστι καὶ σιτικοῖς καρποῖς
αὐτῶν ἡ χώρα καὶ ὀσπρίοις, ἔτι δὲ ἀμπέλῳ καὶ μέλιτι πολλῷ. τὰ
μὲν τῶν ἄλλων ἀκροδρύων καὶ φοινίκων οὐδ᾽ ἀριθμεῖται παρ᾽ αὐτοῖς.
κτήνη τε πολλὰ παμμιγῆ, καὶ δαψιλὴς ἡ τούτων νομή· διὸ καλῶς 113
10 ἔβλεψαν, ὅτι πολυανθρωπίας οἱ τόποι προσδέονται, καὶ τὴν κατασκευὴν τῆς πόλεως καὶ τῶν κωμῶν ἔθεντο κατὰ λόγον. πολὺ δὲ 114
πλῆθος καὶ τῶν ἀρωμάτων καὶ λίθων πολυτελῶν καὶ χρυσοῦ παρα-
κομίζεται διὰ τῶν Ἀράβων εἰς τὸν τόπον. ἐργάσιμος γὰρ καὶ πρὸς
τὴν ἐμπορίαν ἐστὶ κατεσκευασμένη ἡ χώρα, καὶ πολύτεχνος ἡ πόλις,
15 οὐ σπανίζει δὲ οὐδὲν τῶν διακομιζομένων διὰ τῆς θαλάσσης. ἔχει 115
γὰρ καὶ λιμένας εὐκαίρους χορηγοῦντας, τόν τε κατὰ τὴν Ἀσκαλῶνα
καὶ Ἰόππην καὶ Γάζαν, ὁμοίως δὲ καὶ Πτολεμαΐδα τὴν ὑπὸ τοῦ
βασιλέως ἐκτισμένην. μέση δὲ κεῖται πρὸς τοὺς προειρημένους
τόπους, οὐκ ἀπέχουσα τούτων πολύ. ἔχει δὲ πάντα δαψιλῆ κάθυγρος
20 οὖσα πάντοθεν ἡ χώρα καὶ μεγάλην ἀσφάλειαν ἔχουσα. περιρρεῖ 116
δ᾽ αὐτὴν ὁ λεγόμενος Ἰορδάνης ποταμὸς ἀείρρους. <τῆς δὲ χώρας>
οὐκ ἔλαττον ἑξακισχιλίων μυριάδων ἀρουρῶν κατὰ τὸ ἀρχαῖον οὔσης
(μετέπειτα δὲ οἱ γειτνιῶντες ἐπέβησαν αὐτῆς) ἑξήκοντα μυριάδες
ἀνδρῶν ἔγκληροι καθεστήκεισαν ἑκατοντάρουροι. πληρούμενος δὲ
25 ὁ ποταμός, καθὼς ὁ Νεῖλος, ἐν ταῖς πρὸς τὸν θερισμὸν ἡμέραις,
πολλὴν ἀρδεύει τῆς γῆς· ὃς εἰς ἕτερον ποταμὸν ἐκβάλλει τὸ ῥεῦμα 117
κατὰ τὴν Πτολεμαίων χώραν, οὗτος δὲ ἔξεισιν εἰς θάλασσαν.

23 εξηκ. μυρ. cf Ex 39³ LXX (12³⁷ Num 11²¹)   25 cf Jos 3¹⁵

6 ε λαικοις (sic) H εν λαικ. GIT ευλαικ. B εν ελαικ. ΚΑΡΖ   7 om ΗΚΑGΙΒΡ
αυτων ΒΡΤΖ   9 τε] τα ΗΑGΙΖ   10 προσδεονται ΒΡΤΖ] δεονται cett TΖ
14 εστιν η χ. κατεσκ. (κατασκ. Τ*) ΒΡΤΖ | πολις]+εστιν Ρ   16 τον Β]
των cett τα edd   17 om του Ρ   18 εκτισμενην] κατεσκευασμενην Ρ |
ειρημ. ΒΤ   19 καθυγρατος GΙPΖ pr και Ρ   21 verba inserui   23 υπε-
βησαν Ρ (cod Mon) απεβ. edd pr | μυριαδων Τ   24 εκατονταρουροις codd
txt ex papyris corr Mahaffy   26 πολυν Β | εμβαλλει GΒΡΖ   27—2 p 540
ουτος δε—Αζ. χωραν om Α

ἄλλοι δὲ χείμαρροι λεγόμενοι κατίασι, περιλαμβάνοντες τὰ πρὸς
118 τὴν Γάζαν μέρη καὶ τὴν Ἀζωτίων χώραν. περιέχεται δὲ ἀσφαλείαις
αὐτοφυέσι, δυσείσβολος οὖσα καὶ πλήθεσιν ἀπραγμάτευτος, διὰ τὸ
στενὰς εἶναι τὰς παρόδους, κρημνῶν παρακειμένων καὶ φαράγγων
βαθέων, ἔτι δὲ τραχείας οὔσης πάσης τῆς περιεχούσης πᾶσαν τὴν 5
119 χώραν ὀρεινῆς. Ἐλέγετο δὲ καὶ ἐκ τῶν παρακειμένων ὀρέων
τῆς Ἀραβίας μέταλλα χαλκοῦ καὶ σιδήρου συνίστασθαι πρότερον. ἐκλέλειπται δὲ ταῦτα, καθ᾽ ὃν ἐπεκράτησαν Πέρσαι χρόνον,
τῶν τότε προστατούντων ποιησαμένων διαβολήν, ὡς ἄχρηστος ἡ
120 κατεργασία γίνεται καὶ πολυδάπανος, ὅπως μὴ διὰ τὴν μεταλ- 10
λείαν τῶν εἰρημένων συμβῇ καὶ τὴν χώραν καταφθείρεσθαι, καὶ
σχεδὸν διὰ τὴν ἐκείνων δυναστείαν ἀλλοτριωθῆναι, παρεύρεσιν
λαβόντων εἰς τοὺς τόπους εἰσόδου, διὰ τὸ τὴν διαβολὴν γεγονέναι
ταύτην.

Ὅσον οὖν καὶ περὶ τούτων ἔδει, κεφαλαιωδῶς σεσήμαγκά σοι, 15
ὦ Φιλόκρατες ἀδελφέ· τὰ δὲ τῆς ἑρμηνείας ἑπομένως δηλώσομεν.
121 Ἐπιλέξας γὰρ τοὺς ἀρίστους ἄνδρας καὶ παιδείᾳ διαφέροντας, ἅτε δὴ
γονέων τετευχότας ἐνδόξων, οἵτινες οὐ μόνον τὴν τῶν Ἰουδαϊκῶν
γραμμάτων ἕξιν περιεποίησαν αὑτοῖς, ἀλλὰ καὶ τῆς τῶν Ἑλληνικῶν
122 ἐφρόντισαν οὐ παρέργως κατασκευῆς· διὸ καὶ πρὸς τὰς πρεσβείας 20
εὔθετοι καθεστήκεισαν, καὶ τοῦτ᾽ ἐπετέλουν ὅτε δέοι, καὶ πρὸς τὰς
ὁμιλίας καὶ τὰς ἐπερωτήσεις τὰς διὰ τοῦ νόμου μεγάλην εὐφυΐαν
εἶχον, τὸ μέσον ἐζηλωκότες κατάστημα (τοῦτο γὰρ κάλλιστόν ἐστιν),
ἀποτεθειμένοι τὸ τραχὺ καὶ βάρβαρον τῆς διανοίας, ὁμοίως δὲ καὶ
τὸ κατοίεσθαι καὶ νομίζειν ὑπερφρονεῖν ἑτέρους ὑπερβεβηκότες, τὴν 25
δ᾽ ὁμιλίαν καὶ τὸ συνακούειν καὶ πρὸς ἕκαστον ἀποκρίνεσθαι δεόντως
παραδεδεγμένοι, καὶ πάντες ταῦτα συντηροῦντες καὶ μᾶλλον ἐν
τούτοις βουλόμενοι ὑπερφέρειν ἕτερος ἑτέρου, καὶ τοῦ καθηγουμένου

πάντες ἄξιοι καὶ τῆς περὶ αὐτὸν ἀρετῆς. νοῆσαι δ᾽ ἦν, ὡς ἠγάπησαν 123
τὸν Ἐλεάζαρον δυσαποσπάστως ἔχοντες, καὶ ἐκεῖνος αὐτούς· χωρὶς
καὶ τοῦ πρὸς τὸν βασιλέα γεγραφέναι περὶ τῆς ἀποκαταστάσεως
αὐτῶν πολλὰ παρεκάλεσε τὸν Ἀνδρέαν ποιῆσαι, συναντιλαμβάνεσθαι
5 παρακαλῶν, καθ᾽ ὃ ἂν δυνώμεθα. καὶ ἡμῶν ἐπαγγελλομένων <εὖ φρον- 124
τίσειν> περὶ τούτων, ἔφη καὶ λίαν διαγωνιᾶν· εἰδέναι γάρ, ὅτι
φιλάγαθος ὢν ὁ βασιλεὺς πάντων μέγιστον ἡγεῖται τὸ μεταπέμ-
πεσθαι, καθ᾽ ὃν ἂν τόπον ὀνομασθῇ τις ἄνθρωπος διαφέρων ἀγωγῇ
καὶ φρονήσει παρ᾽ ἑτέρους. μετείληφα γὰρ καλῶς αὐτὸν λέγειν, ὅτι 125
10 περὶ ἑαυτὸν ἔχων ἄνδρας δικαίους καὶ σώφρονας τὴν μεγίστην ἂν
φυλακὴν τῆς βασιλείας ἕξειν, συμβουλευόντων παρρησίᾳ πρὸς τὸ
συμφέρον τῶν φίλων· ὃ δὴ σύνεστι τοῖς ἀποστελλομένοις ὑπ᾽
αὐτοῦ. καὶ δι᾽ ὅρκων ἐπιστοῦτο, μὴ προΐεσθαι τοὺς ἀνθρώπους, εἴ 126
τις ἑτέρα χρεία πρὸς τὰ κατ᾽ ἰδίαν αὐτῷ κατεπείγοι, πρὸς δὲ τὴν
15 κοινὴν πᾶσι τοῖς πολίταις ἐπανόρθωσιν ἐξαποστέλλειν αὐτούς. τὸ 127
γὰρ καλῶς ζῆν ἐν τῷ τὰ νόμιμα συντηρεῖν εἶναι· τοῦτο δὲ ἐπιτε-
λεῖσθαι διὰ τῆς ἀκροάσεως πολλῷ μᾶλλον ἢ διὰ τῆς ἀναγνώσεως.
προτιθέμενος οὖν ταῦτα καὶ τὰ τούτοις παραπλήσια φανερὸς ἦν τὴν
διάθεσιν, ὃς ἦν πρὸς αὐτούς.

20 ⁵Ἄξιον δὲ ἐπιμνησθῆναι <διὰ> βραχέων τῶν ὑποδειχθέντων ὑπ᾽ 128 § Eus
αὐτοῦ πρὸς τὰ δι᾽ ἡμῶν ἐπιζητηθέντα. νομίζω γὰρ τοὺς πολλοὺς
περιεργίαν ἔχειν τινὰ τῶν ἐν τῇ νομοθεσίᾳ περί τε τῶν βρωτῶν καὶ
ποτῶν καὶ τῶν νομιζομένων ἀκαθάρτων εἶναι κνωδάλων. πυνθανομένων 129

20 ff Lev 11. Deut 14^{3-19}

2 δυσαποσπ.]+αυτου B | εκεινος]+δηλονοτι ηγαπησεν B | αυτους]+ος B HKAGIBP
TZ Eus
αυτος sine puncto sequente Wend.   3 om και P | γεγραπται I   4 τον
ανδρα B   5 ευ φροντ. Wend.] αφροντισειν codd   6 τουτου P   7 φι-
λανος BT   9 αυτον καλως BTZ   10 αυτον BT | εχων]+ο Πτολεμαιος B
11 εξει B   12 συνεστη Z   14 om ιδιαν B (in fin lin fort evanuit) | αυτων
BT   18 φανερως P   20 δια βραχεων ap Eus conj Vigerus] βραχεων
codd et Eus (bis scr Eus°) | επιδειχθεντων Eusⁱ   21 προς ημων επι-
ζητηθεντα HKA προς δι ημων επιζητ. GIZ* προς δε ημων επιζητηθεντων
BPTZᶜᵒʳʳ txt Eus | νομιζειν γαρ τοις πολλοις Ar codd (B excepto) Eus
txt B   22 τινα εχειν BPT | περι] pr λεγω δε Eus | των 2°] om Eus |
βρωματων GIBPTZ txt cett Eus   23 om και BPTZ

574 ΑΡΙΣΤΕΑΣ

γὰρ ἡμῶν, διὰ τί, μιᾶς καταβολῆς οὔσης, τὰ μὲν ἀκάθαρτα νομίζεται
πρὸς βρῶσιν, τὰ δὲ καὶ πρὸς τὴν ἀφὴν (δεισιδαιμόνως γὰρ τὰ
πλεῖστα τὴν νομοθεσίαν ἔχειν, ἐν δὲ τούτοις †πάνυ† δεισιδαιμόνως)
130 πρὸς ταῦτα οὕτως ἐνήρξατο   Θεωρεῖς, ἔφη, τὰς ἀναστροφὰς
καὶ τὰς ὁμιλίας, οἷον ἐνεργάζονται πρᾶγμα, διότι κακοῖς ὁμιλήσαντες 5
διαστροφὰς ἐπιλαμβάνουσιν ἄνθρωποι, καὶ ταλαίπωροι δι᾽ ὅλου τοῦ
ζῆν εἰσιν· ἐὰν δὲ σοφοῖς καὶ φρονίμοις συζῶσιν, ἐξ ἀγνοίας ἐπανορ-
131 θώσεως εἰς τὸν βίον ἔτυχον.   διαστειλάμενος οὖν τὰ τῆς εὐσεβείας
καὶ δικαιοσύνης πρῶτον ὁ νομοθέτης ἡμῶν, καὶ διδάξας ἕκαστα περὶ
τούτων, οὐκ ἀπαγορευτικῶς μόνον ἀλλ᾽ ἐνδεικτικῶς, καὶ τὰς βλάβας 10
προδήλους καὶ τὰς ὑπὸ τοῦ θεοῦ γινομένας ἐπιπομπὰς τοῖς αἰτίοις—
132 προϋπέδειξε γὰρ πάντων πρῶτον, ὅτι μόνος ὁ θεός ἐστι, καὶ διὰ
πάντων ἡ δύναμις αὐτοῦ φανερὰ γίνεται, πεπληρωμένου παντὸς
τόπου τῆς δυναστείας, καὶ οὐθὲν αὐτὸν λανθάνει τῶν ἐπὶ γῆς γινομένων ὑπ᾽ ἀνθρώπων κρυφίως, ἀλλ᾽ ὅσα ποιεῖ τις αὐτῷ φανερὰ 15
133 καθέστηκε, καὶ τὰ μέλλοντα γίνεσθαι— ταῦτ᾽ οὖν ἐξεργαζόμενος
ἀκριβῶς καὶ πρόδηλα θεὶς ἔδειξεν ὅτι, κἂν ἐννοηθῇ τις κακίαν
ἐπιτελεῖν, οὐκ ἂν λάθοι, μὴ ὅτι καὶ πράξας, διὰ πάσης τῆς νομο-
134 θεσίας τὸ τοῦ θεοῦ δυνατὸν ἐνδεικνύμενος.   ποιησάμενος οὖν τὴν
καταρχὴν ταύτην, καὶ δείξας ὅτι πάντες οἱ λοιποὶ παρ᾽ ἡμᾶς 20
ἄνθρωποι πολλοὺς θεοὺς εἶναι νομίζουσιν, αὐτοὶ δυναμικώτεροι
135 πολλῷ καθεστῶτες ὧν σέβονται ματαίως—ἀγάλματα γὰρ ποιήσαντες
ἐκ λίθων καὶ ξύλων, εἰκόνας φασὶν εἶναι τῶν ἐξευρόντων τι πρὸς τὸ
ζῆν αὐτοῖς χρήσιμον, οἷς προσκυνοῦσι, παρὰ πόδας ἔχοντες τὴν ἀναι-
136 σθησίαν. εἴ τι γὰρ κατ᾽ ἐκεῖνό τις <θεὸς εἴη>, κατὰ τὴν ἐξεύρεσιν, 25

HKAGIBP
TZ Eus
3 της νομοθεσιας B | πανυ] πασι B παλιν πανυ HKA παλιν cett Eus
5 εργαζονται AIBP Eus^codd det   6 δια του ζην Eus^i δι ολου την ζωην Eus^o
8 ενετυχον BT | ουν Eus] δε εστι B om cett   9 πρωτον ο νομ. Eus.] ο
πρωτονομοθετης Ar codd   10 ενδικως Ar codd txt Eus   11 προδηλως I
?προδηλωσας | υπο] επι P Eus^codd | om του P Eus | γενομ. P Eus^codd (γιγν.
Eus^i)   12 πρωτον παντων Eus P | om ο BPTZ | η δυν. αυτ. δια παντ.
Eus^o   13 δυναμις]+εστιν GIZ | παντος] pr του B   14 ουδεν B | των
επιγινομενων (-νωμ. Z) PT*Z (γης suprascr T^1)   15 υπ] υπο των B | κρυ-
φεως GI κρυφαιως Eus^i   16 εργαζομενος B εξεργασαμενος Eus^o   17 προ-
δηλωθεις HKA   18 λανθανοι B λαθη P | δια πασης] δι ολης Eus^i εξ ολης
Eus^o   22 πολλω Eus P] πολλων Ar codd cett   23 και] η Eus   25 ει
τι HKAG^vid I] ειτε cett Eus | θεος ειη ex conj] θειη codd Eus θεωθειη conj
Wend.

παντελῶς ἀνόητον· τῶν γὰρ ἐν τῇ κτίσει λαβόντες τινὰ συνέθηκαν
καὶ προσυπέδειξαν εὔχρηστα, τὴν κατασκευὴν αὐτῶν οὐ ποιήσαντες
αὐτοί· διὸ κενὸν καὶ μάταιον τοὺς ὁμοίους ἀποθεοῦν. καὶ γὰρ ἔτι 137
καὶ νῦν εὑρεματικώτεροι καὶ πολυμαθέστεροι τῶν ἀνθρώπων τῶν πρίν
5 εἰσι πολλοί, καὶ οὐκ ἂν φθάνοιεν αὐτοὺς προσκυνοῦντες. καὶ νομίζουσιν οἱ ταῦτα διαπλάσαντες καὶ μυθοποιήσαντες τῶν Ἑλλήνων
οἱ σοφώτατοι καθεστάναι. τῶν γὰρ ἄλλων πολυματαίων τί δεῖ καὶ 138
λέγειν, Αἰγυπτίων τε καὶ τῶν παραπλησίων, οἵτινες ἐπὶ θηρία καὶ
τῶν ἑρπετῶν τὰ πλεῖστα καὶ κνωδάλων τὴν ἀπέρεισιν πεποίηνται,
10 καὶ ταῦτα προσκυνοῦσι, καὶ θύουσι τούτοις καὶ ζῶσι καὶ τελευτήσασι;— συνθεωρήσας οὖν ἕκαστα σοφὸς ὢν ὁ νομοθέτης, 139
ὑπὸ θεοῦ κατεσκευασμένος εἰς ἐπίγνωσιν τῶν ἁπάντων, περιέφραξεν
ἡμᾶς ἀδιακόποις χάραξι καὶ σιδηροῖς τείχεσιν, ὅπως μηθενὶ τῶν
ἄλλων ἐθνῶν ἐπιμισγώμεθα κατὰ μηδέν, ἁγνοὶ καθεστῶτες κατὰ σῶμα
15 καὶ κατὰ ψυχήν, ἀπολελυμένοι ματαίων δοξῶν, τὸν μόνον θεὸν καὶ
δυνατὸν σεβόμενοι παρ᾽ ὅλην τὴν πᾶσαν κτίσιν. ὅθεν οἱ Αἰγυπτίων 140
καθηγεμόνες ἱερεῖς, ἐγκεκυφότες εἰς πολλὰ καὶ μετεσχηκότες
πραγμάτων, ἀνθρώπους θεοῦ προσονομάζουσιν ἡμᾶς· ὃ τοῖς λοιποῖς
οὐ πρόσεστιν, εἰ μή τις σέβεται τὸν κατὰ ἀλήθειαν θεόν, ἀλλ᾽ εἰσὶν
20 ἄνθρωποι βρωτῶν καὶ ποτῶν καὶ σκέπης· ἡ γὰρ πᾶσα διάθεσις 141
αὐτῶν ἐπὶ ταῦτα καταφεύγει. τοῖς δὲ παρ᾽ ἡμῶν ἐν οὐδενὶ ταῦτα λε-
λόγισται, περὶ δὲ τῆς τοῦ θεοῦ δυναστείας δι᾽ ὅλου τοῦ ζῆν ἡ σκέψις
αὐτοῖς ἐστιν. ὅπως οὖν μηθενὶ συναλισγούμενοι μηδ᾽ ὁμιλοῦν- 142
τες φαύλοις διαστροφὰς λαμβάνωμεν, πάντοθεν ἡμᾶς περιέφραξεν
25 ἁγνείαις καὶ διὰ βρωτῶν καὶ ποτῶν καὶ ἁφῶν καὶ ἀκοῆς καὶ ὁράσεως

---

1 ανοητον Eus] ανοητοι codd   2 ευχρηστοτατην (+την Eus⁰) κατ. Eus HKAGIBP
3 om αυτοι P   4 ευρημ. ΑΒ ευρετικωτεροι Eus   5 φθανοιεν Eus] φθα- TZ Eus
σειαν Β (-σοιαν Τ) φθανοισαν cett   7 των]+μεν Eus | δει] δη HAGI
9 κνωδ.] pr επι Eusⁱ | απερ εισι PT*Z   11 ουν] τοιγαρουν Eusⁱ | om
εκαστα P | ο νομ. υπο θ. σοφ. ων P   12 κατεσκευασμενα Η (α 3⁰ sup lin)
Eus^codd det   13 μηδενι Eus Z μηθεν HKAGI   14 και σωμα και ψυχην
Eus⁰   15 απολελυμενοι Eus P] -μενων cett   16 πασαν την κτ. P | Αι-
γυπτιων οι Eus   18 εις πραγματα I   19 τις] τι ΗΑ (s postea suprascr
H*vidΑ*vid) KGI   21 ημιν ΒΤΖ Eus⁰   22 om δε HAGI | om της του
Eusⁱ   23 αυτων Β* | ουν Eus] τε εν Β εν cett | μηδενι ΒΡ Eus | συνα-
λισγομ. Τ Eus ex quo συμμισγομ. Wend.   24 φαυλω Eus⁰ γαμοις P |
λαμβανοιμεν Eus | περιεφραξαν Eus⁰   25 αφης Eus⁰

143 νομικῶς. τὸ γὰρ καθόλου πάντα πρὸς τὸν φυσικὸν λόγον ὅμοια
καθέστηκεν, ὑπὸ μιᾶς δυνάμεως οἰκονομούμενα, καὶ καθ' ἓν ἕκαστον
ἔχει λόγον βαθύν, ἀφ' ὧν ἀπεχόμεθα κατὰ τὴν χρῆσιν, καὶ οἷς
συγχρώμεθα. χάριν δὲ ὑποδείγματος ἓν ἢ δεύτερον ἐπιδραμών σοι
144 σημανῶ. Μὴ γὰρ εἰς τὸν καταπεπτωκότα λόγον ἔλθῃς, ὅτι ΜΥῶΝ 5
καὶ ΓΑΛῆΣ ἢ τῶν τοιούτων χάριν περιεργίαν ποιούμενος ἐνομοθέτει
ταῦτα Μωϋσῆς· ἀλλὰ πρὸς ἁγνὴν ἐπίσκεψιν καὶ τρόπων ἐξαρτισμὸν
145 δικαιοσύνης ἕνεκεν σεμνῶς πάντα ἀνατέτακται. τῶν γὰρ πτηνῶν,
οἷς χρώμεθα, πάντα ἥμερα καθέστηκε καὶ διαφέρει καθαριότητι,
πυροῖς καὶ ὀσπρίοις χρώμενα πρὸς τὴν τροφήν, οἷον περιστεραὶ 10
τρυγόνες ἀττακοὶ πέρδικες ἔτι δὲ χῆνες καὶ τὰ ἄλλα ὅσα τοιαῦτα.
146 περὶ ὧν δὲ ἀπηγόρευται πτηνῶν, εὑρήσεις ἄγριά τε καὶ σαρκοφάγα
καὶ καταδυναστεύοντα τῇ περὶ ἑαυτὰ δυνάμει τὰ λοιπά, καὶ τὴν
τροφὴν ἔχοντα δαπάνησιν τῶν προειρημένων ἡμέρων μετὰ ἀδικίας·
οὐ μόνον δὲ ταῦτα, ἀλλὰ καὶ τοὺς ἄρνας καὶ ἐρίφους ἀναρπάζουσι, 15
147 καὶ τοὺς ἀνθρώπους δὲ ἀδικοῦσι νεκρούς τε καὶ ζῶντας. παράσημον
οὖν ἔθετο διὰ τούτων, ἀκάθαρτα προσονομάσας, ὅτι δέον ἐστὶ κατὰ
ψυχήν, οἷς ἡ νομοθεσία διατέτακται, δικαιοσύνῃ συγχρῆσθαι καὶ
μηδένα καταδυναστεύειν, πεποιθότας ἰσχύι τῇ καθ' ἑαυτούς, μηδὲ
ἀφαιρεῖσθαι μηδέν, ἀλλ' ἐκ δικαίου τὰ τοῦ βίου κυβερνᾶν, ὡς τὰ 20
τῶν προειρημένων πτηνῶν ἥμερα ζῷα τὰ φυόμενα τῶν ὀσπρίων ἐπὶ
γῆς δαπανᾷ, καὶ οὐ καταδυναστεύει πρὸς τὴν ἐπαναίρεσιν τῶν συγ-
148 γενικῶν. διὰ τῶν τοιούτων οὖν παραδέδωκεν ὁ νομοθέτης σημειοῦ-

5 f Lev 11²⁹   11 Lev 11²²   17 Deut 14¹⁸

HKAGIBP   1 νομικης G Eusᵒ -κοις P | το] τω T Eusⁱ   2 δυναμεως]+οικονομικως
TZ Eus
P | εκαστα Eusᵒ   3 λογον εχει BT | απεσχομεθα ΚΑΙ   5 εισελθης
Eusⁱ (ελθηςᵒ)   6 περιεργιας Eus περιεργασιαν Z   7 Μωσης ΑP Eus |
τροπων]+ εξαιρετον Eusᵒ   8 παντα] ταυτα BPTZ | πετεινων Eus
9 καθεστηκε και Eus] καθεστηκεν a B καθεστηκε cett | καθαροτητι HKBPTZ
10 χρωμεθα Κ | om την Κ Eusᵒ   11 ατταγοι Eusⁱ | om ετι Κ   12 πε-
τεινων Eus   13 περι] παρ Κ | αυτα Eus εαυτων GI | τα πολλα Z* (τα λ.
Zᶜᵒʳʳ) των λοιπων B   14 δαπανησιν] pr την Eus   15 αρπαζουσι Eus
17 δεον] δε Eusⁱ   19 μηδενι IB μηδενος T | πεποιθοτας Eus] -θοσιν B
·θοτες (-θωτ. P) cett | τη εαυτων Eusᵒ   20 μηθεν Eusᵒ | εκ δικαιοτατου
βιου Eus | διακυβερναν Eusᵒ   21 ζωα ημερα B   22 επαναιρεσιν]+ουτε
των υποβεβηκοτων ουτε Eusⁱ (om 20 ως τα—22 συγγεν. Eusᵒ)   23 των
τοιουτ.] τουτων Eusᵒ | παρεδωκεν Eus P | ομοιουσθαι BT

σθαι τοῖς συνετοῖς, εἶναι δικαίους τε καὶ μηδὲν ἐπιτελεῖν βίᾳ, μηδὲ
τῇ περὶ ἑαυτοὺς ἰσχύϊ πεποιθότας ἑτέρους καταδυναστεύειν. ὅπου 149
γὰρ οὐδ᾽ ἅψασθαι καθῆκε τῶν προειρημένων διὰ τὴν περὶ ἕκαστα διάθεσιν, πῶς οὐ φυλακτέον παντάπασι τοὺς τρόπους εἰς τοῦτο κατακλα-
5 σθῆναι; πάντα οὖν τὰ τῆς συγχωρήσεως ἡμῖν ἐπὶ τούτων καὶ τῶν 150
κτηνῶν τροπολογῶν ἐκτέθειται. τὸ γὰρ ΔΙΧΗΛΕΥΕΙΝ καὶ διαστέλλειν
ὁπλῆς ὄνυχας σημεῖόν ἐστι τοῦ διαστέλλειν ἕκαστα τῶν πράξεων
ἐπὶ τὸ καλῶς ἔχον· ἡ γὰρ ἰσχὺς τῶν ὅλων σωμάτων μετ᾽ ἐνεργείας 151
ἀπέρεισιν ἐπὶ τοὺς ὤμους ἔχει καὶ τὰ σκέλη. μετὰ διαστολῆς οὖν
10 ἅπαντα ἐπιτελεῖν πρὸς δικαιοσύνην ἀναγκάζει †τὸ σημειοῦσθαι† διὰ
τούτων· ἔτι δὲ καὶ διότι παρὰ πάντας ἀνθρώπους διεστάλμεθα. οἱ 152
γὰρ πλείονες τῶν λοιπῶν ἀνθρώπων ἑαυτοὺς μολύνουσιν ἐπιμισγό-
μενοι, συντελοῦντες μεγάλην ἀδικίαν, καὶ χῶραι καὶ πόλεις ὅλαι
σεμνύνονται ἐπὶ τούτοις. οὐ μόνον γὰρ <προάγουσι> τοὺς ἄρσενας,
15 ἀλλὰ καὶ τεκούσας ἔτι δὲ θυγατέρας μολύνουσιν. ἡμεῖς δὲ ἀπὸ
τούτων διεστάλμεθα. περὶ ὃν δὲ ἐστιν ὁ προειρημένος τῆς δια- 153
στολῆς τρόπος, περὶ τοῦτον εἶναι καὶ τὸν τῆς μνήμης κεχαρακτή-
ρικεν. ΠΑΝΤΑ γὰρ ὅσα ΔΙΧΗΛΕΙ καὶ ΜΗΡΥΚΙΣΜΟΝ ΑΝΑΓΕΙ σαφῶς
τοῖς νοοῦσιν ἐκτίθεται τὸ τῆς μνήμης. ἡ γὰρ ἀναμηρύκησις οὐθὲν 154
20 ἕτερον, ἀλλὰ τῆς ζωῆς καὶ συστάσεως ἐπίμνησις. τὸ γὰρ ζῆν διὰ

6 Lev 11³ ff (Deut 14⁶ ff)   18 Lev 11³ ff

1 om τε P Eusº vid   2 αυτους Eus | ετερων BT   4 ου] ουν ΚΑΙGᵗˣᵗ ΗΚΑGΙΒΡ
(corr Gᵐᵍ)   5 παντα ουν Eus] παντων (+ δε B) Ar codd | τα Eus] om Ar ᵀᶻ Eus
codd | της συγχ. Eusⁱ Ar codd] τα συγχωρηθεντα Eusº | ημιν] om Eusº
ημων ενεκα B txt Eusⁱ Ar cett   6 εκτεθειται Eusⁱ] εξεθετο B εκθεοιται (-τε
GI) Ar codd cett εκτεθεικε Eusº | διχηλιζειν Κ   7 οπλας B | σημεια B |
εκαστην P   10 το σημειουσθαι ΗΚΑGΙΖ (το σημ. και Eusⁱ) το ομοιουσθαι
Τ (τω ομ. B) τω σημ. Eusº, pro απαντα 10—μολυνουσιν 12 exhibens βιωσκο-
μεν· τω σημειουσθαι οτι παρα παντας ανθρωπους διαστελλομεθα· οι γαρ αλλοι
μολυνουσιν εαυτους. Fortasse legendum ο σημειουται   12 ανθρωπων] om
Eus   13 ολαι] οσαι B   14 επι τουτ. σεμν. Eusº | προαγουσι conj
Schmidt] προσαγουσι codd et Eus qui legit προς αρσενας (αρρ.º) προσαγουσιν
15 δε] + και ΗΚΑ Eusº   16 εσταλμεθα BPTZ | ον] ων BPT   17 τροπος
BPT Eus] τοπος cett | τουτων BPT | και τ. τ. μν. ειναι Eusº | το την μνημην
P | κεχαρακτηρικεναι (-τηκεναι Z) codd Ar txt Eus   18 παντα] ειπας
Eusⁱ   19 εκτιθεται Eus] εκτιθεμαι (εκτιθημι P) Ar codd | ουδεν B
20 αλλ η Eusº | συστασεως] pr της B | υπομνησις εστι Eus

155 τῆς τροφῆς συνεστάναι νομίζει. διὸ παρακελεύεται καὶ διὰ τῆς
γραφῆς ὁ λέγων οὕτως· ΜΝΕΊᾼ ΜΝΗCΘΉCΗ ΚΥΡΙΟΥ ΤΟΥ̑ ΠΟΙΉCΑΝΤΟC
ΕΝ CΟΙ ΤᾺ ΜΕΓΆΛΑ ΚᾺΙ ΘΑΥΜΑCΤΆ. κατανοούμενα γὰρ καὶ ΜΕΓΆΛΑ
ΚᾺΙ ἜΝΔΟΖΑ φαίνεται· πρῶτον μὲν ἡ σύμπηξις τοῦ σώματος καὶ ἡ
156 τῆς τροφῆς διοίκησις καὶ ἡ περὶ ἕκαστον μέλος διαστολή· πολλῷ 5
δὲ μᾶλλον ἡ τῶν αἰσθήσεων διακόσμησις, διανοίας ἐνέργημα καὶ
κίνησις ἀόρατος, ἥ τε ὀξύτης τοῦ πρὸς ἕκαστόν τι πράσσειν καὶ
157 τεχνῶν εὕρεσις ἀπέραστον περιέχει τρόπον. διὸ παρακελεύεται
μνείαν ἔχειν, ὡς συντηρεῖται τὰ προειρημένα θείᾳ δυνάμει σὺν
κατασκευῇ. πάντα γὰρ χρόνον καὶ τόπον ὥρικε πρὸς τὸ διὰ 10
158 παντὸς μνημονεύειν τοῦ κρατοῦντος θεοῦ καὶ συντηροῦντος. καὶ
γὰρ ἐπὶ τῶν βρωτῶν καὶ ποτῶν ἀπαρξαμένους εὐθέως τότε †συγ-
χρῆσθαι† κελεύει. καὶ μὴν καὶ ἐκ τῶν περιβολαίων παράσημον
ἡμῖν μνείας δέδωκεν, ὡσαύτως δὲ καὶ ἐπὶ ΤΩ̑Ν ΠΥΛΩ̑Ν καὶ θυρῶν
προστέταχε μὲν ἡμῖν τιθέναι τὰ λόγια, πρὸς τὸ μνείαν εἶναι θεοῦ· 15
159 καὶ ἐπὶ ΤΩ̑Ν ΧΕΙΡΩ̑Ν δὲ διαρρήδην τὸ σημεῖον κελεύει ΠΕΡΙΗ̑ΦΘΑΙ,
σαφῶς ἀποδεικνὺς ὅτι πᾶσαν ἐνέργειαν μετὰ δικαιοσύνης ἐπιτελεῖν
δεῖ, μνήμην ἔχοντας τῆς ἑαυτῶν κατασκευῆς, ἐπὶ πᾶσι δὲ τὸν περὶ
160 θεοῦ φόβον. κελεύει δὲ ΚᾺΙ ΚΟΙΤΑΖΟΜΈΝΟΥC ΚᾺΙ ΔΙΑΝΙCΤΑΜΈΝΟΥC
μελετᾶν τὰς τοῦ θεοῦ κατασκευάς, οὐ μόνον λόγῳ, ἀλλὰ διαλήψει 20

2 ff Deut 7¹⁸; 10²¹   14 ff Deut 6⁷ ff

HKAGIBP   **1** om και Eus   **2** om ο Eus | κυριου]+του θεου Eus   **3** και μεγ.
TZ Eus
(+και θαυμαστα P) και ενδ.] και ενδοξα και μεγαλα Eusⁱ ενδοξα Eusᵒ
4 πρωτα Eusᵒ | η συμπ. η του σ. Eusⁱ η του σ. συμπ.. Eusᵒ | και 2ᵒ] om
BPTZ   **5** μερος Eusᵒ   **6** η των BP] η της των cett Eusⁱ   **8** επε-
ραστον περιεχει K Eus απεραντον παρεχει BPTZ txt HAGI   **9** τα
προειρ.] om BT +συνεχομενα Eusⁱ | θειας δυναμεως P | συν κατασκευη K]
συγκατασκευη (και συγκ. BT¹Aᶜᵒʳʳ) codd cett Eusⁱ (om Eusᵒ)   **10** τοπον και
χρονον Eusⁱ χρονων και τροπον P   **11** και συντηρουντος] συντηρουντας και
τας αρχας και μεσοτητας και τελευτας Eusⁱ (om και συντηρ.—κελενει 13 Eusᵒ)
12 ποτων] pr των GI | απαρξ.] αρξαμενους I αρπαζομενους K om BT | συγ-
χρησθαι Eus] συγχωρησαι Ar codd   **14** επι] pr επι των πολεων και
οικησεων δια το σκεπαζεσθαι και Eus   **15** προστεταχε μεν] προστεταχεν
Eus   **16** το σημ. διαρρ. P | περιειληφθαι PZ περι...ηφθαι (ras 3 litt) T
18 της εαυτων κατασκευης Eus] αυτης B τοις P και τοις Z της codd cett
(cum seqq conj) της ημων συστασεως edd pr | om δε Z | περι] του P Eusᵒ
19 διανισταμενους]+και πορευομενους Eus   **20** λογω μονον Eus | αλλα]
+και KP Eus

θεωροῦντας τὴν κίνησιν καὶ ὑπόληψιν ἑαυτῶν, ὅταν εἰς ὕπνον
ἔρχωνται, καὶ τὴν ἔγερσιν, ὡς θεία τίς ἐστι καὶ ἀκατάληπτος τούτων
ἡ μετάθεσις. Δέδεικται δέ σοι καὶ τὸ περισσὸν τῆς λογίας τῆς 161
κατὰ τὴν διαστολὴν καὶ μνείαν, ὡς ἐξεθέμεθα τὴν διχηλίαν καὶ τὸν
5 μηρυκισμόν. οὐ γὰρ εἰκῇ καὶ κατὰ τὸ ἐμπεσὸν εἰς ψυχὴν νενομο-
θέτηται, πρὸς δ᾽ ἀλήθειαν καὶ σημείωσιν ὀρθοῦ λόγου. διατάξας 162
γὰρ ἐπὶ βρωτῶν καὶ ποτῶν καὶ τῶν κατὰ τὰς ἁφὰς ἕκαστα, κελεύει
μηθὲν εἰκῇ μήτε πράσσειν μήτε ἀκούειν, μήτε τῇ τοῦ λόγου
δυναστείᾳ συγχρωμένους ἐπὶ τὴν ἀδικίαν τρέπεσθαι. καὶ ἐπὶ τῶν 163
10 κνωδάλων δὲ ταὐτὸν ἔστιν εὑρεῖν. κακοποιητικὸς γὰρ ὁ τρόπος
ἐστὶ καὶ ΓΑΛΗC καὶ ΜΥΩΝ καὶ τῶν τούτοις ὁμοίων, ὅσα διηγόρευται.
πάντα γὰρ λυμαίνονται καὶ κακοποιοῦσι μύες, οὐ μόνον πρὸς τὴν 164
ἑαυτῶν τροφήν, ἀλλὰ καὶ εἰς τὸ παντελῶς ἄχρηστον γίνεσθαι ἀνθρώπῳ, ὅ τι ἂν δή ποτ᾽ οὖν ἐπιβάληται κακοποιεῖν. τό τε τῆς γαλῆς 165
15 γένος ἰδιάζον ἐστί· χωρὶς γὰρ τοῦ προειρημένου ἔχει λυμαντικὸν κατά-
στημα· διὰ γὰρ τῶν ὤτων συλλαμβάνει, τεκνοποιεῖ δὲ τῷ στόματι.
καὶ διὰ τοῦτο ὁ τοιοῦτος τρόπος τῶν ἀνθρώπων ἀκάθαρτός ἐστιν· 166
ὅσα γὰρ δι᾽ ἀκοῆς λαβόντες, ταῦτα τῷ λόγῳ σωματοποιήσαντες,
κακοῖς ἑτέρους ἐνεκύλισαν, ἀκαθαρσίαν οὐ τὴν τυχοῦσαν ἐπετέλεσαν,
20 μιανθέντες αὐτοὶ παντάπασι τῷ τῆς ἀσεβείας μολυσμῷ. καλῶς δὲ
ποιῶν ὁ βασιλεὺς ὑμῶν τοὺς τοιούτους ἀναιρεῖ, καθὼς μεταλαμβάνομεν.—Ἐγὼ δ᾽ εἶπα Τοὺς ἐμφανιστὰς οἴομαί σε λέγειν· καὶ γὰρ 167
αἰκίαις καὶ θανάτοις ἐπαλγέσιν αὐτοὺς περιβάλλει συνεχῶς.—Ὁ δέ
Τούτους γὰρ καὶ λέγω· ἡ γὰρ ἐπαγρύπνησις ἀνθρώπων ἀπωλείᾳ

11 Lev 11²⁹

1 τα κινηματα Eus° | υποληψιν] pr την Eus   2 ερχονται GIZ   2 f. η   ΗΚΑGΙΒΡ
τουτων μεταθεσις Eus   3 ευλογιας fort recte A αλογιας Ρ   4 εξεθεσθαι   ΤΖ Eus
Eusⁱ | om τον Eusⁱ   5 και Eus] om Ar codd   7 και ποτων GIPZ Eusⁱ]
om Ar codd cett Eus°   8 τη Eus] om Ar codd   9 χρωμενους Ι
10 ff. εστιν ο τροπος Eus°   12 λυμαινεται Β | και κακοπ.—τροφην αλλα (13)
om ΒΡΤΖ   13 εις το Eusⁱ] om Ar Eusᶜᵒᵈᵈ ᶜᵉᵗᵗ | γινεται ΒΡΖ   14 επι-
βαλληται Eus°   17 τουτο] τουτ ουν Eusⁱᵒ | τοις ανθρωποις Eusⁱ   19 ετε-
ροις Τ | ακαθαρσιαν]+τε Eus | απετελεσαν Β* Eusⁱ   21 ημων Τ Eusⁱᵒ |
αναιρειν GI   23 επαλγεσι (om αυτους) Κ | παραβαλλει Eusⁱ (περιβ. Eus°)
24 τουτους—επαγρυπνησις] τουτοις γαρ επαγρ. Eusⁱ επαγρυπ. γαρ Eus° | εις
ανθρωπων απωλειαν Eus txt (cf Diod 14. 68 επηγρυπνηκως τη τουτων απω-
λεια) ex Ar codd (ἀπώλεια)

37—2

168 ἀνόσιος. ὁ δὲ νόμος ἡμῶν κελεύει μήτε λόγῳ μήτε ἔργῳ μηδένα
κακοποιεῖν. καὶ περὶ τούτων οὖν, ὅσον ἐπὶ βραχὺ <διεξῆλθον,
προσυποδείξας> σοι διότι πάντα κεκανόνισται πρὸς δικαιοσύνην,
καὶ οὐδὲν εἰκῆ κατατέτακται διὰ τῆς γραφῆς οὐδὲ μυθωδῶς, ἀλλ᾽
ἵνα δι᾽ ὅλου τοῦ ζῆν καὶ ἐν ταῖς πράξεσιν ἀσκῶμεν δικαιοσύνην 5
169 πρὸς πάντας ἀνθρώπους, μεμνημένοι τοῦ δυναστεύοντος θεοῦ. περὶ
βρωτῶν οὖν καὶ τῶν ἀκαθάρτων ἑρπετῶν καὶ κνωδάλων καὶ πᾶς
λόγος ἀνατείνει πρὸς δικαιοσύνην καὶ τὴν τῶν ἀνθρώπων συνανα-
170 στροφὴν δικαίαν. Ἐμοὶ μὲν οὖν καλῶς ἐνόμιζε περὶ
ἑκάστων ἀπολογεῖσθαι· καὶ γὰρ ἐπὶ τῶν προσφερομένων ἔλεγε 10
μόσχων τε καὶ κριῶν καὶ χιμάρων, ὅτι δεῖ ταῦτα ἐκ βουκολίων καὶ
ποιμνίων λαμβάνοντας ἥμερα θυσιάζειν, καὶ μηθὲν ἄγριον, ὅπως οἱ
προσφέροντες τὰς θυσίας μηθὲν ὑπερήφανον ἑαυτοῖς συνιστορῶσι,
σημειώσει κεχρημένοι τοῦ διατάξαντος. τῆς γὰρ ἑαυτοῦ ψυχῆς
τοῦ παντὸς τρόπου τὴν προσφορὰν ποιεῖται ὁ τὴν θυσίαν προσάγων. 15
171 καὶ περὶ τούτων οὖν νομίζω τὰ τῆς ὁμιλίας ἄξια λόγου καθεστάναι·
διὸ τὴν σεμνότητα καὶ φυσικὴν διάνοιαν τοῦ νόμου προῆγμαι δια-
¶ Eus σαφῆσαί σοι, Φιλόκρατες, δι᾽ ἣν ἔχεις φιλομάθειαν.¶

§ Jos 172 ⁵Ὁ δὲ Ἐλεάζαρος ποιησάμενος θυσίαν καὶ τοὺς ἄνδρας ἐπιλέξας
καὶ πολλὰ δῶρα τῷ βασιλεῖ κατασκευάσας προέπεμψεν ἡμᾶς μετὰ 20
173 ἀσφαλείας πολλῆς. ὡς δὲ παρεγενήθημεν εἰς Ἀλεξάνδρειαν, προσ-

HKAGIBP   1 ανοσιον Eus° | λογω] νομω BTZ   1 f. κακοποιειν μηδενα Eus
TZ Eus Jos
2 ουν] δε P | οσον—διεξηλθον] διεξηλθον βραχυ Eus° | διεξελθειν Ar codd
(-ελθη P) Eusⁱ   3 προσυποδειξαντα Ar codd Eusⁱ δεικνυων Eus° | διοτι]
οτι Eus°   4 μυθωδως B Eus] θυμωδως codd cett | αλλ ινα] αλλα H
6 μεμνημενους BPTZ   7 ουν] ον P | και 3°] ο Eus   8 αναστροφην P
9 ? ενομιζετο   10 υπολογεισθαι G απολελογησθαι Eus | επι Ar codd Eusⁱ]
και περι Eus°   11 om τε Eusⁱ | δει Eus] αει Ar codd   12 λαμβανοντες
omissis ημερα—προσφεροντες (13) BPTZ | θυσιαζειν] κατασκευαζειν Eus
13 συνιστορουσι P   14 κεχρημενοι Eus] κεχρημενου Ar codd   16 και
περι—σεμνοτητα (17)] om K | αξιολογου καθ. HAGTZ αξιολογως καθ. P αξια
καθεσταναι λογου Eus°   17 διο] δια Eus | και φυσ. διαν. om Eus | νομου]+
ην Eus   18 om σοι BPTZ Eus° | Φιλοκρατες BT Eus] Φιλοκρατη codd cett
20 παρασκευασας P   21 Αλεξανδ.]+και P | προσαγγελλει G (-ελει I
-ηγγελει ATZ) txt HKP (B προσηγγελλη)

ἠγγέλη τῷ βασιλεῖ περὶ τῆς ἀφίξεως ἡμῶν. <παρειμένοι> δ᾽ εἰς
τὴν αὐλὴν Ἀνδρέας τε καὶ ἐγώ, φιλοφρόνως ἠσπασάμεθα τὸν βασιλέα καὶ τὰς ἐπιστολὰς ἀποδεδώκαμεν τὰς παρὰ τοῦ Ἐλεαζάρου.
περὶ πολλοῦ δὲ ποιούμενος τοῖς ἀπεσταλμένοις ἀνδράσιν ἐντυχεῖν, 174
5 ἐκέλευσε τοὺς λοιποὺς πάντας ἀπολῦσαι τοὺς ἐπὶ τῶν χρειῶν,
καλεῖν δὲ τοὺς ἀνθρώπους. οὗ πᾶσι παραδόξου φανέντος—διὰ τὸ 175
κατὰ ἔθος εἶναι, πεμπταίους εἰς πρόσωπον ἔρχεσθαι βασιλεῖ τοὺς
περὶ χρήσιμον ἀφικνουμένους, τοὺς δὲ παρὰ βασιλέων ἢ πόλεων ἐν
ὑπεροχαῖς μόλις ἐν τριάκοντα εἰς τὴν αὐλὴν παρίεσθαι—τοὺς δὲ
10 ἥκοντας τιμῆς καταξιῶν μείζονος, καὶ τὴν ὑπεροχὴν κρίνων τοῦ
πέμψαντος, ἀπολύσας οὓς ἐνόμιζε περισσούς, ὑπέμενε περιπατῶν,
ἕως ἂν παραγινομένους ἀσπάσηται. παρελθόντων δὲ σὺν τοῖς 176
ἀπεσταλμένοις δώροις καὶ ταῖς διαφόροις διφθέραις, ἐν αἷς ἡ
νομοθεσία γεγραμμένη χρυσογραφίᾳ τοῖς Ἰουδαϊκοῖς γράμμασι, θαυ-
15 μασίως <εἰργασμένου τοῦ ὑμένος>, καὶ τῆς πρὸς ἄλληλα συμβολῆς
ἀνεπαισθήτου κατεσκευασμένης, ὡς εἶδεν ὁ βασιλεὺς τοὺς ἄνδρας,
ἐπηρώτα περὶ τῶν βιβλίων. ὡς δὲ ἀπεκάλυψαν τὰ τῶν ἐνειλημάτων 177
καὶ τοὺς ὑμένας ἀνείλιξαν, πολὺν ἐπιστὰς χρόνον καὶ προσκυνήσας
σχεδὸν ἑπτάκις εἶπεν Εὐχαριστῶ μέν, ἄνδρες, ὑμῖν, τῷ δ᾽ ἀποστεί-
20 λαντι μᾶλλον, μέγιστον δὲ τῷ θεῷ, οὗτινός ἐστι τὰ λόγια
ταῦτα. ὁμοθυμαδὸν δὲ πάντων εἰπόντων ὑπὸ μίαν φωνήν, τῶν 178
τε παραγεγονότων καὶ τῶν συμπαρόντων, Εὖ βασιλεῦ, προήχθη
δακρῦσαι τῇ χαρᾷ πεπληρωμένος. ἡ γὰρ τῆς ψυχῆς ἔντασις καὶ τὸ

1 παρειμεν δ HGIZ παρημεν δ ΚΑΡΤ ως δε παρημεν Β txt ex conj HKAGIBP
Schmidt 3 επιδεδωκαμεν ΒΖ Fort leg απεδωκ. (απεδοσαν Jos) | τας 2° TZ Jos
GIP] om cett 4 περι] pr και ΡΤΖ | ποιουμενος]+ο βασιλευς ΒΡ 5 απαν-
τας Ρ 7 κατα εθνος HKAGIPT κατα εθνους Ζ απο εθνους Β txt ex Jos
(παρα το εθος) 8 περι]+τι Β | χρησιμον] fort χρηματισμον | om εν ΗΡ
9 υπεροχης Ρ | τριακοντα] λ ημεραις Β 10 του] τους Κ 11 υπεμεινε Β
txt cett cum Josvid (περιεμενεν) 12 παραγενομενους ΒΤ 14 om τοις Ζ
15 εργασαμενου Κ (ειργ. Ι) ειργασμενης ΒΤcorr (-ου Τ*) εργασμενης Ρ | της
υμενου HKcorrGIBPTcorr του υμενου Α | της] τοις Ρ | συμπλοκης Ζ 16 ανε-
παισθητως ΒΤcorr | κατεσκευασμενη HKAGI 17 επερωτα GIB*Ρ | εν-
ειληματων Jos] ανειληματων (-λημμ. GIPTZ) Ar codd 20 ουτινος ΒΤ]
τινος cett (ου Jos) 21 ειποντων δε παντ. ομ. Κ 23 της χαρας ΒΤ |
εντασις ΡΖ] εκστασις Β ενστασις cett

τῆς τιμῆς ὑπερτεῖνον δακρύειν ἀναγκάζει κατὰ τὰς ἐπιτυχίας.
179 κελεύσας δὲ εἰς τάξιν ἀποδοῦναι τὰ τεύχη, τὸ τηνικαῦτα ἀσπασά-
μενος τοὺς ἄνδρας εἶπε Δίκαιον ἦν, θεοσεβεῖς ἄνδρες, ὧν χάριν ὑμᾶς
μετεπεμψάμην, ἐκείνοις πρῶτον σεβασμὸν ἀποδοῦναι, μετὰ ταῦτα
180 τὴν δεξιὰν ὑμῖν προτεῖναι· διὸ πεποίηκα τοῦτο πρῶτον. μεγάλην 5
δὲ τέθειμαι τὴν ἡμέραν ταύτην, ἐν ᾗ παραγεγόνατε, καὶ κατ' ἐνιαυτὸν
ἐπίσημος ἔσται πάντα τὸν τῆς ζωῆς ἡμῶν χρόνον· συντέτυχε γὰρ
καὶ τὰ κατὰ τὴν νίκην ἡμῖν προσπεπτωκέναι τῆς πρὸς Ἀντίγονον
ναυμαχίας. διὸ καὶ δειπνῆσαι σήμερον μεθ' ὑμῶν βουλήσομαι.
181 πάντα <δ' ὑμῖν>, εἶπε, παρέσται καθηκόντως, οἷς συγχρήσησθε, 10
κἀμοὶ μεθ' ὑμῶν. τῶν δὲ ἀσμενισάντων ἐκέλευσε καταλύ-
ματα δοθῆναι τὰ κάλλιστα πλησίον τῆς ἄκρας αὐτοῖς, καὶ τὰ κατὰ
τὸ συμπόσιον ἑτοιμάζειν.
182 Ὁ δὲ <ἀρχεδέατρος> Νικάνωρ Δωρόθεον προσκαλεσάμενος, ὃς
<ἦν> ἐπὶ τούτων ἀποτεταγμένος, ἐκέλευσε τὴν ἑτοιμασίαν εἰς ἕκαστον 15
ἐπιτελεῖν. ἦν γὰρ οὕτω διατεταγμένον ὑπὸ τοῦ βασιλέως, ἃ μὲν ἔτι
καὶ νῦν ὁρᾷς· ὅσαι γὰρ πόλεις εἰσίν, <αἳ τοῖς αὐτοῖς> συγχρῶνται
πρὸς τὰ ποτὰ καὶ βρωτὰ καὶ στρωμνάς, τοσοῦτοι καὶ προεστῶτες
ἦσαν· καὶ κατὰ τοὺς ἐθισμοὺς οὕτως ἐσκευάζετο, ὅταν παραγένοιντο
πρὸς τοὺς βασιλεῖς, ἵνα κατὰ μηθὲν δυσχεραίνοντες ἱλαρῶς διεξά- 20
183 γωσιν· ὃ καὶ περὶ τούτους ἐγεγόνει. προσεχέστατος γὰρ ὢν
ἄνθρωπος ὁ Δωρόθεος εἶχε τὴν τῶν τοιούτων προστασίαν. συνέ-
στρωσε δὲ πάντα τὰ δι' αὐτοῦ χειριζόμενα, πρὸς τὰς τοιαύτας ὑποδοχὰς
διαμεμερισμένα. διμερῆ τε ἐποίησε τὰ τῶν κλισιῶν, καθὼς προσέ-

1 τιμης] ψυχης ΑΖ | υπερ τινων Ρ 4 σεβασμον—πρωτον (5)] om Ptxt
ins Ping | μεταδουναι Ζ | μετα] pr και Β 5 προτειναι] προδουναι Β
6 τιθεμαι Β 8 τα] om PZ hab Bvid T* sup lin cett 9 om και Β | ημων
BZ | βουλησωμαι Ρ 10 παντα δ υμιν ex conj Mend.] παντα δυναμιν
HKAGI παντα δυναιμην Ρ πασαν δυναμιν BTZ | παρεσταναι ΒΤ | συγχρη-
σησθε HKGI] συγχρησεσθε (-σεσθαι Ζ) cett 11 καμε ΒΤ 12 τα 2°]
om TZ 14 αρχεδεατρος (cf C. I. G. 4678) conj Letronne (ο επι της των
ξενων αποδοχης τεταγμενος Jos)] αρχιητρος codd | ος ην] ος (ως Ρ) ων codd
16 αποτελειν ΒΤ επιτελη Ρ txt cett 17 αι τοις αυτοις] αις ΒΤ οις cett
txt ex Jos (οσαι τοις αυτοις χρωνται) correxi (οσ. γαρ πολ. εθεσιν ιδιοις Wend.)
18 βρωτα και ποτα Κ | βρωματα BPTZ | στρωμνας ΒΤ] στρωμναις cett | το-
σουταις Ρ τοσουτο Ζ 19 παραγενωνται ΒΤ 20 μηδεν Β 21 προσ-
εχεστατα et om γαρ ων—παντα (23) Α 21 f. ων ανθρωπος] ανθρ. ων Β ων Ρ
23 αποδοχας Ρ 24 διαμεμετρημενα BPTZ | διμερη BZT (sed ras 1 litt int
ε et ρ in T) Jos] διμετρη Ρ διαμερη cett

ταξεν ὁ βασιλεύς· τοὺς γὰρ ἡμίσεις ἐκέλευσεν ἀνὰ χεῖρα κατα-
κλῖναι, τοὺς δὲ λοιποὺς μετὰ τὴν ἑαυτοῦ κλισίαν, οὐδὲν ἐλλιπὼν εἰς
τὸ τιμᾶν τοὺς ἄνδρας. Ὡς δὲ κατεκλίθησαν, ἐκέλευσε τῷ 184
Δωροθέῳ τοῖς ἐθισμοῖς οἷς χρῶνται πάντες οἱ παραγινόμενοι πρὸς
5 αὐτὸν ἀπὸ τῆς Ἰουδαίας, οὕτως ἐπιτελεῖν. διὸ τοὺς ἱεροκήρυκας
καὶ θύτας καὶ τοὺς ἄλλους, οἷς ἔθος ἦν τὰς κατευχὰς ποιεῖσθαι,
παρῃτήσατο· τῶν δὲ παραγεγονότων σὺν ἡμῖν Ἐλισσαῖον ὄντα
τῶν ἱερέων πρεσβύτερον παρεκάλεσε ποιήσασθαι κατευχήν, ὃς
ἀξιολόγως στὰς εἶπε Πληρώσαι σε, βασιλεῦ, πάντων τῶν ἀγαθῶν 185
10 ὧν ἔκτισεν ὁ παντοκράτωρ θεός· καὶ δῴη σοι ταῦτ᾽ ἔχειν καὶ γυναικὶ
καὶ τέκνοις καὶ τοῖς ὁμονοοῦσι πάντα ἀνέκλειπτα τὸν τῆς ζωῆς
χρόνον. Εἰπόντος δὲ ταῦτα τούτου κατερράγη κρότος μετὰ κραυγῆς 186
καὶ χαρᾶς εὐφροσύνου πλείονα χρόνον· καὶ τὸ τηνικαῦτα πρὸς τὸ
τέρπεσθαι διὰ τῶν ἡτοιμασμένων ἐτράπησαν, τῶν λειτουργιῶν
15 ἁπασῶν διὰ τῆς τοῦ Δωροθέου συντάξεως ἐπιτελουμένων· ἐν οἷς καὶ
βασιλικοὶ παῖδες ἦσαν, καὶ τῶν τιμωμένων ὑπὸ τοῦ βασιλέως.⁋   ⁋ Jos

Ὅτε δὲ καιρὸν ἔλαβεν ἐκ διαστήματος, ἠρώτησε τὸν ἔχοντα τὴν 187
πρώτην ἀνάκλισιν (ἦσαν γὰρ καθ᾽ ἡλικίαν τὴν ἀνάπτωσιν πεποιη-
μένοι) Πῶς ἂν τὴν βασιλείαν μέχρι τέλους ἄπταιστον ἔχων
20 διατελοῖ; βραχὺ δὲ ἐπισχὼν εἶπεν Οὕτως ἂν μάλιστα διευθύνοις, 188
μιμούμενος τὸ τοῦ θεοῦ διὰ παντὸς ἐπιεικές. μακροθυμίᾳ γὰρ
χρώμενος, καὶ βλιμάζων τοὺς ἀξίους ἐπιεικέστερον, καθώς εἰσιν

1 εκελευσεν] προσεταξεν P | ανα χειρα Jos] αναρχα Ar codd   3 f. τον HKAGIBP
Δωροθεον Jos   4 τους εθισμους BT | παραγενομενοι BPTZ   6 οις] ους H   TZ Jos
7 Ελισσαιον Jos] Ελεαζαρον codd   8 παρεκαλεσε A Jos (-σεν)] παρεκαλε-
σαν cett | ποιησεσθαι P   9 ειπε] ad hoc add †εὔ† Gᵗˣᵗ εὐ Iᵐᵍ ευχη Bᵐᵍ |
βασιλευς I   10 και 2°] om A   11 ζωης]+σου BPTZ   12 om τουτου
BTZ   18 γαρ] δε K | αναπτω A* (σιν sup lin in H)   19 απταιστον μ.
τελους I   19 f εχω διατελοι H*AGI εχων διατελοιη Hᶜᵒʳʳ εχω διατελειν K
διατελοιη εχων BT txt Z   20 μαλιστα] καλλιστα P | διευθυνεις HK*A
-νης P   22 βλημαζων codd (βληζων suprascripto μα P). A* βλημαζων
habuisse videtur, sed βλημ in ετοιμᵛⁱᵈ mutatum est. Hinc δοκιμαζων F ετοι-
μαζων L κριματαζων D¹ (αζων cum lacuna D*)   22 καθως] η καθως conj
Schmidt

189 ἄξιοι, μετατιθεὶς ἐκ τῆς κακίας καὶ εἰς μετάνοιαν ἄξεις. Ἐπαινέσας δὲ ὁ βασιλεὺς τὸν ἐχόμενον ἠρώτα Πῶς ἂν ἕκαστα πράττοι;
ὁ δὲ ἀπεκρίθη Τὸ δίκαιον εἰ πρὸς ἅπαντας διατηροῖ, ἑαυτῷ καλῶς
τὰ ἕκαστα πράξει, διαλαμβάνων ὅτι πᾶν ἐννόημα σαφές ἐστι θεῷ·
190 καταρχὴν δὲ θείου φόβου λαμβάνων ἐν οὐδενὶ διαπίπτοις.   Καὶ 5
τοῦτον δὲ εὖ μάλα παραδεξάμενος ἕτερον ἐπηρώτα Πῶς ἂν ὁμοίους
ἑαυτῷ ἔχοι τοὺς φίλους; κἀκεῖνος εἶπεν Εἰ θεωροίησαν πολλήν σε
πρόνοιαν ποιούμενον ὧν ἄρχεις ὄχλων· σὺ δὲ τοῦτο πράξεις ἐπι-
βλέπων ὡς ὁ θεὸς εὐεργετεῖ τὸ τῶν ἀνθρώπων γένος, ὁ ὑγίειαν
αὐτοῖς καὶ τροφὴν καὶ τὰ λοιπὰ κατὰ καιρὸν παρασκευάζων 10
191 ἅπαντα.   Συνεπιμαρτυρήσας δὲ τούτῳ τὸν ἐχόμενον ἠρώτα
Πῶς ἂν ἐν τοῖς χρηματισμοῖς καὶ διακρίσεσιν εὐφημίας <τυγχάνοι>
καὶ ὑπὸ τῶν ἀποτυγχανόντων; ὁ δὲ εἶπεν Εἰ πᾶσιν ἴσος γένοιο τῷ
λόγῳ, καὶ μηδὲν ὑπερηφάνως μηδὲ τῇ περὶ σεαυτὸν ἰσχύι πράσσοις
192 κατὰ τῶν ἁμαρτανόντων. τοῦτο δὲ ποιήσεις τὴν διάταξιν βλέπων 15
τὴν ὑπὸ τοῦ θεοῦ· τὰ γὰρ ἱκετευόμενα συντελεῖσθαι τοῖς ἀξίοις,
τοῖς δὲ ἀποτυγχάνουσιν ἢ δι' ὀνείρων ἢ πράξεων σημαίνεσθαι τὸ
βλαβερὸν αὐτοῖς, οὐ κατὰ τὰς ἁμαρτίας οὐδὲ <κατὰ> τὴν μεγαλω-
σύνην τῆς ἰσχύος τύπτοντος αὐτούς, ἀλλ' ἐπιεικείᾳ χρωμένου τοῦ
193 θεοῦ.   Εὖ δὲ καὶ τοῦτον κατεπαινέσας ἠρώτα τὸν ἐξῆς Πῶς 20
ἂν ἐν ταῖς πολεμικαῖς χρείαις ἀήττητος εἴη; ὁ δὲ εἶπεν Εἰ μὴ
πεποιθὼς ὑπάρχοι τοῖς ὄχλοις μηδὲ ταῖς δυνάμεσιν, ἀλλὰ τὸν θεὸν
ἐπικαλοῖτο διὰ πάντων, ἵνα τὰς ἐπιβολὰς αὐτῷ κατευθύνῃ δικαίως
194 διεξάγοντι πάντα.   Ἀποδεξάμενος δὲ καὶ τοῦτον τὸν ἕτερον
ἠρώτα Πῶς ἂν φοβερὸς εἴη τοῖς ἐχθροῖς; ὁ δὲ εἶπεν Εἰ τῇ τῶν 25
ὅπλων καὶ δυνάμεων παρασκευῇ πολλῇ χρώμενος <εἰδείη> ταῦτα

---

1 μετατιθεις]+τε Β μετατιθης Α*   2 εκαστα <καλλιστα> Wend.
3 παντας Ρ | διατηρει ΒΡΤΖ -ροιη Αcorr | εαυτω ΒΡΤΖ (·το)] εαυτον cett
4 πραξοι Κ   6 τουτο Α | επηρωτα ΒΤ] επερωτα cett | ομοιως Β   7 εαυτω]
εαυτου Η om Ζ   10 κατασκευαζων Ρ   12 διαρισεσιν Ζtxt διαιρεσιν Ζmg |
τυγχανω codd corr Schmidt   13 ισως ΒΡΤ | γενοιο—σεαυτον (14)] om
ΒΡΤΖ   14 πραττεις Ρ πρασοις Η* (σ altera suprascr) Κ   18 κατα 2°]
om codd   19 αυτοις GI   21 om ταις ΒΡΤΖ | ειην Ζ | ο ΒΡΤΖΚcorr τω
cett   22 υπαρχοι Κ] υπαρχοις HAGI υπαρχεις ΒΡΤΖ | οχλοις] οπλοις Ρ
23 επικαλη Β | επιβουλας Ι   25 τη] τω Τ   26 οπλιων Ρ | και δυναμεων]
om Ζ και δυναμενων G | ειδειη ex conj] ειη ει δε ειη (οιει Β) codd

ὄντα κενὰ ἐπὶ πλείονα χρόνον πρὸς τὸ συμπέρασμα δρᾶν τι· καὶ
γὰρ ὁ θεὸς διδοὺς ἀνοχὰς καὶ ἐνδεικνύμενος τὸν τῆς δυναστείας
φόβον ἐγκατασκευάζει πάσῃ διανοίᾳ.   Καὶ τοῦτον δὲ ἐπαι- 195
νέσας εἶπε πρὸς τὸν ἐχόμενον Τί κάλλιστον αὐτῷ πρὸς τὸ ζῆν ἂν
5 εἴη; κἀκεῖνος ἔφη Τὸ γινώσκειν ὅτι θεὸς δυναστεύει τῶν ἁπάντων,
καὶ ἐπὶ τῶν καλλίστων πράξεων οὐκ αὐτοὶ κατευθύνομεν τὰ βουλευ-
θέντα· θεὸς δὲ τελειοῖ τὰ πάντων καὶ καθηγεῖται δυναστεύων.   Ἐπι- 196
φωνήσας δὲ καὶ τούτῳ καλῶς λέγειν τὸν ἕτερον ἠρώτα Πῶς ἂν
ἀκέραια συντηρήσας ἅπαντα τοῖς ἐγγόνοις τὴν αὐτὴν παραδιδοῖ
10 διάθεσιν ἐπὶ τέλει;   §ὁ δὲ εἶπεν Εὐχόμενος ἀεὶ πρὸς τὸν θεὸν §C
ἀγαθὰς ἐπινοίας λαμβάνειν πρὸς τὰ μέλλοντα πράσσεσθαι, καὶ τοῖς
ἐγγόνοις παρακελευόμενος μὴ ἐκπλήττεσθαι τῇ δόξῃ μηδὲ τῷ
πλούτῳ· θεὸν γὰρ εἶναι τὸν χαριζόμενον ταῦτα, καὶ οὐ δι᾽ ἑαυτοὺς
ἔχειν τὴν ὑπεροχὴν ἁπάντων.   Ἐπιμαρτυρήσας δὲ τούτοις 197
15 τοῦ μετὰ ταῦτα ἐπυνθάνετο Πῶς ἂν τὰ συμβαίνοντα μετρίως
φέροι; ἐκεῖνος δὲ ἔφησεν Εἰ πρόληψιν λαμβάνοις, ὅτι γέγοναν
ὑπὸ τοῦ θεοῦ πάντες ἄνθρωποι μετασχεῖν τῶν μεγίστων κακῶν,
ὡσαύτως δὲ καὶ ἀγαθῶν, καὶ οὐκ ἔστιν ἄνθρωπον ὄντα τούτων ἀμιγῆ
γενέσθαι· ὁ θεὸς δὲ τὴν εὐψυχίαν δίδωσιν, ὃν ἱκετεύειν ἀναγ-
20 καῖον.   Φιλοφρονηθεὶς δὲ καὶ τοῦτον καλῶς εἶπεν ἅπαντας 198
ἀποφαίνεσθαι· ἐπερωτήσας δὲ ἔτι ἕνα καταλήξω τὸ νῦν ἔχον, ἵνα
καὶ πρὸς τὸ τέρπεσθαι τραπέντες ἡδέως διεξάγωμεν. ἐν δὲ ταῖς
μετὰ ταῦτα ἐξ ἑξῆς ἡμέραις καὶ παρὰ τῶν λοιπῶν ἑξῆς μαθήσομαί
τι πλέον. εἶτ᾽ ἐπηρώτα τὸν ἄνδρα Τί πέρας ἀνδρείας ἐστίν;   ὁ 199
25 δὲ εἶπεν Εἰ τὸ βουλευθὲν ὀρθῶς ἐν ταῖς τῶν κινδύνων πράξεσιν
ἐπιτελοῖτο κατὰ πρόθεσιν. τελειοῦται δὲ ὑπὸ τοῦ θεοῦ πάντα σοι
καλῶς βουλευομένῳ, βασιλεῦ, συμφερόντως.   §Ἐπιφωνησάντων 200 §Jos
δὲ πάντων καὶ κρότῳ σημηναμένων πρὸς τοὺς φιλοσόφους εἶπεν ὁ
βασιλεὺς (οὐκ ὀλίγοι γὰρ παρῆσαν τούτοις) Οἴομαι διαφέρειν τοὺς

2 τον] τα recte ut vid Wend.   8 om και BPTZ | τουτο Z   9 εκγο- HKAGIB
νοις ABT   10 επι τελει P] επιτελειν BZ^corr επιτελη Τ επιτελοι cett CPTZ Jos
12 εκγονοις AB*T   13 om ου Β   14 απαντων] pr των Η | τουτους I
16 φερει P | λαμβανεις BT | γεγονασιν BPT   18 αγαθων] pr των BT
19 om δε C   20 τουτω P   21 αποκρινεσθαι B | om δε C   23 ημερας
GI | εξης 2°] om BPTZ   24 ειτ επηρωτα BCTZ (ειτα BC)] ειτ επερωτα
cett   27 βουλευομενω BT] βουλομενω cett   28 σημαναμενων CTZ
29 ολιγοις Z

ἄνδρας ἀρετῇ καὶ συνιέναι πλεῖον, οἵτινες ἐκ τοῦ καιροῦ τοιαύτας
ἐρωτήσεις λαμβάνοντες, ὡς δέον ἐστὶν ἀποκέκρινται, πάντες ἀπὸ
201 θεοῦ τοῦ λόγου τὴν καταρχὴν ποιούμενοι. Μενέδημος δὲ ὁ
Ἐρετριεὺς φιλόσοφος εἶπε Ναί, βασιλεῦ· προνοίᾳ γὰρ τῶν ὅλων
διοικουμένων, καὶ ὑπειληφότων ὀρθῶς τοῦτο, ὅτι θεόκτιστόν ἐστιν 5
ἄνθρωπος, ἀκολουθεῖ πᾶσαν δυναστείαν καὶ λόγου καλλονὴν ἀπὸ
202 θεοῦ κατάρχεσθαι. τοῦ δὲ βασιλέως ἐπινεύσαντος τὰ περὶ τούτων
¶ Jos ἔληξεν,¶ ἐτράπησαν δὲ πρὸς εὐφροσύνην. ἐπιλαβούσης δὲ τῆς
ἑσπέρας τὸ συμπόσιον ἐλύθη.

203 Τῇ δὲ μετὰ ταῦτα πάλιν κατὰ τὴν αὐτὴν διάταξιν τὰ τῆς 10
ἀναπτώσεως καὶ συμποσίας ἐπετελεῖτο. καθὸ δὲ ἐνόμιζεν ὁ
βασιλεὺς εὔκαιρον εἶναι πρὸς τὸ πυνθάνεσθαί τι τῶν ἀνδρῶν,
204 ἐπηρώτα τοὺς ἑξῆς τῶν ἀποκεκριμένων τῇ προτέρᾳ ἡμέρᾳ. πρὸς
τὸν ἑνδέκατον δὲ ἤρξατο τὴν κοινολογίαν ποιεῖσθαι· δέκα γὰρ ἦσαν
οἱ ἠρωτημένοι τῇ προτέρᾳ. σιγῆς δὲ γενομένης ἐπυνθάνετο Πῶς 15
205 ἂν πλούσιος διαμένοι; βραχὺ δὲ ἐπισχὼν ὁ τὴν ἐρώτησιν ἐκδεχό-
μενος εἶπεν Εἰ μηδὲν ἀνάξιον τῆς ἀρχῆς μηδὲ ἀσελγὲς πράσσοι,
μηδὲ δαπάνῃ εἰς τὰ κενὰ καὶ μάταια συντελοῖ, τοὺς <δὲ> ὑποτεταγμένους εὐεργεσίᾳ πρὸς εὔνοιαν ἄγοι τὴν ἑαυτοῦ· καὶ γὰρ ὁ θεὸς πᾶσιν
206 αἴτιος ἀγαθῶν ἐστιν, ᾧ κατακολουθεῖν ἀναγκαῖον. Ἐπαι- 20
νέσας δὲ ὁ βασιλεὺς τοῦτον ἕτερον ἐπηρώτα Πῶς ἂν τὴν ἀλήθειαν
διατηροῖ; ὁ δὲ πρὸς τοῦτο ἀπεκρίθη Γινώσκων ὅτι μεγάλην
αἰσχύνην ἐπιφέρει τὸ ψεῦδος πᾶσιν ἀνθρώποις, πολλῷ δὲ μᾶλλον
τοῖς βασιλεῦσιν· ἐξουσίαν γὰρ ἔχοντες ὃ βούλονται πράσσειν, τίνος
ἕνεκεν ἂν ψεύσαιντο; προσλαμβάνειν δὲ δεῖ τοῦτό σε, βασιλεῦ, διότι 25
207 φιλαλήθης ὁ θεός ἐστιν. Ἀποδεξάμενος δὲ εὖ μάλα καὶ
τοῦτον ἐπιβλέψας εἶπεν Τί ἐστι σοφίας διδαχή; ὁ δὲ ἕτερος

HKAGIB   3 om του Β | Μενεδιμος ΒΤ Βενεδημος Ζ | om δε ΒΤ   8 δε 1° Β] δε
CPTZ Jos   τα cett | προς ευφροσ.—τη δε (10)] om A   13 πρωτη Κ | προς τον ενδεκ.—
προτερα (15) om Βtxt ins Βmg   15 om οι ΚΒ | προτερα] προτερεα Α*
(-ραια Αcorr) +ημερα Βmg   16 διαμελλοι Ρ   18 δαπανην Mend. | συν-
τελει ΒCΤ συντελη Ζ ασυντελει Ρ | δε Mend. (et sic L)] om codd cett
19 ενεργεσια]+δε Β | αγει ΒΤ   21 επηρωτα ΒΤ] επερωτα cett   22 δια-
τηροιη ΒΑcorr   23 επιφερει ΚΒ επιφεροι cett   24 εξουσιαν—πρασσειν]
om C | ο] ων Β   25 αν ενεκεν Ζ | προσλαμβανειν ΒΤ] προλαμβανειν cett |
σε] σοι Α   26 om ο θεος Ρ   27 post τουτον fort επι τον μετ αυτον vel
aliquid simile excidit

ἀπεφήνατο Καθὼς οὐ βούλει σεαυτῷ τὰ κακὰ παρεῖναι, μέτοχος δὲ
τῶν ἀγαθῶν ὑπάρχειν ἁπάντων, εἰ πράσσοις τοῦτο πρὸς τοὺς ὑποτεταγμένους καὶ τοὺς ἁμαρτάνοντας, εἰ τοὺς καλοὺς καὶ ἀγαθοὺς τῶν
ἀνθρώπων ἐπιεικέστερον νουθετοῖς· καὶ γὰρ ὁ θεὸς τοὺς ἀνθρώπους
5 ἅπαντας ἐπιεικείᾳ ἄγει. Ἐπαινέσας αὐτὸν τῷ μετ᾽ αὐτὸν 208
εἶπε Πῶς ἂν φιλάνθρωπος εἴη; κἀκεῖνος ἔφη Θεωρῶν ὡς ἐν
πολλῷ χρόνῳ καὶ κακοπαθείαις μεγίσταις αὔξει τε καὶ γεννᾶται τὸ
τῶν ἀνθρώπων γένος· ὅθεν οὔτε εὐκόπως δεῖ κολάζειν, οὔτε αἰκίαις
περιβάλλειν· γινώσκων ὅτι τὸ τῶν ἀνθρώπων ζῆν ἐν ὀδύναις τε καὶ
10 τιμωρίαις καθέστηκεν. ἐπινοῶν οὖν ἕκαστα πρὸς τὸν ἔλεον τραπήσῃ·
καὶ γὰρ ὁ θεὸς ἐλεήμων ἐστίν. Ἀποδεξάμενος δὲ τοῦτον 209
ἐπυνθάνετο τοῦ κατὰ τὸ ἑξῆς Τίς ἀναγκαιότατος τρόπος βασιλείας;
Τὸ συντηρεῖν, εἶπεν, αὐτὸν ἀδωροδόκητον, καὶ νήφειν τὸ πλεῖον μέρος
τοῦ βίου, καὶ δικαιοσύνην προτιμᾶν, καὶ τοὺς τοιούτους φιλοποιεῖ-
15 σθαι· καὶ γὰρ ὁ θεὸς φιλοδίκαιός ἐστιν. Ἐπισημήνας καὶ 210
τοῦτον πρὸς τὸν ἕτερον εἶπε Τί τὸ τῆς εὐσεβείας ἐστὶ κατάστημα;
ἐκεῖνος δὲ ἔφη Τὸ διαλαμβάνειν ὅτι πάντα διὰ παντὸς ὁ θεὸς ἐνεργεῖ
καὶ γινώσκει, καὶ οὐθὲν ἂν λάθοι ἄδικον ποιήσας ἢ κακὸν ἐργασά-
μενος ἄνθρωπος· ὡς γὰρ θεὸς εὐεργετεῖ τὸν ὅλον κόσμον, οὕτως καὶ
20 σὺ μιμούμενος ἀπρόσκοπος ἂν εἴης. Ἐπιφωνήσας δὲ τούτῳ 211
πρὸς τὸν ἕτερον εἶπε Τίς ὅρος τοῦ βασιλεύειν ἐστίν; ὁ δὲ ἔφη Τὸ
καλῶς ἄρχειν ἑαυτοῦ, καὶ μὴ τῷ πλούτῳ καὶ τῇ δόξῃ φερόμενον
ὑπερήφανον καὶ ἄσχημόν τι ἐπιθυμῆσαι, εἰ καλῶς λογίζοιο. πάντα
γάρ σοι πάρεστιν ὡς οὐδέν. ὁ θεὸς δὲ ἀπροσδεής ἐστι καὶ ἐπιεικής.

---

1 απεφηνατο] ειπε B απεκρινατο P | βουλη HGCZ | om τα BCTZ HKAGIB
2 πρασσεις KBCP   2 f αμαρτ. και τους υποτεταγ. P   3 om τους 1º B CPTZ
4 νουθετεις KBPT   6 om αν Z* ins Zcorr   7 om τε I   8 ουτε 1º]
ουδε Z | αικιαις (cf 3 Macc 6. 26) BT] αιτιαις HKCPZ αιτιας GIA
9 τον α̅ν̅ο̅ν̅ HKB | om τε KB   11 δε]+και GI   12 om επυνθανετο
Ktxt ins post εξης Kmg | το] τον K | βασιλειας] pr της P   13 εαυτον P
14 φιλοπονεισθαι H   16 om τον BT | om της B | καταστημα εστιν Z
17 om δε K | διαπαντος]+οτι K | ενεργει και γινωσκει ο θ̅σ̅ P   19 θεος]
pr ο P | om ολον P   20 τουτον CPZ   22 εαυτου]+και βασιλευειν εστι K
23 υπερηφανον]+τι BT*? (ras 2 litt) | om τι B | επιθυμησαι P] εννοησα-
σθαι B επινοησαιο Z επιθυμησαιο cett   24 ως ουδεν] οσα δεον conj
Wend.

καὶ σὺ καθόσον ἄνθρωπος ἐννόει, καὶ μὴ πολλῶν ὀρέγου, τῶν δὲ
212 ἱκανῶν πρὸς τὸ βασιλεύειν.   Κατεπαινέσας δὲ αὐτόν, ἐπηρώτα
τὸν ἕτερον Πῶς ἂν τὰ κάλλιστα διαλογίζοιτο; ἀπεκρίθη δὲ ἐκεῖνος
Εἰ τὸ δίκαιον ἐπὶ παντὸς προβάλλοι συνεχῶς, καὶ νομίζοι τὴν
ἀδικίαν τοῦ ζῆν στέρησιν εἶναι· καὶ γὰρ .ὁ θεὸς διὰ παντὸς τοῖς 5
213 δικαίοις ἀγαθὰ προσημαίνει μέγιστα.   Τοῦτον δὲ ἐπαινέσας
εἶπε πρὸς τὸν ἐξῆς Πῶς ἂν ἐν τοῖς ὕπνοις ἀτάραχος εἴη; ὁ δὲ ἔφη
Δυσαπολόγητον ἠρώτηκας πρᾶγμα. συναναφέρειν γὰρ οὐ δυνάμεθα
ἐν τούτοις τοῖς κατὰ τὸν ὕπνον ἑαυτούς, ἀλλὰ περιεχόμεθα ἀλογίστω
214 κατὰ <τάδε> αἰσθήσει. πάσχομεν γὰρ κατὰ τὴν ψυχὴν ἐπὶ τοῖς 10
ὑποπίπτουσιν ὡς θεωρουμένοις· ἀλογιστοῦμεν δέ, καθόσον ὑπολαμ-
βάνομεν καὶ ἐπὶ πέλαγος καὶ ἐν πλοίοις ἢ πολεῖν, ἢ πέτασθαι φερο-
μένους καὶ διαίρειν εἰς ἑτέρους τόπους, καὶ τοιαῦτα ἕτερα, †καὶ ὁ ταῦθ᾽
215 ὑπολαμβάνων μὴ καθεστάναι†. πλὴν ὅσον ἔμοιγε ἐφικτόν, οὕτω
διείληφα· κατὰ πάντα τρόπον σέ, βασιλεῦ, καὶ τὰ λεγόμενα καὶ τὰ 15
πραττόμενα πρὸς εὐσέβειαν ἐπανάγειν, ὅπως <ἑαυτῷ> συνιστορῇς, ὅτι
τὸ κατ᾽ ἀρετὴν συντηρῶν οὔτε χαρίζεσθαι προαιρῇ παρὰ λόγον, οὐδὲ
216 ἐξουσίᾳ χρώμενος τὸ δίκαιον αἴρεις. ἐπὶ πλεῖον γάρ, ἐν οἷς ἕκαστος
πράγμασιν ἐγρηγορὼς τὴν διαγωγὴν ποιεῖται, καὶ καθ᾽ ὕπνον ἐν τοῖς
αὐτοῖς ἡ διάνοια τὴν ἀναστροφὴν ἔχει, †ὡς δὲ† πάντα διαλογισμὸν 20
καὶ πρᾶξιν ἐπὶ τὰ κάλλιστα τρεπομένην κατευθύνει καὶ ἐγρηγορὼς
217 καὶ ἐν ὕπνῳ. διὸ καὶ περὶ σὲ διὰ παντός ἐστιν εὐστάθεια.   Κατ-
ευφημήσας δὲ καὶ τοῦτον εἶπε πρὸς τὸν ἕτερον Ἐπεὶ σὺ δέκατος
τὴν ἀπόκρισιν ἔχεις, ὡς ἂν ἀποφήνῃ, πρὸς τὸ δεῖπνον τραπησόμεθα.

HKAGIB   3 om τα B   4 ει] εις G | προβαλοι P προβαλλει C προβαλοις G προ-
CPTZ   βαλλοις I | νομιζει P   5 om του ζην Z   9 τους υπνους P   10 ταδε]
τηδε HKAPT τι δε GICZ τα τηδε B (τα excurrit in mg sed prima manu) |
πασχωμεν GIP | om την I   11 υπολαμβανομεν BCPT] υπολαμβανομενοι
cett   12 και 1°] om B | πολειν KGIBT] πωλειν HCPZ πλειν A (η πολ.]
περιπολειν Wend.) | πετασθαι]+ημας B   13 και ο ταυθ—βασιλευ (15) om
Btxt ins in mg Brubr | ο] om K το P   14 υπολαμβανειν KGICPZ | καθιστα-
ναι I Locus perobscurus ? κατα ταυθ υπολαμβανομεν καθεσταναι   15 τρο-
πον παντα Z | σε] σοι KBT   16 εαυτω] εαυτου codd   17 om το B
18 αιρεις] αναιρεις P αιρης Z ερεις A   19 ποιηται P | η διανοια εν τοις
αυτοις BT   20 ως δε codd] Fortasse ως δ εχει vel ος δ εχει   21 κατευ-
θυνεις Zcorr   24 τραπησωμεθα GICPZ

ἠρώτα δέ Πῶς ἂν μηδὲν ἀνάξιον ἑαυτῶν πράσσοιμεν; ὁ δὲ εἶπεν 218
Ἐπίβλεπε διὰ παντὸς εἰς τὴν σεαυτοῦ δόξαν καὶ τὴν ὑπεροχήν, ἵνα
τούτοις ἀκόλουθα καὶ λέγῃς καὶ διανοῇ, γινώσκων ὅτι πάντες ὧν
ἄρχεις περὶ σοῦ καὶ διανοοῦνται καὶ λαλοῦσιν. οὐ γὰρ ἐλάχιστόν 219
5 σε δεῖ τῶν ὑποκριτῶν φαίνεσθαι· τὸ γὰρ πρόσωπον, <ὃ δέον αὐτοῖς>
ἐστιν ὑποκρίνεσθαι, τοῦτο συνθεωροῦντες ἀκόλουθα πάντα πράσ-
σουσι· σὺ δὲ οὐχ ὑπόκρισιν ἔχεις, ἀλλ᾽ ἀληθῶς βασιλεύεις, θεοῦ
δόντος σοι καταξίως τῶν τρόπων τὴν ἡγεμονίαν.   Τοῦ δὲ 220
βασιλέως εὖ μάλα συγκροτήσαντος μετὰ φιλοφροσύνης ἐπὶ πλείονα
10 χρόνον, τοὺς ἀνθρώπους καθυπνοῦν παρεκάλουν. καὶ τὰ μὲν πρὸς
τούτους ὡς ἔληξεν, ἐπὶ τὴν ἑξῆς ἐτράπησαν τῆς συμποσίας
διάταξιν.

Τῇ δὲ ἐχομένῃ, τῆς αὐτῆς διατάξεως γενηθείσης, ὅτε καιρὸν ὑπε- 221
λάμβανεν ὁ βασιλεὺς εἶναι τοῦ πυνθάνεσθαί τι τῶν ἀνδρῶν, ἠρώτα
15 τὸν πρῶτον τῶν ἀπολιπόντων πρὸς τὴν ἑξῆς ἐρώτησιν Τίς ἐστιν
ἀρχὴ κρατίστη; ἐκεῖνος δὲ ἔφη Τὸ κρατεῖν ἑαυτοῦ καὶ μὴ συγκατα- 222
φέρεσθαι ταῖς ὁρμαῖς. πᾶσι γὰρ ἀνθρώποις φυσικὸν εἶναι τὸ πρός
τι τὴν διάνοιαν ῥέπειν· τοῖς μὲν οὖν πολλοῖς ἐπὶ τὰ βρωτὰ καὶ 223
ποτὰ καὶ τὰς ἡδονὰς εἰκός ἐστι κεκλίσθαι, τοῖς δὲ βασιλεῦσιν ἐπὶ
20 χώρας κατάκτησιν, κατὰ τὸ τῆς δόξης μέγεθος· πλὴν ἐν πᾶσι
μετριότης καλόν. ἃ δὲ ὁ θεὸς δίδωσι, ταῦτα λαμβάνων σύνεχε·
τῶν δ᾽ ἀνεφίκτων μὴ ἐπιθύμει.   Τοῖς δὲ ῥηθεῖσιν ἀρεσθεὶς 224
πρὸς τὸν ἐχόμενον εἶπε Πῶς ἂν ἐκτὸς εἴη φθόνου; διαλιπὼν δὲ
ἐκεῖνος ἔφη Πρῶτον εἰ νοῆσαι, ὅτι ὁ θεὸς πᾶσι μερίζει δόξαν τε
25 καὶ πλούτου μέγεθος τοῖς βασιλεῦσι, καὶ οὐδεὶς περὶ ἑαυτόν ἐστι

---

1 αυτων CZ   3 λεγεις PZ   5 δει B] δια cett | ο δεον αυτοις conj HKAGIB
Schmidt] ουδε αυτο (αυτος B) codd   6 τουτο]+γαρ GI | συν (in συνθεω- CPTZ
ρουντες) sup lin T¹   8 τον τροπον Zᵗˣᵗ | ηγεμονειαν H   10 καθυπνουντας
C υπνουν GI | παρεκ. καθ. Z   11 τουτοις Z | εληξεν Schard] ελεξεν codd |
επι]+τουτοις (post ras) Z | ως εληξεν—εχομενη (13)] om H   13 υπελαβεν
CTZ   14 ηρωτα ex conj] πρωτα codd (επηρωτα Zᶜᵒʳʳ)   15 των απο-
λιποντων (-λειπ. P)] τον απολιποντα BCTZ +ηγε B | ερωτησιν]+εφη P
18 om την διαν. Z | βρωματα P   19 κεκλεισθαι PB*ᵛⁱᵈ   20 κατα] και
Wend. | om το C   21 om ταυτα P | συνεχε λαμβανων B* (corr B¹)
23 πως] ως Z | διαλειπων I   24 ει νοησαις ZᶜᵒʳʳP (-ησσ.) εννοησας B
25 πλουτον HGI | παρ εαυτον Wend.

βασιλεύς· πάντες γὰρ θέλουσι μετασχεῖν ταύτης τῆς δόξης, ἀλλ᾽ οὐ
225 δύνανται· θεοῦ γάρ ἐστι δόμα.   Ἐπαινέσας δὲ τὸν ἄνδρα
διὰ πλειόνων ἐπηρώτα τὸν ἕτερον Πῶς ἂν καταφρονοίη τῶν ἐχθρῶν;
ὁ δὲ εἶπεν Ἡσκηκὼς πρὸς πάντας ἀνθρώπους εὔνοιαν καὶ κατεργα-
σάμενος φιλίας, λόγον οὐθενὸς ἂν ἔχοις· τὸ δὲ κεχαριτῶσθαι πρὸς 5
πάντας ἀνθρώπους καὶ καλὸν δῶρον εἰληφέναι παρὰ θεοῦ τοῦτ᾽ ἔστι
226 κράτιστον.   Συναινέσας δὲ τούτοις τὸν ἑξῆς ἐκέλευσεν
ἀποκριθῆναι, πρὸς αὐτὸν εἰπών Πῶς ἂν δοξαζόμενος διαμένοι; εἶπε
δέ Τῇ προθυμίᾳ καὶ ταῖς χάρισι πρὸς τοὺς ἄλλους μεταδοτικὸς ὢν
καὶ μεγαλομερὴς οὐδέποτ᾽ ἂν ἀπολίποι δόξης· ἵνα δὲ τὰ προειρη- 10
227 μένα σοι διαμένῃ, τὸν θεὸν ἐπικαλοῦ διὰ παντός.   Εὐφη-
μήσας δὲ τοῦτον ἕτερον ἠρώτα Πῶς τινα δεῖ φιλότιμον εἶναι;
ἐκεῖνος δὲ ἔφη Πρὸς τοὺς φιλικῶς ἔχοντας ἡμῖν οἴονται πάντες ὅτι
πρὸς τούτους δέον· ἐγὼ δ᾽ ὑπολαμβάνω, πρὸς τοὺς ἀντιδοξοῦντας
φιλοτιμίαν δεῖν χαριστικὴν ἔχειν, ἵνα τούτῳ τῷ τρόπῳ μετάγωμεν 15
αὐτοὺς ἐπὶ τὸ καθῆκον καὶ συμφέρον ἑαυτοῖς. δεῖ δὲ τὸν θεὸν
λιτανεύειν, ἵνα ταῦτ᾽ ἐπιτελῆται· τὰς γὰρ ἁπάντων διανοίας
228 κρατεῖ.   Συνομολογήσας δὲ τούτοις τὸν ἕκτον ἐκέλευσεν
ἀποφήνασθαι πυνθανόμενος Τίσι δεῖ χαρίζεσθαι; ἐκεῖνος δ᾽
ἀπεκρίθη Γονεῦσι διὰ παντός, καὶ γὰρ ὁ θεὸς πεποίηται ἐντολὴν 20
μεγίστην περὶ τῆς τῶν γονέων τιμῆς. ἐπομένως δὲ τὴν τῶν φίλων
ἐγκρίνει διάθεσιν, προσονομάσας ΙΣΟΝ ΤΗ ΨΥΧΗ ΤΟΝ ΦΙΛΟΝ. σὺ
δὲ καλῶς ποιεῖς ἅπαντας ἀνθρώπους εἰς φιλίαν πρὸς ἑαυτὸν καθ-
229 ιστῶν.   Παρακαλέσας δὲ καὶ τοῦτον ἐπυνθάνετο καὶ τοῦ
μετέπειτα Τί καλλονῆς ἄξιόν ἐστιν; ὁ δὲ εἶπεν Εὐσέβεια. καὶ 25
γὰρ αὕτη καλλονή τίς ἐστι πρωτεύουσα. τὸ δὲ δυνατὸν αὐτῆς

22 Deut 13⁶

HKAGIB   2 δυναντ αν Z   5 φιλιαν Z   6 om και GI   8 ειπων] ειπεν GIC
CPTZ   ειπας Z | πως] ως Z   9 προμηθεια K | μεταδοτ ων προς τους αλλους B
10 απολειποι P   11 διαμενοι A   12 πως] προς Wend. | δει sup lin scr
Z* vid   13 οιονται] οιον και K   15 δει BP | εχειν] ειναι B | τροπω]
προσωπω CZ   17 επιτελειται C   18 συνομολογησασθαι P et (δε omisso)
Z*   19 om δ Z   20 απεκριθη] ειπε Z   21 επομενος P   22 εγκρινειν Z
23 προς εαυτον] εαυτω P   24 και 1°] om B   26 om τις PZ | προτερευ-
ουσα H προτευουσα GI | ἐστιν αὐτῆς B* (corr B¹)

ἐστιν ἀγάπη· αὕτη γὰρ θεοῦ δόσις ἐστίν· ἣν καὶ σὺ κέκτησαι πάντα
περιέχων ἐν αὐτῇ τὰ ἀγαθά.   Λίαν δὲ φιλοφρόνως ἐπικρο- 230
τήσας εἶπε πρὸς τὸν ἕτερον Πῶς ἂν πταίσας πάλιν τῆς αὐτῆς
κρατῆσαι δόξης; ὁ δὲ ἔφη Σὲ μὲν οὐ δυνατόν ἐστι πταῖσαι, πᾶσι
5 γὰρ χάριτας ἔσπαρκας, αἳ βλαστάνουσιν εὔνοιαν, ἣ τὰ μέγιστα τῶν
ὅπλων κατισχύουσα περιλαμβάνει τὴν μεγίστην ἀσφάλειαν· εἰ δέ 231
τινες πταίουσιν, ἐφ᾽ οἷς πταίουσιν, οὐκέτι χρὴ ταῦτα πράσσειν, ἀλλὰ
φιλίαν κατακτησαμένους δικαιοπραγεῖν. θεοῦ δὲ δῶρον ἀγαθῶν
ἐργάτην εἶναι καὶ μὴ τῶν ἐναντίων.   Συναρεσθεὶς δὲ τούτοις 232
10 πρὸς τὸν ἕτερον εἶπε Πῶς ἂν ἐκτὸς γένοιτο λύπης; ὁ δὲ ἔφησεν Εἰ
μηδένα βλάπτοι, πάντας δὲ ὠφελοῖ, τῇ δικαιοσύνῃ κατακολουθῶν·
τοὺς γὰρ ἀπ᾽ αὐτῆς καρποὺς ἀλυπίαν κατασκευάζειν. ἱκετεύειν δὲ 233
τὸν θεόν, ἵνα μὴ τὰ παρὰ τὴν προαίρεσιν ἡμῶν ἀνακύπτοντα
βλάπτῃ, λέγω δὴ οἷον θάνατοί τε καὶ νόσοι καὶ λῦπαι καὶ τὰ
15 τοιαῦτα. <αὐτῷ> δὲ σοὶ εὐσεβεῖ καθεστῶτι τούτων οὐδὲν ἂν
προσέλθοι.   Καλῶς δὲ καὶ τοῦτον ἐπαινέσας τὸν δέκατον ἠρώτα 234
Τί μέγιστόν ἐστι δόξης; ὁ δὲ εἶπε Τὸ τιμᾶν τὸν θεόν· τοῦτο δ᾽
ἐστὶν οὐ δώροις οὐδὲ θυσίαις, ἀλλὰ ψυχῆς καθαρότητι καὶ διαλήψεως
ὁσίας, καθὼς ὑπὸ τοῦ θεοῦ πάντα κατασκευάζεται καὶ διοικεῖται
20 κατὰ τὴν αὐτοῦ βούλησιν· ἣν καὶ σὺ διατελεῖς ἔχων γνώμην, ᾗ
πάρεστι σημειοῦσθαι πᾶσιν ἐκ τῶν ὑπὸ σοῦ συντετελεσμένων καὶ
συντελουμένων.   Μετὰ μείζονος δὲ φωνῆς πάντας αὐτοὺς ὁ 235
βασιλεὺς ἠσπάζετο καὶ παρεκάλει, συνεπιφωνούντων τῶν παρόντων,
μάλιστα δὲ τῶν φιλοσόφων. καὶ γὰρ ταῖς ἀγωγαῖς καὶ τῷ λόγῳ
25 πολὺ προέχοντες αὐτῶν ἦσαν, ὡς ἂν ἀπὸ θεοῦ τὴν καταρχὴν ποιούμενοι. μετὰ δὲ ταῦτα ὁ βασιλεὺς εἰς τὸ φιλοφρονεῖσθαι προῆλθε
διὰ τῶν προπόσεων.

1 γαρ] δε Β | θῦ δοσις BCPT] θεοδοσιος cett   2 αυτη] εαυτη Κ αυτω   HKAGIB
Β* εαυτω Β¹ txt cett   3 της αυτης παλιν Ρ   5 εσπερκας ΗΑ | ευνοιαν]   CPTZ
+ει δε τινες πταιουσιν εφ οις πταιουσι Κ* (del rubricator)   8 κτησα-
μενους ΒΤ | αγαθον CT*Z   9 συναρκεσθεις Β   10 εφησεν] εφη ΑΡ
11 βλαπτοι] λυπειται Ζᵛⁱᵈ (fin ex corr) | ωφελει ΚΤ οφελοιη Ρ   12 αυτους
Κ   13 om τα KBCTZ   14 βλαπτοι CPZ | λεγω δη (δε Ζ)] om Ρ | om
τε Ρ   15 τοιαυτα δε σοι codd (cum lacuna post τοιαυτα BC) αυτω inserui |
αυτω—καθεστωτι] ευσεβει δε σοι οντι Ρ   19 καθως—κατα (20)] om
ΗΚΑGΙ   22 δε μειζονος Ζ   25 προσεχοντες ΒΖ | αυτω Β* | ησαν Ρ]
om cett   27 προποσεων ΒΤΗᶜᵒʳʳ] πραιποσιτων ΡΚᶜᵒʳʳ προποσετων cett

236 　Τῇ δὲ ἐπιούσῃ κατὰ τὰ αὐτὰ τῆς διατάξεως τοῦ συμποσίου
γενομένης, καθὼς εὔκαιρον ἐγένετο τῷ βασιλεῖ, τοὺς ἑξῆς ἠρώτα τῶν
προαποκεκριμένων, εἶπε δὲ τῷ πρώτῳ Τὸ φρονεῖν εἰ διδακτόν ἐστιν;
ὃς δ᾽ εἶπε Ψυχῆς ἐστι κατασκευὴ διὰ θείας δυνάμεως ἐπιδέχεσθαι
237 πᾶν τὸ καλόν, ἀποστρέφεσθαι δὲ τἀναντία. 　　　Συνομολογήσας 5
δὲ τὸν ἐχόμενον ἠρώτα Τί πρὸς ὑγείαν μάλιστα συντείνει; ἐκεῖνος
δὲ ἔφη Σωφροσύνη· ταύτης δὲ οὐκ ἔστι τυχεῖν, ἐὰν μὴ θεὸς κατα-
238 σκευάσῃ τὴν διάνοιαν εἰς τοῦτο. 　　　Παρακαλέσας δὲ τοῦτον πρὸς
τὸν ἕτερον ἔφη Πῶς ἂν γονεῦσι τὰς ἀξίας ἀποδῷη χάριτας; ὃς δὲ
εἶπε Μηδὲν αὐτοὺς λυπήσας· τοῦτο δ᾽ οὐκ ἔστιν, εἰ μὴ θεὸς τῆς δια- 10
239 νοίας ἡγεμὼν γένοιτο πρὸς τὰ κάλλιστα. 　　　Προσεπινεύσας δὲ
τούτῳ τὸν ἑξῆς ἠρώτα Πῶς ἂν φιλήκοος εἴη; ἐκεῖνος δὲ εἶπε Διαλαμβάνων ὅτι πάντα συμφέρει γινώσκειν, ὅπως ἂν πρὸς τὰ συμβαίνοντα ἐκλεγόμενός τι τῶν ἠκροαμένων ἀνθυποτιθεὶς πρὸς τὰ τῶν
καιρῶν †ἂν ἀντιπράσσηται†, σὺν χειραγωγίᾳ θεοῦ· τοῦτο δ᾽ ἐστίν, 15
240 αἱ τῶν πράξεων τελειώσεις ὑπ᾽ αὐτοῦ. 　　　Τοῦτον δὲ ἐπαινέσας
πρὸς τὸν ἕτερον εἶπε Πῶς ἂν μηθὲν παράνομον πράσσοι; πρὸς τοῦτο
ἔφησε Γινώσκων ὅτι τὰς ἐπινοίας ὁ θεὸς ἔδωκε τοῖς νομοθετήσασι
πρὸς τὸ σώζεσθαι τοὺς βίους τῶν ἀνθρώπων, ἀκόλουθος εἴης
241 ἂν αὐτοῖς. 　　　Ἀποδεξάμενος δὲ αὐτὸν πρὸς ἕτερον εἶπε Τίς 20
ὠφέλεια συγγενείας ἐστίν; ὁ δὲ ἀπεφήνατο Ἐὰν τοῖς συμβαίνουσι
νομίζωμεν ἀτυχοῦσι μὲν ἐλαττοῦσθαι, καὶ κακοπαθῶμεν ὡς αὐτοί,
242 φαίνεται τὸ συγγενὲς ὅσον ἰσχῦόν ἐστι—τελουμένων δὲ τούτων καὶ
δόξα καὶ προκοπὴ παρὰ τοῖς τοιούτοις ὑπάρξει· τὸ γὰρ συνεργὲς

HKAGIB
CPTZ
　　2 γενομενου BT | τους] τοις I 　　3 αποκεκριμενων T 　　4 δια] και P
6 εκεινο B* εκεινος B¹ 　　7 εαν] ει A | κατασκευασει HAGCZ* 　　8 om δε
BCPTZ 　　9 ειπε Z | αποδων G αποδωση Z | γονευσιν αποδωη τας αξ. χαρ.
B 　　10 λυπησας P] λυπησαι cett | της διανοιας ηγεμων bis scripsit K
12 om αν C | ειη] pr αν Z | διαλαμβανειν B 　　13 συμφερει T 　　14 ανθυ-
ποτιθης T (Wend.) txt (αντ. GICZ) cett 　　15 αν αντιπρασσηται] αντιπρασ-
σηται G (αν τι πρασσ.) IB txt (fort recte) cett (ἂν ἀντ. Wend.) | συγχειρα-
γωγια A*GITZ | εστιν αι] εστι και P 　　16 η των πρ. τελειωσις T* | ? εισιν
υπ αυτου 　　17 πρασσοι παρα τον νομον BCPTZ 　　18 δεδωκε P 　　19 ειης]
pr αν BTZ* (post ras) 　　20 om αν BT | αυτου] τουτον P | ετερον] pr τον
HPZ 　　22 νομιζωμεν KA^corr B^corr T] νομιζομεν cett | ατυχουσι KA^corr BPT]
ατυχωσι cett | ως αυτοι BC^corr T^corr] ως αυτον PC*T* vid ως αυτων cett
(? ωσαυτως) 　　23 οσον—συνεργες (24)] om B^txt ins B^mg | om και P
24 υπαρχει GI | συγγενες B^corr T

εὐνόως γινόμενον ὡς ἐξ ἑαυτοῦ ἀδιάλυτον πρὸς ἅπαντα—μετὰ δὲ εὐημερίας, μηδὲν προσδεῖσθαι τῶν ἐκείνων· ἀλλὰ δέον <θεὸν> ἱκετεύειν,
πάντα ἀγαθοποιεῖν.   Ὡσαύτως δὲ ἐκείνοις ἀποδεξάμενος 243
αὐτὸν ἄλλον ἠρώτα Πῶς ἀφοβία γίνεται; εἶπε δέ Συνιστορούσης
5 τῆς διανοίας μηδὲν κακὸν πεπραχέναι, θεοῦ κατευθύνοντος εἰς τὸ
καλῶς ἅπαντα βουλεύεσθαι.   Τούτῳ δὲ ἐπιφωνήσας πρὸς 244
ἄλλον εἶπε Πῶς ἂν προχείρως ἔχοι τὸν ὀρθὸν λόγον; ὁ δὲ εἶπεν
Εἰ τὰ τῶν ἀνθρώπων ἀτυχήματα διὰ παντὸς ἐπιβλέποι· γινώσκων
ὅτι ὁ θεὸς ἀφαιρεῖται τὰς εὐημερίας, ἑτέρους δὲ δοξάζων εἰς τὸ
10 τιμᾶσθαι προάγει.   Καλῶς δὲ καὶ τοῦτον ἀποδεξάμενος τὸν 245
ἑξῆς ἀποκριθῆναι παρεκάλει Πῶς ἂν μὴ εἰς ῥαθυμίαν, μηδὲ ἐπὶ τὰς
ἡδονὰς τρέποιτο; ὁ δέ Προχείρως ἔχων, εἶπεν, ὅτι μεγάλης
βασιλείας κατάρχει καὶ πολλῶν ὄχλων ἀφηγεῖται, καὶ οὐ δεῖ περὶ
ἕτερόν τι τὴν διάνοιαν εἶναι, τῆς δὲ τούτων ἐπιμελείας φροντίζειν·
15 θεὸν δὲ ἀξιοῦν, ὅπως μηθὲν ἐλλίπῃ τῶν καθηκόντων.   Ἐπαι- 246
νέσας δὲ καὶ τοῦτον τὸν δέκατον <ἠρώτα Πῶς ἂν ἐπιγινώσκοι> τοὺς
δόλῳ τινὶ πρὸς αὐτὸν πράσσοντας; ὁ δὲ ἀπεφήνατο πρὸς τοῦτο Εἰ
παρατηροῖτο τὴν ἀγωγὴν ἐλευθέριον οὖσαν, καὶ τὴν εὐταξίαν διαμέ-
νουσαν ἐν τοῖς ἀσπασμοῖς καὶ συμβουλίαις καὶ τῇ λοιπῇ συνανα-
20 στροφῇ τῶν σὺν αὐτῷ, καὶ μηθὲν ὑπερτείνοντας τοῦ δέοντος ἐν ταῖς
φιλοφρονήσεσι καὶ τοῖς λοιποῖς τοῖς κατὰ τὴν ἀγωγήν. θεὸς δὲ 247
τὴν διάνοιαν <ἄξει> σοι, βασιλεῦ, πρὸς τὰ κάλλιστα.   Συγ-
κροτήσας πάντας τ᾽ ἐπαινέσας κατ᾽ ὄνομα, καὶ τῶν παρόντων ταὐτὰ
ποιούντων, ἐπὶ τὸ μέλπειν ἐτράπησαν.

---

1 διαλυτον Z   **2** θεον ins. Mend.   **3** ις in εκεινοις sup HKAGIB
ras T   **4** πως ex οπως Tᵛⁱᵈ | om ειπε δε K   **6** απαντας G | τουτο   CPTZ

P   **7** εχῃ τον ορθον λογον προχειρως B | εχει CZ   **8** επιβλεπει BP
13 καταρχῃ Z | om οχλων B   **15** ελλειπει B* ελλειπῃ BᶜᵒʳʳPT
16 ερωτα codd | αν επιγινωσκοι] επιγινωσκοι B επιγινωσκει (-εις Z) cett
17 δολον τινα Aᶜᵒʳʳ | πρασσοντας προς αυτον BT | προς τουτο (τουτον B*
Tᶜᵒʳʳ ᵛⁱᵈ) απεφηνατο P   **18** αυταξιαν KI (ευ sup ras H)   **19** συμβουλ-
λιαις (-ειαις GICZ)] συμβουλιας HK (-ειας) A*   **20** μηδεν HKBP | υπερ-
τεινειν P υπερτεινοντ B* (as add Bᶜᵒʳʳ) υπερτεινωνται Zᶜᵒʳʳ   **22** διανοιαν]
δι ανοι C | εξει codd | συγκροτησας] + δε B +ουν και P cum praecedd conj
cett ο δε βασιλευς συγκροτησας edd pr (cod Mon)   **23** τ (τε C)] om P | τα
αυτα BᵛⁱᵈT

S S   38

248 Τῇ δὲ ἐχομένῃ τὸν καιρὸν λαβὼν ἐπηρώτα τὸν ἑξῆς Τίς ἐστιν
ἀμέλεια μεγίστη; πρὸς τοῦτ᾽ ἔφη Εἰ τέκνων ἀφροντίς τις εἴη, καὶ μὴ
κατὰ πάντα τρόπον ἀγαγεῖν <σπεύδοι>· εὐχόμεθα γὰρ ἀεὶ πρὸς τὸν
θεόν, οὐχ οὕτως περὶ ἑαυτῶν ὡς περὶ τῶν ἐγγόνων, ἵνα παρῇ πάντα
αὐτοῖς τὰ ἀγαθά. τὸ δὲ ἐπιδεῖσθαι παιδία σωφροσύνης μετασχεῖν, 5
249 θεοῦ δυνάμει τοῦτο γίνεται. Φήσας δὲ εὐλογεῖν ἄλλον
ἠρώτα Πῶς ἂν φιλόπατρις εἴη; Προτιθέμενος, εἶπεν, ὅτι καλὸν ἐν
ἰδίᾳ καὶ ζῆν καὶ τελευτᾶν. ἡ δὲ ξενία τοῖς μὲν πένησι καταφρόνησιν
ἐργάζεται, τοῖς δὲ πλουσίοις ὄνειδος, ὡς διὰ κακίαν ἐκπεπτωκόσιν.
εὐεργετῶν οὖν ἅπαντας, καθὼς συνεχῶς τοῦτ᾽ ἐπιτελεῖς, θεοῦ διδόντος 10
250 σοὶ πρὸς πάντας χάριν, φιλόπατρις φανήσῃ. Τούτου δὲ
ἀκούσας τοῦ κατὰ τὸ ἑξῆς ἐπυνθάνετο Πῶς <ἂν> ἁρμόσαι γυναικί;
<Γινώσκων> ὅτι μὲν θρασύ ἐστιν, ἔφη, τὸ θῆλυ γένος, καὶ δραστικὸν
ἐφ᾽ ὃ βούλεται πρᾶγμα, καὶ μεταπῖπτον εὐκόπως διὰ παραλογισμοῦ,
καὶ τῇ φύσει κατεσκεύασται ἀσθενές· δέον δ᾽ ἐστὶ κατὰ τὸ ὑγιὲς 15
251 χρῆσθαι, καὶ μὴ πρὸς ἔριν ἀντιπράσσειν. κατορθοῦται γὰρ βίος,
ὅταν ὁ κυβερνῶν εἰδῇ, πρὸς τίνα σκοπὸν δεῖ τὴν διέξοδον ποιεῖ-
252 σθαι. θεοῦ δ᾽ ἐπικλήσει καὶ βίος κυβερνᾶται κατὰ πάντα. Συν-
ανθομολογησάμενος δὲ τούτῳ τὸν ἑξῆς ἠρώτα Πῶς <ἂν> ἀναμάρτητος εἴη; ὁ δὲ ἔφησεν Ὡς ἅπαντα πράσσων καὶ μετὰ διαλογισμοῦ 20
καὶ μὴ πειθόμενος διαβολαῖς, ἀλλ᾽ αὐτὸς ὢν δοκιμαστὴς τῶν λεγομένων καὶ κρίσει κατευθύνων τὰ τῶν ἐντεύξεων καὶ διὰ κρίσεως
ἐπιτελῶν ταῦτα ἀναμάρτητος, ἔφησεν, ἂν εἴης, ὦ βασιλεῦ. τὸ δ᾽
ἐπινοεῖν ταῦτα καὶ ἐν τούτοις ἀναστρέφεσθαι θείας δυνάμεώς ἐστιν

2 αφροντις τις ειη P] αφροντις (αφροστις G) τις ει GIK αφροντις τις η
cett   3 σπευδοι] σπευδη B om cett (spat 5 vel 6 litt hab T)   4 εκγονων
A | om παρη P   5 επιδεσθαι conj Wend. | παιδια P teste Wend.] παι-
δειαν cett   7 προστιθεμενος B   8 ξενιτεια Wend. (ξενητια cod Mon)
9 εκπεπτωκασιν C   11 φανησει P | om δε P   12 κατα το (κατα τον H)]
om P | om αν codd | αρμωσει P   13 γινωσκων] om codd ex conj sup-
plevi | θρασυ—γενος] φησι θρασυ το θηλυ γενος εστι P | εστιν εφη TB^rubricator
(εστι B*)] εστι cett   14 om και P | μεταπιπτων GI | ευκολως P
15 και] καν K | κατεσκευασθη P -σθαι CZ   16 εριν] αιρειν GI ερριν PZ
17 ο κυβερνων K] om P κυβερνων cett | ηδη H ιδη KA | διεξοδον BCTZ]
εξοδον cett   18 κατα] και τα I | παν C | συναντομ. AGICZ   19 τουτω]
τουτον PCZ | om αν codd   20 εφησεν Ωs] εφη Σεμνως conj Mend. |
απαν H*A (απαν H^corr) | om και P | μετα partim sup ras I   23 om
εφησεν P

ἔργον.   Διαχυθεὶς δὲ τοῖς εἰρημένοις τὸν ἕτερον ἠρώτα 253
Πῶς ἂν ἐκτὸς θυμοῦ γένοιτο; πρὸς τοῦτ' εἶπε Γινώσκων ὅτι πάντων
ἐξουσίαν ἔχει, καί, εἰ χρήσαιτο θυμῷ, θάνατον ἐπιφέρει· ὅπερ ἀνω-
φελὲς καὶ ἀλγεινόν ἐστιν, εἰ τὸ ζῆν ἀφελεῖται πολλῶν, διὰ τὸ κύριον
5 εἶναι.   πάντων δ' ὑπηκόων ὄντων καὶ μηδενὸς ἐναντιουμένου, τίνος 254
χάριν θυμωθήσεται; γινώσκειν δὲ δεῖ, διότι θεὸς τὸν πάντα κόσμον
διοικεῖ μετ' εὐμενείας καὶ χωρὶς ὀργῆς ἀπάσης· τούτῳ δὲ κατακολουθεῖν ἀναγκαῖόν ἐστί σε, ἔφησεν, ὦ βασιλεῦ.   Καλῶς 255
δὲ ἀποκεκρίσθαι φήσας τοῦτον ἐπυνθάνετο τοῦ μετέπειτα Τί ἐστιν
10 εὐβουλία; Τὸ καλῶς ἅπαντα πράσσειν, ἀπεφήνατο, μετὰ διαλογισμοῦ, κατὰ τὴν βουλὴν παρατιθέντα καὶ <τὰ> βλαβερὰ τῶν κατὰ
τὸ ἐναντίον τοῦ λόγου διάστημα, ἵνα πρὸς ἕκαστον ἐπινοήσαντες
ὦμεν εὖ βεβουλευμένοι, καὶ τὸ προτεθὲν ἡμῖν ἐπιτελῆται. τὸ δ' αὖ
κράτιστον, θεοῦ δυναστείᾳ πᾶν βούλευμα <τελείωσιν ἕξει> σοι
15 τὴν εὐσέβειαν ἀσκοῦντι.   Κατωρθωκέναι δὲ καὶ τοῦτον εἰπὼν 256
ἄλλον ἠρώτα¶ Τί ἐστι φιλοσοφία; Τὸ καλῶς διαλογίζεσθαι πρὸς ¶ C
ἕκαστον τῶν συμβαινόντων, ἀπεφήνατο, καὶ μὴ ἐκφέρεσθαι ταῖς
ὁρμαῖς, ἀλλὰ τὰς βλάβας καταμελετᾶν τὰς ἐκ τῶν ἐπιθυμιῶν ἐκβαι-
νούσας, καὶ τὰ πρὸς τὸν καιρὸν πράσσειν δεόντως μετριοπαθῆ καθε-
20 στῶτα. ἵνα δ' ἐπίστασιν τούτων λαμβάνωμεν, θεραπεύειν δεῖ τὸν
θεόν.   Ἐπισημήνας δὲ καὶ τοῦτον ἕτερον ἠρώτα Πῶς ἂν 257
ἀποδοχῆς <ἐν ξενιτείᾳ> τυγχάνοι; Πᾶσιν ἴσος γινόμενος, ἔφη, καὶ
μᾶλλον ἥττων ἢ καθυπερέχων φαινόμενος πρὸς οὓς ξενιτεύει.
κοινῶς γὰρ ὁ θεὸς τὸ ταπεινούμενον προσδέχεται κατὰ φύσιν, καὶ τὸ
25 τῶν ἀνθρώπων γένος τοὺς ὑποτασσομένους φιλανθρωπεῖ.   Ἐπι- 258
μαρτυρήσας δὲ τούτοις ἄλλον ἠρώτα Πῶς <ἃ> ἂν κατασκευάσῃ καὶ

---

2 γινωσκειν I   3 εχεις A | χρησαι τω P | θυμου HKAGICZ | επι- HKAGIB
φερειν B   6 δε P] om cett | διοτι] οτι KBT   7 τουτο PZ | κατακολου- CPTZ
θειν]+σε P   8 σε] om P σοι Hᶜᵒʳʳ | om εφησεν ω K   10 πραττειν B |
μετα]+δε Z   11 τα κατα την ιδιαν βουλην παρατιθεντας B | om τα
codd | om των B   13 επιτελειται CPZ   14 τελειωσιν εξει σοι conj
Mend.] τεως συνεξει σοι BT ιν εξισοι Z τεως ιν (ινα C) εξισοι cett   15 κατ-
ορθωκεναι HKGICZ | ειπας HGICZ   17 εκαστα BPTZ   19 τα] τας B*
20 δειν B* δε (pro δεον?) K txt cett   21 επισημανας P (-μειν. Z*)
22 εν ξενιτ. Mend.] η ξενιτεια codd | τυγχανη PT -νει Z | γινομενος P] γενομ.
cett   23 ηττον GIZ* | ξενιτευη BT   24 om και B   25 γενος]+και
B | φιλοφρονει B   26 α αν] ἃν codd ἃν Wend.

38—2

μετὰ τοῦτο διαμένῃ; πρὸς τοῦτ᾽ εἶπεν Εἰ μεγάλα καὶ σεμνὰ ταῖς
ποιήσεσιν ἐπιτελοῖ, πρὸς τὸ φείσασθαι τοὺς θεωροῦντας διὰ τὴν
καλλονήν, καὶ μηθένα τῶν κατεργαζομένων τὰ τοιαῦτα παραπέμποι,
μηδὲ τοὺς ἄλλους ἀμισθὶ συντελεῖν ἀναγκάζοι τὰ πρὸς τὴν χρείαν.
259 διανοούμενος γὰρ ὡς θεὸς πολυωρεῖ τὸ τῶν ἀνθρώπων γένος, χορη- 5
γῶν αὐτοῖς καὶ ὑγείαν καὶ εὐαισθησίαν καὶ τὰ λοιπά, καὶ αὐτὸς
ἀκόλουθόν τι πράξει τῶν κακοπαθειῶν ἀποδιδοὺς τὴν ἀντάμειψιν.
260 τὰ γὰρ ἐκ δικαιοσύνης τελούμενα, ταῦτα καὶ διαμένει.   Εὖ
δὲ καὶ τοῦτον εἰρηκέναι φήσας τὸν δέκατον ἠρώτα Τί ἐστι σοφίας
καρπός; ὁ δὲ εἶπε Τὸ μὴ συνιστορεῖν ἑαυτῷ κακὸν πεπραχότι, τὸν 10
261 δὲ βίον ἐν ἀληθείᾳ διεξάγειν. ἐκ τούτων γὰρ κρατίστη χαρὰ καὶ
ψυχῆς εὐστάθειά σοι γίνεται, μέγιστε βασιλεῦ, καὶ ἐλπίδες ἐπὶ θεῷ
καλαὶ κρατοῦντί σοι τῆς ἀρχῆς εὐσεβῶς.   Ὡς δὲ συνήκουσαν
πάντες ἐπεφώνησαν σὺν κρότῳ πλείονι. καὶ μετὰ ταῦτα πρὸς τὸ
προπιεῖν ὁ βασιλεὺς [λαμβάνειν] ἐτράπη, χαρᾷ πεπληρωμένος.   15
262   Τῇ δ᾽ ἑξῆς καθὼς πρότερον ἡ διάταξις ἦν τῶν κατὰ τὸν πότον
ἐπιτελουμένων, καιροῦ δὲ γενομένου τοὺς ἀπολιπόντας ὁ βασιλεὺς
ἐπηρώτα. πρὸς τὸν πρῶτον δὲ ἔφη Πῶς ἂν μὴ τραπείη τις εἰς
263 ὑπερηφανίαν; ἀπεκρίθη δέ Εἰ τὴν ἰσότητα τηροῖ, καὶ παρ᾽ ἕκαστον
ἑαυτὸν ὑπομιμνήσκοι, καθὼς ἄνθρωπος ὢν ἀνθρώπων ἡγεῖται. καὶ 20
ὁ θεὸς τοὺς ὑπερηφάνους καθαιρεῖ, τοὺς δὲ ἐπιεικεῖς καὶ ταπεινοὺς
264 ὑψοῖ.   Παρακαλέσας δὲ αὐτὸν τὸν ἑξῆς ἐπηρώτα Τίσι δεῖ
συμβούλοις χρῆσθαι; τοῖς διὰ πολλῶν, ἔφη, πεπειραμένοις πραγμάτων καὶ τὴν εὔνοιαν συντηροῦσιν ἀκέραιον πρὸς αὐτὸν καὶ τῶν
τρόπων ὅσοι μετέχουσιν αὐτῷ. θεοῦ δὲ ἐπιφάνεια γίνεται πρὸς τὰ 25

HKAGIB   1 διαμενει Wend. | προς τουτ—επιτελοι (2)] om HKA   2 επιτελοιη P |
PTZ   τας θ. Z   3 μηδενα GI | παραπεμπει P   4 αμισθοι Z | αναγκαζει P
6 αυτος] αυτοις A   8 διαμενοι B   11 διεξαγειν P] διαγειν B διεξαγαγειν
cett | χαρα κρατιστη B   13 κρατουν Z*   15 πιειν AB | λαμβανειν (-νην
P)] hab codd omn   Fort cf πιειν δουναι etc vel προποσιν pro προπιειν legen-
dum | χαρας KBP χαρα τι Z   16 το δ εξης B | καθως]+και B | κατα των
τοπων Z   17 γινομενου KAGI   18 επηρωτα BPT] επερωτα cett | τρα-
πειη BT] τραποιη PZ τραπη K τραποι cett | om εις P   19 τηρει BPT
20 υπομιμνησκει BPT   21 ο] ως B   22 ηρωτα B επερωτα Z txt cett |
δει ex δε vel δη fact in B   23 εφη P] om cett post πραγματων ins
Zcorr   24 f τον τροπον H   25 θεου—αξιοις (1, pag 565)] om BPTZ

τοιαῦτα τοῖς ἀξίοις.   Ἐπαινέσας δὲ αὐτὸν ἄλλον ἠρώτα Τίς 265
ἐστι βασιλεῖ κτῆσις ἀναγκαιοτάτη; Τῶν ὑποτεταγμένων φιλαν-
θρωπία καὶ ἀγάπησις, ἀπεκρίνατο. διὰ γὰρ τούτων ἄλυτος εὐνοίας
δεσμὸς γίνεται. τὸ δὲ γίνεσθαι κατὰ προαίρεσιν ταῦτα ὁ θεὸς
5 ἐπιτελεῖ.   Κατεπαινέσας δὲ αὐτὸν ἑτέρου διεπυνθάνετο 266
Τί πέρας ἐστὶ λόγου; κἀκεῖνος δὲ ἔφησε Τὸ πεῖσαι τὸν ἀντιλέγοντα,
διὰ τῆς ὑποτεταγμένης τάξεως τὰς βλάβας ἐπιδεικνύντα· οὕτω γὰρ
λήψῃ τὸν ἀκροατὴν οὐκ ἀντικείμενος, συγχρώμενος δὲ ἐπαίνῳ πρὸς
τὸ πεῖσαι. θεοῦ δὲ ἐνεργείᾳ κατευθύνεται πειθώ.   Εὖ δὲ 267
10 λέγειν φήσας αὐτὸν ἕτερον ἠρώτα Πῶς ἄν, παμμιγῶν ὄχλων ὄντων
ἐν τῇ βασιλείᾳ, τούτοις <ἁρμόσαι>; Τὸ πρέπον ἑκάστῳ συνυποκρινό-
μενος, εἶπε, καθηγεμόνα λαμβάνων δικαιοσύνην· ὡς καὶ ποιεῖς θεοῦ
σοι διδόντος εὖ λογίζεσθαι.   Φιλοφρονηθεὶς δὲ τούτῳ πρὸς 268
τὸν ἕτερον εἶπεν Ἐπὶ τίσι δεῖ λυπεῖσθαι; πρὸς ταῦτα ἀπεκρίθη Τὰ
15 συμβαίνοντα τοῖς φίλοις ὅταν θεωρῶμεν πολυχρόνια καὶ ἀνέκφευκτα
γινόμενα. τελευτήσασι μὲν γὰρ καὶ κακῶν ἀπολελυμένοις οὐχ
ὑπογράφει λύπην ὁ λόγος· ἀλλὰ ἐφ᾽ ἑαυτοὺς ἀναφέροντες καὶ τὸ
πρὸς ἑαυτοὺς συμφέρον λυποῦνται πάντες ἄνθρωπου. τὸ δ᾽ ἐκφυγεῖν
πᾶν κακὸν θεοῦ δυνάμει γίνεται.   Ὡς ἔδει δὲ φήσας αὐτὸν 269
20 ἀποκρίνεσθαι πρὸς ἕτερον εἶπε Πῶς ἀδοξία γίνεται; ἐκεῖνος δὲ
ἔφησεν Ὅταν ὑπερηφανία καθηγῆται καὶ θράσος ἄληκτον, ἀτιμα-
σμὸς ἐπιφύεται καὶ δόξης ἀναίρεσις. θεὸς δὲ δόξης πάσης κυριεύει,
ῥέπων οὗ βούλεται.   Καὶ τούτῳ δ᾽ ἐπικυρώσας τὰ τῆς ἀπο- 270
κρίσεως τὸν ἑξῆς ἠρώτα Τίσι δεῖ πιστεύειν ἑαυτόν; Τοῖς διὰ τὴν
25 εὔνοιαν, εἶπε, συνοῦσί σοι, καὶ μὴ διὰ τὸν φόβον μηδὲ διὰ πολυ-

---

1 τίς] τι I   2 βασιλει] βασιλικη A | κτισις GI   4 ταυτα κατα HKAGIB
προαιρεσιν B   5 επιτελοι Z | ετερου] τον ετερον BTZ | επυνθανετο BZ PTZ
7 επιδεικνυντας HGIPZ υποδεικνυντας K   8 ληψει AP ληψ Zᵗˣᵗ (ληψαι
Zᵐᵍ) | αντικειμενον BPTZ   10 φησας] πεισας Zᵗˣᵗ ειπας Zᵐᵍ | ετερον] pr
τον K   11 αρμοσει B* (-ση Bᶜᵒʳʳ) αρμοση cett   13 τουτο PZᵗˣᵗ (τουτον
Zᵐᵍ fort recte cf 198) txt cett   14 λυπησθαι P   15 ανευφευκτα HGI
ανεκφευτα T ανεφευκτα Z ανεκφυκτα B txt KAP   17 f το προς εαυ-
τους] προς το εαυτοις P   19 δυναμεως BT   20 αποκρινασθαι
GIBᵛⁱᵈ Tᶠᵒʳᵗ ᵉˣ ᶜᵒʳʳ   21 καθηγειται GIA   22 αναιρεσις BPT] αιρεσις
cett | απασης P   23 τουτο Z | τα] τας GI   25 ειπε] εφη
BT

ὡρίαν, ἐπανάγουσι πάντα πρὸς τὸ κερδαίνειν. τὸ μὲν γὰρ ἀγαπήσεως σημεῖον, τὸ δὲ δυσνοίας καὶ καιροτηρησίας· ὃς γὰρ ἐπὶ
τὸ πλεονεκτεῖν <ὁρμᾶται> προδότης πέφυκε. σὺ δὲ πάντας εὐνόους
271 ἔχεις θεοῦ σοι καλὴν βουλὴν διδόντος. Σοφῶς δὲ αὐτὸν
εἰπὼν ἀποκεκρίσθαι, ἑτέρῳ εἶπε Τί βασιλείαν διατηρεῖ; πρὸς τοῦτ' 5
ἔφη Μέριμνα καὶ φροντίς, ὡς οὐδὲν κακουργηθήσεται διὰ τῶν ἀπο-
τεταγμένων εἰς τοὺς ὄχλους ταῖς χρείαις· καθὼς σὺ τοῦτο πράσσεις
272 θεοῦ σοι τὴν σεμνὴν ἐπίνοιαν διδόντος. Θαρσύνας δὲ τοῦτον
ἕτερον ἐπηρώτα Τί διαφυλάσσει χάριτα καὶ τιμήν; ὁ δὲ εἶπεν
'Αρετή. καλῶν γὰρ ἔργων ἐστὶν ἐπιτέλεια, τὸ δὲ κακὸν ἀποτρίβε- 10
ται· καθὼς σὺ διατηρεῖς τὴν πρὸς ἅπαντας καλοκἀγαθίαν παρὰ
273 θεοῦ δῶρον τοῦτ' ἔχων. Κεχαρισμένως δὲ καὶ τοῦτον ἀποδεξάμενος τὸν ἑνδέκατον ἐπηρώτα (διὰ τὸ δύο πλεονάζειν τῶν ἑβδομήκοντα) Πῶς ἂν κατὰ ψυχὴν καὶ ἐν τοῖς πολέμοις εἰρηνικῶς ἔχοι;
ὁ δὲ ἀπεφήνατο Διαλαμβάνων ὅτι κακὸν οὐδὲν εἴργασται τῶν ὑπο- 15
τεταγμένων οὐθενί, πάντες δὲ ἀγωνιοῦνται περὶ τῶν εὐεργετημά-
των, εἰδότες, κἂν ἐκ τοῦ ζῆν ἀποτρέχωσιν, ἐπιμελητήν σε τῶν
274 βίων. οὐ γὰρ διαλείπεις ἐπανορθῶν ἅπαντας τοῦ θεοῦ σοι καλο-
φροσύνην δεδωκότος. Ἐπισημήνας δὲ κρότῳ πάντας αὐτοὺς
ἀπεδέξατο φιλοφρονούμενος, καὶ προπίνων ἑκάστῳ πλεῖόν τι πρὸς 20
τὸ τερφθῆναι <ἐτράπη>, μετ' εὐφροσύνης τοῖς ἀνδράσι συνὼν καὶ
χαρᾶς πλείονος.

275 Τῇ ἑβδόμῃ δὲ τῶν ἡμερῶν, πλείονος παρασκευῆς γενομένης,
προσπαραγινομένων πλειόνων ἑτέρων ἀπὸ τῶν πόλεων (ἦσαν γὰρ

HKAGIB 1 επαναγουσι B] επαναγαγουσι Z^corr επαναγων P επαναγοντας cett |
PTZ   παντας P   3 το] τω B* (το B^corr) T (ex το fact vid) | ορμαται bene Mend.]
ορα BT^corr οραται cett   4 διδουντος Z* | σοφως BT] σαφως cett   5 ειπας
GIZ | διατηροι G   8 θρασυνας KB   9 διαφυλασση I (-λαττει B)
10 καλον γαρ εργον K | εστιν—διατηρεις την (11) om HKA   12 κεχαρισ-
μενος AZ* κεχαριτωμενως I   13 των B] τους cett | εβδομηκοντα] ο KGIBT.
Scholium hab τον ενδεκατον δε ερωτα δια το δυο πλεοναζειν των εβδομηκοντα
οπισθεν γαρ ανα δεκα ηρωτα B^mg (rubricator)   16 ουθενι KPT] ουδενι B ουθεν
IIAGI | δε] γαρ B*   17 απορεχουσιν GIH (-σι) Z*^vid   20 προπινων
B] προσπινων cett   21 ετραπη ins Mend. | τ. ανδ. συν. μετ ευφ. Z   23 δε
BPT] om cett   24 προσπαραγενομενων ετ. πλειονων K | om ησαν—πρεσ-
βεις (1, pag 567) BPTZ

ἱκανοὶ πρέσβεις), ἐπηρώτησεν ὁ βασιλεὺς καιροῦ γενομένου τὸν
πρωτεύοντα τῶν ἀπολιπόντων τῆς ἐρωτήσεως Πῶς ἂν ἀπαραλό-
γιστος <εἴη>; ἐκεῖνος δὲ ἔφη Δοκιμάζων καὶ τὸν λέγοντα καὶ τὸ 276
λεγόμενον καὶ περὶ τίνος λέγει, καὶ ἐν πλείονι χρόνῳ τὰ αὐτὰ δι'
5 ἑτέρων τρόπων ἐπερωτῶν. τὸ δὲ νοῦν ἔχειν ὀξὺν καὶ δύνασθαι
κρίνειν ἕκαστα θεοῦ δώρημα καλόν ἐστιν· ὡς σὺ τοῦτο κέκτησαι,
βασιλεῦ. Κρότῳ δὲ ἐπισημηνάμενος ὁ βασιλεὺς ἕτερον 277 § C
ἐπηρώτα Διὰ τί τὴν ἀρετὴν οὐ παραδέχονται τῶν ἀνθρώπων
οἱ πλείονες; Ὅτι φυσικῶς ἅπαντες, εἶπεν, ἀκρατεῖς καὶ ἐπὶ τὰς
10 ἡδονὰς τρεπόμενοι γεγόνασιν· ὧν χάριν ἀδικία πέφυκε καὶ τὸ τῆς
πλεονεξίας χύμα. τὸ δὲ τῆς ἀρετῆς κατάστημα κωλύει τοὺς ἐπιφε- 278
ρομένους ἐπὶ τὴν ἡδονοκρασίαν, ἐγκράτειαν δὲ κελεύει καὶ δικαιοσύνην προτιμᾶν. ὁ δὲ θεὸς πάντων ἡγεῖται τούτων. Εὖ δὲ 279
ἀποκεκρίσθαι τοῦτον εἰπὼν ὁ βασιλεὺς ἠρώτα Τίσι δεῖ κατακολου-
15 θεῖν τοὺς βασιλεῖς; ὁ δὲ ἔφη Τοῖς νόμοις, ἵνα δικαιοπραγοῦντες
ἀνακτῶνται τοὺς βίους τῶν ἀνθρώπων· καθὼς σὺ τοῦτο πράσσων
ἀένναον μνήμην καταβέβλησαι σεαυτοῦ, θείῳ προστάγματι κατα-
κολουθῶν. Εἰπὼν δὲ καὶ τοῦτον καλῶς λέγειν τὸν ἐχόμενον 280
ἠρώτα Τίνας δεῖ καθιστάνειν στρατηγούς; ὃς δὲ εἶπεν Ὅσοι
20 μισοπονηρίαν ἔχουσι, καὶ τὴν ἀγωγὴν αὐτοῦ μιμούμενοι, πρὸς τὸ
διὰ παντὸς εὐδοξίαν ἔχειν αὐτούς, τὰ δίκαια πράσσουσι· καθὼς σὺ
τοῦτο ἐπιτελεῖς, εἶπε, μέγιστε βασιλεῦ, θεοῦ σοι στέφανον δικαιοσύνης δεδωκότος. Ἀποδεξάμενος δὲ αὐτὸν μετὰ φωνῆς ἐπὶ τὸν 281
ἐχόμενον ἐπιβλέψας εἶπε Τίνας δεῖ καθιστάνειν ἐπὶ τῶν δυνάμεων
25 ἄρχοντας; ὁ δὲ ἀπεφήνατο Τοὺς ἀνδρείᾳ διαφέροντας καὶ δικαιοσύνῃ, καὶ περὶ πολλοῦ ποιουμένους τὸ σώζειν τοὺς ἄνδρας ἢ τὸ

---

1 επερωτησεν Z | γινομενου HAIPZ | τον] των Z*   **2** απολειποντων P HKAGI
3 ειη ex corr] η codd omn | δοκιμαζοντα Z | το] τον codd omn   **4** χρονων BCPTZ
G   **5** επερωτων τροπων A   **6** ως] ο HKA | τουτο bis scr T   **8** επε-
ρωτα Z | om ου C | των ανθρωπων BPT] τινες των ανθρωπων cett   **9** ειπεν]
ωσπερ BT ειπερ CZ*   **11** διαστημα CPZ (κατα- sup ras T)   **12** και
δικ. κελευει B   **14** αποκρινασθαι BPT -εσθαι Z | ειπας GICZ | ηρωτα]
αλλον ηρ. H ηρ. ετερον BT ηρ. τον εξης P txt KAGIC τον μετ αυτον ηρ.
edd pr   **18** ειπας GIC ειπε Z   **21** αυτοις H   **22** ειπε μεγιστε BT]
om P ειπεν ο (sic) C ειπε (-πεν Z) cett | δικαιοσυνην C   **26** το 2°] τω
ABCT (fort ex το T)

¶ P νικᾷν, τῷ θράσει <παραβάλλοντας> τὸ ζῆν. ὥς⸌ γὰρ ὁ θεὸς εὖ
ἐργάζεται πᾶσι, καὶ σὺ τοῦτον μιμούμενος εὐεργετεῖς τοὺς ὑπὸ
282 σεαυτόν.   Ὁ δὲ ἀποκεκρίσθαι φήσας αὐτὸν εὖ, ἄλλον ἠρώτα
Τίνα θαυμάζειν ἄξιόν ἐστιν ἄνθρωπον; ὁ δὲ ἔφη Τὸν κεχορηγημένον
δόξῃ καὶ πλούτῳ καὶ δυνάμει, καὶ ψυχὴν ἴσον πᾶσιν ὄντα· καθὼς 5
σὺ τοῦτο ποιῶν ἀξιοθαύμαστος εἶ τοῦ θεοῦ σοι διδόντος εἰς ταῦτα
283 τὴν ἐπιμέλειαν.   Ἐπιφωνήσας δὲ καὶ τούτῳ πρὸς τὸν ἕτερον
εἶπεν Ἐν τίσι δεῖ πράγμασι τοὺς βασιλεῖς τὸν πλείω χρόνον διά-
γειν; ὁ δὲ εἶπεν Ἐν ταῖς ἀναγνώσεσι καὶ ἐν ταῖς τῶν πορειῶν
ἀπογραφαῖς διατρίβειν, ὅσαι πρὸς τὰς βασιλείας ἀναγεγραμμέναι 10
τυγχάνουσι πρὸς ἐπανόρθωσιν καὶ διαμονὴν ἀνθρώπων. ὃ σὺ
πράσσων ἀνέφικτον ἄλλοις δόξαν κέκτησαι θεοῦ σοι τὰ βουλή-
284 ματα συντελοῦντος.   Ἐνεργῶς δὲ καὶ τοῦτον προσειπὼν
ἕτερον ἠρώτα Τίνας δεῖ ποιεῖσθαι τὰς διαγωγὰς ἐν ταῖς ἀνέσεσι
καὶ ῥαθυμίαις; ὁ δὲ ἔφη Θεωρεῖν ὅσα <παίζεται> μετὰ περι- 15
στολῆς καὶ πρὸ ὀφθαλμῶν τιθέναι τὰ τοῦ βίου μετ᾽ εὐσχημο-
σύνης καὶ καταστολῆς γινόμενα <βίῳ συμφέρον καὶ καθῆκον>·
285 ἔνεστι γὰρ καὶ ἐν τούτοις ἐπισκευή τις. πολλάκις γὰρ καὶ ἐκ τῶν
ἐλαχίστων αἱρετόν τι δείκνυται. σὺ δὲ πᾶσαν ἠσκηκὼς καταστολὴν
διὰ τῶν ἐνεργειῶν φιλοσοφεῖς διὰ καλοκἀγαθίαν ὑπὸ θεοῦ τιμώ- 20
286 μενος.   Εὐαρεστήσας δὲ τοῖς προειρημένοις πρὸς τὸν ἔνατον
εἶπε Πῶς δεῖ διὰ τῶν συμποσίων διεξάγειν; ὁ δὲ ἔφησε Παραλαμ-
βάνοντα τοὺς φιλομαθεῖς καὶ δυναμένους ὑπομιμνήσκειν τὰ <χρήσιμα
τῇ βασιλείᾳ> καὶ τοῖς τῶν ἀρχομένων βίοις—ἐμμελέστερον ἢ μου-
287 σικώτερον οὐκ ἂν εὕροις τι τούτων· οὗτοι γὰρ θεοφιλεῖς εἰσι πρὸς τὰ 25
κάλλιστα πεπαιδευκότες τὰς διανοίας—καθὼς καὶ σὺ τοῦτο πράσσεις,
288 ὡς ἂν ὑπὸ θεοῦ σοι κατευθυνομένων ἁπάντων.   Διαχυθεὶς

1 τω] τα P | παραβαλλοντας conj Schmidt] περιβαλλοντας codd
2 πασι] παλιν B   5 ψυχηι πασιν ισον H   7 τουτο Z   8 δει] δε Z |
πλειονα A (πλειωι GI)   9 om εν 2° BT   12 πρασσων] πρασσων (-σως
K*) ως K | ανεφικτον Z^mg] ουκ εφικτον K εφικτον cett   13 τελουντος H
συντελουμενος CZ | εναργως B | τουτω AB | προσειπας GICZ   14 ποιειν
K   15 om ο δε εφη K | οσα παιζεται (corr Schmidt)] οσα πλιζεται
HGICTZ* οσα οπλιζεται KAZ^mg ος οπλ. B   16 τιθεμενος B   17 βιω—
καθηκον bene Wend.] βιοι (βιοις K) σωφρονων και κατεχων codd   21 ενα-
τον HB*] εννατον cett   22 om δει C   23 f χρησιμα τη βασιλεια Mend.]
χρηματα της βασιλειας codd   24 τους των αρχ. βιους B   27 σου Z^txt

δὲ ἐπὶ τοῖς εἰρημένοις, ἐπυνθάνετο τοῦ μετέπειτα Τί κάλλιστόν ἐστι
τοῖς ὄχλοις, ἐξ ἰδιώτου βασιλέα κατασταθῆναι <ἐπ'> αὐτῶν, ἢ ἐκ
βασιλέως βασιλέα; ἐκεῖνος δὲ ἔφη Τὸ ἄοιστον τῇ φύσει. καὶ γὰρ 289
ἐκ βασιλέων βασιλεῖς γινόμενοι πρὸς τοὺς ὑποτεταγμένους ἀνήμε-
5 ροί τε καὶ σκληροὶ καθίστανται· πολλῷ δὲ μᾶλλον καί τινες τῶν
ἰδιωτῶν καὶ κακῶν πεπειραμένοι καὶ πενίας μετεσχηκότες ἄρξαντες
ὄχλων χαλεπώτεροι τῶν ἀνοσίων τυράννων ἐξέβησαν. ἀλλὰ ὡς 290
προεῖπον, ἦθος χρηστὸν καὶ παιδείας κεκοινωνηκὸς δυνατὸν ἄρχειν
ἐστί· καθὼς σὺ βασιλεὺς μέγας ὑπάρχεις, οὐ τοσοῦτον τῇ δόξῃ τῆς
10 ἀρχῆς καὶ πλούτῳ προσχών, ὅσον ἐπιεικείᾳ καὶ φιλανθρωπίᾳ πάντας
ἀνθρώπους ὑπερῆρκας τοῦ θεοῦ σοι δεδωρημένου ταῦτα. Ἐπὶ 291
πλείονα χρόνον καὶ τοῦτον ἐπαινέσας τὸν ἐπὶ πᾶσιν ἠρώτα Τί
μέγιστόν ἐστι βασιλείας; πρὸς τοῦτο εἶπε Τὸ διὰ παντὸς ἐν εἰρήνῃ
καθεστάναι τοὺς ὑποτεταγμένους, καὶ κομίζεσθαι τὸ δίκαιον ταχέως
15 ἐν ταῖς διακρίσεσι. ταῦτα δὲ γίνεται διὰ τὸν ἡγούμενον, ὅταν 292
μισοπόνηρος ᾖ καὶ φιλάγαθος καὶ περὶ πολλοῦ ποιούμενος ψυχὴν
ἀνθρώπου σώζειν· καθὼς καὶ σὺ μέγιστον κακὸν ἥγησαι τὴν
ἀδικίαν, δικαίως δὲ πάντα κυβερνῶν ἀέναον τὴν περὶ σεαυτὸν δόξαν
κατεσκεύασας, τοῦ θεοῦ σοι διδόντος ἔχειν ἁγνὴν καὶ ἀμιγῆ παντὸς
20 κακοῦ τὴν διάνοιαν. Καταλήξαντος δὲ τούτου κατερράγη 293
κρότος μετὰ φωνῆς καὶ χαρᾶς ἐπὶ πλείονα χρόνον. ὡς δὲ ἐπαύσατο,
ὁ βασιλεὺς λαβὼν ποτήριον ἐπεχέατο καὶ τῶν παρόντων ἁπάντων
καὶ τῶν εἰρημένων λόγων. §ἐπὶ πᾶσι δὲ εἶπε Τὰ μέγιστά μοι §Jos
γέγονεν ἀγαθὰ παραγενηθέντων ὑμῶν· πολλὰ γὰρ ὠφέλημαι, κατα- 294
25 βεβλημένων ὑμῶν διδαχὴν ἐμοὶ πρὸς τὸ βασιλεύειν. ἑκάστῳ
δὲ τρία τάλαντα προσέταξεν ἀργυρίου δοθῆναι καὶ τὸν ὑποκαταστή-

1 om δε K   2 επ Mend.] υπ codd   3 τον Schmidt | αρεστον HKAGIB
HKAGI   4 εκ] pr οι K | βασιλεων] βασιλεως B | om βασιλεις HA | γενο-   CTZ Jos
μενοι K   5 om δε Z | των ιδιωτων τινες BT   6 ιδιωτικων Z   8 παι-
δειας KB (πεδιας B*) TZ (ex -ειαν)] παιδεια (-δια C) cett   9 βασιλευ T* vid
11 υπερηρας KB* | επι πλειονα χρονον] cum praecedd conj Schmidt Wend.
(sic HKA). Cf autem §§ 220, 293   13 τουτο GICT*] τουτον HKABTcorr
14 νομιζεσθαι C   17 κακον B] om cett   18 σεαυτου CBvid   19 κατα-
σκευασας HI | om εχειν Z | αμιγην C   22 λαβων cum cod M restitui]
λαλων codd cett   23 τον ειρημενον λογον K | λογον Zmg | μεγιστα] παμ-
μεγιστα A   24 παραγεγενημενων B | ωφελημα GI | καταβεβληκοτων B

¶ Jos σοντα παῖδα.¶ συνεπιφωνησάντων δὲ πάντων, χαρᾶς ἐπληρώθη τὸ
συμπόσιον, ἀδιαλείπτως τοῦ βασιλέως εἰς εὐφροσύνην τραπέντος.

295   Ἐγὼ δὲ <εἰ πεπλεόνακα,> τούτοις, ὦ Φιλόκρατες, συγγνώμην
ἔχειν. τεθαυμακὼς γὰρ τοὺς ἄνδρας ὑπὲρ τὸ δέον, ὡς ἐκ τοῦ καιροῦ τὰς
296 ἀποκρίσεις ἐποιοῦντο πολλοῦ χρόνου δεομένας, καὶ τοῦ μὲν ἐρωτῶντος 5
μεμεριμνηκότος ἕκαστα, τῶν δὲ ἀποκρινομένων καταλλήλως ἐχόντων
τὰ πρὸς τὰς ἐρωτήσεις, ἄξιοι θαυμασμοῦ κατεφαίνοντό μοι καὶ τοῖς
παροῦσι, μάλιστα δὲ τοῖς φιλοσόφοις. οἴομαι δὲ καὶ πᾶσι τοῖς
297 παραληψομένοις τὴν ἀναγραφὴν ἄπιστον φανεῖται. ψεύσασθαι μὲν
οὖν οὐ καθῆκόν ἐστι περὶ τῶν ἀναγραφομένων· εἰ δὲ καί τι παρα- 10
βαίην, οὐχ ὅσιον ἐν τούτοις· ἀλλ᾽, ὡς γέγονεν, οὕτως διασαφοῦμεν
ἀφοσιούμενοι πᾶν ἁμάρτημα. διόπερ ἐπειράθην ἀποδεξάμενος αὐτῶν
τὴν τοῦ λόγου δύναμιν παρὰ τῶν ἀναγραφομένων ἕκαστα τῶν
γινομένων ἔν τε τοῖς χρηματισμοῖς τοῦ βασιλέως καὶ ταῖς συμ-
298 ποσίαις μεταλαβεῖν. ἔθος γάρ ἐστι, καθὼς καὶ σὺ γινώσκεις, ἀφ᾽ 15
ἧς ἂν [ἡμέρας] ὁ βασιλεὺς ἄρξηται χρηματίζειν, μέχρις οὗ κατα-
κοιμηθῇ, πάντα ἀναγράφεσθαι τὰ λεγόμενα καὶ πρασσόμενα, καλῶς
299 γινομένου καὶ συμφερόντως. τῇ γὰρ ἐπιούσῃ τὰ τῇ πρότερον
πεπραγμένα καὶ λελαλημένα πρὸ τοῦ χρηματισμοῦ παραναγινώ-
σκεται, καί, εἴ τι μὴ δεόντως γέγονε, διορθώσεως τυγχάνει τὸ 20
300 πεπραγμένον. πάντ᾽ οὖν ἀκριβῶς <παρὰ τῶν> ἀναγεγραμμένων, ὡς
ἐλέχθη, μεταλαβόντες κατακεχωρίκαμεν, εἰδότες ἣν ἔχεις φιλομάθειαν εἰς τὰ χρήσιμα.

§ Jos 301   ᾽Μετὰ δὲ τρεῖς ἡμέρας ὁ Δημήτριος παραλαβὼν αὐτούς, καὶ
διελθὼν τὸ τῶν ἑπτὰ σταδίων ἀνάχωμα τῆς θαλάσσης πρὸς τὴν 25
νῆσον, καὶ διαβὰς τὴν γέφυραν, καὶ προσελθὼν ὡς ἐπὶ τὰ βόρεια

HKAGIB
CTZ Jos

3 ει πεπλεονακα (cf Diod I. 90. 4) bene Mend.] ειτα πλειονα και codd
6 καταλληλως BT] αλληλως cett   7 τα] τας C   8 δε 2°]+ως B
9 απιστα K   12 αφοσιωμενοι HGICZ (αφωσιωμενοι A)   15 om και I
16 om αν B | ημερας codd] omittendum vid ημερας ωρας Wend. ωρας Mend. |
αρξεται B   18 γενομενου I | τη 2°] om H   19 λαλημενα Z | παραναγιν.
BT] παραγινωσκεται cett   20 δεοντος CZ | γεγονε BT] γεγονος (-νως GI)
cett | om το πεπραγμενον BT   21 παντ] παντες C | παρα των Wend.]
παντων codd | παντ—μεταλαβοντες (22)] παντων ουν ακριβως των αναγεγραμ-
μενων μεταλαβοντες παντες BT   22 ελεγχθη Z | κεχωρηκαμεν CZ κατα-
κεχωρηκαμεν codd cett   26 διαβας προς την γεφυραν Jos | προελθων Jos |
om ως Z

μέρη, συνέδριον ποιησάμενος εἰς κατεσκευασμένον οἶκον παρὰ τὴν
ἠϊόνα, διαπρεπῶς ἔχοντα καὶ πολλῆς ἡσυχίας ἔφεδρον, παρεκάλει
τοὺς ἄνδρας τὰ τῆς ἑρμηνείας ἐπιτελεῖν, παρόντων ὅσα πρὸς τὴν
χρείαν ἔδει καλῶς. οἱ δὲ ἐπετέλουν ἕκαστα σύμφωνα ποιοῦντες 302
5 πρὸς ἑαυτοὺς ταῖς ἀντιβολαῖς· τὸ δὲ ἐκ τῆς συμφωνίας γινόμενον
πρεπόντως ἀναγραφῆς οὕτως ἐτύγχανε παρὰ τοῦ Δημητρίου. καὶ 303
μέχρι μὲν ὥρας ἐνάτης τὰ τῆς συνεδρείας ἐγίνετο· μετὰ δὲ ταῦτα
περὶ τὴν τοῦ σώματος θεραπείαν ἀπελύοντο γίνεσθαι, χορηγουμένων
αὐτοῖς δαψιλῶς ὧν προῃροῦντο πάντων. ἐκτὸς δὲ καὶ καθ᾽ ἡμέραν, 304
10 ὅσα βασιλεῖ παρεσκευάζετο, καὶ τούτοις ὁ Δωρόθεος ἐπετέλει·
προστεταγμένον γὰρ ἦν αὐτῷ διὰ τοῦ βασιλέως. ἅμα δὲ τῇ πρωΐᾳ
παρεγίνοντο εἰς τὴν αὐλὴν καθ᾽ ἡμέραν, καὶ ποιησάμενοι τὸν
ἀσπασμὸν τοῦ βασιλέως, ἀπελύοντο πρὸς τὸν ἑαυτῶν τόπον. ὡς δὲ 305
ἔθος ἐστὶ πᾶσι τοῖς Ἰουδαίοις, <ἀπονιψάμενοι> τῇ θαλάσσῃ τὰς
15 χεῖρας, ὡς ἂν εὔξωνται πρὸς τὸν θεόν, ἐτρέποντο πρὸς τὴν ἀνάγνωσιν
καὶ τὴν ἑκάστου διασάφησιν.¶ Ἐπηρώτησα δὲ καὶ τοῦτο 306 ¶ Jos
Τίνος χάριν ἀπονιζόμενοι τὰς χεῖρας τὸ τηνικαῦτα εὔχονται; διεσά-
φουν δέ, ὅτι μαρτύριόν ἐστι τοῦ μηδὲν εἰργάσθαι κακόν· πᾶσα γὰρ
ἐνέργεια διὰ τῶν χειρῶν γίνεται· καλῶς καὶ ὁσίως μεταφέροντες ἐπὶ
20 τὴν δικαιοσύνην καὶ τὴν ἀλήθειαν πάντα. καθὼς δὲ προειρήκαμεν, 307
οὕτως καθ᾽ ἑκάστην εἰς τὸν τόπον, ἔχοντα τερπνότητα διὰ τὴν
ἡσυχίαν καὶ καταύγειαν, συναγόμενοι τὸ προκείμενον ἐπετέλουν.
συνέτυχε δὲ οὕτως, ὥστε ἐν ἡμέραις ἑβδομήκοντα δυσὶ τελειωθῆναι
τὰ τῆς μεταγραφῆς, οἱονεὶ κατὰ πρόθεσίν τινα τοῦ τοιούτου γεγενη-
25 μένου. §Τελείωσιν δὲ ὅτε ἔλαβε, συναγαγὼν ὁ Δημήτριος 308 § Jos

---

1 κατασκευασμενον CZ   2 ηιον (ηιων Z) αδιαπρεπως H*GICZ ηιον HKAGIB
διαπρεπως A   3 τα της] τας BTZ   5 ταις αντιβολαις part sup ras B | CTZ Jos
γενομενον BCTZ   7 ενατης HC] θ Κ εννατης cett | συνεδριας BCTZ
9 αυτοις KBT Jos] αυτων cett   10 Δοροθεος C   13 προς] εις BT (sed B
primum aliud scripsit quod postea erasit) | τον εαυτων KBT] εαυτων codd
cett τον αυτον Jos   14 απονιψαμενους AIC^{vid}Z απονιψαμενη B* -μενοις
cett   15 ευξωνται Κ] ηυξαντο (ευξ- GI) cett   16 επηρωτησα CT]
επηρωτα B επερωτησα cett | τουτον G   18 μηθεν Κ   20 ειρηκαμεν I
21 τερπνοτητα BTZ (-νωτ.)] τερπω τινα HKΛ*GIC (τερπωλην τινα Μ τερ-
ποτητα A^{corr vid})   23 εβδομηκοντα συν δυσιν Κ εβδ. και δυσιν Jos εβδομηκοντα δυο Τ ο̅β̅ BZ   24 γραφης I   25 οτε δε ελαβε τελειωσιν B

τὸ πλῆθος τῶν Ἰουδαίων εἰς τὸν τόπον, οὗ καὶ τὰ τῆς ἑρμηνείας
ἐτελέσθη, παρανέγνω πᾶσι, παρόντων καὶ τῶν διερμηνευσάντων, οἵτινες μεγάλης ἀποδοχῆς καὶ παρὰ τοῦ πλήθους ἔτυχον, ὡς ἂν
309 μεγάλων ἀγαθῶν παραίτιοι γεγονότες. ὡσαύτως δὲ καὶ τὸν
Δημήτριον ἀποδεξάμενοι παρεκάλεσαν μεταδοῦναι τοῖς ἡγουμένοις 5
§ Eus 310 αὐτῶν, μεταγράψαντα τὸν πάντα νόμον. ⁵καθὼς δὲ ἀνεγνώσθη τὰ
τεύχη, στάντες οἱ ἱερεῖς καὶ τῶν ἑρμηνέων οἱ πρεσβύτεροι καὶ
τῶν ἀπὸ τοῦ πολιτεύματος οἵ τε ἡγούμενοι τοῦ πλήθους εἶπον
Ἐπεὶ καλῶς καὶ ὁσίως διηρμήνευται καὶ κατὰ πᾶν ἠκριβωμένως,
καλῶς ἔχον ἐστίν, ἵνα διαμείνῃ ταῦθ᾽ οὕτως ἔχοντα, καὶ μὴ γένηται 10
311 μηδεμία διασκευή.   πάντων δ᾽ ἐπιφωνησάντων τοῖς εἰρημένοις, ἐκέλευσαν διαράσασθαι, καθὼς ἔθος αὐτοῖς ἐστιν, εἴ τις
διασκευάσει προστιθεὶς ἢ μεταφέρων τι τὸ σύνολον τῶν γεγραμμένων ἢ ποιούμενος ἀφαίρεσιν, καλῶς τοῦτο πράσσοντες, ἵνα διὰ
παντὸς ἀέννα καὶ μένοντα φυλάσσηται.   15
312   Προσφωνηθέντων δὲ καὶ τούτων τῷ βασιλεῖ μεγάλως ἐχάρη·
τὴν γὰρ πρόθεσιν, ἣν εἶχεν, ἀσφαλῶς ἔδοξε τετελειῶσθαι. παραν-
εγνώσθη δὲ αὐτῷ καὶ πάντα, καὶ λίαν ἐξεθαύμασε τὴν τοῦ
νομοθέτου διάνοιαν. καὶ πρὸς τὸν Δημήτριον εἶπε Πῶς τηλικούτων
συντετελεσμένων οὐδεὶς ἐπεβάλετο τῶν ἱστορικῶν ἢ ποιητῶν ἐπι- 20
313 μνησθῆναι; ἐκεῖνος δὲ ἔφη Διὰ τὸ σεμνὴν εἶναι τὴν νομοθεσίαν
καὶ διὰ θεοῦ γεγονέναι· καὶ τῶν ἐπιβαλλομένων τινὲς ὑπὸ τοῦ θεοῦ
314 πληγέντες τῆς ἐπιβολῆς ἀπέστησαν. καὶ γὰρ ἔφησεν ἀκηκοέναι
Θεοπόμπου, διότι μέλλων τινὰ τῶν προηρμηνευμένων ἐπισφα-

1 και τα] κατα Z*   6 om δε Eusᵒ | τα] pr ταυτα Eusᵒ   9 om καλως
Eusⁱ | και 2ᵒ] om I | ακριβως Eus   10 διαμενη Eusⁱ (διαμενει Eusᵒ vid) txt
ex Jos confirmatur (διαμειναι) | om μη Eusⁱ | γινηται Eusⁱ   12 εκελευσαν
Jos Eusᵉᵈᵈ] εκελευσε (-σεν Eus) Ar codd Eusⁱᵒ | επαρασθαι Eus | καθω I
καθο A | εστιν αυτοις Eusᵒ   13 μεταφερον GI | om τι Eusᵒ   14 πρασ-
σοντος HKA txt codd cett Jos (πραττ.) Eus   15 και μενοντα] μενοντα
Eusᵒ μενοντες Eusⁱ vid   17 παρανεγνωσθη KBCT Eus] παρεγνωσθη HAGI
19 τηλικουτων]+πραγματων fort recte Eus   20 επεβαλετο ΠKBCT Eus]
επελαβετο AGI | η] ουδε Eus | ποιητων B Eus Jos] ποιητικως HK ποιητικων
cett   22 επιβαλομενων Eusⁱ | om του Eusᵒ   23 επιβουλης H* vid KAGI |
εφησαν Eusᵒ   24 Θεοπεμπτου Ar codd txt Jos Eus | προερμηνευμενων
HKGIC

λέστερον ἐκ τοῦ νόμου προσιστορεῖν ταραχὴν λάβοι τῆς διανοίας
πλεῖον ἡμερῶν τριάκοντα· κατὰ δὲ τὴν ἄνεσιν ἐξιλάσκεσθαι τὸν
θεόν, σαφὲς αὐτῷ γενέσθαι, τίνος χάριν τὸ συμβαῖνόν ἐστι. δι' 315
ὀνείρου δὲ σημανθέντος, ὅτι τὰ θεῖα βούλεται περιεργασάμενος εἰς
5 κοινοὺς ἀνθρώπους ἐκφέρειν, ἀποσχόμενον δὲ οὕτως ἀποκαταστῆναι.
καὶ παρὰ Θεοδέκτου δὲ τοῦ τῶν τραγῳδιῶν ποιητοῦ μετέλαβον ἐγώ, 316
διότι παραφέρειν μέλλοντός τι τῶν ἀναγεγραμμένων ἐν τῇ βίβλῳ
πρός τι δρᾶμα τὰς ὄψεις ἀπεγλαυκώθη· καὶ λαβὼν ὑπόνοιαν, ὅτι
διὰ τοῦτ' αὐτῷ τὸ σύμπτωμα γέγονεν, ἐξιλασάμενος τὸν θεὸν ἐν
10 πολλαῖς ἡμέραις ἀποκατέστη. Μεταλαβὼν δὲ ὁ βασιλεύς, 317
καθὼς προεῖπον, περὶ τούτων τὰ παρὰ τοῦ Δημητρίου, προσκυνήσας
ἐκέλευσε μεγάλην ἐπιμέλειαν ποιεῖσθαι τῶν βιβλίων καὶ συντηρεῖν
ἁγνῶς.¶ παρακαλέσας δὲ καὶ τοὺς ἑρμηνεῖς, ἵνα παραγίνωνται 318 ¶ Eus
πυκνότερον πρὸς αὐτόν, ἐὰν ἀποκατασταθῶσιν εἰς τὴν Ἰουδαίαν,—
15 δίκαιον γὰρ εἶπε τὴν ἐκπομπὴν αὐτῶν γενέσθαι· παραγενηθέντας δέ,
ὡς θέμις, ἕξειν αὐτοὺς φίλους, καὶ <πολυωρίας> τῆς μεγίστης τεύξε-
σθαι παρ' αὐτοῦ. τὰ δὲ πρὸς τὴν ἐκπομπὴν αὐτῶν ἐκέλευσεν ἑτοι- 319
μάζειν, μεγαλομερῶς τοῖς ἀνδράσι χρησάμενος. ἑκάστῳ γὰρ στολὰς
ἔδωκε τῶν κρατίστων τρεῖς καὶ χρυσίου τάλαντα δύο καὶ κυλίκιον
20 ταλάντου καὶ τρικλίνου πᾶσαν κατάστρωσιν. ἔπεμψε δὲ καὶ τῷ 320
Ἐλεαζάρῳ μετὰ τῆς ἐκπομπῆς αὐτῶν ἀργυρόποδας κλίνας δέκα καὶ
τὰ ἀκόλουθα πάντα καὶ κυλίκιον ταλάντων τριάκοντα καὶ στολὰς
δέκα καὶ πορφύραν καὶ στέφανον διαπρεπῆ καὶ βυσσίνων ὀθονίων

---

1 προιστορειν HKAGI txt BCT Eus | λαβοι Eus] λαβειν Ar codd HKAGIB
2 τριακοντα] λ̄ ΚΑ | ανεσιν Ar codd Jos] αιτησιν Eus   3 om το Eusᵒ CTZ Jos
4 σημανθεντος] μαθοντος Eus   5 δε ουτως] ωσαυτως ΒΤ δε αυτως CZ   Eus
8 οψις C | απεγλαυκωθη Eus Aᶜᵒʳʳ] απεγλυκωθη ΗΚΑ*GI επεγλυκωθη
Β*CTZ* (-γλαυκ. Βᶜᵒʳʳ Zᵐᵍ γλαυκωθειη Jos)   9 ταυτ Eusⁱ | αυτω BAᶜᵒʳʳ
Eus] αυτο cett | om το συμπτωμα Eus   11 προειπε Eusⁱᵒ | περι—Δημητριου
em Cobet] περι τουτων τα περι του Δ. Eus περι των (om των C) του Δ. Ar
codd (ταυτα παρα του Δ. Jos)   12 συντηρεισθαι Eusᵒ   13 αγνων CTZ*
αγνα Β | τοις I | παραγινονται GIC   14 αποκαταστωσιν Κ | Ιουδαιαν]
ιδιαν Α   15 om γαρ Β (hab Jos)   16 ως θεμις] ωσαυθις Aᶜᵒʳʳ | εξειν
Aᶜᵒʳʳ (cod Mon ap Wend.)] εξεις Η εξει cett | πολυωριας (cf 270) Mahaffy]
πολυδωριας codd et Jos | τευξασθαι BCTZ txt cett Jos   18 μεγαλοπρεπως
Κ | χαρισαμενος Wend.   19 κυλικιον ABT Jos] κυλιδιον cett κυλικειον hic
et 22 Wend.   22 τριακοντα] λ̄ ΚΑ   23 στεφον Τ

ἱστοὺς ἑκατὸν καὶ φιάλας καὶ τρυβλία καὶ κρατῆρας χρυσοῦς δύο
321 πρὸς ἀνάθεσιν. ἔγραψε δὲ καὶ παρακαλῶν, ἵνα, ἐάν τινες τῶν
ἀνδρῶν προαιρῶνται πρὸς αὐτὸν ἀνακομισθῆναι, μὴ κωλύσῃ, περὶ
πολλοῦ ποιούμενος τοῖς πεπαιδευμένοις συνεῖναι, καὶ εἰς τοιούτους
¶ Jos τὸν πλοῦτον κατατίθεσθαι δαψιλῶς, καὶ οὐκ εἰς μάταια.¶   5

322   Σὺ δέ, καθὼς ἐπηγγειλάμην, ἀπέχεις τὴν διήγησιν, ὦ Φιλόκρατες.
τέρπειν γὰρ οἴομαί σε ταῦτα ἢ τὰ τῶν μυθολόγων βιβλία. νένευκας
γὰρ πρὸς περιεργίαν τῶν δυναμένων ὠφελεῖν διάνοιαν, καὶ ἐν τούτοις
τὸν πλείονα χρόνον διατελεῖς. πειράσομαι δὲ καὶ τὰ λοιπὰ τῶν
ἀξιολόγων ἀναγράφειν, ἵνα διαπορευόμενος αὐτὰ κομίζῃ τοῦ βουλή- 10
ματος τὸ κάλλιστον ἔπαθλον.

HKAGIB   1 ιστους Jos] εις τους Ar codd | τρυβλια]+και σπονδεια Jos   3 προαι-
CTZ Jos
ρουνται Z   4 om και HKGICZ | τοιουτοις I   7 σε] om B* ins B¹
adnotat ισως μαλλον Z^{mg}   9 πλειον KGICZ πλειω HA | διατελειν Z |
λοιπα bis scr C   10 κομιζει GI   11 om το καλλιστον T

INDICES.

INDEX I.

S. S.

INDEX II.

DATE DUE

JA 28 '75			
MR 4 '75			